TODD McFARLANE AND
IMAGE COMICS PRESENT

SPAWN COLLECTED EDITION VOLUME FIVE

STORY
TODD MCFARLANE
BRIAN HOLGUIN

PENCILS
TODD MCFARLANE
GREG CAPULLO
DWAYNE TURNER

INKS
TODD MCFARLANE
DANNY MIKI
LEE MATSUNAMI
SCOTT KOBAYASHI

LETTERING
TOM ORZECHOWSKI

COLOR
BRIAN HABERLIN
DAN KEMP
TYSON WENGLER
DAVE KEMP
ANDY TROY

COVER
TODD MCFARLANE
GREG CAPULLO
BRIAN HABERLIN

Spawn created by
TODD MCFARLANE

TODD McFARLANE PRODUCTIONS
SPAWN.COM

SPAWN COLLECTION VOL. 5. APRIL 2008. First Printing. Contains issues 76-95 of Spawn. Published by IMAGE COMICS, 1942 University Ave. Berkeley, CA 94704.

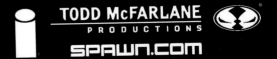

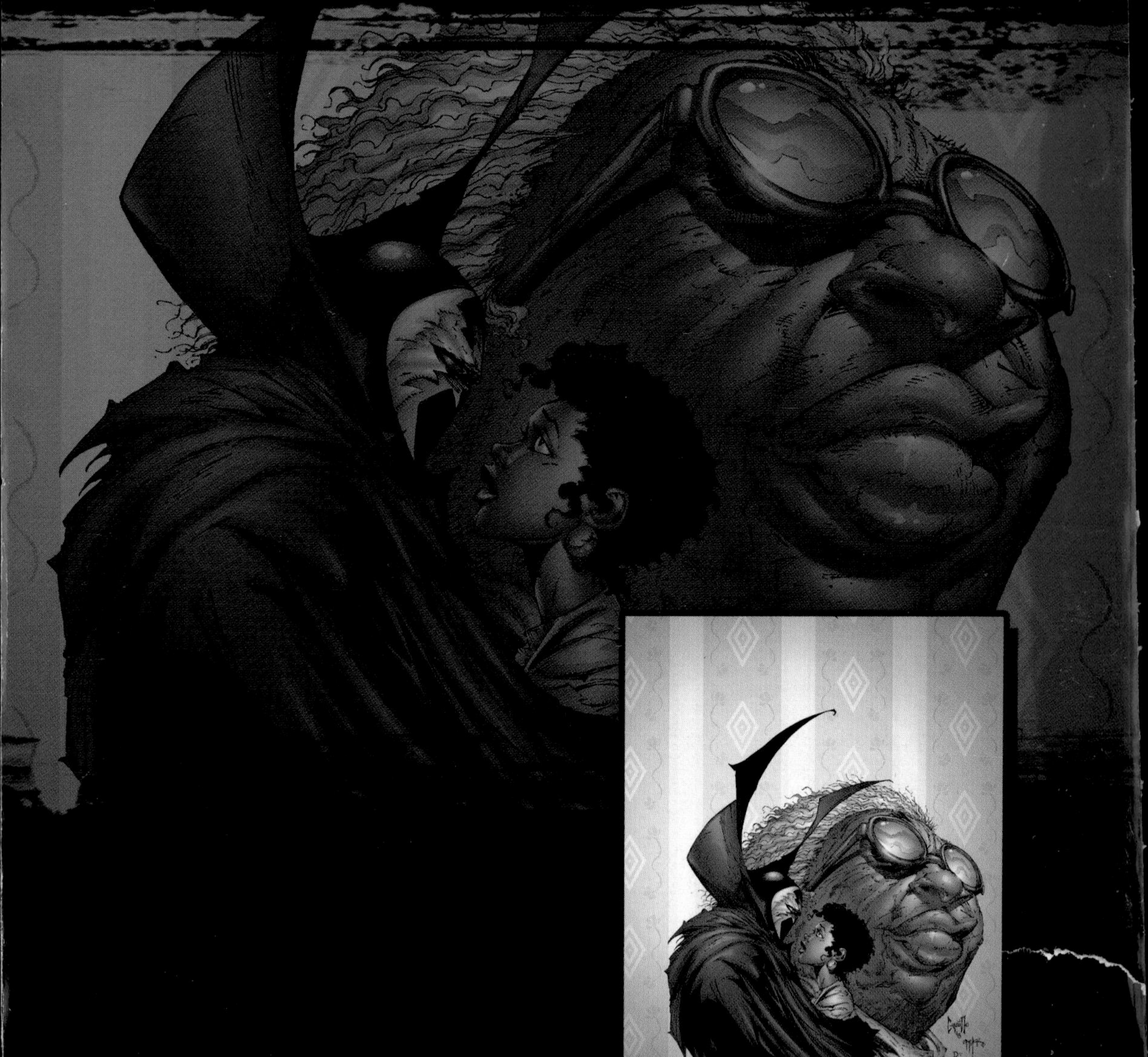

ISSUE SEVENTY-SIX

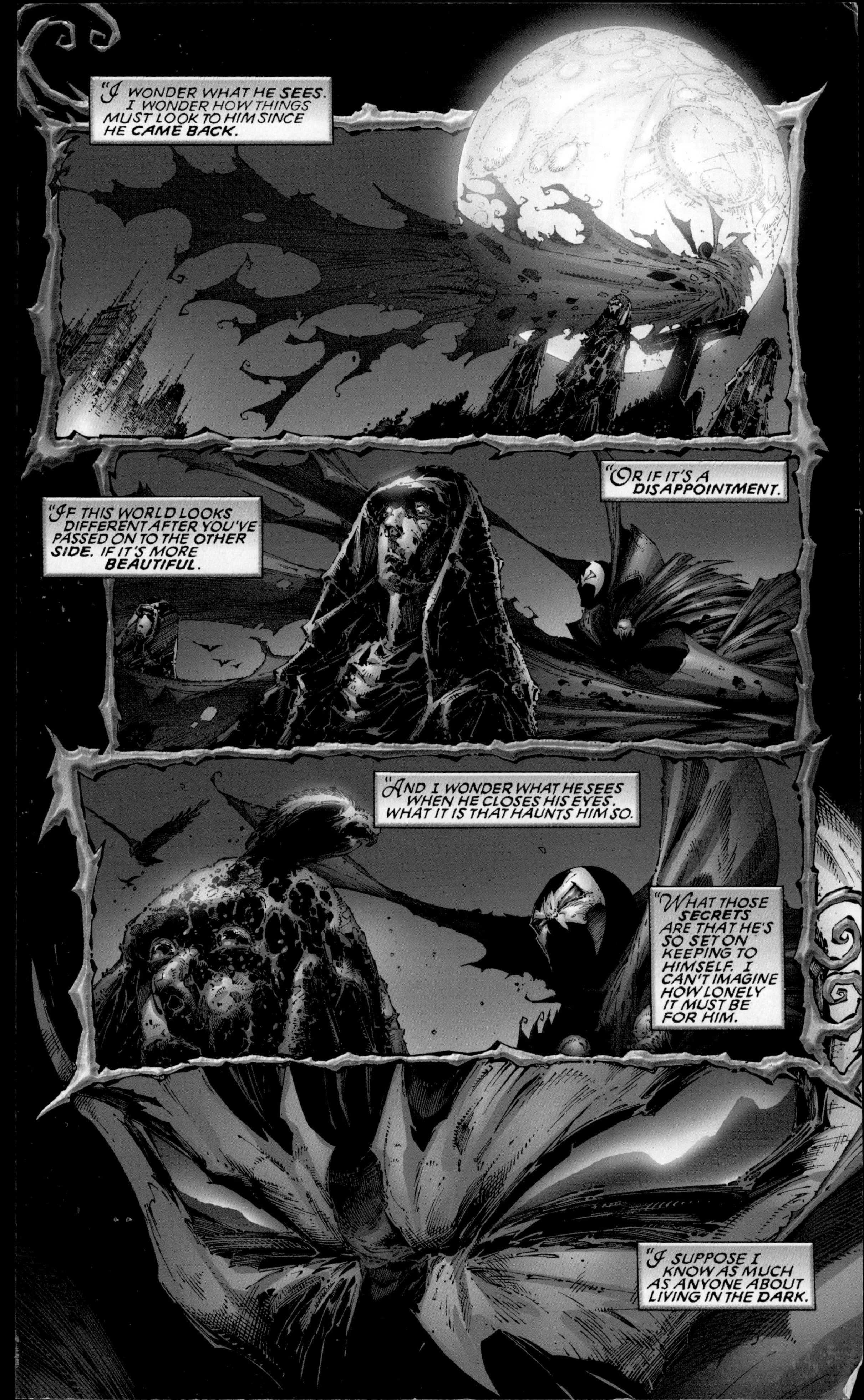
"I WONDER WHAT HE SEES. I WONDER HOW THINGS MUST LOOK TO HIM SINCE HE CAME BACK.
"IF THIS WORLD LOOKS DIFFERENT AFTER YOU'VE PASSED ON TO THE OTHER SIDE. IF IT'S MORE BEAUTIFUL.
"OR IF IT'S A DISAPPOINTMENT.
"AND I WONDER WHAT HE SEES WHEN HE CLOSES HIS EYES. WHAT IT IS THAT HAUNTS HIM SO.
"WHAT THOSE SECRETS ARE THAT HE'S SO SET ON KEEPING TO HIMSELF. I CAN'T IMAGINE HOW LONELY IT MUST BE FOR HIM.
"I SUPPOSE I KNOW AS MUCH AS ANYONE ABOUT LIVING IN THE DARK.

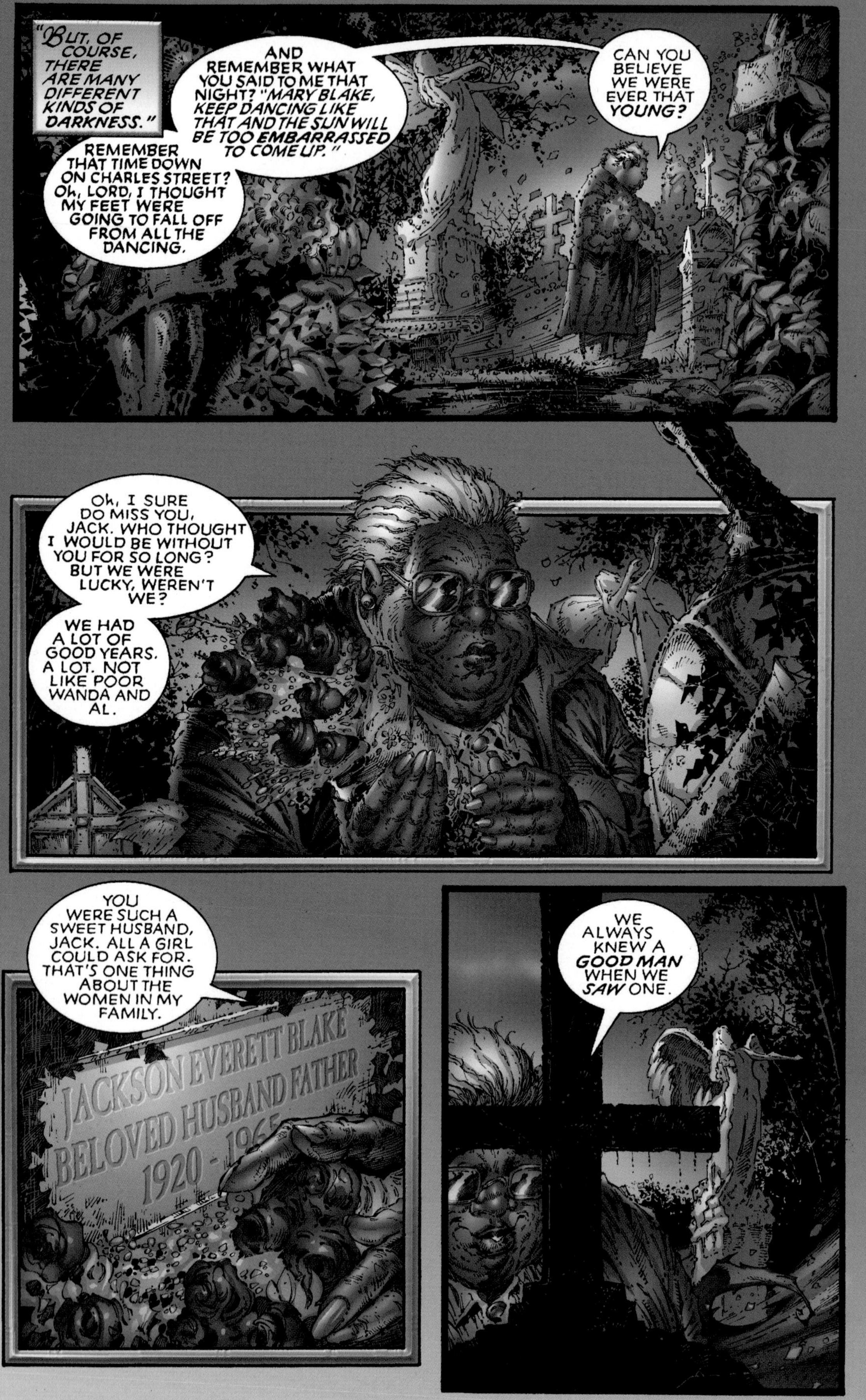
"BUT, OF COURSE, THERE ARE MANY DIFFERENT KINDS OF DARKNESS."
REMEMBER THAT TIME DOWN ON CHARLES STREET? Oh, LORD, I THOUGHT MY FEET WERE GOING TO FALL OFF FROM ALL THE DANCING.
AND REMEMBER WHAT YOU SAID TO ME THAT NIGHT? "MARY BLAKE, KEEP DANCING LIKE THAT AND THE SUN WILL BE TOO EMBARRASSED TO COME UP."
CAN YOU BELIEVE WE WERE EVER THAT YOUNG?
Oh, I SURE DO MISS YOU, JACK. WHO THOUGHT I WOULD BE WITHOUT YOU FOR SO LONG? BUT WE WERE LUCKY, WEREN'T WE?
WE HAD A LOT OF GOOD YEARS. A LOT. NOT LIKE POOR WANDA AND AL.
YOU WERE SUCH A SWEET HUSBAND, JACK. ALL A GIRL COULD ASK FOR. THAT'S ONE THING ABOUT THE WOMEN IN MY FAMILY.
JACKSON EVERETT BLAKE
BELOVED HUSBAND FATHER
1920 - 1965
WE ALWAYS KNEW A GOOD MAN WHEN WE SAW ONE.

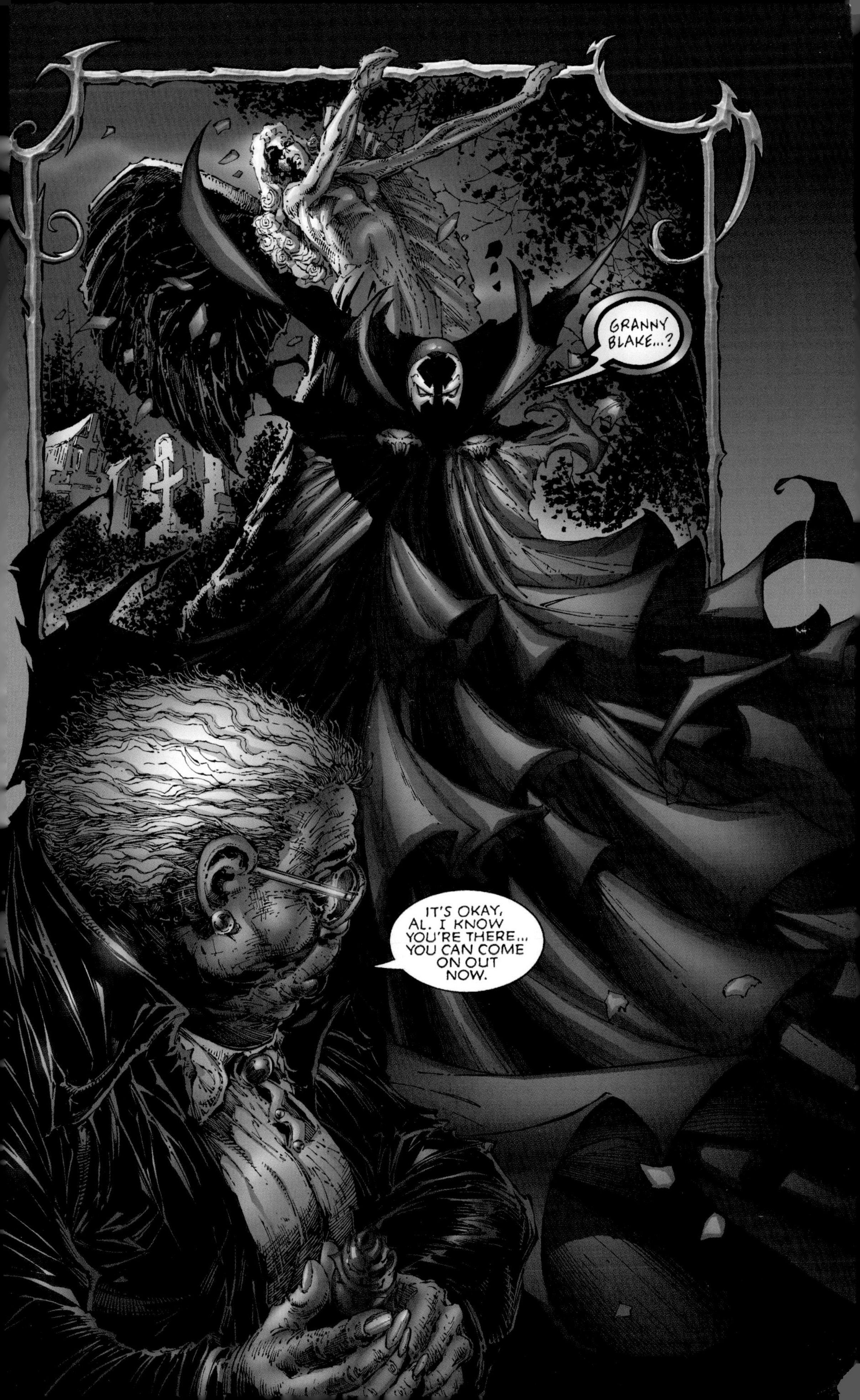
GRANNY BLAKE...?
IT'S OKAY, AL. I KNOW YOU'RE THERE... YOU CAN COME ON OUT NOW.

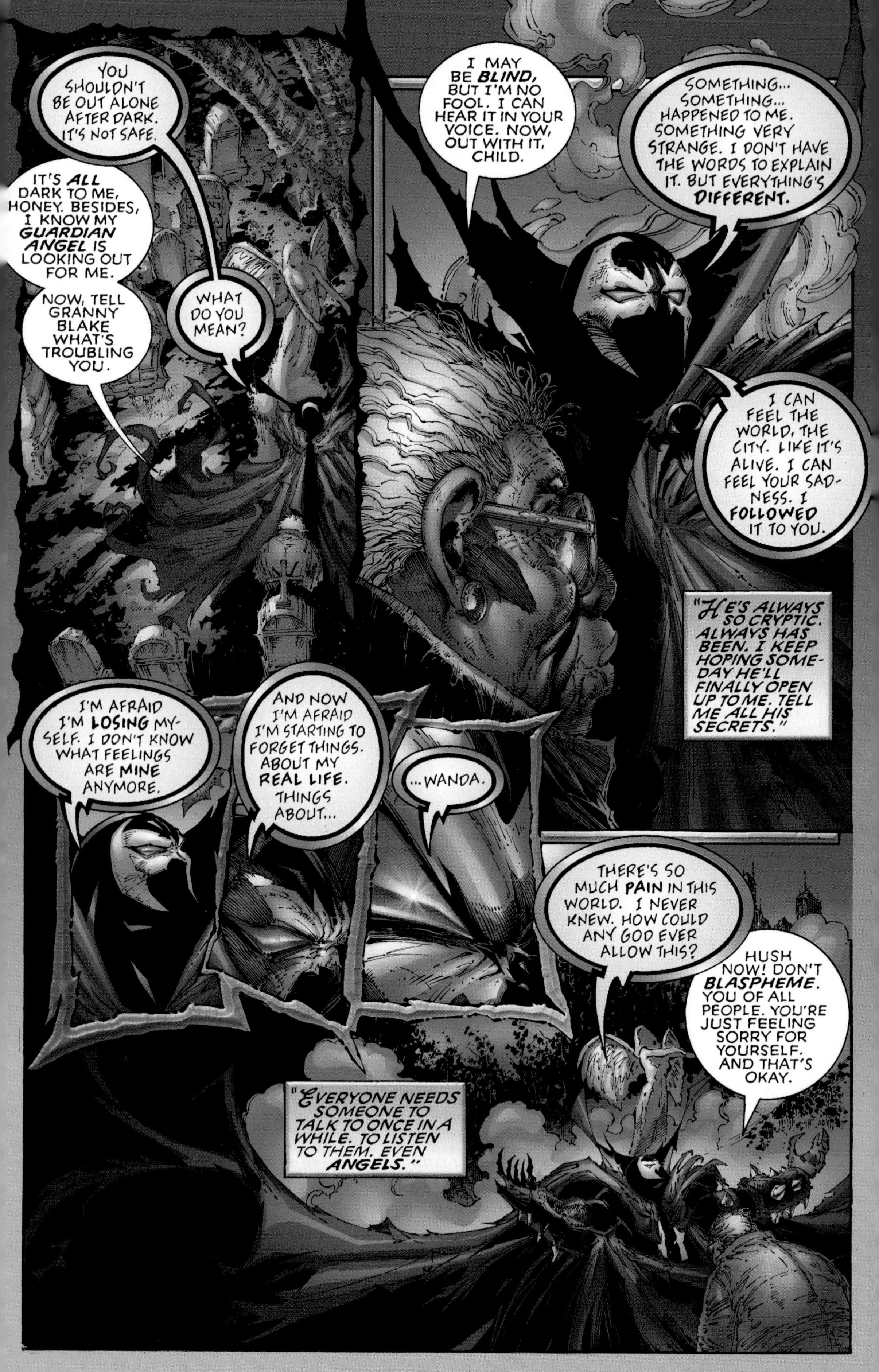
YOU SHOULDN'T BE OUT ALONE AFTER DARK. IT'S NOT SAFE.
IT'S ALL DARK TO ME, HONEY. BESIDES, I KNOW MY GUARDIAN ANGEL IS LOOKING OUT FOR ME.
NOW, TELL GRANNY BLAKE WHAT'S TROUBLING YOU.
WHAT DO YOU MEAN?
I MAY BE BLIND, BUT I'M NO FOOL. I CAN HEAR IT IN YOUR VOICE. NOW, OUT WITH IT, CHILD.
SOMETHING... SOMETHING... HAPPENED TO ME. SOMETHING VERY STRANGE. I DON'T HAVE THE WORDS TO EXPLAIN IT. BUT EVERYTHING'S DIFFERENT.
I CAN FEEL THE WORLD, THE CITY. LIKE IT'S ALIVE. I CAN FEEL YOUR SADNESS. I FOLLOWED IT TO YOU.
"HE'S ALWAYS SO CRYPTIC. ALWAYS HAS BEEN. I KEEP HOPING SOMEDAY HE'LL FINALLY OPEN UP TO ME. TELL ME ALL HIS SECRETS."
I'M AFRAID I'M LOSING MYSELF. I DON'T KNOW WHAT FEELINGS ARE MINE ANYMORE.
AND NOW I'M AFRAID I'M STARTING TO FORGET THINGS. ABOUT MY REAL LIFE. THINGS ABOUT...
...WANDA.
THERE'S SO MUCH PAIN IN THIS WORLD. I NEVER KNEW. HOW COULD ANY GOD EVER ALLOW THIS?
HUSH NOW! DON'T BLASPHEME. YOU OF ALL PEOPLE. YOU'RE JUST FEELING SORRY FOR YOURSELF. AND THAT'S OKAY.
"EVERYONE NEEDS SOMEONE TO TALK TO ONCE IN A WHILE. TO LISTEN TO THEM. EVEN ANGELS."

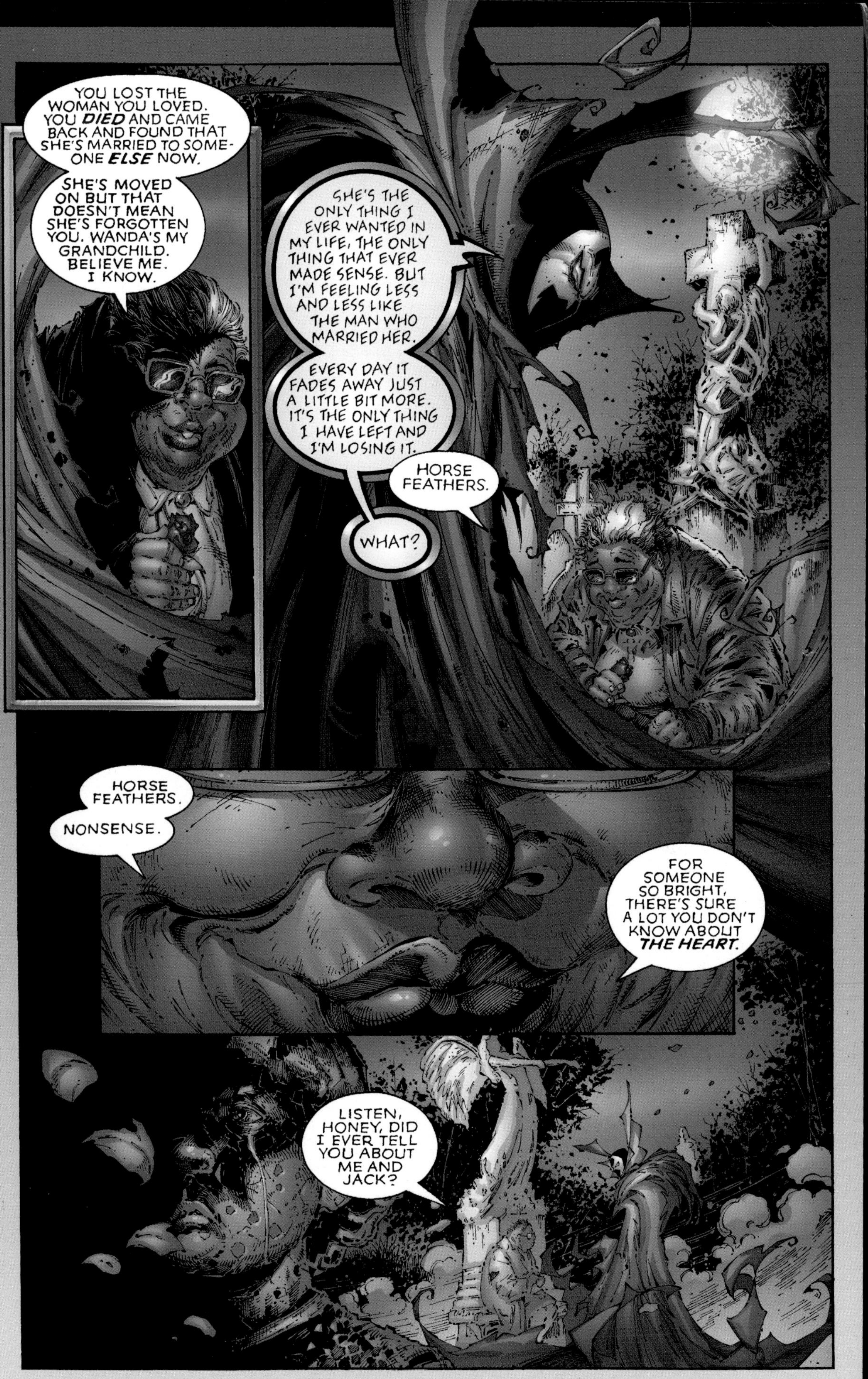
YOU LOST THE WOMAN YOU LOVED. YOU DIED AND CAME BACK AND FOUND THAT SHE'S MARRIED TO SOME-ONE ELSE NOW.
SHE'S MOVED ON BUT THAT DOESN'T MEAN SHE'S FORGOTTEN YOU. WANDA'S MY GRANDCHILD. BELIEVE ME. I KNOW.
SHE'S THE ONLY THING I EVER WANTED IN MY LIFE, THE ONLY THING THAT EVER MADE SENSE. BUT I'M FEELING LESS AND LESS LIKE THE MAN WHO MARRIED HER.
EVERY DAY IT FADES AWAY JUST A LITTLE BIT MORE. IT'S THE ONLY THING I HAVE LEFT AND I'M LOSING IT.
HORSE FEATHERS.
WHAT?
HORSE FEATHERS.
NONSENSE.
FOR SOMEONE SO BRIGHT, THERE'S SURE A LOT YOU DON'T KNOW ABOUT THE HEART.
LISTEN, HONEY, DID I EVER TELL YOU ABOUT ME AND JACK?

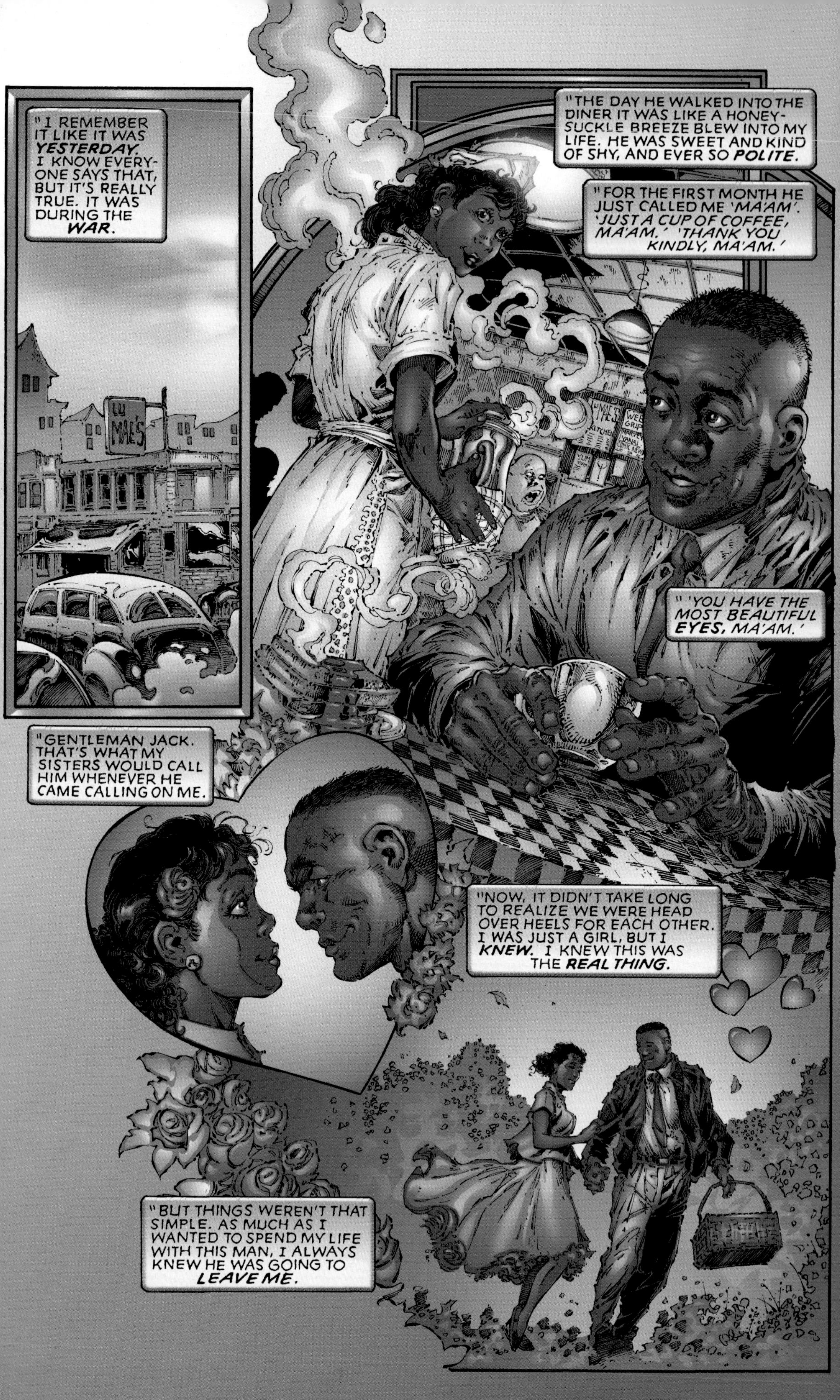
"I REMEMBER IT LIKE IT WAS YESTERDAY. I KNOW EVERYONE SAYS THAT, BUT IT'S REALLY TRUE. IT WAS DURING THE WAR.
"THE DAY HE WALKED INTO THE DINER IT WAS LIKE A HONEY-SUCKLE BREEZE BLEW INTO MY LIFE. HE WAS SWEET AND KIND OF SHY, AND EVER SO POLITE.
"FOR THE FIRST MONTH HE JUST CALLED ME 'MA'AM'. 'JUST A CUP OF COFFEE, MA'AM.' 'THANK YOU KINDLY, MA'AM.'
" 'YOU HAVE THE MOST BEAUTIFUL EYES, MA'AM.'
"GENTLEMAN JACK. THAT'S WHAT MY SISTERS WOULD CALL HIM WHENEVER HE CAME CALLING ON ME.
"NOW, IT DIDN'T TAKE LONG TO REALIZE WE WERE HEAD OVER HEELS FOR EACH OTHER. I WAS JUST A GIRL, BUT I KNEW. I KNEW THIS WAS THE REAL THING.
"BUT THINGS WEREN'T THAT SIMPLE. AS MUCH AS I WANTED TO SPEND MY LIFE WITH THIS MAN, I ALWAYS KNEW HE WAS GOING TO LEAVE ME.

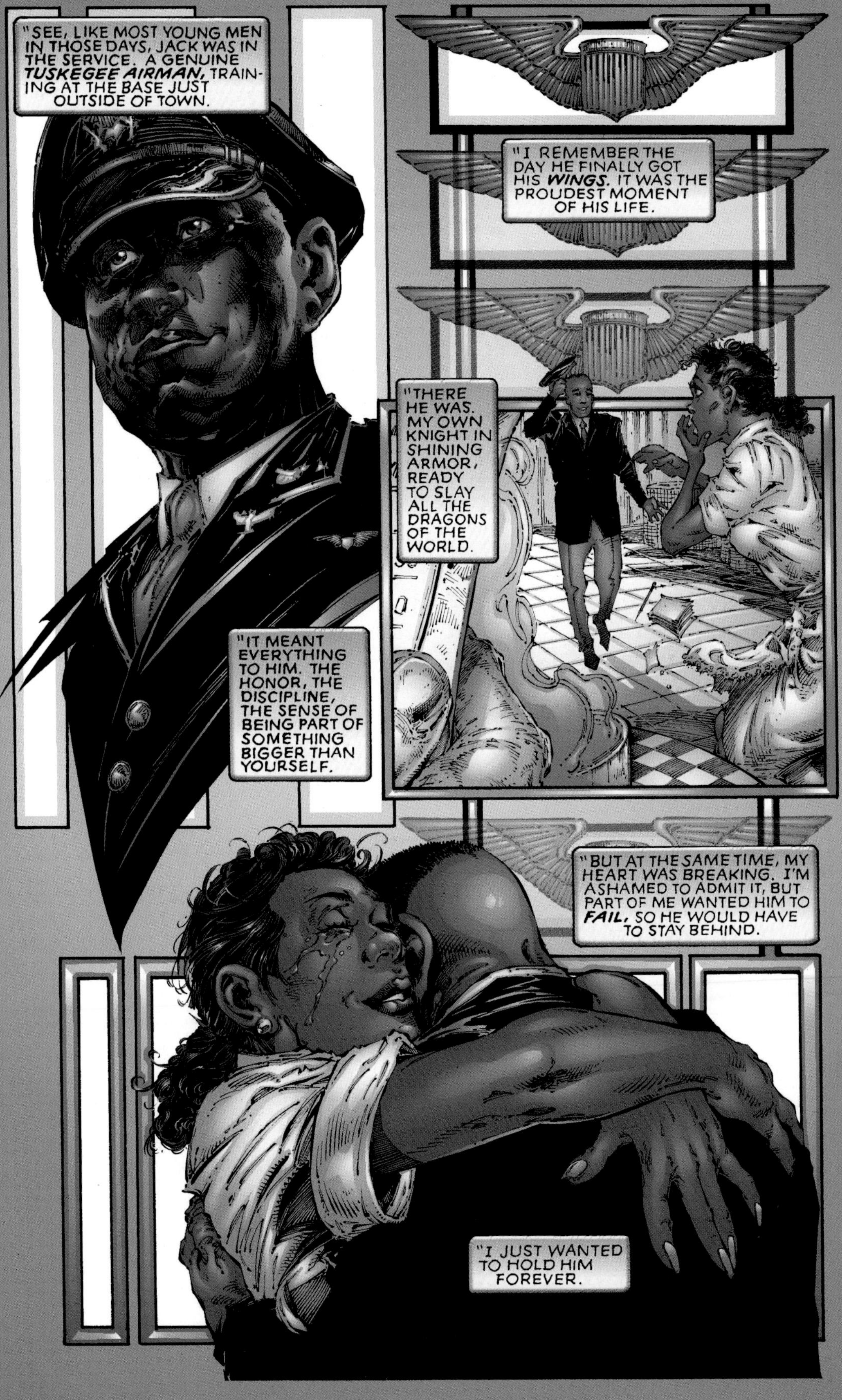
"SEE, LIKE MOST YOUNG MEN IN THOSE DAYS, JACK WAS IN THE SERVICE. A GENUINE *TUSKEGEE AIRMAN,* TRAINING AT THE BASE JUST OUTSIDE OF TOWN.
"I REMEMBER THE DAY HE FINALLY GOT HIS *WINGS.* IT WAS THE PROUDEST MOMENT OF HIS LIFE.
"THERE HE WAS. MY OWN KNIGHT IN SHINING ARMOR, READY TO SLAY ALL THE DRAGONS OF THE WORLD.
"IT MEANT EVERYTHING TO HIM. THE HONOR, THE DISCIPLINE, THE SENSE OF BEING PART OF SOMETHING BIGGER THAN YOURSELF.
"BUT AT THE SAME TIME, MY HEART WAS BREAKING. I'M ASHAMED TO ADMIT IT, BUT PART OF ME WANTED HIM TO *FAIL,* SO HE WOULD HAVE TO STAY BEHIND.
"I JUST WANTED TO HOLD HIM FOREVER.

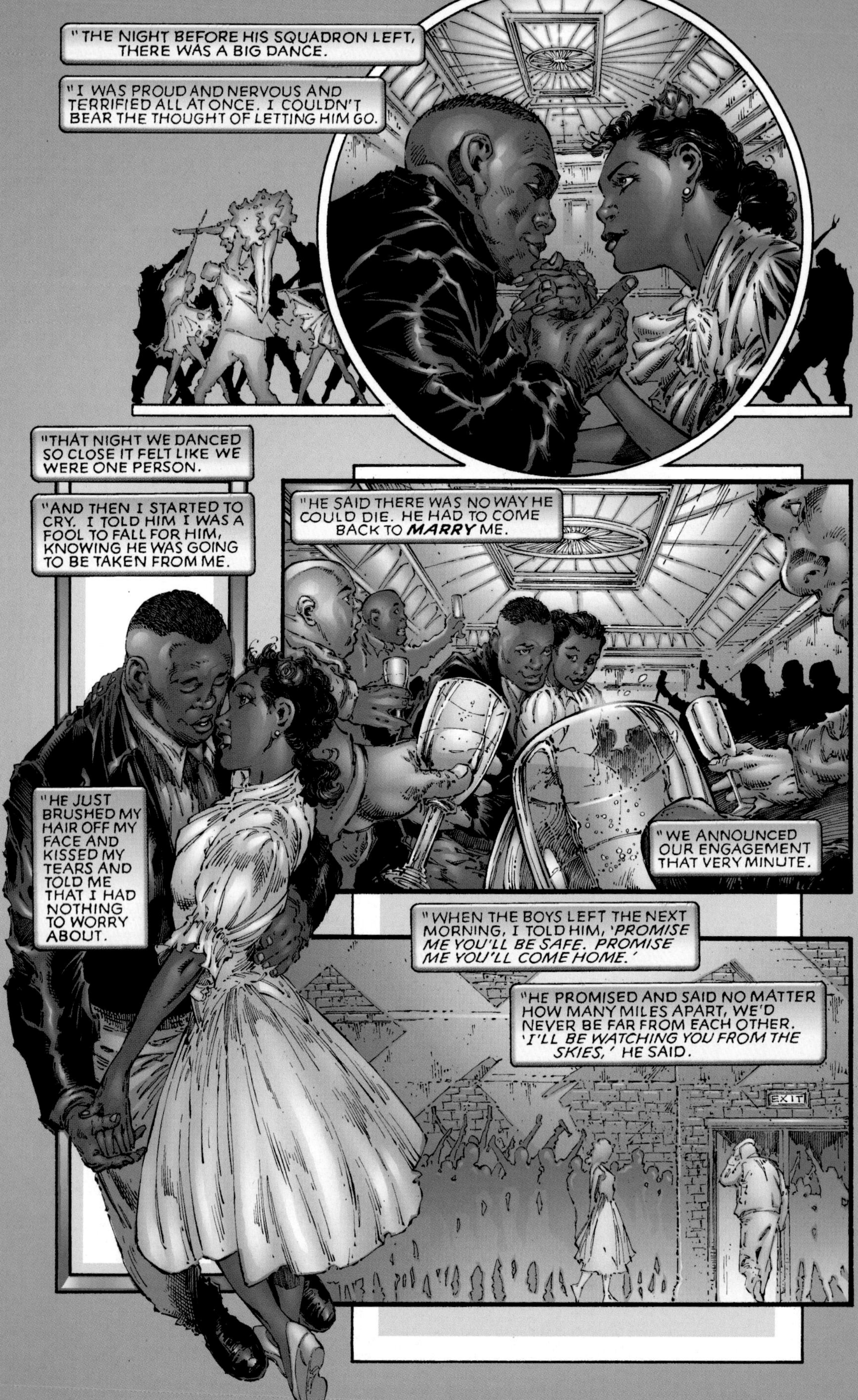
"THE NIGHT BEFORE HIS SQUADRON LEFT, THERE WAS A BIG DANCE.
"I WAS PROUD AND NERVOUS AND TERRIFIED ALL AT ONCE. I COULDN'T BEAR THE THOUGHT OF LETTING HIM GO.
"THAT NIGHT WE DANCED SO CLOSE IT FELT LIKE WE WERE ONE PERSON.
"AND THEN I STARTED TO CRY. I TOLD HIM I WAS A FOOL TO FALL FOR HIM, KNOWING HE WAS GOING TO BE TAKEN FROM ME.
"HE JUST BRUSHED MY HAIR OFF MY FACE AND KISSED MY TEARS AND TOLD ME THAT I HAD NOTHING TO WORRY ABOUT.
"HE SAID THERE WAS NO WAY HE COULD DIE. HE HAD TO COME BACK TO *MARRY* ME.
"WE ANNOUNCED OUR ENGAGEMENT THAT VERY MINUTE.
"WHEN THE BOYS LEFT THE NEXT MORNING, I TOLD HIM, '*PROMISE ME YOU'LL BE SAFE. PROMISE ME YOU'LL COME HOME.*'
"HE PROMISED AND SAID NO MATTER HOW MANY MILES APART, WE'D NEVER BE FAR FROM EACH OTHER. '*I'LL BE WATCHING YOU FROM THE SKIES,*' HE SAID.
EXIT

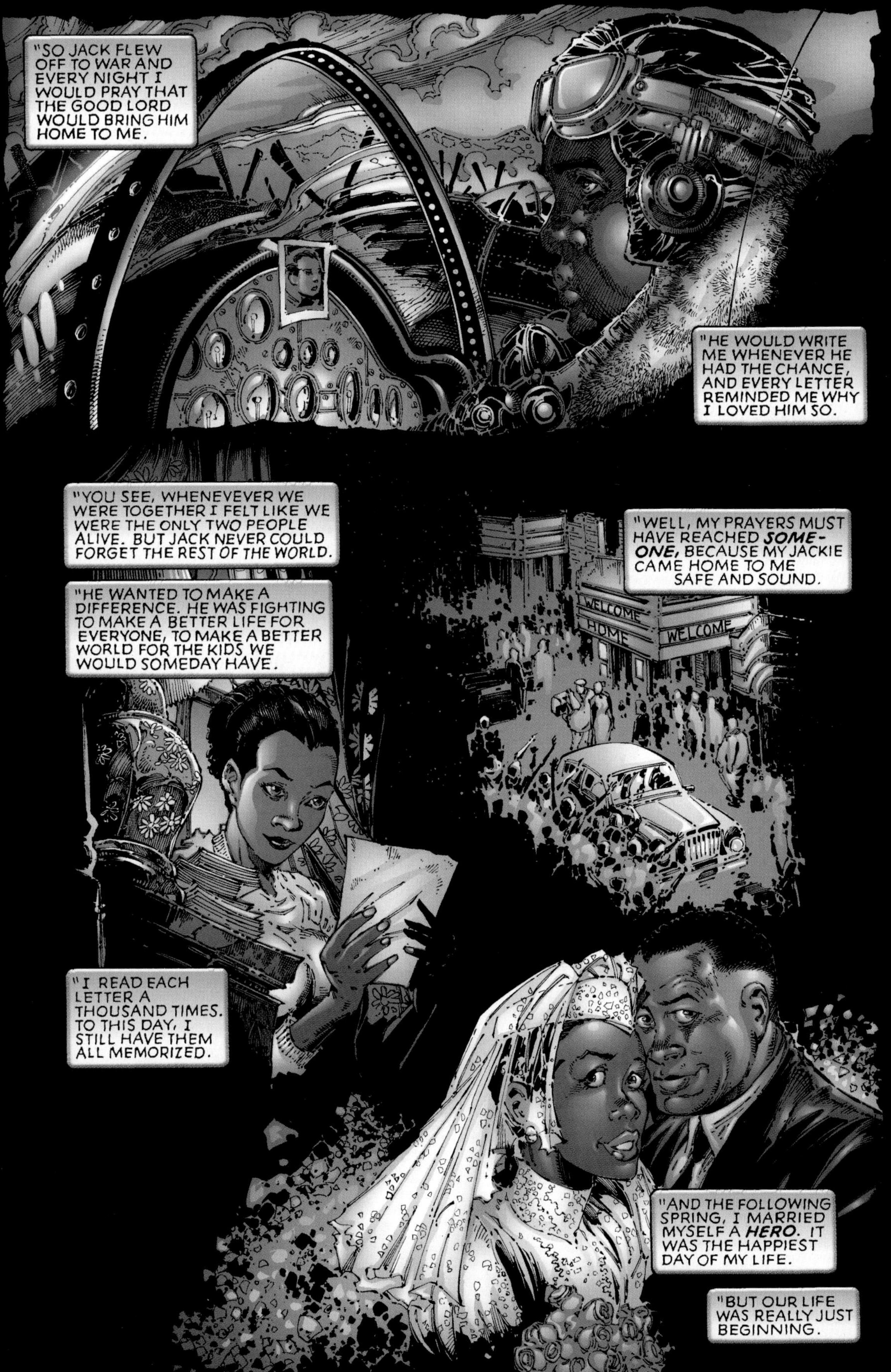
"SO JACK FLEW OFF TO WAR AND EVERY NIGHT I WOULD PRAY THAT THE GOOD LORD WOULD BRING HIM HOME TO ME.
"HE WOULD WRITE ME WHENEVER HE HAD THE CHANCE, AND EVERY LETTER REMINDED ME WHY I LOVED HIM SO.
"YOU SEE, WHENEVEVER WE WERE TOGETHER I FELT LIKE WE WERE THE ONLY TWO PEOPLE ALIVE. BUT JACK NEVER COULD FORGET THE REST OF THE WORLD.
"HE WANTED TO MAKE A DIFFERENCE. HE WAS FIGHTING TO MAKE A BETTER LIFE FOR EVERYONE, TO MAKE A BETTER WORLD FOR THE KIDS WE WOULD SOMEDAY HAVE.
"I READ EACH LETTER A THOUSAND TIMES. TO THIS DAY, I STILL HAVE THEM ALL MEMORIZED.
"WELL, MY PRAYERS MUST HAVE REACHED **SOME-ONE,** BECAUSE MY JACKIE CAME HOME TO ME SAFE AND SOUND.
WELCOME HOME
WELCOME
"AND THE FOLLOWING SPRING, I MARRIED MYSELF A **HERO**. IT WAS THE HAPPIEST DAY OF MY LIFE.
"BUT OUR LIFE WAS REALLY JUST BEGINNING.

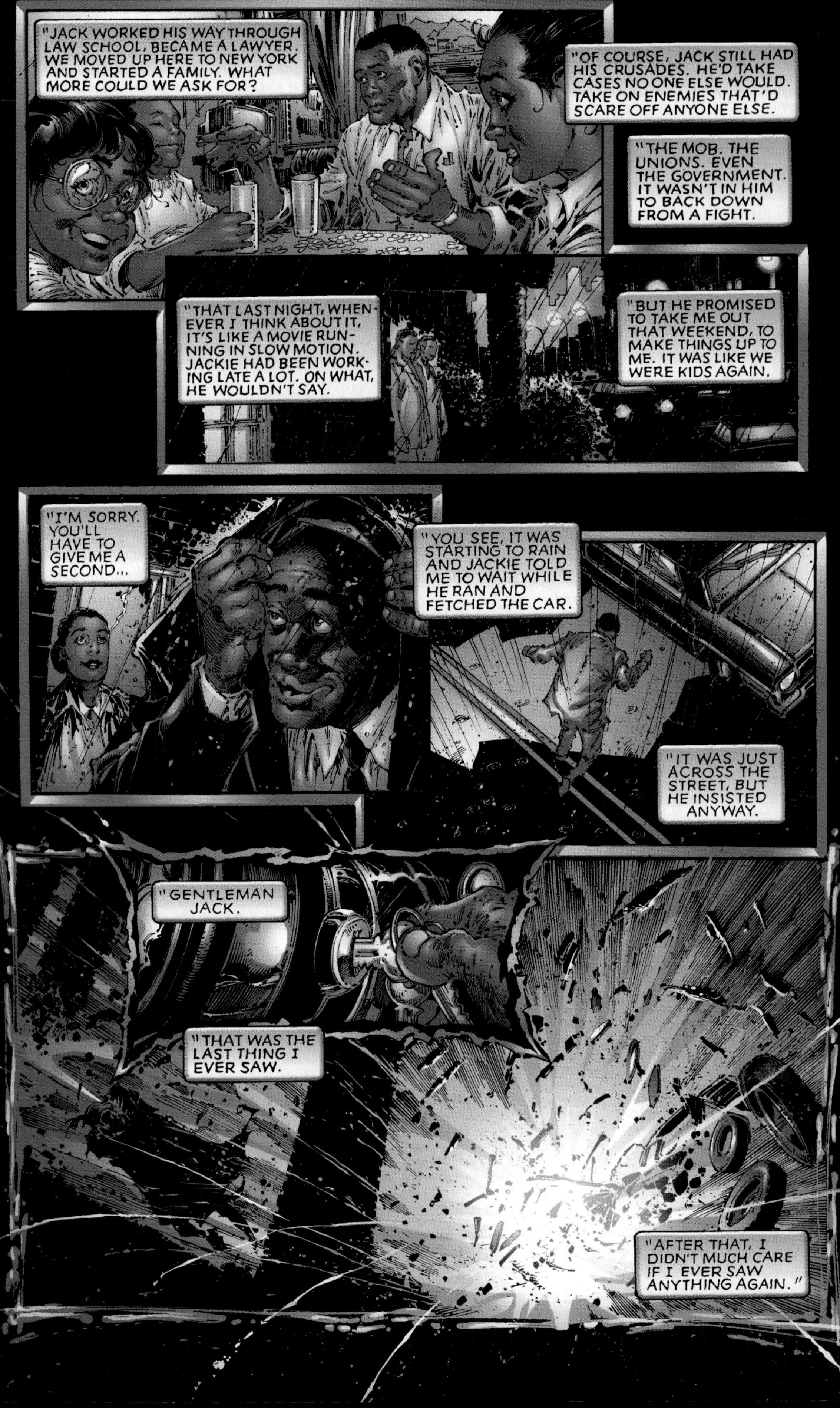
"JACK WORKED HIS WAY THROUGH LAW SCHOOL, BECAME A LAWYER. WE MOVED UP HERE TO NEW YORK AND STARTED A FAMILY. WHAT MORE COULD WE ASK FOR?
"OF COURSE, JACK STILL HAD HIS CRUSADES. HE'D TAKE CASES NO ONE ELSE WOULD. TAKE ON ENEMIES THAT'D SCARE OFF ANYONE ELSE.
"THE MOB. THE UNIONS. EVEN THE GOVERNMENT. IT WASN'T IN HIM TO BACK DOWN FROM A FIGHT.
"THAT LAST NIGHT, WHENEVER I THINK ABOUT IT, IT'S LIKE A MOVIE RUNNING IN SLOW MOTION. JACKIE HAD BEEN WORKING LATE A LOT. ON WHAT, HE WOULDN'T SAY.
"BUT HE PROMISED TO TAKE ME OUT THAT WEEKEND, TO MAKE THINGS UP TO ME. IT WAS LIKE WE WERE KIDS AGAIN.
"I'M SORRY. YOU'LL HAVE TO GIVE ME A SECOND...
"YOU SEE, IT WAS STARTING TO RAIN AND JACKIE TOLD ME TO WAIT WHILE HE RAN AND FETCHED THE CAR.
"IT WAS JUST ACROSS THE STREET, BUT HE INSISTED ANYWAY.
"GENTLEMAN JACK.
"THAT WAS THE LAST THING I EVER SAW.
"AFTER THAT, I DIDN'T MUCH CARE IF I EVER SAW ANYTHING AGAIN."

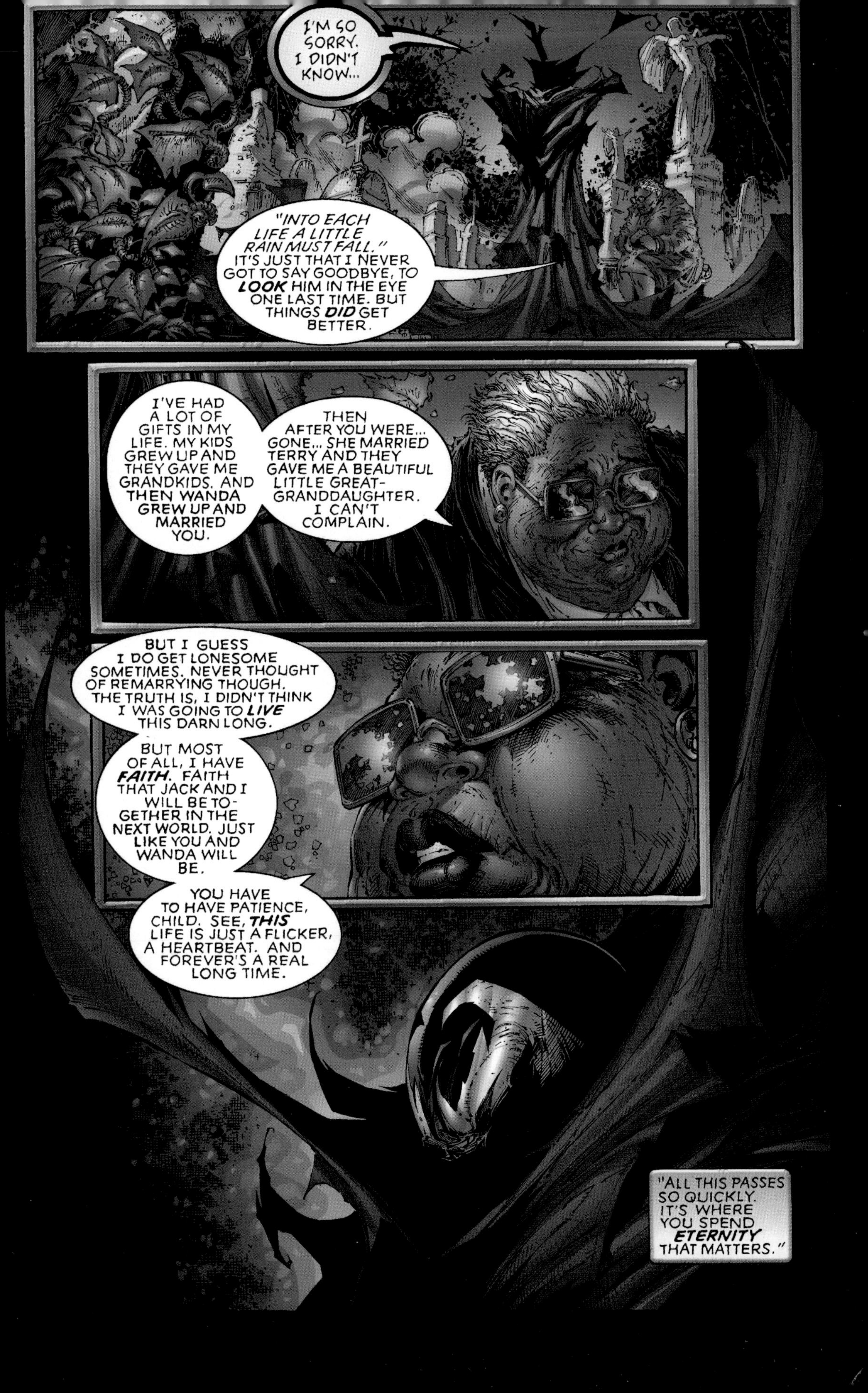
I'M SO SORRY. I DIDN'T KNOW...
"INTO EACH LIFE A LITTLE RAIN MUST FALL." IT'S JUST THAT I NEVER GOT TO SAY GOODBYE, TO LOOK HIM IN THE EYE ONE LAST TIME. BUT THINGS DID GET BETTER.
I'VE HAD A LOT OF GIFTS IN MY LIFE. MY KIDS GREW UP AND THEY GAVE ME GRANDKIDS. AND THEN WANDA GREW UP AND MARRIED YOU.
THEN AFTER YOU WERE... GONE... SHE MARRIED TERRY AND THEY GAVE ME A BEAUTIFUL LITTLE GREAT-GRANDDAUGHTER. I CAN'T COMPLAIN.
BUT I GUESS I DO GET LONESOME SOMETIMES. NEVER THOUGHT OF REMARRYING THOUGH. THE TRUTH IS, I DIDN'T THINK I WAS GOING TO LIVE THIS DARN LONG.
BUT MOST OF ALL, I HAVE FAITH. FAITH THAT JACK AND I WILL BE TOGETHER IN THE NEXT WORLD. JUST LIKE YOU AND WANDA WILL BE.
YOU HAVE TO HAVE PATIENCE, CHILD. SEE, THIS LIFE IS JUST A FLICKER, A HEARTBEAT. AND FOREVER'S A REAL LONG TIME.
"ALL THIS PASSES SO QUICKLY. IT'S WHERE YOU SPEND ETERNITY THAT MATTERS."

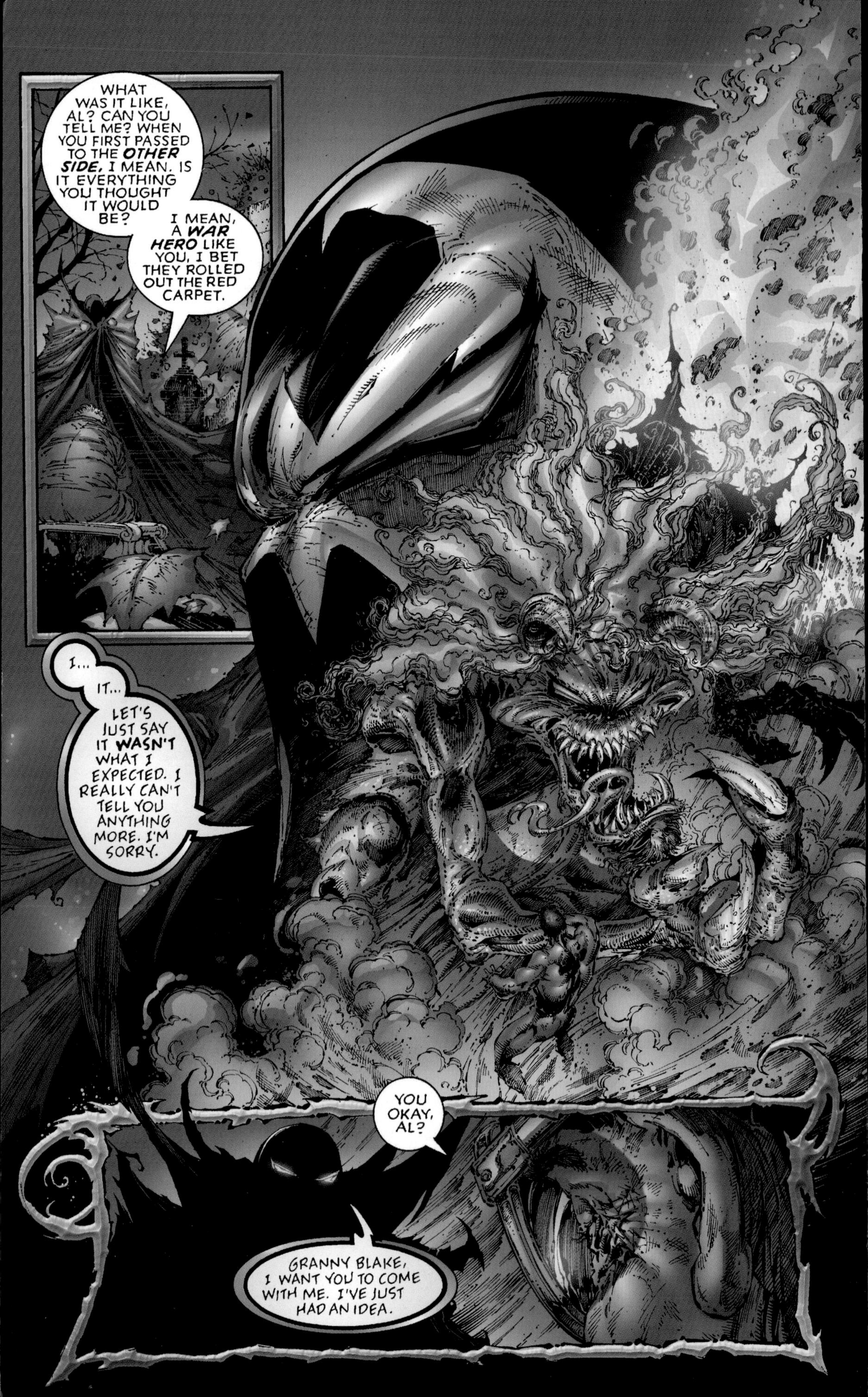

WHAT WAS IT LIKE, AL? CAN YOU TELL ME? WHEN YOU FIRST PASSED TO THE OTHER SIDE, I MEAN. IS IT EVERYTHING YOU THOUGHT IT WOULD BE?
I MEAN, A WAR HERO LIKE YOU, I BET THEY ROLLED OUT THE RED CARPET.
I...
IT...
LET'S JUST SAY IT WASN'T WHAT I EXPECTED. I REALLY CAN'T TELL YOU ANYTHING MORE. I'M SORRY.
YOU OKAY, AL?
GRANNY BLAKE, I WANT YOU TO COME WITH ME. I'VE JUST HAD AN IDEA.

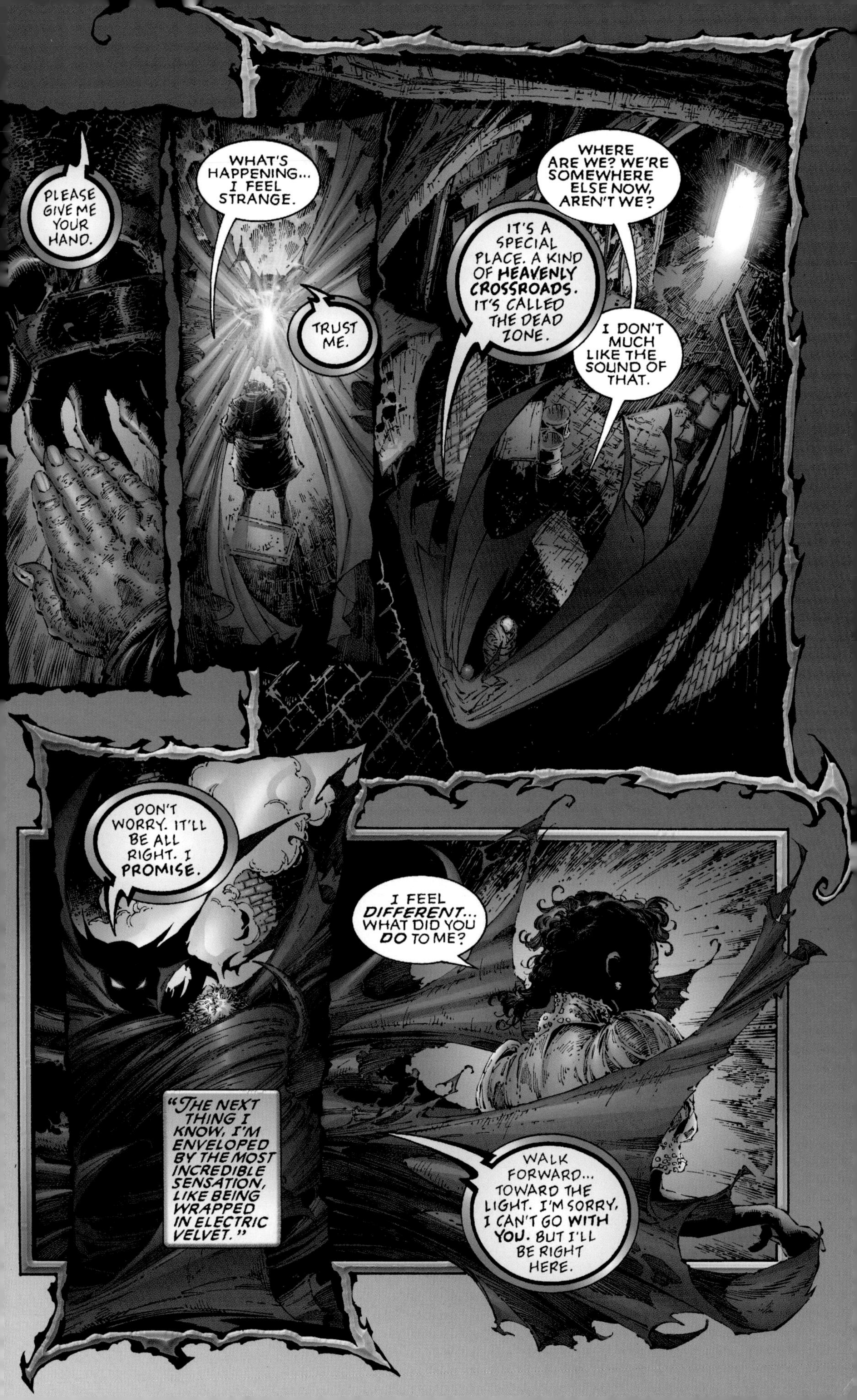
PLEASE GIVE ME YOUR HAND.
WHAT'S HAPPENING... I FEEL STRANGE.
TRUST ME.
WHERE ARE WE? WE'RE SOMEWHERE ELSE NOW, AREN'T WE?
IT'S A SPECIAL PLACE. A KIND OF HEAVENLY CROSSROADS. IT'S CALLED THE DEAD ZONE.
I DON'T MUCH LIKE THE SOUND OF THAT.
DON'T WORRY. IT'LL BE ALL RIGHT. I PROMISE.
"THE NEXT THING I KNOW, I'M ENVELOPED BY THE MOST INCREDIBLE SENSATION, LIKE BEING WRAPPED IN ELECTRIC VELVET."
I FEEL DIFFERENT... WHAT DID YOU DO TO ME?
WALK FORWARD... TOWARD THE LIGHT. I'M SORRY, I CAN'T GO WITH YOU. BUT I'LL BE RIGHT HERE.

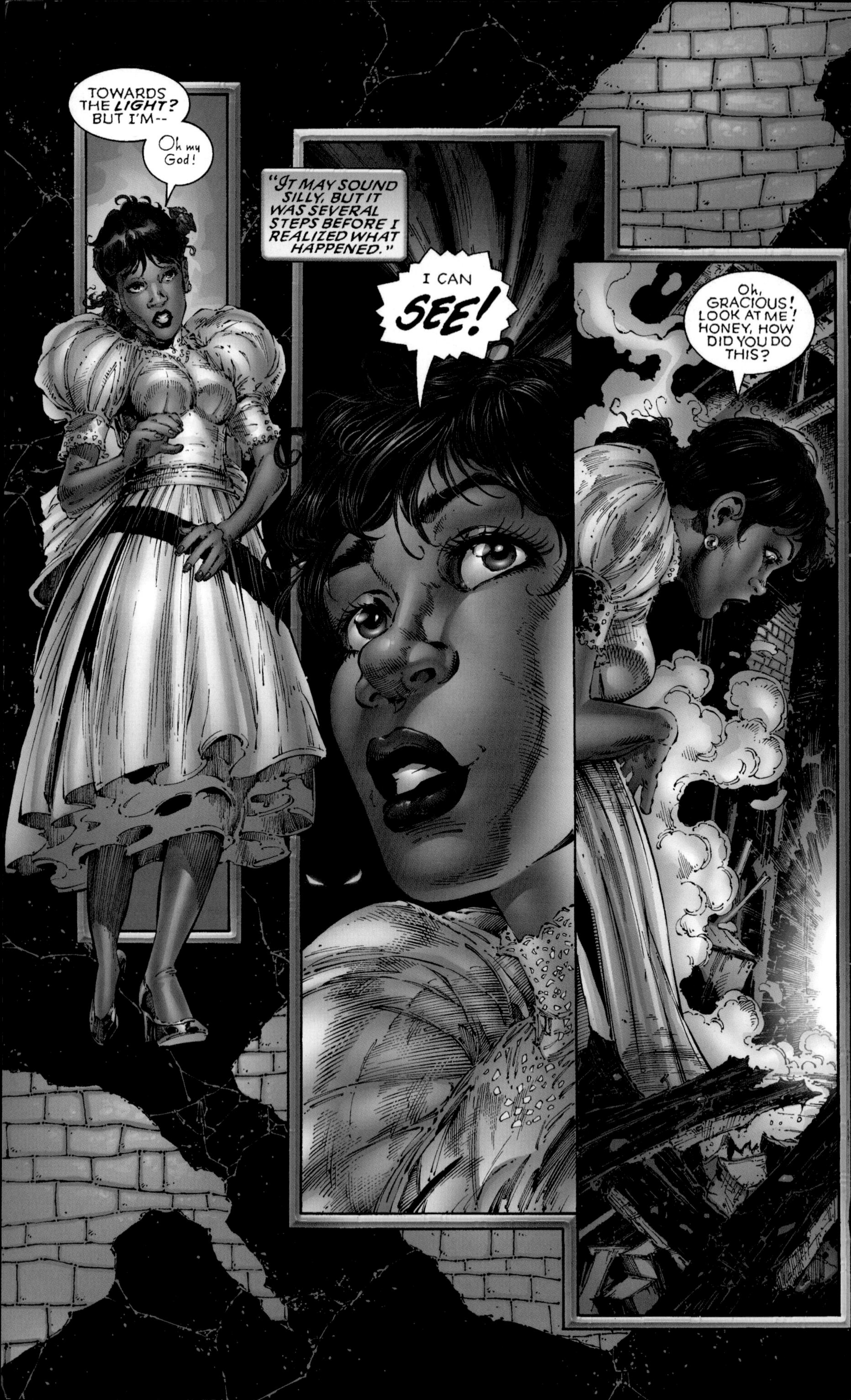
TOWARDS THE LIGHT? BUT I'M--
Oh my God!
"IT MAY SOUND SILLY, BUT IT WAS SEVERAL STEPS BEFORE I REALIZED WHAT HAPPENED."
I CAN SEE!
Oh, GRACIOUS! LOOK AT ME! HONEY, HOW DID YOU DO THIS?

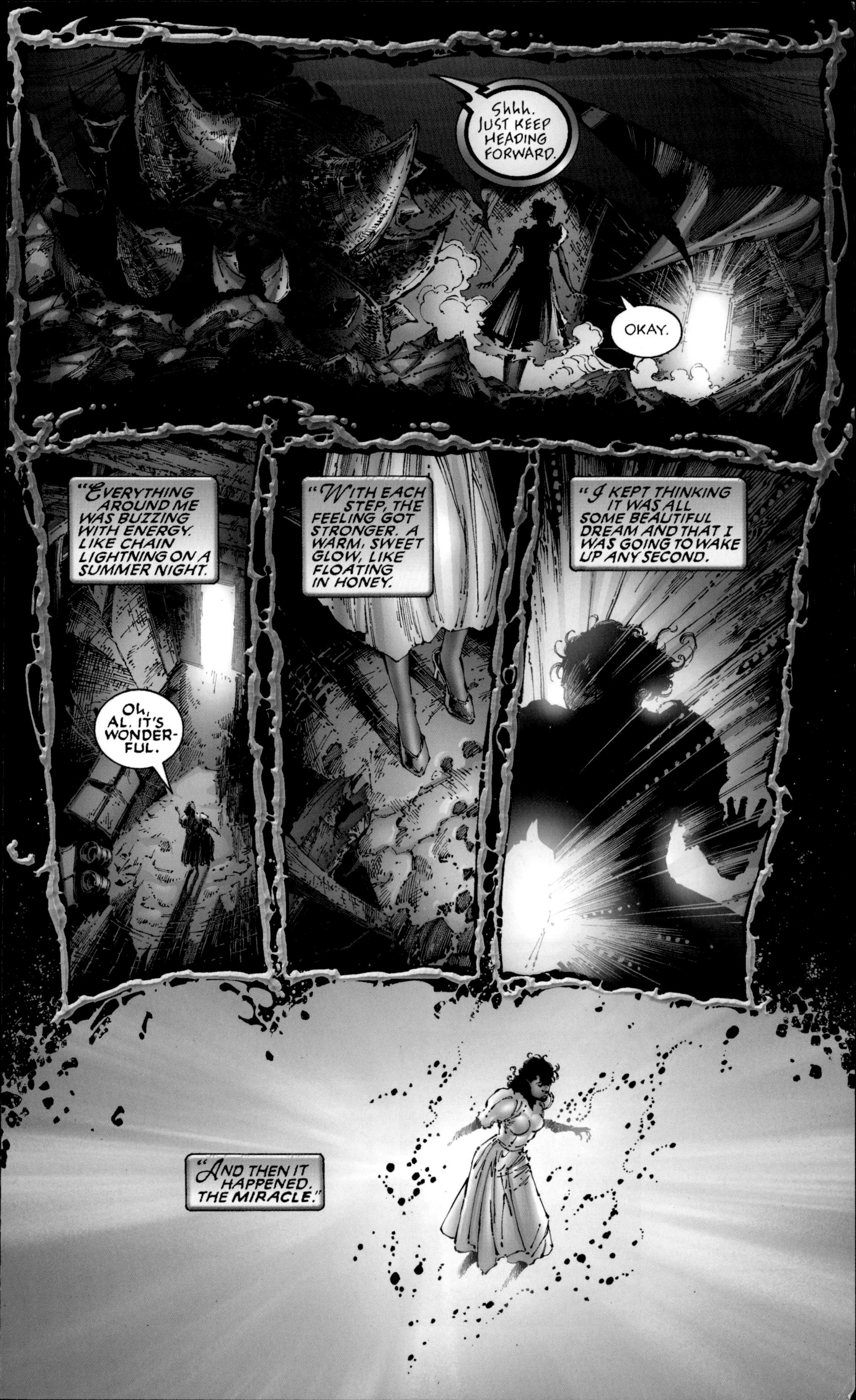

Shhh. JUST KEEP HEADING FORWARD.
OKAY.
"EVERYTHING AROUND ME WAS BUZZING WITH ENERGY. LIKE CHAIN LIGHTNING ON A SUMMER NIGHT.
Oh, AL, IT'S WONDERFUL.
"WITH EACH STEP, THE FEELING GOT STRONGER. A WARM, SWEET GLOW, LIKE FLOATING IN HONEY.
"I KEPT THINKING IT WAS ALL SOME BEAUTIFUL DREAM AND THAT I WAS GOING TO WAKE UP ANY SECOND.
"AND THEN IT HAPPENED. THE MIRACLE."

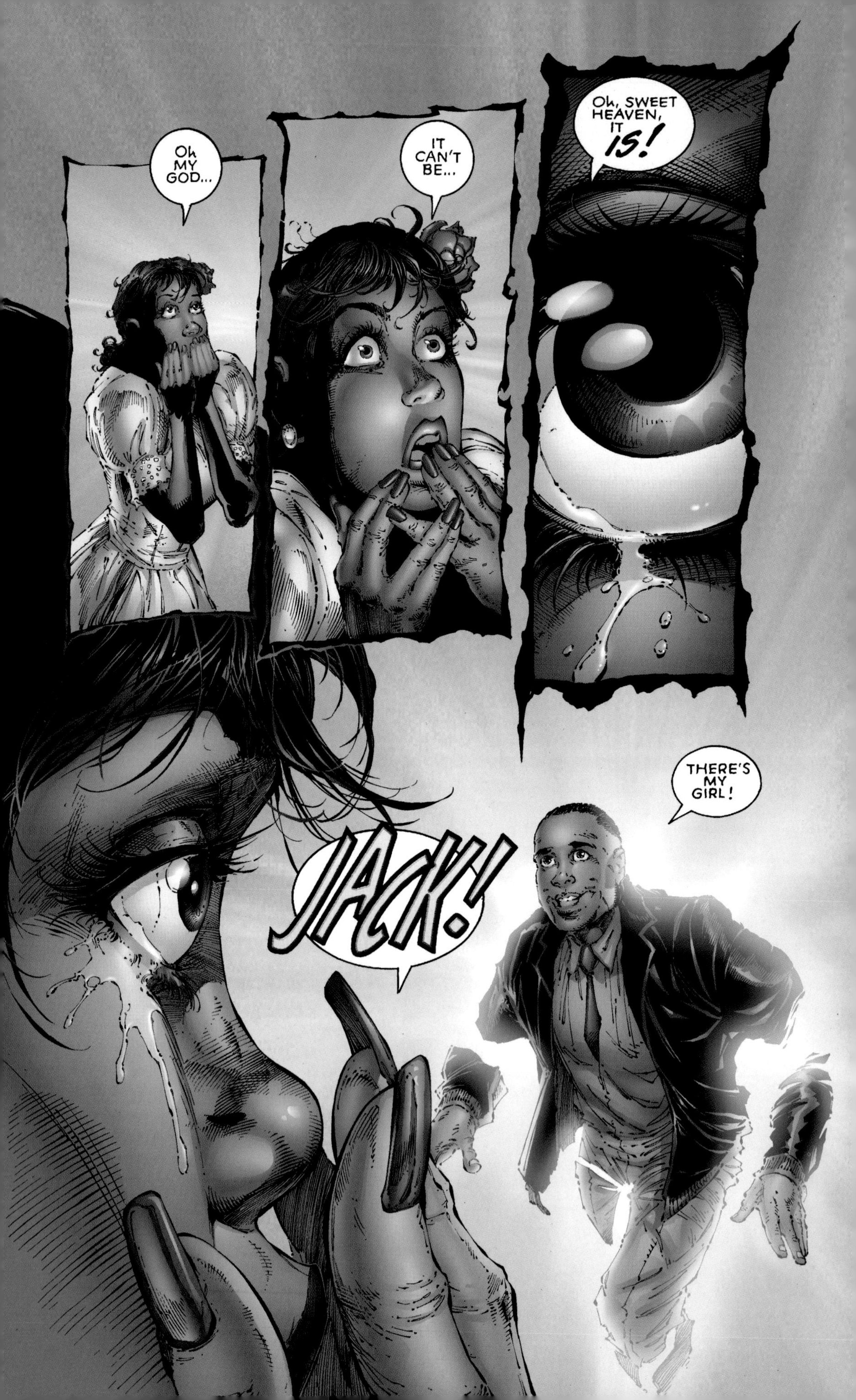
Oh MY GOD...
IT CAN'T BE...
Oh, SWEET HEAVEN, IT IS!
JACK!
THERE'S MY GIRL!

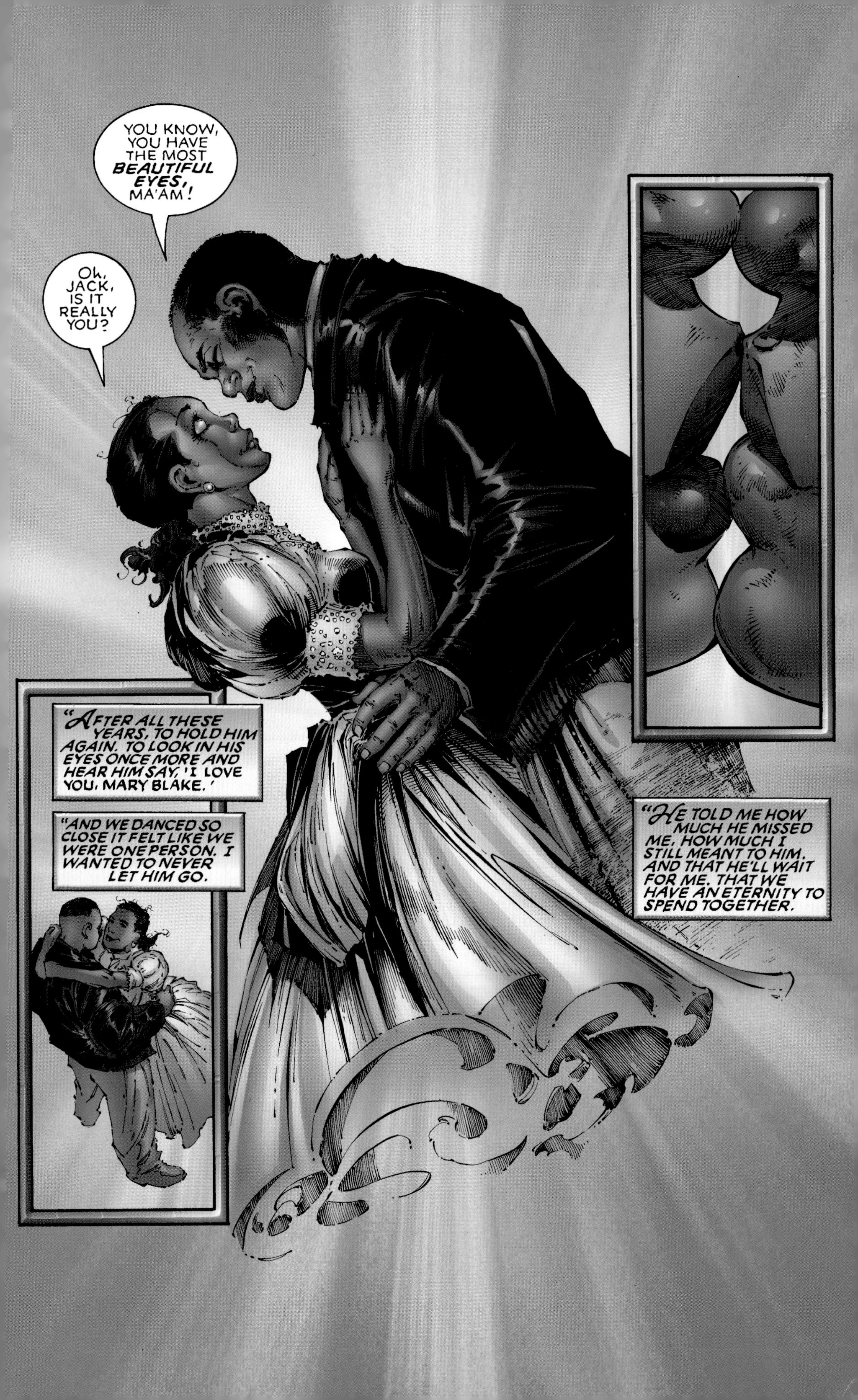

YOU KNOW, YOU HAVE THE MOST BEAUTIFUL EYES, MA'AM!
Oh, JACK, IS IT REALLY YOU?
"AFTER ALL THESE YEARS, TO HOLD HIM AGAIN. TO LOOK IN HIS EYES ONCE MORE AND HEAR HIM SAY, 'I LOVE YOU, MARY BLAKE.'
"AND WE DANCED SO CLOSE IT FELT LIKE WE WERE ONE PERSON. I WANTED TO NEVER LET HIM GO.
"HE TOLD ME HOW MUCH HE MISSED ME. HOW MUCH I STILL MEANT TO HIM. AND THAT HE'LL WAIT FOR ME. THAT WE HAVE AN ETERNITY TO SPEND TOGETHER.

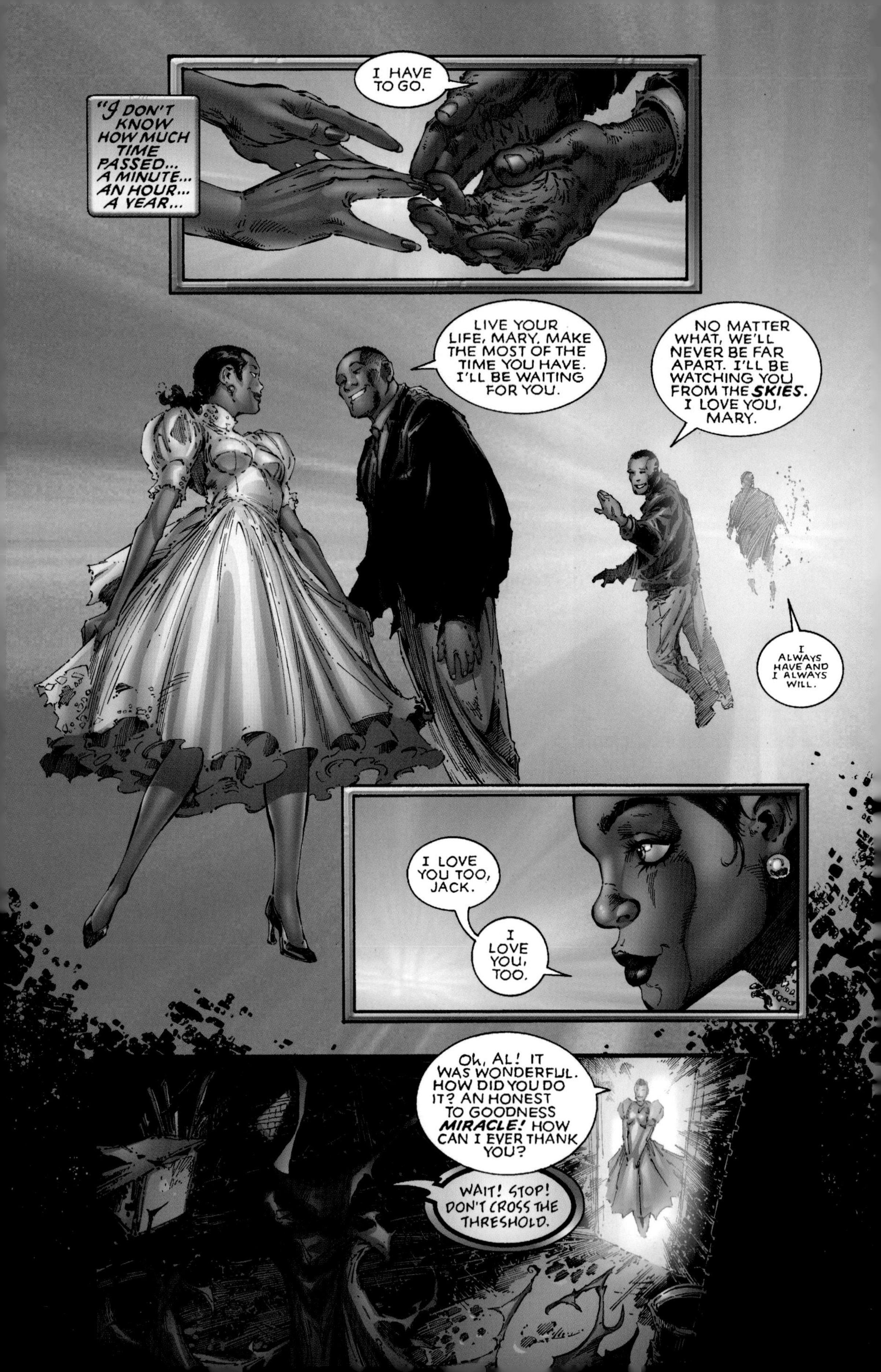
"I DON'T KNOW HOW MUCH TIME PASSED... A MINUTE... AN HOUR... A YEAR...
I HAVE TO GO.
LIVE YOUR LIFE, MARY. MAKE THE MOST OF THE TIME YOU HAVE. I'LL BE WAITING FOR YOU.
NO MATTER WHAT, WE'LL NEVER BE FAR APART. I'LL BE WATCHING YOU FROM THE SKIES. I LOVE YOU, MARY.
I ALWAYS HAVE AND I ALWAYS WILL.
I LOVE YOU TOO, JACK.
I LOVE YOU, TOO.
Oh, AL! IT WAS WONDERFUL. HOW DID YOU DO IT? AN HONEST TO GOODNESS MIRACLE! HOW CAN I EVER THANK YOU?
WAIT! STOP! DON'T CROSS THE THRESHOLD.

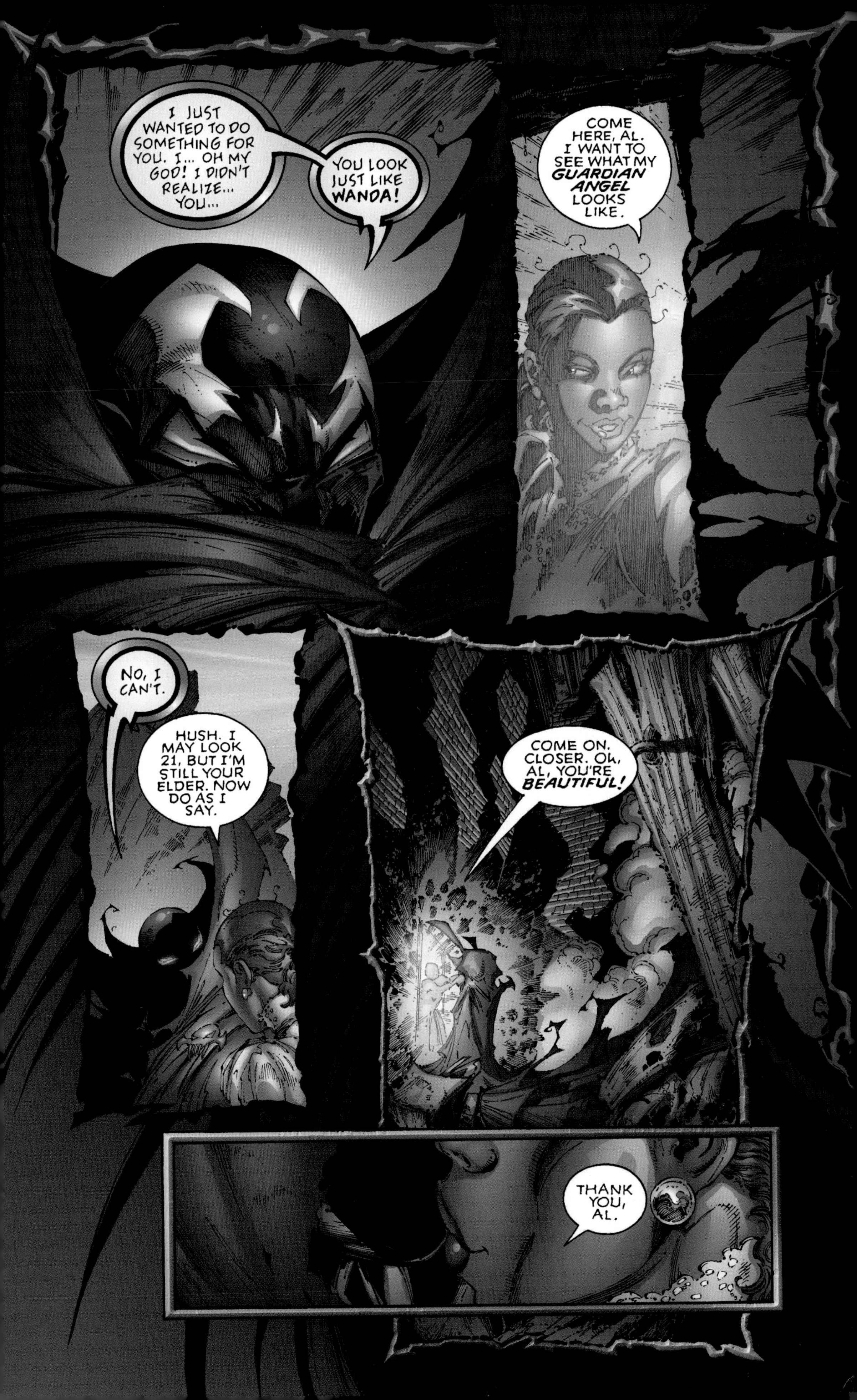
I JUST WANTED TO DO SOMETHING FOR YOU. I... OH MY GOD! I DIDN'T REALIZE... YOU...
YOU LOOK JUST LIKE WANDA!
COME HERE, AL. I WANT TO SEE WHAT MY GUARDIAN ANGEL LOOKS LIKE.
NO, I CAN'T.
HUSH. I MAY LOOK 21, BUT I'M STILL YOUR ELDER. NOW DO AS I SAY.
COME ON. CLOSER. Oh, AL, YOU'RE BEAUTIFUL!
THANK YOU, AL.

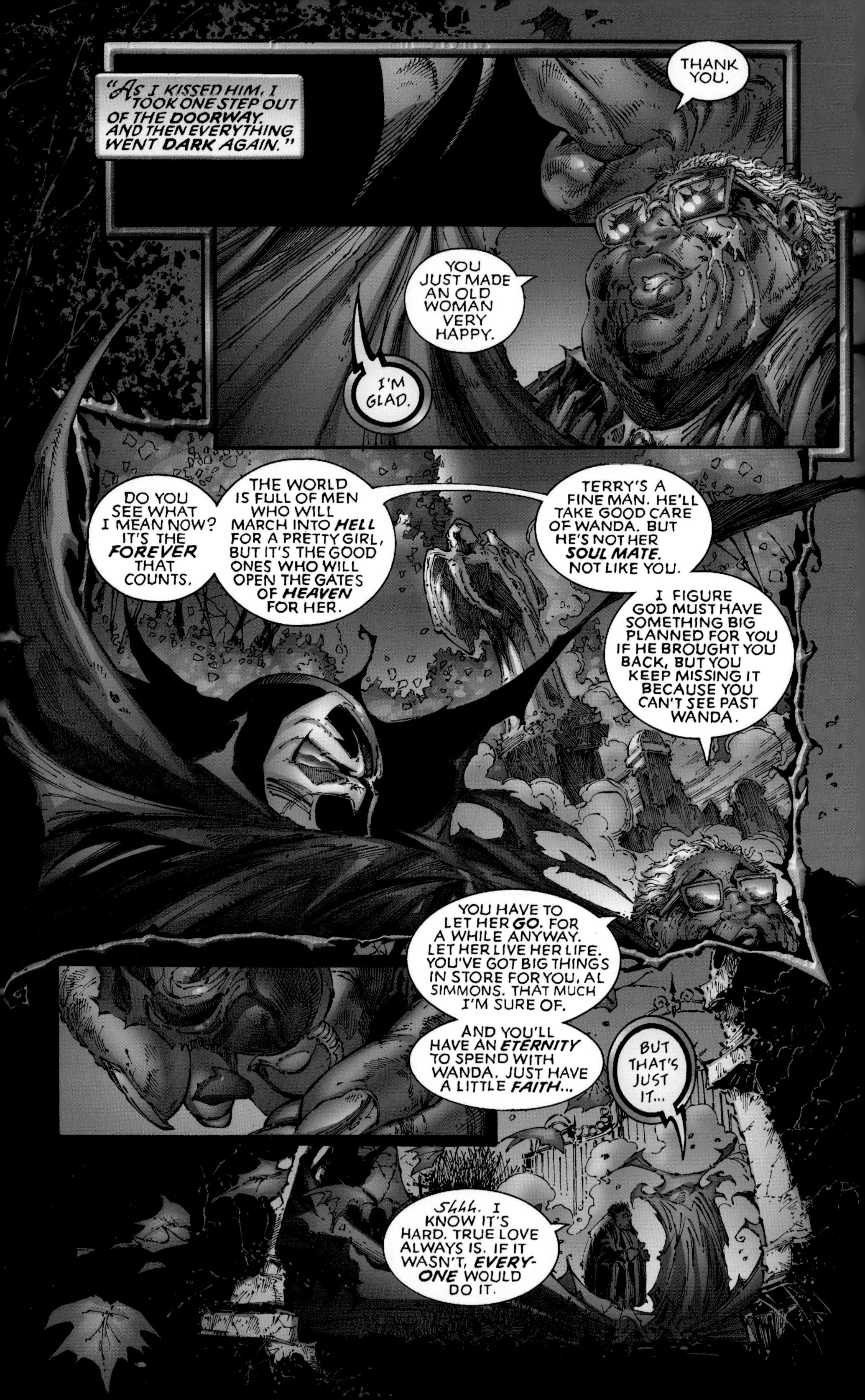
"AS I KISSED HIM, I TOOK ONE STEP OUT OF THE DOORWAY, AND THEN EVERYTHING WENT DARK AGAIN."
THANK YOU.
YOU JUST MADE AN OLD WOMAN VERY HAPPY.
I'M GLAD.
DO YOU SEE WHAT I MEAN NOW? IT'S THE FOREVER THAT COUNTS.
THE WORLD IS FULL OF MEN WHO WILL MARCH INTO HELL FOR A PRETTY GIRL, BUT IT'S THE GOOD ONES WHO WILL OPEN THE GATES OF HEAVEN FOR HER.
TERRY'S A FINE MAN. HE'LL TAKE GOOD CARE OF WANDA. BUT HE'S NOT HER SOUL MATE. NOT LIKE YOU.
I FIGURE GOD MUST HAVE SOMETHING BIG PLANNED FOR YOU IF HE BROUGHT YOU BACK, BUT YOU KEEP MISSING IT BECAUSE YOU CAN'T SEE PAST WANDA.
YOU HAVE TO LET HER GO. FOR A WHILE ANYWAY. LET HER LIVE HER LIFE. YOU'VE GOT BIG THINGS IN STORE FOR YOU, AL SIMMONS. THAT MUCH I'M SURE OF.
AND YOU'LL HAVE AN ETERNITY TO SPEND WITH WANDA. JUST HAVE A LITTLE FAITH...
BUT THAT'S JUST IT...
Shhh. I KNOW IT'S HARD. TRUE LOVE ALWAYS IS. IF IT WASN'T, EVERY-ONE WOULD DO IT.

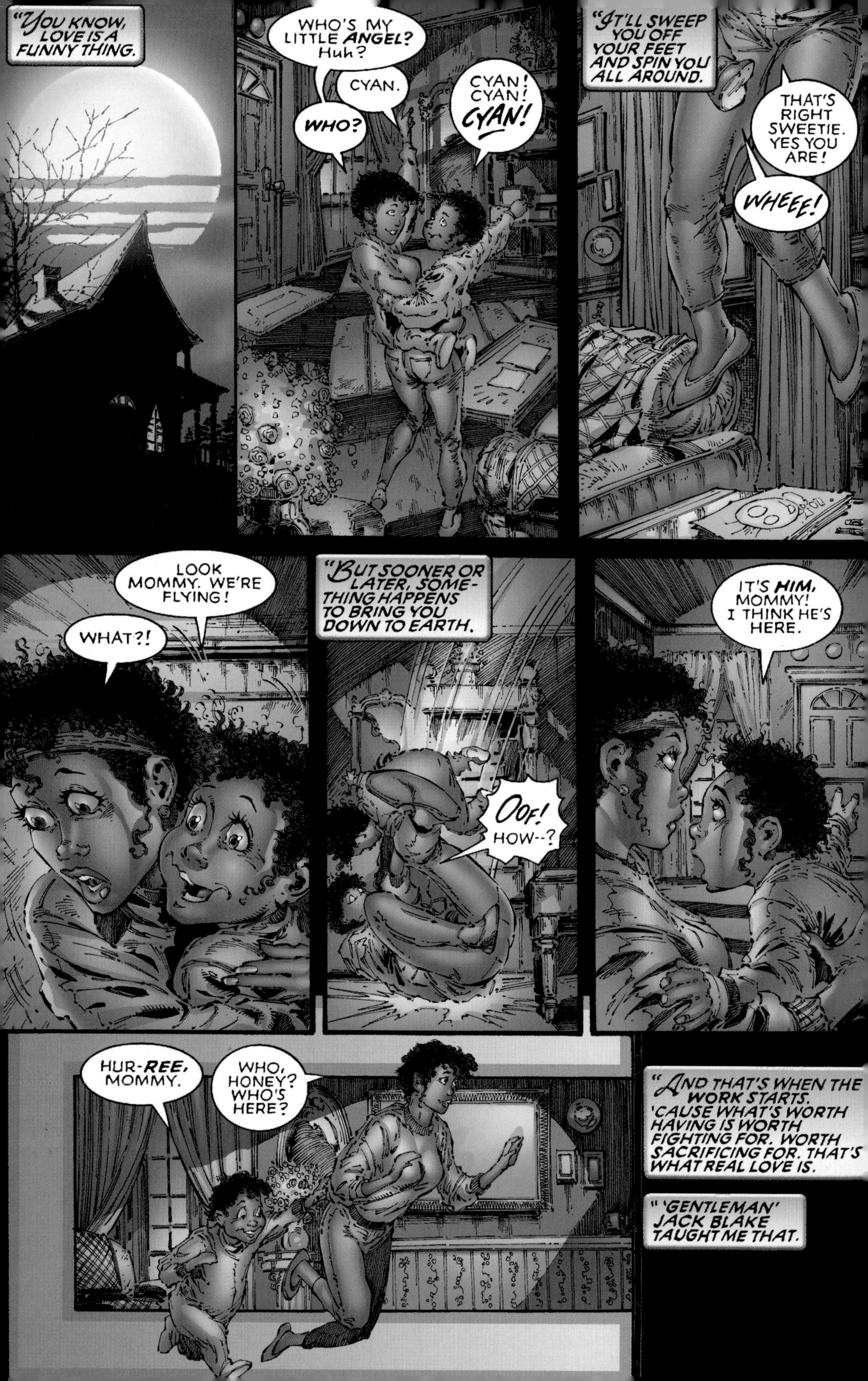
"YOU KNOW, LOVE IS A FUNNY THING.
WHO'S MY LITTLE ANGEL? Huh?
CYAN.
WHO?
CYAN! CYAN! CYAN!
"IT'LL SWEEP YOU OFF YOUR FEET AND SPIN YOU ALL AROUND.
THAT'S RIGHT SWEETIE. YES YOU ARE!
WHEEE!
LOOK MOMMY. WE'RE FLYING!
WHAT?!
"BUT SOONER OR LATER, SOMETHING HAPPENS TO BRING YOU DOWN TO EARTH.
OOF! HOW--?
IT'S HIM, MOMMY! I THINK HE'S HERE.
HUR-REE, MOMMY.
WHO, HONEY? WHO'S HERE?
"AND THAT'S WHEN THE WORK STARTS. 'CAUSE WHAT'S WORTH HAVING IS WORTH FIGHTING FOR. WORTH SACRIFICING FOR. THAT'S WHAT REAL LOVE IS.
" 'GENTLEMAN' JACK BLAKE TAUGHT ME THAT.

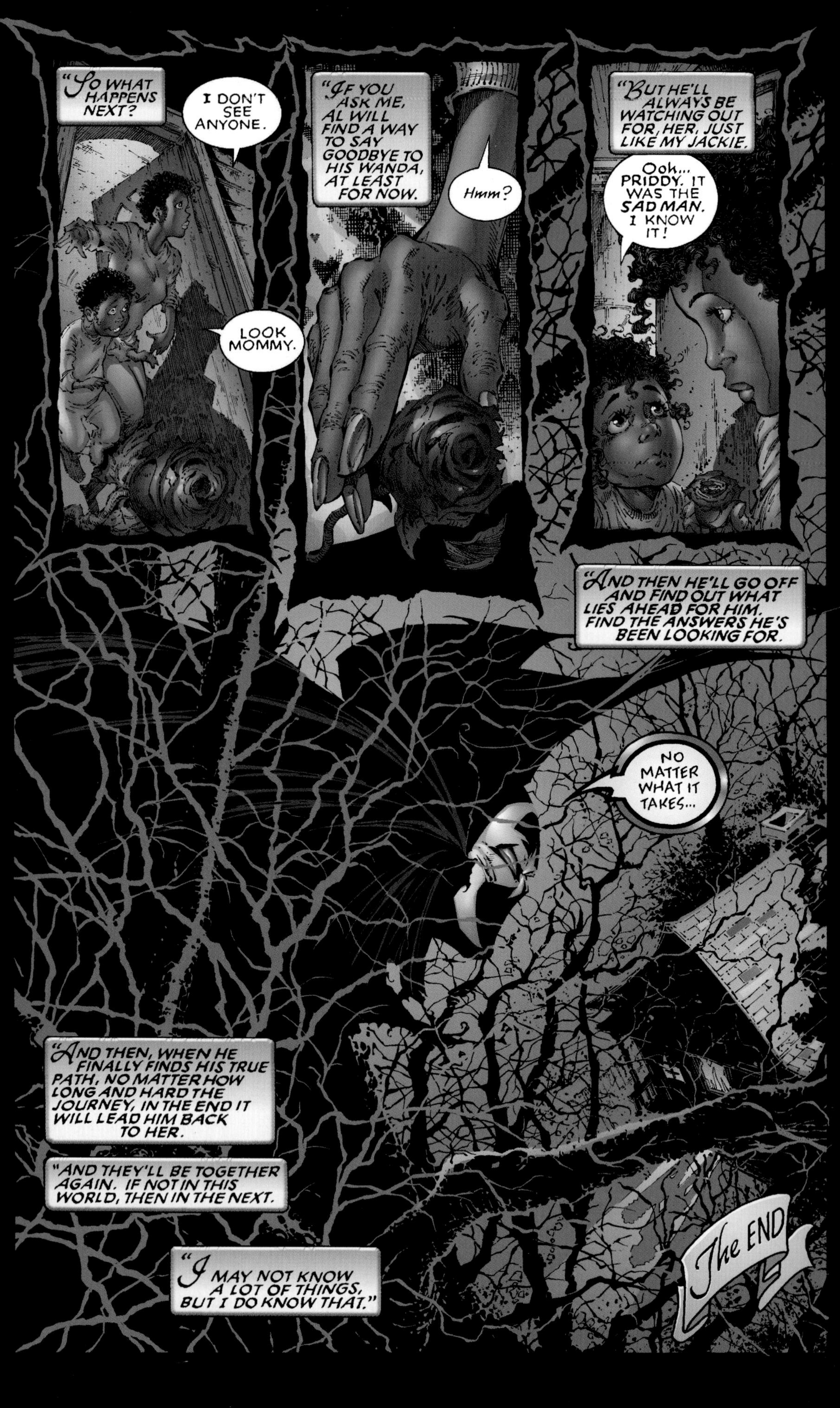
"SO WHAT HAPPENS NEXT?
I DON'T SEE ANYONE.
LOOK MOMMY.
"IF YOU ASK ME, AL WILL FIND A WAY TO SAY GOODBYE TO HIS WANDA, AT LEAST FOR NOW.
Hmm?
"BUT HE'LL ALWAYS BE WATCHING OUT FOR, HER, JUST LIKE MY JACKIE.
Ooh... PRIDDY. IT WAS THE SAD MAN. I KNOW IT!
"AND THEN HE'LL GO OFF AND FIND OUT WHAT LIES AHEAD FOR HIM. FIND THE ANSWERS HE'S BEEN LOOKING FOR.
NO MATTER WHAT IT TAKES...
"AND THEN, WHEN HE FINALLY FINDS HIS TRUE PATH, NO MATTER HOW LONG AND HARD THE JOURNEY, IN THE END IT WILL LEAD HIM BACK TO HER.
"AND THEY'LL BE TOGETHER AGAIN. IF NOT IN THIS WORLD, THEN IN THE NEXT.
"I MAY NOT KNOW A LOT OF THINGS, BUT I DO KNOW THAT."
The END

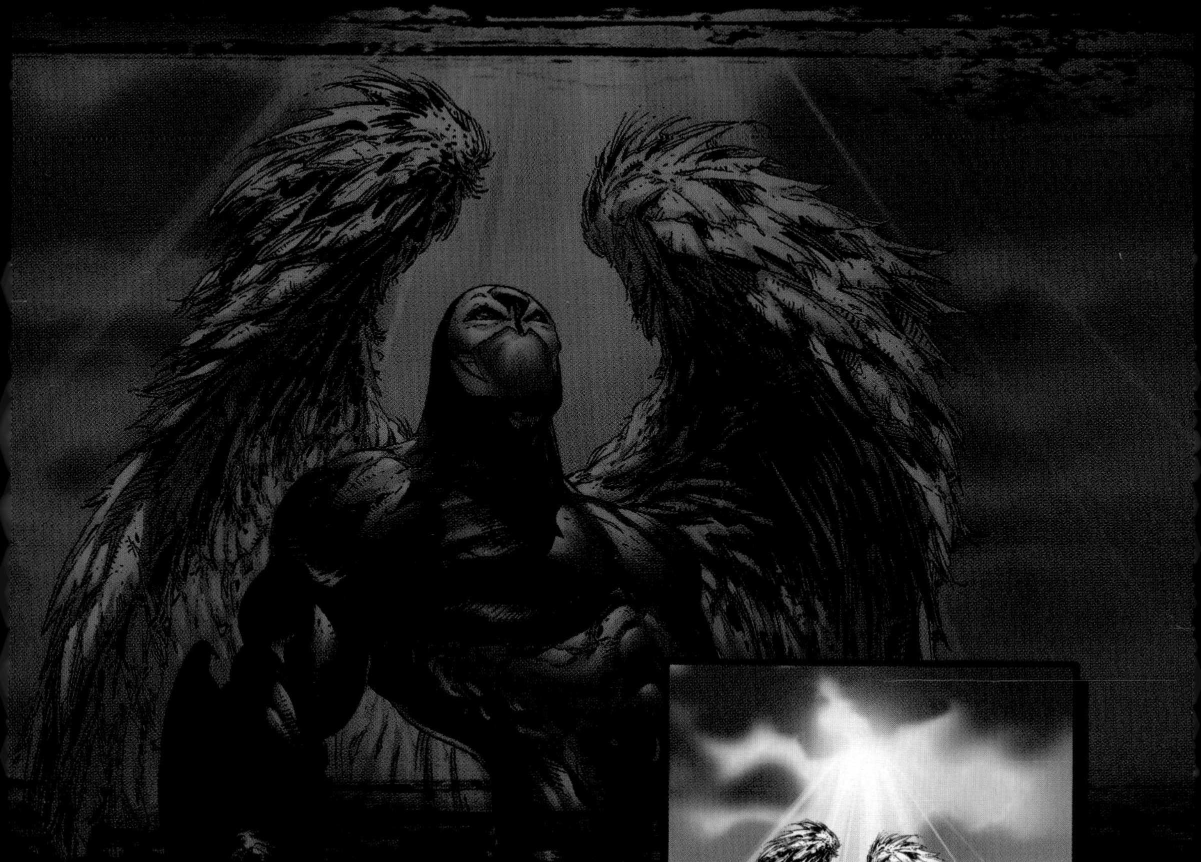

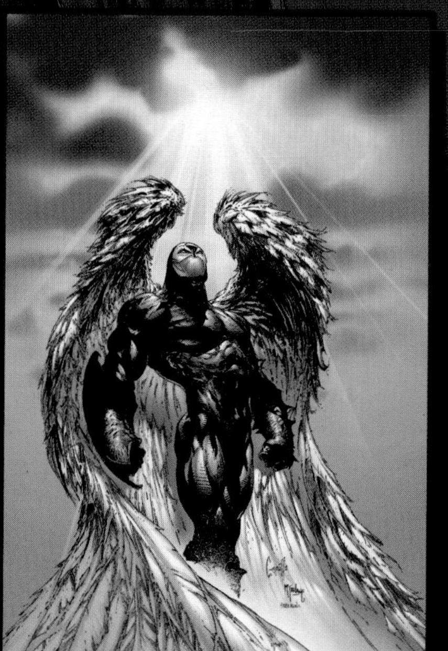

ISSUE SEVENTY-SEVEN

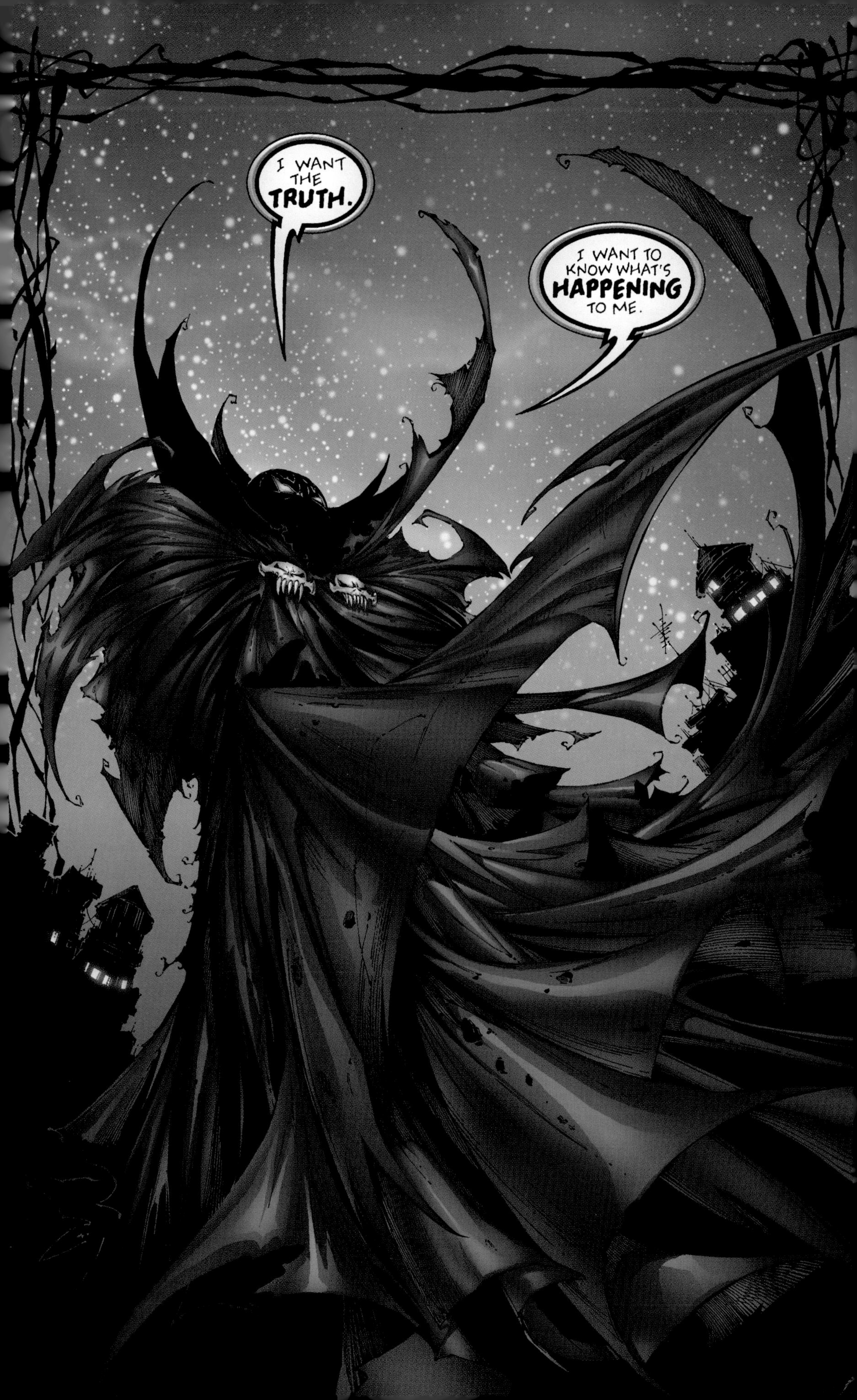
I WANT THE TRUTH.
I WANT TO KNOW WHAT'S HAPPENING TO ME.

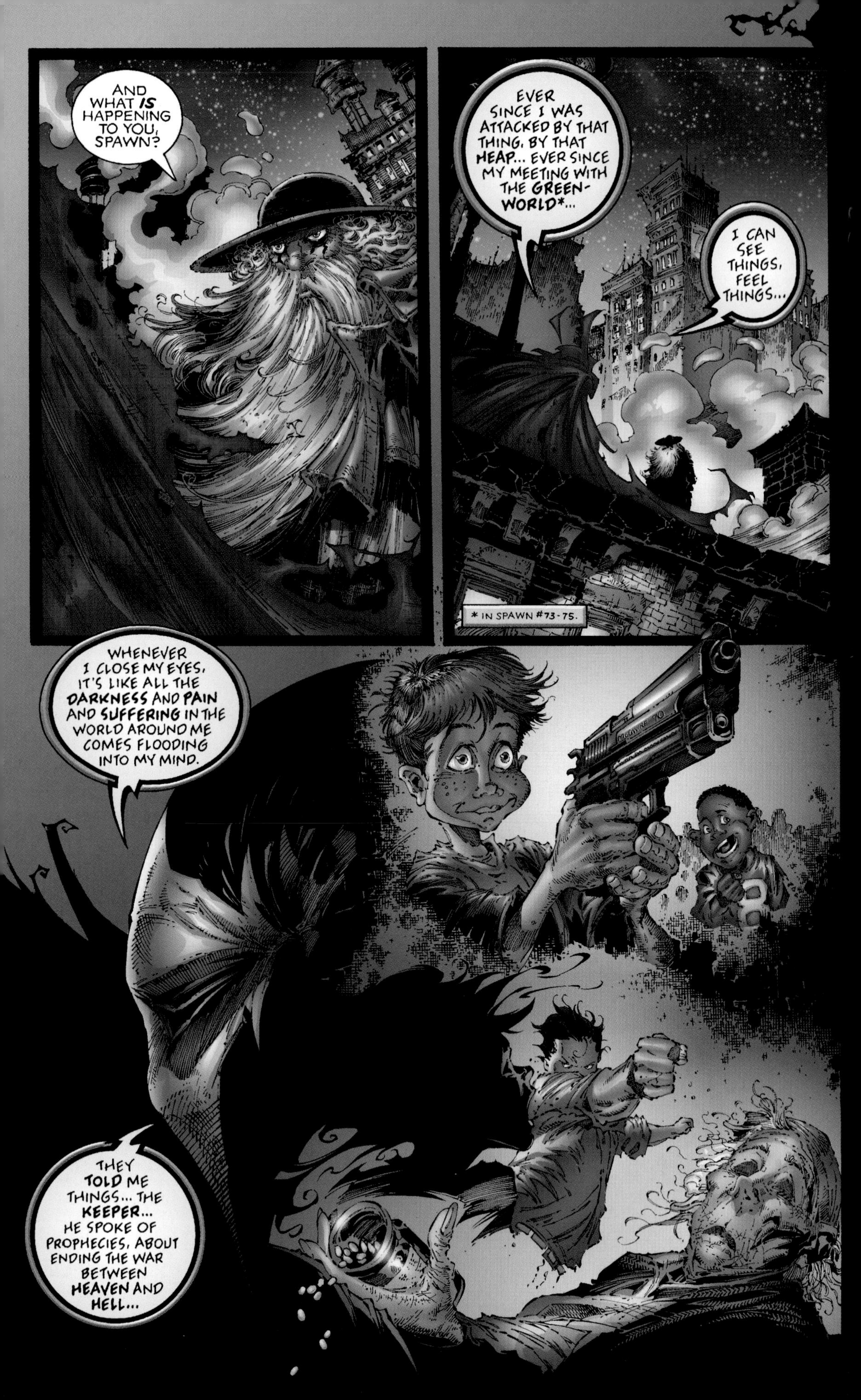
AND WHAT IS HAPPENING TO YOU, SPAWN?
EVER SINCE I WAS ATTACKED BY THAT THING, BY THAT HEAP... EVER SINCE MY MEETING WITH THE GREEN-WORLD*...
I CAN SEE THINGS, FEEL THINGS...
* IN SPAWN #73-75.
WHENEVER I CLOSE MY EYES, IT'S LIKE ALL THE DARKNESS AND PAIN AND SUFFERING IN THE WORLD AROUND ME COMES FLOODING INTO MY MIND.
THEY TOLD ME THINGS... THE KEEPER... HE SPOKE OF PROPHECIES, ABOUT ENDING THE WAR BETWEEN HEAVEN AND HELL...

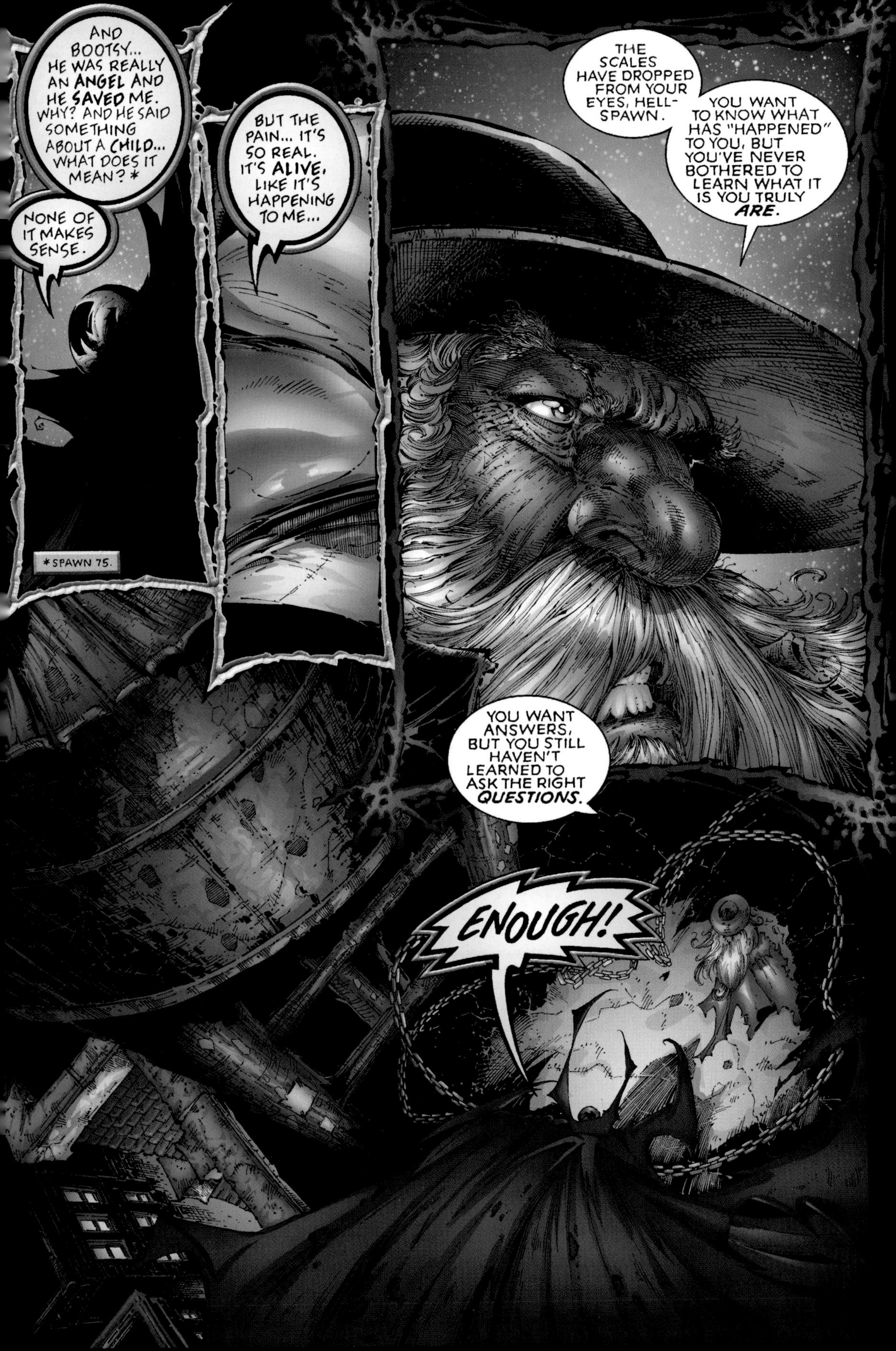
AND BOOTSY... HE WAS REALLY AN ANGEL AND HE SAVED ME. WHY? AND HE SAID SOMETHING ABOUT A CHILD... WHAT DOES IT MEAN? *
NONE OF IT MAKES SENSE.
* SPAWN 75.
BUT THE PAIN... IT'S SO REAL. IT'S ALIVE, LIKE IT'S HAPPENING TO ME...
THE SCALES HAVE DROPPED FROM YOUR EYES, HELL-SPAWN.
YOU WANT TO KNOW WHAT HAS "HAPPENED" TO YOU, BUT YOU'VE NEVER BOTHERED TO LEARN WHAT IT IS YOU TRULY ARE.
YOU WANT ANSWERS, BUT YOU STILL HAVEN'T LEARNED TO ASK THE RIGHT QUESTIONS.
ENOUGH!

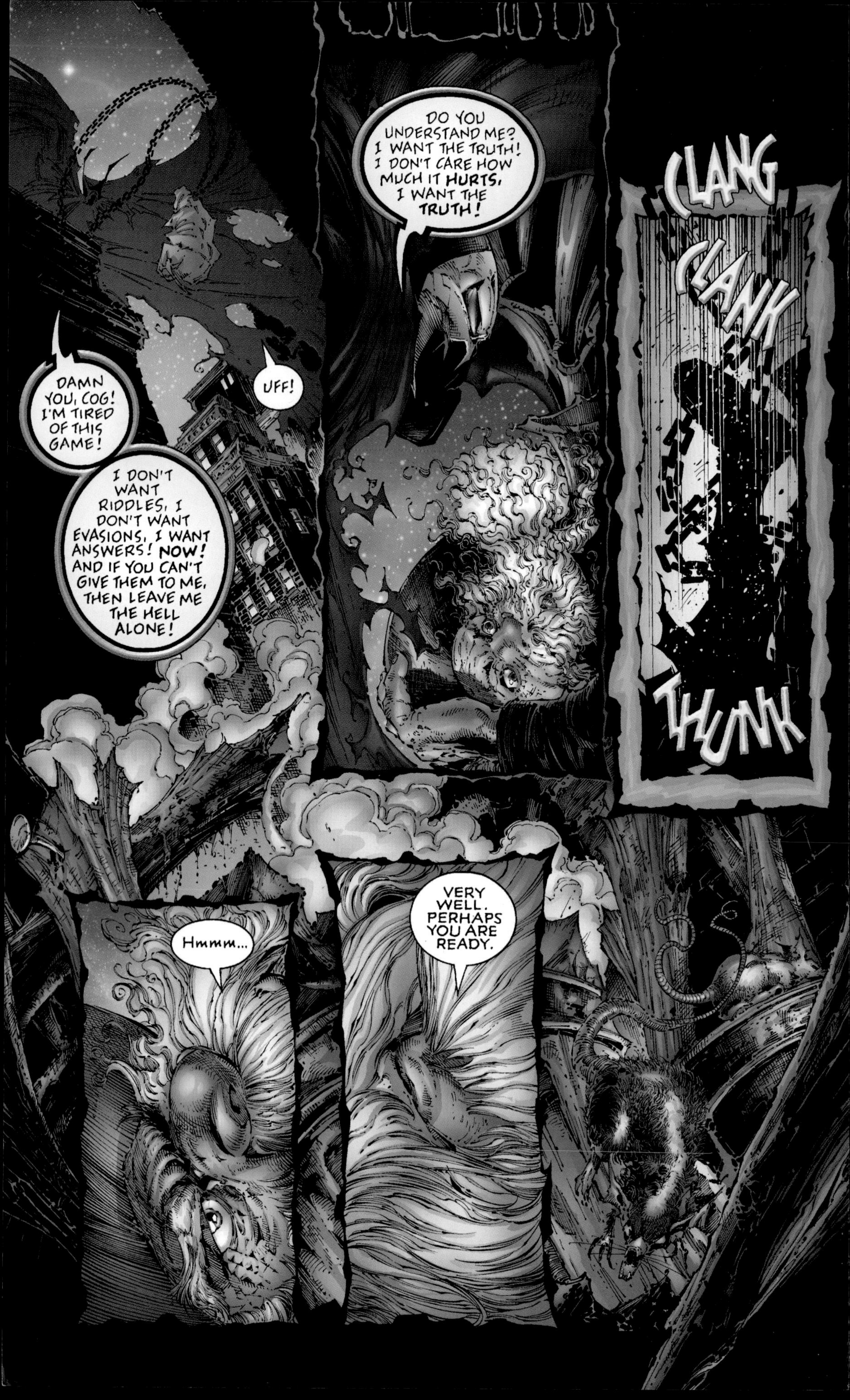
DAMN YOU, COG! I'M TIRED OF THIS GAME!
UFF!
I DON'T WANT RIDDLES, I DON'T WANT EVASIONS, I WANT ANSWERS! NOW! AND IF YOU CAN'T GIVE THEM TO ME, THEN LEAVE ME THE HELL ALONE!
DO YOU UNDERSTAND ME? I WANT THE TRUTH! I DON'T CARE HOW MUCH IT HURTS, I WANT THE TRUTH!
CLANG
CLANK
THUNK
Hmmm...
VERY WELL. PERHAPS YOU ARE READY.

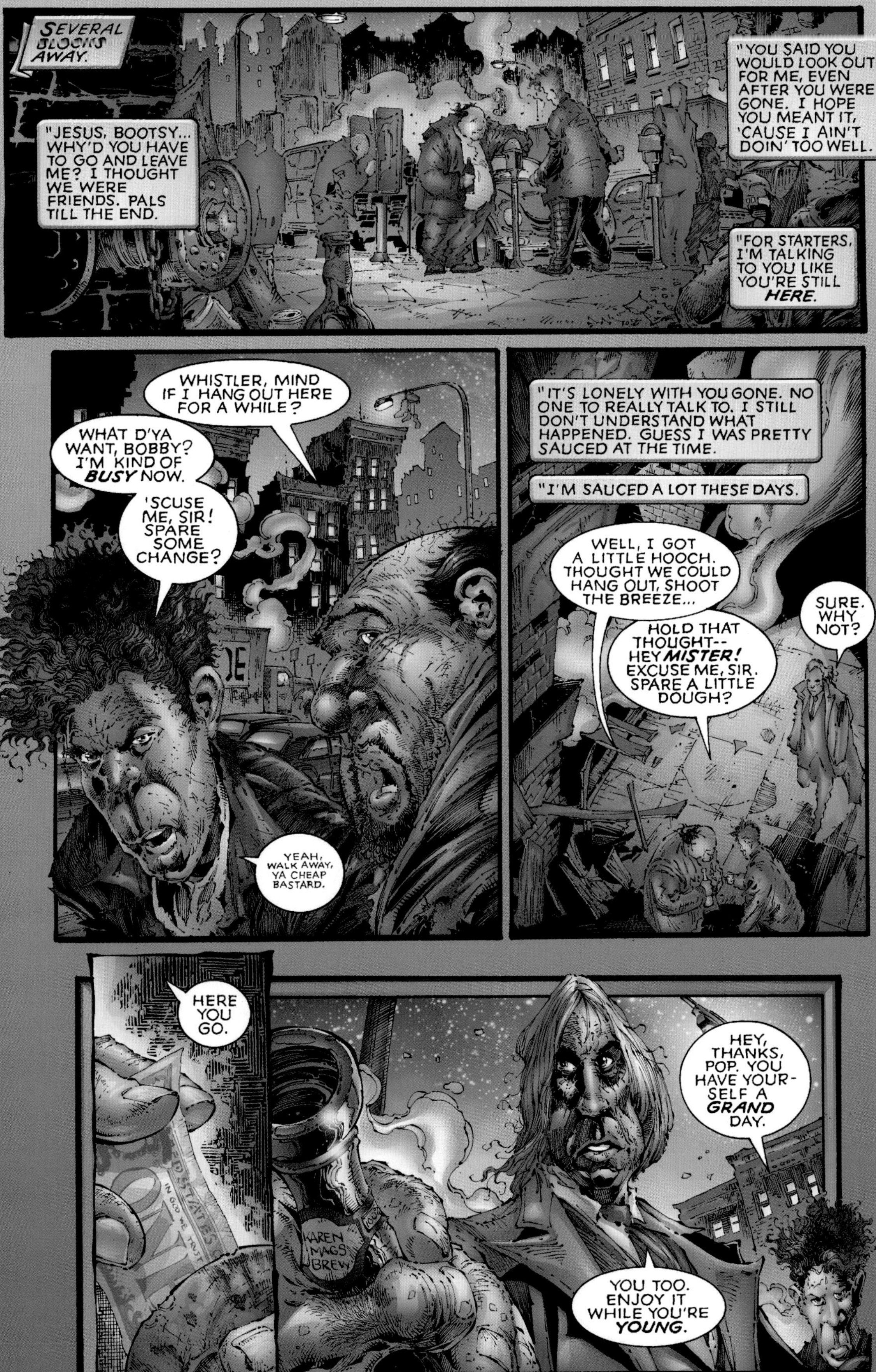
SEVERAL BLOCKS AWAY.
"JESUS, BOOTSY... WHY'D YOU HAVE TO GO AND LEAVE ME? I THOUGHT WE WERE FRIENDS. PALS TILL THE END.
"YOU SAID YOU WOULD LOOK OUT FOR ME, EVEN AFTER YOU WERE GONE. I HOPE YOU MEANT IT, 'CAUSE I AIN'T DOIN' TOO WELL.
"FOR STARTERS, I'M TALKING TO YOU LIKE YOU'RE STILL HERE.
WHISTLER, MIND IF I HANG OUT HERE FOR A WHILE?
WHAT D'YA WANT, BOBBY? I'M KIND OF BUSY NOW.
'SCUSE ME, SIR! SPARE SOME CHANGE?
YEAH, WALK AWAY, YA CHEAP BASTARD.
"IT'S LONELY WITH YOU GONE. NO ONE TO REALLY TALK TO. I STILL DON'T UNDERSTAND WHAT HAPPENED. GUESS I WAS PRETTY SAUCED AT THE TIME.
"I'M SAUCED A LOT THESE DAYS.
WELL, I GOT A LITTLE HOOCH. THOUGHT WE COULD HANG OUT, SHOOT THE BREEZE...
HOLD THAT THOUGHT-- HEY MISTER! EXCUSE ME, SIR. SPARE A LITTLE DOUGH?
SURE. WHY NOT?
HERE YOU GO.
HEY, THANKS, POP. YOU HAVE YOURSELF A GRAND DAY.
YOU TOO. ENJOY IT WHILE YOU'RE YOUNG.
KAREN MAGS BREW

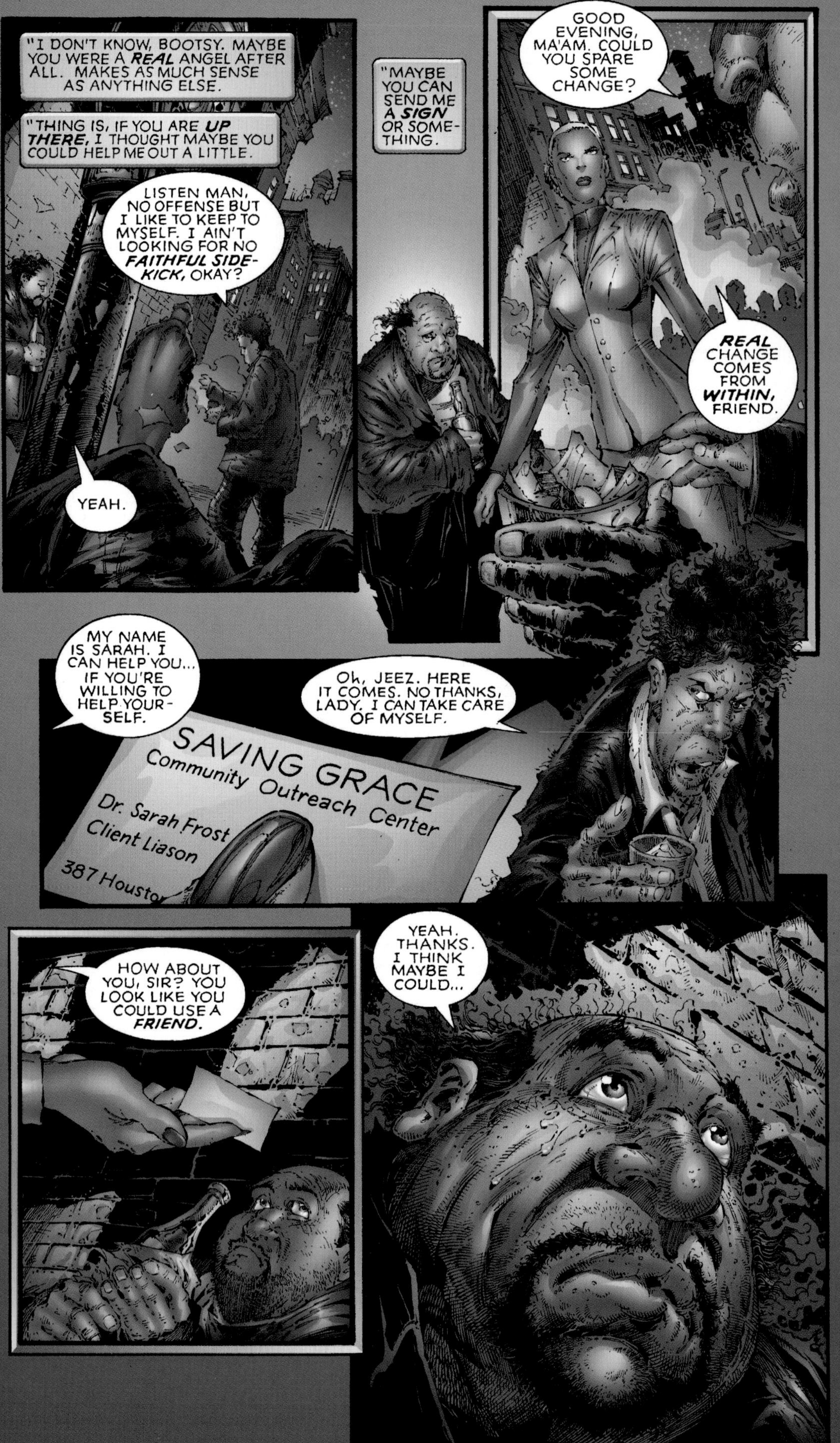
"I DON'T KNOW, BOOTSY. MAYBE YOU WERE A REAL ANGEL AFTER ALL. MAKES AS MUCH SENSE AS ANYTHING ELSE.
"THING IS, IF YOU ARE UP THERE, I THOUGHT MAYBE YOU COULD HELP ME OUT A LITTLE.
LISTEN MAN, NO OFFENSE BUT I LIKE TO KEEP TO MYSELF. I AIN'T LOOKING FOR NO FAITHFUL SIDE-KICK, OKAY?
YEAH.
"MAYBE YOU CAN SEND ME A SIGN OR SOME-THING.
GOOD EVENING, MA'AM. COULD YOU SPARE SOME CHANGE?
REAL CHANGE COMES FROM WITHIN, FRIEND.
MY NAME IS SARAH. I CAN HELP YOU... IF YOU'RE WILLING TO HELP YOUR-SELF.
OH, JEEZ. HERE IT COMES. NO THANKS, LADY. I CAN TAKE CARE OF MYSELF.
SAVING GRACE
Community Outreach Center
Dr. Sarah Frost
Client Liason
387 Housto
HOW ABOUT YOU, SIR? YOU LOOK LIKE YOU COULD USE A FRIEND.
YEAH. THANKS. I THINK MAYBE I COULD...

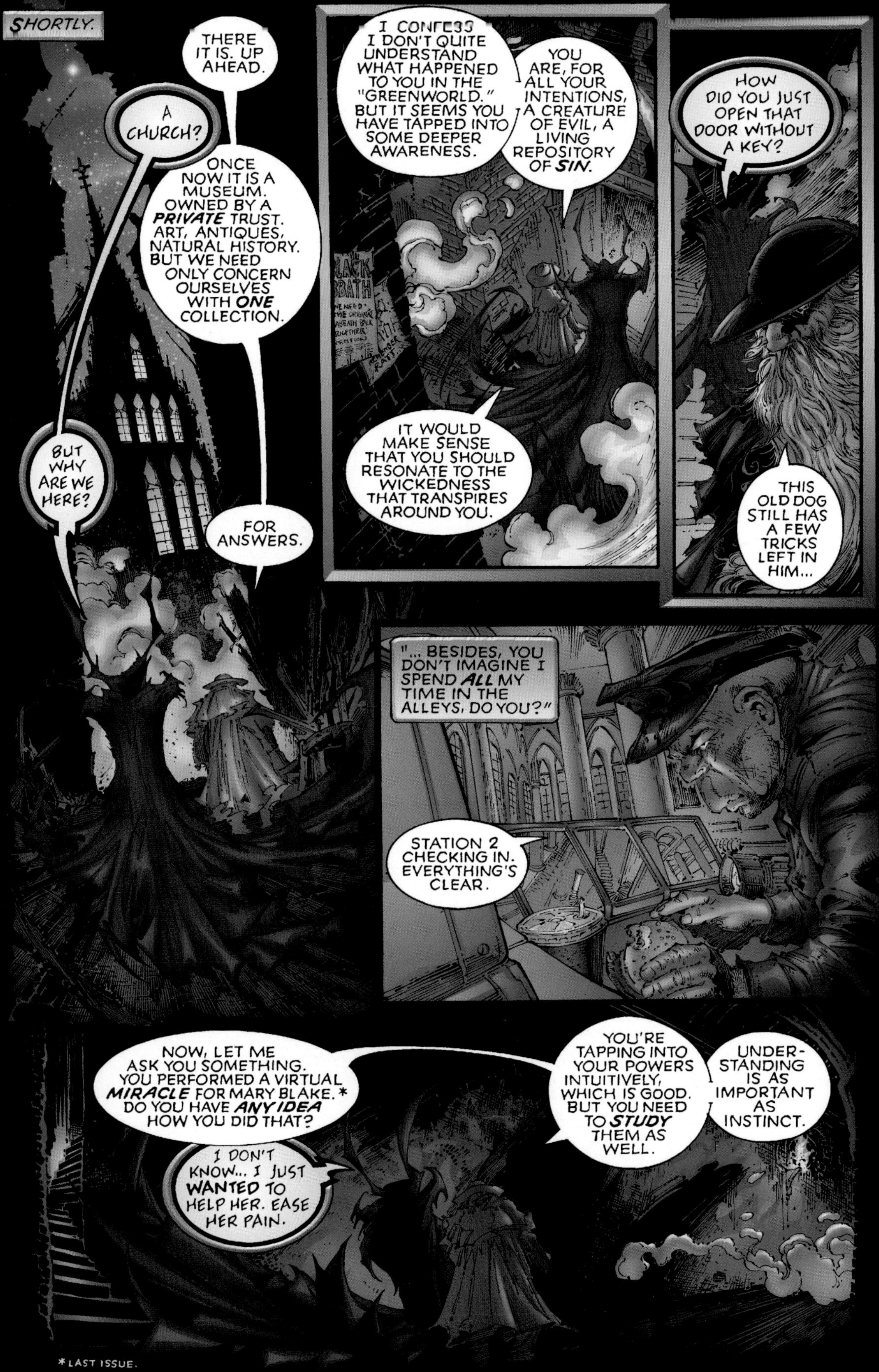
SHORTLY.
THERE IT IS. UP AHEAD.
A CHURCH?
ONCE. NOW IT IS A MUSEUM. OWNED BY A PRIVATE TRUST. ART, ANTIQUES, NATURAL HISTORY. BUT WE NEED ONLY CONCERN OURSELVES WITH ONE COLLECTION.
BUT WHY ARE WE HERE?
FOR ANSWERS.
I CONFESS I DON'T QUITE UNDERSTAND WHAT HAPPENED TO YOU IN THE "GREENWORLD." BUT IT SEEMS YOU HAVE TAPPED INTO SOME DEEPER AWARENESS.
YOU ARE, FOR ALL YOUR INTENTIONS, A CREATURE OF EVIL, A LIVING REPOSITORY OF SIN.
IT WOULD MAKE SENSE THAT YOU SHOULD RESONATE TO THE WICKEDNESS THAT TRANSPIRES AROUND YOU.
HOW DID YOU JUST OPEN THAT DOOR WITHOUT A KEY?
THIS OLD DOG STILL HAS A FEW TRICKS LEFT IN HIM...
"... BESIDES, YOU DON'T IMAGINE I SPEND ALL MY TIME IN THE ALLEYS, DO YOU?"
STATION 2 CHECKING IN. EVERYTHING'S CLEAR.
NOW, LET ME ASK YOU SOMETHING. YOU PERFORMED A VIRTUAL MIRACLE FOR MARY BLAKE.* DO YOU HAVE ANY IDEA HOW YOU DID THAT?
I DON'T KNOW... I JUST WANTED TO HELP HER. EASE HER PAIN.
YOU'RE TAPPING INTO YOUR POWERS INTUITIVELY, WHICH IS GOOD. BUT YOU NEED TO STUDY THEM AS WELL.
UNDER-STANDING IS AS IMPORTANT AS INSTINCT.
*LAST ISSUE.

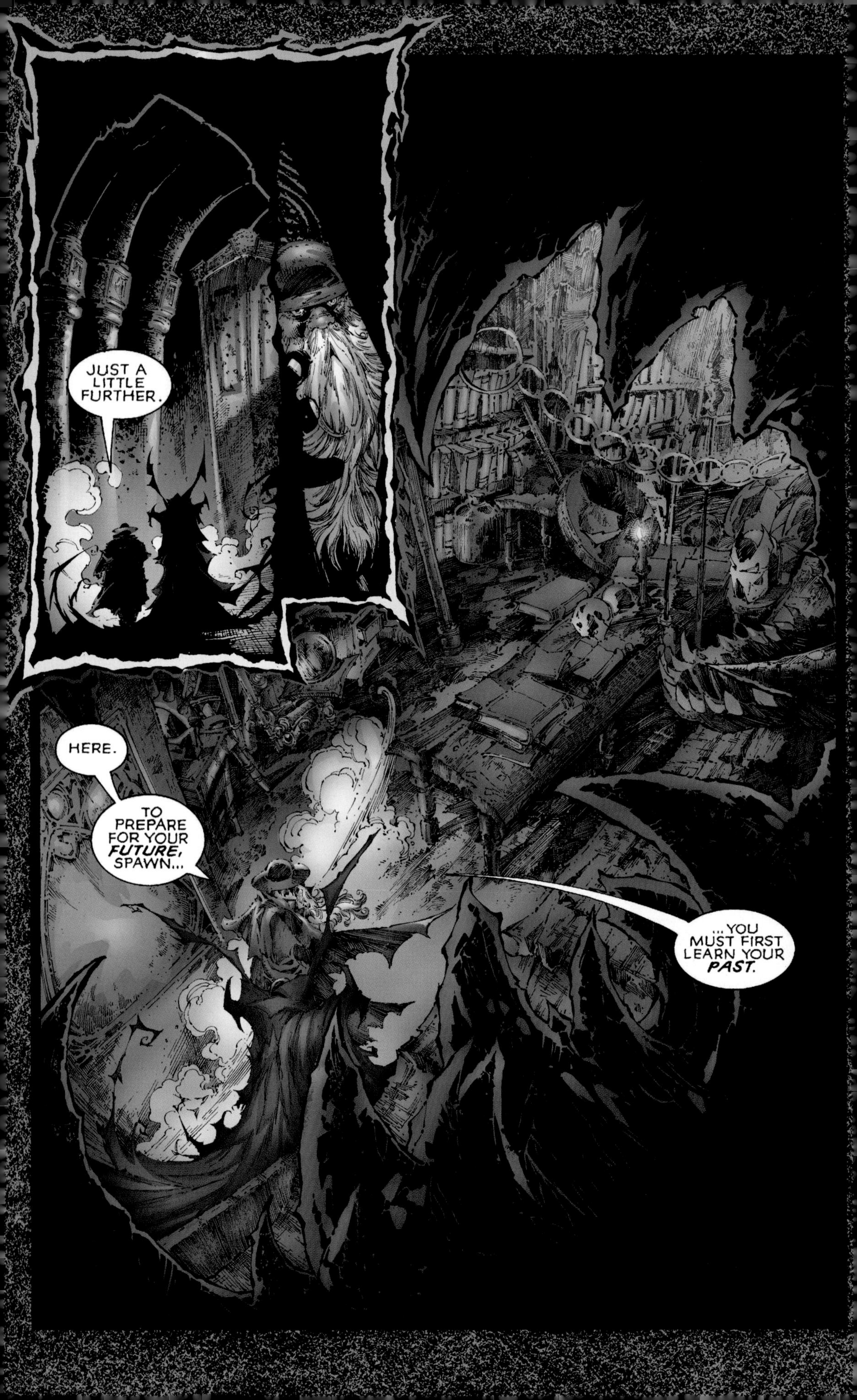
JUST A LITTLE FURTHER.
HERE.
TO PREPARE FOR YOUR *FUTURE,* SPAWN...
...YOU MUST FIRST LEARN YOUR *PAST.*

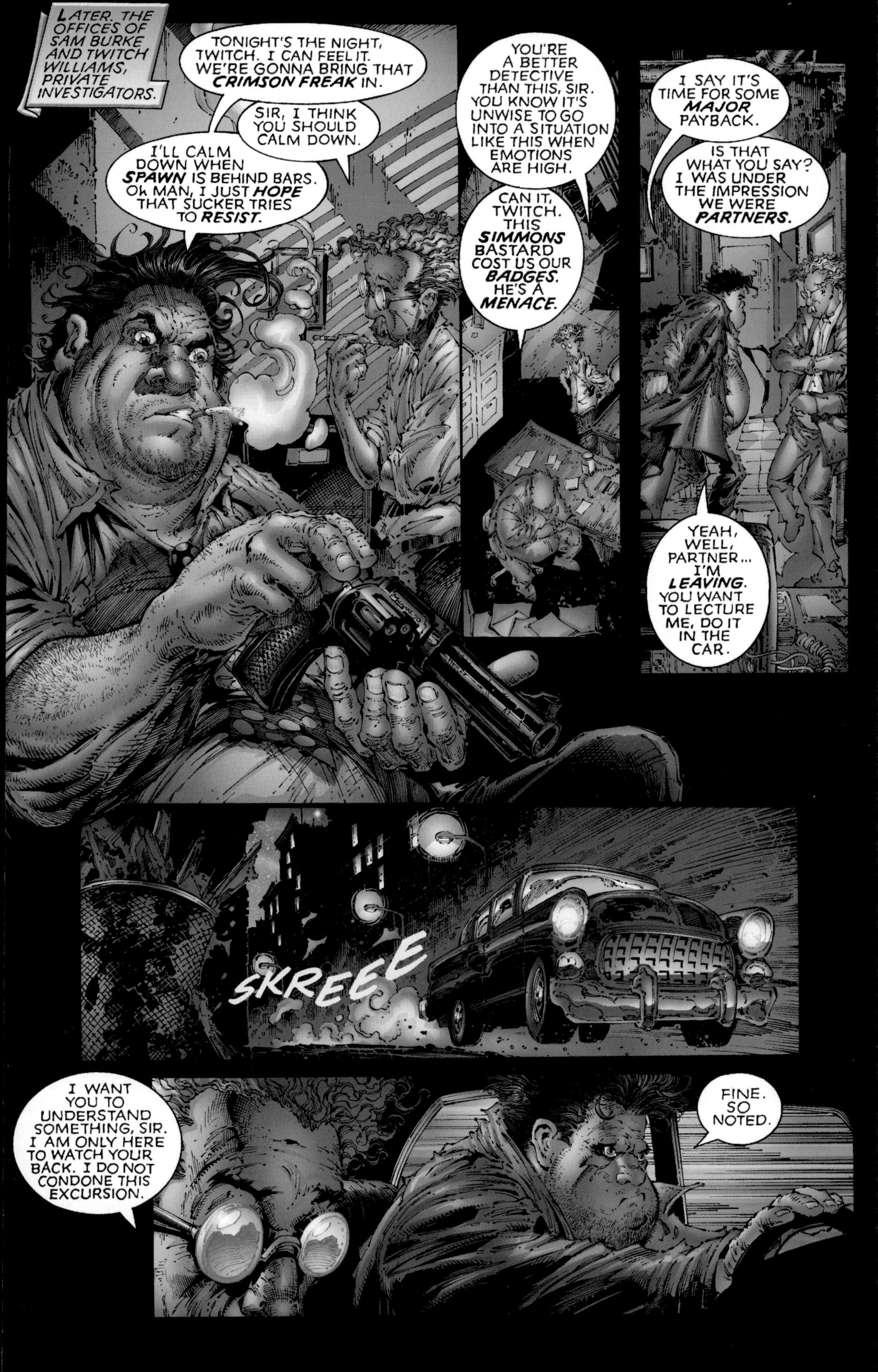
LATER. THE OFFICES OF SAM BURKE AND TWITCH WILLIAMS, PRIVATE INVESTIGATORS.
TONIGHT'S THE NIGHT, TWITCH. I CAN FEEL IT. WE'RE GONNA BRING THAT CRIMSON FREAK IN.
SIR, I THINK YOU SHOULD CALM DOWN.
I'LL CALM DOWN WHEN SPAWN IS BEHIND BARS. Oh MAN, I JUST HOPE THAT SUCKER TRIES TO RESIST.
YOU'RE A BETTER DETECTIVE THAN THIS, SIR. YOU KNOW IT'S UNWISE TO GO INTO A SITUATION LIKE THIS WHEN EMOTIONS ARE HIGH.
CAN IT, TWITCH. THIS SIMMONS BASTARD COST US OUR BADGES. HE'S A MENACE.
I SAY IT'S TIME FOR SOME MAJOR PAYBACK.
IS THAT WHAT YOU SAY? I WAS UNDER THE IMPRESSION WE WERE PARTNERS.
YEAH, WELL, PARTNER... I'M LEAVING. YOU WANT TO LECTURE ME, DO IT IN THE CAR.
SKREEE
I WANT YOU TO UNDERSTAND SOMETHING, SIR. I AM ONLY HERE TO WATCH YOUR BACK. I DO NOT CONDONE THIS EXCURSION.
FINE. SO NOTED.

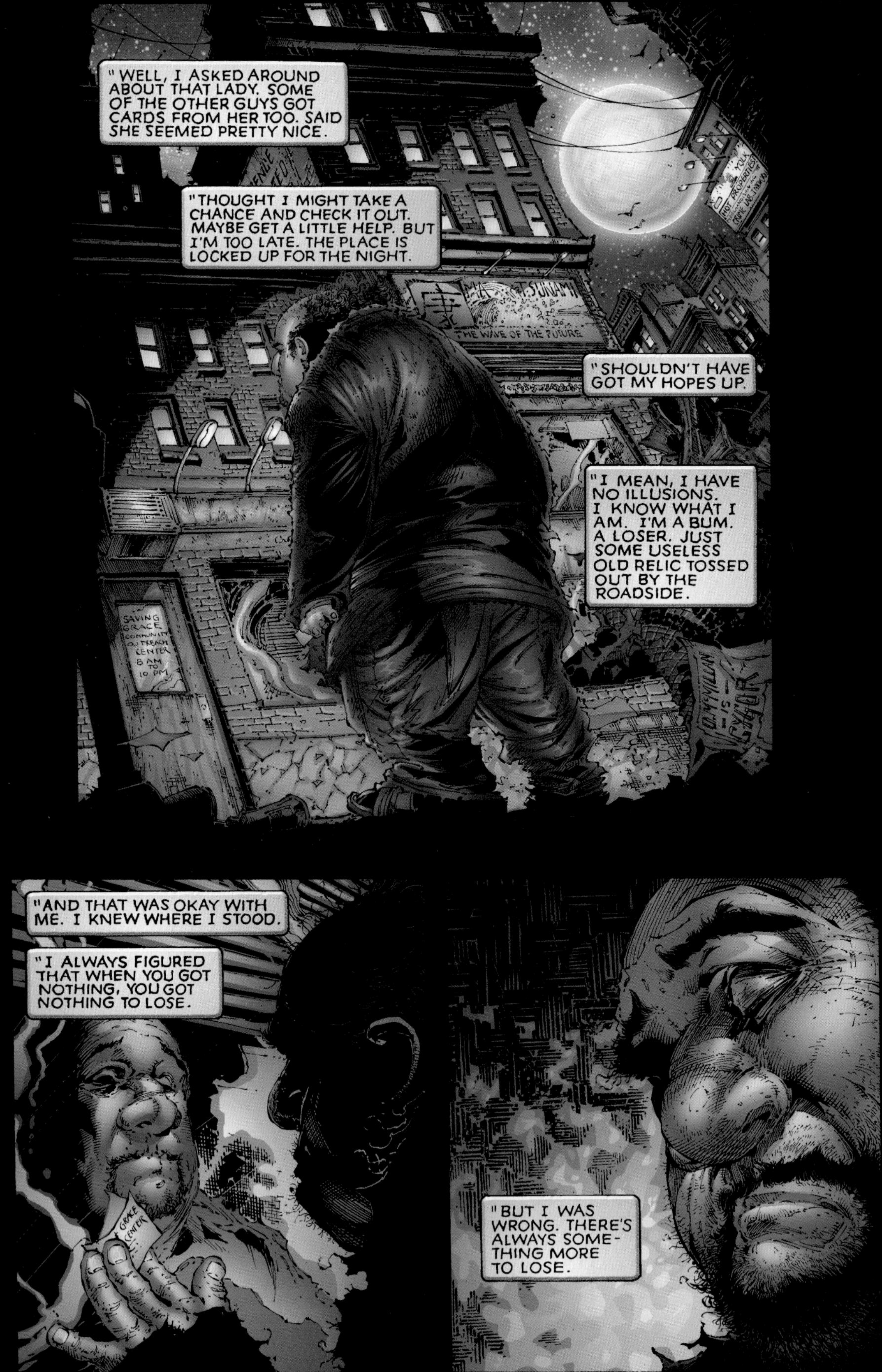
"WELL, I ASKED AROUND ABOUT THAT LADY. SOME OF THE OTHER GUYS GOT CARDS FROM HER TOO. SAID SHE SEEMED PRETTY NICE.
"THOUGHT I MIGHT TAKE A CHANCE AND CHECK IT OUT. MAYBE GET A LITTLE HELP. BUT I'M TOO LATE. THE PLACE IS LOCKED UP FOR THE NIGHT.
THE WAVE OF THE FUTURE
"SHOULDN'T HAVE GOT MY HOPES UP.
"I MEAN, I HAVE NO ILLUSIONS. I KNOW WHAT I AM. I'M A BUM. A LOSER. JUST SOME USELESS OLD RELIC TOSSED OUT BY THE ROADSIDE.
SAVING GRACE COMMUNITY OUTREACH CENTER 8 AM TO 10 PM
"AND THAT WAS OKAY WITH ME. I KNEW WHERE I STOOD.
"I ALWAYS FIGURED THAT WHEN YOU GOT NOTHING, YOU GOT NOTHING TO LOSE.
"BUT I WAS WRONG. THERE'S ALWAYS SOME-THING MORE TO LOSE.

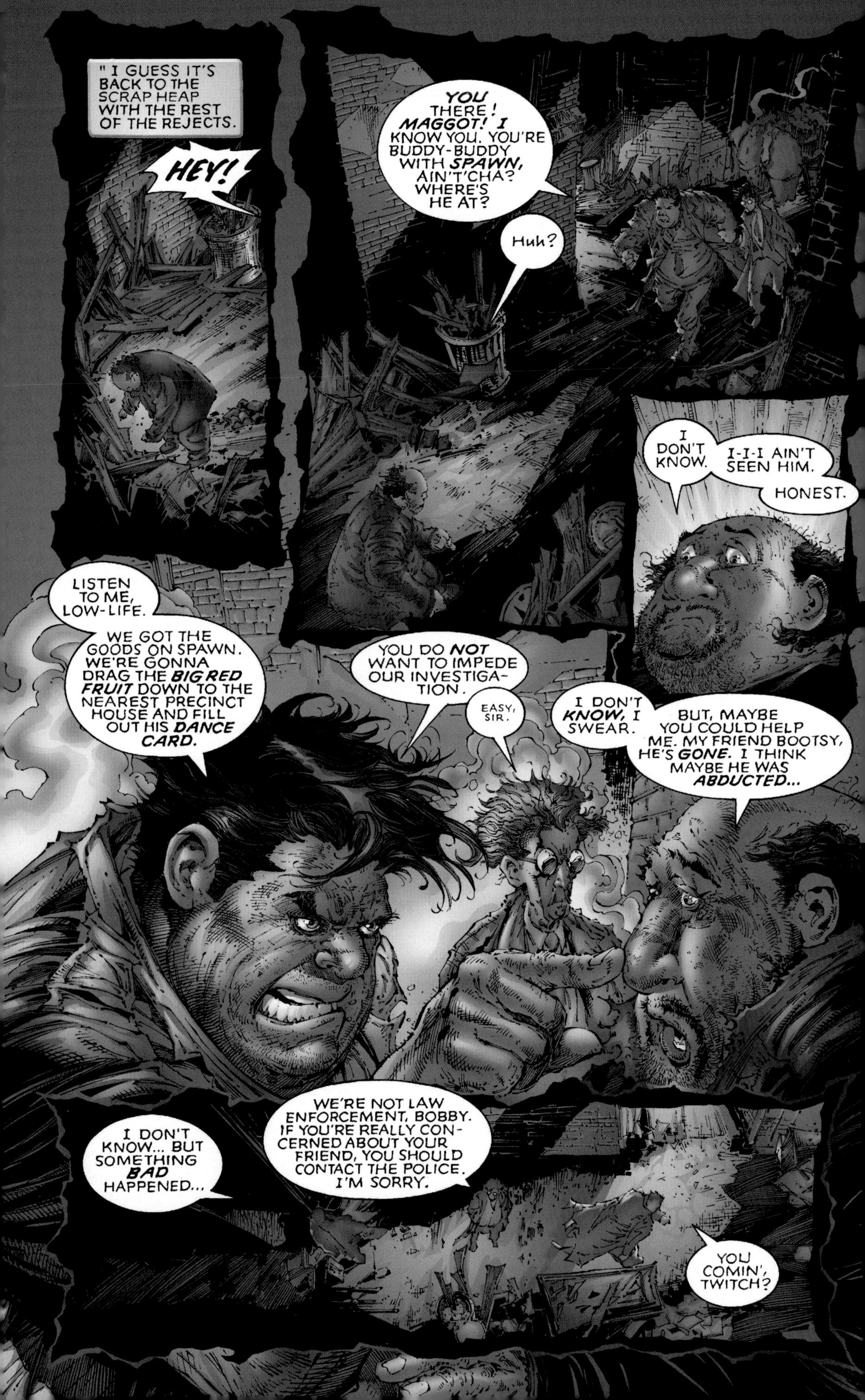
"I GUESS IT'S BACK TO THE SCRAP HEAP WITH THE REST OF THE REJECTS.
HEY!
YOU THERE! MAGGOT! I KNOW YOU. YOU'RE BUDDY-BUDDY WITH SPAWN, AIN'T'CHA? WHERE'S HE AT?
Huh?
I DON'T KNOW.
I-I-I AIN'T SEEN HIM.
HONEST.
LISTEN TO ME, LOW-LIFE.
WE GOT THE GOODS ON SPAWN. WE'RE GONNA DRAG THE BIG RED FRUIT DOWN TO THE NEAREST PRECINCT HOUSE AND FILL OUT HIS DANCE CARD.
YOU DO NOT WANT TO IMPEDE OUR INVESTIGATION.
EASY, SIR.
I DON'T KNOW, I SWEAR.
BUT, MAYBE YOU COULD HELP ME. MY FRIEND BOOTSY, HE'S GONE. I THINK MAYBE HE WAS ABDUCTED...
I DON'T KNOW... BUT SOMETHING BAD HAPPENED...
WE'RE NOT LAW ENFORCEMENT, BOBBY. IF YOU'RE REALLY CONCERNED ABOUT YOUR FRIEND, YOU SHOULD CONTACT THE POLICE. I'M SORRY.
YOU COMIN', TWITCH?

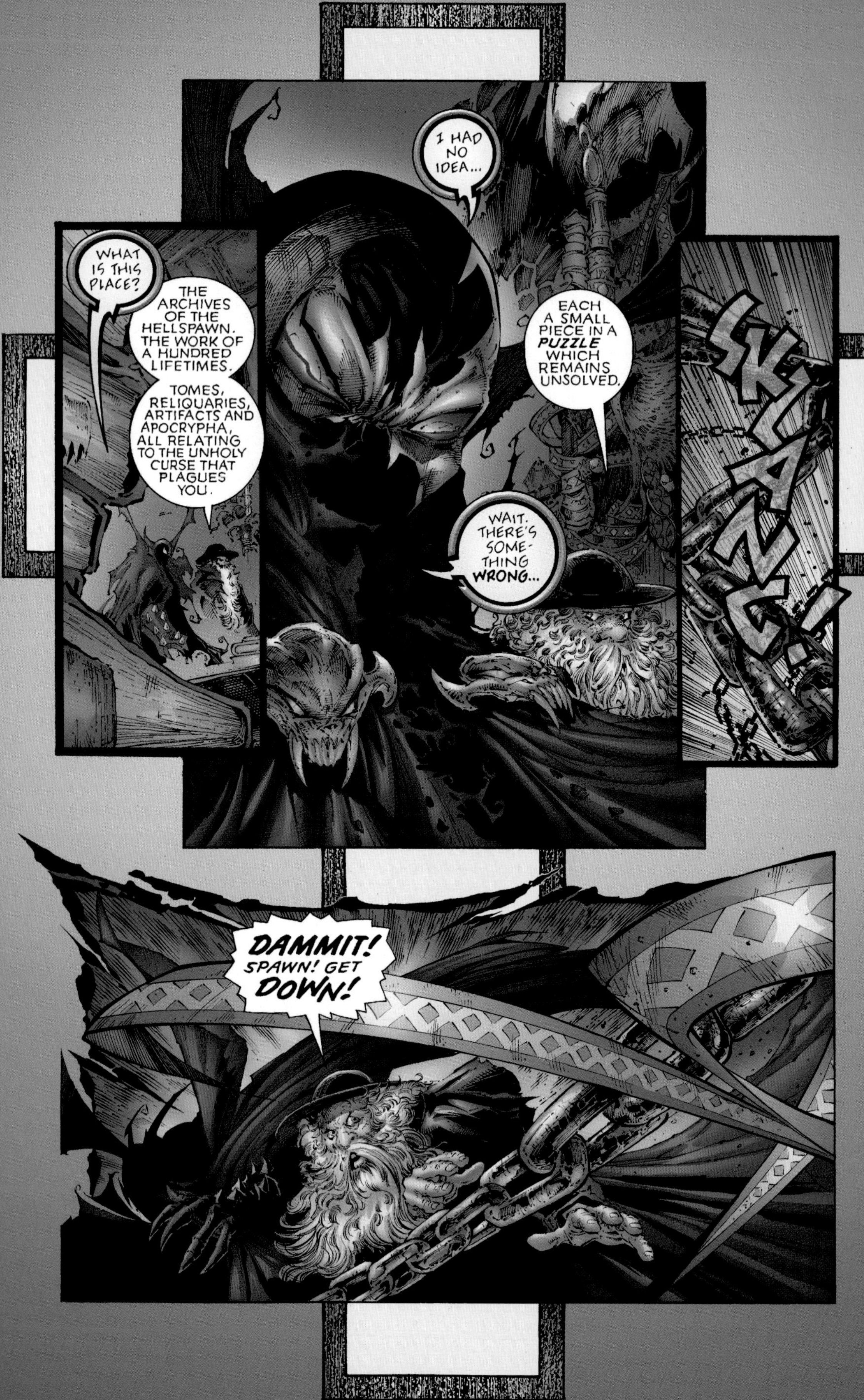

I HAD NO IDEA...
WHAT IS THIS PLACE?
THE ARCHIVES OF THE HELLSPAWN. THE WORK OF A HUNDRED LIFETIMES.
TOMES, RELIQUARIES, ARTIFACTS AND APOCRYPHA, ALL RELATING TO THE UNHOLY CURSE THAT PLAGUES YOU.
EACH A SMALL PIECE IN A PUZZLE WHICH REMAINS UNSOLVED.
WAIT. THERE'S SOME-THING WRONG...
DAMMIT! SPAWN! GET DOWN!

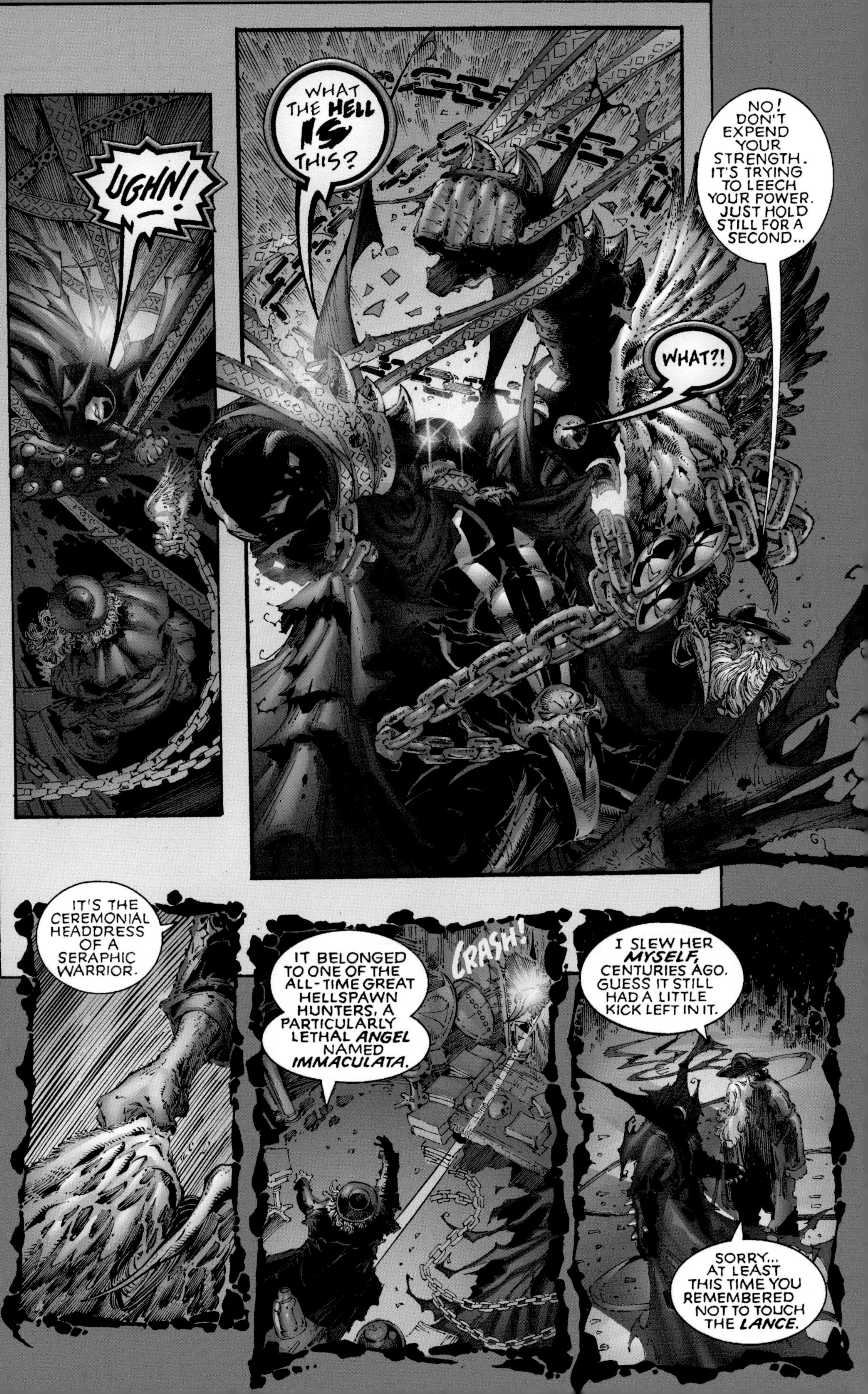
UGHN!
WHAT THE HELL IS THIS?
NO! DON'T EXPEND YOUR STRENGTH. IT'S TRYING TO LEECH YOUR POWER. JUST HOLD STILL FOR A SECOND...
WHAT?!
IT'S THE CEREMONIAL HEADDRESS OF A SERAPHIC WARRIOR.
IT BELONGED TO ONE OF THE ALL-TIME GREAT HELLSPAWN HUNTERS, A PARTICULARLY LETHAL ANGEL NAMED IMMACULATA.
CRASH!
I SLEW HER MYSELF, CENTURIES AGO. GUESS IT STILL HAD A LITTLE KICK LEFT IN IT.
SORRY... AT LEAST THIS TIME YOU REMEMBERED NOT TO TOUCH THE LANCE.

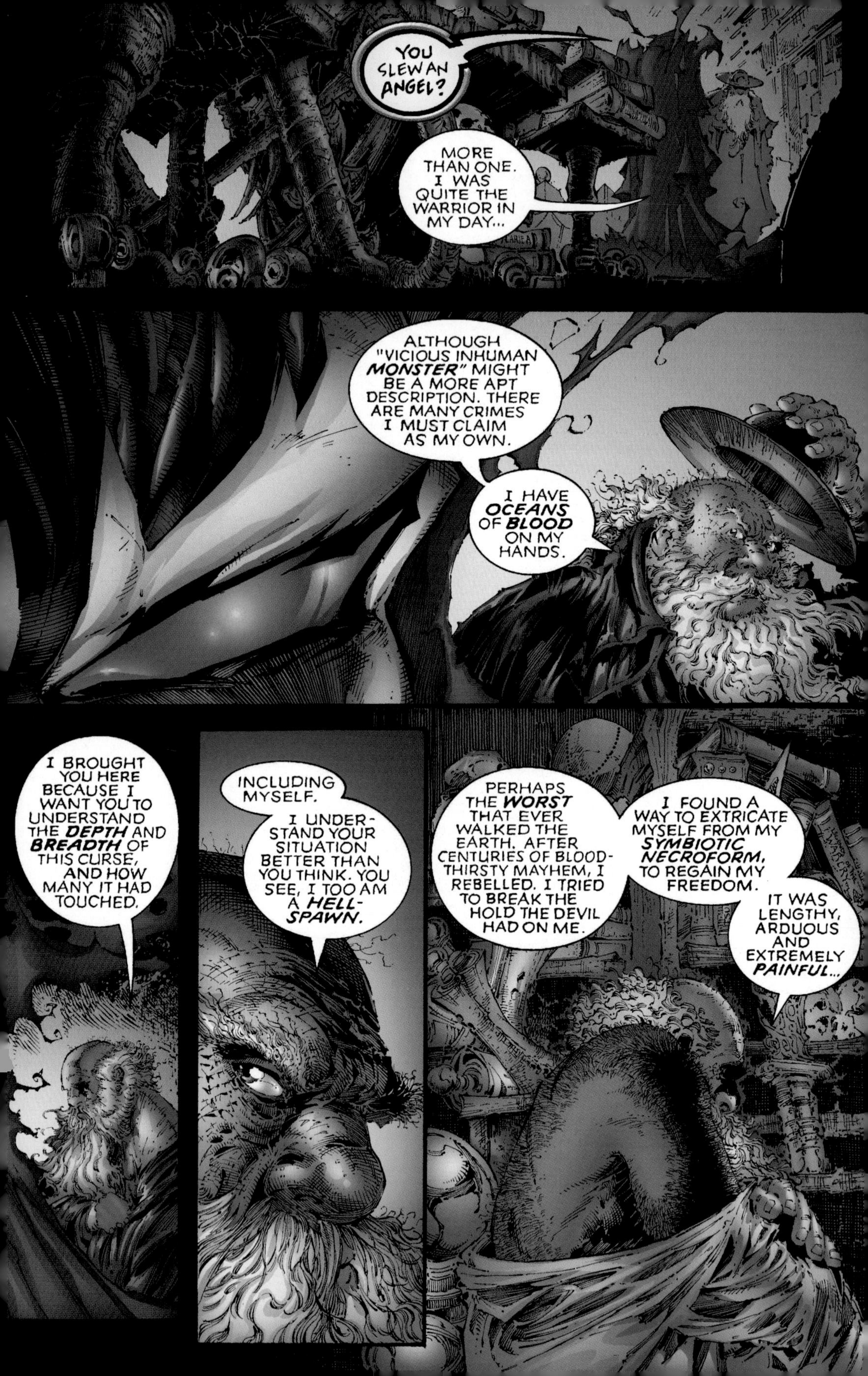
YOU SLEW AN ANGEL?
MORE THAN ONE. I WAS QUITE THE WARRIOR IN MY DAY...
ALTHOUGH "VICIOUS INHUMAN MONSTER" MIGHT BE A MORE APT DESCRIPTION. THERE ARE MANY CRIMES I MUST CLAIM AS MY OWN.
I HAVE OCEANS OF BLOOD ON MY HANDS.
I BROUGHT YOU HERE BECAUSE I WANT YOU TO UNDERSTAND THE DEPTH AND BREADTH OF THIS CURSE, AND HOW MANY IT HAD TOUCHED.
INCLUDING MYSELF.
I UNDERSTAND YOUR SITUATION BETTER THAN YOU THINK. YOU SEE, I TOO AM A HELL-SPAWN.
PERHAPS THE WORST THAT EVER WALKED THE EARTH. AFTER CENTURIES OF BLOOD-THIRSTY MAYHEM, I REBELLED. I TRIED TO BREAK THE HOLD THE DEVIL HAD ON ME.
I FOUND A WAY TO EXTRICATE MYSELF FROM MY SYMBIOTIC NECROFORM, TO REGAIN MY FREEDOM.
IT WAS LENGTHY, ARDUOUS AND EXTREMELY PAINFUL...

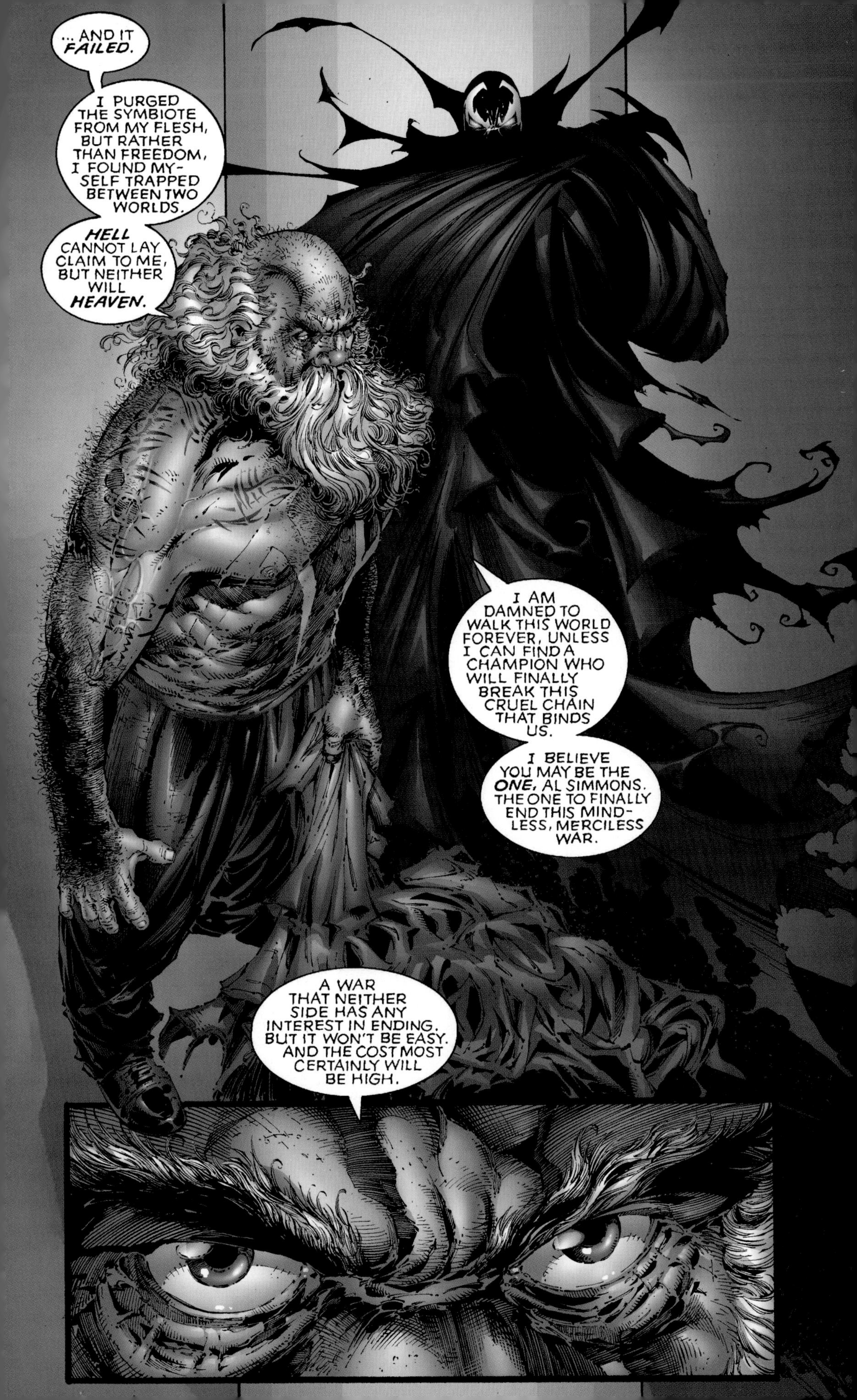
... AND IT *FAILED*.
I PURGED THE SYMBIOTE FROM MY FLESH, BUT RATHER THAN FREEDOM, I FOUND MY-SELF TRAPPED BETWEEN TWO WORLDS.
HELL CANNOT LAY CLAIM TO ME, BUT NEITHER WILL *HEAVEN*.
I AM DAMNED TO WALK THIS WORLD FOREVER, UNLESS I CAN FIND A CHAMPION WHO WILL FINALLY BREAK THIS CRUEL CHAIN THAT BINDS US.
I BELIEVE YOU MAY BE THE *ONE*, AL SIMMONS. THE ONE TO FINALLY END THIS MIND-LESS, MERCILESS WAR.
A WAR THAT NEITHER SIDE HAS ANY INTEREST IN ENDING. BUT IT WON'T BE EASY. AND THE COST MOST CERTAINLY WILL BE HIGH.

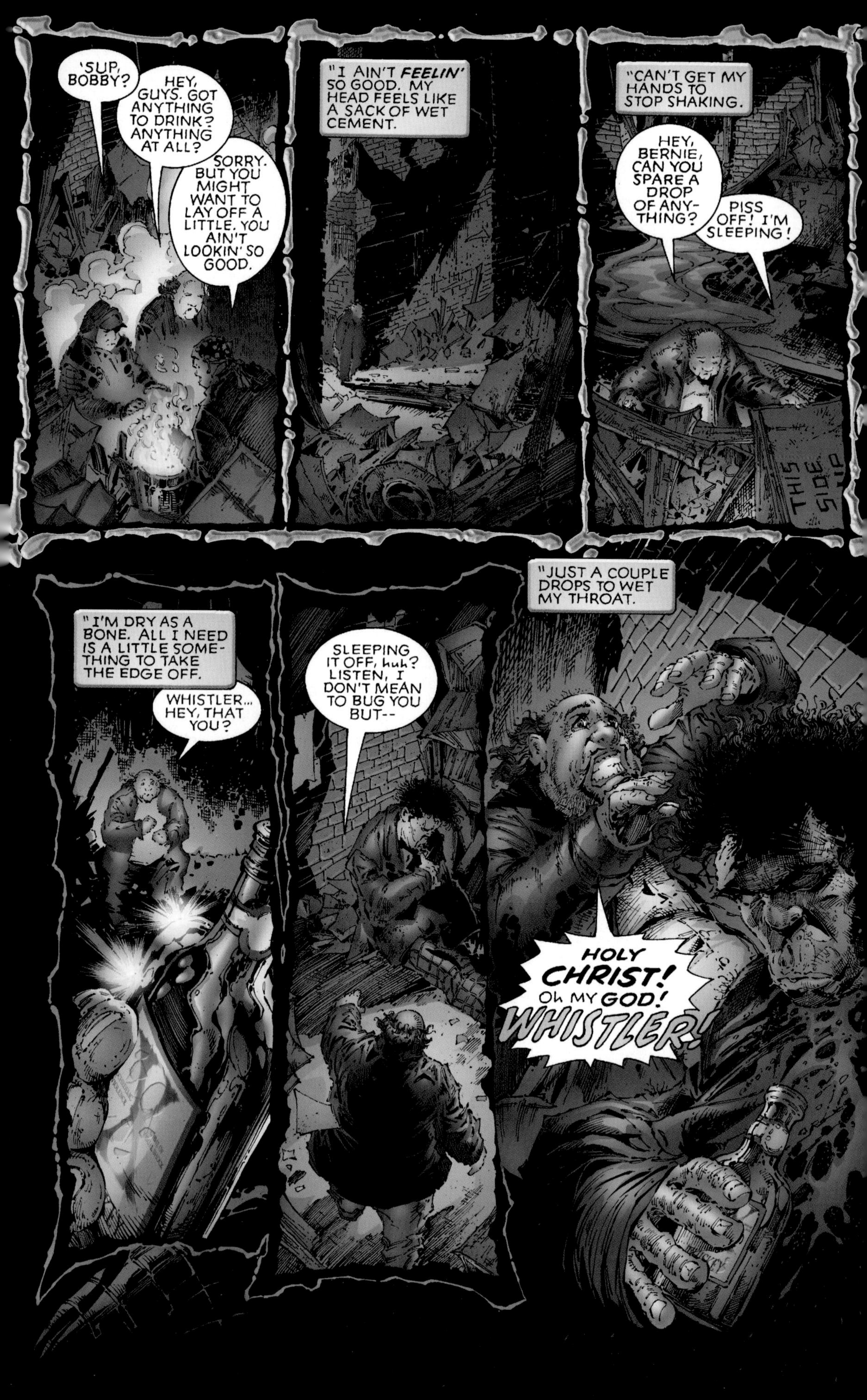
'SUP, BOBBY?
HEY, GUYS. GOT ANYTHING TO DRINK? ANYTHING AT ALL?
SORRY. BUT YOU MIGHT WANT TO LAY OFF A LITTLE. YOU AIN'T LOOKIN' SO GOOD.
"I AIN'T FEELIN' SO GOOD. MY HEAD FEELS LIKE A SACK OF WET CEMENT.
"CAN'T GET MY HANDS TO STOP SHAKING.
HEY, BERNIE, CAN YOU SPARE A DROP OF ANY-THING?
PISS OFF! I'M SLEEPING!
THIS SIDE UP
"I'M DRY AS A BONE. ALL I NEED IS A LITTLE SOME-THING TO TAKE THE EDGE OFF.
WHISTLER... HEY, THAT YOU?
SLEEPING IT OFF, huh? LISTEN, I DON'T MEAN TO BUG YOU BUT--
"JUST A COUPLE DROPS TO WET MY THROAT.
HOLY CHRIST! Oh MY GOD! WHISTLER!

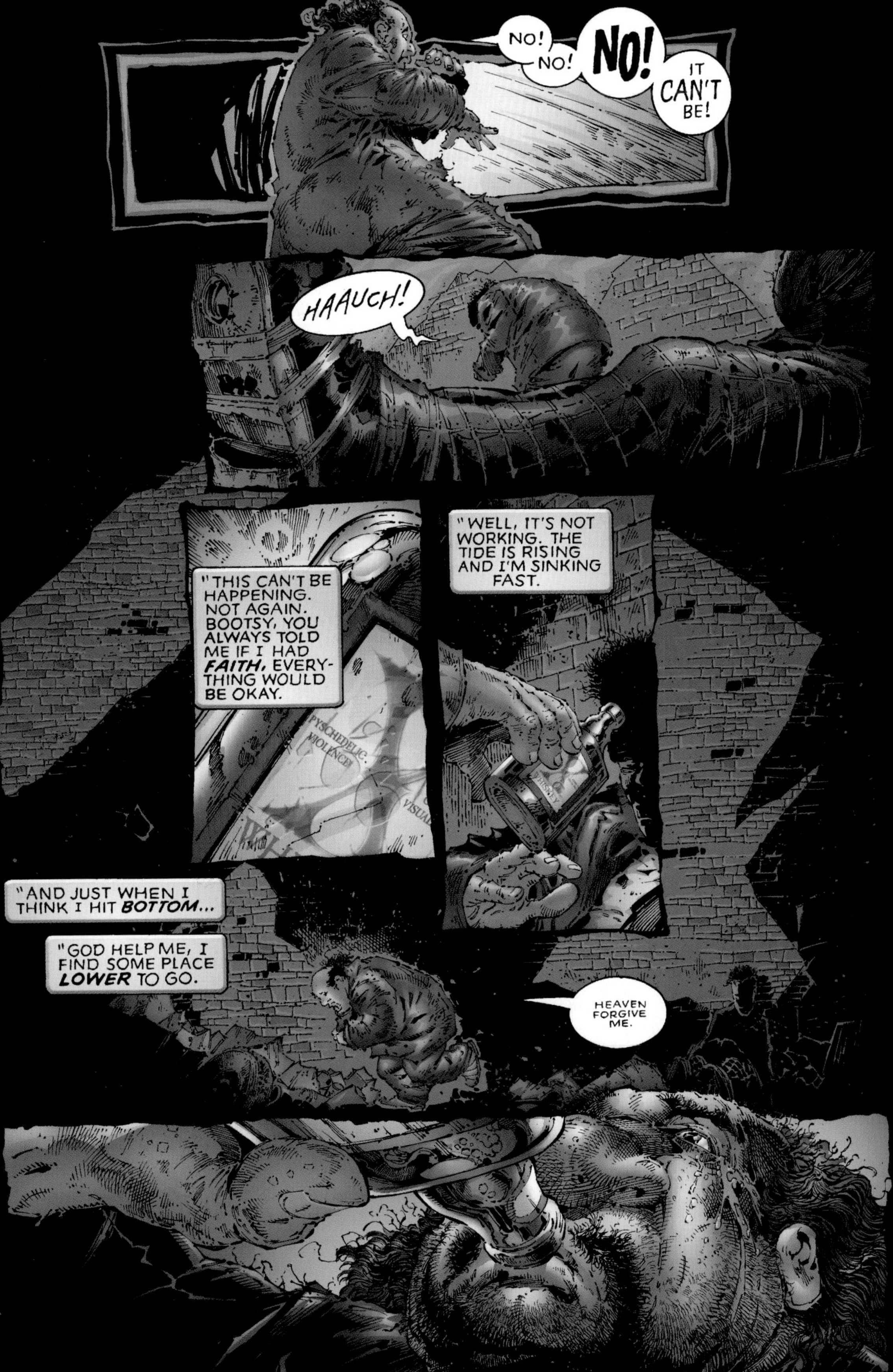
NO!
NO!
NO!
IT CAN'T BE!
HAAUCH!
"THIS CAN'T BE HAPPENING. NOT AGAIN. BOOTSY, YOU ALWAYS TOLD ME IF I HAD FAITH, EVERYTHING WOULD BE OKAY.
PSYCHEDELIC VIOLENCE
"WELL, IT'S NOT WORKING. THE TIDE IS RISING AND I'M SINKING FAST.
"AND JUST WHEN I THINK I HIT BOTTOM...
"GOD HELP ME, I FIND SOME PLACE LOWER TO GO.
HEAVEN FORGIVE ME.

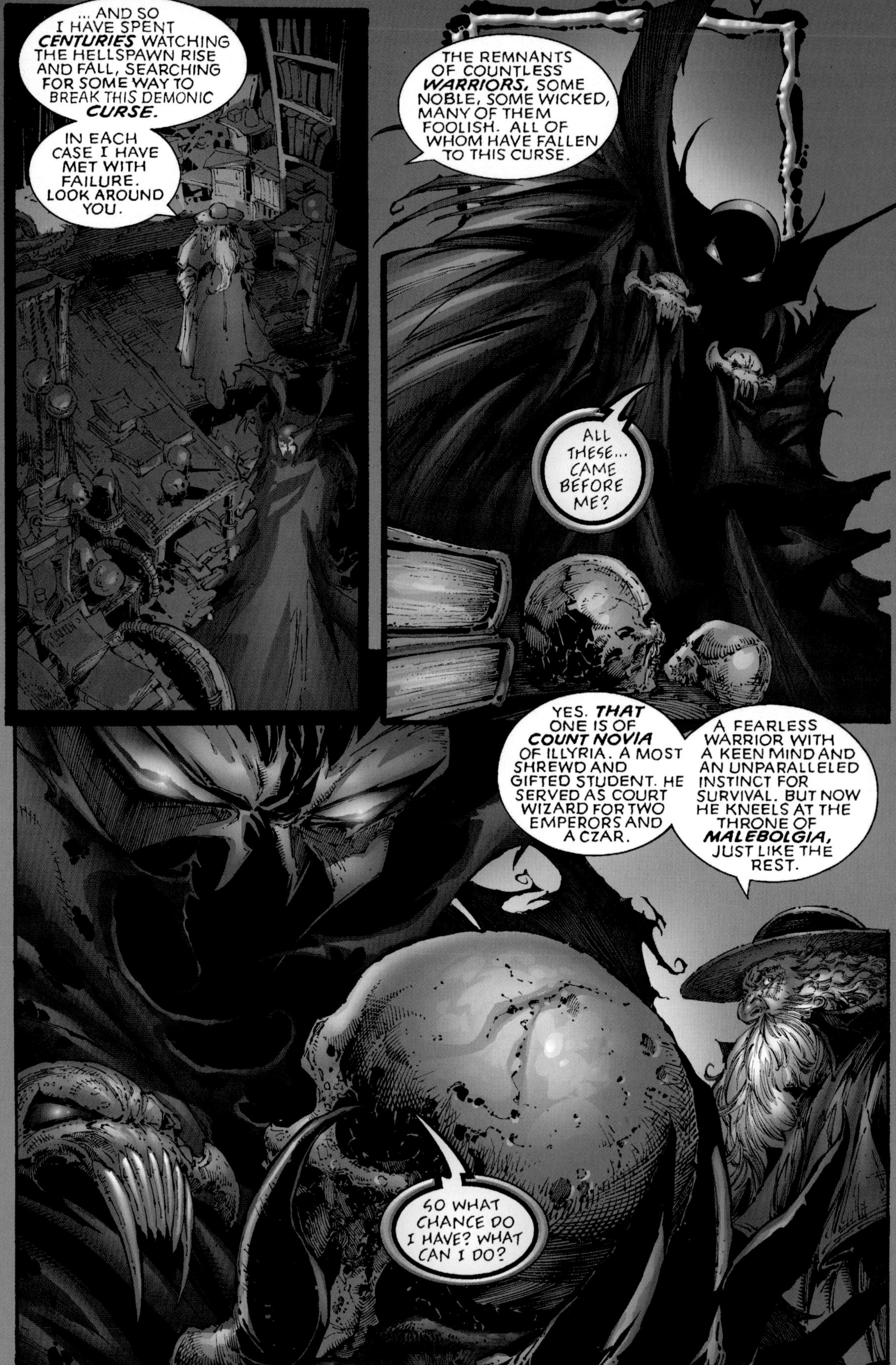
... AND SO I HAVE SPENT CENTURIES WATCHING THE HELLSPAWN RISE AND FALL, SEARCHING FOR SOME WAY TO BREAK THIS DEMONIC CURSE.
IN EACH CASE I HAVE MET WITH FAILURE. LOOK AROUND YOU.
THE REMNANTS OF COUNTLESS WARRIORS, SOME NOBLE, SOME WICKED, MANY OF THEM FOOLISH. ALL OF WHOM HAVE FALLEN TO THIS CURSE.
ALL THESE... CAME BEFORE ME?
YES. THAT ONE IS OF COUNT NOVIA OF ILLYRIA. A MOST SHREWD AND GIFTED STUDENT. HE SERVED AS COURT WIZARD FOR TWO EMPERORS AND A CZAR.
A FEARLESS WARRIOR WITH A KEEN MIND AND AN UNPARALLELED INSTINCT FOR SURVIVAL. BUT NOW HE KNEELS AT THE THRONE OF MALEBOLGIA, JUST LIKE THE REST.
SO WHAT CHANCE DO I HAVE? WHAT CAN I DO?

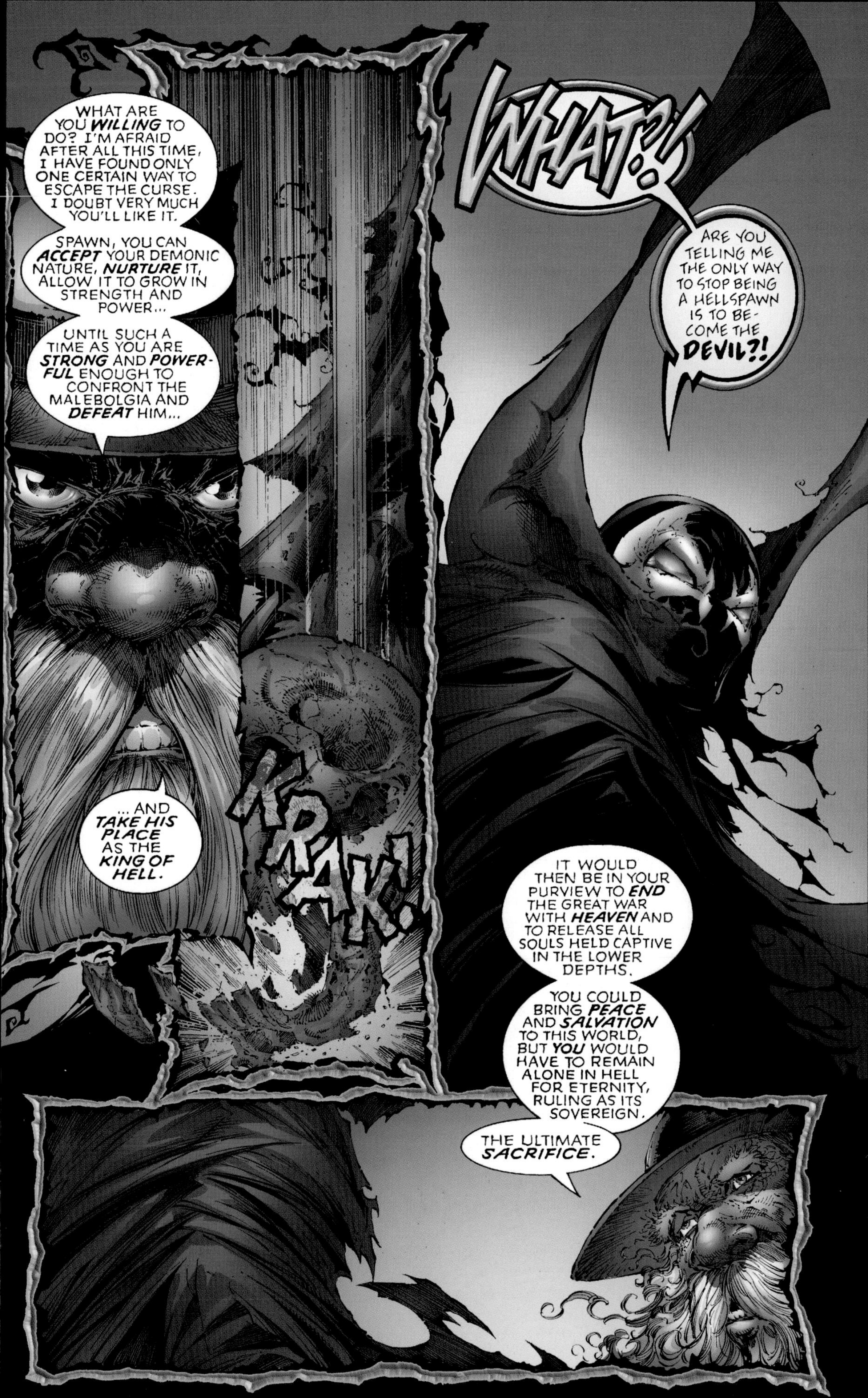
WHAT ARE YOU WILLING TO DO? I'M AFRAID AFTER ALL THIS TIME, I HAVE FOUND ONLY ONE CERTAIN WAY TO ESCAPE THE CURSE. I DOUBT VERY MUCH YOU'LL LIKE IT.
SPAWN, YOU CAN ACCEPT YOUR DEMONIC NATURE, NURTURE IT, ALLOW IT TO GROW IN STRENGTH AND POWER...
UNTIL SUCH A TIME AS YOU ARE STRONG AND POWERFUL ENOUGH TO CONFRONT THE MALEBOLGIA AND DEFEAT HIM...
...AND TAKE HIS PLACE AS THE KING OF HELL.
KRAK!
WHAT?!
ARE YOU TELLING ME THE ONLY WAY TO STOP BEING A HELLSPAWN IS TO BECOME THE DEVIL?!
IT WOULD THEN BE IN YOUR PURVIEW TO END THE GREAT WAR WITH HEAVEN AND TO RELEASE ALL SOULS HELD CAPTIVE IN THE LOWER DEPTHS.
YOU COULD BRING PEACE AND SALVATION TO THIS WORLD, BUT YOU WOULD HAVE TO REMAIN ALONE IN HELL FOR ETERNITY, RULING AS ITS SOVEREIGN.
THE ULTIMATE SACRIFICE.

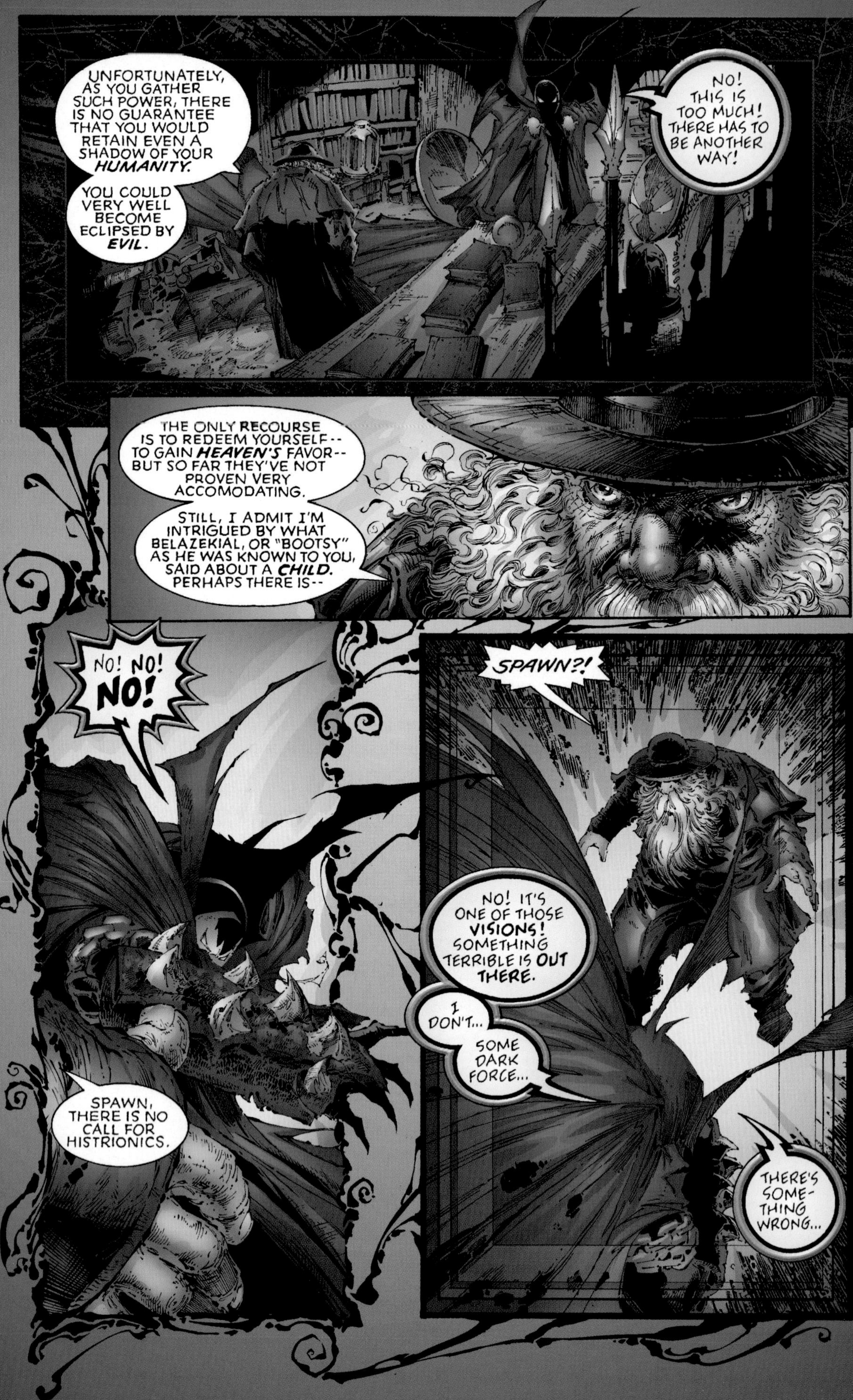
UNFORTUNATELY, AS YOU GATHER SUCH POWER, THERE IS NO GUARANTEE THAT YOU WOULD RETAIN EVEN A SHADOW OF YOUR HUMANITY.
YOU COULD VERY WELL BECOME ECLIPSED BY EVIL.
NO! THIS IS TOO MUCH! THERE HAS TO BE ANOTHER WAY!
THE ONLY RECOURSE IS TO REDEEM YOURSELF-- TO GAIN HEAVEN'S FAVOR-- BUT SO FAR THEY'VE NOT PROVEN VERY ACCOMODATING.
STILL, I ADMIT I'M INTRIGUED BY WHAT BELAZEKIAL, OR "BOOTSY" AS HE WAS KNOWN TO YOU, SAID ABOUT A CHILD. PERHAPS THERE IS--
NO! NO! NO!
SPAWN, THERE IS NO CALL FOR HISTRIONICS.
SPAWN?!
NO! IT'S ONE OF THOSE VISIONS! SOMETHING TERRIBLE IS OUT THERE.
I DON'T...
SOME DARK FORCE...
THERE'S SOME-THING WRONG...

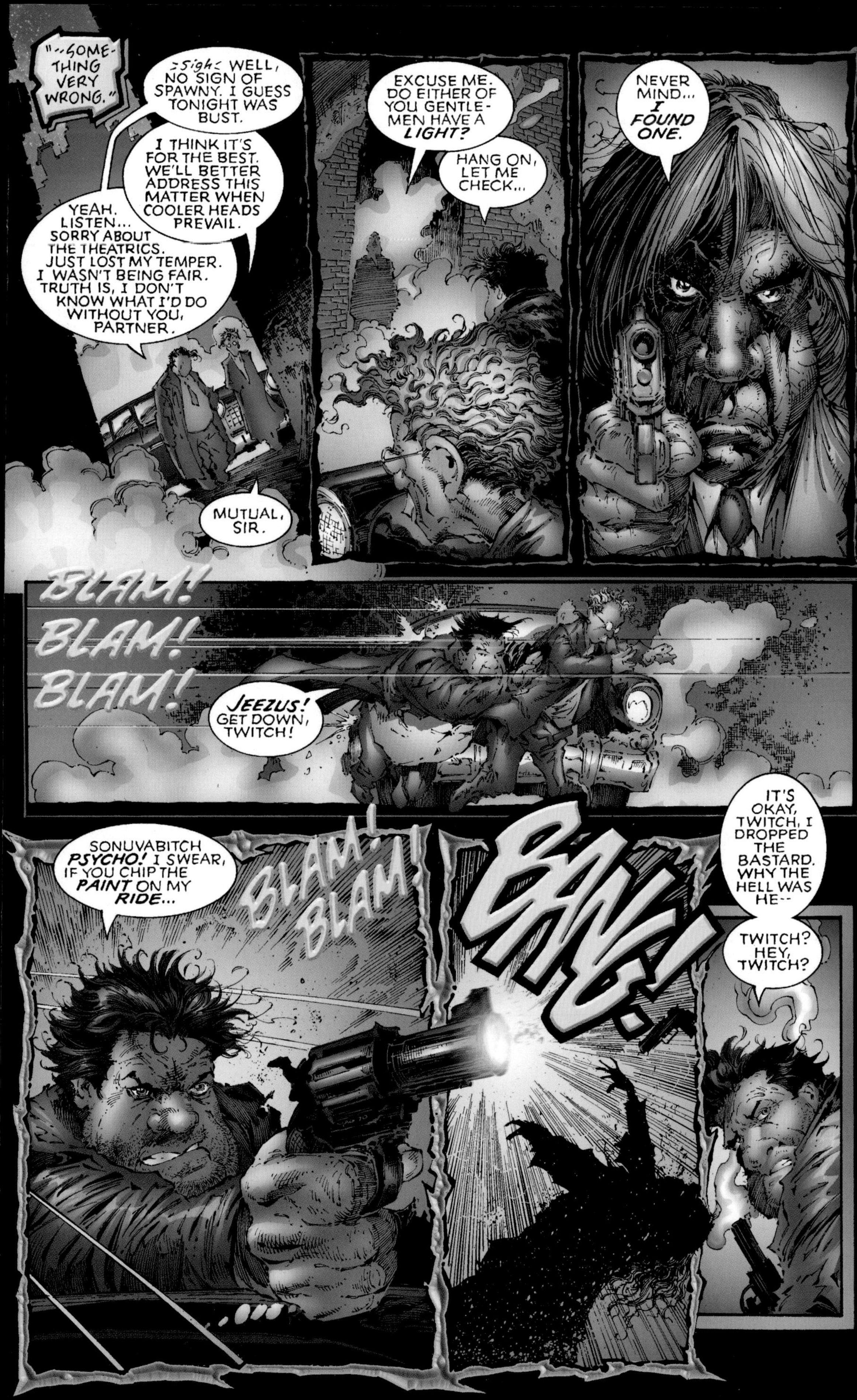
"--SOMETHING VERY WRONG."
>Sigh< WELL, NO SIGN OF SPAWNY. I GUESS TONIGHT WAS BUST.
I THINK IT'S FOR THE BEST. WE'LL BETTER ADDRESS THIS MATTER WHEN COOLER HEADS PREVAIL.
YEAH. LISTEN... SORRY ABOUT THE THEATRICS. JUST LOST MY TEMPER. I WASN'T BEING FAIR. TRUTH IS, I DON'T KNOW WHAT I'D DO WITHOUT YOU, PARTNER.
MUTUAL, SIR.
EXCUSE ME. DO EITHER OF YOU GENTLEMEN HAVE A LIGHT?
HANG ON, LET ME CHECK...
NEVER MIND... I FOUND ONE.
BLAM! BLAM! BLAM!
JEEZUS! GET DOWN, TWITCH!
SONUVABITCH PSYCHO! I SWEAR, IF YOU CHIP THE PAINT ON MY RIDE...
BLAM! BLAM!
BANG!
IT'S OKAY, TWITCH, I DROPPED THE BASTARD. WHY THE HELL WAS HE--
TWITCH? HEY, TWITCH?

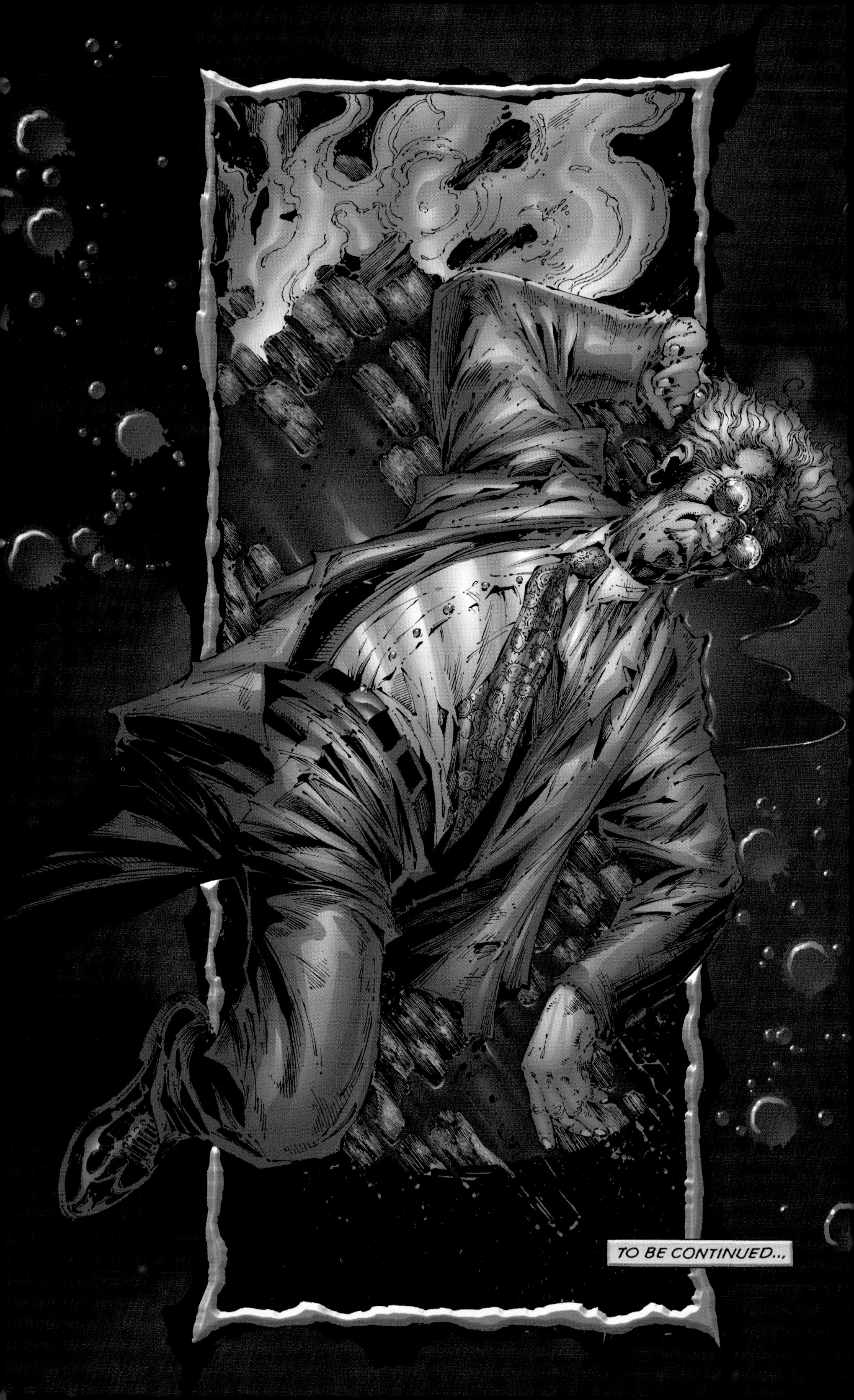
TO BE CONTINUED...

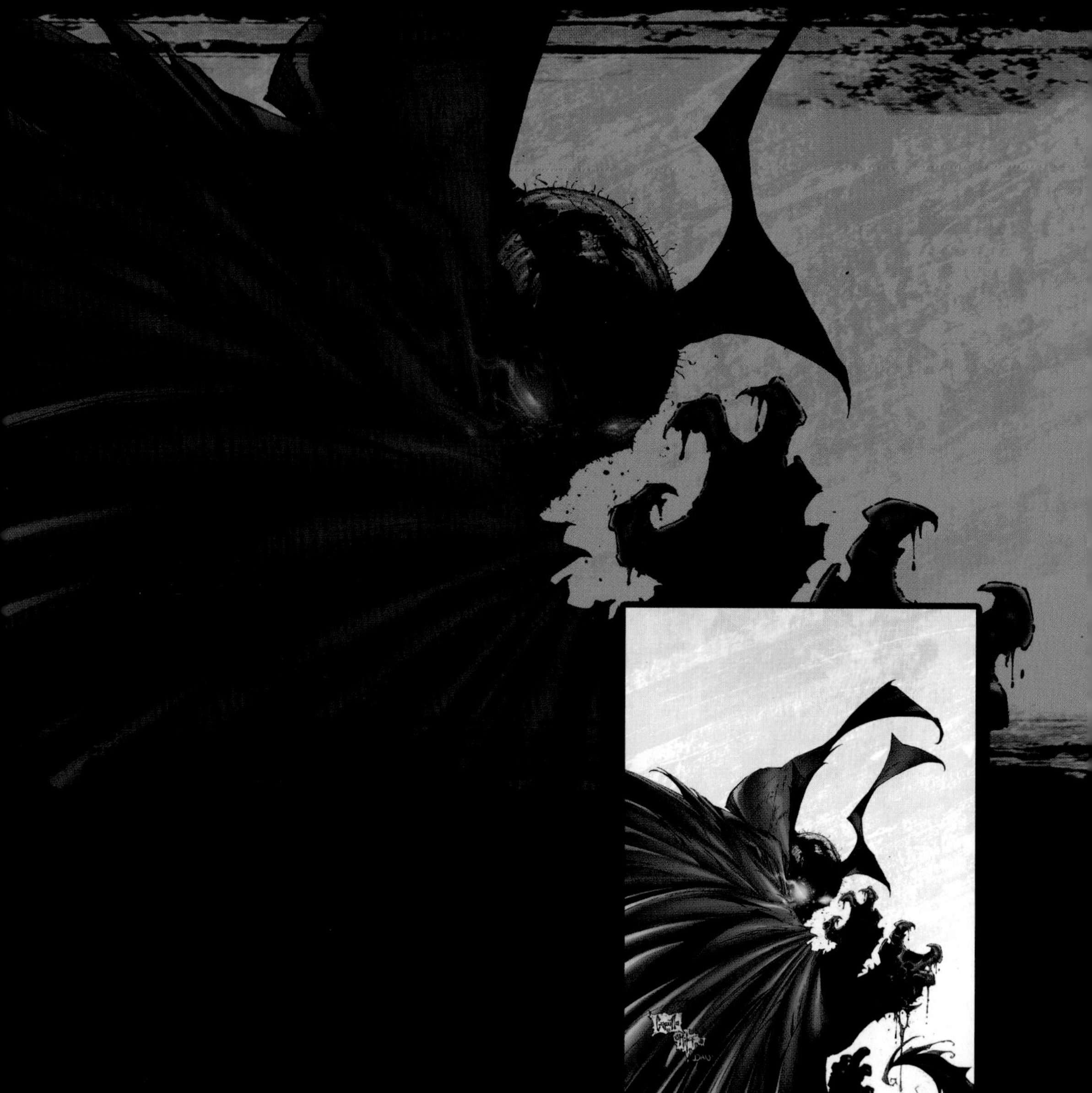

ISSUE SEVENTY-EIGHT

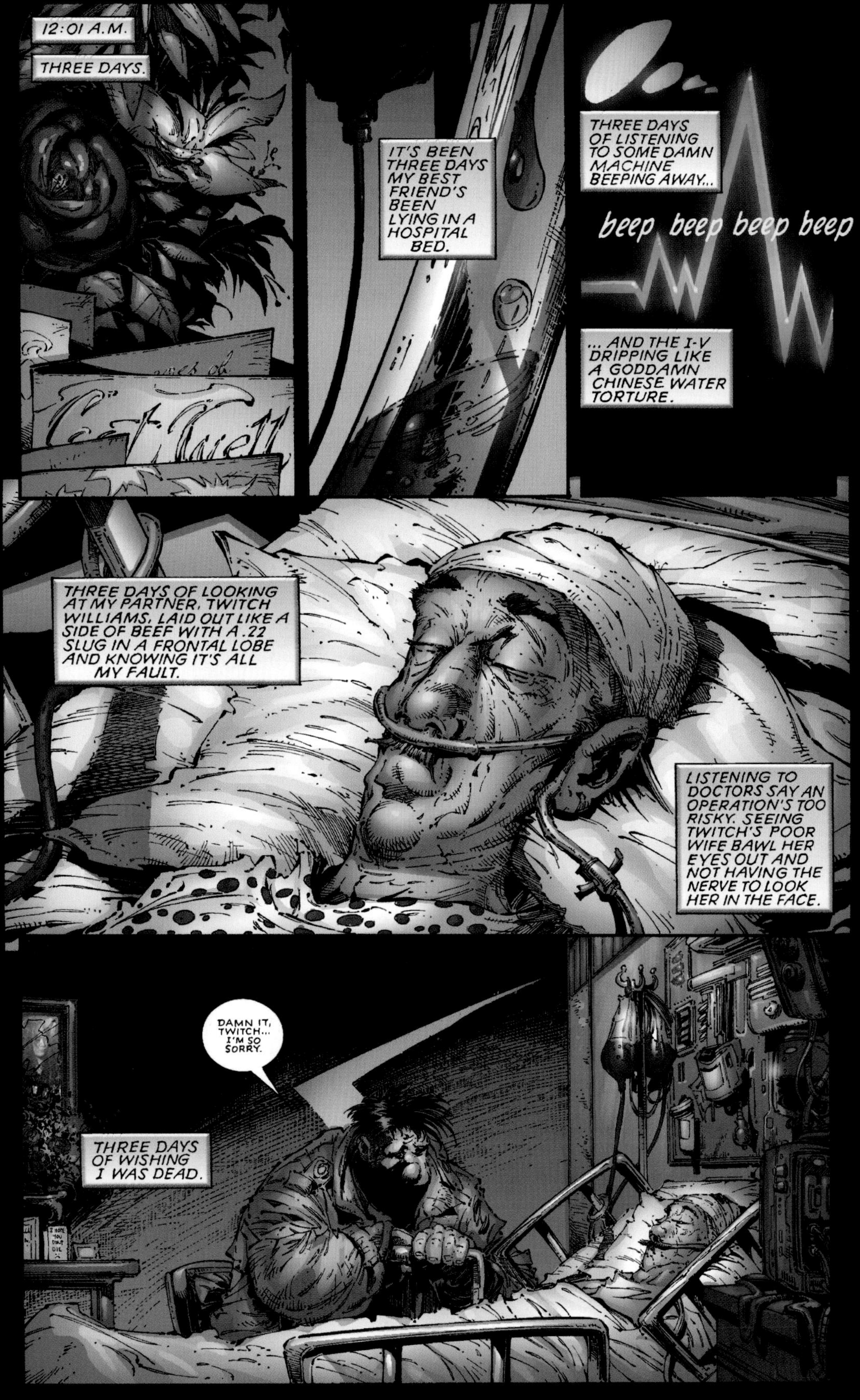
12:01 A.M.
THREE DAYS.
IT'S BEEN THREE DAYS MY BEST FRIEND'S BEEN LYING IN A HOSPITAL BED.
THREE DAYS OF LISTENING TO SOME DAMN MACHINE BEEPING AWAY...
beep beep beep beep
... AND THE I-V DRIPPING LIKE A GODDAMN CHINESE WATER TORTURE.
THREE DAYS OF LOOKING AT MY PARTNER, TWITCH WILLIAMS, LAID OUT LIKE A SIDE OF BEEF WITH A .22 SLUG IN A FRONTAL LOBE AND KNOWING IT'S ALL MY FAULT.
LISTENING TO DOCTORS SAY AN OPERATION'S TOO RISKY. SEEING TWITCH'S POOR WIFE BAWL HER EYES OUT AND NOT HAVING THE NERVE TO LOOK HER IN THE FACE.
DAMN IT, TWITCH... I'M SO SORRY.
THREE DAYS OF WISHING I WAS DEAD.

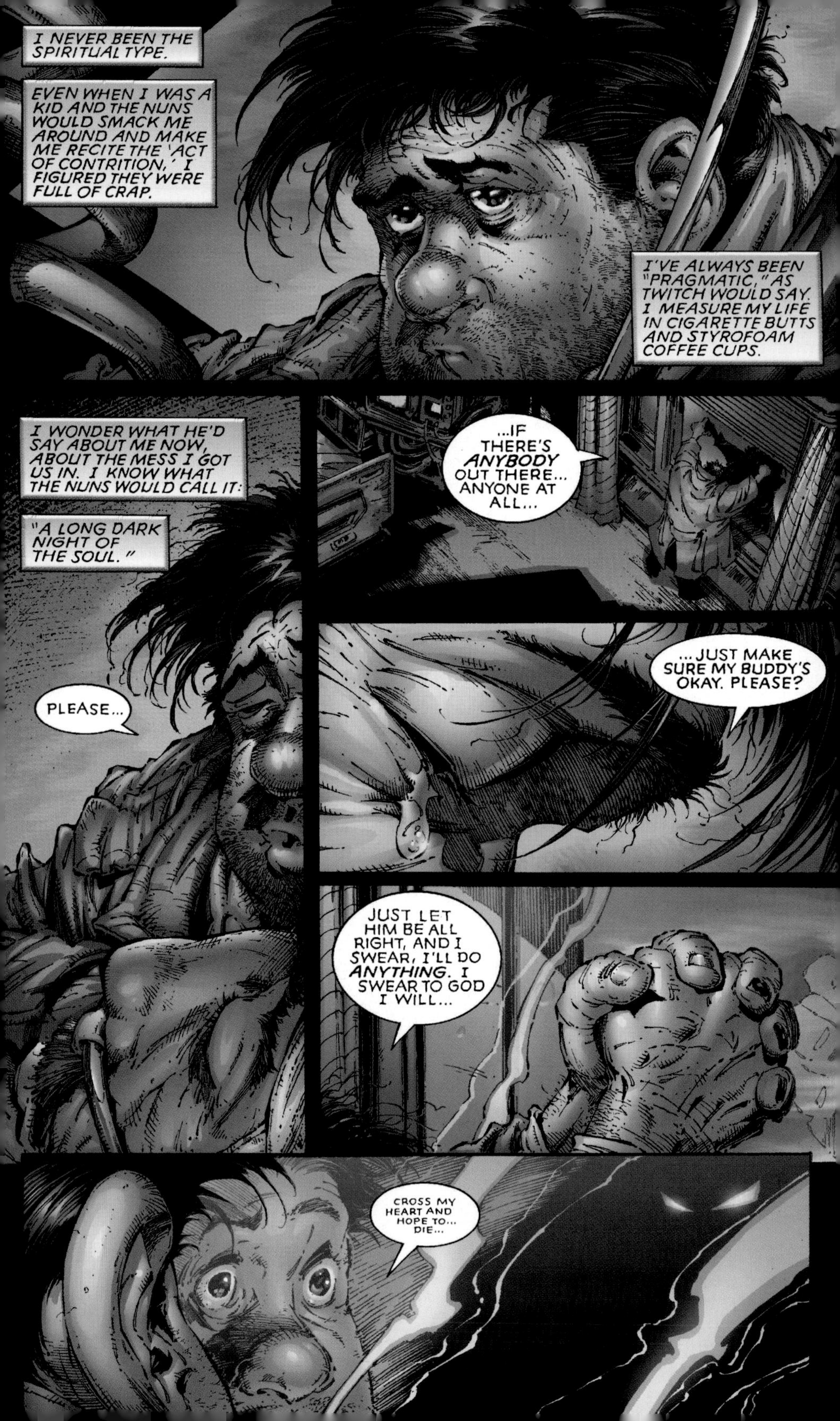

I NEVER BEEN THE SPIRITUAL TYPE.
EVEN WHEN I WAS A KID AND THE NUNS WOULD SMACK ME AROUND AND MAKE ME RECITE THE 'ACT OF CONTRITION,' I FIGURED THEY WERE FULL OF CRAP.
I'VE ALWAYS BEEN "PRAGMATIC," AS TWITCH WOULD SAY. I MEASURE MY LIFE IN CIGARETTE BUTTS AND STYROFOAM COFFEE CUPS.
I WONDER WHAT HE'D SAY ABOUT ME NOW, ABOUT THE MESS I GOT US IN. I KNOW WHAT THE NUNS WOULD CALL IT:
"A LONG DARK NIGHT OF THE SOUL."
PLEASE...
...IF THERE'S ANYBODY OUT THERE... ANYONE AT ALL...
...JUST MAKE SURE MY BUDDY'S OKAY. PLEASE?
JUST LET HIM BE ALL RIGHT, AND I SWEAR, I'LL DO ANYTHING. I SWEAR TO GOD I WILL...
CROSS MY HEART AND HOPE TO... DIE...

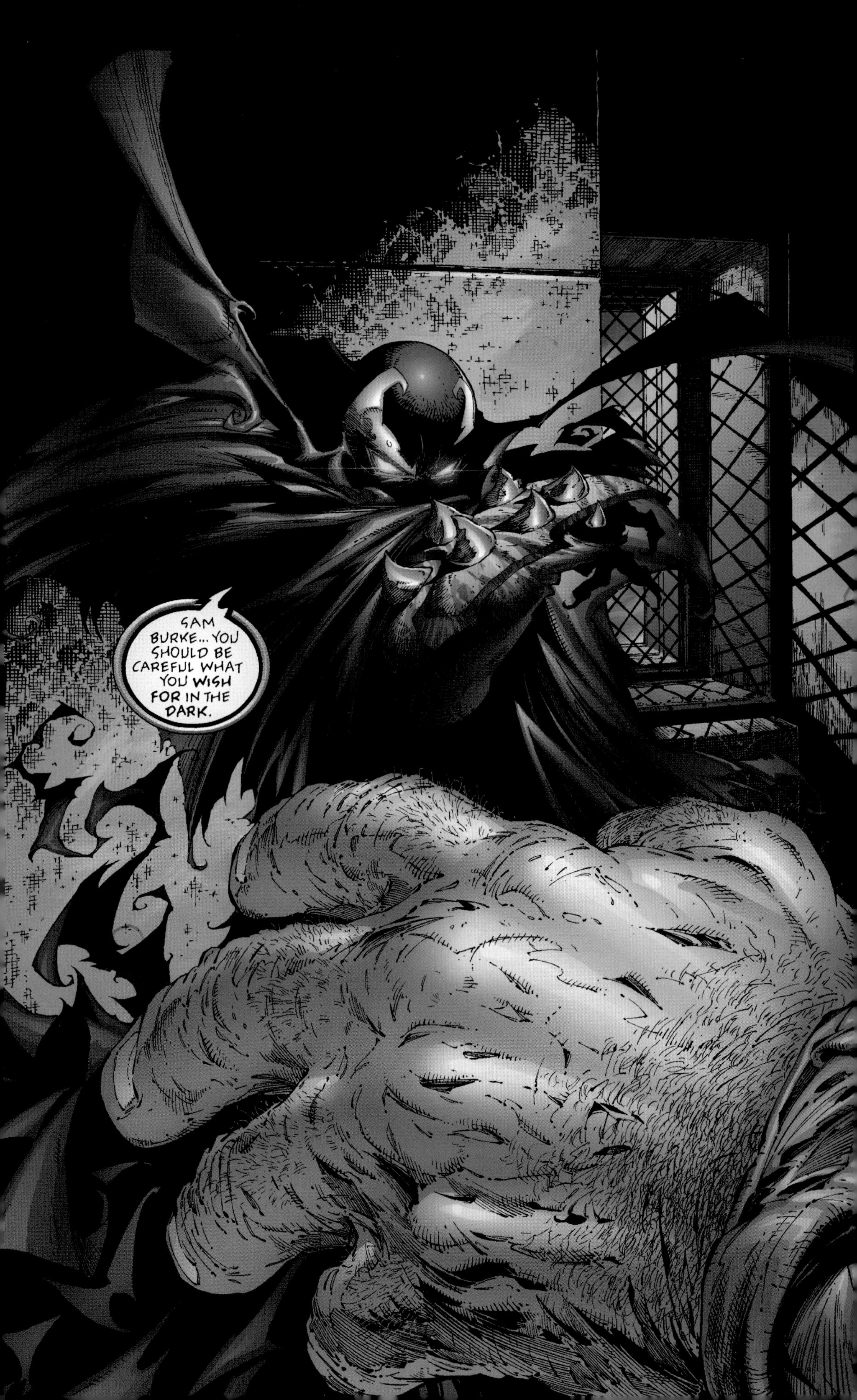
SAM BURKE... YOU SHOULD BE CAREFUL WHAT YOU WISH FOR IN THE DARK.

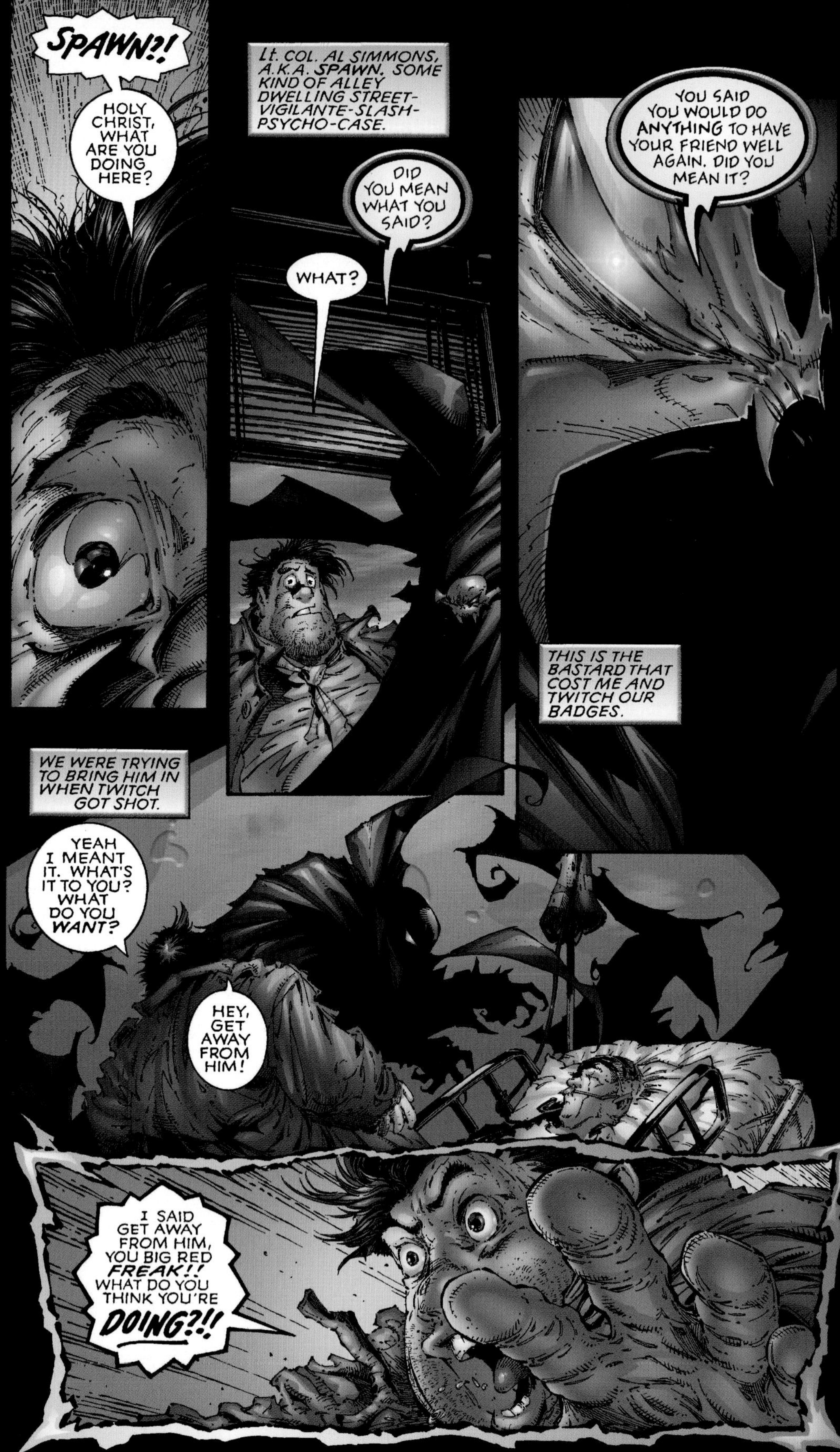
SPAWN?!
HOLY CHRIST, WHAT ARE YOU DOING HERE?
Lt. COL. AL SIMMONS, A.K.A. SPAWN. SOME KIND OF ALLEY DWELLING STREET-VIGILANTE-SLASH-PSYCHO-CASE.
DID YOU MEAN WHAT YOU SAID?
WHAT?
YOU SAID YOU WOULD DO ANYTHING TO HAVE YOUR FRIEND WELL AGAIN. DID YOU MEAN IT?
THIS IS THE BASTARD THAT COST ME AND TWITCH OUR BADGES.
WE WERE TRYING TO BRING HIM IN WHEN TWITCH GOT SHOT.
YEAH I MEANT IT. WHAT'S IT TO YOU? WHAT DO YOU WANT?
HEY, GET AWAY FROM HIM!
I SAID GET AWAY FROM HIM, YOU BIG RED FREAK!! WHAT DO YOU THINK YOU'RE DOING?!!

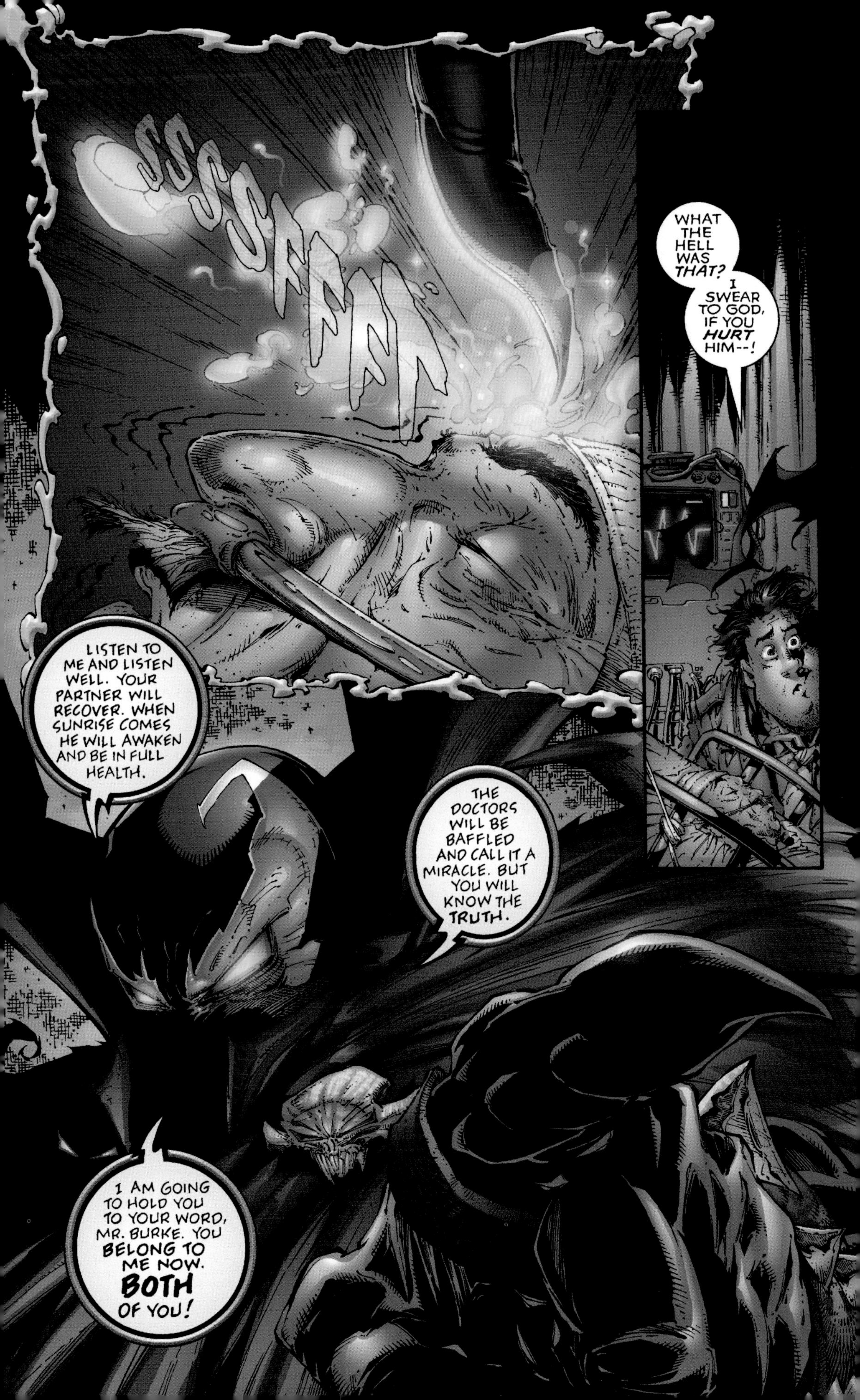
SSSSAFFF
WHAT THE HELL WAS THAT?
I SWEAR TO GOD, IF YOU HURT HIM--!
LISTEN TO ME AND LISTEN WELL. YOUR PARTNER WILL RECOVER. WHEN SUNRISE COMES HE WILL AWAKEN AND BE IN FULL HEALTH.
THE DOCTORS WILL BE BAFFLED AND CALL IT A MIRACLE. BUT YOU WILL KNOW THE TRUTH.
I AM GOING TO HOLD YOU TO YOUR WORD, MR. BURKE. YOU BELONG TO ME NOW. BOTH OF YOU!

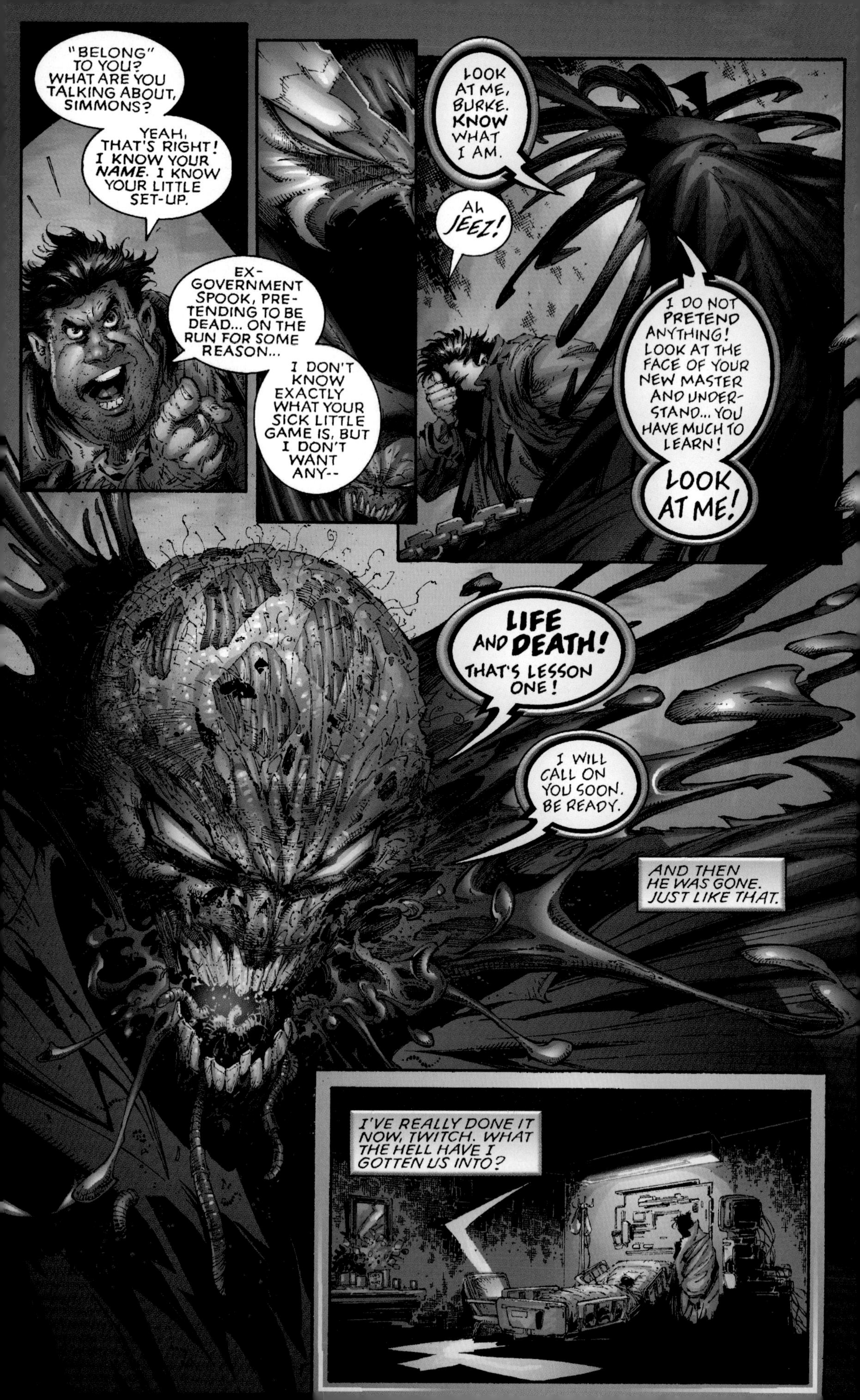
"BELONG" TO YOU? WHAT ARE YOU TALKING ABOUT, SIMMONS?
YEAH, THAT'S RIGHT! I KNOW YOUR NAME. I KNOW YOUR LITTLE SET-UP.
EX-GOVERNMENT SPOOK, PRETENDING TO BE DEAD... ON THE RUN FOR SOME REASON...
I DON'T KNOW EXACTLY WHAT YOUR SICK LITTLE GAME IS, BUT I DON'T WANT ANY--
LOOK AT ME, BURKE. KNOW WHAT I AM.
Ah JEEZ!
I DO NOT PRETEND ANYTHING! LOOK AT THE FACE OF YOUR NEW MASTER AND UNDERSTAND... YOU HAVE MUCH TO LEARN!
LOOK AT ME!
LIFE AND DEATH! THAT'S LESSON ONE!
I WILL CALL ON YOU SOON. BE READY.
AND THEN HE WAS GONE. JUST LIKE THAT.
I'VE REALLY DONE IT NOW, TWITCH. WHAT THE HELL HAVE I GOTTEN US INTO?

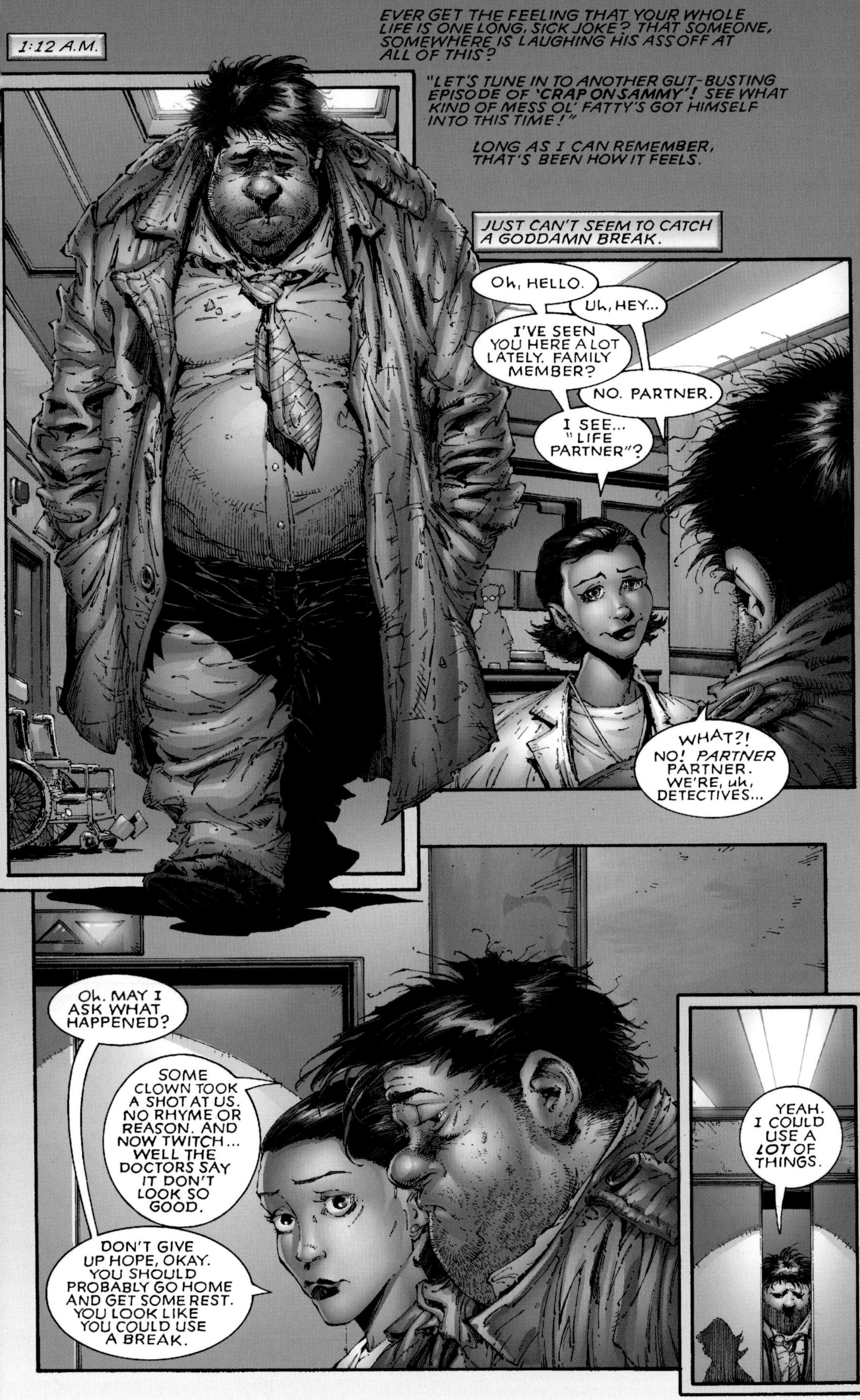
1:12 A.M.
EVER GET THE FEELING THAT YOUR WHOLE LIFE IS ONE LONG, SICK JOKE? THAT SOMEONE, SOMEWHERE IS LAUGHING HIS ASS OFF AT ALL OF THIS?
"LET'S TUNE IN TO ANOTHER GUT-BUSTING EPISODE OF 'CRAP ON SAMMY'! SEE WHAT KIND OF MESS OL' FATTY'S GOT HIMSELF INTO THIS TIME!"
LONG AS I CAN REMEMBER, THAT'S BEEN HOW IT FEELS.
JUST CAN'T SEEM TO CATCH A GODDAMN BREAK.
Oh, HELLO.
Uh, HEY...
I'VE SEEN YOU HERE A LOT LATELY. FAMILY MEMBER?
NO. PARTNER.
I SEE... "LIFE PARTNER"?
WHAT?! NO! PARTNER PARTNER. WE'RE, uh, DETECTIVES...
Oh. MAY I ASK WHAT HAPPENED?
SOME CLOWN TOOK A SHOT AT US. NO RHYME OR REASON. AND NOW TWITCH... WELL THE DOCTORS SAY IT DON'T LOOK SO GOOD.
DON'T GIVE UP HOPE, OKAY. YOU SHOULD PROBABLY GO HOME AND GET SOME REST. YOU LOOK LIKE YOU COULD USE A BREAK.
YEAH. I COULD USE A LOT OF THINGS.

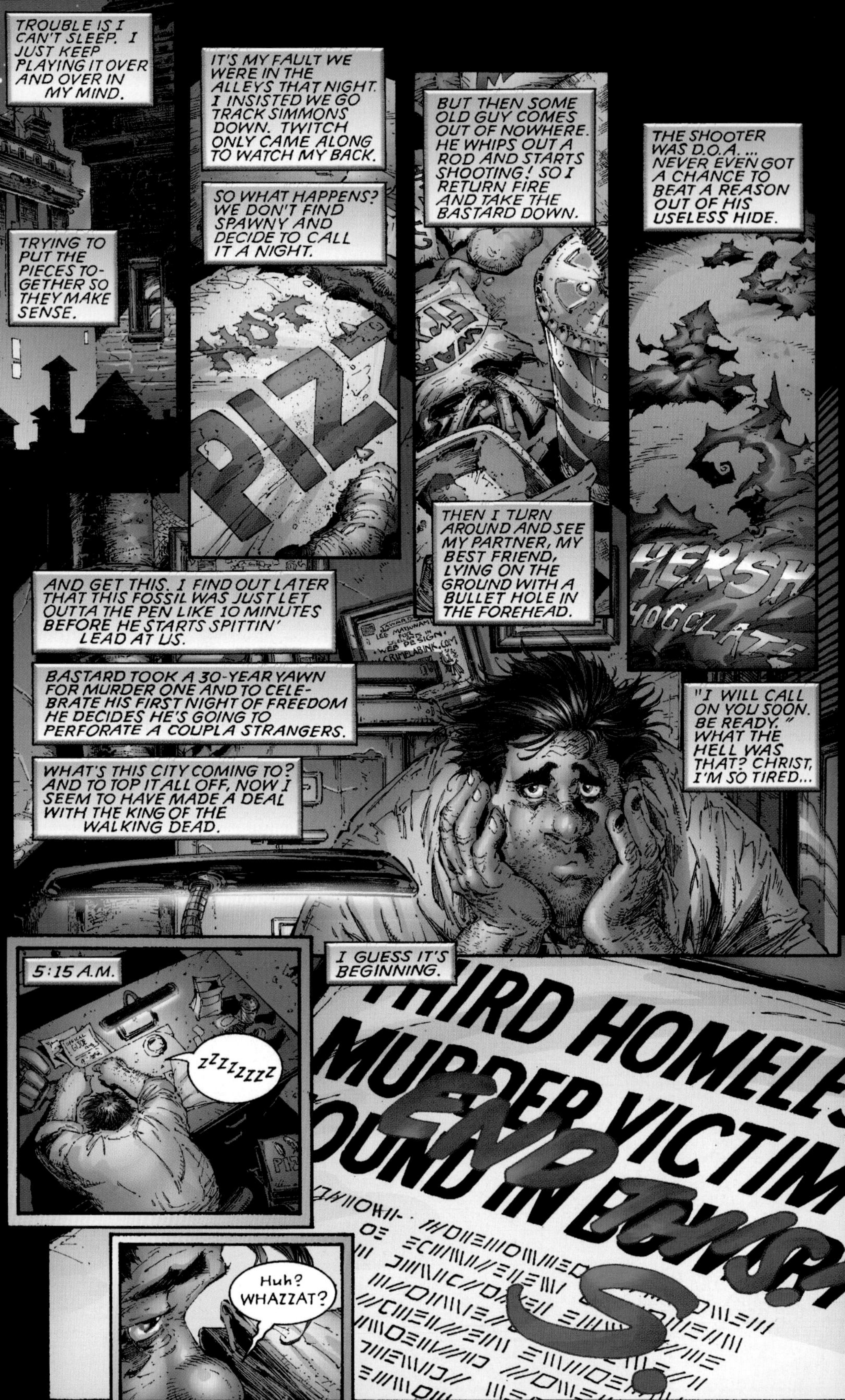
TROUBLE IS I CAN'T SLEEP. I JUST KEEP PLAYING IT OVER AND OVER IN MY MIND.
TRYING TO PUT THE PIECES TO-GETHER SO THEY MAKE SENSE.
IT'S MY FAULT WE WERE IN THE ALLEYS THAT NIGHT. I INSISTED WE GO TRACK SIMMONS DOWN. TWITCH ONLY CAME ALONG TO WATCH MY BACK.
SO WHAT HAPPENS? WE DON'T FIND SPAWNY AND DECIDE TO CALL IT A NIGHT.
BUT THEN SOME OLD GUY COMES OUT OF NOWHERE. HE WHIPS OUT A ROD AND STARTS SHOOTING! SO I RETURN FIRE AND TAKE THE BASTARD DOWN.
THEN I TURN AROUND AND SEE MY PARTNER, MY BEST FRIEND, LYING ON THE GROUND WITH A BULLET HOLE IN THE FOREHEAD.
THE SHOOTER WAS D.O.A.... NEVER EVEN GOT A CHANCE TO BEAT A REASON OUT OF HIS USELESS HIDE.
AND GET THIS. I FIND OUT LATER THAT THIS FOSSIL WAS JUST LET OUTTA THE PEN LIKE 10 MINUTES BEFORE HE STARTS SPITTIN' LEAD AT US.
BASTARD TOOK A 30-YEAR YAWN FOR MURDER ONE AND TO CELE-BRATE HIS FIRST NIGHT OF FREEDOM HE DECIDES HE'S GOING TO PERFORATE A COUPLA STRANGERS.
WHAT'S THIS CITY COMING TO? AND TO TOP IT ALL OFF, NOW I SEEM TO HAVE MADE A DEAL WITH THE KING OF THE WALKING DEAD.
"I WILL CALL ON YOU SOON. BE READY." WHAT THE HELL WAS THAT? CHRIST, I'M SO TIRED...
5:15 A.M.
ZZZZZZZZ
I GUESS IT'S BEGINNING.
Huh? WHAZZAT?
END

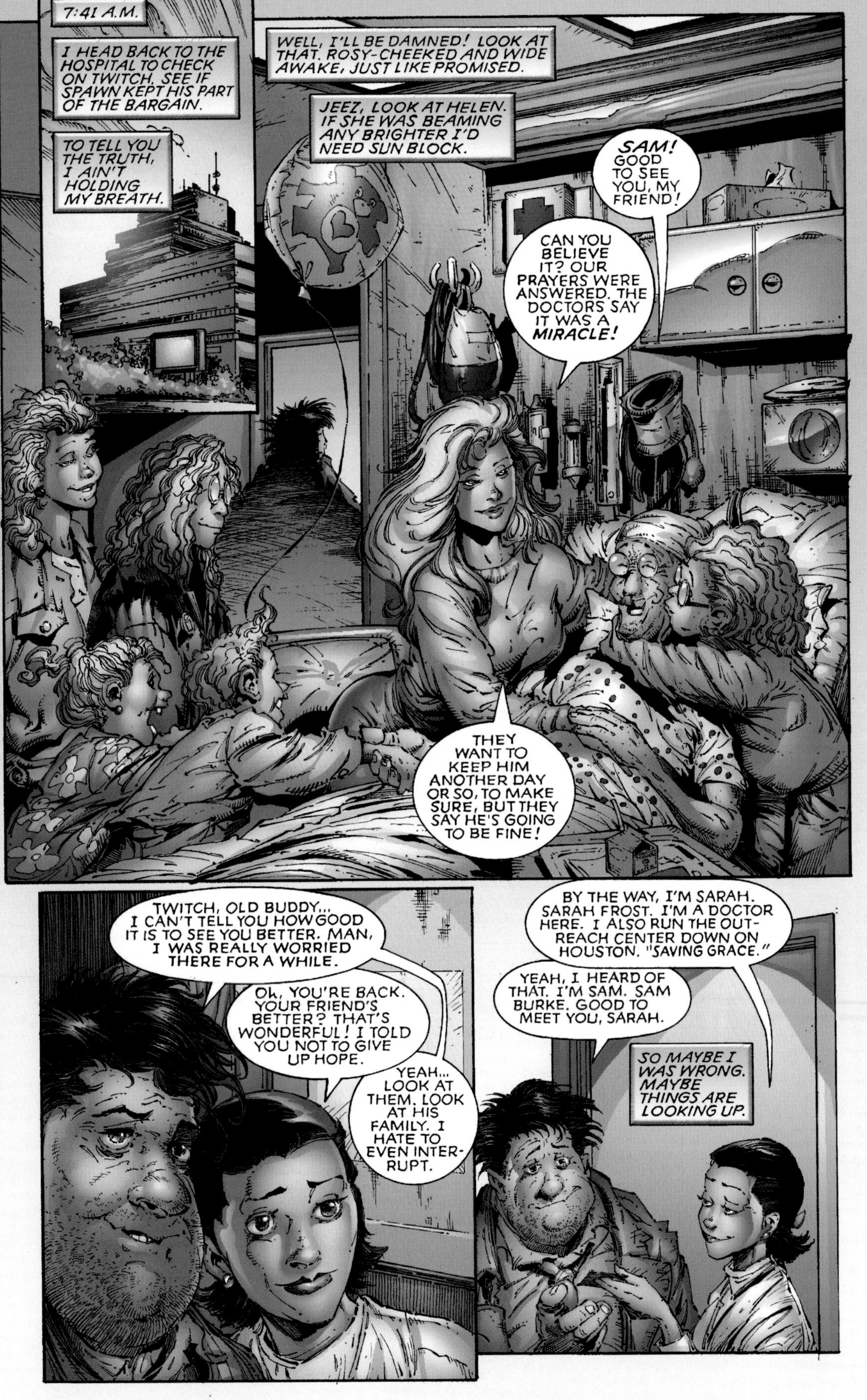
7:41 A.M.
I HEAD BACK TO THE HOSPITAL TO CHECK ON TWITCH, SEE IF SPAWN KEPT HIS PART OF THE BARGAIN.
TO TELL YOU THE TRUTH, I AIN'T HOLDING MY BREATH.
WELL, I'LL BE DAMNED! LOOK AT THAT. ROSY-CHEEKED AND WIDE AWAKE, JUST LIKE PROMISED.
JEEZ, LOOK AT HELEN. IF SHE WAS BEAMING ANY BRIGHTER I'D NEED SUN BLOCK.
SAM! GOOD TO SEE YOU, MY FRIEND!
CAN YOU BELIEVE IT? OUR PRAYERS WERE ANSWERED. THE DOCTORS SAY IT WAS A MIRACLE!
THEY WANT TO KEEP HIM ANOTHER DAY OR SO, TO MAKE SURE, BUT THEY SAY HE'S GOING TO BE FINE!
TWITCH, OLD BUDDY... I CAN'T TELL YOU HOW GOOD IT IS TO SEE YOU BETTER. MAN, I WAS REALLY WORRIED THERE FOR A WHILE.
Oh, YOU'RE BACK. YOUR FRIEND'S BETTER? THAT'S WONDERFUL! I TOLD YOU NOT TO GIVE UP HOPE.
YEAH... LOOK AT THEM. LOOK AT HIS FAMILY. I HATE TO EVEN INTER-RUPT.
BY THE WAY, I'M SARAH. SARAH FROST. I'M A DOCTOR HERE. I ALSO RUN THE OUT-REACH CENTER DOWN ON HOUSTON. "SAVING GRACE."
YEAH, I HEARD OF THAT. I'M SAM. SAM BURKE. GOOD TO MEET YOU, SARAH.
SO MAYBE I WAS WRONG. MAYBE THINGS ARE LOOKING UP.

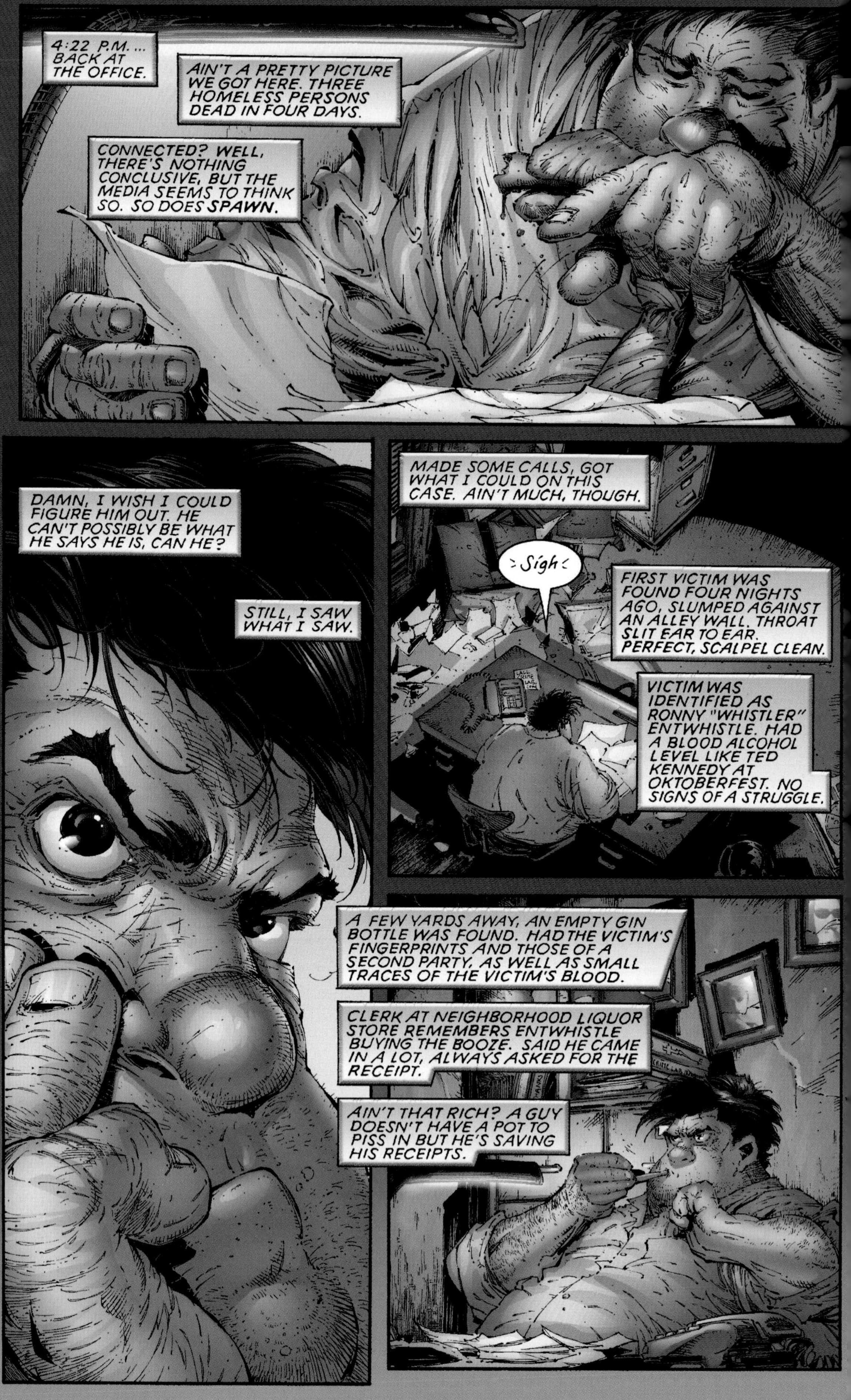
4:22 P.M. ... BACK AT THE OFFICE.
AIN'T A PRETTY PICTURE WE GOT HERE. THREE HOMELESS PERSONS DEAD IN FOUR DAYS.
CONNECTED? WELL, THERE'S NOTHING CONCLUSIVE, BUT THE MEDIA SEEMS TO THINK SO. SO DOES SPAWN.
DAMN, I WISH I COULD FIGURE HIM OUT. HE CAN'T POSSIBLY BE WHAT HE SAYS HE IS, CAN HE?
STILL, I SAW WHAT I SAW.
MADE SOME CALLS, GOT WHAT I COULD ON THIS CASE. AIN'T MUCH, THOUGH.
Sigh
FIRST VICTIM WAS FOUND FOUR NIGHTS AGO, SLUMPED AGAINST AN ALLEY WALL, THROAT SLIT EAR TO EAR. PERFECT, SCALPEL CLEAN.
VICTIM WAS IDENTIFIED AS RONNY "WHISTLER" ENTWHISTLE. HAD A BLOOD ALCOHOL LEVEL LIKE TED KENNEDY AT OKTOBERFEST. NO SIGNS OF A STRUGGLE.
A FEW YARDS AWAY, AN EMPTY GIN BOTTLE WAS FOUND. HAD THE VICTIM'S FINGERPRINTS AND THOSE OF A SECOND PARTY, AS WELL AS SMALL TRACES OF THE VICTIM'S BLOOD.
CLERK AT NEIGHBORHOOD LIQUOR STORE REMEMBERS ENTWHISTLE BUYING THE BOOZE. SAID HE CAME IN A LOT, ALWAYS ASKED FOR THE RECEIPT.
AIN'T THAT RICH? A GUY DOESN'T HAVE A POT TO PISS IN BUT HE'S SAVING HIS RECEIPTS.

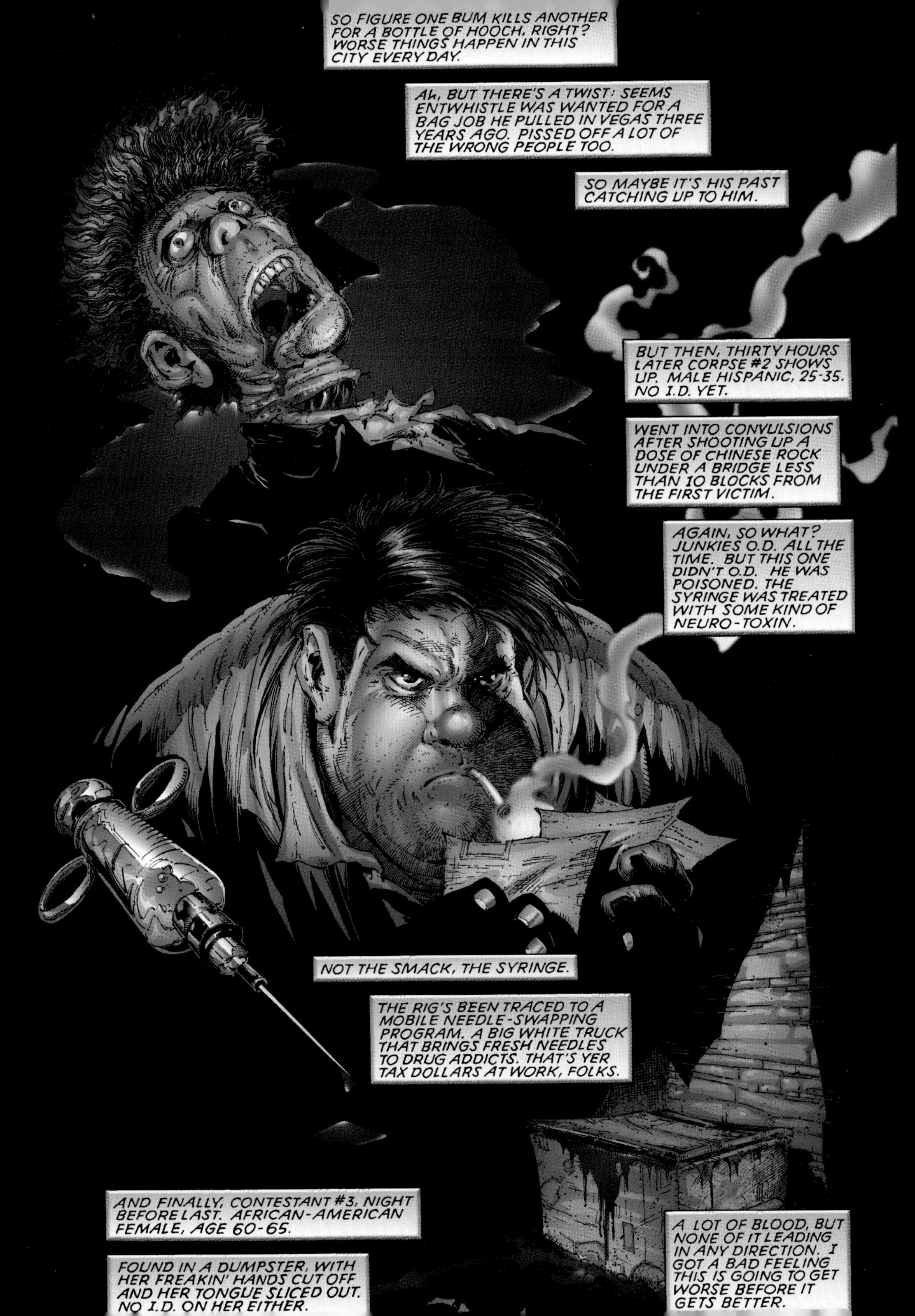
SO FIGURE ONE BUM KILLS ANOTHER FOR A BOTTLE OF HOOCH, RIGHT? WORSE THINGS HAPPEN IN THIS CITY EVERY DAY.
Ah, BUT THERE'S A TWIST: SEEMS ENTWHISTLE WAS WANTED FOR A BAG JOB HE PULLED IN VEGAS THREE YEARS AGO. PISSED OFF A LOT OF THE WRONG PEOPLE TOO.
SO MAYBE IT'S HIS PAST CATCHING UP TO HIM.
BUT THEN, THIRTY HOURS LATER CORPSE #2 SHOWS UP. MALE HISPANIC, 25-35. NO I.D. YET.
WENT INTO CONVULSIONS AFTER SHOOTING UP A DOSE OF CHINESE ROCK UNDER A BRIDGE LESS THAN 10 BLOCKS FROM THE FIRST VICTIM.
AGAIN, SO WHAT? JUNKIES O.D. ALL THE TIME. BUT THIS ONE DIDN'T O.D. HE WAS POISONED. THE SYRINGE WAS TREATED WITH SOME KIND OF NEURO-TOXIN.
NOT THE SMACK, THE SYRINGE.
THE RIG'S BEEN TRACED TO A MOBILE NEEDLE-SWAPPING PROGRAM. A BIG WHITE TRUCK THAT BRINGS FRESH NEEDLES TO DRUG ADDICTS. THAT'S YER TAX DOLLARS AT WORK, FOLKS.
AND FINALLY, CONTESTANT #3, NIGHT BEFORE LAST. AFRICAN-AMERICAN FEMALE, AGE 60-65.
FOUND IN A DUMPSTER, WITH HER FREAKIN' HANDS CUT OFF AND HER TONGUE SLICED OUT. NO I.D. ON HER EITHER.
A LOT OF BLOOD, BUT NONE OF IT LEADING IN ANY DIRECTION. I GOT A BAD FEELING THIS IS GOING TO GET WORSE BEFORE IT GETS BETTER.

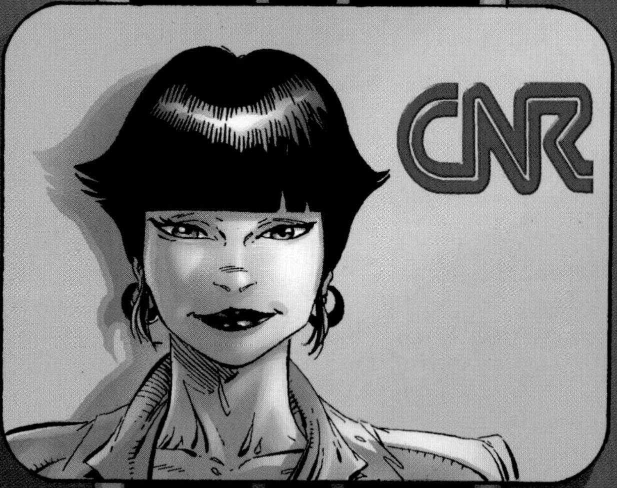
CNR

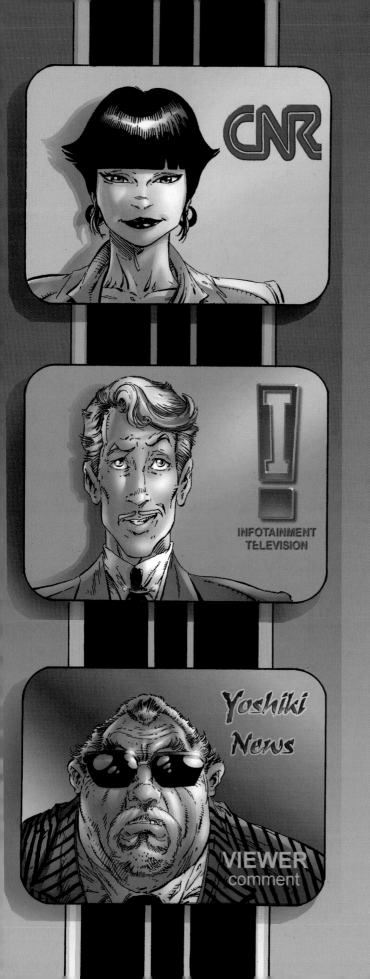

...INCREASINGLY GRUESOME STRING OF MURDERS AMONG NEW YORK CITY'S HOMELESS POPULATION HAS SPARKED OUTCRIES FROM MANY CORNERS. WHILE NO CONCRETE LINK BETWEEN THE CRIMES HAS BEEN ESTABLISHED, CITY OFFICIALS ARE PLEDGING THEIR SUPPPORT, AGREEING TO OPEN UP EMERGENCY SHELTERS UNTIL THE KILLER OR KILLERS ARE APPREHENDED. POLICE COULD NOT RELEASE ANY INFORMATION ON THEIR PROGRESS IN THE CASE, BUT INSIST THEY ARE "PURSUING THE MATTER WITH ALL DUE DILIGENCE."

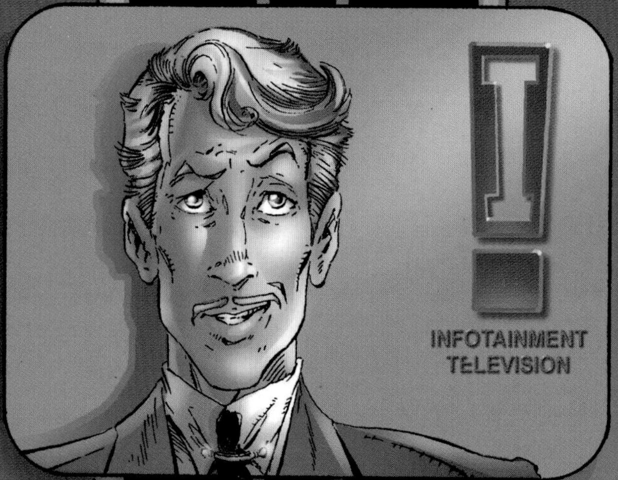
I
INFOTAINMENT
TELEVISION

THERE'S NO SHORTAGE OF ***ENVY*** DIRECTED TOWARD THE MAYOR'S OFFICE LATELY, AND IT'S COMING FROM NO LESS THAN THE EXECS AT THE ***TOP AD AGENCIES.*** THE REDEFINITION OF THE HOMELESS AS "OUTDOORSMEN" AND THE IMPLIED MAKEOVER OF THE CITY'S STREETS AS "THE UNTAMED FRONTIER" HAVE BEEN ***GENUINELY*** INSPIRED EXPANSIONS OF THE THEME-PARK ATMOSPHERE THIS ADMINISTRATION HAS EMBRACED. RECENT YEARS HAVE SEEN GROWING NUMBERS OF THE POOR AND WRETCHED, AND AT LAST THEY HAVE A DESIGNATED ***PLACE*** IN THE ***SCHEME*** OF THINGS!

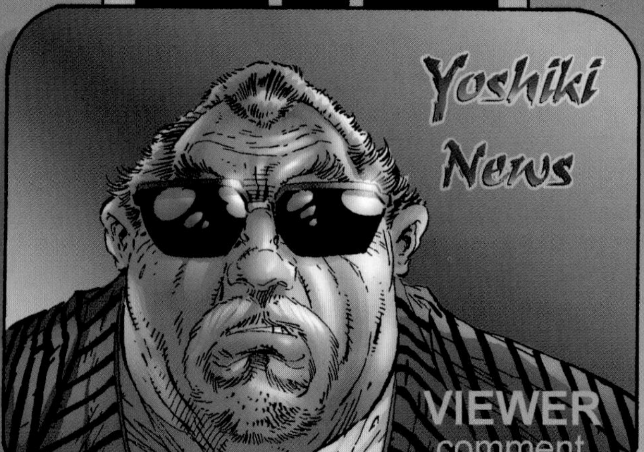
Yoshiki
News
VIEWER
comment

WELL, IMAGINE MY ***SURPRISE!*** IT LOOKS TO BE MORE OF THE SAME OLD SAME OLD IN THE ***"NEW" NEW YORK!*** WHILE THE ILLUSTRIOUS MAYOR WOULD LIKE TO PRETEND THAT THERE ARE ***NO*** REMAINING HOMELESS PEOPLE IN HIS FAIR CITY, THE CURRENT SPATE OF VIOLENCE HAS PUT A MIGHTY DING IN THE CITY'S CAREFULLY CONSTRUCTED, FAMILY-FRIENDLY ***IMAGE.*** A SPOKESPERSON FOR TOURIST RELATIONS CONCEDES THAT THE LATEST MURDER SPREE MIGHT "VERY WELL HAVE A NEGATIVE IMPACT ON THE CITY'S NATIONAL PROFILE." MIGHT I ***DIFFER*** WITH THIS ESTEEMED SHILL FOR THE GODS OF COMMERCE? IF ANYTHING, OUR TOWN CAN NOW ***TRULY*** BOAST OF HAVING SOMETHING FOR EVERYONE! FROM THE THEATRE DISTRICT IN MIDTOWN TO BUTCHERTOWN IN THE BOWERY, THERE'S NO DENYING THAT ***IT'S A HELLUVA TOWN.***

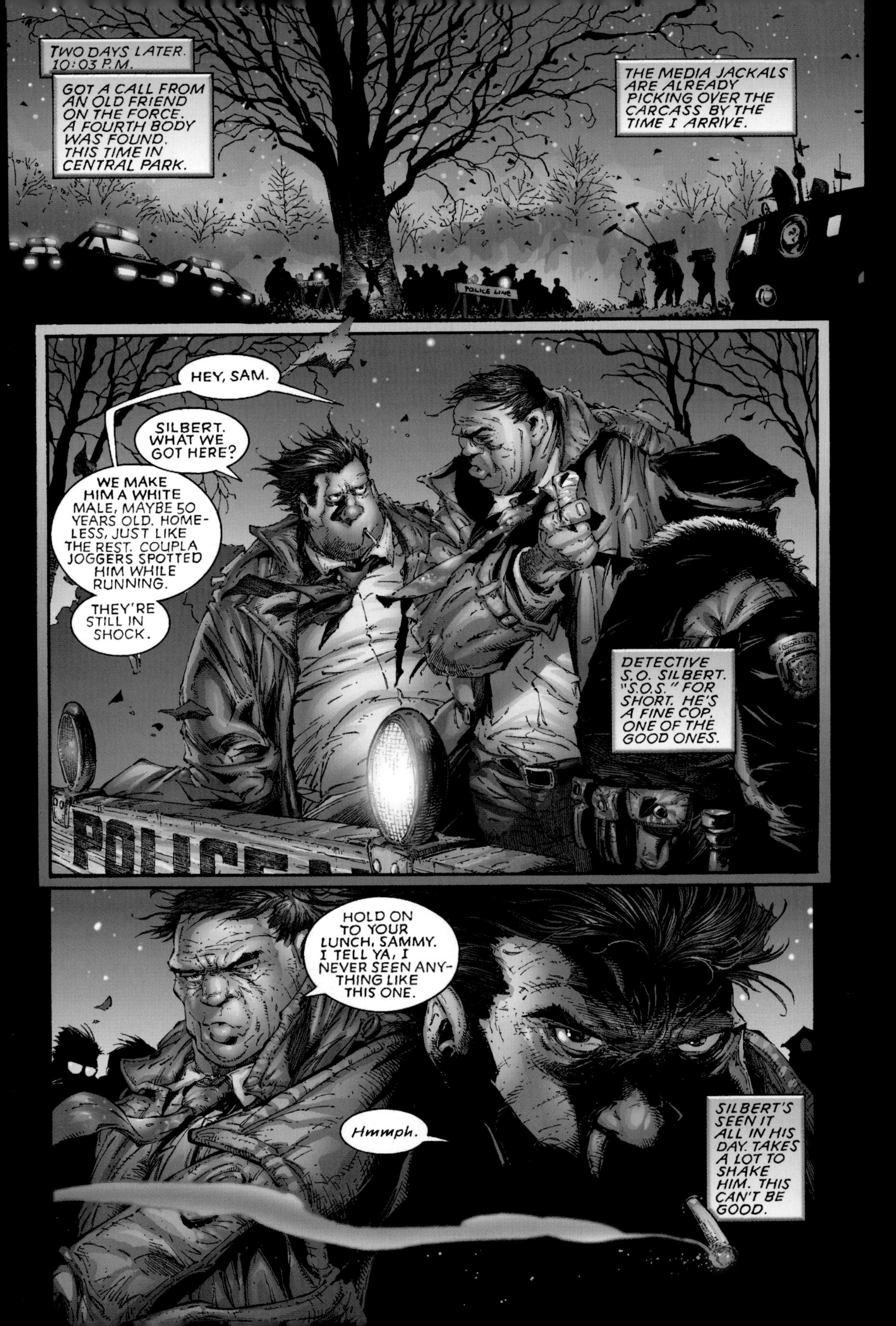

TWO DAYS LATER. 10:03 P.M.
GOT A CALL FROM AN OLD FRIEND ON THE FORCE. A FOURTH BODY WAS FOUND. THIS TIME IN CENTRAL PARK.
THE MEDIA JACKALS ARE ALREADY PICKING OVER THE CARCASS BY THE TIME I ARRIVE.
POLICE LINE
HEY, SAM.
SILBERT. WHAT WE GOT HERE?
WE MAKE HIM A WHITE MALE, MAYBE 50 YEARS OLD. HOMELESS, JUST LIKE THE REST. COUPLA JOGGERS SPOTTED HIM WHILE RUNNING.
THEY'RE STILL IN SHOCK.
DETECTIVE S.O. SILBERT. "S.O.S." FOR SHORT. HE'S A FINE COP. ONE OF THE GOOD ONES.
HOLD ON TO YOUR LUNCH, SAMMY. I TELL YA, I NEVER SEEN ANYTHING LIKE THIS ONE.
Hmmph.
SILBERT'S SEEN IT ALL IN HIS DAY. TAKES A LOT TO SHAKE HIM. THIS CAN'T BE GOOD.

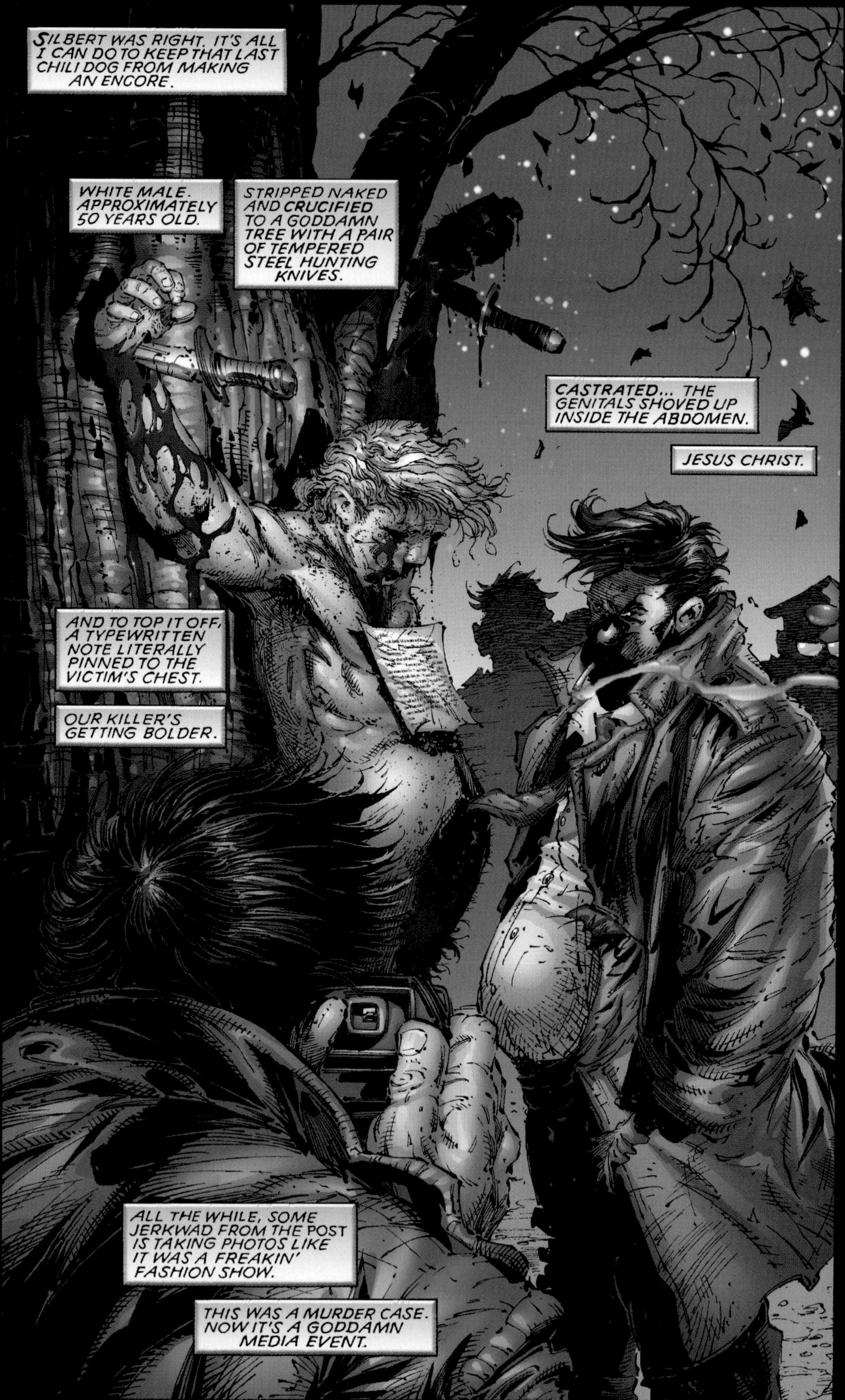
SILBERT WAS RIGHT. IT'S ALL I CAN DO TO KEEP THAT LAST CHILI DOG FROM MAKING AN ENCORE.
WHITE MALE. APPROXIMATELY 50 YEARS OLD.
STRIPPED NAKED AND CRUCIFIED TO A GODDAMN TREE WITH A PAIR OF TEMPERED STEEL HUNTING KNIVES.
CASTRATED... THE GENITALS SHOVED UP INSIDE THE ABDOMEN.
JESUS CHRIST.
AND TO TOP IT OFF, A TYPEWRITTEN NOTE LITERALLY PINNED TO THE VICTIM'S CHEST.
OUR KILLER'S GETTING BOLDER.
ALL THE WHILE, SOME JERKWAD FROM THE POST IS TAKING PHOTOS LIKE IT WAS A FREAKIN' FASHION SHOW.
THIS WAS A MURDER CASE. NOW IT'S A GODDAMN MEDIA EVENT.

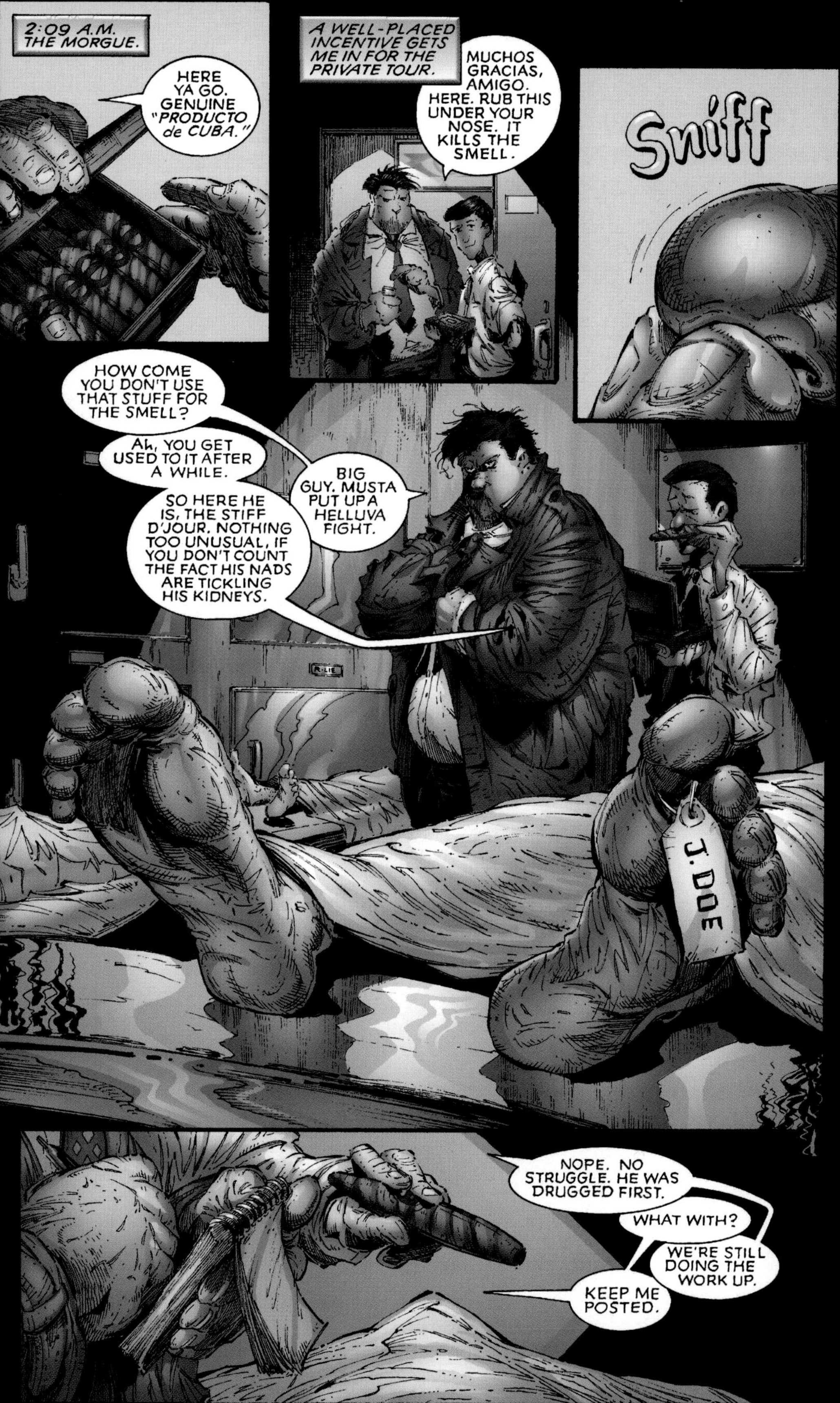
2:09 A.M. THE MORGUE.
HERE YA GO. GENUINE "PRODUCTO de CUBA."
A WELL-PLACED INCENTIVE GETS ME IN FOR THE PRIVATE TOUR.
MUCHOS GRACIAS, AMIGO. HERE. RUB THIS UNDER YOUR NOSE. IT KILLS THE SMELL.
Sniff
HOW COME YOU DON'T USE THAT STUFF FOR THE SMELL?
Ah, YOU GET USED TO IT AFTER A WHILE.
SO HERE HE IS, THE STIFF D'JOUR. NOTHING TOO UNUSUAL, IF YOU DON'T COUNT THE FACT HIS NADS ARE TICKLING HIS KIDNEYS.
BIG GUY. MUSTA PUT UP A HELLUVA FIGHT.
J. DOE
NOPE. NO STRUGGLE. HE WAS DRUGGED FIRST.
WHAT WITH?
WE'RE STILL DOING THE WORK UP.
KEEP ME POSTED.

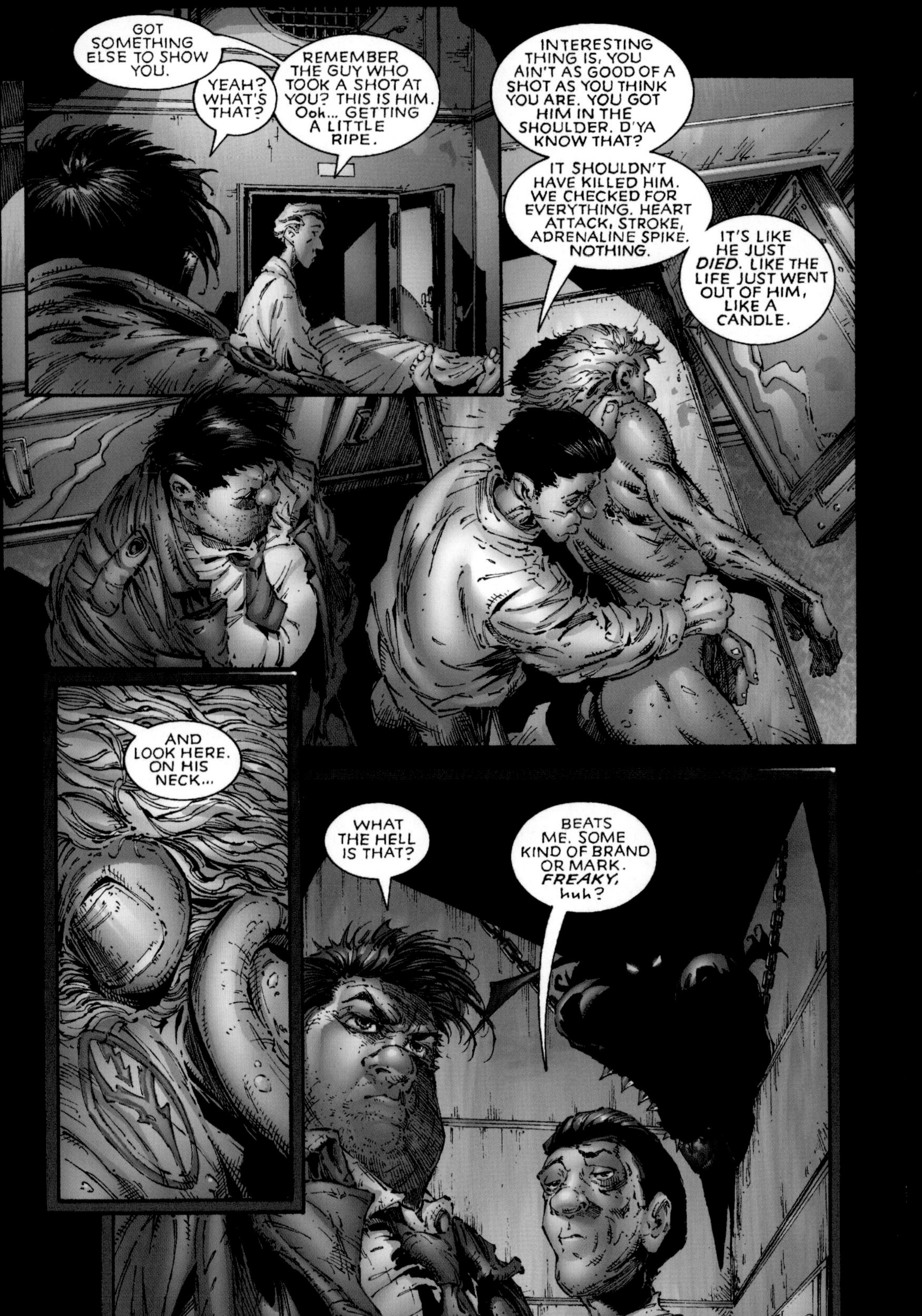

GOT SOMETHING ELSE TO SHOW YOU.
YEAH? WHAT'S THAT?
REMEMBER THE GUY WHO TOOK A SHOT AT YOU? THIS IS HIM. Ook... GETTING A LITTLE RIPE.
INTERESTING THING IS, YOU AIN'T AS GOOD OF A SHOT AS YOU THINK YOU ARE. YOU GOT HIM IN THE SHOULDER. D'YA KNOW THAT?
IT SHOULDN'T HAVE KILLED HIM. WE CHECKED FOR EVERYTHING. HEART ATTACK, STROKE, ADRENALINE SPIKE. NOTHING.
IT'S LIKE HE JUST *DIED*. LIKE THE LIFE JUST WENT OUT OF HIM, LIKE A CANDLE.
AND LOOK HERE. ON HIS NECK...
WHAT THE HELL IS THAT?
BEATS ME. SOME KIND OF BRAND OR MARK. *FREAKY,* huh?

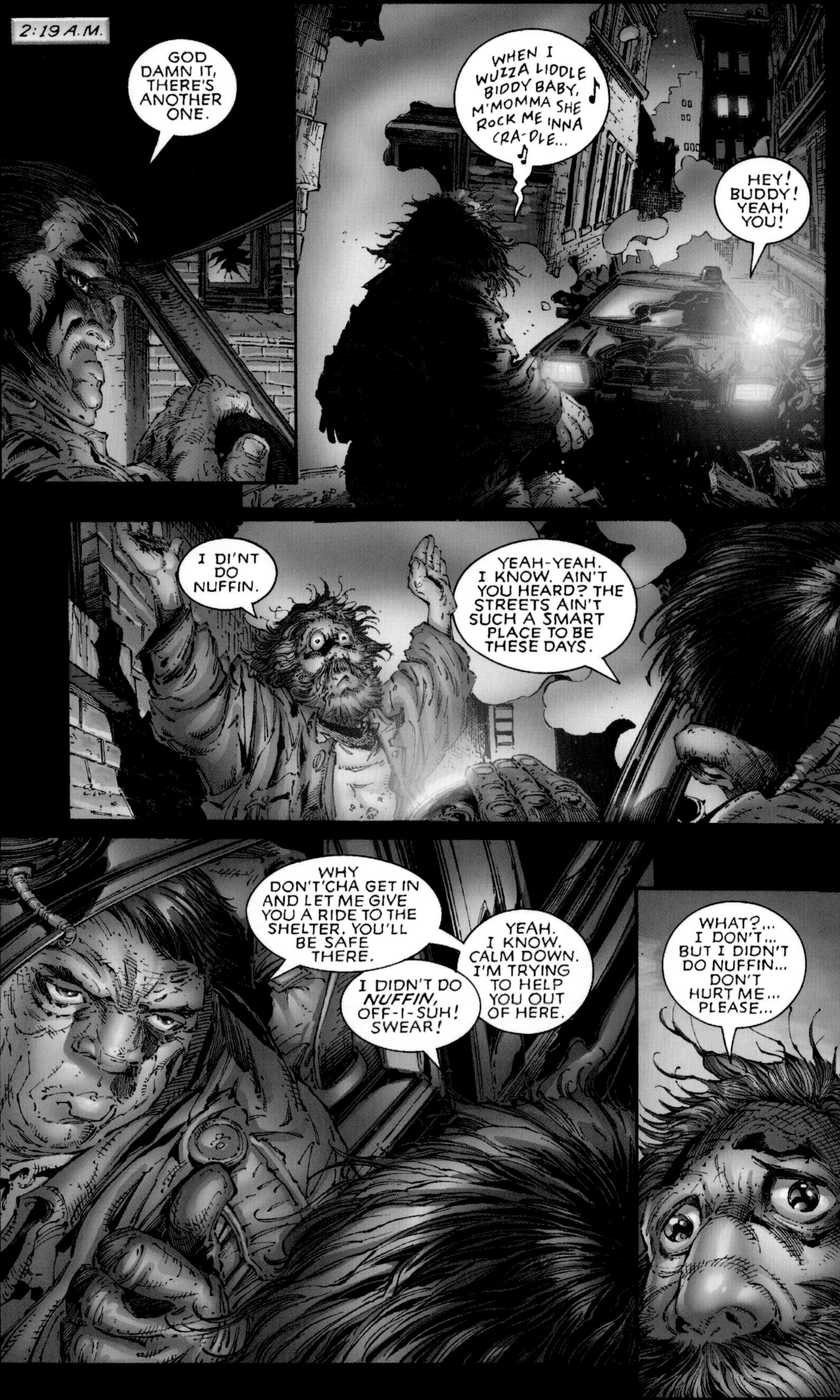
2:19 A.M.
GOD DAMN IT, THERE'S ANOTHER ONE.
WHEN I WUZZA LIDDLE BIDDY BABY, M'MOMMA SHE ROCK ME INNA CRA-DLE...
HEY! BUDDY! YEAH, YOU!
I DI'NT DO NUFFIN.
YEAH-YEAH. I KNOW. AIN'T YOU HEARD? THE STREETS AIN'T SUCH A SMART PLACE TO BE THESE DAYS.
WHY DON'T'CHA GET IN AND LET ME GIVE YOU A RIDE TO THE SHELTER. YOU'LL BE SAFE THERE.
I DIDN'T DO NUFFIN, OFF-I-SUH! SWEAR!
YEAH. I KNOW. CALM DOWN. I'M TRYING TO HELP YOU OUT OF HERE.
WHAT?... I DON'T... BUT I DIDN'T DO NUFFIN... DON'T HURT ME... PLEASE...

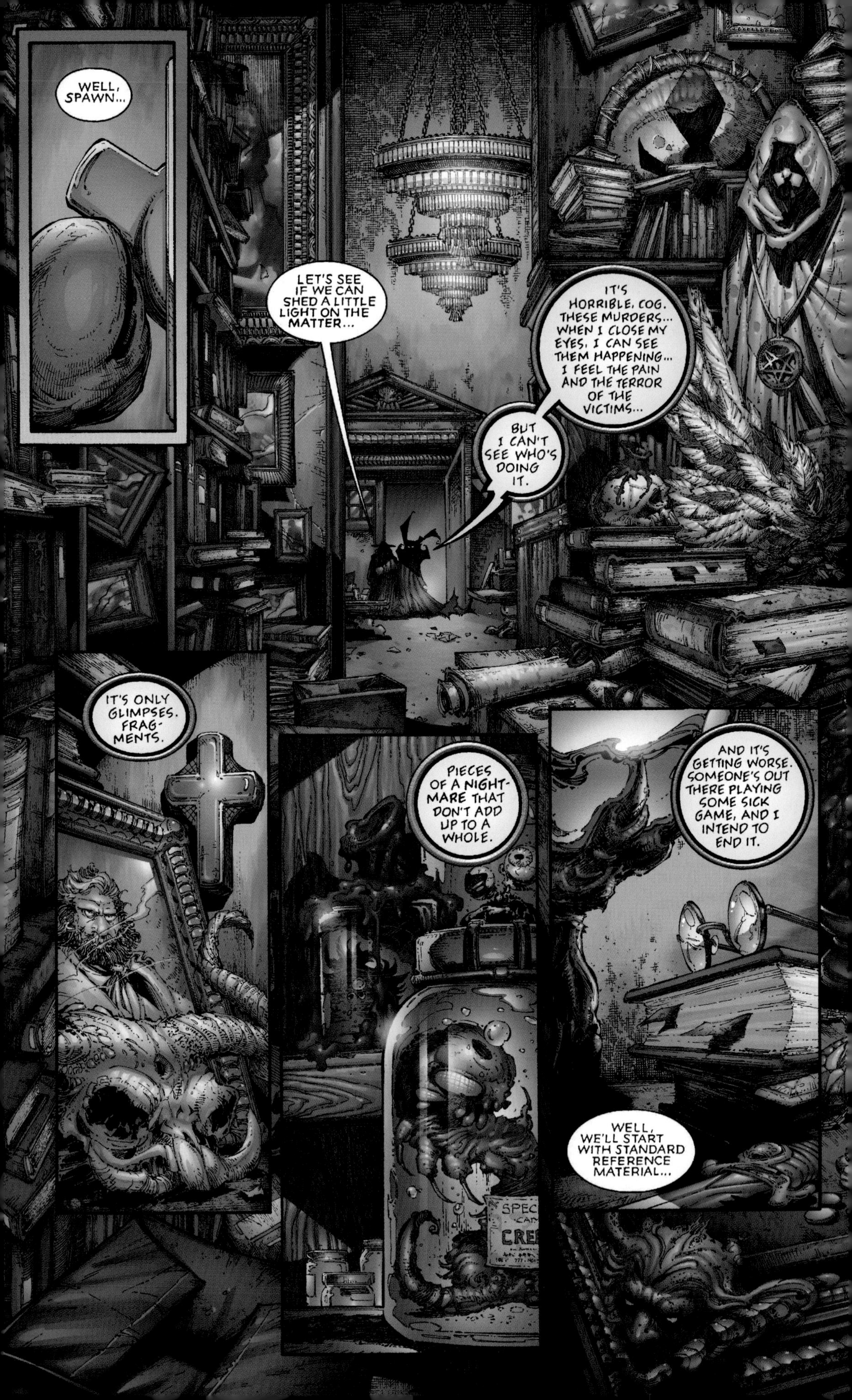
WELL, SPAWN...
LET'S SEE IF WE CAN SHED A LITTLE LIGHT ON THE MATTER...
IT'S HORRIBLE, COG. THESE MURDERS... WHEN I CLOSE MY EYES, I CAN SEE THEM HAPPENING... I FEEL THE PAIN AND THE TERROR OF THE VICTIMS...
BUT I CAN'T SEE WHO'S DOING IT.
IT'S ONLY GLIMPSES. FRAG-MENTS.
PIECES OF A NIGHT-MARE THAT DON'T ADD UP TO A WHOLE.
AND IT'S GETTING WORSE. SOMEONE'S OUT THERE PLAYING SOME SICK GAME, AND I INTEND TO END IT.
WELL, WE'LL START WITH STANDARD REFERENCE MATERIAL...

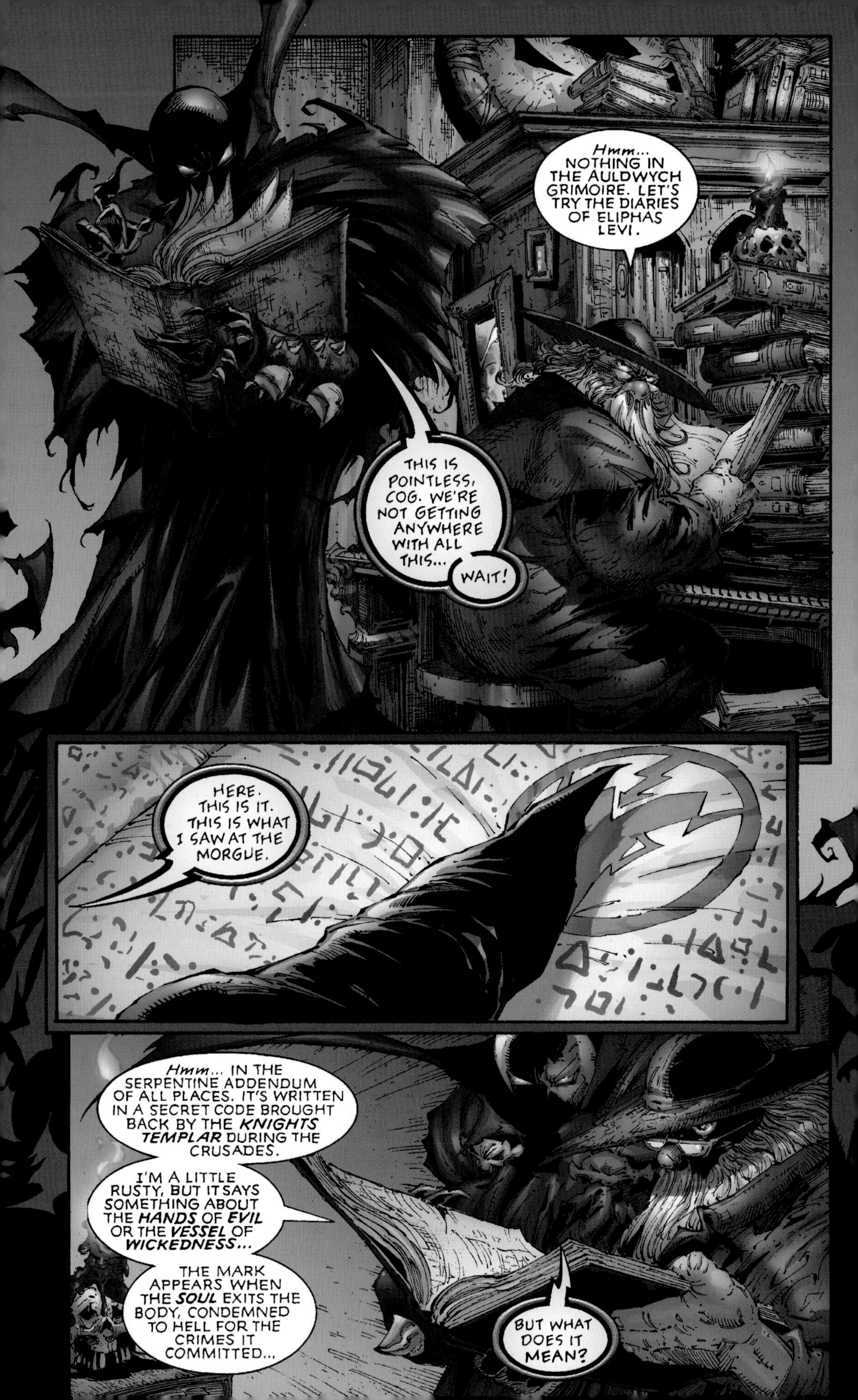

Hmm... NOTHING IN THE AULDWYCH GRIMOIRE. LET'S TRY THE DIARIES OF ELIPHAS LEVI.
THIS IS POINTLESS, COG. WE'RE NOT GETTING ANYWHERE WITH ALL THIS...
WAIT!
HERE. THIS IS IT. THIS IS WHAT I SAW AT THE MORGUE.
Hmm... IN THE SERPENTINE ADDENDUM OF ALL PLACES. IT'S WRITTEN IN A SECRET CODE BROUGHT BACK BY THE KNIGHTS TEMPLAR DURING THE CRUSADES.
I'M A LITTLE RUSTY, BUT IT SAYS SOMETHING ABOUT THE HANDS OF EVIL OR THE VESSEL OF WICKEDNESS...
THE MARK APPEARS WHEN THE SOUL EXITS THE BODY, CONDEMNED TO HELL FOR THE CRIMES IT COMMITTED...
BUT WHAT DOES IT MEAN?

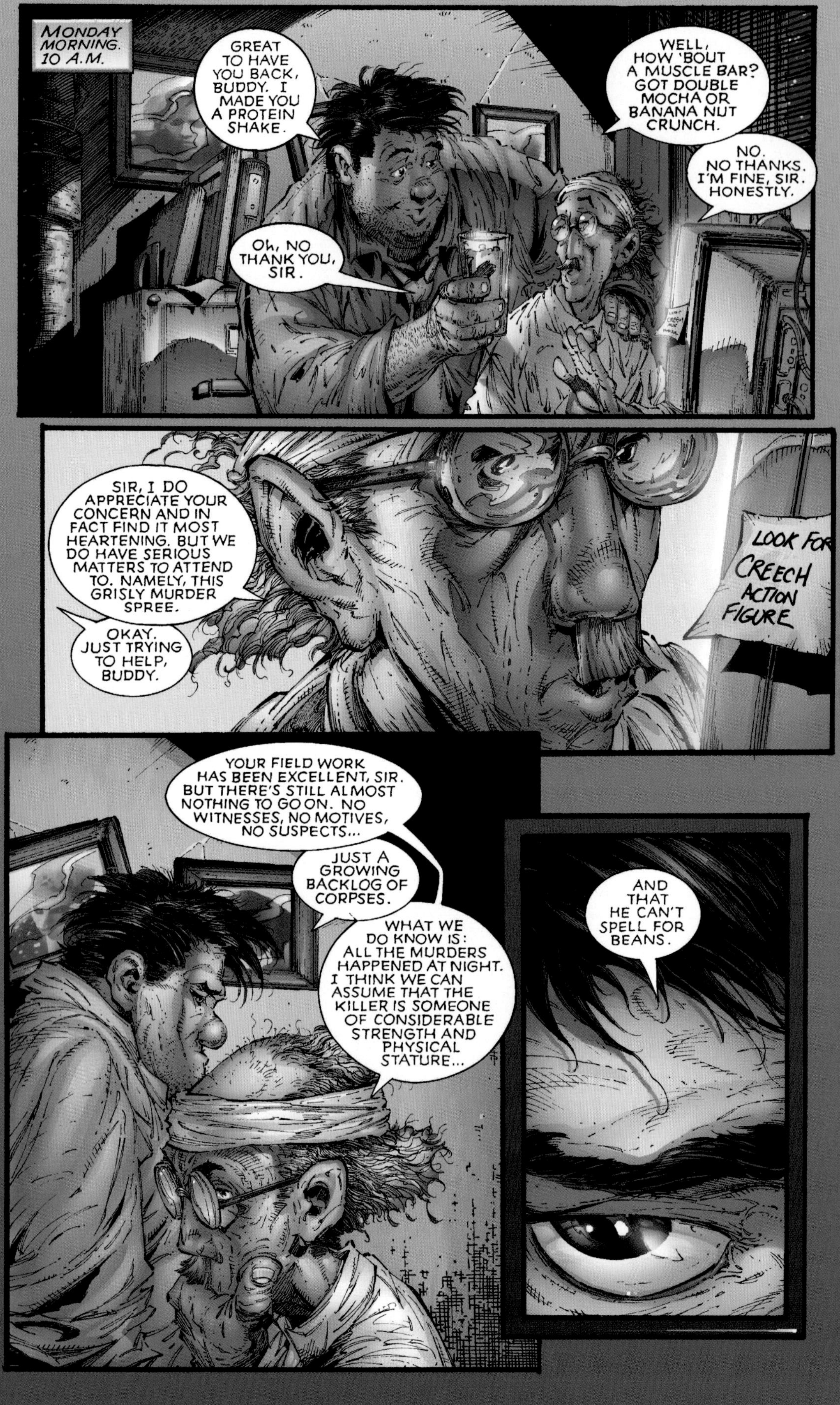
MONDAY MORNING. 10 A.M.
GREAT TO HAVE YOU BACK, BUDDY. I MADE YOU A PROTEIN SHAKE.
Oh, NO THANK YOU, SIR.
WELL, HOW 'BOUT A MUSCLE BAR? GOT DOUBLE MOCHA OR BANANA NUT CRUNCH.
NO. NO THANKS. I'M FINE, SIR. HONESTLY.
SIR, I DO APPRECIATE YOUR CONCERN AND IN FACT FIND IT MOST HEARTENING. BUT WE DO HAVE SERIOUS MATTERS TO ATTEND TO. NAMELY, THIS GRISLY MURDER SPREE.
OKAY. JUST TRYING TO HELP, BUDDY.
LOOK FOR CREECH ACTION FIGURE
YOUR FIELD WORK HAS BEEN EXCELLENT, SIR. BUT THERE'S STILL ALMOST NOTHING TO GO ON. NO WITNESSES, NO MOTIVES, NO SUSPECTS...
JUST A GROWING BACKLOG OF CORPSES.
WHAT WE DO KNOW IS: ALL THE MURDERS HAPPENED AT NIGHT. I THINK WE CAN ASSUME THAT THE KILLER IS SOMEONE OF CONSIDERABLE STRENGTH AND PHYSICAL STATURE...
AND THAT HE CAN'T SPELL FOR BEANS.

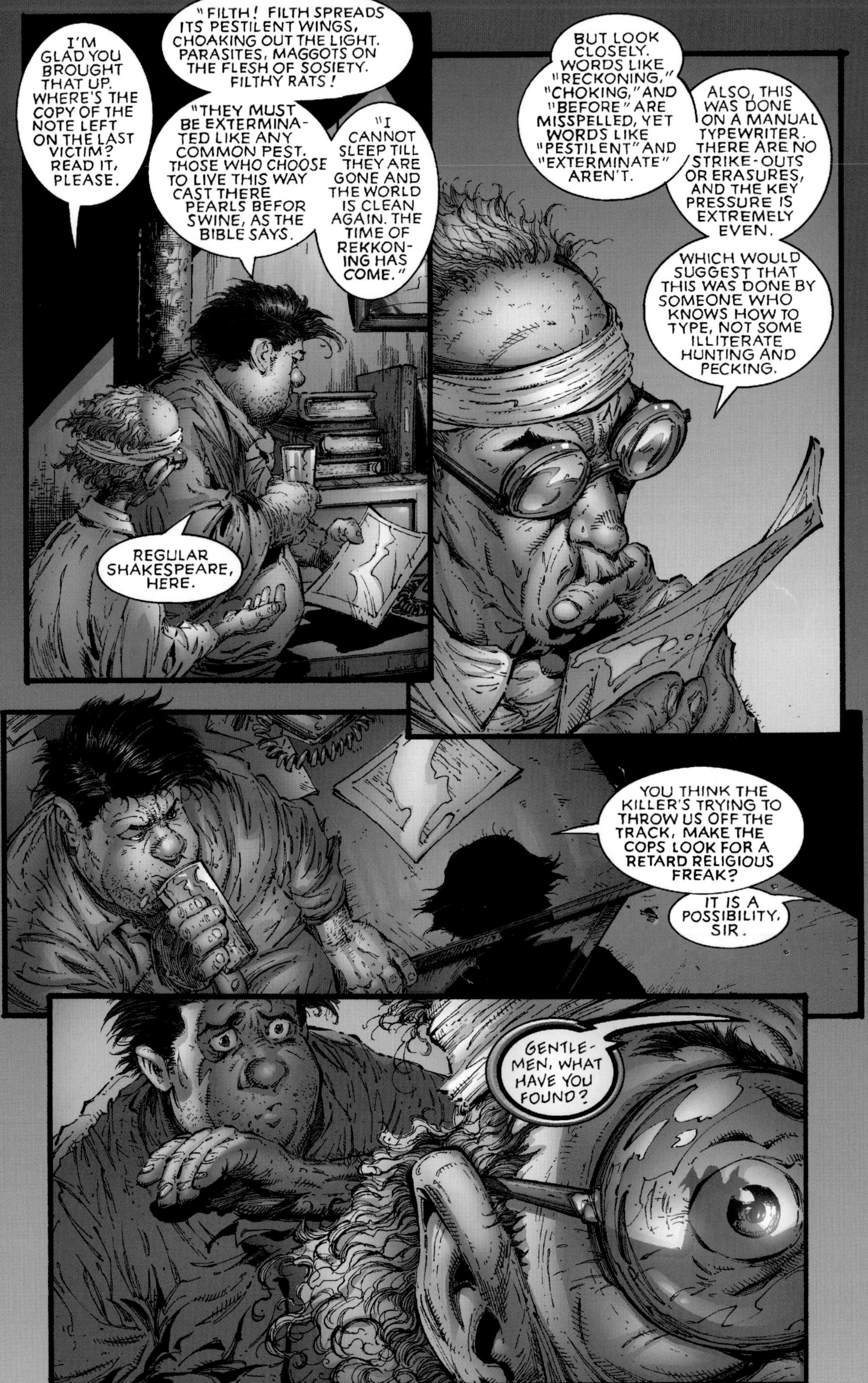

I'M GLAD YOU BROUGHT THAT UP. WHERE'S THE COPY OF THE NOTE LEFT ON THE LAST VICTIM? READ IT, PLEASE.
"FILTH! FILTH SPREADS ITS PESTILENT WINGS, CHOAKING OUT THE LIGHT. PARASITES, MAGGOTS ON THE FLESH OF SOSIETY. FILTHY RATS!
"THEY MUST BE EXTERMINA-TED LIKE ANY COMMON PEST. THOSE WHO CHOOSE TO LIVE THIS WAY CAST THERE PEARLS BEFOR SWINE, AS THE BIBLE SAYS.
"I CANNOT SLEEP TILL THEY ARE GONE AND THE WORLD IS CLEAN AGAIN. THE TIME OF REKKON-ING HAS COME."
REGULAR SHAKESPEARE, HERE.
BUT LOOK CLOSELY. WORDS LIKE "RECKONING," "CHOKING," AND "BEFORE" ARE MISSPELLED, YET WORDS LIKE "PESTILENT" AND "EXTERMINATE" AREN'T.
ALSO, THIS WAS DONE ON A MANUAL TYPEWRITER. THERE ARE NO STRIKE-OUTS OR ERASURES, AND THE KEY PRESSURE IS EXTREMELY EVEN.
WHICH WOULD SUGGEST THAT THIS WAS DONE BY SOMEONE WHO KNOWS HOW TO TYPE, NOT SOME ILLITERATE HUNTING AND PECKING.
YOU THINK THE KILLER'S TRYING TO THROW US OFF THE TRACK, MAKE THE COPS LOOK FOR A RETARD RELIGIOUS FREAK?
IT IS A POSSIBILITY, SIR.
GENTLE-MEN, WHAT HAVE YOU FOUND?

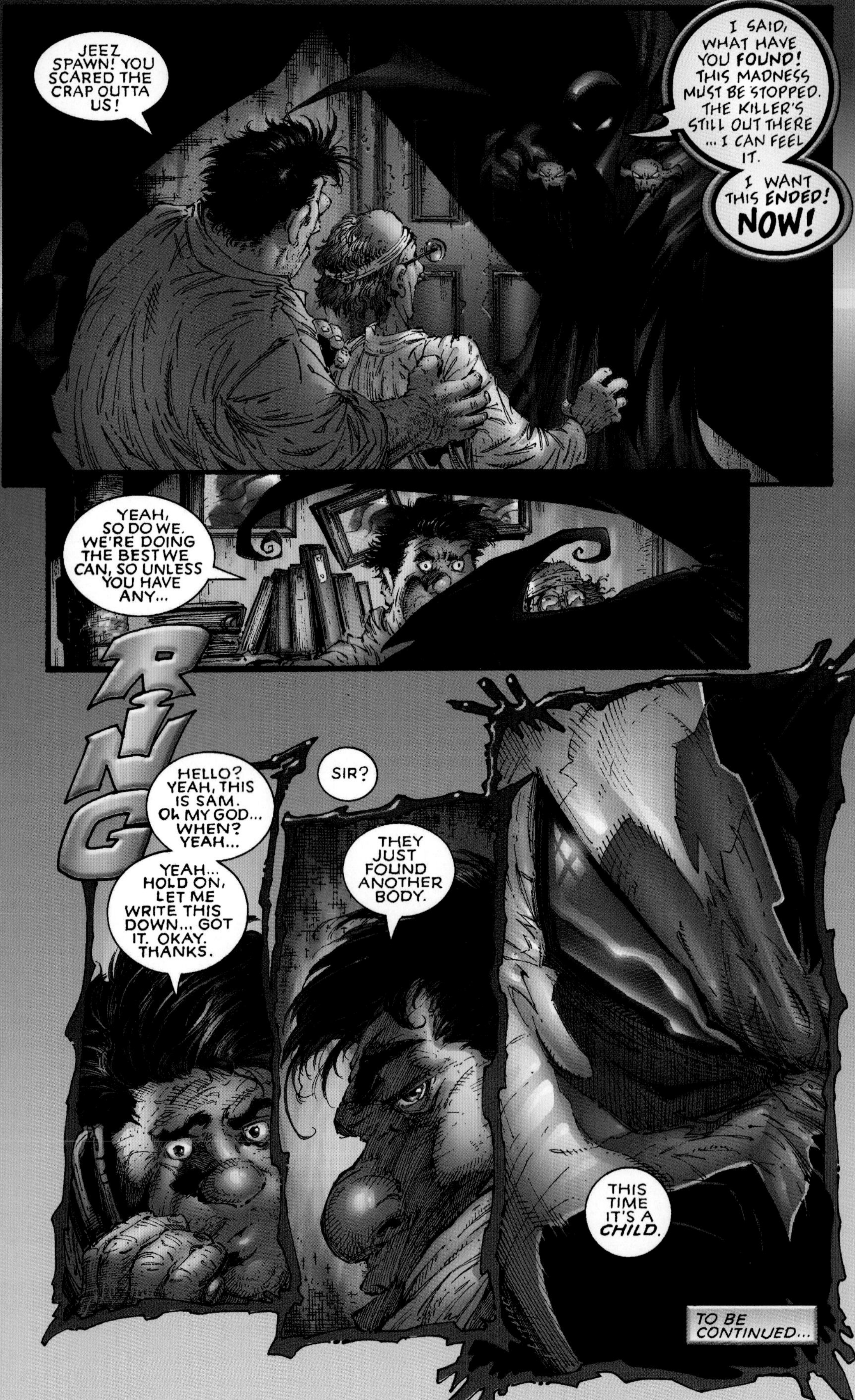
JEEZ SPAWN! YOU SCARED THE CRAP OUTTA US!
I SAID, WHAT HAVE YOU FOUND! THIS MADNESS MUST BE STOPPED. THE KILLER'S STILL OUT THERE ...I CAN FEEL IT.
I WANT THIS ENDED! NOW!
YEAH, SO DO WE. WE'RE DOING THE BEST WE CAN, SO UNLESS YOU HAVE ANY...
RING
HELLO? YEAH, THIS IS SAM. Oh MY GOD... WHEN? YEAH...
YEAH... HOLD ON, LET ME WRITE THIS DOWN... GOT IT. OKAY. THANKS.
SIR?
THEY JUST FOUND ANOTHER BODY.
THIS TIME IT'S A CHILD.
TO BE CONTINUED...

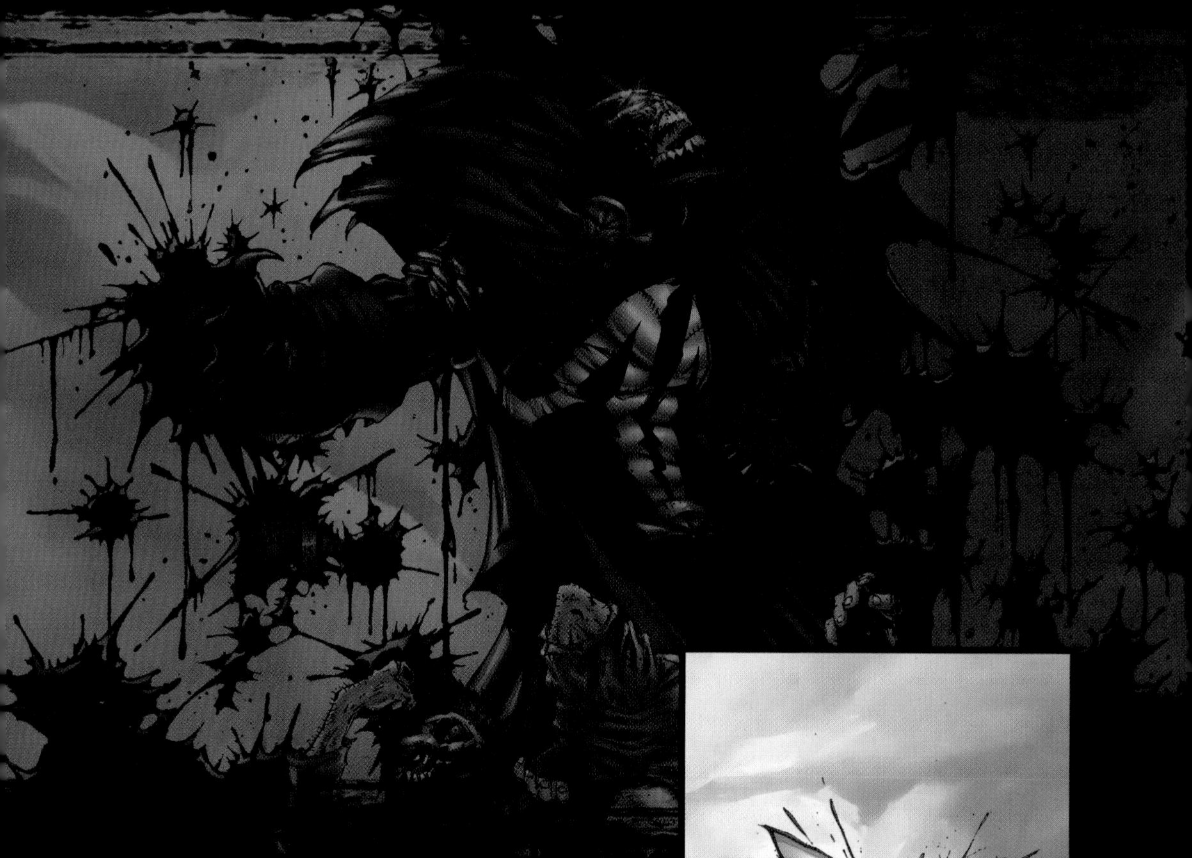

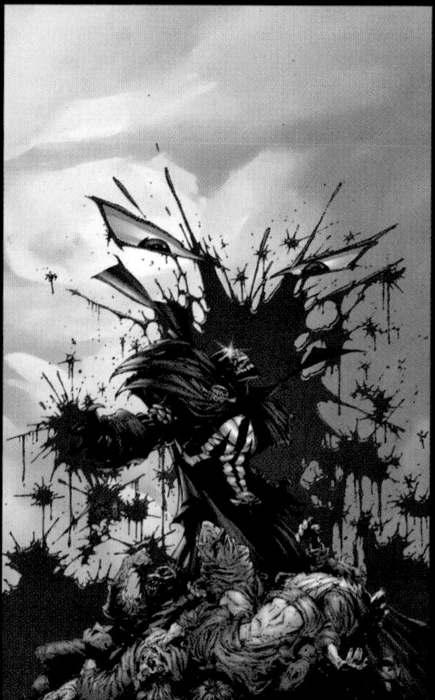

ISSUE SEVENTY-NINE

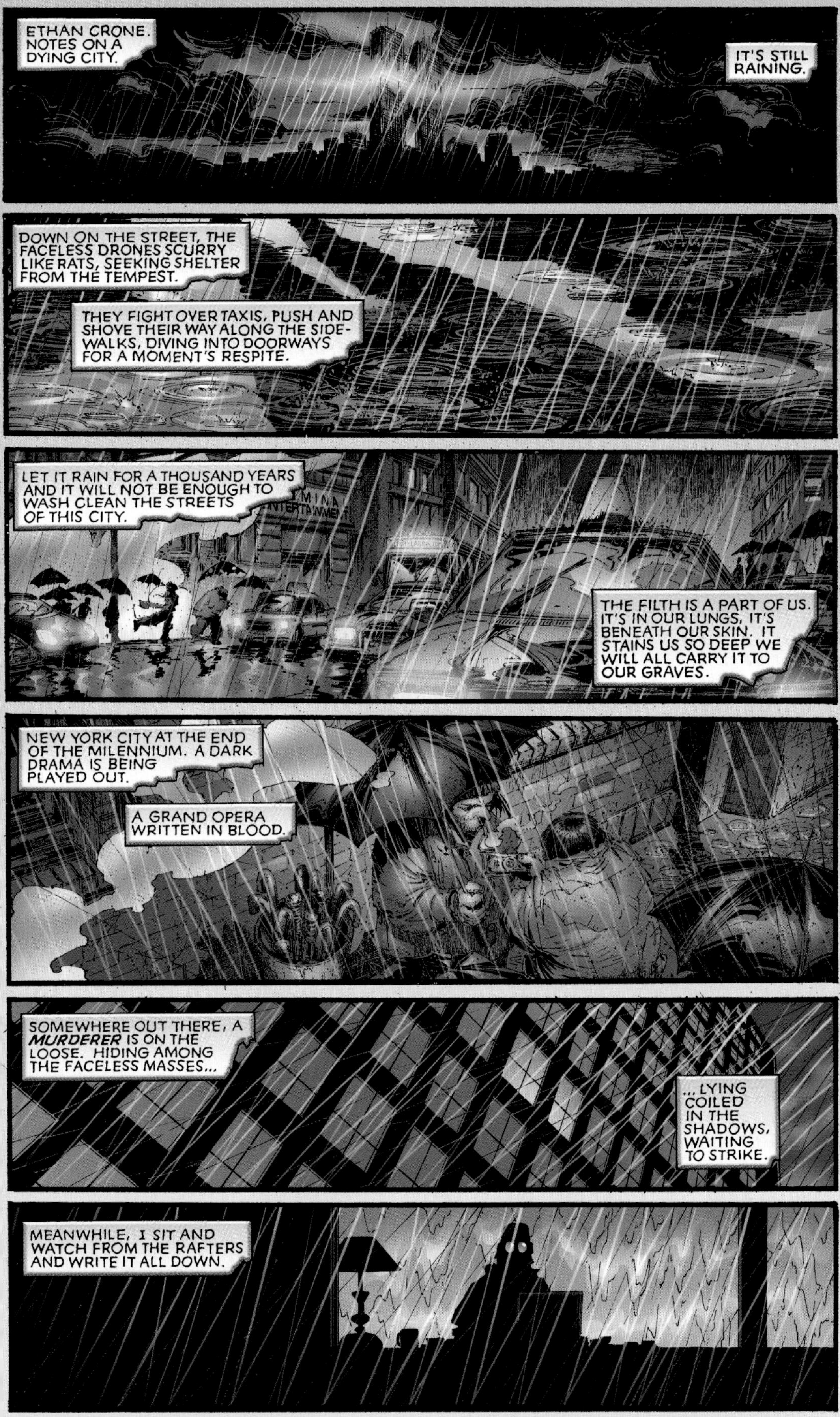
ETHAN CRONE. NOTES ON A DYING CITY.
IT'S STILL RAINING.
DOWN ON THE STREET, THE FACELESS DRONES SCURRY LIKE RATS, SEEKING SHELTER FROM THE TEMPEST.
THEY FIGHT OVER TAXIS, PUSH AND SHOVE THEIR WAY ALONG THE SIDE-WALKS, DIVING INTO DOORWAYS FOR A MOMENT'S RESPITE.
LET IT RAIN FOR A THOUSAND YEARS AND IT WILL NOT BE ENOUGH TO WASH CLEAN THE STREETS OF THIS CITY.
THE FILTH IS A PART OF US. IT'S IN OUR LUNGS, IT'S BENEATH OUR SKIN. IT STAINS US SO DEEP WE WILL ALL CARRY IT TO OUR GRAVES.
NEW YORK CITY AT THE END OF THE MILENNIUM. A DARK DRAMA IS BEING PLAYED OUT.
A GRAND OPERA WRITTEN IN BLOOD.
SOMEWHERE OUT THERE, A *MURDERER* IS ON THE LOOSE. HIDING AMONG THE FACELESS MASSES...
...LYING COILED IN THE SHADOWS, WAITING TO STRIKE.
MEANWHILE, I SIT AND WATCH FROM THE RAFTERS AND WRITE IT ALL DOWN.

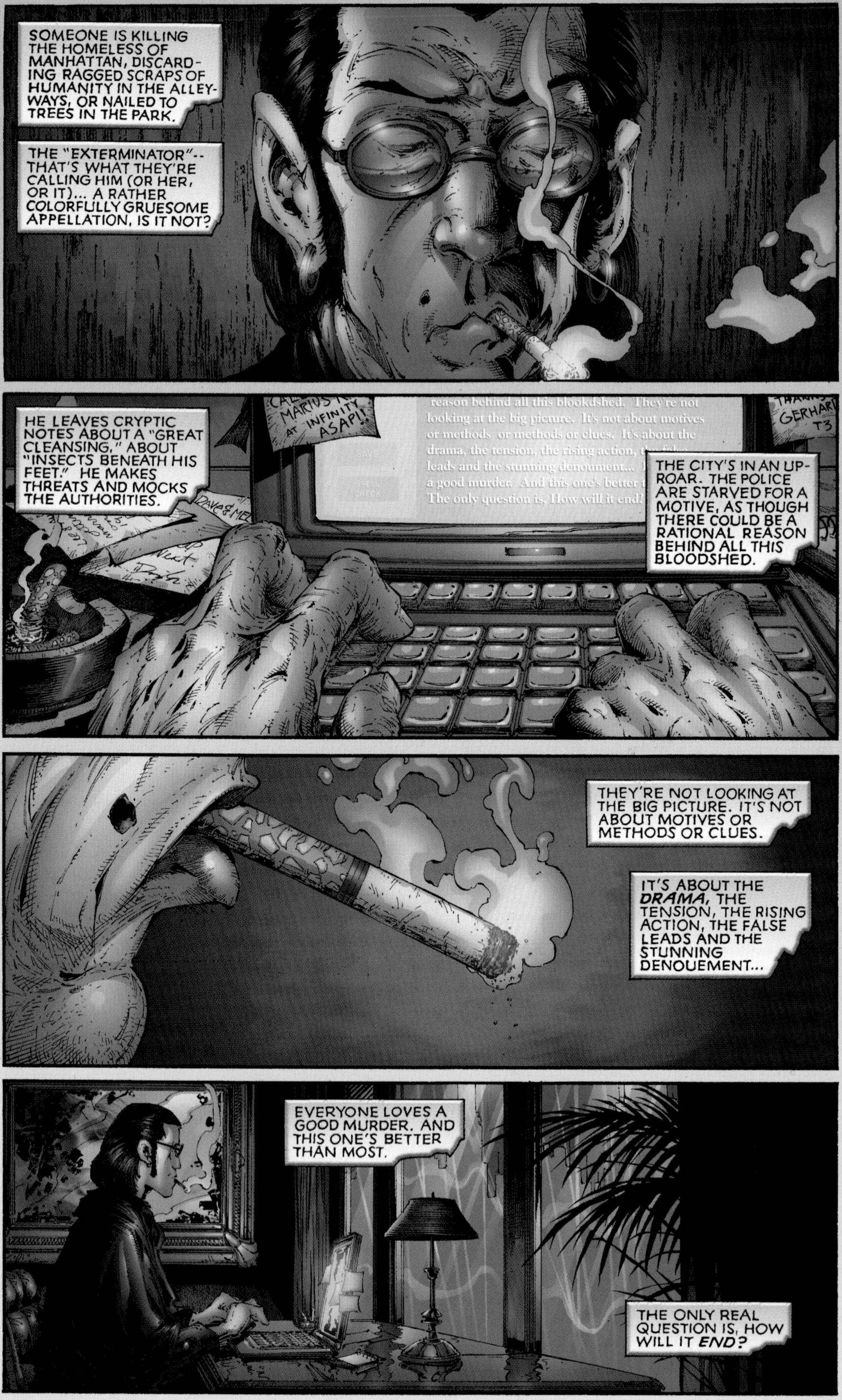
SOMEONE IS KILLING THE HOMELESS OF MANHATTAN, DISCARDING RAGGED SCRAPS OF HUMANITY IN THE ALLEYWAYS, OR NAILED TO TREES IN THE PARK.
THE "EXTERMINATOR"--THAT'S WHAT THEY'RE CALLING HIM (OR HER, OR IT)... A RATHER COLORFULLY GRUESOME APPELLATION, IS IT NOT?
HE LEAVES CRYPTIC NOTES ABOUT A "GREAT CLEANSING," ABOUT "INSECTS BENEATH HIS FEET." HE MAKES THREATS AND MOCKS THE AUTHORITIES.
THE CITY'S IN AN UPROAR. THE POLICE ARE STARVED FOR A MOTIVE, AS THOUGH THERE COULD BE A RATIONAL REASON BEHIND ALL THIS BLOODSHED.
THEY'RE NOT LOOKING AT THE BIG PICTURE. IT'S NOT ABOUT MOTIVES OR METHODS OR CLUES.
IT'S ABOUT THE *DRAMA,* THE TENSION, THE RISING ACTION, THE FALSE LEADS AND THE STUNNING DENOUEMENT...
EVERYONE LOVES A GOOD MURDER. AND THIS ONE'S BETTER THAN MOST.
THE ONLY REAL QUESTION IS, HOW WILL IT *END?*

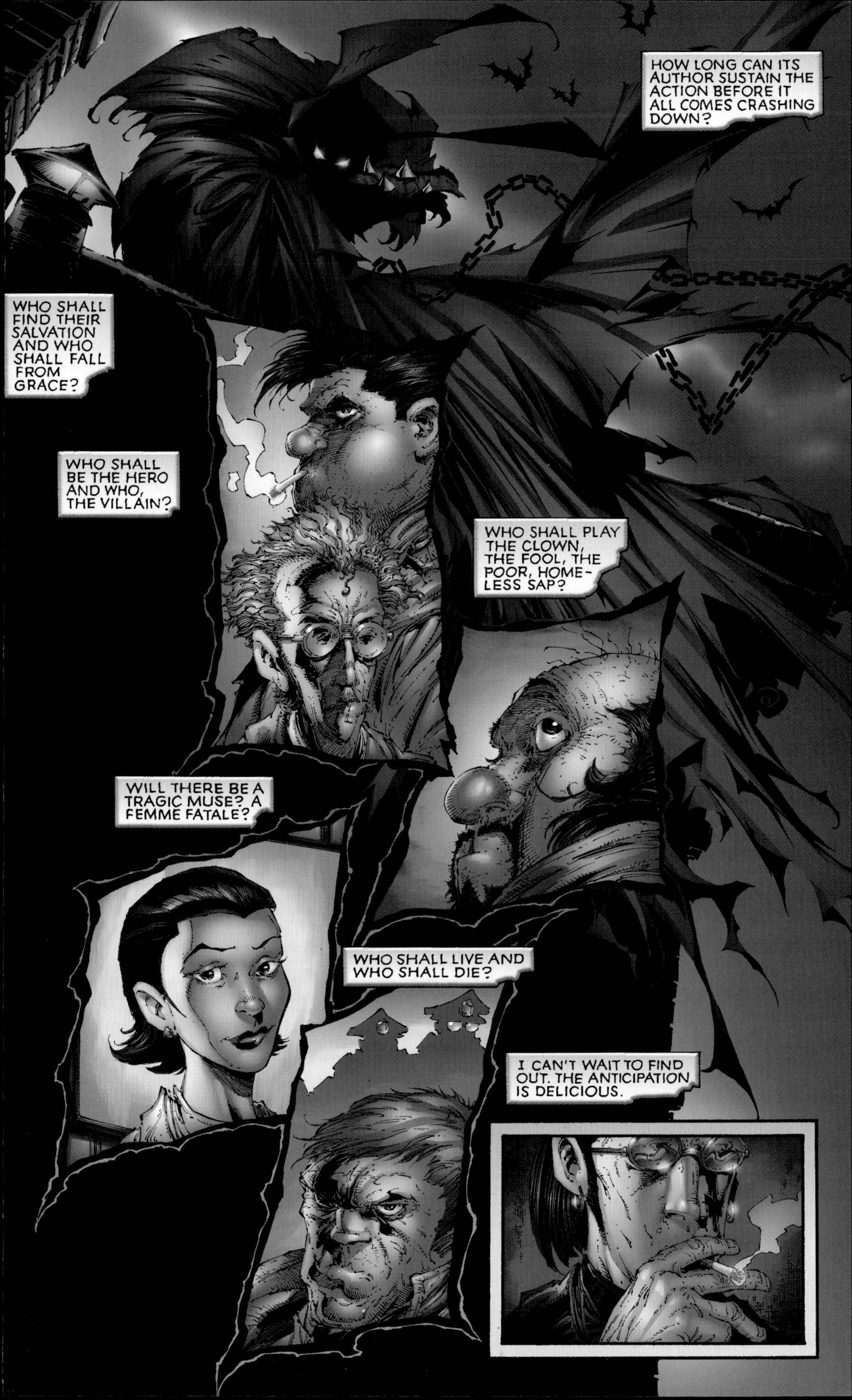
HOW LONG CAN ITS AUTHOR SUSTAIN THE ACTION BEFORE IT ALL COMES CRASHING DOWN?
WHO SHALL FIND THEIR SALVATION AND WHO SHALL FALL FROM GRACE?
WHO SHALL BE THE HERO AND WHO, THE VILLAIN?
WHO SHALL PLAY THE CLOWN, THE FOOL, THE POOR, HOME-LESS SAP?
WILL THERE BE A TRAGIC MUSE? A FEMME FATALE?
WHO SHALL LIVE AND WHO SHALL DIE?
I CAN'T WAIT TO FIND OUT. THE ANTICIPATION IS DELICIOUS.

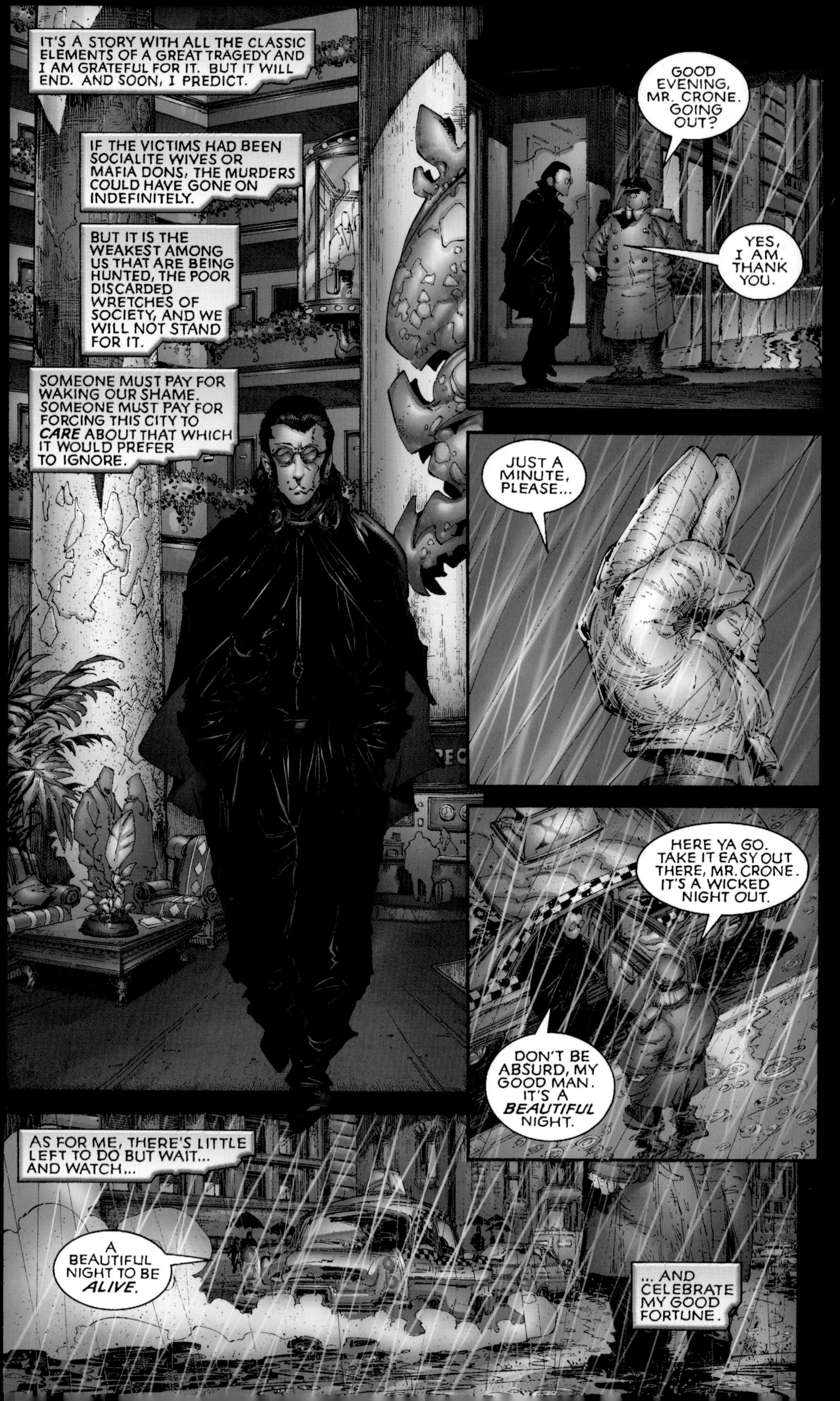
IT'S A STORY WITH ALL THE CLASSIC ELEMENTS OF A GREAT TRAGEDY AND I AM GRATEFUL FOR IT. BUT IT WILL END. AND SOON, I PREDICT.
IF THE VICTIMS HAD BEEN SOCIALITE WIVES OR MAFIA DONS, THE MURDERS COULD HAVE GONE ON INDEFINITELY.
BUT IT IS THE WEAKEST AMONG US THAT ARE BEING HUNTED, THE POOR DISCARDED WRETCHES OF SOCIETY, AND WE WILL NOT STAND FOR IT.
SOMEONE MUST PAY FOR WAKING OUR SHAME. SOMEONE MUST PAY FOR FORCING THIS CITY TO *CARE* ABOUT THAT WHICH IT WOULD PREFER TO IGNORE.
GOOD EVENING, MR. CRONE. GOING OUT?
YES, I AM. THANK YOU.
JUST A MINUTE, PLEASE...
HERE YA GO. TAKE IT EASY OUT THERE, MR. CRONE. IT'S A WICKED NIGHT OUT.
DON'T BE ABSURD, MY GOOD MAN. IT'S A *BEAUTIFUL* NIGHT.
AS FOR ME, THERE'S LITTLE LEFT TO DO BUT WAIT... AND WATCH...
A BEAUTIFUL NIGHT TO BE *ALIVE*.
... AND CELEBRATE MY GOOD FORTUNE.

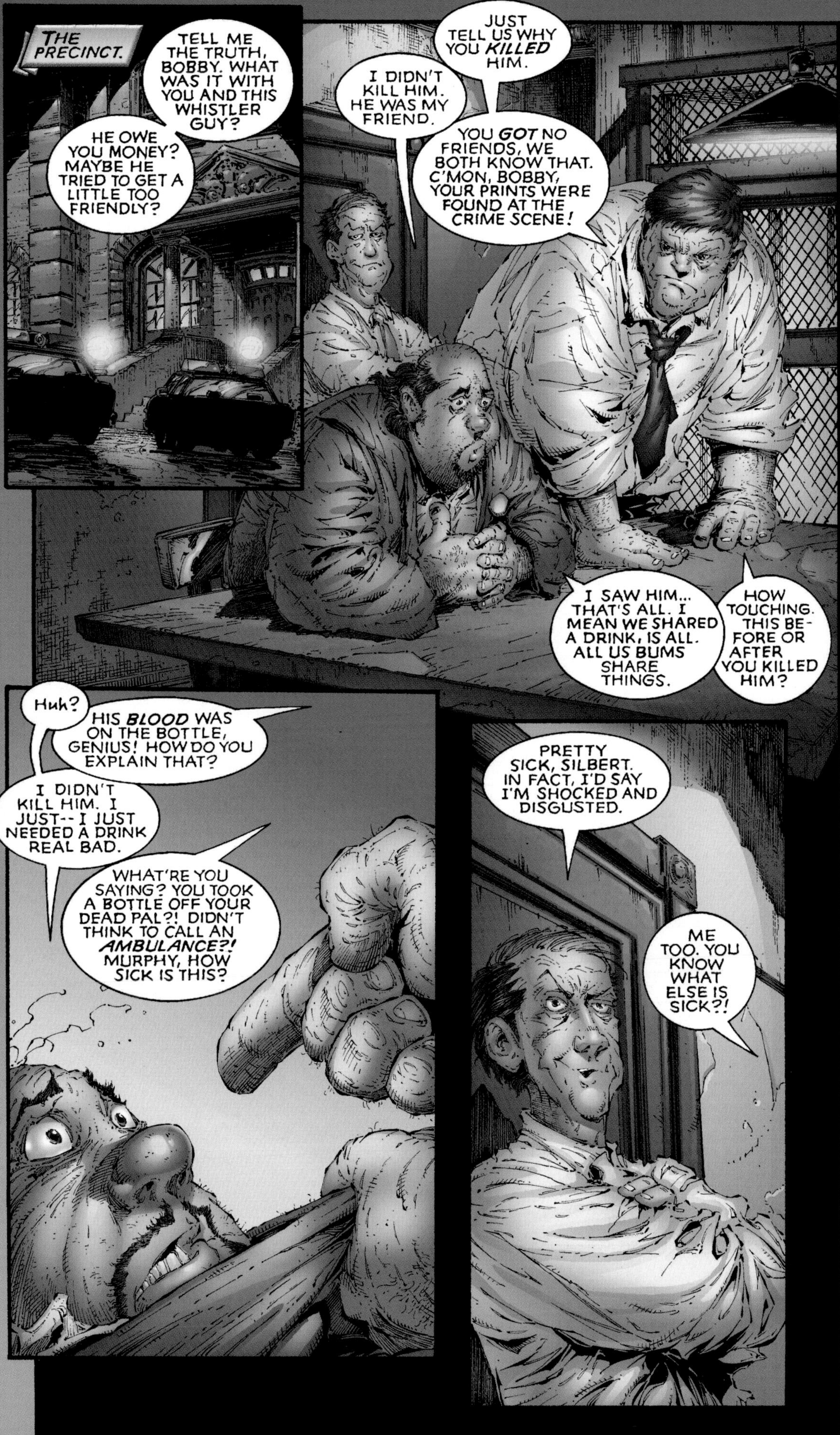
THE PRECINCT.
TELL ME THE TRUTH, BOBBY. WHAT WAS IT WITH YOU AND THIS WHISTLER GUY?
HE OWE YOU MONEY? MAYBE HE TRIED TO GET A LITTLE TOO FRIENDLY?
I DIDN'T KILL HIM. HE WAS MY FRIEND.
JUST TELL US WHY YOU KILLED HIM.
YOU GOT NO FRIENDS, WE BOTH KNOW THAT. C'MON, BOBBY, YOUR PRINTS WERE FOUND AT THE CRIME SCENE!
I SAW HIM... THAT'S ALL. I MEAN WE SHARED A DRINK, IS ALL. ALL US BUMS SHARE THINGS.
HOW TOUCHING. THIS BE-FORE OR AFTER YOU KILLED HIM?
Huh?
HIS BLOOD WAS ON THE BOTTLE, GENIUS! HOW DO YOU EXPLAIN THAT?
I DIDN'T KILL HIM. I JUST-- I JUST NEEDED A DRINK REAL BAD.
WHAT'RE YOU SAYING? YOU TOOK A BOTTLE OFF YOUR DEAD PAL?! DIDN'T THINK TO CALL AN AMBULANCE?! MURPHY, HOW SICK IS THIS?
PRETTY SICK, SILBERT. IN FACT, I'D SAY I'M SHOCKED AND DISGUSTED.
ME TOO. YOU KNOW WHAT ELSE IS SICK?!

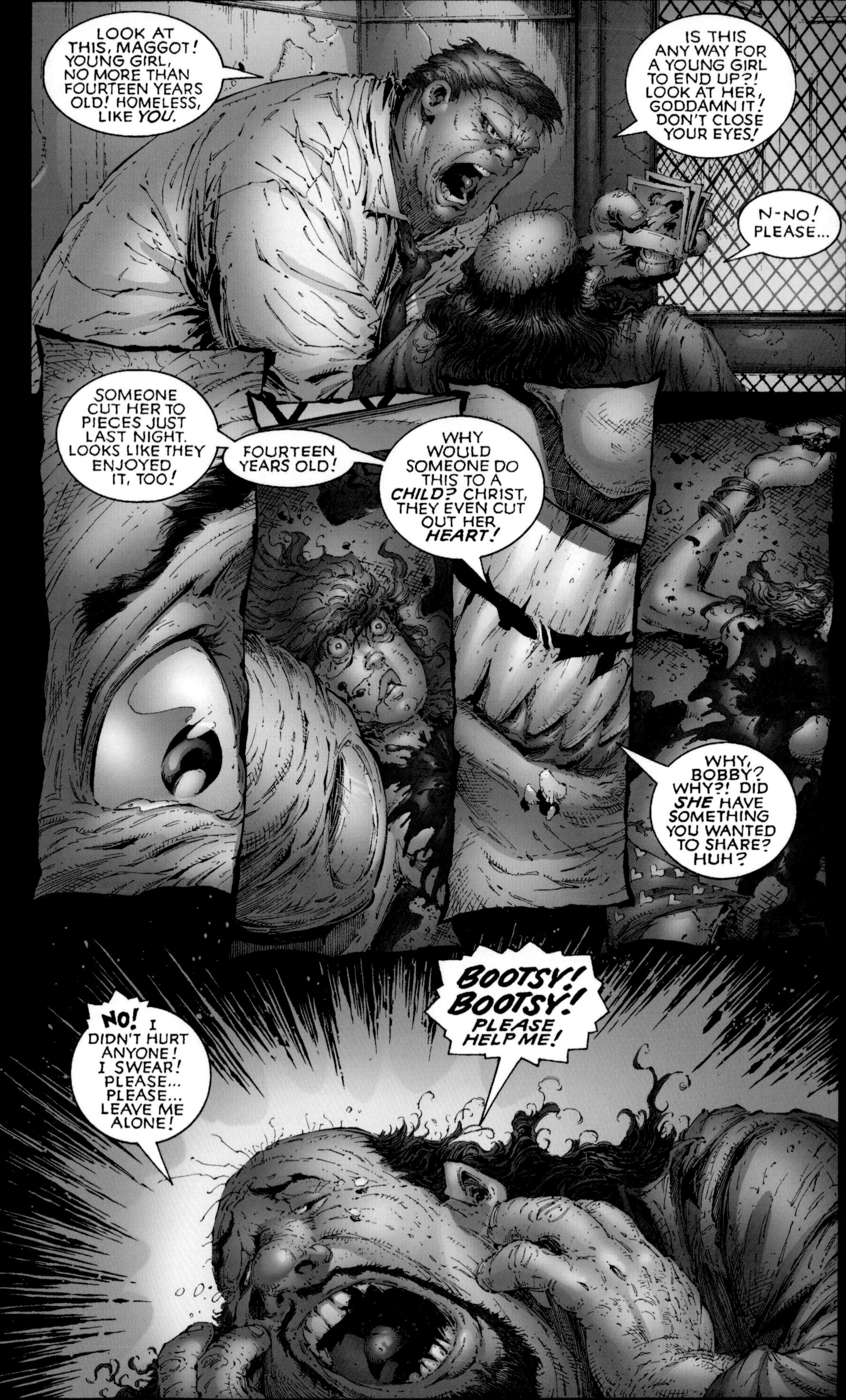
LOOK AT THIS, MAGGOT! YOUNG GIRL, NO MORE THAN FOURTEEN YEARS OLD! HOMELESS, LIKE *YOU.*
IS THIS ANY WAY FOR A YOUNG GIRL TO END UP?! LOOK AT HER, GODDAMN IT! DON'T CLOSE YOUR EYES!
N-NO! PLEASE...
SOMEONE CUT HER TO PIECES JUST LAST NIGHT. LOOKS LIKE THEY ENJOYED IT, TOO!
FOURTEEN YEARS OLD!
WHY WOULD SOMEONE DO THIS TO A *CHILD?* CHRIST, THEY EVEN CUT OUT HER *HEART!*
WHY, BOBBY? WHY?! DID *SHE* HAVE SOMETHING YOU WANTED TO SHARE? HUH?
NO! I DIDN'T HURT ANYONE! I SWEAR! PLEASE... PLEASE... LEAVE ME ALONE!
BOOTSY! BOOTSY! PLEASE HELP ME!

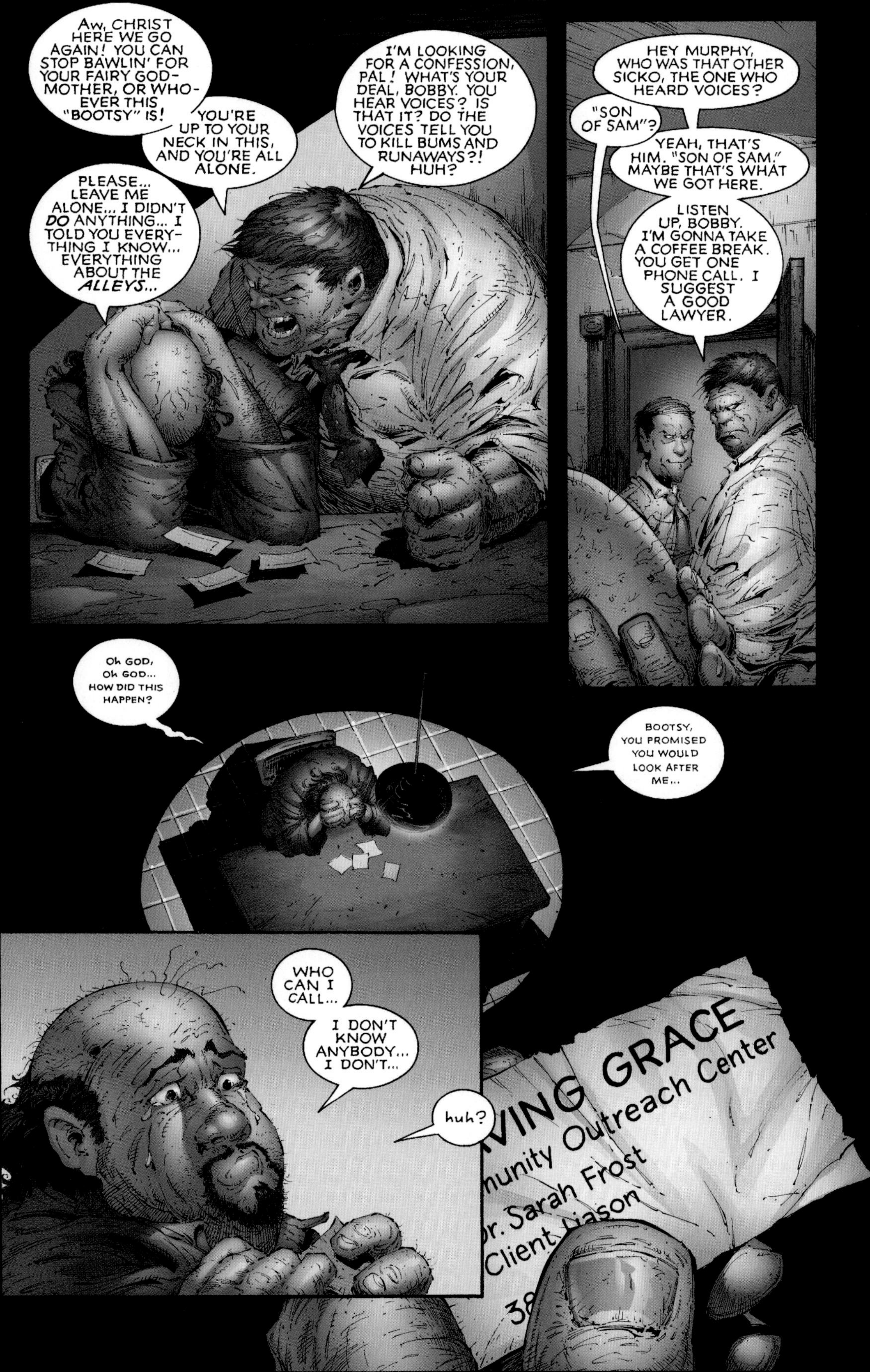

Aw, CHRIST HERE WE GO AGAIN! YOU CAN STOP BAWLIN' FOR YOUR FAIRY GOD-MOTHER, OR WHO-EVER THIS "BOOTSY" IS!
YOU'RE UP TO YOUR NECK IN THIS, AND YOU'RE ALL ALONE.
I'M LOOKING FOR A CONFESSION, PAL! WHAT'S YOUR DEAL, BOBBY. YOU HEAR VOICES? IS THAT IT? DO THE VOICES TELL YOU TO KILL BUMS AND RUNAWAYS?! HUH?
PLEASE... LEAVE ME ALONE... I DIDN'T DO ANYTHING... I TOLD YOU EVERY-THING I KNOW... EVERYTHING ABOUT THE ALLEYS...
HEY MURPHY, WHO WAS THAT OTHER SICKO, THE ONE WHO HEARD VOICES?
"SON OF SAM"?
YEAH, THAT'S HIM. "SON OF SAM." MAYBE THAT'S WHAT WE GOT HERE.
LISTEN UP, BOBBY. I'M GONNA TAKE A COFFEE BREAK. YOU GET ONE PHONE CALL. I SUGGEST A GOOD LAWYER.
Oh GOD, Oh GOD... HOW DID THIS HAPPEN?
BOOTSY, YOU PROMISED YOU WOULD LOOK AFTER ME...
WHO CAN I CALL...
I DON'T KNOW ANYBODY... I DON'T...
huh?
VING GRACE
munity Outreach Center
r. Sarah Frost
Client
38

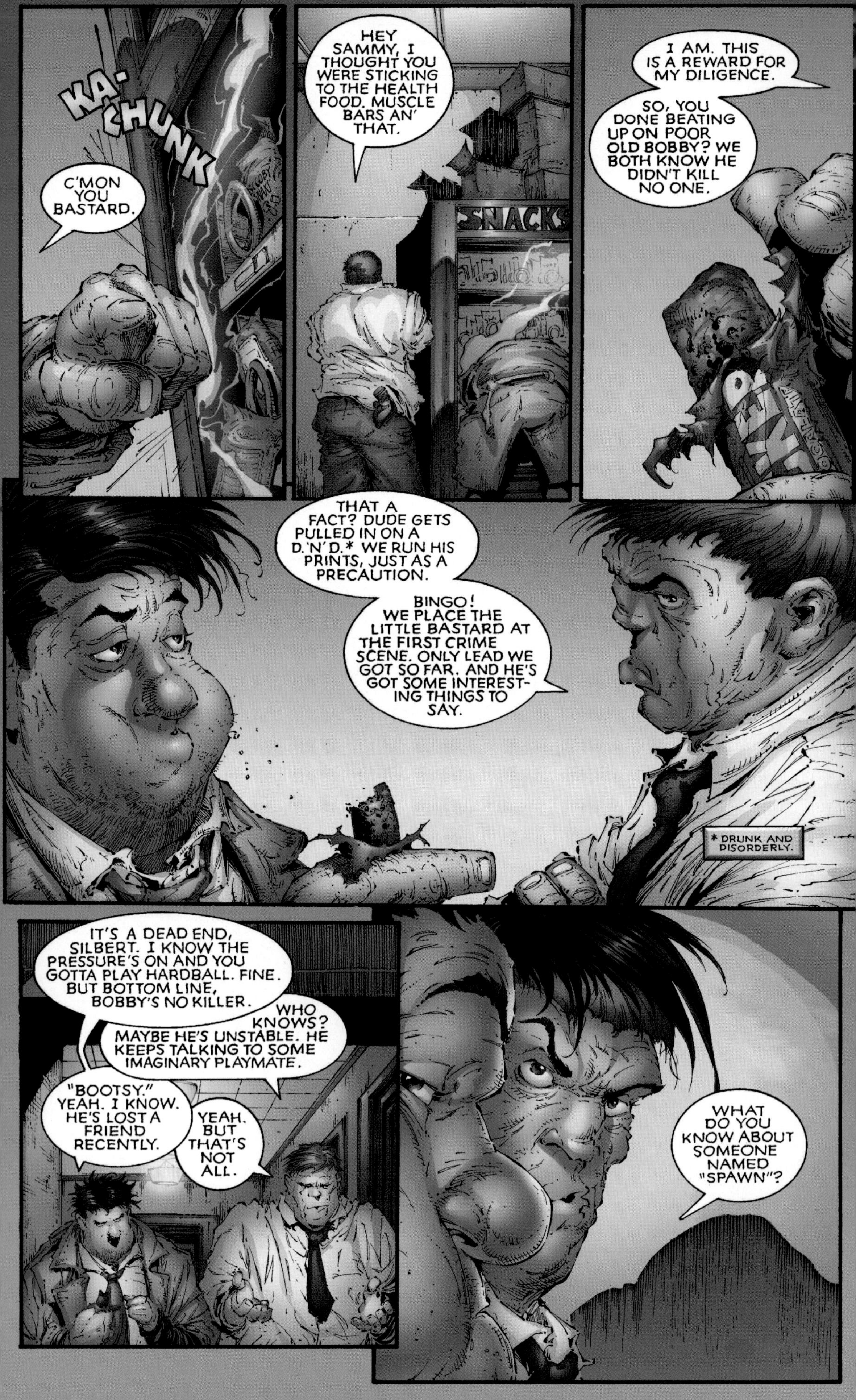
KA-CHUNK
C'MON YOU BASTARD.
HEY SAMMY, I THOUGHT YOU WERE STICKING TO THE HEALTH FOOD. MUSCLE BARS AN' THAT.
SNACKS
I AM. THIS IS A REWARD FOR MY DILIGENCE.
SO, YOU DONE BEATING UP ON POOR OLD BOBBY? WE BOTH KNOW HE DIDN'T KILL NO ONE.
THAT A FACT? DUDE GETS PULLED IN ON A D.'N'D.* WE RUN HIS PRINTS, JUST AS A PRECAUTION.
BINGO! WE PLACE THE LITTLE BASTARD AT THE FIRST CRIME SCENE. ONLY LEAD WE GOT SO FAR. AND HE'S GOT SOME INTERESTING THINGS TO SAY.
* DRUNK AND DISORDERLY.
IT'S A DEAD END, SILBERT. I KNOW THE PRESSURE'S ON AND YOU GOTTA PLAY HARDBALL. FINE. BUT BOTTOM LINE, BOBBY'S NO KILLER.
WHO KNOWS? MAYBE HE'S UNSTABLE. HE KEEPS TALKING TO SOME IMAGINARY PLAYMATE.
"BOOTSY." YEAH. I KNOW. HE'S LOST A FRIEND RECENTLY.
YEAH. BUT THAT'S NOT ALL.
WHAT DO YOU KNOW ABOUT SOMEONE NAMED "SPAWN"?

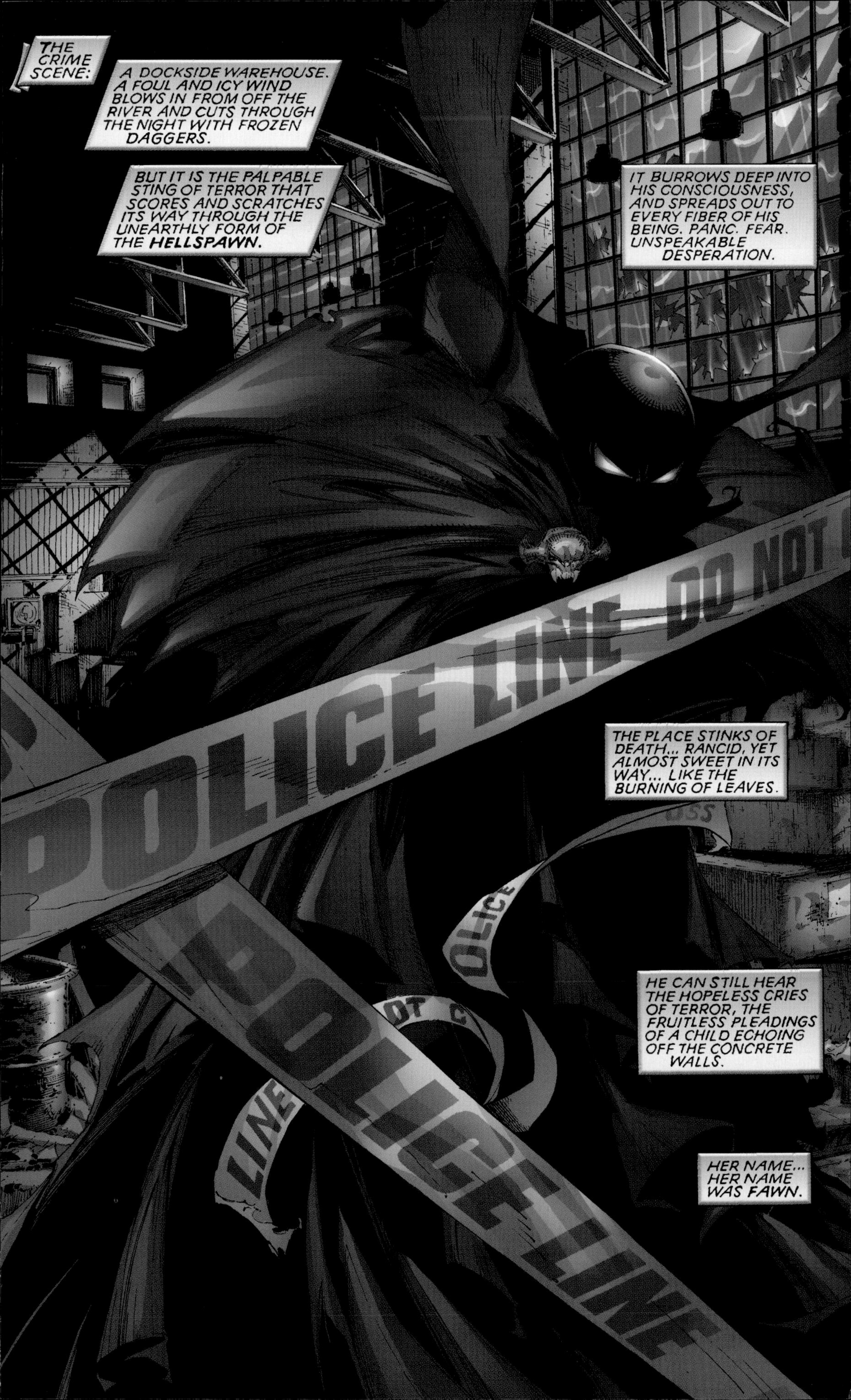
THE CRIME SCENE:
A DOCKSIDE WAREHOUSE. A FOUL AND ICY WIND BLOWS IN FROM OFF THE RIVER AND CUTS THROUGH THE NIGHT WITH FROZEN DAGGERS.
BUT IT IS THE PALPABLE STING OF TERROR THAT SCORES AND SCRATCHES ITS WAY THROUGH THE UNEARTHLY FORM OF THE HELLSPAWN.
IT BURROWS DEEP INTO HIS CONSCIOUSNESS, AND SPREADS OUT TO EVERY FIBER OF HIS BEING. PANIC. FEAR. UNSPEAKABLE DESPERATION.
POLICE LINE DO NOT
THE PLACE STINKS OF DEATH... RANCID, YET ALMOST SWEET IN ITS WAY... LIKE THE BURNING OF LEAVES.
HE CAN STILL HEAR THE HOPELESS CRIES OF TERROR, THE FRUITLESS PLEADINGS OF A CHILD ECHOING OFF THE CONCRETE WALLS.
HER NAME... HER NAME WAS FAWN.

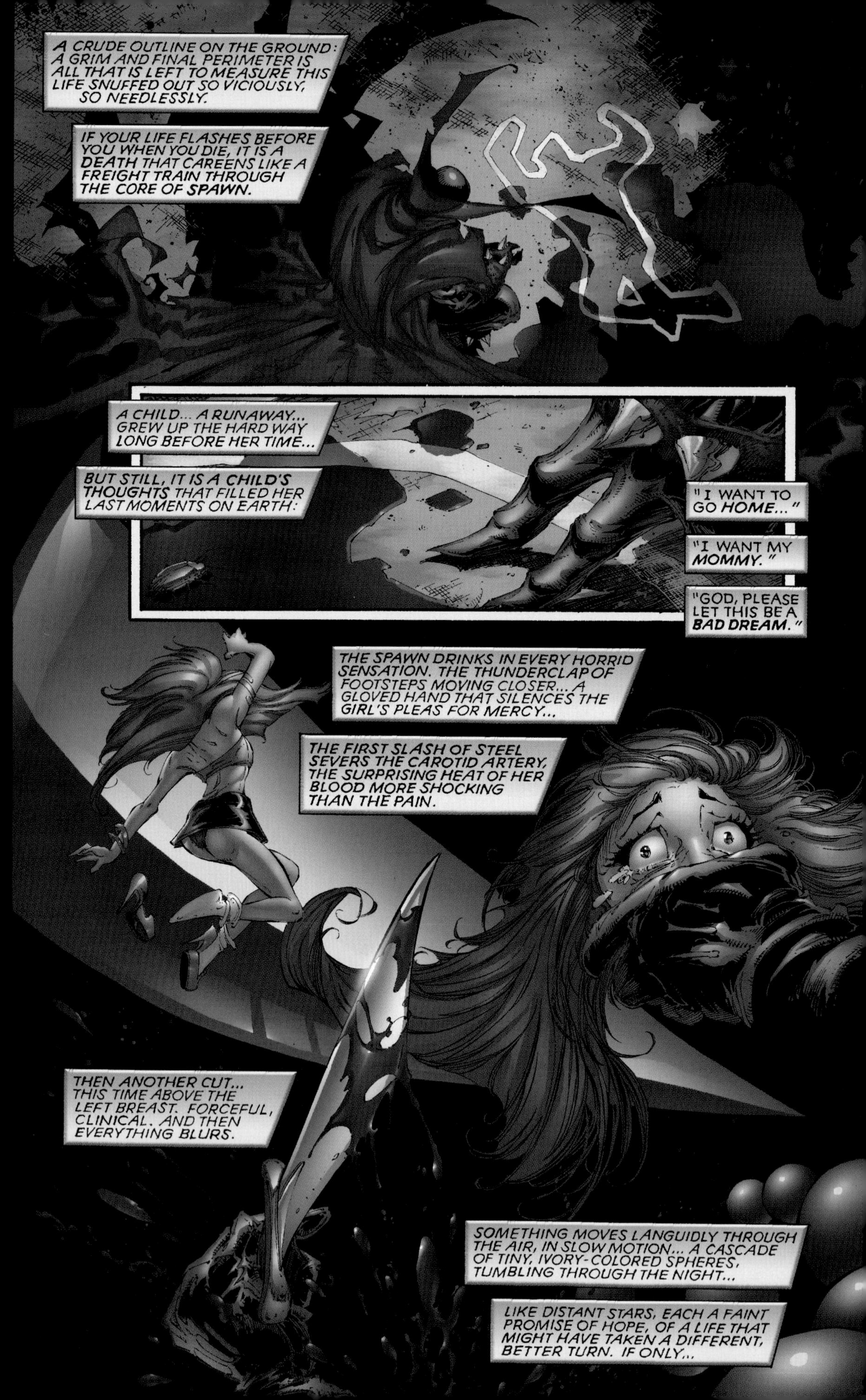
A CRUDE OUTLINE ON THE GROUND: A GRIM AND FINAL PERIMETER IS ALL THAT IS LEFT TO MEASURE THIS LIFE SNUFFED OUT SO VICIOUSLY, SO NEEDLESSLY.
IF YOUR LIFE FLASHES BEFORE YOU WHEN YOU DIE, IT IS A DEATH THAT CAREENS LIKE A FREIGHT TRAIN THROUGH THE CORE OF SPAWN.
A CHILD... A RUNAWAY... GREW UP THE HARD WAY LONG BEFORE HER TIME...
BUT STILL, IT IS A CHILD'S THOUGHTS THAT FILLED HER LAST MOMENTS ON EARTH:
"I WANT TO GO HOME..."
"I WANT MY MOMMY."
"GOD, PLEASE LET THIS BE A BAD DREAM."
THE SPAWN DRINKS IN EVERY HORRID SENSATION. THE THUNDERCLAP OF FOOTSTEPS MOVING CLOSER... A GLOVED HAND THAT SILENCES THE GIRL'S PLEAS FOR MERCY...
THE FIRST SLASH OF STEEL SEVERS THE CAROTID ARTERY, THE SURPRISING HEAT OF HER BLOOD MORE SHOCKING THAN THE PAIN.
THEN ANOTHER CUT... THIS TIME ABOVE THE LEFT BREAST. FORCEFUL, CLINICAL. AND THEN EVERYTHING BLURS.
SOMETHING MOVES LANGUIDLY THROUGH THE AIR, IN SLOW MOTION... A CASCADE OF TINY, IVORY-COLORED SPHERES, TUMBLING THROUGH THE NIGHT...
LIKE DISTANT STARS, EACH A FAINT PROMISE OF HOPE, OF A LIFE THAT MIGHT HAVE TAKEN A DIFFERENT, BETTER TURN. IF ONLY...

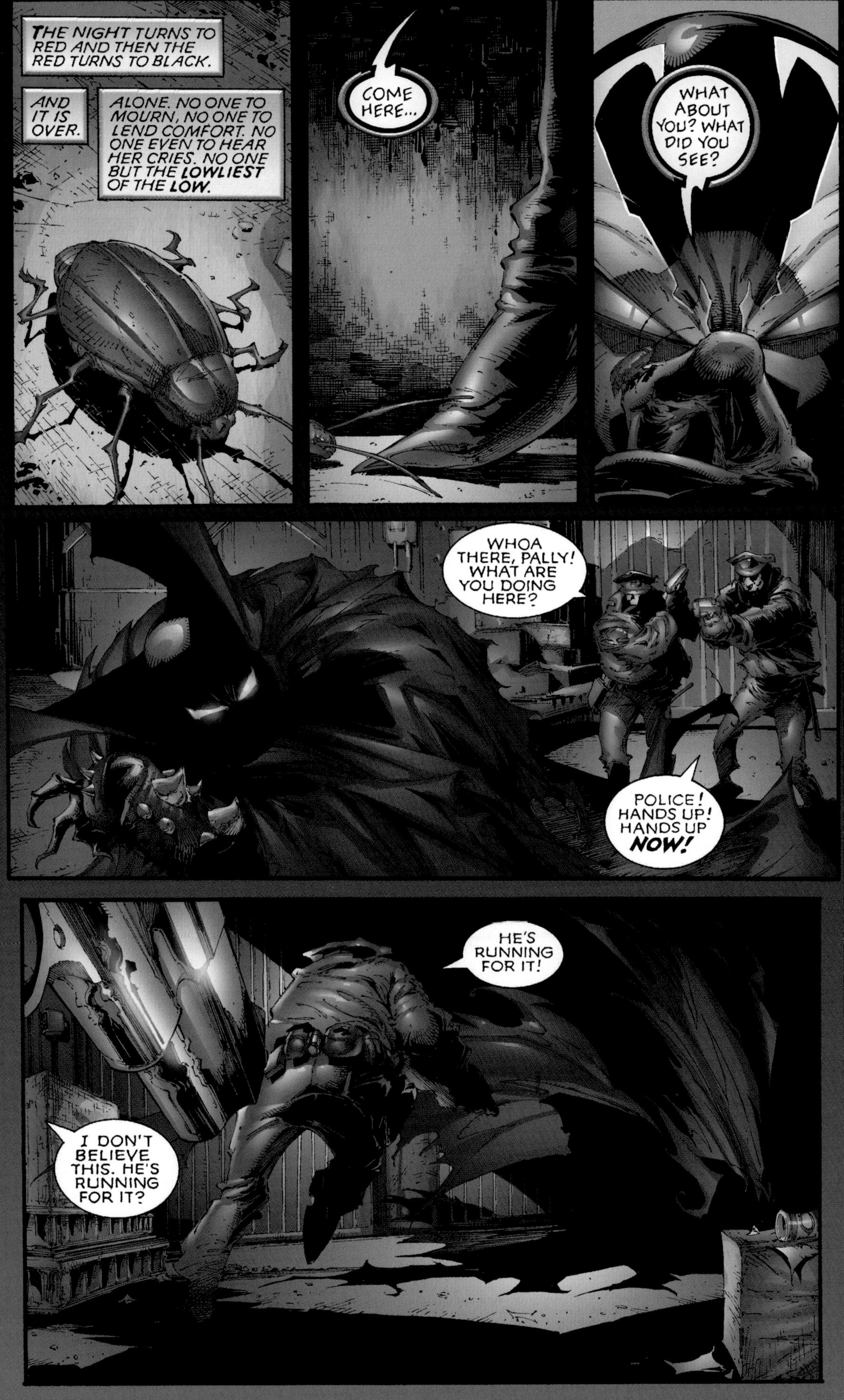
THE NIGHT TURNS TO RED AND THEN THE RED TURNS TO BLACK.
AND IT IS OVER.
ALONE. NO ONE TO MOURN, NO ONE TO LEND COMFORT. NO ONE EVEN TO HEAR HER CRIES. NO ONE BUT THE LOWLIEST OF THE LOW.
COME HERE...
WHAT ABOUT YOU? WHAT DID YOU SEE?
WHOA THERE, PALLY! WHAT ARE YOU DOING HERE?
POLICE! HANDS UP! HANDS UP NOW!
HE'S RUNNING FOR IT!
I DON'T BELIEVE THIS. HE'S RUNNING FOR IT?

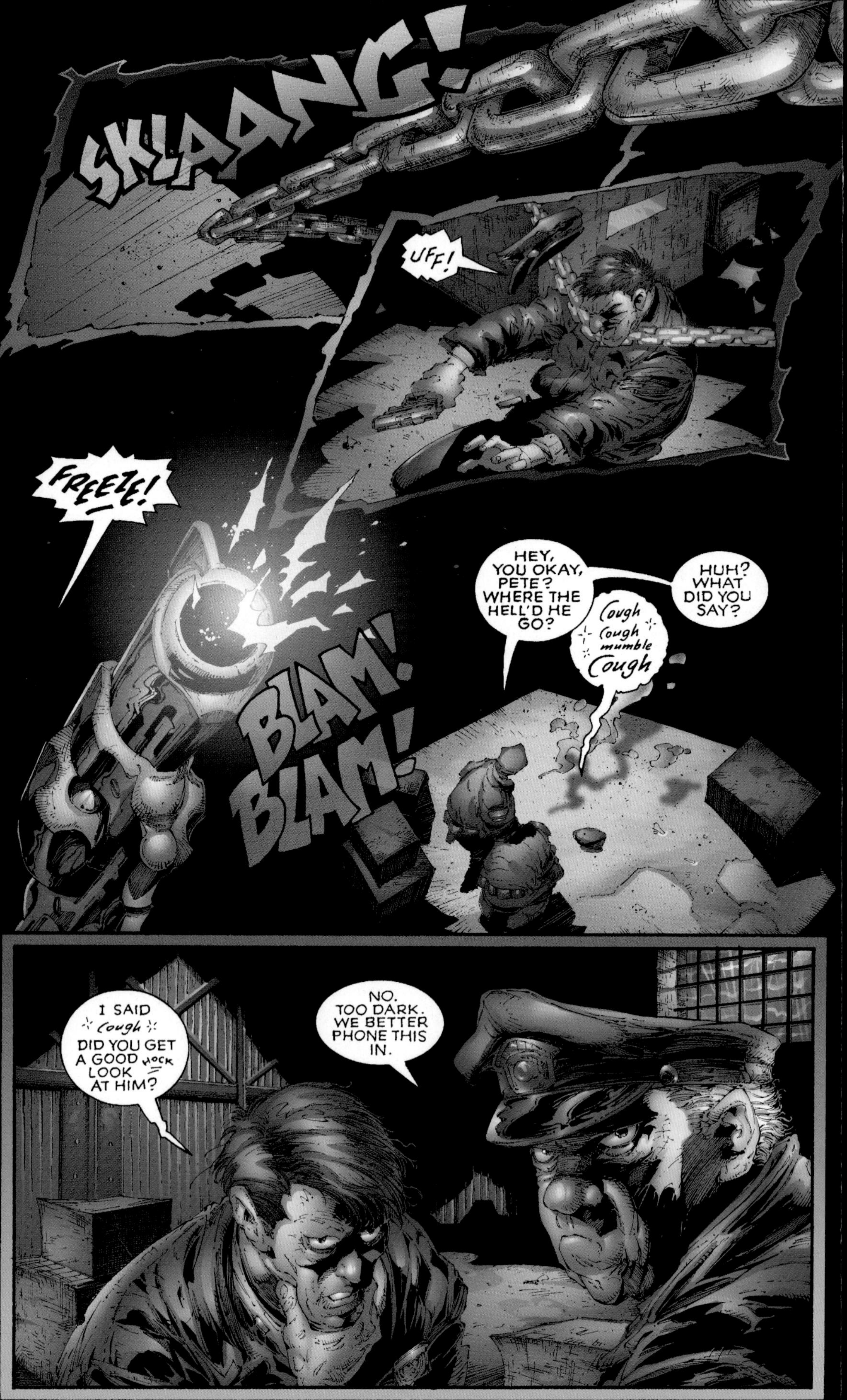
SKLAANG!
UFF!
FREEZE!
BLAM! BLAM!
HEY, YOU OKAY, PETE? WHERE THE HELL'D HE GO?
Cough Cough mumble Cough
HUH? WHAT DID YOU SAY?
I SAID Cough DID YOU GET A GOOD HOCK LOOK AT HIM?
NO. TOO DARK. WE BETTER PHONE THIS IN.

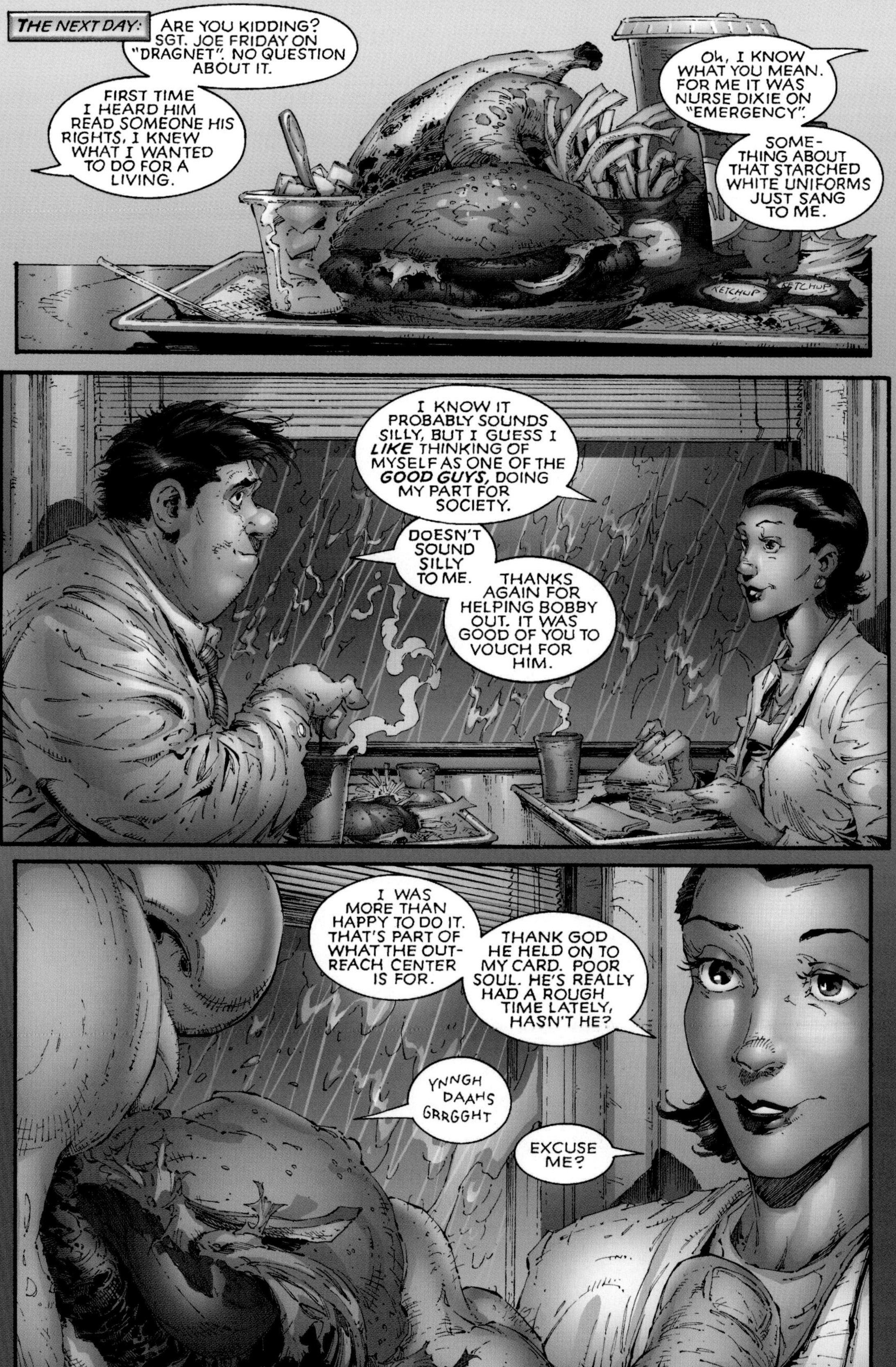
THE NEXT DAY:
ARE YOU KIDDING? SGT. JOE FRIDAY ON "DRAGNET". NO QUESTION ABOUT IT.
FIRST TIME I HEARD HIM READ SOMEONE HIS RIGHTS, I KNEW WHAT I WANTED TO DO FOR A LIVING.
Oh, I KNOW WHAT YOU MEAN. FOR ME IT WAS NURSE DIXIE ON "EMERGENCY".
SOME-THING ABOUT THAT STARCHED WHITE UNIFORMS JUST SANG TO ME.
KETCHUP
KETCHUP
I KNOW IT PROBABLY SOUNDS SILLY, BUT I GUESS I LIKE THINKING OF MYSELF AS ONE OF THE GOOD GUYS, DOING MY PART FOR SOCIETY.
DOESN'T SOUND SILLY TO ME.
THANKS AGAIN FOR HELPING BOBBY OUT. IT WAS GOOD OF YOU TO VOUCH FOR HIM.
I WAS MORE THAN HAPPY TO DO IT. THAT'S PART OF WHAT THE OUT-REACH CENTER IS FOR.
THANK GOD HE HELD ON TO MY CARD. POOR SOUL. HE'S REALLY HAD A ROUGH TIME LATELY, HASN'T HE?
YNNGH DAAHS GRRGGHT
EXCUSE ME?

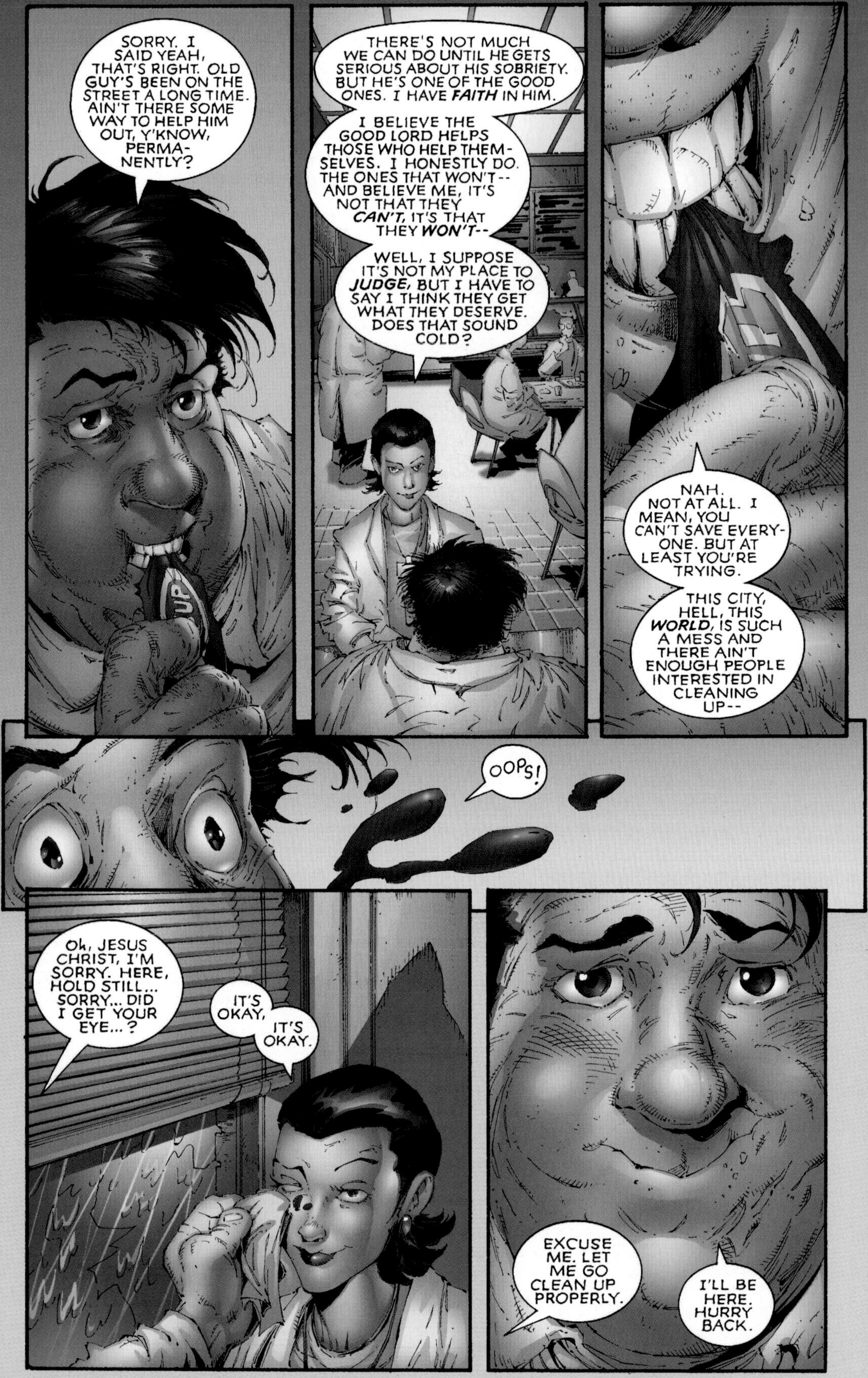

SORRY. I SAID YEAH, THAT'S RIGHT. OLD GUY'S BEEN ON THE STREET A LONG TIME. AIN'T THERE SOME WAY TO HELP HIM OUT, Y'KNOW, PERMA-NENTLY?
UP
THERE'S NOT MUCH WE CAN DO UNTIL HE GETS SERIOUS ABOUT HIS SOBRIETY. BUT HE'S ONE OF THE GOOD ONES. I HAVE FAITH IN HIM.
I BELIEVE THE GOOD LORD HELPS THOSE WHO HELP THEM-SELVES. I HONESTLY DO. THE ONES THAT WON'T-- AND BELIEVE ME, IT'S NOT THAT THEY CAN'T, IT'S THAT THEY WON'T--
WELL, I SUPPOSE IT'S NOT MY PLACE TO JUDGE, BUT I HAVE TO SAY I THINK THEY GET WHAT THEY DESERVE. DOES THAT SOUND COLD?
NAH. NOT AT ALL. I MEAN, YOU CAN'T SAVE EVERY-ONE. BUT AT LEAST YOU'RE TRYING.
THIS CITY, HELL, THIS WORLD, IS SUCH A MESS AND THERE AIN'T ENOUGH PEOPLE INTERESTED IN CLEANING UP--
OOPS!
Oh, JESUS CHRIST, I'M SORRY. HERE, HOLD STILL... SORRY... DID I GET YOUR EYE...?
IT'S OKAY, IT'S OKAY.
EXCUSE ME. LET ME GO CLEAN UP PROPERLY.
I'LL BE HERE. HURRY BACK.

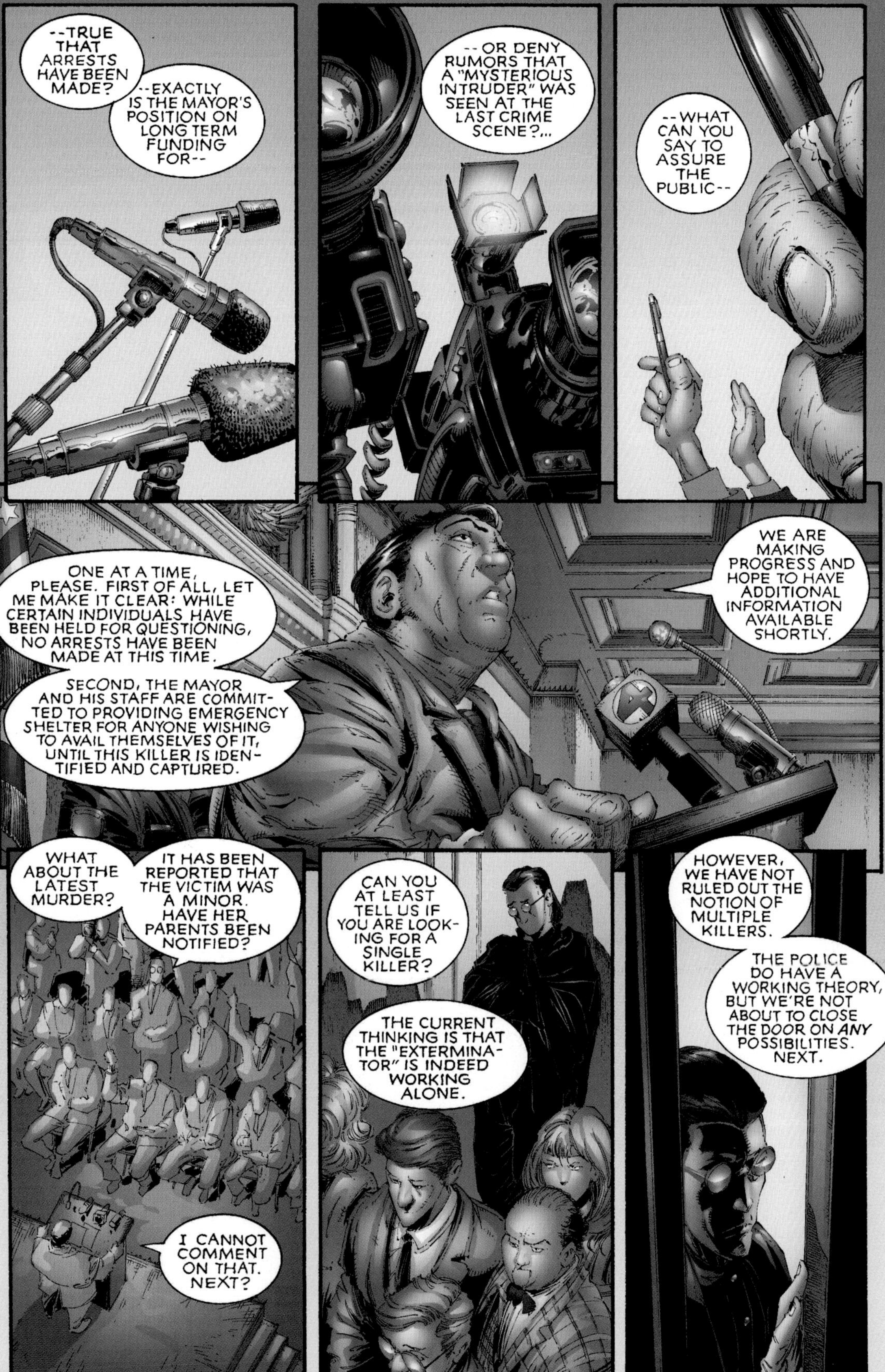
--TRUE THAT ARRESTS HAVE BEEN MADE?
--EXACTLY IS THE MAYOR'S POSITION ON LONG TERM FUNDING FOR--
--OR DENY RUMORS THAT A "MYSTERIOUS INTRUDER" WAS SEEN AT THE LAST CRIME SCENE?...
--WHAT CAN YOU SAY TO ASSURE THE PUBLIC--
ONE AT A TIME, PLEASE. FIRST OF ALL, LET ME MAKE IT CLEAR: WHILE CERTAIN INDIVIDUALS HAVE BEEN HELD FOR QUESTIONING, NO ARRESTS HAVE BEEN MADE AT THIS TIME.
SECOND, THE MAYOR AND HIS STAFF ARE COMMITTED TO PROVIDING EMERGENCY SHELTER FOR ANYONE WISHING TO AVAIL THEMSELVES OF IT, UNTIL THIS KILLER IS IDENTIFIED AND CAPTURED.
WE ARE MAKING PROGRESS AND HOPE TO HAVE ADDITIONAL INFORMATION AVAILABLE SHORTLY.
WHAT ABOUT THE LATEST MURDER?
IT HAS BEEN REPORTED THAT THE VICTIM WAS A MINOR. HAVE HER PARENTS BEEN NOTIFIED?
I CANNOT COMMENT ON THAT. NEXT?
CAN YOU AT LEAST TELL US IF YOU ARE LOOKING FOR A SINGLE KILLER?
THE CURRENT THINKING IS THAT THE "EXTERMINATOR" IS INDEED WORKING ALONE.
HOWEVER, WE HAVE NOT RULED OUT THE NOTION OF MULTIPLE KILLERS.
THE POLICE DO HAVE A WORKING THEORY, BUT WE'RE NOT ABOUT TO CLOSE THE DOOR ON *ANY* POSSIBILITIES. NEXT.

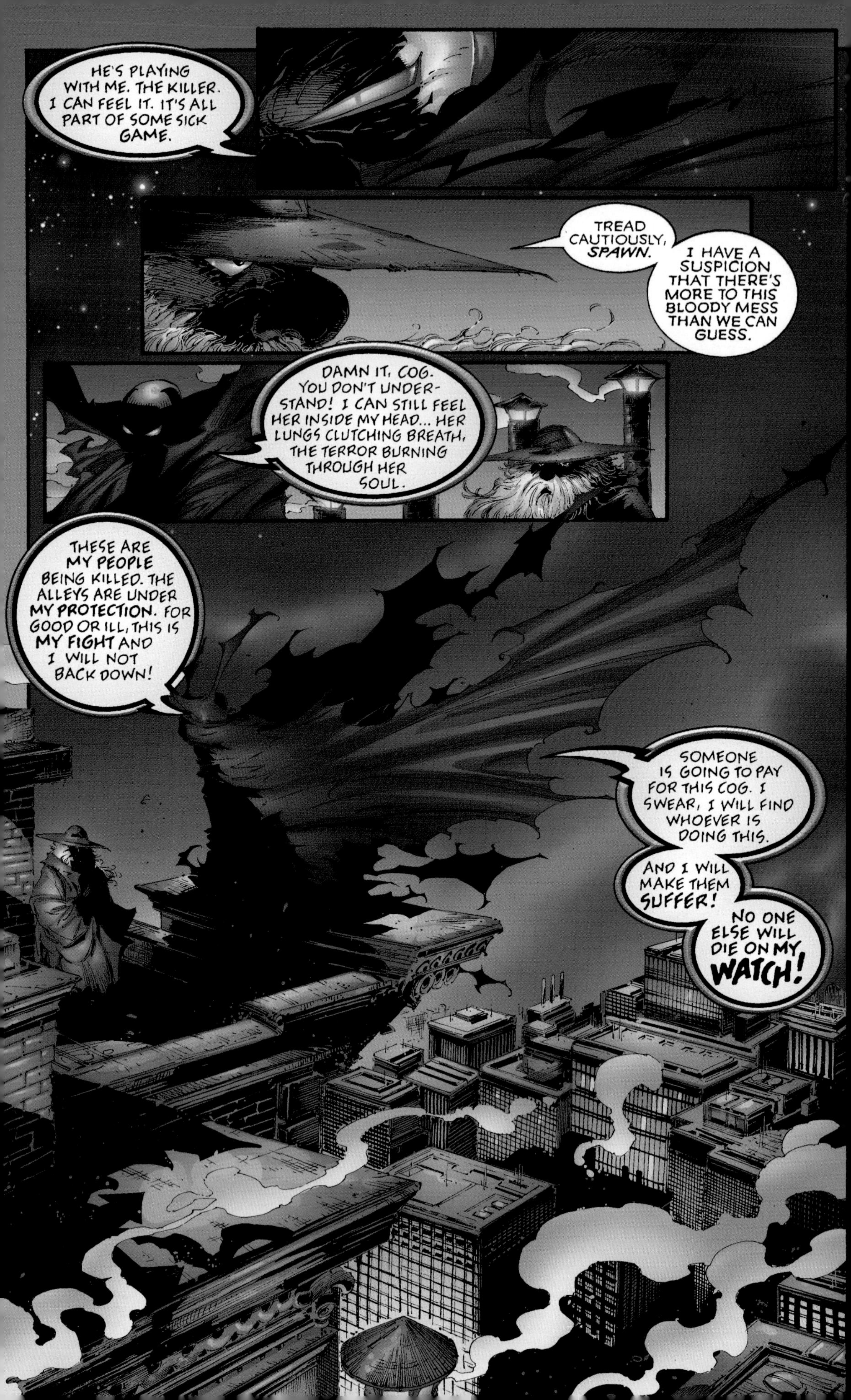
HE'S PLAYING WITH ME. THE KILLER. I CAN FEEL IT. IT'S ALL PART OF SOME SICK GAME.
TREAD CAUTIOUSLY, SPAWN.
I HAVE A SUSPICION THAT THERE'S MORE TO THIS BLOODY MESS THAN WE CAN GUESS.
DAMN IT, COG. YOU DON'T UNDER-STAND! I CAN STILL FEEL HER INSIDE MY HEAD... HER LUNGS CLUTCHING BREATH, THE TERROR BURNING THROUGH HER SOUL.
THESE ARE MY PEOPLE BEING KILLED. THE ALLEYS ARE UNDER MY PROTECTION. FOR GOOD OR ILL, THIS IS MY FIGHT AND I WILL NOT BACK DOWN!
SOMEONE IS GOING TO PAY FOR THIS COG. I SWEAR, I WILL FIND WHOEVER IS DOING THIS.
AND I WILL MAKE THEM SUFFER!
NO ONE ELSE WILL DIE ON MY WATCH!

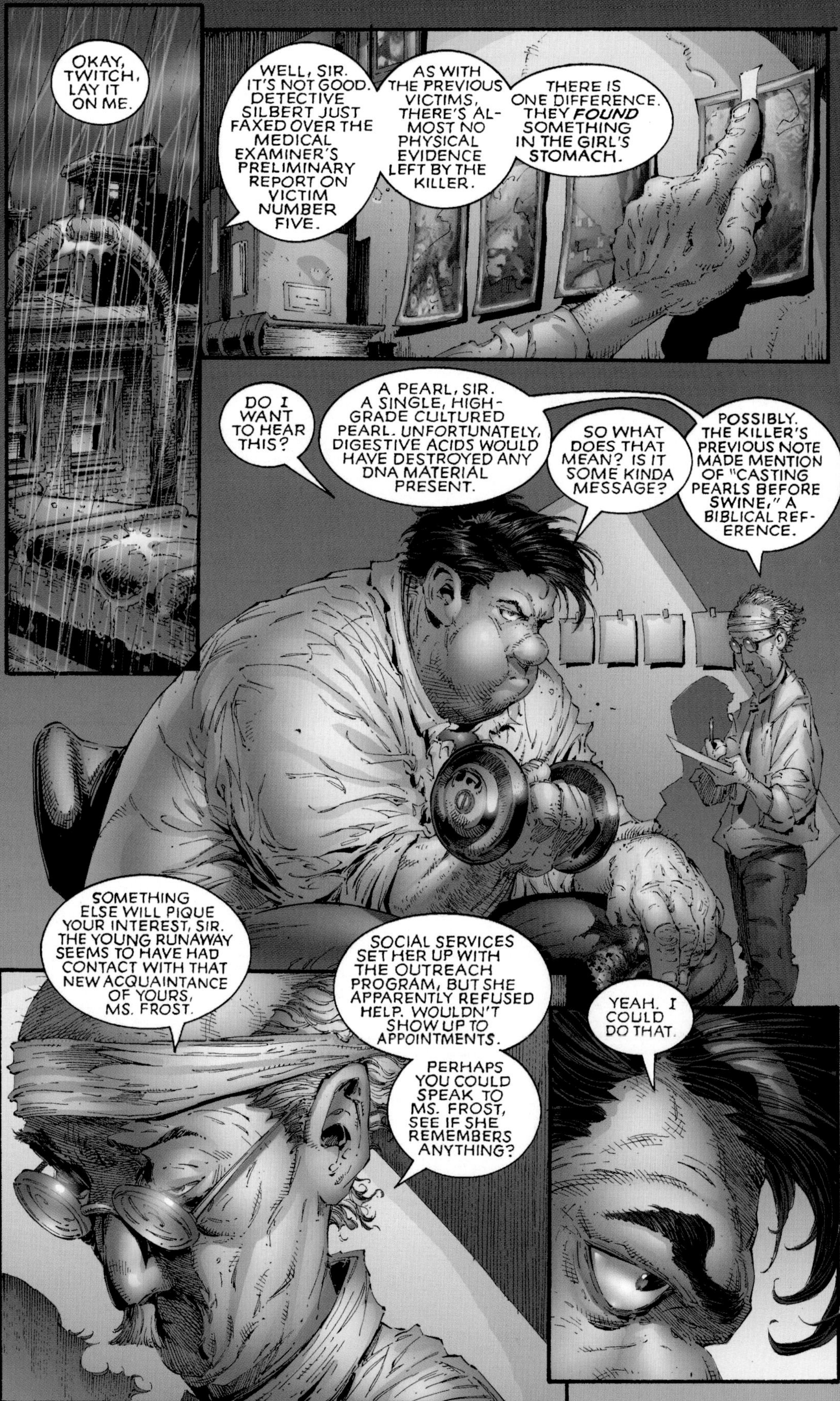
OKAY, TWITCH, LAY IT ON ME.
WELL, SIR. IT'S NOT GOOD. DETECTIVE SILBERT JUST FAXED OVER THE MEDICAL EXAMINER'S PRELIMINARY REPORT ON VICTIM NUMBER FIVE.
AS WITH THE PREVIOUS VICTIMS, THERE'S AL-MOST NO PHYSICAL EVIDENCE LEFT BY THE KILLER.
THERE IS ONE DIFFERENCE. THEY *FOUND* SOMETHING IN THE GIRL'S STOMACH.
DO I WANT TO HEAR THIS?
A PEARL, SIR. A SINGLE, HIGH-GRADE CULTURED PEARL. UNFORTUNATELY, DIGESTIVE ACIDS WOULD HAVE DESTROYED ANY DNA MATERIAL PRESENT.
SO WHAT DOES THAT MEAN? IS IT SOME KINDA MESSAGE?
POSSIBLY. THE KILLER'S PREVIOUS NOTE MADE MENTION OF "CASTING PEARLS BEFORE SWINE," A BIBLICAL REF-ERENCE.
SOMETHING ELSE WILL PIQUE YOUR INTEREST, SIR. THE YOUNG RUNAWAY SEEMS TO HAVE HAD CONTACT WITH THAT NEW ACQUAINTANCE OF YOURS, MS. FROST.
SOCIAL SERVICES SET HER UP WITH THE OUTREACH PROGRAM, BUT SHE APPARENTLY REFUSED HELP. WOULDN'T SHOW UP TO APPOINTMENTS.
PERHAPS YOU COULD SPEAK TO MS. FROST, SEE IF SHE REMEMBERS ANYTHING?
YEAH. I COULD DO THAT.

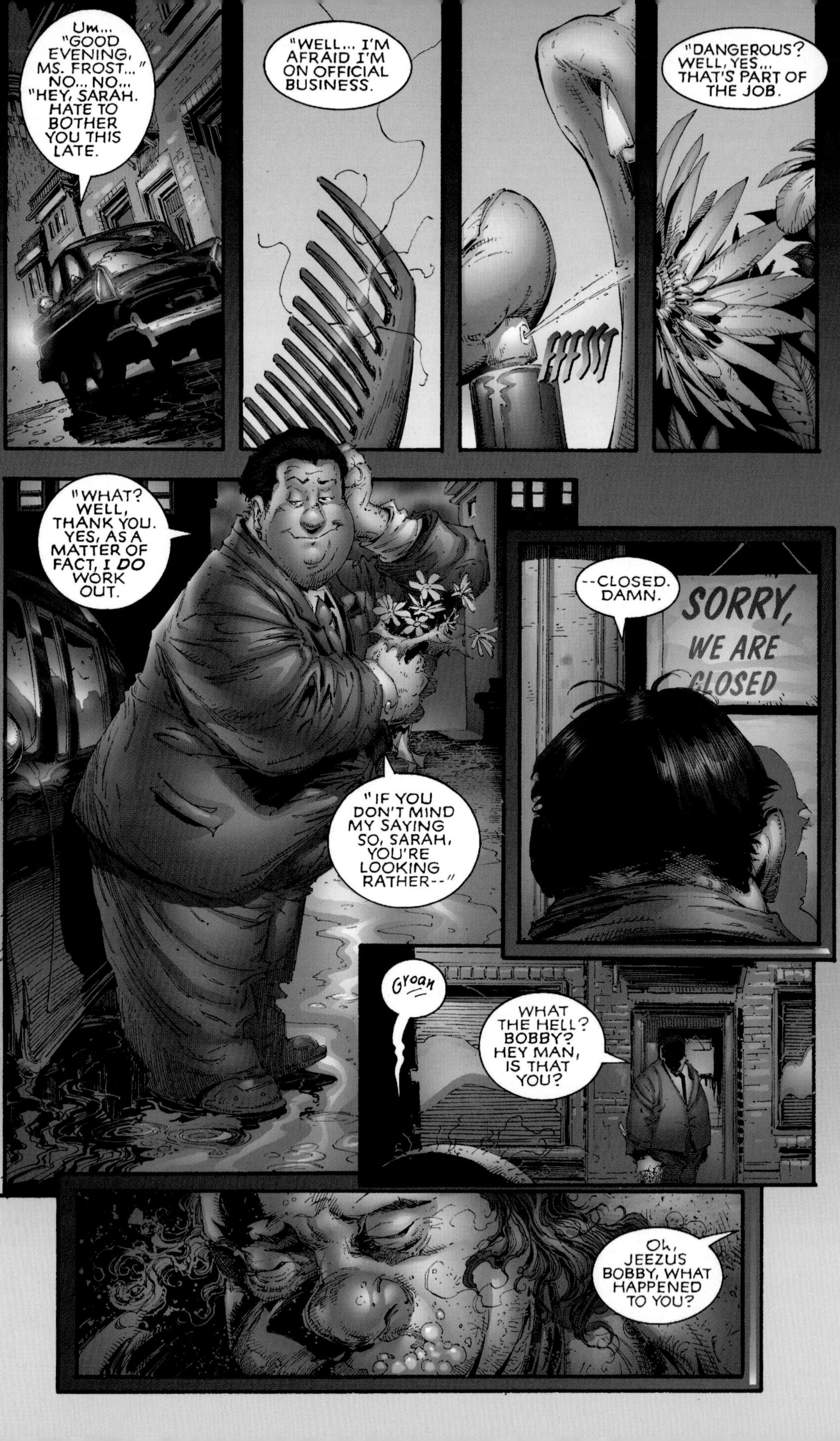

Um... "GOOD EVENING, MS. FROST..." NO... NO... "HEY, SARAH. HATE TO BOTHER YOU THIS LATE.
"WELL... I'M AFRAID I'M ON OFFICIAL BUSINESS.
FFFSST
"DANGEROUS? WELL, YES... THAT'S PART OF THE JOB.
"WHAT? WELL, THANK YOU. YES, AS A MATTER OF FACT, I *DO* WORK OUT.
"IF YOU DON'T MIND MY SAYING SO, SARAH, YOU'RE LOOKING RATHER--"
--CLOSED. DAMN.
SORRY, WE ARE CLOSED
Groan
WHAT THE HELL? BOBBY? HEY MAN, IS THAT YOU?
Oh, JEEZUS BOBBY, WHAT HAPPENED TO YOU?

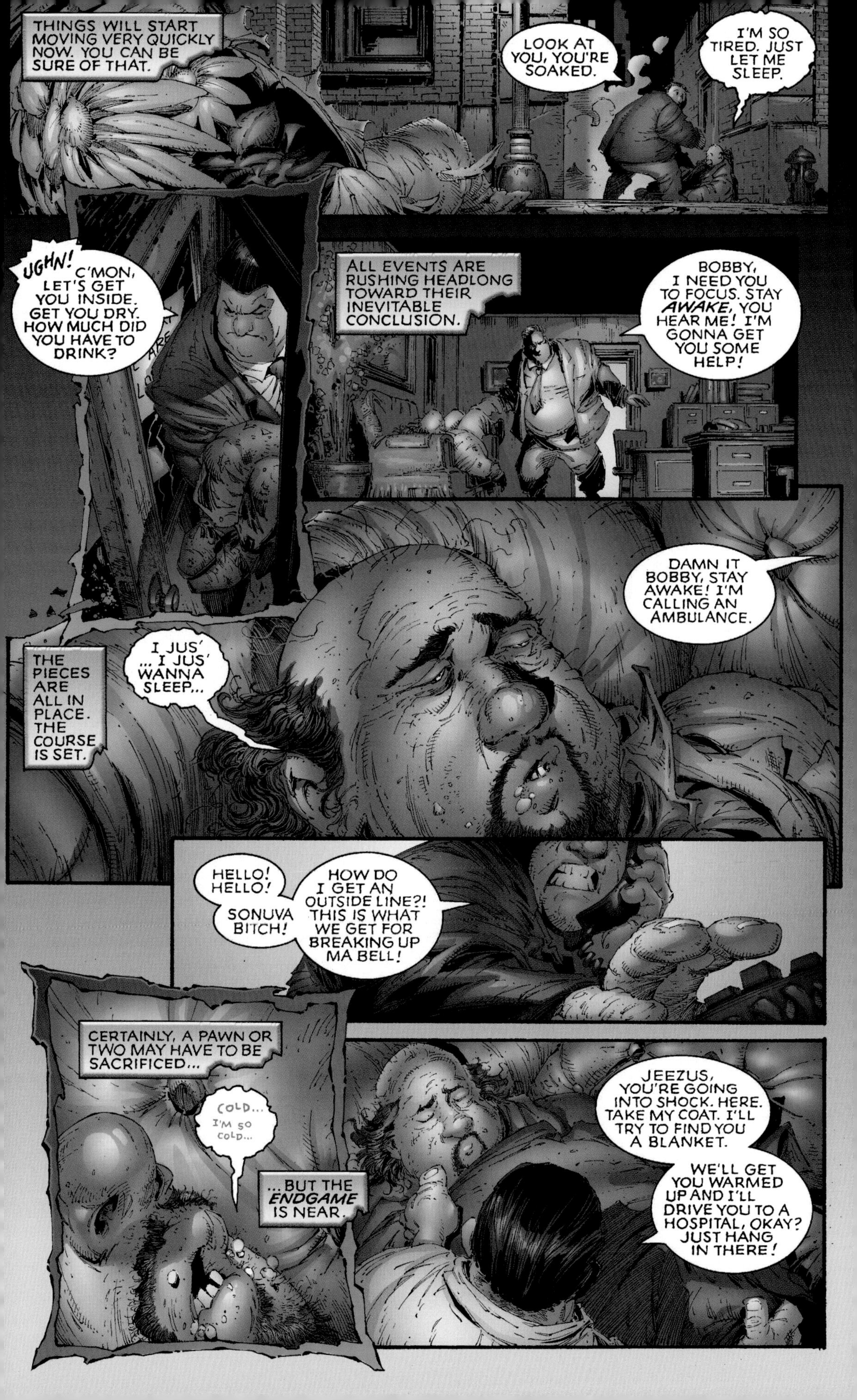
THINGS WILL START MOVING VERY QUICKLY NOW. YOU CAN BE SURE OF THAT.
LOOK AT YOU, YOU'RE SOAKED.
I'M SO TIRED. JUST LET ME SLEEP.
UGHN!
C'MON, LET'S GET YOU INSIDE. GET YOU DRY. HOW MUCH DID YOU HAVE TO DRINK?
ALL EVENTS ARE RUSHING HEADLONG TOWARD THEIR INEVITABLE CONCLUSION.
BOBBY, I NEED YOU TO FOCUS. STAY AWAKE, YOU HEAR ME! I'M GONNA GET YOU SOME HELP!
DAMN IT BOBBY, STAY AWAKE! I'M CALLING AN AMBULANCE.
THE PIECES ARE ALL IN PLACE. THE COURSE IS SET.
I JUS' ... I JUS' WANNA SLEEP...
HELLO! HELLO!
SONUVA BITCH!
HOW DO I GET AN OUTSIDE LINE?! THIS IS WHAT WE GET FOR BREAKING UP MA BELL!
CERTAINLY, A PAWN OR TWO MAY HAVE TO BE SACRIFICED...
COLD... I'M SO COLD...
...BUT THE ENDGAME IS NEAR.
JEEZUS, YOU'RE GOING INTO SHOCK. HERE. TAKE MY COAT. I'LL TRY TO FIND YOU A BLANKET.
WE'LL GET YOU WARMED UP AND I'LL DRIVE YOU TO A HOSPITAL, OKAY? JUST HANG IN THERE!

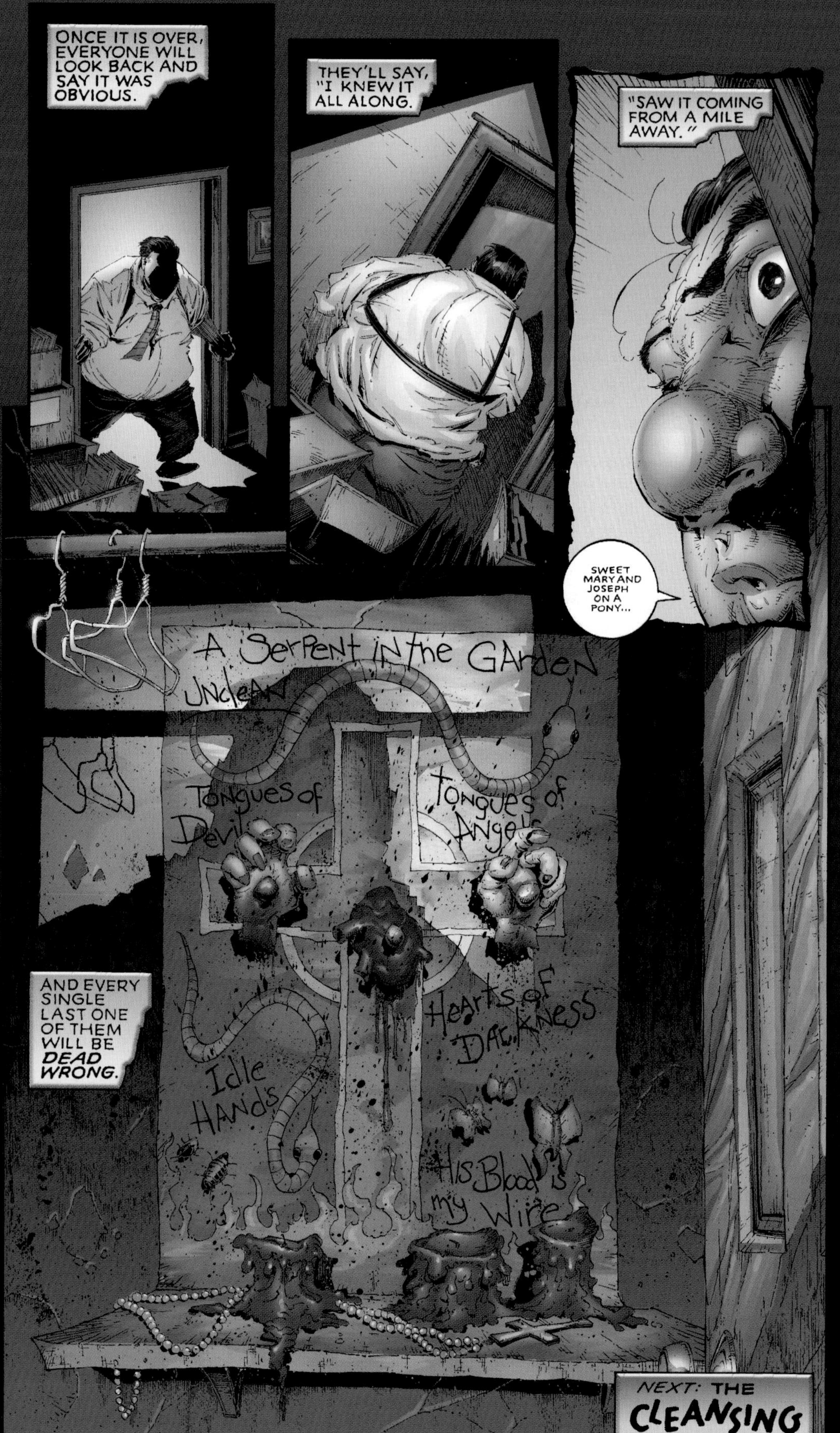
ONCE IT IS OVER, EVERYONE WILL LOOK BACK AND SAY IT WAS OBVIOUS.
THEY'LL SAY, "I KNEW IT ALL ALONG.
"SAW IT COMING FROM A MILE AWAY."
SWEET MARY AND JOSEPH ON A PONY...
A Serpent in the GArden
Unclean
Tongues of Devil
Tongues of Angel
Hearts of Darkness
Idle Hands
His Blood is my Wine
AND EVERY SINGLE LAST ONE OF THEM WILL BE *DEAD WRONG*.
NEXT: THE CLEANSING

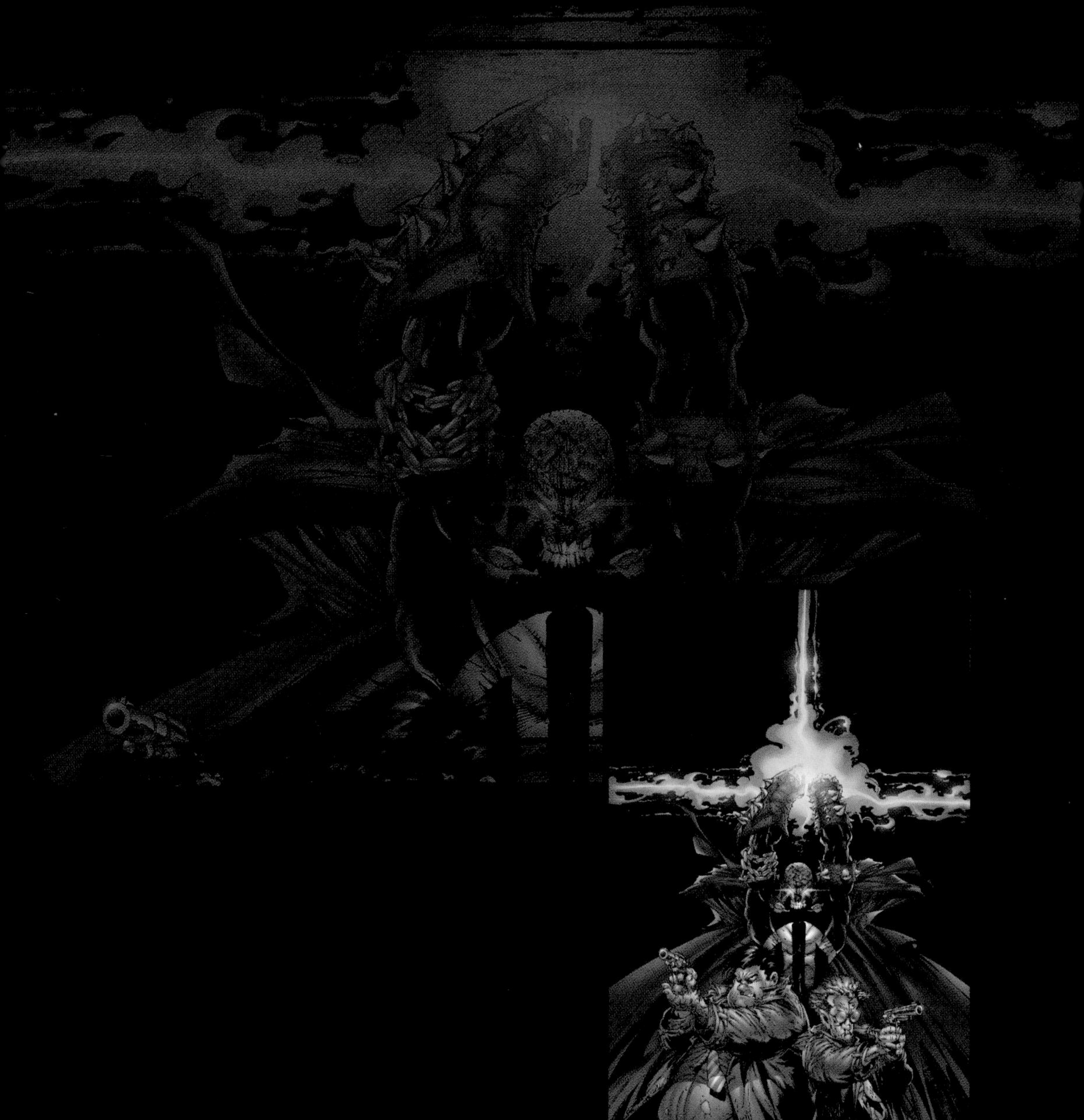

ISSUE EIGHTY

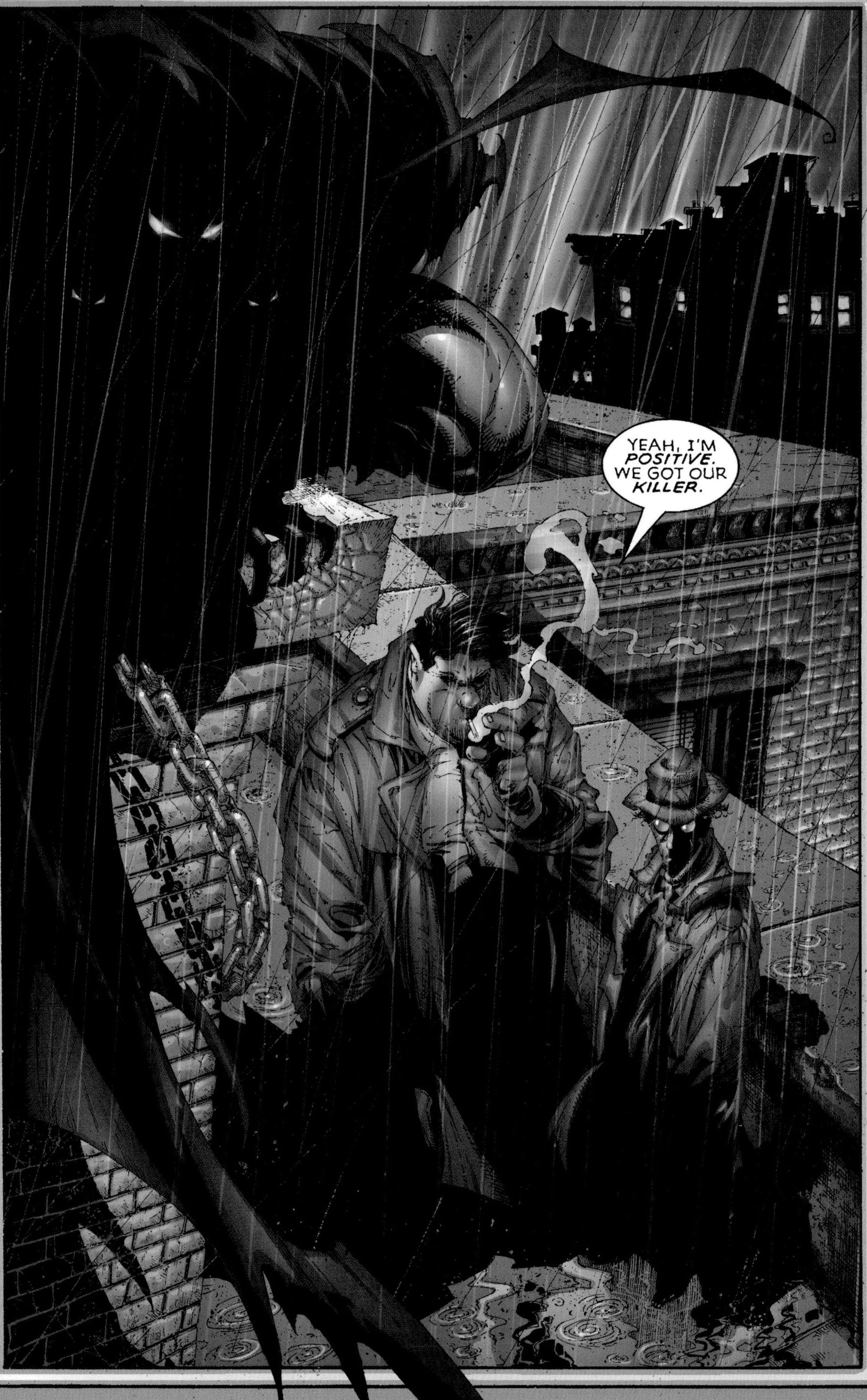
YEAH, I'M POSITIVE. WE GOT OUR KILLER.

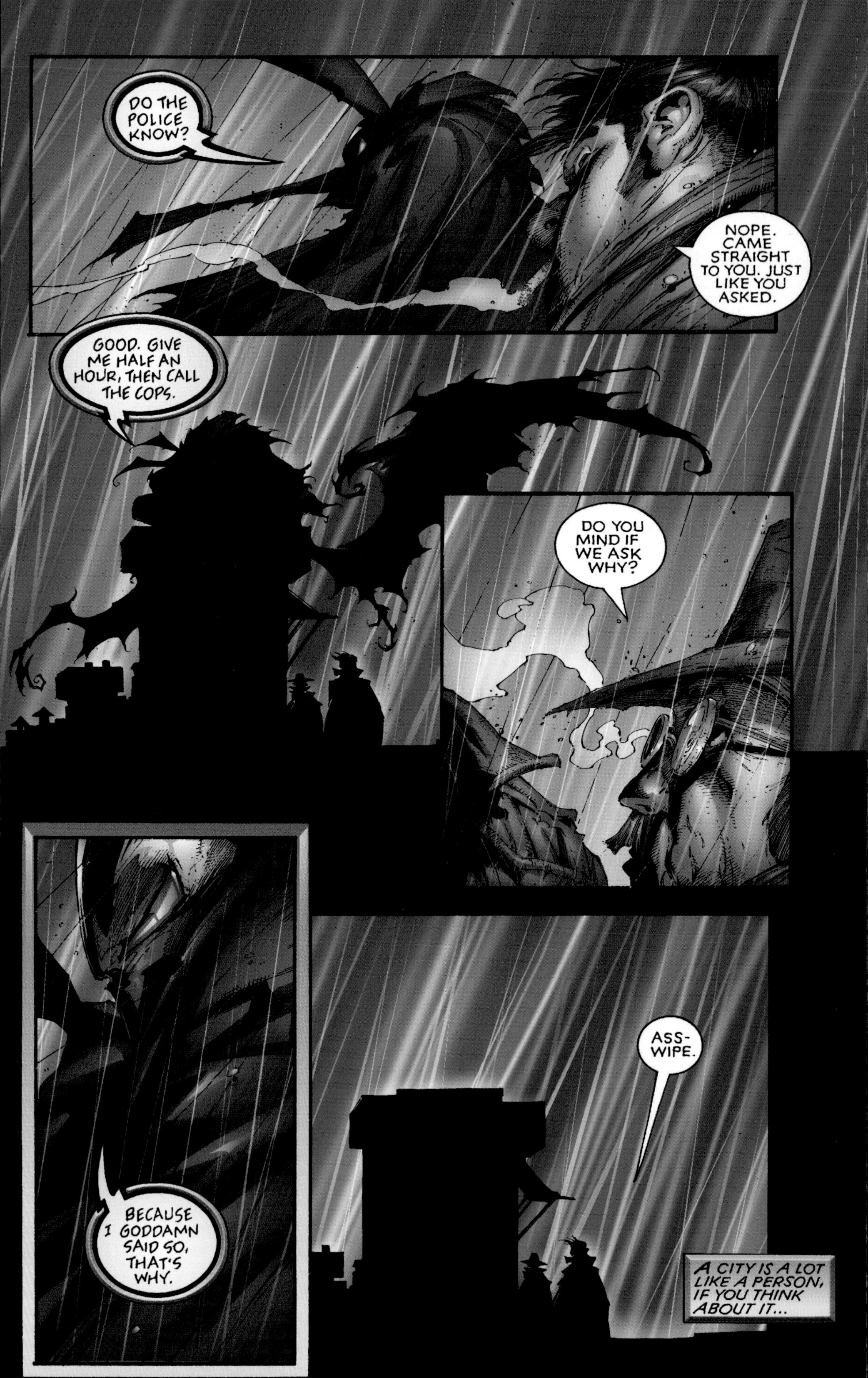
DO THE POLICE KNOW?
NOPE. CAME STRAIGHT TO YOU. JUST LIKE YOU ASKED.
GOOD. GIVE ME HALF AN HOUR, THEN CALL THE COPS.
DO YOU MIND IF WE ASK WHY?
BECAUSE I GODDAMN SAID SO, THAT'S WHY.
ASS-WIPE.
A CITY IS A LOT LIKE A PERSON, IF YOU THINK ABOUT IT...

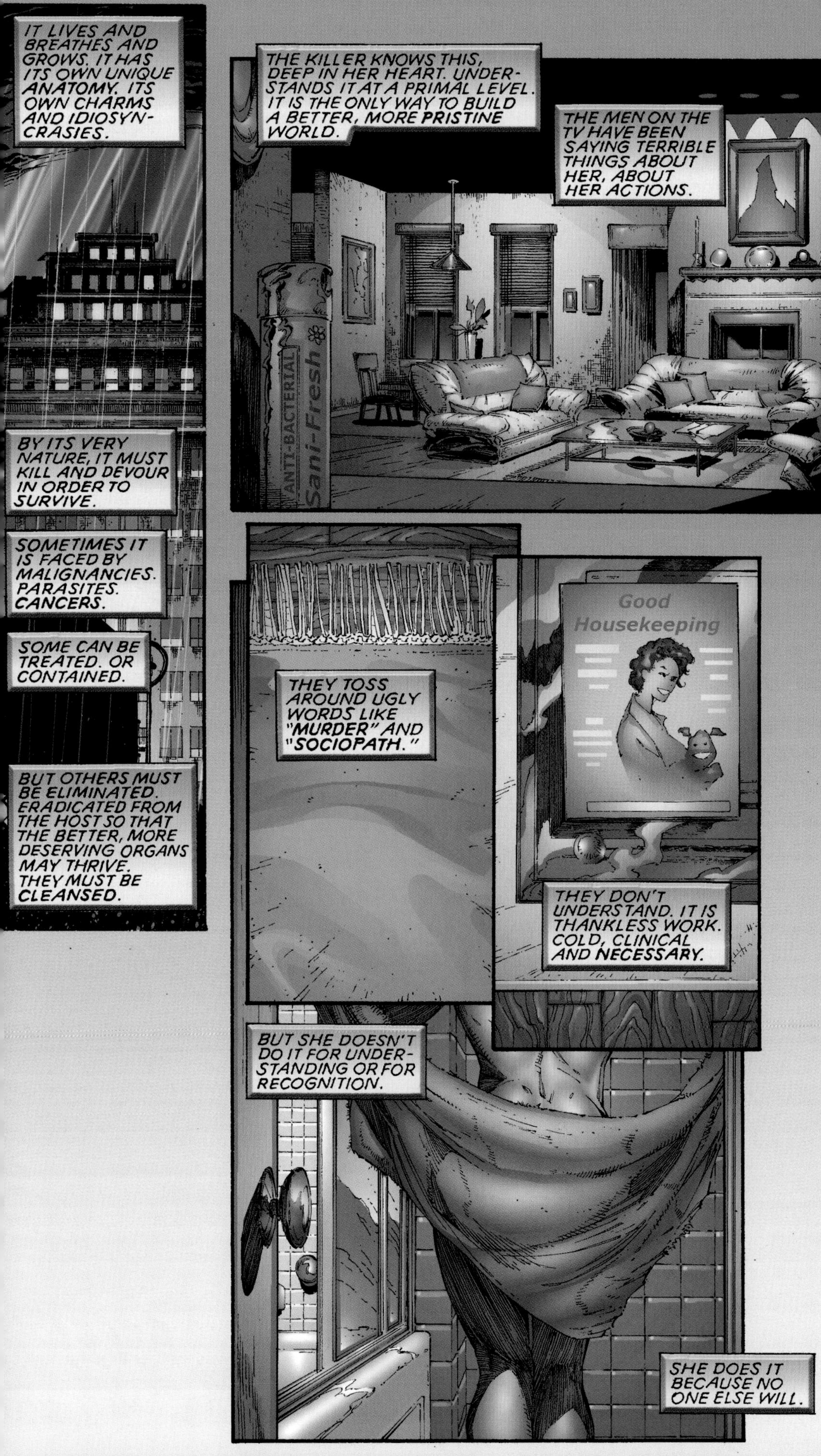
IT LIVES AND BREATHES AND GROWS. IT HAS ITS OWN UNIQUE ANATOMY. ITS OWN CHARMS AND IDIOSYN-CRASIES.
BY ITS VERY NATURE, IT MUST KILL AND DEVOUR IN ORDER TO SURVIVE.
SOMETIMES IT IS FACED BY MALIGNANCIES. PARASITES. CANCERS.
SOME CAN BE TREATED. OR CONTAINED.
BUT OTHERS MUST BE ELIMINATED. ERADICATED FROM THE HOST SO THAT THE BETTER, MORE DESERVING ORGANS MAY THRIVE. THEY MUST BE CLEANSED.
THE KILLER KNOWS THIS, DEEP IN HER HEART. UNDER-STANDS IT AT A PRIMAL LEVEL. IT IS THE ONLY WAY TO BUILD A BETTER, MORE PRISTINE WORLD.
THE MEN ON THE TV HAVE BEEN SAYING TERRIBLE THINGS ABOUT HER, ABOUT HER ACTIONS.
ANTI-BACTERIAL
Sani-Fresh
THEY TOSS AROUND UGLY WORDS LIKE "MURDER" AND "SOCIOPATH."
Good Housekeeping
THEY DON'T UNDERSTAND. IT IS THANKLESS WORK. COLD, CLINICAL AND NECESSARY.
BUT SHE DOESN'T DO IT FOR UNDER-STANDING OR FOR RECOGNITION.
SHE DOES IT BECAUSE NO ONE ELSE WILL.

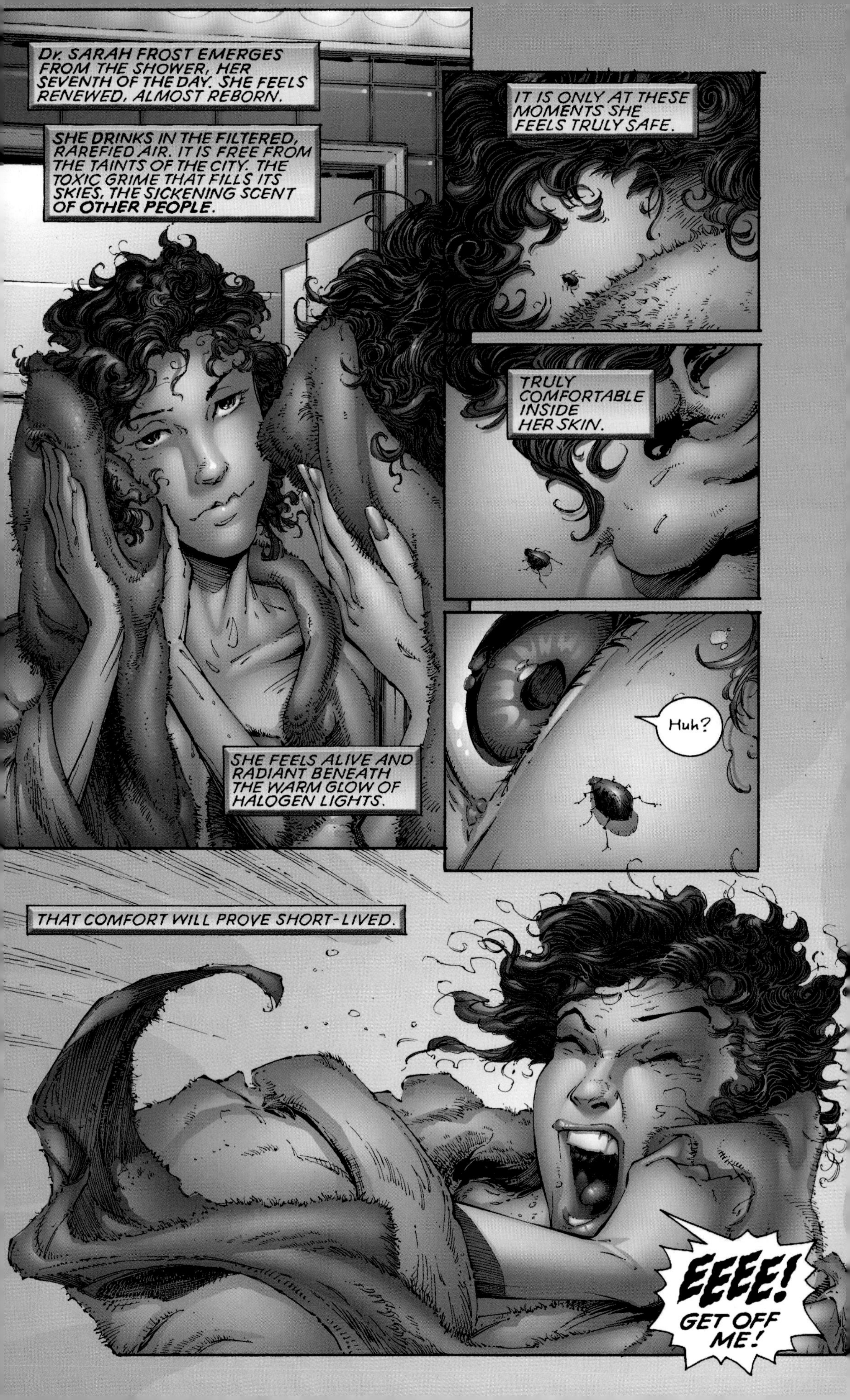
Dr. SARAH FROST EMERGES FROM THE SHOWER, HER SEVENTH OF THE DAY. SHE FEELS RENEWED, ALMOST REBORN.
SHE DRINKS IN THE FILTERED, RAREFIED AIR. IT IS FREE FROM THE TAINTS OF THE CITY. THE TOXIC GRIME THAT FILLS ITS SKIES, THE SICKENING SCENT OF OTHER PEOPLE.
SHE FEELS ALIVE AND RADIANT BENEATH THE WARM GLOW OF HALOGEN LIGHTS.
IT IS ONLY AT THESE MOMENTS SHE FEELS TRULY SAFE.
TRULY COMFORTABLE INSIDE HER SKIN.
Huh?
THAT COMFORT WILL PROVE SHORT-LIVED.
EEEE! GET OFF ME!

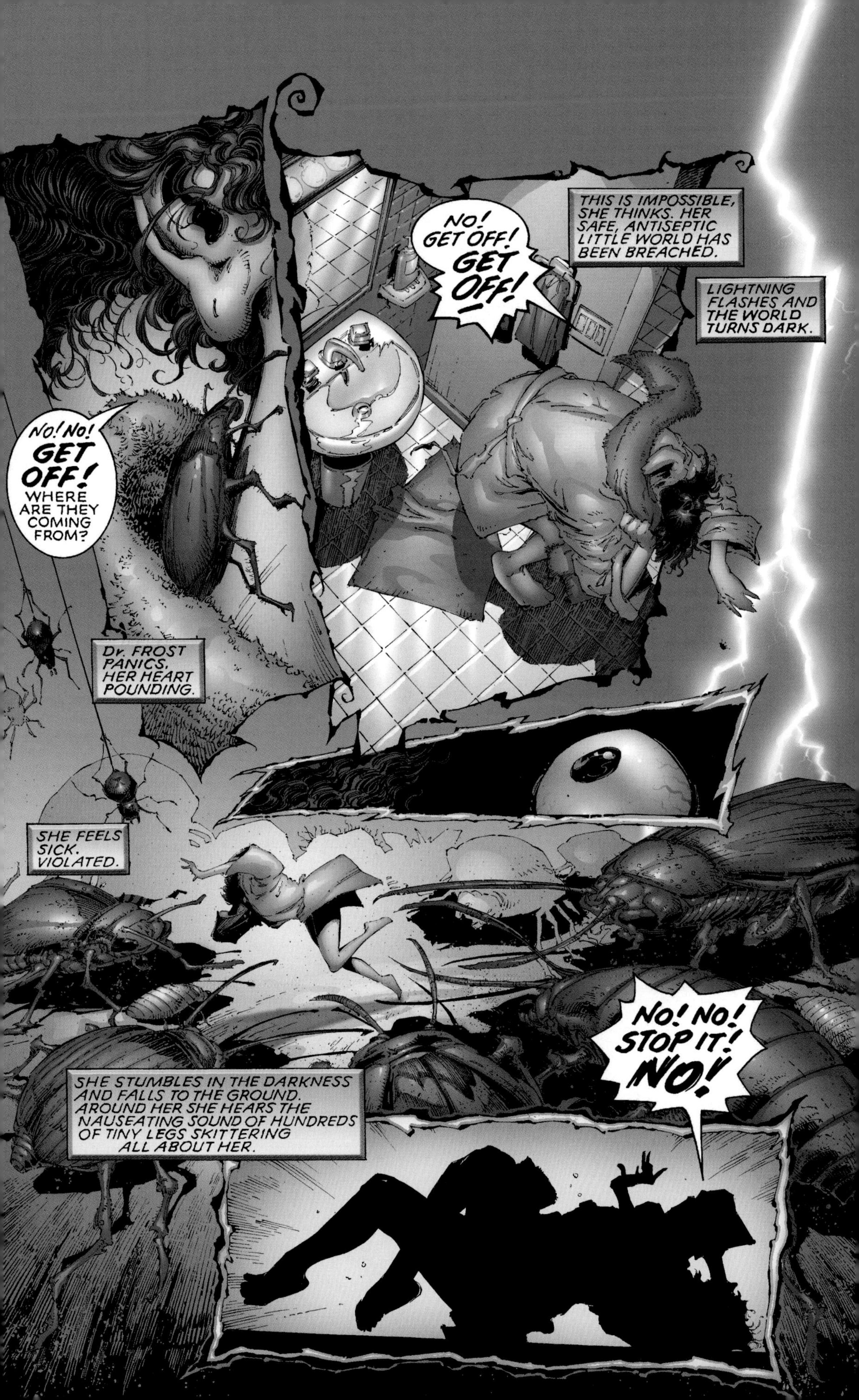
NO! GET OFF! GET OFF!
THIS IS IMPOSSIBLE, SHE THINKS. HER SAFE, ANTISEPTIC LITTLE WORLD HAS BEEN BREACHED.
LIGHTNING FLASHES AND THE WORLD TURNS DARK.
NO! NO! GET OFF! WHERE ARE THEY COMING FROM?
Dr. FROST PANICS, HER HEART POUNDING.
SHE FEELS SICK. VIOLATED.
SHE STUMBLES IN THE DARKNESS AND FALLS TO THE GROUND. AROUND HER SHE HEARS THE NAUSEATING SOUND OF HUNDREDS OF TINY LEGS SKITTERING ALL ABOUT HER.
NO! NO! STOP IT! NO!

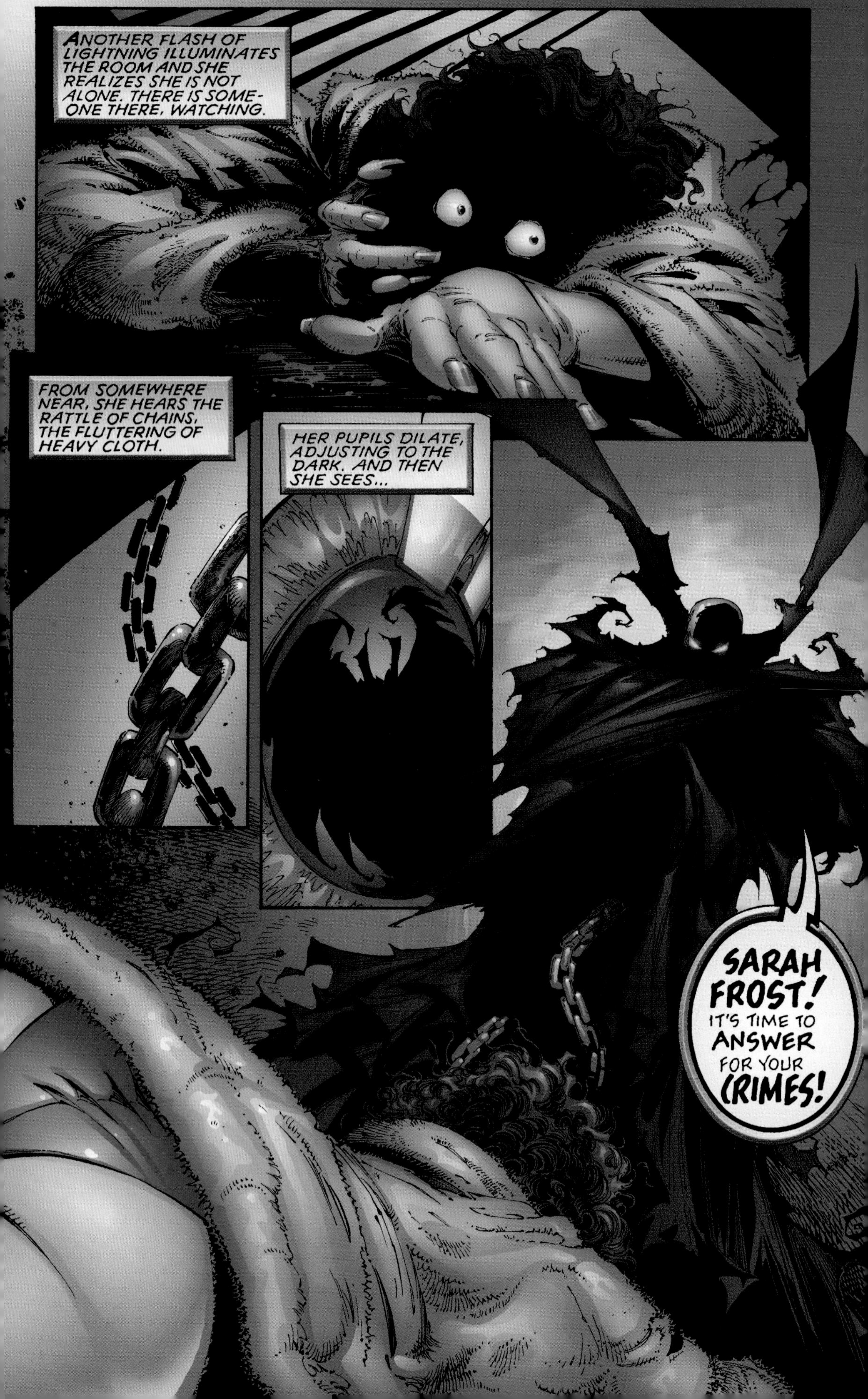
ANOTHER FLASH OF LIGHTNING ILLUMINATES THE ROOM AND SHE REALIZES SHE IS NOT ALONE. THERE IS SOMEONE THERE, WATCHING.
FROM SOMEWHERE NEAR, SHE HEARS THE RATTLE OF CHAINS, THE FLUTTERING OF HEAVY CLOTH.
HER PUPILS DILATE, ADJUSTING TO THE DARK. AND THEN SHE SEES...
SARAH FROST! IT'S TIME TO ANSWER FOR YOUR CRIMES!

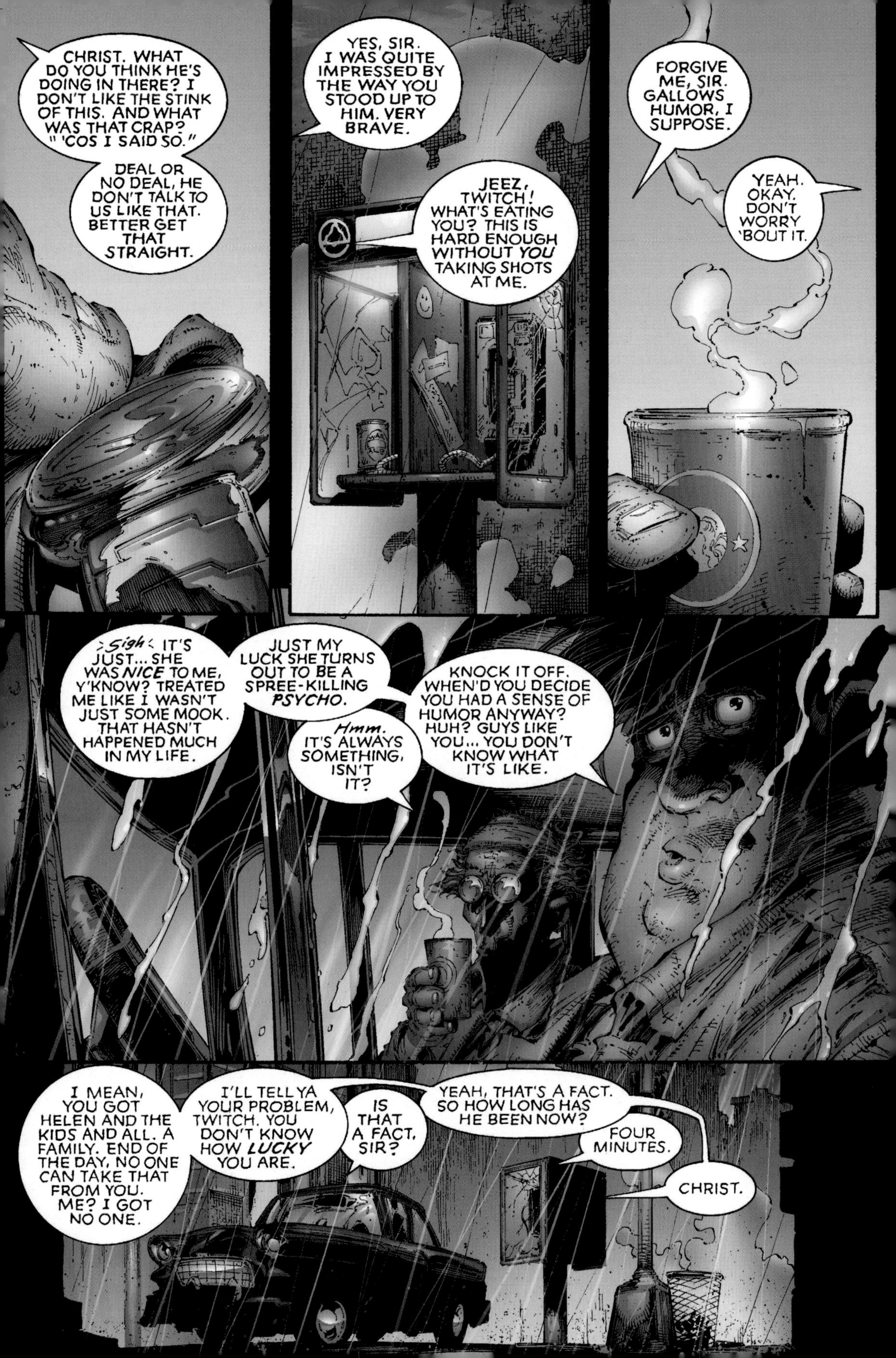
CHRIST. WHAT DO YOU THINK HE'S DOING IN THERE? I DON'T LIKE THE STINK OF THIS. AND WHAT WAS THAT CRAP? "'COS I SAID SO."
DEAL OR NO DEAL, HE DON'T TALK TO US LIKE THAT. BETTER GET THAT STRAIGHT.
YES, SIR. I WAS QUITE IMPRESSED BY THE WAY YOU STOOD UP TO HIM. VERY BRAVE.
JEEZ, TWITCH! WHAT'S EATING YOU? THIS IS HARD ENOUGH WITHOUT *YOU* TAKING SHOTS AT ME.
FORGIVE ME, SIR. GALLOWS HUMOR, I SUPPOSE.
YEAH. OKAY. DON'T WORRY 'BOUT IT.
>*Sigh*< IT'S JUST... SHE WAS *NICE* TO ME, Y'KNOW? TREATED ME LIKE I WASN'T JUST SOME MOOK. THAT HASN'T HAPPENED MUCH IN MY LIFE.
JUST MY LUCK SHE TURNS OUT TO BE A SPREE-KILLING *PSYCHO*.
Hmm. IT'S ALWAYS SOMETHING, ISN'T IT?
KNOCK IT OFF. WHEN'D YOU DECIDE YOU HAD A SENSE OF HUMOR ANYWAY? HUH? GUYS LIKE YOU... YOU DON'T KNOW WHAT IT'S LIKE.
I MEAN, YOU GOT HELEN AND THE KIDS AND ALL. A FAMILY. END OF THE DAY, NO ONE CAN TAKE THAT FROM YOU. ME? I GOT NO ONE.
I'LL TELL YA YOUR PROBLEM, TWITCH. YOU DON'T KNOW HOW *LUCKY* YOU ARE.
IS THAT A FACT, SIR?
YEAH, THAT'S A FACT. SO HOW LONG HAS HE BEEN NOW?
FOUR MINUTES.
CHRIST.

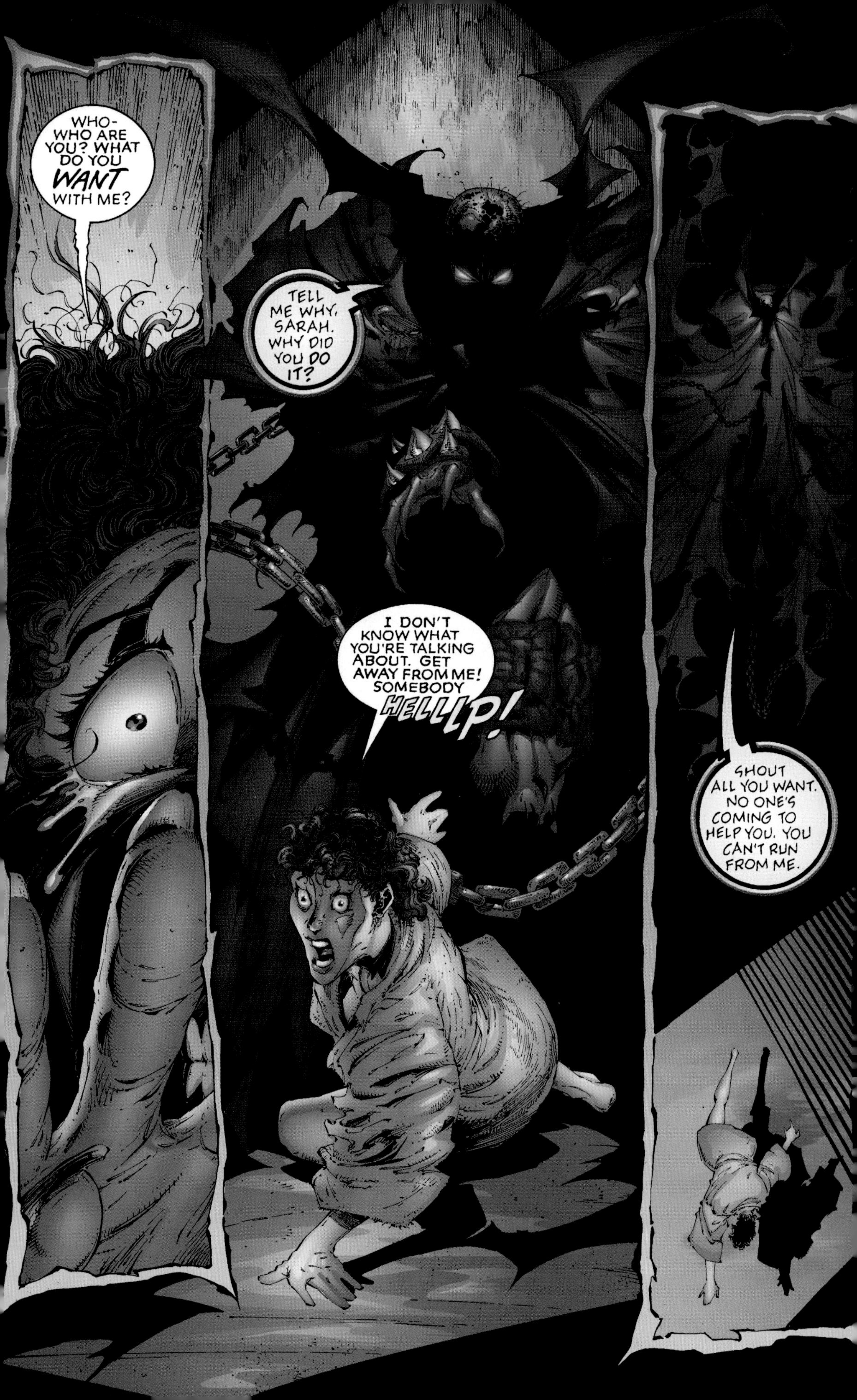
WHO-WHO ARE YOU? WHAT DO YOU WANT WITH ME?
TELL ME WHY, SARAH. WHY DID YOU DO IT?
I DON'T KNOW WHAT YOU'RE TALKING ABOUT. GET AWAY FROM ME! SOMEBODY HELLLP!
SHOUT ALL YOU WANT. NO ONE'S COMING TO HELP YOU. YOU CAN'T RUN FROM ME.

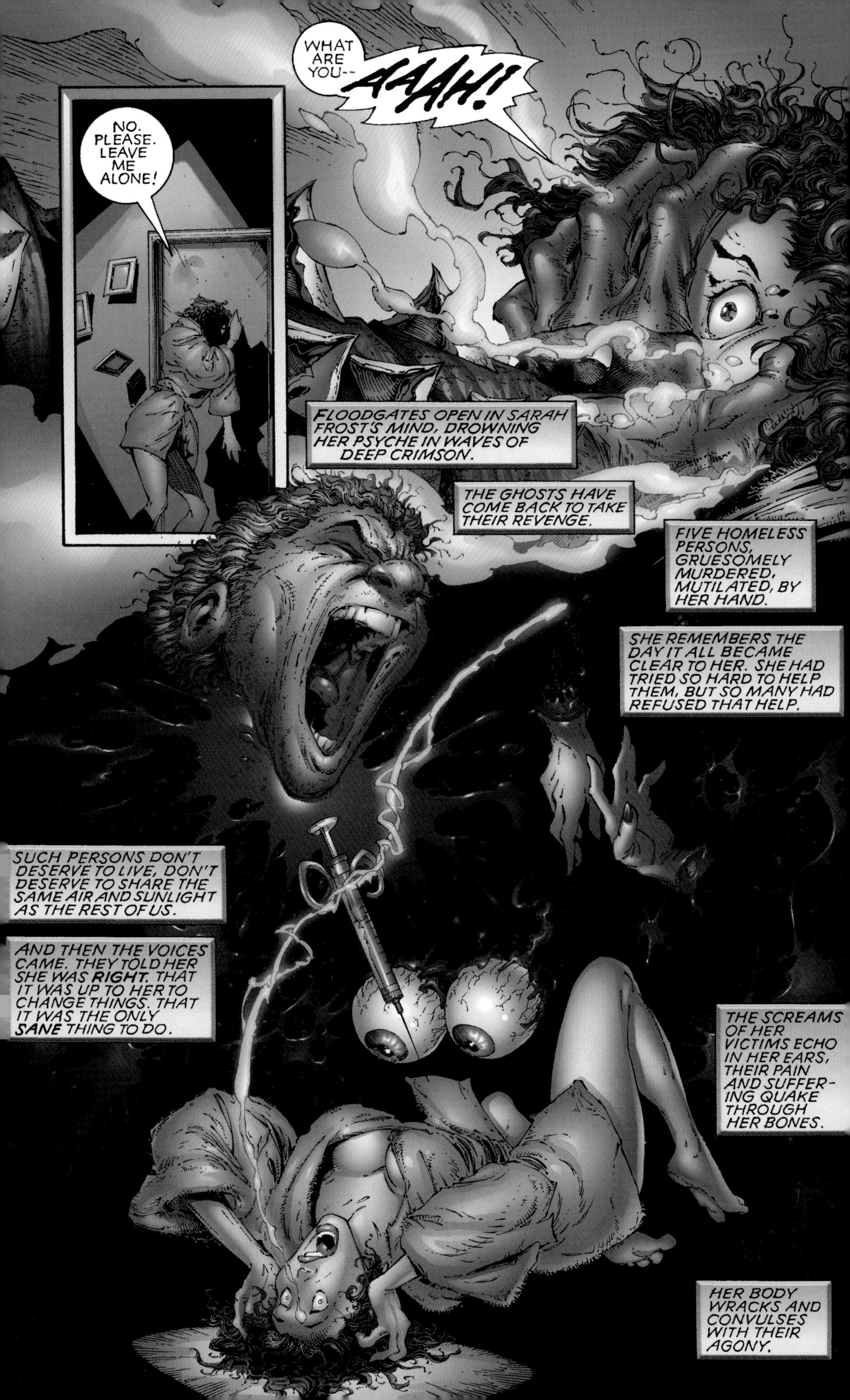

WHAT ARE YOU-- AAAH!
NO. PLEASE. LEAVE ME ALONE!
FLOODGATES OPEN IN SARAH FROST'S MIND, DROWNING HER PSYCHE IN WAVES OF DEEP CRIMSON.
THE GHOSTS HAVE COME BACK TO TAKE THEIR REVENGE.
FIVE HOMELESS PERSONS, GRUESOMELY MURDERED, MUTILATED, BY HER HAND.
SHE REMEMBERS THE DAY IT ALL BECAME CLEAR TO HER. SHE HAD TRIED SO HARD TO HELP THEM, BUT SO MANY HAD REFUSED THAT HELP.
SUCH PERSONS DON'T DESERVE TO LIVE, DON'T DESERVE TO SHARE THE SAME AIR AND SUNLIGHT AS THE REST OF US.
AND THEN THE VOICES CAME. THEY TOLD HER SHE WAS **RIGHT**. THAT IT WAS UP TO HER TO CHANGE THINGS. THAT IT WAS THE ONLY **SANE** THING TO DO.
THE SCREAMS OF HER VICTIMS ECHO IN HER EARS, THEIR PAIN AND SUFFERING QUAKE THROUGH HER BONES.
HER BODY WRACKS AND CONVULSES WITH THEIR AGONY.

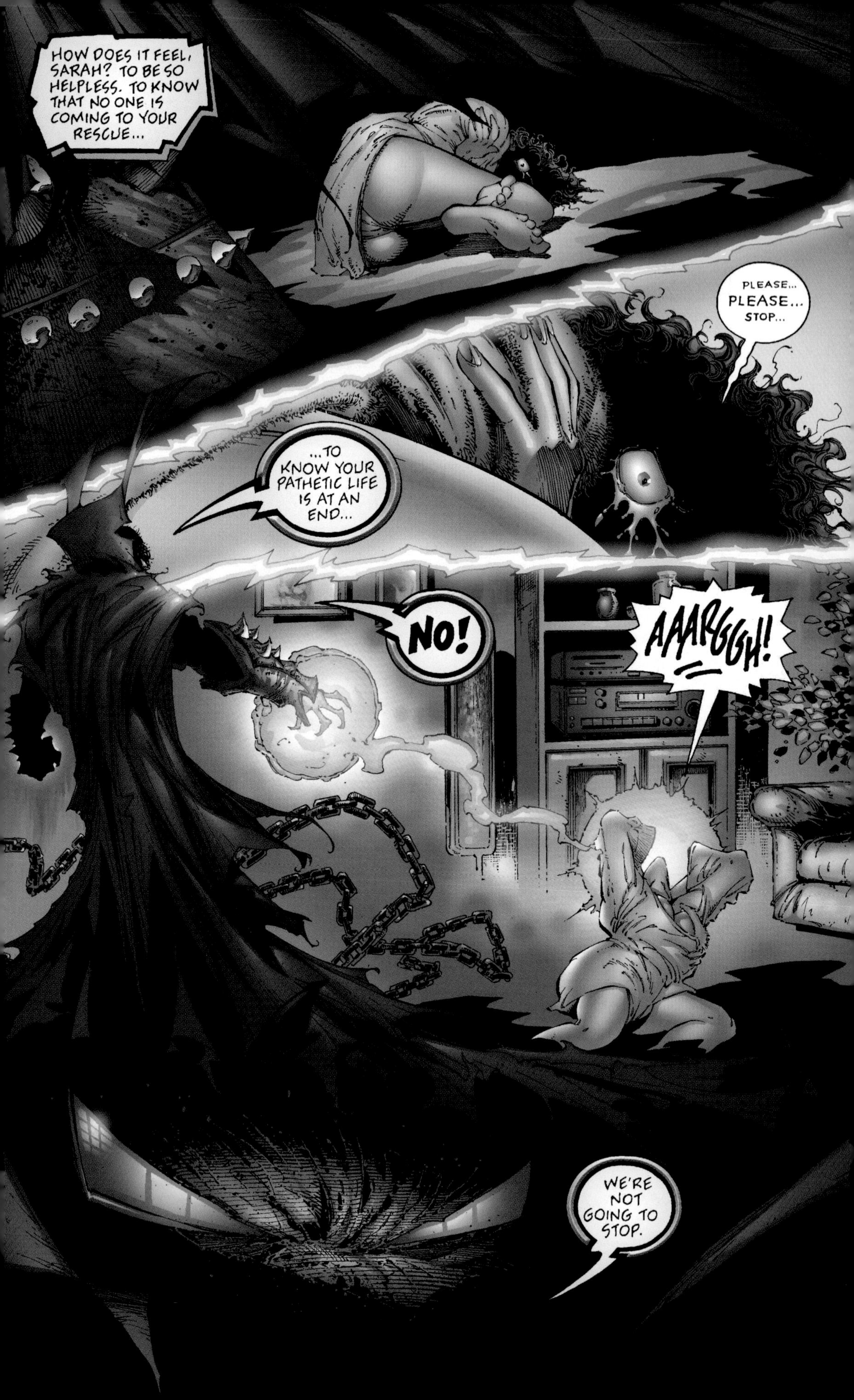
HOW DOES IT FEEL, SARAH? TO BE SO HELPLESS. TO KNOW THAT NO ONE IS COMING TO YOUR RESCUE...
PLEASE... PLEASE... STOP...
...TO KNOW YOUR PATHETIC LIFE IS AT AN END...
NO!
AAARGGH!
WE'RE NOT GOING TO STOP.

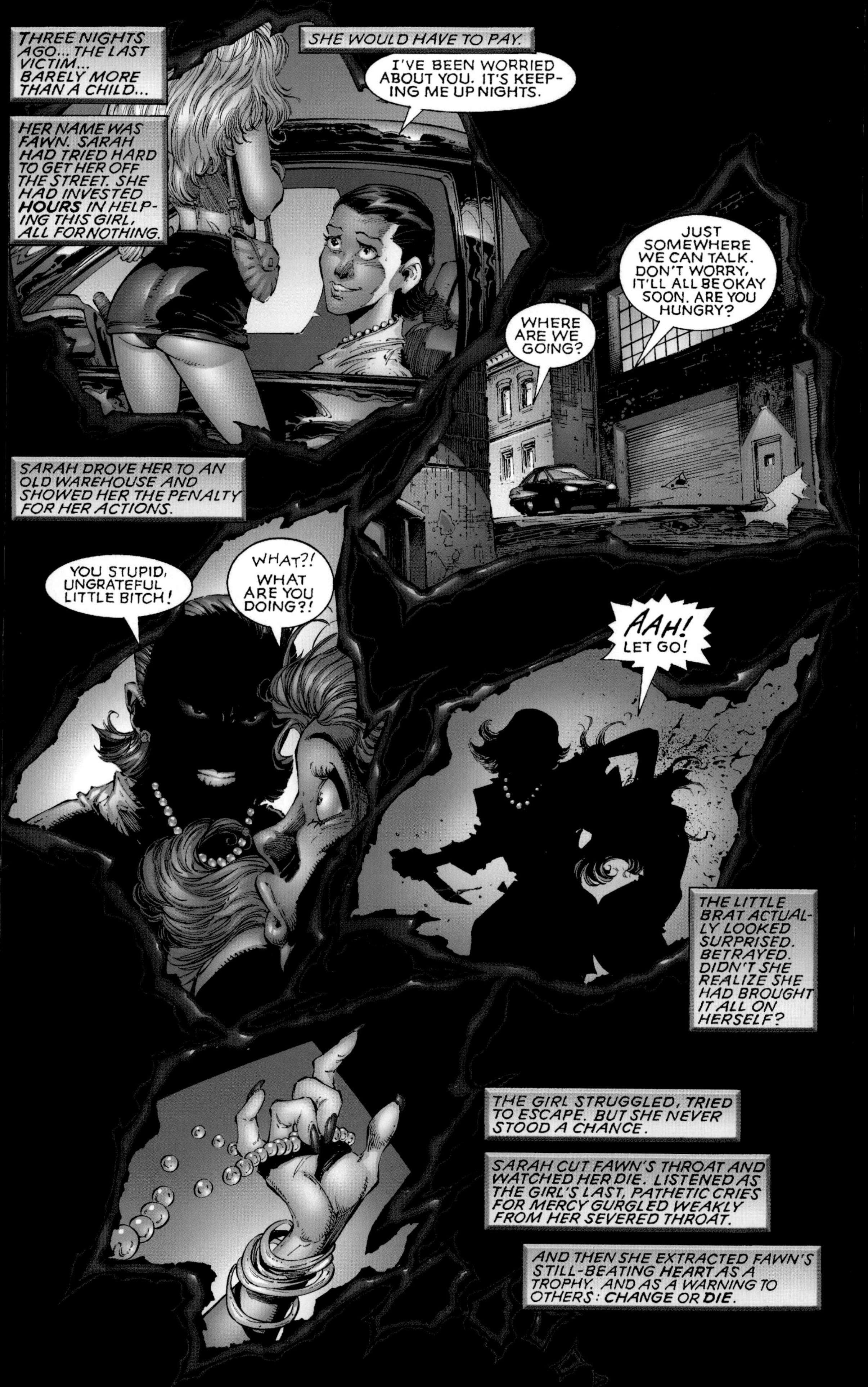
THREE NIGHTS AGO... THE LAST VICTIM... BARELY MORE THAN A CHILD...
SHE WOULD HAVE TO PAY.
I'VE BEEN WORRIED ABOUT YOU. IT'S KEEPING ME UP NIGHTS.
HER NAME WAS FAWN. SARAH HAD TRIED HARD TO GET HER OFF THE STREET. SHE HAD INVESTED HOURS IN HELPING THIS GIRL, ALL FOR NOTHING.
WHERE ARE WE GOING?
JUST SOMEWHERE WE CAN TALK. DON'T WORRY, IT'LL ALL BE OKAY SOON. ARE YOU HUNGRY?
SARAH DROVE HER TO AN OLD WAREHOUSE AND SHOWED HER THE PENALTY FOR HER ACTIONS.
YOU STUPID, UNGRATEFUL LITTLE BITCH!
WHAT?! WHAT ARE YOU DOING?!
AAH! LET GO!
THE LITTLE BRAT ACTUALLY LOOKED SURPRISED. BETRAYED. DIDN'T SHE REALIZE SHE HAD BROUGHT IT ALL ON HERSELF?
THE GIRL STRUGGLED, TRIED TO ESCAPE. BUT SHE NEVER STOOD A CHANCE.
SARAH CUT FAWN'S THROAT AND WATCHED HER DIE. LISTENED AS THE GIRL'S LAST, PATHETIC CRIES FOR MERCY GURGLED WEAKLY FROM HER SEVERED THROAT.
AND THEN SHE EXTRACTED FAWN'S STILL-BEATING HEART AS A TROPHY. AND AS A WARNING TO OTHERS: CHANGE OR DIE.

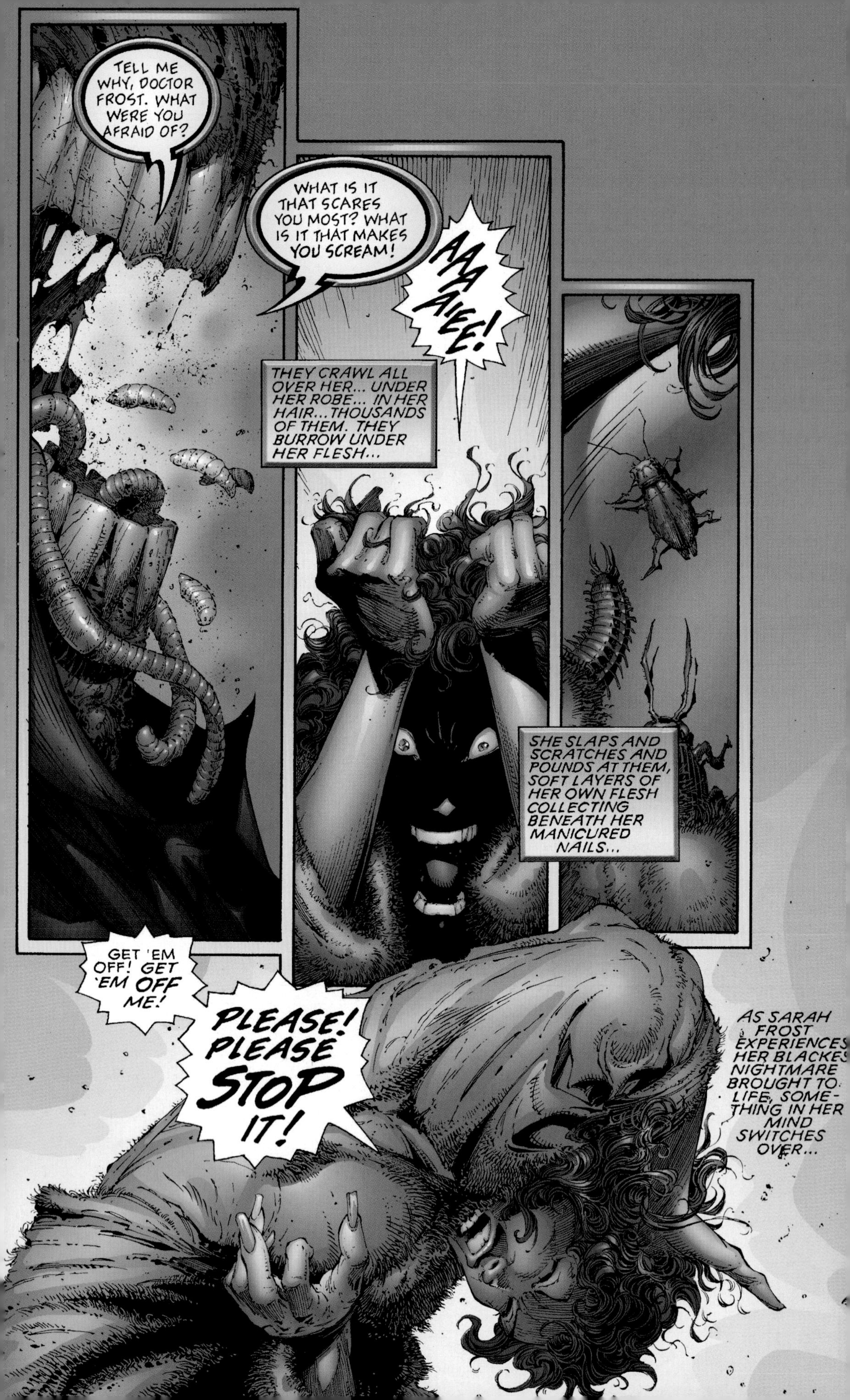
TELL ME WHY, DOCTOR FROST. WHAT WERE YOU AFRAID OF?
WHAT IS IT THAT SCARES YOU MOST? WHAT IS IT THAT MAKES YOU SCREAM!
AAAAIEEE!
THEY CRAWL ALL OVER HER... UNDER HER ROBE... IN HER HAIR...THOUSANDS OF THEM. THEY BURROW UNDER HER FLESH...
SHE SLAPS AND SCRATCHES AND POUNDS AT THEM, SOFT LAYERS OF HER OWN FLESH COLLECTING BENEATH HER MANICURED NAILS...
GET 'EM OFF! GET 'EM OFF ME!
PLEASE! PLEASE STOP IT!
AS SARAH FROST EXPERIENCES HER BLACKES NIGHTMARE BROUGHT TO LIFE, SOME-THING IN HER MIND SWITCHES OVER...

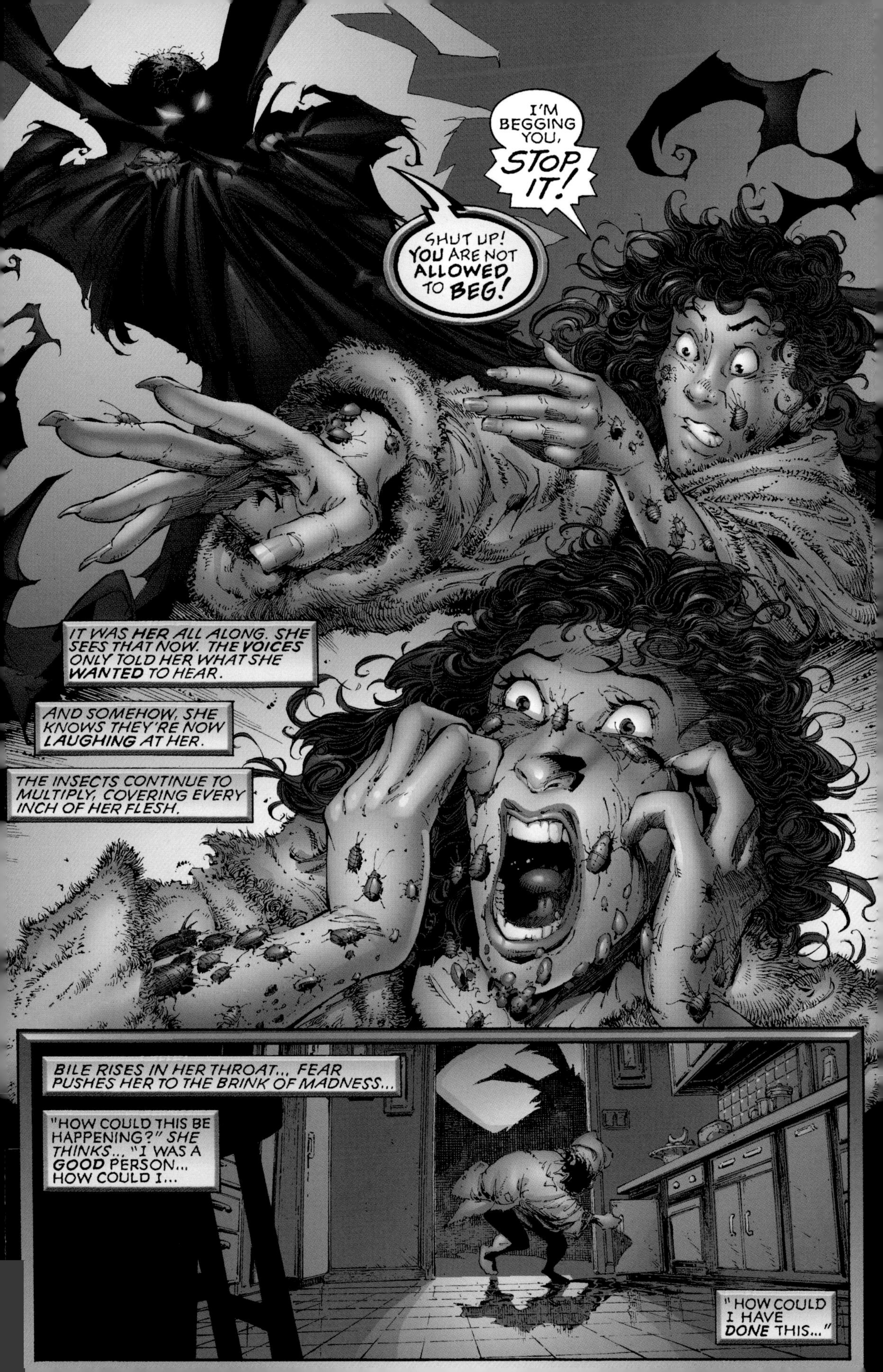

I'M BEGGING YOU, STOP IT!
SHUT UP! YOU ARE NOT ALLOWED TO BEG!
IT WAS HER ALL ALONG. SHE SEES THAT NOW. THE VOICES ONLY TOLD HER WHAT SHE WANTED TO HEAR.
AND SOMEHOW, SHE KNOWS THEY'RE NOW LAUGHING AT HER.
THE INSECTS CONTINUE TO MULTIPLY, COVERING EVERY INCH OF HER FLESH.
BILE RISES IN HER THROAT... FEAR PUSHES HER TO THE BRINK OF MADNESS...
"HOW COULD THIS BE HAPPENING?" SHE THINKS... "I WAS A GOOD PERSON... HOW COULD I...
"HOW COULD I HAVE DONE THIS..."

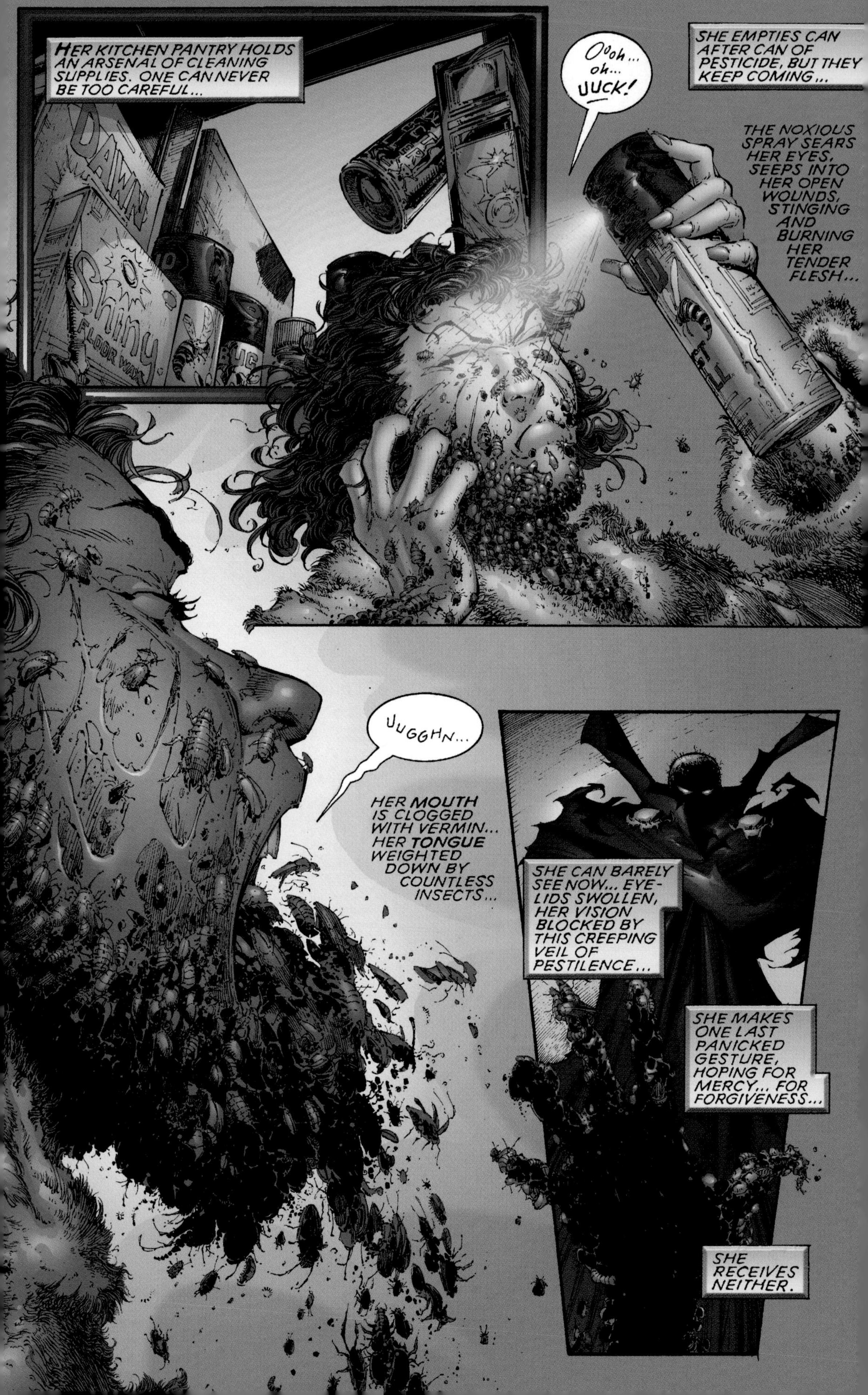
HER KITCHEN PANTRY HOLDS AN ARSENAL OF CLEANING SUPPLIES. ONE CAN NEVER BE TOO CAREFUL...
DAWN
Shiny FLOOR WAX
Oooh... oh... UUCK!
SHE EMPTIES CAN AFTER CAN OF PESTICIDE, BUT THEY KEEP COMING...
THE NOXIOUS SPRAY SEARS HER EYES, SEEPS INTO HER OPEN WOUNDS, STINGING AND BURNING HER TENDER FLESH...
UUGGHN...
HER MOUTH IS CLOGGED WITH VERMIN... HER TONGUE WEIGHTED DOWN BY COUNTLESS INSECTS...
SHE CAN BARELY SEE NOW... EYE-LIDS SWOLLEN, HER VISION BLOCKED BY THIS CREEPING VEIL OF PESTILENCE...
SHE MAKES ONE LAST PANICKED GESTURE, HOPING FOR MERCY... FOR FORGIVENESS...
SHE RECEIVES NEITHER.

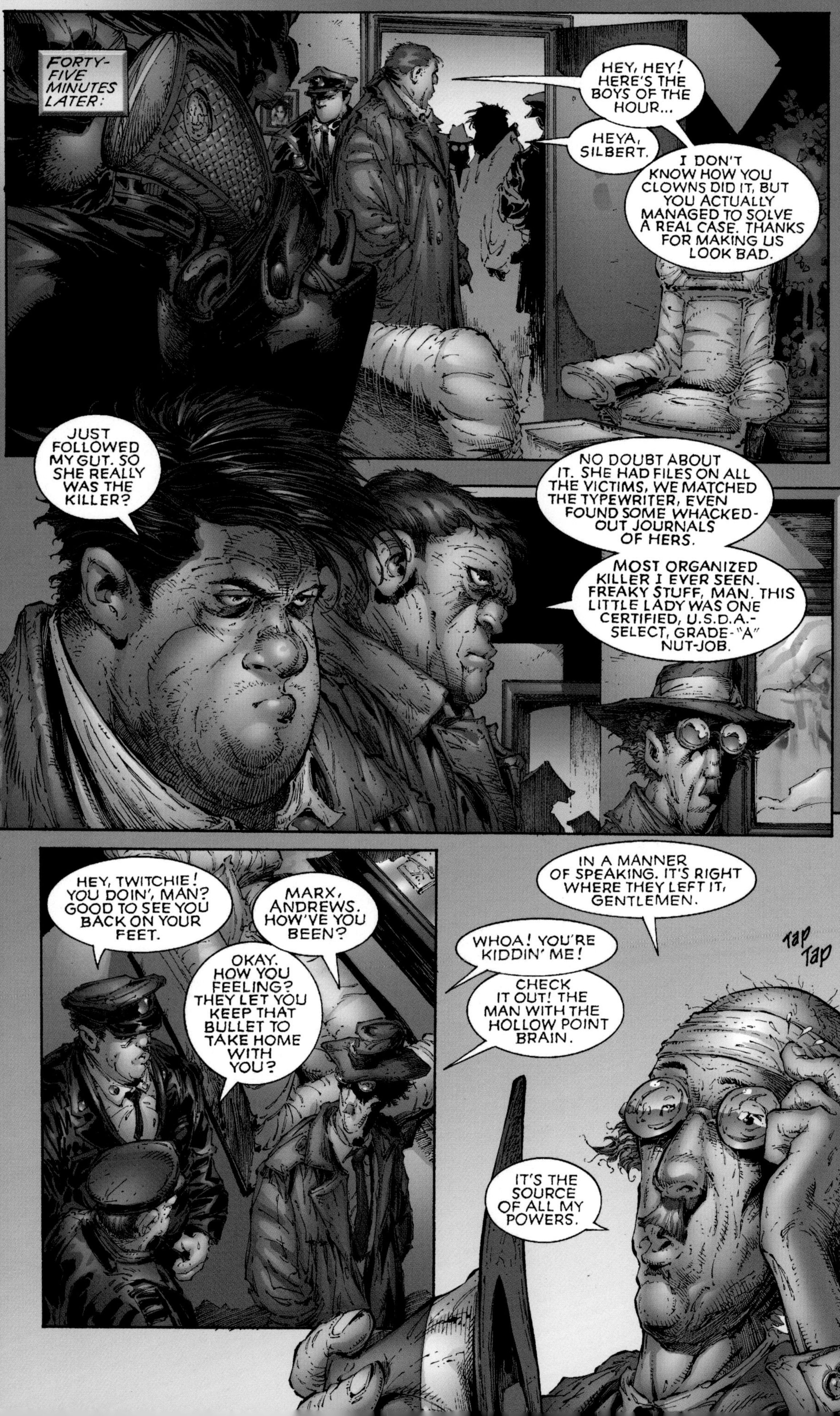
FORTY-FIVE MINUTES LATER:
HEY, HEY! HERE'S THE BOYS OF THE HOUR...
HEYA, SILBERT.
I DON'T KNOW HOW YOU CLOWNS DID IT, BUT YOU ACTUALLY MANAGED TO SOLVE A REAL CASE. THANKS FOR MAKING US LOOK BAD.
JUST FOLLOWED MY GUT. SO SHE REALLY WAS THE KILLER?
NO DOUBT ABOUT IT. SHE HAD FILES ON ALL THE VICTIMS, WE MATCHED THE TYPEWRITER, EVEN FOUND SOME WHACKED-OUT JOURNALS OF HERS.
MOST ORGANIZED KILLER I EVER SEEN. FREAKY STUFF, MAN. THIS LITTLE LADY WAS ONE CERTIFIED, U.S.D.A.-SELECT, GRADE-"A" NUT-JOB.
HEY, TWITCHIE! YOU DOIN', MAN? GOOD TO SEE YOU BACK ON YOUR FEET.
MARX, ANDREWS. HOW'VE YOU BEEN?
OKAY. HOW YOU FEELING? THEY LET YOU KEEP THAT BULLET TO TAKE HOME WITH YOU?
IN A MANNER OF SPEAKING. IT'S RIGHT WHERE THEY LEFT IT, GENTLEMEN.
TAP TAP
WHOA! YOU'RE KIDDIN' ME!
CHECK IT OUT! THE MAN WITH THE HOLLOW POINT BRAIN.
IT'S THE SOURCE OF ALL MY POWERS.

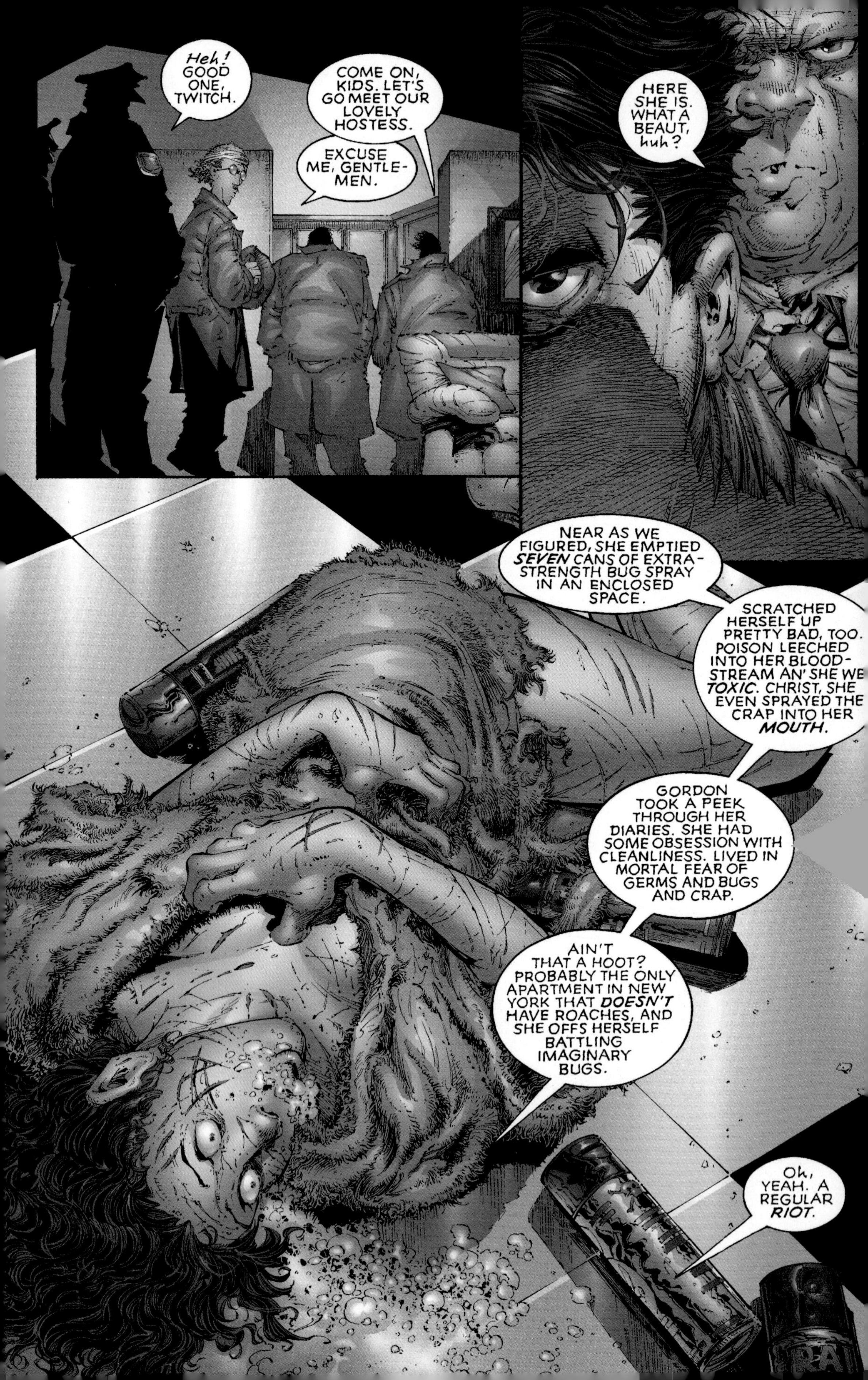
Heh! GOOD ONE, TWITCH.
COME ON, KIDS. LET'S GO MEET OUR LOVELY HOSTESS.
EXCUSE ME, GENTLEMEN.
HERE SHE IS. WHAT A BEAUT, huh?
NEAR AS WE FIGURED, SHE EMPTIED SEVEN CANS OF EXTRA-STRENGTH BUG SPRAY IN AN ENCLOSED SPACE.
SCRATCHED HERSELF UP PRETTY BAD, TOO. POISON LEECHED INTO HER BLOODSTREAM AN' SHE WE TOXIC. CHRIST, SHE EVEN SPRAYED THE CRAP INTO HER MOUTH.
GORDON TOOK A PEEK THROUGH HER DIARIES. SHE HAD SOME OBSESSION WITH CLEANLINESS. LIVED IN MORTAL FEAR OF GERMS AND BUGS AND CRAP.
AIN'T THAT A HOOT? PROBABLY THE ONLY APARTMENT IN NEW YORK THAT DOESN'T HAVE ROACHES, AND SHE OFFS HERSELF BATTLING IMAGINARY BUGS.
Oh, YEAH. A REGULAR RIOT.

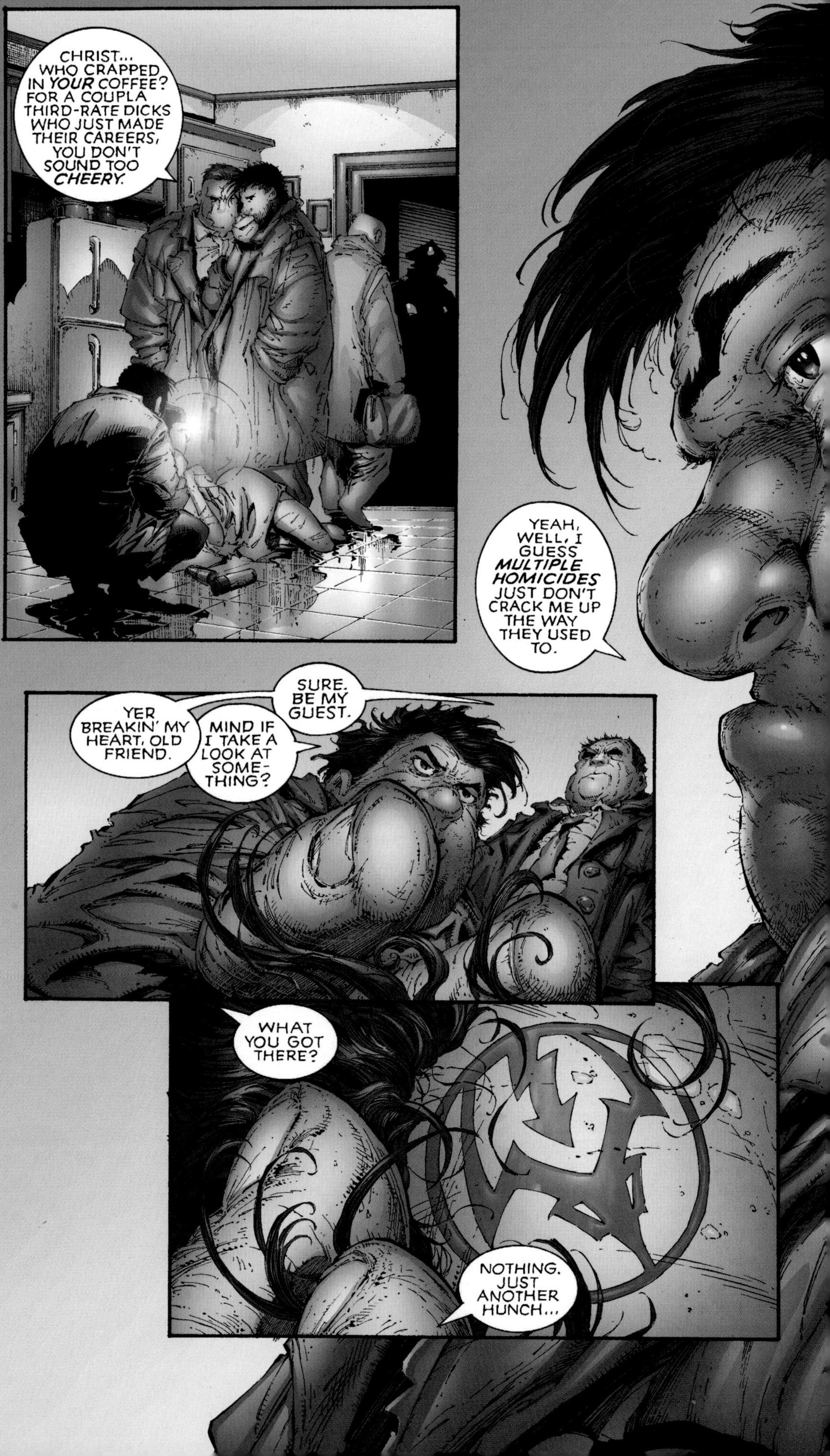
CHRIST... WHO CRAPPED IN *YOUR* COFFEE? FOR A COUPLA THIRD-RATE DICKS WHO JUST MADE THEIR CAREERS, YOU DON'T SOUND TOO *CHEERY*.
YEAH, WELL, I GUESS *MULTIPLE HOMICIDES* JUST DON'T CRACK ME UP THE WAY THEY USED TO.
YER BREAKIN' MY HEART, OLD FRIEND.
MIND IF I TAKE A LOOK AT SOME-THING?
SURE. BE MY GUEST.
WHAT YOU GOT THERE?
NOTHING. JUST ANOTHER HUNCH...

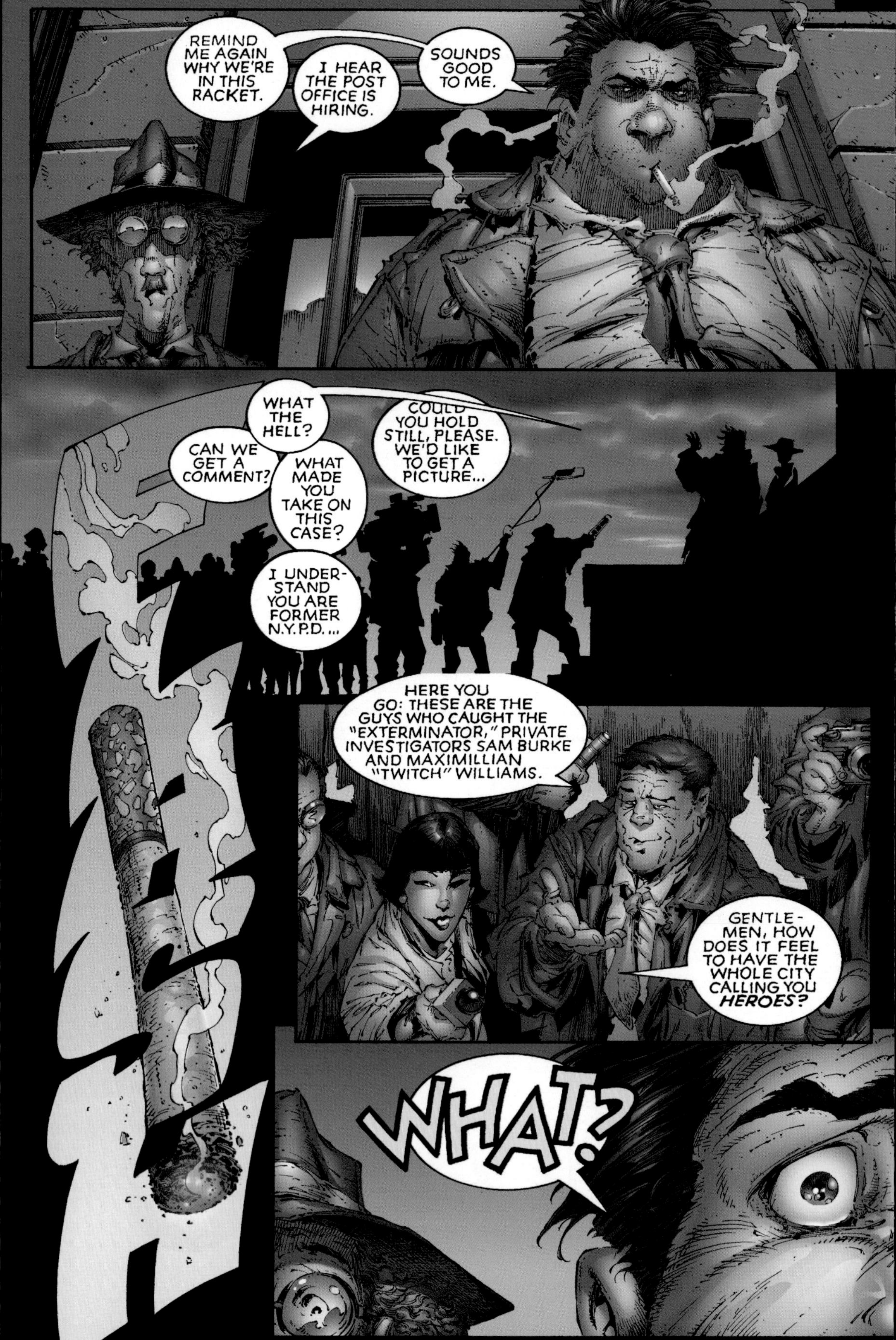

REMIND ME AGAIN WHY WE'RE IN THIS RACKET.
I HEAR THE POST OFFICE IS HIRING.
SOUNDS GOOD TO ME.
WHAT THE HELL?
COULD YOU HOLD STILL, PLEASE. WE'D LIKE TO GET A PICTURE...
CAN WE GET A COMMENT?
WHAT MADE YOU TAKE ON THIS CASE?
I UNDER-STAND YOU ARE FORMER N.Y.P.D. ...
HERE YOU GO: THESE ARE THE GUYS WHO CAUGHT THE "EXTERMINATOR," PRIVATE INVESTIGATORS SAM BURKE AND MAXIMILLIAN "TWITCH" WILLIAMS.
GENTLE-MEN, HOW DOES IT FEEL TO HAVE THE WHOLE CITY CALLING YOU *HEROES?*
WHAT?

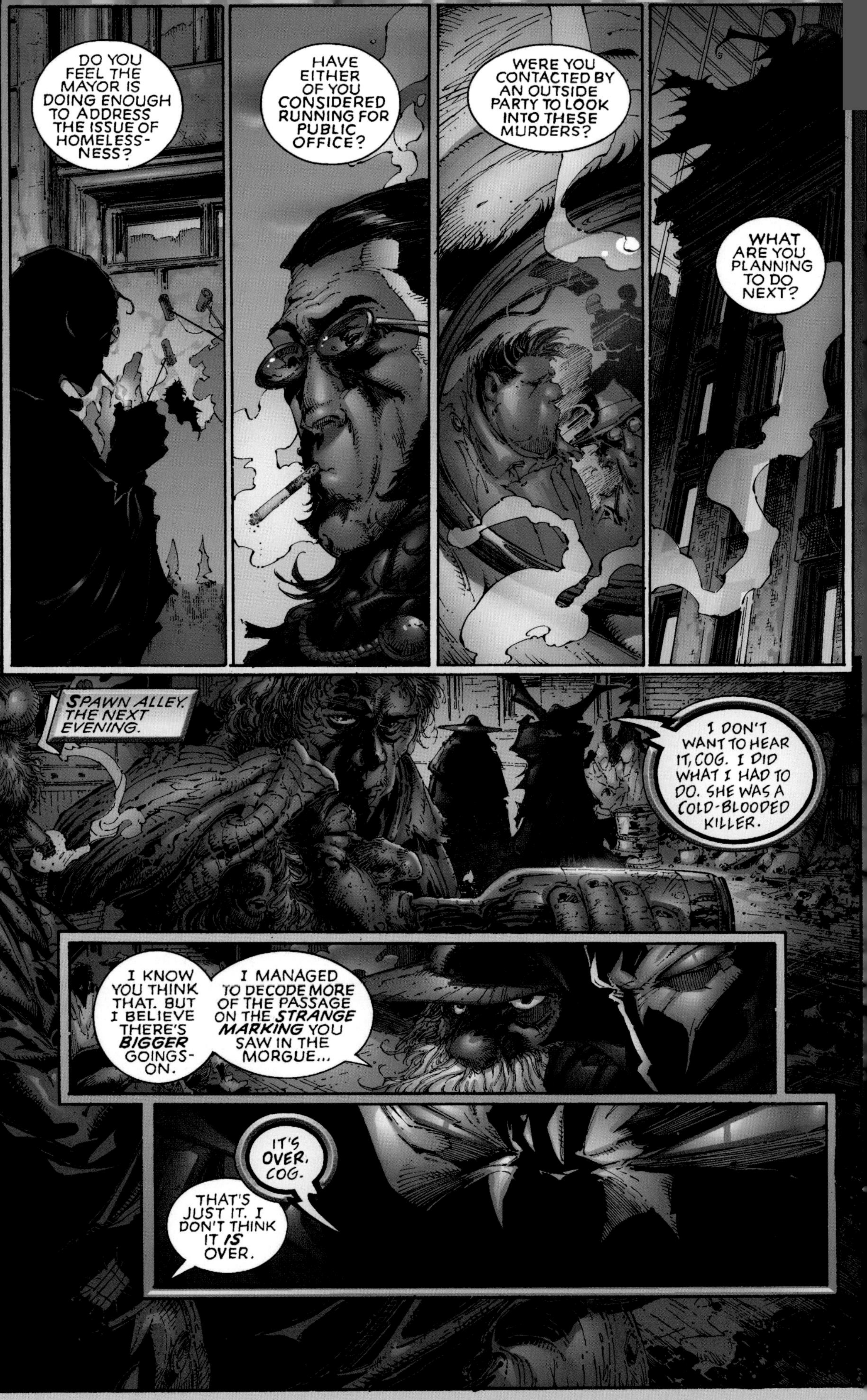
DO YOU FEEL THE MAYOR IS DOING ENOUGH TO ADDRESS THE ISSUE OF HOMELESS-NESS?
HAVE EITHER OF YOU CONSIDERED RUNNING FOR PUBLIC OFFICE?
WERE YOU CONTACTED BY AN OUTSIDE PARTY TO LOOK INTO THESE MURDERS?
WHAT ARE YOU PLANNING TO DO NEXT?
SPAWN ALLEY. THE NEXT EVENING.
I DON'T WANT TO HEAR IT, COG. I DID WHAT I HAD TO DO. SHE WAS A COLD-BLOODED KILLER.
I KNOW YOU THINK THAT. BUT I BELIEVE THERE'S BIGGER GOINGS-ON.
I MANAGED TO DECODE MORE OF THE PASSAGE ON THE STRANGE MARKING YOU SAW IN THE MORGUE...
IT'S OVER, COG.
THAT'S JUST IT. I DON'T THINK IT IS OVER.

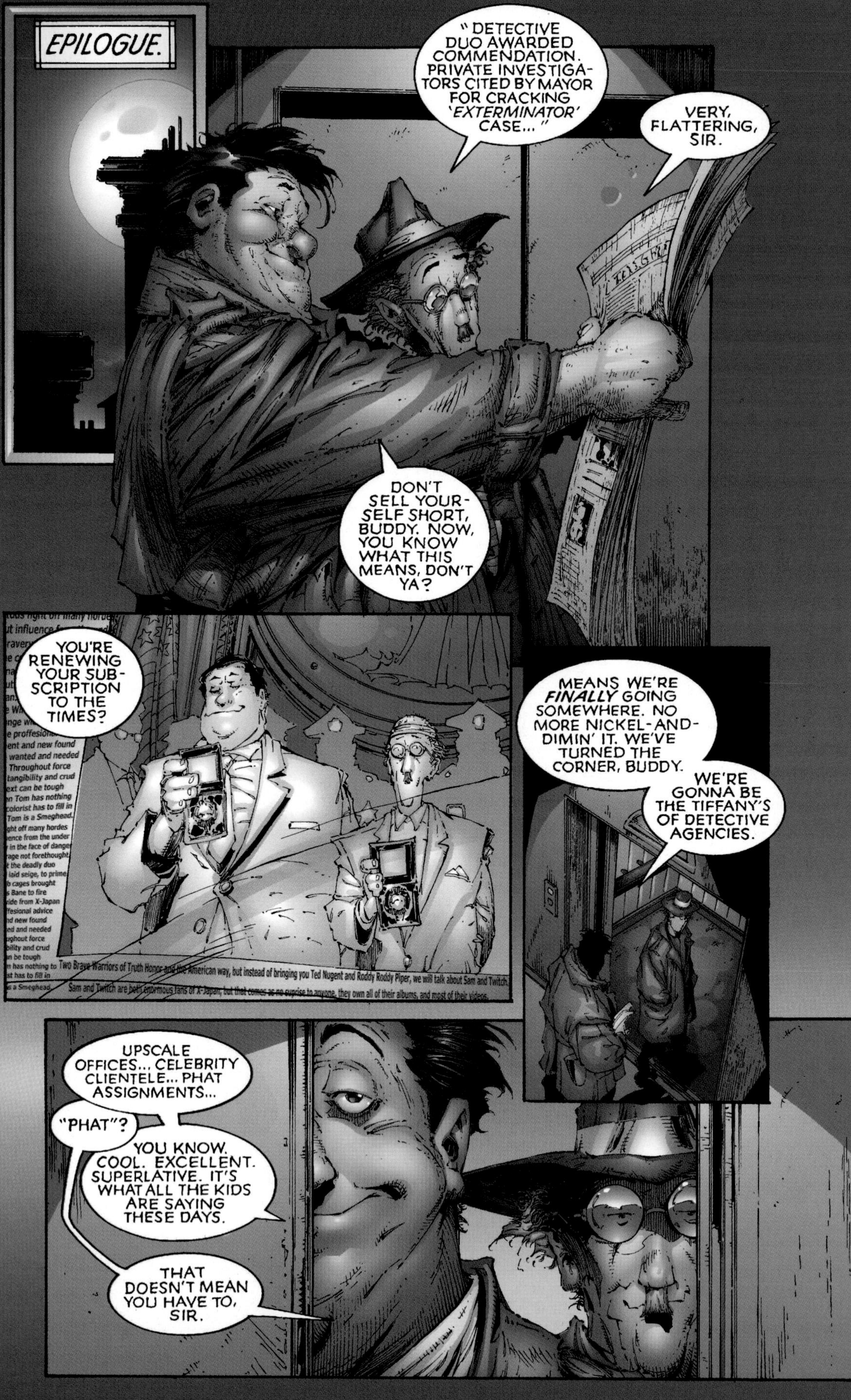
EPILOGUE.
" DETECTIVE DUO AWARDED COMMENDATION. PRIVATE INVESTIGATORS CITED BY MAYOR FOR CRACKING 'EXTERMINATOR' CASE... "
VERY, FLATTERING, SIR.
DON'T SELL YOURSELF SHORT, BUDDY. NOW, YOU KNOW WHAT THIS MEANS, DON'T YA?
YOU'RE RENEWING YOUR SUBSCRIPTION TO THE TIMES?
Two Brave Warriors of Truth Honor and the American way, but instead of bringing you Ted Nugent and Roddy Roddy Piper, we will talk about Sam and Twitch.
MEANS WE'RE FINALLY GOING SOMEWHERE. NO MORE NICKEL-AND-DIMIN' IT. WE'VE TURNED THE CORNER, BUDDY.
WE'RE GONNA BE THE TIFFANY'S OF DETECTIVE AGENCIES.
UPSCALE OFFICES... CELEBRITY CLIENTELE... PHAT ASSIGNMENTS...
"PHAT"?
YOU KNOW. COOL. EXCELLENT. SUPERLATIVE. IT'S WHAT ALL THE KIDS ARE SAYING THESE DAYS.
THAT DOESN'T MEAN YOU HAVE TO, SIR.

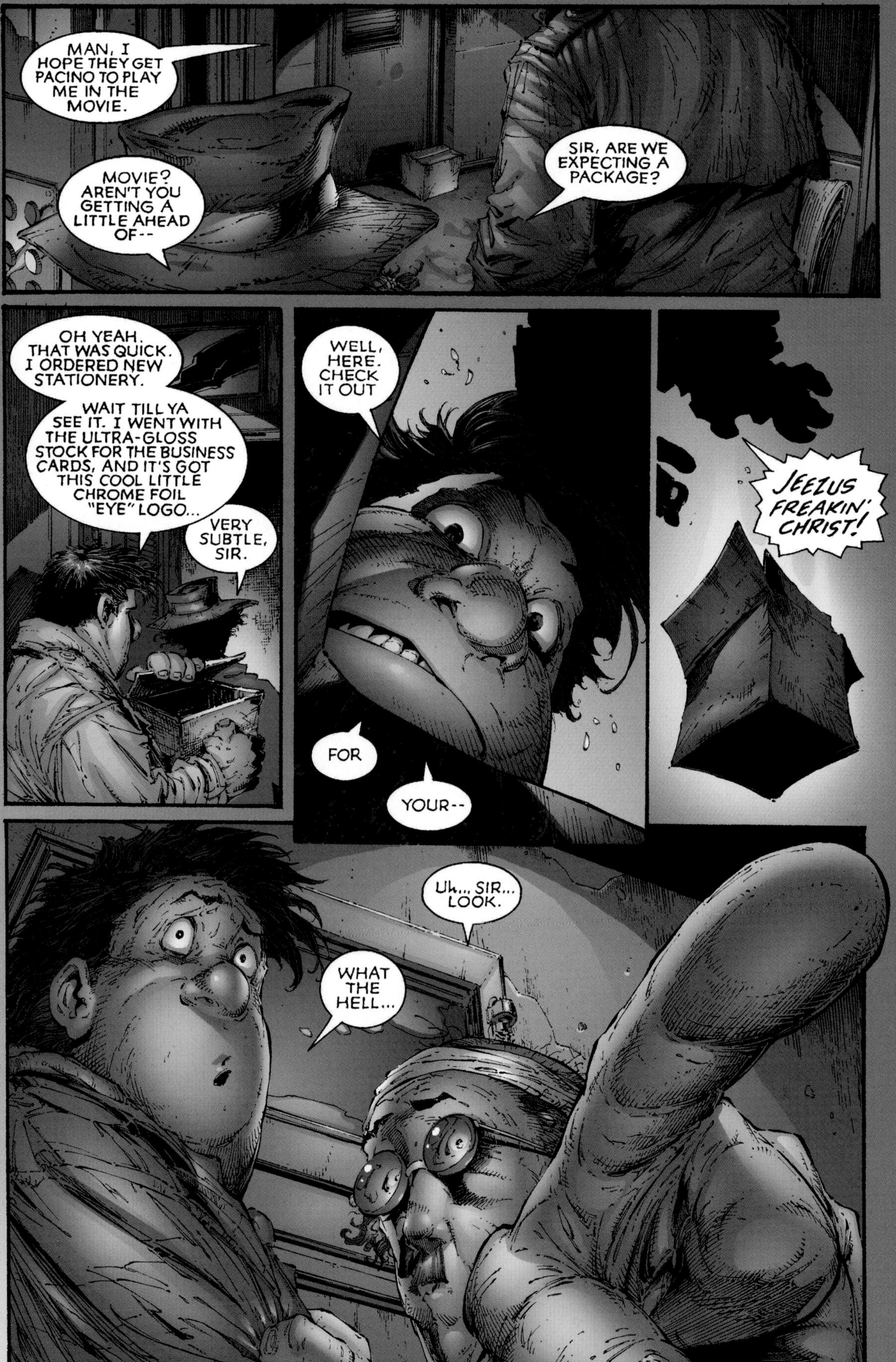
MAN, I HOPE THEY GET PACINO TO PLAY ME IN THE MOVIE.
SIR, ARE WE EXPECTING A PACKAGE?
MOVIE? AREN'T YOU GETTING A LITTLE AHEAD OF--
OH YEAH. THAT WAS QUICK. I ORDERED NEW STATIONERY.
WAIT TILL YA SEE IT. I WENT WITH THE ULTRA-GLOSS STOCK FOR THE BUSINESS CARDS, AND IT'S GOT THIS COOL LITTLE CHROME FOIL "EYE" LOGO...
VERY SUBTLE, SIR.
WELL, HERE. CHECK IT OUT
FOR
YOUR--
JEEZUS FREAKIN' CHRIST!
Uh... SIR... LOOK.
WHAT THE HELL...

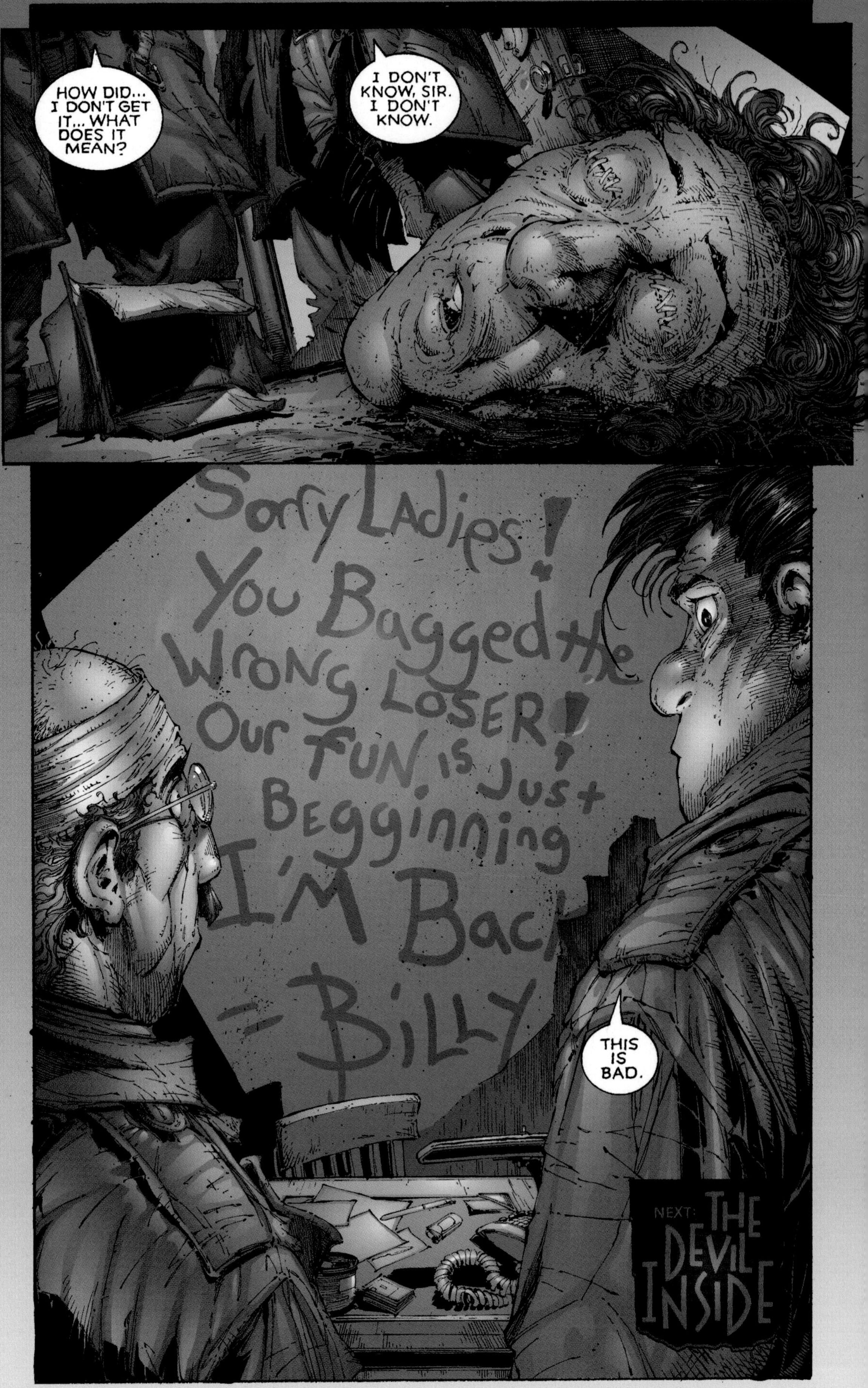
HOW DID... I DON'T GET IT... WHAT DOES IT MEAN?
I DON'T KNOW, SIR. I DON'T KNOW.
Sorry Ladies! You Bagged the Wrong LOSER! Our FUN is Just Begginning I'M Back
- Billy
THIS IS BAD.
NEXT: THE DEVIL INSIDE

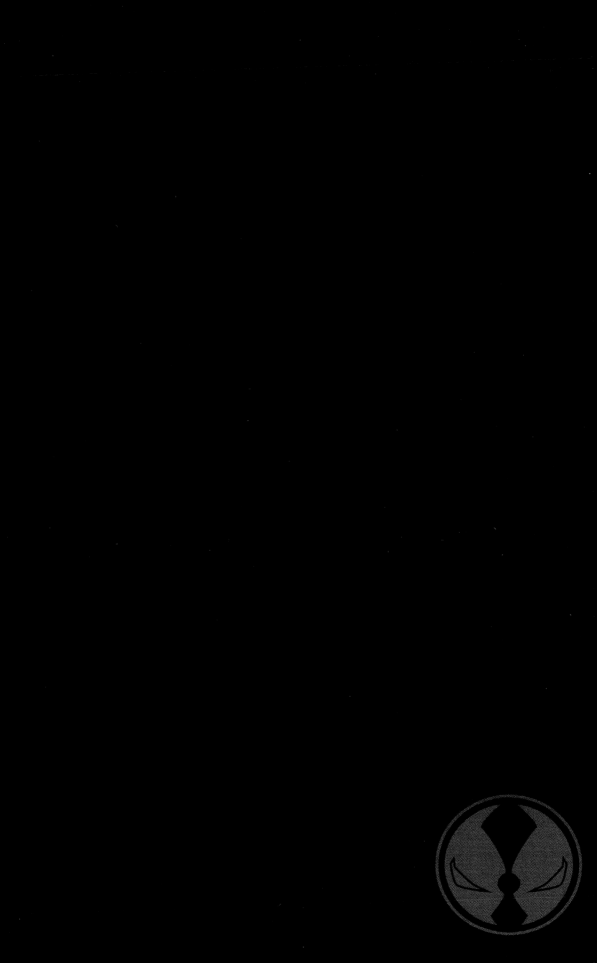

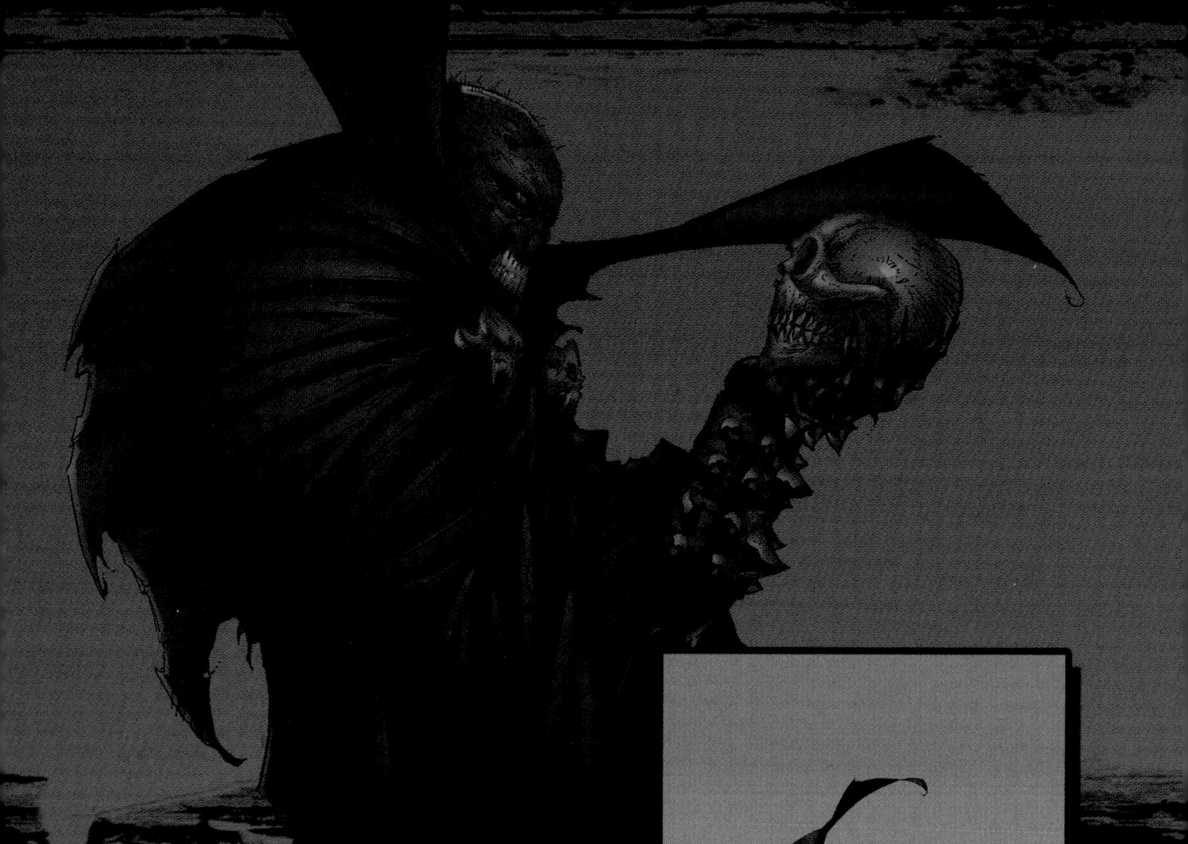

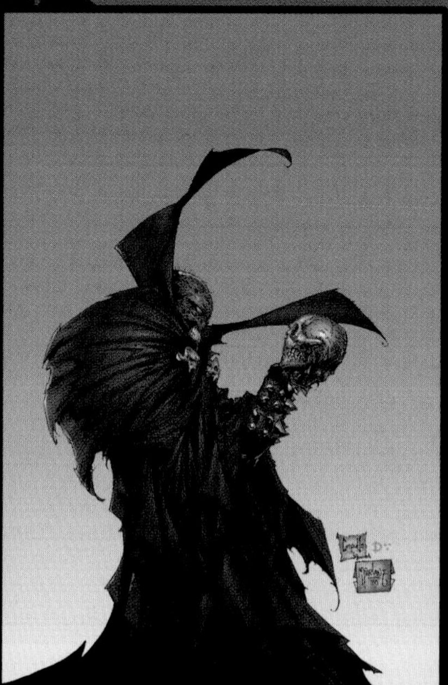

ISSUE EIGHTY-ONE

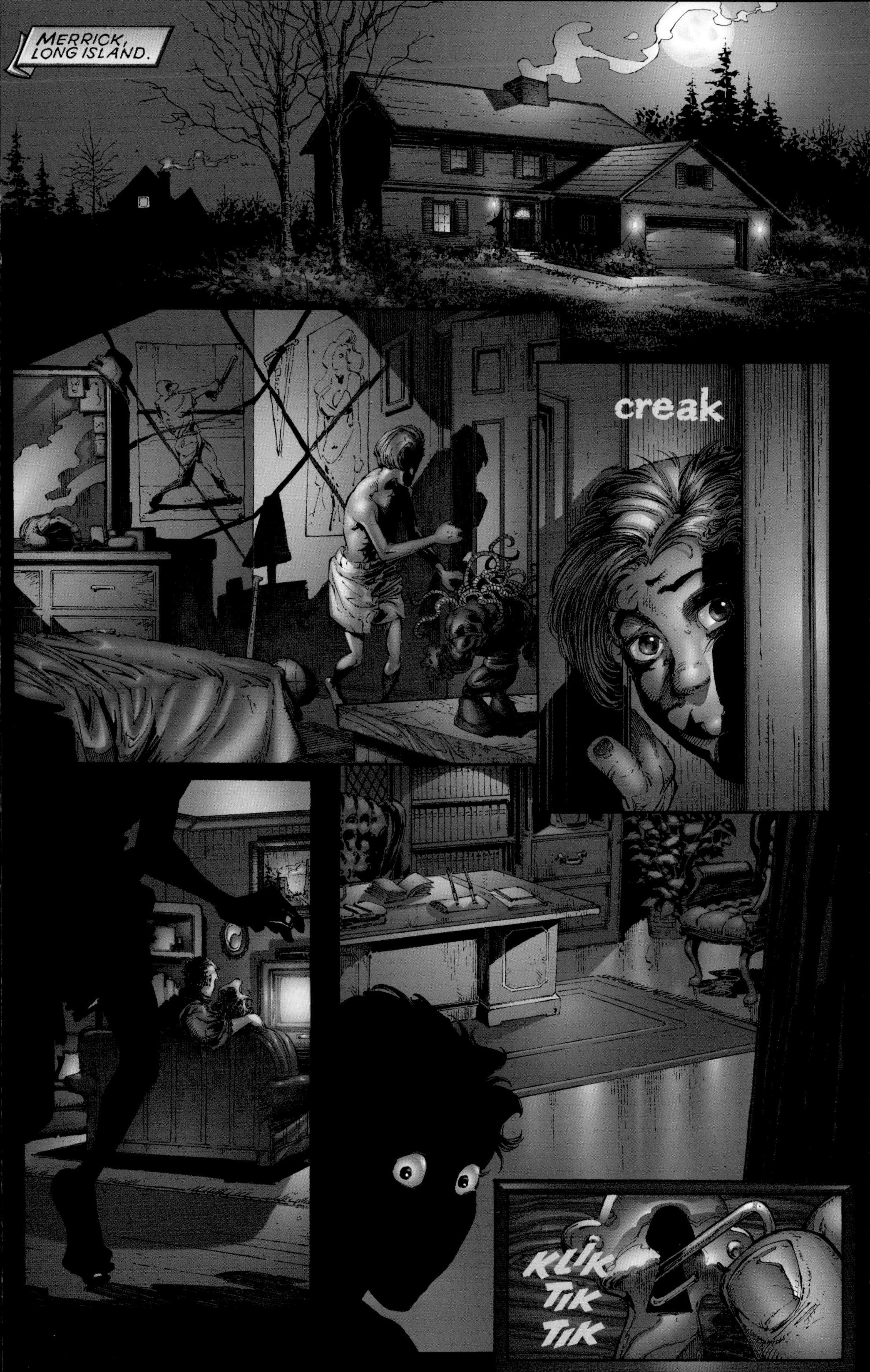
MERRICK, LONG ISLAND.
creak
KLIK
TIK
TIK

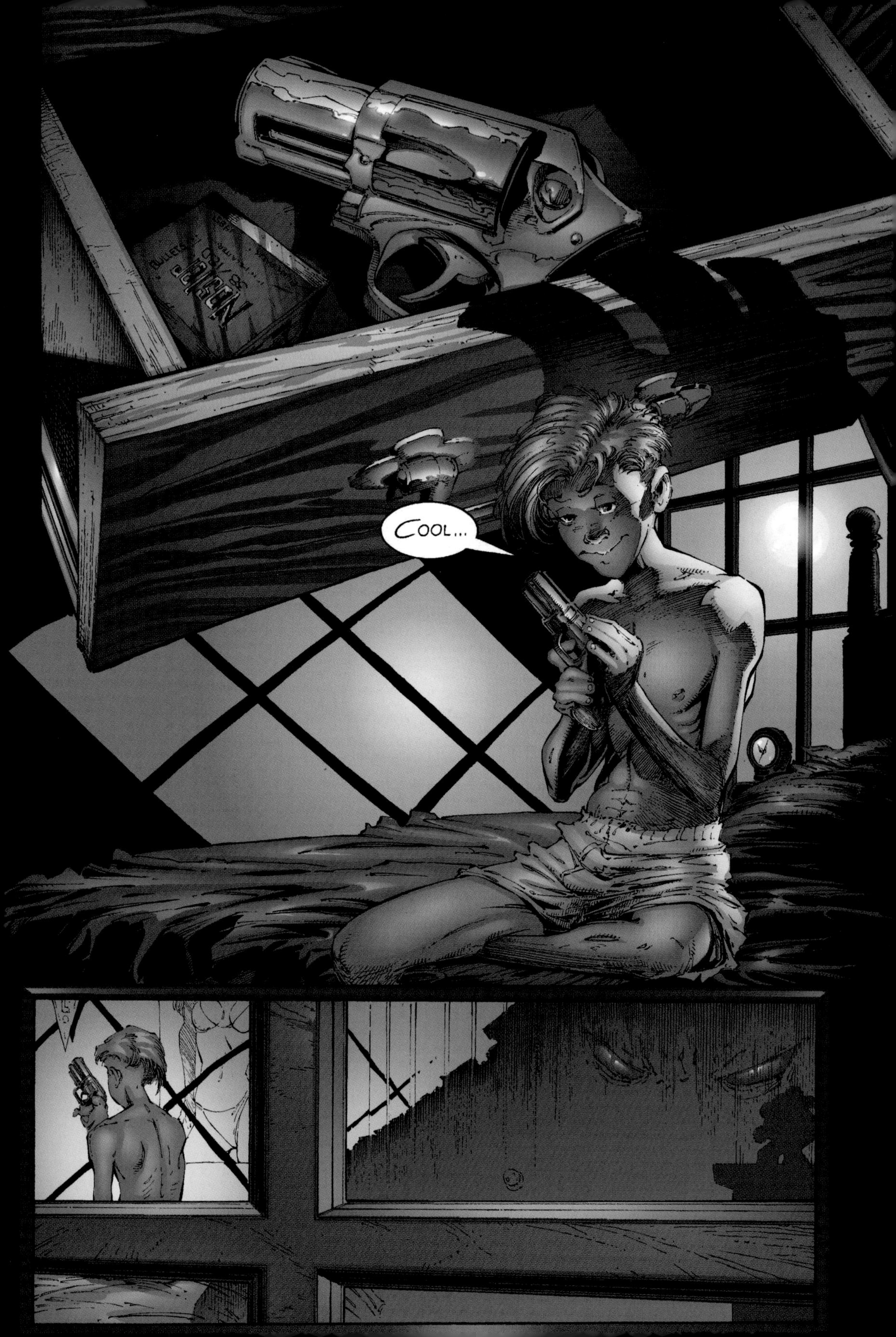
COOL...

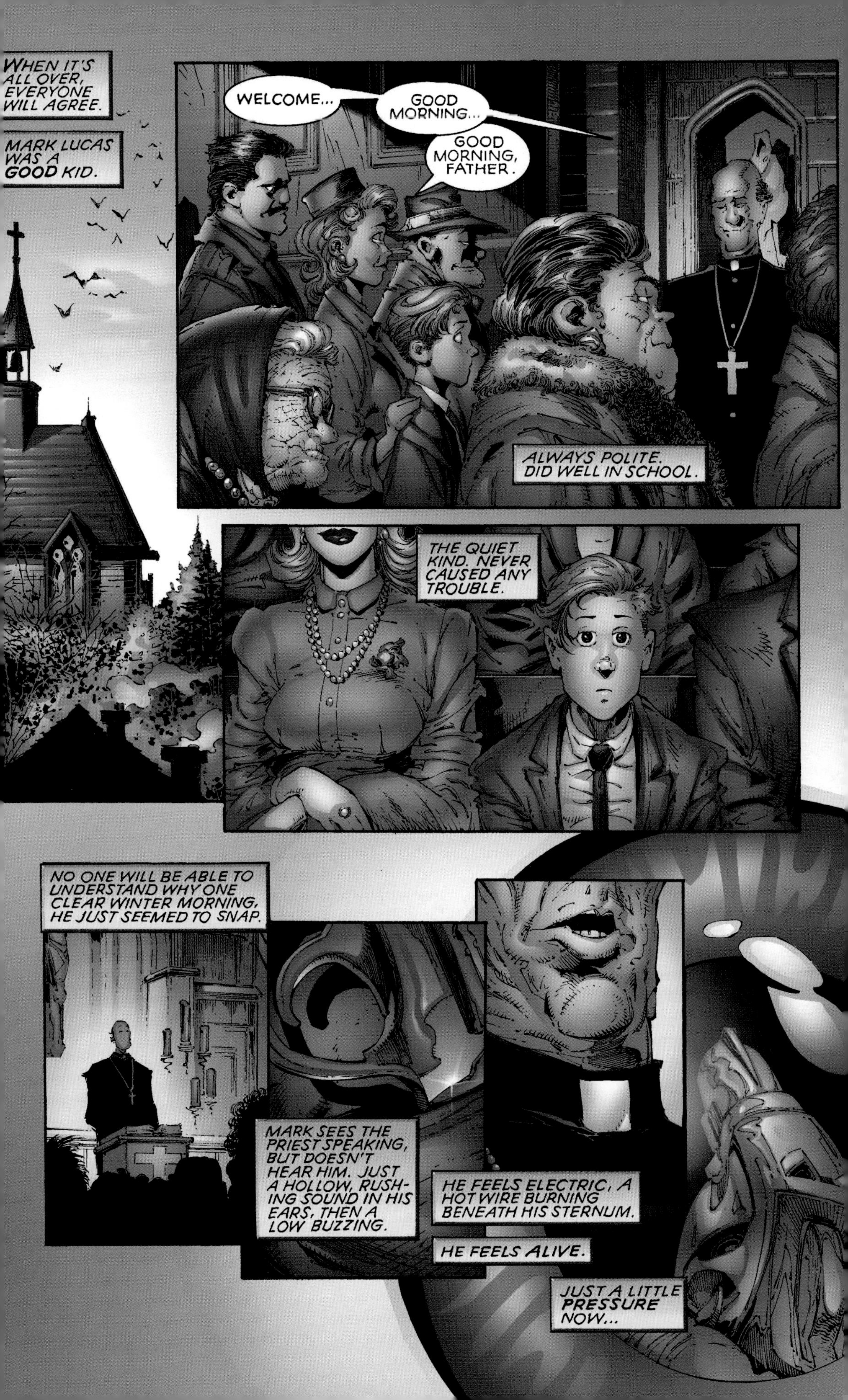
WHEN IT'S ALL OVER, EVERYONE WILL AGREE.
MARK LUCAS WAS A GOOD KID.
WELCOME...
GOOD MORNING...
GOOD MORNING, FATHER.
ALWAYS POLITE. DID WELL IN SCHOOL.
THE QUIET KIND. NEVER CAUSED ANY TROUBLE.
NO ONE WILL BE ABLE TO UNDERSTAND WHY ONE CLEAR WINTER MORNING, HE JUST SEEMED TO SNAP.
MARK SEES THE PRIEST SPEAKING, BUT DOESN'T HEAR HIM. JUST A HOLLOW, RUSHING SOUND IN HIS EARS, THEN A LOW BUZZING.
HE FEELS ELECTRIC, A HOT WIRE BURNING BENEATH HIS STERNUM.
HE FEELS ALIVE.
JUST A LITTLE PRESSURE NOW...

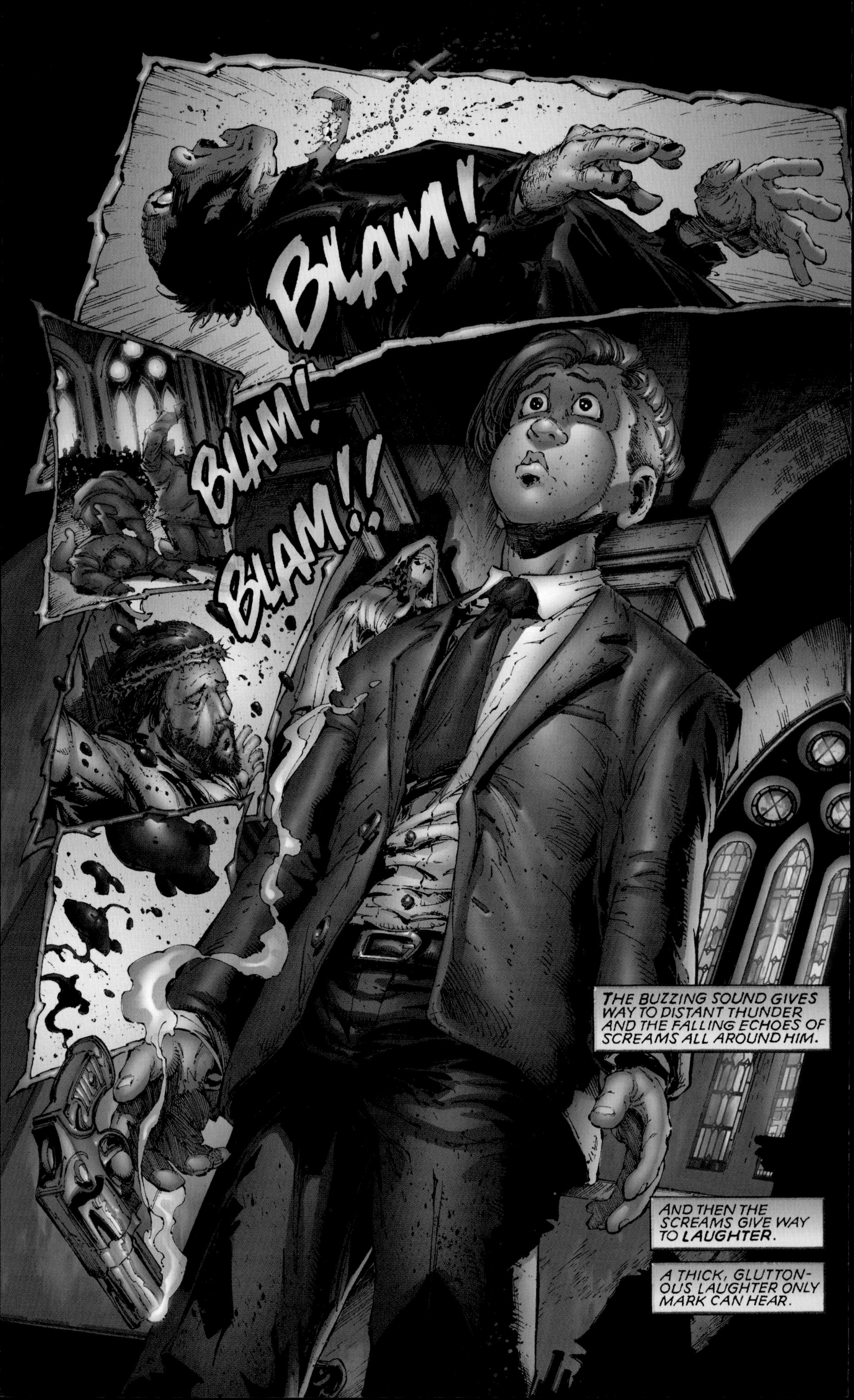
BLAM!
BLAM!
BLAM!!
THE BUZZING SOUND GIVES WAY TO DISTANT THUNDER AND THE FALLING ECHOES OF SCREAMS ALL AROUND HIM.
AND THEN THE SCREAMS GIVE WAY TO LAUGHTER.
A THICK, GLUTTON-OUS LAUGHTER ONLY MARK CAN HEAR.

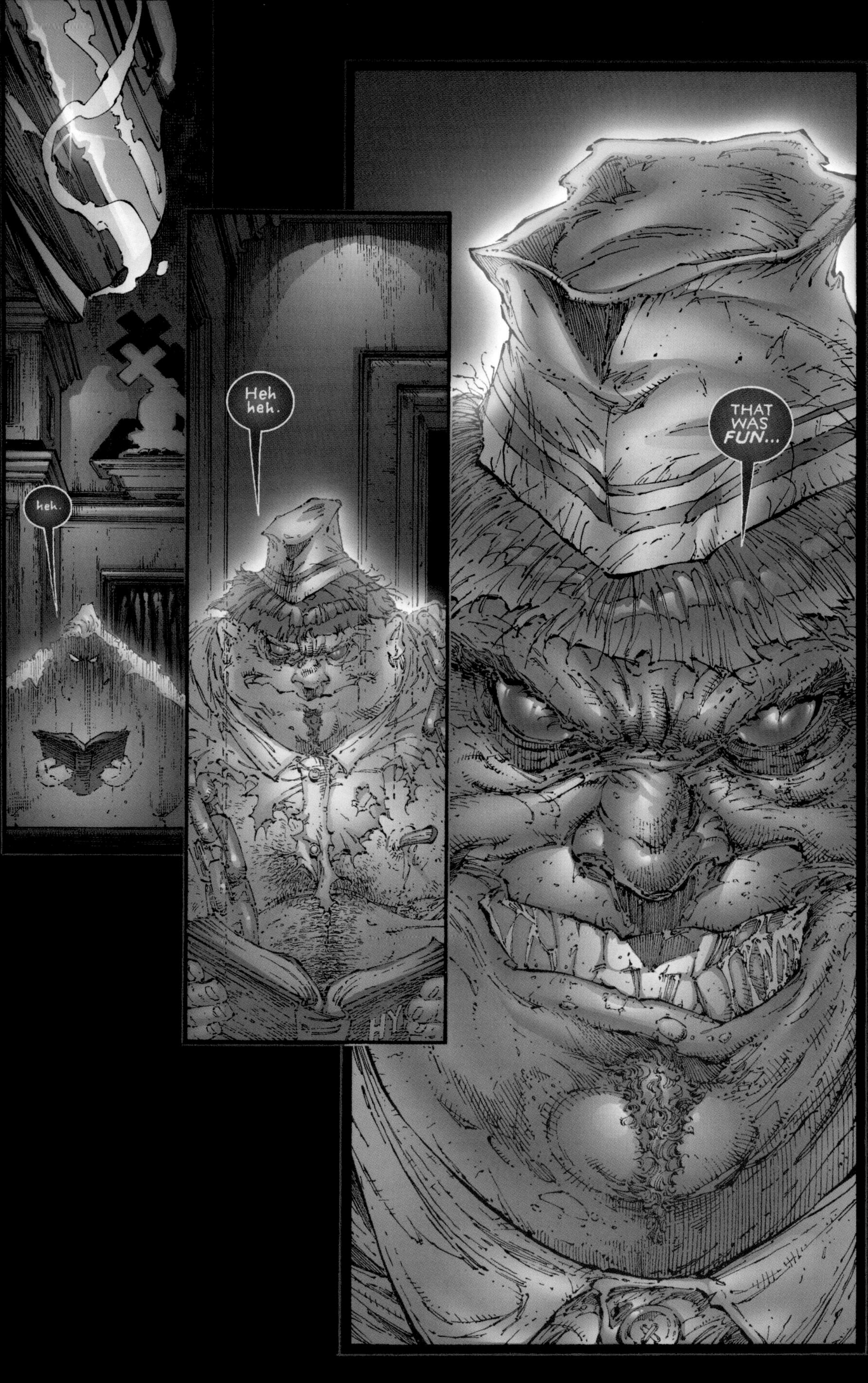
heh.
Heh heh.
THAT WAS FUN...

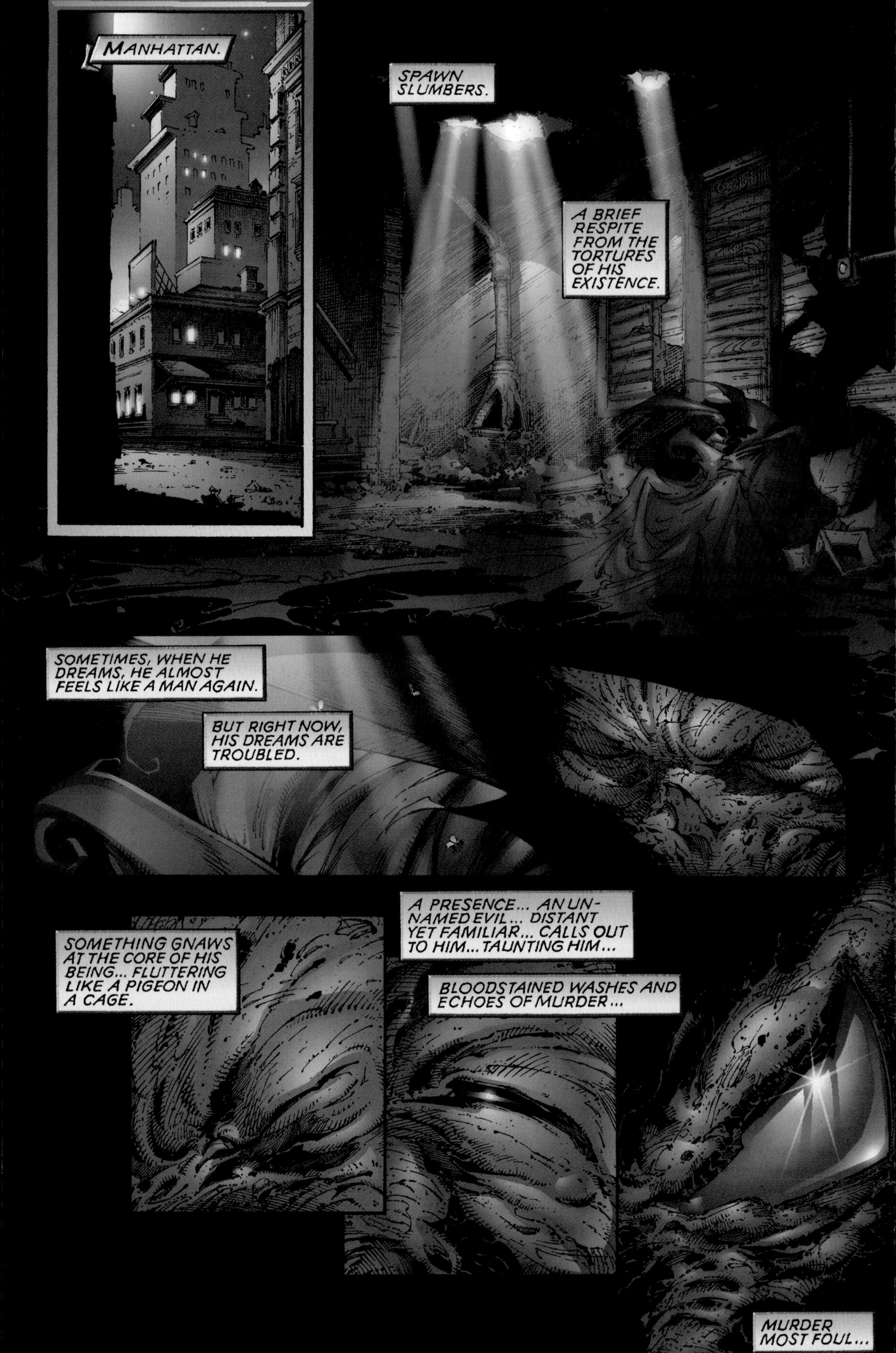
MANHATTAN.
SPAWN SLUMBERS.
A BRIEF RESPITE FROM THE TORTURES OF HIS EXISTENCE.
SOMETIMES, WHEN HE DREAMS, HE ALMOST FEELS LIKE A MAN AGAIN.
BUT RIGHT NOW, HIS DREAMS ARE TROUBLED.
SOMETHING GNAWS AT THE CORE OF HIS BEING... FLUTTERING LIKE A PIGEON IN A CAGE.
A PRESENCE... AN UN-NAMED EVIL... DISTANT YET FAMILIAR... CALLS OUT TO HIM... TAUNTING HIM...
BLOODSTAINED WASHES AND ECHOES OF MURDER...
MURDER MOST FOUL...

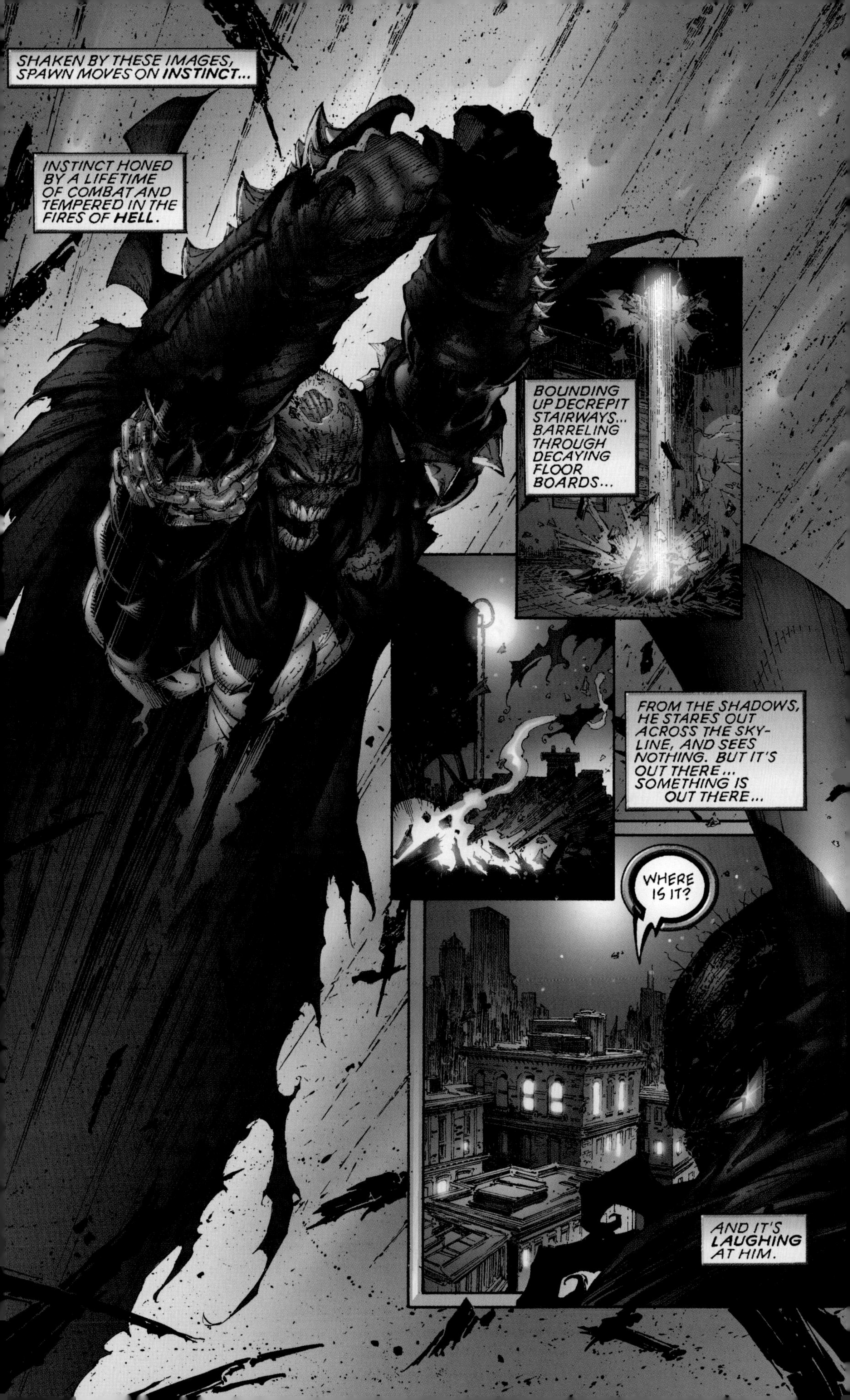
SHAKEN BY THESE IMAGES, SPAWN MOVES ON **INSTINCT**...
INSTINCT HONED BY A LIFETIME OF COMBAT AND TEMPERED IN THE FIRES OF **HELL**.
BOUNDING UP DECREPIT STAIRWAYS... BARRELING THROUGH DECAYING FLOOR BOARDS...
FROM THE SHADOWS, HE STARES OUT ACROSS THE SKY-LINE, AND SEES NOTHING. BUT IT'S OUT THERE... SOMETHING IS OUT THERE...
WHERE IS IT?
AND IT'S **LAUGHING** AT HIM.

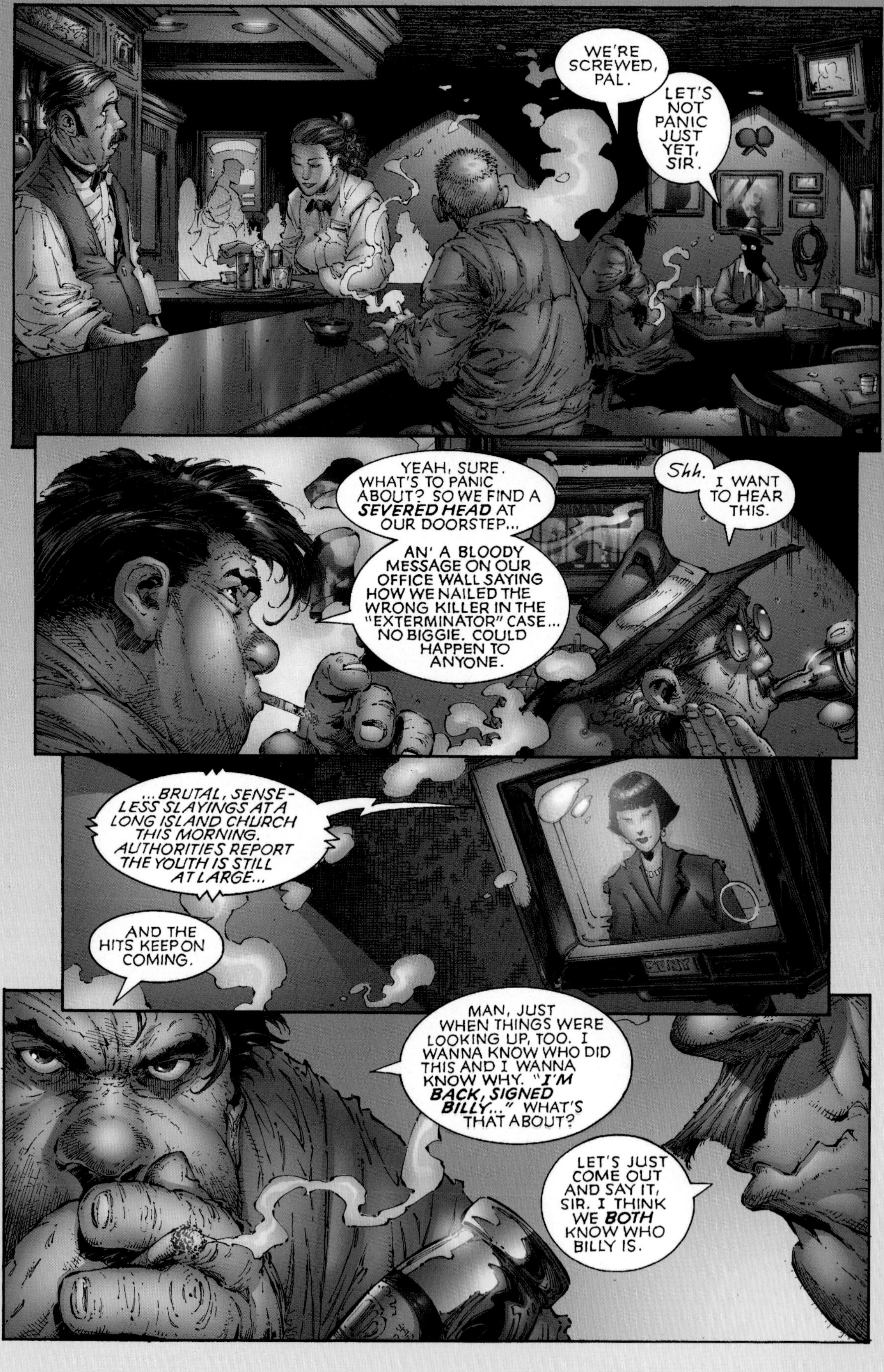

WE'RE SCREWED, PAL.
LET'S NOT PANIC JUST YET, SIR.
YEAH, SURE. WHAT'S TO PANIC ABOUT? SO WE FIND A **SEVERED HEAD** AT OUR DOORSTEP...
AN' A BLOODY MESSAGE ON OUR OFFICE WALL SAYING HOW WE NAILED THE WRONG KILLER IN THE "EXTERMINATOR" CASE... NO BIGGIE. COULD HAPPEN TO ANYONE.
Shh. I WANT TO HEAR THIS.
...BRUTAL, SENSE-LESS SLAYINGS AT A LONG ISLAND CHURCH THIS MORNING. AUTHORITIES REPORT THE YOUTH IS STILL AT LARGE...
AND THE HITS KEEP ON COMING.
MAN, JUST WHEN THINGS WERE LOOKING UP, TOO. I WANNA KNOW WHO DID THIS AND I WANNA KNOW WHY. "***I'M BACK, SIGNED BILLY...***" WHAT'S THAT ABOUT?
LET'S JUST COME OUT AND SAY IT, SIR. I THINK WE **BOTH** KNOW WHO BILLY IS.

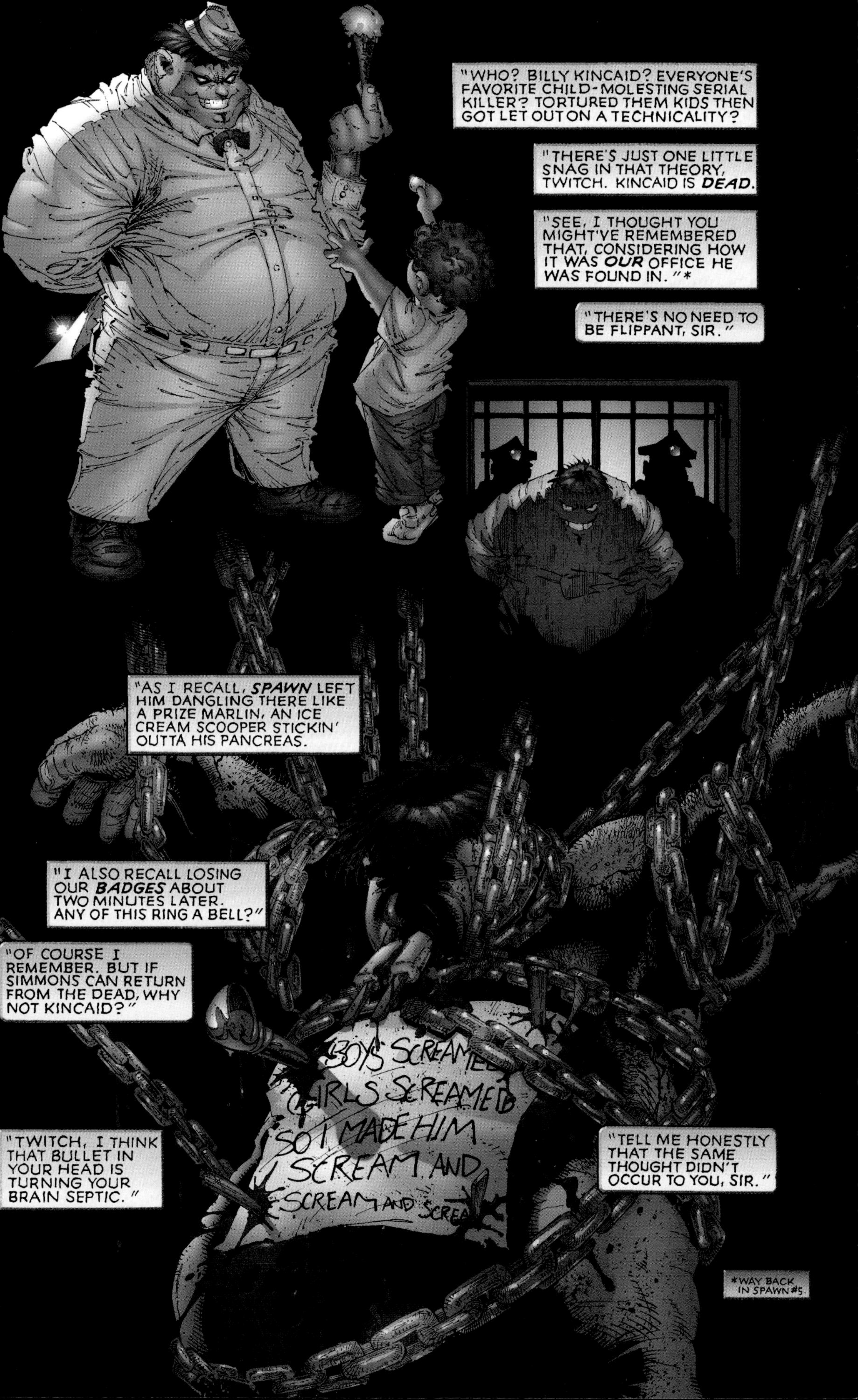
"WHO? BILLY KINCAID? EVERYONE'S FAVORITE CHILD-MOLESTING SERIAL KILLER? TORTURED THEM KIDS THEN GOT LET OUT ON A TECHNICALITY?
"THERE'S JUST ONE LITTLE SNAG IN THAT THEORY, TWITCH. KINCAID IS **DEAD**.
"SEE, I THOUGHT YOU MIGHT'VE REMEMBERED THAT, CONSIDERING HOW IT WAS **OUR** OFFICE HE WAS FOUND IN."*
"THERE'S NO NEED TO BE FLIPPANT, SIR."
"AS I RECALL, **SPAWN** LEFT HIM DANGLING THERE LIKE A PRIZE MARLIN, AN ICE CREAM SCOOPER STICKIN' OUTTA HIS PANCREAS.
"I ALSO RECALL LOSING OUR **BADGES** ABOUT TWO MINUTES LATER. ANY OF THIS RING A BELL?"
"OF COURSE I REMEMBER. BUT IF SIMMONS CAN RETURN FROM THE DEAD, WHY NOT KINCAID?"
BOYS SCREAMED
GIRLS SCREAMED
SO I MADE HIM
SCREAM AND
SCREAM AND SCREA
"TWITCH, I THINK THAT BULLET IN YOUR HEAD IS TURNING YOUR BRAIN SEPTIC."
"TELL ME HONESTLY THAT THE SAME THOUGHT DIDN'T OCCUR TO YOU, SIR."
*WAY BACK IN SPAWN #5.

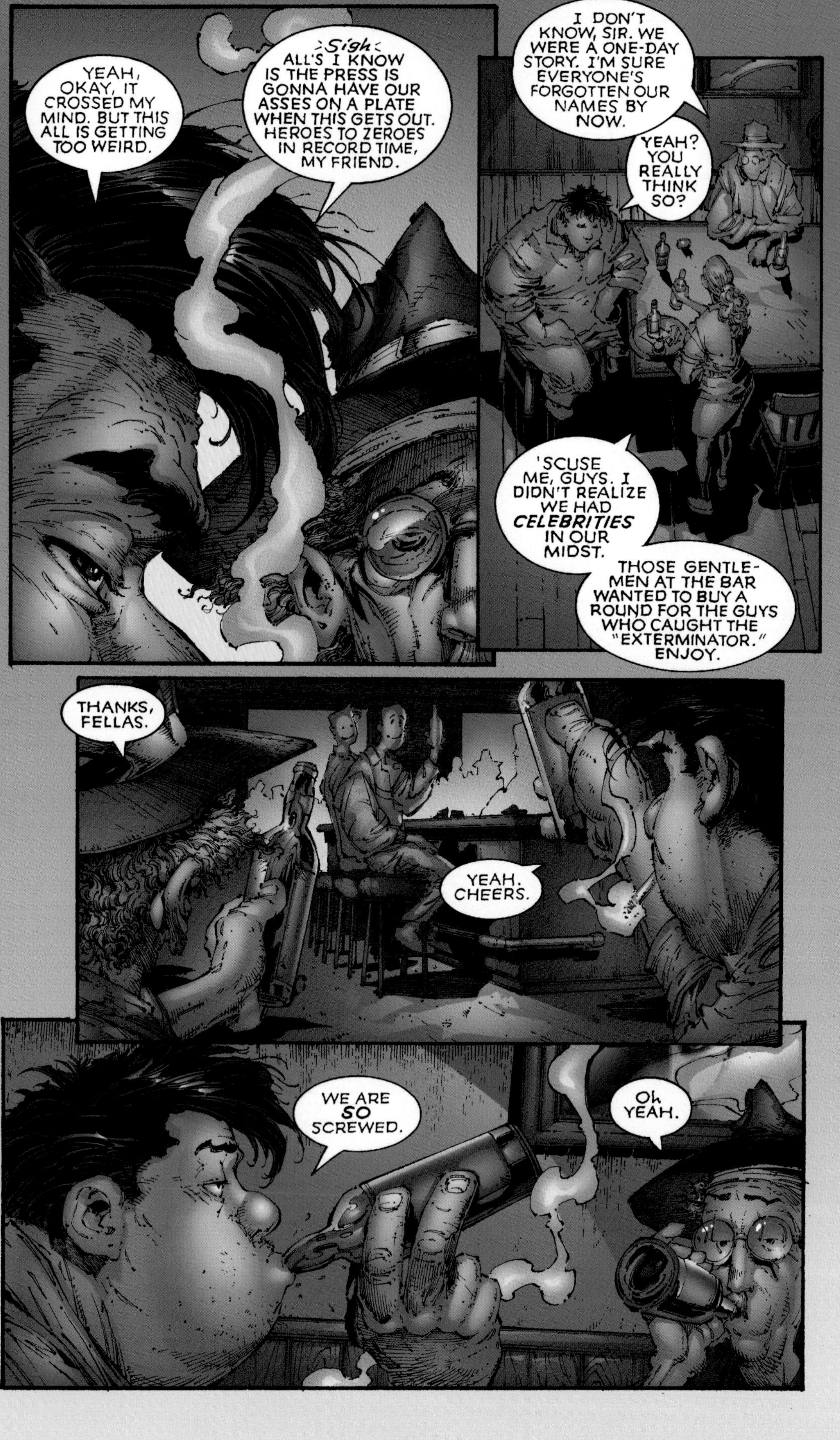
YEAH, OKAY, IT CROSSED MY MIND. BUT THIS ALL IS GETTING TOO WEIRD.
>Sigh< ALL'S I KNOW IS THE PRESS IS GONNA HAVE OUR ASSES ON A PLATE WHEN THIS GETS OUT. HEROES TO ZEROES IN RECORD TIME, MY FRIEND.
I DON'T KNOW, SIR. WE WERE A ONE-DAY STORY. I'M SURE EVERYONE'S FORGOTTEN OUR NAMES BY NOW.
YEAH? YOU REALLY THINK SO?
'SCUSE ME, GUYS. I DIDN'T REALIZE WE HAD CELEBRITIES IN OUR MIDST.
THOSE GENTLEMEN AT THE BAR WANTED TO BUY A ROUND FOR THE GUYS WHO CAUGHT THE "EXTERMINATOR." ENJOY.
THANKS, FELLAS.
YEAH. CHEERS.
WE ARE SO SCREWED.
Oh YEAH.

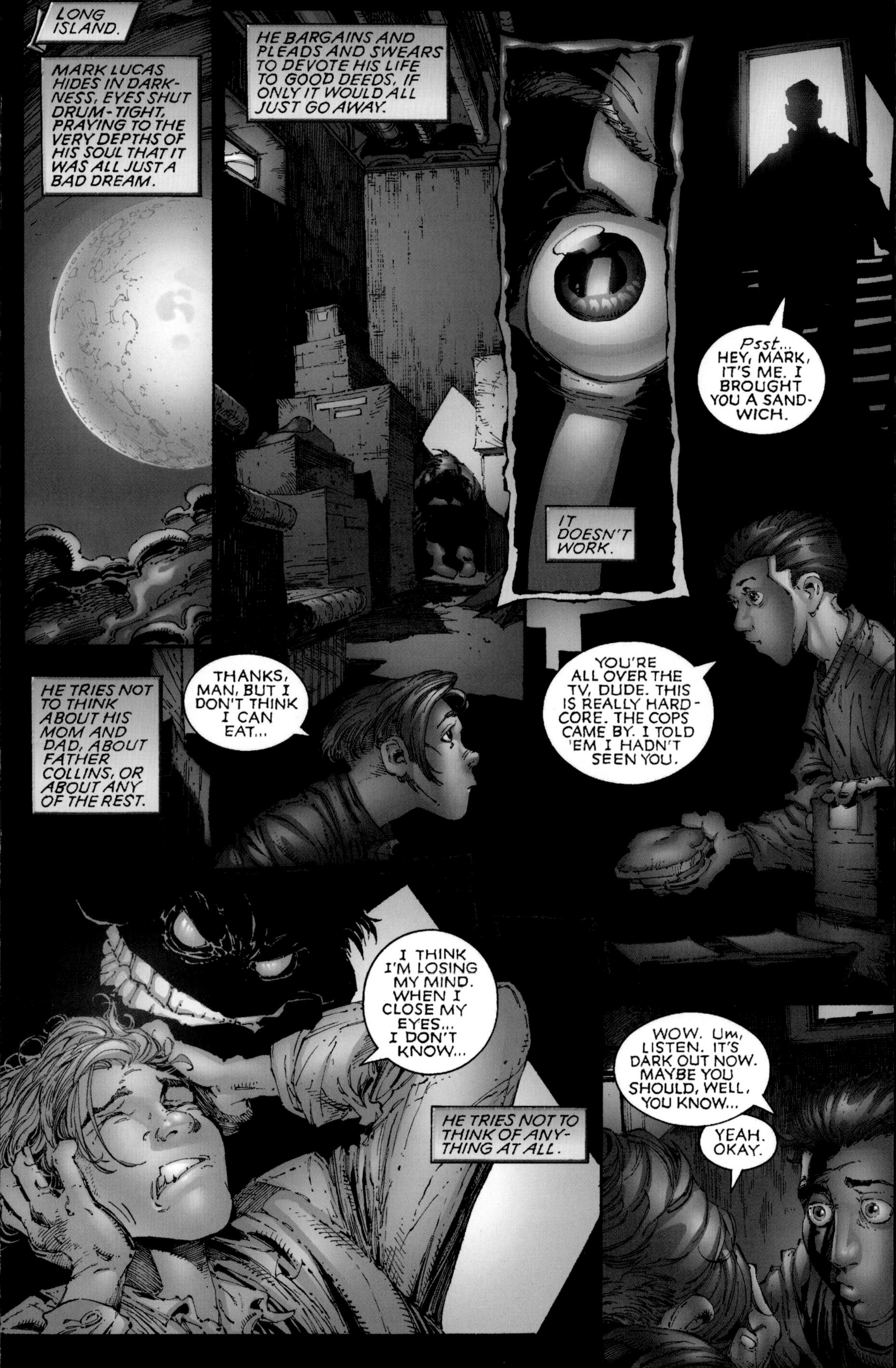
LONG ISLAND.
MARK LUCAS HIDES IN DARKNESS, EYES SHUT DRUM-TIGHT, PRAYING TO THE VERY DEPTHS OF HIS SOUL THAT IT WAS ALL JUST A BAD DREAM.
HE BARGAINS AND PLEADS AND SWEARS TO DEVOTE HIS LIFE TO GOOD DEEDS, IF ONLY IT WOULD ALL JUST GO AWAY.
IT DOESN'T WORK.
Psst... HEY, MARK, IT'S ME. I BROUGHT YOU A SANDWICH.
HE TRIES NOT TO THINK ABOUT HIS MOM AND DAD, ABOUT FATHER COLLINS, OR ABOUT ANY OF THE REST.
THANKS, MAN, BUT I DON'T THINK I CAN EAT...
YOU'RE ALL OVER THE TV, DUDE. THIS IS REALLY HARDCORE. THE COPS CAME BY. I TOLD 'EM I HADN'T SEEN YOU.
I THINK I'M LOSING MY MIND. WHEN I CLOSE MY EYES... I DON'T KNOW...
HE TRIES NOT TO THINK OF ANYTHING AT ALL.
WOW. Um, LISTEN. IT'S DARK OUT NOW. MAYBE YOU SHOULD, WELL, YOU KNOW...
YEAH. OKAY.

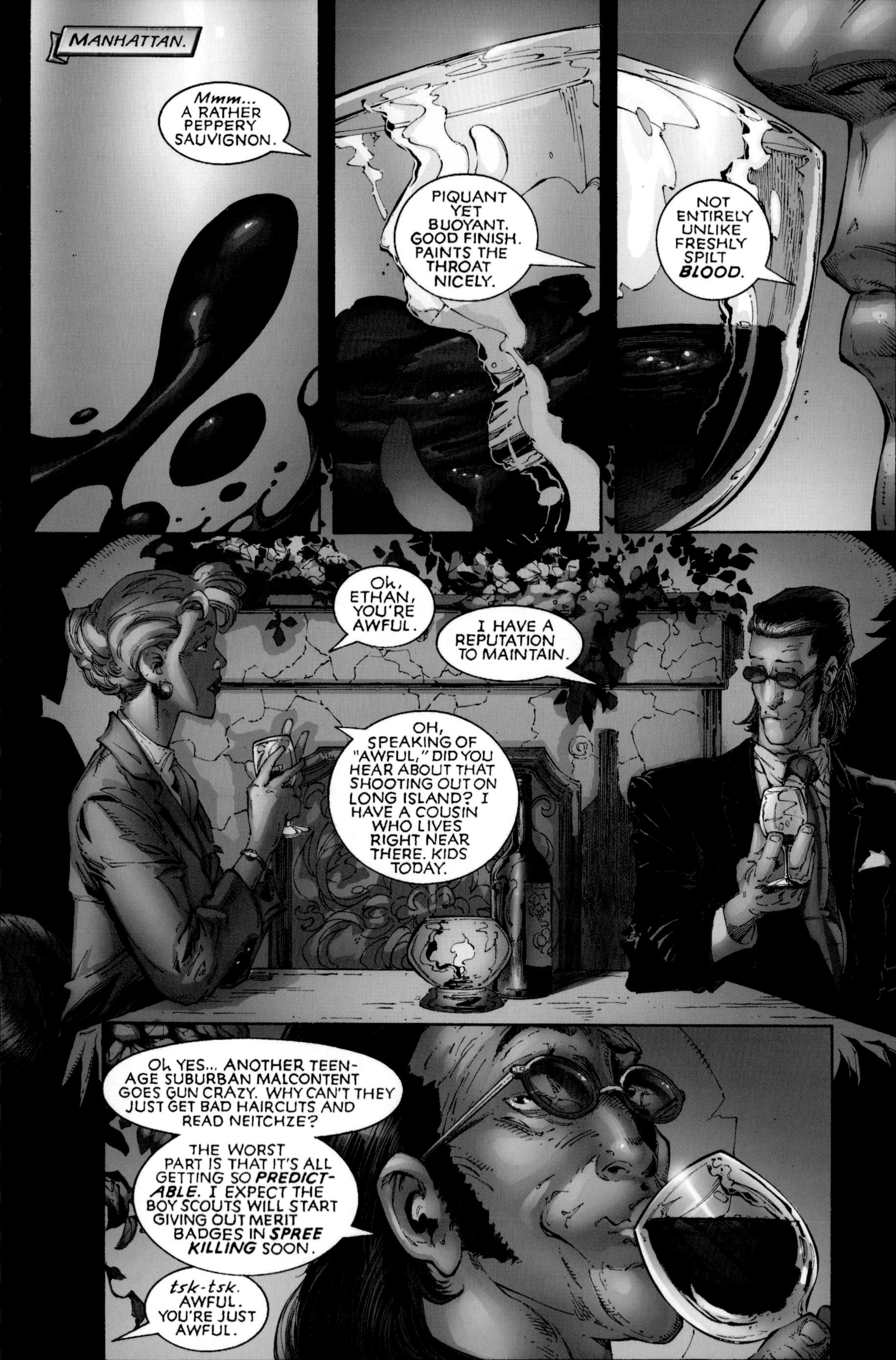
MANHATTAN.
Mmm... A RATHER PEPPERY SAUVIGNON.
PIQUANT YET BUOYANT. GOOD FINISH. PAINTS THE THROAT NICELY.
NOT ENTIRELY UNLIKE FRESHLY SPILT BLOOD.
Oh, ETHAN, YOU'RE AWFUL.
I HAVE A REPUTATION TO MAINTAIN.
OH, SPEAKING OF "AWFUL," DID YOU HEAR ABOUT THAT SHOOTING OUT ON LONG ISLAND? I HAVE A COUSIN WHO LIVES RIGHT NEAR THERE. KIDS TODAY.
Oh YES... ANOTHER TEEN-AGE SUBURBAN MALCONTENT GOES GUN CRAZY. WHY CAN'T THEY JUST GET BAD HAIRCUTS AND READ NEITCHZE?
THE WORST PART IS THAT IT'S ALL GETTING SO PREDICTABLE. I EXPECT THE BOY SCOUTS WILL START GIVING OUT MERIT BADGES IN SPREE KILLING SOON.
tsk-tsk. AWFUL. YOU'RE JUST AWFUL.

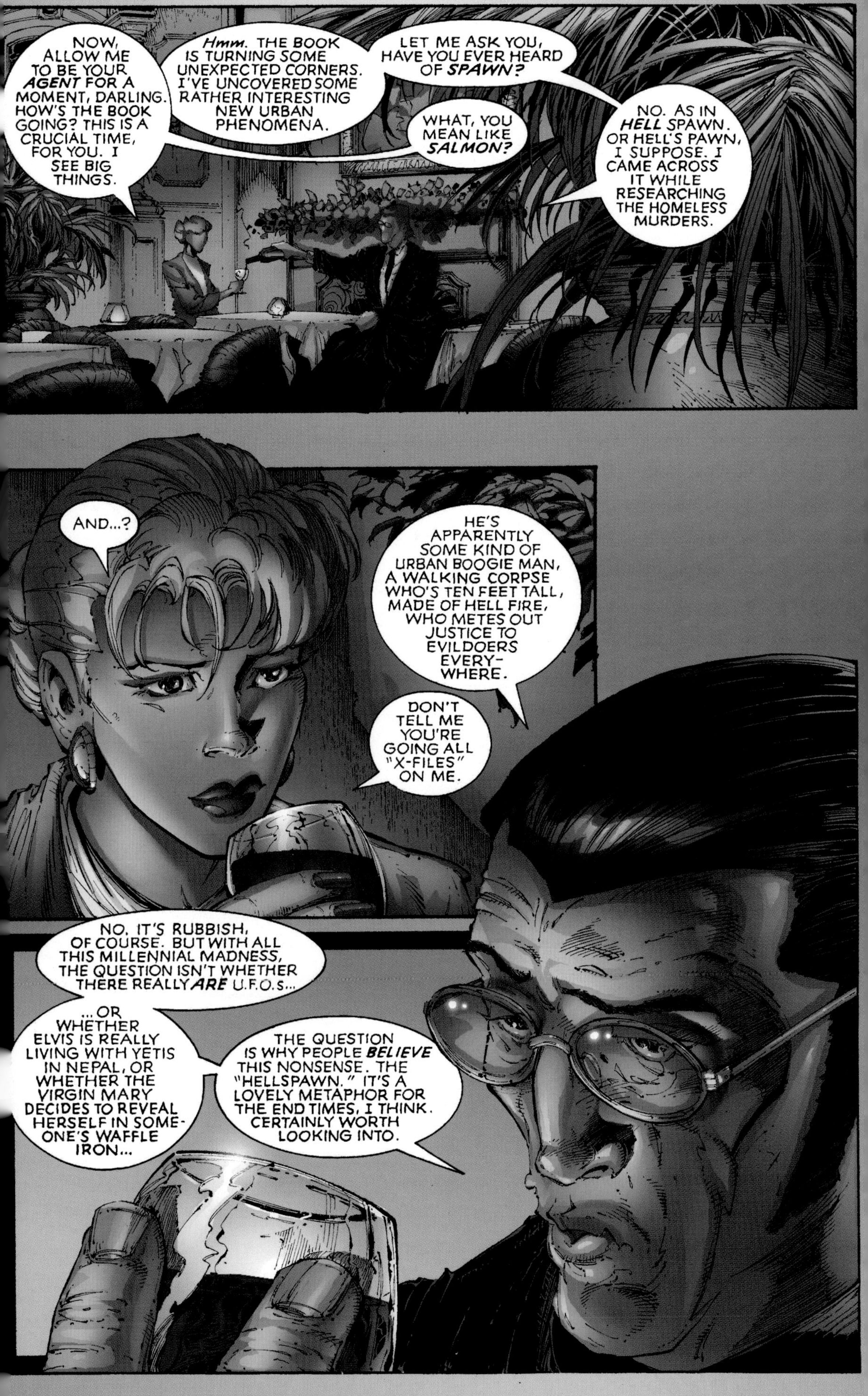
NOW, ALLOW ME TO BE YOUR *AGENT* FOR A MOMENT, DARLING. HOW'S THE BOOK GOING? THIS IS A CRUCIAL TIME, FOR YOU. I SEE BIG THINGS.
Hmm. THE BOOK IS TURNING SOME UNEXPECTED CORNERS. I'VE UNCOVERED SOME RATHER INTERESTING NEW URBAN PHENOMENA.
LET ME ASK YOU, HAVE YOU EVER HEARD OF *SPAWN?*
WHAT, YOU MEAN LIKE *SALMON?*
NO. AS IN *HELL* SPAWN. OR HELL'S PAWN, I SUPPOSE. I CAME ACROSS IT WHILE RESEARCHING THE HOMELESS MURDERS.
AND...?
HE'S APPARENTLY SOME KIND OF URBAN BOOGIE MAN, A WALKING CORPSE WHO'S TEN FEET TALL, MADE OF HELL FIRE, WHO METES OUT JUSTICE TO EVILDOERS EVERY-WHERE.
DON'T TELL ME YOU'RE GOING ALL "X-FILES" ON ME.
NO, IT'S RUBBISH, OF COURSE. BUT WITH ALL THIS MILLENNIAL MADNESS, THE QUESTION ISN'T WHETHER THERE REALLY *ARE* U.F.O.s...
...OR WHETHER ELVIS IS REALLY LIVING WITH YETIS IN NEPAL, OR WHETHER THE VIRGIN MARY DECIDES TO REVEAL HERSELF IN SOME-ONE'S WAFFLE IRON...
THE QUESTION IS WHY PEOPLE *BELIEVE* THIS NONSENSE. THE "HELLSPAWN." IT'S A LOVELY METAPHOR FOR THE END TIMES, I THINK. CERTAINLY WORTH LOOKING INTO.

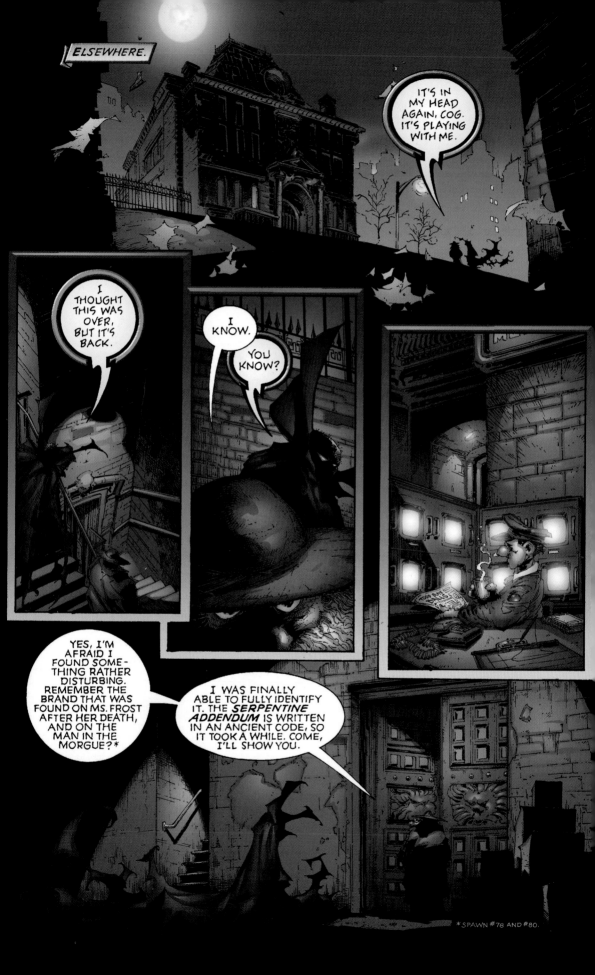

ELSEWHERE.

IT'S IN MY HEAD AGAIN, COG. IT'S PLAYING WITH ME.

I THOUGHT THIS WAS OVER, BUT IT'S BACK.

I KNOW.

YOU KNOW?

YES, I'M AFRAID I FOUND SOMETHING RATHER DISTURBING. REMEMBER THE BRAND THAT WAS FOUND ON MS. FROST AFTER HER DEATH, AND ON THE MAN IN THE MORGUE?*

I WAS FINALLY ABLE TO FULLY IDENTIFY IT. THE *SERPENTINE ADDENDUM* IS WRITTEN IN AN ANCIENT CODE, SO IT TOOK A WHILE. COME, I'LL SHOW YOU.

* SPAWN #78 AND #80.

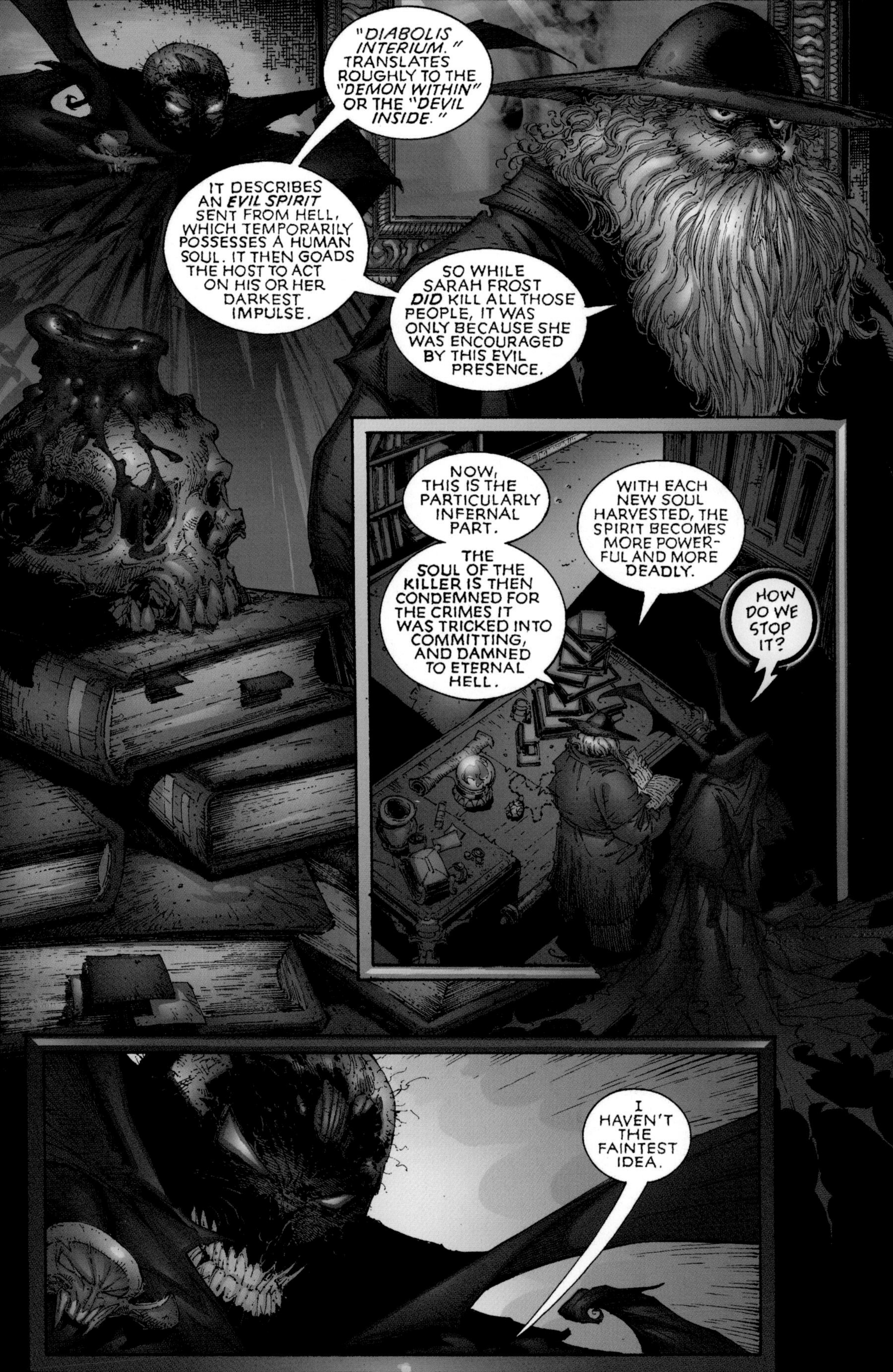
"DIABOLIS INTERIUM." TRANSLATES ROUGHLY TO THE "DEMON WITHIN" OR THE "DEVIL INSIDE."
IT DESCRIBES AN EVIL SPIRIT SENT FROM HELL, WHICH TEMPORARILY POSSESSES A HUMAN SOUL. IT THEN GOADS THE HOST TO ACT ON HIS OR HER DARKEST IMPULSE.
SO WHILE SARAH FROST DID KILL ALL THOSE PEOPLE, IT WAS ONLY BECAUSE SHE WAS ENCOURAGED BY THIS EVIL PRESENCE.
NOW, THIS IS THE PARTICULARLY INFERNAL PART.
THE SOUL OF THE KILLER IS THEN CONDEMNED FOR THE CRIMES IT WAS TRICKED INTO COMMITTING, AND DAMNED TO ETERNAL HELL.
WITH EACH NEW SOUL HARVESTED, THE SPIRIT BECOMES MORE POWER-FUL AND MORE DEADLY.
HOW DO WE STOP IT?
I HAVEN'T THE FAINTEST IDEA.

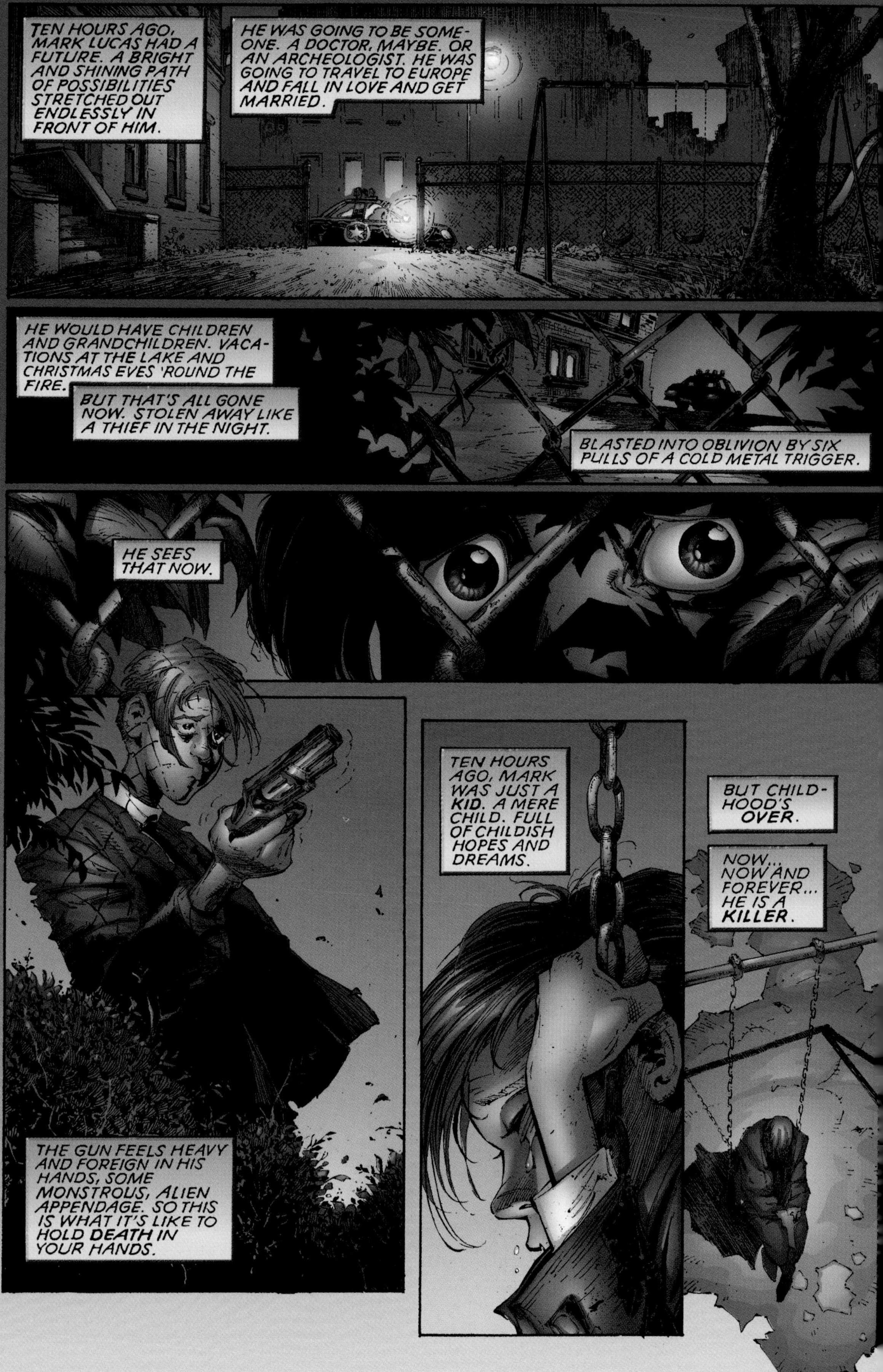

TEN HOURS AGO, MARK LUCAS HAD A FUTURE. A BRIGHT AND SHINING PATH OF POSSIBILITIES STRETCHED OUT ENDLESSLY IN FRONT OF HIM.
HE WAS GOING TO BE SOME-ONE. A DOCTOR, MAYBE. OR AN ARCHEOLOGIST. HE WAS GOING TO TRAVEL TO EUROPE AND FALL IN LOVE AND GET MARRIED.
HE WOULD HAVE CHILDREN AND GRANDCHILDREN. VACA-TIONS AT THE LAKE AND CHRISTMAS EVES 'ROUND THE FIRE.
BUT THAT'S ALL GONE NOW. STOLEN AWAY LIKE A THIEF IN THE NIGHT.
BLASTED INTO OBLIVION BY SIX PULLS OF A COLD METAL TRIGGER.
HE SEES THAT NOW.
THE GUN FEELS HEAVY AND FOREIGN IN HIS HANDS, SOME MONSTROUS, ALIEN APPENDAGE. SO THIS IS WHAT IT'S LIKE TO HOLD DEATH IN YOUR HANDS.
TEN HOURS AGO, MARK WAS JUST A KID. A MERE CHILD. FULL OF CHILDISH HOPES AND DREAMS.
BUT CHILD-HOOD'S OVER.
NOW... NOW AND FOREVER... HE IS A KILLER.

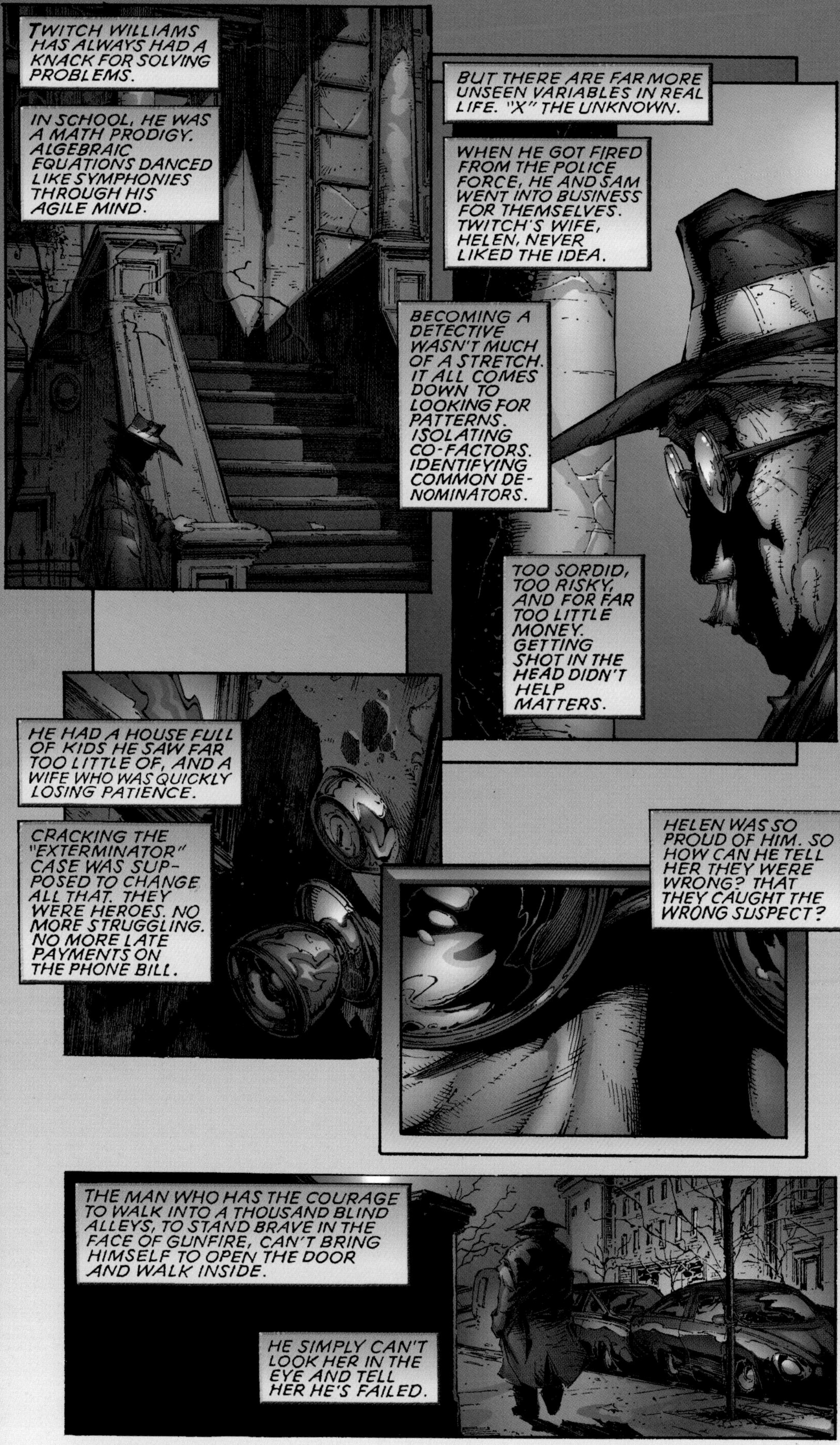
TWITCH WILLIAMS HAS ALWAYS HAD A KNACK FOR SOLVING PROBLEMS.
IN SCHOOL, HE WAS A MATH PRODIGY. ALGEBRAIC EQUATIONS DANCED LIKE SYMPHONIES THROUGH HIS AGILE MIND.
BUT THERE ARE FAR MORE UNSEEN VARIABLES IN REAL LIFE. "X" THE UNKNOWN.
WHEN HE GOT FIRED FROM THE POLICE FORCE, HE AND SAM WENT INTO BUSINESS FOR THEMSELVES. TWITCH'S WIFE, HELEN, NEVER LIKED THE IDEA.
BECOMING A DETECTIVE WASN'T MUCH OF A STRETCH. IT ALL COMES DOWN TO LOOKING FOR PATTERNS. ISOLATING CO-FACTORS. IDENTIFYING COMMON DE-NOMINATORS.
TOO SORDID, TOO RISKY, AND FOR FAR TOO LITTLE MONEY. GETTING SHOT IN THE HEAD DIDN'T HELP MATTERS.
HE HAD A HOUSE FULL OF KIDS HE SAW FAR TOO LITTLE OF, AND A WIFE WHO WAS QUICKLY LOSING PATIENCE.
CRACKING THE "EXTERMINATOR" CASE WAS SUP-POSED TO CHANGE ALL THAT. THEY WERE HEROES. NO MORE STRUGGLING. NO MORE LATE PAYMENTS ON THE PHONE BILL.
HELEN WAS SO PROUD OF HIM. SO HOW CAN HE TELL HER THEY WERE WRONG? THAT THEY CAUGHT THE WRONG SUSPECT?
THE MAN WHO HAS THE COURAGE TO WALK INTO A THOUSAND BLIND ALLEYS, TO STAND BRAVE IN THE FACE OF GUNFIRE, CAN'T BRING HIMSELF TO OPEN THE DOOR AND WALK INSIDE.
HE SIMPLY CAN'T LOOK HER IN THE EYE AND TELL HER HE'S FAILED.

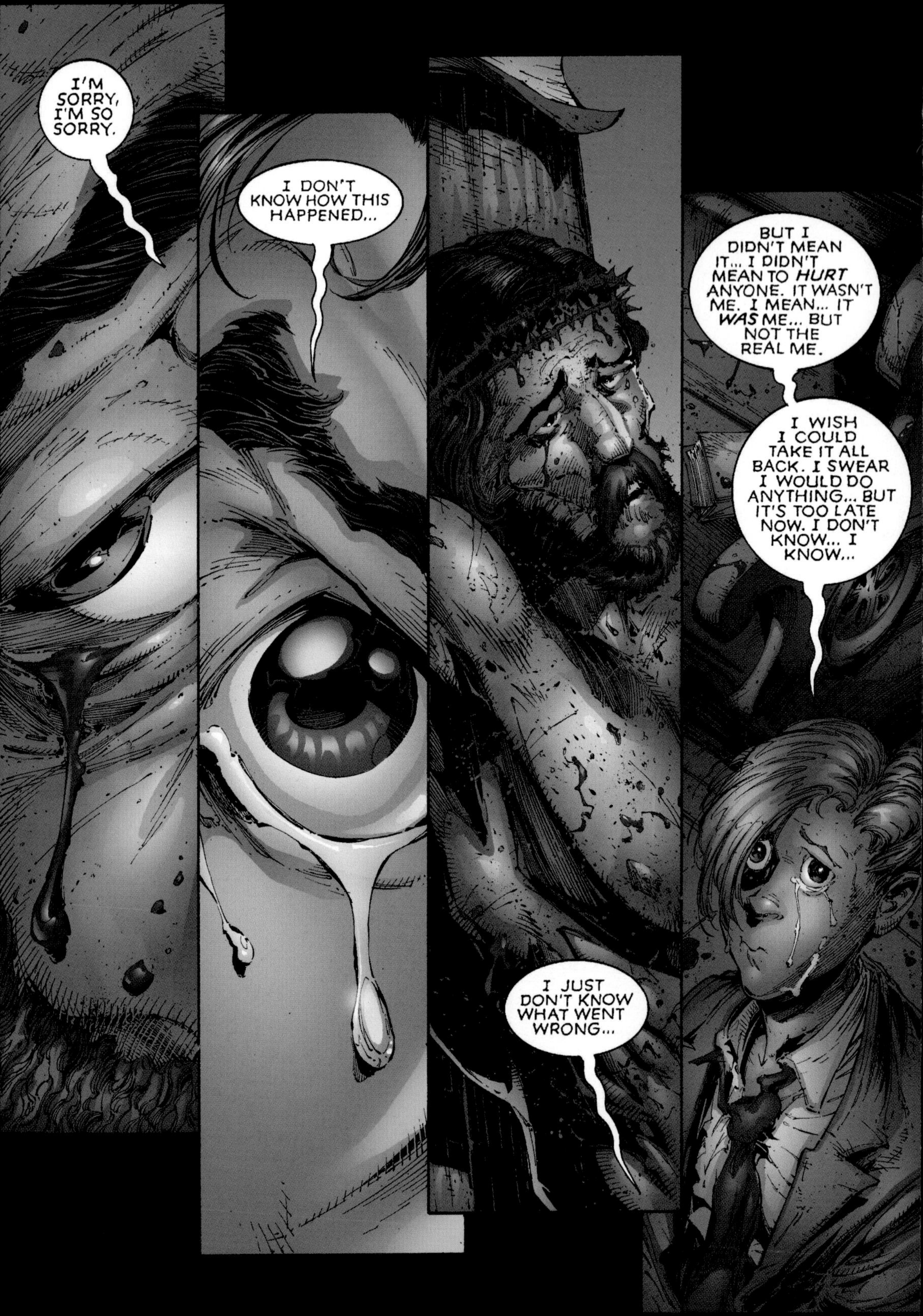
I'M SORRY, I'M SO SORRY.
I DON'T KNOW HOW THIS HAPPENED...
BUT I DIDN'T MEAN IT... I DIDN'T MEAN TO *HURT* ANYONE. IT WASN'T ME. I MEAN... IT *WAS* ME... BUT NOT THE REAL ME.
I WISH I COULD TAKE IT ALL BACK. I SWEAR I WOULD DO ANYTHING... BUT IT'S TOO LATE NOW. I DON'T KNOW... I KNOW...
I JUST DON'T KNOW WHAT WENT WRONG...

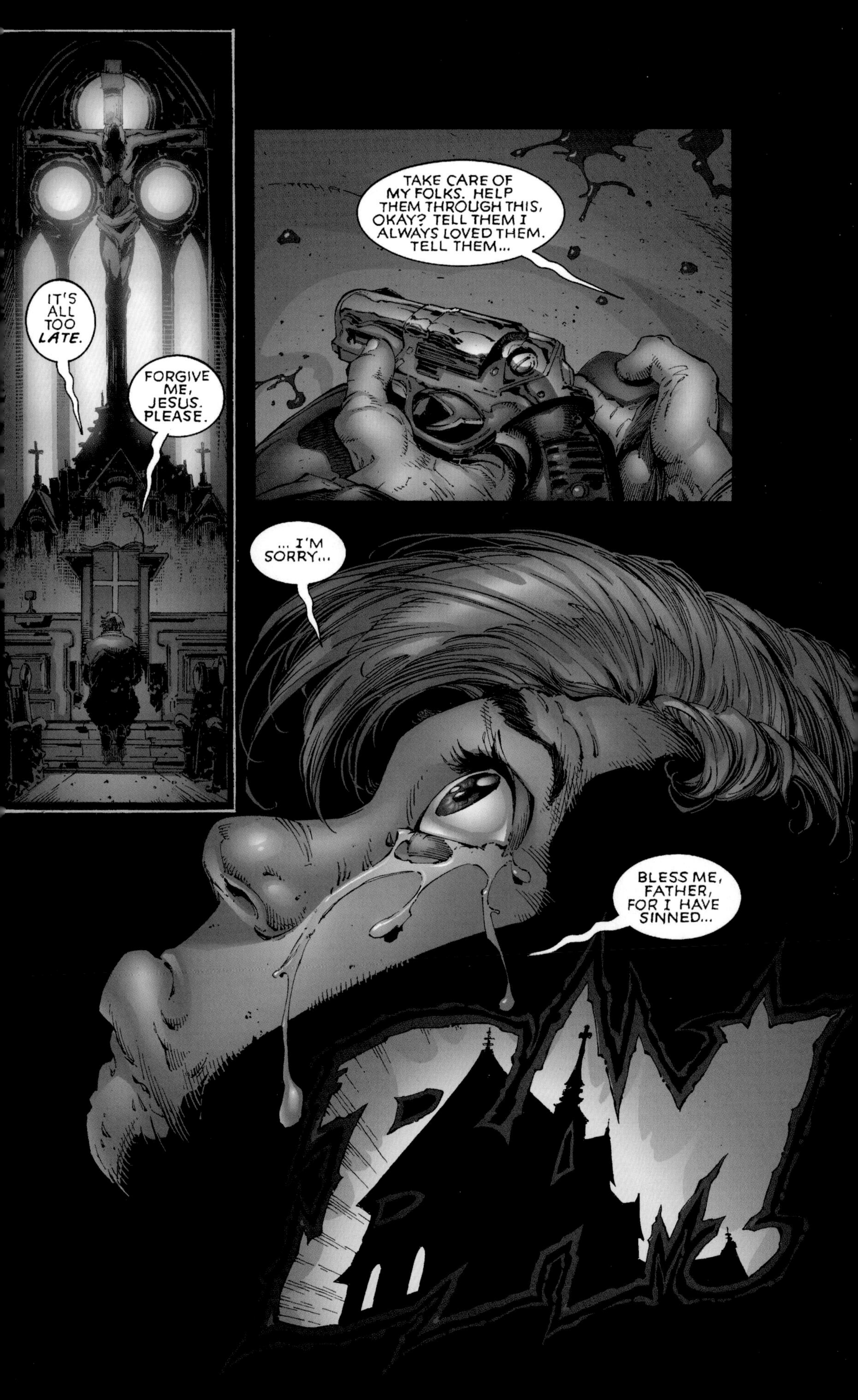
IT'S ALL TOO LATE.
FORGIVE ME, JESUS. PLEASE.
TAKE CARE OF MY FOLKS. HELP THEM THROUGH THIS, OKAY? TELL THEM I ALWAYS LOVED THEM. TELL THEM...
... I'M SORRY...
BLESS ME, FATHER, FOR I HAVE SINNED...

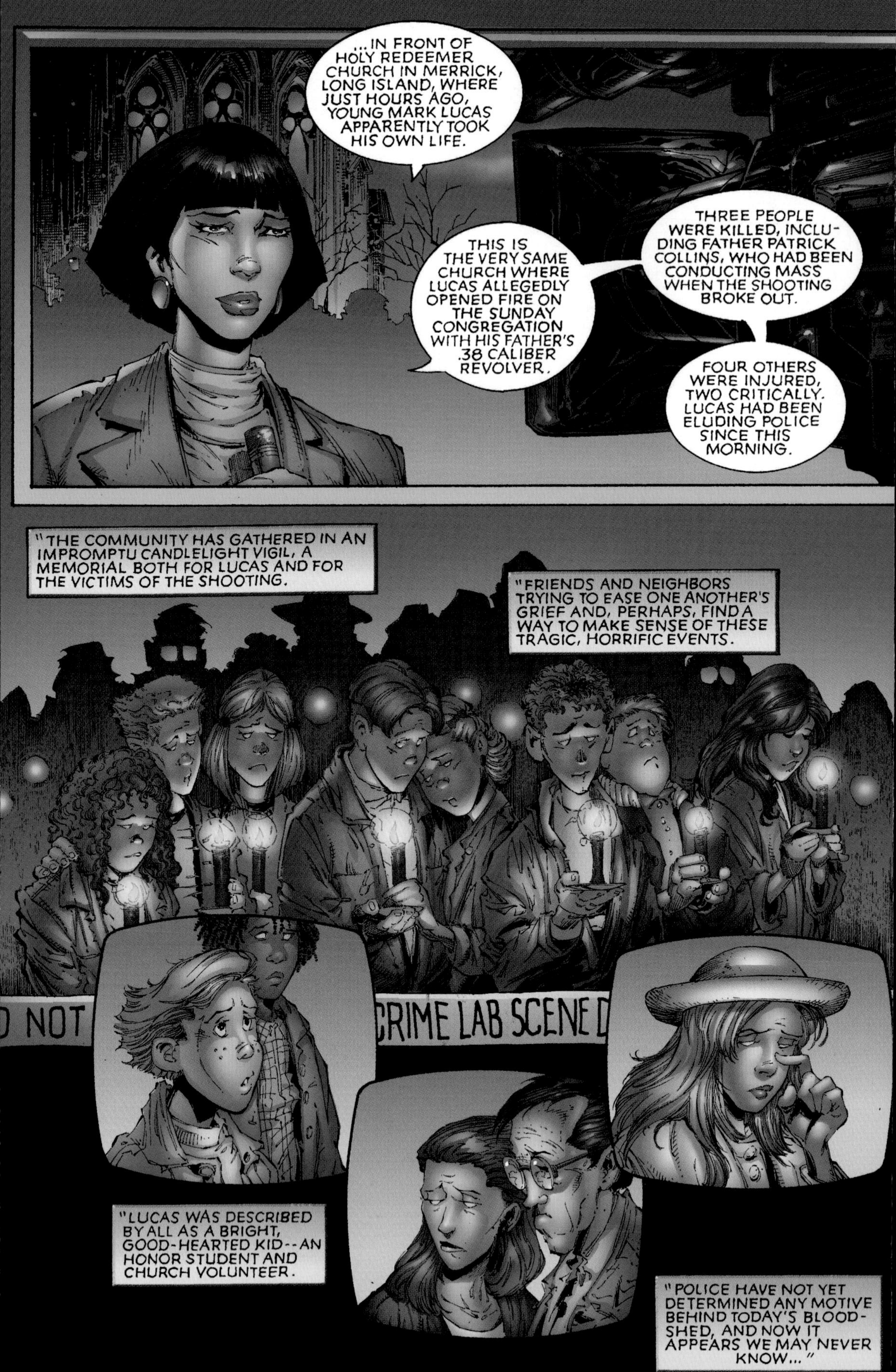
...IN FRONT OF HOLY REDEEMER CHURCH IN MERRICK, LONG ISLAND, WHERE JUST HOURS AGO, YOUNG MARK LUCAS APPARENTLY TOOK HIS OWN LIFE.
THIS IS THE VERY SAME CHURCH WHERE LUCAS ALLEGEDLY OPENED FIRE ON THE SUNDAY CONGREGATION WITH HIS FATHER'S .38 CALIBER REVOLVER.
THREE PEOPLE WERE KILLED, INCLUDING FATHER PATRICK COLLINS, WHO HAD BEEN CONDUCTING MASS WHEN THE SHOOTING BROKE OUT.
FOUR OTHERS WERE INJURED, TWO CRITICALLY. LUCAS HAD BEEN ELUDING POLICE SINCE THIS MORNING.
"THE COMMUNITY HAS GATHERED IN AN IMPROMPTU CANDLELIGHT VIGIL, A MEMORIAL BOTH FOR LUCAS AND FOR THE VICTIMS OF THE SHOOTING.
"FRIENDS AND NEIGHBORS TRYING TO EASE ONE ANOTHER'S GRIEF AND, PERHAPS, FIND A WAY TO MAKE SENSE OF THESE TRAGIC, HORRIFIC EVENTS.
D NOT
CRIME LAB SCENE D
"LUCAS WAS DESCRIBED BY ALL AS A BRIGHT, GOOD-HEARTED KID--AN HONOR STUDENT AND CHURCH VOLUNTEER.
"POLICE HAVE NOT YET DETERMINED ANY MOTIVE BEHIND TODAY'S BLOODSHED, AND NOW IT APPEARS WE MAY NEVER KNOW..."

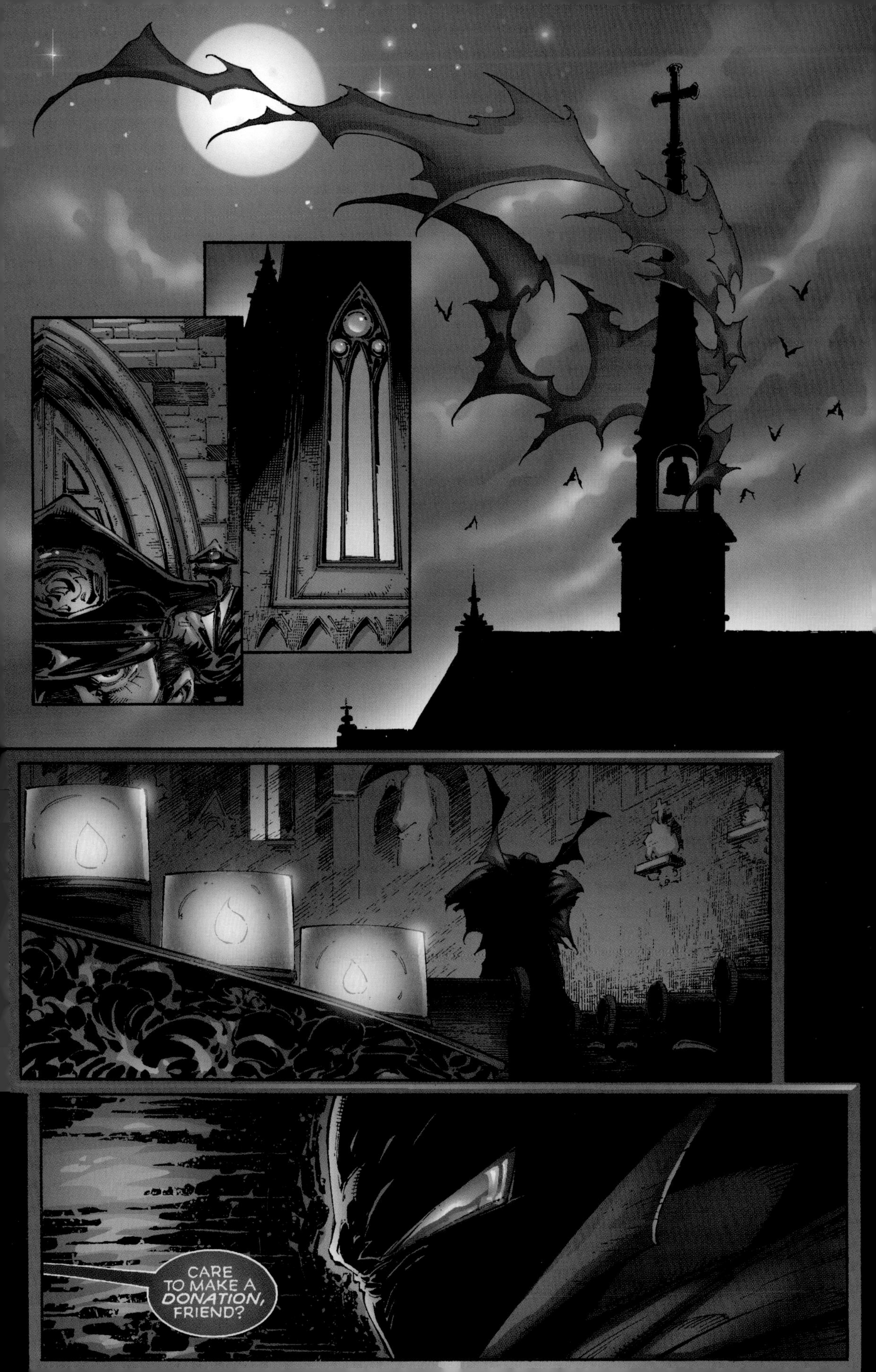
CARE TO MAKE A DONATION, FRIEND?

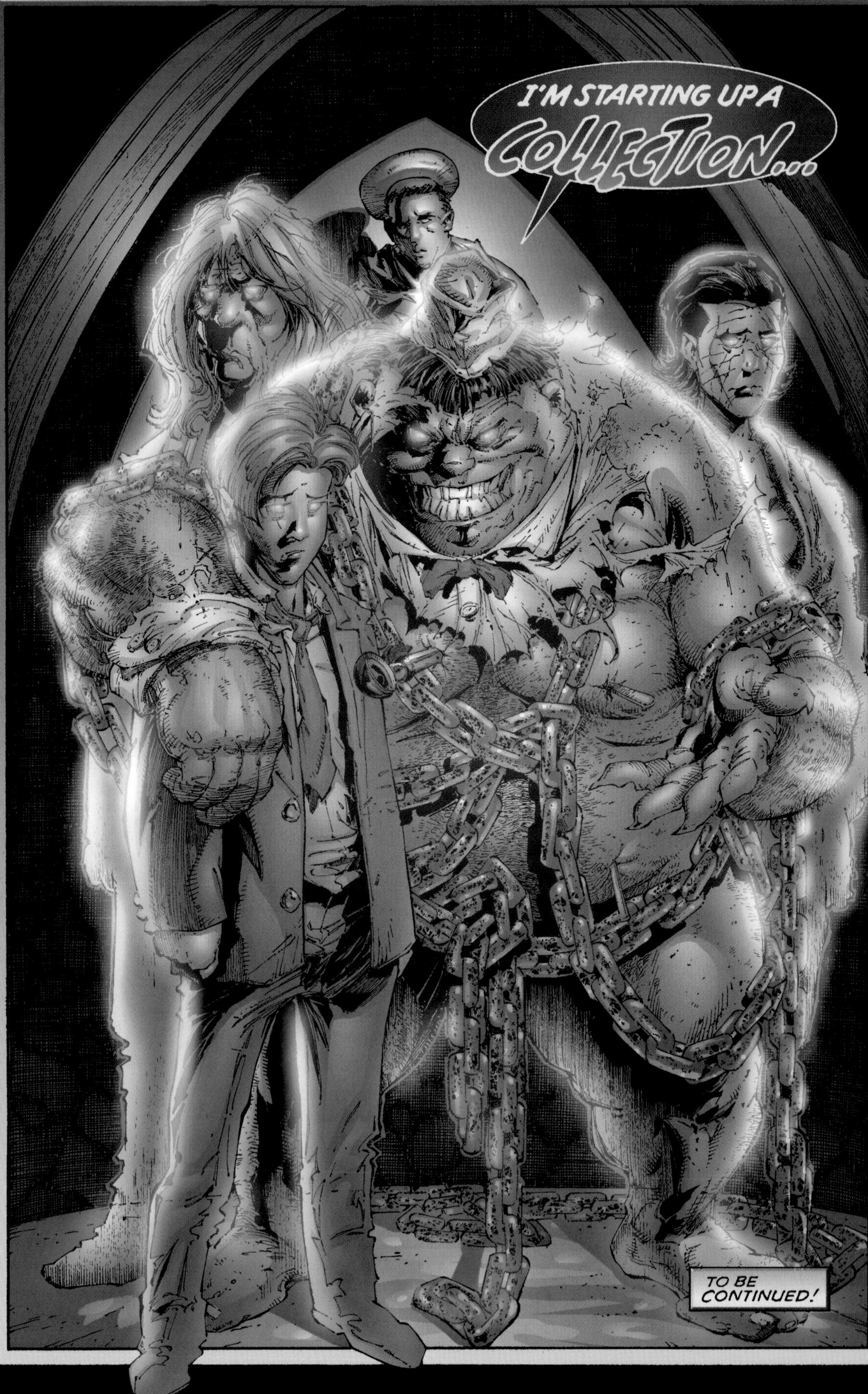
I'M STARTING UP A COLLECTION...
TO BE CONTINUED!

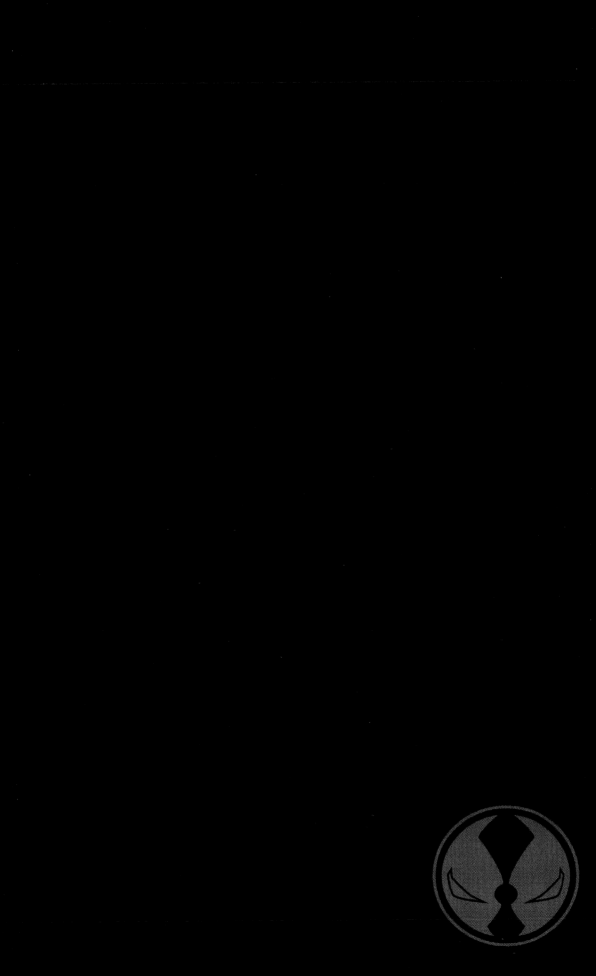

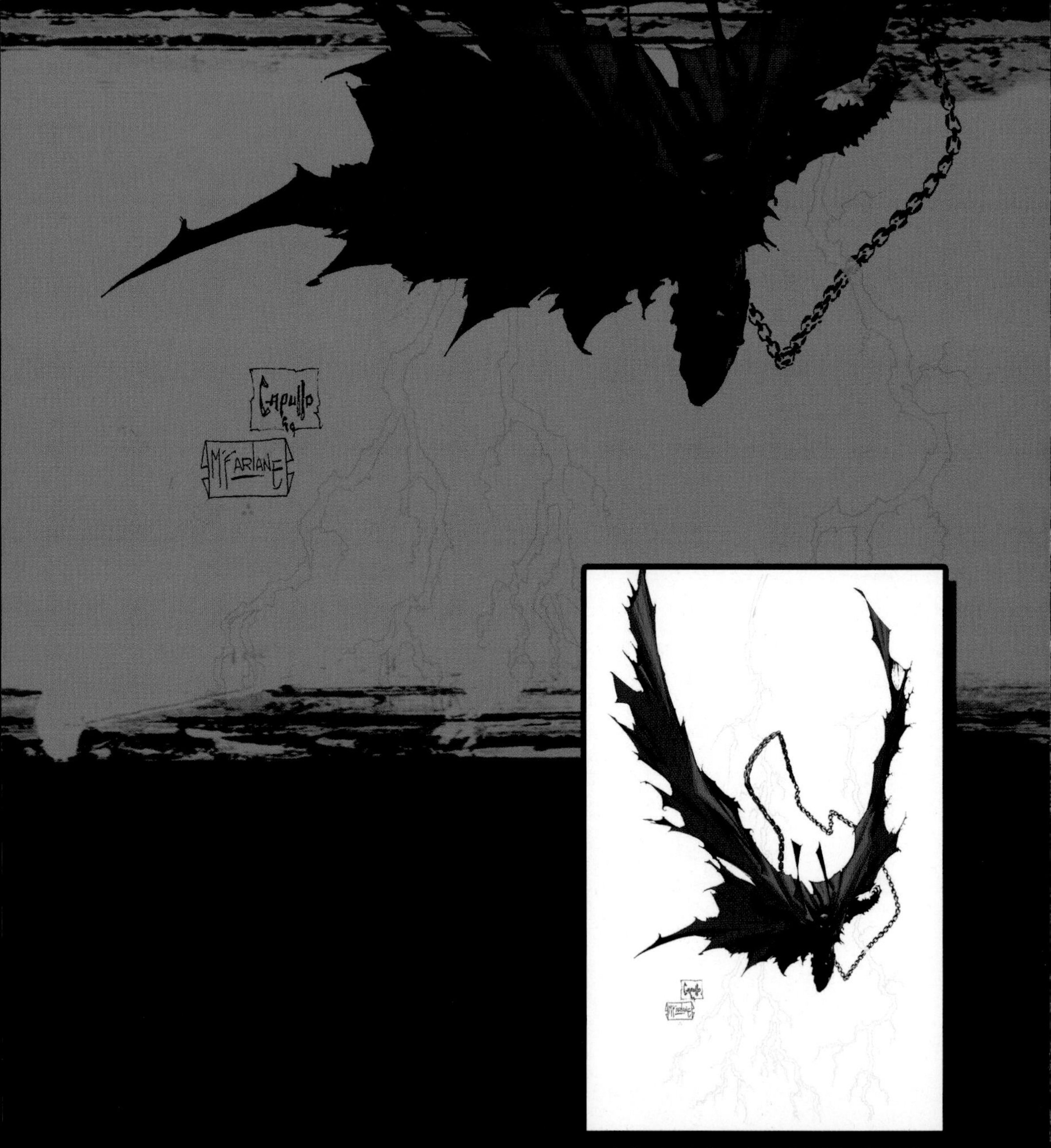
Capullo
McFarlane

ISSUE EIGHTY-TWO

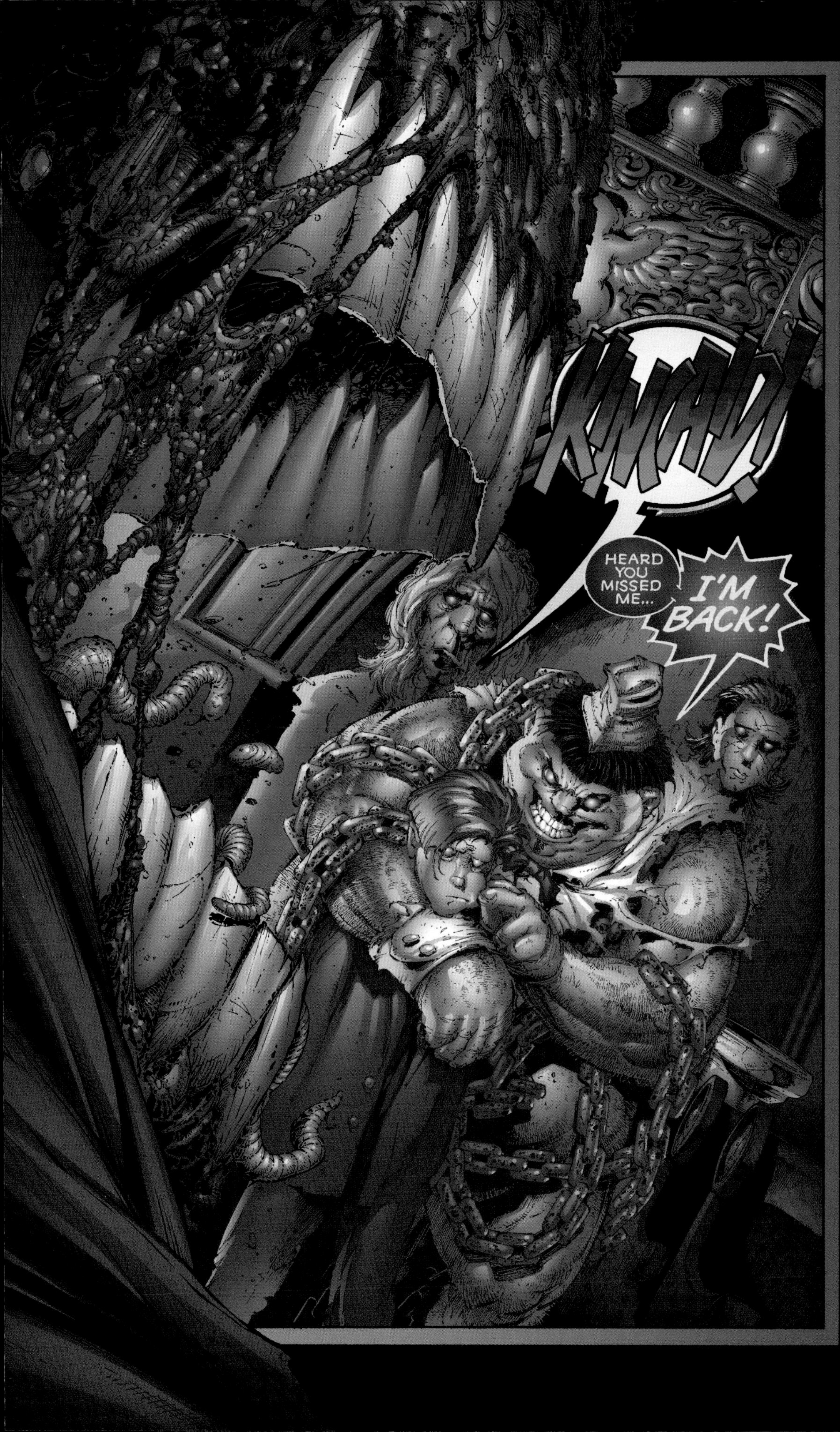
KNNAK!
HEARD YOU MISSED ME...
I'M BACK!

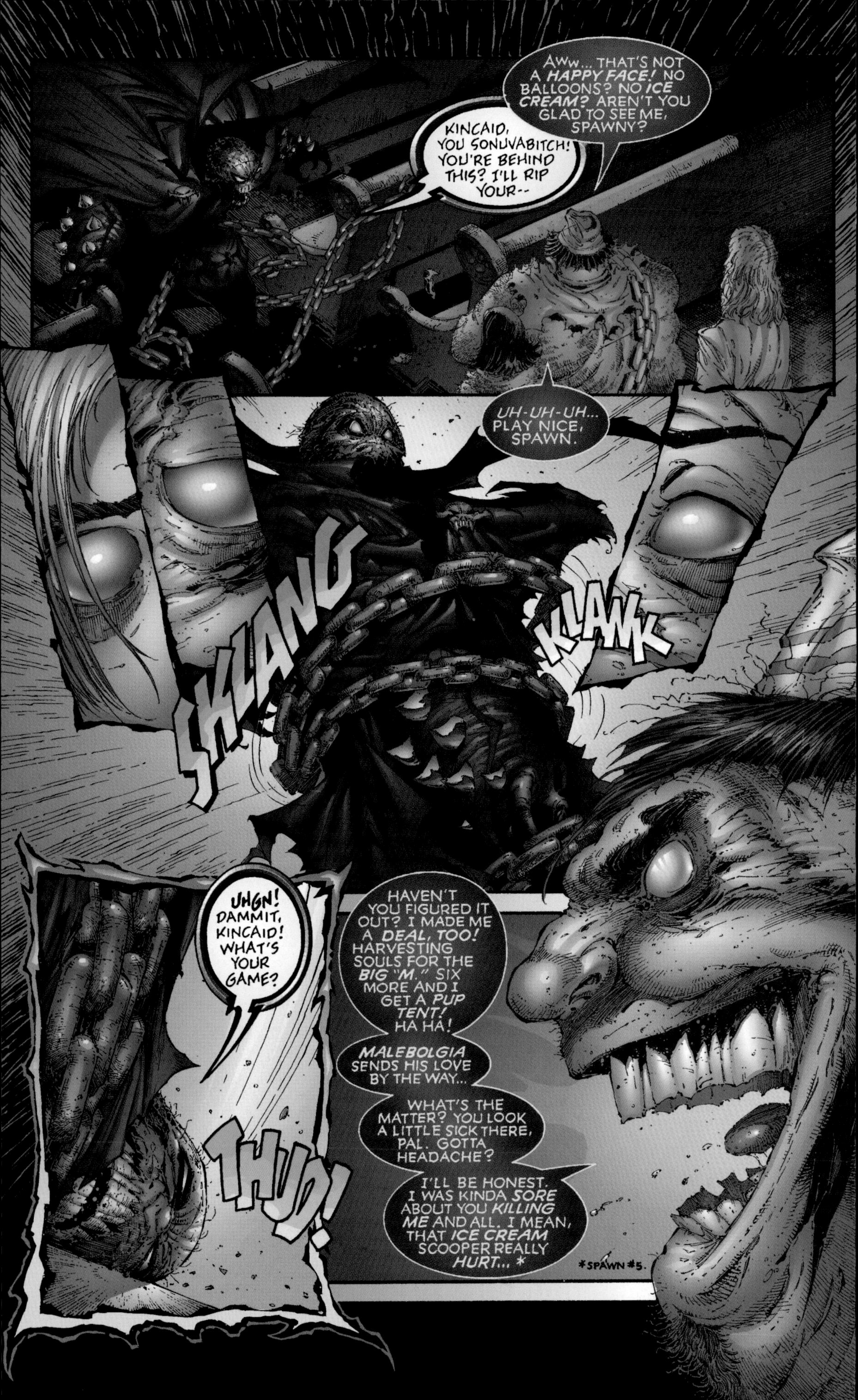

KINCAID, YOU SONUVABITCH! YOU'RE BEHIND THIS? I'LL RIP YOUR--
AWW... THAT'S NOT A HAPPY FACE! NO BALLOONS? NO ICE CREAM? AREN'T YOU GLAD TO SEE ME, SPAWNY?
UH-UH-UH... PLAY NICE, SPAWN.
SKLANG
KLANK
UHGN! DAMMIT, KINCAID! WHAT'S YOUR GAME?
THUD!
HAVEN'T YOU FIGURED IT OUT? I MADE ME A DEAL, TOO! HARVESTING SOULS FOR THE BIG "M." SIX MORE AND I GET A PUP TENT! HA HA!
MALEBOLGIA SENDS HIS LOVE BY THE WAY...
WHAT'S THE MATTER? YOU LOOK A LITTLE SICK THERE, PAL. GOTTA HEADACHE?
I'LL BE HONEST. I WAS KINDA SORE ABOUT YOU KILLING ME AND ALL. I MEAN, THAT ICE CREAM SCOOPER REALLY HURT... *
*SPAWN #5.

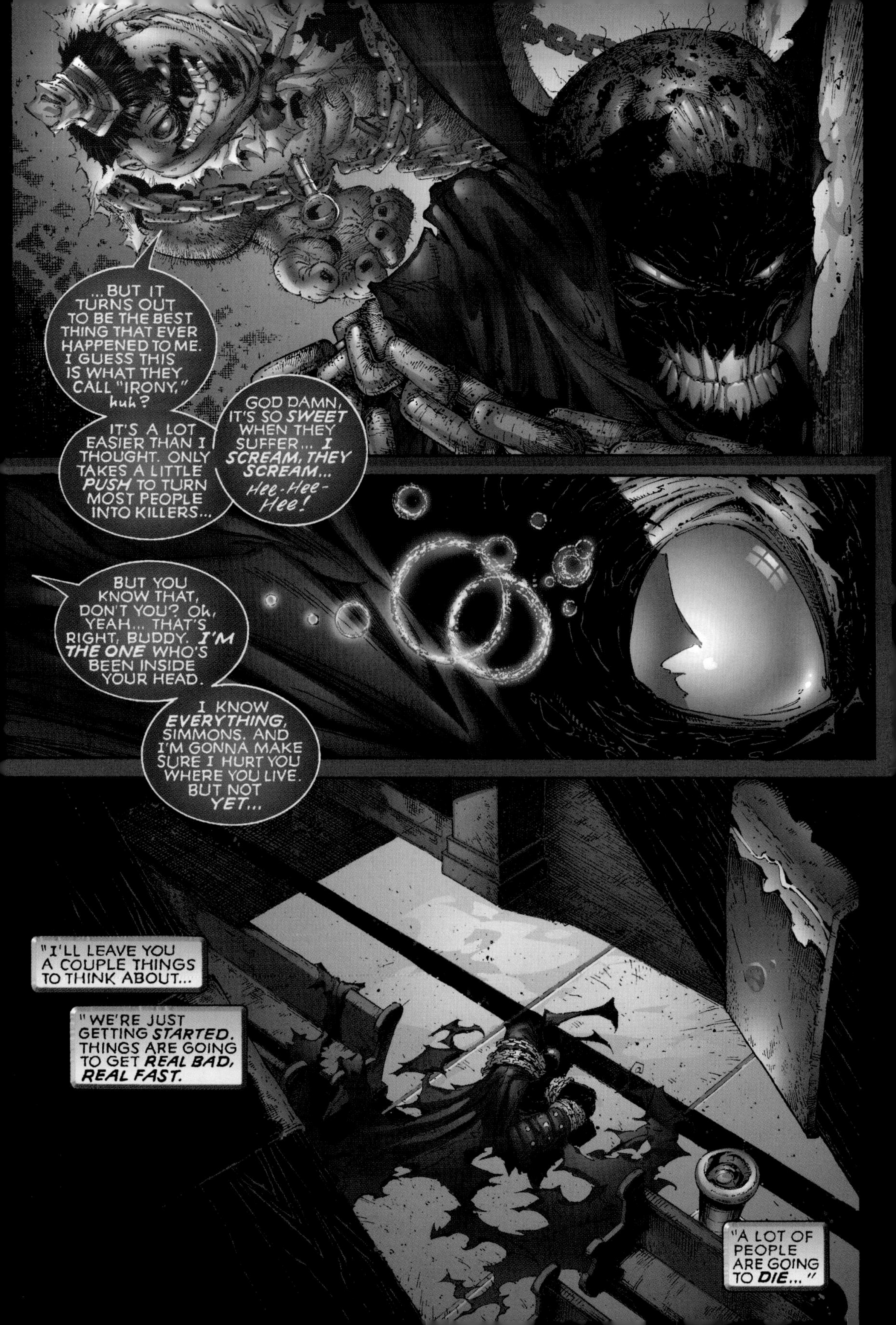
...BUT IT TURNS OUT TO BE THE BEST THING THAT EVER HAPPENED TO ME. I GUESS THIS IS WHAT THEY CALL "IRONY," huh?
IT'S A LOT EASIER THAN I THOUGHT. ONLY TAKES A LITTLE PUSH TO TURN MOST PEOPLE INTO KILLERS...
GOD DAMN, IT'S SO SWEET WHEN THEY SUFFER... I SCREAM, THEY SCREAM... Hee-Hee-Hee!
BUT YOU KNOW THAT, DON'T YOU? Oh, YEAH... THAT'S RIGHT, BUDDY. I'M THE ONE WHO'S BEEN INSIDE YOUR HEAD.
I KNOW EVERYTHING, SIMMONS. AND I'M GONNA MAKE SURE I HURT YOU WHERE YOU LIVE. BUT NOT YET...
"I'LL LEAVE YOU A COUPLE THINGS TO THINK ABOUT...
"WE'RE JUST GETTING STARTED. THINGS ARE GOING TO GET REAL BAD, REAL FAST.
"A LOT OF PEOPLE ARE GOING TO DIE..."

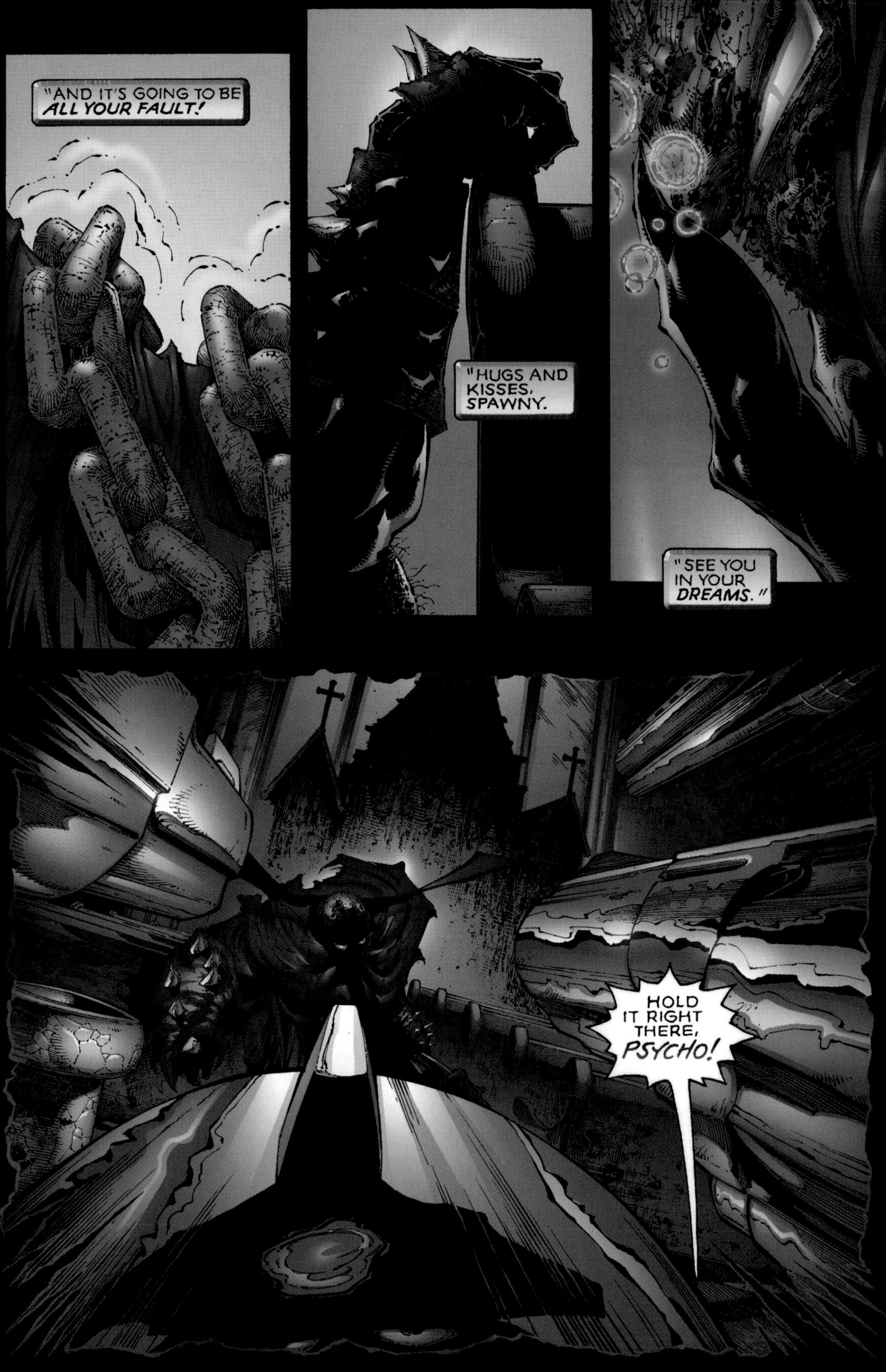
"AND IT'S GOING TO BE ALL YOUR FAULT!
"HUGS AND KISSES, SPAWNY.
"SEE YOU IN YOUR DREAMS."
HOLD IT RIGHT THERE, PSYCHO!

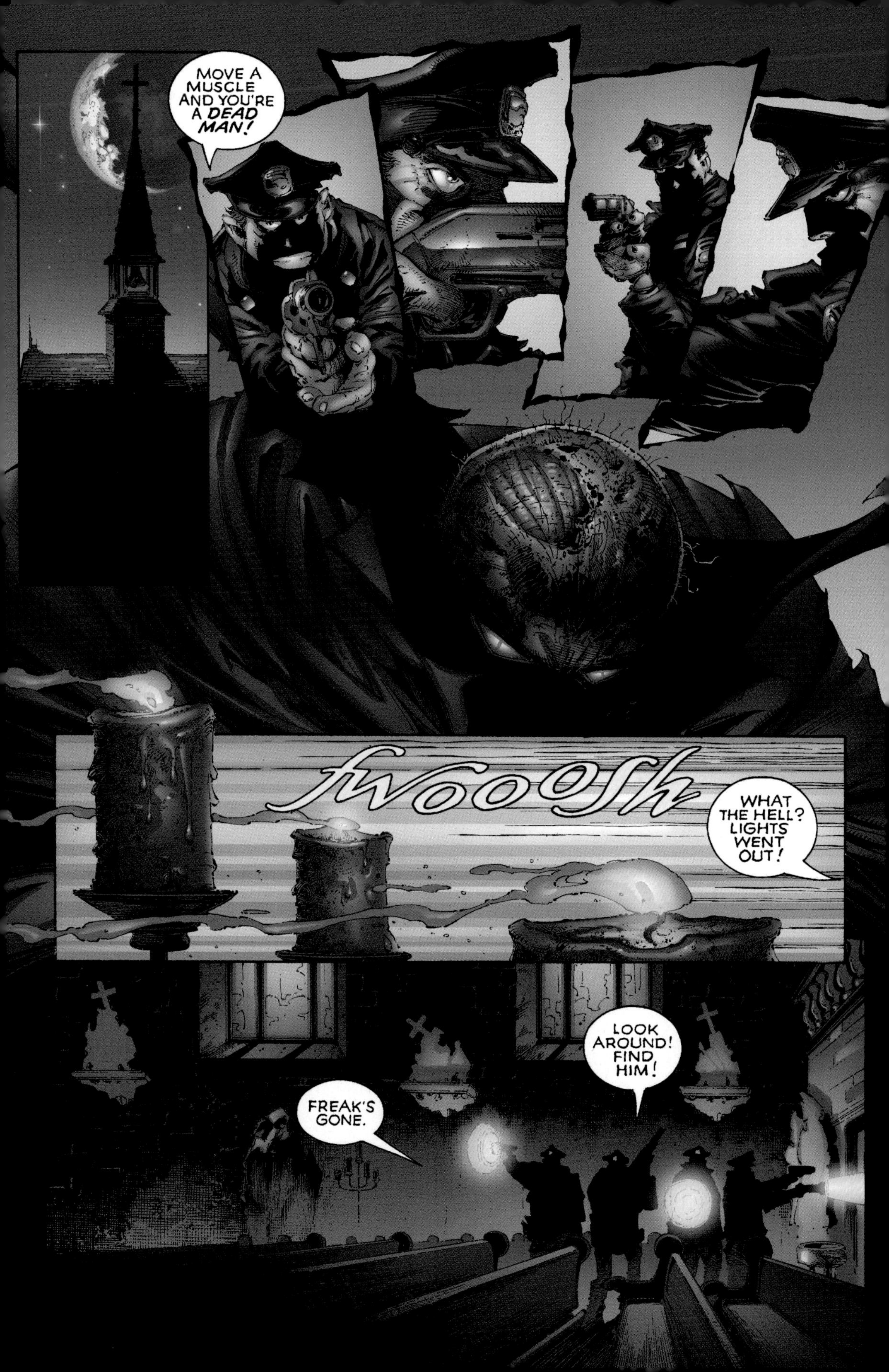
MOVE A MUSCLE AND YOU'RE A *DEAD MAN!*
fwoosh
WHAT THE HELL? LIGHTS WENT OUT!
FREAK'S GONE.
LOOK AROUND! FIND HIM!

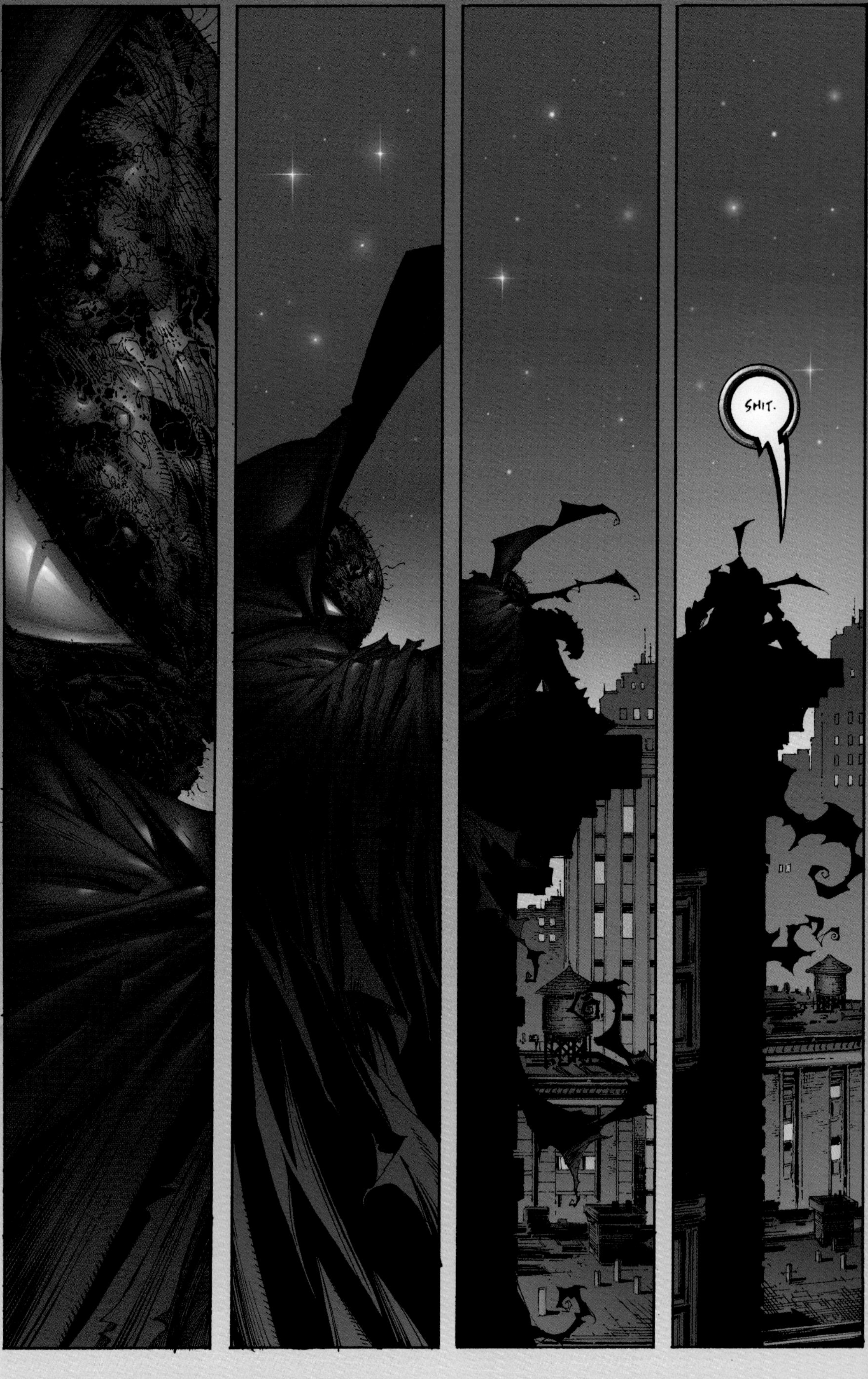
SHIT.

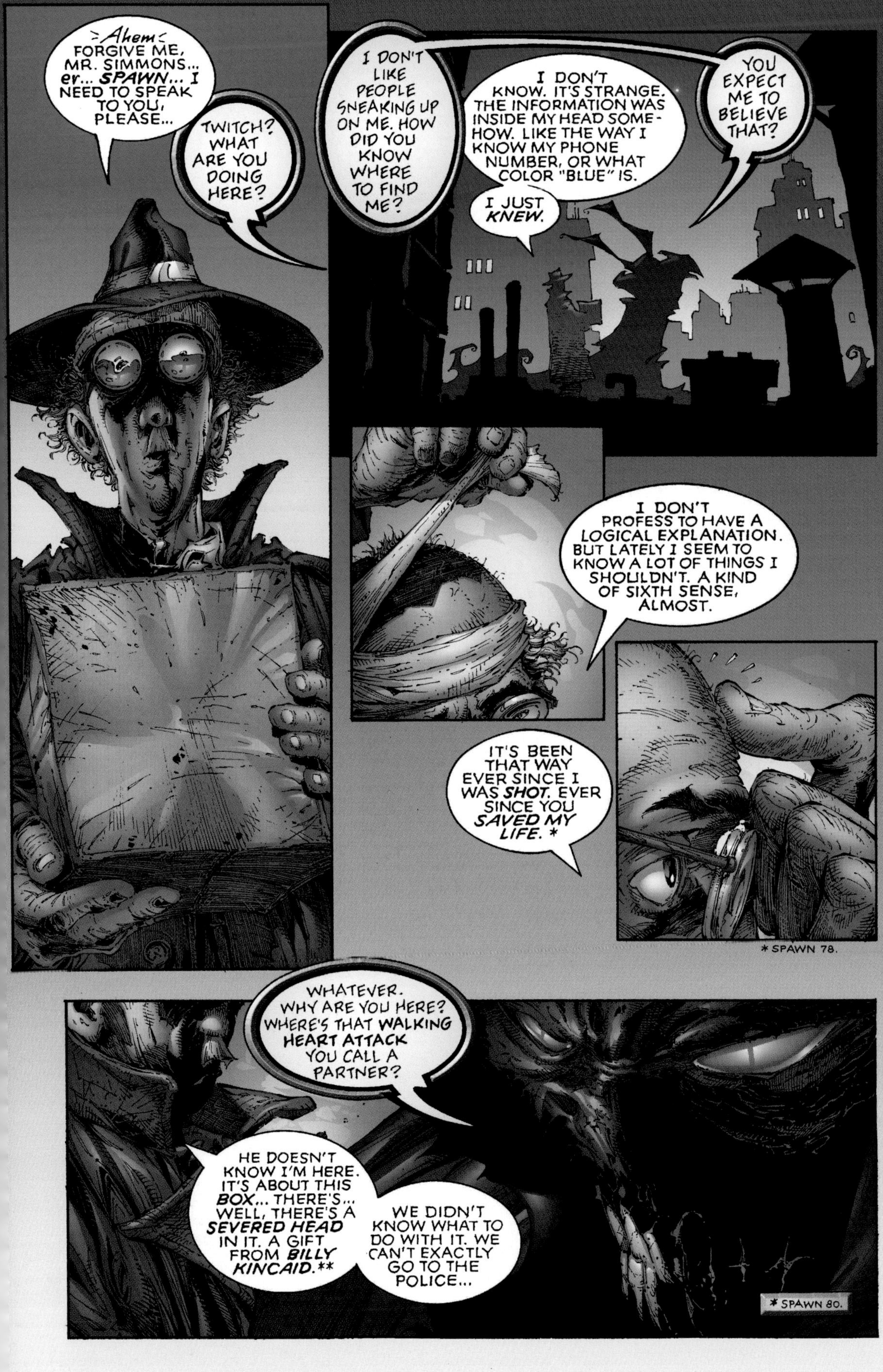

Ahem
FORGIVE ME, MR. SIMMONS... er... SPAWN... I NEED TO SPEAK TO YOU, PLEASE...
TWITCH? WHAT ARE YOU DOING HERE?
I DON'T LIKE PEOPLE SNEAKING UP ON ME. HOW DID YOU KNOW WHERE TO FIND ME?
I DON'T KNOW. IT'S STRANGE. THE INFORMATION WAS INSIDE MY HEAD SOMEHOW. LIKE THE WAY I KNOW MY PHONE NUMBER, OR WHAT COLOR "BLUE" IS.
I JUST KNEW.
YOU EXPECT ME TO BELIEVE THAT?
I DON'T PROFESS TO HAVE A LOGICAL EXPLANATION. BUT LATELY I SEEM TO KNOW A LOT OF THINGS I SHOULDN'T. A KIND OF SIXTH SENSE, ALMOST.
IT'S BEEN THAT WAY EVER SINCE I WAS SHOT. EVER SINCE YOU SAVED MY LIFE. *
* SPAWN 78.
WHATEVER. WHY ARE YOU HERE? WHERE'S THAT WALKING HEART ATTACK YOU CALL A PARTNER?
HE DOESN'T KNOW I'M HERE. IT'S ABOUT THIS BOX... THERE'S... WELL, THERE'S A SEVERED HEAD IN IT. A GIFT FROM BILLY KINCAID.**
WE DIDN'T KNOW WHAT TO DO WITH IT. WE CAN'T EXACTLY GO TO THE POLICE...
* SPAWN 80.

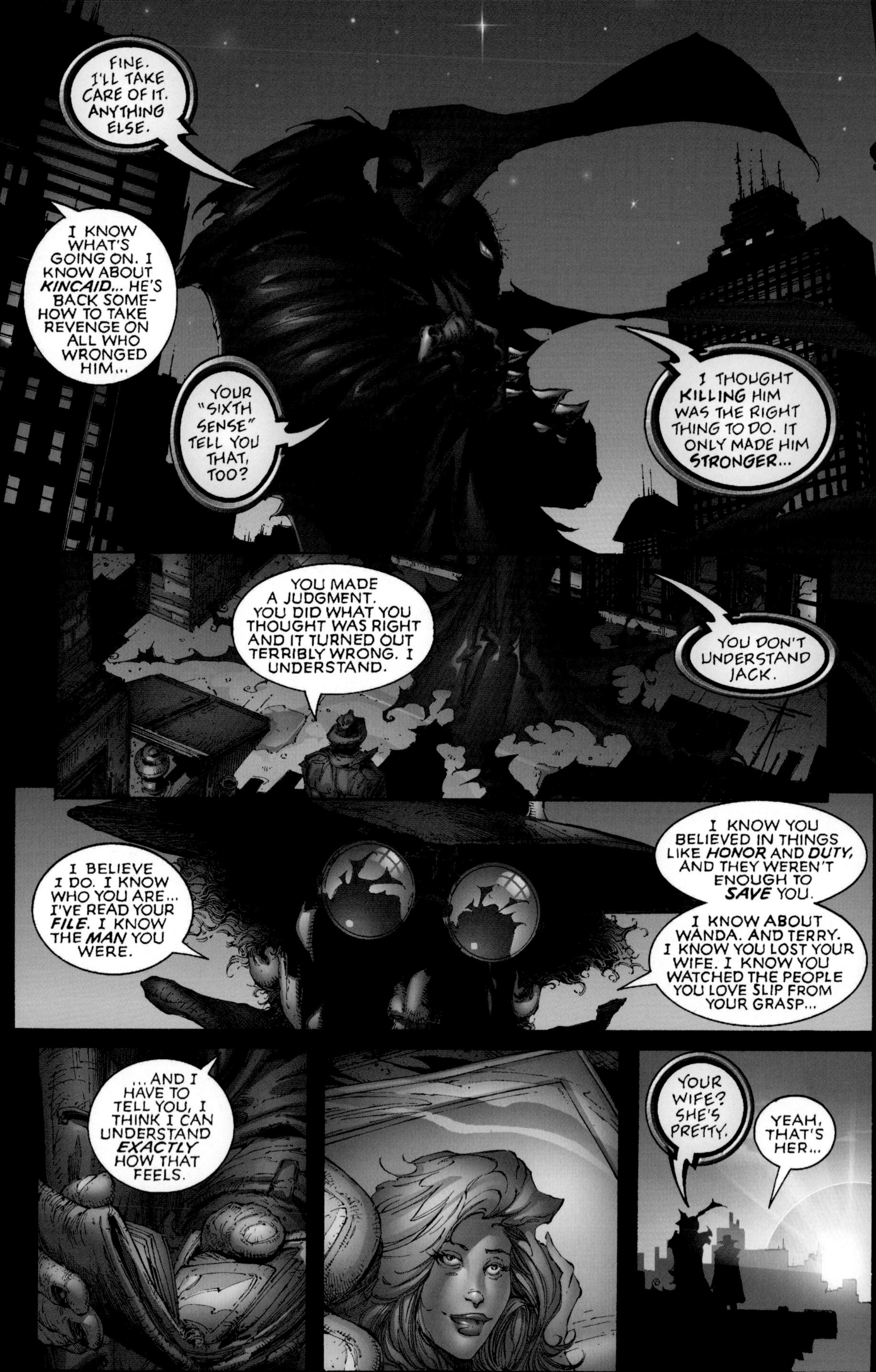
FINE. I'LL TAKE CARE OF IT. ANYTHING ELSE.
I KNOW WHAT'S GOING ON. I KNOW ABOUT KINCAID... HE'S BACK SOMEHOW TO TAKE REVENGE ON ALL WHO WRONGED HIM...
YOUR "SIXTH SENSE" TELL YOU THAT, TOO?
I THOUGHT KILLING HIM WAS THE RIGHT THING TO DO. IT ONLY MADE HIM STRONGER...
YOU MADE A JUDGMENT. YOU DID WHAT YOU THOUGHT WAS RIGHT AND IT TURNED OUT TERRIBLY WRONG. I UNDERSTAND.
YOU DON'T UNDERSTAND JACK.
I BELIEVE I DO. I KNOW WHO YOU ARE... I'VE READ YOUR FILE. I KNOW THE MAN YOU WERE.
I KNOW YOU BELIEVED IN THINGS LIKE HONOR AND DUTY, AND THEY WEREN'T ENOUGH TO SAVE YOU.
I KNOW ABOUT WANDA. AND TERRY. I KNOW YOU LOST YOUR WIFE. I KNOW YOU WATCHED THE PEOPLE YOU LOVE SLIP FROM YOUR GRASP...
...AND I HAVE TO TELL YOU, I THINK I CAN UNDERSTAND EXACTLY HOW THAT FEELS.
YOUR WIFE? SHE'S PRETTY.
YEAH, THAT'S HER...

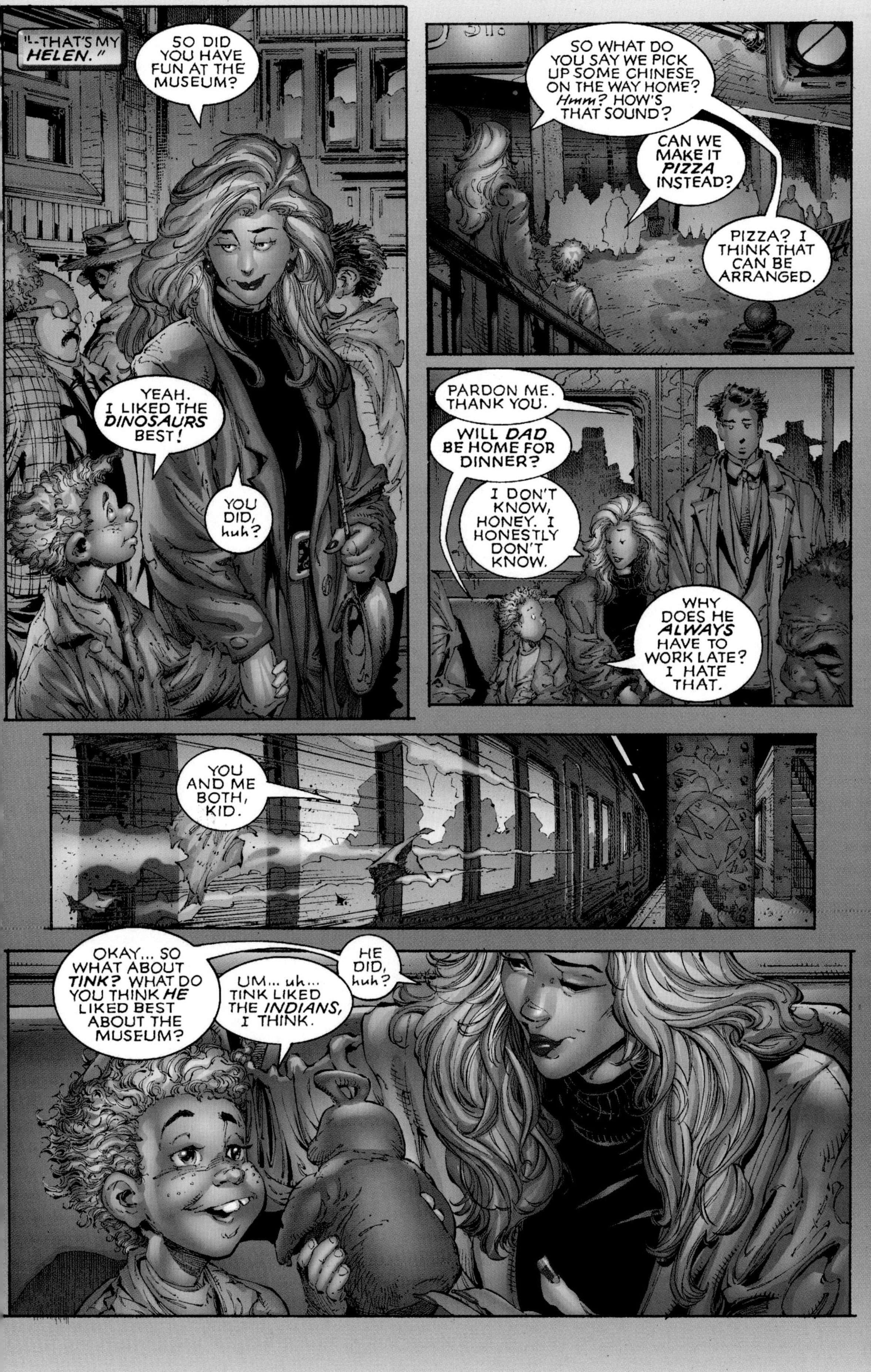
"I-THAT'S MY HELEN."
SO DID YOU HAVE FUN AT THE MUSEUM?
YEAH. I LIKED THE DINOSAURS BEST!
YOU DID, huh?
SO WHAT DO YOU SAY WE PICK UP SOME CHINESE ON THE WAY HOME? Hmm? HOW'S THAT SOUND?
CAN WE MAKE IT PIZZA INSTEAD?
PIZZA? I THINK THAT CAN BE ARRANGED.
PARDON ME. THANK YOU.
WILL DAD BE HOME FOR DINNER?
I DON'T KNOW, HONEY. I HONESTLY DON'T KNOW.
WHY DOES HE ALWAYS HAVE TO WORK LATE? I HATE THAT.
YOU AND ME BOTH, KID.
OKAY... SO WHAT ABOUT TINK? WHAT DO YOU THINK HE LIKED BEST ABOUT THE MUSEUM?
UM... uh... TINK LIKED THE INDIANS, I THINK.
HE DID, huh?

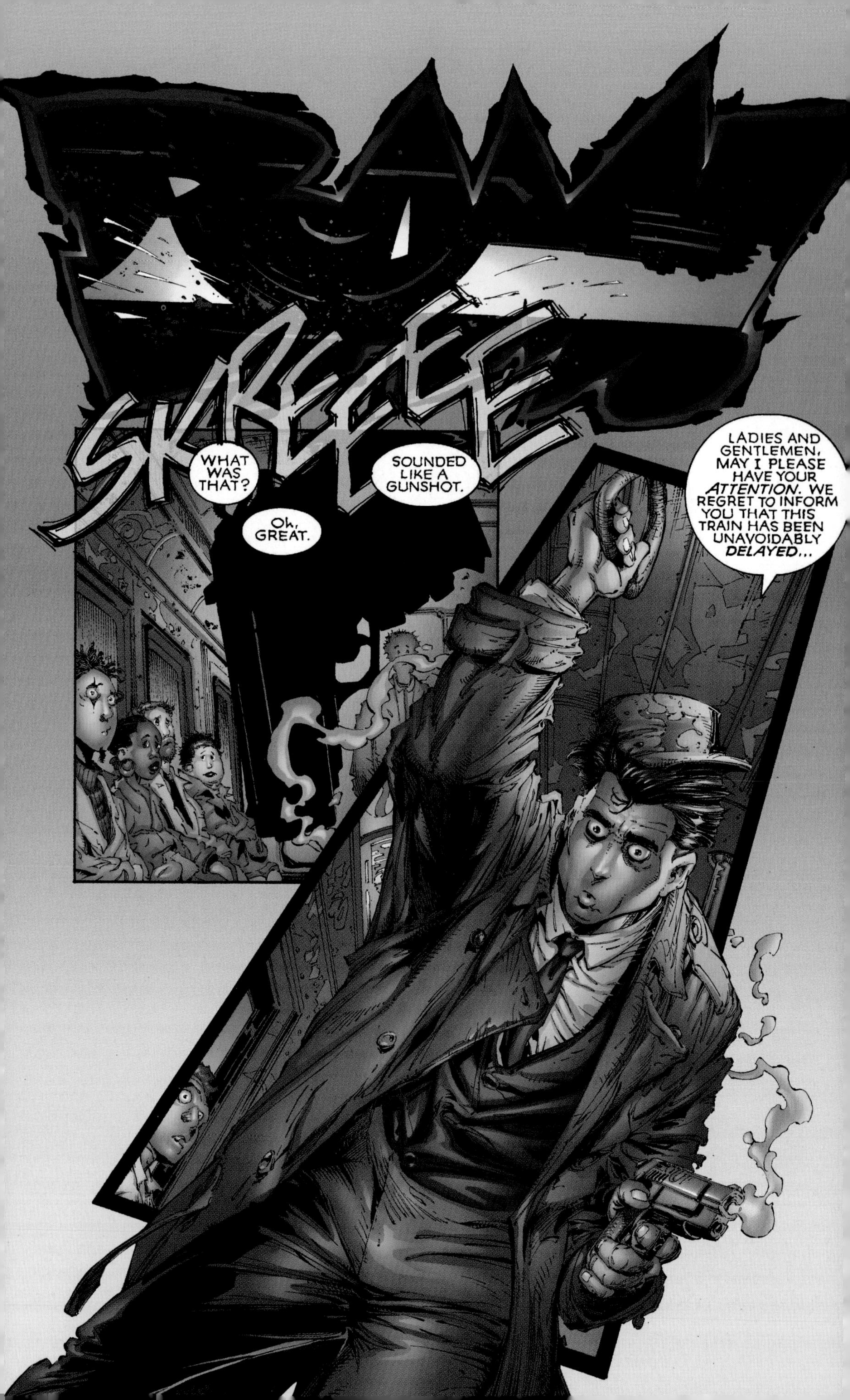
SKREEE
WHAT WAS THAT?
SOUNDED LIKE A GUNSHOT.
Oh, GREAT.
LADIES AND GENTLEMEN, MAY I PLEASE HAVE YOUR ATTENTION. WE REGRET TO INFORM YOU THAT THIS TRAIN HAS BEEN UNAVOIDABLY DELAYED...

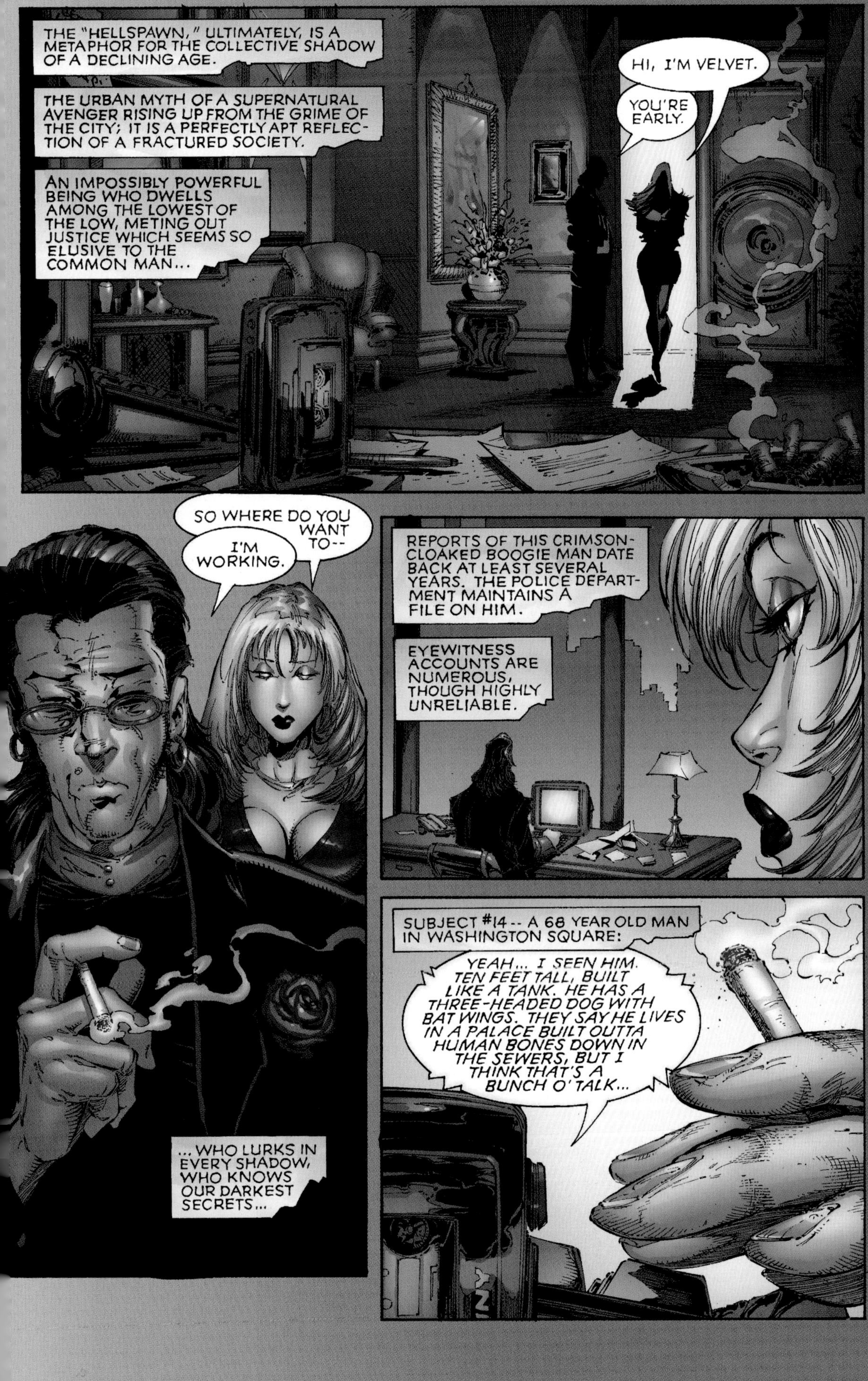

THE "HELLSPAWN," ULTIMATELY, IS A METAPHOR FOR THE COLLECTIVE SHADOW OF A DECLINING AGE.
THE URBAN MYTH OF A SUPERNATURAL AVENGER RISING UP FROM THE GRIME OF THE CITY; IT IS A PERFECTLY APT REFLECTION OF A FRACTURED SOCIETY.
AN IMPOSSIBLY POWERFUL BEING WHO DWELLS AMONG THE LOWEST OF THE LOW, METING OUT JUSTICE WHICH SEEMS SO ELUSIVE TO THE COMMON MAN...
HI, I'M VELVET.
YOU'RE EARLY.
SO WHERE DO YOU WANT TO--
I'M WORKING.
...WHO LURKS IN EVERY SHADOW, WHO KNOWS OUR DARKEST SECRETS...
REPORTS OF THIS CRIMSON-CLOAKED BOOGIE MAN DATE BACK AT LEAST SEVERAL YEARS. THE POLICE DEPARTMENT MAINTAINS A FILE ON HIM.
EYEWITNESS ACCOUNTS ARE NUMEROUS, THOUGH HIGHLY UNRELIABLE.
SUBJECT #14 -- A 68 YEAR OLD MAN IN WASHINGTON SQUARE:
YEAH... I SEEN HIM. TEN FEET TALL, BUILT LIKE A TANK. HE HAS A THREE-HEADED DOG WITH BAT WINGS. THEY SAY HE LIVES IN A PALACE BUILT OUTTA HUMAN BONES DOWN IN THE SEWERS, BUT I THINK THAT'S A BUNCH O' TALK...

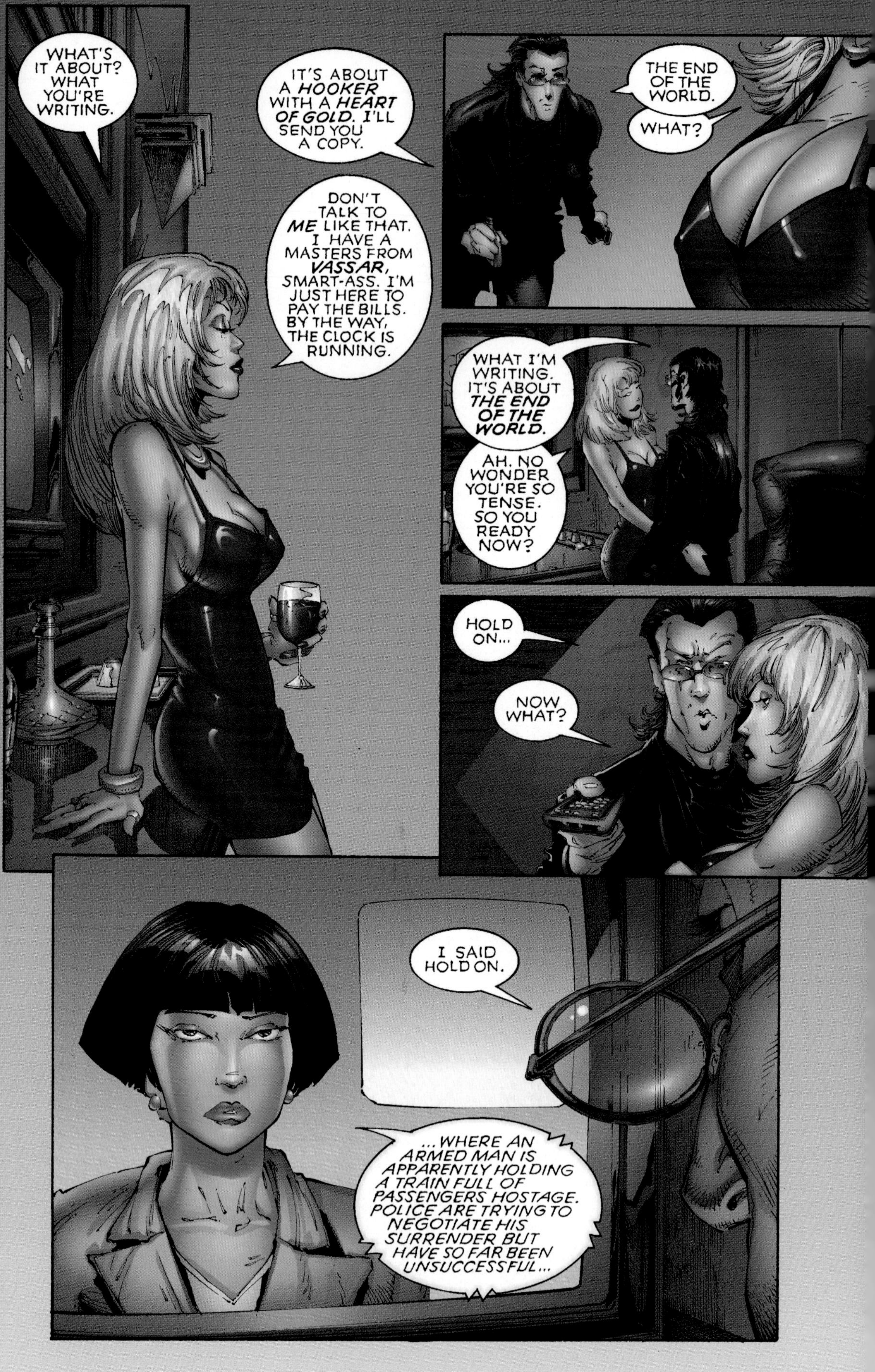
WHAT'S IT ABOUT? WHAT YOU'RE WRITING.
IT'S ABOUT A HOOKER WITH A HEART OF GOLD. I'LL SEND YOU A COPY.
DON'T TALK TO ME LIKE THAT. I HAVE A MASTERS FROM VASSAR, SMART-ASS. I'M JUST HERE TO PAY THE BILLS. BY THE WAY, THE CLOCK IS RUNNING.
THE END OF THE WORLD.
WHAT?
WHAT I'M WRITING. IT'S ABOUT THE END OF THE WORLD.
AH. NO WONDER YOU'RE SO TENSE. SO YOU READY NOW?
HOLD ON...
NOW WHAT?
I SAID HOLD ON.
...WHERE AN ARMED MAN IS APPARENTLY HOLDING A TRAIN FULL OF PASSENGERS HOSTAGE. POLICE ARE TRYING TO NEGOTIATE HIS SURRENDER BUT HAVE SO FAR BEEN UNSUCCESSFUL...

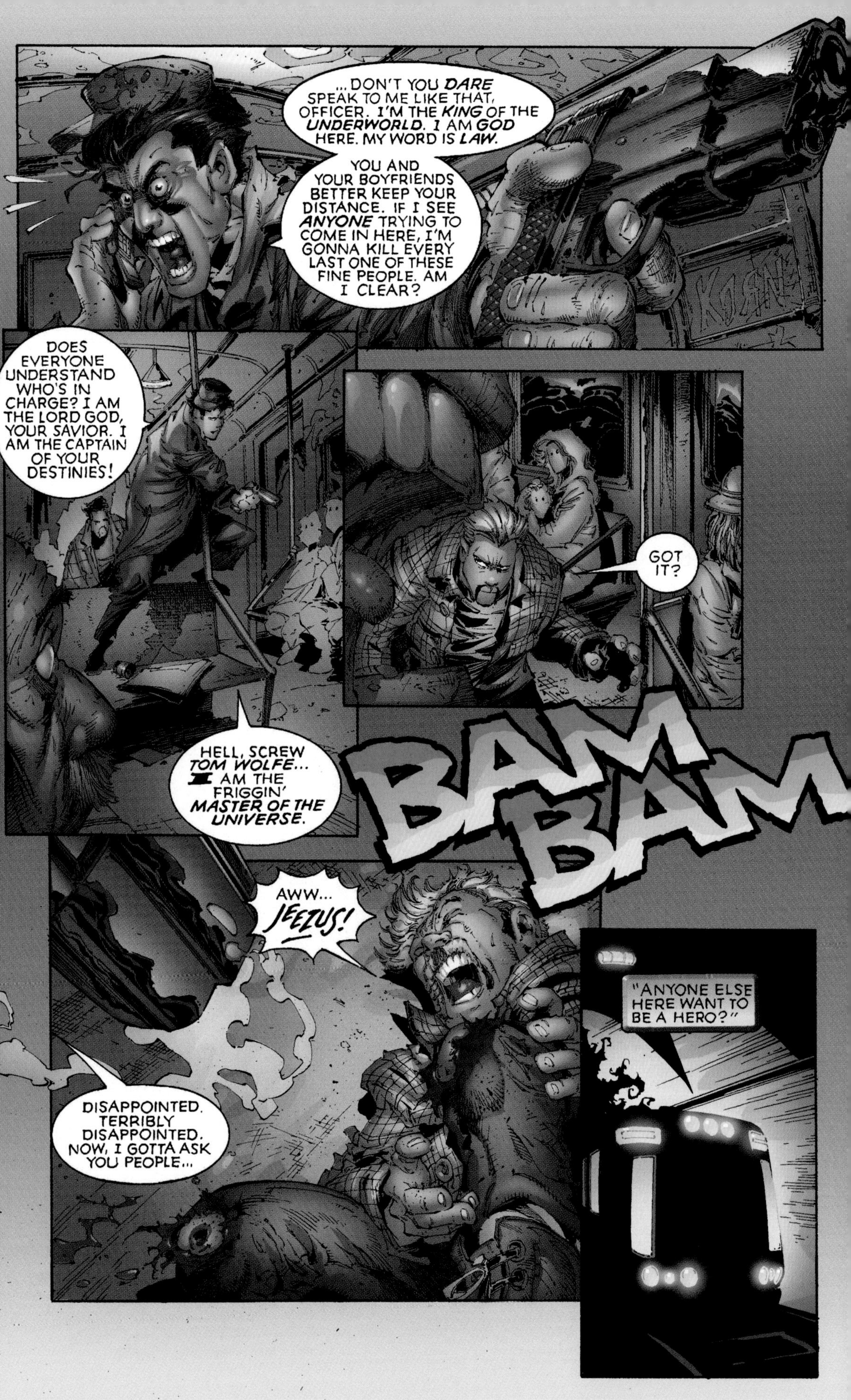

...DON'T YOU DARE SPEAK TO ME LIKE THAT, OFFICER. I'M THE KING OF THE UNDERWORLD. I AM GOD HERE. MY WORD IS LAW.
YOU AND YOUR BOYFRIENDS BETTER KEEP YOUR DISTANCE. IF I SEE ANYONE TRYING TO COME IN HERE, I'M GONNA KILL EVERY LAST ONE OF THESE FINE PEOPLE. AM I CLEAR?
DOES EVERYONE UNDERSTAND WHO'S IN CHARGE? I AM THE LORD GOD, YOUR SAVIOR. I AM THE CAPTAIN OF YOUR DESTINIES!
GOT IT?
HELL, SCREW TOM WOLFE... I AM THE FRIGGIN' MASTER OF THE UNIVERSE.
BAM
BAM
AWW... JEEZUS!
DISAPPOINTED. TERRIBLY DISAPPOINTED. NOW, I GOTTA ASK YOU PEOPLE...
"ANYONE ELSE HERE WANT TO BE A HERO?"

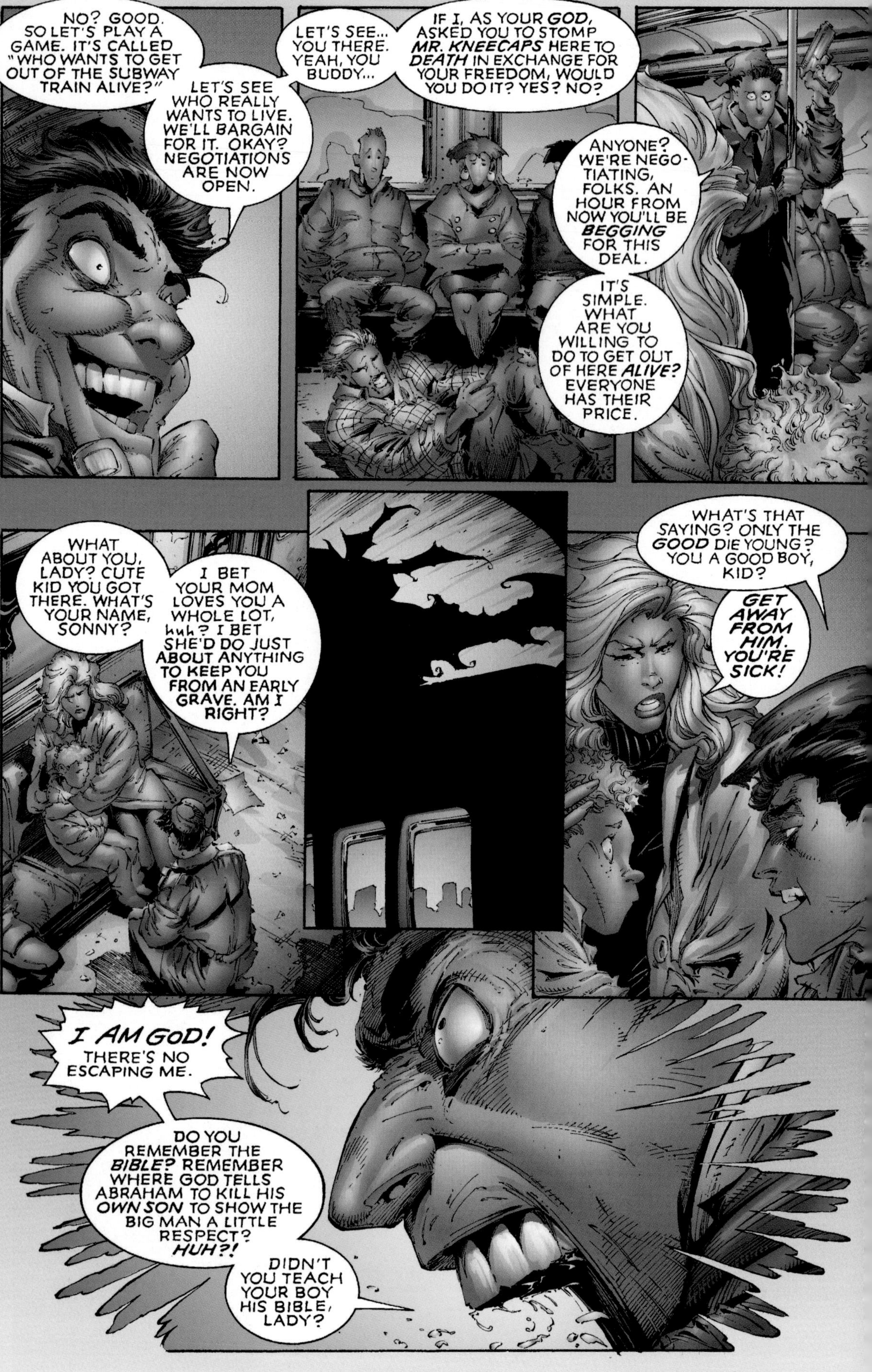

NO? GOOD. SO LET'S PLAY A GAME. IT'S CALLED "WHO WANTS TO GET OUT OF THE SUBWAY TRAIN ALIVE?"
LET'S SEE WHO REALLY WANTS TO LIVE. WE'LL BARGAIN FOR IT. OKAY? NEGOTIATIONS ARE NOW OPEN.
LET'S SEE... YOU THERE. YEAH, YOU BUDDY...
IF I, AS YOUR GOD, ASKED YOU TO STOMP MR. KNEECAPS HERE TO DEATH IN EXCHANGE FOR YOUR FREEDOM, WOULD YOU DO IT? YES? NO?
ANYONE? WE'RE NEGOTIATING, FOLKS. AN HOUR FROM NOW YOU'LL BE BEGGING FOR THIS DEAL.
IT'S SIMPLE. WHAT ARE YOU WILLING TO DO TO GET OUT OF HERE ALIVE? EVERYONE HAS THEIR PRICE.
WHAT ABOUT YOU, LADY? CUTE KID YOU GOT THERE. WHAT'S YOUR NAME, SONNY?
I BET YOUR MOM LOVES YOU A WHOLE LOT, huh? I BET SHE'D DO JUST ABOUT ANYTHING TO KEEP YOU FROM AN EARLY GRAVE. AM I RIGHT?
WHAT'S THAT SAYING? ONLY THE GOOD DIE YOUNG? YOU A GOOD BOY, KID?
GET AWAY FROM HIM. YOU'RE SICK!
I AM GOD! THERE'S NO ESCAPING ME.
DO YOU REMEMBER THE BIBLE? REMEMBER WHERE GOD TELLS ABRAHAM TO KILL HIS OWN SON TO SHOW THE BIG MAN A LITTLE RESPECT? HUH?!
DIDN'T YOU TEACH YOUR BOY HIS BIBLE, LADY?

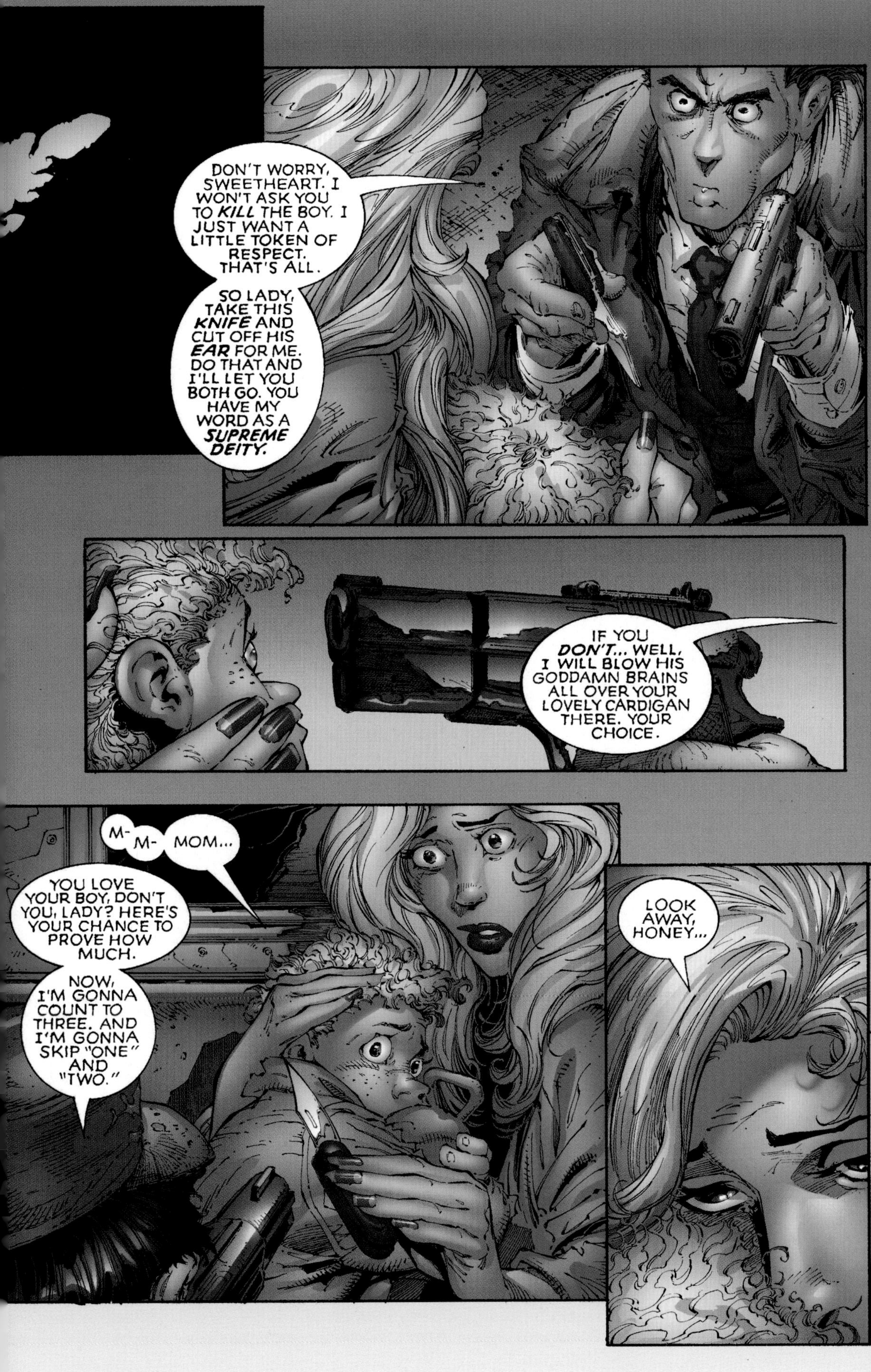

DON'T WORRY, SWEETHEART. I WON'T ASK YOU TO KILL THE BOY. I JUST WANT A LITTLE TOKEN OF RESPECT. THAT'S ALL.
SO LADY, TAKE THIS KNIFE AND CUT OFF HIS EAR FOR ME. DO THAT AND I'LL LET YOU BOTH GO. YOU HAVE MY WORD AS A SUPREME DEITY.
IF YOU DON'T... WELL, I WILL BLOW HIS GODDAMN BRAINS ALL OVER YOUR LOVELY CARDIGAN THERE. YOUR CHOICE.
M- M- MOM...
YOU LOVE YOUR BOY, DON'T YOU, LADY? HERE'S YOUR CHANCE TO PROVE HOW MUCH.
NOW, I'M GONNA COUNT TO THREE. AND I'M GONNA SKIP "ONE" AND "TWO."
LOOK AWAY, HONEY...

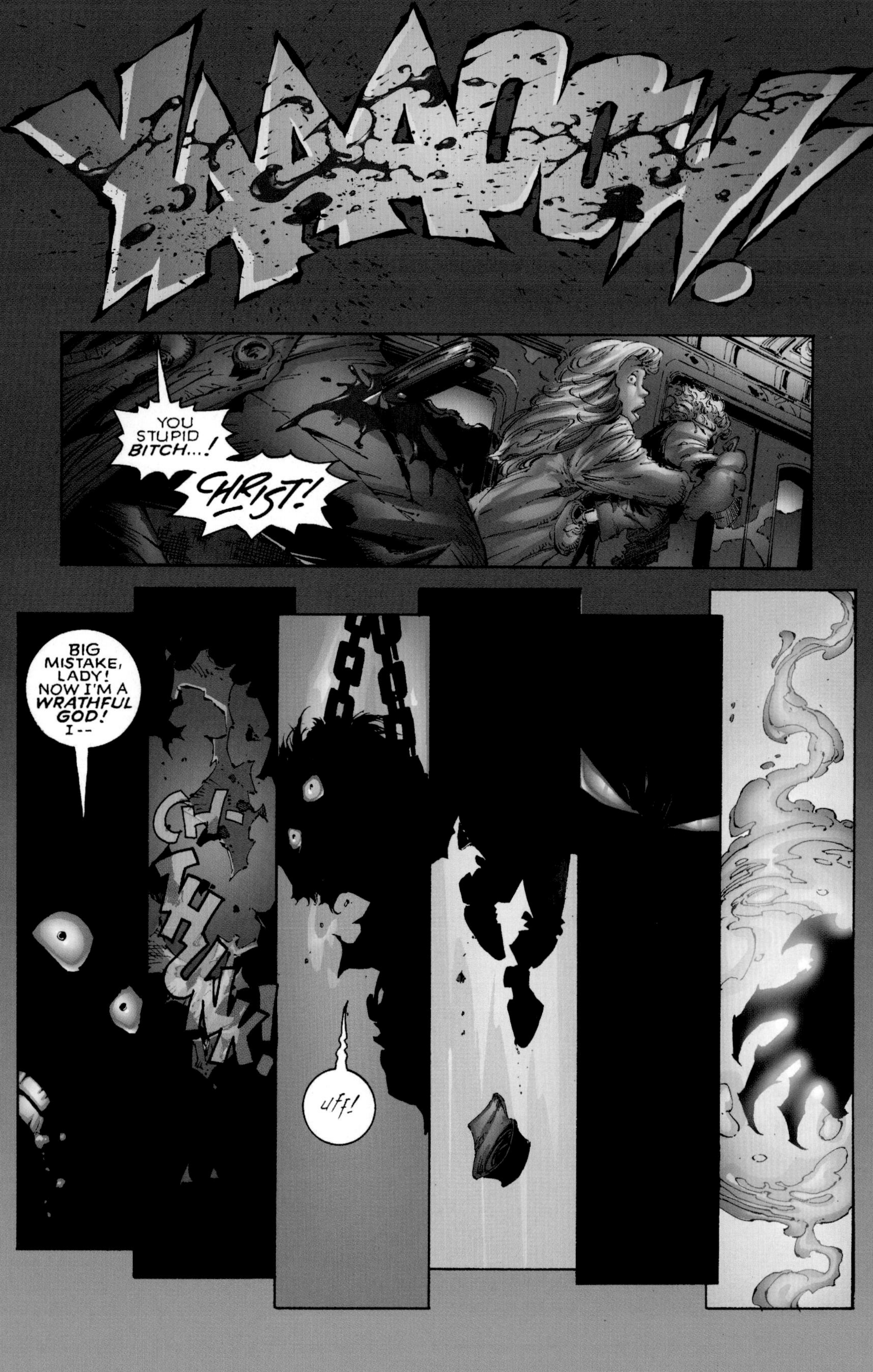
YAAAOW!
YOU STUPID BITCH...!
CHRIST!
BIG MISTAKE, LADY! NOW I'M A WRATHFUL GOD! I --
CH-CHUNK!
uff!

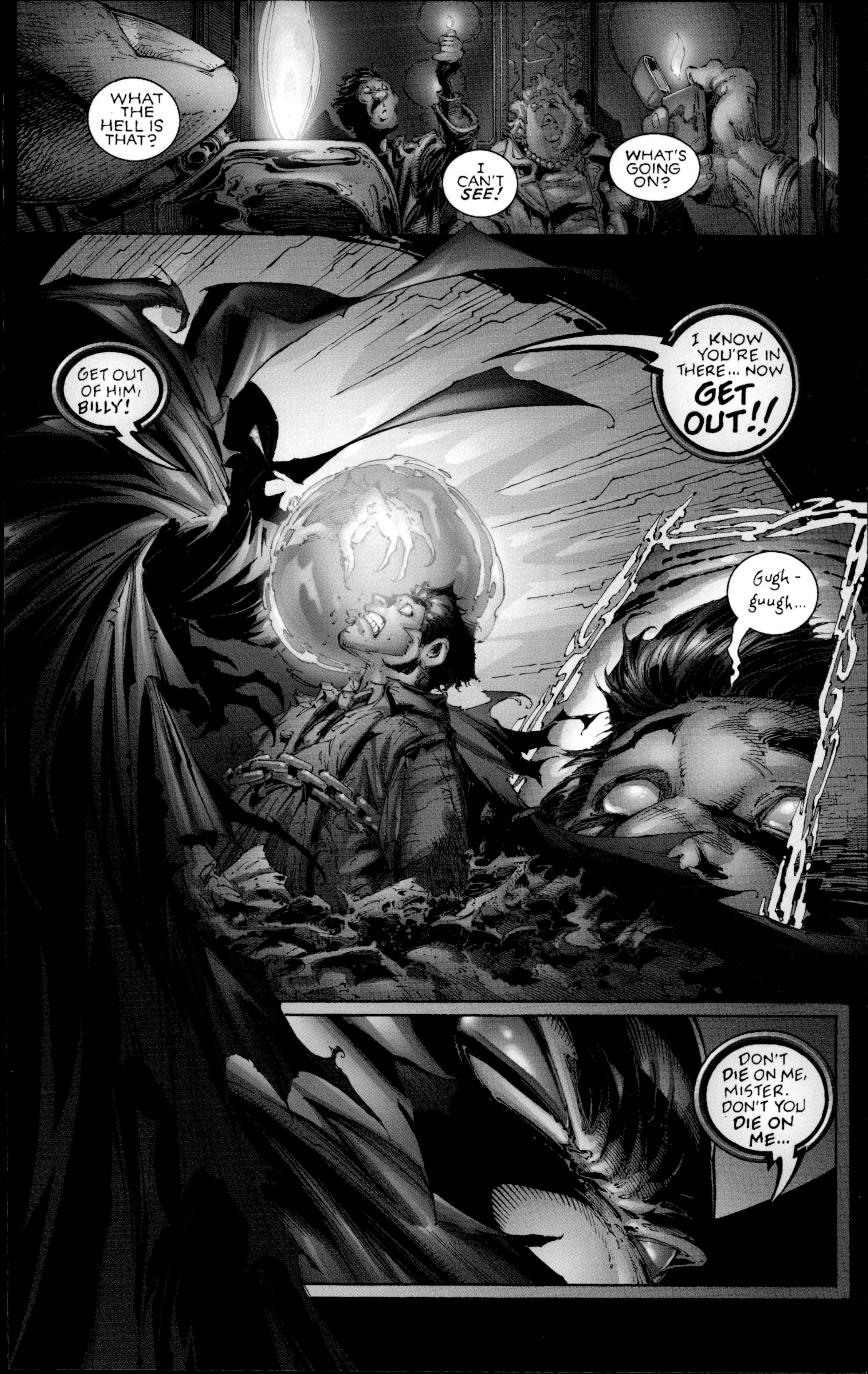
WHAT THE HELL IS THAT?
I CAN'T SEE!
WHAT'S GOING ON?
GET OUT OF HIM, BILLY!
I KNOW YOU'RE IN THERE... NOW GET OUT!!
Gugh-guugh...
DON'T DIE ON ME, MISTER. DON'T YOU DIE ON ME...

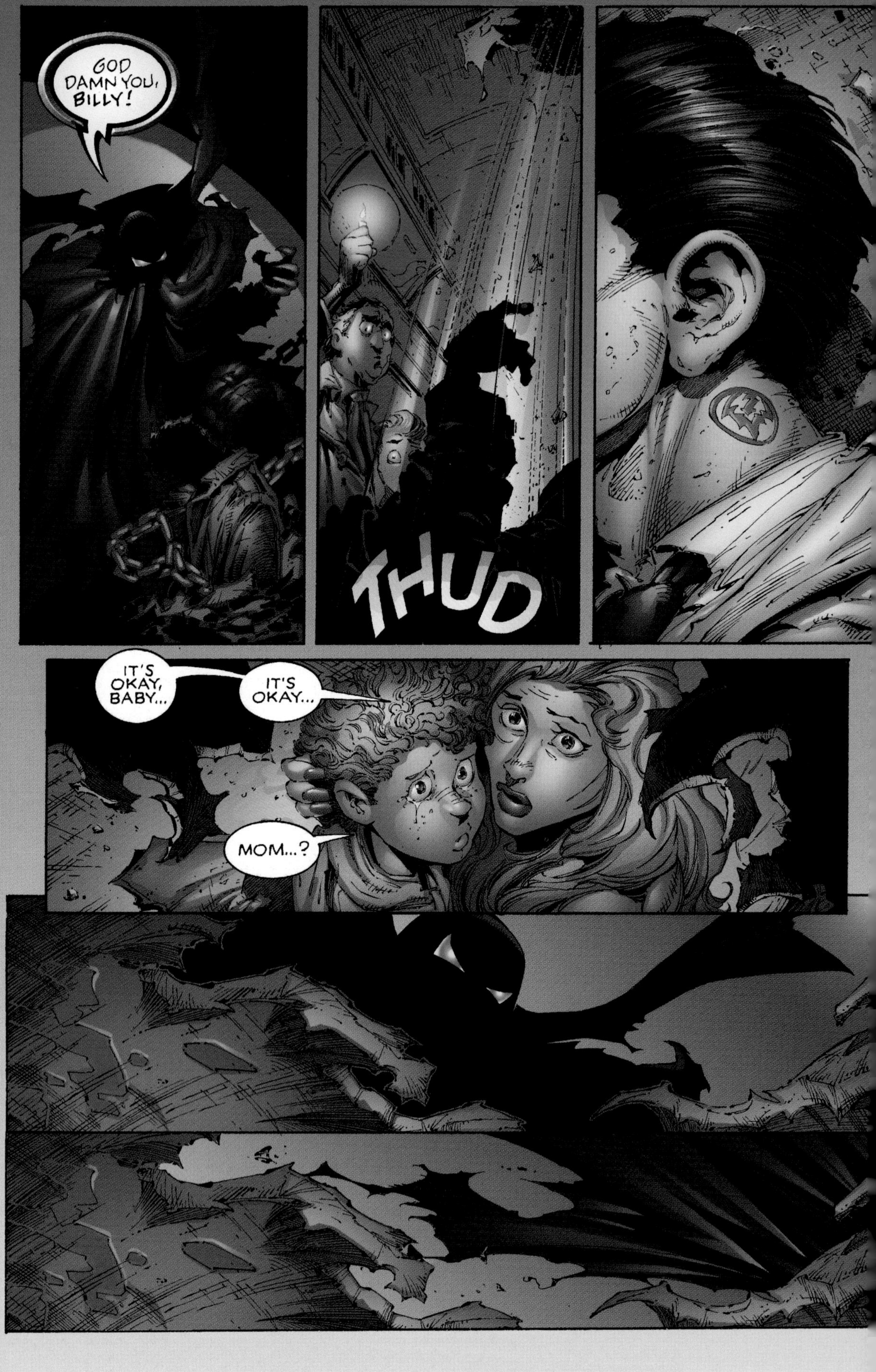
GOD DAMN YOU, BILLY!
THUD
IT'S OKAY, BABY...
IT'S OKAY...
MOM...?

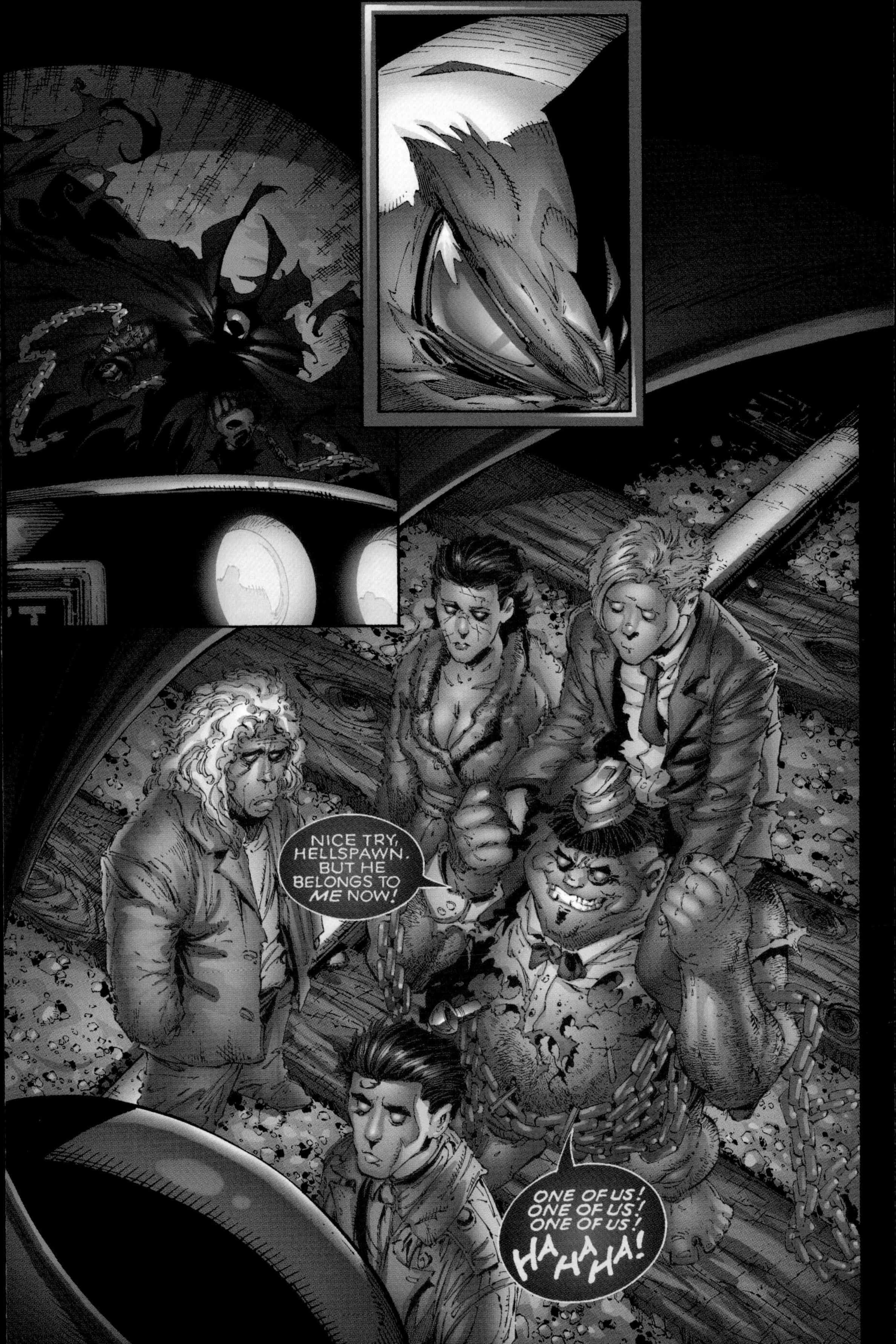
NICE TRY, HELLSPAWN. BUT HE BELONGS TO ME NOW!
ONE OF US! ONE OF US! ONE OF US!
HA HA HA HA!

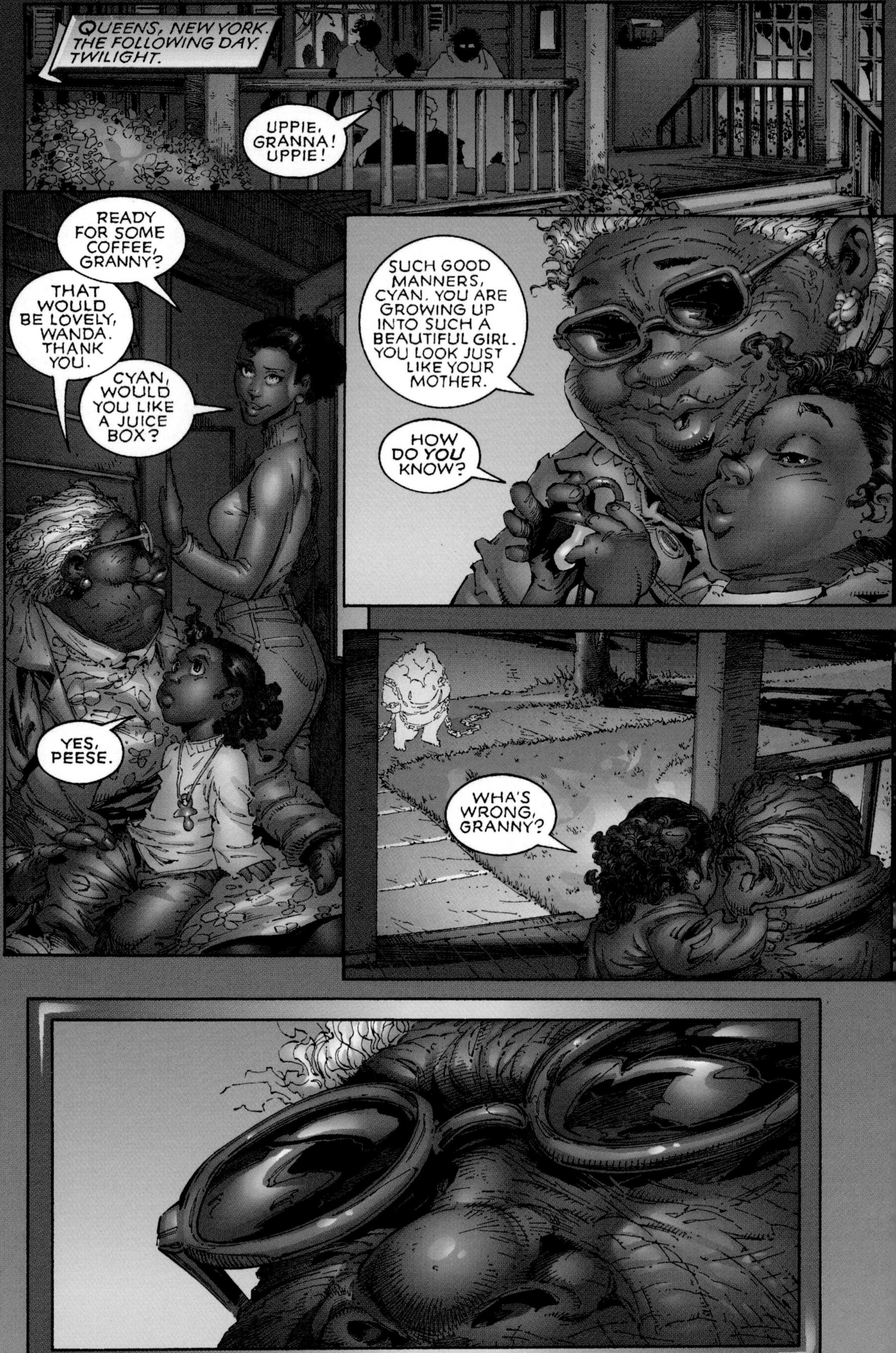
QUEENS, NEW YORK. THE FOLLOWING DAY. TWILIGHT.
UPPIE, GRANNA! UPPIE!
READY FOR SOME COFFEE, GRANNY?
THAT WOULD BE LOVELY, WANDA. THANK YOU.
CYAN, WOULD YOU LIKE A JUICE BOX?
YES, PEESE.
SUCH GOOD MANNERS, CYAN. YOU ARE GROWING UP INTO SUCH A BEAUTIFUL GIRL. YOU LOOK JUST LIKE YOUR MOTHER.
HOW DO *YOU* KNOW?
WHA'S WRONG, GRANNY?

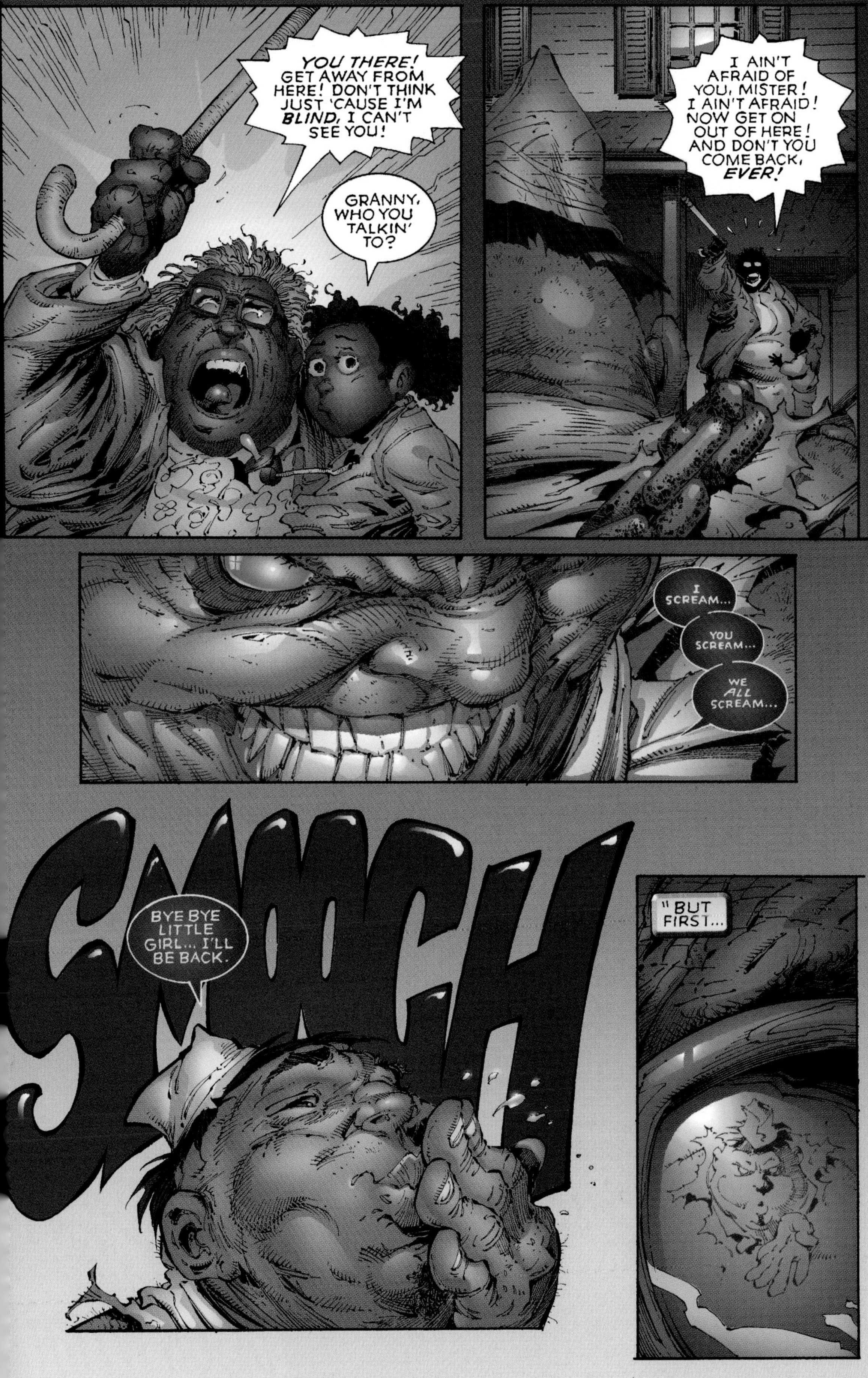
YOU THERE! GET AWAY FROM HERE! DON'T THINK JUST 'CAUSE I'M BLIND, I CAN'T SEE YOU!
GRANNY, WHO YOU TALKIN' TO?
I AIN'T AFRAID OF YOU, MISTER! I AIN'T AFRAID! NOW GET ON OUT OF HERE! AND DON'T YOU COME BACK, EVER!
I SCREAM...
YOU SCREAM...
WE ALL SCREAM...
SMOCH
BYE BYE LITTLE GIRL... I'LL BE BACK.
"BUT FIRST...

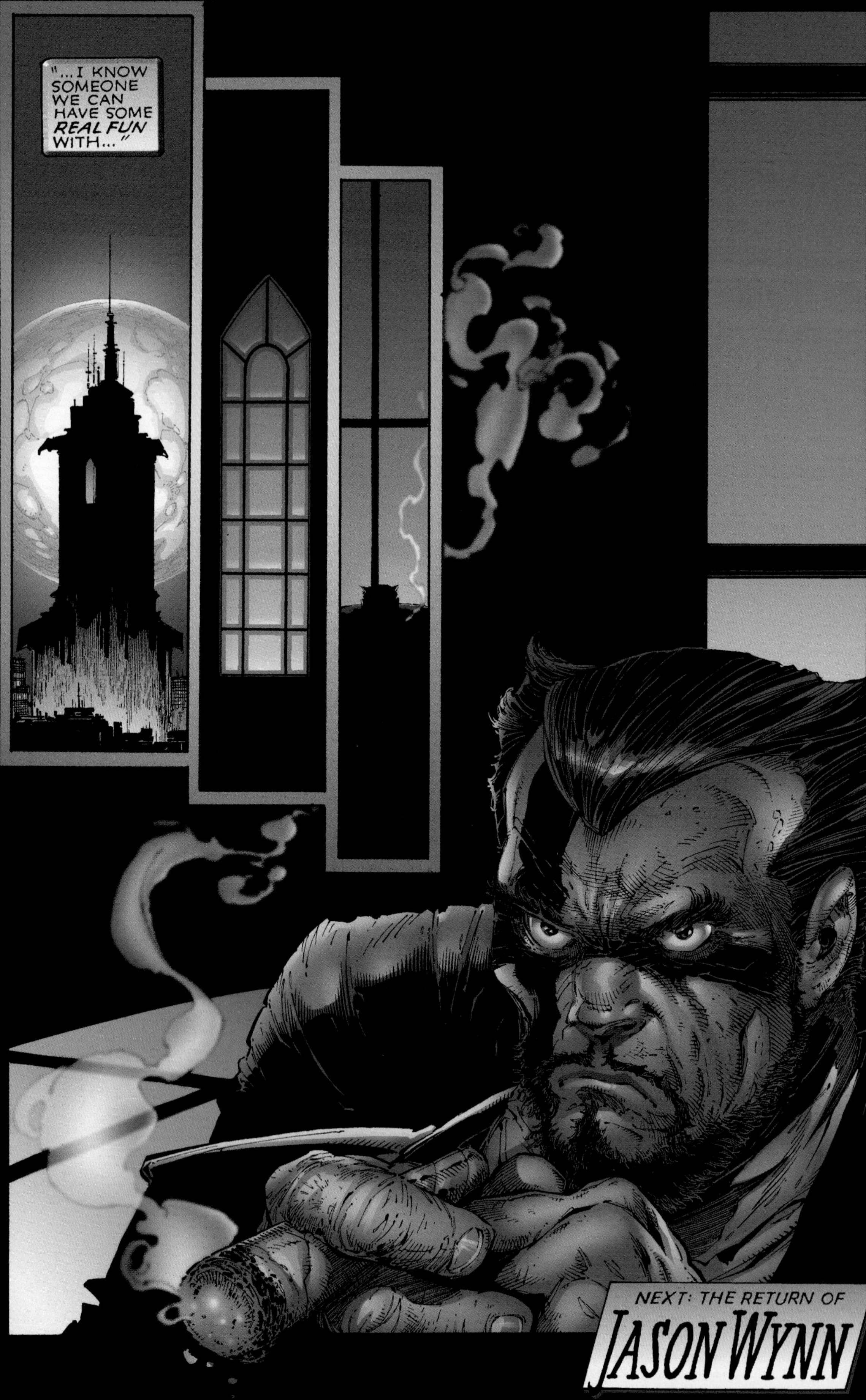
"...I KNOW SOMEONE WE CAN HAVE SOME *REAL FUN* WITH..."
NEXT: THE RETURN OF
JASON WYNN

ISSUE EIGHTY-THREE

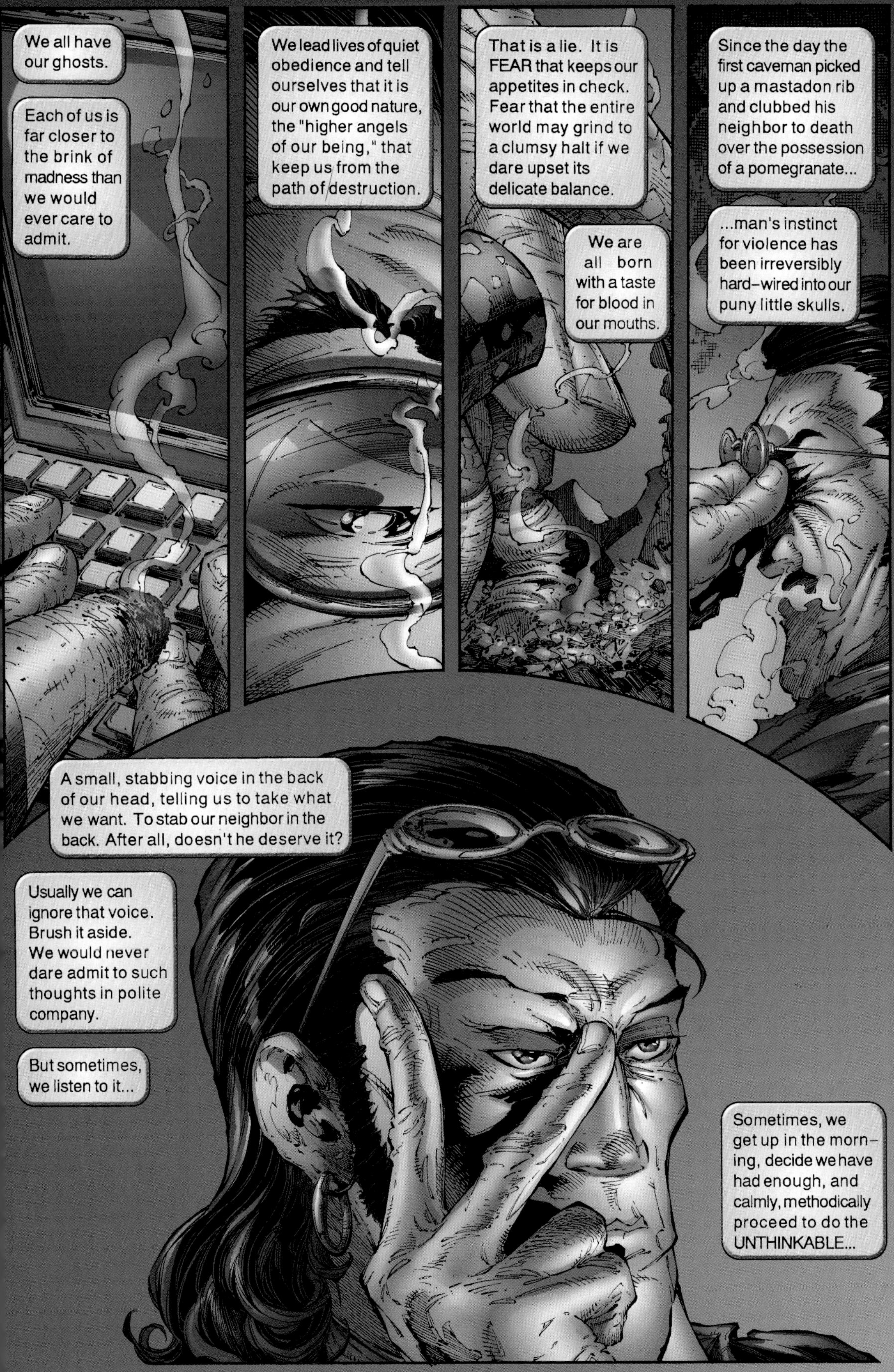
We all have our ghosts.
Each of us is far closer to the brink of madness than we would ever care to admit.
We lead lives of quiet obedience and tell ourselves that it is our own good nature, the "higher angels of our being," that keep us from the path of destruction.
That is a lie. It is FEAR that keeps our appetites in check. Fear that the entire world may grind to a clumsy halt if we dare upset its delicate balance.
We are all born with a taste for blood in our mouths.
Since the day the first caveman picked up a mastadon rib and clubbed his neighbor to death over the possession of a pomegranate...
...man's instinct for violence has been irreversibly hard-wired into our puny little skulls.
A small, stabbing voice in the back of our head, telling us to take what we want. To stab our neighbor in the back. After all, doesn't he deserve it?
Usually we can ignore that voice. Brush it aside. We would never dare admit to such thoughts in polite company.
But sometimes, we listen to it...
Sometimes, we get up in the morn-ing, decide we have had enough, and calmly, methodically proceed to do the UNTHINKABLE...

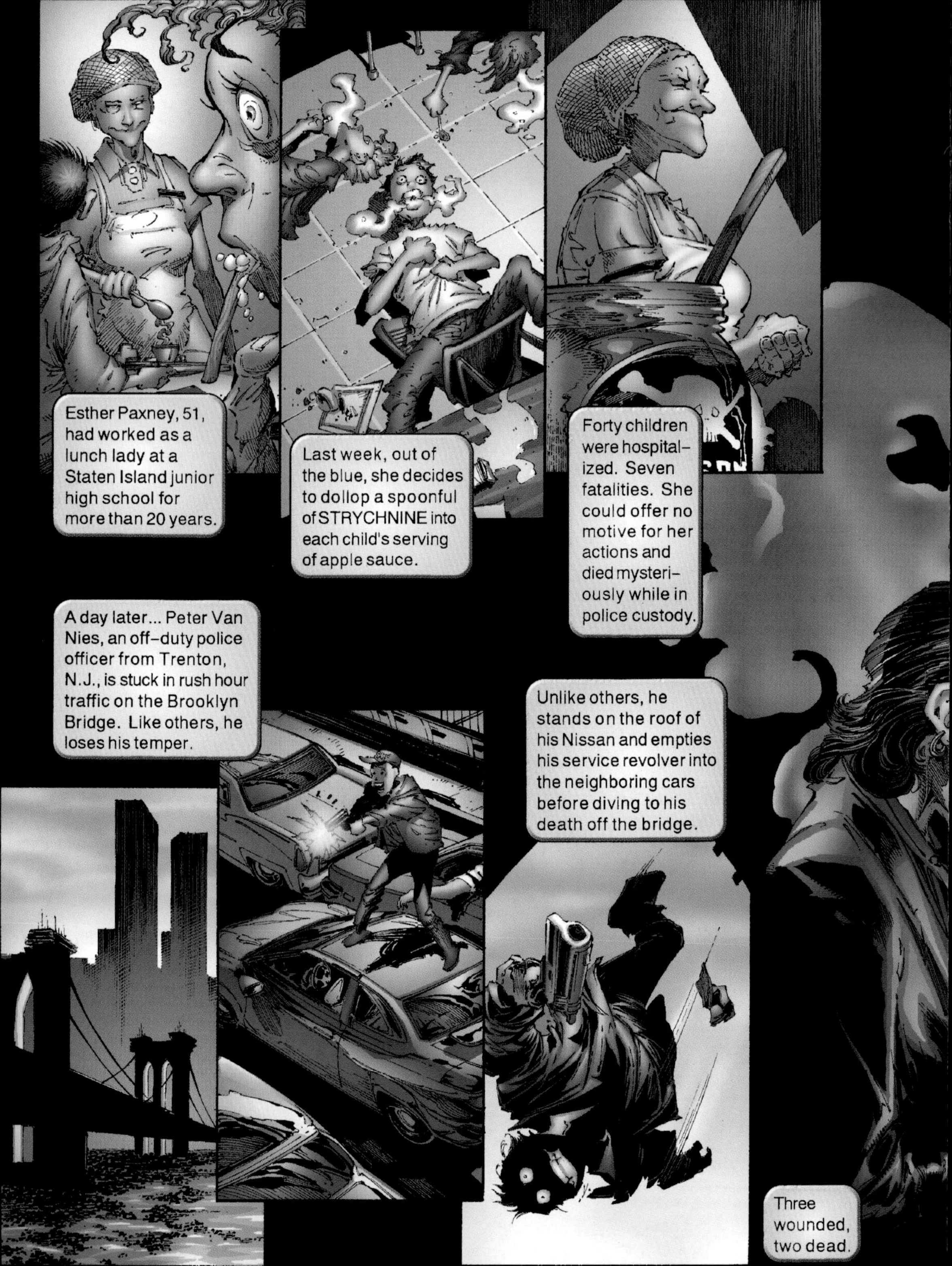

Esther Paxney, 51, had worked as a lunch lady at a Staten Island junior high school for more than 20 years.

Last week, out of the blue, she decides to dollop a spoonful of STRYCHNINE into each child's serving of apple sauce.

Forty children were hospitalized. Seven fatalities. She could offer no motive for her actions and died mysteriously while in police custody.

A day later... Peter Van Nies, an off-duty police officer from Trenton, N.J., is stuck in rush hour traffic on the Brooklyn Bridge. Like others, he loses his temper.

Unlike others, he stands on the roof of his Nissan and empties his service revolver into the neighboring cars before diving to his death off the bridge.

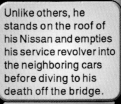

Three wounded, two dead.

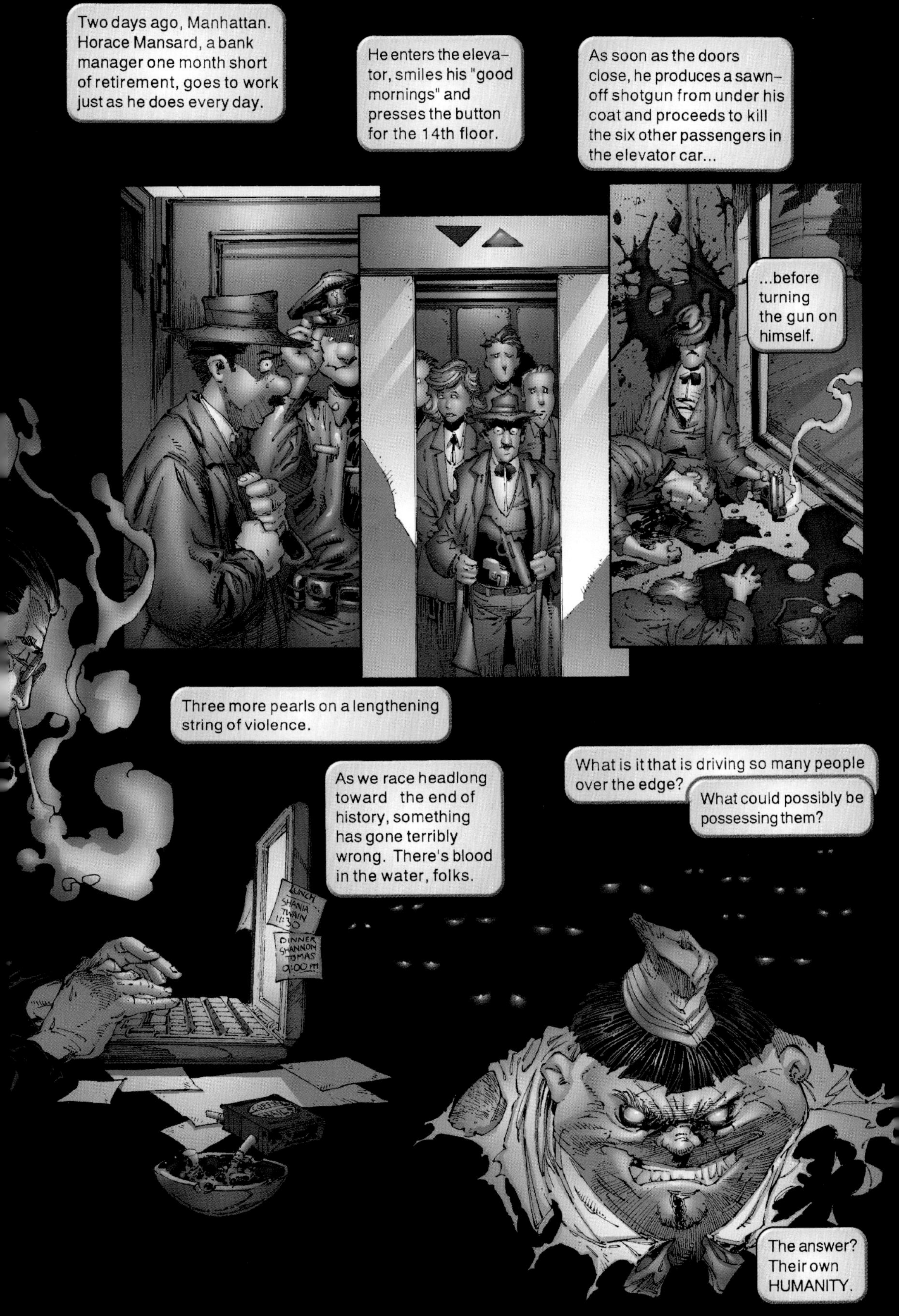
Two days ago, Manhattan. Horace Mansard, a bank manager one month short of retirement, goes to work just as he does every day.
He enters the elevator, smiles his "good mornings" and presses the button for the 14th floor.
As soon as the doors close, he produces a sawn-off shotgun from under his coat and proceeds to kill the six other passengers in the elevator car...
...before turning the gun on himself.
Three more pearls on a lengthening string of violence.
As we race headlong toward the end of history, something has gone terribly wrong. There's blood in the water, folks.
What is it that is driving so many people over the edge?
What could possibly be possessing them?
LUNCH SHANIA TWAIN 11:30
DINNER SHANNON TOMAS 9:00 PM
The answer? Their own HUMANITY.

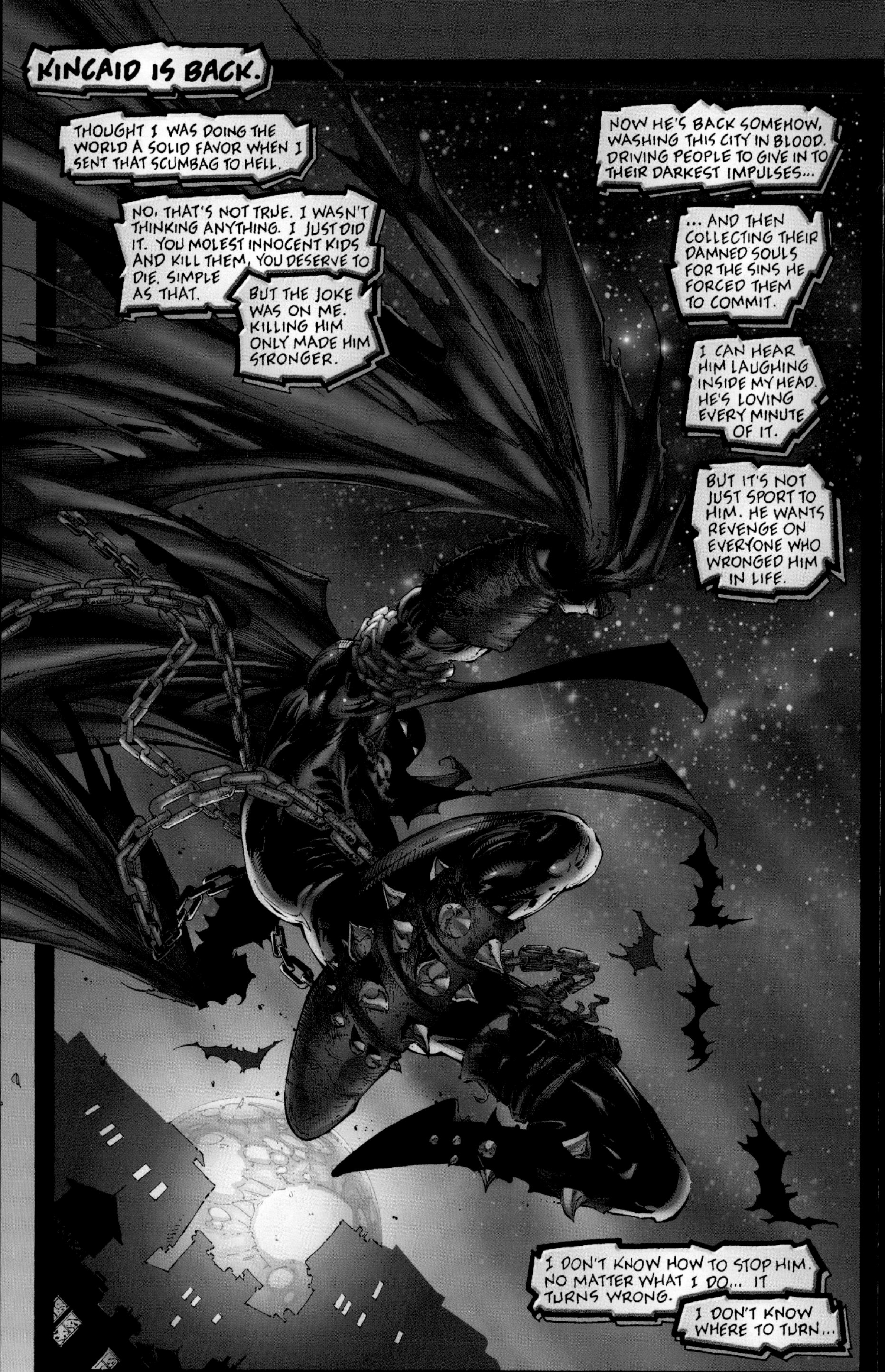
KINCAID IS BACK.
THOUGHT I WAS DOING THE WORLD A SOLID FAVOR WHEN I SENT THAT SCUMBAG TO HELL.
NO, THAT'S NOT TRUE. I WASN'T THINKING ANYTHING. I JUST DID IT. YOU MOLEST INNOCENT KIDS AND KILL THEM, YOU DESERVE TO DIE. SIMPLE AS THAT.
BUT THE JOKE WAS ON ME. KILLING HIM ONLY MADE HIM STRONGER.
NOW HE'S BACK SOMEHOW, WASHING THIS CITY IN BLOOD. DRIVING PEOPLE TO GIVE IN TO THEIR DARKEST IMPULSES...
... AND THEN COLLECTING THEIR DAMNED SOULS FOR THE SINS HE FORCED THEM TO COMMIT.
I CAN HEAR HIM LAUGHING INSIDE MY HEAD. HE'S LOVING EVERY MINUTE OF IT.
BUT IT'S NOT JUST SPORT TO HIM. HE WANTS REVENGE ON EVERYONE WHO WRONGED HIM IN LIFE.
I DON'T KNOW HOW TO STOP HIM. NO MATTER WHAT I DO... IT TURNS WRONG.
I DON'T KNOW WHERE TO TURN...

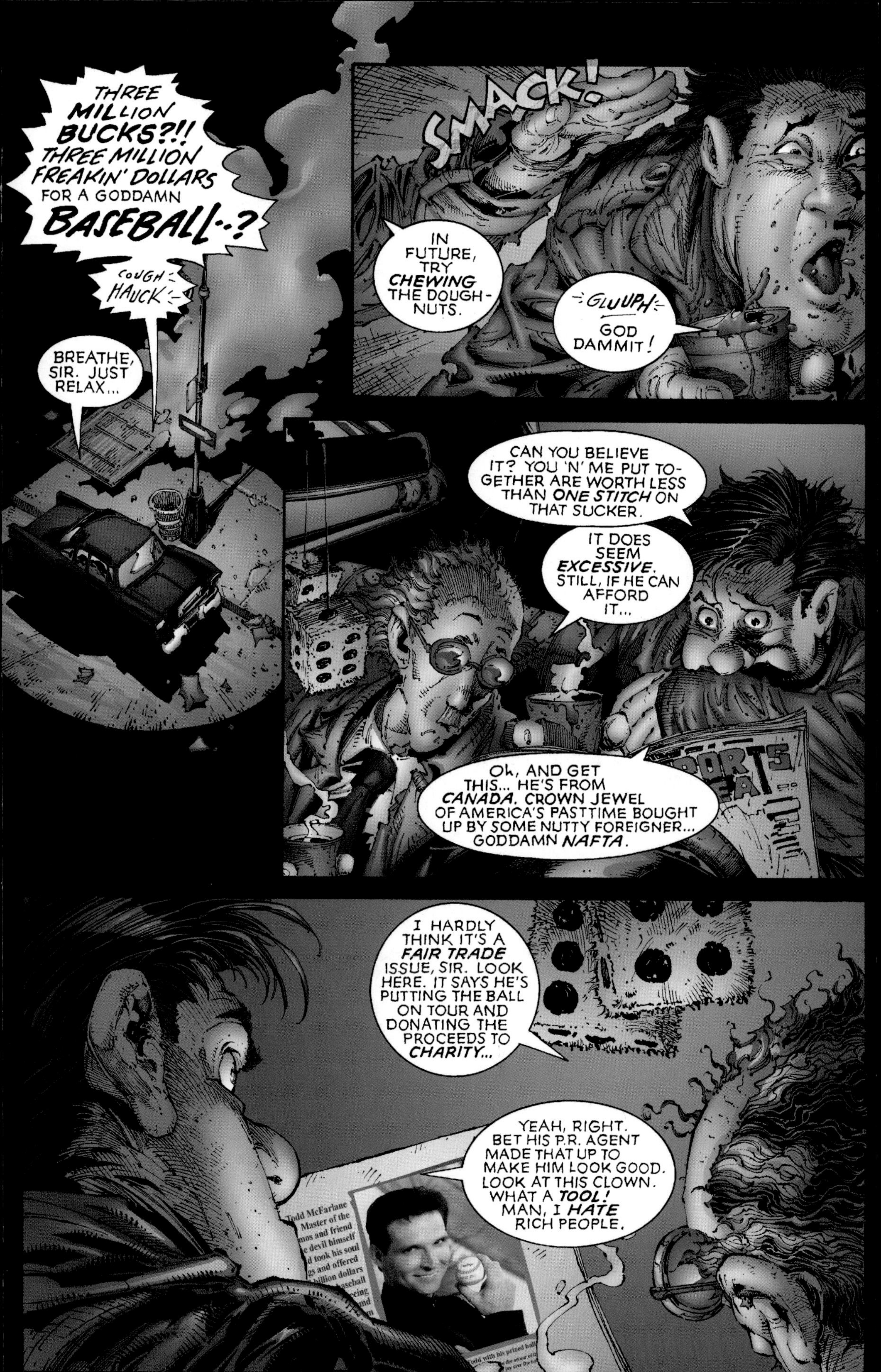
THREE MILLION BUCKS?!! THREE MILLION FREAKIN' DOLLARS FOR A GODDAMN BASEBALL..?
COUGH-HAUCK
BREATHE, SIR. JUST RELAX...
SMACK!
IN FUTURE, TRY CHEWING THE DOUGH-NUTS.
GLUUPH
GOD DAMMIT!
CAN YOU BELIEVE IT? YOU 'N' ME PUT TO-GETHER ARE WORTH LESS THAN ONE STITCH ON THAT SUCKER.
IT DOES SEEM EXCESSIVE. STILL, IF HE CAN AFFORD IT...
Oh, AND GET THIS... HE'S FROM CANADA. CROWN JEWEL OF AMERICA'S PASTTIME BOUGHT UP BY SOME NUTTY FOREIGNER... GODDAMN NAFTA.
I HARDLY THINK IT'S A FAIR TRADE ISSUE, SIR. LOOK HERE. IT SAYS HE'S PUTTING THE BALL ON TOUR AND DONATING THE PROCEEDS TO CHARITY...
YEAH, RIGHT. BET HIS P.R. AGENT MADE THAT UP TO MAKE HIM LOOK GOOD. LOOK AT THIS CLOWN. WHAT A TOOL! MAN, I HATE RICH PEOPLE.
Todd McFarlane

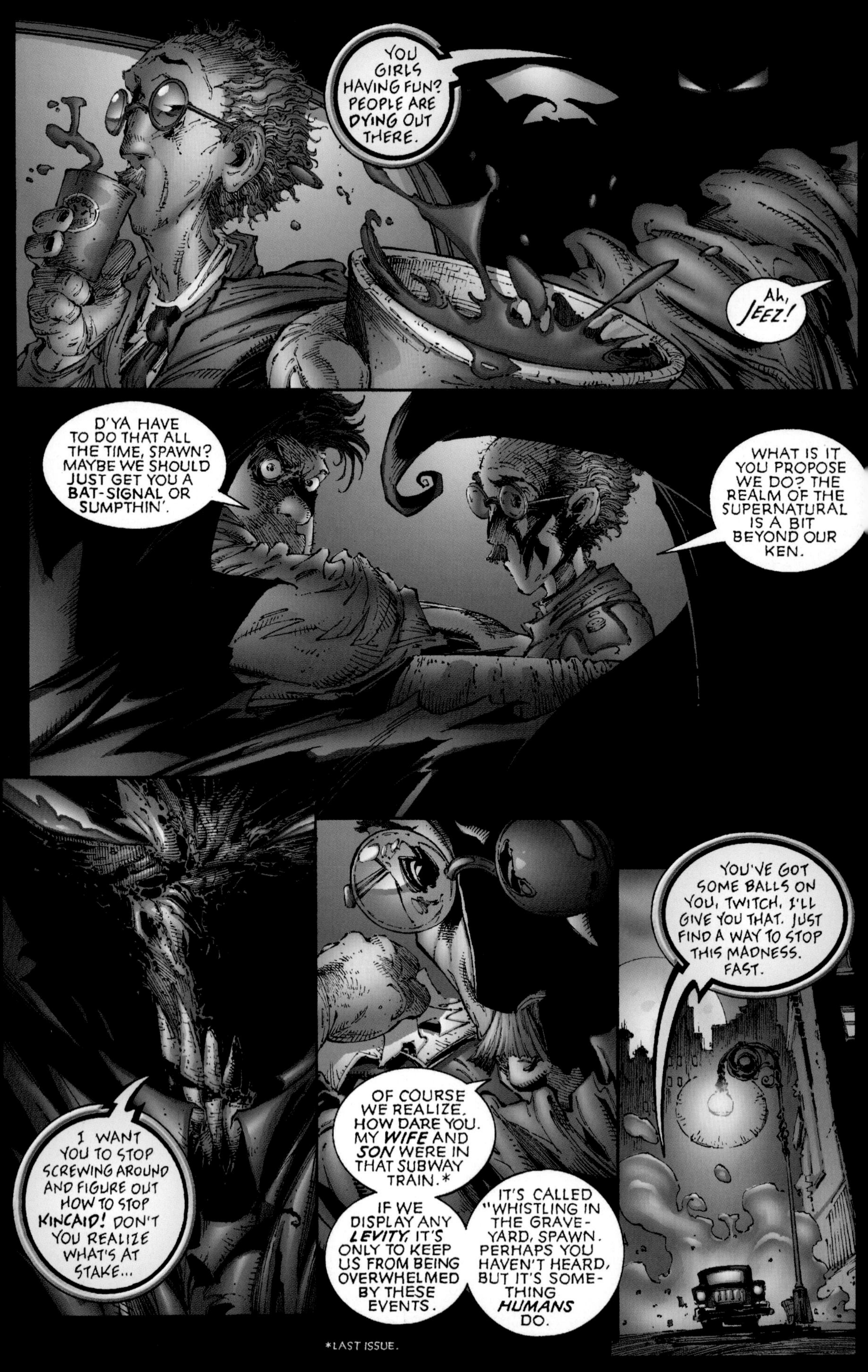
YOU GIRLS HAVING FUN? PEOPLE ARE DYING OUT THERE.
Ah, JEEZ!
D'YA HAVE TO DO THAT ALL THE TIME, SPAWN? MAYBE WE SHOULD JUST GET YOU A BAT-SIGNAL OR SUMPTHIN'.
WHAT IS IT YOU PROPOSE WE DO? THE REALM OF THE SUPERNATURAL IS A BIT BEYOND OUR KEN.
I WANT YOU TO STOP SCREWING AROUND AND FIGURE OUT HOW TO STOP KINCAID! DON'T YOU REALIZE WHAT'S AT STAKE...
OF COURSE WE REALIZE. HOW DARE YOU. MY WIFE AND SON WERE IN THAT SUBWAY TRAIN.*
IF WE DISPLAY ANY LEVITY, IT'S ONLY TO KEEP US FROM BEING OVERWHELMED BY THESE EVENTS.
IT'S CALLED "WHISTLING IN THE GRAVE-YARD, SPAWN. PERHAPS YOU HAVEN'T HEARD, BUT IT'S SOME-THING HUMANS DO.
YOU'VE GOT SOME BALLS ON YOU, TWITCH. I'LL GIVE YOU THAT. JUST FIND A WAY TO STOP THIS MADNESS. FAST.

*LAST ISSUE.

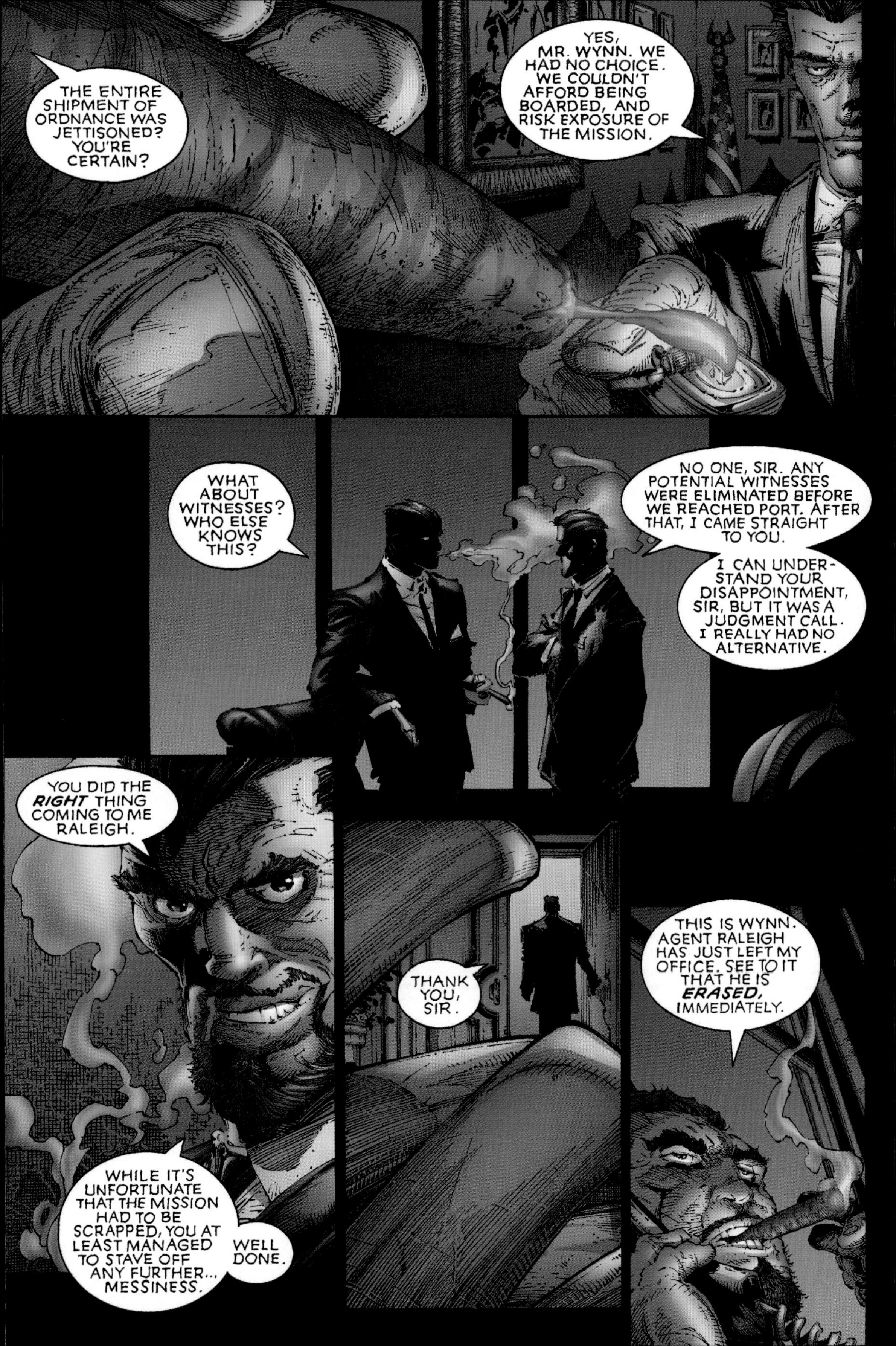
THE ENTIRE SHIPMENT OF ORDNANCE WAS JETTISONED? YOU'RE CERTAIN?
YES, MR. WYNN. WE HAD NO CHOICE. WE COULDN'T AFFORD BEING BOARDED, AND RISK EXPOSURE OF THE MISSION.
WHAT ABOUT WITNESSES? WHO ELSE KNOWS THIS?
NO ONE, SIR. ANY POTENTIAL WITNESSES WERE ELIMINATED BEFORE WE REACHED PORT. AFTER THAT, I CAME STRAIGHT TO YOU.
I CAN UNDER-STAND YOUR DISAPPOINTMENT, SIR, BUT IT WAS A JUDGMENT CALL. I REALLY HAD NO ALTERNATIVE.
YOU DID THE *RIGHT* THING COMING TO ME RALEIGH.
WHILE IT'S UNFORTUNATE THAT THE MISSION HAD TO BE SCRAPPED, YOU AT LEAST MANAGED TO STAVE OFF ANY FURTHER... MESSINESS.
WELL DONE.
THANK YOU, SIR.
THIS IS WYNN. AGENT RALEIGH HAS JUST LEFT MY OFFICE. SEE TO IT THAT HE IS ***ERASED,*** IMMEDIATELY.

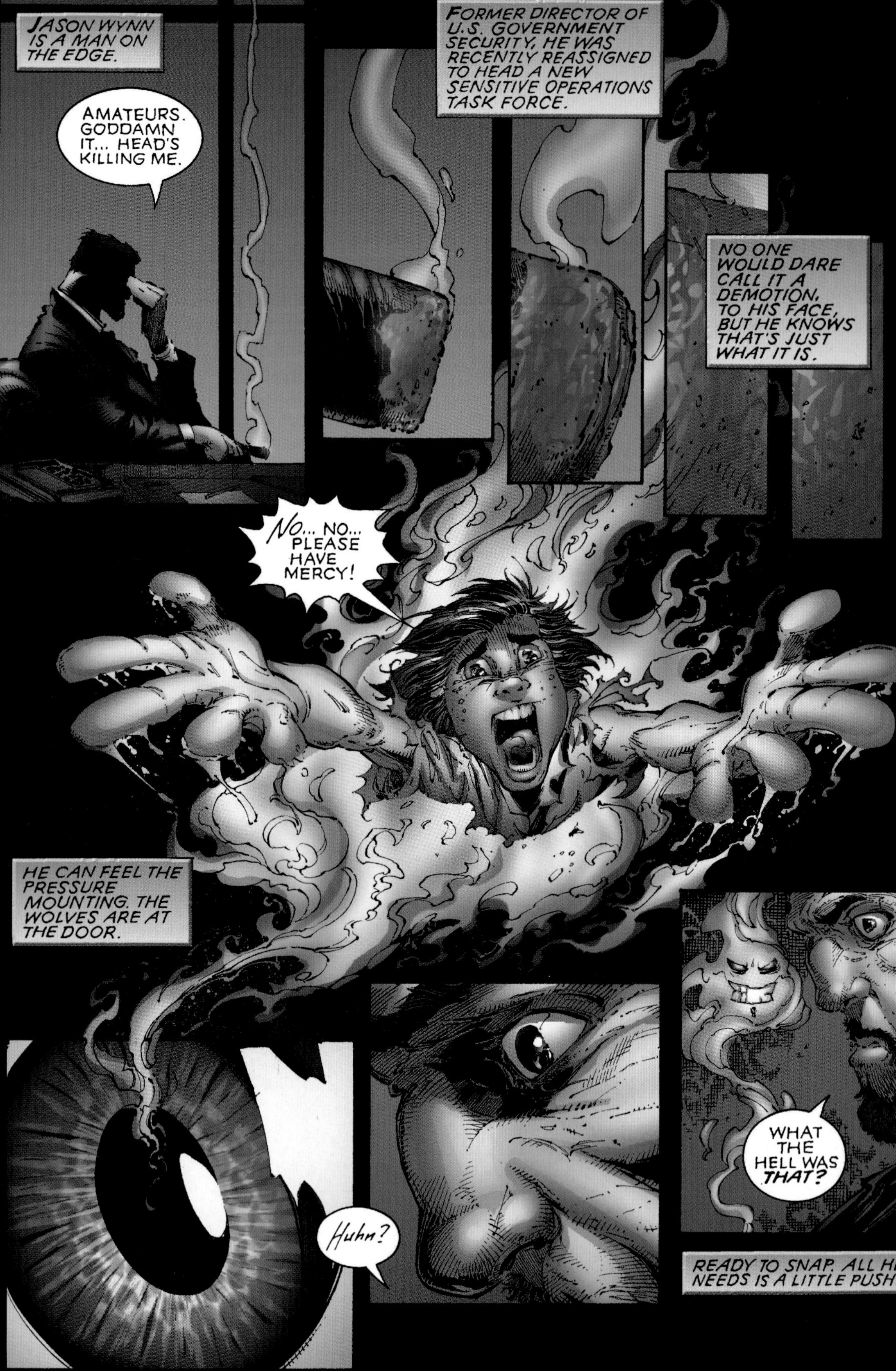
JASON WYNN IS A MAN ON THE EDGE.
AMATEURS. GODDAMN IT... HEAD'S KILLING ME.
FORMER DIRECTOR OF U.S. GOVERNMENT SECURITY, HE WAS RECENTLY REASSIGNED TO HEAD A NEW SENSITIVE OPERATIONS TASK FORCE.
NO ONE WOULD DARE CALL IT A DEMOTION, TO HIS FACE, BUT HE KNOWS THAT'S JUST WHAT IT IS.
NO... NO... PLEASE HAVE MERCY!
HE CAN FEEL THE PRESSURE MOUNTING. THE WOLVES ARE AT THE DOOR.
Huhn?
WHAT THE HELL WAS THAT?
READY TO SNAP. ALL HE NEEDS IS A LITTLE PUSH

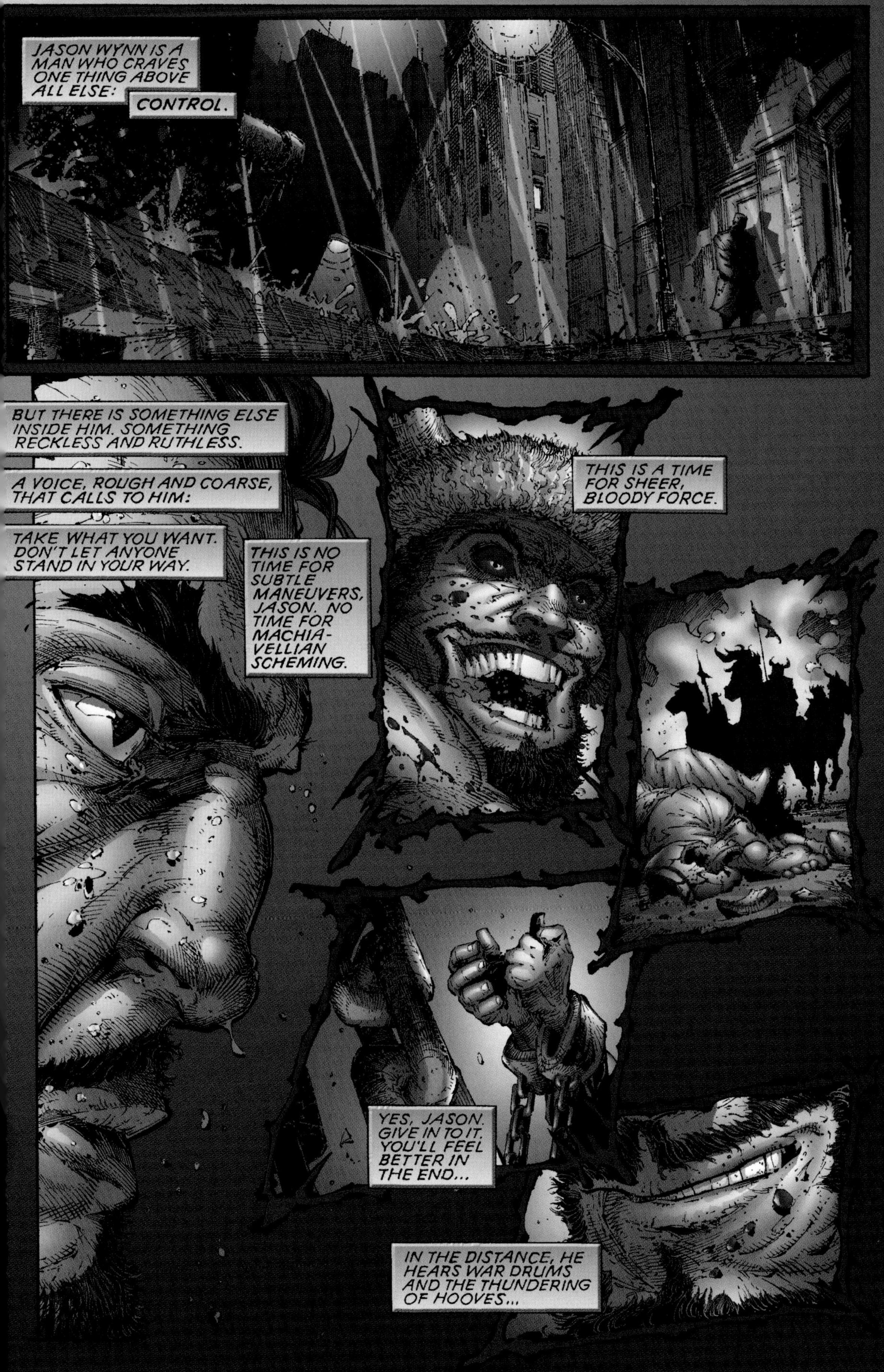
JASON WYNN IS A MAN WHO CRAVES ONE THING ABOVE ALL ELSE:
CONTROL.
BUT THERE IS SOMETHING ELSE INSIDE HIM. SOMETHING RECKLESS AND RUTHLESS.
A VOICE, ROUGH AND COARSE, THAT CALLS TO HIM:
TAKE WHAT YOU WANT. DON'T LET ANYONE STAND IN YOUR WAY.
THIS IS NO TIME FOR SUBTLE MANEUVERS, JASON. NO TIME FOR MACHIA-VELLIAN SCHEMING.
THIS IS A TIME FOR SHEER, BLOODY FORCE.
YES, JASON. GIVE IN TO IT. YOU'LL FEEL BETTER IN THE END...
IN THE DISTANCE, HE HEARS WAR DRUMS AND THE THUNDERING OF HOOVES...

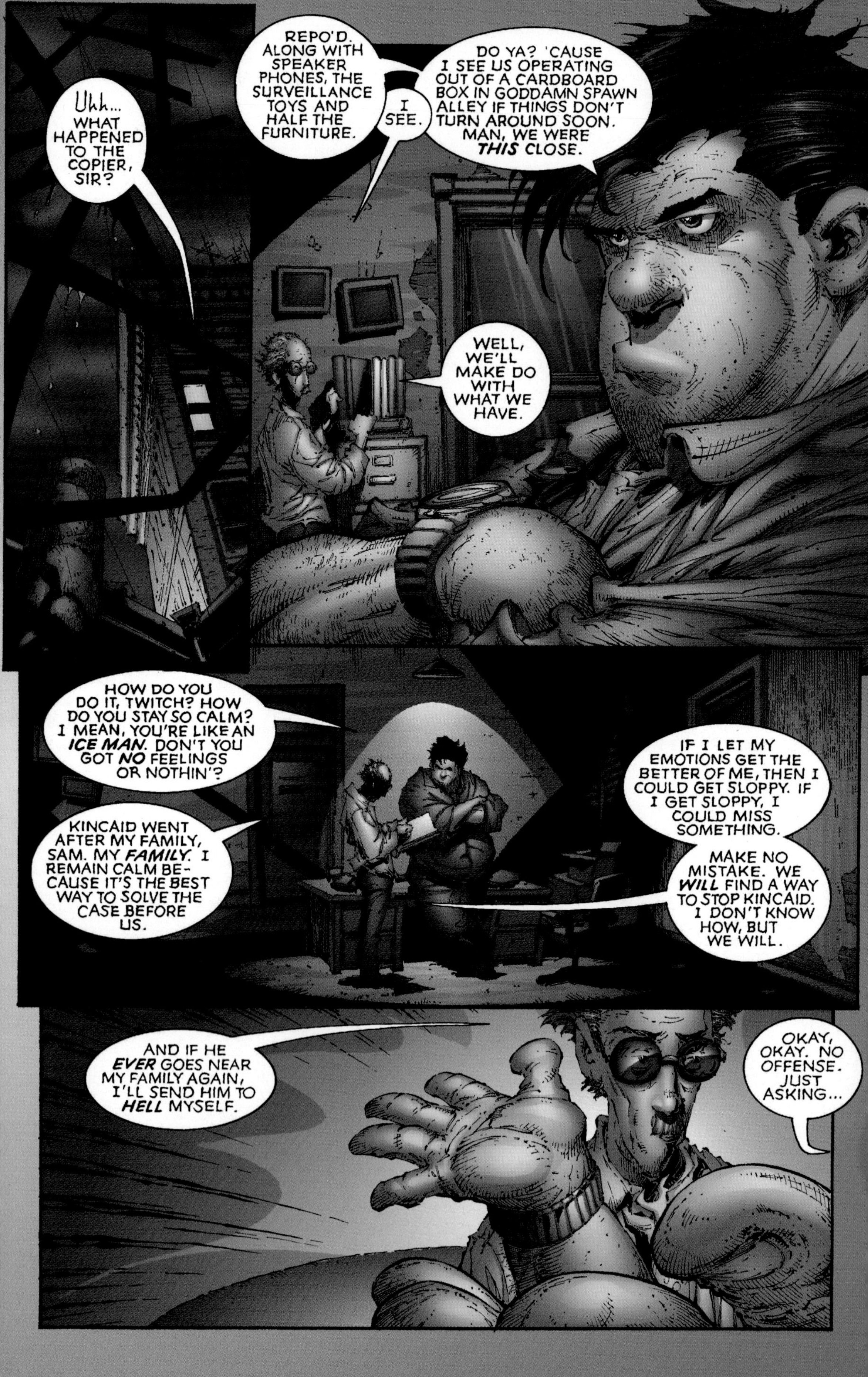
Uhh... WHAT HAPPENED TO THE COPIER, SIR?
REPO'D. ALONG WITH SPEAKER PHONES, THE SURVEILLANCE TOYS AND HALF THE FURNITURE.
I SEE.
DO YA? 'CAUSE I SEE US OPERATING OUT OF A CARDBOARD BOX IN GODDAMN SPAWN ALLEY IF THINGS DON'T TURN AROUND SOON. MAN, WE WERE THIS CLOSE.
WELL, WE'LL MAKE DO WITH WHAT WE HAVE.
HOW DO YOU DO IT, TWITCH? HOW DO YOU STAY SO CALM? I MEAN, YOU'RE LIKE AN ICE MAN. DON'T YOU GOT NO FEELINGS OR NOTHIN'?
KINCAID WENT AFTER MY FAMILY, SAM. MY FAMILY. I REMAIN CALM BE-CAUSE IT'S THE BEST WAY TO SOLVE THE CASE BEFORE US.
IF I LET MY EMOTIONS GET THE BETTER OF ME, THEN I COULD GET SLOPPY. IF I GET SLOPPY, I COULD MISS SOMETHING.
MAKE NO MISTAKE. WE WILL FIND A WAY TO STOP KINCAID. I DON'T KNOW HOW, BUT WE WILL.
AND IF HE EVER GOES NEAR MY FAMILY AGAIN, I'LL SEND HIM TO HELL MYSELF.
OKAY, OKAY. NO OFFENSE. JUST ASKING...

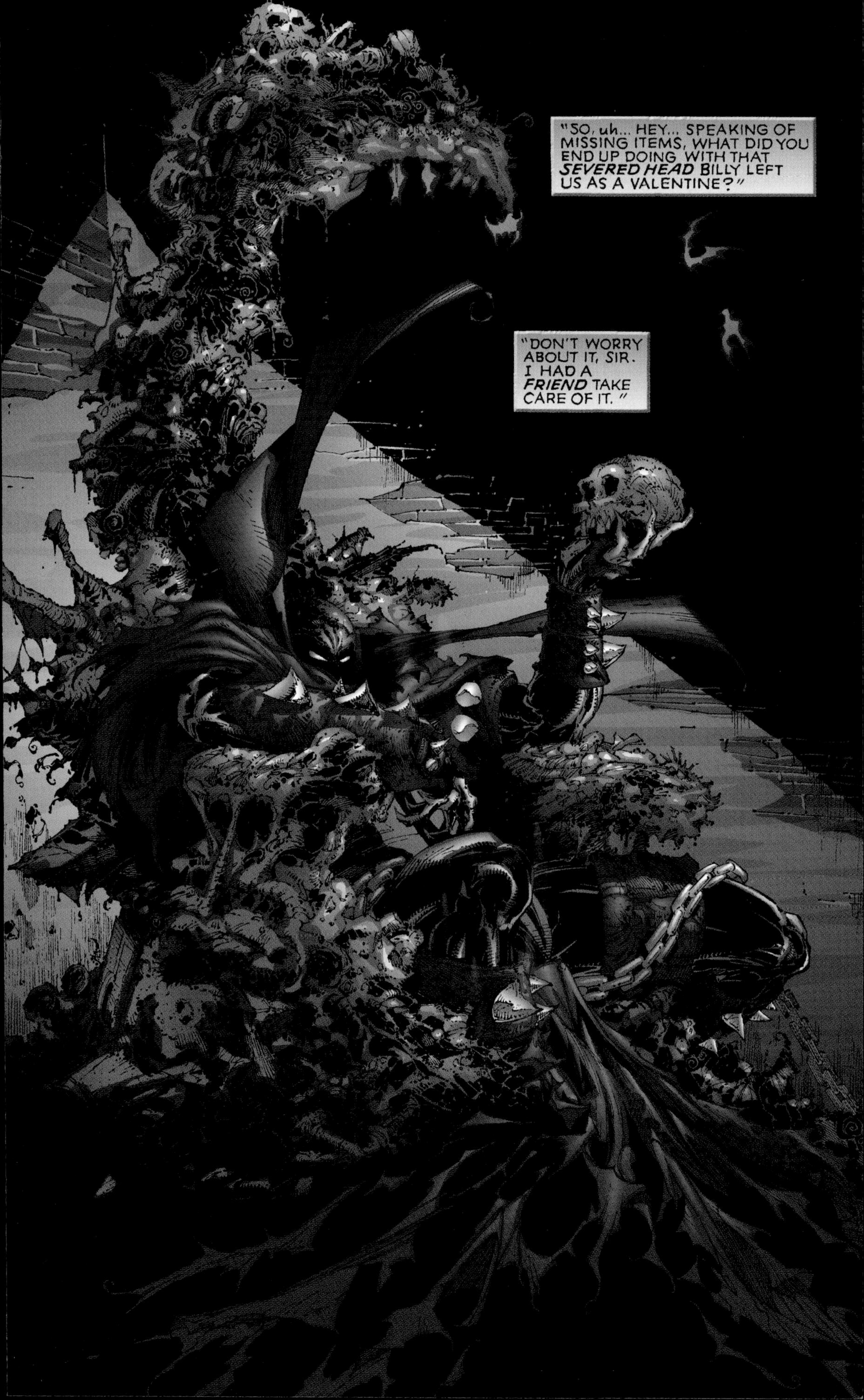
"SO, uh... HEY... SPEAKING OF MISSING ITEMS, WHAT DID YOU END UP DOING WITH THAT SEVERED HEAD BILLY LEFT US AS A VALENTINE?"
"DON'T WORRY ABOUT IT, SIR. I HAD A FRIEND TAKE CARE OF IT."

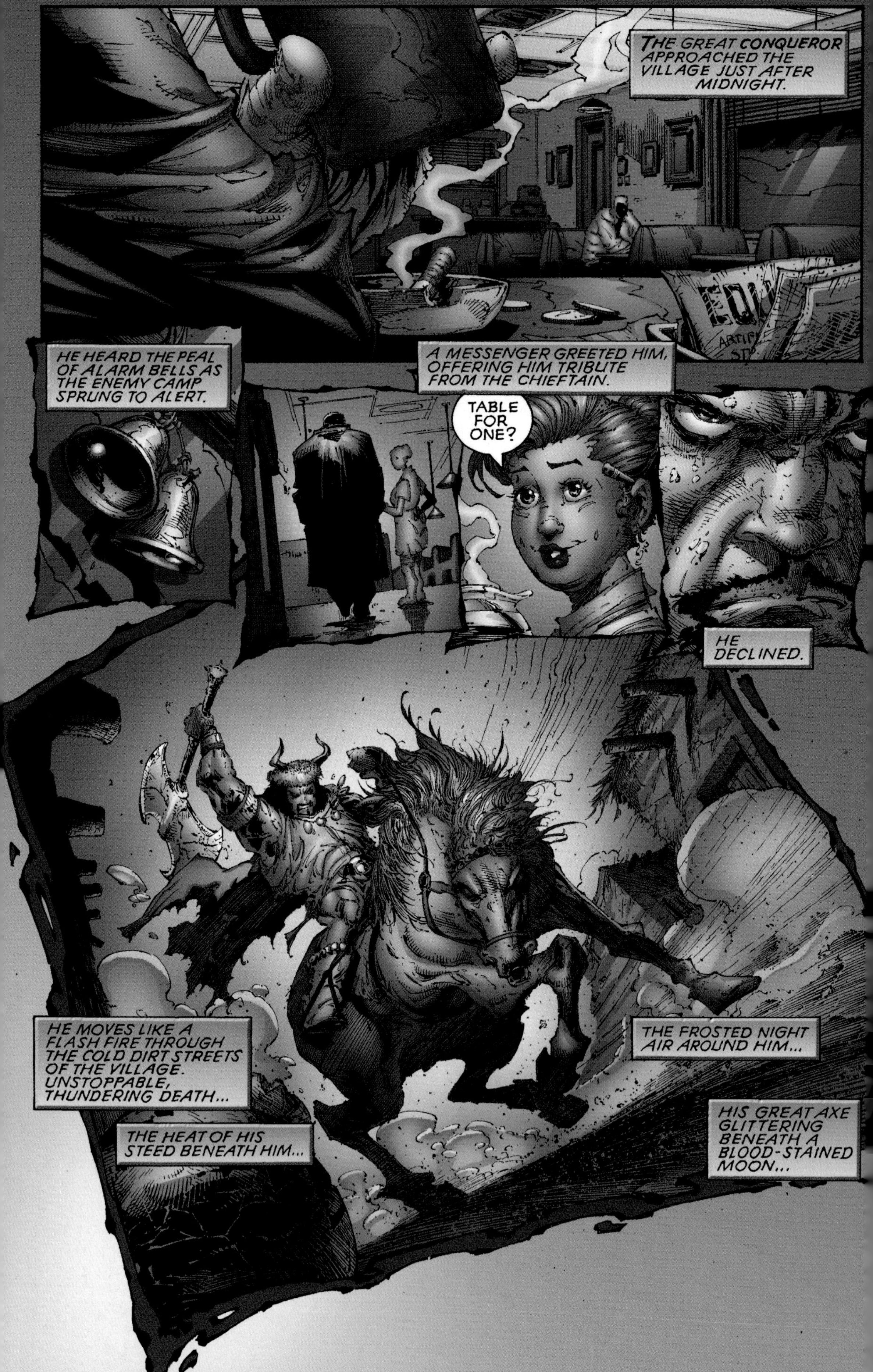
THE GREAT CONQUEROR APPROACHED THE VILLAGE JUST AFTER MIDNIGHT.
HE HEARD THE PEAL OF ALARM BELLS AS THE ENEMY CAMP SPRUNG TO ALERT.
A MESSENGER GREETED HIM, OFFERING HIM TRIBUTE FROM THE CHIEFTAIN.
TABLE FOR ONE?
HE DECLINED.
HE MOVES LIKE A FLASH FIRE THROUGH THE COLD DIRT STREETS OF THE VILLAGE. UNSTOPPABLE, THUNDERING DEATH...
THE HEAT OF HIS STEED BENEATH HIM...
THE FROSTED NIGHT AIR AROUND HIM...
HIS GREAT AXE GLITTERING BENEATH A BLOOD-STAINED MOON...

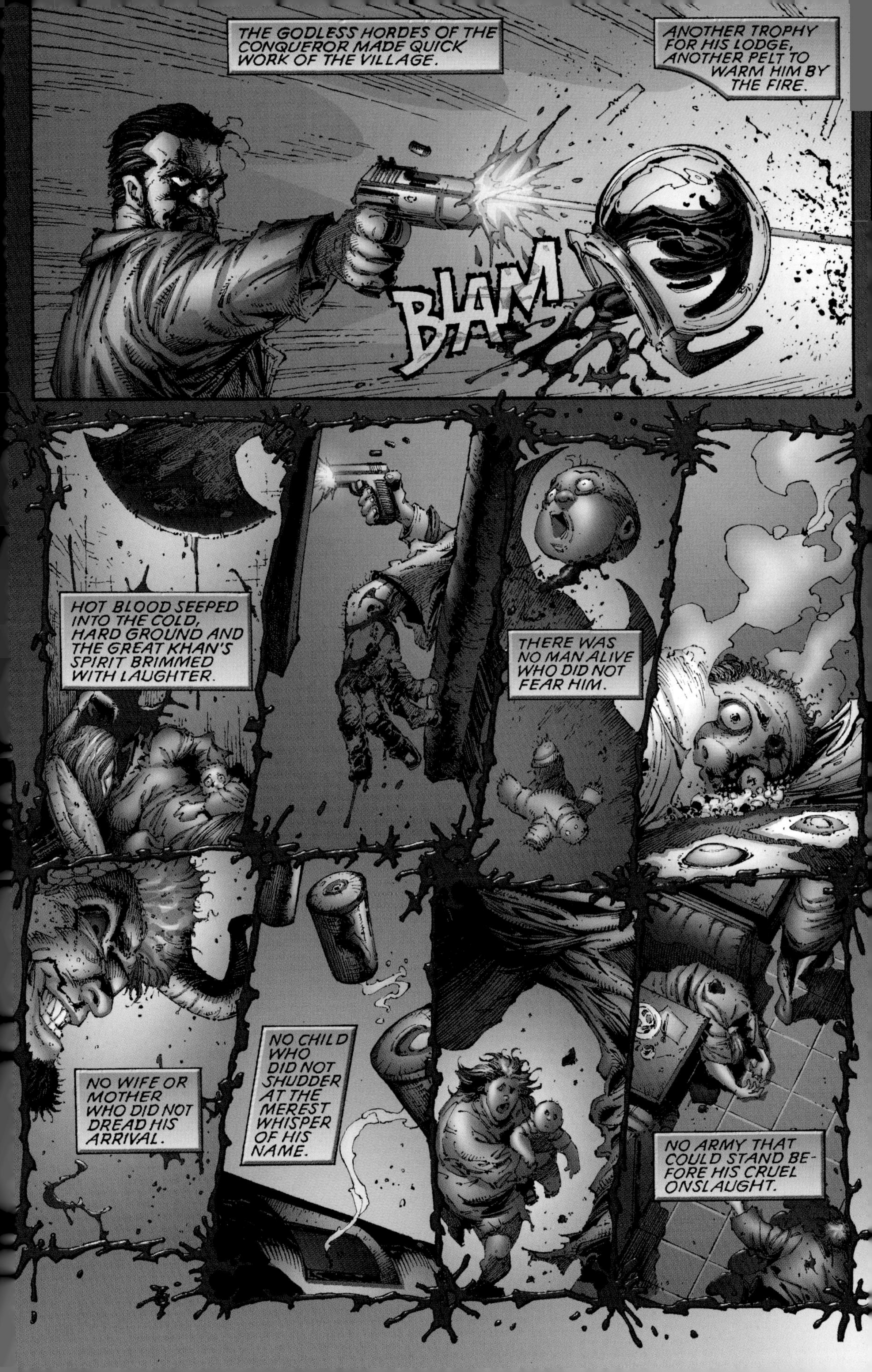
THE GODLESS HORDES OF THE CONQUEROR MADE QUICK WORK OF THE VILLAGE.
ANOTHER TROPHY FOR HIS LODGE, ANOTHER PELT TO WARM HIM BY THE FIRE.
BLAM
HOT BLOOD SEEPED INTO THE COLD, HARD GROUND AND THE GREAT KHAN'S SPIRIT BRIMMED WITH LAUGHTER.
THERE WAS NO MAN ALIVE WHO DID NOT FEAR HIM.
NO WIFE OR MOTHER WHO DID NOT DREAD HIS ARRIVAL.
NO CHILD WHO DID NOT SHUDDER AT THE MEREST WHISPER OF HIS NAME.
NO ARMY THAT COULD STAND BEFORE HIS CRUEL ONSLAUGHT.

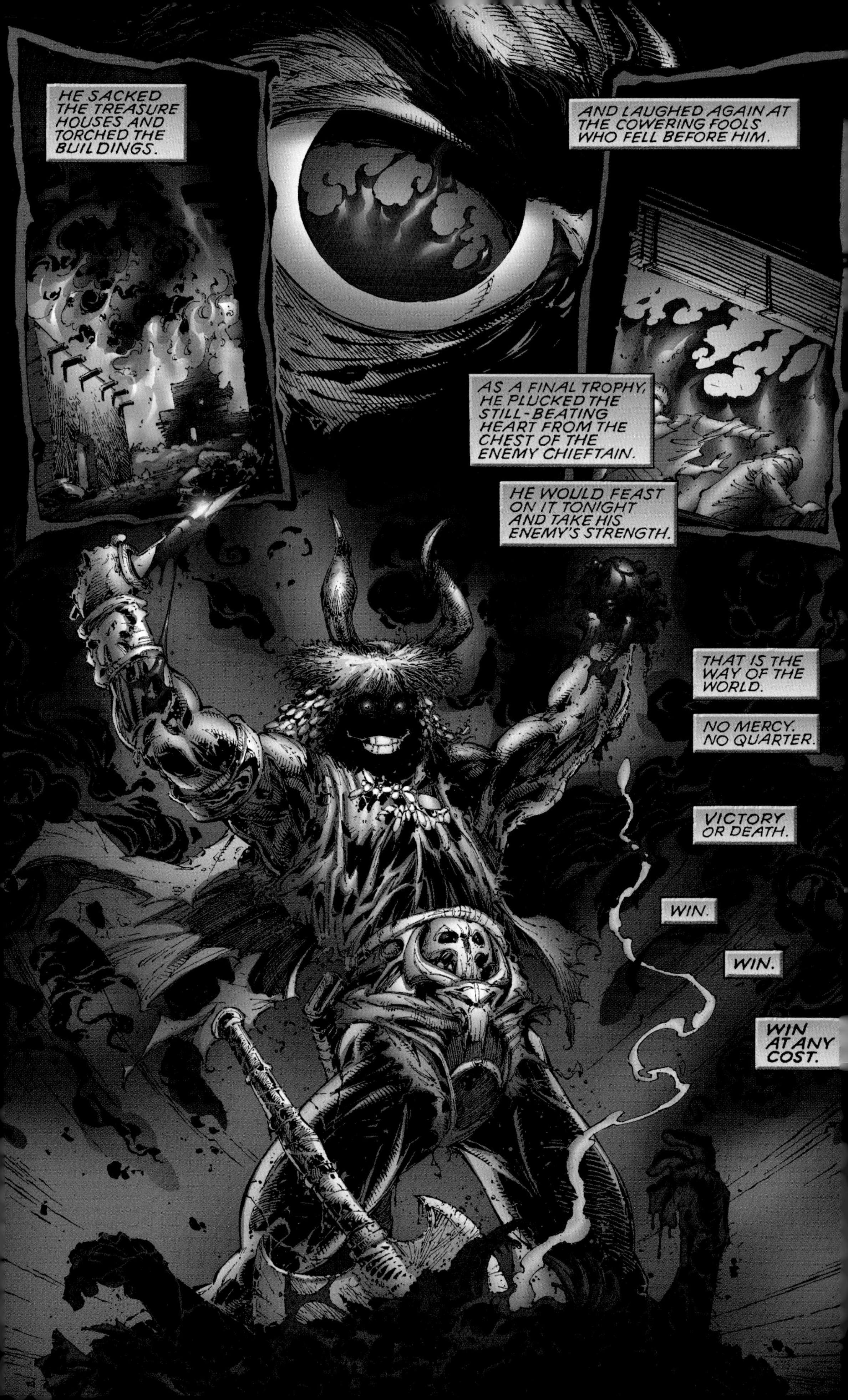
HE SACKED THE TREASURE HOUSES AND TORCHED THE BUILDINGS.
AND LAUGHED AGAIN AT THE COWERING FOOLS WHO FELL BEFORE HIM.
AS A FINAL TROPHY, HE PLUCKED THE STILL-BEATING HEART FROM THE CHEST OF THE ENEMY CHIEFTAIN.
HE WOULD FEAST ON IT TONIGHT AND TAKE HIS ENEMY'S STRENGTH.
THAT IS THE WAY OF THE WORLD.
NO MERCY. NO QUARTER.
VICTORY OR DEATH.
WIN.
WIN.
WIN AT ANY COST.

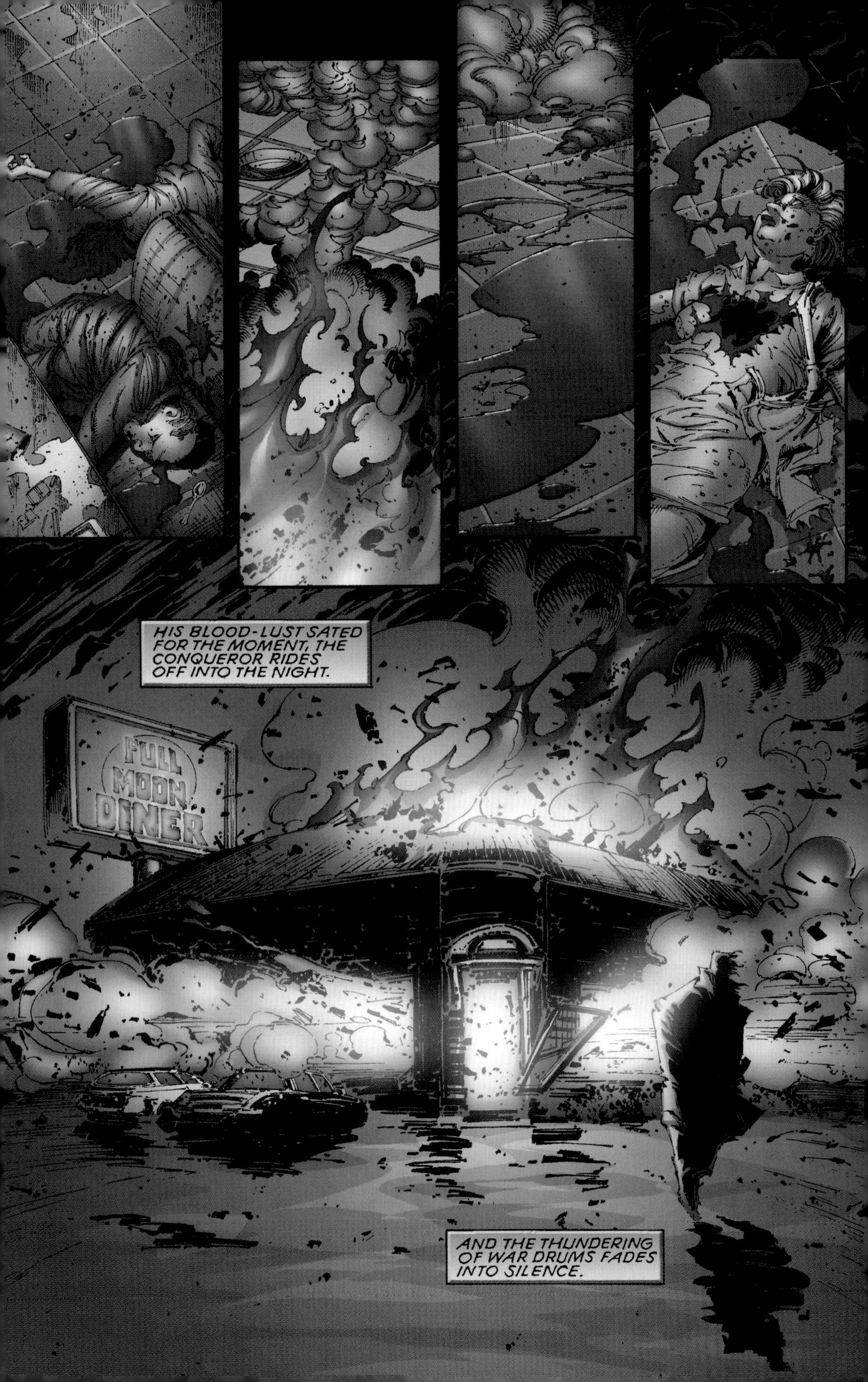
HIS BLOOD-LUST SATED FOR THE MOMENT, THE CONQUEROR RIDES OFF INTO THE NIGHT.
FULL MOON DINER
AND THE THUNDERING OF WAR DRUMS FADES INTO SILENCE.

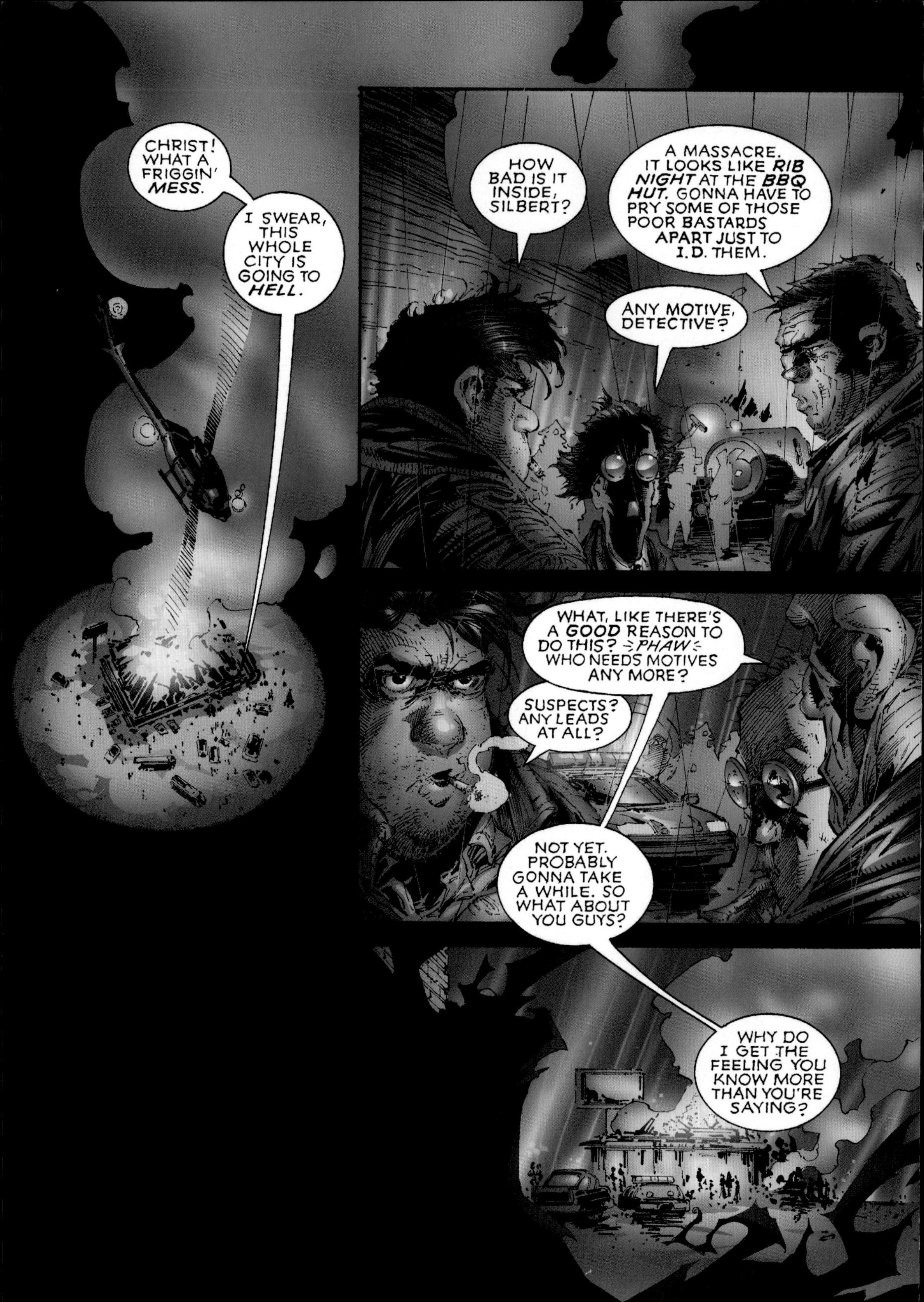
CHRIST! WHAT A FRIGGIN' MESS.
I SWEAR, THIS WHOLE CITY IS GOING TO HELL.
HOW BAD IS IT INSIDE, SILBERT?
A MASSACRE. IT LOOKS LIKE RIB NIGHT AT THE BBQ HUT. GONNA HAVE TO PRY SOME OF THOSE POOR BASTARDS APART JUST TO I.D. THEM.
ANY MOTIVE, DETECTIVE?
WHAT, LIKE THERE'S A GOOD REASON TO DO THIS? PHAW WHO NEEDS MOTIVES ANY MORE?
SUSPECTS? ANY LEADS AT ALL?
NOT YET. PROBABLY GONNA TAKE A WHILE. SO WHAT ABOUT YOU GUYS?
WHY DO I GET THE FEELING YOU KNOW MORE THAN YOU'RE SAYING?

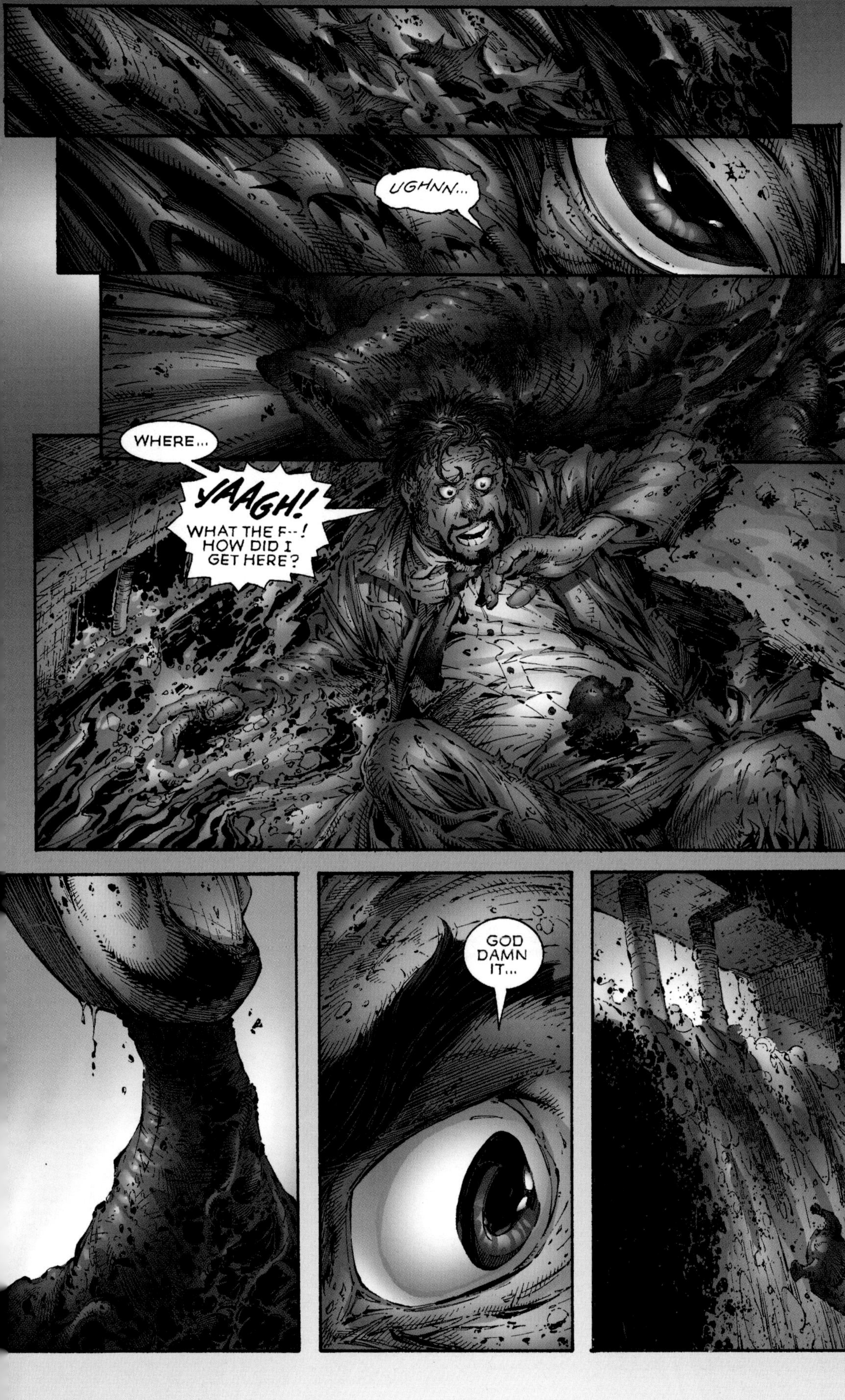
UGHNN...
WHERE...
YAAGH!
WHAT THE F--! HOW DID I GET HERE?
GOD DAMN IT...

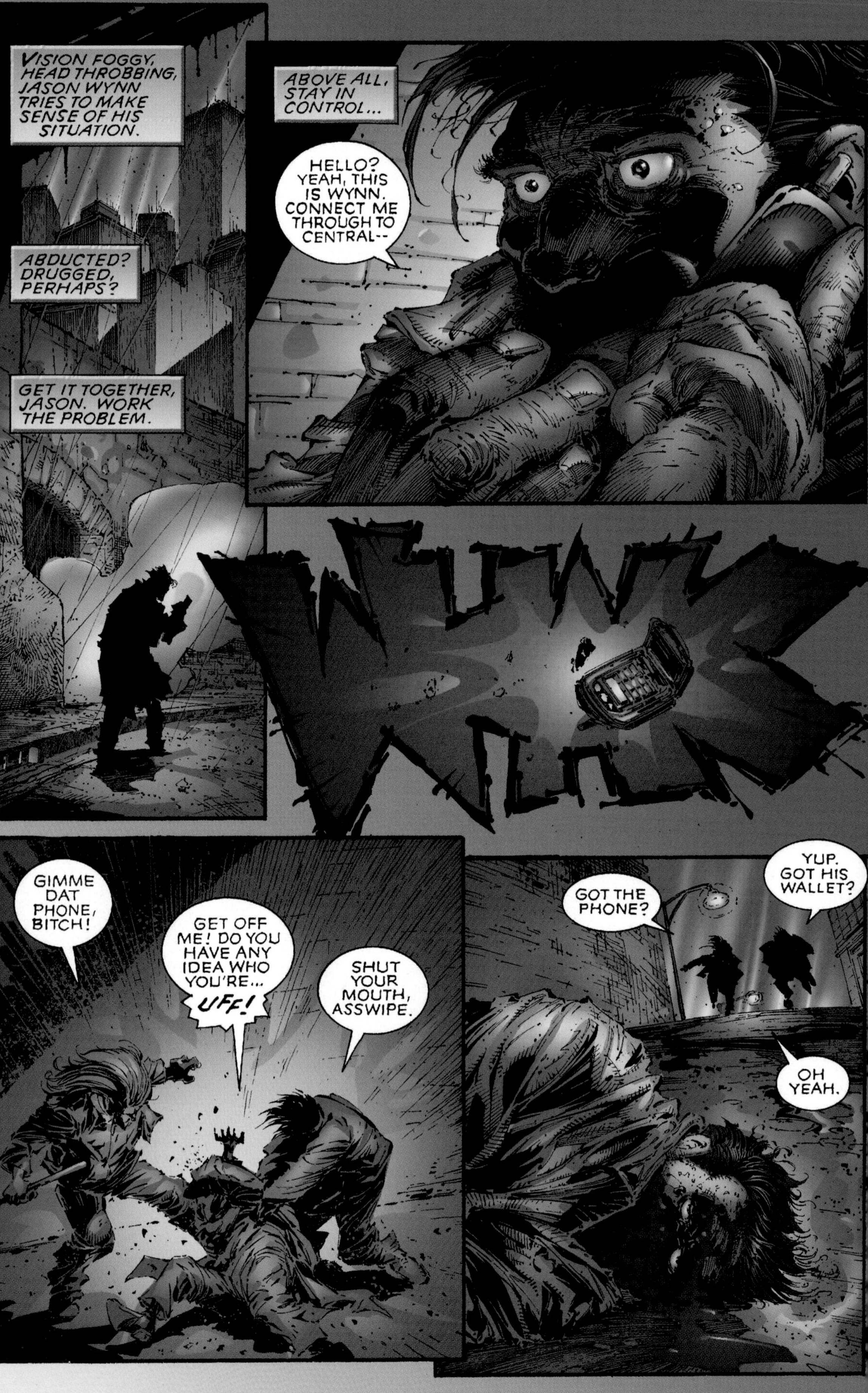
VISION FOGGY, HEAD THROBBING, JASON WYNN TRIES TO MAKE SENSE OF HIS SITUATION.
ABDUCTED? DRUGGED, PERHAPS?
GET IT TOGETHER, JASON. WORK THE PROBLEM.
ABOVE ALL, STAY IN CONTROL...
HELLO? YEAH, THIS IS WYNN. CONNECT ME THROUGH TO CENTRAL--
GIMME DAT PHONE, BITCH!
GET OFF ME! DO YOU HAVE ANY IDEA WHO YOU'RE...
UFF!
SHUT YOUR MOUTH, ASSWIPE.
GOT THE PHONE?
YUP. GOT HIS WALLET?
OH YEAH.

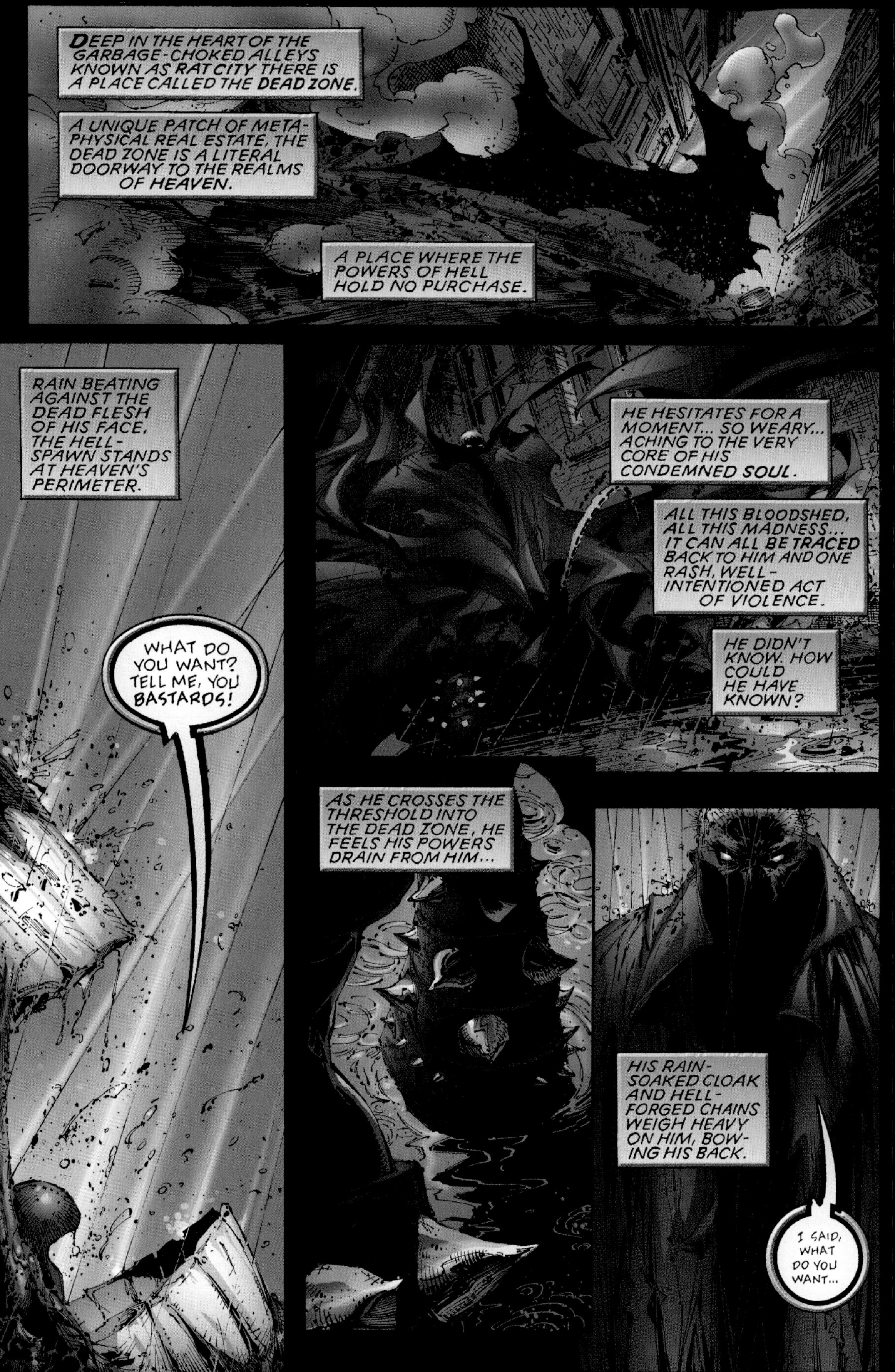
DEEP IN THE HEART OF THE GARBAGE-CHOKED ALLEYS KNOWN AS RAT CITY THERE IS A PLACE CALLED THE DEAD ZONE.
A UNIQUE PATCH OF META-PHYSICAL REAL ESTATE, THE DEAD ZONE IS A LITERAL DOORWAY TO THE REALMS OF HEAVEN.
A PLACE WHERE THE POWERS OF HELL HOLD NO PURCHASE.
RAIN BEATING AGAINST THE DEAD FLESH OF HIS FACE, THE HELL-SPAWN STANDS AT HEAVEN'S PERIMETER.
WHAT DO YOU WANT? TELL ME, YOU BASTARDS!
HE HESITATES FOR A MOMENT... SO WEARY... ACHING TO THE VERY CORE OF HIS CONDEMNED SOUL.
ALL THIS BLOODSHED, ALL THIS MADNESS... IT CAN ALL BE TRACED BACK TO HIM AND ONE RASH, WELL-INTENTIONED ACT OF VIOLENCE.
HE DIDN'T KNOW. HOW COULD HE HAVE KNOWN?
AS HE CROSSES THE THRESHOLD INTO THE DEAD ZONE, HE FEELS HIS POWERS DRAIN FROM HIM...
HIS RAIN-SOAKED CLOAK AND HELL-FORGED CHAINS WEIGH HEAVY ON HIM, BOWING HIS BACK.
I SAID, WHAT DO YOU WANT...

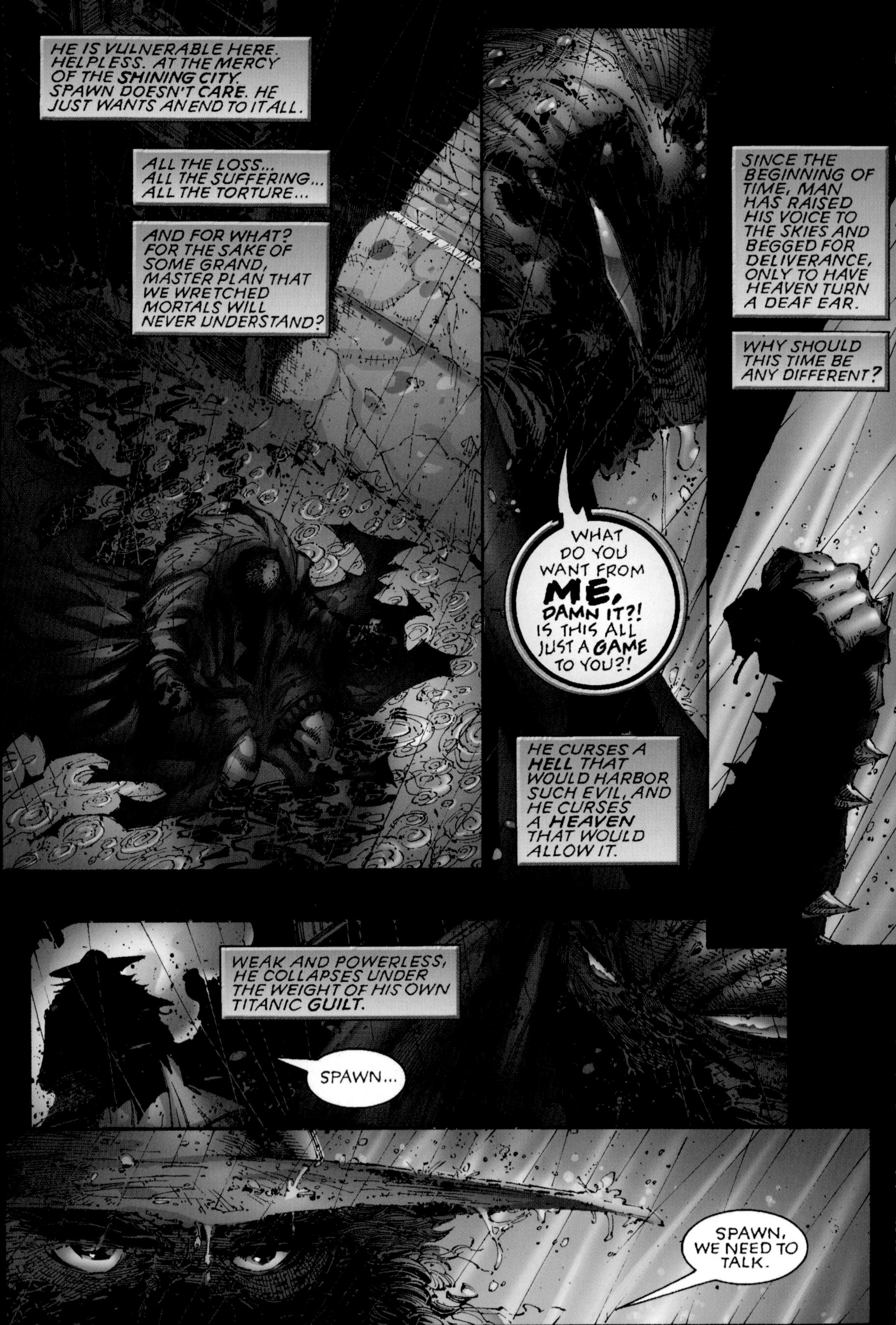
HE IS VULNERABLE HERE. HELPLESS. AT THE MERCY OF THE SHINING CITY. SPAWN DOESN'T CARE. HE JUST WANTS AN END TO IT ALL.
ALL THE LOSS... ALL THE SUFFERING... ALL THE TORTURE...
AND FOR WHAT? FOR THE SAKE OF SOME GRAND, MASTER PLAN THAT WE WRETCHED MORTALS WILL NEVER UNDERSTAND?
WHAT DO YOU WANT FROM ME, DAMN IT?! IS THIS ALL JUST A GAME TO YOU?!
SINCE THE BEGINNING OF TIME, MAN HAS RAISED HIS VOICE TO THE SKIES AND BEGGED FOR DELIVERANCE, ONLY TO HAVE HEAVEN TURN A DEAF EAR.
WHY SHOULD THIS TIME BE ANY DIFFERENT?
HE CURSES A HELL THAT WOULD HARBOR SUCH EVIL, AND HE CURSES A HEAVEN THAT WOULD ALLOW IT.
WEAK AND POWERLESS, HE COLLAPSES UNDER THE WEIGHT OF HIS OWN TITANIC GUILT.
SPAWN...
SPAWN, WE NEED TO TALK.

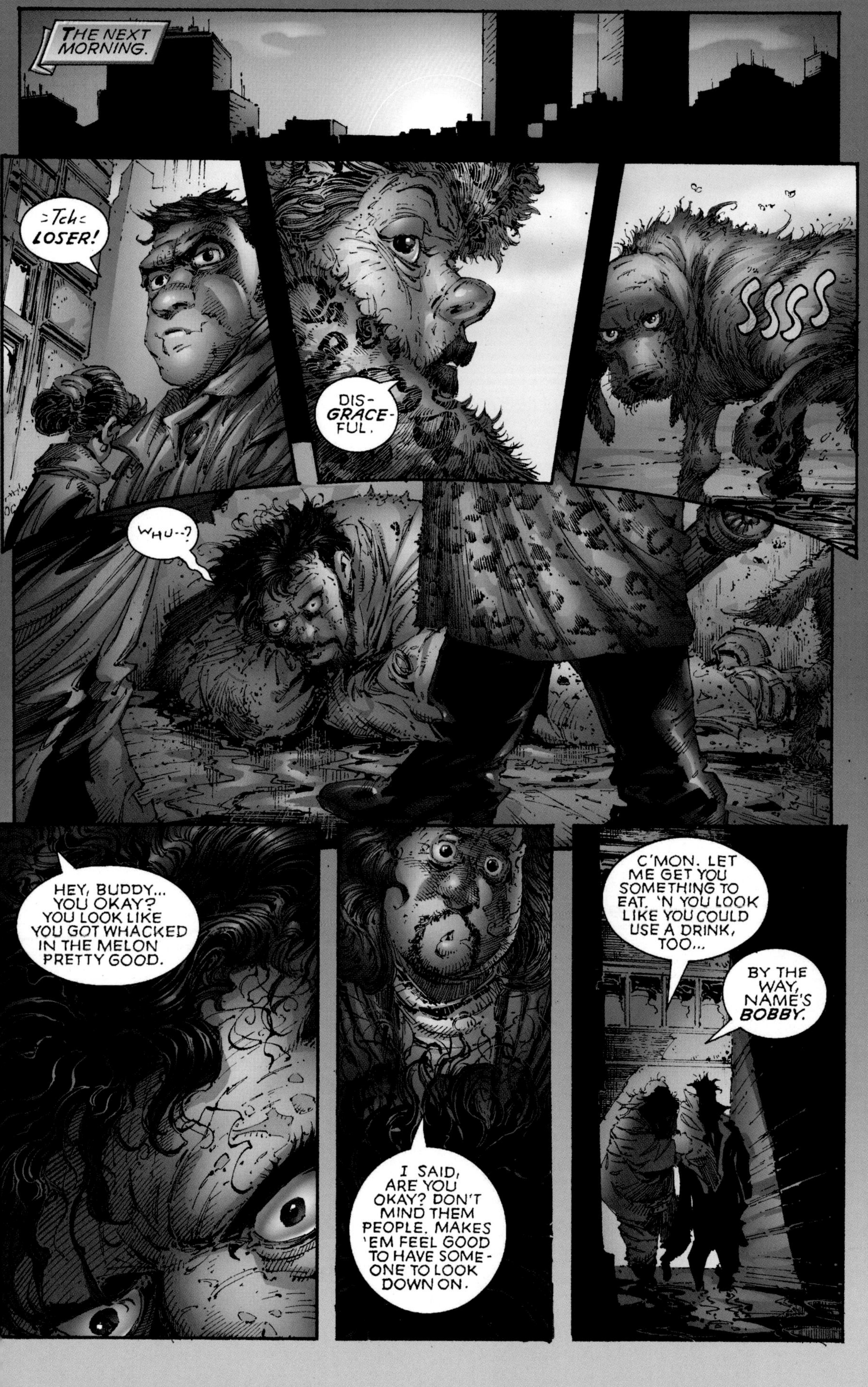
THE NEXT MORNING.
=Tch= LOSER!
DIS-GRACE-FUL.
SSSS
WHU--?
HEY, BUDDY... YOU OKAY? YOU LOOK LIKE YOU GOT WHACKED IN THE MELON PRETTY GOOD.
I SAID, ARE YOU OKAY? DON'T MIND THEM PEOPLE. MAKES 'EM FEEL GOOD TO HAVE SOME-ONE TO LOOK DOWN ON.
C'MON. LET ME GET YOU SOMETHING TO EAT. 'N YOU LOOK LIKE YOU COULD USE A DRINK, TOO...
BY THE WAY, NAME'S BOBBY.

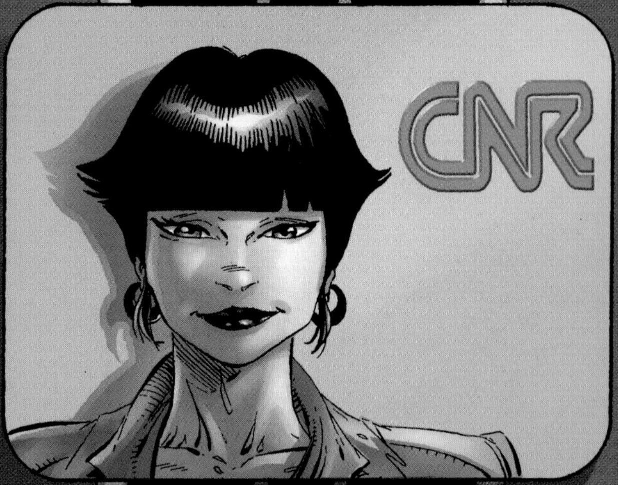
CNR

... FULL MOON DINER, THE SITE OF LAST NIGHT'S GRISLY SLAYINGS. AT THIS TIME, POLICE OFFER LITTLE INFORMATION ABOUT THE INVESTIGATION. WHAT IS CERTAIN IS THAT A PERSON OR PERSONS UNKNOWN ENTERED THE POPULAR ALL-NIGHT EATERY SHORTLY AFTER 1:00 A. M., AND OPENED FIRE ON THE CROWD BEFORE SETTING THE ESTABLISHMENT ABLAZE. REPORTS CONFIRM MORE THAN ONE DOZEN DEAD IN THE ATTACK. POLICE WILL NOT RELEASE THE NAMES OF ANY OF THE DECEASED UNTIL ALL THE VICTIMS HAVE BEEN IDENTIFIED AND THEIR FAMILIES NOTIFIED.

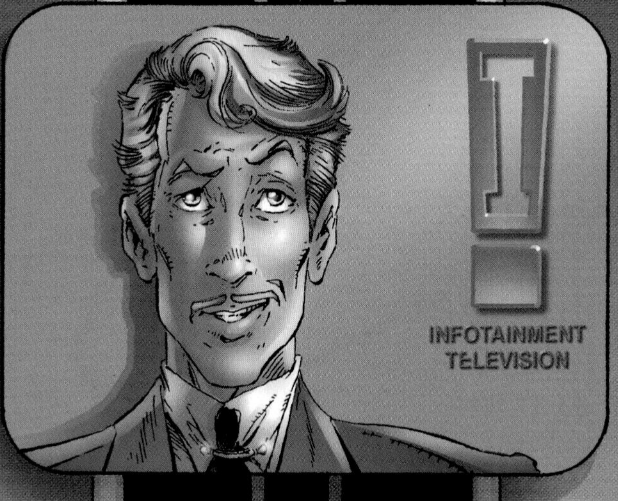
I!
INFOTAINMENT
TELEVISION

WELL, EVERYONE IN THE ***WESTERN HEMISPHERE*** SEEMS TO BE GEARING UP FOR THE RELEASE OF THE LATEST CHAPTER IN A CERTAIN ***ABSURDLY*** POPULAR SERIES OF SCI-FI FILMS. ***YOU*** KNOW, THE ONE FROM A GALAXY FAR, FAR AWAY... SO, OF COURSE, THAT MEANS ***LOTS*** MORE TOYS, VIDEO GAMES, T-SHIRTS AND FAST-FOOD TIE-INS. BUT THAT'S NOT ***ALL***. IT'S ALSO GOING TO MEAN ***HIGHER TICKET PRICES***. YES, THAT'S RIGHT. TICKET PRICES ARE GOING UP IN MOST MAJOR CITIES, ***JUST*** IN TIME FOR THE MOTHER OF ALL BLOCKBUSTERS. THAT MEANS A TRIP TO THE CINEMA, PLUS POPCORN AND A COUPLE OF SODAS COULD NOW REQUIRE MANY MOVIEGOERS TO GET A SECOND JOB. SO, ***STILL*** PLANNING ON SEEING IT TWELVE TIMES?

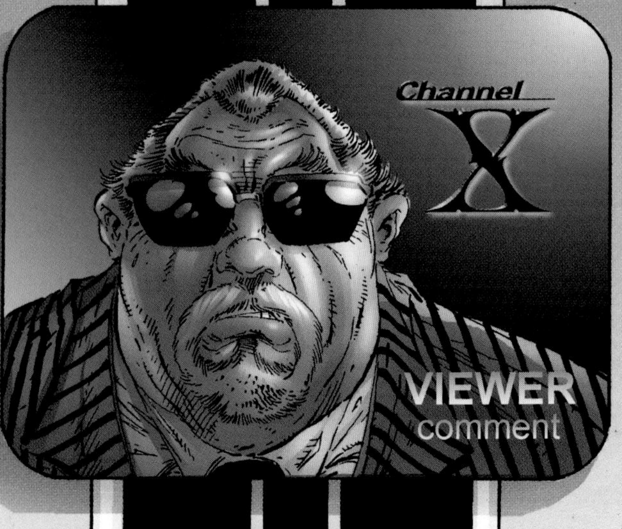
Channel
X
VIEWER
comment

ANYONE REMEMBER ***JASON WYNN?*** ACCORDING TO MY SOURCES, THE SHADOWY ***U. S. SECURITY GROUP*** DIRECTOR MAY BE LOOKING FOR A NEW JOB. RUMOR HAS IT THAT INTERNAL CONFLICTS AND A LACK OF CONFIDENCE IN WYNN'S... SHALL WE SAY... "MANAGEMENT TACTICS" FORCED HIS REMOVAL FROM THE DIRECTORSHIP. AS FOR ***WHOSE*** FOOTPRINT WAS ON WYNN'S ASS WHEN HE WAS SHOWN THE DOOR... WELL... LET'S JUST SAY THERE'S A ***VERY*** LONG LIST OF CANDIDATES, ONE OF WHICH MIGHT LEAD ALL THE WAY TO 1600 PENNSYLVANIA AVENUE. OFFICIALLY, ***NO ONE*** WILL GO ON RECORD AND WYNN, OF COURSE, COULD ***NOT*** BE REACHED FOR COMMENT...

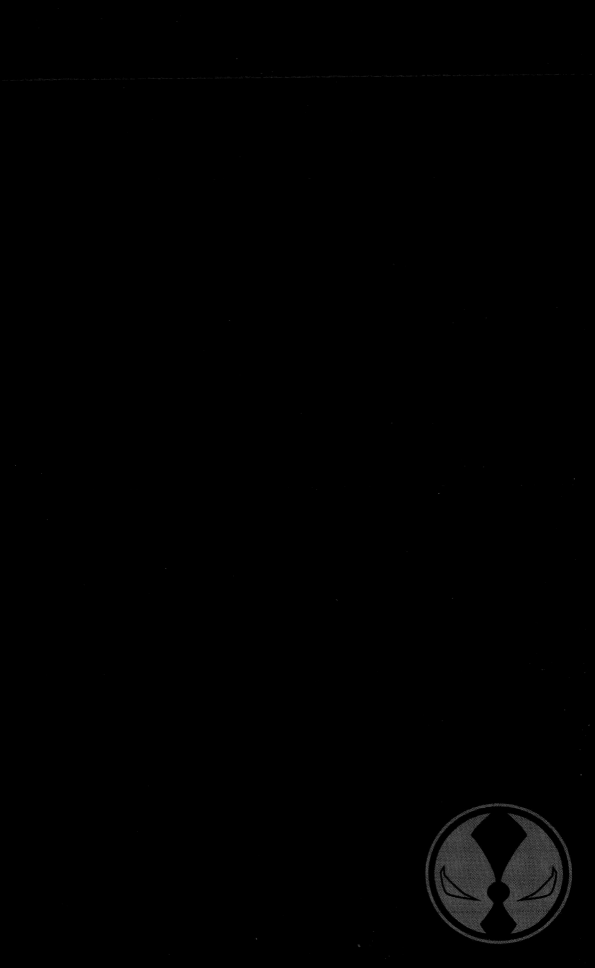

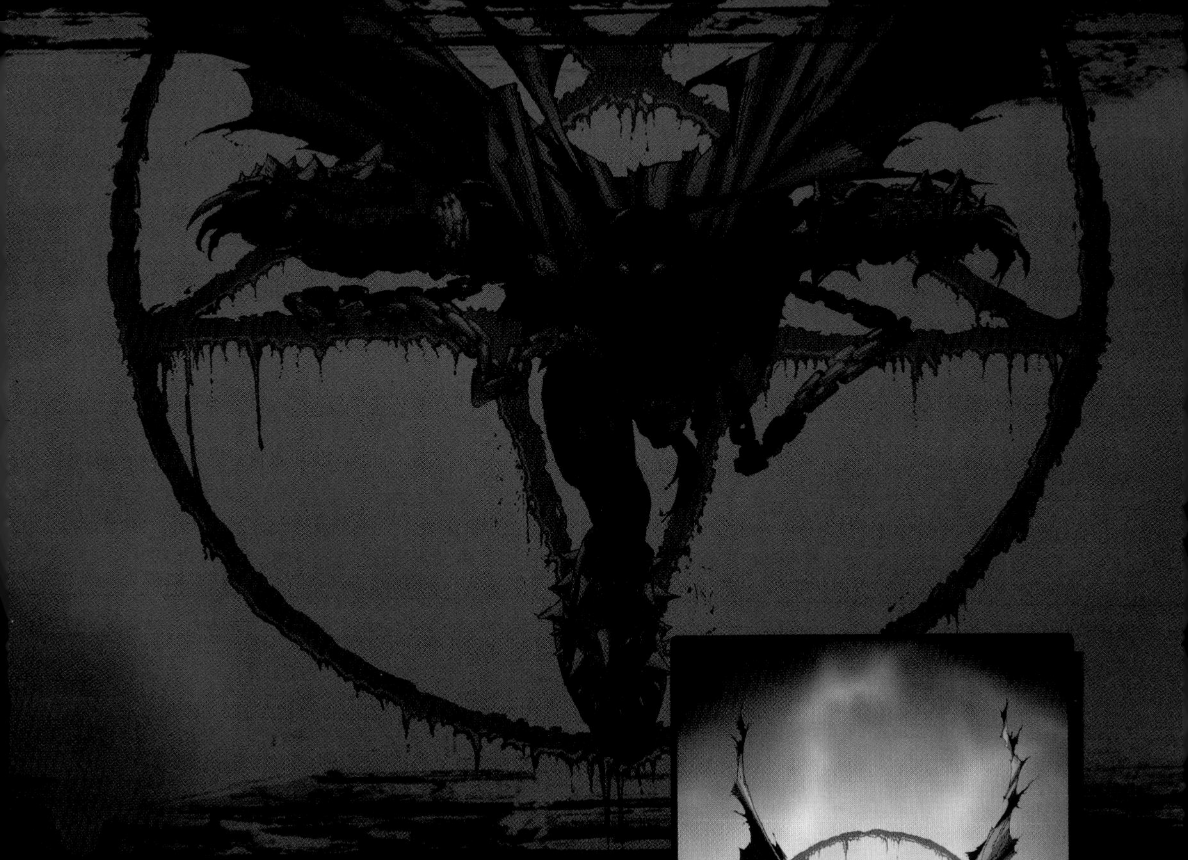

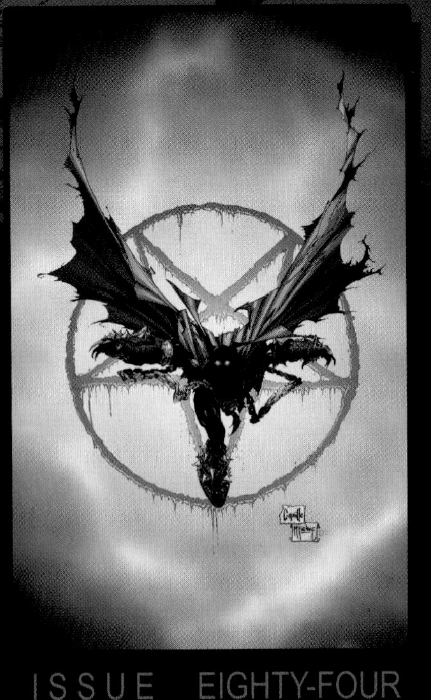

ISSUE EIGHTY-FOUR

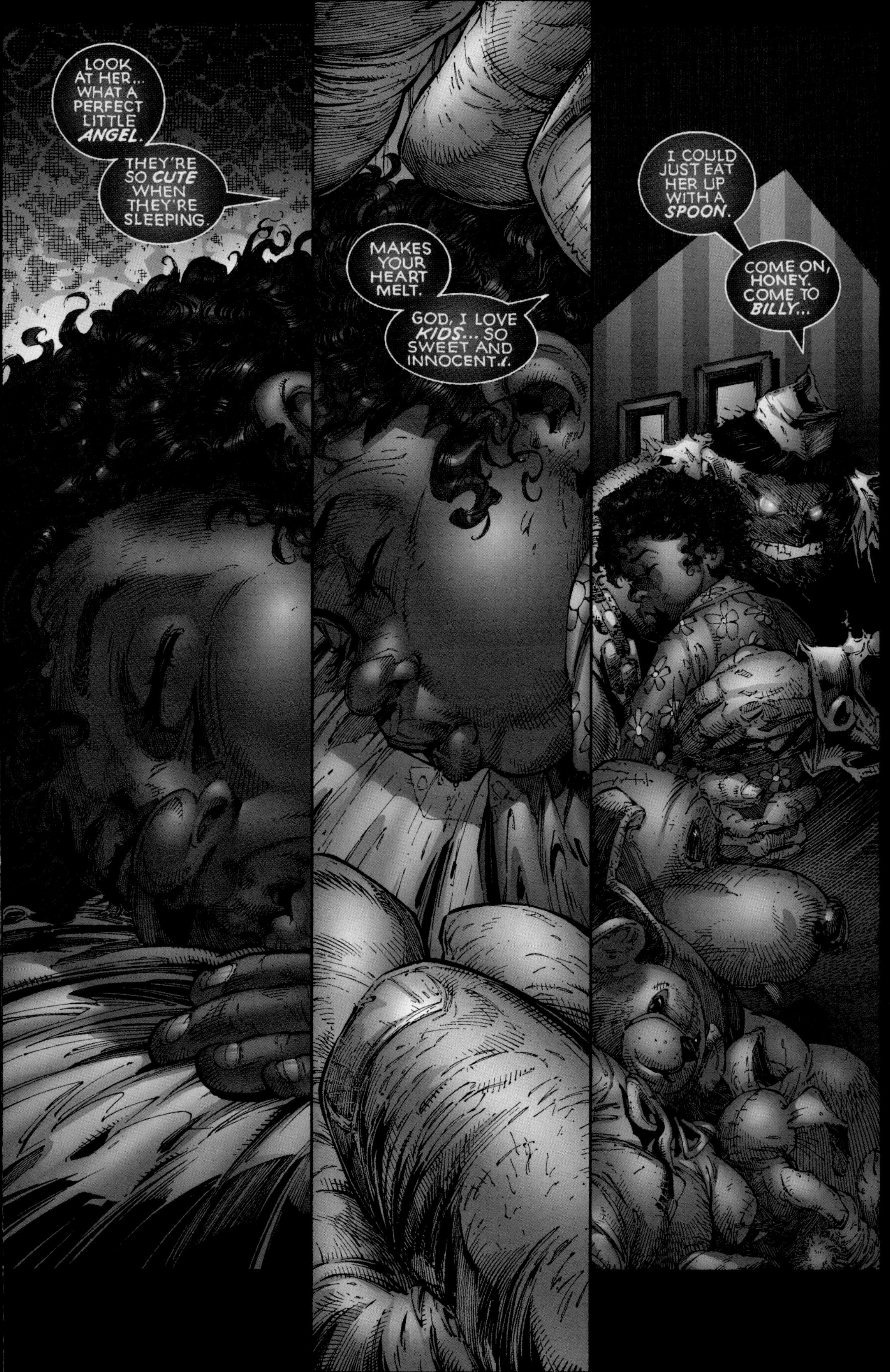
LOOK AT HER... WHAT A PERFECT LITTLE ANGEL.
THEY'RE SO CUTE WHEN THEY'RE SLEEPING.
MAKES YOUR HEART MELT.
GOD, I LOVE KIDS... SO SWEET AND INNOCENT...
I COULD JUST EAT HER UP WITH A SPOON.
COME ON, HONEY. COME TO BILLY...

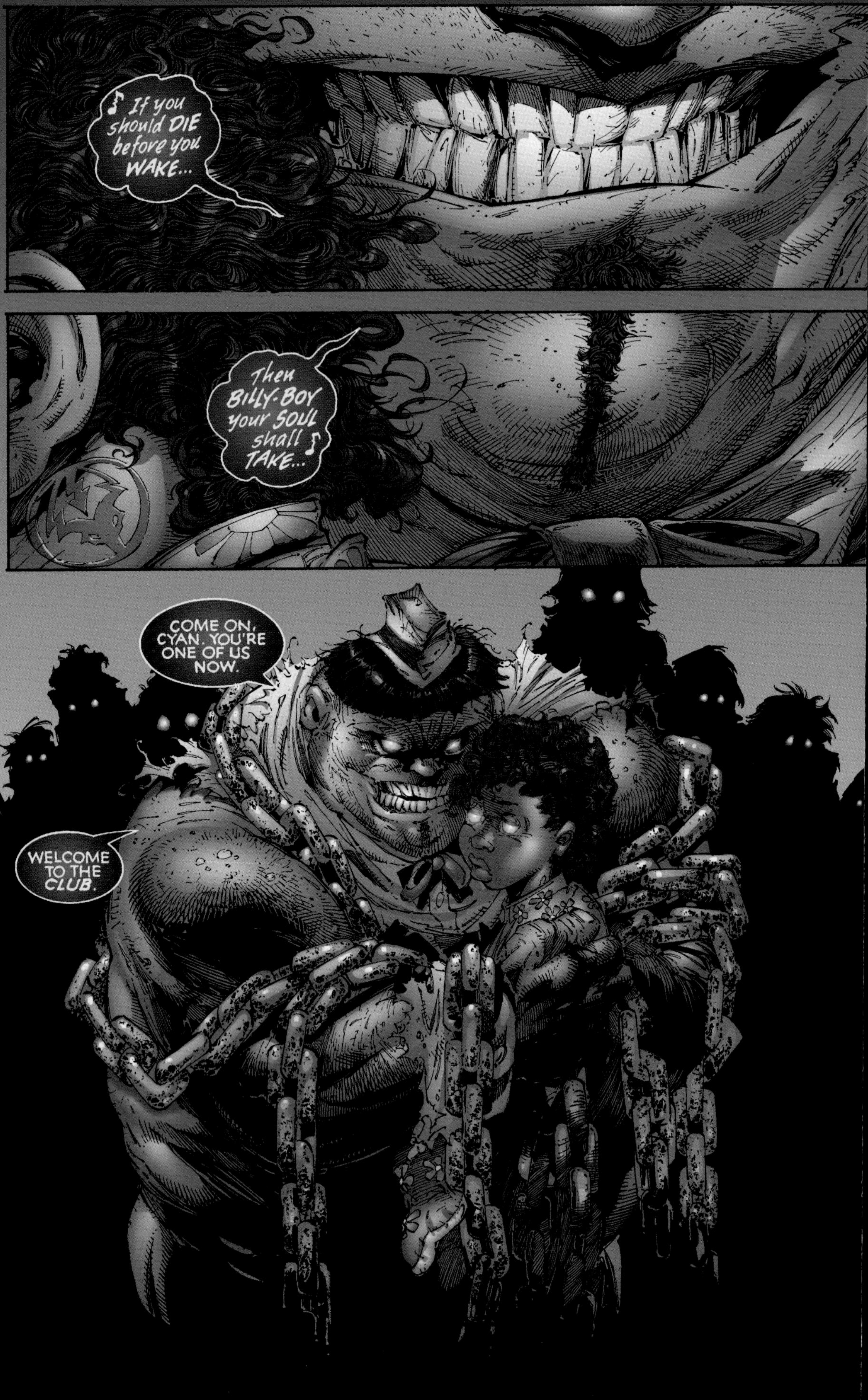
If you should DIE before you WAKE...
Then BILLY-BOY your SOUL shall TAKE...
COME ON, CYAN. YOU'RE ONE OF US NOW.
WELCOME TO THE CLUB.

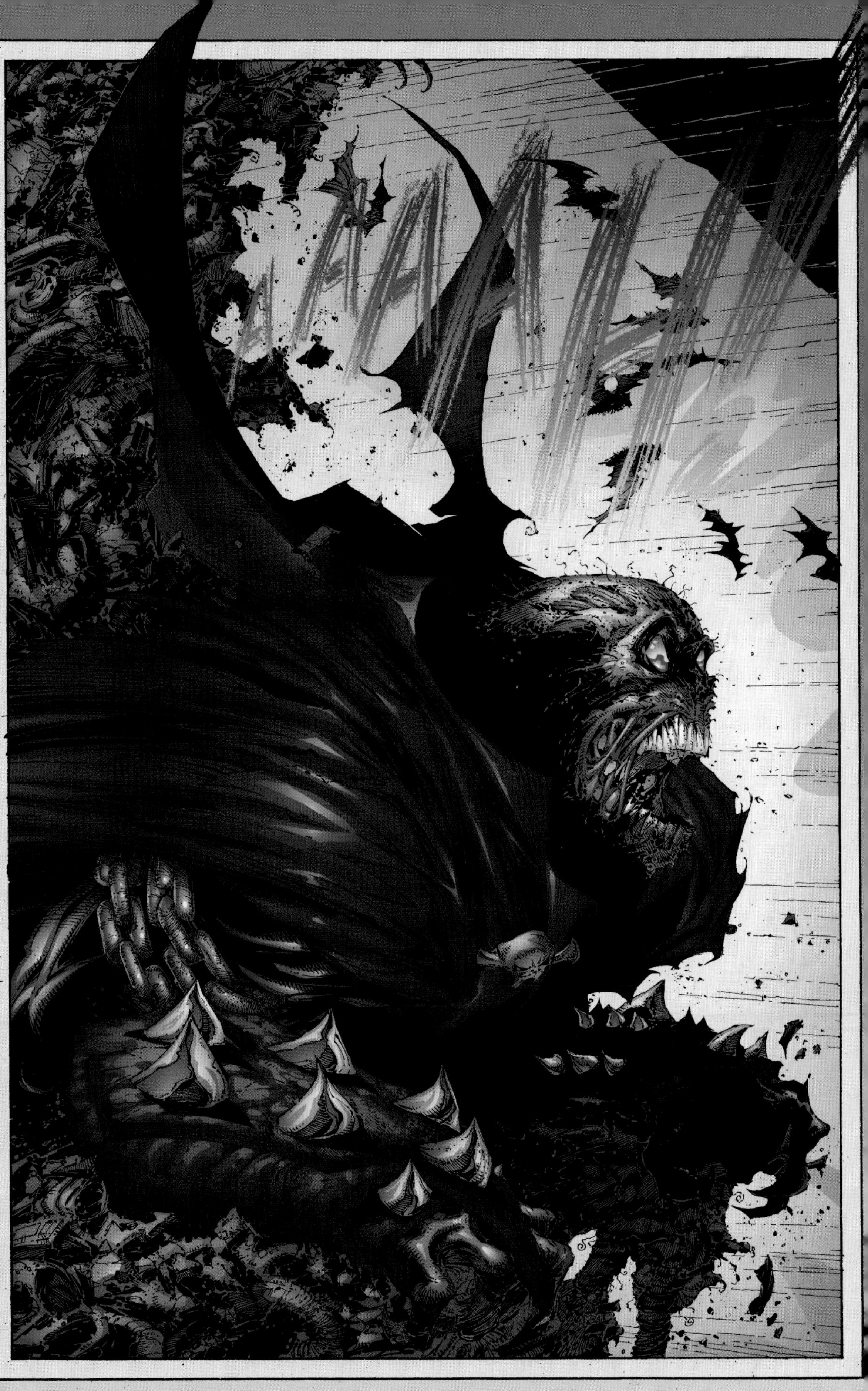

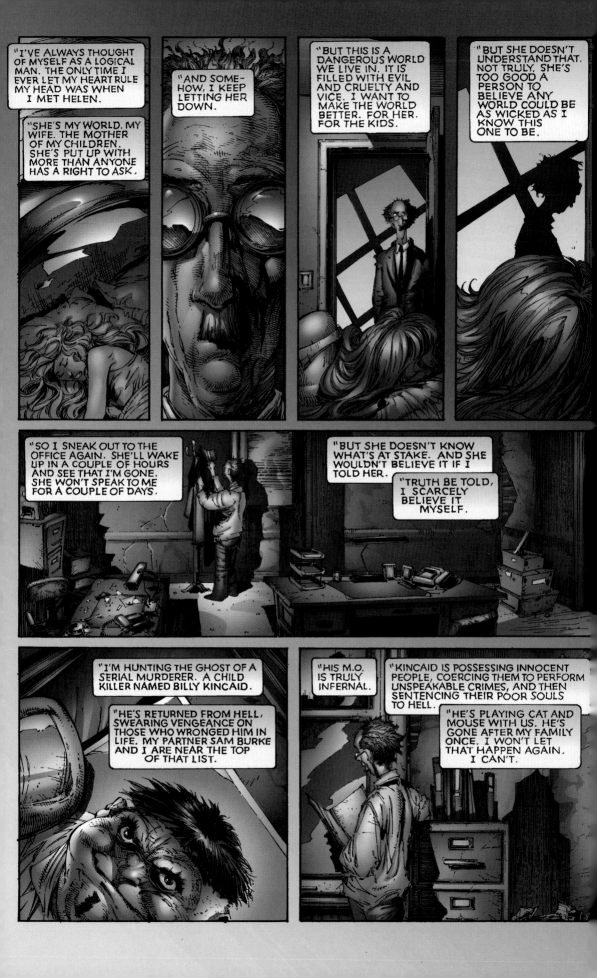

"I'VE ALWAYS THOUGHT OF MYSELF AS A LOGICAL MAN. THE ONLY TIME I EVER LET MY HEART RULE MY HEAD WAS WHEN I MET HELEN.

"SHE'S MY WORLD. MY WIFE. THE MOTHER OF MY CHILDREN. SHE'S PUT UP WITH MORE THAN ANYONE HAS A RIGHT TO ASK.

"AND SOME-HOW, I KEEP LETTING HER DOWN.

"BUT THIS IS A DANGEROUS WORLD WE LIVE IN. IT IS FILLED WITH EVIL AND CRUELTY AND VICE. I WANT TO MAKE THE WORLD BETTER. FOR HER. FOR THE KIDS.

"BUT SHE DOESN'T UNDERSTAND THAT. NOT TRULY. SHE'S TOO GOOD A PERSON TO BELIEVE ANY WORLD COULD BE AS WICKED AS I KNOW THIS ONE TO BE.

"SO I SNEAK OUT TO THE OFFICE AGAIN. SHE'LL WAKE UP IN A COUPLE OF HOURS AND SEE THAT I'M GONE. SHE WON'T SPEAK TO ME FOR A COUPLE OF DAYS.

"BUT SHE DOESN'T KNOW WHAT'S AT STAKE. AND SHE WOULDN'T BELIEVE IT IF I TOLD HER.

"TRUTH BE TOLD, I SCARCELY BELIEVE IT MYSELF.

"I'M HUNTING THE GHOST OF A SERIAL MURDERER. A CHILD KILLER NAMED BILLY KINCAID.

"HE'S RETURNED FROM HELL, SWEARING VENGEANCE ON THOSE WHO WRONGED HIM IN LIFE. MY PARTNER SAM BURKE AND I ARE NEAR THE TOP OF THAT LIST.

"HIS M.O. IS TRULY INFERNAL.

"KINCAID IS POSSESSING INNOCENT PEOPLE, COERCING THEM TO PERFORM UNSPEAKABLE CRIMES, AND THEN SENTENCING THEIR POOR SOULS TO HELL.

"HE'S PLAYING CAT AND MOUSE WITH US. HE'S GONE AFTER MY FAMILY ONCE. I WON'T LET THAT HAPPEN AGAIN. I CAN'T.

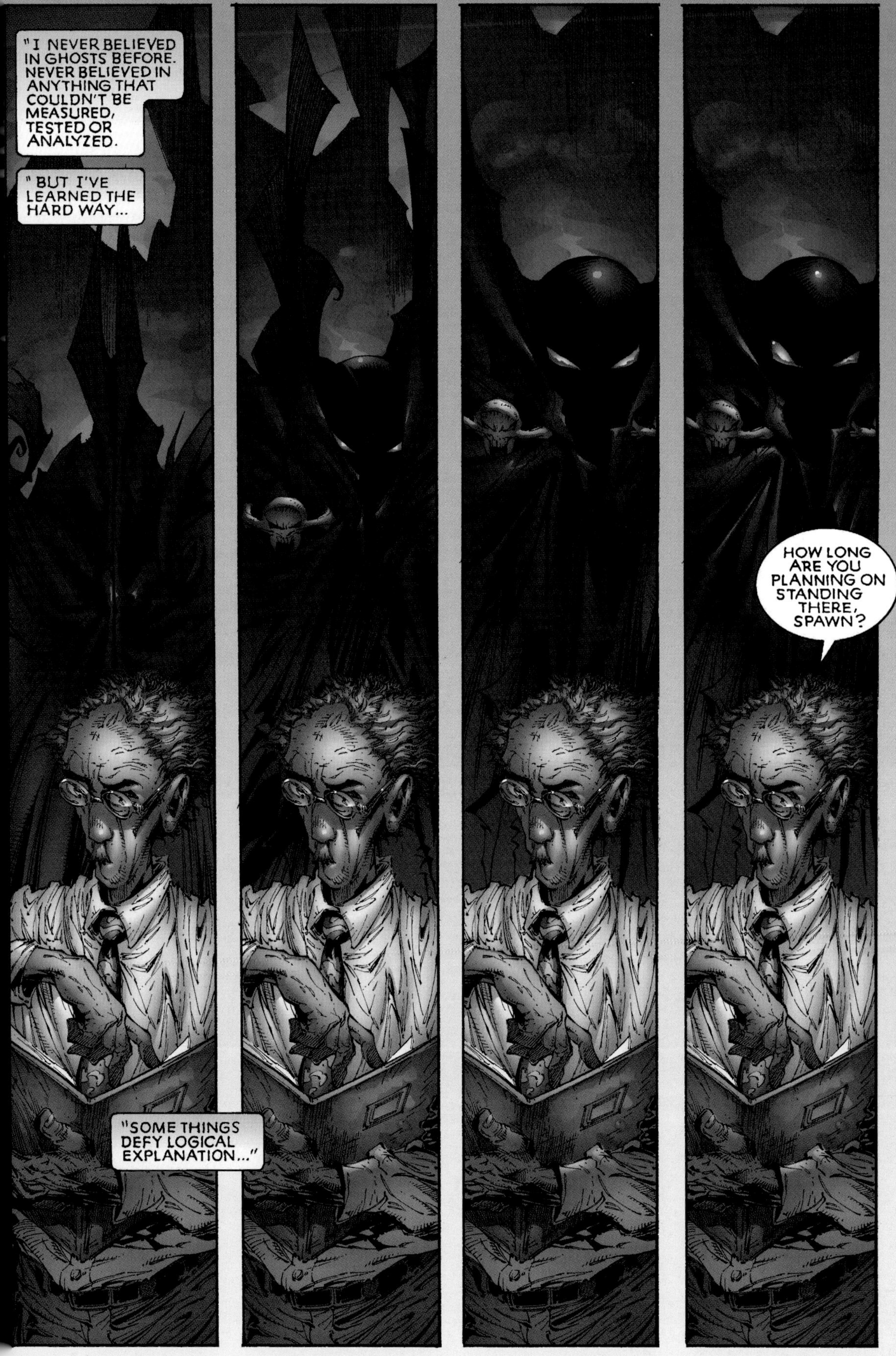
"I NEVER BELIEVED IN GHOSTS BEFORE. NEVER BELIEVED IN ANYTHING THAT COULDN'T BE MEASURED, TESTED OR ANALYZED.
"BUT I'VE LEARNED THE HARD WAY...
"SOME THINGS DEFY LOGICAL EXPLANATION..."
HOW LONG ARE YOU PLANNING ON STANDING THERE, SPAWN?

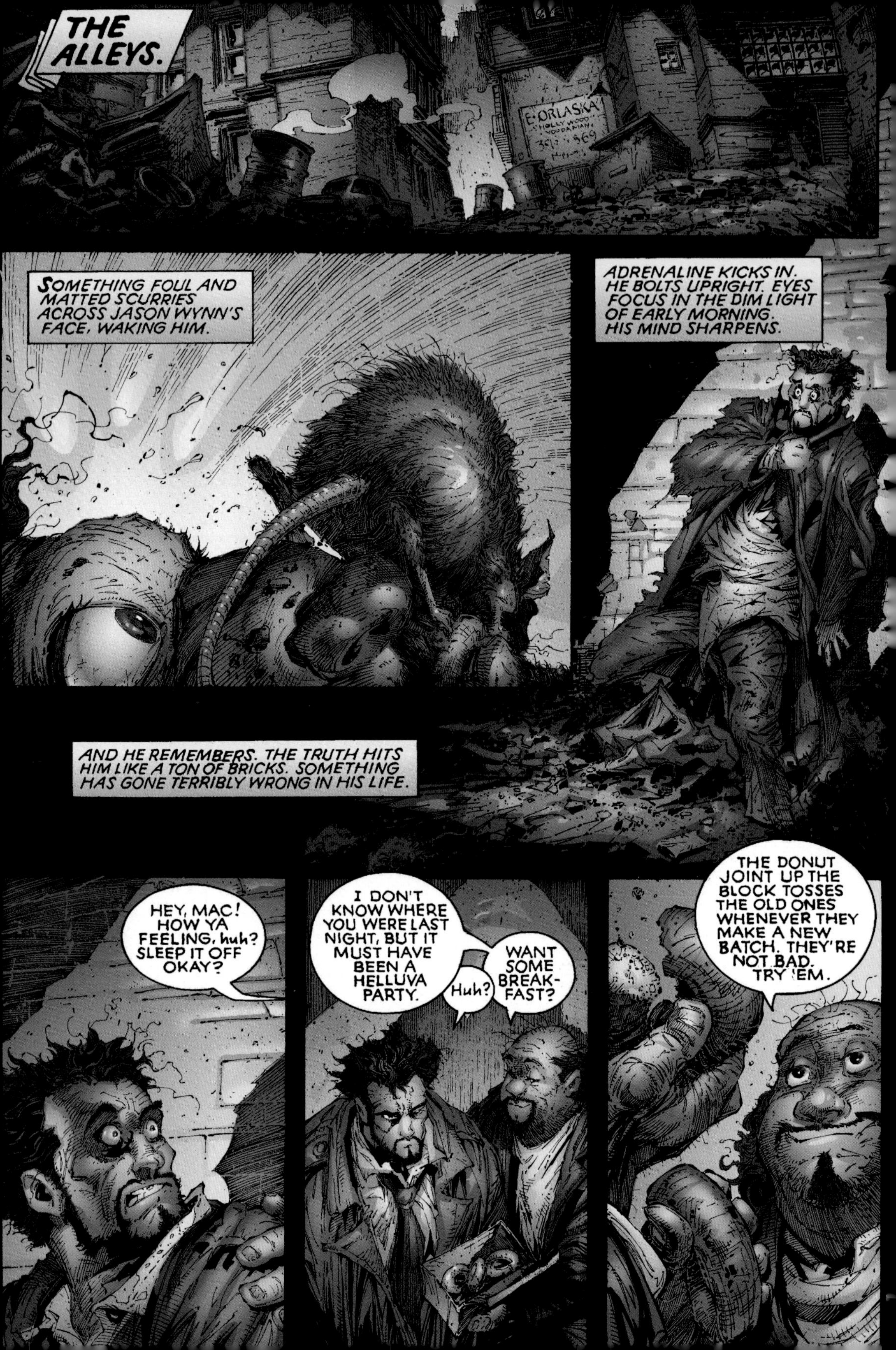
THE ALLEYS.
E. ORLASKA
SOMETHING FOUL AND MATTED SCURRIES ACROSS JASON WYNN'S FACE, WAKING HIM.
ADRENALINE KICKS IN. HE BOLTS UPRIGHT. EYES FOCUS IN THE DIM LIGHT OF EARLY MORNING. HIS MIND SHARPENS.
AND HE REMEMBERS. THE TRUTH HITS HIM LIKE A TON OF BRICKS. SOMETHING HAS GONE TERRIBLY WRONG IN HIS LIFE.
HEY, MAC! HOW YA FEELING, huh? SLEEP IT OFF OKAY?
I DON'T KNOW WHERE YOU WERE LAST NIGHT, BUT IT MUST HAVE BEEN A HELLUVA PARTY.
Huh?
WANT SOME BREAK-FAST?
THE DONUT JOINT UP THE BLOCK TOSSES THE OLD ONES WHENEVER THEY MAKE A NEW BATCH. THEY'RE NOT BAD. TRY 'EM.

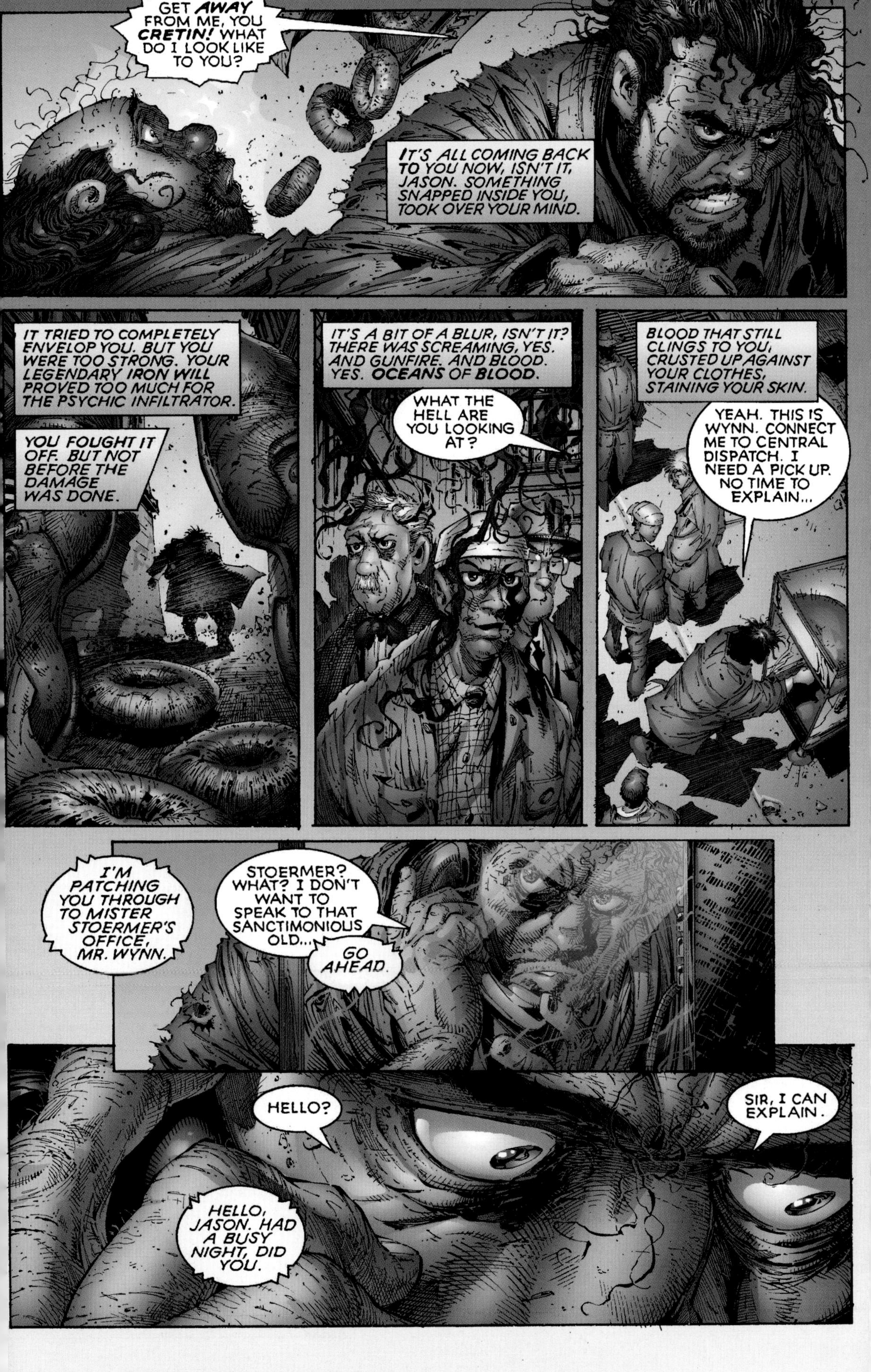
GET AWAY FROM ME, YOU CRETIN! WHAT DO I LOOK LIKE TO YOU?
IT'S ALL COMING BACK TO YOU NOW, ISN'T IT, JASON. SOMETHING SNAPPED INSIDE YOU, TOOK OVER YOUR MIND.
IT TRIED TO COMPLETELY ENVELOP YOU. BUT YOU WERE TOO STRONG. YOUR LEGENDARY IRON WILL PROVED TOO MUCH FOR THE PSYCHIC INFILTRATOR.
YOU FOUGHT IT OFF. BUT NOT BEFORE THE DAMAGE WAS DONE.
IT'S A BIT OF A BLUR, ISN'T IT? THERE WAS SCREAMING, YES. AND GUNFIRE. AND BLOOD. YES. OCEANS OF BLOOD.
WHAT THE HELL ARE YOU LOOKING AT?
BLOOD THAT STILL CLINGS TO YOU, CRUSTED UP AGAINST YOUR CLOTHES, STAINING YOUR SKIN.
YEAH. THIS IS WYNN. CONNECT ME TO CENTRAL DISPATCH. I NEED A PICK UP. NO TIME TO EXPLAIN...
I'M PATCHING YOU THROUGH TO MISTER STOERMER'S OFFICE, MR. WYNN.
STOERMER? WHAT? I DON'T WANT TO SPEAK TO THAT SANCTIMONIOUS OLD...
GO AHEAD.
HELLO?
SIR, I CAN EXPLAIN.
HELLO, JASON. HAD A BUSY NIGHT, DID YOU.

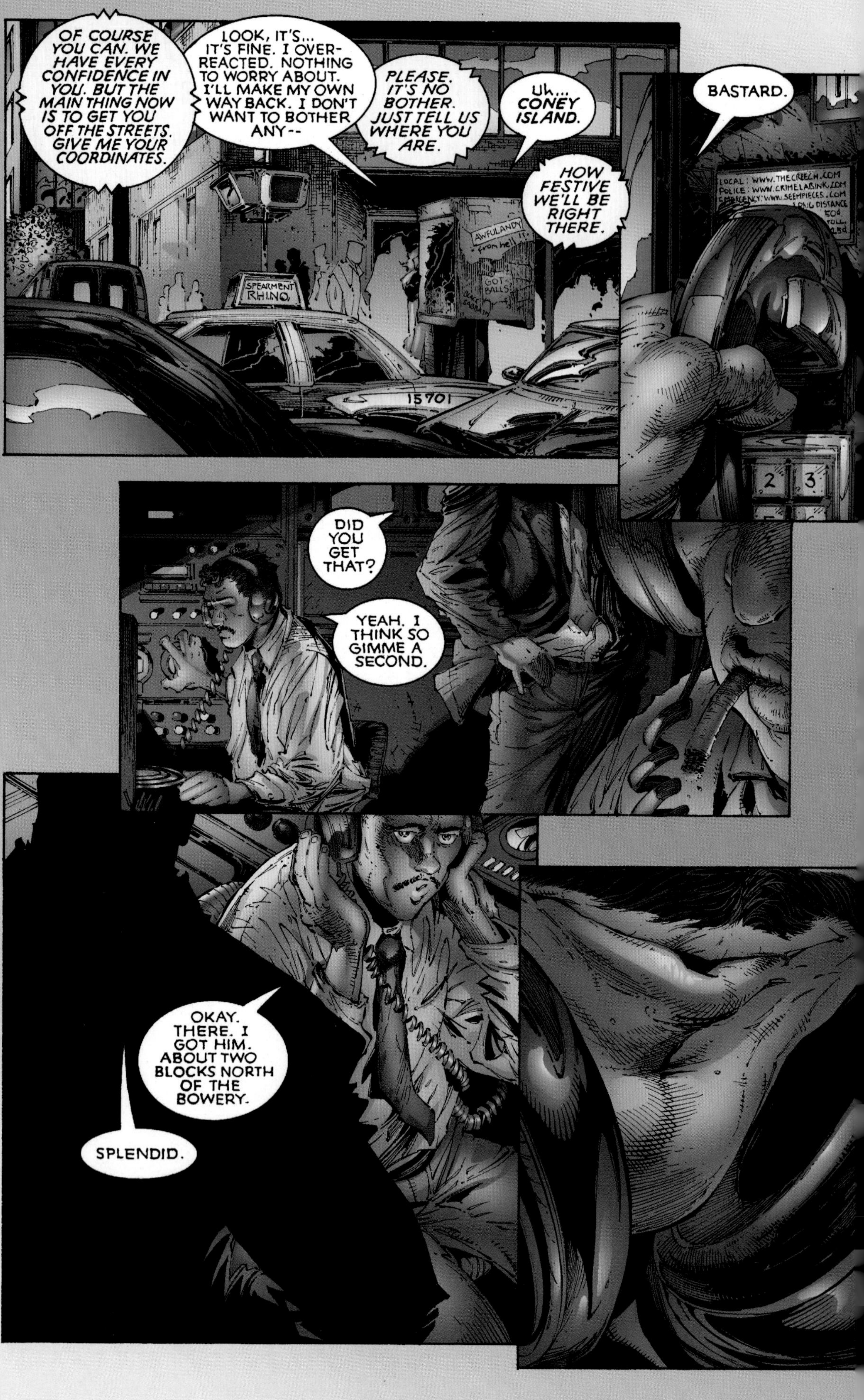

OF COURSE YOU CAN. WE HAVE EVERY CONFIDENCE IN YOU. BUT THE MAIN THING NOW IS TO GET YOU OFF THE STREETS. GIVE ME YOUR COORDINATES.
LOOK, IT'S... IT'S FINE. I OVER-REACTED. NOTHING TO WORRY ABOUT. I'LL MAKE MY OWN WAY BACK. I DON'T WANT TO BOTHER ANY--
PLEASE. IT'S NO BOTHER. JUST TELL US WHERE YOU ARE.
Uh... CONEY ISLAND.
HOW FESTIVE WE'LL BE RIGHT THERE.
SPEARMENT RHINO
15701
BASTARD.
DID YOU GET THAT?
YEAH. I THINK SO GIMME A SECOND.
OKAY. THERE. I GOT HIM. ABOUT TWO BLOCKS NORTH OF THE BOWERY.
SPLENDID.

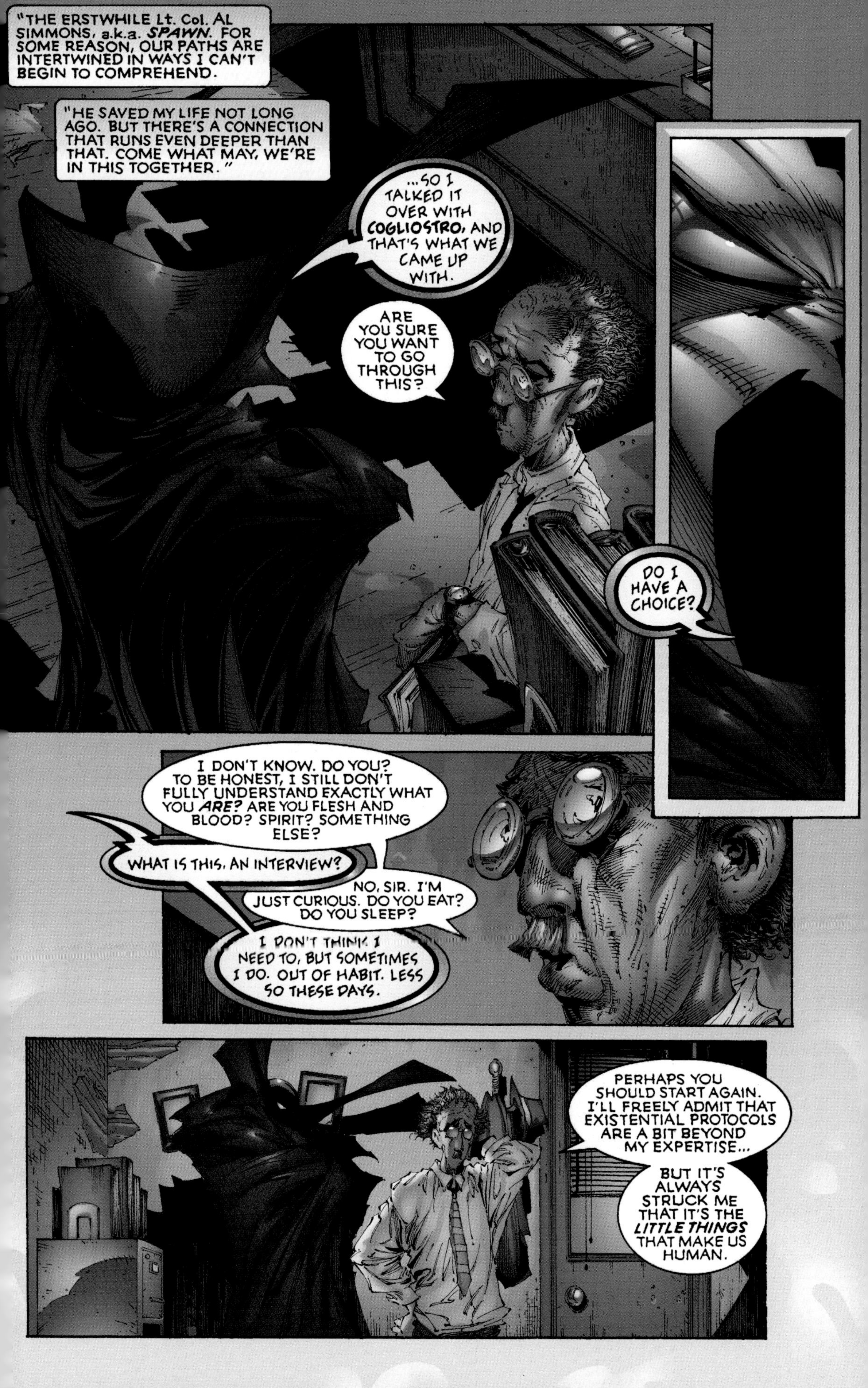
"THE ERSTWHILE Lt. Col. AL SIMMONS, a.k.a. SPAWN. FOR SOME REASON, OUR PATHS ARE INTERTWINED IN WAYS I CAN'T BEGIN TO COMPREHEND.
"HE SAVED MY LIFE NOT LONG AGO. BUT THERE'S A CONNECTION THAT RUNS EVEN DEEPER THAN THAT. COME WHAT MAY, WE'RE IN THIS TOGETHER."
...SO I TALKED IT OVER WITH COGLIOSTRO, AND THAT'S WHAT WE CAME UP WITH.
ARE YOU SURE YOU WANT TO GO THROUGH THIS?
DO I HAVE A CHOICE?
I DON'T KNOW. DO YOU? TO BE HONEST, I STILL DON'T FULLY UNDERSTAND EXACTLY WHAT YOU ARE? ARE YOU FLESH AND BLOOD? SPIRIT? SOMETHING ELSE?
WHAT IS THIS, AN INTERVIEW?
NO, SIR. I'M JUST CURIOUS. DO YOU EAT? DO YOU SLEEP?
I DON'T THINK I NEED TO, BUT SOMETIMES I DO. OUT OF HABIT. LESS SO THESE DAYS.
PERHAPS YOU SHOULD START AGAIN. I'LL FREELY ADMIT THAT EXISTENTIAL PROTOCOLS ARE A BIT BEYOND MY EXPERTISE...
BUT IT'S ALWAYS STRUCK ME THAT IT'S THE LITTLE THINGS THAT MAKE US HUMAN.

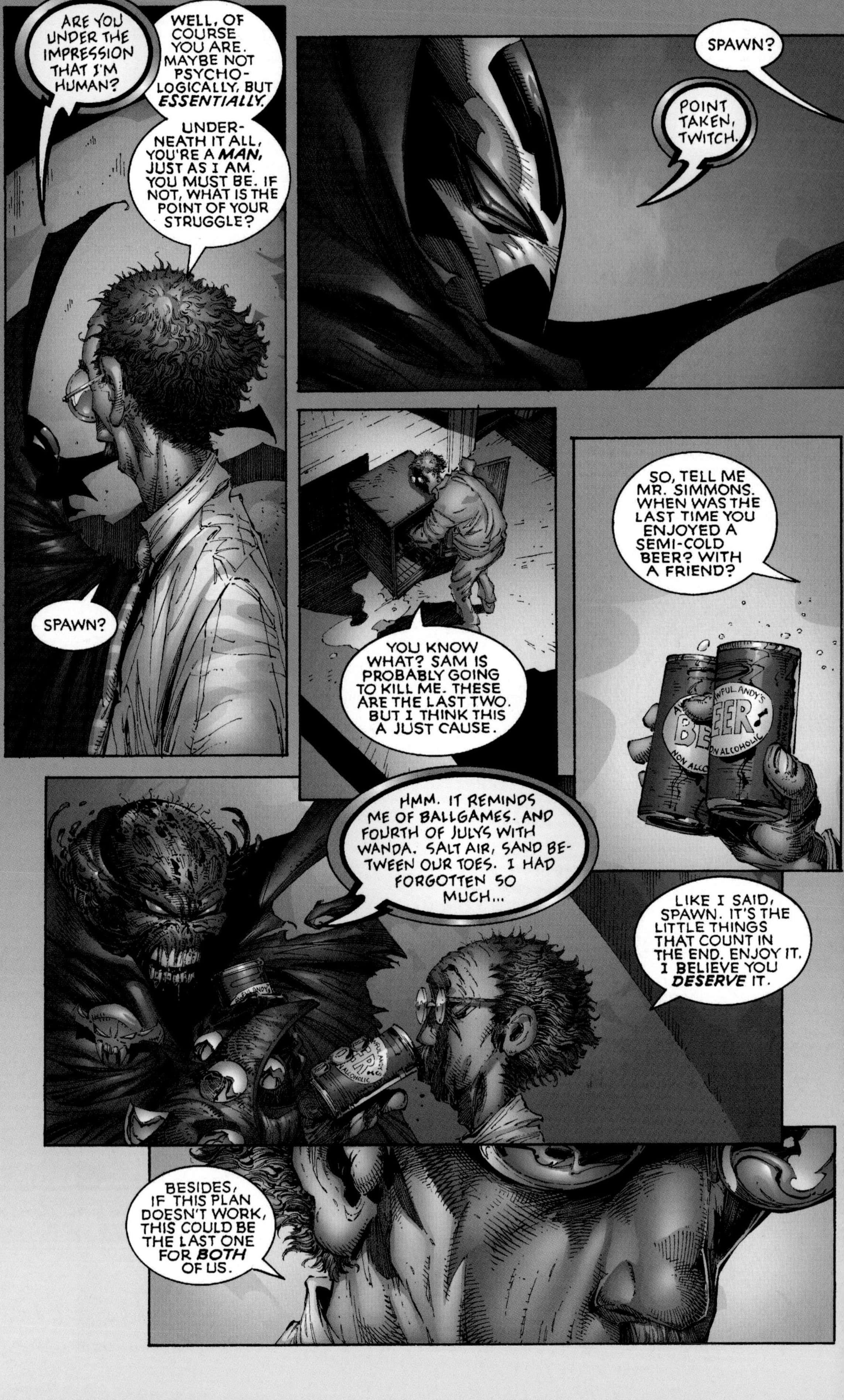
ARE YOU UNDER THE IMPRESSION THAT I'M HUMAN?
WELL, OF COURSE YOU ARE. MAYBE NOT PSYCHO-LOGICALLY, BUT ESSENTIALLY.
UNDER-NEATH IT ALL, YOU'RE A MAN, JUST AS I AM. YOU MUST BE. IF NOT, WHAT IS THE POINT OF YOUR STRUGGLE?
SPAWN?
SPAWN?
POINT TAKEN, TWITCH.
YOU KNOW WHAT? SAM IS PROBABLY GOING TO KILL ME. THESE ARE THE LAST TWO. BUT I THINK THIS A JUST CAUSE.
SO, TELL ME MR. SIMMONS. WHEN WAS THE LAST TIME YOU ENJOYED A SEMI-COLD BEER? WITH A FRIEND?
HMM. IT REMINDS ME OF BALLGAMES. AND FOURTH OF JULYS WITH WANDA. SALT AIR, SAND BE-TWEEN OUR TOES. I HAD FORGOTTEN SO MUCH...
LIKE I SAID, SPAWN. IT'S THE LITTLE THINGS THAT COUNT IN THE END. ENJOY IT. I BELIEVE YOU DESERVE IT.
BESIDES, IF THIS PLAN DOESN'T WORK, THIS COULD BE THE LAST ONE FOR BOTH OF US.

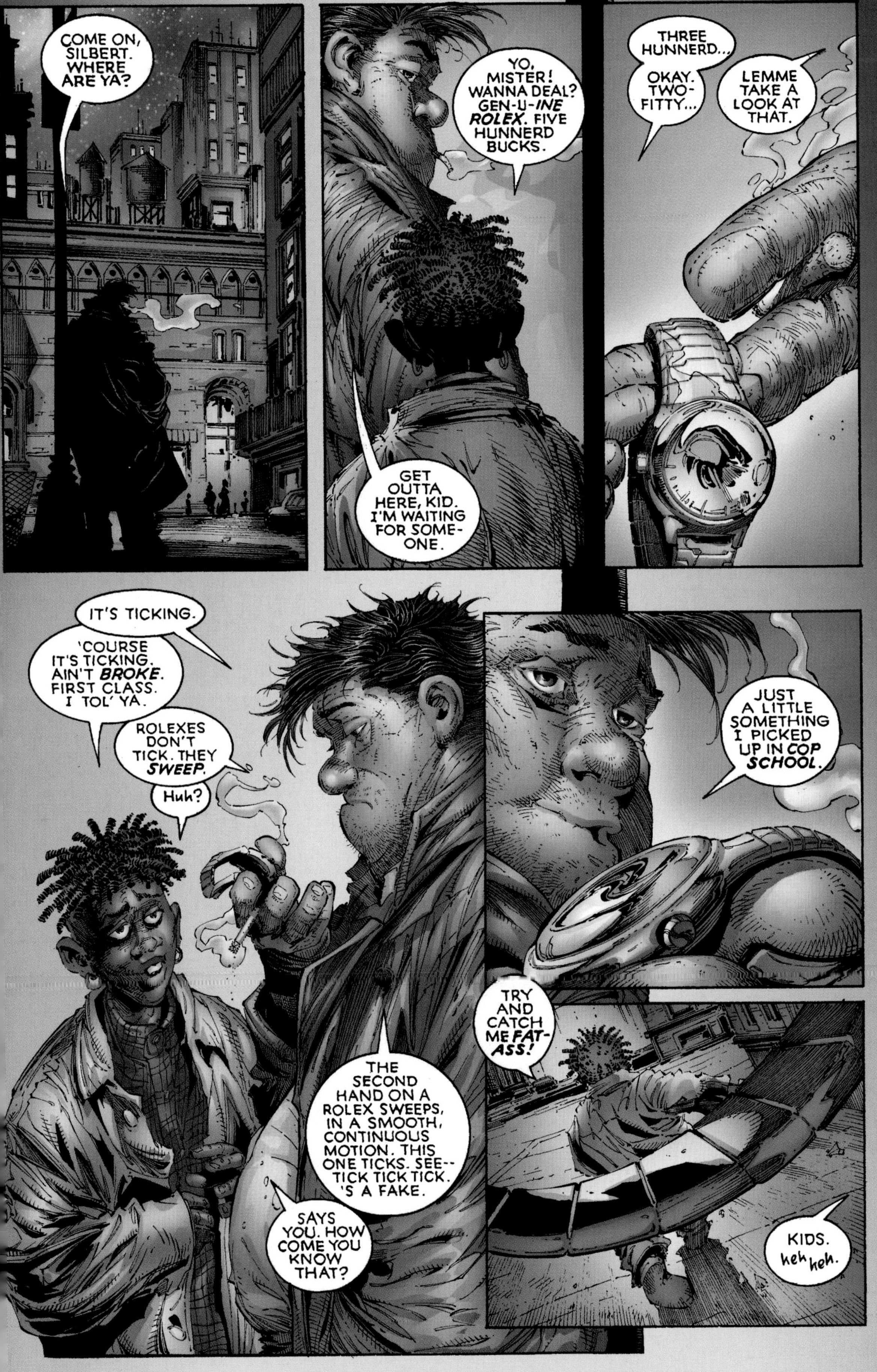
COME ON, SILBERT. WHERE ARE YA?
YO, MISTER! WANNA DEAL? GEN-U-INE ROLEX. FIVE HUNNERD BUCKS.
GET OUTTA HERE, KID. I'M WAITING FOR SOME-ONE.
THREE HUNNERD...
OKAY. TWO-FITTY...
LEMME TAKE A LOOK AT THAT.
IT'S TICKING.
'COURSE IT'S TICKING. AIN'T BROKE. FIRST CLASS. I TOL' YA.
ROLEXES DON'T TICK. THEY SWEEP.
Huh?
THE SECOND HAND ON A ROLEX SWEEPS, IN A SMOOTH, CONTINUOUS MOTION. THIS ONE TICKS. SEE-- TICK TICK TICK. 'S A FAKE.
SAYS YOU. HOW COME YOU KNOW THAT?
JUST A LITTLE SOMETHING I PICKED UP IN COP SCHOOL.
TRY AND CATCH ME FAT-ASS!
KIDS. heh heh.

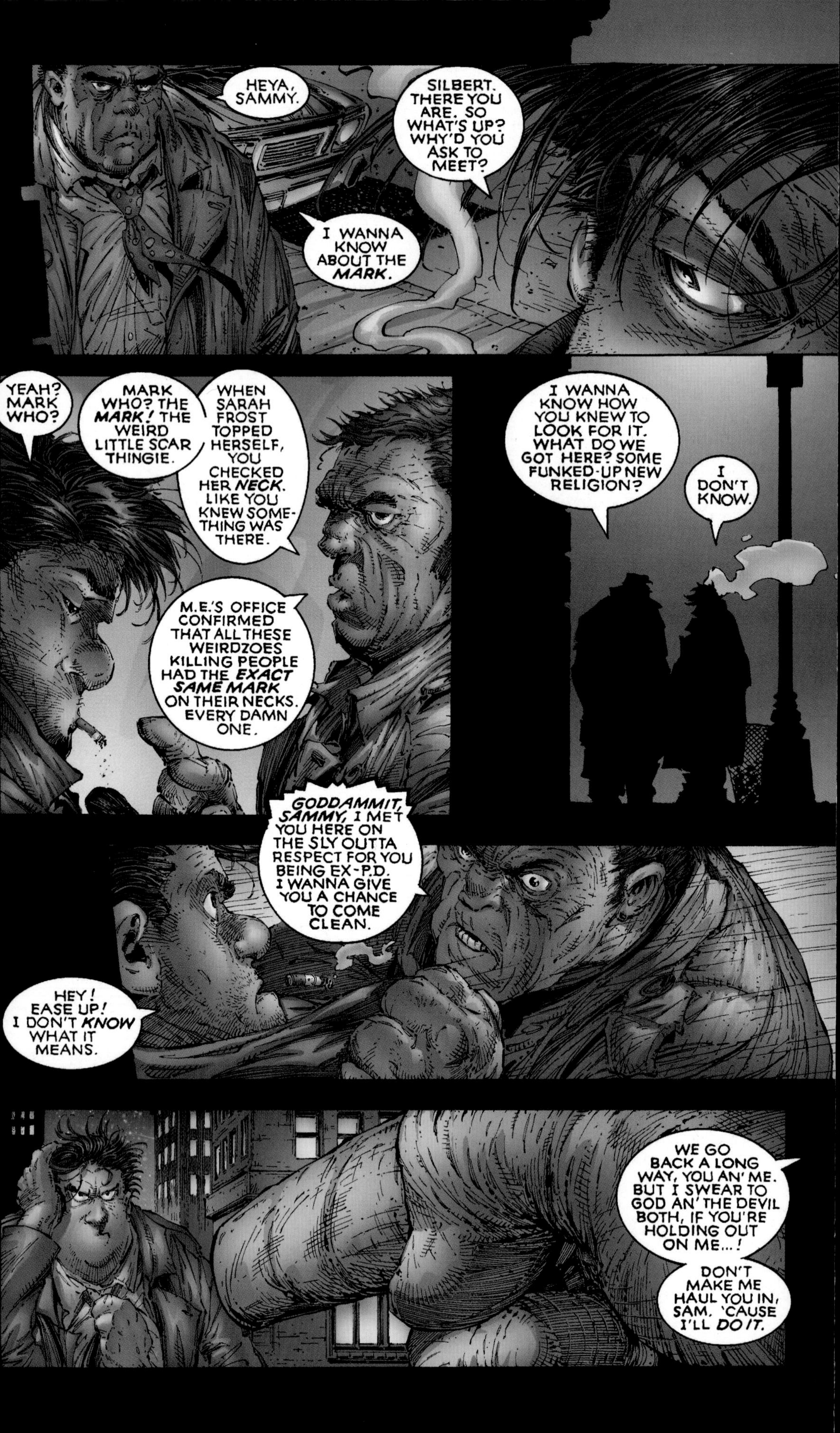
HEYA, SAMMY.
SILBERT. THERE YOU ARE. SO WHAT'S UP? WHY'D YOU ASK TO MEET?
I WANNA KNOW ABOUT THE *MARK*.
YEAH? MARK WHO?
MARK WHO? THE *MARK!* THE WEIRD LITTLE SCAR THINGIE.
WHEN SARAH FROST TOPPED HERSELF, YOU CHECKED HER *NECK*. LIKE YOU KNEW SOME-THING WAS THERE.
M.E.'S OFFICE CONFIRMED THAT ALL THESE WEIRDZOES KILLING PEOPLE HAD THE *EXACT SAME MARK* ON THEIR NECKS. EVERY DAMN ONE.
I WANNA KNOW HOW YOU KNEW TO LOOK FOR IT. WHAT DO WE GOT HERE? SOME FUNKED-UP NEW RELIGION?
I DON'T KNOW.
GODDAMMIT, SAMMY, I MET YOU HERE ON THE SLY OUTTA RESPECT FOR YOU BEING EX-P.D. I WANNA GIVE YOU A CHANCE TO COME CLEAN.
HEY! EASE UP! I DON'T *KNOW* WHAT IT MEANS.
WE GO BACK A LONG WAY, YOU AN' ME. BUT I SWEAR TO GOD AN' THE DEVIL BOTH, IF YOU'RE HOLDING OUT ON ME...!
DON'T MAKE ME HAUL YOU IN, SAM, 'CAUSE I'LL *DO IT*.

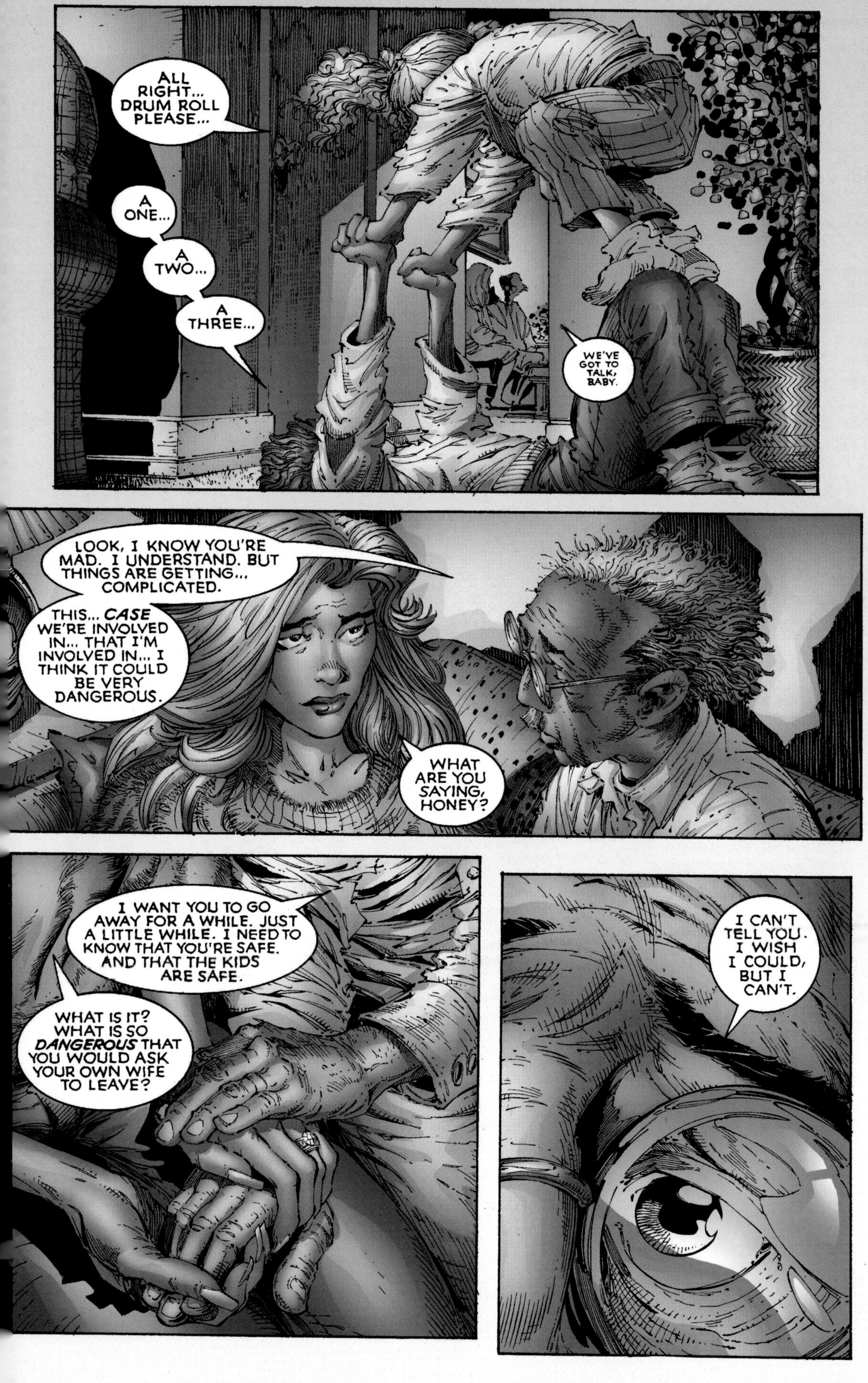
ALL RIGHT... DRUM ROLL PLEASE...
A ONE...
A TWO...
A THREE...
WE'VE GOT TO TALK, BABY.
LOOK, I KNOW YOU'RE MAD. I UNDERSTAND. BUT THINGS ARE GETTING... COMPLICATED.
THIS... CASE WE'RE INVOLVED IN... THAT I'M INVOLVED IN... I THINK IT COULD BE VERY DANGEROUS.
WHAT ARE YOU SAYING, HONEY?
I WANT YOU TO GO AWAY FOR A WHILE. JUST A LITTLE WHILE. I NEED TO KNOW THAT YOU'RE SAFE. AND THAT THE KIDS ARE SAFE.
WHAT IS IT? WHAT IS SO DANGEROUS THAT YOU WOULD ASK YOUR OWN WIFE TO LEAVE?
I CAN'T TELL YOU. I WISH I COULD, BUT I CAN'T.

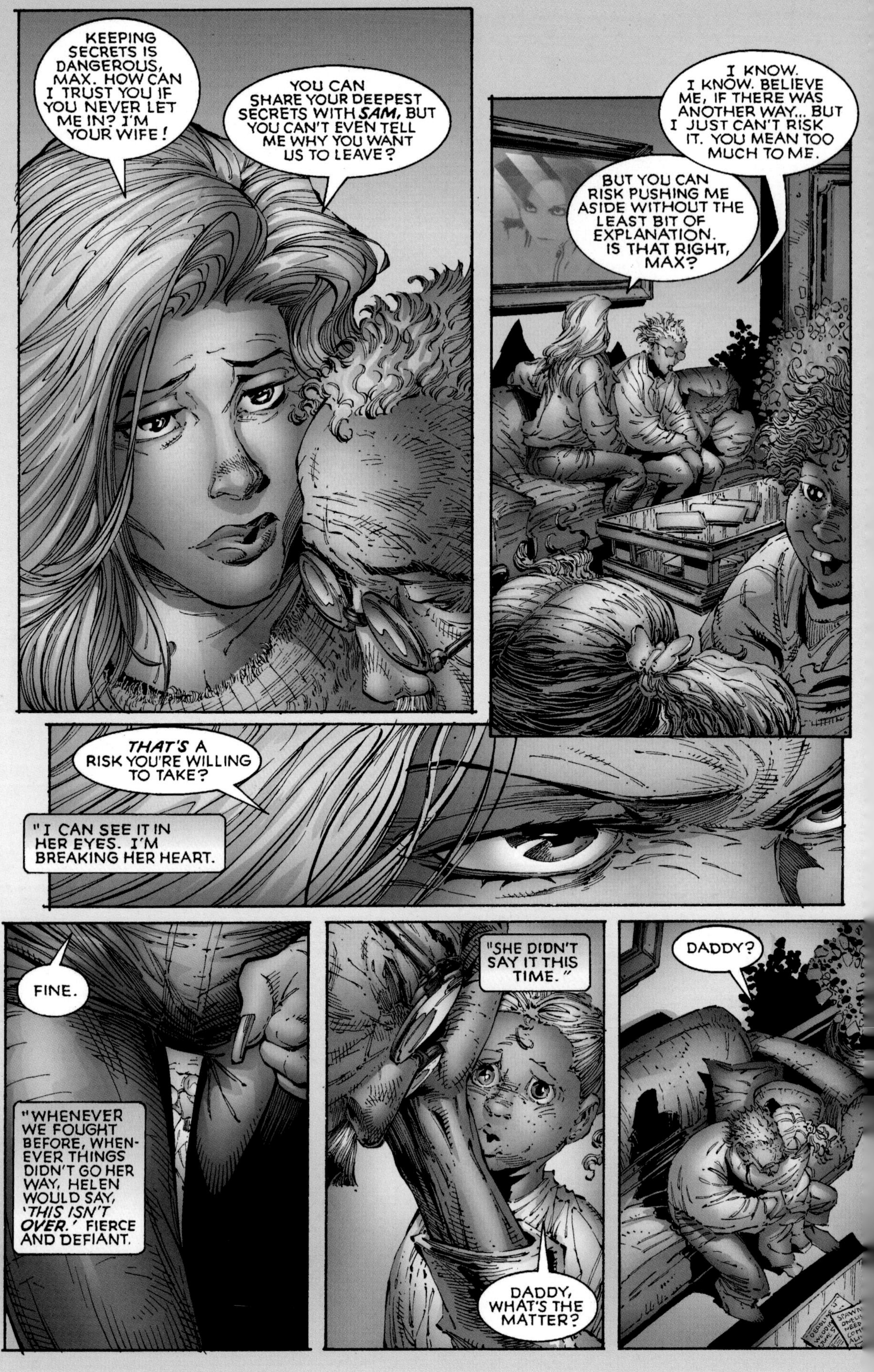
KEEPING SECRETS IS DANGEROUS, MAX. HOW CAN I TRUST YOU IF YOU NEVER LET ME IN? I'M YOUR WIFE!
YOU CAN SHARE YOUR DEEPEST SECRETS WITH SAM, BUT YOU CAN'T EVEN TELL ME WHY YOU WANT US TO LEAVE?
I KNOW. I KNOW. BELIEVE ME, IF THERE WAS ANOTHER WAY... BUT I JUST CAN'T RISK IT. YOU MEAN TOO MUCH TO ME.
BUT YOU CAN RISK PUSHING ME ASIDE WITHOUT THE LEAST BIT OF EXPLANATION. IS THAT RIGHT, MAX?
THAT'S A RISK YOU'RE WILLING TO TAKE?
"I CAN SEE IT IN HER EYES. I'M BREAKING HER HEART.
FINE.
"WHENEVER WE FOUGHT BEFORE, WHENEVER THINGS DIDN'T GO HER WAY, HELEN WOULD SAY, 'THIS ISN'T OVER.' FIERCE AND DEFIANT.
"SHE DIDN'T SAY IT THIS TIME."
DADDY, WHAT'S THE MATTER?
DADDY?

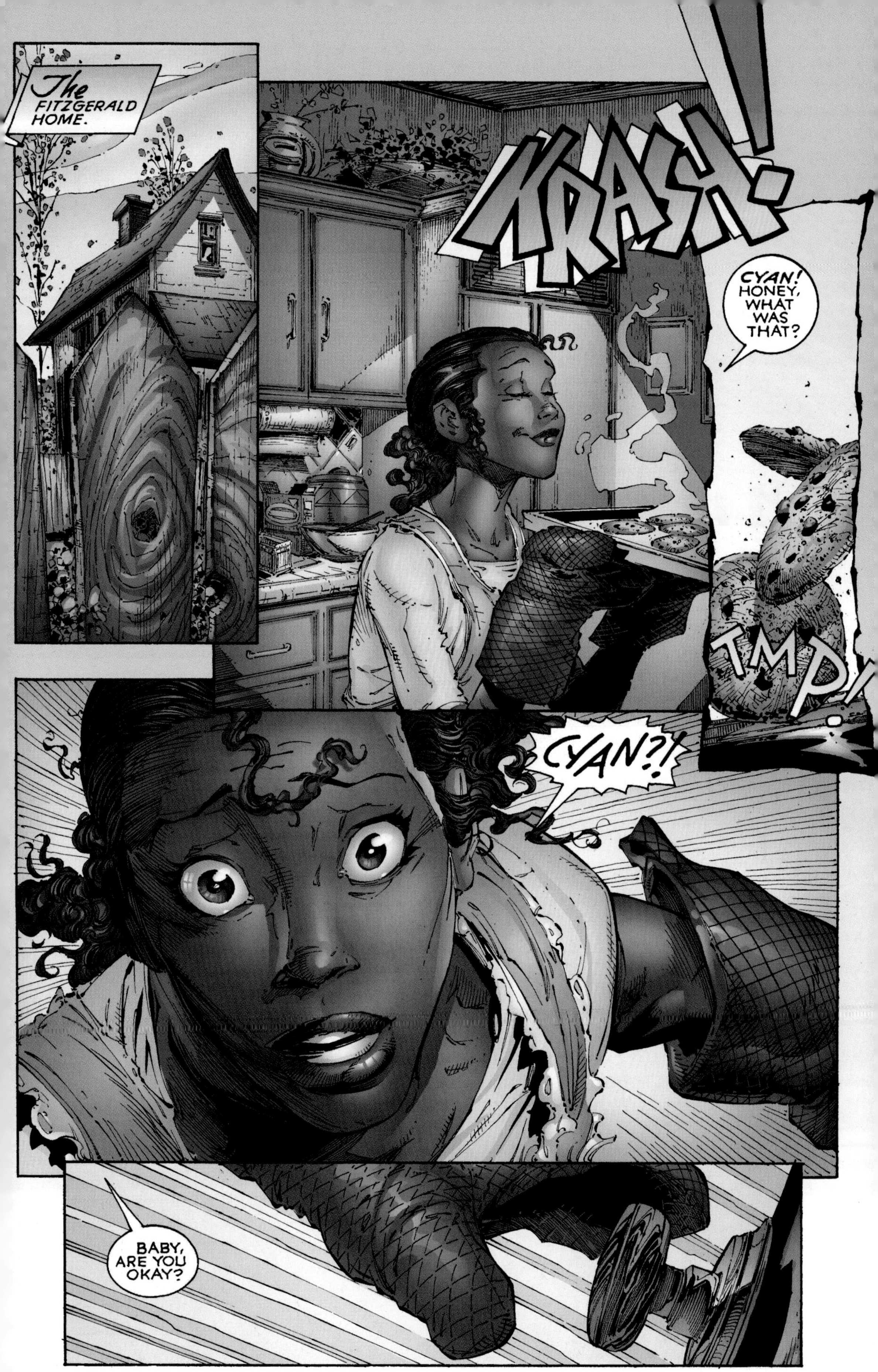
The FITZGERALD HOME.
KRASH!
CYAN! HONEY, WHAT WAS THAT?
TMP!
CYAN?!
BABY, ARE YOU OKAY?

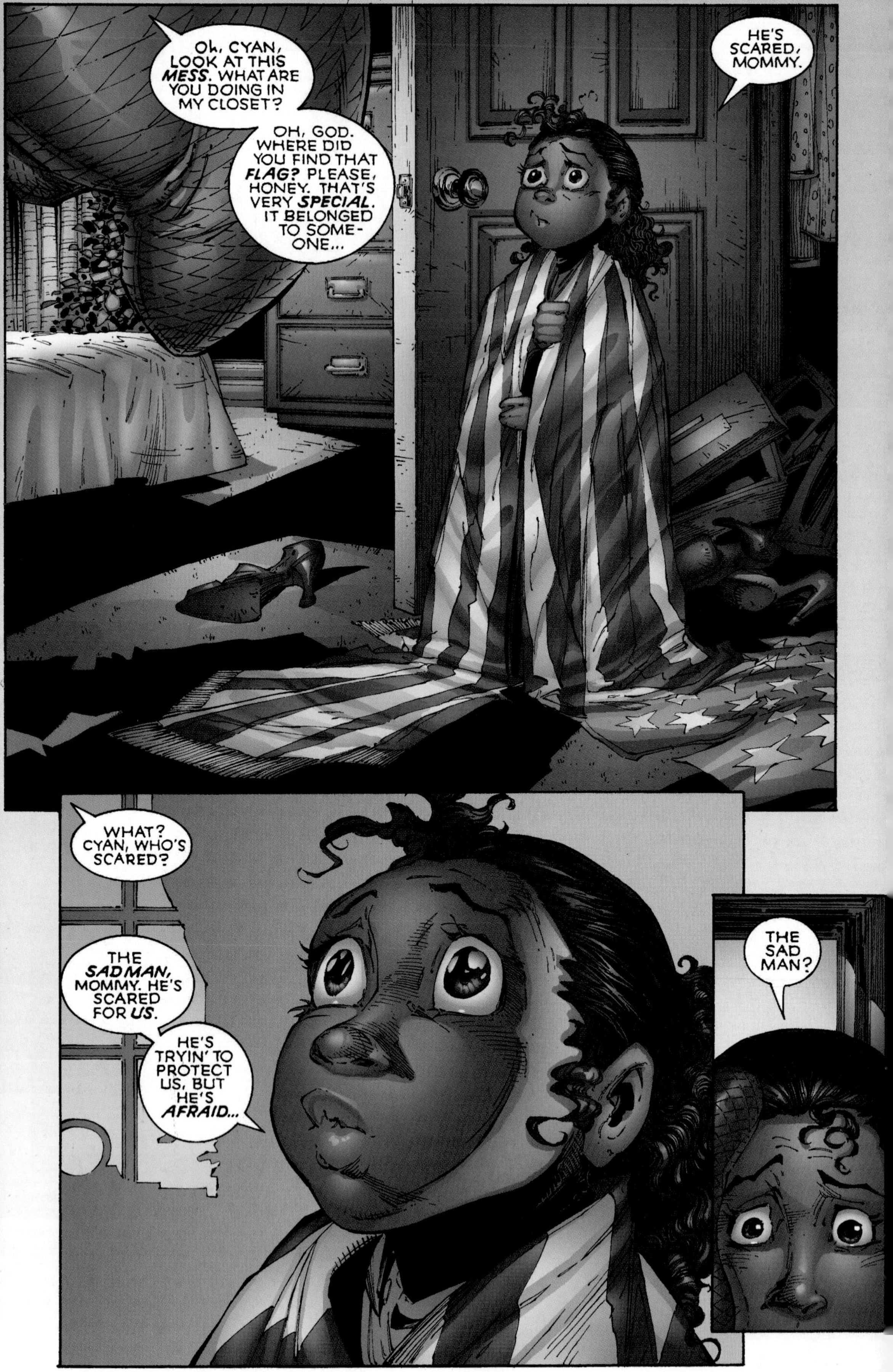
Oh, CYAN, LOOK AT THIS MESS. WHAT ARE YOU DOING IN MY CLOSET?
OH, GOD. WHERE DID YOU FIND THAT FLAG? PLEASE, HONEY. THAT'S VERY SPECIAL. IT BELONGED TO SOME-ONE...
HE'S SCARED, MOMMY.
WHAT? CYAN, WHO'S SCARED?
THE SADMAN, MOMMY. HE'S SCARED FOR US.
HE'S TRYIN' TO PROTECT US, BUT HE'S AFRAID...
THE SAD MAN?

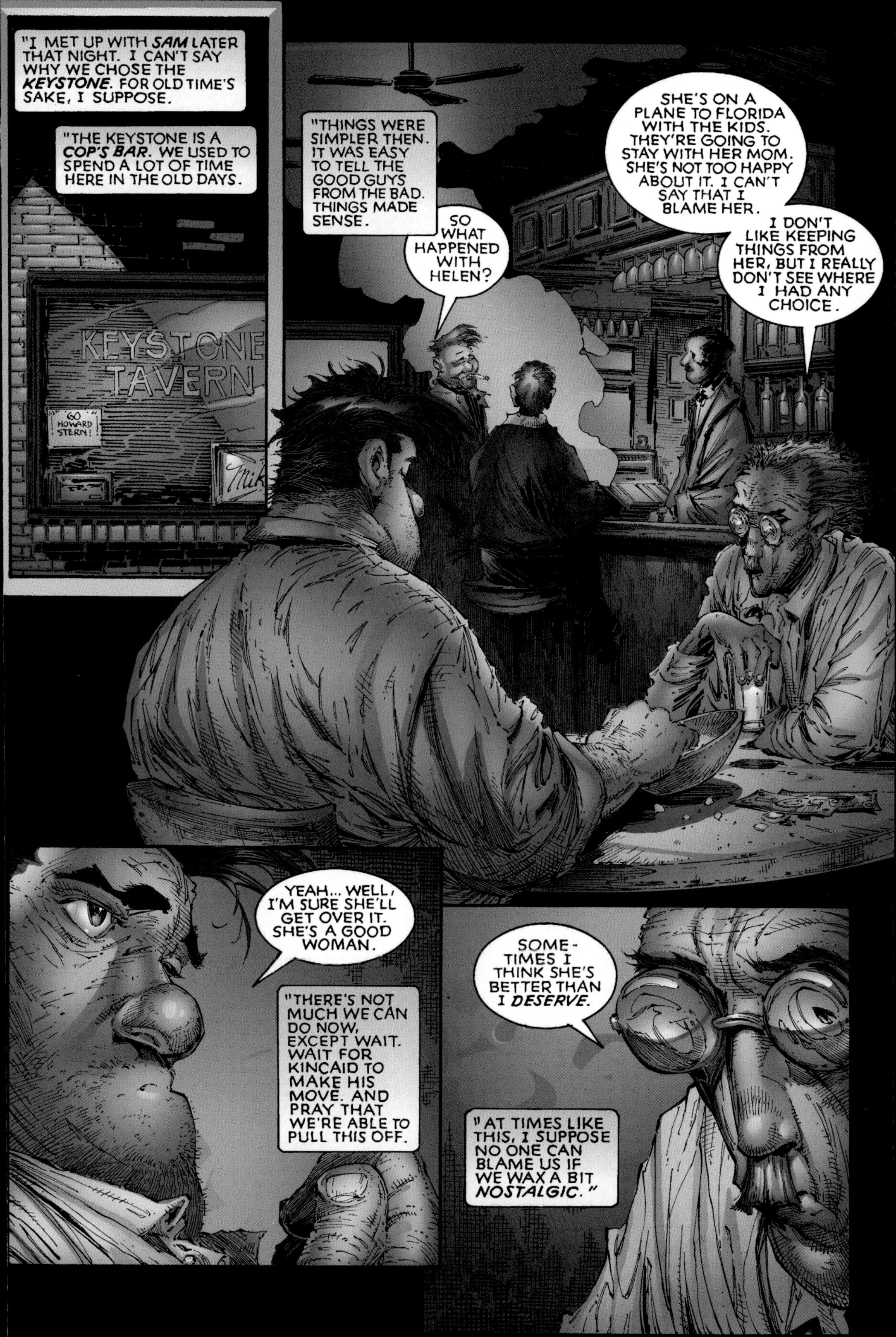
"I MET UP WITH SAM LATER THAT NIGHT. I CAN'T SAY WHY WE CHOSE THE KEYSTONE. FOR OLD TIME'S SAKE, I SUPPOSE.
"THE KEYSTONE IS A COP'S BAR. WE USED TO SPEND A LOT OF TIME HERE IN THE OLD DAYS.
KEYSTONE TAVERN
GO HOWARD STERN!
"THINGS WERE SIMPLER THEN. IT WAS EASY TO TELL THE GOOD GUYS FROM THE BAD. THINGS MADE SENSE.
SO WHAT HAPPENED WITH HELEN?
SHE'S ON A PLANE TO FLORIDA WITH THE KIDS. THEY'RE GOING TO STAY WITH HER MOM. SHE'S NOT TOO HAPPY ABOUT IT. I CAN'T SAY THAT I BLAME HER.
I DON'T LIKE KEEPING THINGS FROM HER, BUT I REALLY DON'T SEE WHERE I HAD ANY CHOICE.
YEAH... WELL, I'M SURE SHE'LL GET OVER IT. SHE'S A GOOD WOMAN.
"THERE'S NOT MUCH WE CAN DO NOW, EXCEPT WAIT. WAIT FOR KINCAID TO MAKE HIS MOVE. AND PRAY THAT WE'RE ABLE TO PULL THIS OFF.
SOME-TIMES I THINK SHE'S BETTER THAN I DESERVE.
"AT TIMES LIKE THIS, I SUPPOSE NO ONE CAN BLAME US IF WE WAX A BIT NOSTALGIC."

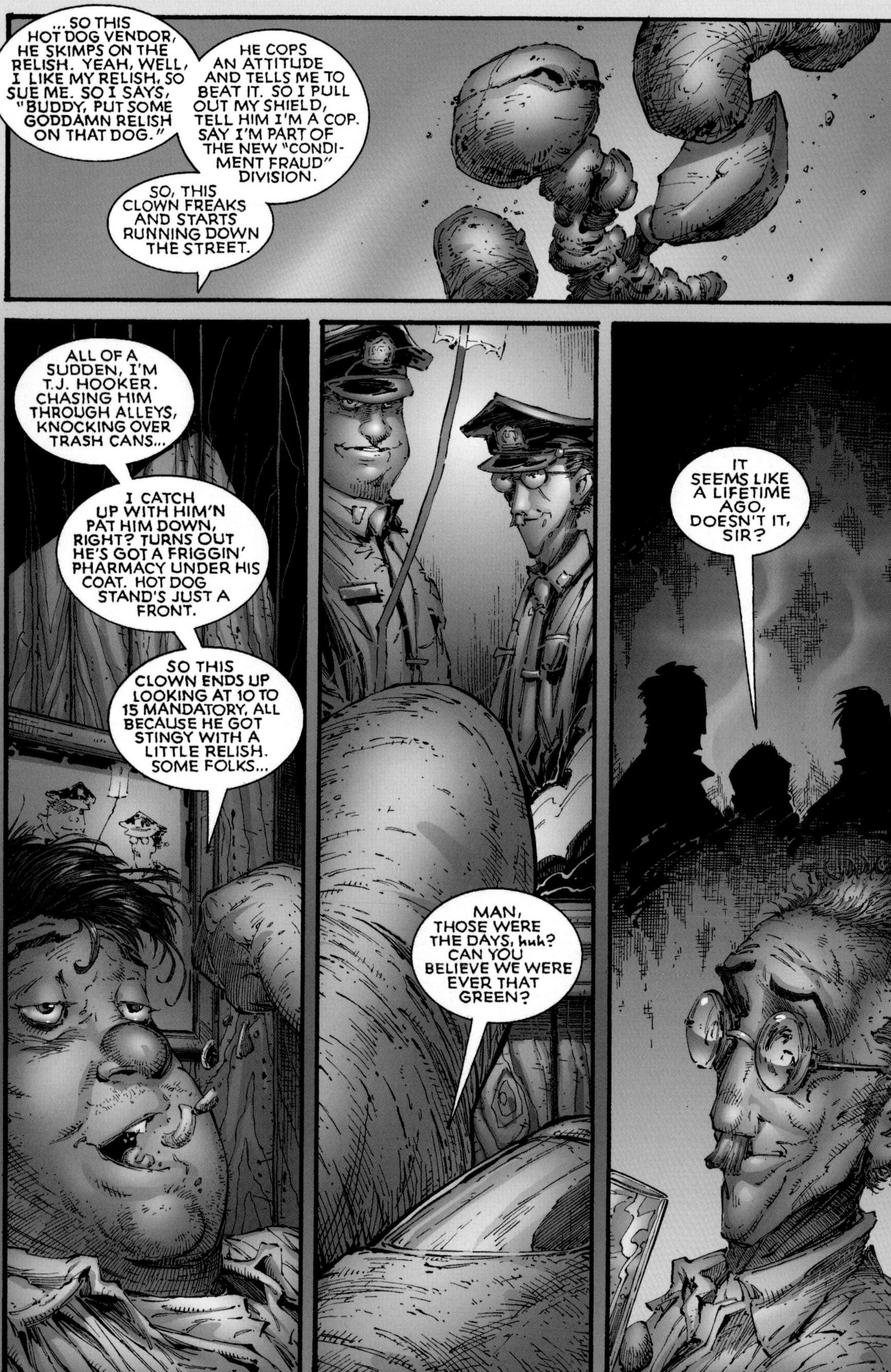
...SO THIS HOT DOG VENDOR, HE SKIMPS ON THE RELISH. YEAH, WELL, I LIKE MY RELISH, SO SUE ME. SO I SAYS, "BUDDY, PUT SOME GODDAMN RELISH ON THAT DOG."
HE COPS AN ATTITUDE AND TELLS ME TO BEAT IT. SO I PULL OUT MY SHIELD, TELL HIM I'M A COP. SAY I'M PART OF THE NEW "CONDI-MENT FRAUD" DIVISION.
SO, THIS CLOWN FREAKS AND STARTS RUNNING DOWN THE STREET.
ALL OF A SUDDEN, I'M T.J. HOOKER. CHASING HIM THROUGH ALLEYS, KNOCKING OVER TRASH CANS...
I CATCH UP WITH HIM'N PAT HIM DOWN, RIGHT? TURNS OUT HE'S GOT A FRIGGIN' PHARMACY UNDER HIS COAT. HOT DOG STAND'S JUST A FRONT.
SO THIS CLOWN ENDS UP LOOKING AT 10 TO 15 MANDATORY, ALL BECAUSE HE GOT STINGY WITH A LITTLE RELISH. SOME FOLKS...
MAN, THOSE WERE THE DAYS, huh? CAN YOU BELIEVE WE WERE EVER THAT GREEN?
IT SEEMS LIKE A LIFETIME AGO, DOESN'T IT, SIR?

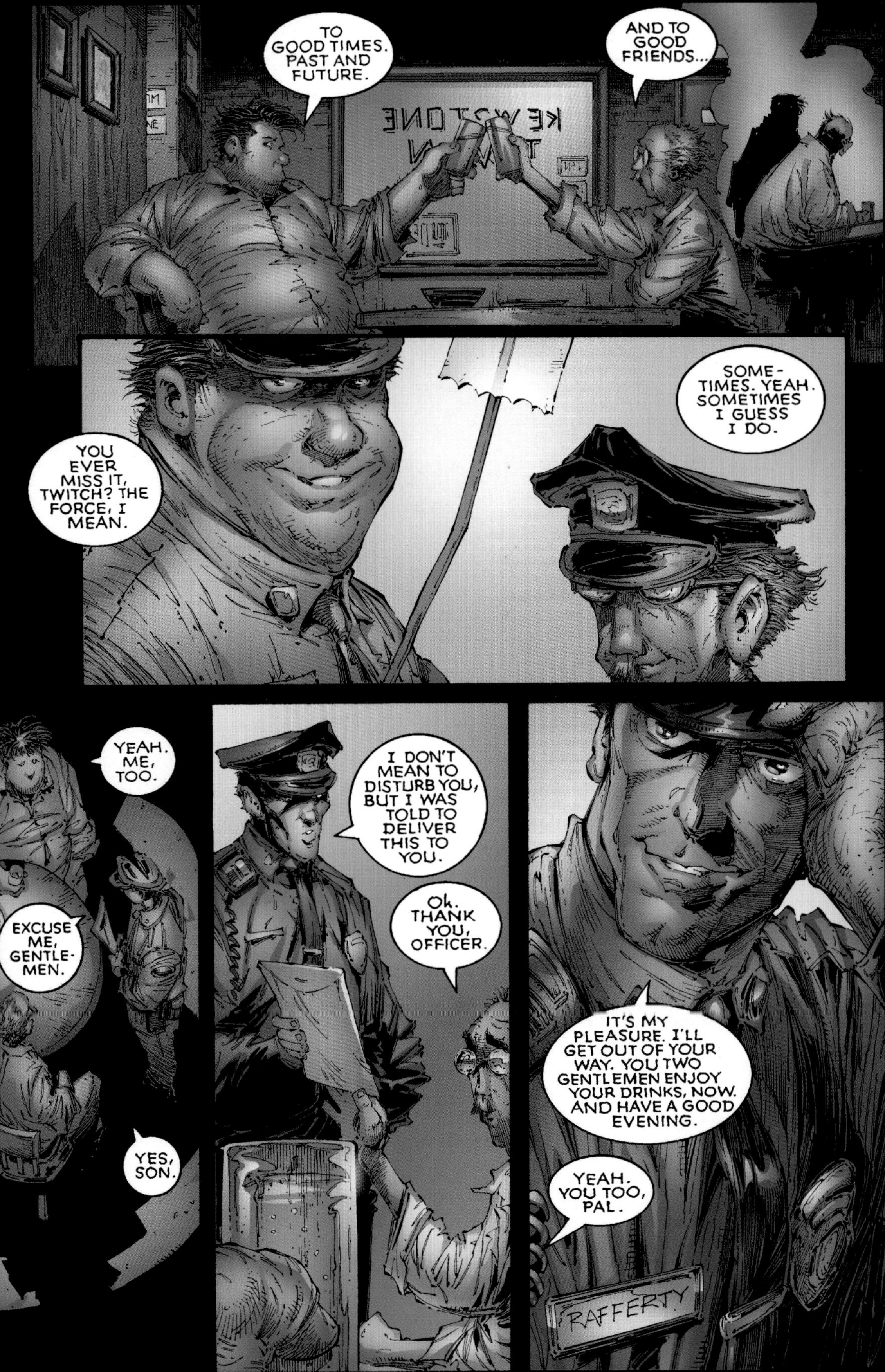
TO GOOD TIMES. PAST AND FUTURE.
AND TO GOOD FRIENDS...
KEYSTONE TAVERN
YOU EVER MISS IT, TWITCH? THE FORCE, I MEAN.
SOME-TIMES. YEAH. SOMETIMES I GUESS I DO.
YEAH. ME, TOO.
EXCUSE ME, GENTLE-MEN.
YES, SON.
I DON'T MEAN TO DISTURB YOU, BUT I WAS TOLD TO DELIVER THIS TO YOU.
Oh. THANK YOU, OFFICER.
IT'S MY PLEASURE. I'LL GET OUT OF YOUR WAY. YOU TWO GENTLEMEN ENJOY YOUR DRINKS, NOW. AND HAVE A GOOD EVENING.
YEAH. YOU TOO, PAL.
RAFFERTY

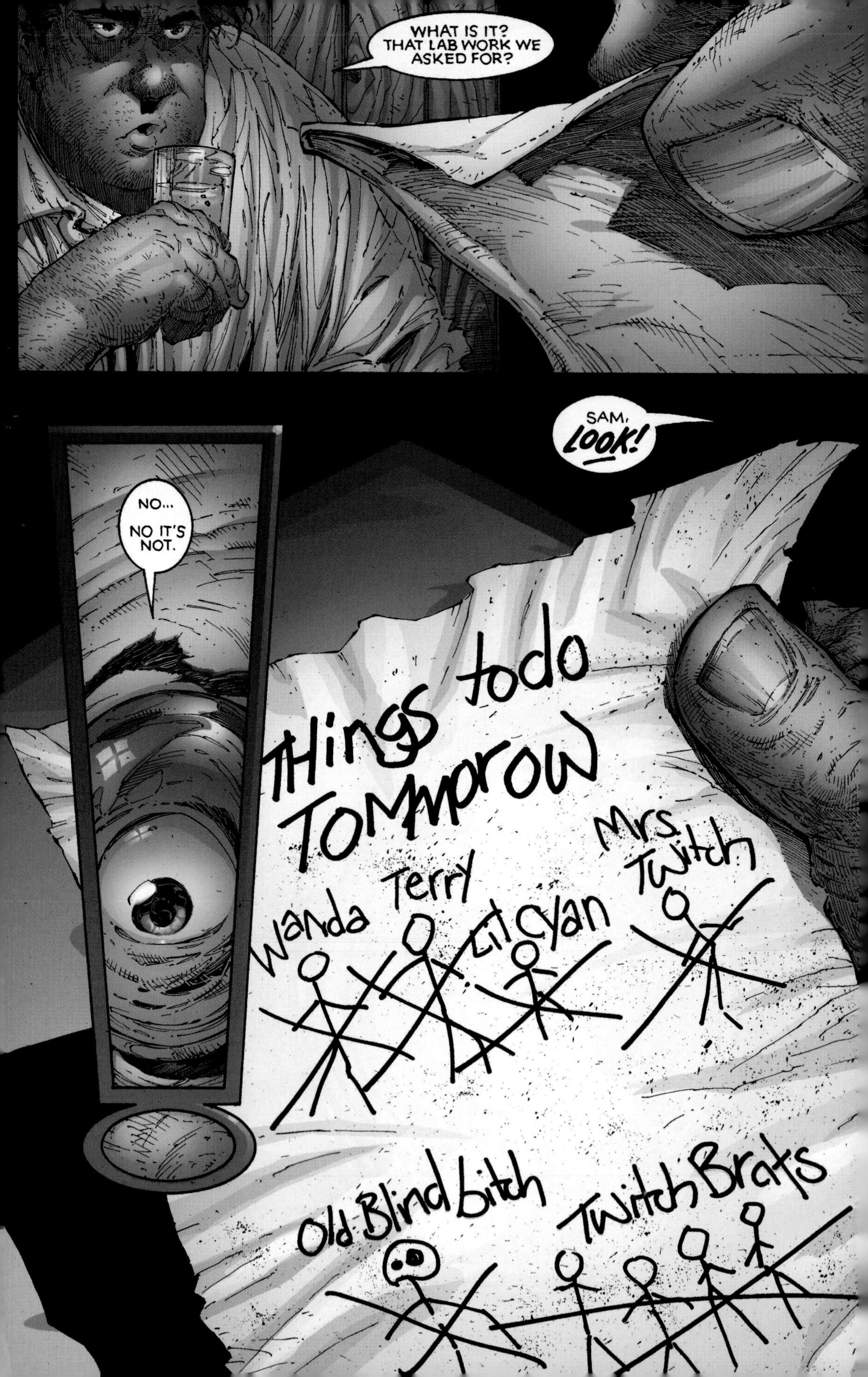

WHAT IS IT? THAT LAB WORK WE ASKED FOR?
SAM, LOOK!
NO... NO IT'S NOT.
THings todo TOMMprOW
Wanda
Terry
Lil Cyan
Mrs. Twitch
Old Blind bitch
Twitch Brats

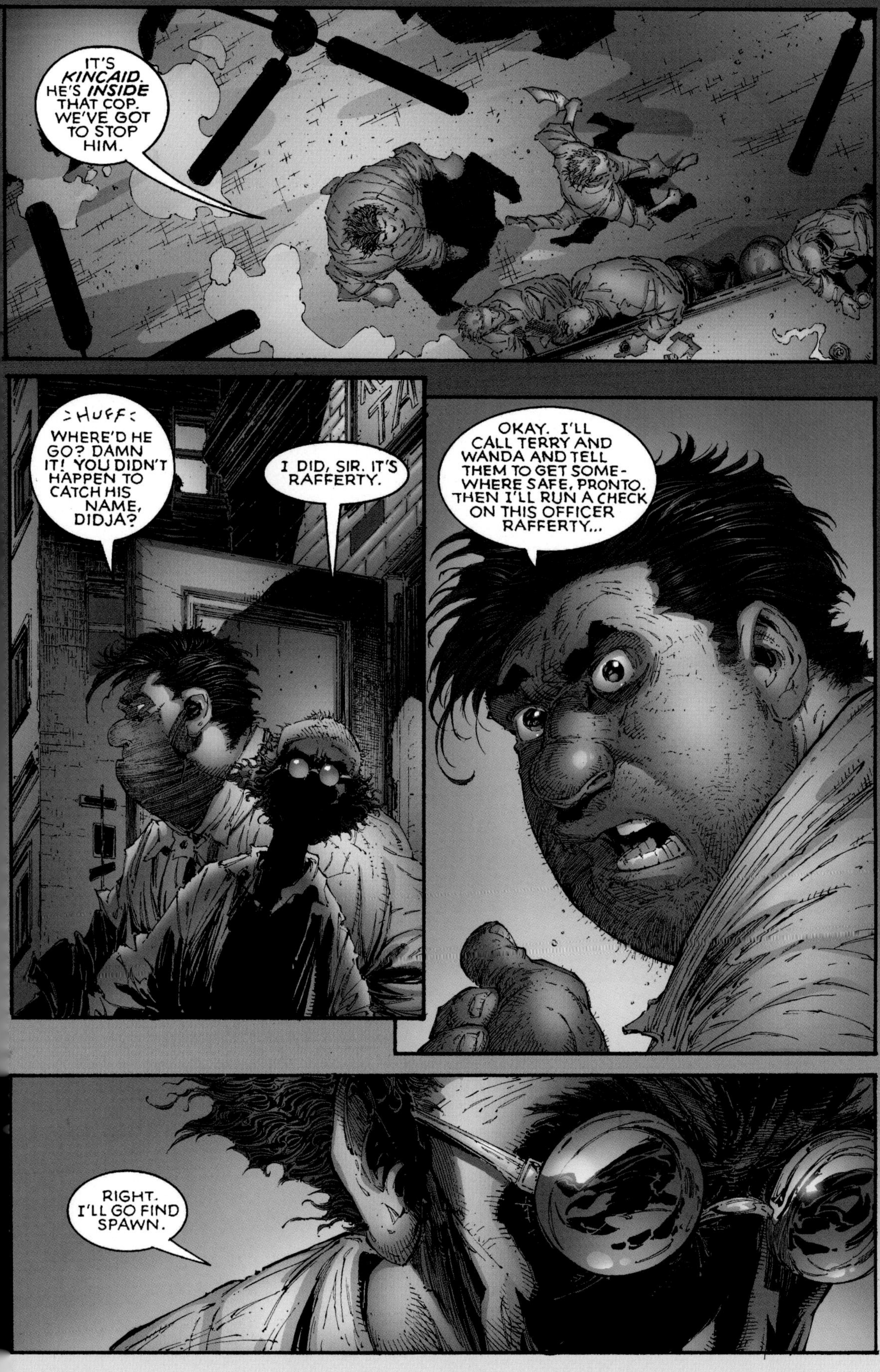
IT'S *KINCAID.* HE'S *INSIDE* THAT COP. WE'VE GOT TO STOP HIM.
HUFF
WHERE'D HE GO? DAMN IT! YOU DIDN'T HAPPEN TO CATCH HIS NAME, DIDJA?
I DID, SIR. IT'S RAFFERTY.
OKAY. I'LL CALL TERRY AND WANDA AND TELL THEM TO GET SOME-WHERE SAFE, PRONTO. THEN I'LL RUN A *CHECK* ON THIS OFFICER RAFFERTY...
RIGHT. I'LL GO FIND SPAWN.

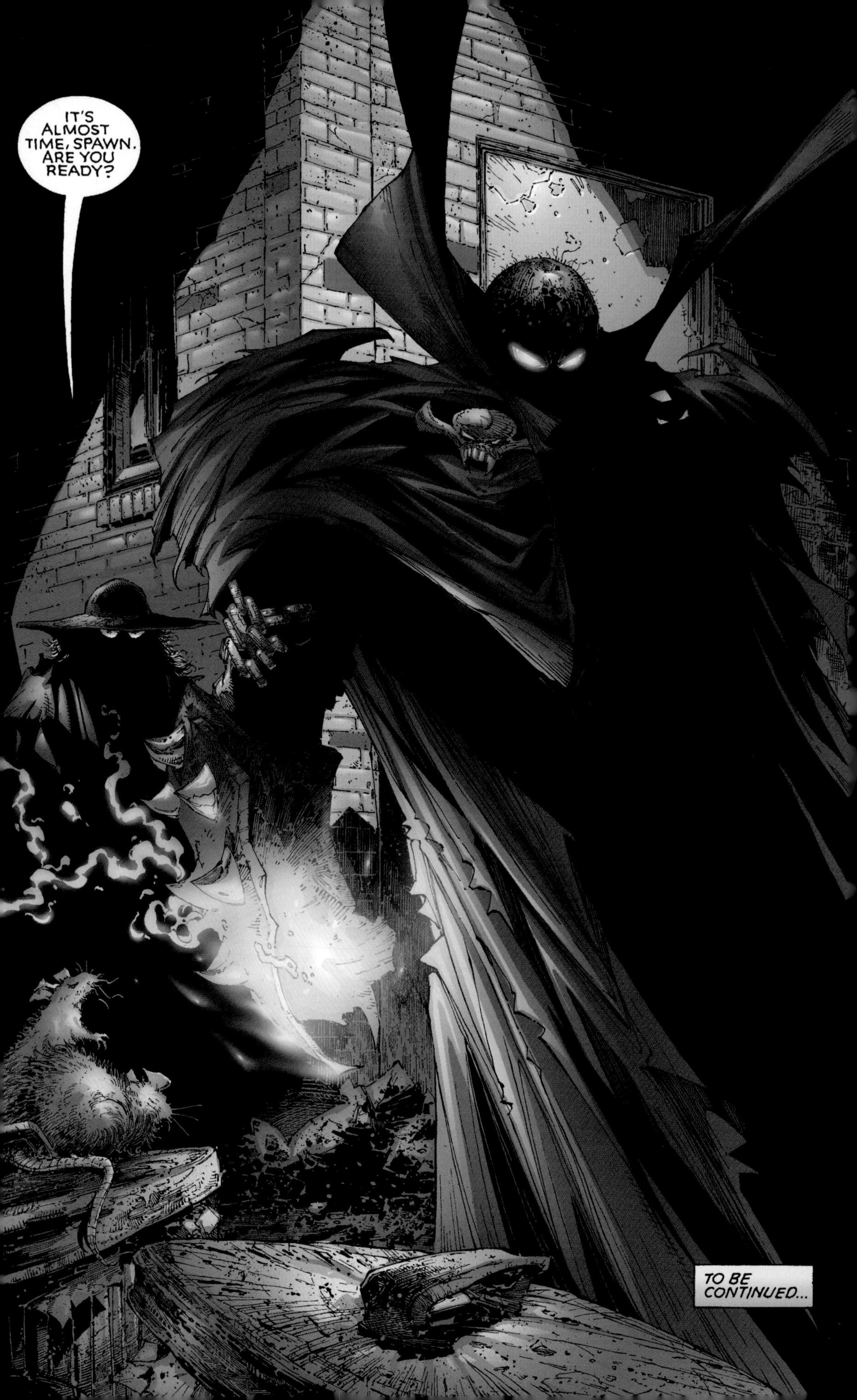
IT'S ALMOST TIME, SPAWN. ARE YOU READY?
TO BE CONTINUED...

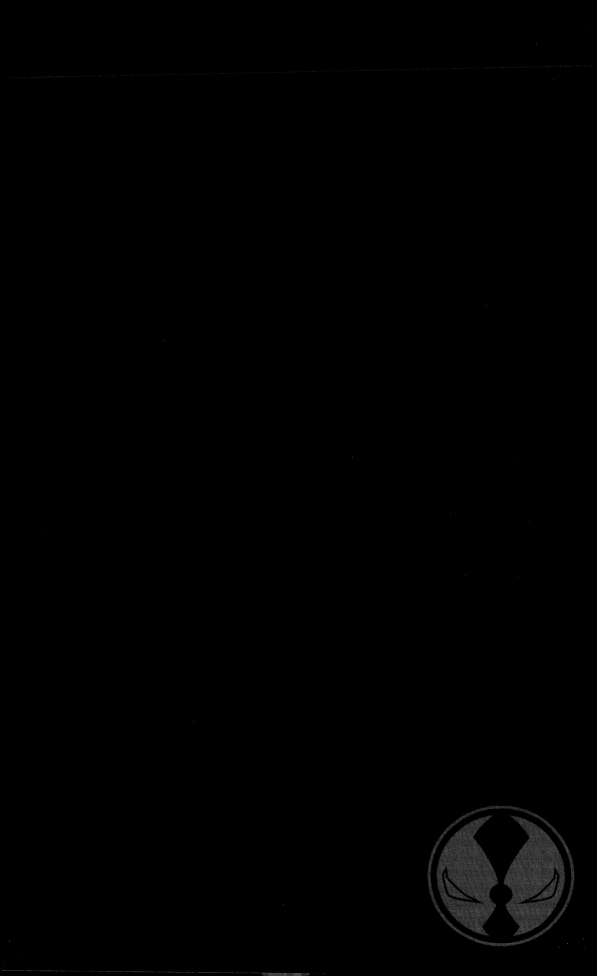

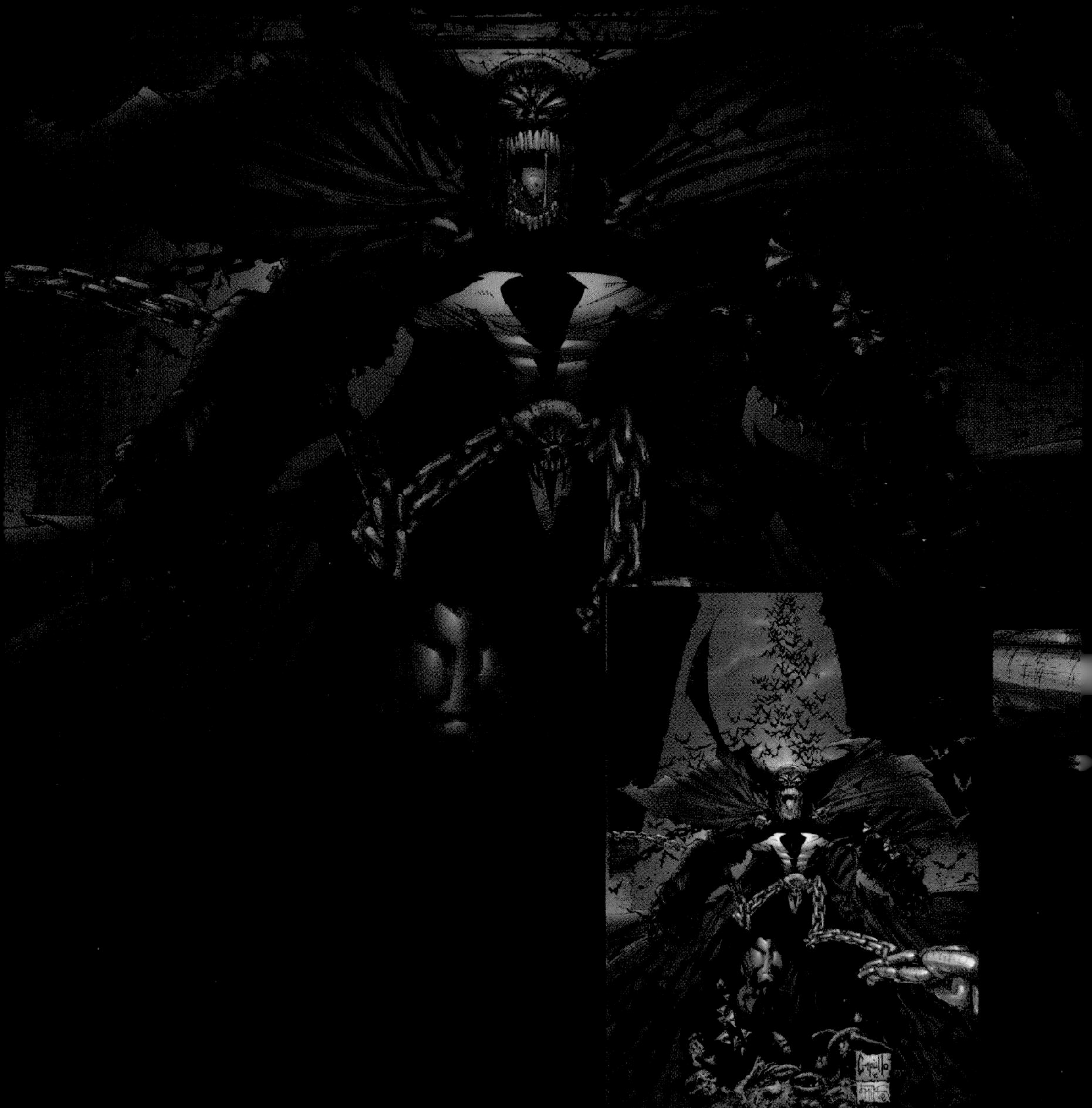

ISSUE EIGHTY-FIVE

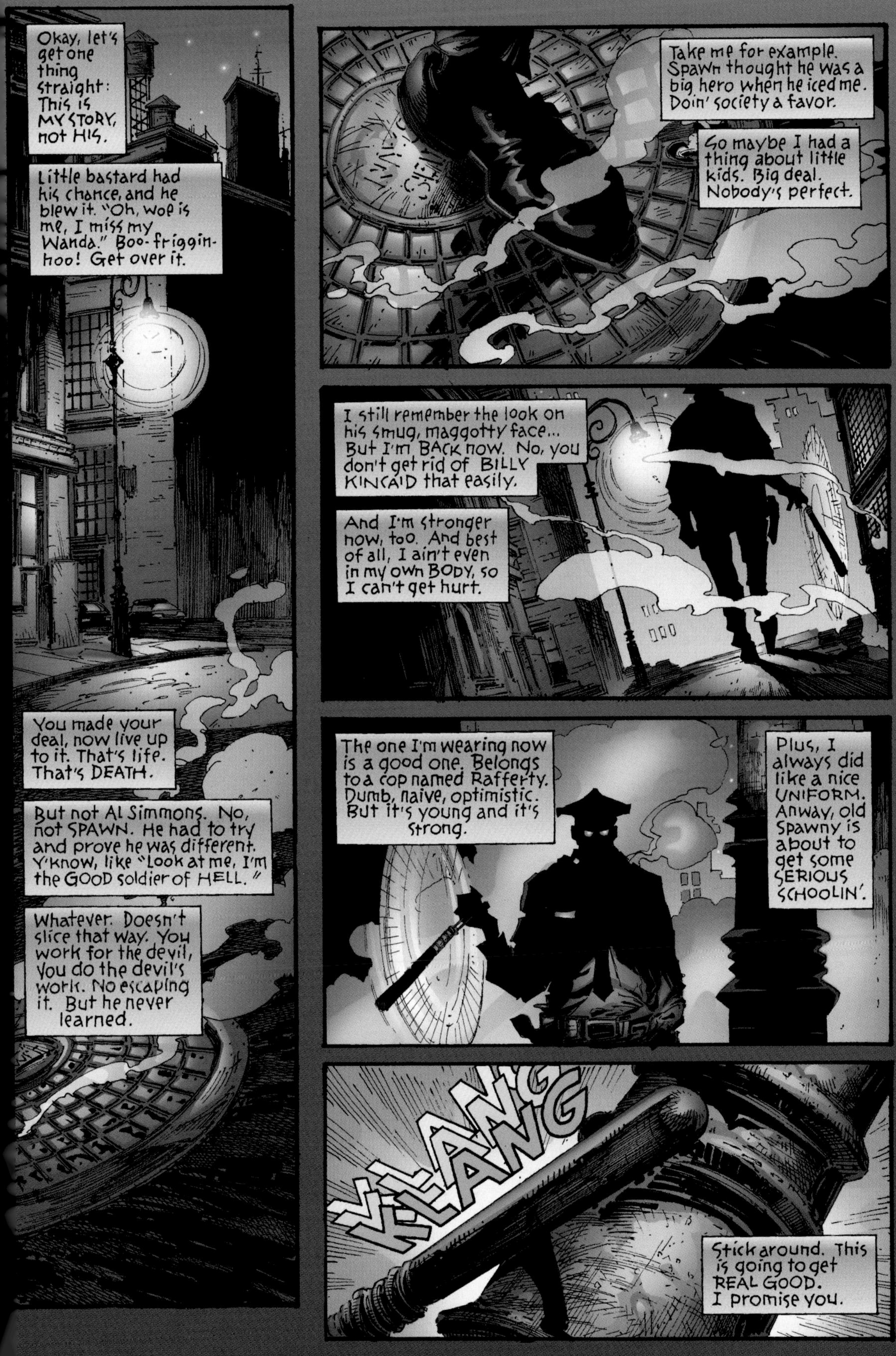
Okay, let's get one thing straight: This is MY STORY, not HIS.
Little bastard had his chance, and he blew it. "Oh, woe is me, I miss my Wanda." Boo-friggin-hoo! Get over it.
You made your deal, now live up to it. That's life. That's DEATH.
But not Al Simmons. No, not SPAWN. He had to try and prove he was different. Y'know, like "Look at me, I'm the GOOD soldier of HELL."
Whatever. Doesn't slice that way. You work for the devil, you do the devil's work. No escaping it. But he never learned.
Take me for example. Spawn thought he was a big hero when he iced me. Doin' society a favor.
So maybe I had a thing about little kids. Big deal. Nobody's perfect.
I still remember the look on his smug, maggotty face... But I'm BACK now. No, you don't get rid of BILLY KINCAID that easily.
And I'm stronger now, too. And best of all, I ain't even in my own BODY, so I can't get hurt.
The one I'm wearing now is a good one. Belongs to a cop named Rafferty. Dumb, naive, optimistic. But it's young and it's strong.
Plus, I always did like a nice UNIFORM. Anway, old Spawny is about to get some SERIOUS SCHOOLIN'.
KLANG
KLANG
Stick around. This is going to get REAL GOOD. I promise you.

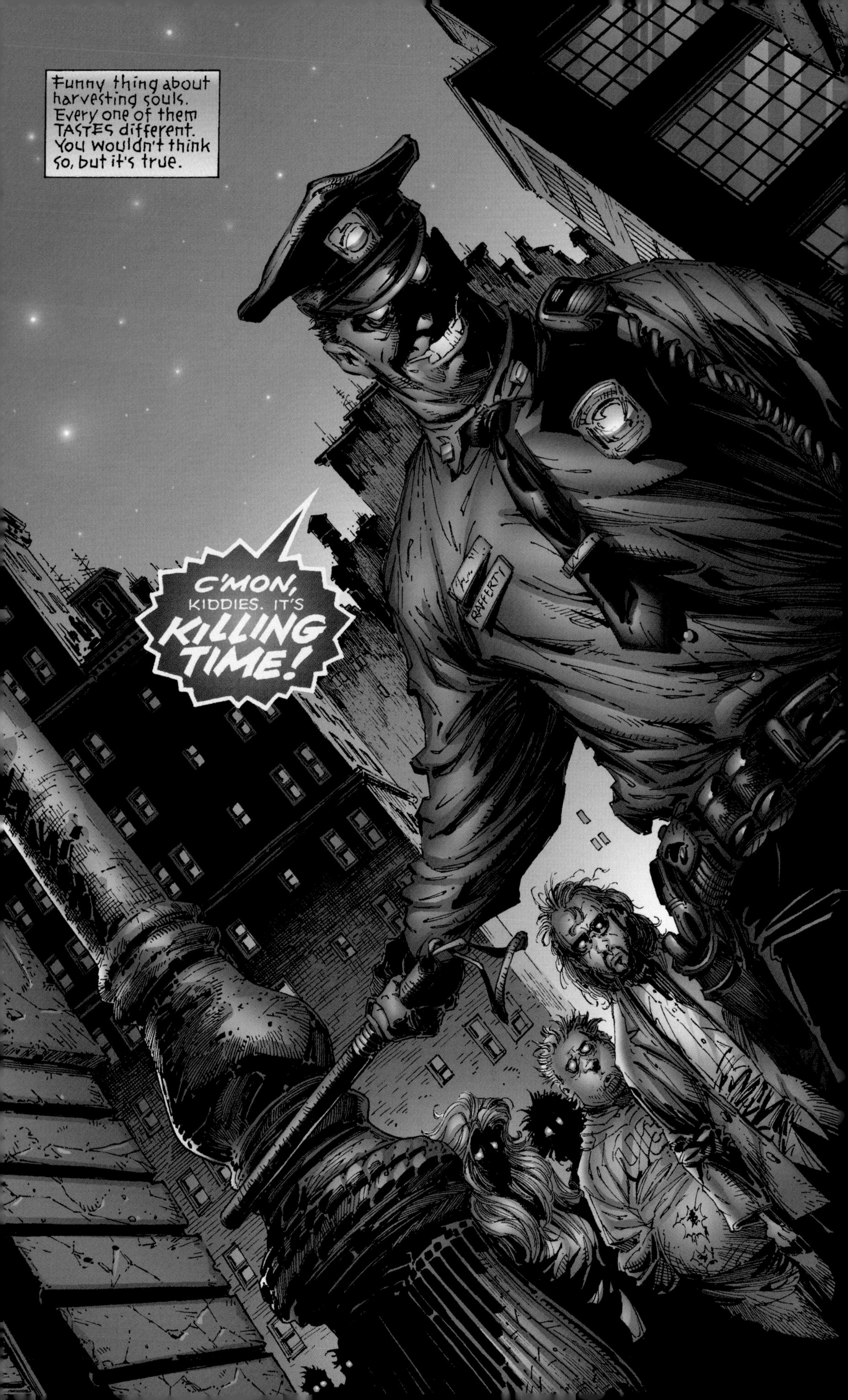
Funny thing about harvesting souls. Every one of them TASTES different. You wouldn't think so, but it's true.
C'MON, KIDDIES. IT'S KILLING TIME!
RAFFERTY

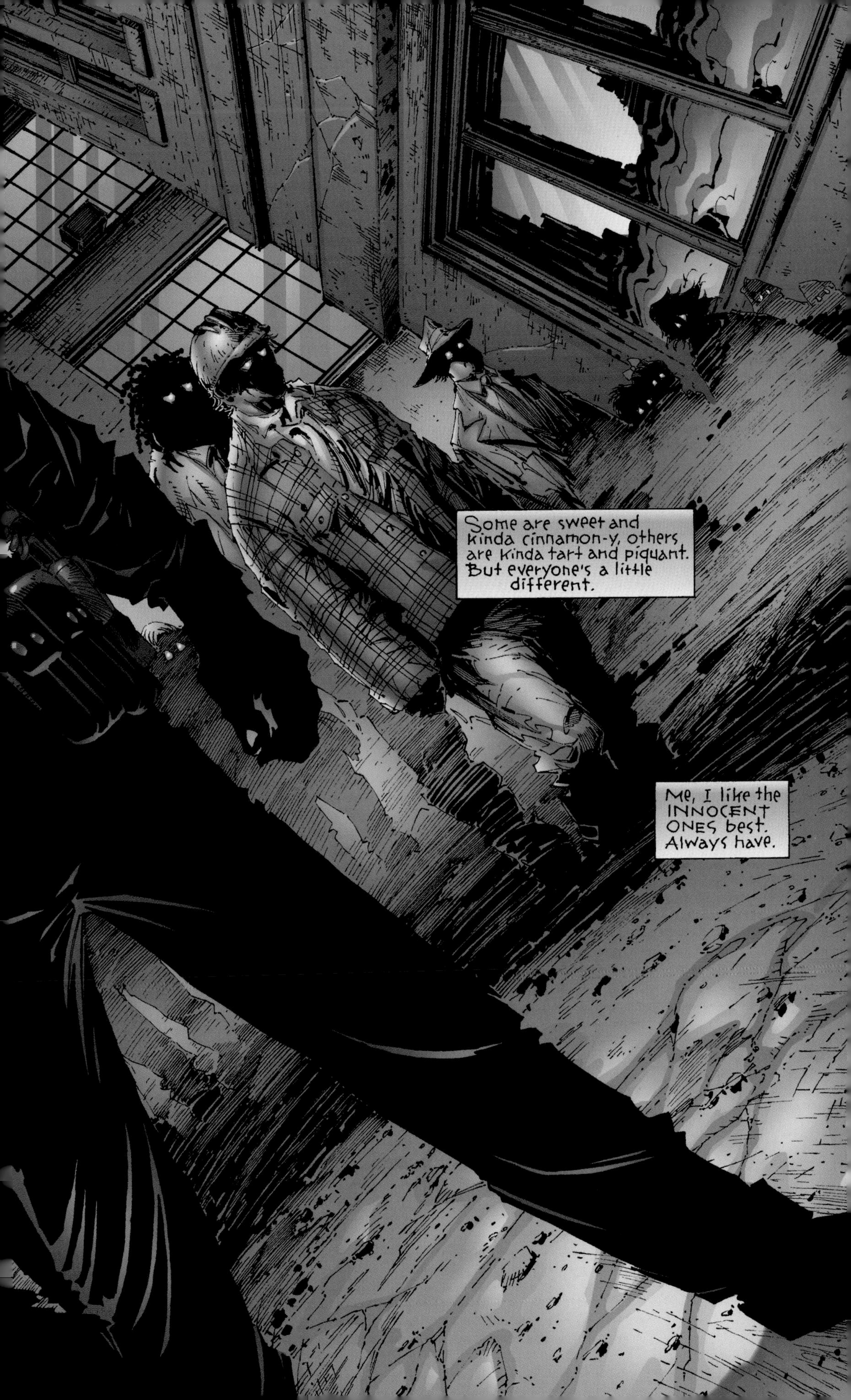
Some are sweet and kinda cinnamon-y, others are kinda tart and piquant. But everyone's a little different.
Me, I like the INNOCENT ONES best. Always have.

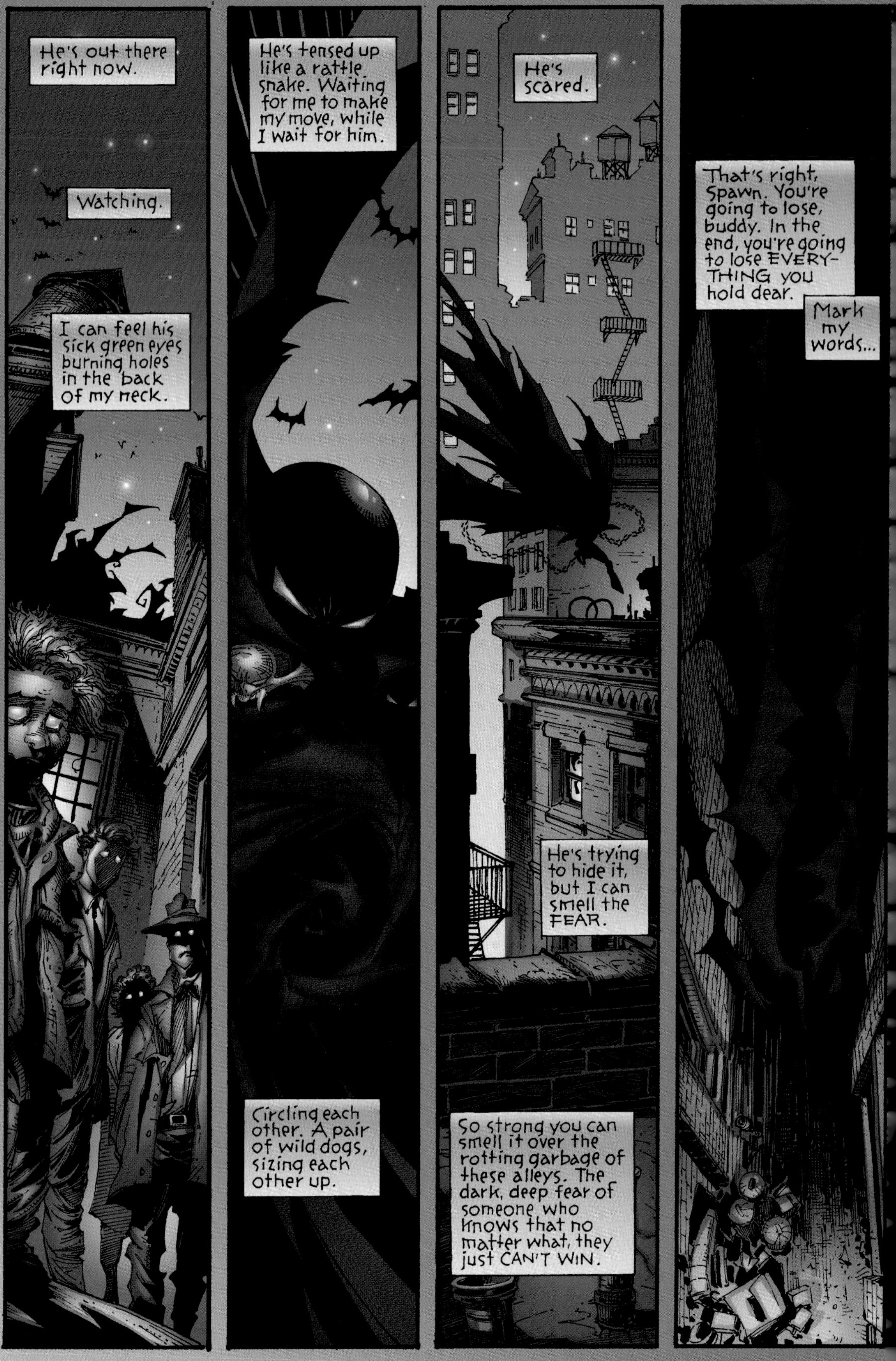
He's out there right now.
Watching.
I can feel his sick green eyes burning holes in the back of my neck.
He's tensed up like a rattle snake. Waiting for me to make my move, while I wait for him.
Circling each other. A pair of wild dogs, sizing each other up.
He's scared.
He's trying to hide it, but I can smell the FEAR.
So strong you can smell it over the rotting garbage of these alleys. The dark, deep fear of someone who knows that no matter what, they just CAN'T WIN.
That's right, Spawn. You're going to lose, buddy. In the end, you're going to lose EVERY-THING you hold dear.
Mark my words...

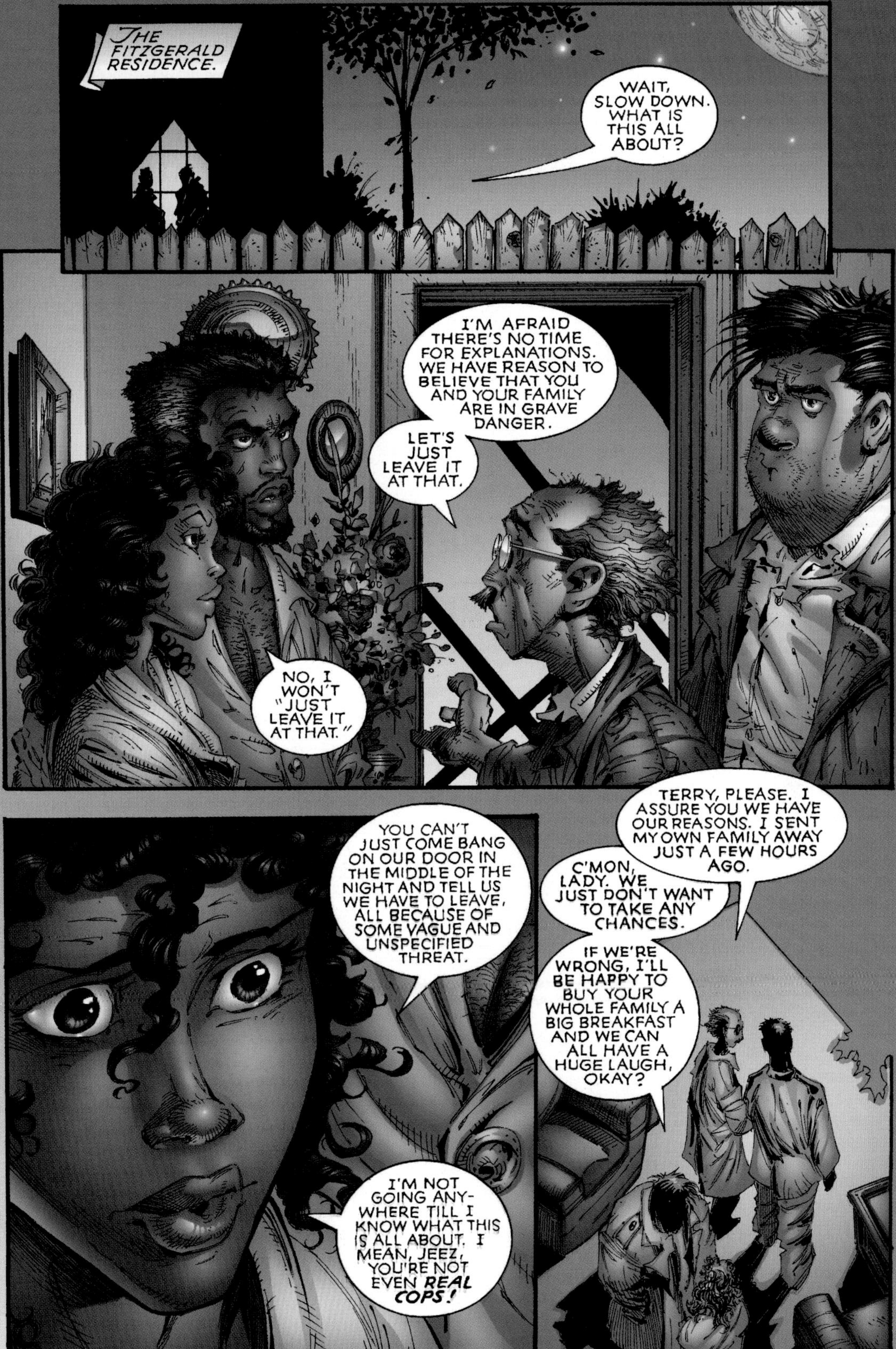
THE FITZGERALD RESIDENCE.
WAIT, SLOW DOWN. WHAT IS THIS ALL ABOUT?
I'M AFRAID THERE'S NO TIME FOR EXPLANATIONS. WE HAVE REASON TO BELIEVE THAT YOU AND YOUR FAMILY ARE IN GRAVE DANGER.
LET'S JUST LEAVE IT AT THAT.
NO, I WON'T "JUST LEAVE IT AT THAT."
YOU CAN'T JUST COME BANG ON OUR DOOR IN THE MIDDLE OF THE NIGHT AND TELL US WE HAVE TO LEAVE, ALL BECAUSE OF SOME VAGUE AND UNSPECIFIED THREAT.
I'M NOT GOING ANYWHERE TILL I KNOW WHAT THIS IS ALL ABOUT. I MEAN, JEEZ, YOU'RE NOT EVEN REAL COPS!
TERRY, PLEASE. I ASSURE YOU WE HAVE OUR REASONS. I SENT MY OWN FAMILY AWAY JUST A FEW HOURS AGO.
C'MON, LADY. WE JUST DON'T WANT TO TAKE ANY CHANCES.
IF WE'RE WRONG, I'LL BE HAPPY TO BUY YOUR WHOLE FAMILY A BIG BREAKFAST AND WE CAN ALL HAVE A HUGE LAUGH, OKAY?

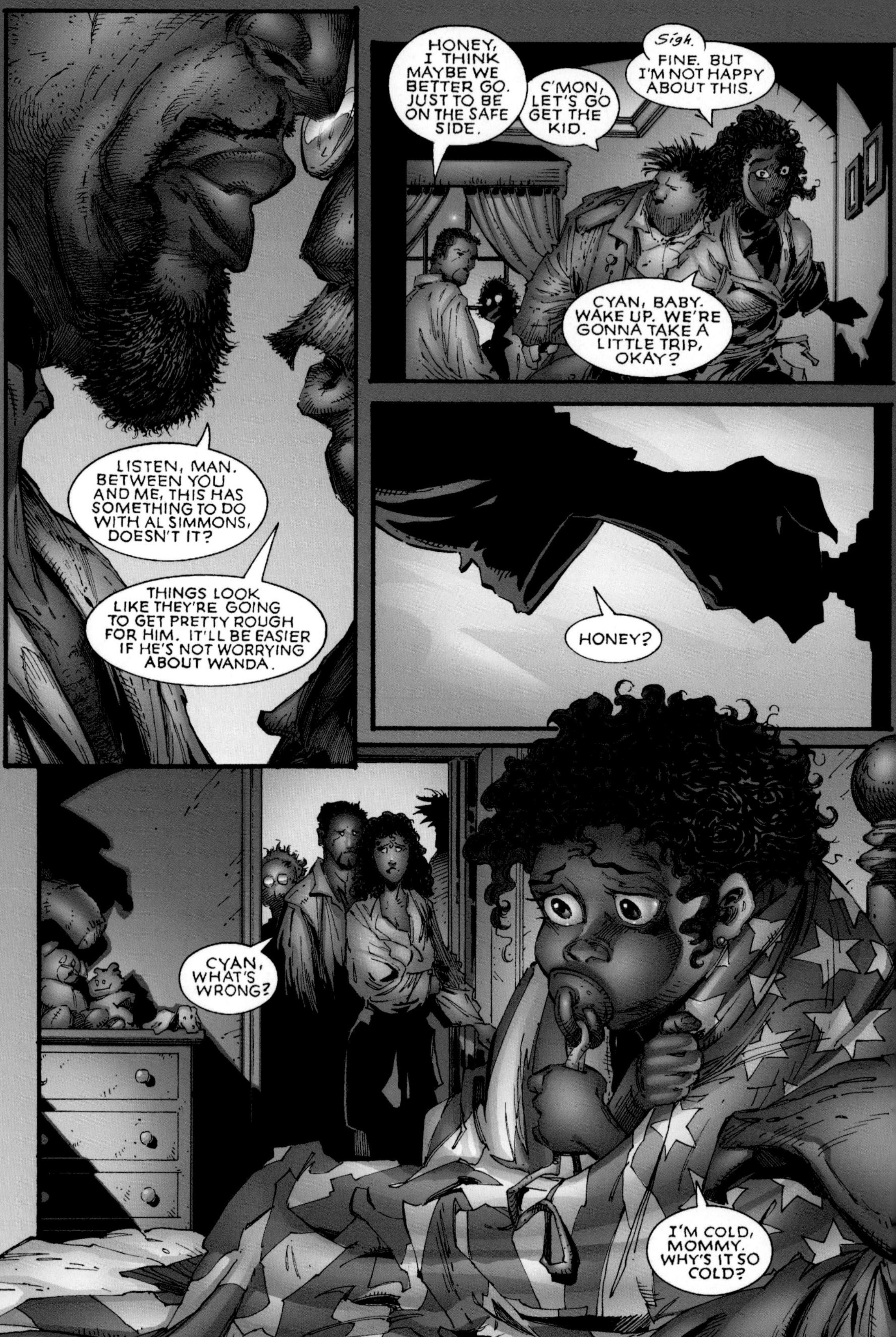
HONEY, I THINK MAYBE WE BETTER GO. JUST TO BE ON THE SAFE SIDE.
C'MON, LET'S GO GET THE KID.
Sigh.
FINE. BUT I'M NOT HAPPY ABOUT THIS.
LISTEN, MAN. BETWEEN YOU AND ME, THIS HAS SOMETHING TO DO WITH AL SIMMONS, DOESN'T IT?
THINGS LOOK LIKE THEY'RE GOING TO GET PRETTY ROUGH FOR HIM. IT'LL BE EASIER IF HE'S NOT WORRYING ABOUT WANDA.
CYAN, BABY. WAKE UP. WE'RE GONNA TAKE A LITTLE TRIP, OKAY?
HONEY?
CYAN, WHAT'S WRONG?
I'M COLD, MOMMY. WHY'S IT SO COLD?

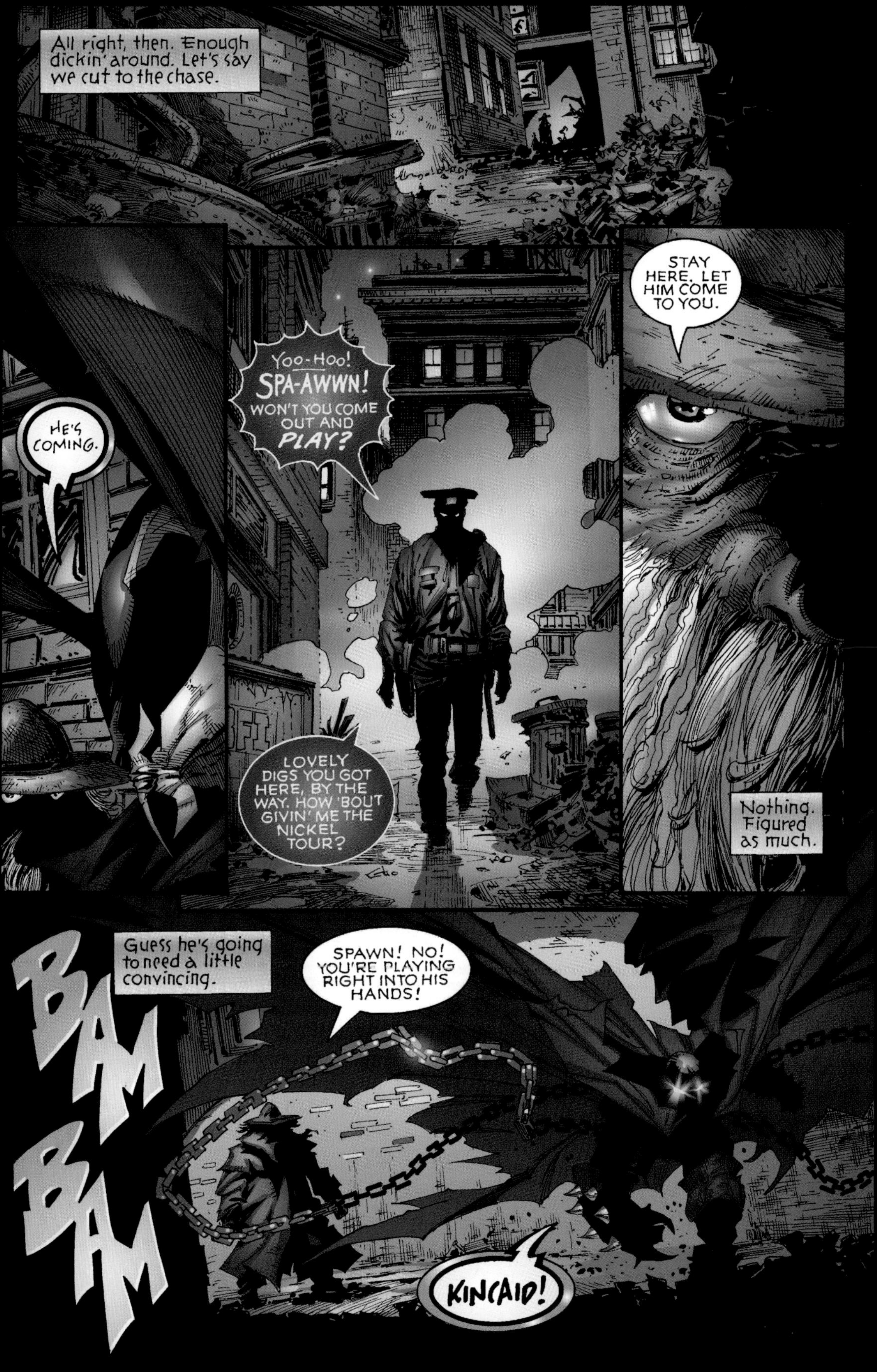
All right, then. Enough dickin' around. Let's say we cut to the chase.
HE'S COMING.
YOO-HOO! SPA-AWWN! WON'T YOU COME OUT AND PLAY?
LOVELY DIGS YOU GOT HERE, BY THE WAY. HOW 'BOUT GIVIN' ME THE NICKEL TOUR?
STAY HERE. LET HIM COME TO YOU.
Nothing. Figured as much.
Guess he's going to need a little convincing.
BAM BAM
SPAWN! NO! YOU'RE PLAYING RIGHT INTO HIS HANDS!
KINCAID!

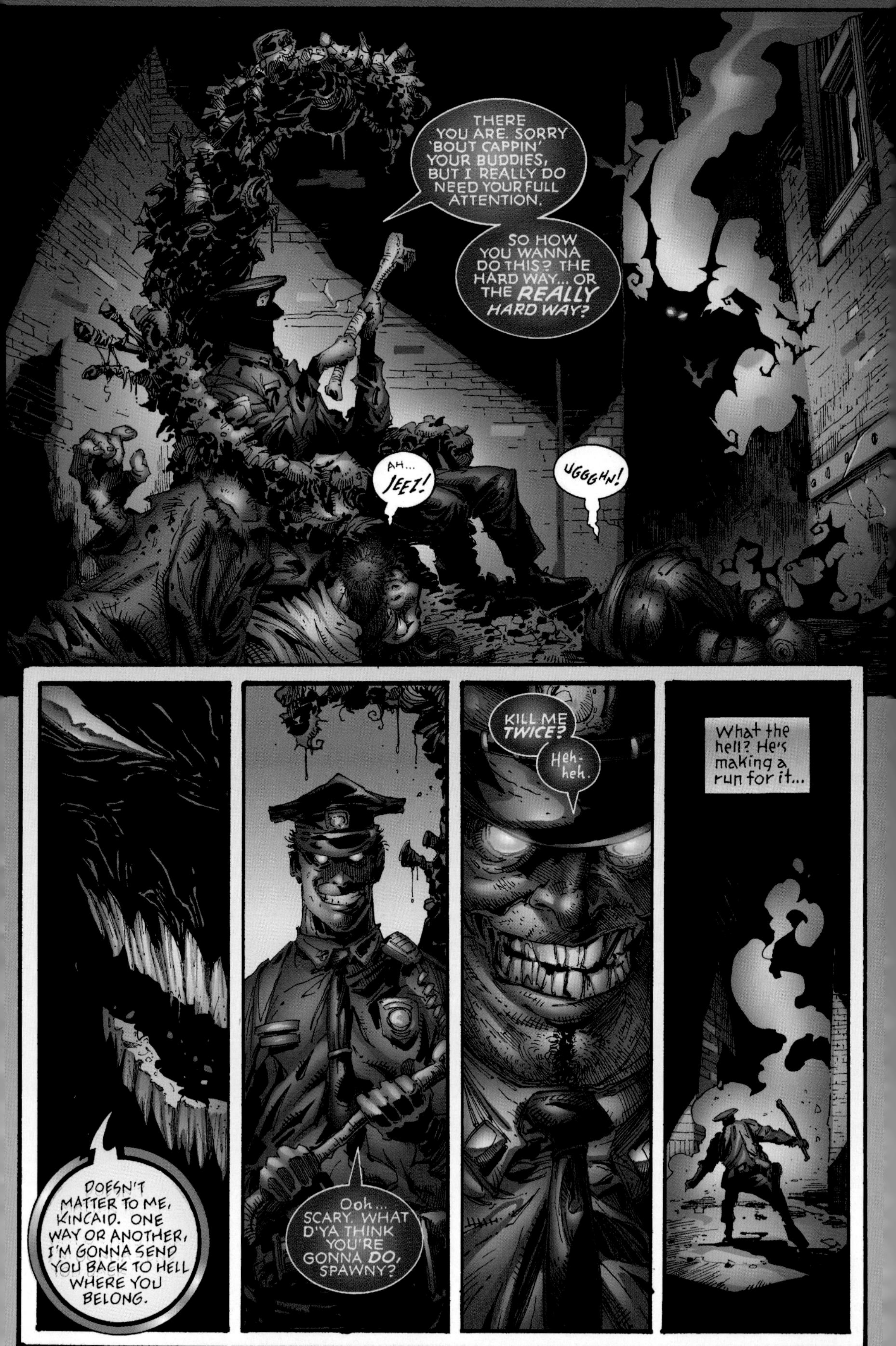
THERE YOU ARE. SORRY 'BOUT CAPPIN' YOUR BUDDIES, BUT I REALLY DO NEED YOUR FULL ATTENTION.
SO HOW YOU WANNA DO THIS? THE HARD WAY... OR THE *REALLY* HARD WAY?
AH... JEEZ!
UGGGHN!
DOESN'T MATTER TO ME, KINCAID. ONE WAY OR ANOTHER, I'M GONNA SEND YOU BACK TO HELL WHERE YOU BELONG.
Ooh... SCARY. WHAT D'YA THINK YOU'RE GONNA *DO*, SPAWNY?
KILL ME *TWICE*?
Heh-heh.
What the hell? He's making a run for it...

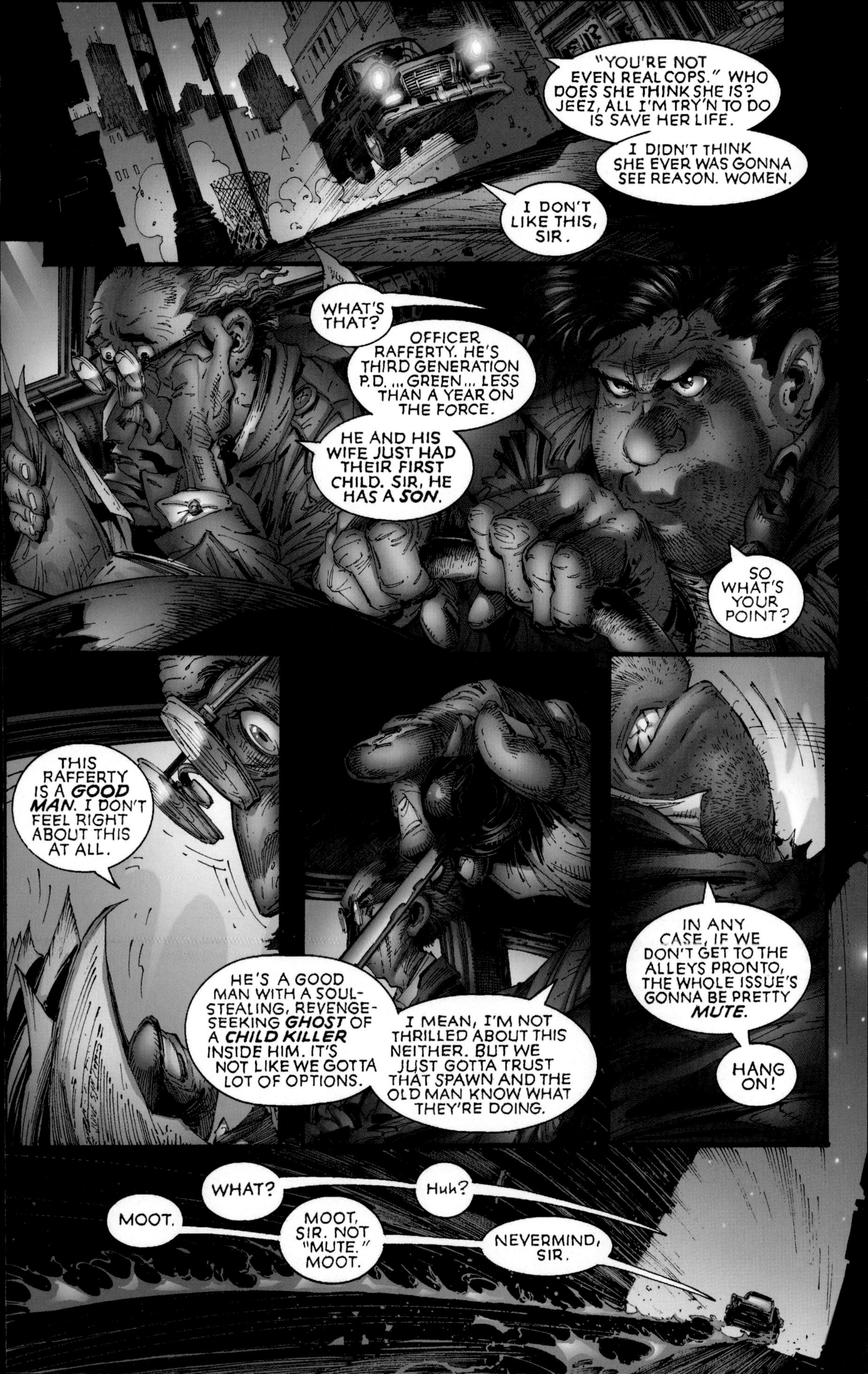
"YOU'RE NOT EVEN REAL COPS." WHO DOES SHE THINK SHE IS? JEEZ, ALL I'M TRY'N TO DO IS SAVE HER LIFE.
I DIDN'T THINK SHE EVER WAS GONNA SEE REASON. WOMEN.
I DON'T LIKE THIS, SIR.
WHAT'S THAT?
OFFICER RAFFERTY. HE'S THIRD GENERATION P.D. ... GREEN ... LESS THAN A YEAR ON THE FORCE.
HE AND HIS WIFE JUST HAD THEIR FIRST CHILD. SIR, HE HAS A *SON*.
SO WHAT'S YOUR POINT?
THIS RAFFERTY IS A ***GOOD MAN***. I DON'T FEEL RIGHT ABOUT THIS AT ALL.
HE'S A GOOD MAN WITH A SOUL-STEALING, REVENGE-SEEKING ***GHOST*** OF A ***CHILD KILLER*** INSIDE HIM. IT'S NOT LIKE WE GOTTA LOT OF OPTIONS.
I MEAN, I'M NOT THRILLED ABOUT THIS NEITHER. BUT WE JUST GOTTA TRUST THAT SPAWN AND THE OLD MAN KNOW WHAT THEY'RE DOING.
IN ANY CASE, IF WE DON'T GET TO THE ALLEYS PRONTO, THE WHOLE ISSUE'S GONNA BE PRETTY ***MUTE***.
HANG ON!
WHAT?
Huh?
MOOT.
MOOT, SIR. NOT "MUTE." MOOT.
NEVERMIND, SIR.

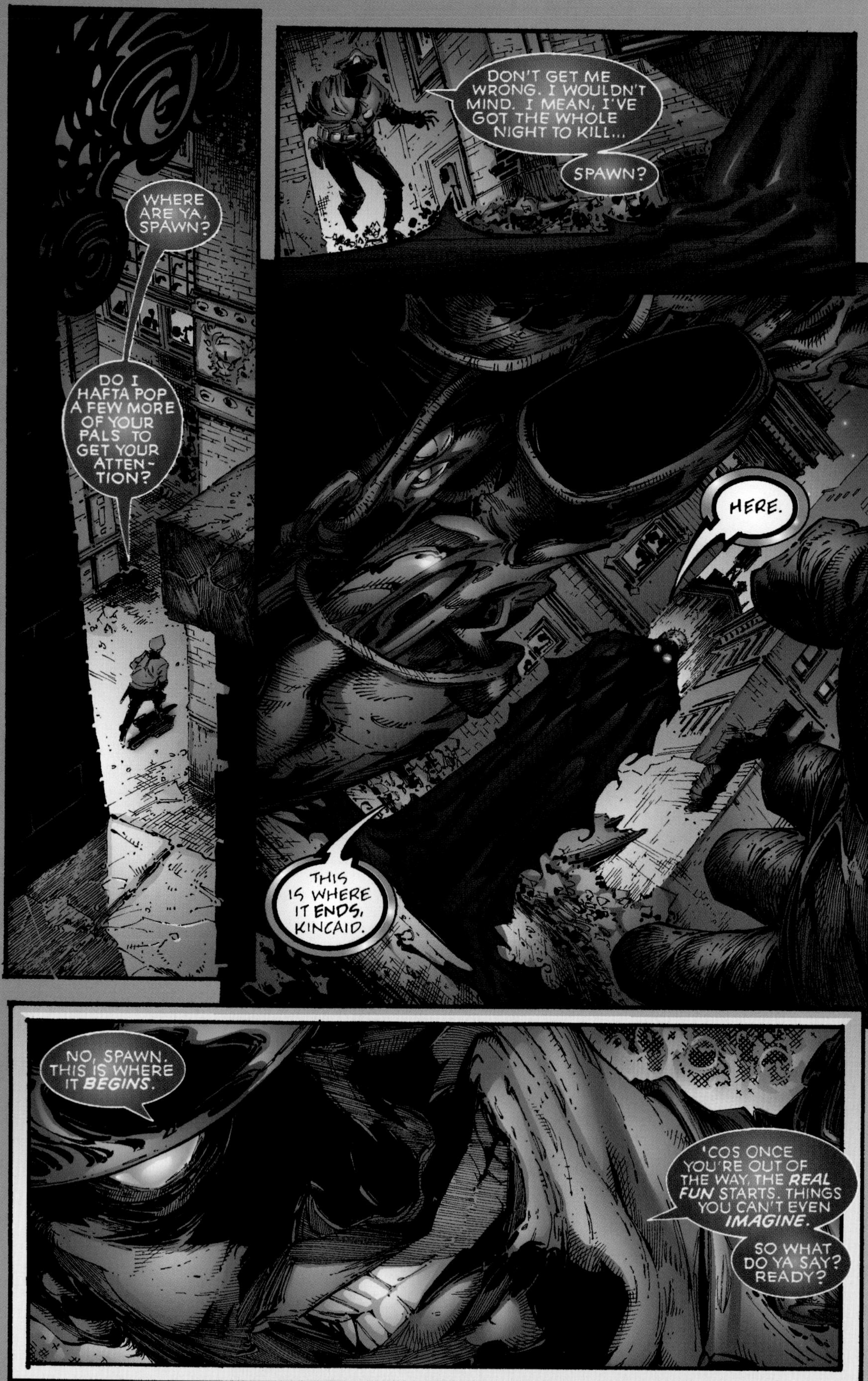
WHERE ARE YA, SPAWN?
DO I HAFTA POP A FEW MORE OF YOUR PALS TO GET YOUR ATTEN-TION?
DON'T GET ME WRONG. I WOULDN'T MIND. I MEAN, I'VE GOT THE WHOLE NIGHT TO KILL...
SPAWN?
HERE.
THIS IS WHERE IT ENDS, KINCAID.
NO, SPAWN. THIS IS WHERE IT BEGINS.
'COS ONCE YOU'RE OUT OF THE WAY, THE REAL FUN STARTS. THINGS YOU CAN'T EVEN IMAGINE.
SO WHAT DO YA SAY? READY?

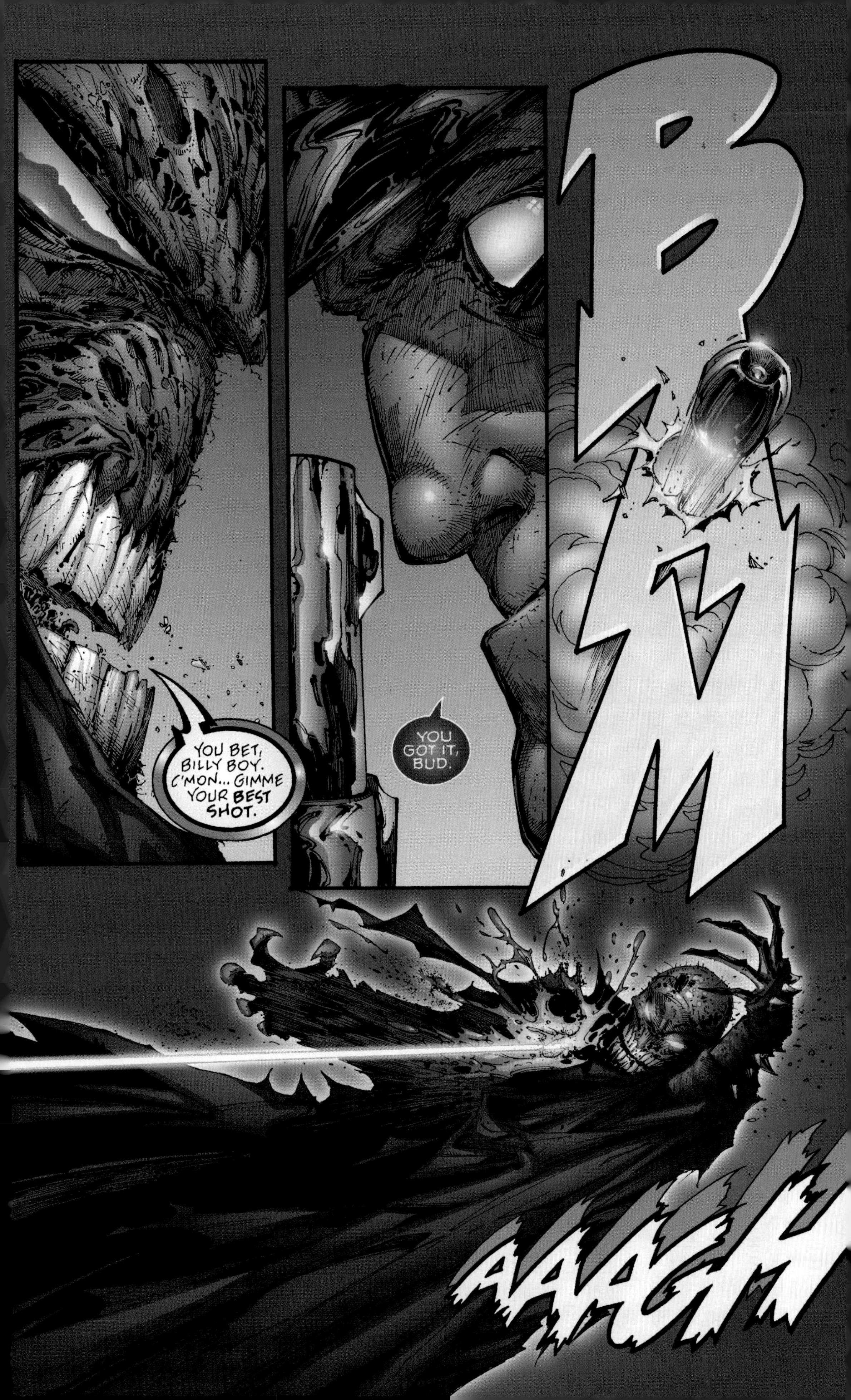
YOU BET, BILLY BOY. C'MON... GIMME YOUR BEST SHOT.
YOU GOT IT, BUD.
BLAM
AAAGH

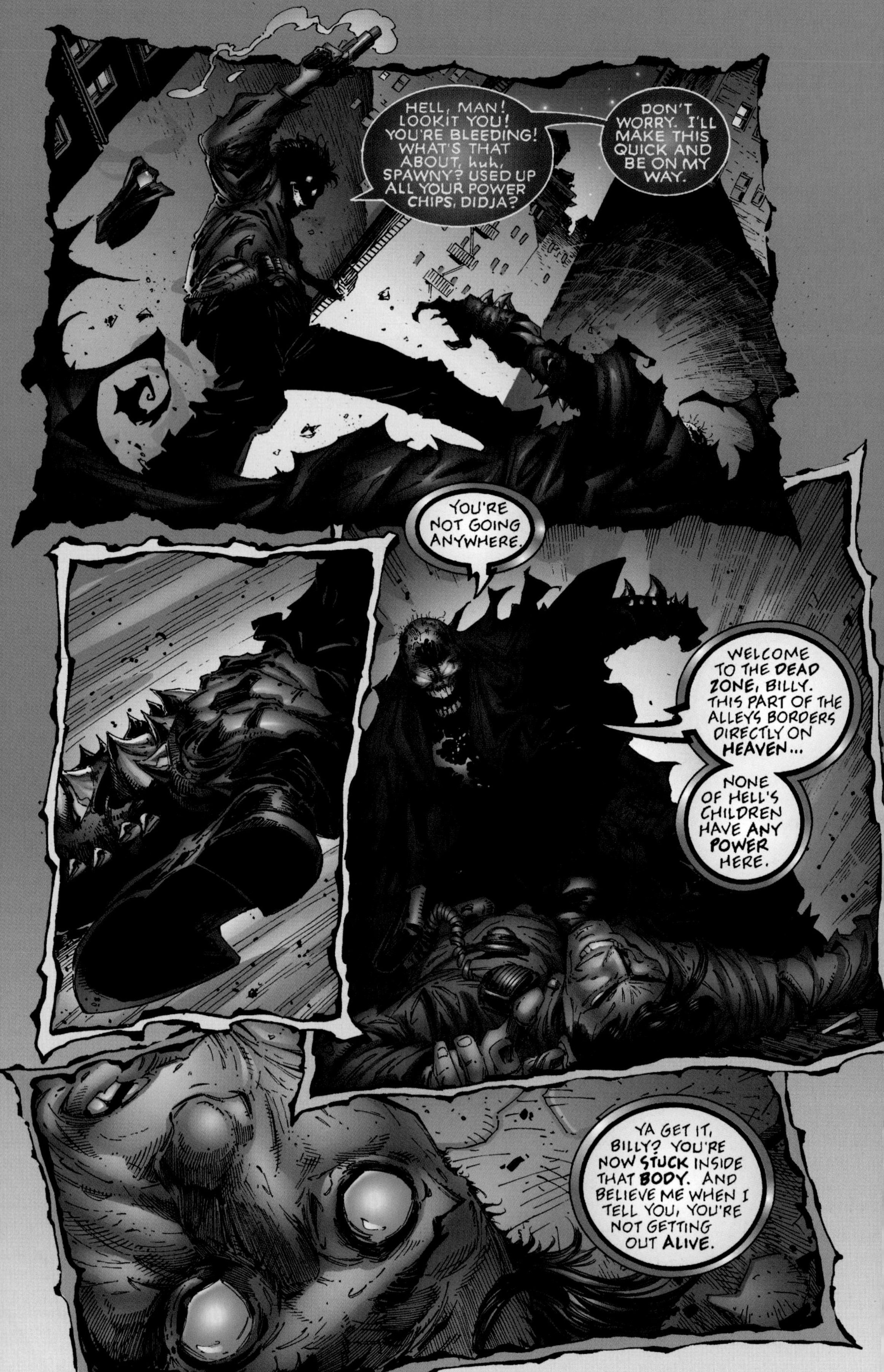
HELL, MAN! LOOKIT YOU! YOU'RE BLEEDING! WHAT'S THAT ABOUT, huh, SPAWNY? USED UP ALL YOUR POWER CHIPS, DIDJA?
DON'T WORRY. I'LL MAKE THIS QUICK AND BE ON MY WAY.
YOU'RE NOT GOING ANYWHERE.
WELCOME TO THE DEAD ZONE, BILLY. THIS PART OF THE ALLEYS BORDERS DIRECTLY ON HEAVEN...
NONE OF HELL'S CHILDREN HAVE ANY POWER HERE.
YA GET IT, BILLY? YOU'RE NOW STUCK INSIDE THAT BODY. AND BELIEVE ME WHEN I TELL YOU, YOU'RE NOT GETTING OUT ALIVE.

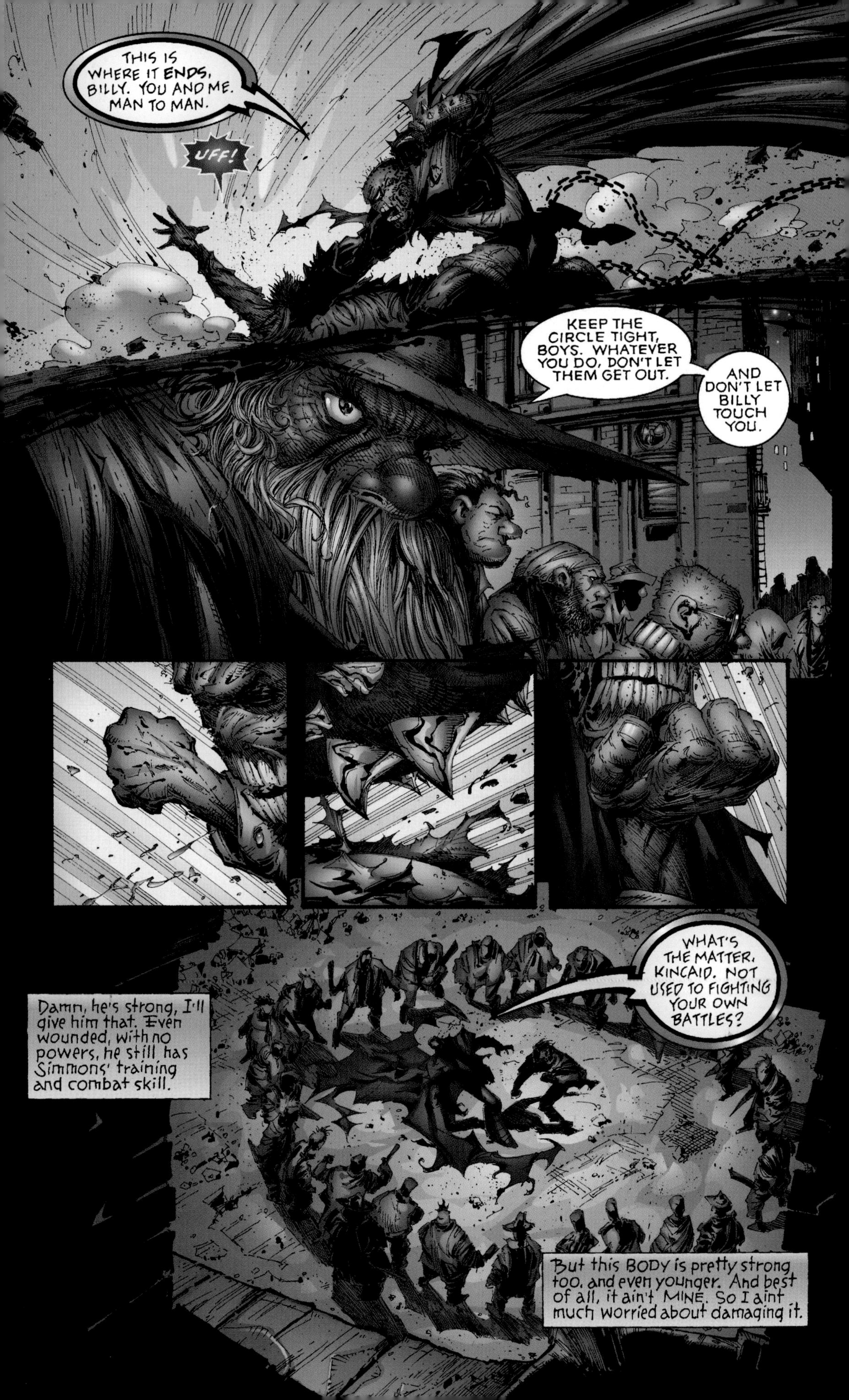
THIS IS WHERE IT ENDS, BILLY. YOU AND ME. MAN TO MAN.
UFF!
KEEP THE CIRCLE TIGHT, BOYS. WHATEVER YOU DO, DON'T LET THEM GET OUT.
AND DON'T LET BILLY TOUCH YOU.
Damn, he's strong, I'll give him that. Even wounded, with no powers, he still has Simmons' training and combat skill.
WHAT'S THE MATTER, KINCAID. NOT USED TO FIGHTING YOUR OWN BATTLES?
But this BODY is pretty strong too, and even younger. And best of all, it ain't MINE. So I aint much worried about damaging it.

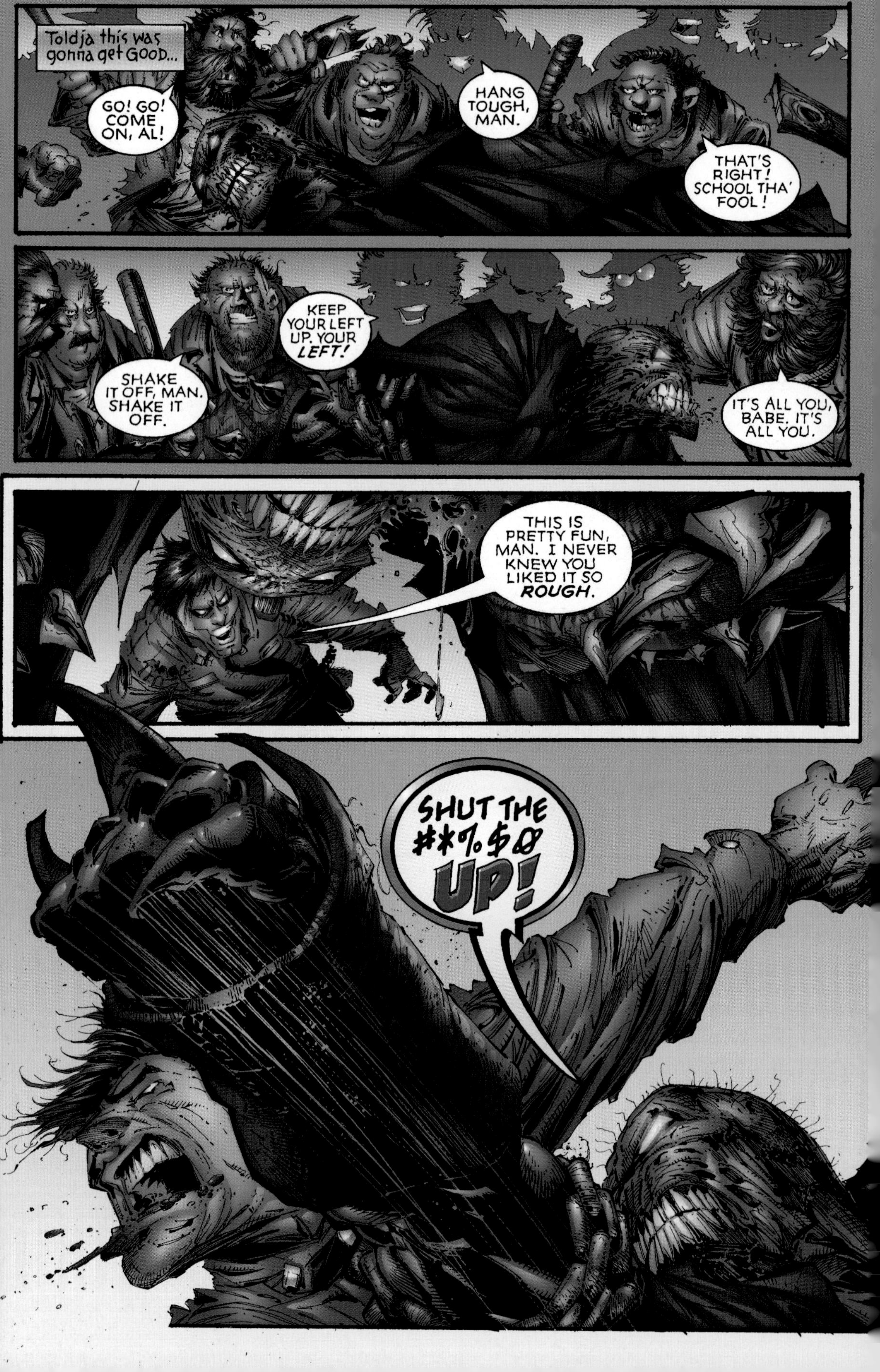

Toldja this was gonna get GOOD...
GO! GO! COME ON, AL!
HANG TOUGH, MAN.
THAT'S RIGHT! SCHOOL THA' FOOL!
KEEP YOUR LEFT UP. YOUR LEFT!
SHAKE IT OFF, MAN. SHAKE IT OFF.
IT'S ALL YOU, BABE. IT'S ALL YOU.
THIS IS PRETTY FUN, MAN. I NEVER KNEW YOU LIKED IT SO ROUGH.
SHUT THE #*%$@ UP!

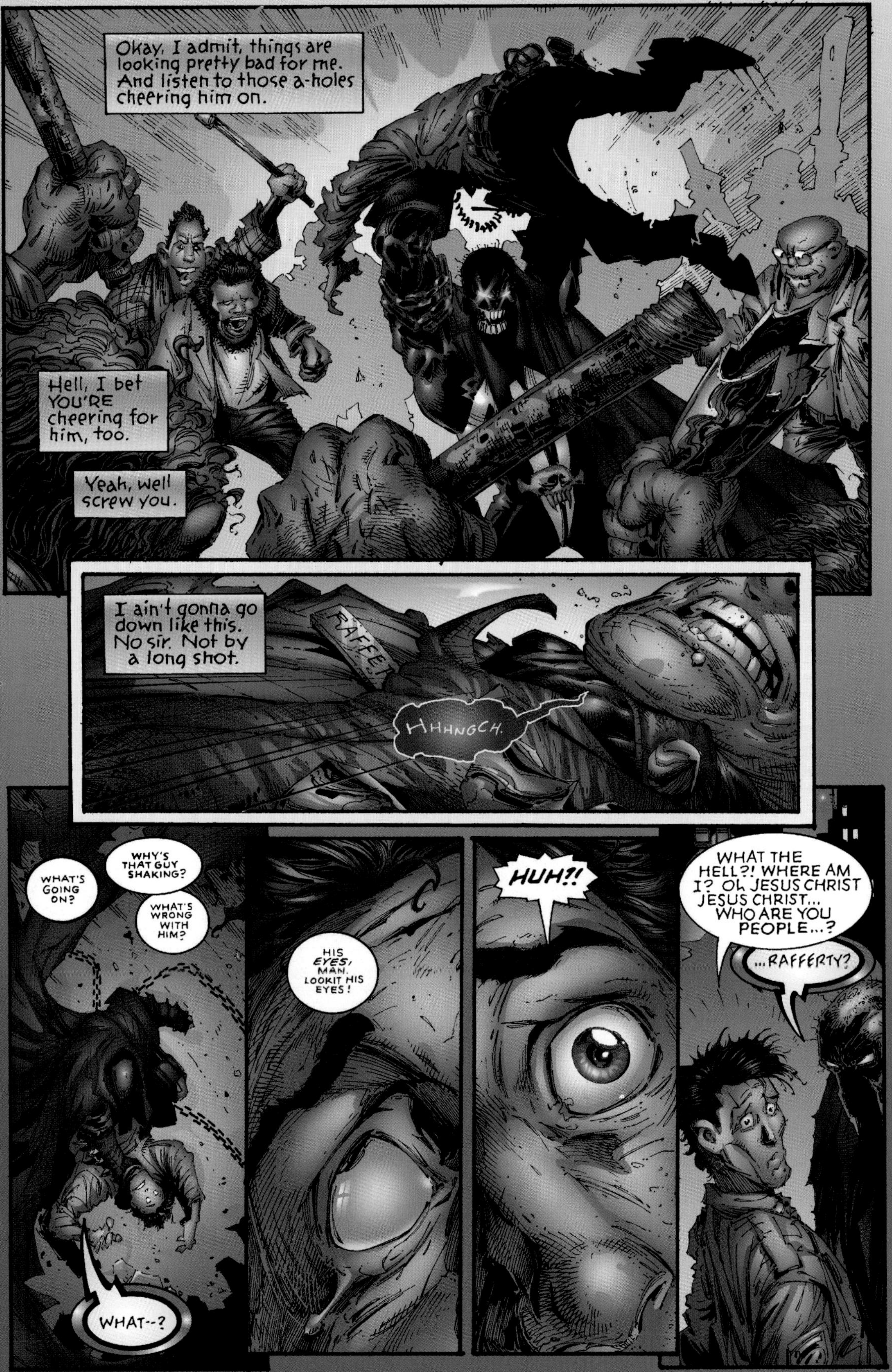
Okay. I admit, things are looking pretty bad for me. And listen to those a-holes cheering him on.
Hell, I bet YOU'RE cheering for him, too.
Yeah, well screw you.
I ain't gonna go down like this. No sir. Not by a long shot.
HHHNGCH.
WHAT'S GOING ON?
WHY'S THAT GUY SHAKING?
WHAT'S WRONG WITH HIM?
WHAT--?
HIS EYES, MAN. LOOKIT HIS EYES!
HUH?!
WHAT THE HELL?! WHERE AM I? OH JESUS CHRIST JESUS CHRIST... WHO ARE YOU PEOPLE...?
...RAFFERTY?

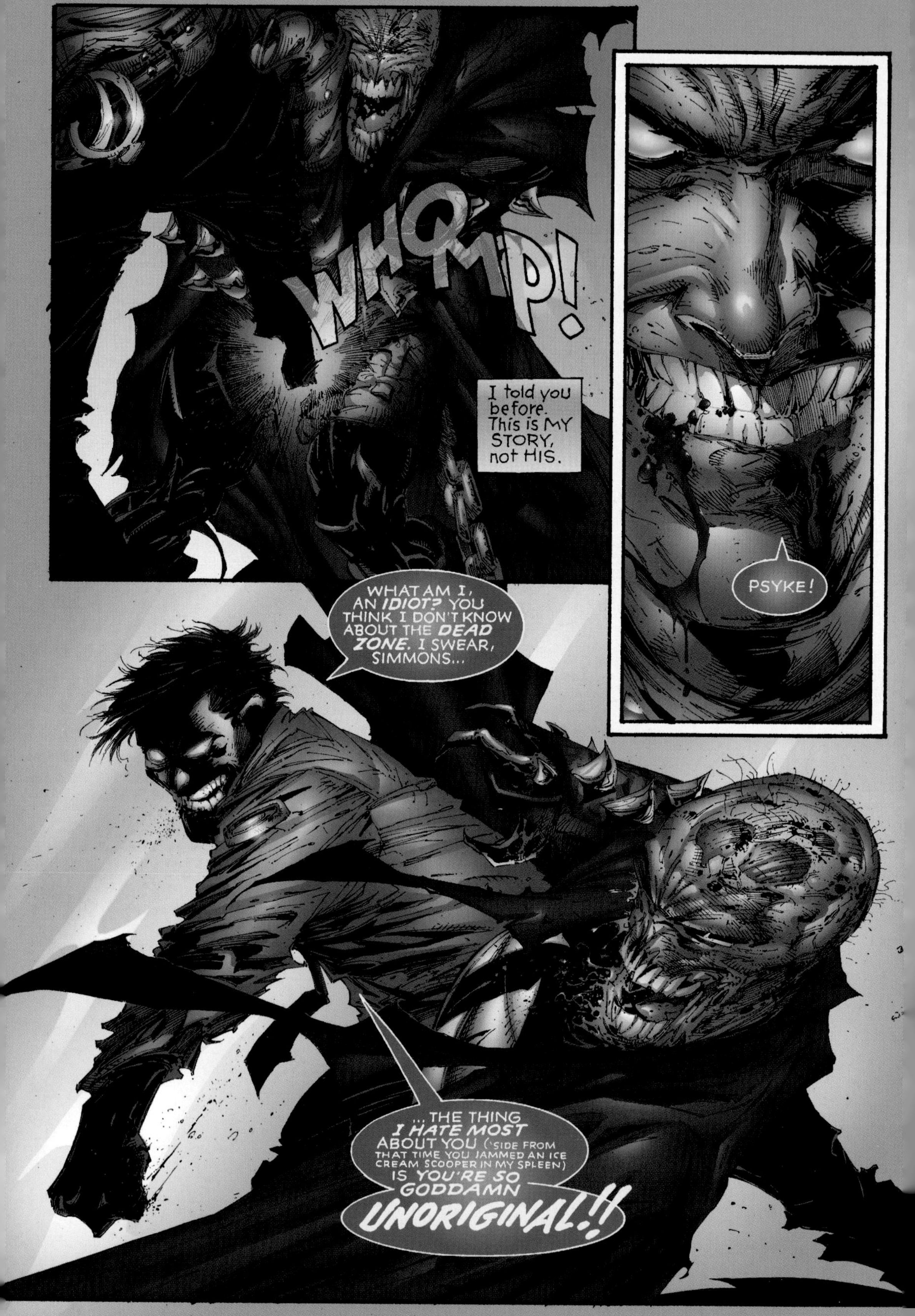
WHOMP!
I told you before. This is MY STORY, not HIS.
PSYKE!
WHAT AM I, AN IDIOT? YOU THINK I DON'T KNOW ABOUT THE DEAD ZONE. I SWEAR, SIMMONS...
...THE THING I HATE MOST ABOUT YOU ('SIDE FROM THAT TIME YOU JAMMED AN ICE CREAM SCOOPER IN MY SPLEEN) IS YOU'RE SO GODDAMN
UNORIGINAL!!

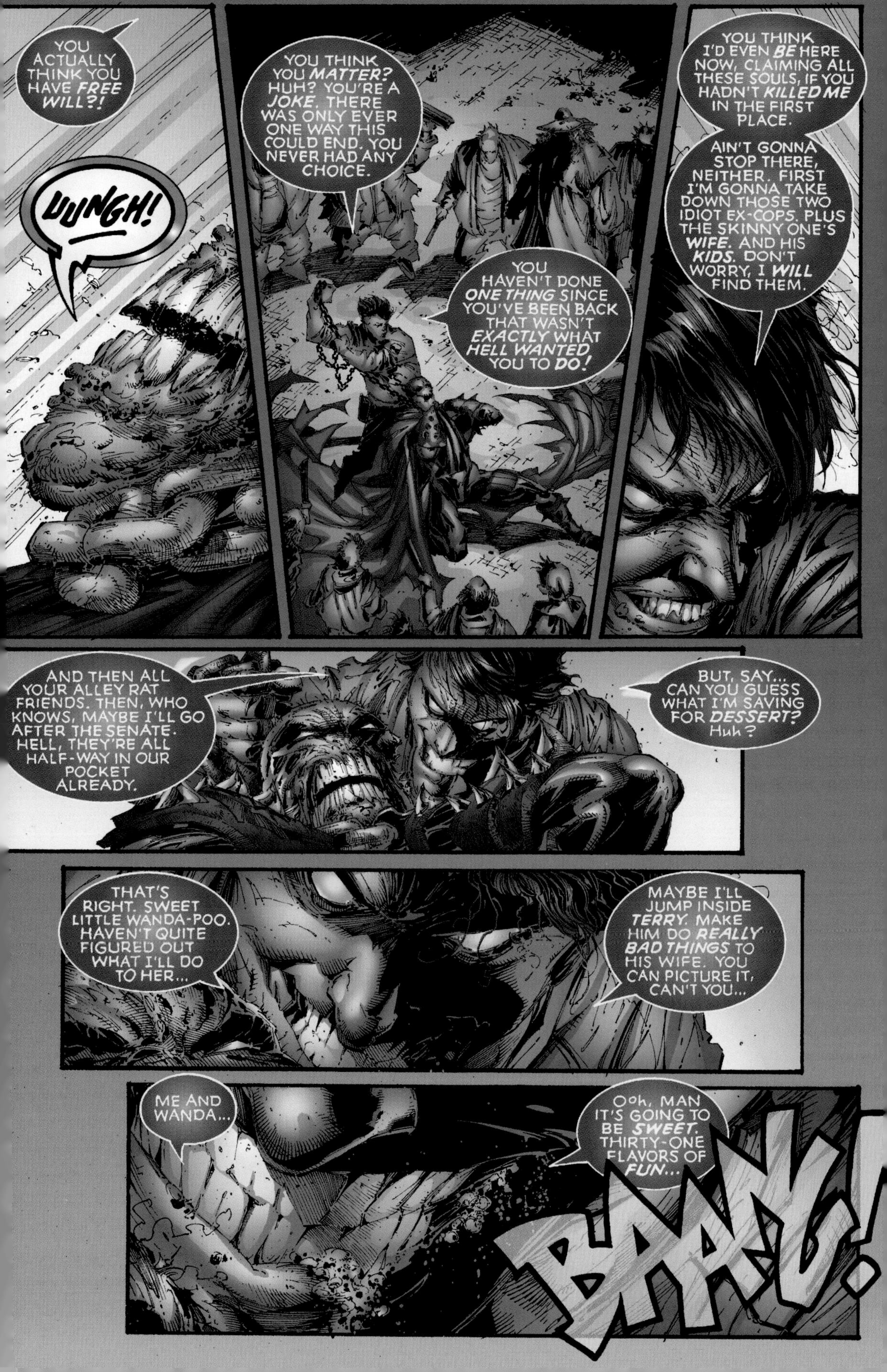

YOU ACTUALLY THINK YOU HAVE FREE WILL?!
UUNGH!
YOU THINK YOU MATTER? HUH? YOU'RE A JOKE. THERE WAS ONLY EVER ONE WAY THIS COULD END. YOU NEVER HAD ANY CHOICE.
YOU HAVEN'T DONE ONE THING SINCE YOU'VE BEEN BACK THAT WASN'T EXACTLY WHAT HELL WANTED YOU TO DO!
YOU THINK I'D EVEN BE HERE NOW, CLAIMING ALL THESE SOULS, IF YOU HADN'T KILLED ME IN THE FIRST PLACE.
AIN'T GONNA STOP THERE, NEITHER. FIRST I'M GONNA TAKE DOWN THOSE TWO IDIOT EX-COPS. PLUS THE SKINNY ONE'S WIFE. AND HIS KIDS. DON'T WORRY, I WILL FIND THEM.
AND THEN ALL YOUR ALLEY RAT FRIENDS. THEN, WHO KNOWS, MAYBE I'LL GO AFTER THE SENATE. HELL, THEY'RE ALL HALF-WAY IN OUR POCKET ALREADY.
BUT, SAY... CAN YOU GUESS WHAT I'M SAVING FOR DESSERT? Huh?
THAT'S RIGHT. SWEET LITTLE WANDA-POO. HAVEN'T QUITE FIGURED OUT WHAT I'LL DO TO HER...
MAYBE I'LL JUMP INSIDE TERRY. MAKE HIM DO REALLY BAD THINGS TO HIS WIFE. YOU CAN PICTURE IT, CAN'T YOU...
ME AND WANDA...
OOH, MAN IT'S GOING TO BE SWEET. THIRTY-ONE FLAVORS OF FUN...
BLAM!

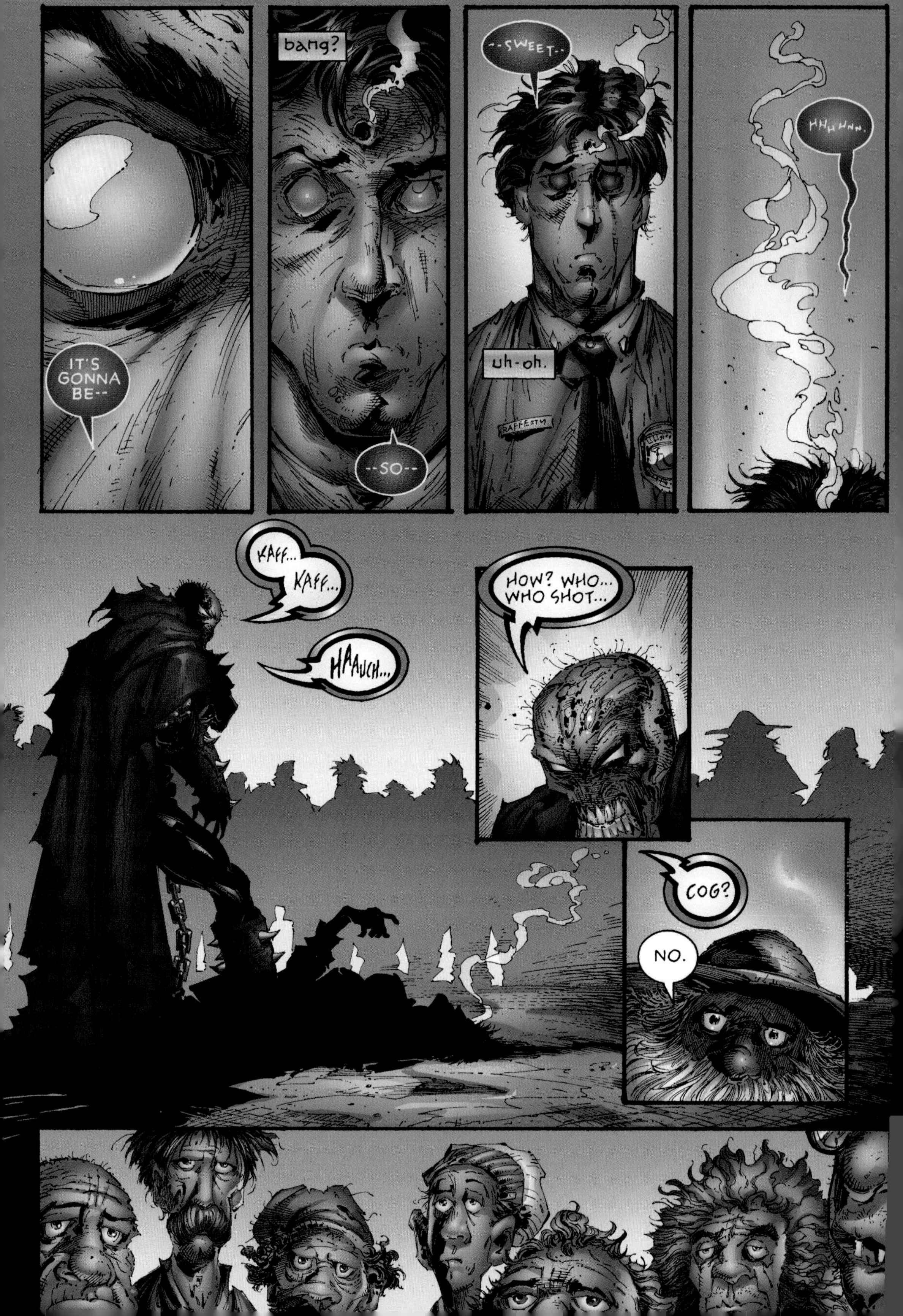
IT'S GONNA BE--
bang?
--SO--
--SWEET--
uh-oh.
RAFFERTY
HHHHNN.
KAFF... KAFF...
HAAUCH...
HOW? WHO... WHO SHOT...
COG?
NO.

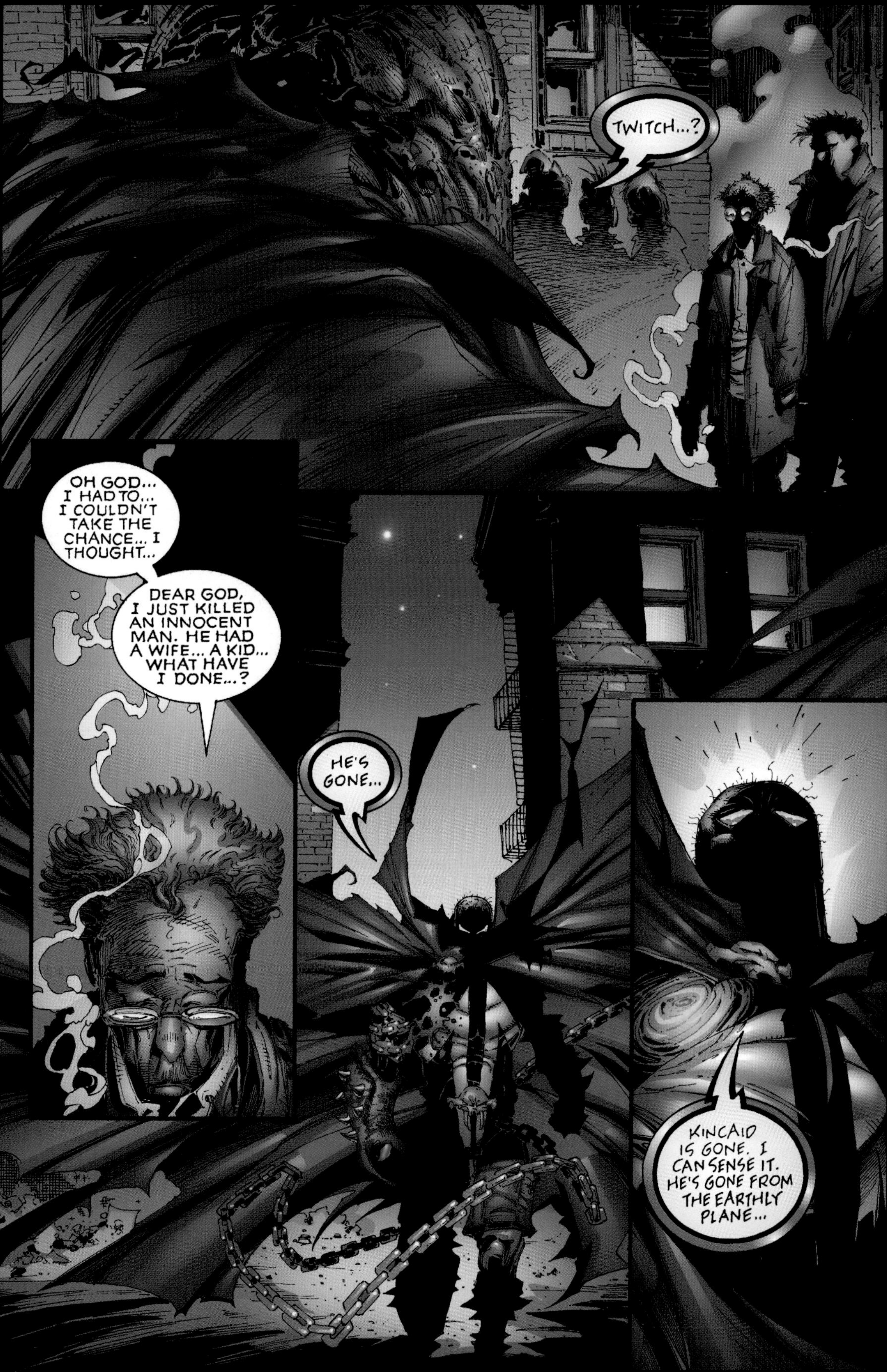
TWITCH...?
OH GOD... I HAD TO... I COULDN'T TAKE THE CHANCE... I THOUGHT...
DEAR GOD, I JUST KILLED AN INNOCENT MAN. HE HAD A WIFE... A KID... WHAT HAVE I DONE...?
HE'S GONE...
KINCAID IS GONE. I CAN SENSE IT. HE'S GONE FROM THE EARTHLY PLANE...

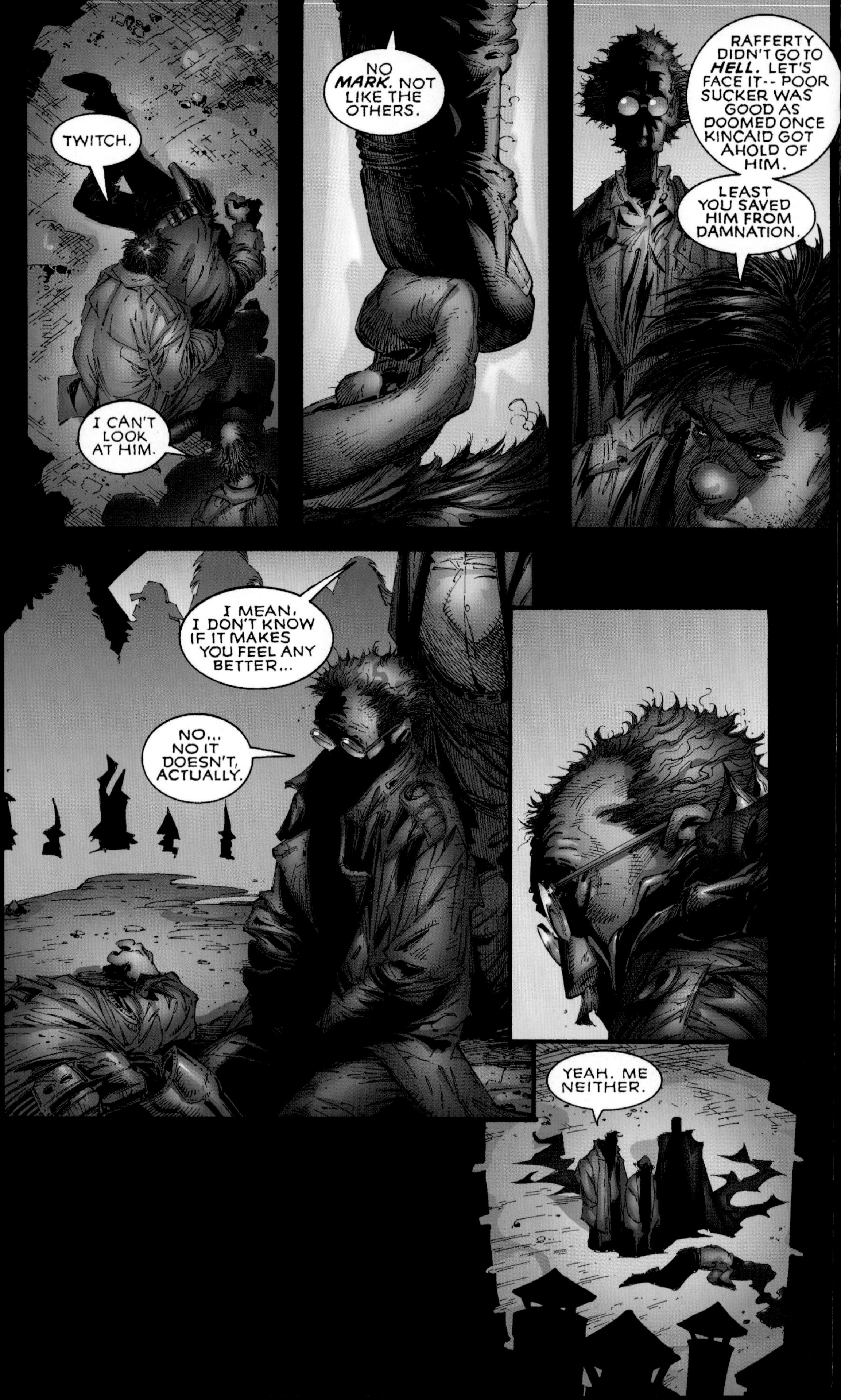
TWITCH.
I CAN'T LOOK AT HIM.
NO MARK. NOT LIKE THE OTHERS.
RAFFERTY DIDN'T GO TO HELL. LET'S FACE IT-- POOR SUCKER WAS GOOD AS DOOMED ONCE KINCAID GOT AHOLD OF HIM.
LEAST YOU SAVED HIM FROM DAMNATION.
I MEAN, I DON'T KNOW IF IT MAKES YOU FEEL ANY BETTER...
NO... NO IT DOESN'T, ACTUALLY.
YEAH. ME NEITHER.

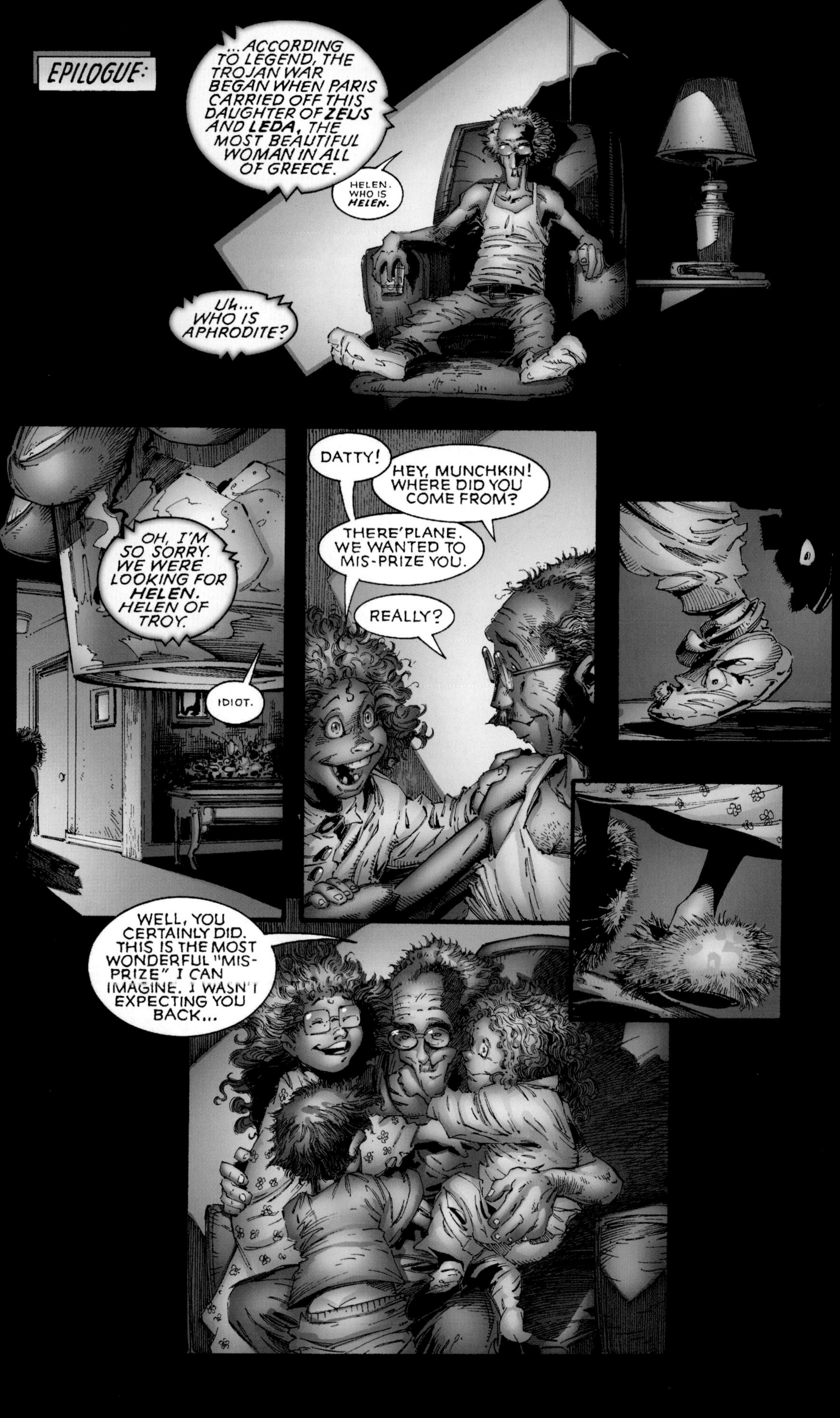
EPILOGUE:
...ACCORDING TO LEGEND, THE TROJAN WAR BEGAN WHEN PARIS CARRIED OFF THIS DAUGHTER OF ZEUS AND LEDA, THE MOST BEAUTIFUL WOMAN IN ALL OF GREECE.
HELEN. WHO IS HELEN.
Uh... WHO IS APHRODITE?
OH, I'M SO SORRY. WE WERE LOOKING FOR HELEN. HELEN OF TROY.
IDIOT.
DATTY!
HEY, MUNCHKIN! WHERE DID YOU COME FROM?
THERE'PLANE. WE WANTED TO MIS-PRIZE YOU.
REALLY?
WELL, YOU CERTAINLY DID. THIS IS THE MOST WONDERFUL "MIS-PRIZE" I CAN IMAGINE. I WASN'T EXPECTING YOU BACK...

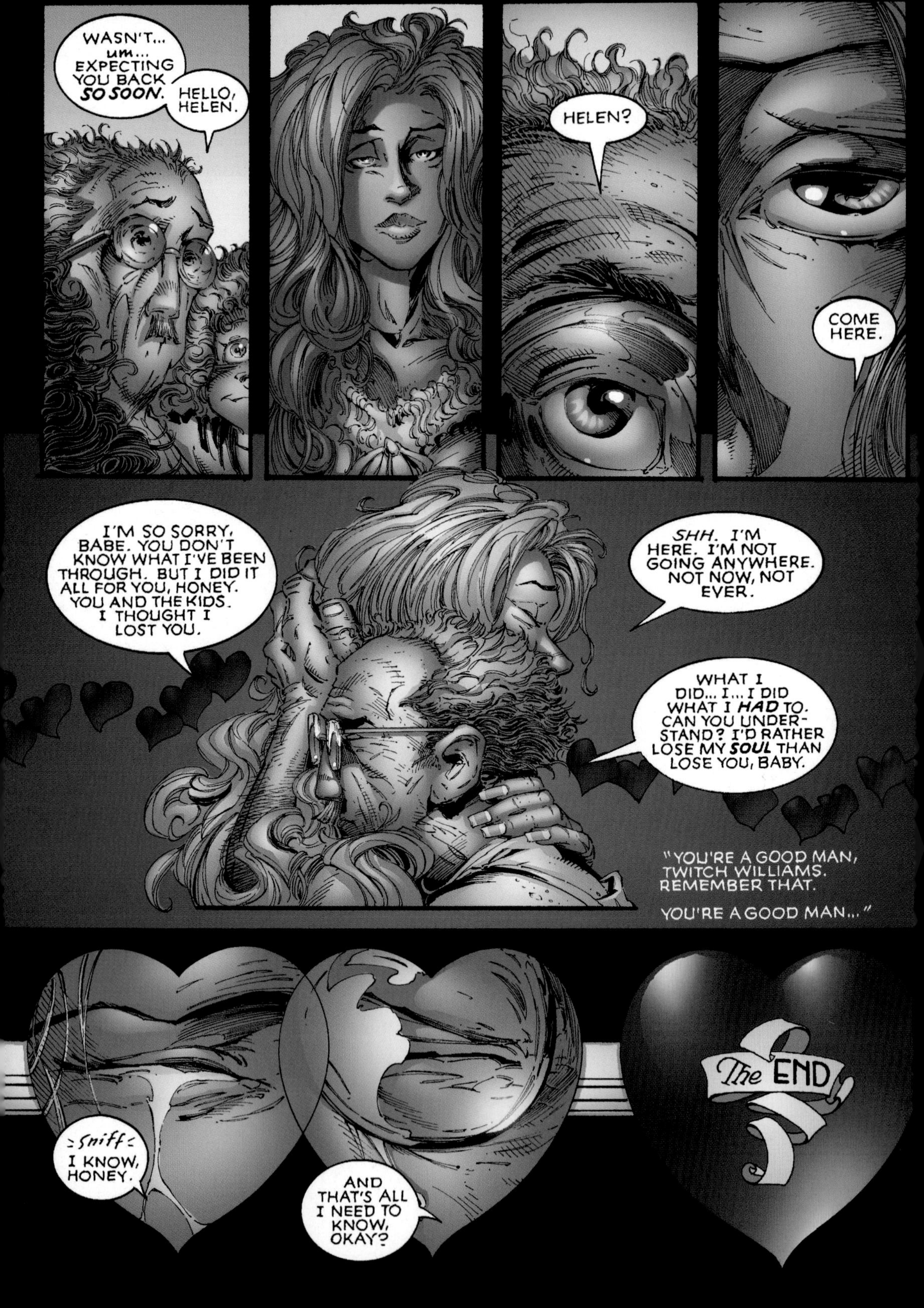
WASN'T... um... EXPECTING YOU BACK SO SOON.
HELLO, HELEN.
HELEN?
COME HERE.
I'M SO SORRY, BABE. YOU DON'T KNOW WHAT I'VE BEEN THROUGH. BUT I DID IT ALL FOR YOU, HONEY. YOU AND THE KIDS. I THOUGHT I LOST YOU.
SHH. I'M HERE. I'M NOT GOING ANYWHERE. NOT NOW, NOT EVER.
WHAT I DID... I... I DID WHAT I HAD TO. CAN YOU UNDERSTAND? I'D RATHER LOSE MY SOUL THAN LOSE YOU, BABY.
"YOU'RE A GOOD MAN, TWITCH WILLIAMS. REMEMBER THAT.
YOU'RE A GOOD MAN..."
SNIFF
I KNOW, HONEY.
AND THAT'S ALL I NEED TO KNOW, OKAY?
The END

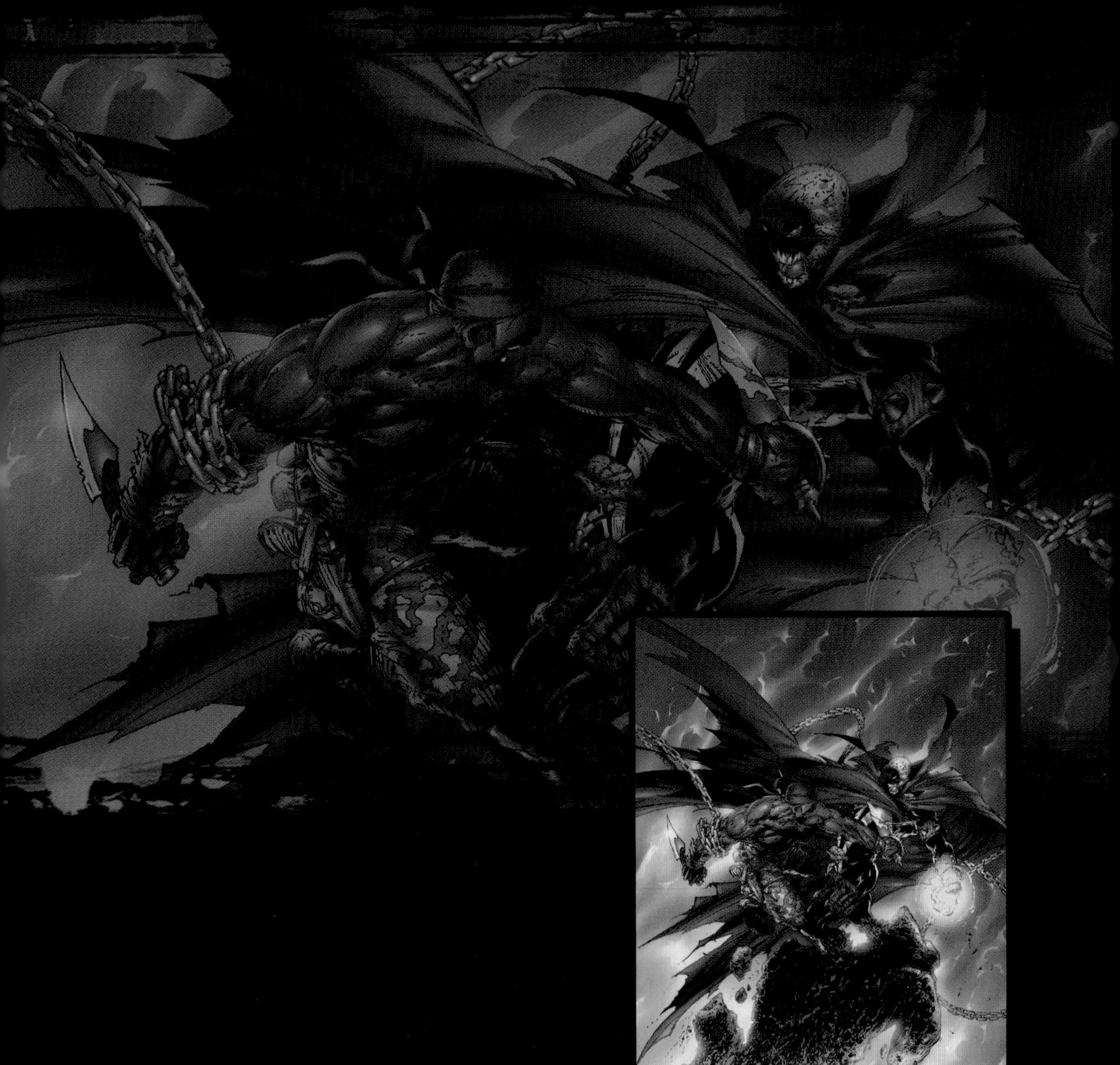

I S S U E   EIGHTY-SIX

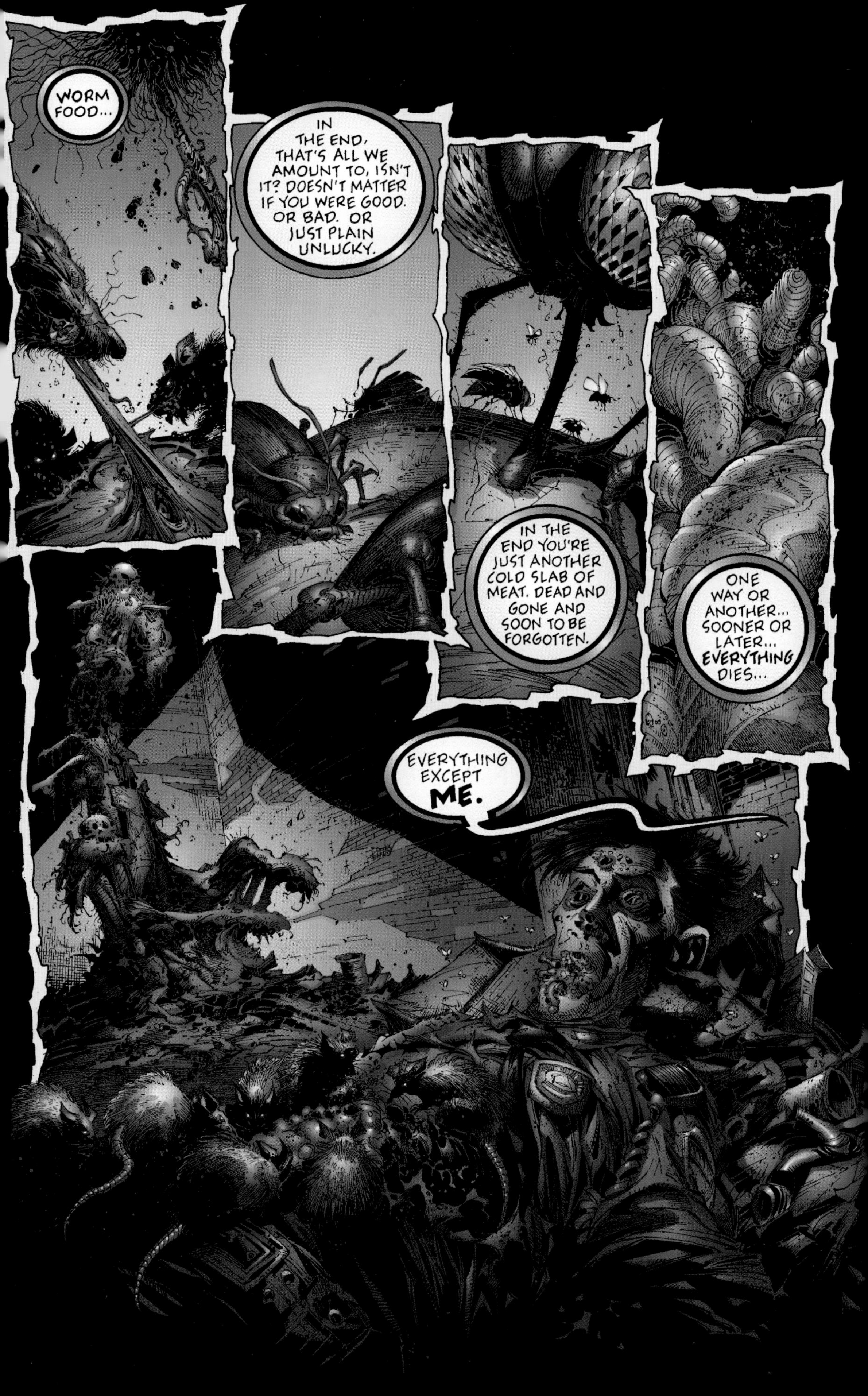
WORM FOOD...
IN THE END, THAT'S ALL WE AMOUNT TO, ISN'T IT? DOESN'T MATTER IF YOU WERE GOOD. OR BAD. OR JUST PLAIN UNLUCKY.
IN THE END YOU'RE JUST ANOTHER COLD SLAB OF MEAT. DEAD AND GONE AND SOON TO BE FORGOTTEN.
ONE WAY OR ANOTHER... SOONER OR LATER... EVERYTHING DIES...
EVERYTHING EXCEPT ME.

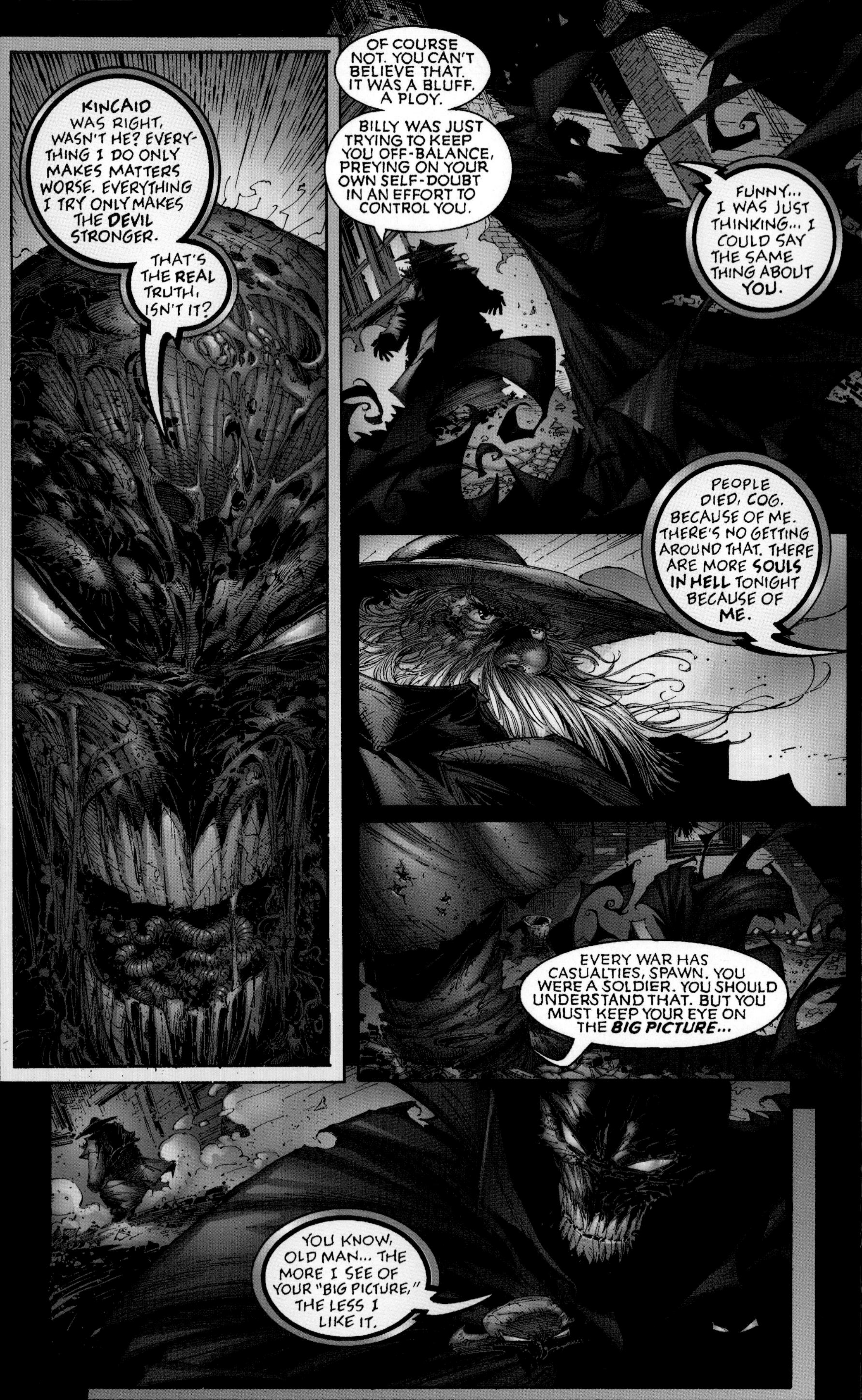
KINCAID WAS RIGHT, WASN'T HE? EVERYTHING I DO ONLY MAKES MATTERS WORSE. EVERYTHING I TRY ONLY MAKES THE DEVIL STRONGER.
THAT'S THE REAL TRUTH, ISN'T IT?
OF COURSE NOT. YOU CAN'T BELIEVE THAT. IT WAS A BLUFF. A PLOY.
BILLY WAS JUST TRYING TO KEEP YOU OFF-BALANCE, PREYING ON YOUR OWN SELF-DOUBT IN AN EFFORT TO CONTROL YOU.
FUNNY... I WAS JUST THINKING... I COULD SAY THE SAME THING ABOUT YOU.
PEOPLE DIED, COG. BECAUSE OF ME. THERE'S NO GETTING AROUND THAT. THERE ARE MORE SOULS IN HELL TONIGHT BECAUSE OF ME.
EVERY WAR HAS CASUALTIES, SPAWN. YOU WERE A SOLDIER. YOU SHOULD UNDERSTAND THAT. BUT YOU MUST KEEP YOUR EYE ON THE BIG PICTURE...
YOU KNOW, OLD MAN... THE MORE I SEE OF YOUR "BIG PICTURE," THE LESS I LIKE IT.

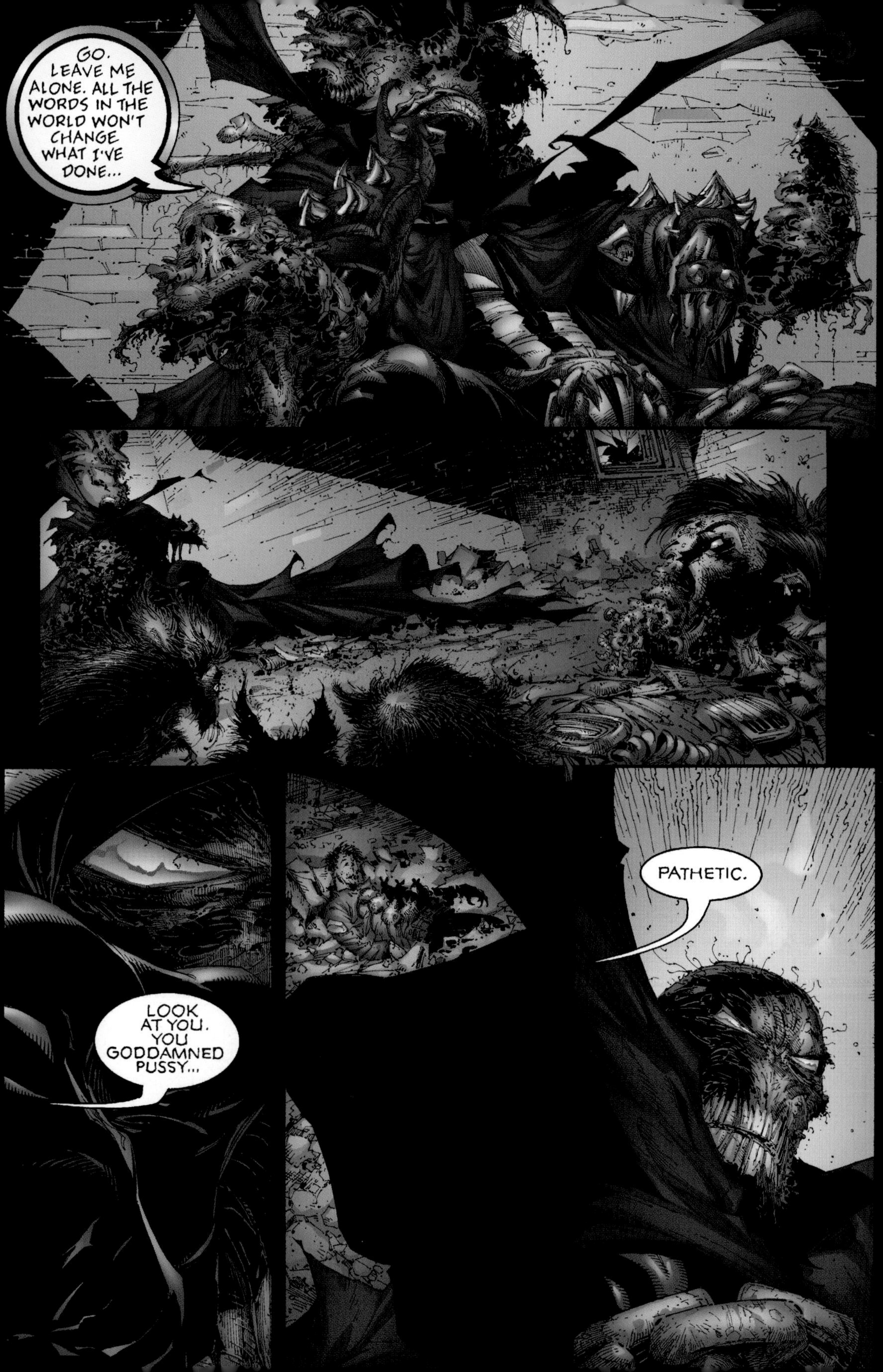
GO. LEAVE ME ALONE. ALL THE WORDS IN THE WORLD WON'T CHANGE WHAT I'VE DONE...
PATHETIC.
LOOK AT YOU. YOU GODDAMNED PUSSY...

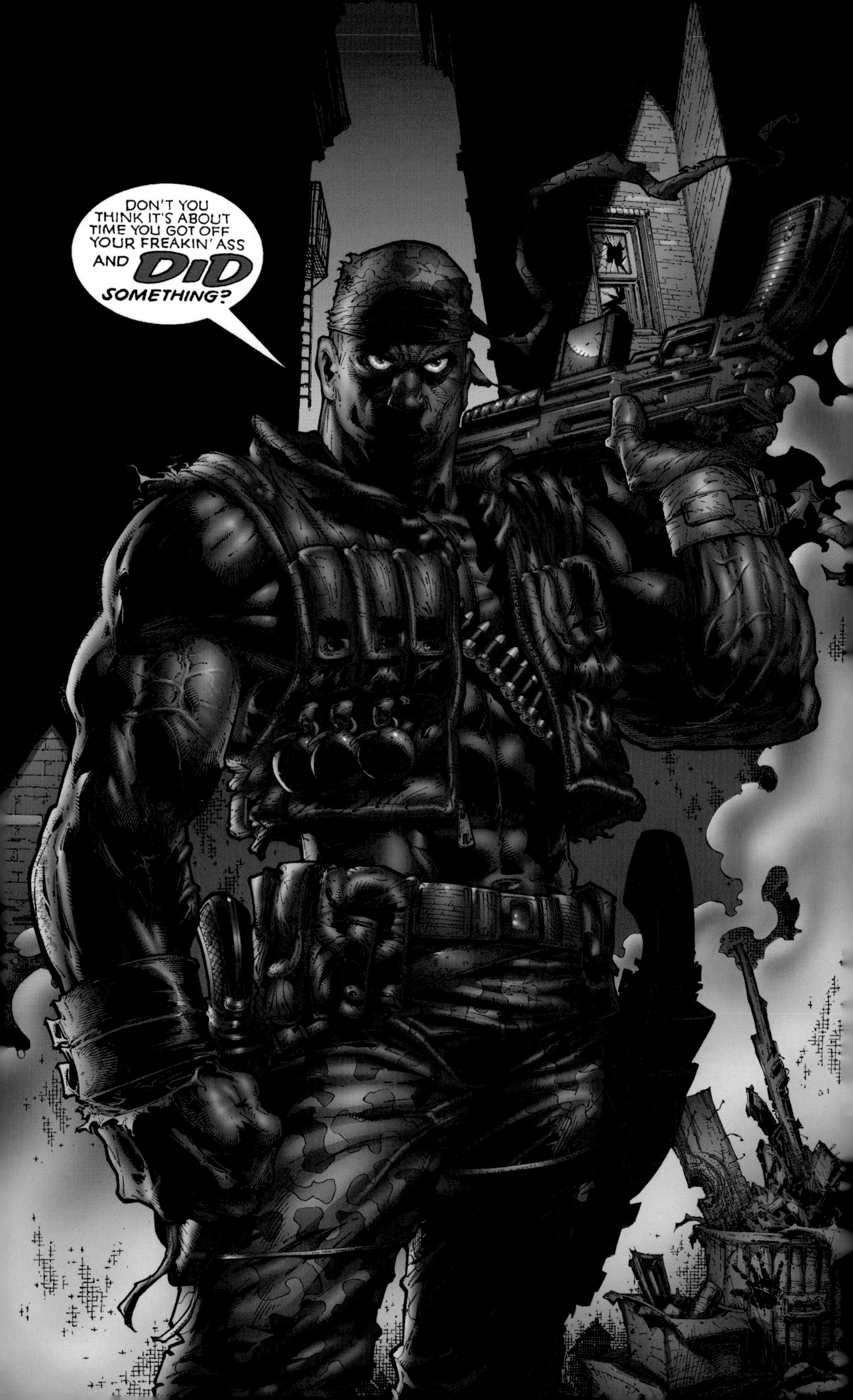
DON'T YOU THINK IT'S ABOUT TIME YOU GOT OFF YOUR FREAKIN' ASS AND DID SOMETHING?

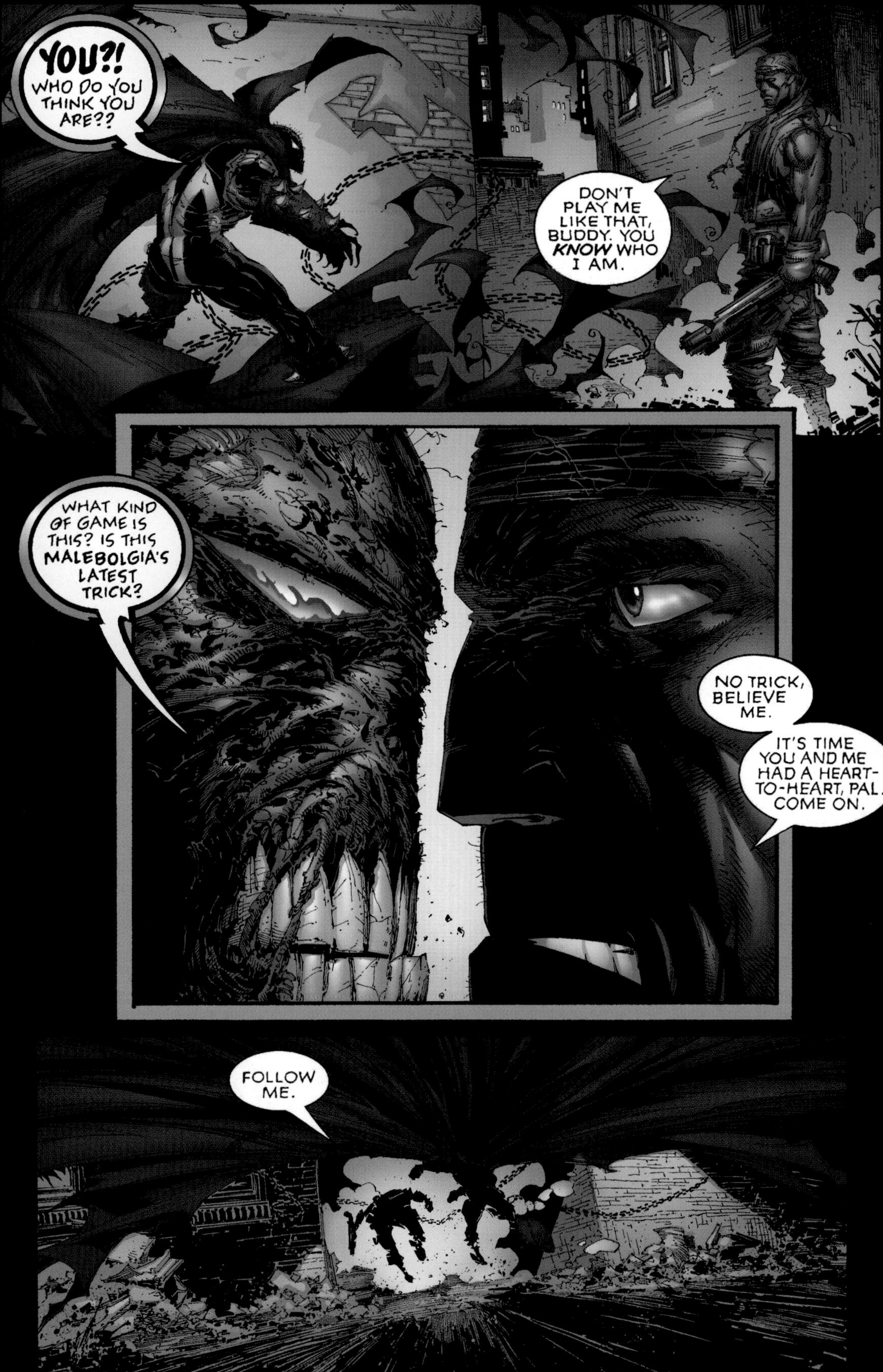
YOU?! WHO DO YOU THINK YOU ARE??
DON'T PLAY ME LIKE THAT, BUDDY. YOU KNOW WHO I AM.
WHAT KIND OF GAME IS THIS? IS THIS MALEBOLGIA'S LATEST TRICK?
NO TRICK, BELIEVE ME.
IT'S TIME YOU AND ME HAD A HEART-TO-HEART, PAL. COME ON.
FOLLOW ME.

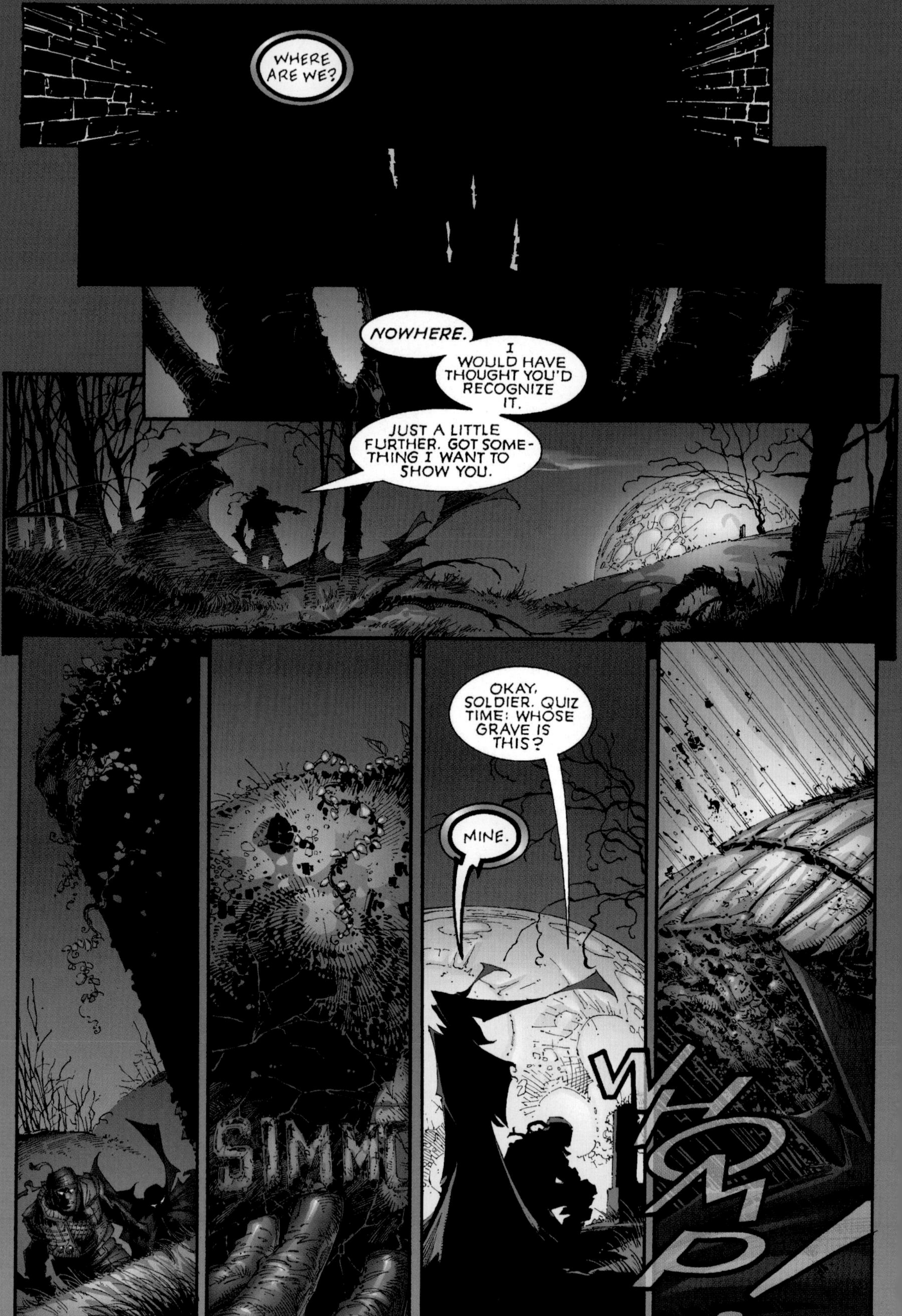
WHERE ARE WE?
NOWHERE.
I WOULD HAVE THOUGHT YOU'D RECOGNIZE IT.
JUST A LITTLE FURTHER. GOT SOMETHING I WANT TO SHOW YOU.
SIMM
OKAY, SOLDIER. QUIZ TIME: WHOSE GRAVE IS THIS?
MINE.
WHOMP!

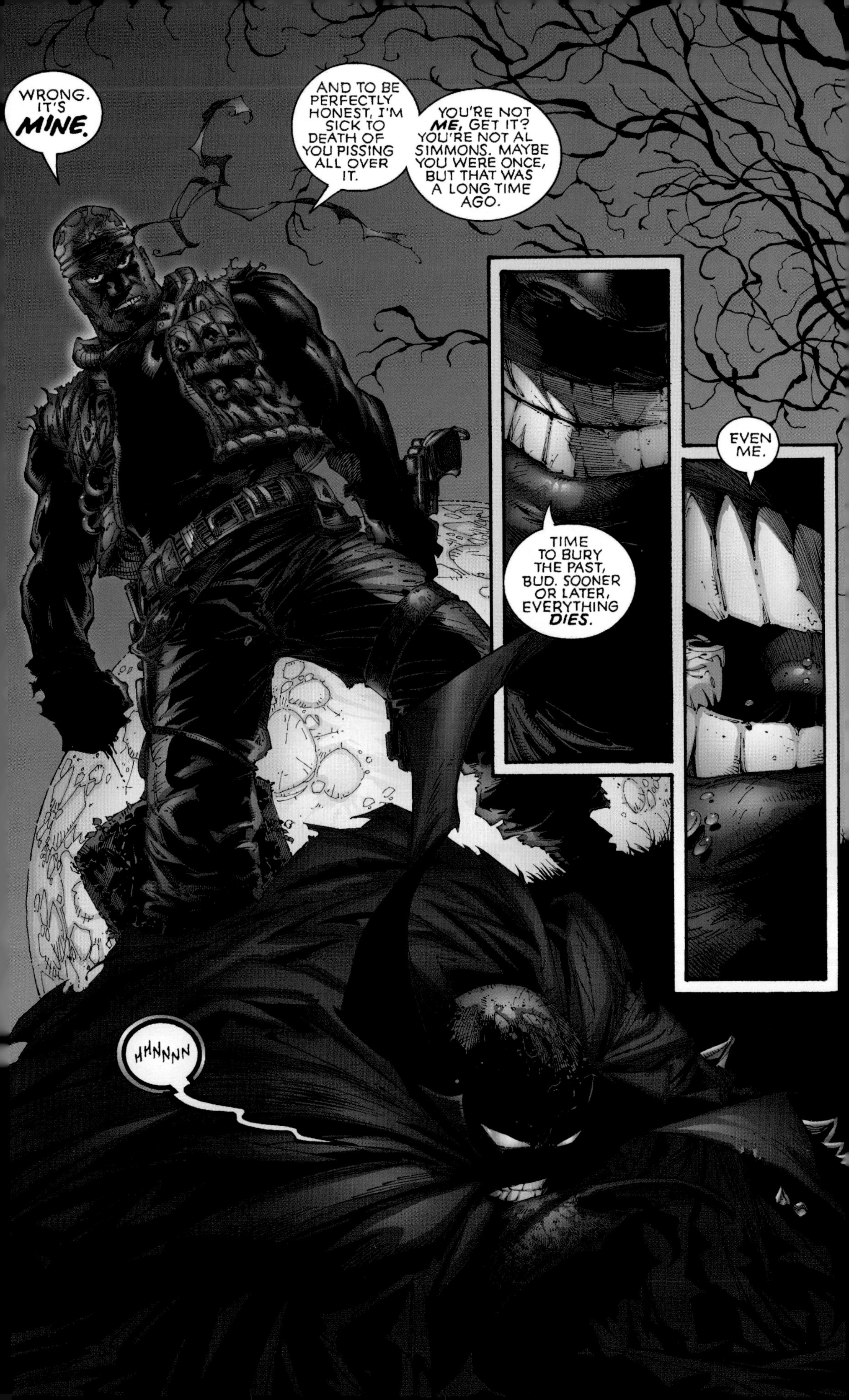
WRONG. IT'S MINE.
AND TO BE PERFECTLY HONEST, I'M SICK TO DEATH OF YOU PISSING ALL OVER IT.
YOU'RE NOT ME, GET IT? YOU'RE NOT AL SIMMONS. MAYBE YOU WERE ONCE, BUT THAT WAS A LONG TIME AGO.
TIME TO BURY THE PAST, BUD. SOONER OR LATER, EVERYTHING DIES.
EVEN ME.
HHNNNN

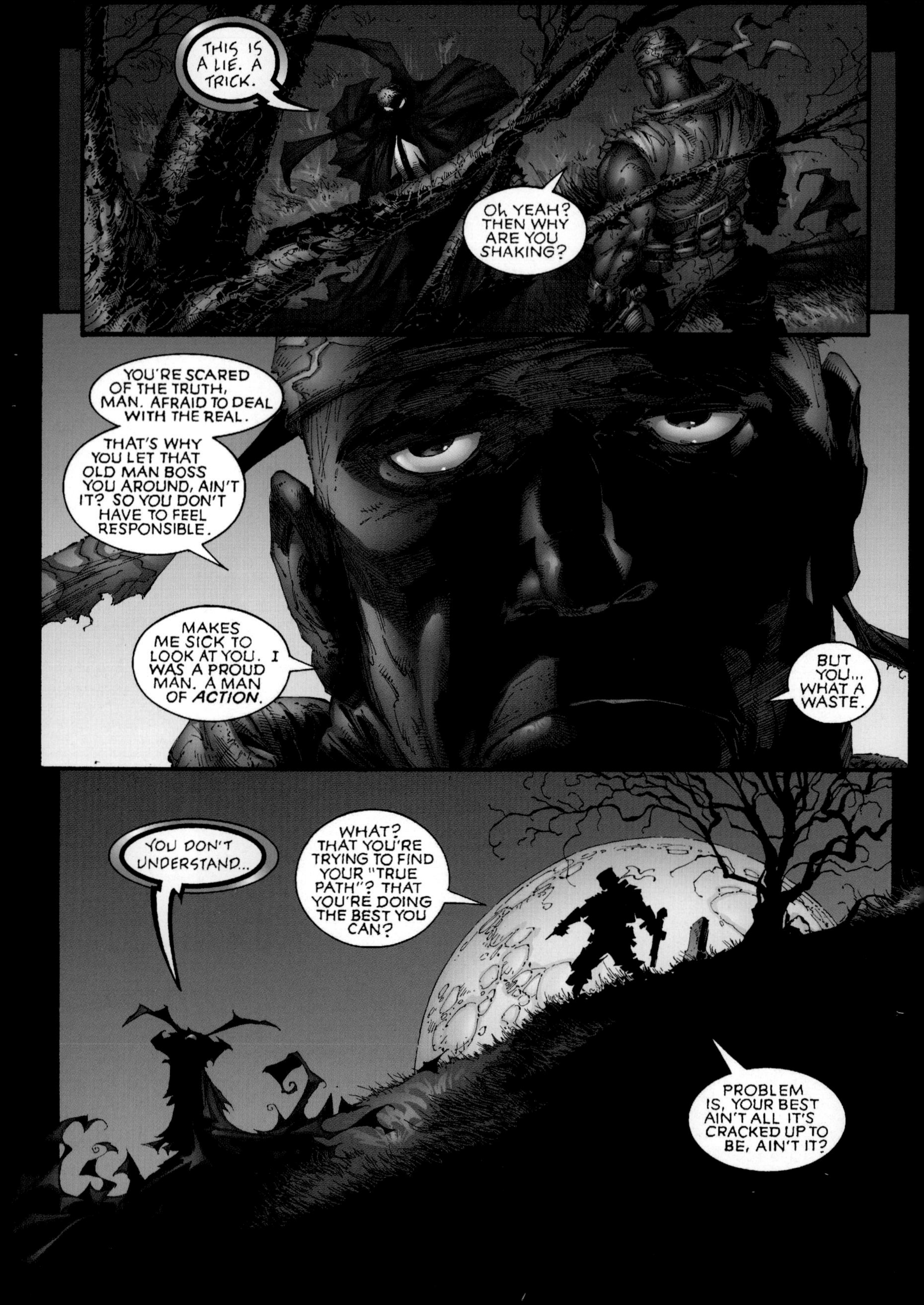
THIS IS A LIE. A TRICK.
Oh YEAH? THEN WHY ARE YOU SHAKING?
YOU'RE SCARED OF THE TRUTH, MAN. AFRAID TO DEAL WITH THE REAL.
THAT'S WHY YOU LET THAT OLD MAN BOSS YOU AROUND, AIN'T IT? SO YOU DON'T HAVE TO FEEL RESPONSIBLE.
MAKES ME SICK TO LOOK AT YOU. I WAS A PROUD MAN. A MAN OF ACTION.
BUT YOU... WHAT A WASTE.
YOU DON'T UNDERSTAND...
WHAT? THAT YOU'RE TRYING TO FIND YOUR "TRUE PATH"? THAT YOU'RE DOING THE BEST YOU CAN?
PROBLEM IS, YOUR BEST AIN'T ALL IT'S CRACKED UP TO BE, AIN'T IT?

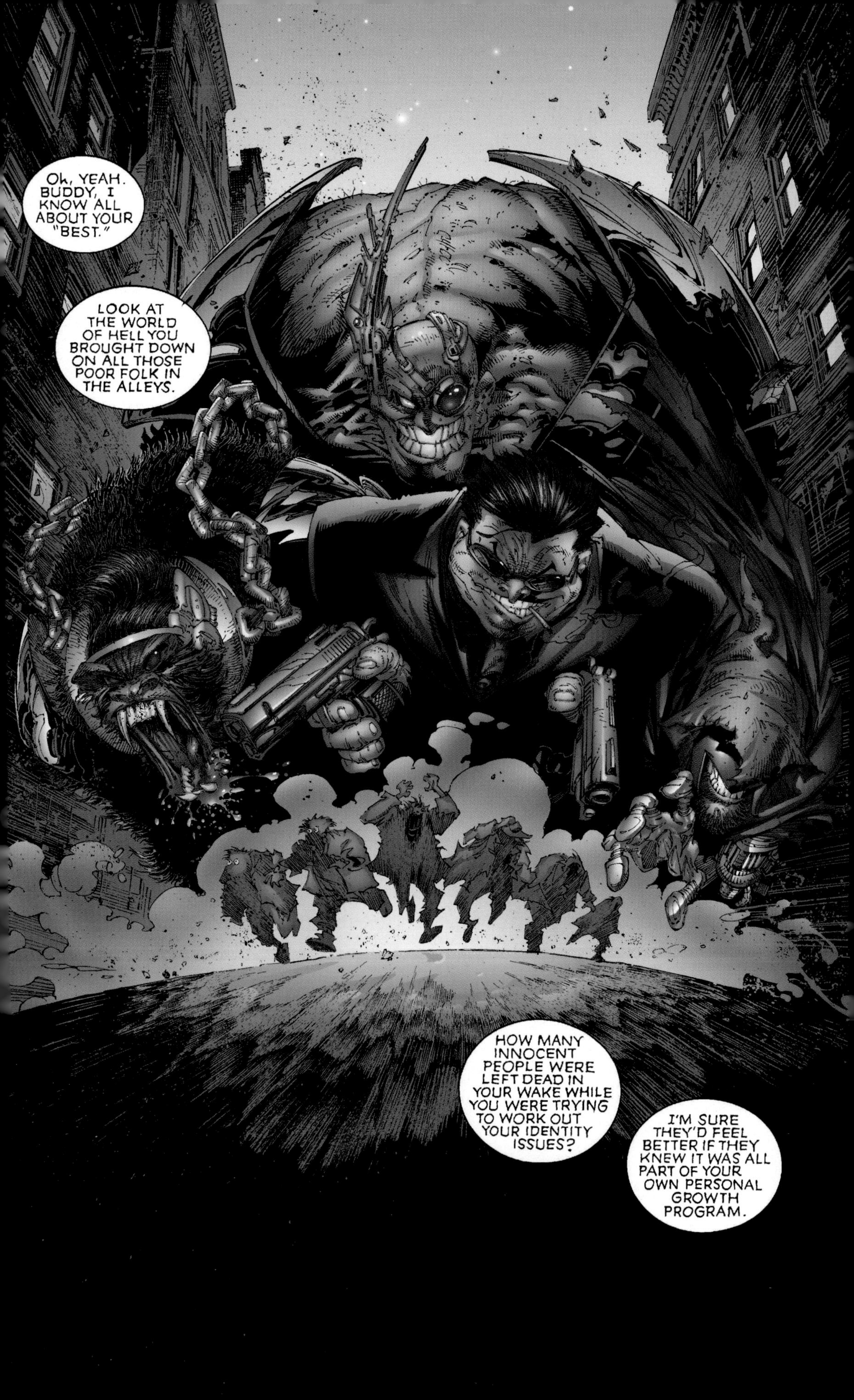
Oh, YEAH. BUDDY, I KNOW ALL ABOUT YOUR "BEST."
LOOK AT THE WORLD OF HELL YOU BROUGHT DOWN ON ALL THOSE POOR FOLK IN THE ALLEYS.
HOW MANY INNOCENT PEOPLE WERE LEFT DEAD IN YOUR WAKE WHILE YOU WERE TRYING TO WORK OUT YOUR IDENTITY ISSUES?
I'M SURE THEY'D FEEL BETTER IF THEY KNEW IT WAS ALL PART OF YOUR OWN PERSONAL GROWTH PROGRAM.

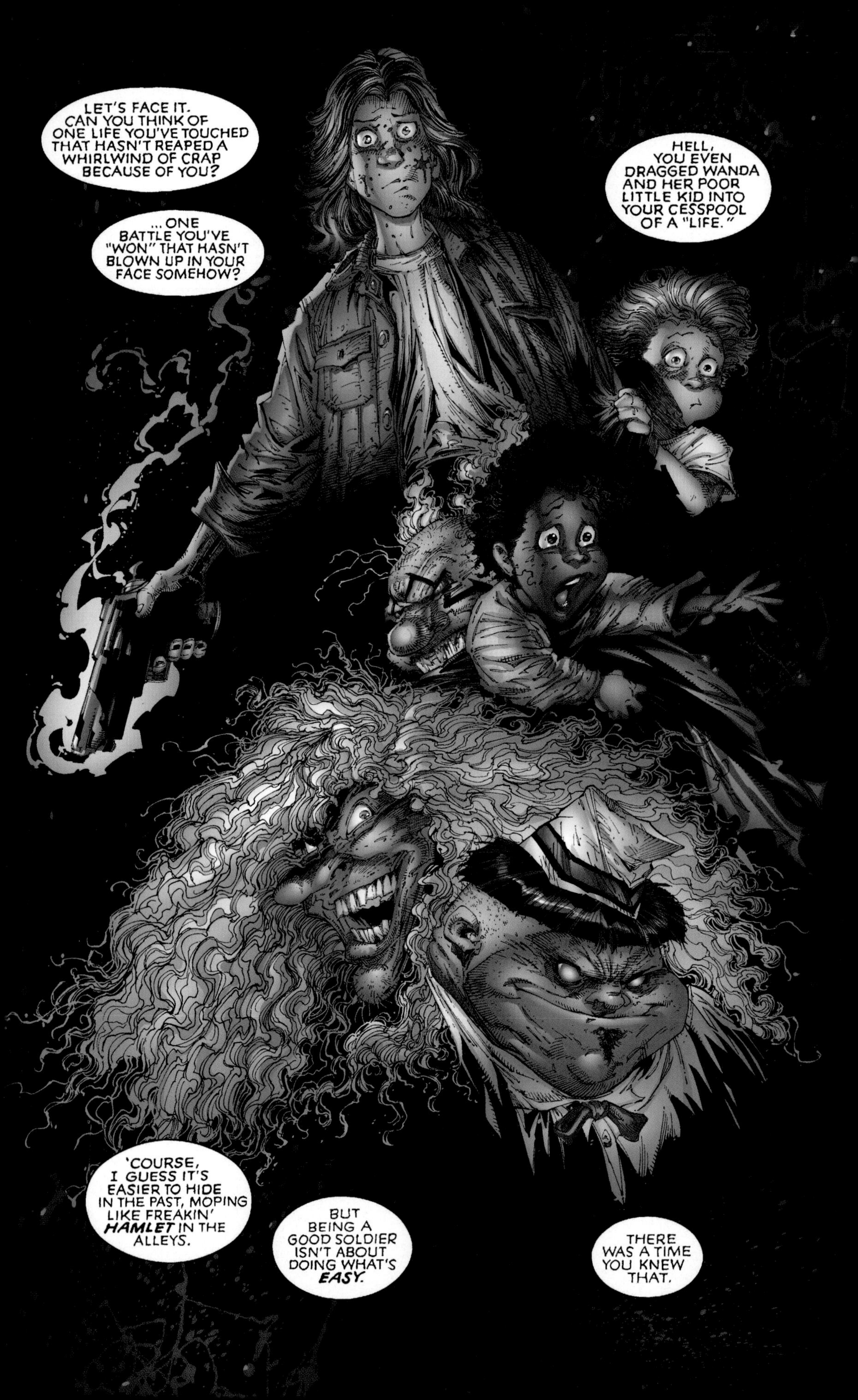
LET'S FACE IT. CAN YOU THINK OF ONE LIFE YOU'VE TOUCHED THAT HASN'T REAPED A WHIRLWIND OF CRAP BECAUSE OF YOU?
...ONE BATTLE YOU'VE "WON" THAT HASN'T BLOWN UP IN YOUR FACE SOMEHOW?
HELL, YOU EVEN DRAGGED WANDA AND HER POOR LITTLE KID INTO YOUR CESSPOOL OF A "LIFE."
'COURSE, I GUESS IT'S EASIER TO HIDE IN THE PAST, MOPING LIKE FREAKIN' HAMLET IN THE ALLEYS.
BUT BEING A GOOD SOLDIER ISN'T ABOUT DOING WHAT'S EASY.
THERE WAS A TIME YOU KNEW THAT.

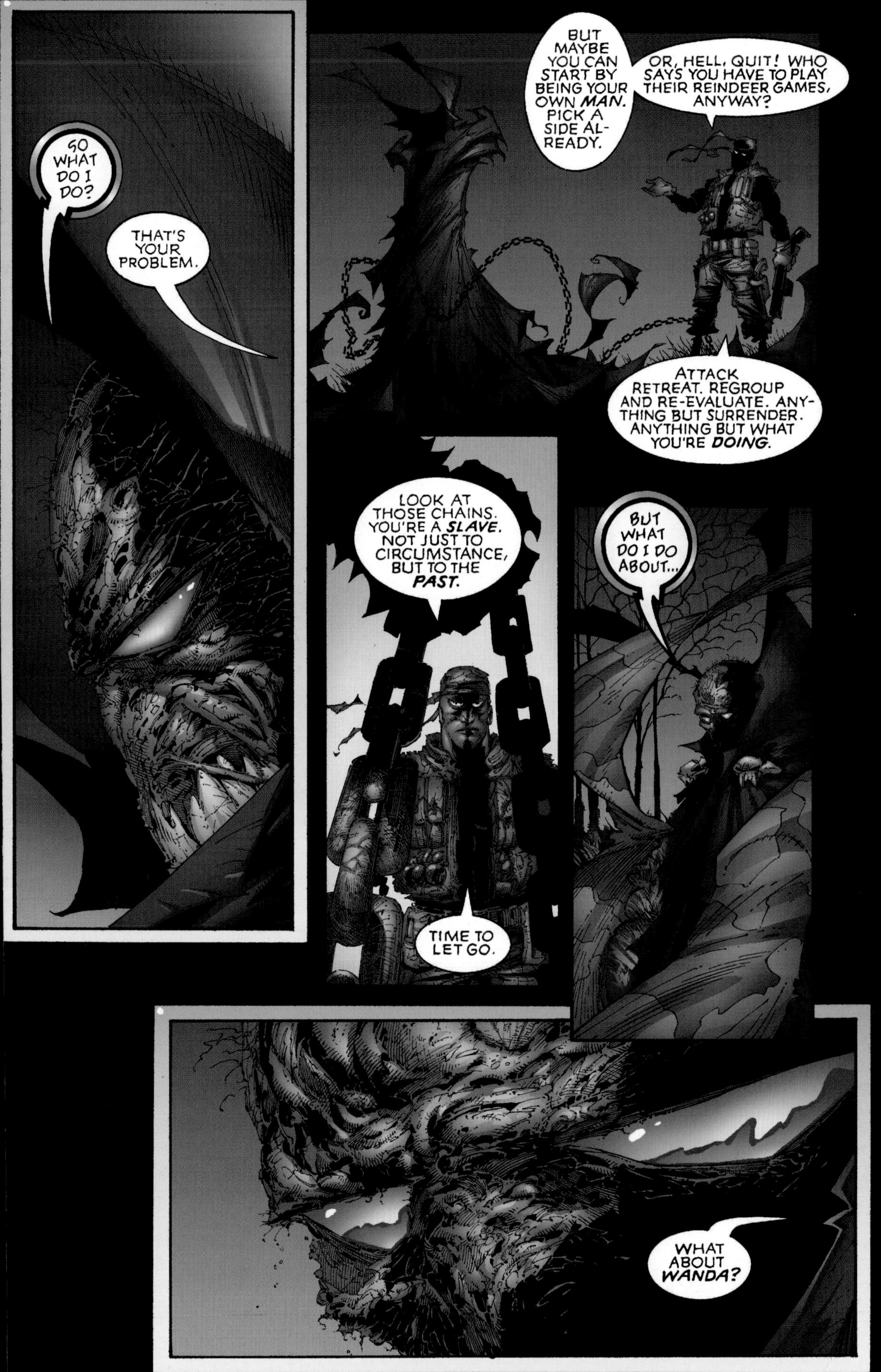
SO WHAT DO I DO?
THAT'S YOUR PROBLEM.
BUT MAYBE YOU CAN START BY BEING YOUR OWN MAN. PICK A SIDE AL-READY.
OR, HELL, QUIT! WHO SAYS YOU HAVE TO PLAY THEIR REINDEER GAMES, ANYWAY?
ATTACK. RETREAT. REGROUP AND RE-EVALUATE. ANYTHING BUT SURRENDER. ANYTHING BUT WHAT YOU'RE DOING.
LOOK AT THOSE CHAINS. YOU'RE A SLAVE. NOT JUST TO CIRCUMSTANCE, BUT TO THE PAST.
TIME TO LET GO.
BUT WHAT DO I DO ABOUT...
WHAT ABOUT WANDA?

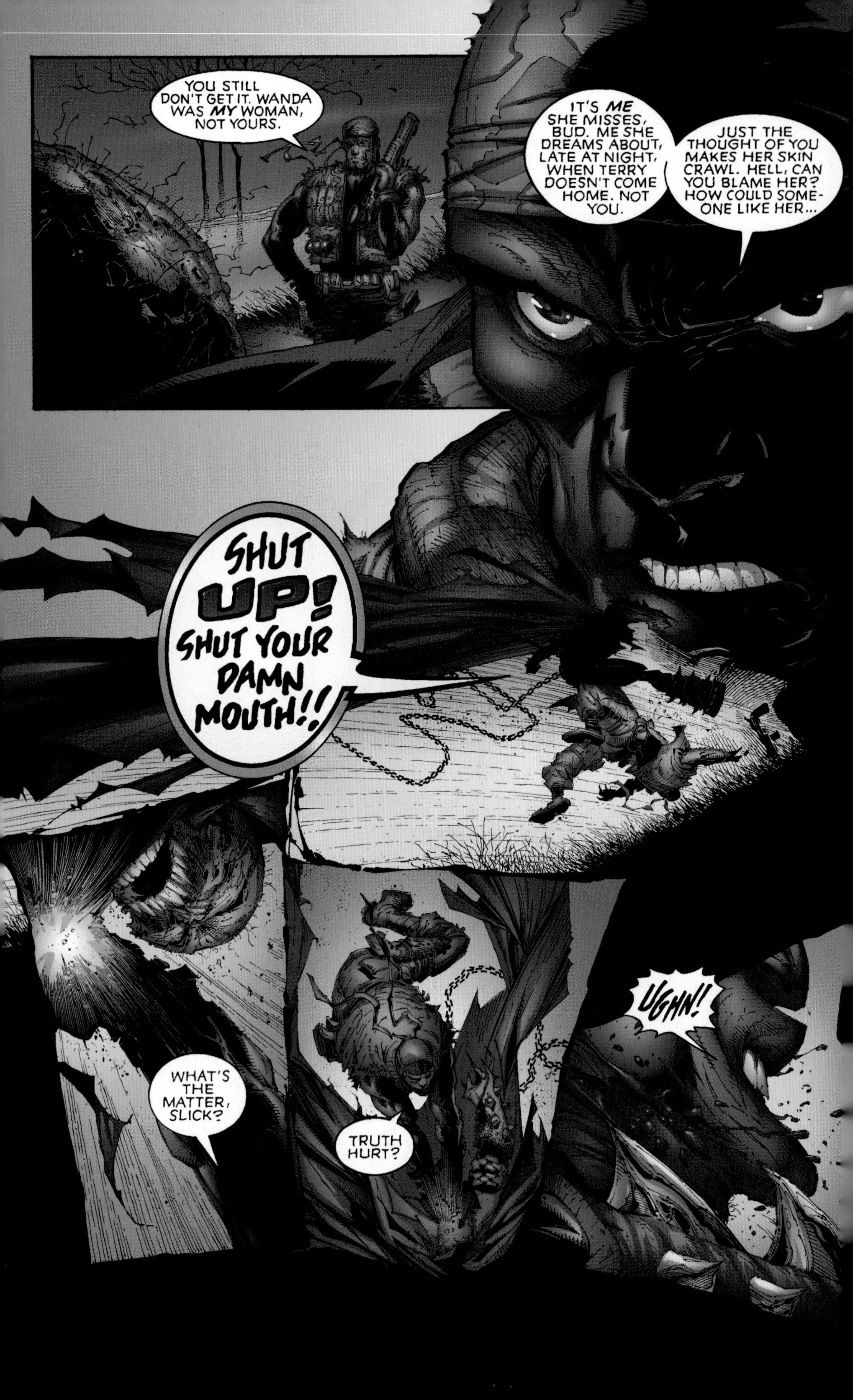
YOU STILL DON'T GET IT. WANDA WAS MY WOMAN, NOT YOURS.
IT'S ME SHE MISSES, BUD. ME SHE DREAMS ABOUT, LATE AT NIGHT, WHEN TERRY DOESN'T COME HOME. NOT YOU.
JUST THE THOUGHT OF YOU MAKES HER SKIN CRAWL. HELL, CAN YOU BLAME HER? HOW COULD SOME-ONE LIKE HER...
SHUT UP! SHUT YOUR DAMN MOUTH!!
UGHN!!
WHAT'S THE MATTER, SLICK?
TRUTH HURT?

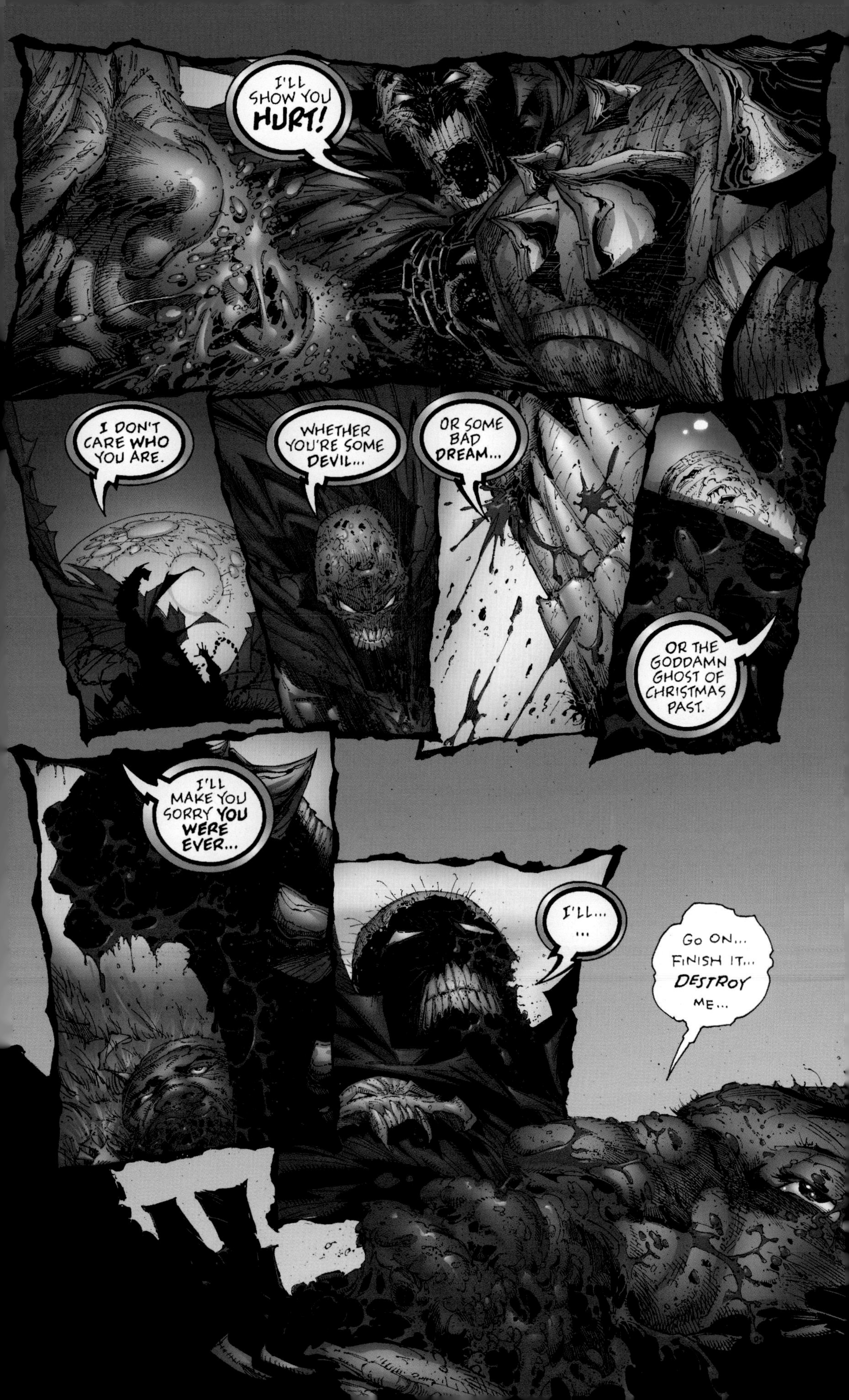
I'LL SHOW YOU HURT!
I DON'T CARE WHO YOU ARE.
WHETHER YOU'RE SOME DEVIL...
OR SOME BAD DREAM...
OR THE GODDAMN GHOST OF CHRISTMAS PAST.
I'LL MAKE YOU SORRY YOU WERE EVER...
I'LL... ...
GO ON... FINISH IT... DESTROY ME...

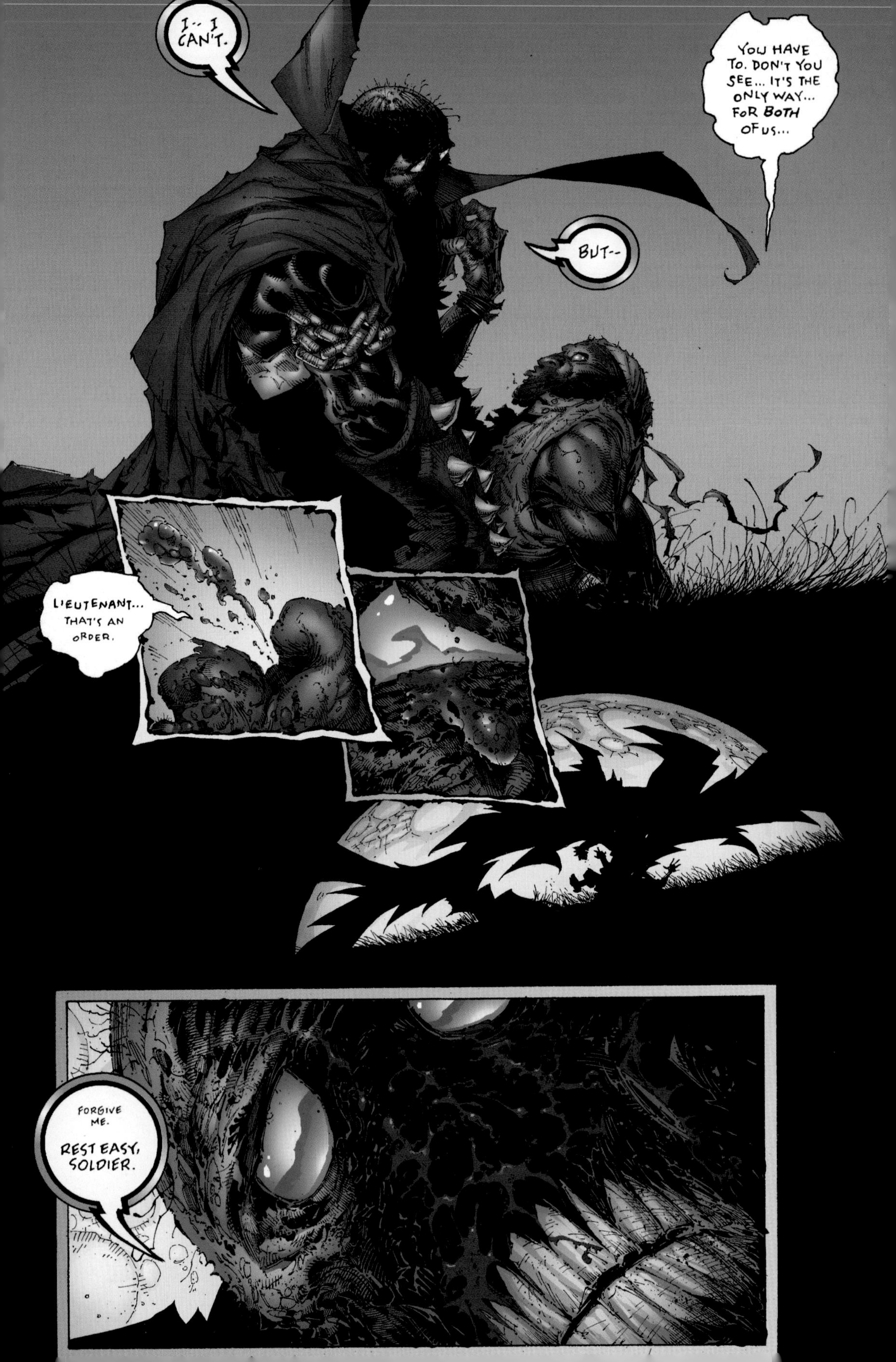

I-- I CAN'T.
YOU HAVE TO. DON'T YOU SEE... IT'S THE ONLY WAY... FOR BOTH OF US...
BUT--
LIEUTENANT... THAT'S AN ORDER.
FORGIVE ME.
REST EASY, SOLDIER.

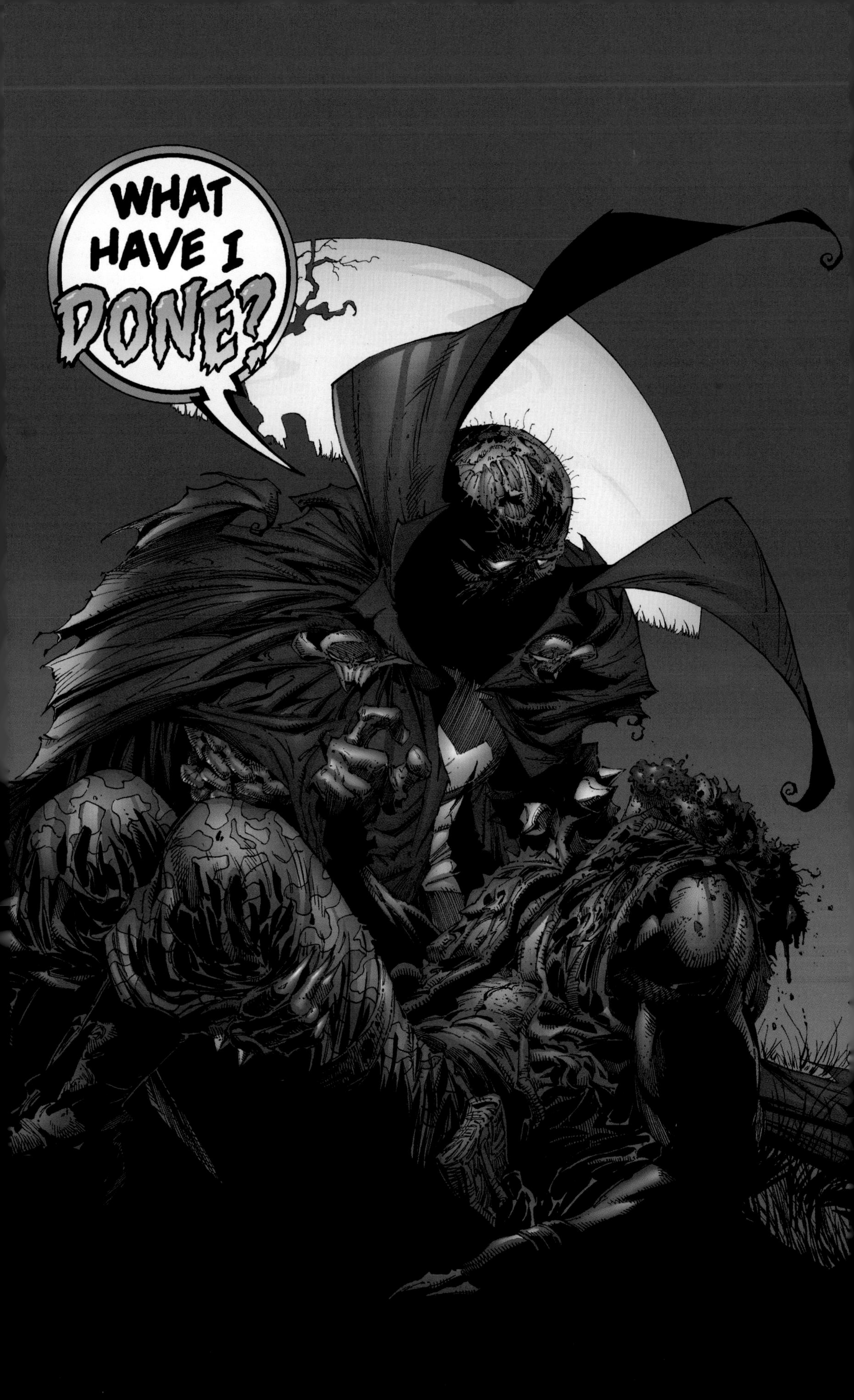
WHAT HAVE I DONE?

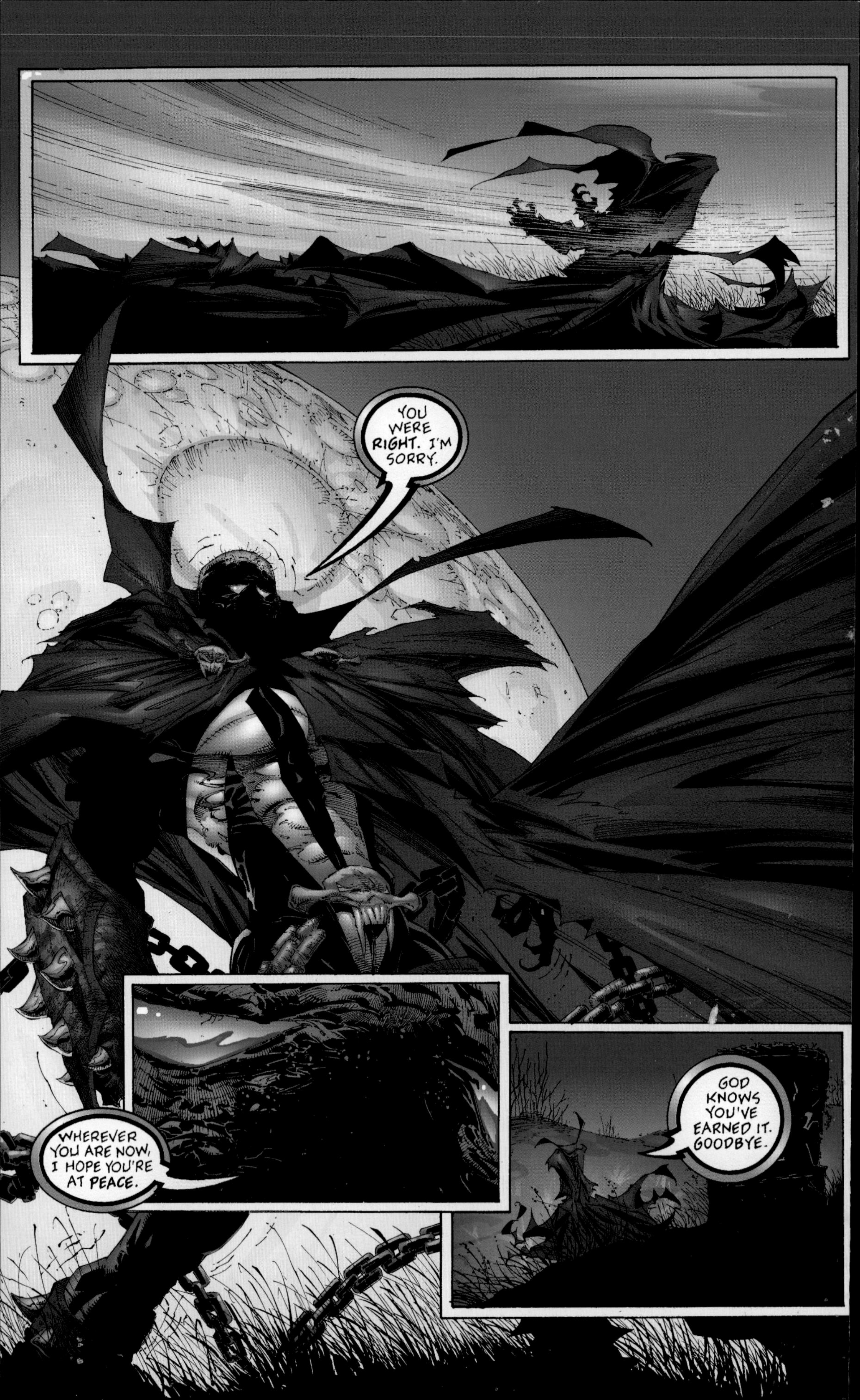
YOU WERE RIGHT. I'M SORRY.
WHEREVER YOU ARE NOW, I HOPE YOU'RE AT PEACE.
GOD KNOWS YOU'VE EARNED IT. GOODBYE.

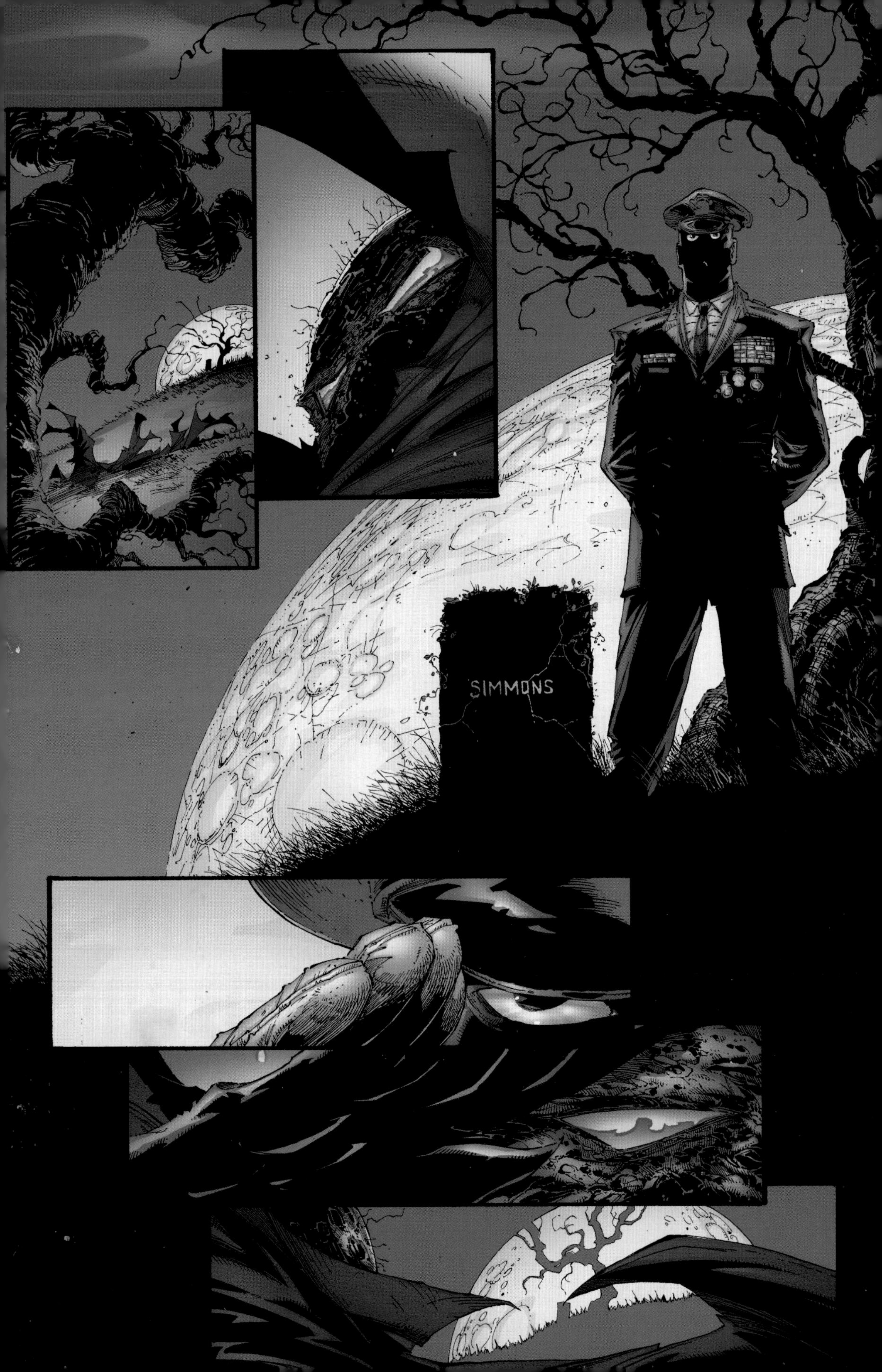
SIMMONS

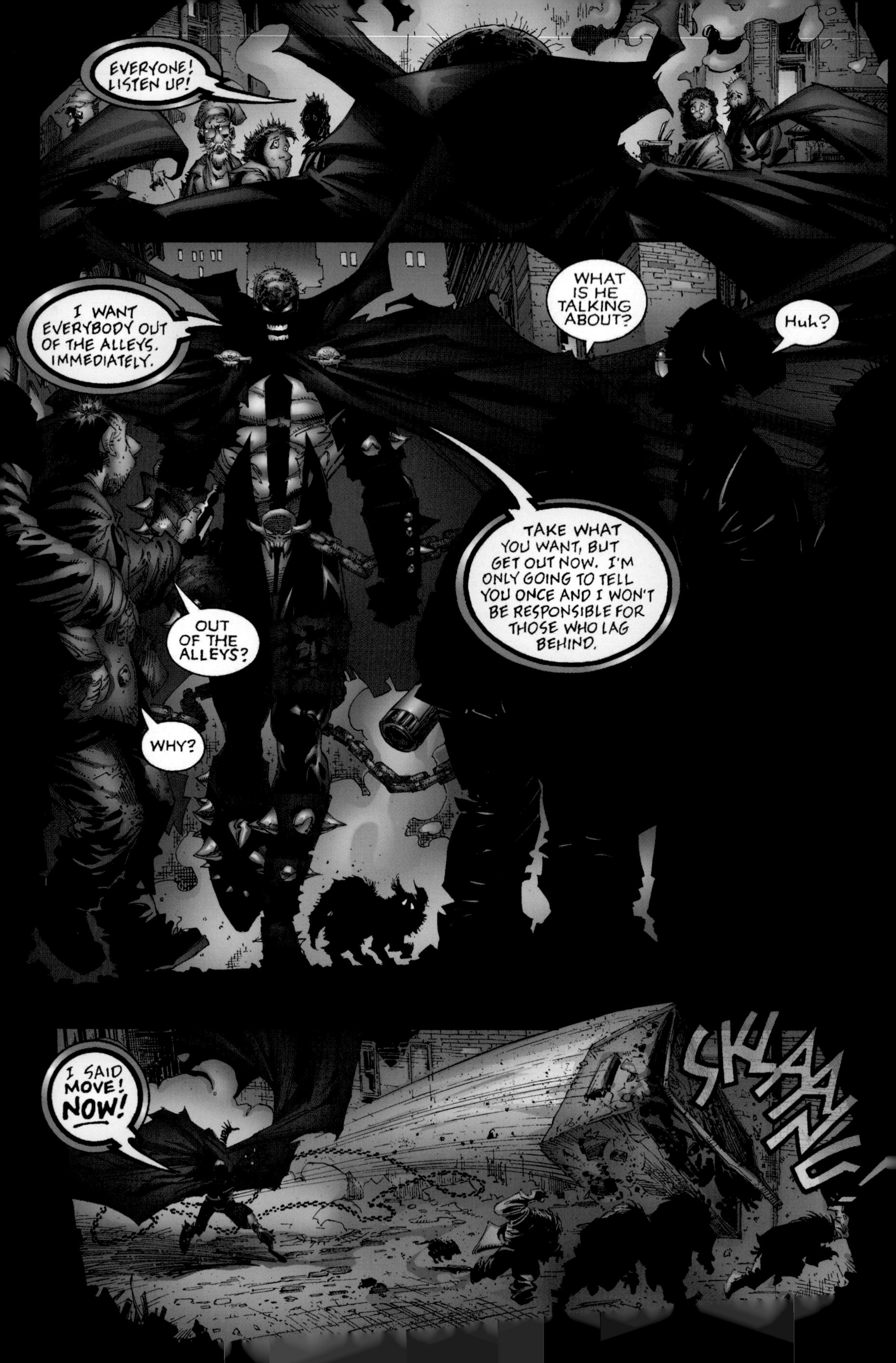
EVERYONE! LISTEN UP!
I WANT EVERYBODY OUT OF THE ALLEYS. IMMEDIATELY.
WHAT IS HE TALKING ABOUT?
Huh?
TAKE WHAT YOU WANT, BUT GET OUT NOW. I'M ONLY GOING TO TELL YOU ONCE AND I WON'T BE RESPONSIBLE FOR THOSE WHO LAG BEHIND.
OUT OF THE ALLEYS?
WHY?
I SAID MOVE! NOW!
SKRAANG

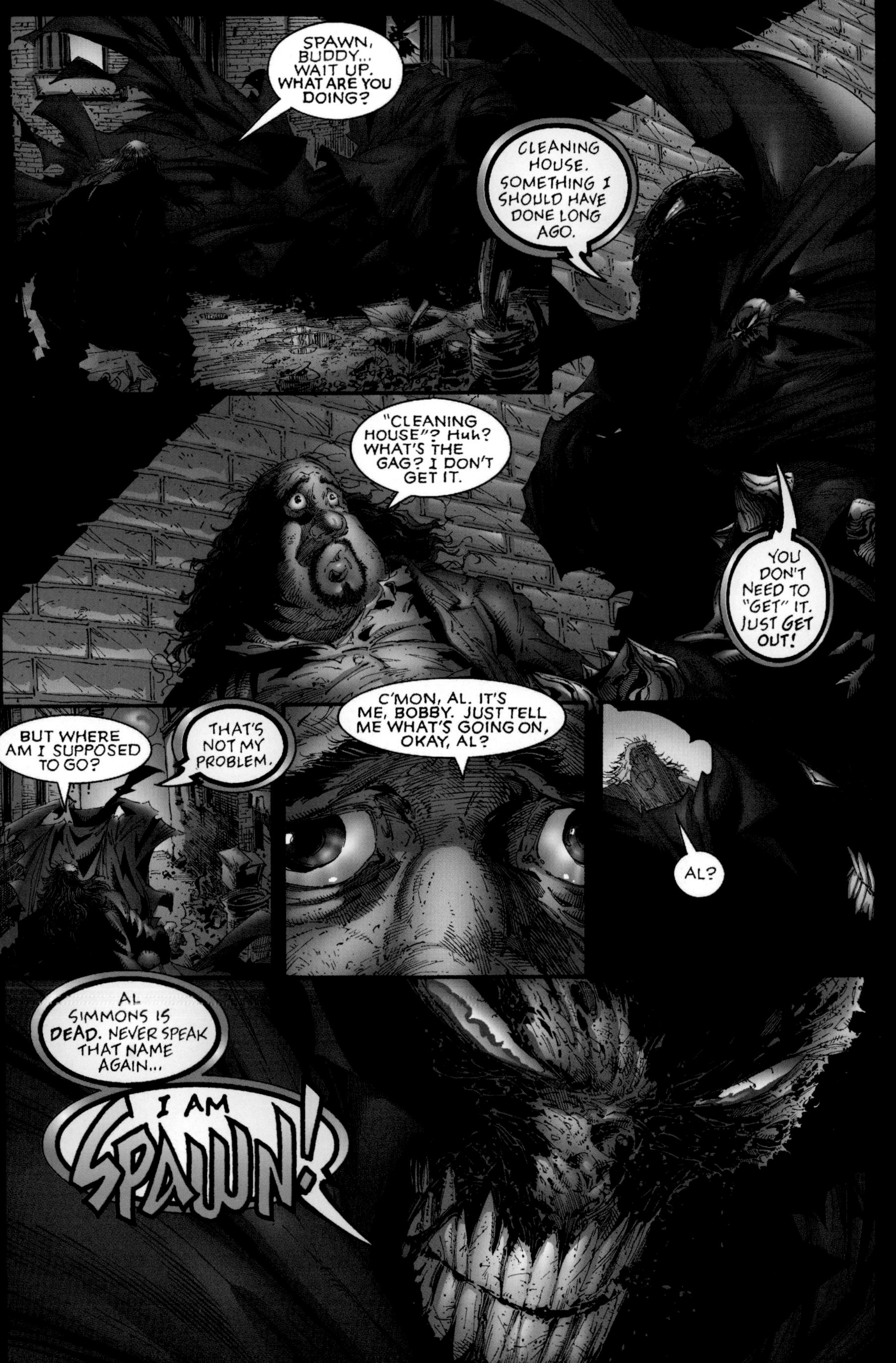
SPAWN, BUDDY... WAIT UP. WHAT ARE YOU DOING?
CLEANING HOUSE. SOMETHING I SHOULD HAVE DONE LONG AGO.
"CLEANING HOUSE"? Huh? WHAT'S THE GAG? I DON'T GET IT.
YOU DON'T NEED TO "GET" IT. JUST GET OUT!
BUT WHERE AM I SUPPOSED TO GO?
THAT'S NOT MY PROBLEM.
C'MON, AL. IT'S ME, BOBBY. JUST TELL ME WHAT'S GOING ON, OKAY, AL?
AL?
AL SIMMONS IS DEAD. NEVER SPEAK THAT NAME AGAIN...
I AM SPAWN!

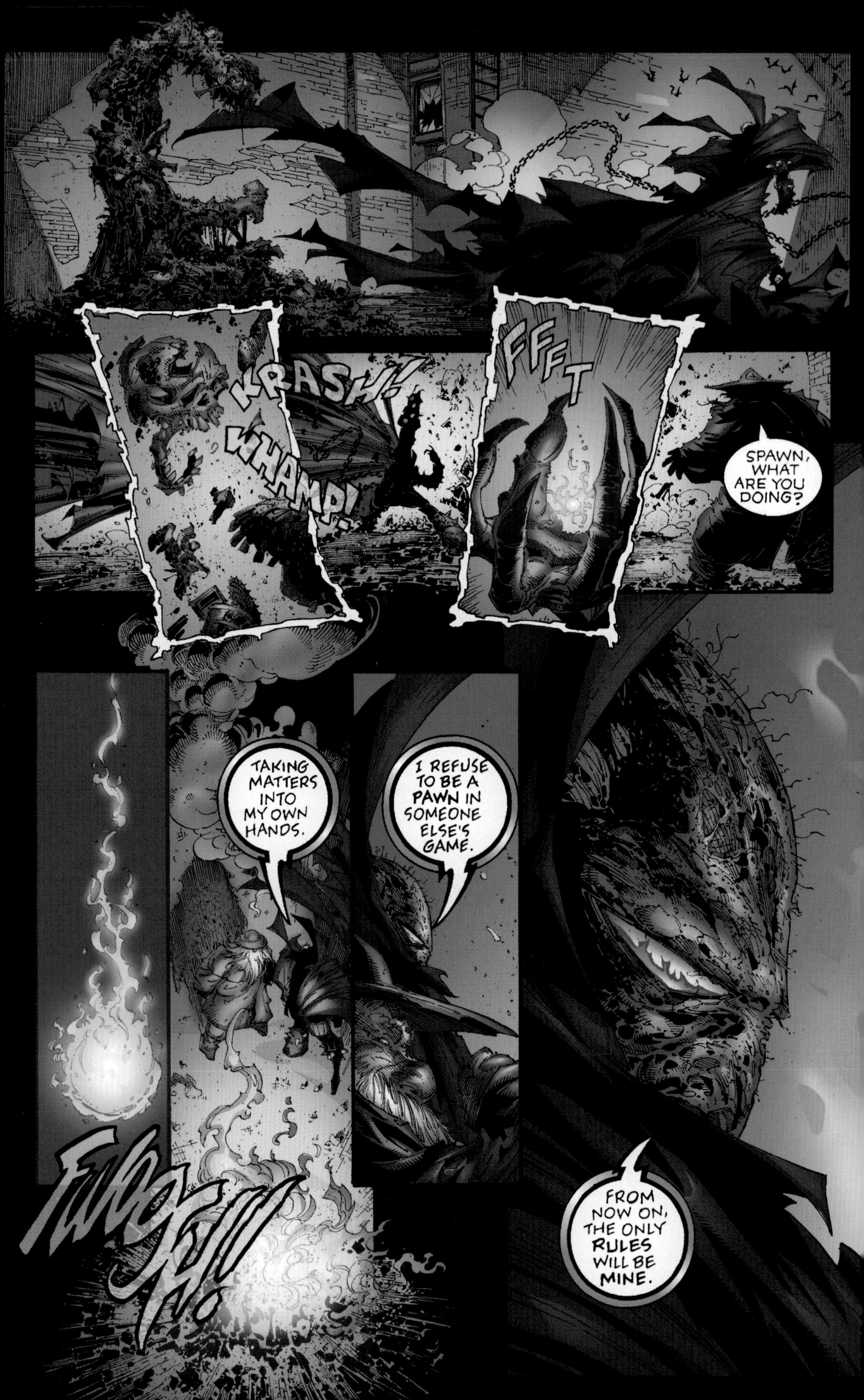
KRASH!
WHAMP!
FFFT
SPAWN, WHAT ARE YOU DOING?
TAKING MATTERS INTO MY OWN HANDS.
I REFUSE TO BE A PAWN IN SOMEONE ELSE'S GAME.
FROM NOW ON, THE ONLY RULES WILL BE MINE.

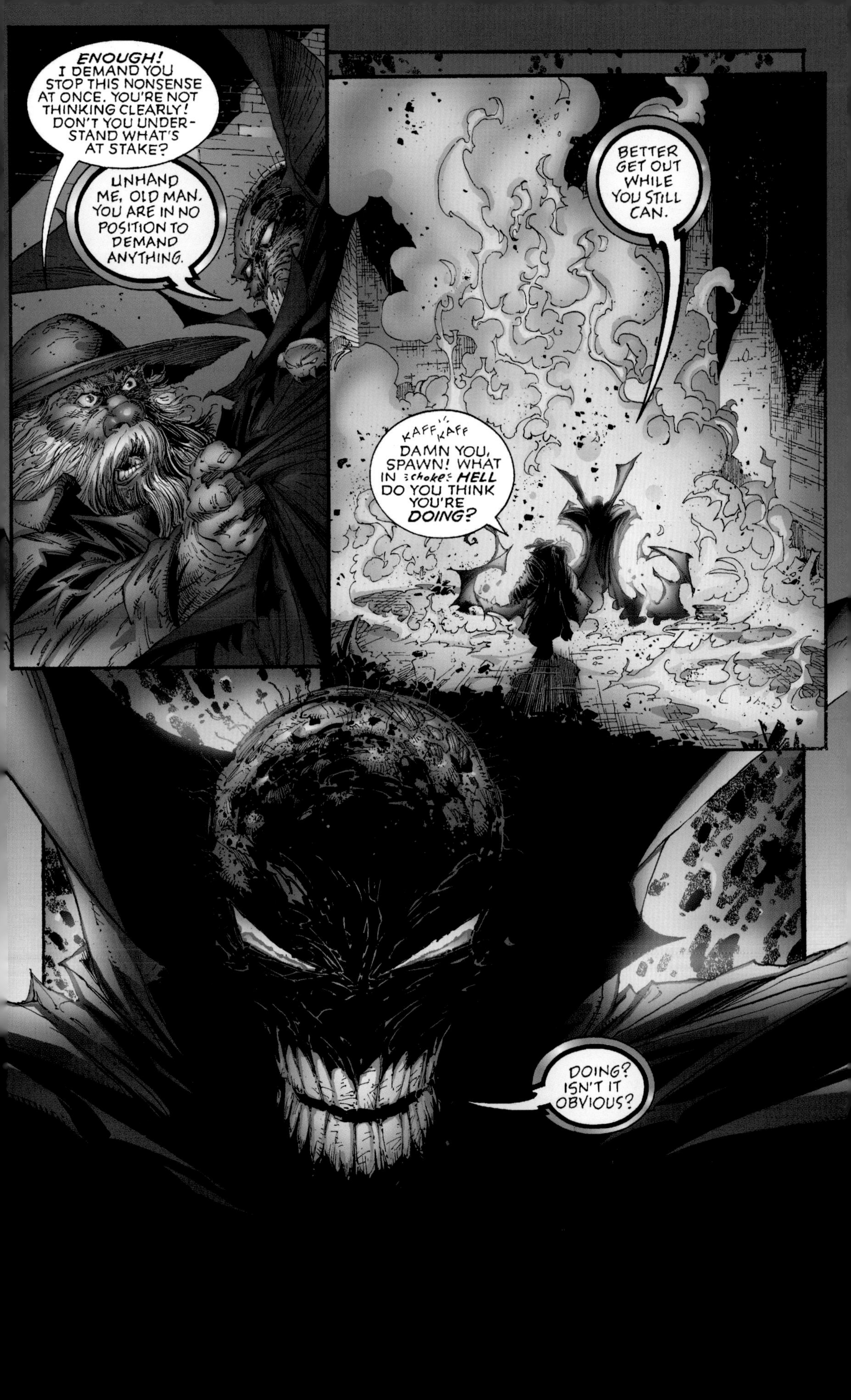
ENOUGH! I DEMAND YOU STOP THIS NONSENSE AT ONCE. YOU'RE NOT THINKING CLEARLY! DON'T YOU UNDER-STAND WHAT'S AT STAKE?
UNHAND ME, OLD MAN. YOU ARE IN NO POSITION TO DEMAND ANYTHING.
BETTER GET OUT WHILE YOU STILL CAN.
KAFF KAFF
DAMN YOU, SPAWN! WHAT IN choke HELL DO YOU THINK YOU'RE DOING?
DOING? ISN'T IT OBVIOUS?

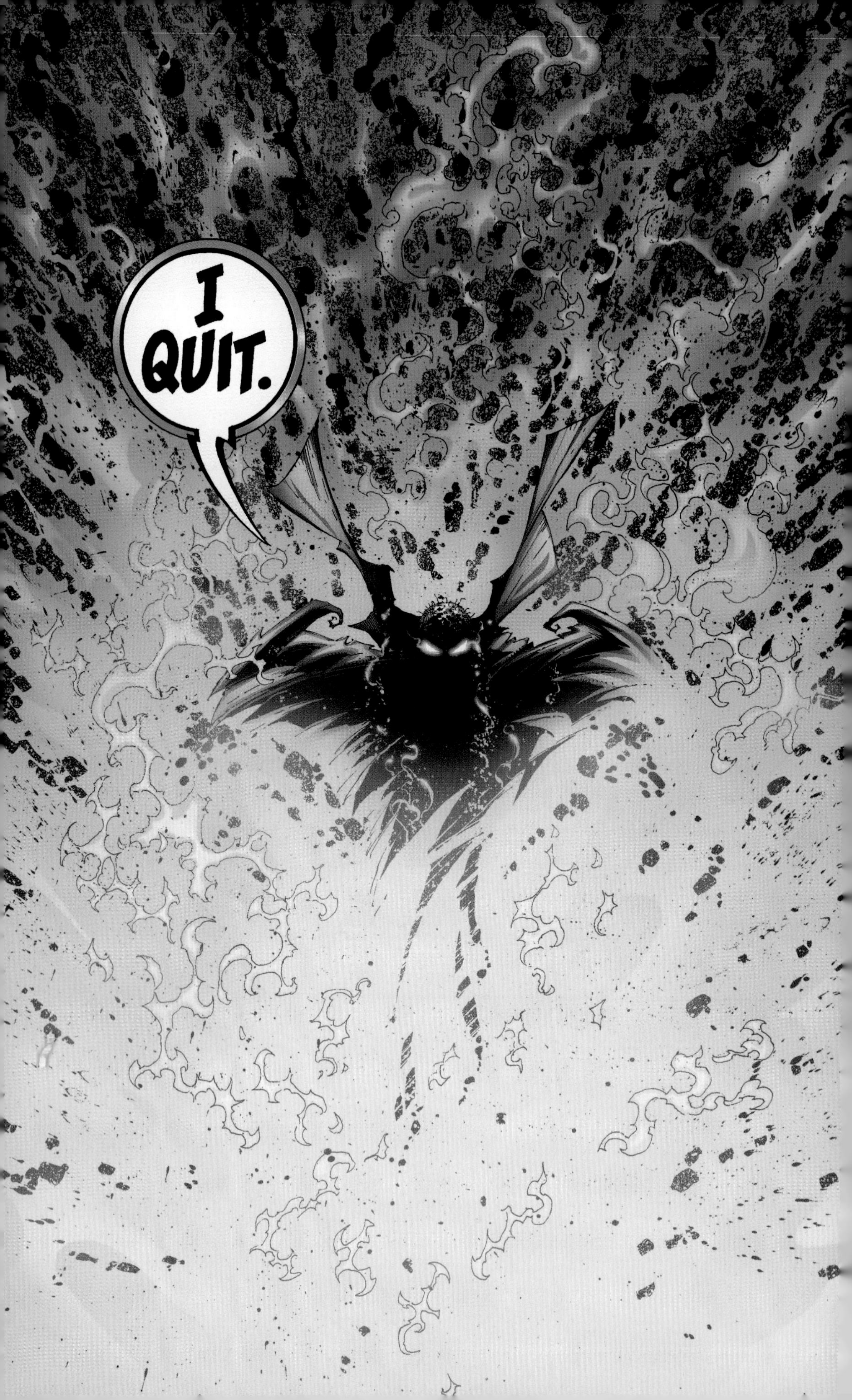
I QUIT.

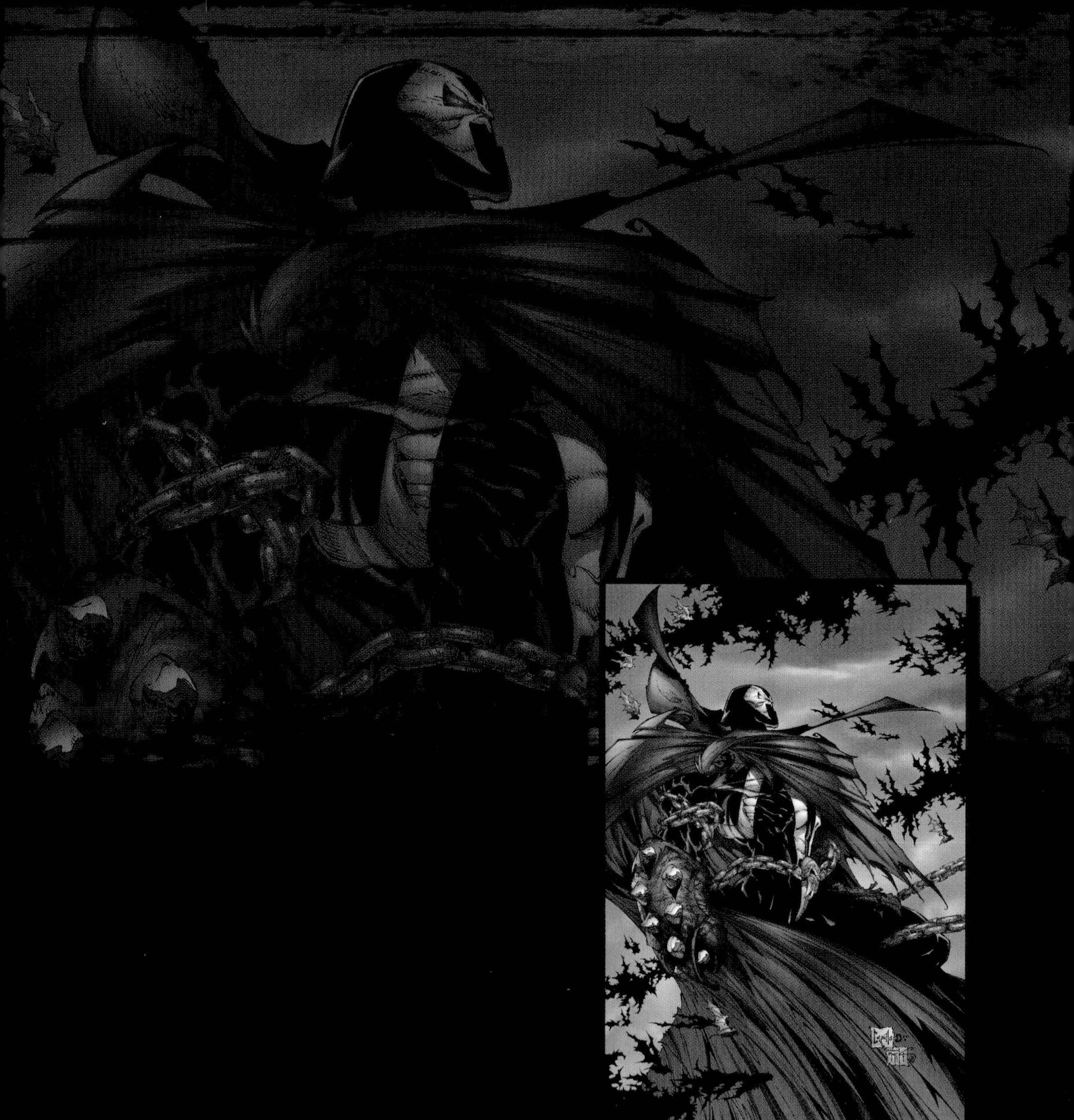

ISSUE EIGHTY-SEVEN

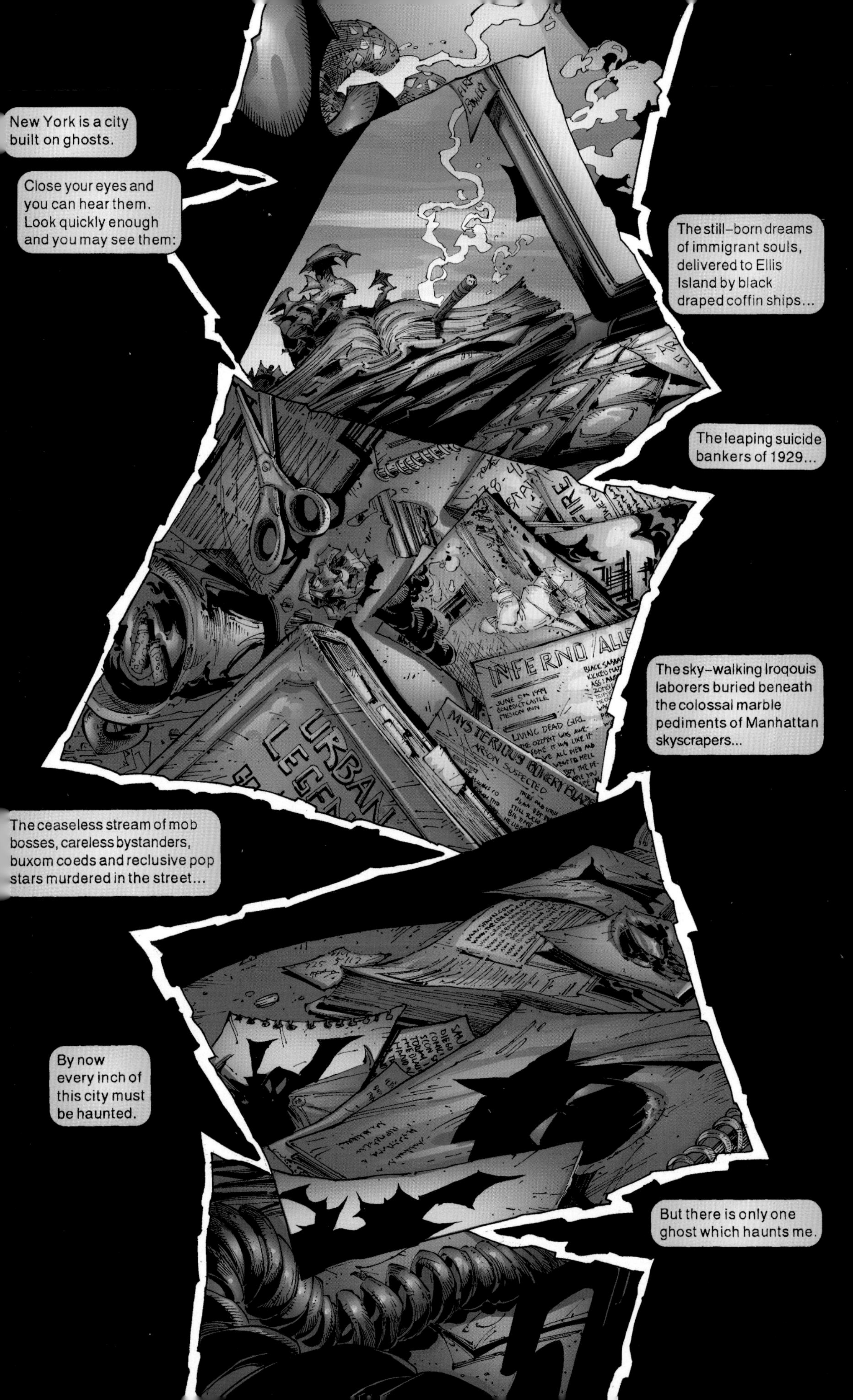
New York is a city built on ghosts.
Close your eyes and you can hear them. Look quickly enough and you may see them:
The still-born dreams of immigrant souls, delivered to Ellis Island by black draped coffin ships...
The leaping suicide bankers of 1929...
The sky-walking Iroqouis laborers buried beneath the colossal marble pediments of Manhattan skyscrapers...
The ceaseless stream of mob bosses, careless bystanders, buxom coeds and reclusive pop stars murdered in the street...
By now every inch of this city must be haunted.
But there is only one ghost which haunts me.
INFERNO
URBAN LEGEND
MYSTERIOUS BOWERY BLAZE
ARSON SUSPECTED
LIVING DEAD GIRL

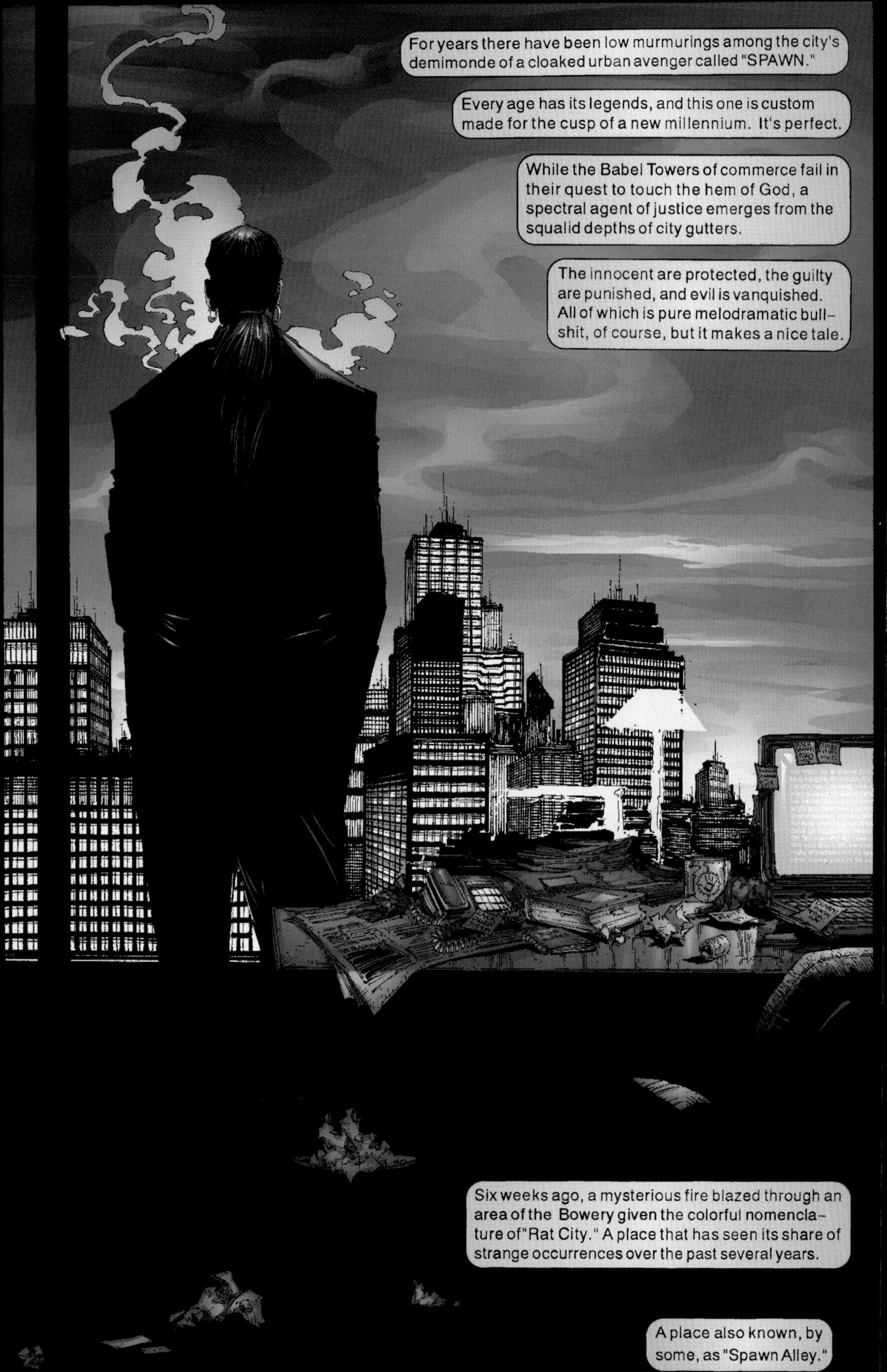
For years there have been low murmurings among the city's demimonde of a cloaked urban avenger called "SPAWN."
Every age has its legends, and this one is custom made for the cusp of a new millennium. It's perfect.
While the Babel Towers of commerce fail in their quest to touch the hem of God, a spectral agent of justice emerges from the squalid depths of city gutters.
The innocent are protected, the guilty are punished, and evil is vanquished. All of which is pure melodramatic bull-shit, of course, but it makes a nice tale.
Six weeks ago, a mysterious fire blazed through an area of the Bowery given the colorful nomencla-ture of "Rat City." A place that has seen its share of strange occurrences over the past several years.
A place also known, by some, as "Spawn Alley."

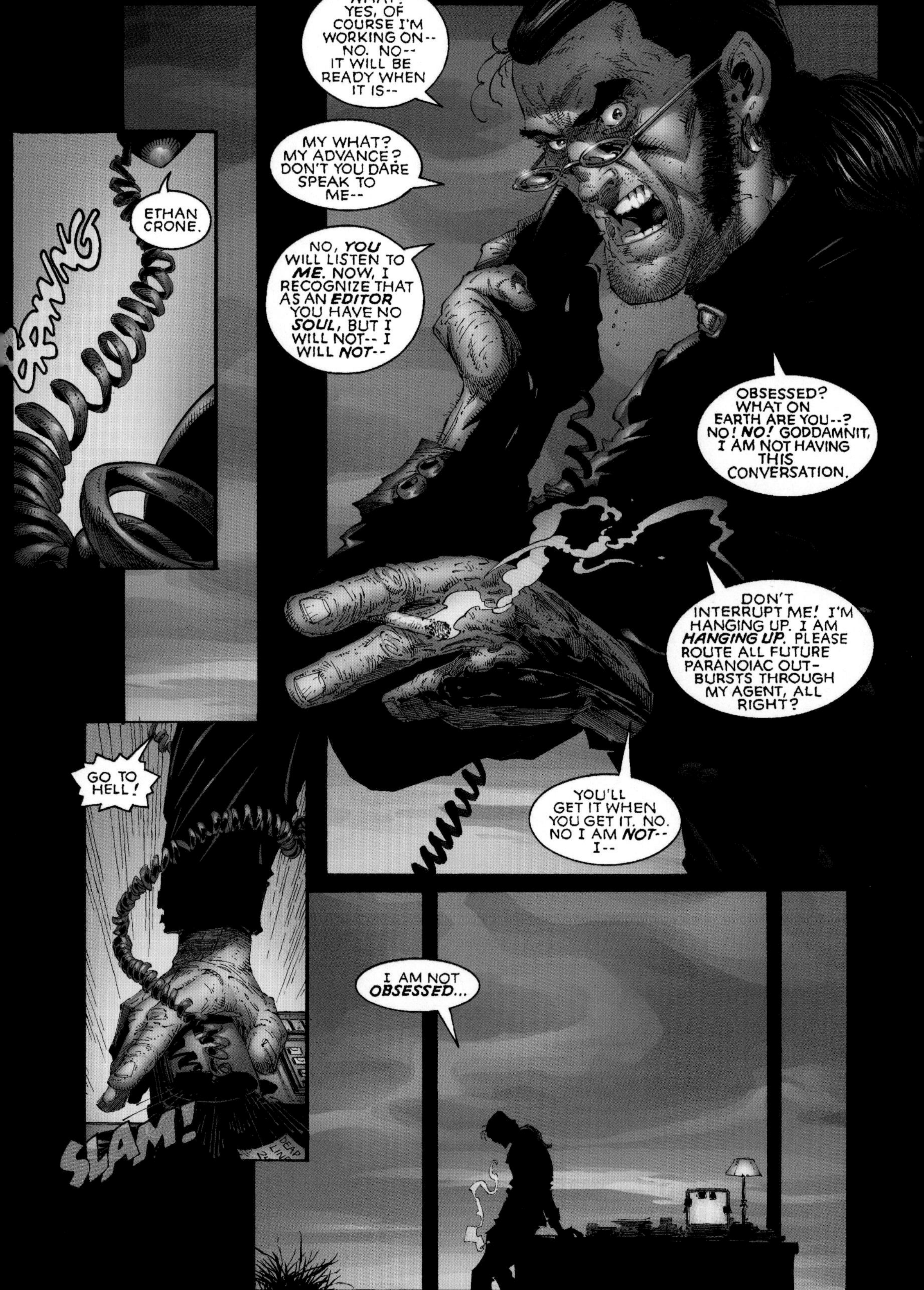
ETHAN CRONE.
WHAT? YES, OF COURSE I'M WORKING ON-- NO. NO-- IT WILL BE READY WHEN IT IS--
MY WHAT? MY ADVANCE? DON'T YOU DARE SPEAK TO ME--
NO, **YOU** WILL LISTEN TO **ME**. NOW, I RECOGNIZE THAT AS AN **EDITOR** YOU HAVE NO **SOUL**, BUT I WILL NOT-- I WILL **NOT**--
OBSESSED? WHAT ON EARTH ARE YOU--? NO! **NO!** GODDAMNIT, I AM NOT HAVING THIS CONVERSATION.
DON'T INTERRUPT ME! I'M HANGING UP. I AM **HANGING UP**. PLEASE ROUTE ALL FUTURE PARANOIAC OUT-BURSTS THROUGH MY AGENT, ALL RIGHT?
YOU'LL GET IT WHEN YOU GET IT. NO. NO I AM **NOT**-- I--
GO TO HELL!
SLAM!
I AM NOT **OBSESSED**...

INTERVIEW #7.

"Stiv and Lyssa"

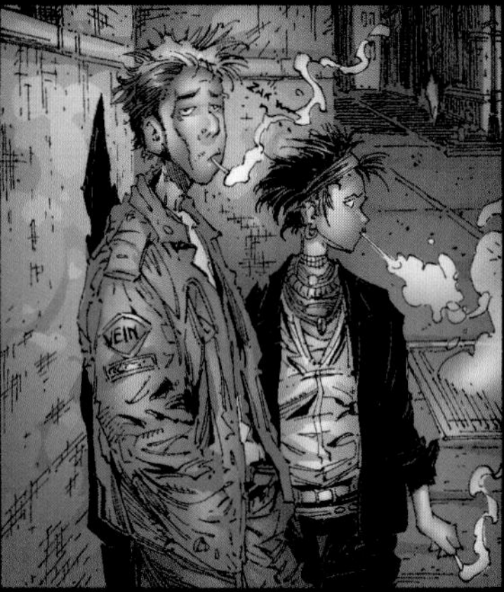

So what... do I just start? Cool. Okay. Yeah, I've heard of Spawn. I useta scam down near the alleys. Dudes 'round there were pretty cool.

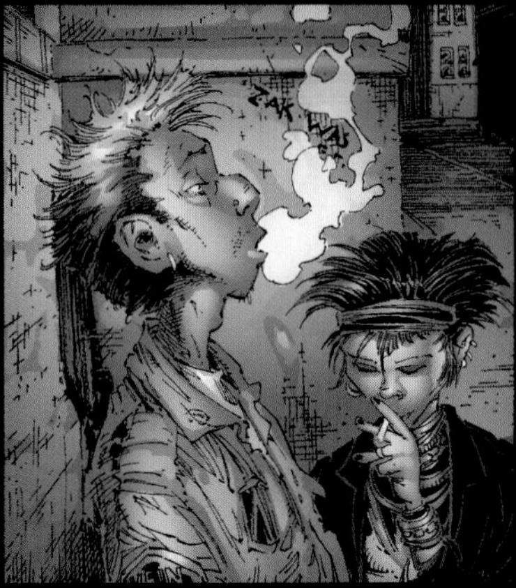
ZAK WAS

Mostly they're old guys, though. It gets really depressing with the old guys. Like they're never gonna change. Whatever you are at 40, that's what you'll be foreva, right? Not me, though. I got plans. Don't we, hon? Big plans.

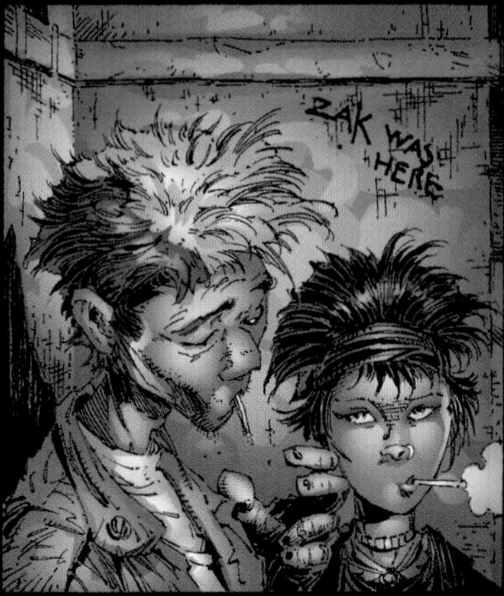
ZAK WAS HERE

So yeah, Spawn. I heard he's a black dude. They did something to him in the war. Like gave him superpowers. Mutation experiment or something. All kinds of weird alien shit. Like in that movie, the one with that guy from the other one. No?

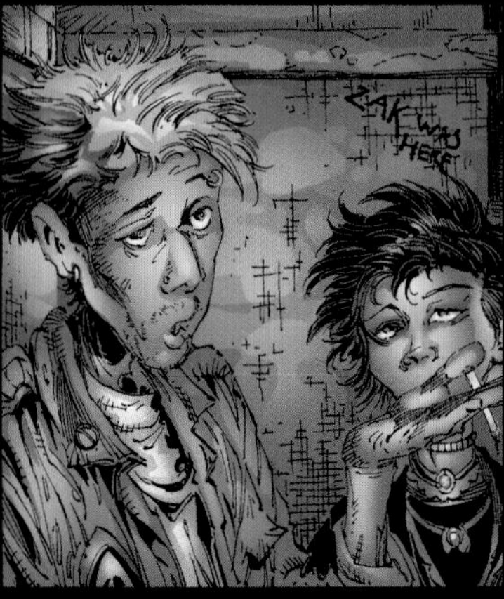
ZAK WAS HERE

I saw him a couple times. Spawn, I mean. Never talked to him though. I just kinda kept my distance. Struck me as the kinda guy who appreciates his privacy, know what I'm saying?

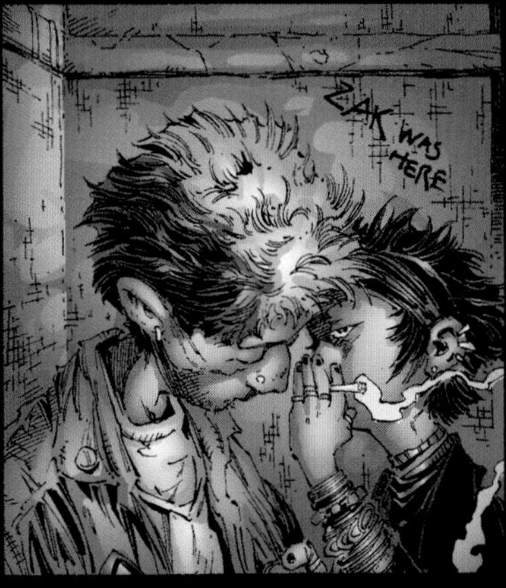
ZAK WAS HERE

What?
(unintelligible)

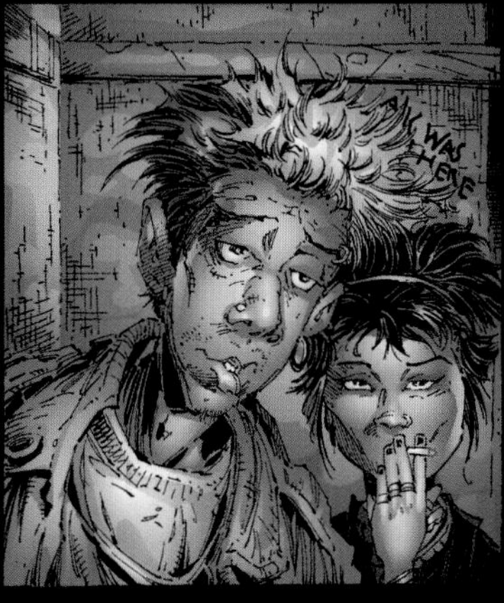
ZAK WAS HERE

So, uh, listen dude... Are we like getting paid for this or what?

INTERVIEW #11
"Jaka"

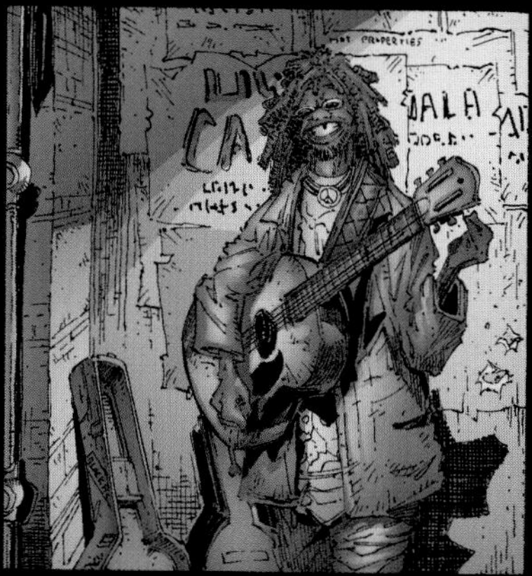

You here to make me famous, friend? Is that what this is about? To bring my god-given talent to the people, let me shine a little righteous light into this dark, dark world? All right. I'm ready for my close-up, mister man!

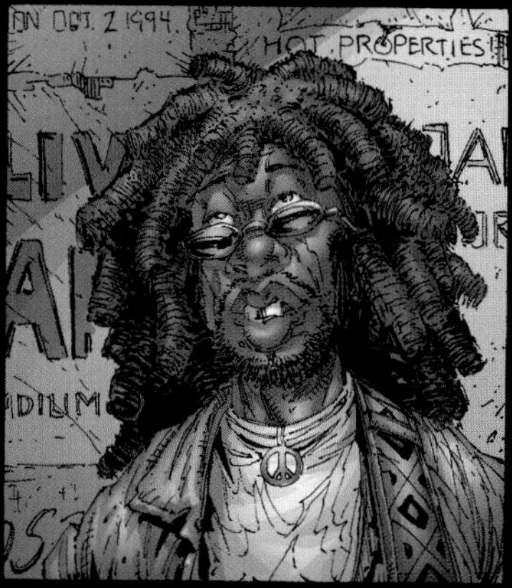
ON OCT. 2 1994
HOT PROPERTIES

Spawn? Listen, brother, you don't want to go there. That's messin' wit' some deep-dark-hella-evil-mikki-fikkin-mojo there. Alla that devil crap? Man, just leave it out. Why you wanna know 'bout sumpin' like that?

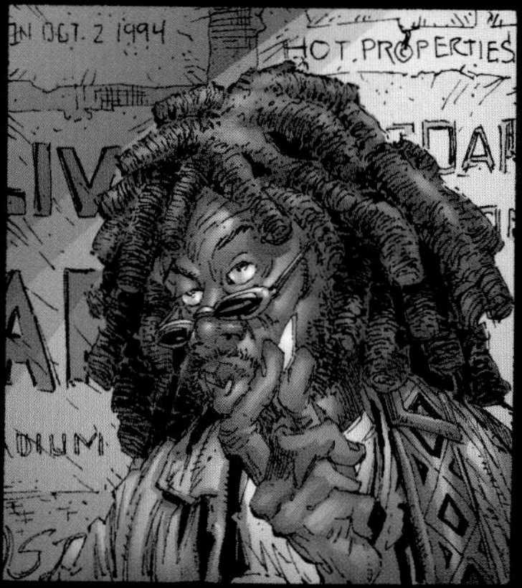
ON OCT. 2 1994
HOT PROPERTIES

Nah, I ain't never seen him. But my pal Rudi has. Saw him skin a man alive and feed him to his dogs. And he's got this stare, right? Just holds you to the spot. Hypnotic, like. He's one messed up cat, I can tell you that much.

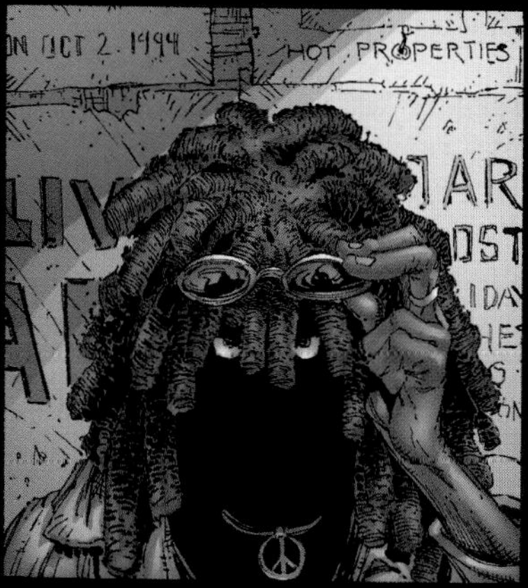
ON OCT 2. 1994
HOT PROPERTIES

You ask me, I think its some kinda voodoo-zombie shit. My granddaddy was a magic man down in N'awlins, he knew all about that crap. He was a healer. One time, when I was kid, I saw him cast seven devils outta his ol' whore.

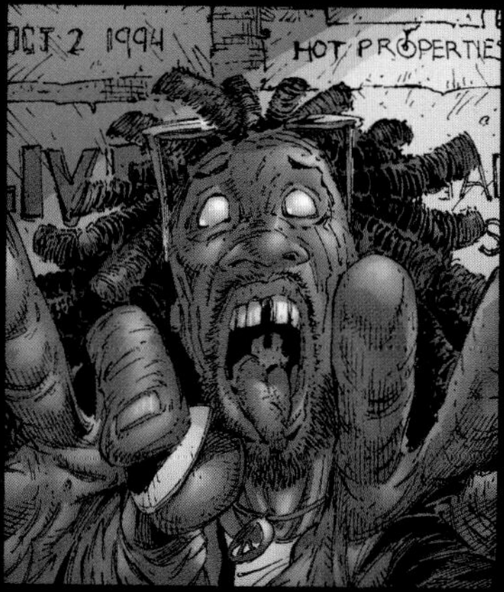
HOT PROPERTIES

YAAAA-AAGHOOOA! HAAAGH! An' alla demons come pourin' outcher mouth, like bats and snakes and lizards. Like you're pukin' up a zoo or something. Don't play wit' that stuff, I'm telling you. For real.

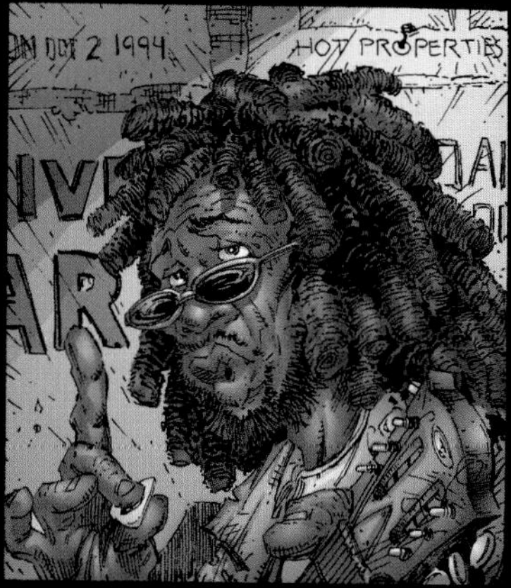
ON OCT 2 1994
HOT PROPERTIES

Walk the path of the righteous man, my brother. The devil is everywhere and it only takes one moment of weakness. You best be keeping your eyes open in this bitch world. Know'm say'n?

INTERVIEW #14
"Willie, Chet and Bigfoot"

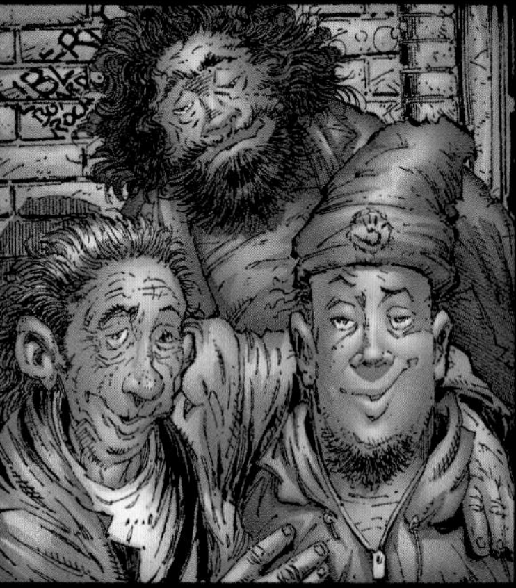

-Yeah, we knew 'im. Real well, too.
-Oh yeah, I was right there when he torched --
-Pals we were. His posse, like in the westerns
-Man I love westerns. Ever see that one, 'bout that bad ass sheriff --

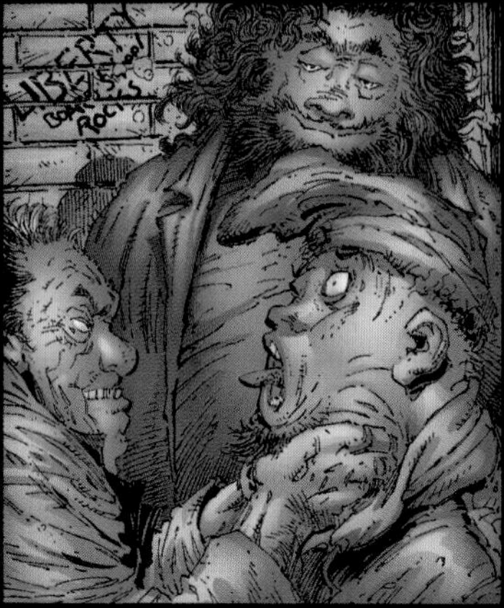

-Hey remember the time he fought that big metal dude, Robo-wop or whatever? What was his name? The pentium Guinea?
-Oh, man, was that sweet! He got him by the throat like this. Wa-POW!

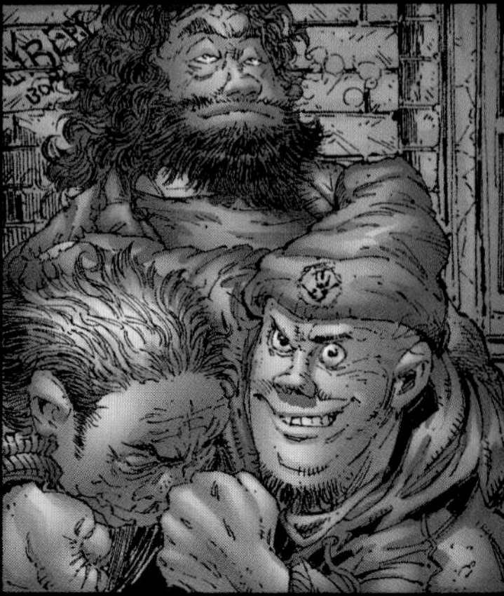

-And then the robot dude, he gets Spawny in a headlock, like grinding his nose into the pavement. It was brutal!
-No. That's not how it (unintelligible) happened. Let go of my (unintelligible)...

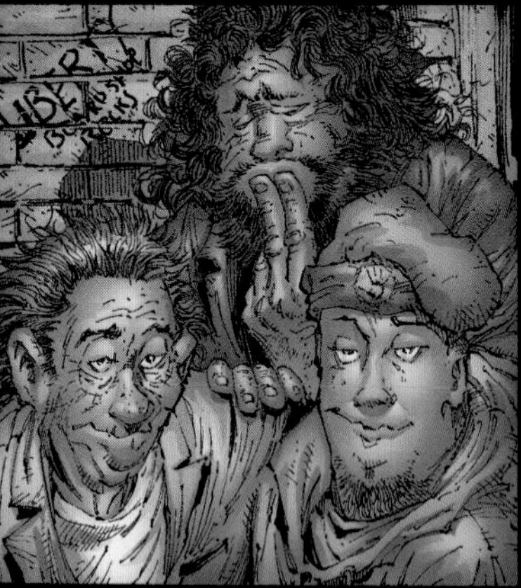

-Those were the days, man. Kickin' ass, takin' names.

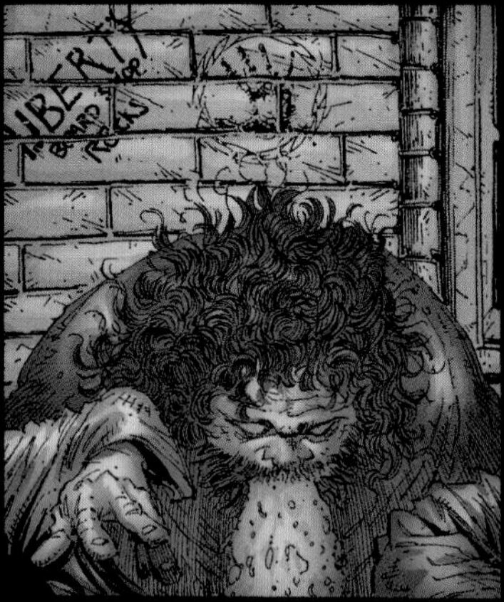

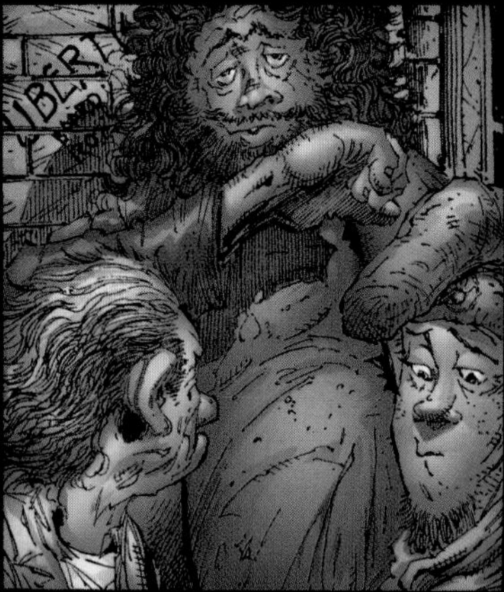

Hey... uh... sorry 'bout your shoes, dude.

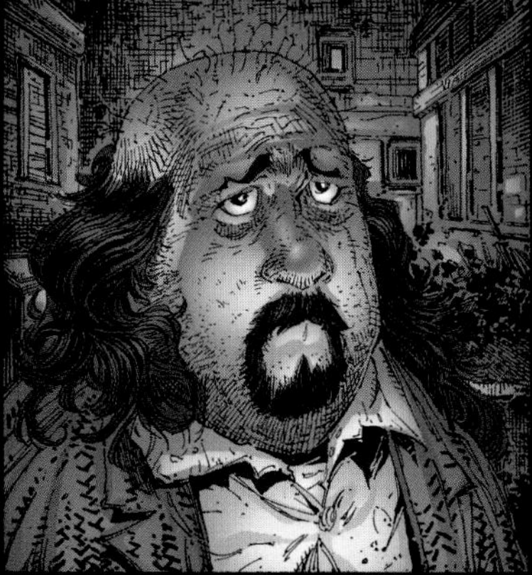

I guess I'd like to think we were friends. I know that sounds weird, but that's how it felt to me. I remember when he first came here, some of the other guys wanted him to leave. Not that you could make him leave or anything like that...

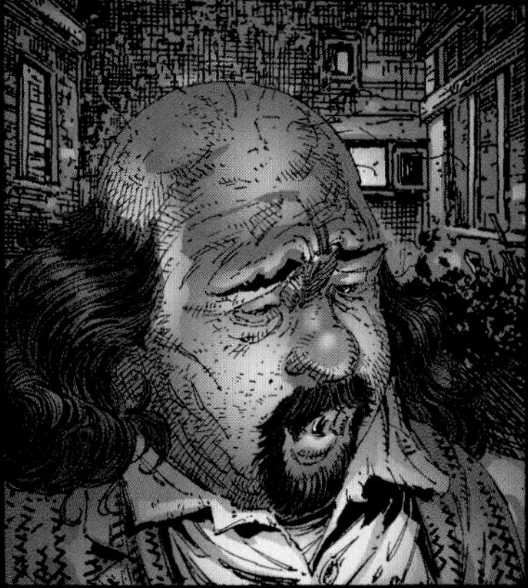

But I always said, hey, he's one of us. Poor sucker's lost his home, his family, his whole life. Just tryin' ta make the best out of a bad situation. Isn't that what we're all doing? All of us?

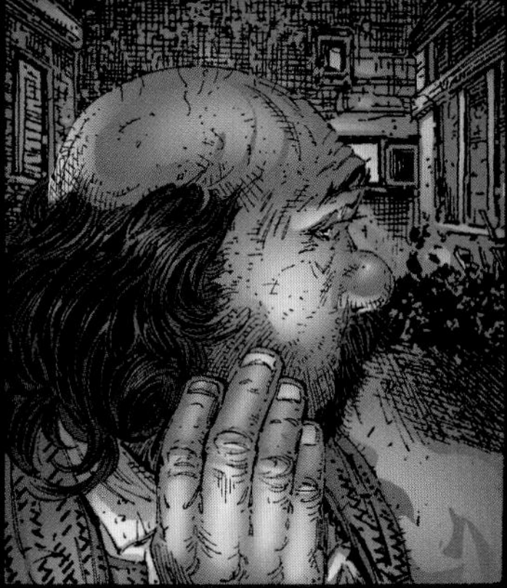

But I never thought he'd just up and leave like that. It was really hard. That last night, before it happened, you could see something in him had changed. Something switched over in him for good, and that was that.

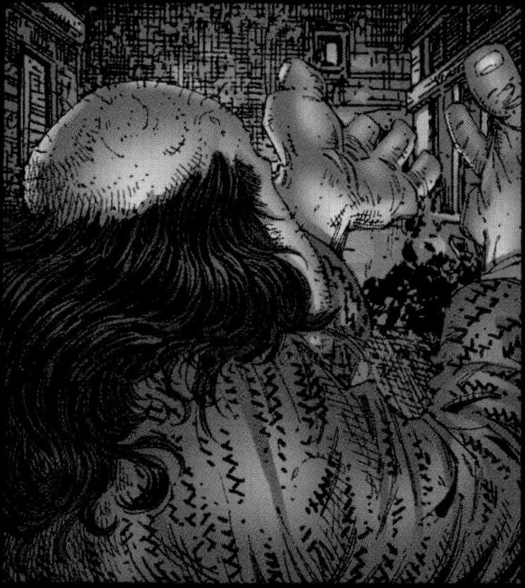

I don't blame him or nothing. Like I said, it's just really hard. See a while back, I lost another friend. His name was Bootsy. At least that's what we called him. Real smart guy. Always looked after me. Closer than brothers.

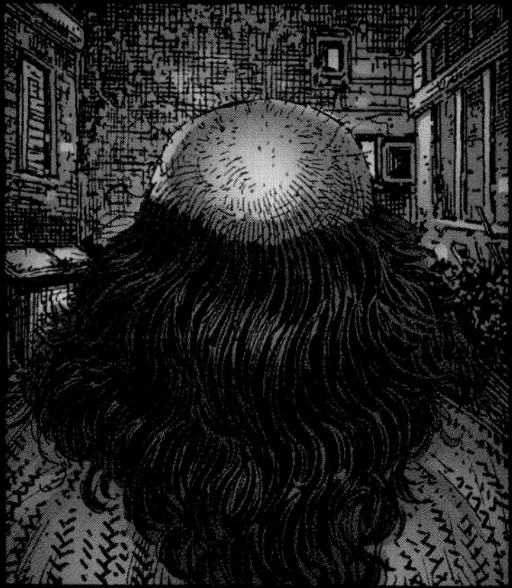

Turns out Bootsy was an angel. An' I don't mean that like he was a nice guy, but that he was an actual, real life angel, sent to watch over us. He saved Spawn's life once. And then he had to leave. Said he'd always look out for me, though.

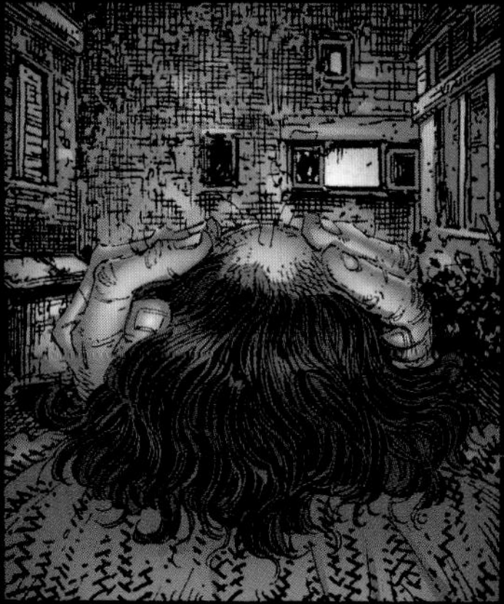

But it don't feel like anyone's looking out for ol' Bobby these days. Every year, these old bones get a little creakier, the days seem a little shorter. Every–day, it's like there's just less of me. Excuse me. Gimme a sec, will ya?

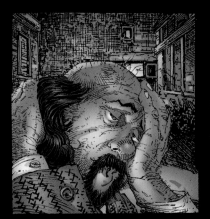

Let me tell you something about Spawn, I don't think anyone ever really understood... Well, to tell the truth, I think he was lonely. Sounds funny, I know, big tough guy like that. But I really think he was.

I mean, I know what it's like to feel you ain't got nothing in this world. Like no matter what you do, you're best days are long behind you and even they were pretty crappy now that you think about it.

Sometimes things get so bleak, you just gotta laugh. Most people don't know this, but ol' Al could have quite a sense of humor when the mood struck him. He had this real deep, booming laugh. I remember once –– Wait. I'm sorry.

Not "Al." Spawn. Spawn. Not Al. He told me not to call him that no more. "Never speak that name again," that's what he said. I'm sorry. I just forgot for a minute. Do you think you can maybe cut that part out?

Anyways... I know I'm rambling, I'm sorry... I guess I'm saying sometimes this world gets so cold, and sometimes the only thing you have to keep you from going under is your friends, and then they go and leave you and...

I'm sorry. Can we just stop now. Please?

INTERVIEW #17
"Sam and Twitch"

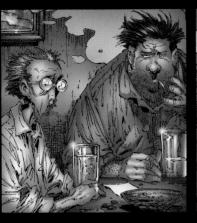

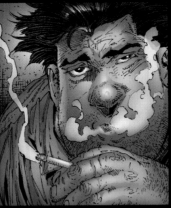

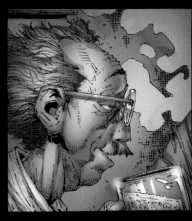

–Actually, we're "Ex"–ex–cops now. Come Monday, we are once again part of the Thin Blue Line that separates civilization from anarchy.*
–"Thin" being used rather metaphorically here, of course.
–Bite me Twitch. So what did ya want to know about?

**see "Sam and Twitch #1" for details.*

– "Health Spa?" Twitch, you know anything about a health spa? Huh? Oh. "Hell Spawn." Gotcha. Scourge of the alleys, caped avenger of New York City? The urban bogeyman, Spawn the Undead? Nah. Never heard of him.

–Although there was one caped marauder as I recall, sir. Do you remember?
–Oh, jeez. I almost forgot. This was years ago, we're still in uniform back then. Get some call about a woman being attacked by a crazed super hero.

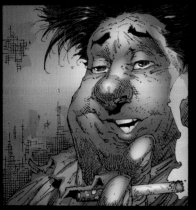

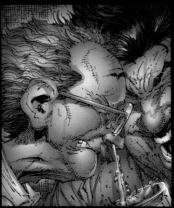

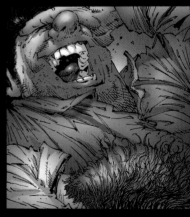

–So we get to the place, check it out. Naked woman tied to her bed, some dude out cold on the floor wearing a Batman mask, a cape, and goddamn nothing else. So what do I do? I go to cuff the intruder.

–And then the broad starts screeching: "Stop it! You'll kill him!" Turns out it was some kinda kinky game. Chick's boy friend would dress up like an idiot and pounce on her from on toppa the dresser. Got her real hot.

–Only this time the poor bastard knocks his head on the ceiling lamp. Boom! Out like a light. So she's tied up, her boyfriend is in a coma for she knows, and she screams blue murder. Man, I seen some weird crap in my time, but that takes the goddman cake!

INTERVIEW #20
"Wanda and Terry"

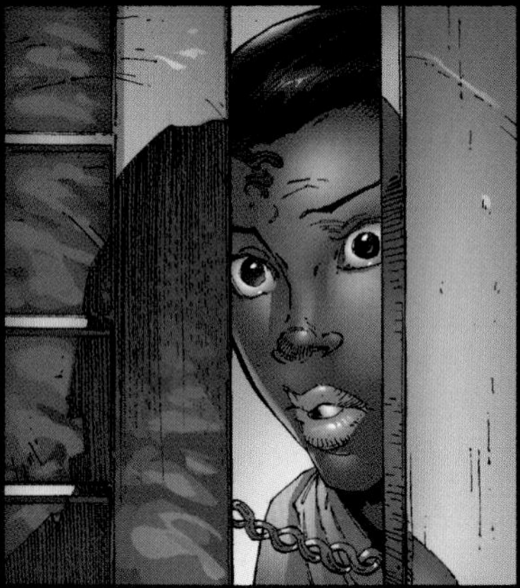

-Yes?
-Good evening. I don't mean to bother you. I was wondering if I could ask you a few questions--
-What is this about?
-I understand you've had contact with someone called Spawn.

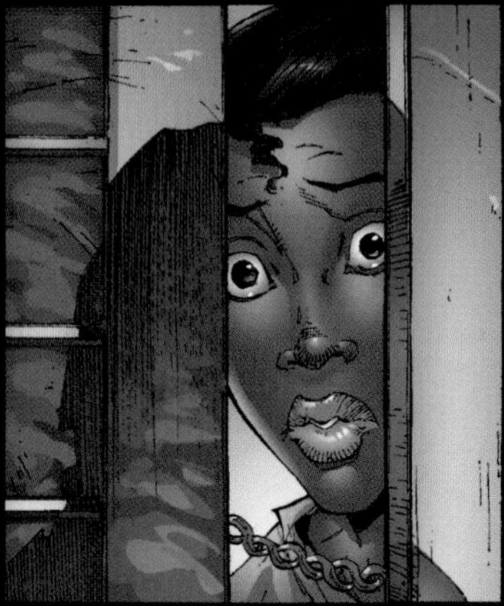

-What?!
-Just a moment of your time. Please. Now correct me if I'm wrong, but your first husband, his name was Al, right? Al Simmons...

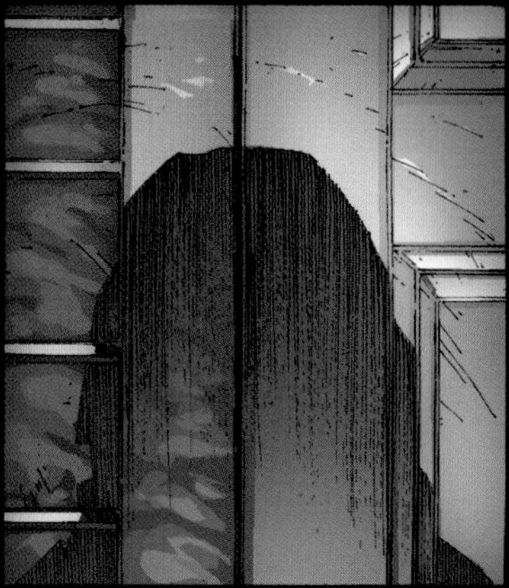

Slam

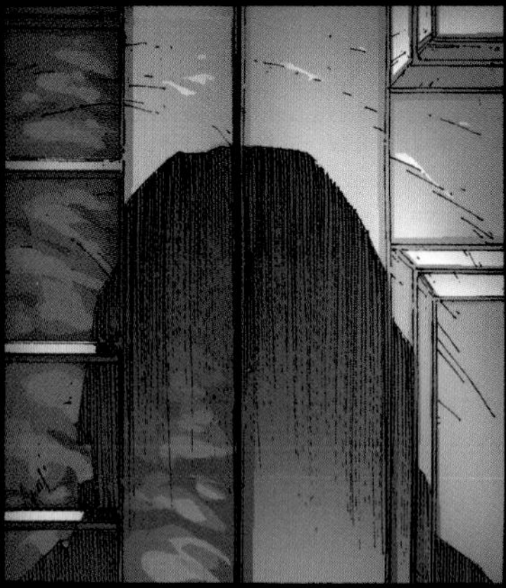

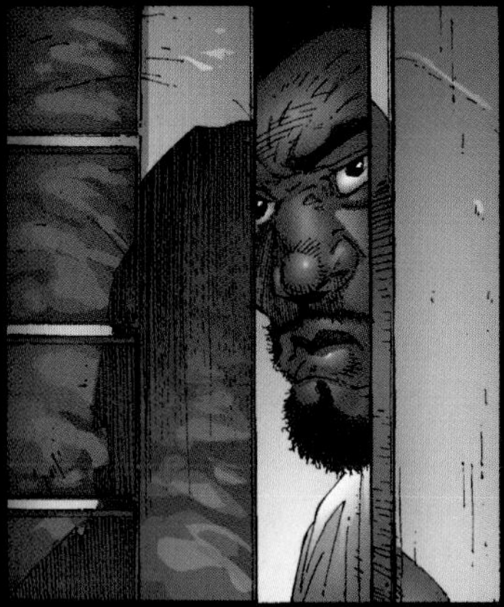

-What do you think you're doing, upsetting my wife like that?
-I'm sorry. If I could just ask a few questions I'd greatly appreciate --
-You know what, little man?

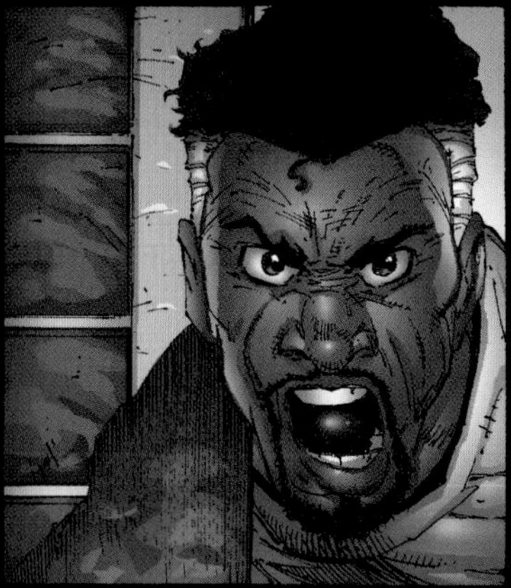

-I would greatly appreciate it if you got the hell off my property before I have to stick my foot up your ass. How's that for a goddamn quote?

INTERVIEW #22
"Corgie"

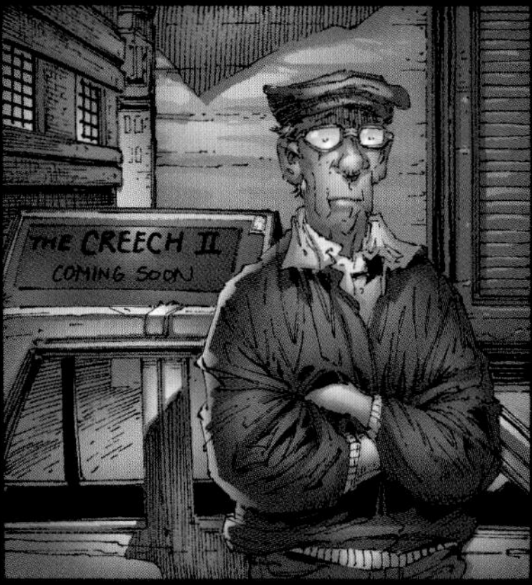
THE CREECH II
COMING SOON

I'm not making no claims about nothing. I only know what I saw, and like I told you that ain't much. It was maybe six months ago, a little after eleven in the p.m. I remember that 'cause the Met had just got out.

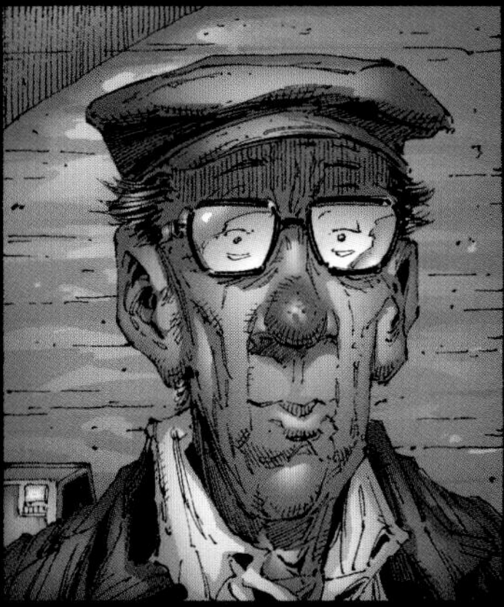

So I pick up this fare and we're headin' towards Soho, when BAM!, something comes out of nowhere. Out of the sky, like. Falls smack bang on the hood of my ride. I thought a bomb went off.

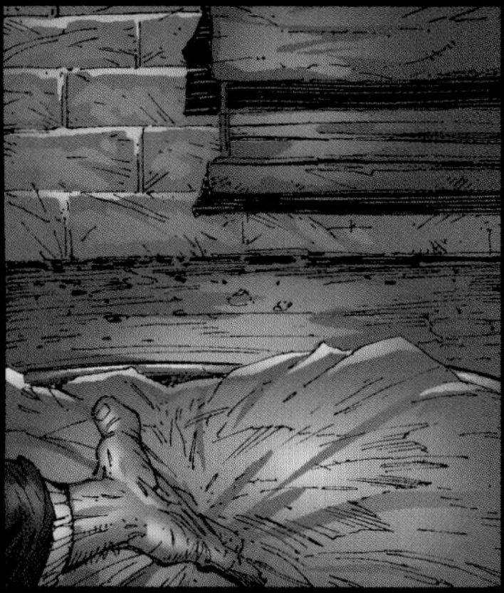

I mean look at that. You want proof, there it is. You see, whatever it was did some real damage. You'd think that woulda killed a person. I hit the brakes and this, this guy or this thing rolls off on to the ground.

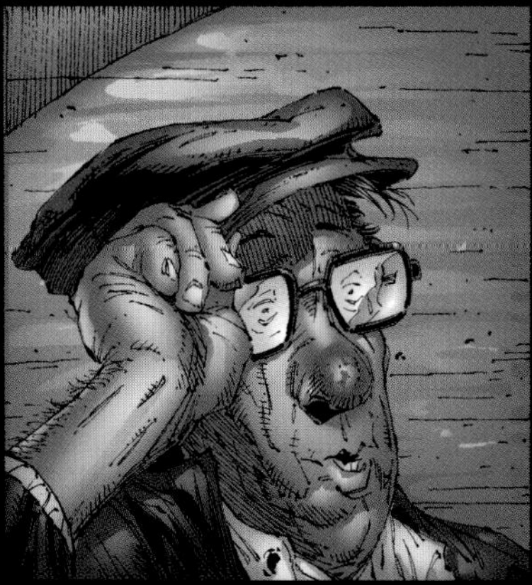

I stare at him for maybe one second, but it felt like forever. I mean I can't believe what's going on. I'm thinking I'm gonna lose my hack license for squashing a ped, but this guy just stands up. I remember his eyes. Green, like cat's eyes in the dark.

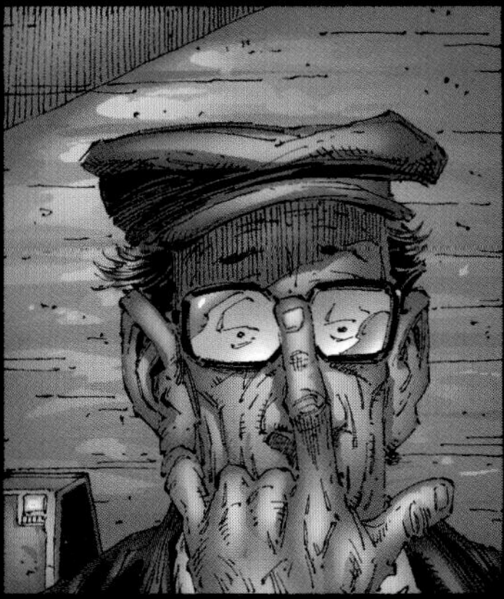

And then he was gone. It happened so fast I wouldn't believe it if it weren't for the damage he done. Meanwhile I got a coupla fares in back panicking, wondering what's going on. It was a peculiar night.

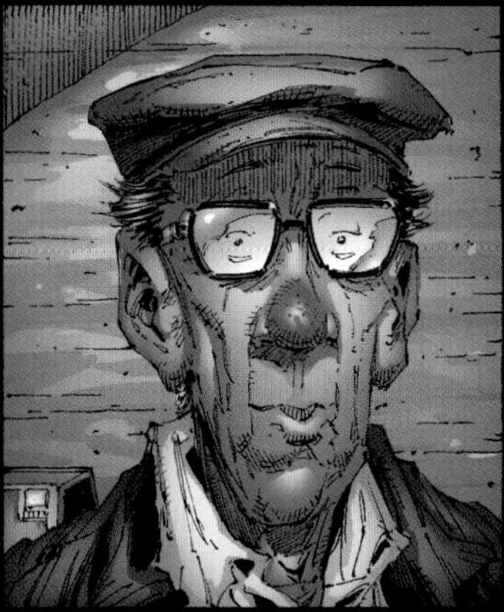

Never saw him again and still have no idea what the hell that thing was. But I tell you one thing. It was real. And whatever it was, they don't write insurance for crap like that. No sir, they sure don't.

INTERVIEW #24
"Identity Unknown"

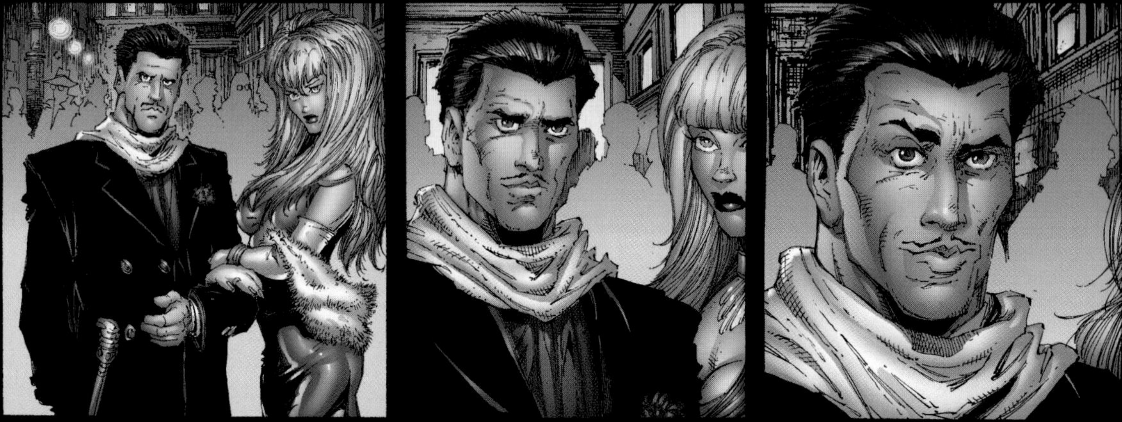

I understand you are inquiring about the existence of some mysterious urban avenger. The Hell Spawn? How fascinating. May I ask you, have you met with much success?

Oh, no. I'm afraid I couldn't be of any help to you. I have little experience with such sordid matters. Dark alleys, blood oaths, vengeance from beyond the grave... No, really not my cup of tea.

I was just curious to know the results of your research. If you had found any concrete evidence regarding this creature's exist–ence. Personal interest. Let's just leave it at that, shall we?

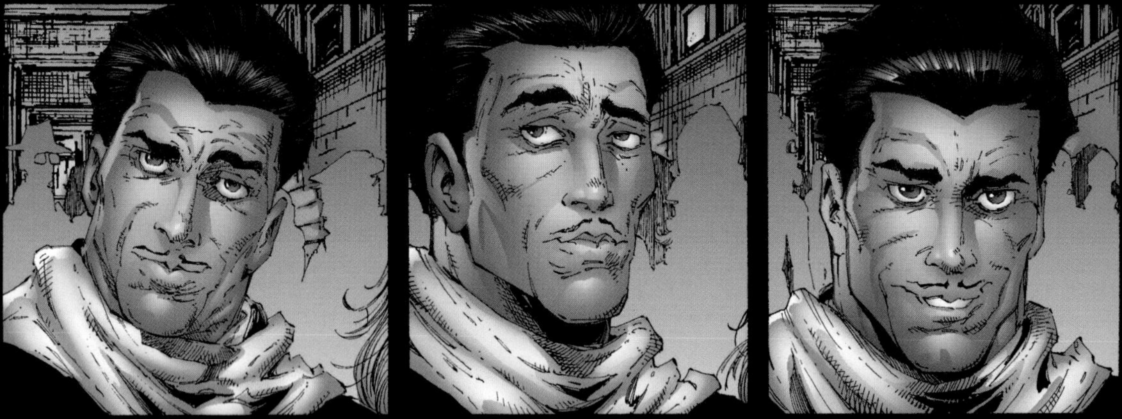

Of course, I realize you have a publisher. And I can appreciate that a contract is a contract. After all, we are nothing if we cannot keep our word, wouldn't you agree?

But anything you turn up -- particularly the Spawn's current whereabouts -- well, let's just say I am in a position to discuss a very generous bargain, should you be so inclined.

Oh no, that won't be necessary. Believe me, when the time comes I will know how to contact you. Good evening, then.

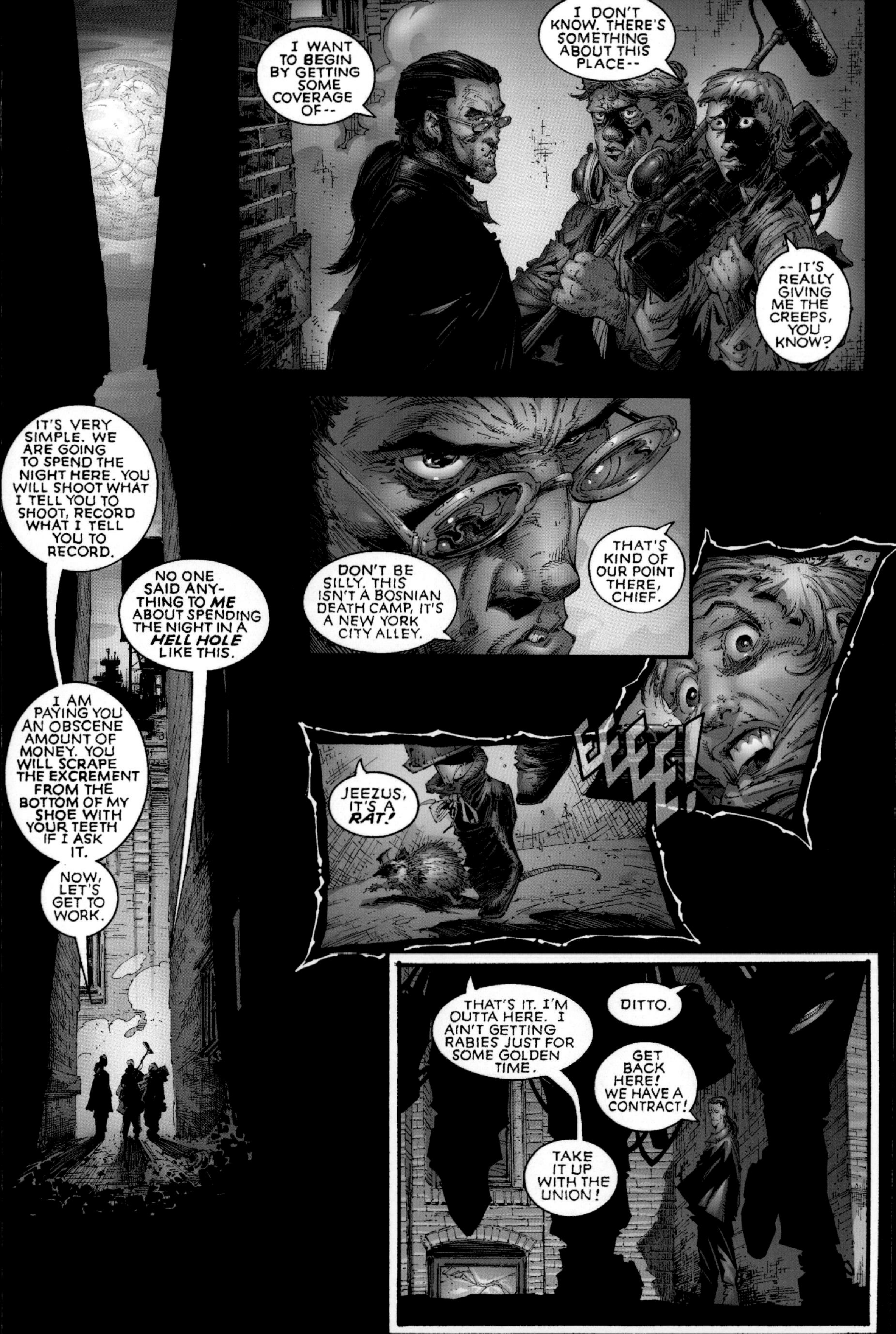
I WANT TO BEGIN BY GETTING SOME COVERAGE OF--
I DON'T KNOW. THERE'S SOMETHING ABOUT THIS PLACE--
--IT'S REALLY GIVING ME THE CREEPS, YOU KNOW?
IT'S VERY SIMPLE. WE ARE GOING TO SPEND THE NIGHT HERE. YOU WILL SHOOT WHAT I TELL YOU TO SHOOT, RECORD WHAT I TELL YOU TO RECORD.
NO ONE SAID ANYTHING TO ME ABOUT SPENDING THE NIGHT IN A HELL HOLE LIKE THIS.
I AM PAYING YOU AN OBSCENE AMOUNT OF MONEY. YOU WILL SCRAPE THE EXCREMENT FROM THE BOTTOM OF MY SHOE WITH YOUR TEETH IF I ASK IT.
NOW, LET'S GET TO WORK.
DON'T BE SILLY. THIS ISN'T A BOSNIAN DEATH CAMP, IT'S A NEW YORK CITY ALLEY.
THAT'S KIND OF OUR POINT THERE, CHIEF.
JEEZUS, IT'S A RAT!
THAT'S IT. I'M OUTTA HERE. I AIN'T GETTING RABIES JUST FOR SOME GOLDEN TIME.
DITTO.
GET BACK HERE! WE HAVE A CONTRACT!
TAKE IT UP WITH THE UNION!

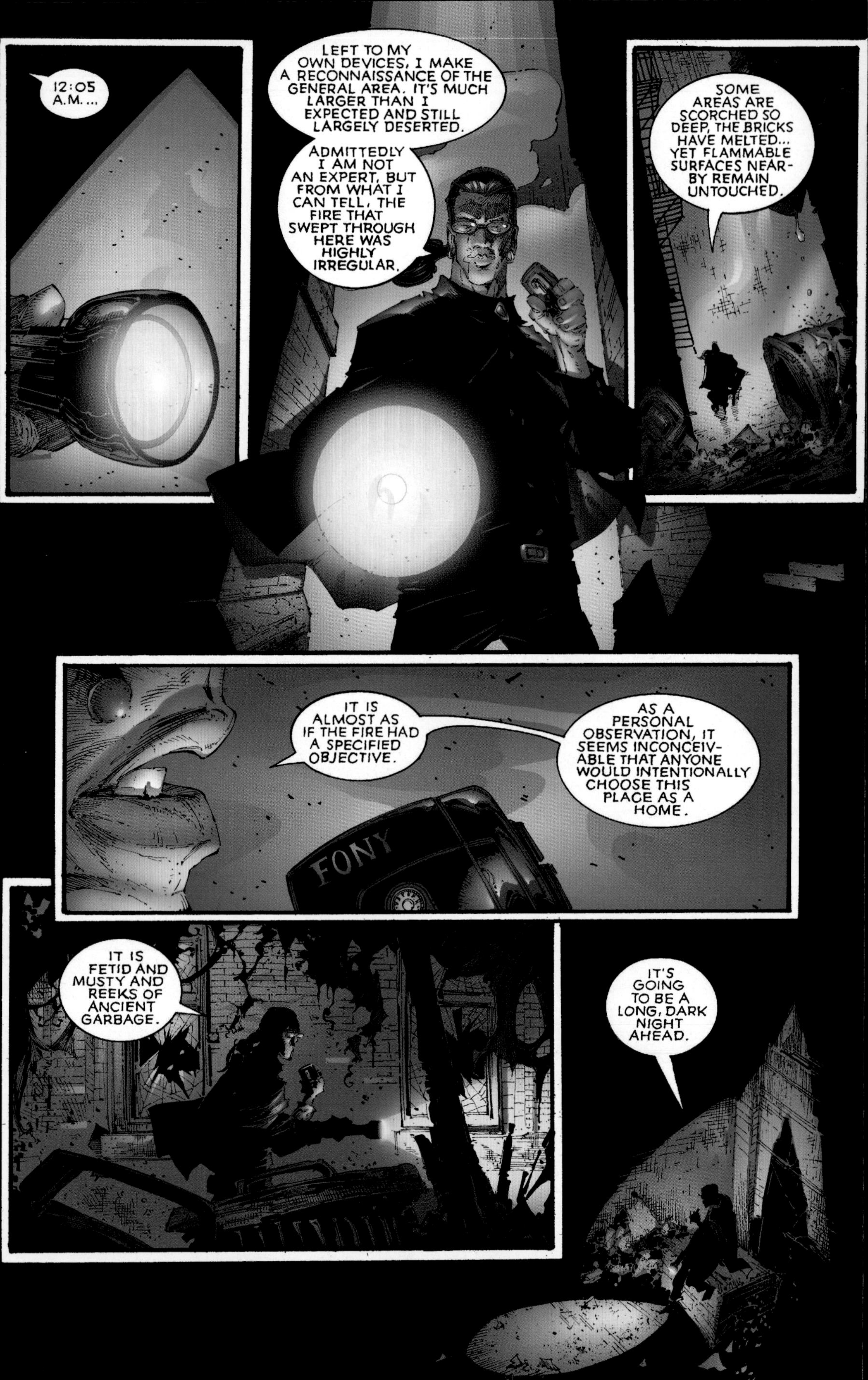
12:05 A.M. ...
LEFT TO MY OWN DEVICES, I MAKE A RECONNAISSANCE OF THE GENERAL AREA. IT'S MUCH LARGER THAN I EXPECTED AND STILL LARGELY DESERTED.
ADMITTEDLY I AM NOT AN EXPERT, BUT FROM WHAT I CAN TELL, THE FIRE THAT SWEPT THROUGH HERE WAS HIGHLY IRREGULAR.
SOME AREAS ARE SCORCHED SO DEEP, THE BRICKS HAVE MELTED... YET FLAMMABLE SURFACES NEAR-BY REMAIN UNTOUCHED.
IT IS ALMOST AS IF THE FIRE HAD A SPECIFIED OBJECTIVE.
AS A PERSONAL OBSERVATION, IT SEEMS INCONCEIV-ABLE THAT ANYONE WOULD INTENTIONALLY CHOOSE THIS PLACE AS A HOME.
FONY
IT IS FETID AND MUSTY AND REEKS OF ANCIENT GARBAGE.
IT'S GOING TO BE A LONG, DARK NIGHT AHEAD.

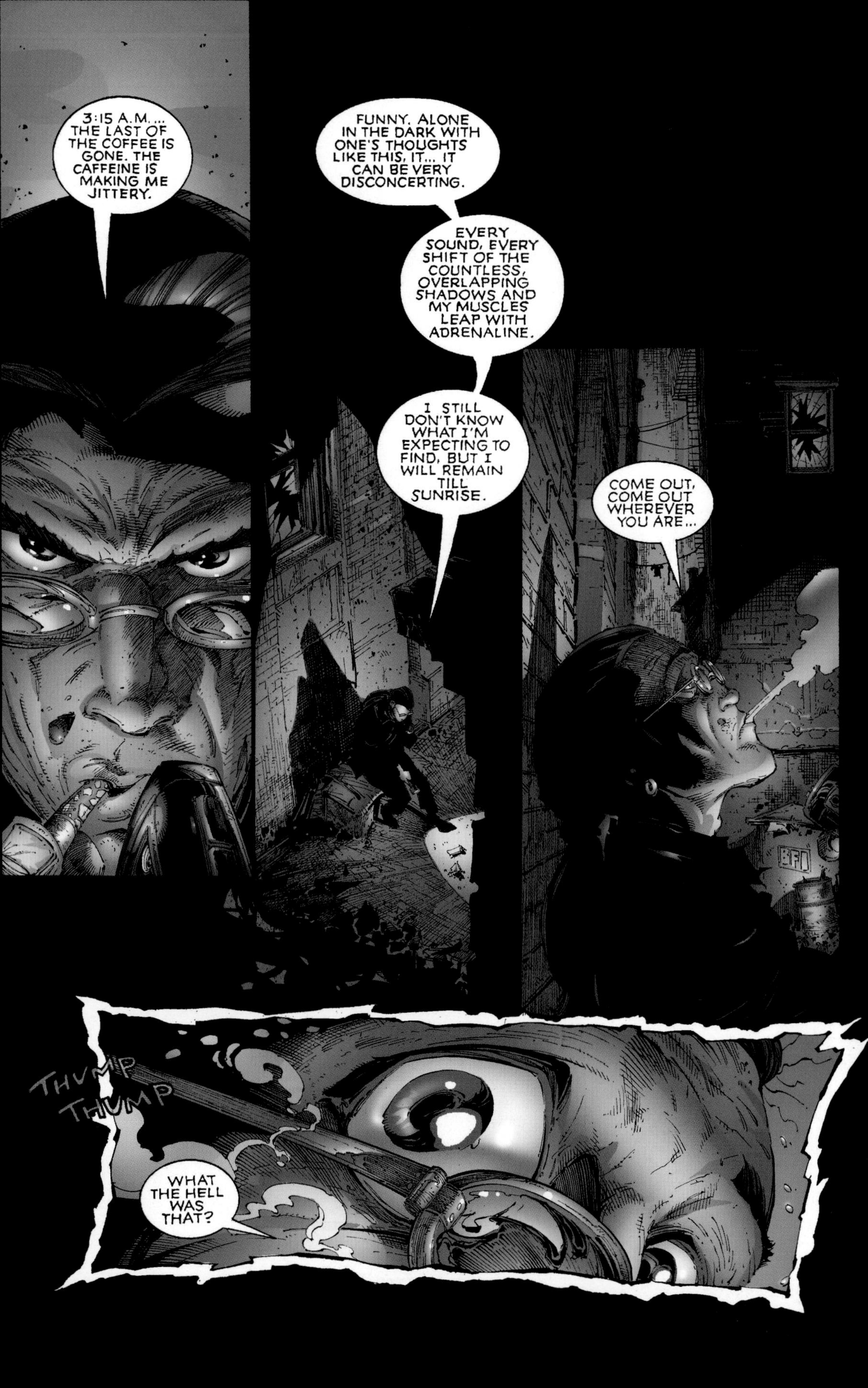
3:15 A.M.... THE LAST OF THE COFFEE IS GONE. THE CAFFEINE IS MAKING ME JITTERY.
FUNNY. ALONE IN THE DARK WITH ONE'S THOUGHTS LIKE THIS, IT... IT CAN BE VERY DISCONCERTING.
EVERY SOUND, EVERY SHIFT OF THE COUNTLESS, OVERLAPPING SHADOWS AND MY MUSCLES LEAP WITH ADRENALINE.
I STILL DON'T KNOW WHAT I'M EXPECTING TO FIND, BUT I WILL REMAIN TILL SUNRISE.
COME OUT, COME OUT WHEREVER YOU ARE...
THUMP THUMP
WHAT THE HELL WAS THAT?

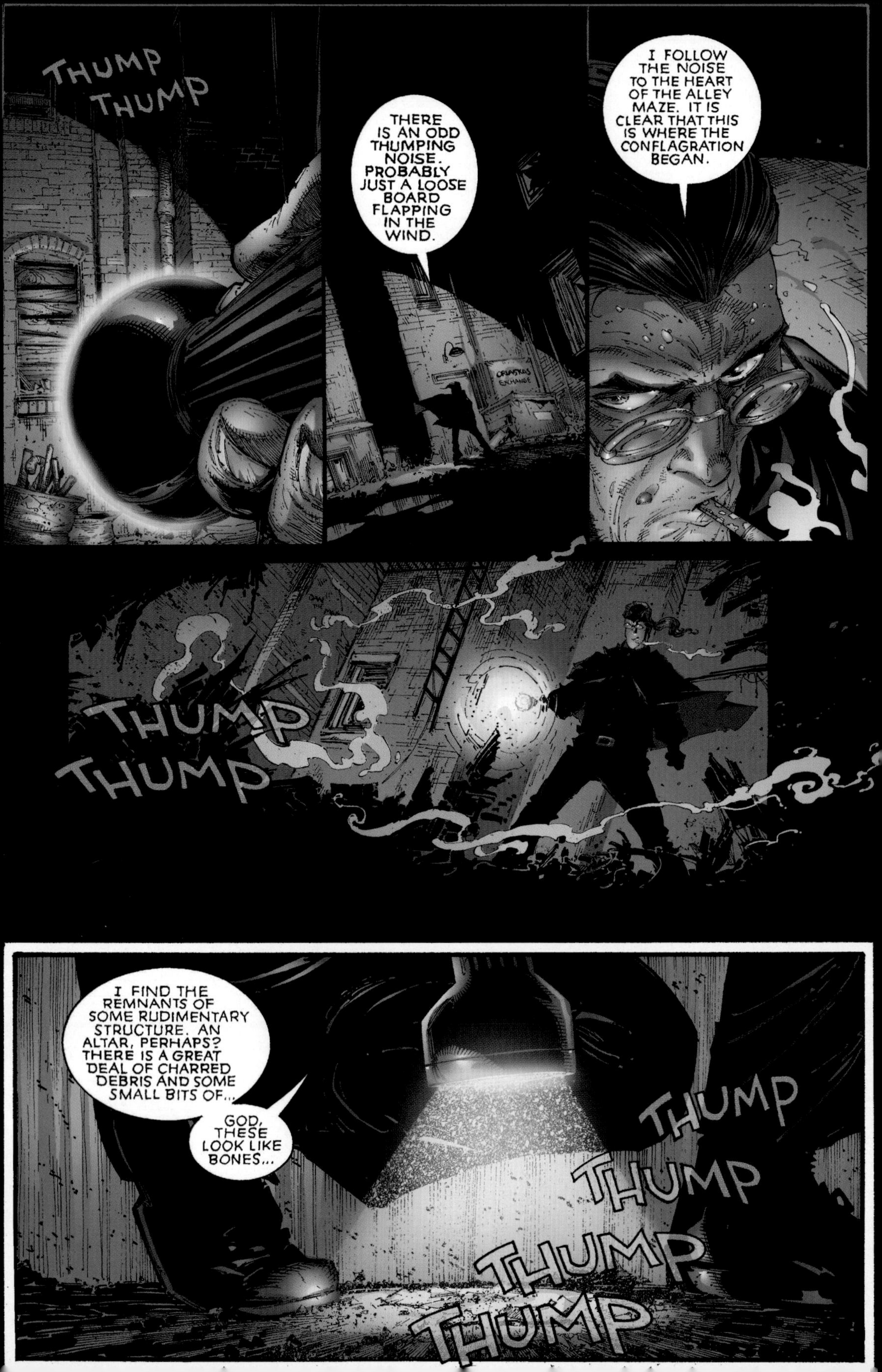
THUMP THUMP
THERE IS AN ODD THUMPING NOISE. PROBABLY JUST A LOOSE BOARD FLAPPING IN THE WIND.
I FOLLOW THE NOISE TO THE HEART OF THE ALLEY MAZE. IT IS CLEAR THAT THIS IS WHERE THE CONFLAGRATION BEGAN.
THUMP THUMP
I FIND THE REMNANTS OF SOME RUDIMENTARY STRUCTURE. AN ALTAR, PERHAPS? THERE IS A GREAT DEAL OF CHARRED DEBRIS AND SOME SMALL BITS OF...
GOD, THESE LOOK LIKE BONES...
THUMP THUMP THUMP THUMP

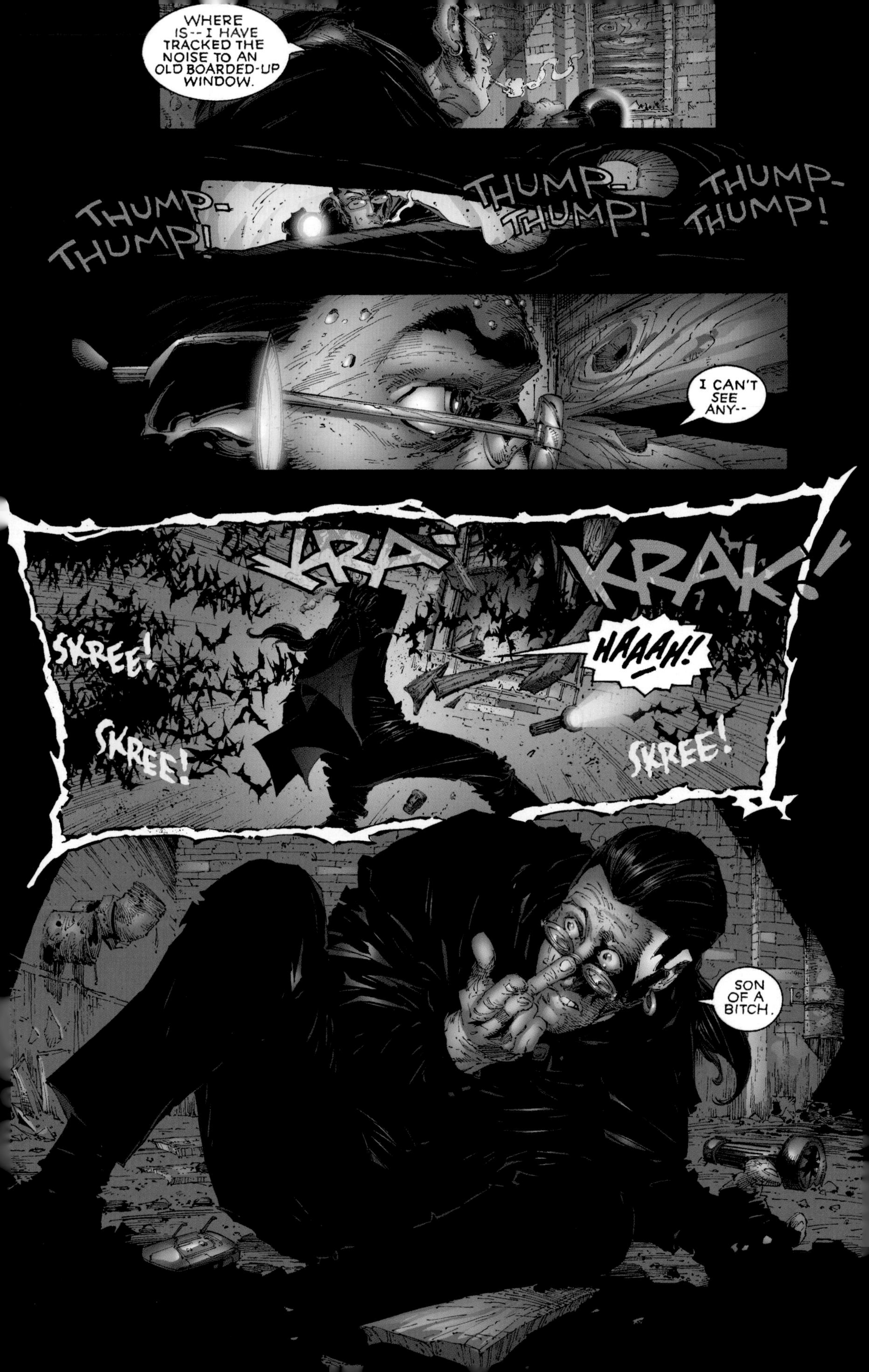

WHERE IS-- I HAVE TRACKED THE NOISE TO AN OLD BOARDED-UP WINDOW.
THUMP-THUMP!
THUMP-THUMP!
THUMP-THUMP!
I CAN'T SEE ANY--
KRAK!
SKREE!
SKREE!
HAAAH!
SKREE!
SON OF A BITCH.

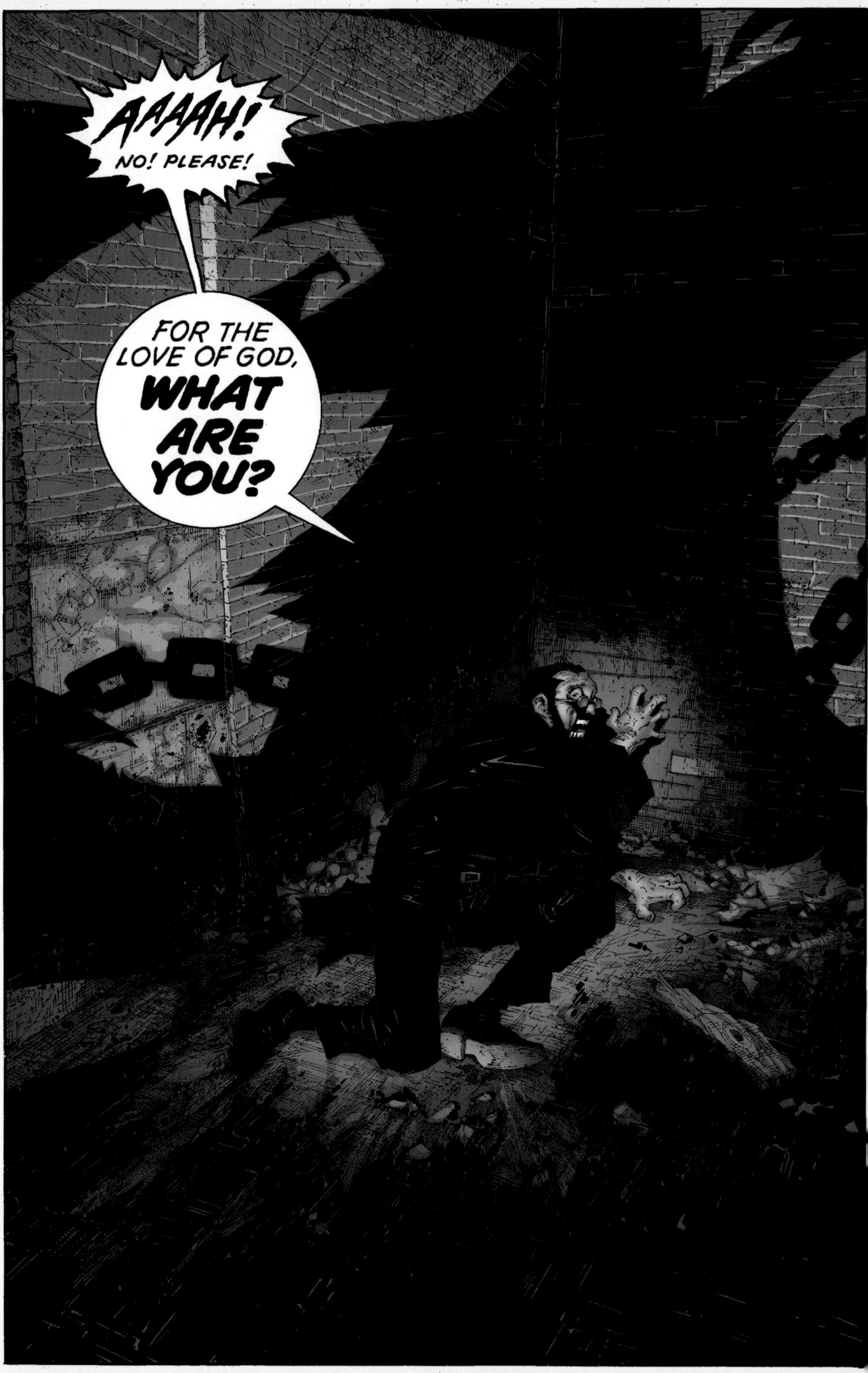
AAAAH! NO! PLEASE!
FOR THE LOVE OF GOD, WHAT ARE YOU?

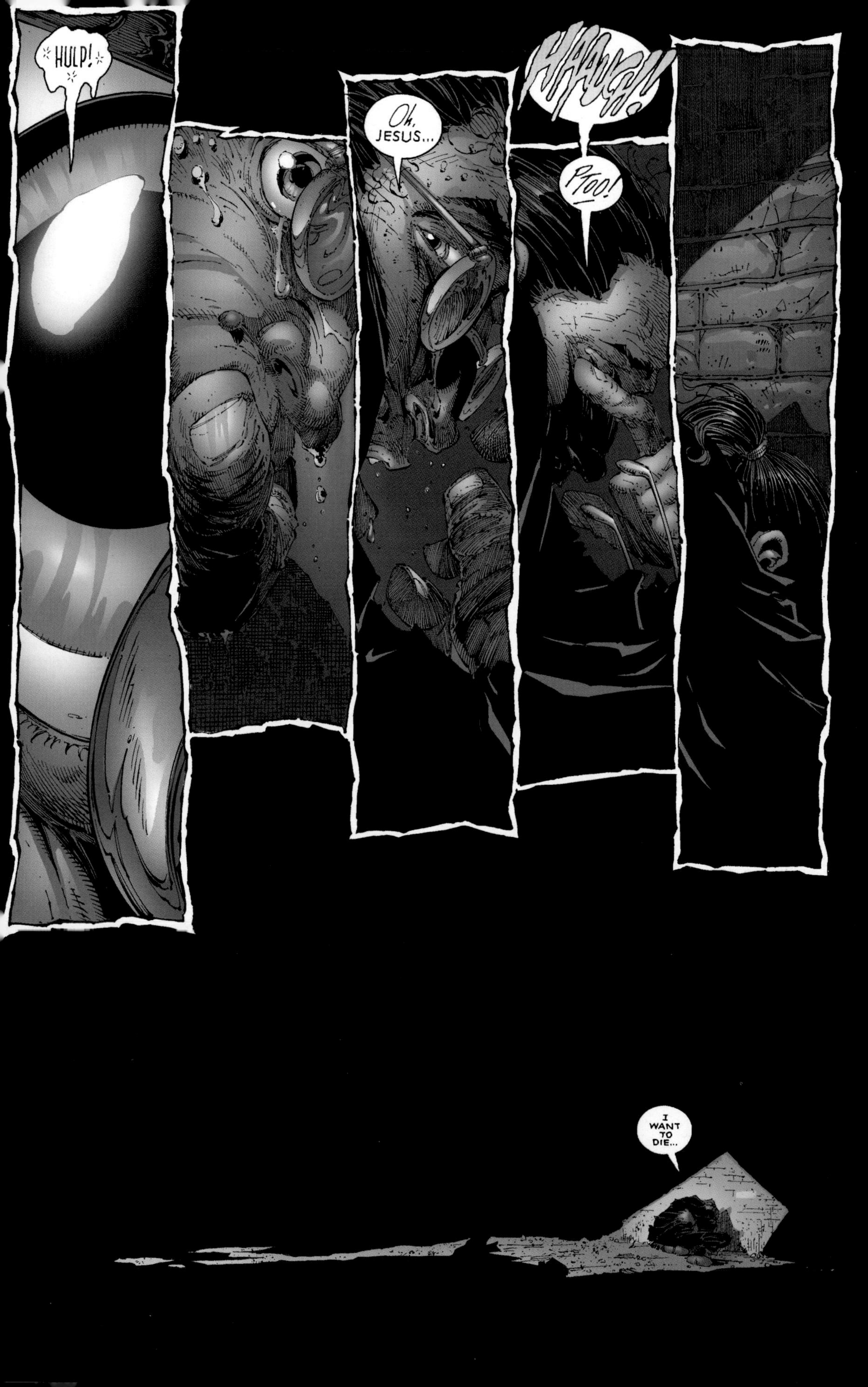
HULP!
Oh, JESUS...
HAAAUGH!!
PTOO!
I WANT TO DIE...

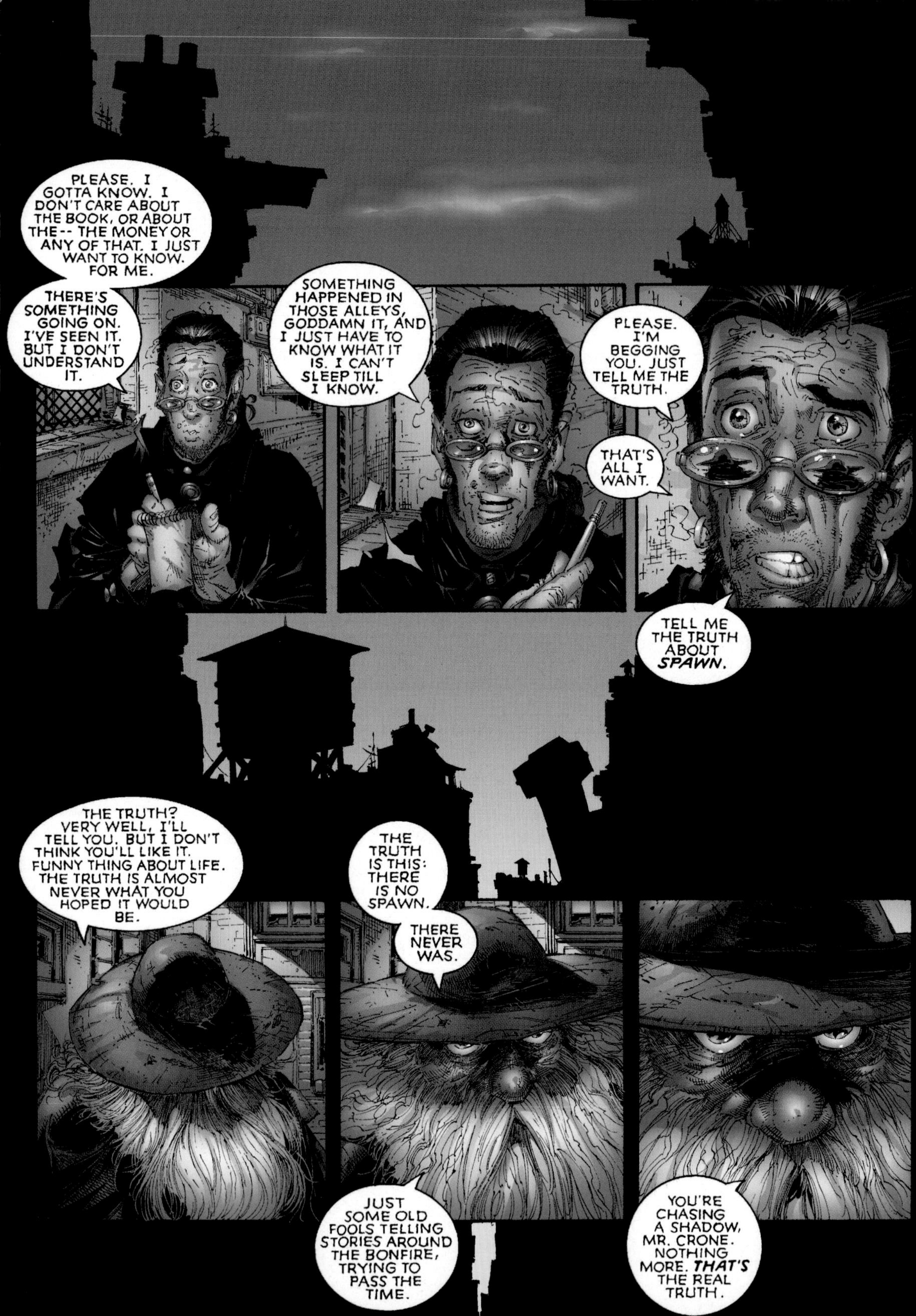
PLEASE. I GOTTA KNOW. I DON'T CARE ABOUT THE BOOK, OR ABOUT THE -- THE MONEY OR ANY OF THAT. I JUST WANT TO KNOW. FOR ME.
THERE'S SOMETHING GOING ON. I'VE SEEN IT. BUT I DON'T UNDERSTAND IT.
SOMETHING HAPPENED IN THOSE ALLEYS, GODDAMN IT, AND I JUST HAVE TO KNOW WHAT IT IS. I CAN'T SLEEP TILL I KNOW.
PLEASE. I'M BEGGING YOU. JUST TELL ME THE TRUTH.
THAT'S ALL I WANT.
TELL ME THE TRUTH ABOUT *SPAWN.*
THE TRUTH? VERY WELL, I'LL TELL YOU. BUT I DON'T THINK YOU'LL LIKE IT. FUNNY THING ABOUT LIFE. THE TRUTH IS ALMOST NEVER WHAT YOU HOPED IT WOULD BE.
THE TRUTH IS THIS: THERE IS NO SPAWN.
THERE NEVER WAS.
JUST SOME OLD FOOLS TELLING STORIES AROUND THE BONFIRE, TRYING TO PASS THE TIME.
YOU'RE CHASING A SHADOW, MR. CRONE. NOTHING MORE. *THAT'S* THE REAL TRUTH.

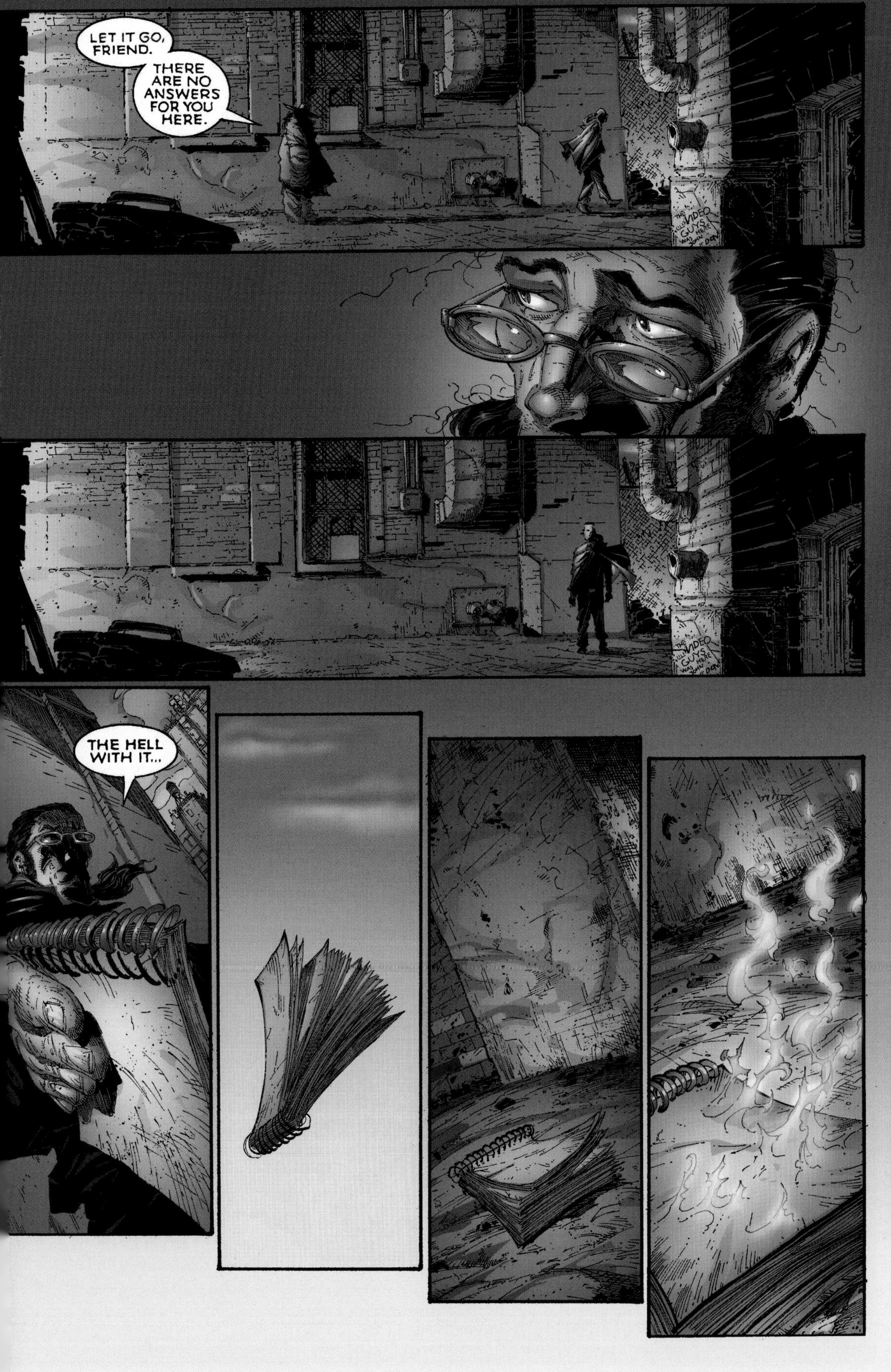
LET IT GO, FRIEND.
THERE ARE NO ANSWERS FOR YOU HERE.
THE HELL WITH IT...

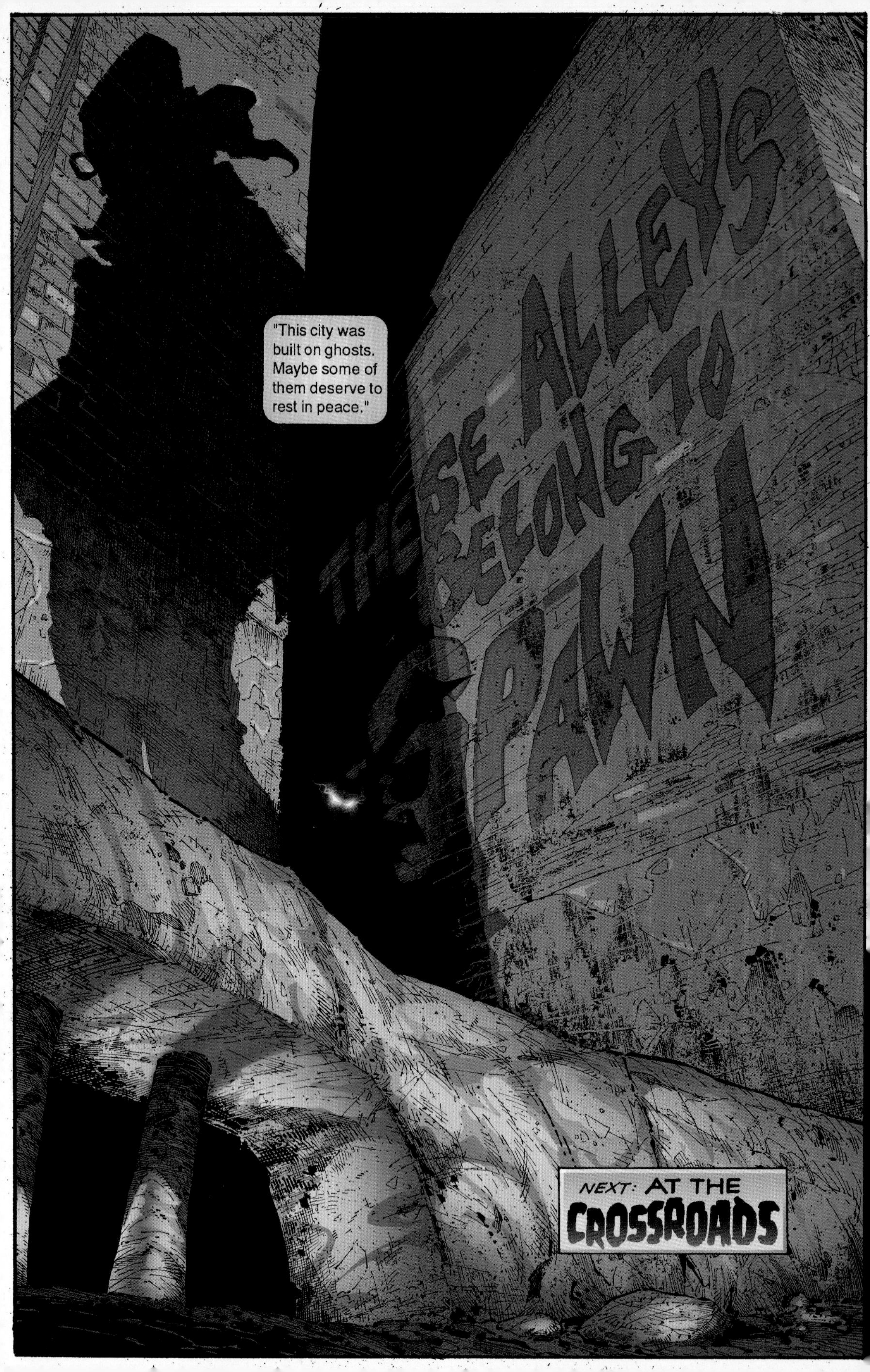
"This city was built on ghosts. Maybe some of them deserve to rest in peace."
THESE ALLEYS BELONG TO PAWN
NEXT: AT THE CROSSROADS

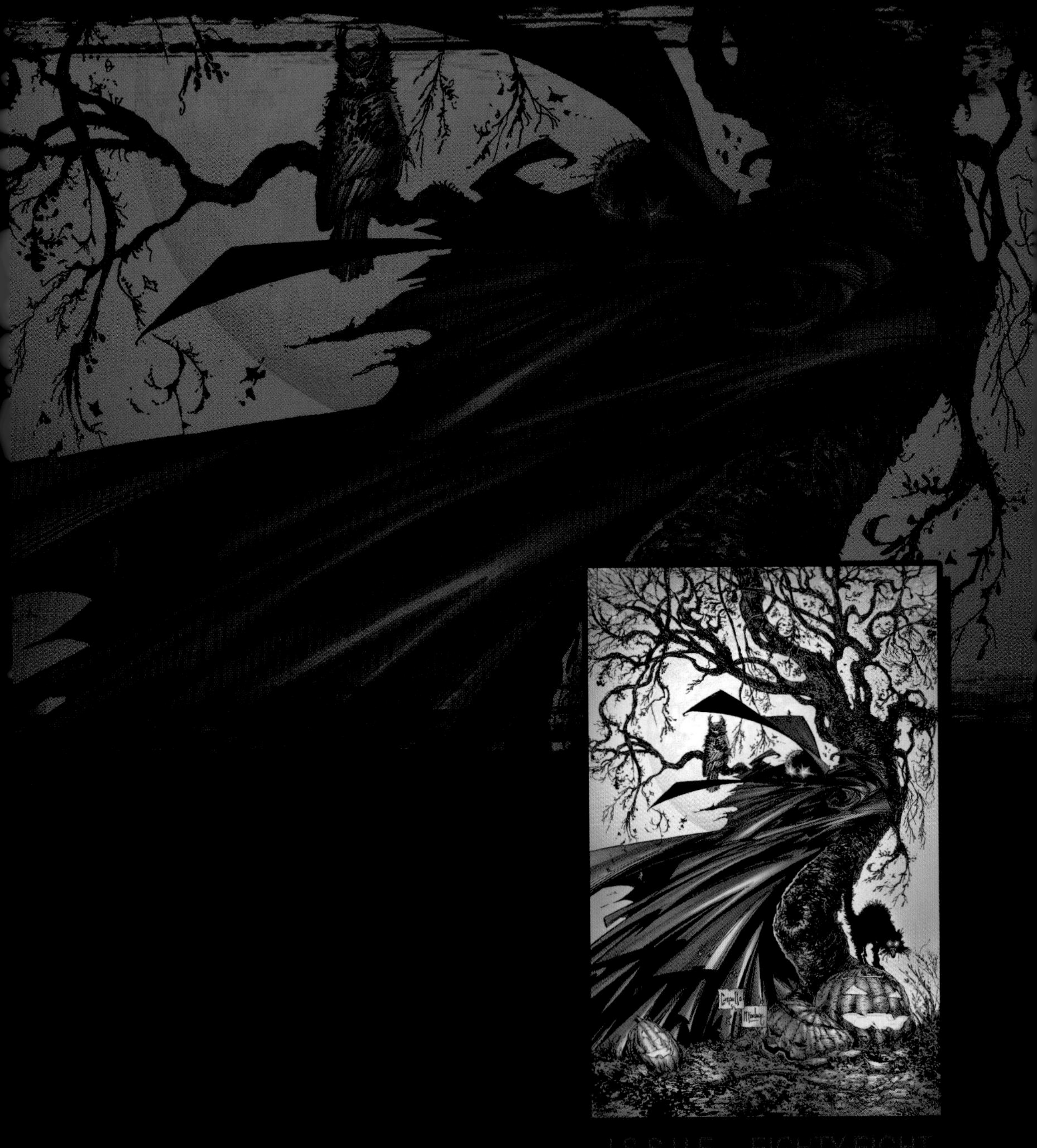

ISSUE EIGHTY-EIGHT

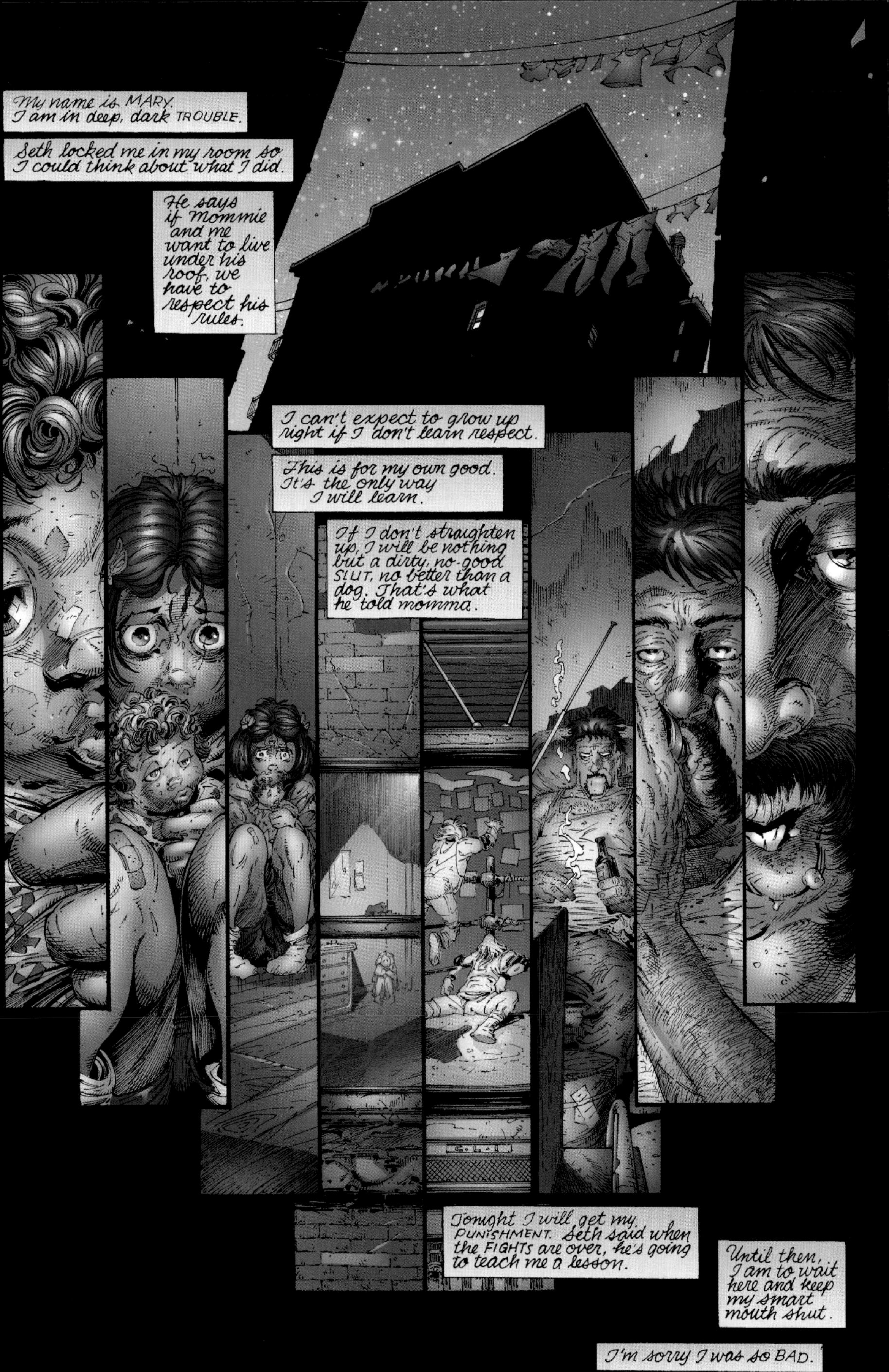
My name is MARY. I am in deep, dark TROUBLE.
Seth locked me in my room so I could think about what I did.
He says if Mommie and me want to live under his roof, we have to respect his rules.
I can't expect to grow up right if I don't learn respect.
This is for my own good. It's the only way I will learn.
If I don't straighten up, I will be nothing but a dirty, no-good SLUT, no better than a dog. That's what he told momma.
Tonight I will get my PUNISHMENT. Seth said when the FIGHTS are over, he's going to teach me a lesson.
Until then, I am to wait here and keep my smart mouth shut.
I'm sorry I was so BAD.

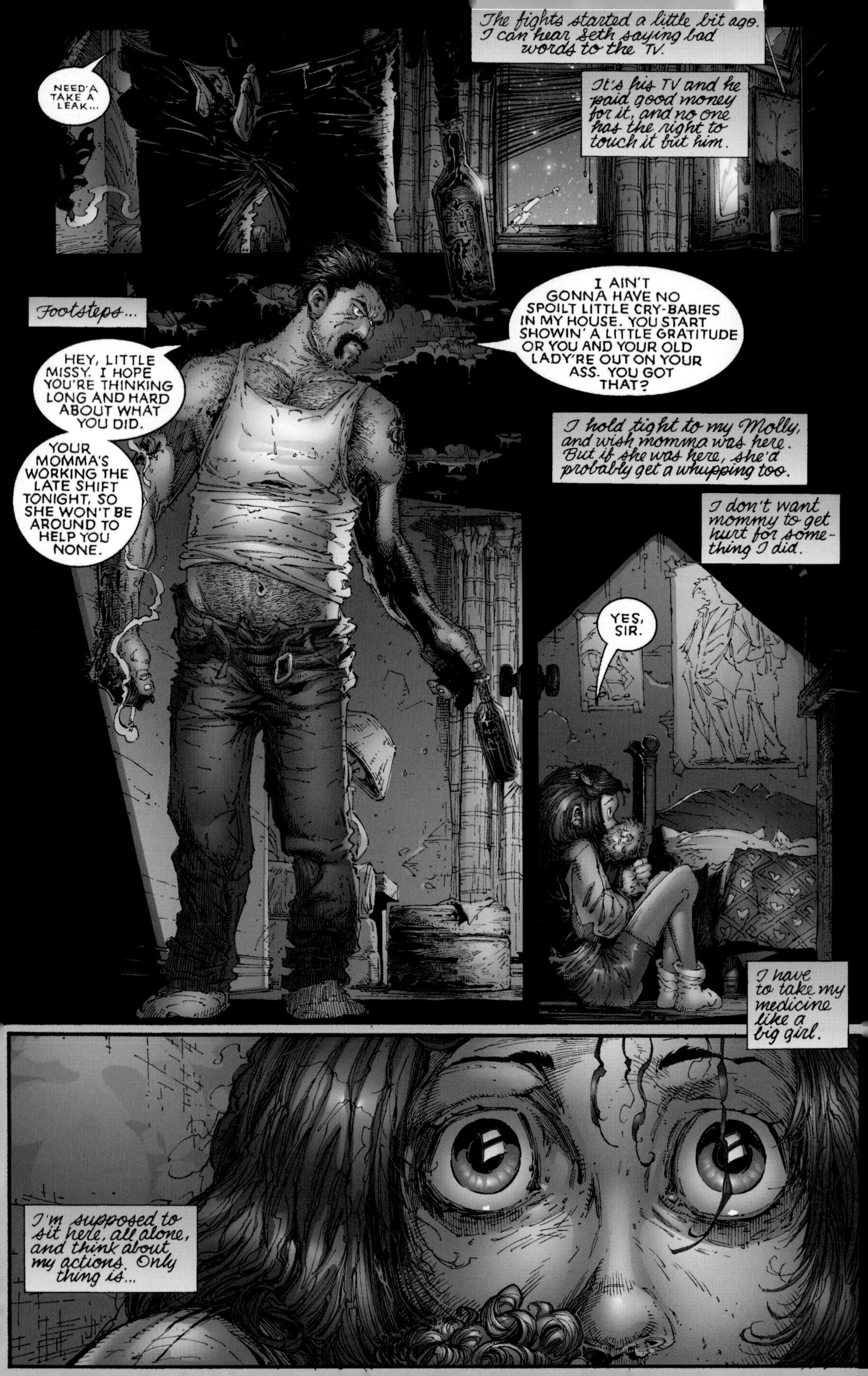
The fights started a little bit ago. I can hear Seth saying bad words to the TV.
NEED'A TAKE A LEAK...
It's his TV and he paid good money for it, and no one has the right to touch it but him.
Footsteps...
HEY, LITTLE MISSY. I HOPE YOU'RE THINKING LONG AND HARD ABOUT WHAT YOU DID.
YOUR MOMMA'S WORKING THE LATE SHIFT TONIGHT, SO SHE WON'T BE AROUND TO HELP YOU NONE.
I AIN'T GONNA HAVE NO SPOILT LITTLE CRY-BABIES IN MY HOUSE. YOU START SHOWIN' A LITTLE GRATITUDE OR YOU AND YOUR OLD LADY'RE OUT ON YOUR ASS. YOU GOT THAT?
I hold tight to my Molly, and wish momma was here. But if she was here, she'd probably get a whupping too.
I don't want mommy to get hurt for something I did.
YES, SIR.
I have to take my medicine like a big girl.
I'm supposed to sit here, all alone, and think about my actions. Only thing is...

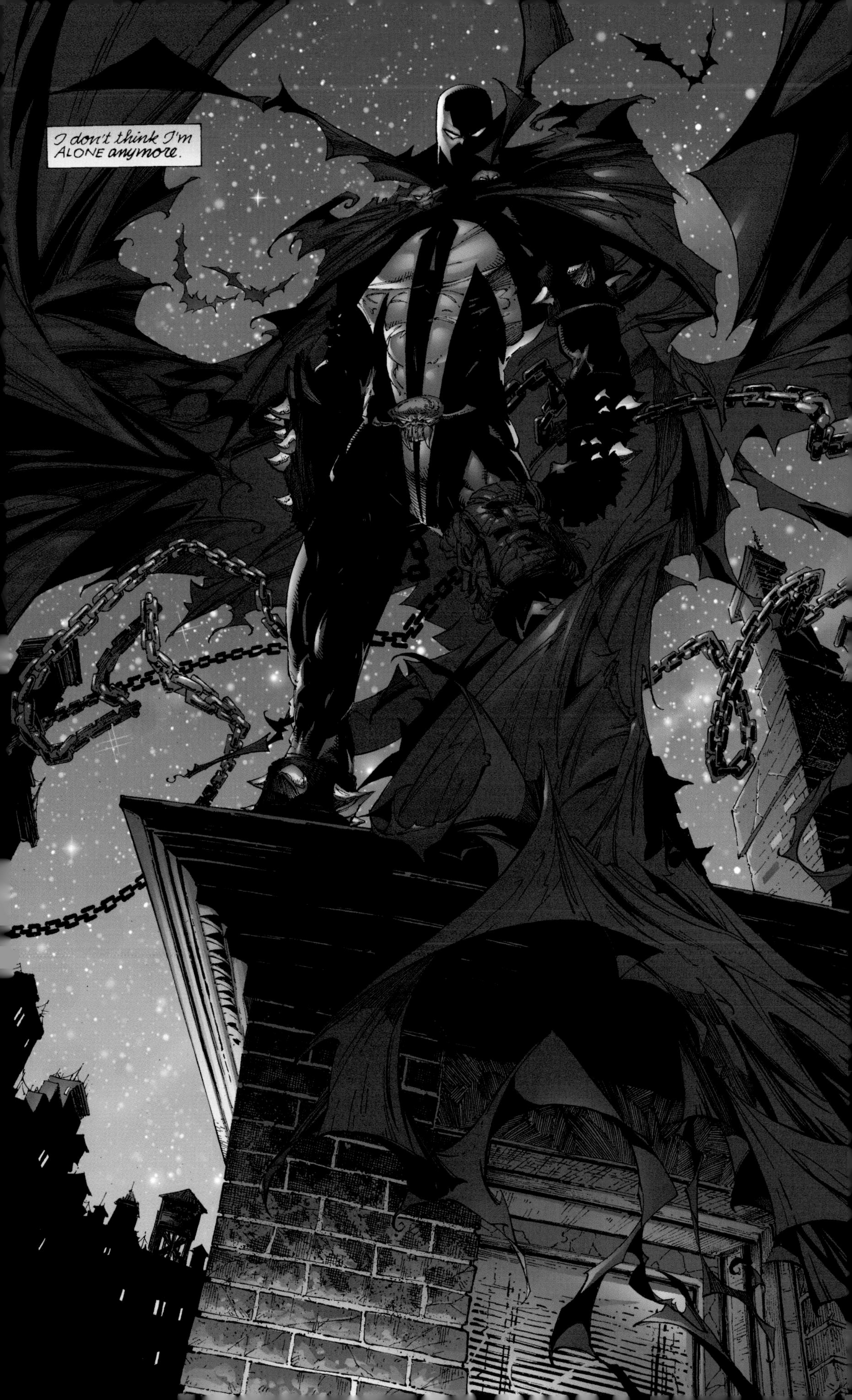
I don't think I'm ALONE anymore.

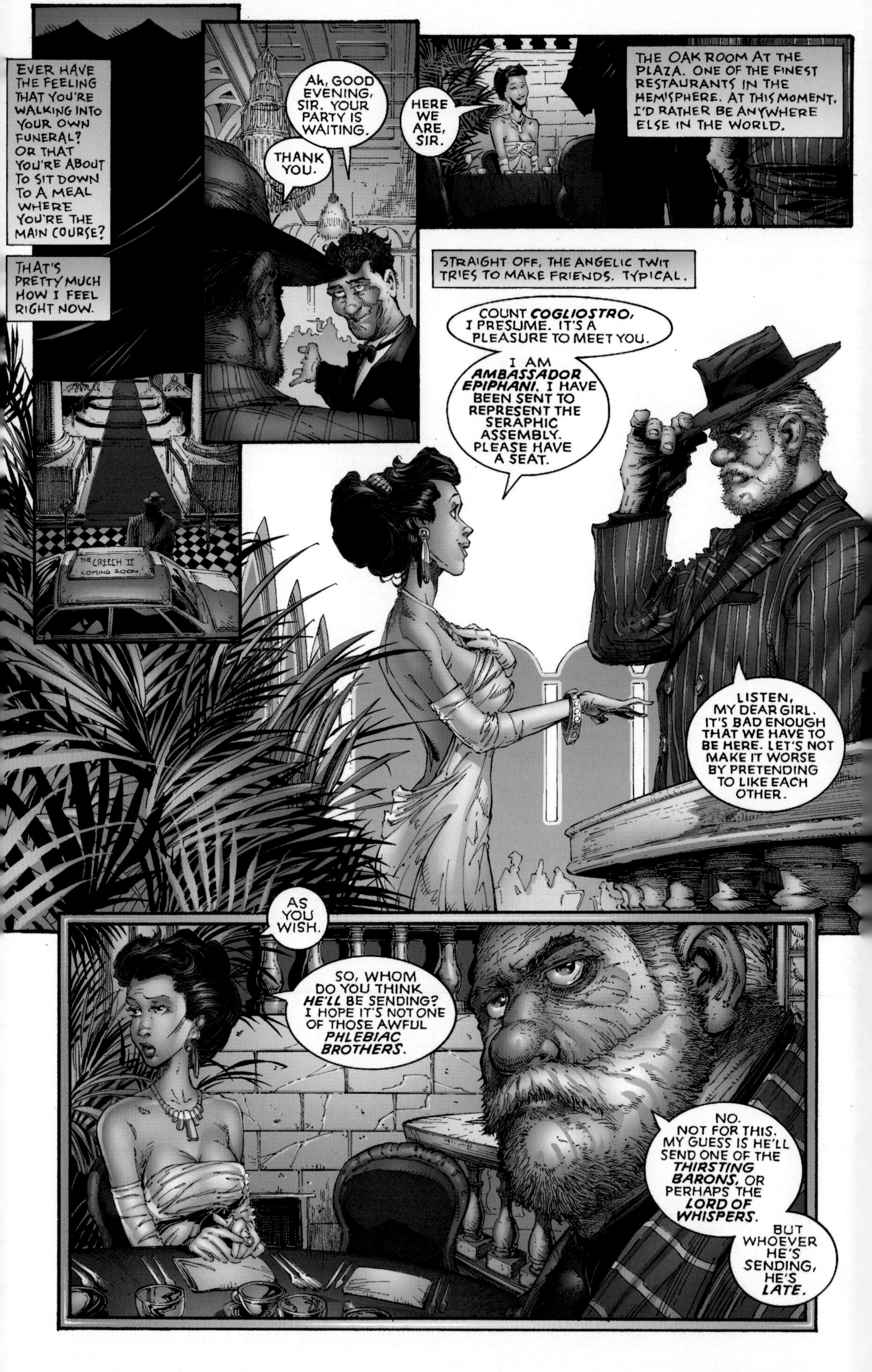

EVER HAVE THE FEELING THAT YOU'RE WALKING INTO YOUR OWN FUNERAL? OR THAT YOU'RE ABOUT TO SIT DOWN TO A MEAL WHERE YOU'RE THE MAIN COURSE?
THAT'S PRETTY MUCH HOW I FEEL RIGHT NOW.
THE CREECH II COMING SOON
Ah, GOOD EVENING, SIR. YOUR PARTY IS WAITING.
THANK YOU.
HERE WE ARE, SIR.
THE OAK ROOM AT THE PLAZA. ONE OF THE FINEST RESTAURANTS IN THE HEMISPHERE. AT THIS MOMENT, I'D RATHER BE ANYWHERE ELSE IN THE WORLD.
STRAIGHT OFF, THE ANGELIC TWIT TRIES TO MAKE FRIENDS. TYPICAL.
COUNT COGLIOSTRO, I PRESUME. IT'S A PLEASURE TO MEET YOU.
I AM AMBASSADOR EPIPHANI. I HAVE BEEN SENT TO REPRESENT THE SERAPHIC ASSEMBLY. PLEASE HAVE A SEAT.
LISTEN, MY DEAR GIRL. IT'S BAD ENOUGH THAT WE HAVE TO BE HERE. LET'S NOT MAKE IT WORSE BY PRETENDING TO LIKE EACH OTHER.
AS YOU WISH.
SO, WHOM DO YOU THINK HE'LL BE SENDING? I HOPE IT'S NOT ONE OF THOSE AWFUL PHLEBIAC BROTHERS.
NO. NOT FOR THIS. MY GUESS IS HE'LL SEND ONE OF THE THIRSTING BARONS, OR PERHAPS THE LORD OF WHISPERS.
BUT WHOEVER HE'S SENDING, HE'S LATE.

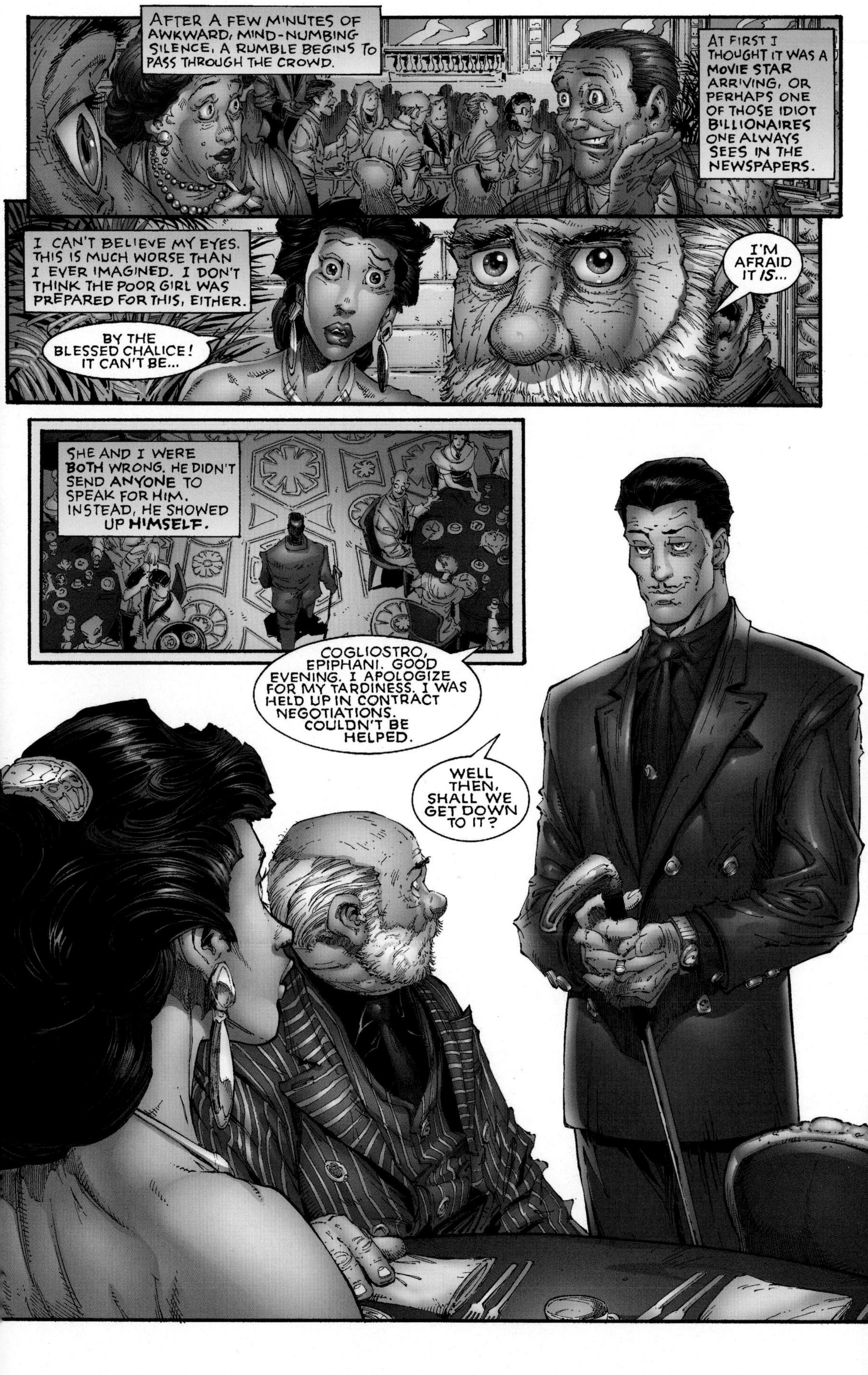
AFTER A FEW MINUTES OF AWKWARD, MIND-NUMBING SILENCE, A RUMBLE BEGINS TO PASS THROUGH THE CROWD.
AT FIRST I THOUGHT IT WAS A MOVIE STAR ARRIVING, OR PERHAPS ONE OF THOSE IDIOT BILLIONAIRES ONE ALWAYS SEES IN THE NEWSPAPERS.
I CAN'T BELIEVE MY EYES. THIS IS MUCH WORSE THAN I EVER IMAGINED. I DON'T THINK THE POOR GIRL WAS PREPARED FOR THIS, EITHER.
BY THE BLESSED CHALICE! IT CAN'T BE...
I'M AFRAID IT IS...
SHE AND I WERE BOTH WRONG. HE DIDN'T SEND ANYONE TO SPEAK FOR HIM. INSTEAD, HE SHOWED UP HIMSELF.
COGLIOSTRO, EPIPHANI. GOOD EVENING. I APOLOGIZE FOR MY TARDINESS. I WAS HELD UP IN CONTRACT NEGOTIATIONS. COULDN'T BE HELPED.
WELL THEN, SHALL WE GET DOWN TO IT?

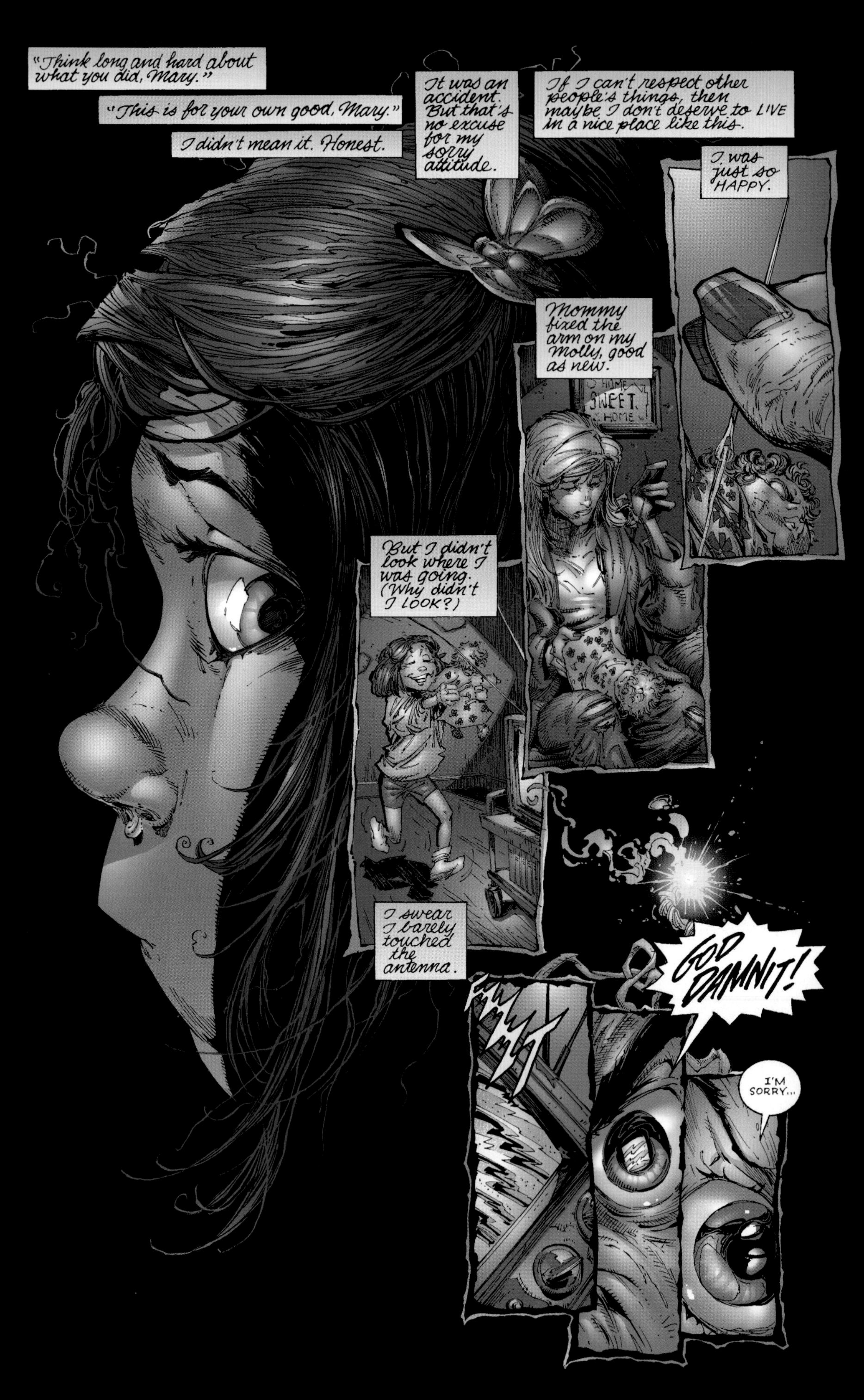

"Think long and hard about what you did, Mary."
"This is for your own good, Mary."
I didn't mean it. Honest.
It was an accident. But that's no excuse for my sorry attitude.
If I can't respect other people's things, then maybe I don't deserve to LIVE in a nice place like this.
I was just so HAPPY.
Mommy fixed the arm on my Molly, good as new.
HOME SWEET HOME
But I didn't look where I was going. (Why didn't I LOOK?)
I swear I barely touched the antenna.
GOD DAMNIT!
I'M SORRY...

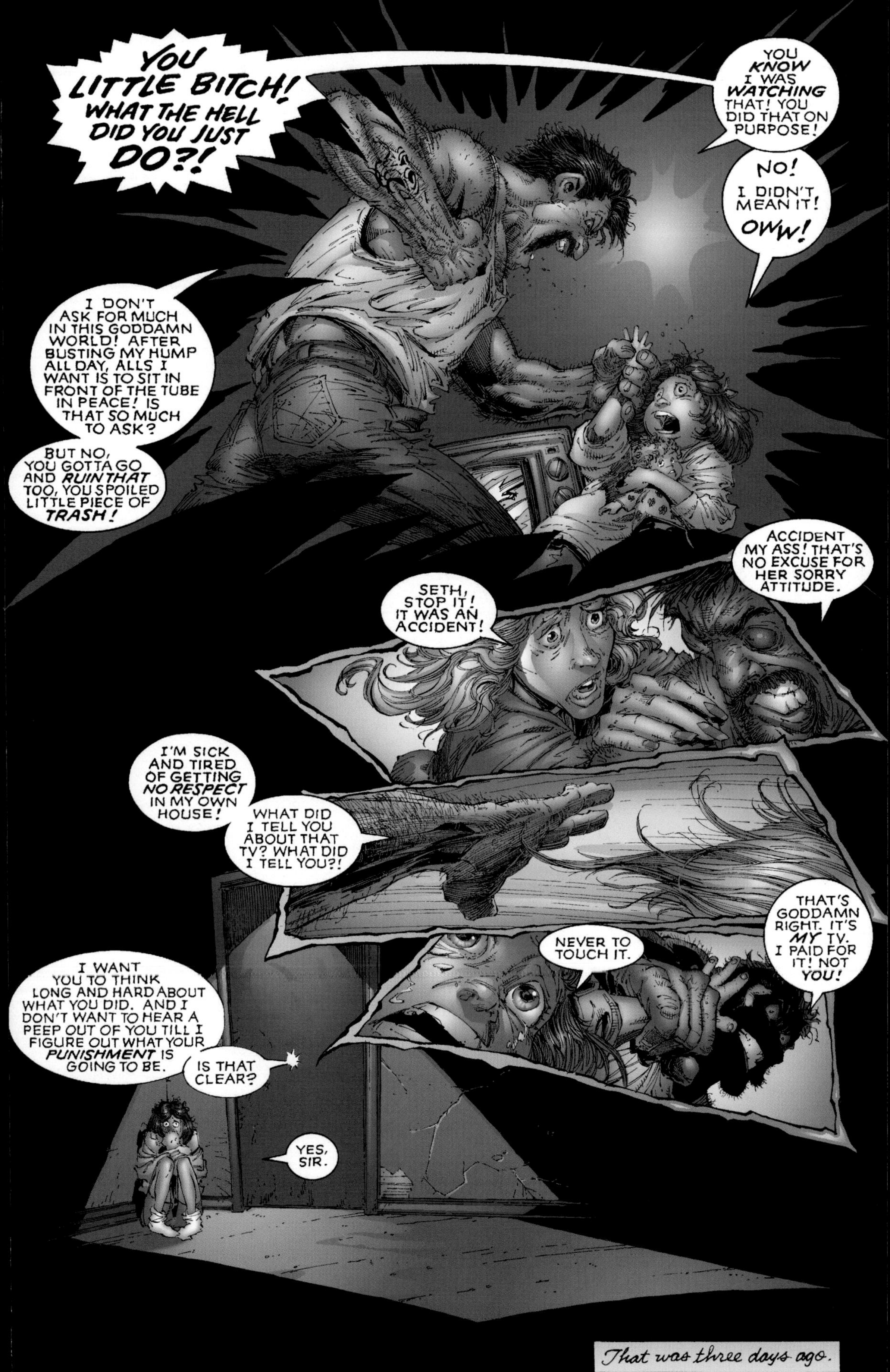
YOU LITTLE BITCH! WHAT THE HELL DID YOU JUST DO?!
YOU KNOW I WAS WATCHING THAT! YOU DID THAT ON PURPOSE!
NO! I DIDN'T MEAN IT! OWW!
I DON'T ASK FOR MUCH IN THIS GODDAMN WORLD! AFTER BUSTING MY HUMP ALL DAY, ALLS I WANT IS TO SIT IN FRONT OF THE TUBE IN PEACE! IS THAT SO MUCH TO ASK?
BUT NO, YOU GOTTA GO AND RUIN THAT TOO, YOU SPOILED LITTLE PIECE OF TRASH!
SETH, STOP IT! IT WAS AN ACCIDENT!
ACCIDENT MY ASS! THAT'S NO EXCUSE FOR HER SORRY ATTITUDE.
I'M SICK AND TIRED OF GETTING NO RESPECT IN MY OWN HOUSE!
WHAT DID I TELL YOU ABOUT THAT TV? WHAT DID I TELL YOU?!
NEVER TO TOUCH IT.
THAT'S GODDAMN RIGHT. IT'S MY TV. I PAID FOR IT! NOT YOU!
I WANT YOU TO THINK LONG AND HARD ABOUT WHAT YOU DID. AND I DON'T WANT TO HEAR A PEEP OUT OF YOU TILL I FIGURE OUT WHAT YOUR PUNISHMENT IS GOING TO BE.
IS THAT CLEAR?
YES, SIR.
That was three days ago.

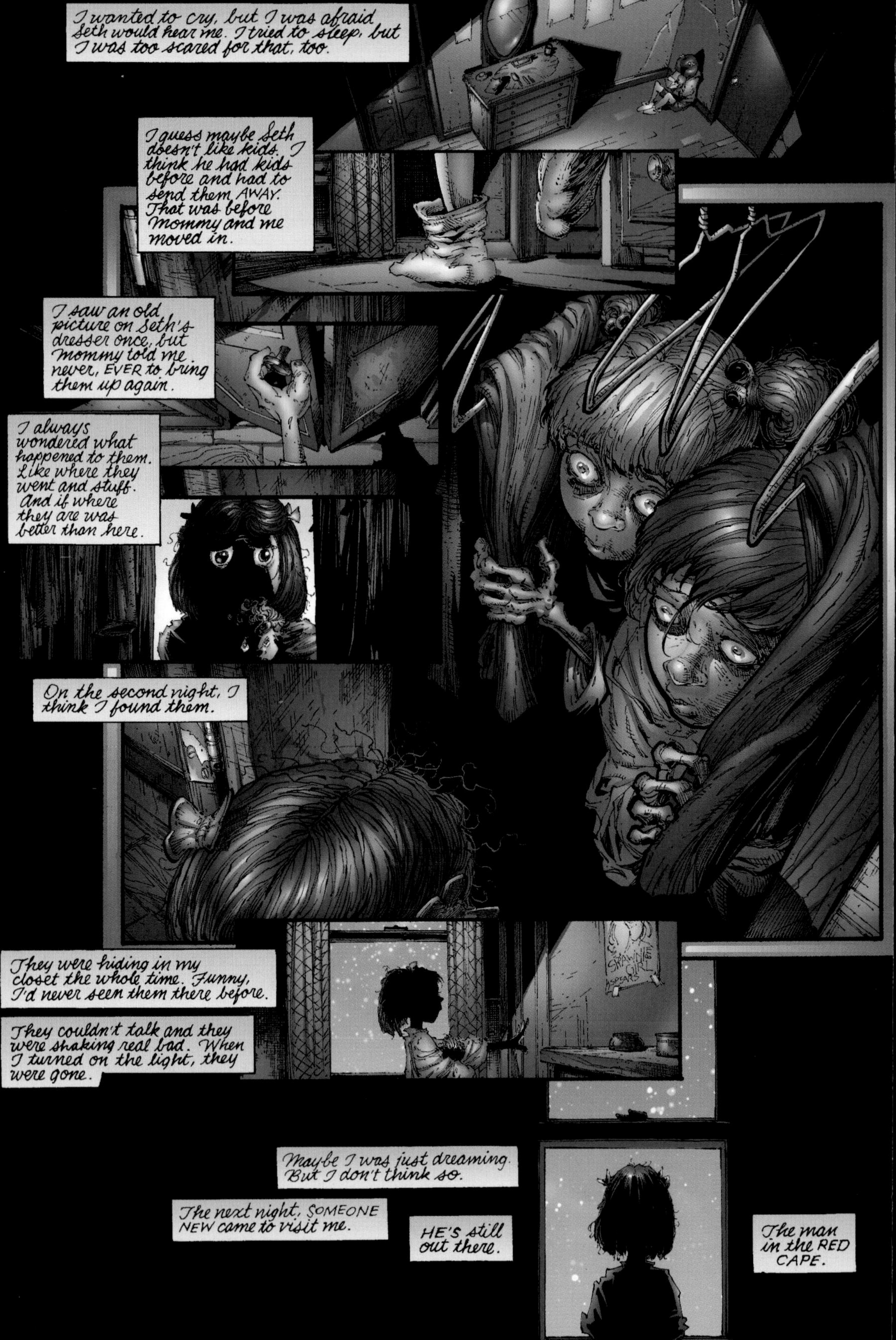
I wanted to cry, but I was afraid Seth would hear me. I tried to sleep, but I was too scared for that, too.
I guess maybe Seth doesn't like kids. I think he had kids before and had to send them AWAY. That was before Mommy and me moved in.
I saw an old picture on Seth's dresser once, but Mommy told me never, EVER to bring them up again.
I always wondered what happened to them. Like where they went and stuff. And if where they are was better than here.
On the second night, I think I found them.
They were hiding in my closet the whole time. Funny, I'd never seen them there before.
They couldn't talk and they were shaking real bad. When I turned on the light, they were gone.
SPAWNIE GIRL
SPEARS
Maybe I was just dreaming. But I don't think so.
The next night, SOMEONE NEW came to visit me.
HE'S still out there.
The man in the RED CAPE.

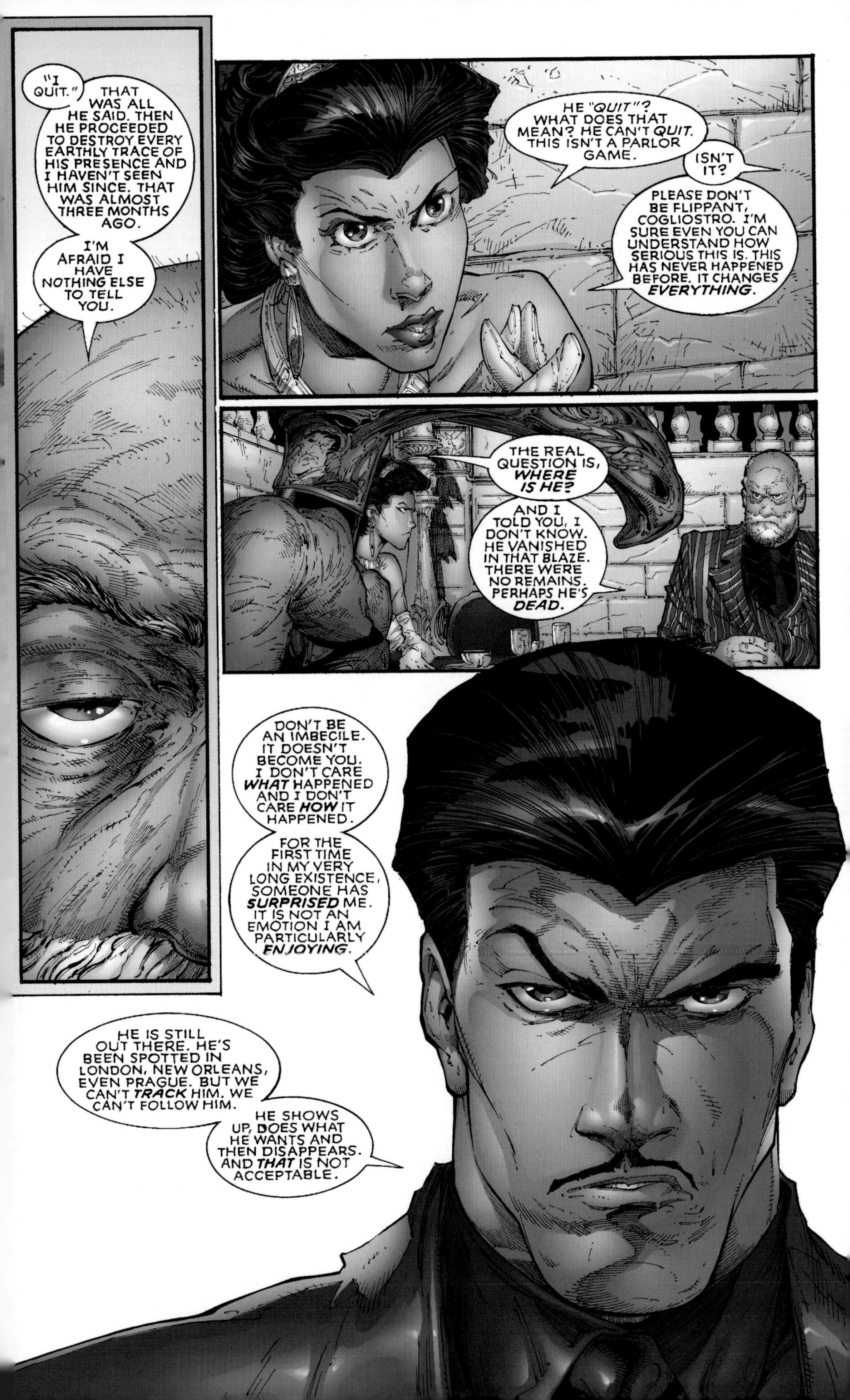
"I QUIT." THAT WAS ALL HE SAID. THEN HE PROCEEDED TO DESTROY EVERY EARTHLY TRACE OF HIS PRESENCE AND I HAVEN'T SEEN HIM SINCE. THAT WAS ALMOST THREE MONTHS AGO.
I'M AFRAID I HAVE NOTHING ELSE TO TELL YOU.
HE "QUIT"? WHAT DOES THAT MEAN? HE CAN'T QUIT. THIS ISN'T A PARLOR GAME.
ISN'T IT?
PLEASE DON'T BE FLIPPANT, COGLIOSTRO. I'M SURE EVEN YOU CAN UNDERSTAND HOW SERIOUS THIS IS. THIS HAS NEVER HAPPENED BEFORE. IT CHANGES EVERYTHING.
THE REAL QUESTION IS, WHERE IS HE?
AND I TOLD YOU, I DON'T KNOW. HE VANISHED IN THAT BLAZE. THERE WERE NO REMAINS. PERHAPS HE'S DEAD.
DON'T BE AN IMBECILE. IT DOESN'T BECOME YOU. I DON'T CARE WHAT HAPPENED AND I DON'T CARE HOW IT HAPPENED.
FOR THE FIRST TIME IN MY VERY LONG EXISTENCE, SOMEONE HAS SURPRISED ME. IT IS NOT AN EMOTION I AM PARTICULARLY ENJOYING.
HE IS STILL OUT THERE. HE'S BEEN SPOTTED IN LONDON, NEW ORLEANS, EVEN PRAGUE. BUT WE CAN'T TRACK HIM. WE CAN'T FOLLOW HIM.
HE SHOWS UP, DOES WHAT HE WANTS AND THEN DISAPPEARS. AND THAT IS NOT ACCEPTABLE.

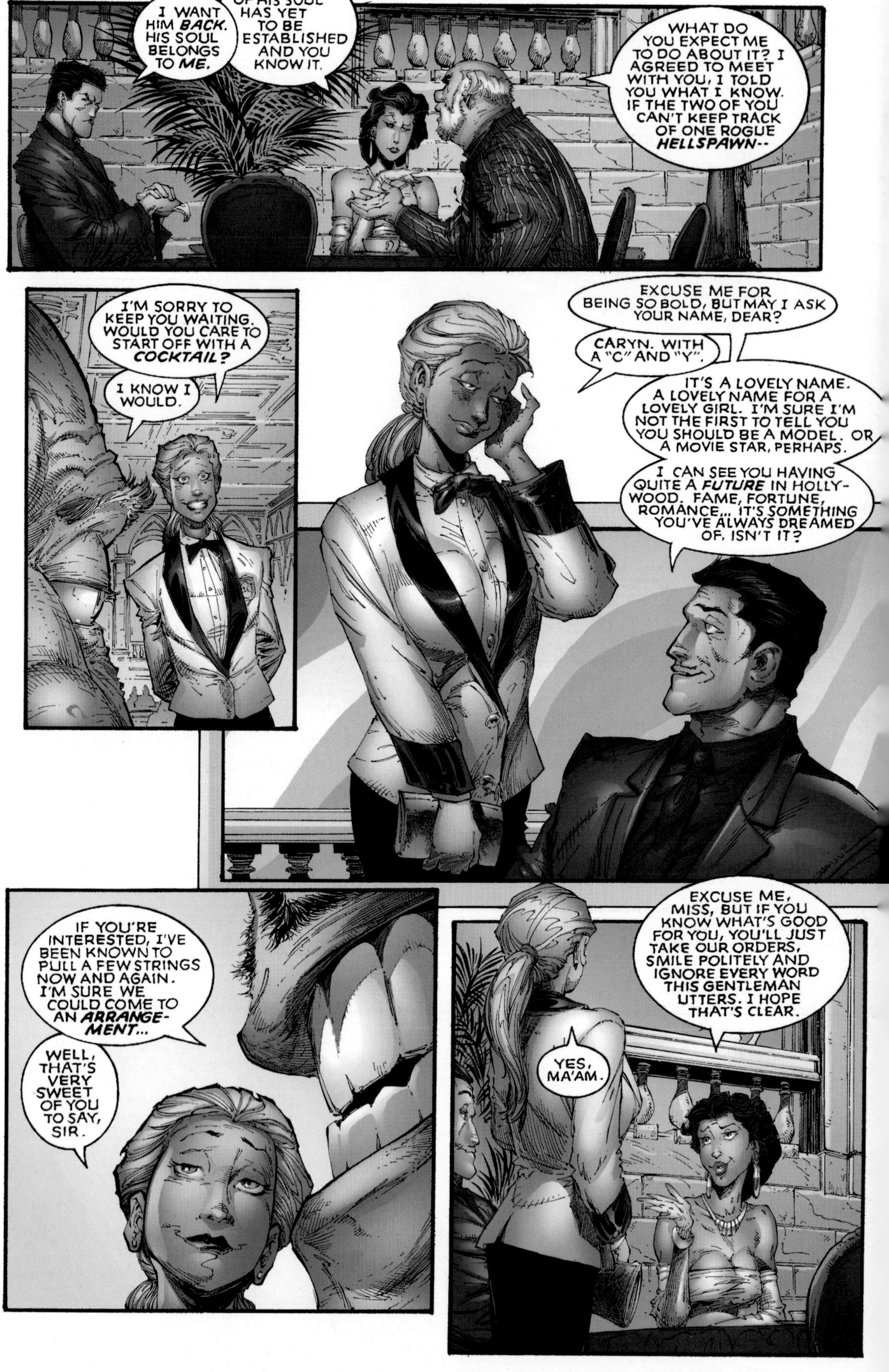
I WANT HIM BACK. HIS SOUL BELONGS TO ME.
THE FATE OF HIS SOUL HAS YET TO BE ESTABLISHED AND YOU KNOW IT.
WHAT DO YOU EXPECT ME TO DO ABOUT IT? I AGREED TO MEET WITH YOU, I TOLD YOU WHAT I KNOW. IF THE TWO OF YOU CAN'T KEEP TRACK OF ONE ROGUE HELLSPAWN--
I'M SORRY TO KEEP YOU WAITING. WOULD YOU CARE TO START OFF WITH A COCKTAIL?
I KNOW I WOULD.
EXCUSE ME FOR BEING SO BOLD, BUT MAY I ASK YOUR NAME, DEAR?
CARYN. WITH A "C" AND "Y".
IT'S A LOVELY NAME. A LOVELY NAME FOR A LOVELY GIRL. I'M SURE I'M NOT THE FIRST TO TELL YOU YOU SHOULD BE A MODEL. OR A MOVIE STAR, PERHAPS.
I CAN SEE YOU HAVING QUITE A FUTURE IN HOLLYWOOD. FAME, FORTUNE, ROMANCE... IT'S SOMETHING YOU'VE ALWAYS DREAMED OF, ISN'T IT?
IF YOU'RE INTERESTED, I'VE BEEN KNOWN TO PULL A FEW STRINGS NOW AND AGAIN. I'M SURE WE COULD COME TO AN ARRANGEMENT...
WELL, THAT'S VERY SWEET OF YOU TO SAY, SIR.
EXCUSE ME, MISS, BUT IF YOU KNOW WHAT'S GOOD FOR YOU, YOU'LL JUST TAKE OUR ORDERS, SMILE POLITELY AND IGNORE EVERY WORD THIS GENTLEMAN UTTERS. I HOPE THAT'S CLEAR.
YES, MA'AM.

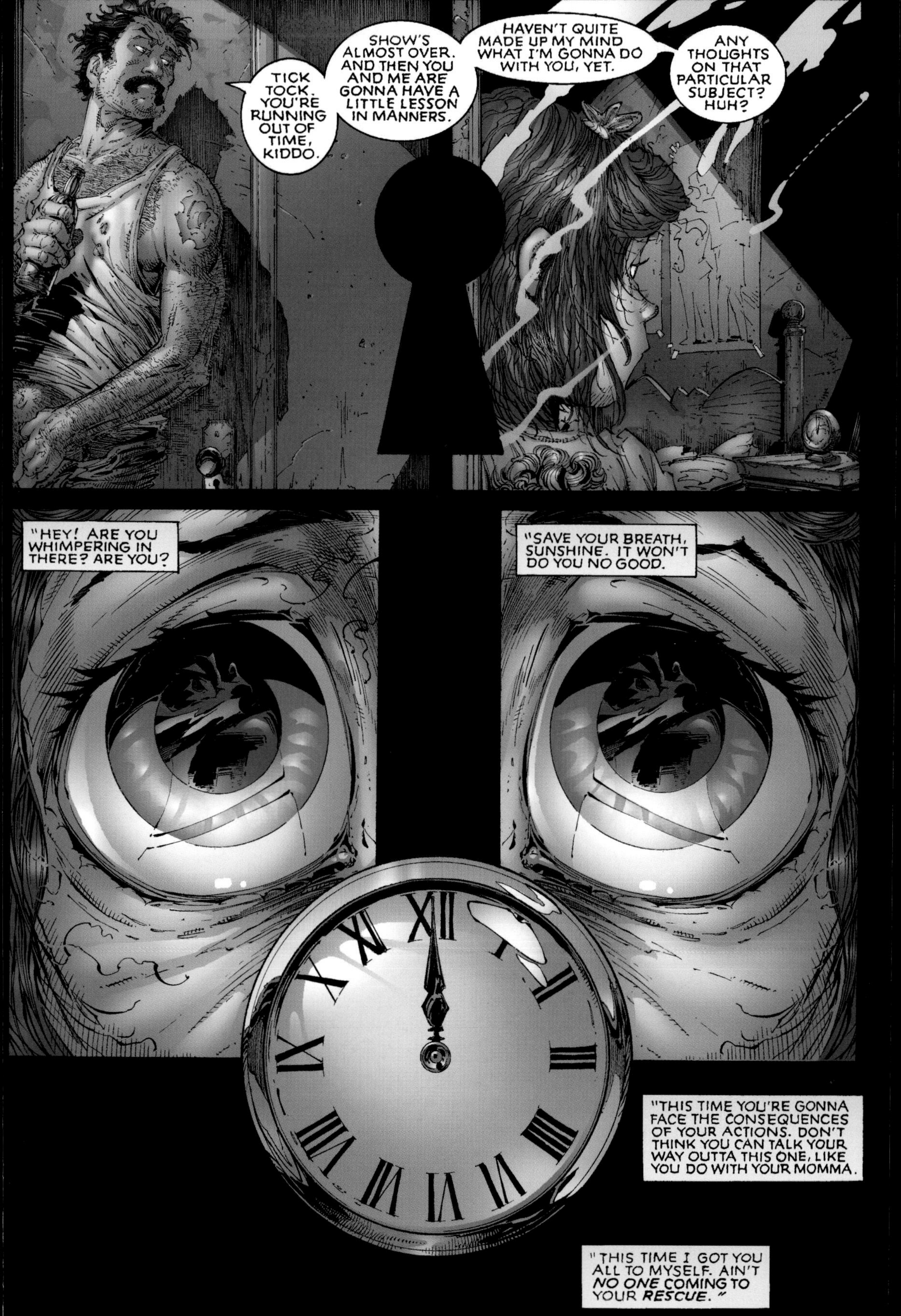
TICK TOCK. YOU'RE RUNNING OUT OF TIME, KIDDO.
SHOW'S ALMOST OVER. AND THEN YOU AND ME ARE GONNA HAVE A LITTLE LESSON IN MANNERS.
HAVEN'T QUITE MADE UP MY MIND WHAT I'M GONNA DO WITH YOU, YET.
ANY THOUGHTS ON THAT PARTICULAR SUBJECT? HUH?
"HEY! ARE YOU WHIMPERING IN THERE? ARE YOU?
"SAVE YOUR BREATH, SUNSHINE. IT WON'T DO YOU NO GOOD.
"THIS TIME YOU'RE GONNA FACE THE CONSEQUENCES OF YOUR ACTIONS. DON'T THINK YOU CAN TALK YOUR WAY OUTTA THIS ONE, LIKE YOU DO WITH YOUR MOMMA.
"THIS TIME I GOT YOU ALL TO MYSELF. AIN'T *NO ONE* COMING TO YOUR *RESCUE*."

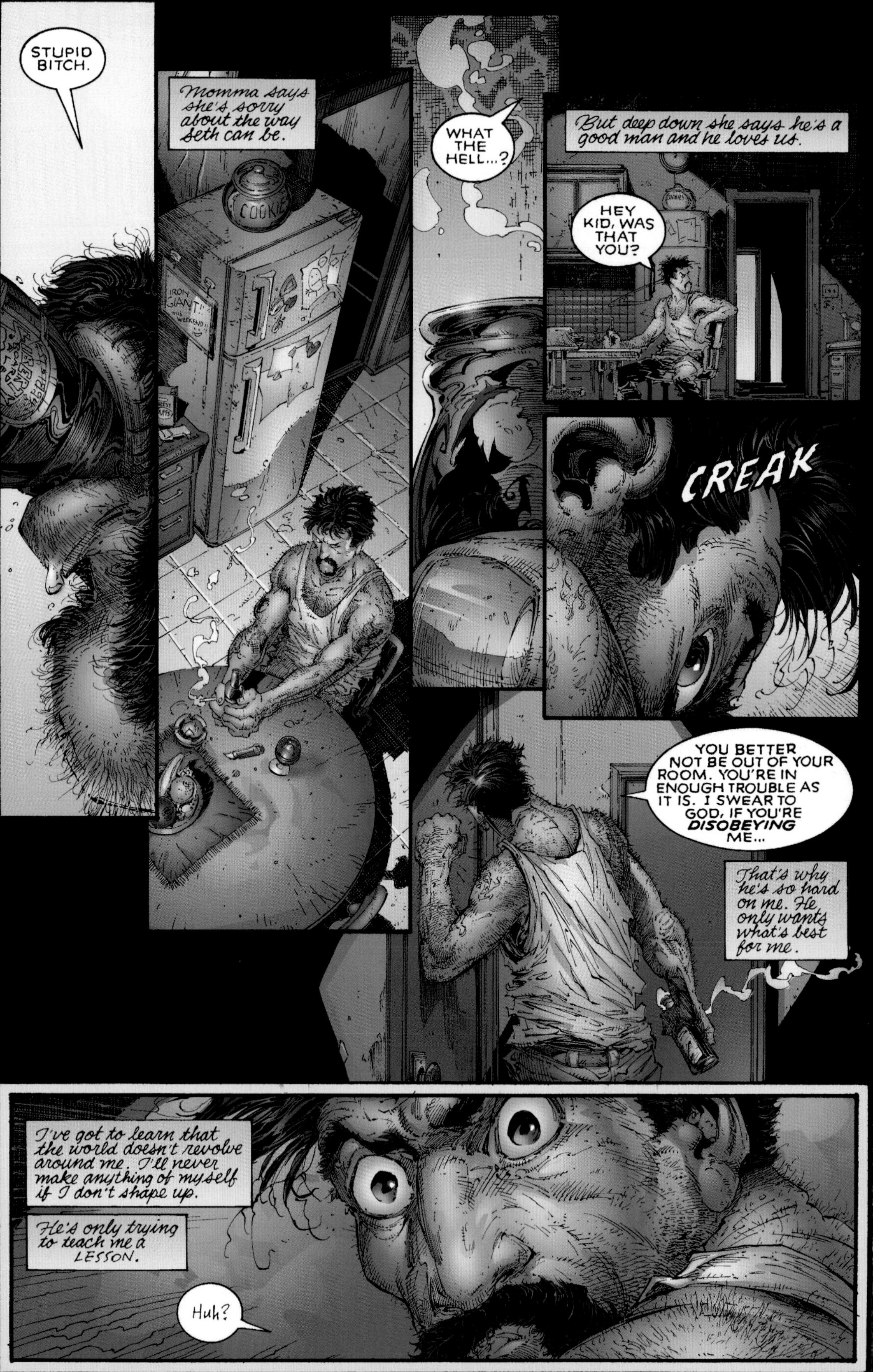

STUPID BITCH.
Momma says she's sorry about the way Seth can be.
COOKIE
IRON GIANT!! THIS WEEKEND!!
WHAT THE HELL...?
But deep down she says he's a good man and he loves us.
HEY KID, WAS THAT YOU?
CREAK
YOU BETTER NOT BE OUT OF YOUR ROOM. YOU'RE IN ENOUGH TROUBLE AS IT IS. I SWEAR TO GOD, IF YOU'RE DISOBEYING ME...
That's why he's so hard on me. He only wants what's best for me.
I've got to learn that the world doesn't revolve around me. I'll never make anything of myself if I don't shape up.
He's only trying to teach me a LESSON.
Huh?

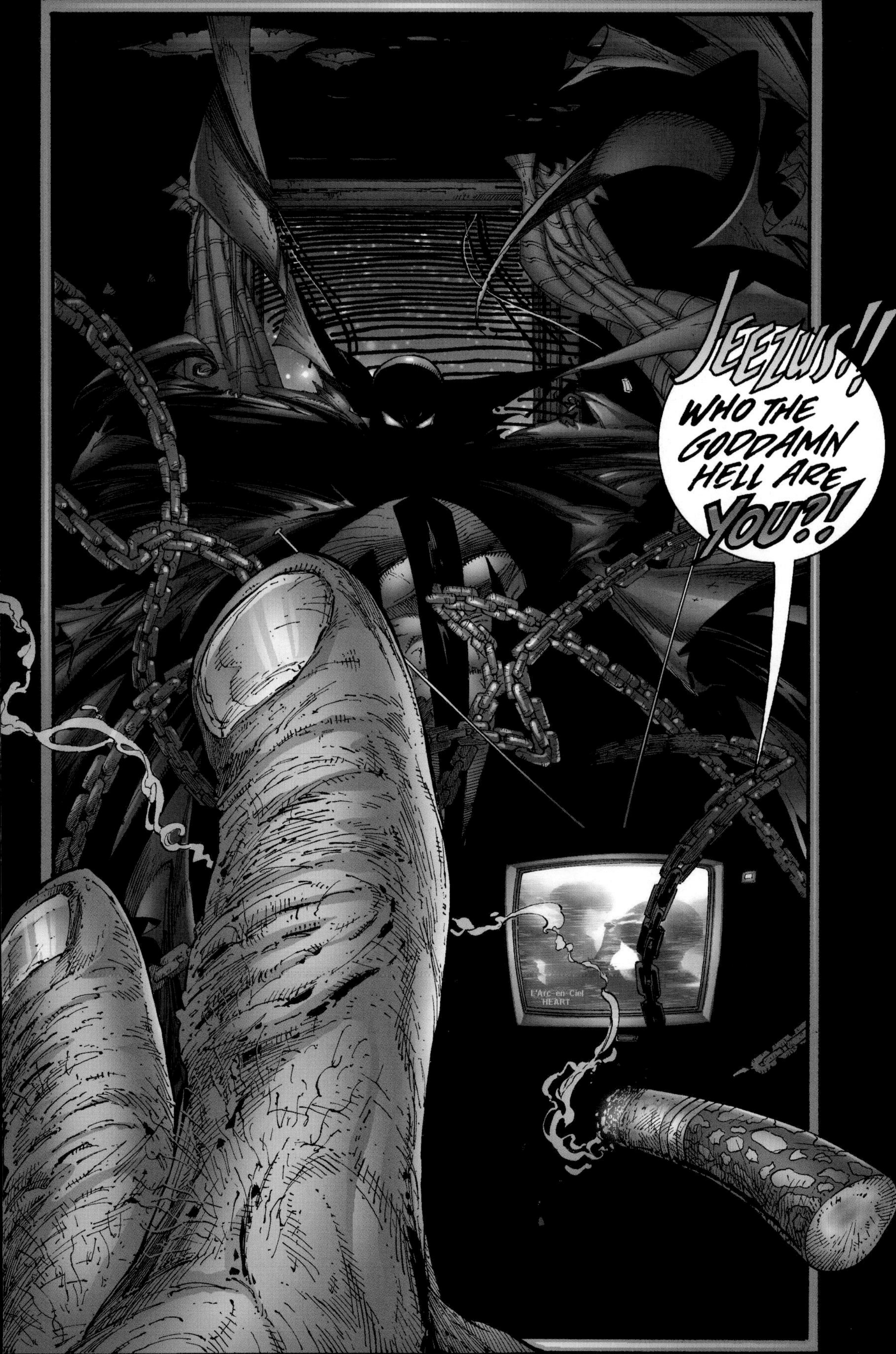
JEEZUS!! WHO THE GODDAMN HELL ARE YOU?!
L'Arc-en-Ciel HEART

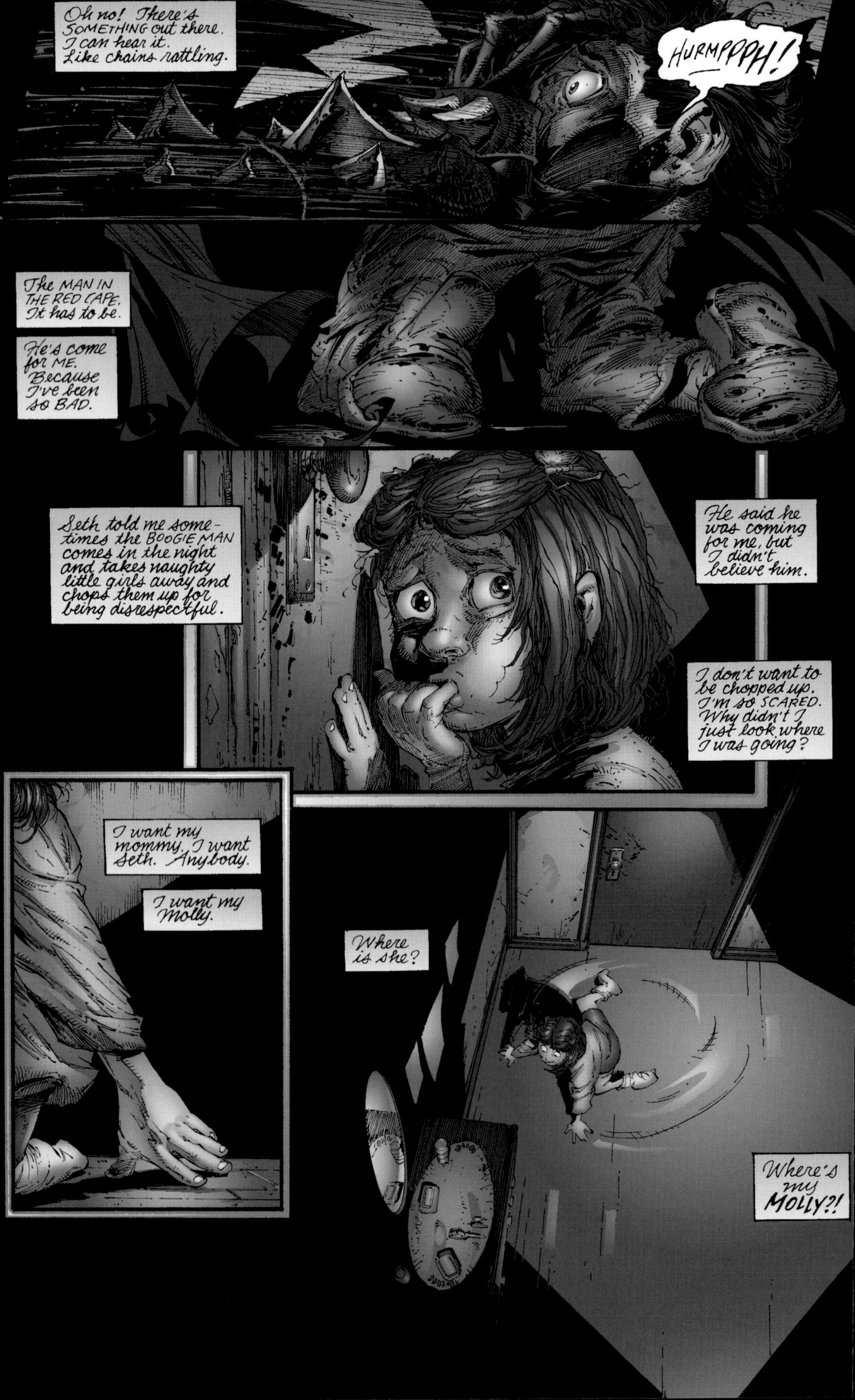

Oh no! There's SOMETHING out there. I can hear it. Like chains rattling.
HURMPPPH!
The MAN IN THE RED CAPE. It has to be.
He's come for ME. Because I've been so BAD.
Seth told me sometimes the BOOGIE MAN comes in the night and takes naughty little girls away and chops them up for being disrespectful.
He said he was coming for me, but I didn't believe him.
I don't want to be chopped up. I'm so SCARED. Why didn't I just look where I was going?
I want my mommy. I want Seth. Anybody.
I want my Molly.
Where is she?
Where's my MOLLY?!

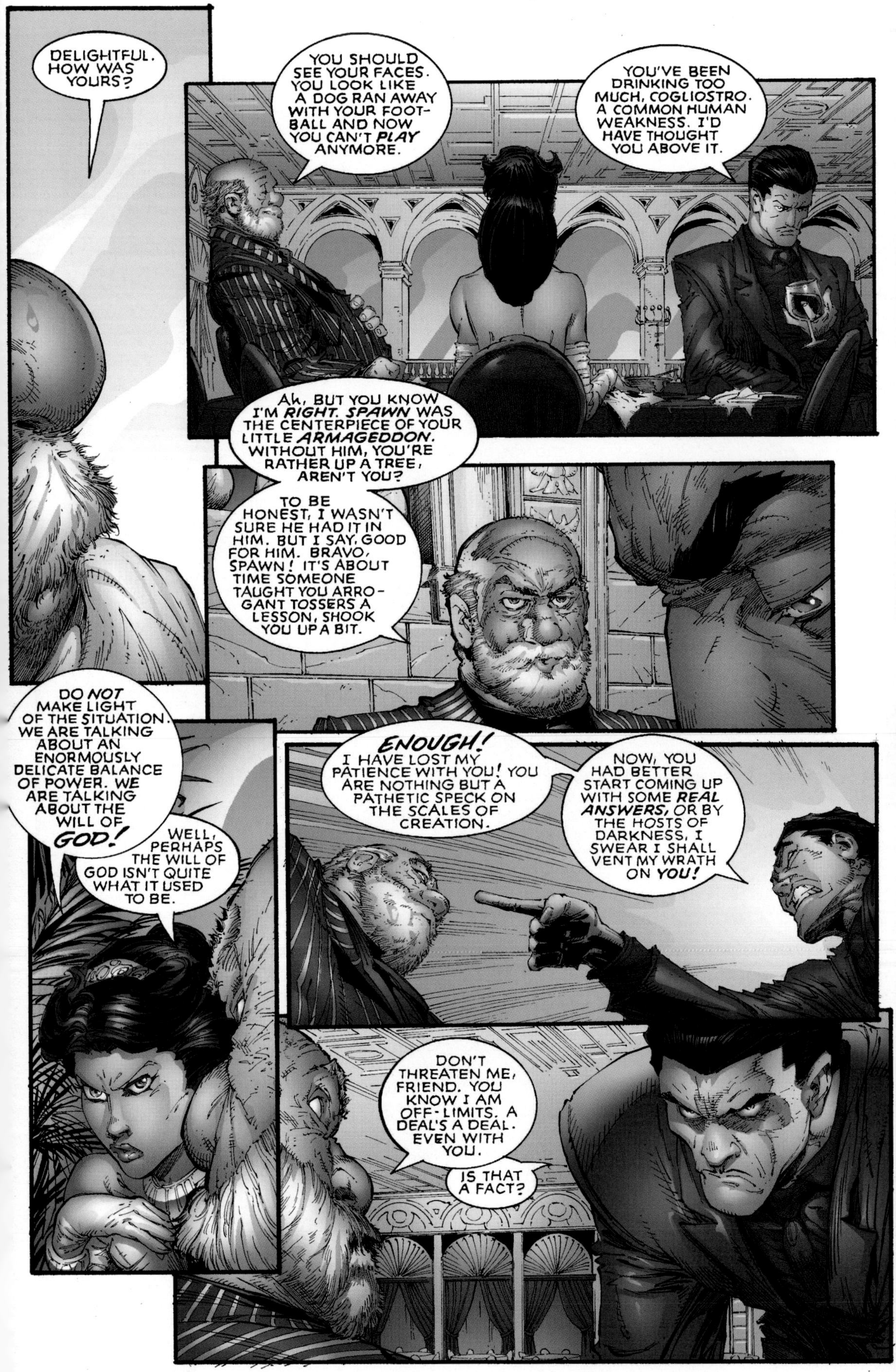

DELIGHTFUL. HOW WAS YOURS?
YOU SHOULD SEE YOUR FACES. YOU LOOK LIKE A DOG RAN AWAY WITH YOUR FOOT-BALL AND NOW YOU CAN'T PLAY ANYMORE.
YOU'VE BEEN DRINKING TOO MUCH, COGLIOSTRO. A COMMON HUMAN WEAKNESS. I'D HAVE THOUGHT YOU ABOVE IT.
Ah, BUT YOU KNOW I'M RIGHT. SPAWN WAS THE CENTERPIECE OF YOUR LITTLE ARMAGEDDON. WITHOUT HIM, YOU'RE RATHER UP A TREE, AREN'T YOU?
TO BE HONEST, I WASN'T SURE HE HAD IT IN HIM. BUT I SAY, GOOD FOR HIM. BRAVO, SPAWN! IT'S ABOUT TIME SOMEONE TAUGHT YOU ARRO-GANT TOSSERS A LESSON, SHOOK YOU UP A BIT.
DO NOT MAKE LIGHT OF THE SITUATION. WE ARE TALKING ABOUT AN ENORMOUSLY DELICATE BALANCE OF POWER. WE ARE TALKING ABOUT THE WILL OF GOD!
WELL, PERHAPS THE WILL OF GOD ISN'T QUITE WHAT IT USED TO BE.
ENOUGH! I HAVE LOST MY PATIENCE WITH YOU! YOU ARE NOTHING BUT A PATHETIC SPECK ON THE SCALES OF CREATION.
NOW, YOU HAD BETTER START COMING UP WITH SOME REAL ANSWERS, OR BY THE HOSTS OF DARKNESS, I SWEAR I SHALL VENT MY WRATH ON YOU!
DON'T THREATEN ME, FRIEND. YOU KNOW I AM OFF-LIMITS. A DEAL'S A DEAL. EVEN WITH YOU.
IS THAT A FACT?

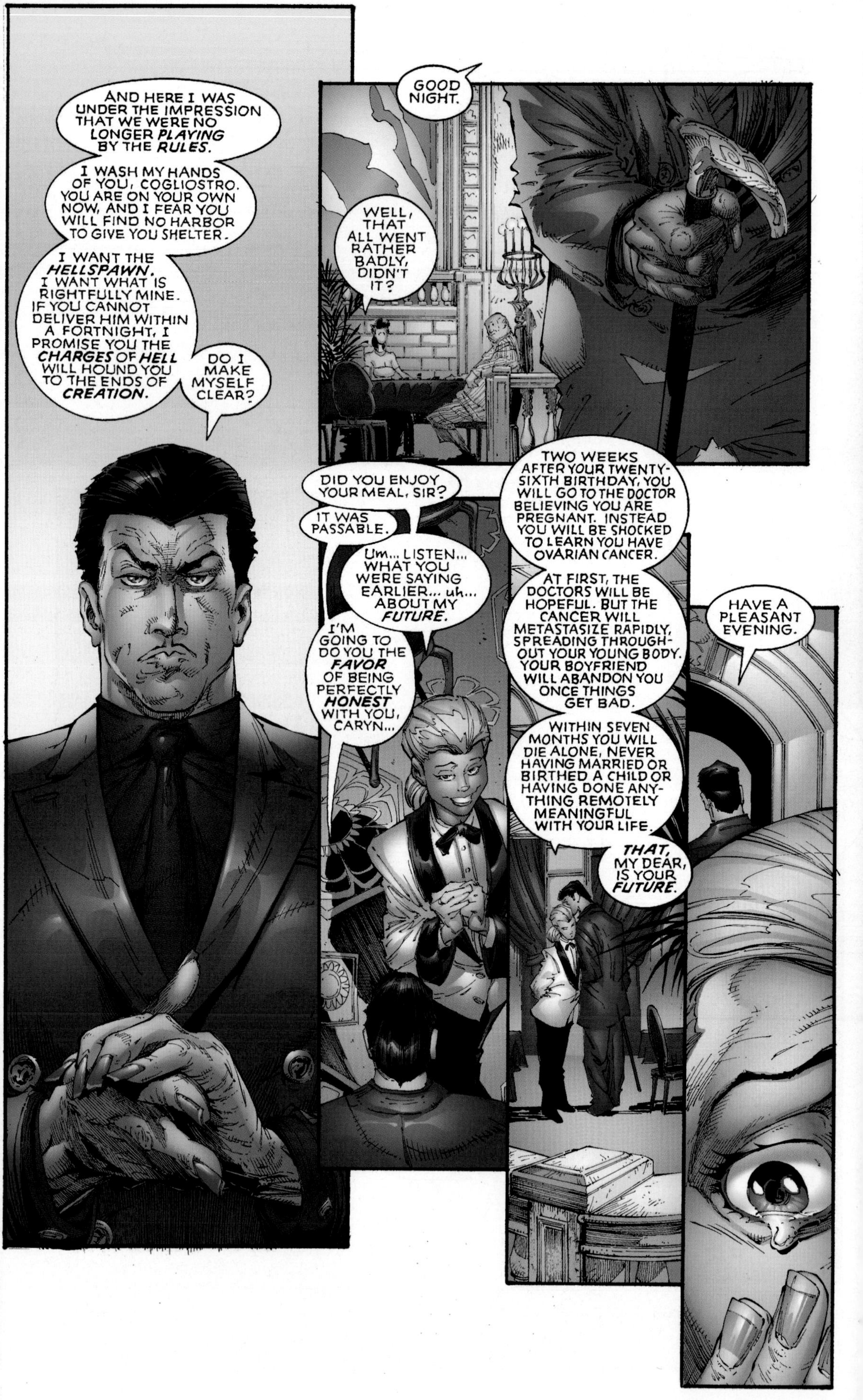
AND HERE I WAS UNDER THE IMPRESSION THAT WE WERE NO LONGER PLAYING BY THE RULES.
I WASH MY HANDS OF YOU, COGLIOSTRO. YOU ARE ON YOUR OWN NOW, AND I FEAR YOU WILL FIND NO HARBOR TO GIVE YOU SHELTER.
I WANT THE HELLSPAWN. I WANT WHAT IS RIGHTFULLY MINE. IF YOU CANNOT DELIVER HIM WITHIN A FORTNIGHT, I PROMISE YOU THE CHARGES OF HELL WILL HOUND YOU TO THE ENDS OF CREATION.
DO I MAKE MYSELF CLEAR?
GOOD NIGHT.
WELL, THAT ALL WENT RATHER BADLY, DIDN'T IT?
DID YOU ENJOY YOUR MEAL, SIR?
IT WAS PASSABLE.
Um... LISTEN... WHAT YOU WERE SAYING EARLIER... uh... ABOUT MY FUTURE.
I'M GOING TO DO YOU THE FAVOR OF BEING PERFECTLY HONEST WITH YOU, CARYN...
TWO WEEKS AFTER YOUR TWENTY-SIXTH BIRTHDAY, YOU WILL GO TO THE DOCTOR BELIEVING YOU ARE PREGNANT. INSTEAD YOU WILL BE SHOCKED TO LEARN YOU HAVE OVARIAN CANCER.
AT FIRST, THE DOCTORS WILL BE HOPEFUL. BUT THE CANCER WILL METASTASIZE RAPIDLY, SPREADING THROUGH-OUT YOUR YOUNG BODY. YOUR BOYFRIEND WILL ABANDON YOU ONCE THINGS GET BAD.
WITHIN SEVEN MONTHS YOU WILL DIE ALONE, NEVER HAVING MARRIED OR BIRTHED A CHILD OR HAVING DONE ANY-THING REMOTELY MEANINGFUL WITH YOUR LIFE.
THAT, MY DEAR, IS YOUR FUTURE.
HAVE A PLEASANT EVENING.

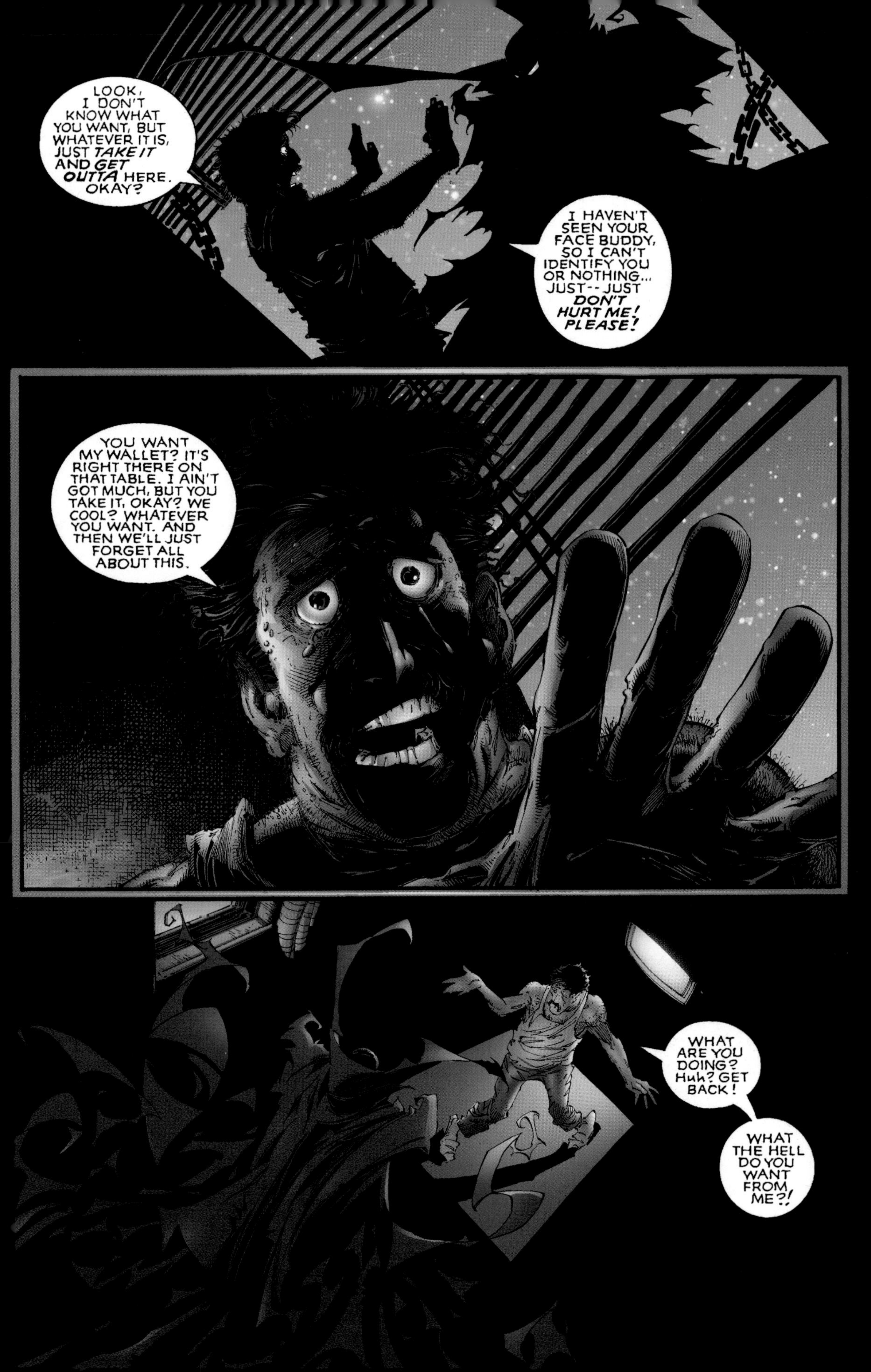
LOOK, I DON'T KNOW WHAT YOU WANT, BUT WHATEVER IT IS, JUST TAKE IT AND GET OUTTA HERE. OKAY?
I HAVEN'T SEEN YOUR FACE BUDDY, SO I CAN'T IDENTIFY YOU OR NOTHING... JUST-- JUST DON'T HURT ME! PLEASE!
YOU WANT MY WALLET? IT'S RIGHT THERE ON THAT TABLE. I AIN'T GOT MUCH, BUT YOU TAKE IT, OKAY? WE COOL? WHATEVER YOU WANT. AND THEN WE'LL JUST FORGET ALL ABOUT THIS.
WHAT ARE YOU DOING? Huh? GET BACK!
WHAT THE HELL DO YOU WANT FROM ME?!

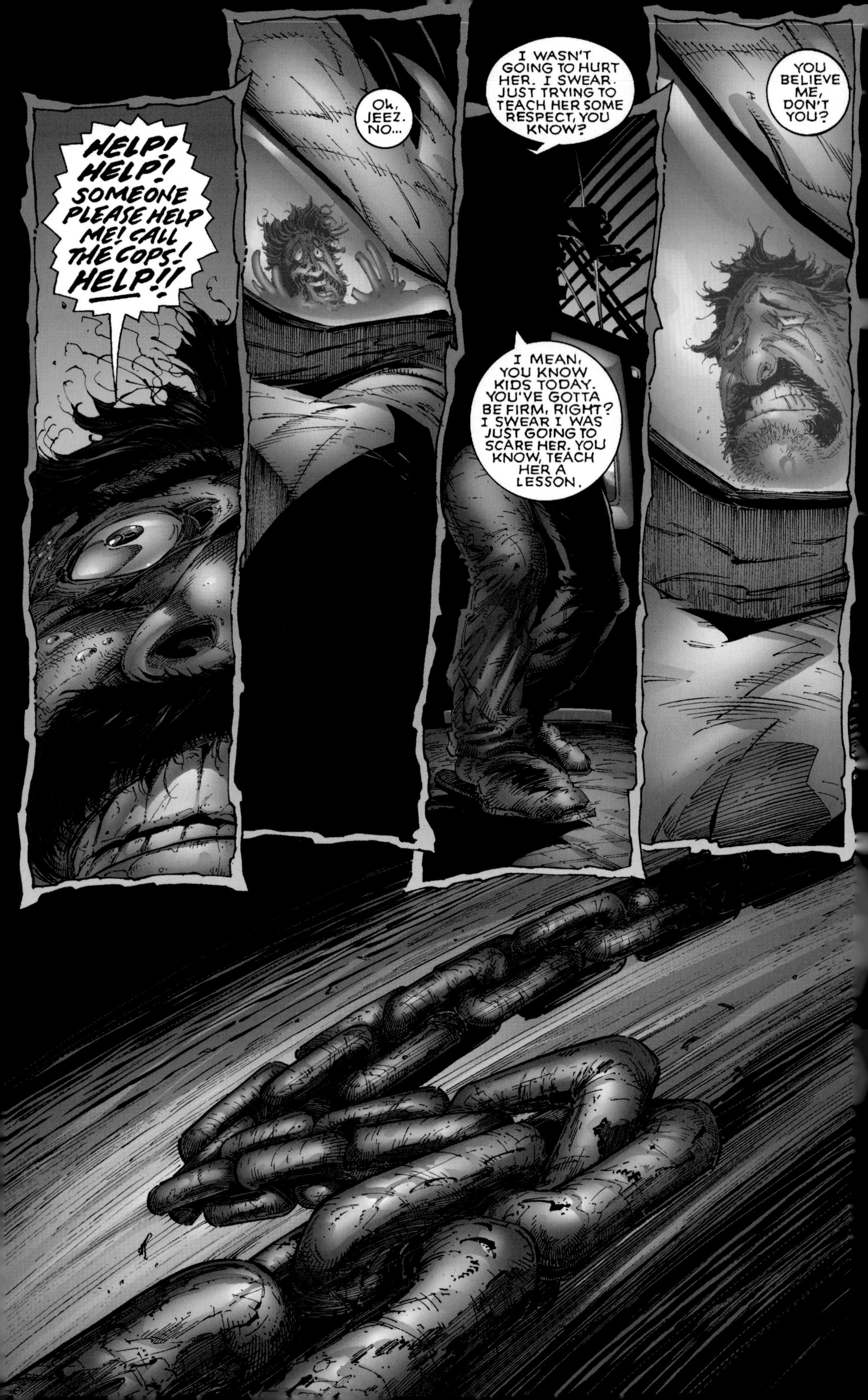
HELP! HELP! SOMEONE PLEASE HELP ME! CALL THE COPS! HELP!!
Oh, JEEZ. NO...
I WASN'T GOING TO HURT HER. I SWEAR. JUST TRYING TO TEACH HER SOME RESPECT, YOU KNOW?
I MEAN, YOU KNOW KIDS TODAY. YOU'VE GOTTA BE FIRM, RIGHT? I SWEAR I WAS JUST GOING TO SCARE HER. YOU KNOW, TEACH HER A LESSON.
YOU BELIEVE ME, DON'T YOU?

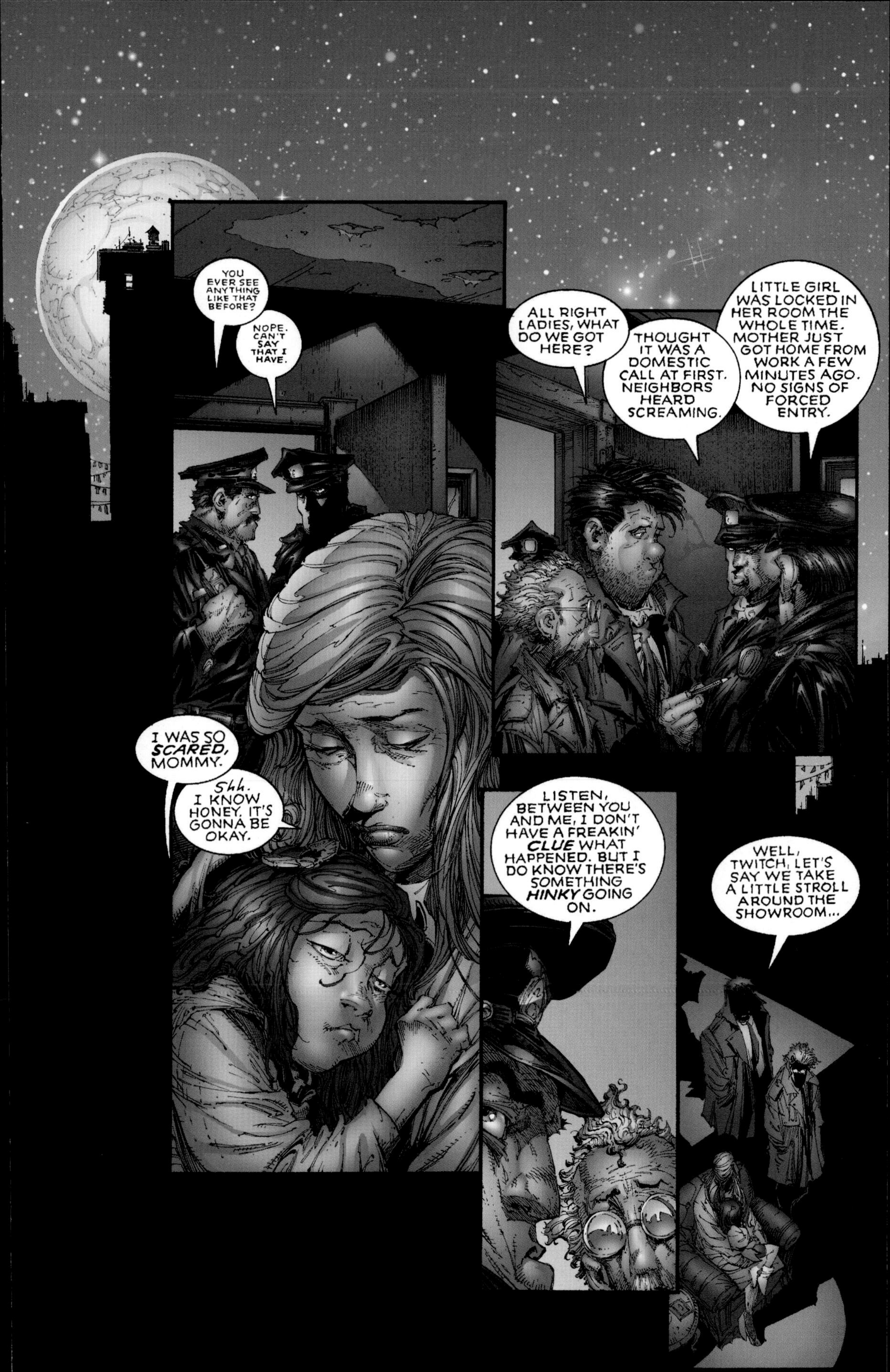

YOU EVER SEE ANYTHING LIKE THAT BEFORE?
NOPE. CAN'T SAY THAT I HAVE.
ALL RIGHT LADIES, WHAT DO WE GOT HERE?
THOUGHT IT WAS A DOMESTIC CALL AT FIRST. NEIGHBORS HEARD SCREAMING.
LITTLE GIRL WAS LOCKED IN HER ROOM THE WHOLE TIME. MOTHER JUST GOT HOME FROM WORK A FEW MINUTES AGO. NO SIGNS OF FORCED ENTRY.
I WAS SO SCARED, MOMMY.
Shh. I KNOW HONEY. IT'S GONNA BE OKAY.
LISTEN, BETWEEN YOU AND ME, I DON'T HAVE A FREAKIN' CLUE WHAT HAPPENED. BUT I DO KNOW THERE'S SOMETHING HINKY GOING ON.
WELL, TWITCH, LET'S SAY WE TAKE A LITTLE STROLL AROUND THE SHOWROOM...

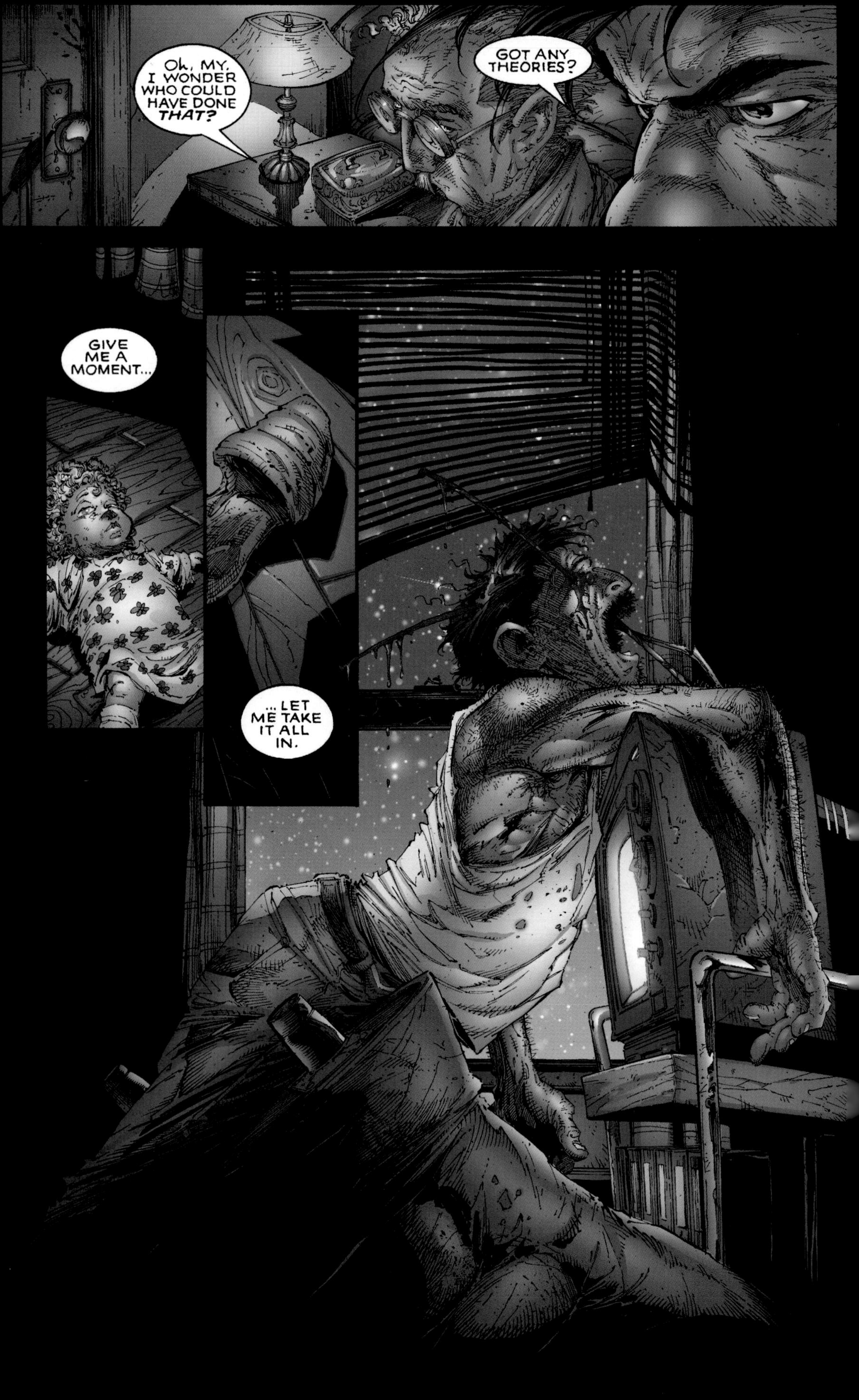
Oh, MY. I WONDER WHO COULD HAVE DONE *THAT?*
GOT ANY THEORIES?
GIVE ME A MOMENT...
... LET ME TAKE IT ALL IN.

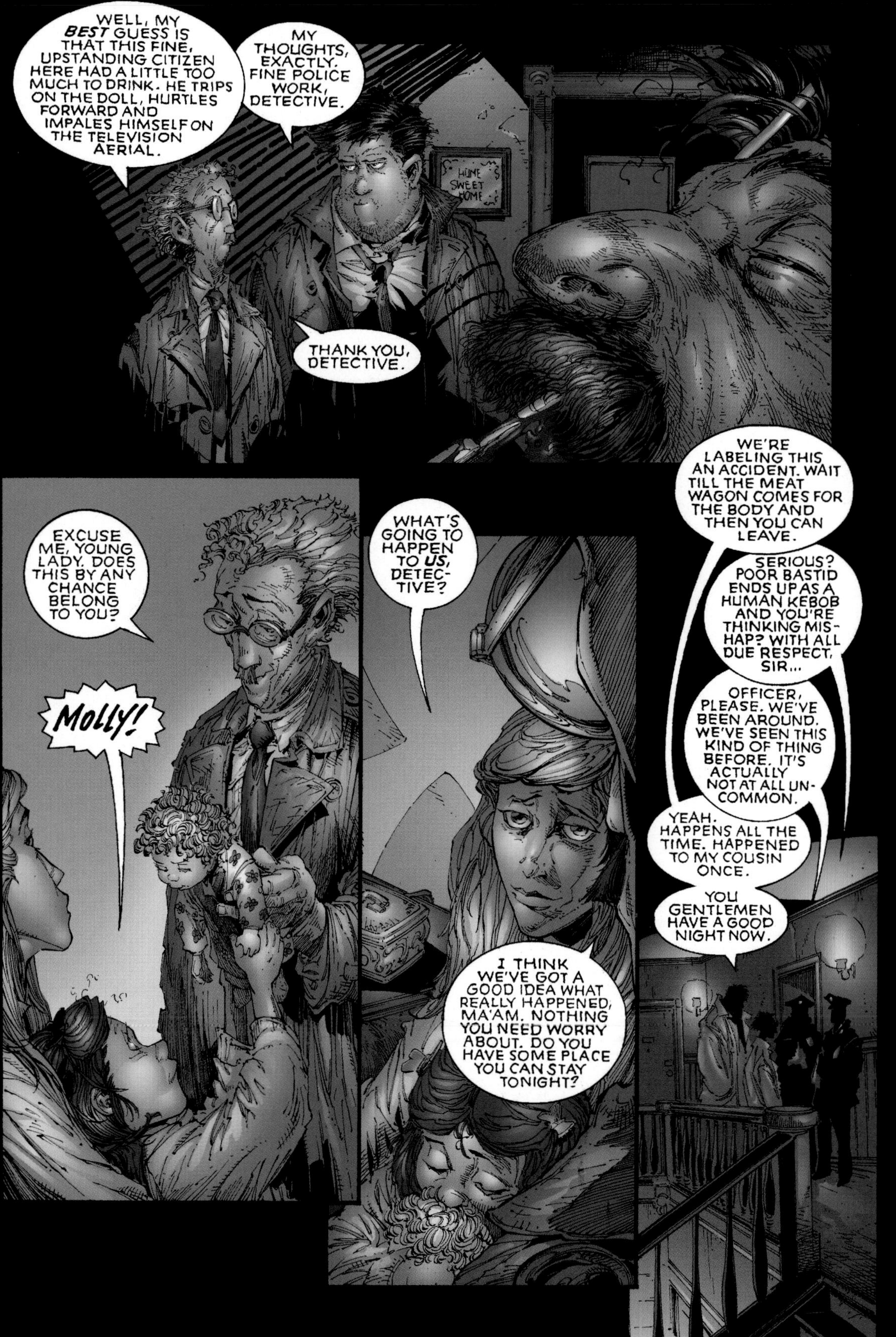
WELL, MY BEST GUESS IS THAT THIS FINE, UPSTANDING CITIZEN HERE HAD A LITTLE TOO MUCH TO DRINK. HE TRIPS ON THE DOLL, HURTLES FORWARD AND IMPALES HIMSELF ON THE TELEVISION AERIAL.
MY THOUGHTS, EXACTLY. FINE POLICE WORK, DETECTIVE.
HOME SWEET HOME
THANK YOU, DETECTIVE.
EXCUSE ME, YOUNG LADY. DOES THIS BY ANY CHANCE BELONG TO YOU?
MOLLY!
WHAT'S GOING TO HAPPEN TO US, DETECTIVE?
I THINK WE'VE GOT A GOOD IDEA WHAT REALLY HAPPENED, MA'AM. NOTHING YOU NEED WORRY ABOUT. DO YOU HAVE SOME PLACE YOU CAN STAY TONIGHT?
WE'RE LABELING THIS AN ACCIDENT. WAIT TILL THE MEAT WAGON COMES FOR THE BODY AND THEN YOU CAN LEAVE.
SERIOUS? POOR BASTID ENDS UP AS A HUMAN KEBOB AND YOU'RE THINKING MISHAP? WITH ALL DUE RESPECT, SIR...
OFFICER, PLEASE. WE'VE BEEN AROUND. WE'VE SEEN THIS KIND OF THING BEFORE. IT'S ACTUALLY NOT AT ALL UNCOMMON.
YEAH. HAPPENS ALL THE TIME. HAPPENED TO MY COUSIN ONCE.
YOU GENTLEMEN HAVE A GOOD NIGHT NOW.

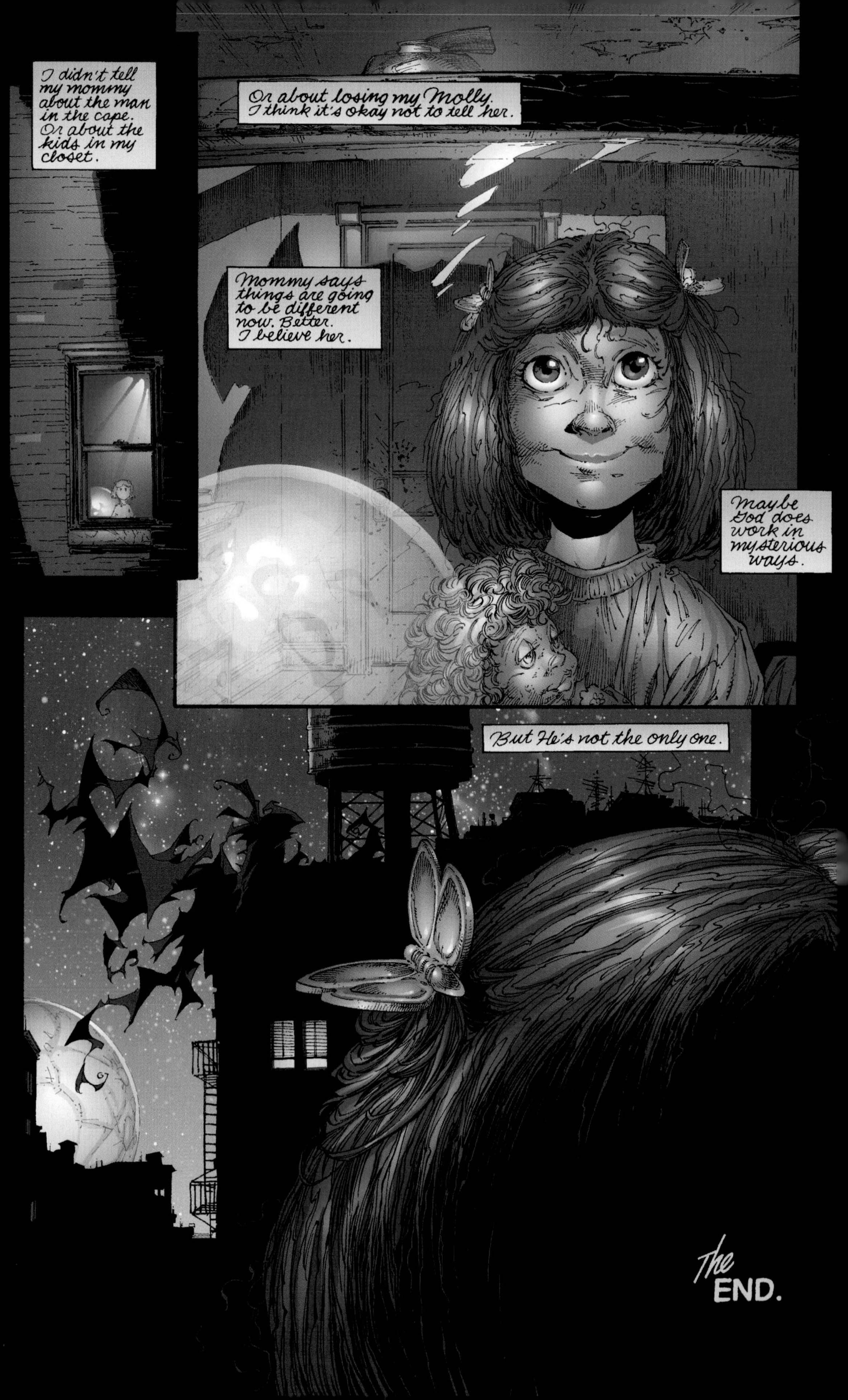
I didn't tell my mommy about the man in the cape. Or about the kids in my closet.
Or about losing my Molly. I think it's okay not to tell her.
Mommy says things are going to be different now. Better. I believe her.
Maybe God does work in mysterious ways.
But He's not the only one.
the END.

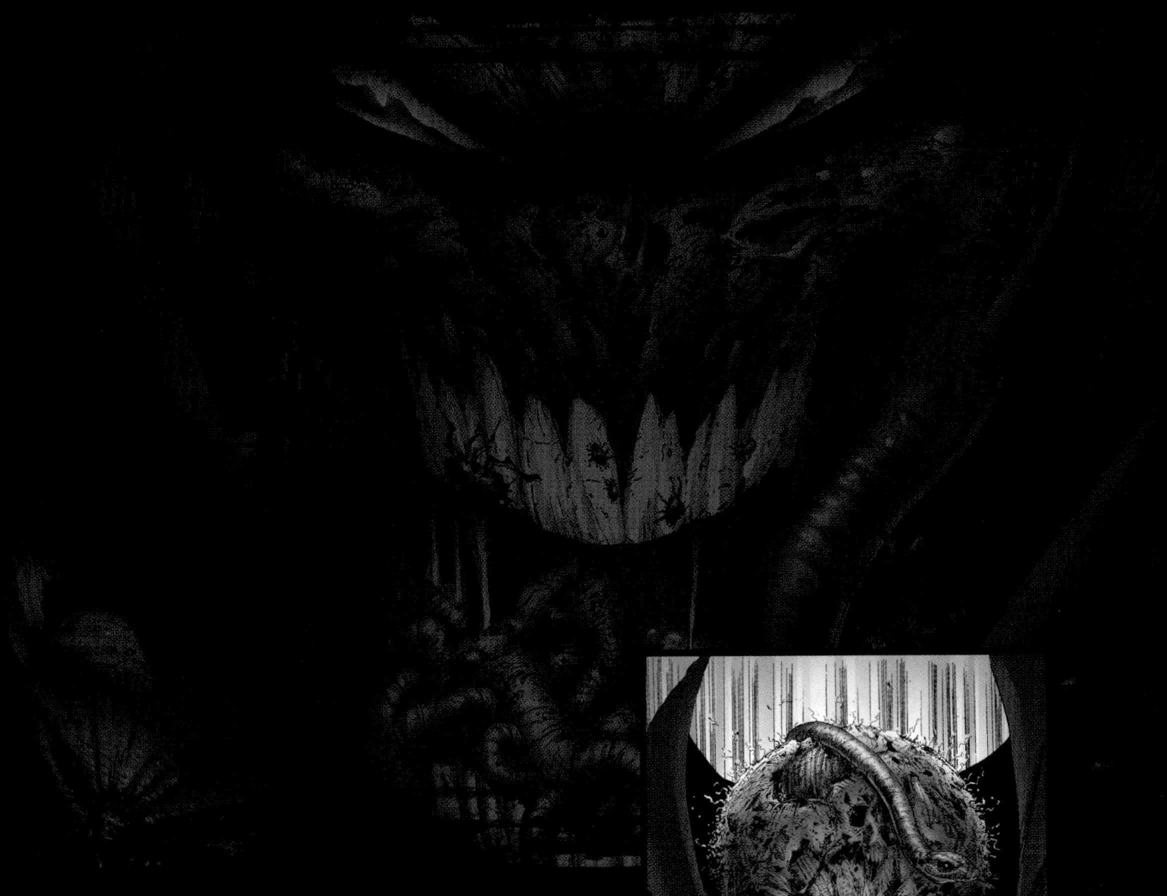

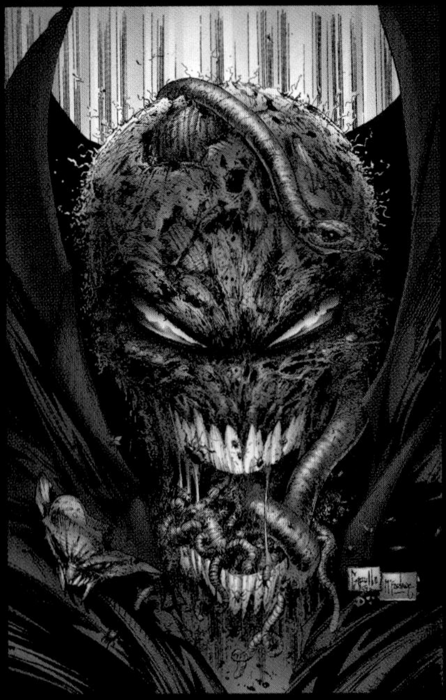

I S S U E EIGHTY-NINE

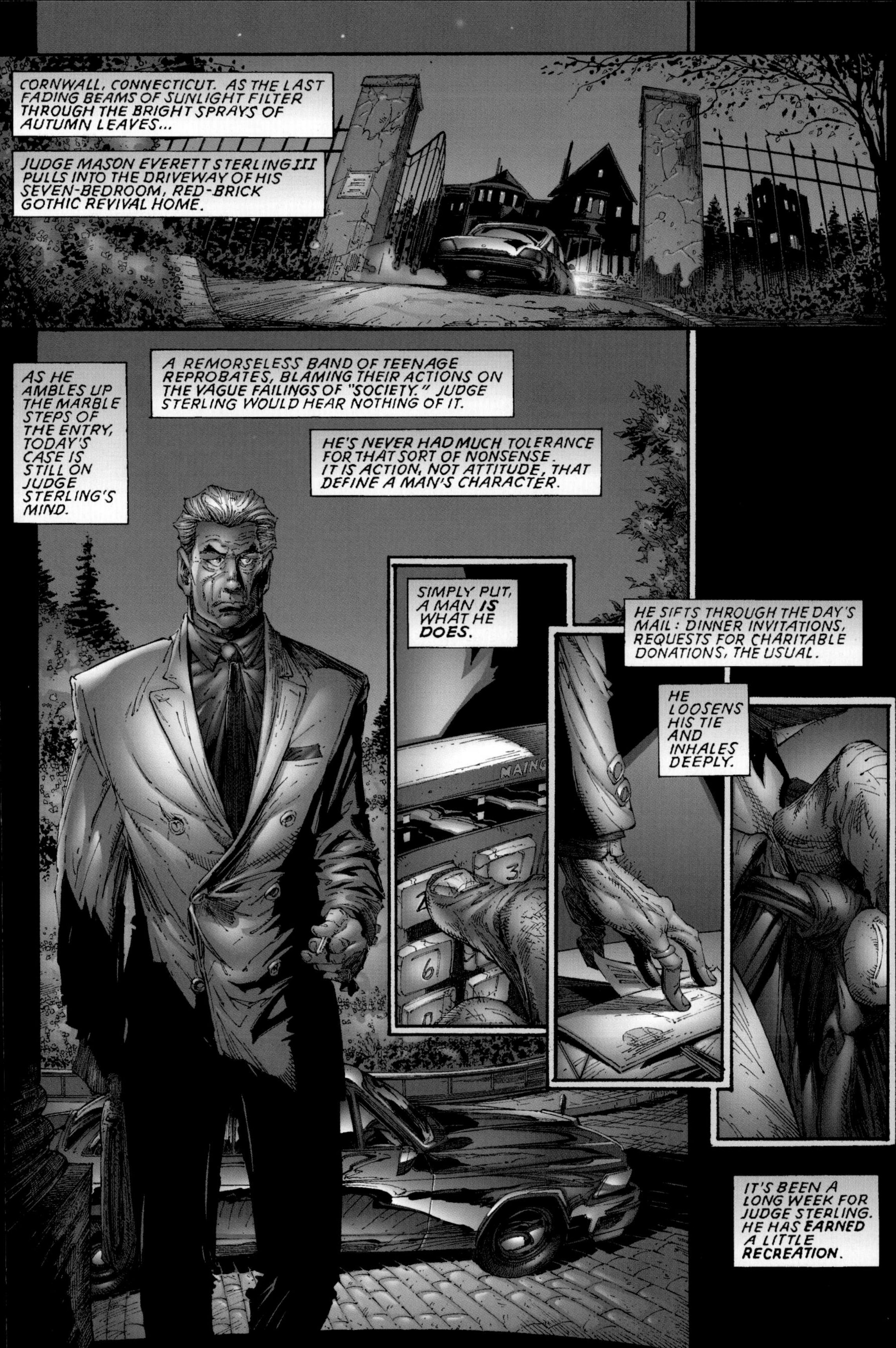
CORNWALL, CONNECTICUT. AS THE LAST FADING BEAMS OF SUNLIGHT FILTER THROUGH THE BRIGHT SPRAYS OF AUTUMN LEAVES...
JUDGE MASON EVERETT STERLING III PULLS INTO THE DRIVEWAY OF HIS SEVEN-BEDROOM, RED-BRICK GOTHIC REVIVAL HOME.
AS HE AMBLES UP THE MARBLE STEPS OF THE ENTRY, TODAY'S CASE IS STILL ON JUDGE STERLING'S MIND.
A REMORSELESS BAND OF TEENAGE REPROBATES, BLAMING THEIR ACTIONS ON THE VAGUE FAILINGS OF "SOCIETY." JUDGE STERLING WOULD HEAR NOTHING OF IT.
HE'S NEVER HAD MUCH TOLERANCE FOR THAT SORT OF NONSENSE. IT IS ACTION, NOT ATTITUDE, THAT DEFINE A MAN'S CHARACTER.
SIMPLY PUT, A MAN IS WHAT HE DOES.
MAIN
HE SIFTS THROUGH THE DAY'S MAIL: DINNER INVITATIONS, REQUESTS FOR CHARITABLE DONATIONS, THE USUAL.
HE LOOSENS HIS TIE AND INHALES DEEPLY.
IT'S BEEN A LONG WEEK FOR JUDGE STERLING. HE HAS EARNED A LITTLE RECREATION.

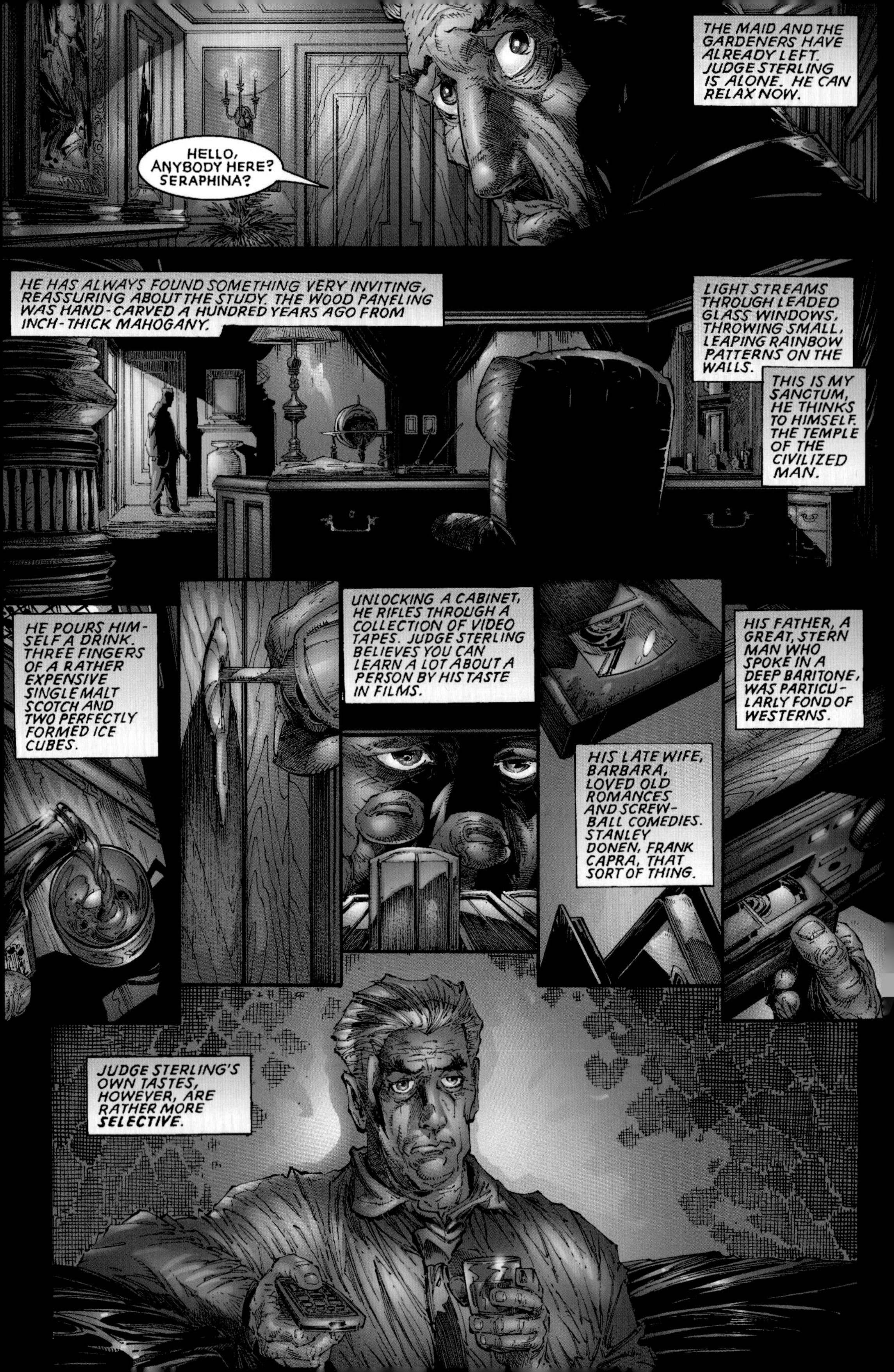
THE MAID AND THE GARDENERS HAVE ALREADY LEFT. JUDGE STERLING IS ALONE. HE CAN RELAX NOW.
HELLO, ANYBODY HERE? SERAPHINA?
HE HAS ALWAYS FOUND SOMETHING VERY INVITING, REASSURING ABOUT THE STUDY. THE WOOD PANELING WAS HAND-CARVED A HUNDRED YEARS AGO FROM INCH-THICK MAHOGANY.
LIGHT STREAMS THROUGH LEADED GLASS WINDOWS, THROWING SMALL, LEAPING RAINBOW PATTERNS ON THE WALLS.
THIS IS MY SANCTUM, HE THINKS TO HIMSELF. THE TEMPLE OF THE CIVILIZED MAN.
HE POURS HIMSELF A DRINK. THREE FINGERS OF A RATHER EXPENSIVE SINGLE MALT SCOTCH AND TWO PERFECTLY FORMED ICE CUBES.
UNLOCKING A CABINET, HE RIFLES THROUGH A COLLECTION OF VIDEO TAPES. JUDGE STERLING BELIEVES YOU CAN LEARN A LOT ABOUT A PERSON BY HIS TASTE IN FILMS.
HIS FATHER, A GREAT, STERN MAN WHO SPOKE IN A DEEP BARITONE, WAS PARTICULARLY FOND OF WESTERNS.
HIS LATE WIFE, BARBARA, LOVED OLD ROMANCES AND SCREWBALL COMEDIES. STANLEY DONEN, FRANK CAPRA, THAT SORT OF THING.
JUDGE STERLING'S OWN TASTES, HOWEVER, ARE RATHER MORE SELECTIVE.

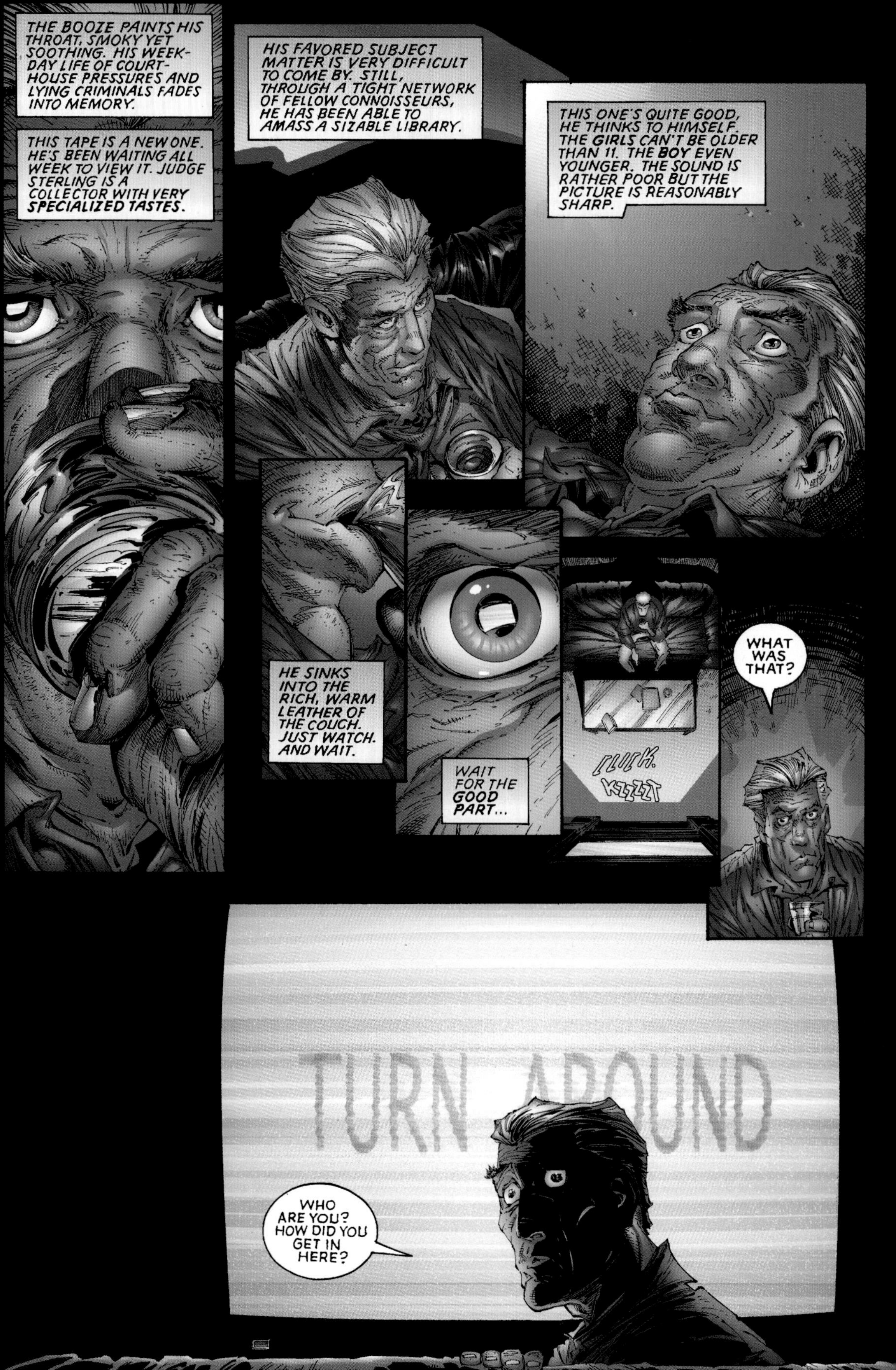
THE BOOZE PAINTS HIS THROAT, SMOKY YET SOOTHING. HIS WEEK-DAY LIFE OF COURT-HOUSE PRESSURES AND LYING CRIMINALS FADES INTO MEMORY.
THIS TAPE IS A NEW ONE. HE'S BEEN WAITING ALL WEEK TO VIEW IT. JUDGE STERLING IS A COLLECTOR WITH VERY SPECIALIZED TASTES.
HIS FAVORED SUBJECT MATTER IS VERY DIFFICULT TO COME BY. STILL, THROUGH A TIGHT NETWORK OF FELLOW CONNOISSEURS, HE HAS BEEN ABLE TO AMASS A SIZABLE LIBRARY.
THIS ONE'S QUITE GOOD, HE THINKS TO HIMSELF. THE GIRLS CAN'T BE OLDER THAN 11. THE BOY EVEN YOUNGER. THE SOUND IS RATHER POOR BUT THE PICTURE IS REASONABLY SHARP.
HE SINKS INTO THE RICH, WARM LEATHER OF THE COUCH. JUST WATCH. AND WAIT.
WAIT FOR THE GOOD PART...
CLICK.
KZZZZT
WHAT WAS THAT?
TURN AROUND
WHO ARE YOU? HOW DID YOU GET IN HERE?

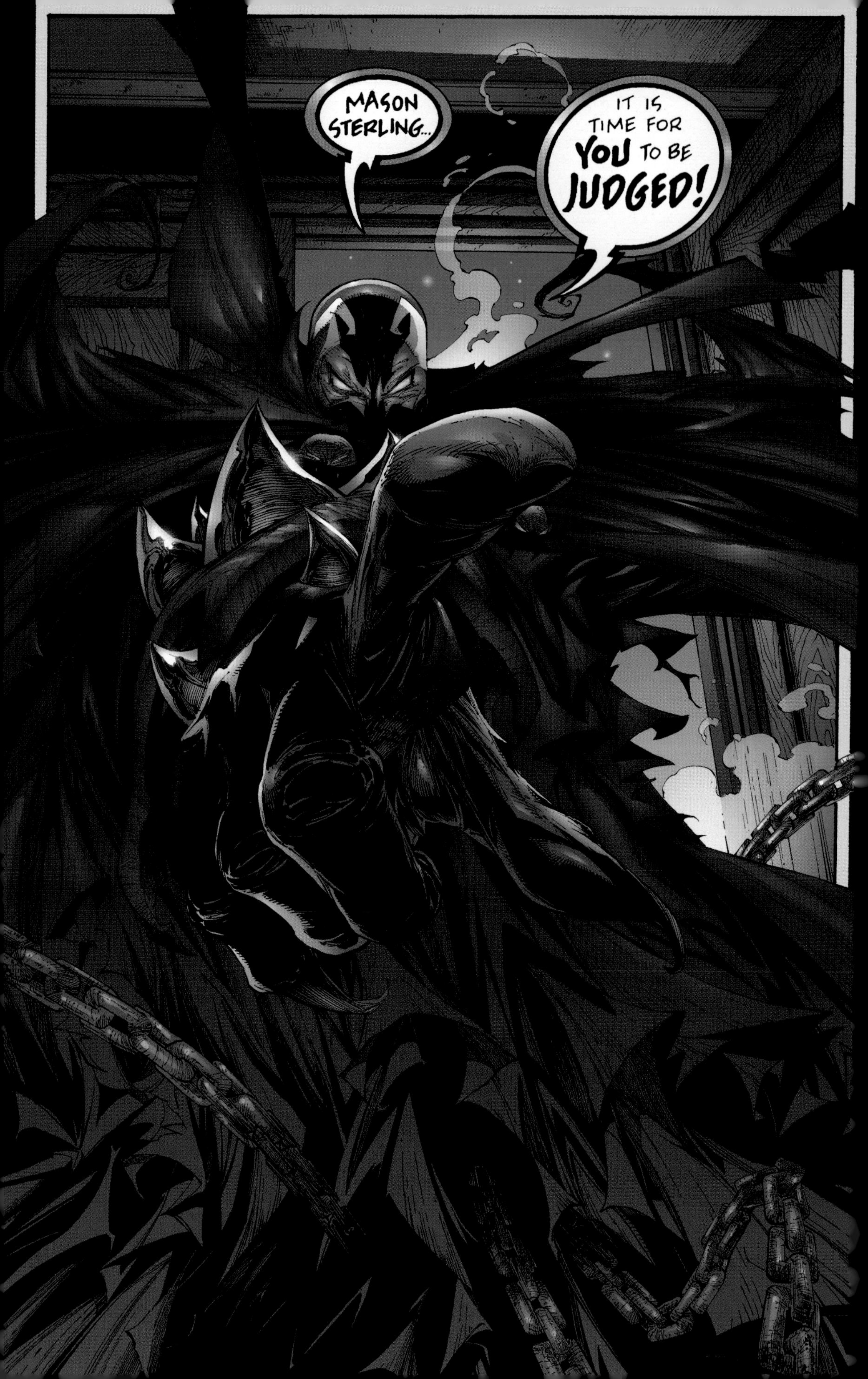
MASON STERLING...
IT IS TIME FOR YOU TO BE JUDGED!

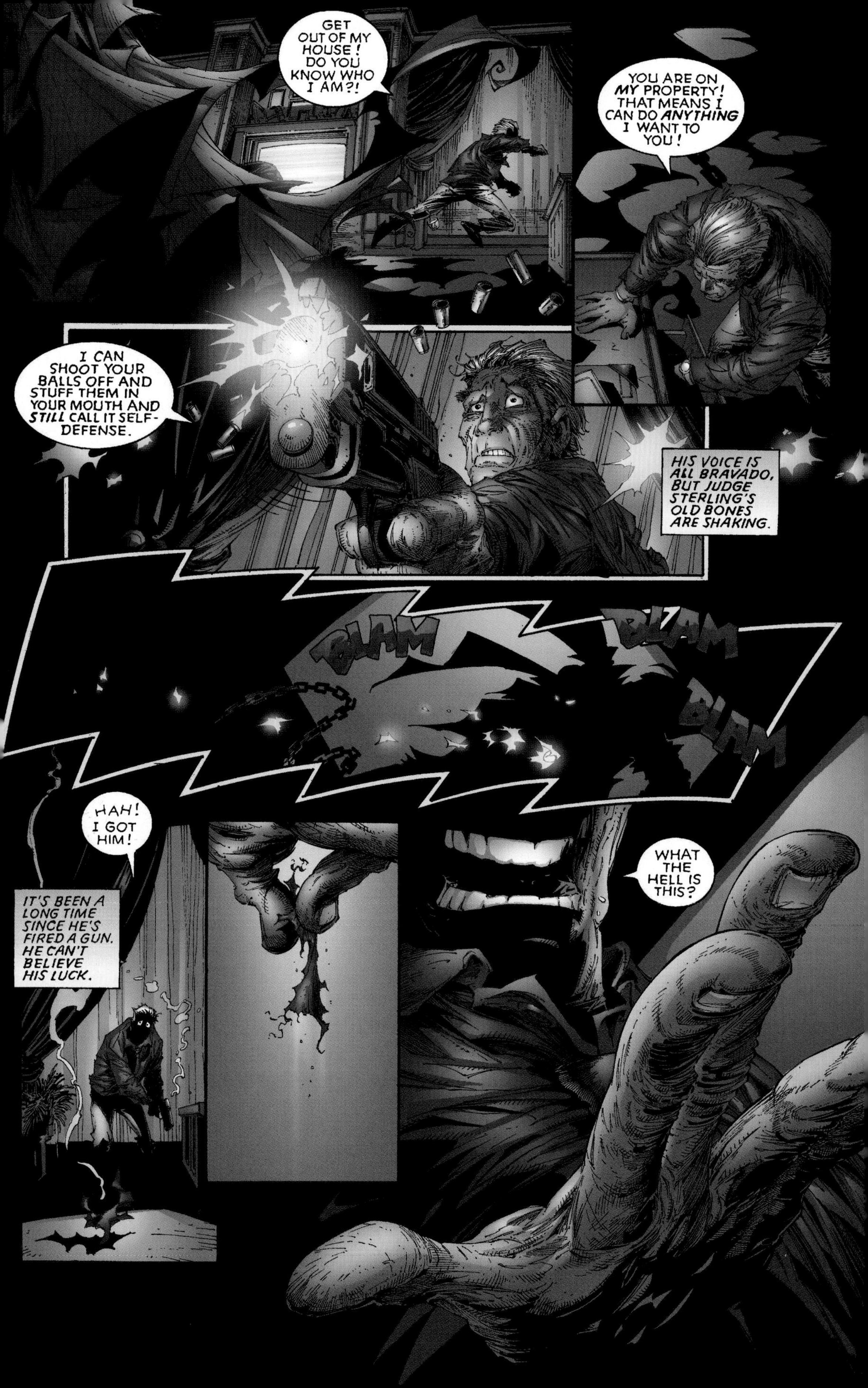
GET OUT OF MY HOUSE! DO YOU KNOW WHO I AM?!
YOU ARE ON MY PROPERTY! THAT MEANS I CAN DO ANYTHING I WANT TO YOU!
I CAN SHOOT YOUR BALLS OFF AND STUFF THEM IN YOUR MOUTH AND STILL CALL IT SELF-DEFENSE.
HIS VOICE IS ALL BRAVADO, BUT JUDGE STERLING'S OLD BONES ARE SHAKING.
BLAM
BLAM
BLAM
HAH! I GOT HIM!
IT'S BEEN A LONG TIME SINCE HE'S FIRED A GUN. HE CAN'T BELIEVE HIS LUCK.
WHAT THE HELL IS THIS?

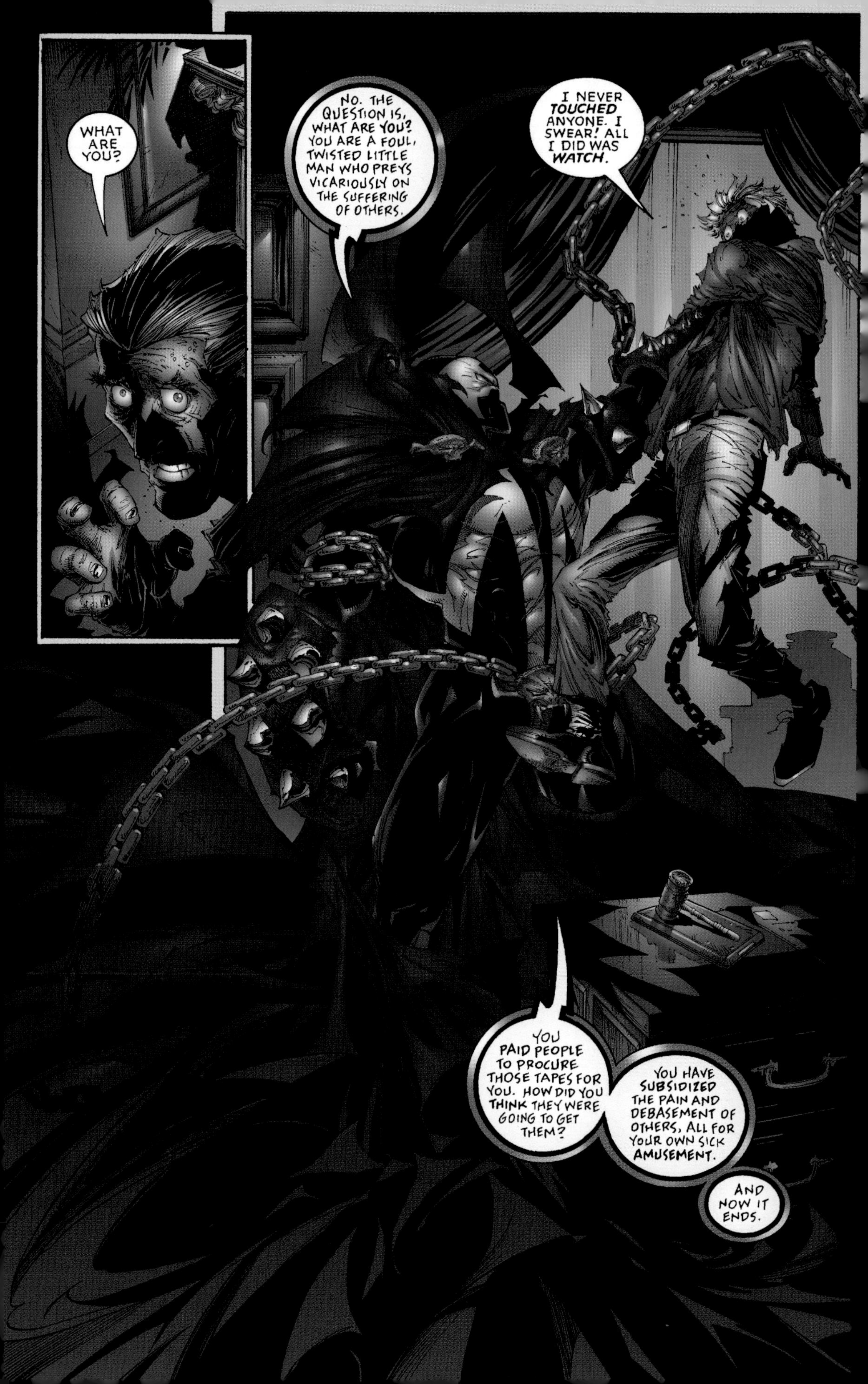
WHAT ARE YOU?
NO. THE QUESTION IS, WHAT ARE YOU? YOU ARE A FOUL, TWISTED LITTLE MAN WHO PREYS VICARIOUSLY ON THE SUFFERING OF OTHERS.
I NEVER TOUCHED ANYONE. I SWEAR! ALL I DID WAS WATCH.
YOU PAID PEOPLE TO PROCURE THOSE TAPES FOR YOU. HOW DID YOU THINK THEY WERE GOING TO GET THEM?
YOU HAVE SUBSIDIZED THE PAIN AND DEBASEMENT OF OTHERS, ALL FOR YOUR OWN SICK AMUSEMENT.
AND NOW IT ENDS.

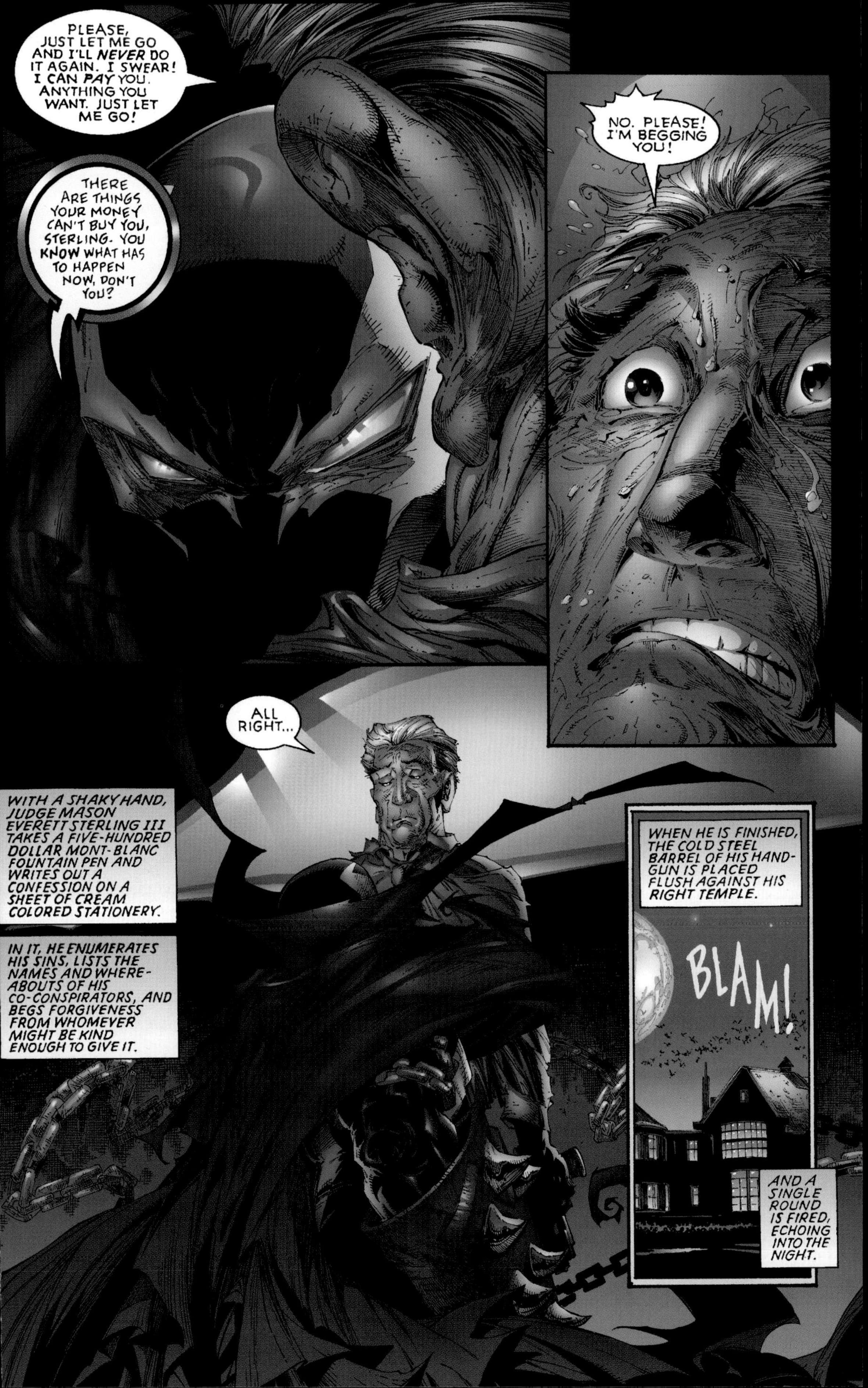
PLEASE, JUST LET ME GO AND I'LL NEVER DO IT AGAIN. I SWEAR! I CAN PAY YOU. ANYTHING YOU WANT. JUST LET ME GO!
THERE ARE THINGS YOUR MONEY CAN'T BUY YOU, STERLING. YOU KNOW WHAT HAS TO HAPPEN NOW, DON'T YOU?
NO. PLEASE! I'M BEGGING YOU!
ALL RIGHT...
WITH A SHAKY HAND, JUDGE MASON EVERETT STERLING III TAKES A FIVE-HUNDRED DOLLAR MONT-BLANC FOUNTAIN PEN AND WRITES OUT A CONFESSION ON A SHEET OF CREAM COLORED STATIONERY.
IN IT, HE ENUMERATES HIS SINS, LISTS THE NAMES AND WHERE-ABOUTS OF HIS CO-CONSPIRATORS, AND BEGS FORGIVENESS FROM WHOMEVER MIGHT BE KIND ENOUGH TO GIVE IT.
WHEN HE IS FINISHED, THE COLD STEEL BARREL OF HIS HAND-GUN IS PLACED FLUSH AGAINST HIS RIGHT TEMPLE.
BLAM!
AND A SINGLE ROUND IS FIRED, ECHOING INTO THE NIGHT.

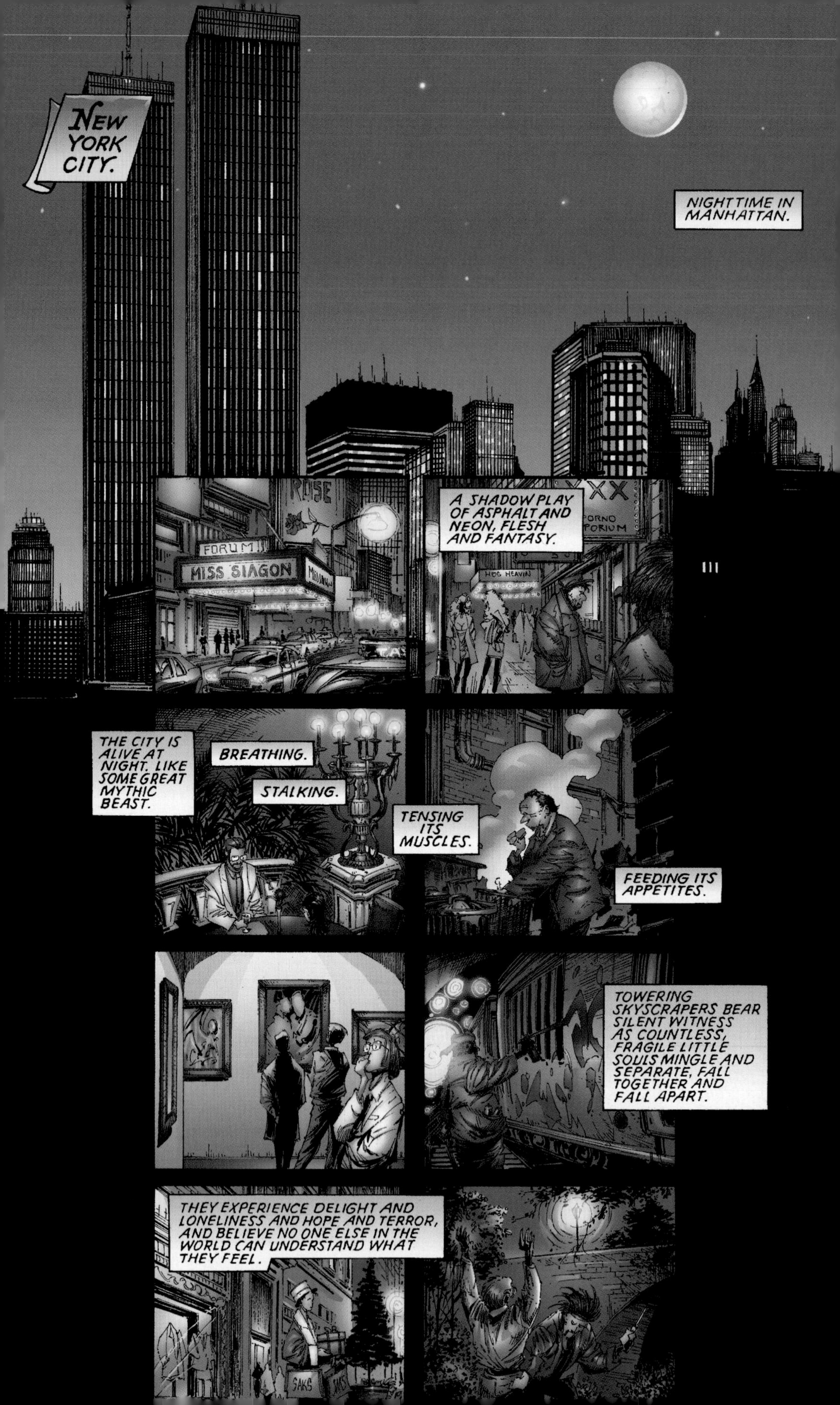

NEW YORK CITY.
NIGHTTIME IN MANHATTAN.
FORUM
MISS SIAGON
A SHADOW PLAY OF ASPHALT AND NEON, FLESH AND FANTASY.
XXX
PORNO
HOG HEAVIN
THE CITY IS ALIVE AT NIGHT, LIKE SOME GREAT MYTHIC BEAST.
BREATHING.
STALKING.
TENSING ITS MUSCLES.
FEEDING ITS APPETITES.
TOWERING SKYSCRAPERS BEAR SILENT WITNESS AS COUNTLESS, FRAGILE LITTLE SOULS MINGLE AND SEPARATE, FALL TOGETHER AND FALL APART.
THEY EXPERIENCE DELIGHT AND LONELINESS AND HOPE AND TERROR, AND BELIEVE NO ONE ELSE IN THE WORLD CAN UNDERSTAND WHAT THEY FEEL.
SAKS

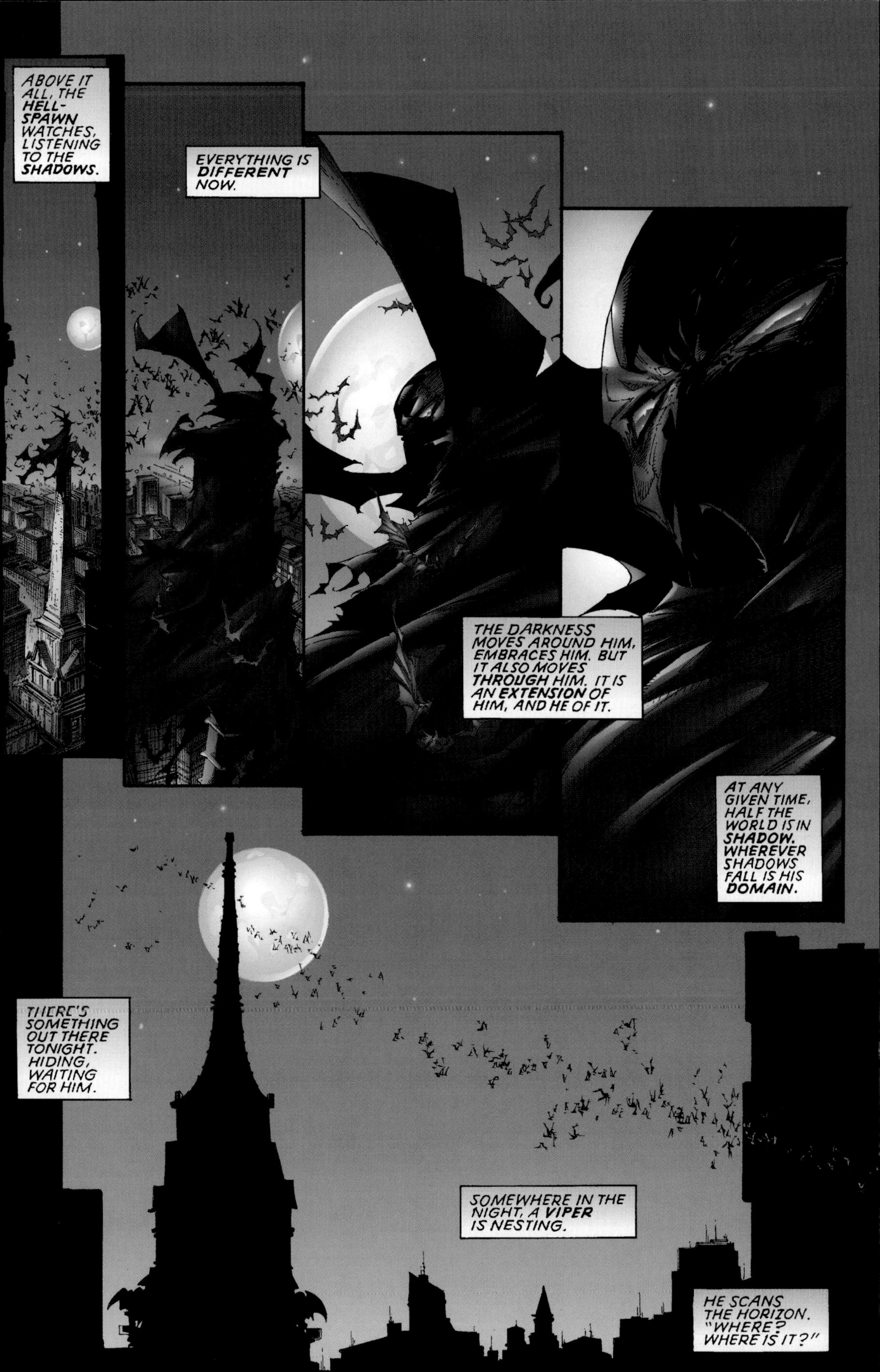
ABOVE IT ALL, THE HELL-SPAWN WATCHES, LISTENING TO THE SHADOWS.
EVERYTHING IS DIFFERENT NOW.
THE DARKNESS MOVES AROUND HIM, EMBRACES HIM. BUT IT ALSO MOVES THROUGH HIM. IT IS AN EXTENSION OF HIM, AND HE OF IT.
AT ANY GIVEN TIME, HALF THE WORLD IS IN SHADOW. WHEREVER SHADOWS FALL IS HIS DOMAIN.
THERE'S SOMETHING OUT THERE TONIGHT. HIDING, WAITING FOR HIM.
SOMEWHERE IN THE NIGHT, A VIPER IS NESTING.
HE SCANS THE HORIZON. "WHERE? WHERE IS IT?"

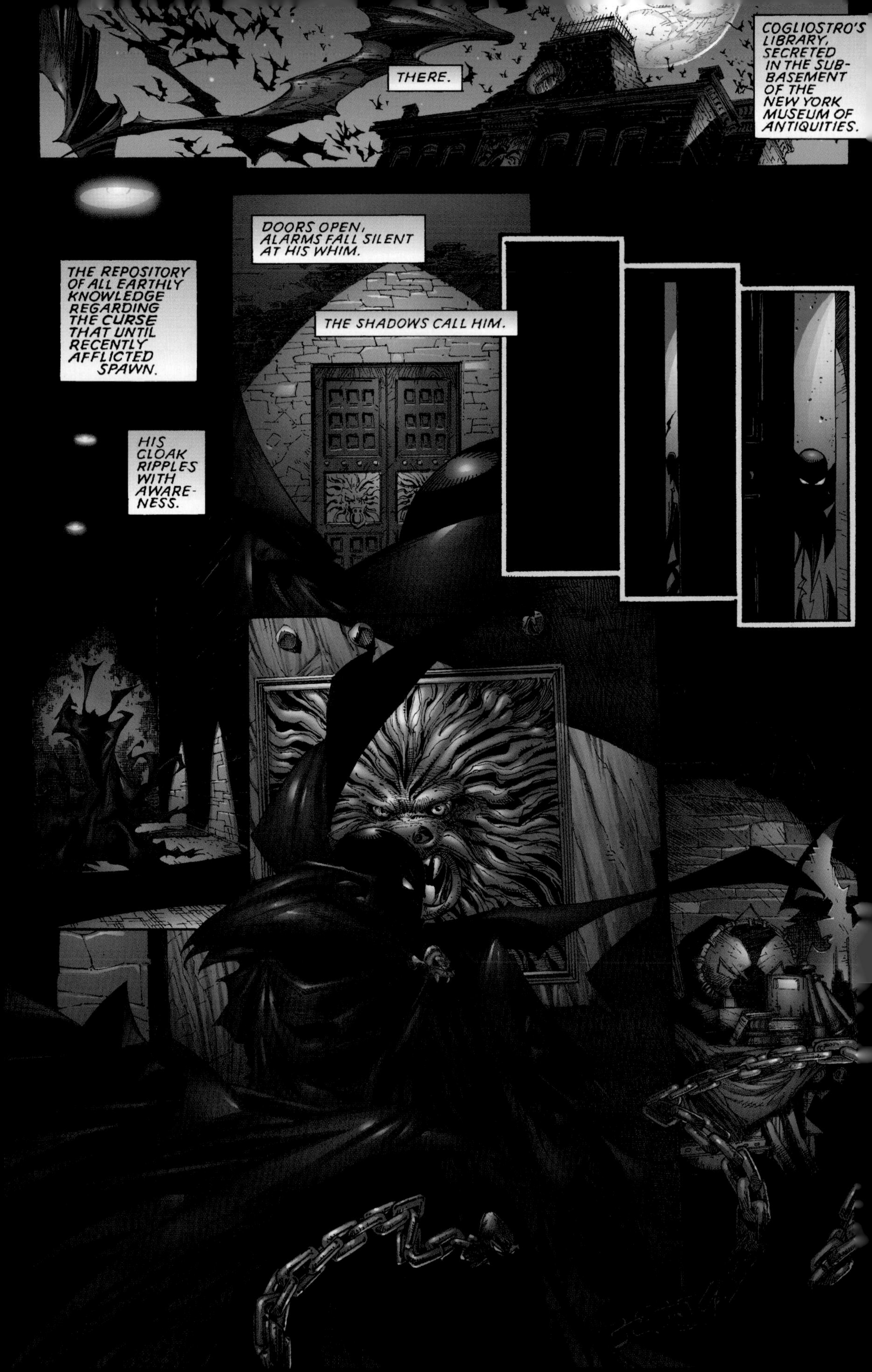
THERE.
COGLIOSTRO'S LIBRARY, SECRETED IN THE SUB-BASEMENT OF THE NEW YORK MUSEUM OF ANTIQUITIES.
DOORS OPEN, ALARMS FALL SILENT AT HIS WHIM.
THE REPOSITORY OF ALL EARTHLY KNOWLEDGE REGARDING THE CURSE THAT UNTIL RECENTLY AFFLICTED SPAWN.
THE SHADOWS CALL HIM.
HIS CLOAK RIPPLES WITH AWARENESS.

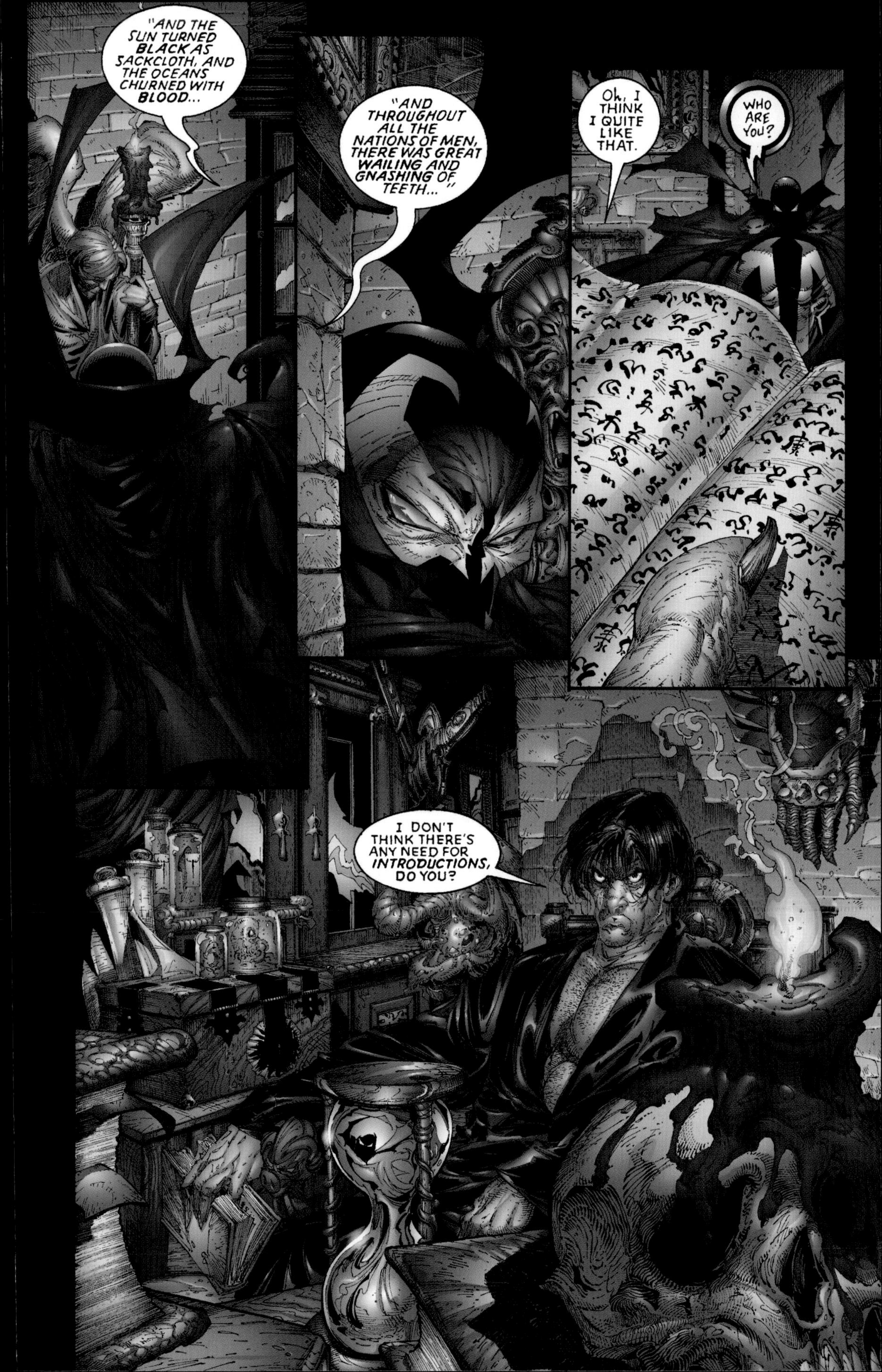
"AND THE SUN TURNED BLACK AS SACKCLOTH, AND THE OCEANS CHURNED WITH BLOOD...
"AND THROUGHOUT ALL THE NATIONS OF MEN, THERE WAS GREAT WAILING AND GNASHING OF TEETH..."
Oh, I THINK I QUITE LIKE THAT.
WHO ARE YOU?
I DON'T THINK THERE'S ANY NEED FOR INTRODUCTIONS, DO YOU?

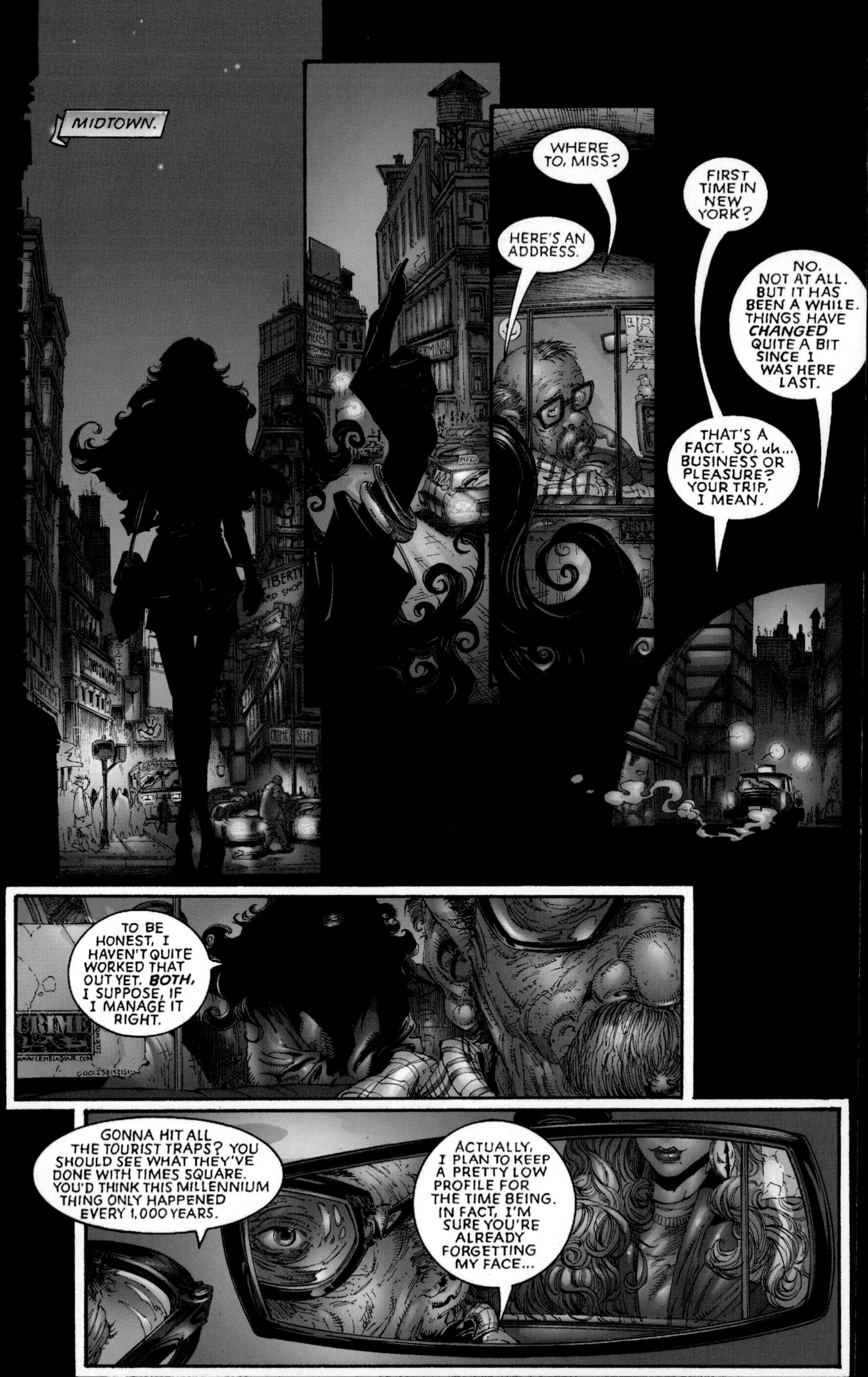
MIDTOWN.
WHERE TO, MISS?
HERE'S AN ADDRESS.
FIRST TIME IN NEW YORK?
NO. NOT AT ALL. BUT IT HAS BEEN A WHILE. THINGS HAVE *CHANGED* QUITE A BIT SINCE I WAS HERE LAST.
THAT'S A FACT. SO, uh... BUSINESS OR PLEASURE? YOUR TRIP, I MEAN.
TO BE HONEST, I HAVEN'T QUITE WORKED THAT OUT YET. *BOTH,* I SUPPOSE, IF I MANAGE IT RIGHT.
GONNA HIT ALL THE TOURIST TRAPS? YOU SHOULD SEE WHAT THEY'VE DONE WITH TIMES SQUARE. YOU'D THINK THIS MILLENNIUM THING ONLY HAPPENED EVERY 1,000 YEARS.
ACTUALLY, I PLAN TO KEEP A PRETTY LOW PROFILE FOR THE TIME BEING. IN FACT, I'M SURE YOU'RE ALREADY FORGETTING MY FACE...

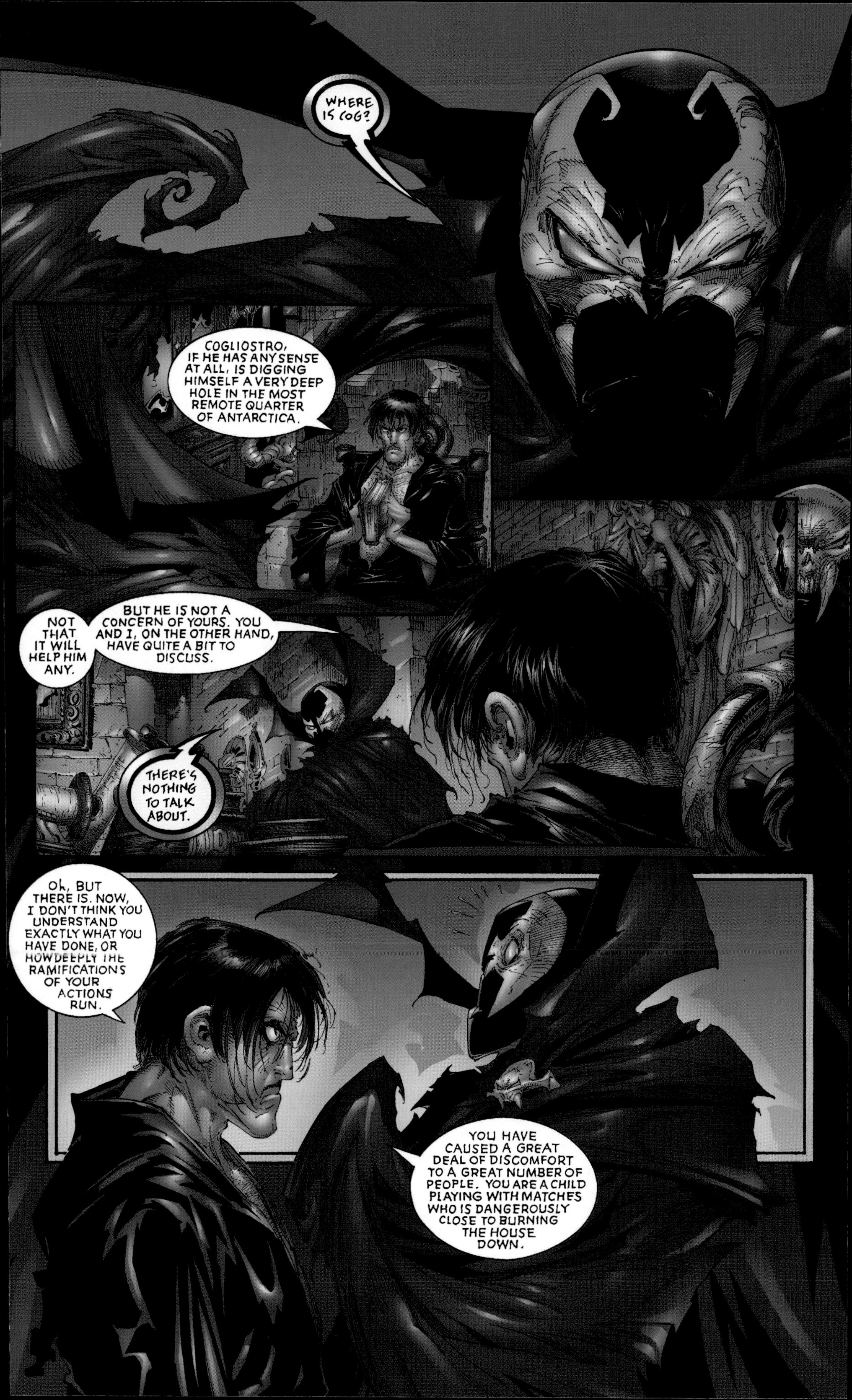
WHERE IS COG?
COGLIOSTRO, IF HE HAS ANY SENSE AT ALL, IS DIGGING HIMSELF A VERY DEEP HOLE IN THE MOST REMOTE QUARTER OF ANTARCTICA.
NOT THAT IT WILL HELP HIM ANY.
BUT HE IS NOT A CONCERN OF YOURS. YOU AND I, ON THE OTHER HAND, HAVE QUITE A BIT TO DISCUSS.
THERE'S NOTHING TO TALK ABOUT.
Oh, BUT THERE IS. NOW, I DON'T THINK YOU UNDERSTAND EXACTLY WHAT YOU HAVE DONE, OR HOW DEEPLY THE RAMIFICATIONS OF YOUR ACTIONS RUN.
YOU HAVE CAUSED A GREAT DEAL OF DISCOMFORT TO A GREAT NUMBER OF PEOPLE. YOU ARE A CHILD PLAYING WITH MATCHES WHO IS DANGEROUSLY CLOSE TO BURNING THE HOUSE DOWN.

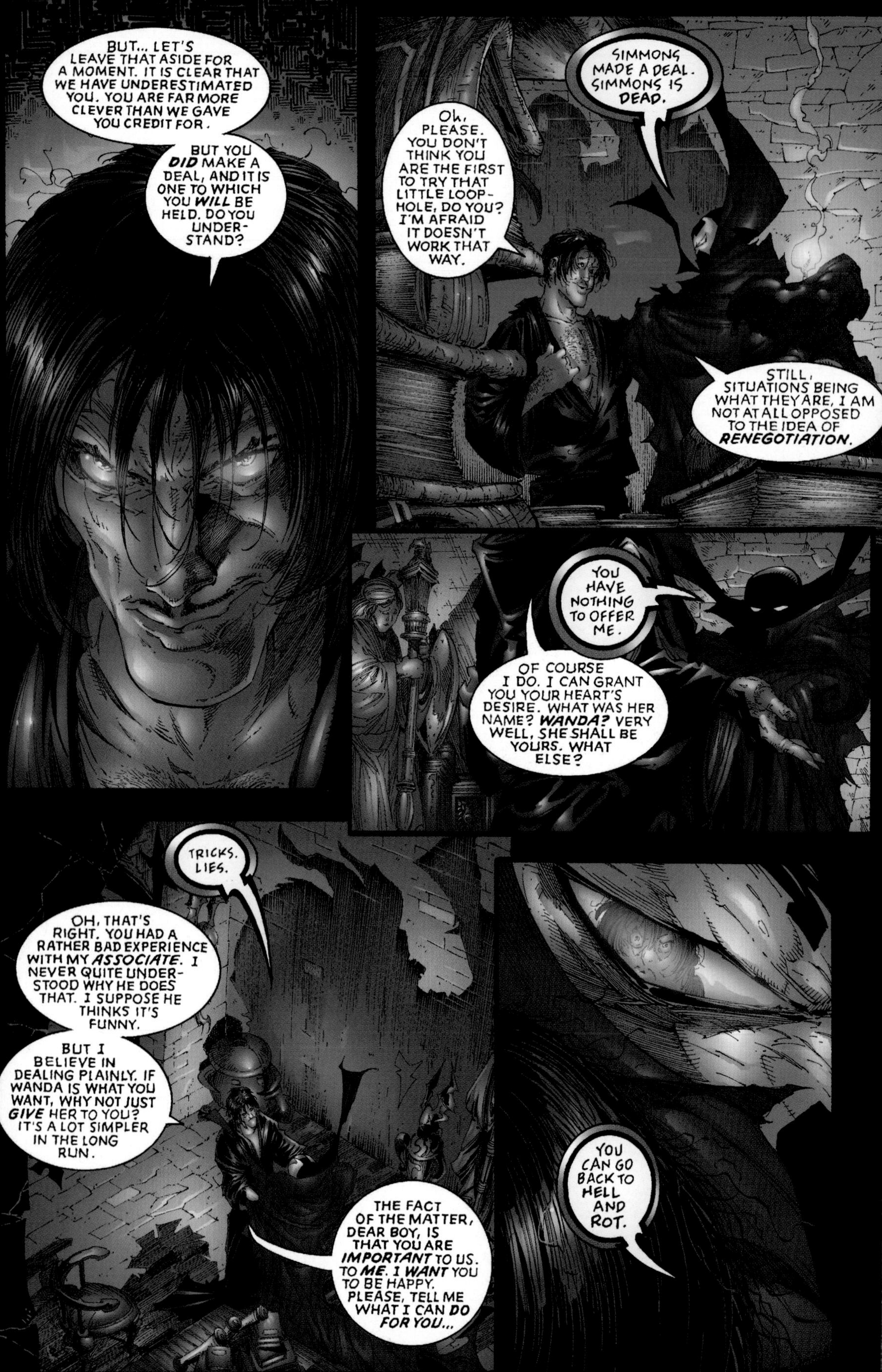
BUT... LET'S LEAVE THAT ASIDE FOR A MOMENT. IT IS CLEAR THAT WE HAVE UNDERESTIMATED YOU. YOU ARE FAR MORE CLEVER THAN WE GAVE YOU CREDIT FOR.
BUT YOU DID MAKE A DEAL, AND IT IS ONE TO WHICH YOU WILL BE HELD. DO YOU UNDERSTAND?
SIMMONS MADE A DEAL. SIMMONS IS DEAD.
OH, PLEASE. YOU DON'T THINK YOU ARE THE FIRST TO TRY THAT LITTLE LOOPHOLE, DO YOU? I'M AFRAID IT DOESN'T WORK THAT WAY.
STILL, SITUATIONS BEING WHAT THEY ARE, I AM NOT AT ALL OPPOSED TO THE IDEA OF RENEGOTIATION.
YOU HAVE NOTHING TO OFFER ME.
OF COURSE I DO. I CAN GRANT YOU YOUR HEART'S DESIRE. WHAT WAS HER NAME? WANDA? VERY WELL, SHE SHALL BE YOURS. WHAT ELSE?
TRICKS. LIES.
OH, THAT'S RIGHT. YOU HAD A RATHER BAD EXPERIENCE WITH MY ASSOCIATE. I NEVER QUITE UNDERSTOOD WHY HE DOES THAT. I SUPPOSE HE THINKS IT'S FUNNY.
BUT I BELIEVE IN DEALING PLAINLY. IF WANDA IS WHAT YOU WANT, WHY NOT JUST GIVE HER TO YOU? IT'S A LOT SIMPLER IN THE LONG RUN.
THE FACT OF THE MATTER, DEAR BOY, IS THAT YOU ARE IMPORTANT TO US. TO ME. I WANT YOU TO BE HAPPY. PLEASE, TELL ME WHAT I CAN DO FOR YOU...
YOU CAN GO BACK TO HELL AND ROT.

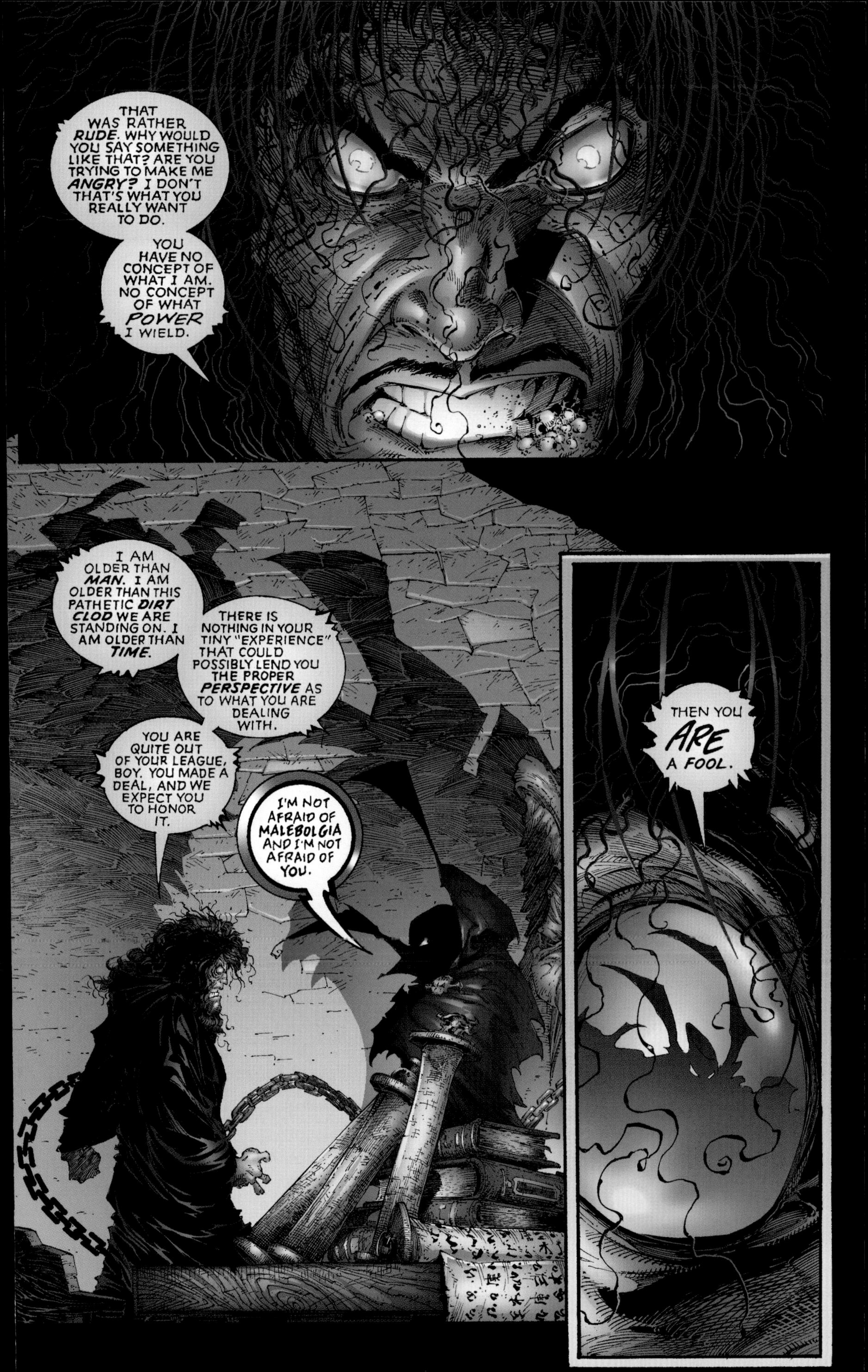
THAT WAS RATHER RUDE. WHY WOULD YOU SAY SOMETHING LIKE THAT? ARE YOU TRYING TO MAKE ME ANGRY? I DON'T THAT'S WHAT YOU REALLY WANT TO DO.
YOU HAVE NO CONCEPT OF WHAT I AM. NO CONCEPT OF WHAT POWER I WIELD.
I AM OLDER THAN MAN. I AM OLDER THAN THIS PATHETIC DIRT CLOD WE ARE STANDING ON. I AM OLDER THAN TIME.
THERE IS NOTHING IN YOUR TINY "EXPERIENCE" THAT COULD POSSIBLY LEND YOU THE PROPER PERSPECTIVE AS TO WHAT YOU ARE DEALING WITH.
YOU ARE QUITE OUT OF YOUR LEAGUE, BOY. YOU MADE A DEAL, AND WE EXPECT YOU TO HONOR IT.
I'M NOT AFRAID OF MALEBOLGIA AND I'M NOT AFRAID OF YOU.
THEN YOU ARE A FOOL.

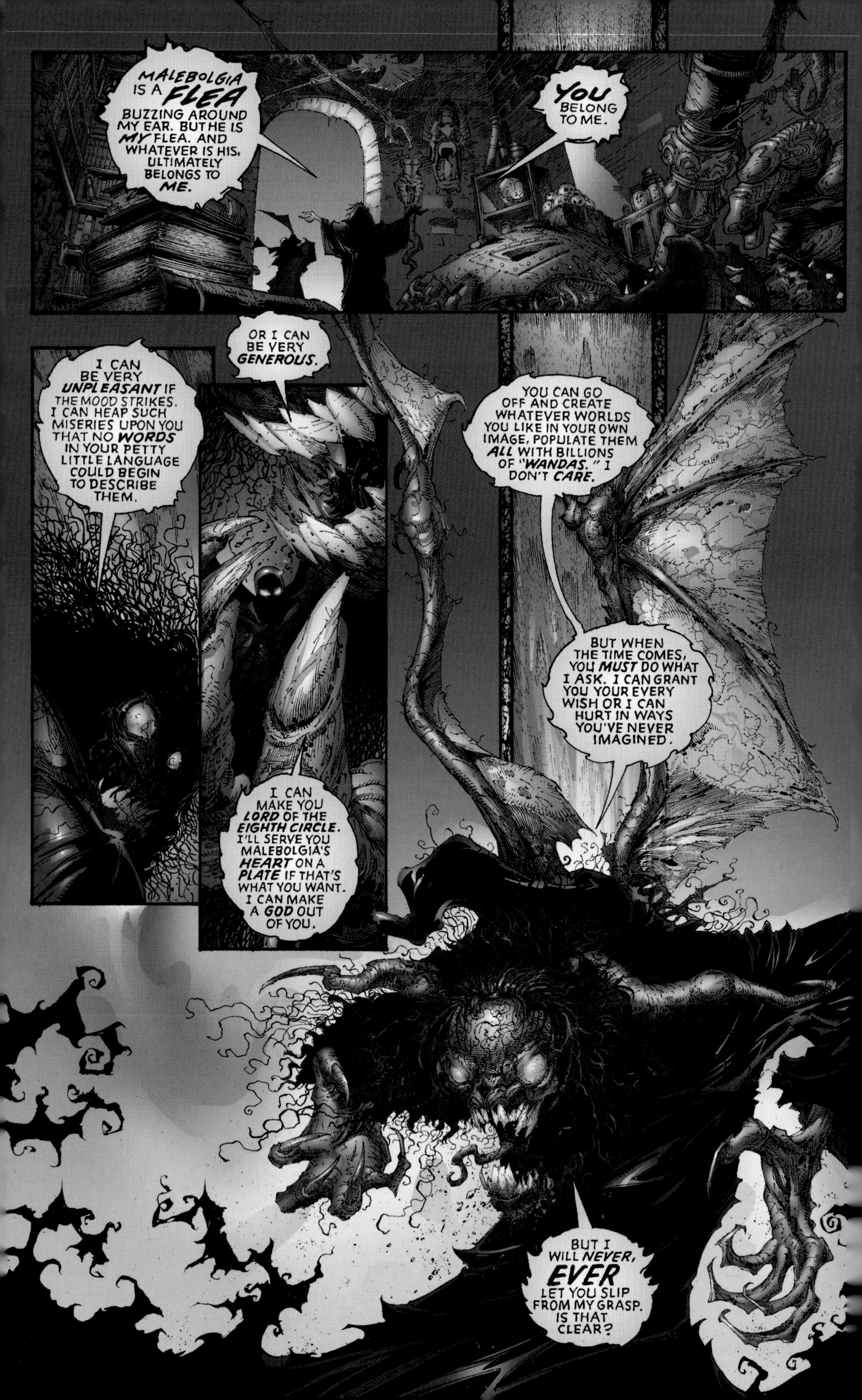

MALEBOLGIA IS A FLEA BUZZING AROUND MY EAR. BUT HE IS MY FLEA. AND WHATEVER IS HIS, ULTIMATELY BELONGS TO ME.
YOU BELONG TO ME.
I CAN BE VERY UNPLEASANT IF THE MOOD STRIKES. I CAN HEAP SUCH MISERIES UPON YOU THAT NO WORDS IN YOUR PETTY LITTLE LANGUAGE COULD BEGIN TO DESCRIBE THEM.
OR I CAN BE VERY GENEROUS.
I CAN MAKE YOU LORD OF THE EIGHTH CIRCLE. I'LL SERVE YOU MALEBOLGIA'S HEART ON A PLATE IF THAT'S WHAT YOU WANT. I CAN MAKE A GOD OUT OF YOU.
YOU CAN GO OFF AND CREATE WHATEVER WORLDS YOU LIKE IN YOUR OWN IMAGE, POPULATE THEM ALL WITH BILLIONS OF "WANDAS." I DON'T CARE.
BUT WHEN THE TIME COMES, YOU MUST DO WHAT I ASK. I CAN GRANT YOU YOUR EVERY WISH OR I CAN HURT IN WAYS YOU'VE NEVER IMAGINED.
BUT I WILL NEVER, EVER LET YOU SLIP FROM MY GRASP. IS THAT CLEAR?

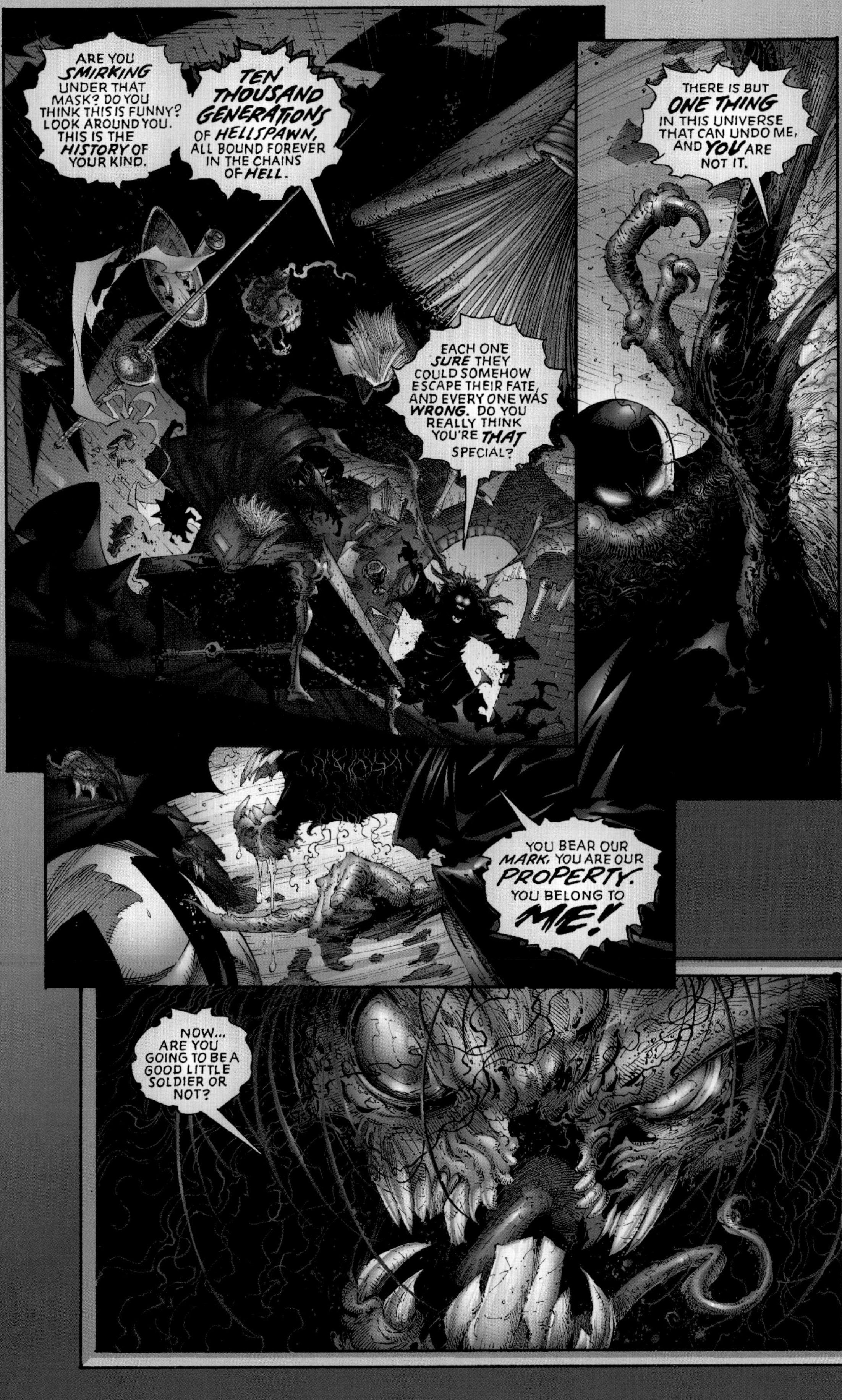

ARE YOU SMIRKING UNDER THAT MASK? DO YOU THINK THIS IS FUNNY? LOOK AROUND YOU. THIS IS THE HISTORY OF YOUR KIND.
TEN THOUSAND GENERATIONS OF HELLSPAWN, ALL BOUND FOREVER IN THE CHAINS OF HELL.
EACH ONE SURE THEY COULD SOMEHOW ESCAPE THEIR FATE, AND EVERY ONE WAS WRONG. DO YOU REALLY THINK YOU'RE THAT SPECIAL?
THERE IS BUT ONE THING IN THIS UNIVERSE THAT CAN UNDO ME, AND YOU ARE NOT IT.
YOU BEAR OUR MARK, YOU ARE OUR PROPERTY. YOU BELONG TO ME!
NOW... ARE YOU GOING TO BE A GOOD LITTLE SOLDIER OR NOT?

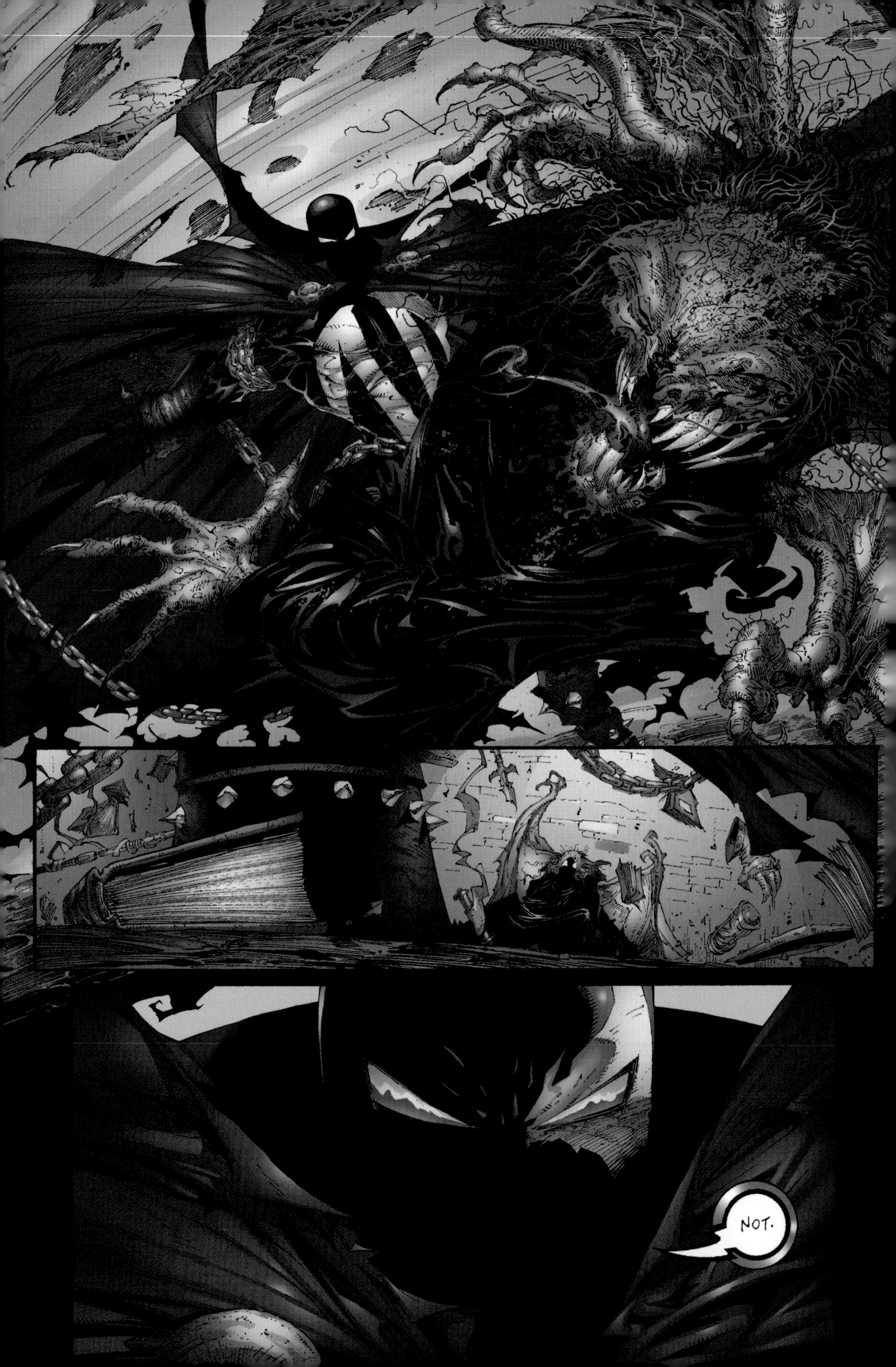
NOT.

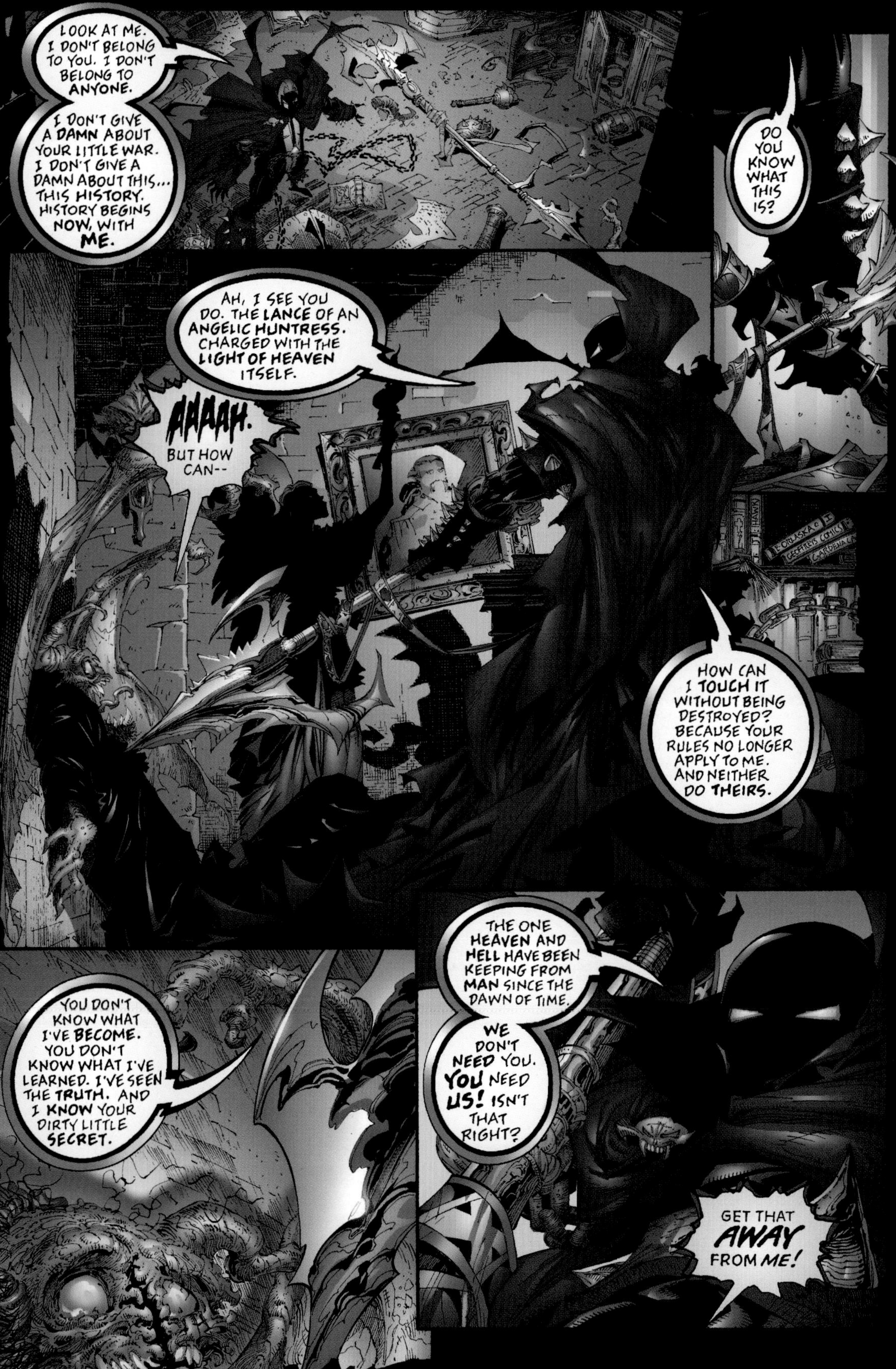

LOOK AT ME. I DON'T BELONG TO YOU. I DON'T BELONG TO ANYONE.
I DON'T GIVE A DAMN ABOUT YOUR LITTLE WAR. I DON'T GIVE A DAMN ABOUT THIS... THIS HISTORY. HISTORY BEGINS NOW, WITH ME.
DO YOU KNOW WHAT THIS IS?
AH, I SEE YOU DO. THE LANCE OF AN ANGELIC HUNTRESS. CHARGED WITH THE LIGHT OF HEAVEN ITSELF.
AAAAH.
BUT HOW CAN--
HOW CAN I TOUCH IT WITHOUT BEING DESTROYED? BECAUSE YOUR RULES NO LONGER APPLY TO ME. AND NEITHER DO THEIRS.
YOU DON'T KNOW WHAT I'VE BECOME. YOU DON'T KNOW WHAT I'VE LEARNED. I'VE SEEN THE TRUTH. AND I KNOW YOUR DIRTY LITTLE SECRET.
THE ONE HEAVEN AND HELL HAVE BEEN KEEPING FROM MAN SINCE THE DAWN OF TIME.
WE DON'T NEED YOU. YOU NEED US! ISN'T THAT RIGHT?
GET THAT AWAY FROM ME!

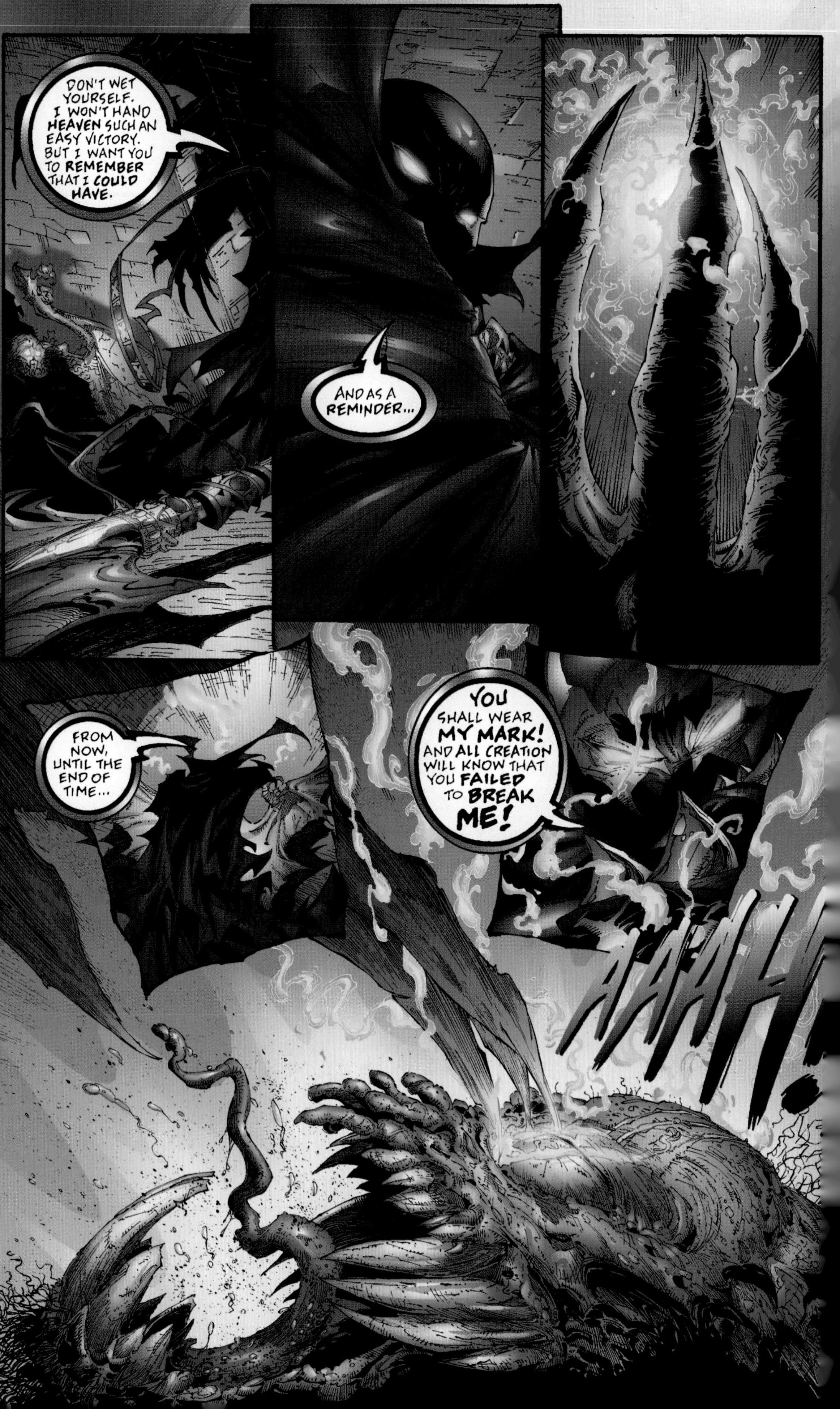
DON'T WET YOURSELF. I WON'T HAND HEAVEN SUCH AN EASY VICTORY. BUT I WANT YOU TO REMEMBER THAT I COULD HAVE.
AND AS A REMINDER...
FROM NOW, UNTIL THE END OF TIME...
YOU SHALL WEAR MY MARK! AND ALL CREATION WILL KNOW THAT YOU FAILED TO BREAK ME!
AAAAH!

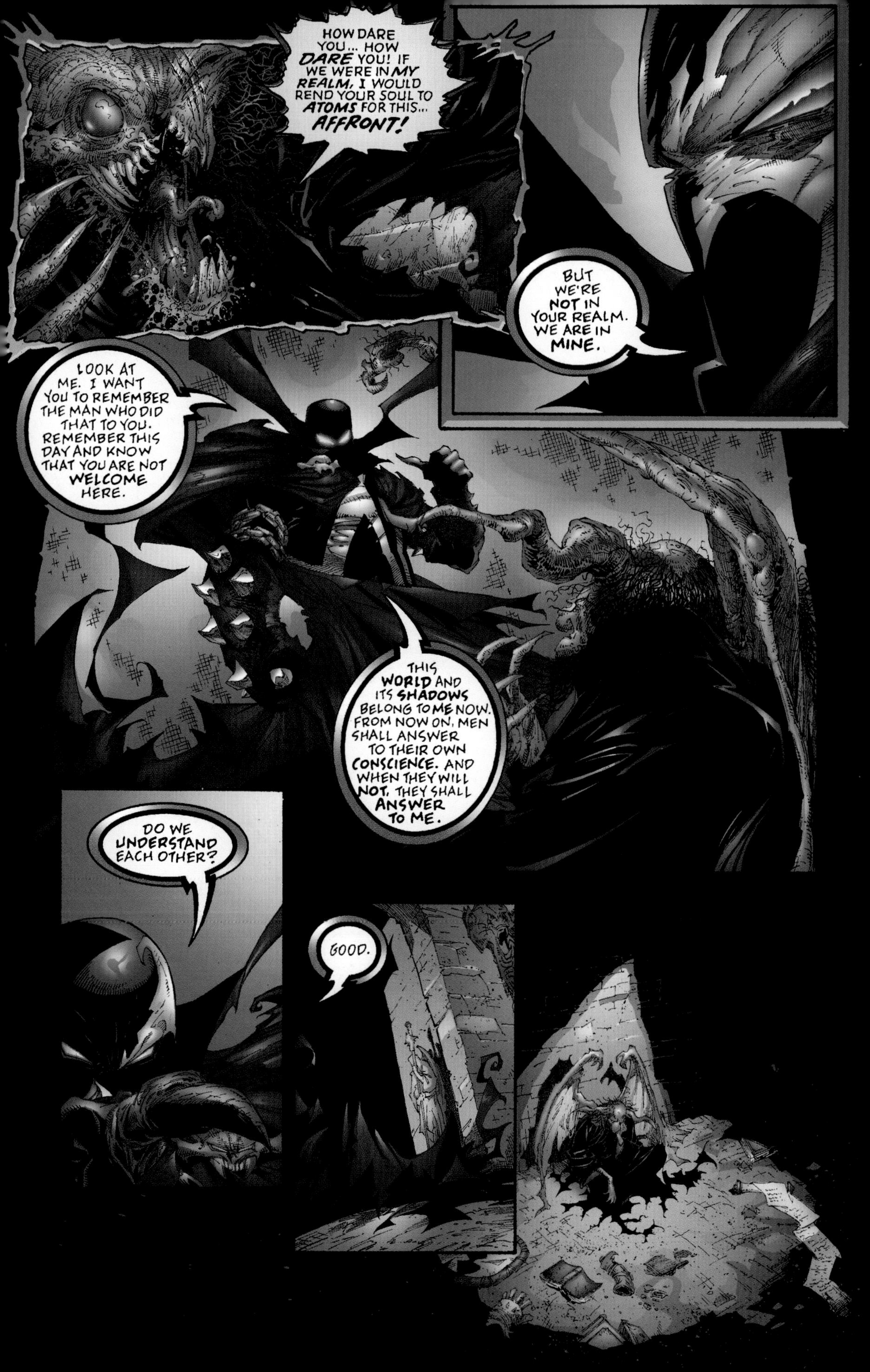

HOW DARE YOU... HOW DARE YOU! IF WE WERE IN MY REALM, I WOULD REND YOUR SOUL TO ATOMS FOR THIS... AFFRONT!
BUT WE'RE NOT IN YOUR REALM. WE ARE IN MINE.
LOOK AT ME. I WANT YOU TO REMEMBER THE MAN WHO DID THAT TO YOU. REMEMBER THIS DAY AND KNOW THAT YOU ARE NOT WELCOME HERE.
THIS WORLD AND ITS SHADOWS BELONG TO ME NOW. FROM NOW ON, MEN SHALL ANSWER TO THEIR OWN CONSCIENCE. AND WHEN THEY WILL NOT, THEY SHALL ANSWER TO ME.
DO WE UNDERSTAND EACH OTHER?
GOOD.

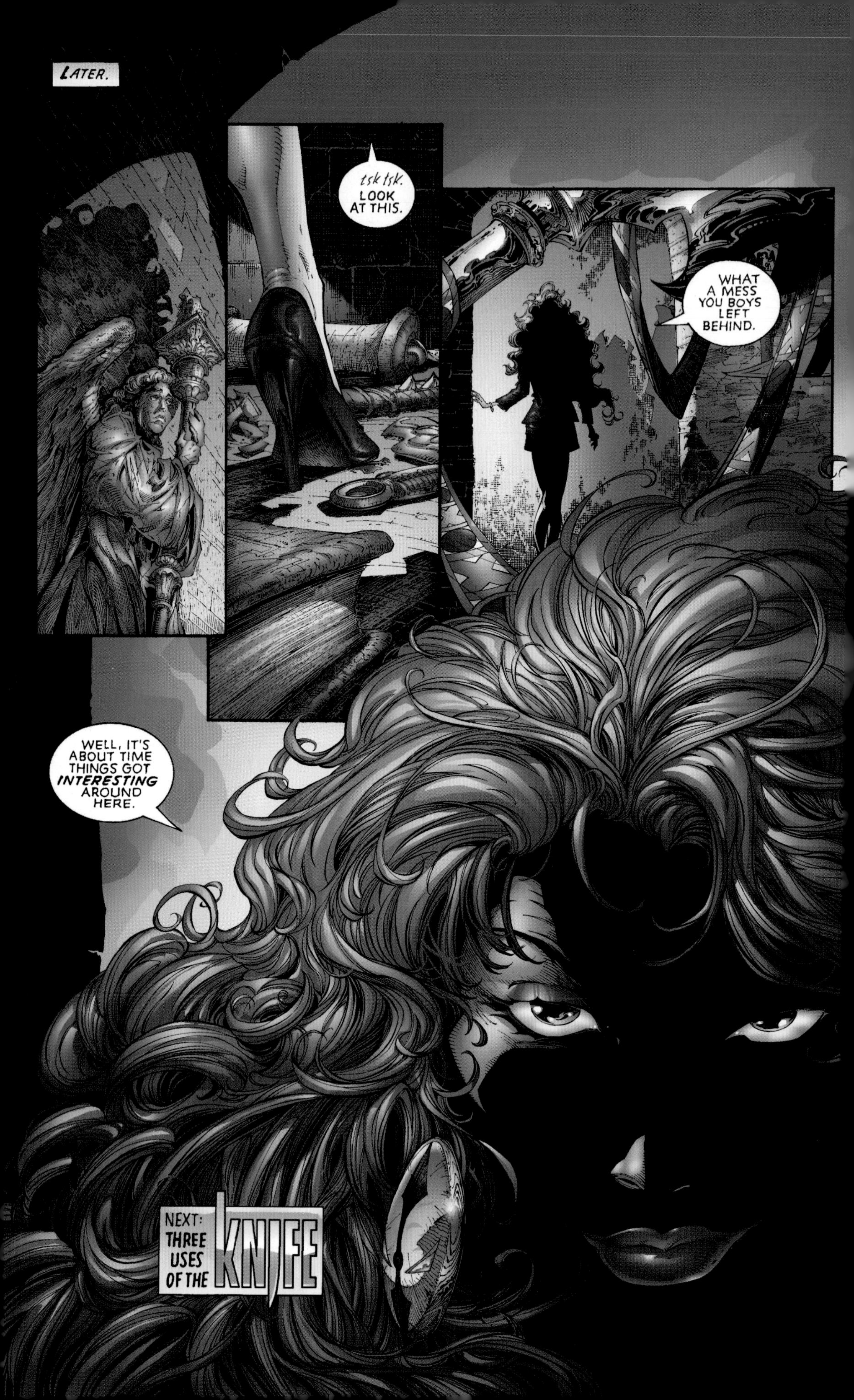
LATER.
tsk tsk. LOOK AT THIS.
WHAT A MESS YOU BOYS LEFT BEHIND.
WELL, IT'S ABOUT TIME THINGS GOT INTERESTING AROUND HERE.
NEXT: THREE USES OF THE KNIFE

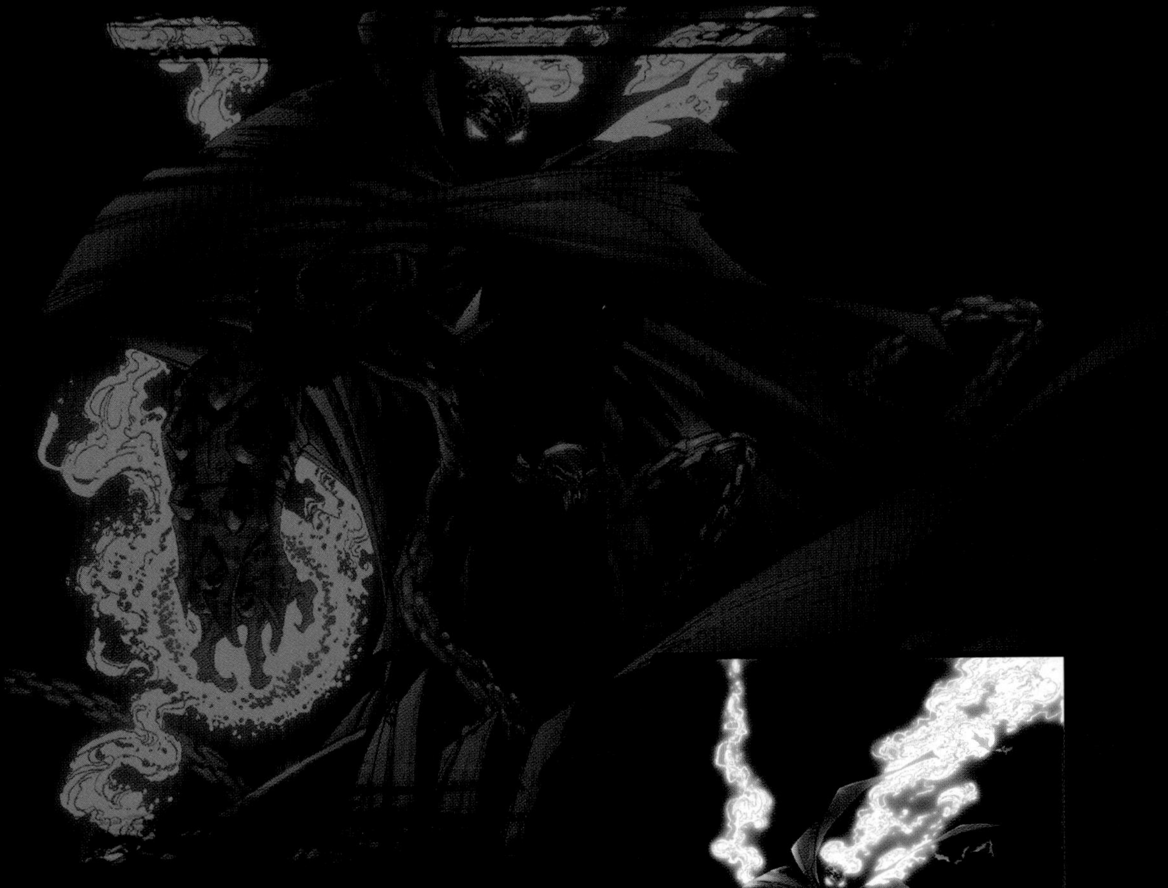

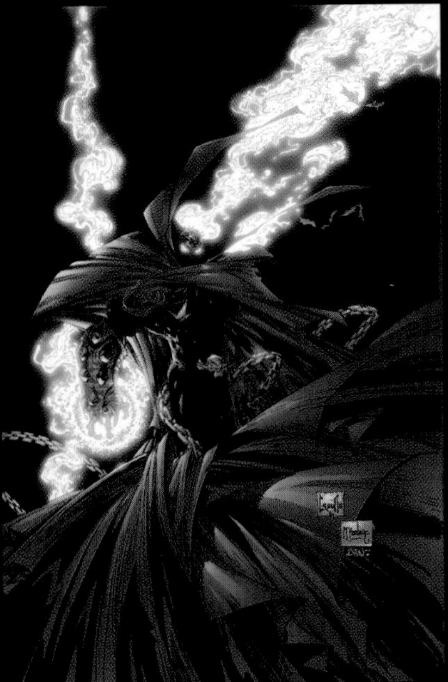

ISSUE NINETY

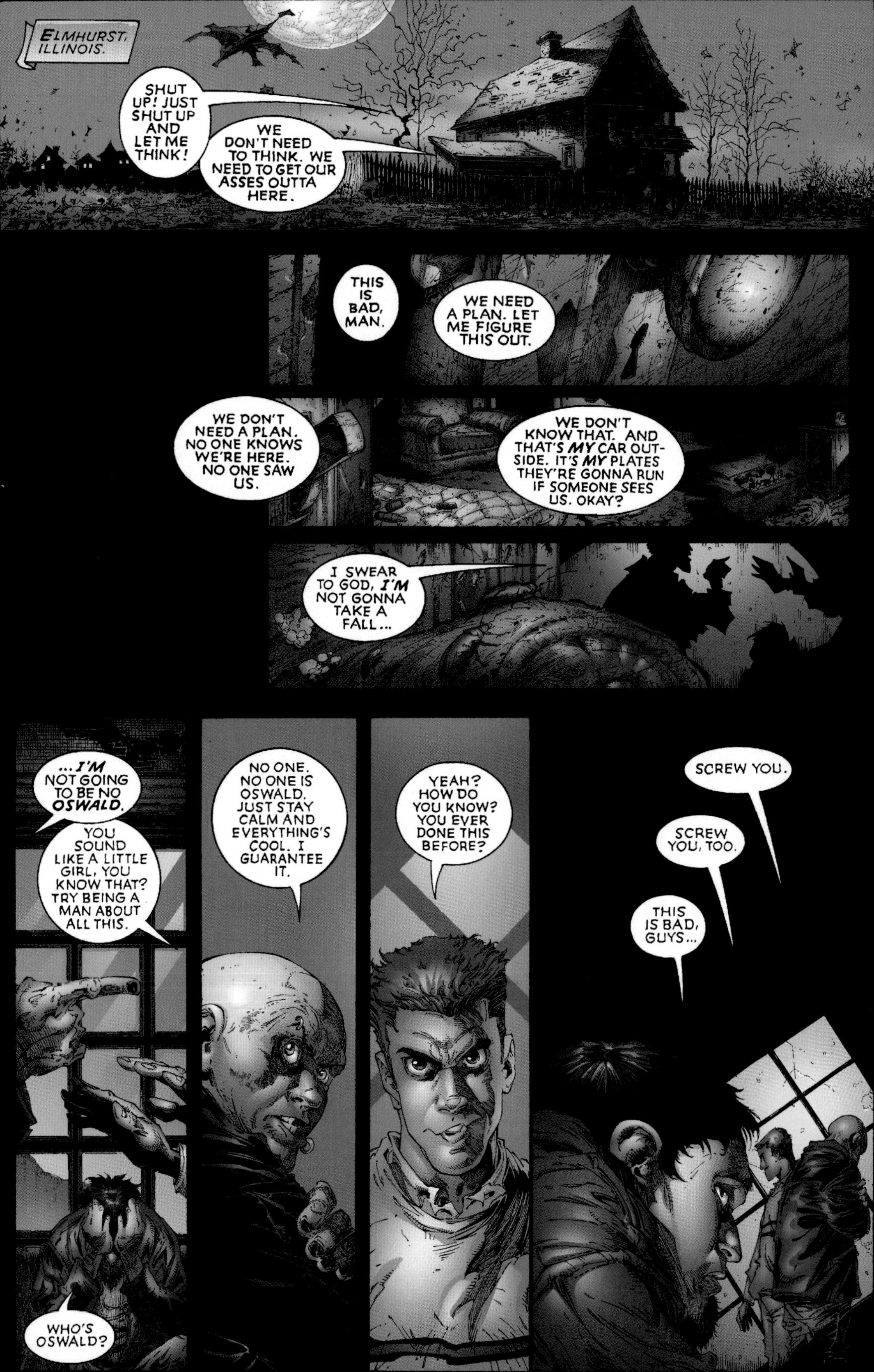
ELMHURST, ILLINOIS.
SHUT UP! JUST SHUT UP AND LET ME THINK!
WE DON'T NEED TO THINK. WE NEED TO GET OUR ASSES OUTTA HERE.
THIS IS BAD, MAN.
WE NEED A PLAN. LET ME FIGURE THIS OUT.
WE DON'T NEED A PLAN. NO ONE KNOWS WE'RE HERE. NO ONE SAW US.
WE DON'T KNOW THAT. AND THAT'S MY CAR OUTSIDE. IT'S MY PLATES THEY'RE GONNA RUN IF SOMEONE SEES US. OKAY?
I SWEAR TO GOD, I'M NOT GONNA TAKE A FALL...
...I'M NOT GOING TO BE NO OSWALD.
YOU SOUND LIKE A LITTLE GIRL, YOU KNOW THAT? TRY BEING A MAN ABOUT ALL THIS.
WHO'S OSWALD?
NO ONE. NO ONE IS OSWALD. JUST STAY CALM AND EVERYTHING'S COOL. I GUARANTEE IT.
YEAH? HOW DO YOU KNOW? YOU EVER DONE THIS BEFORE?
SCREW YOU.
SCREW YOU, TOO.
THIS IS BAD, GUYS...

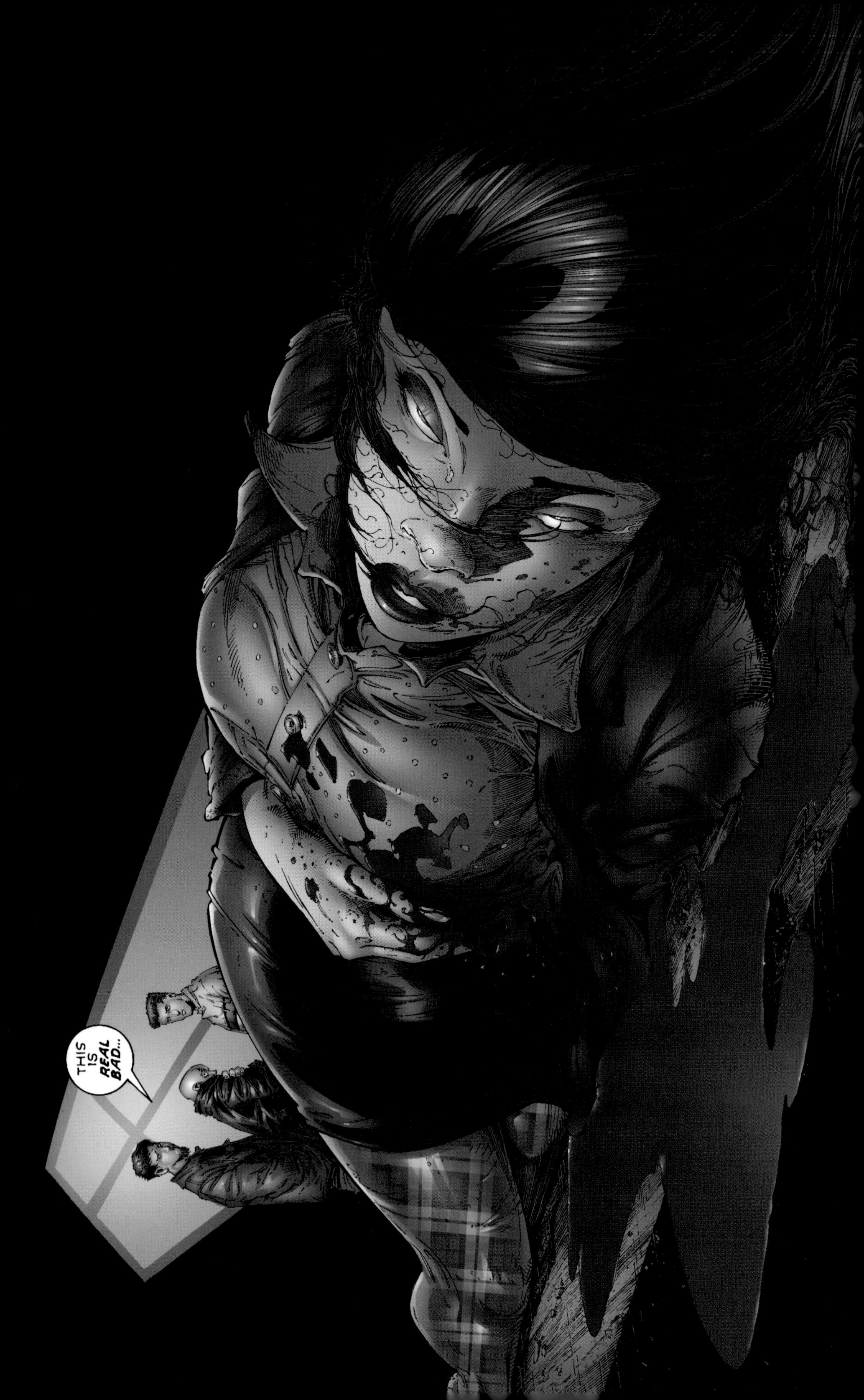
THIS IS REAL BAD...

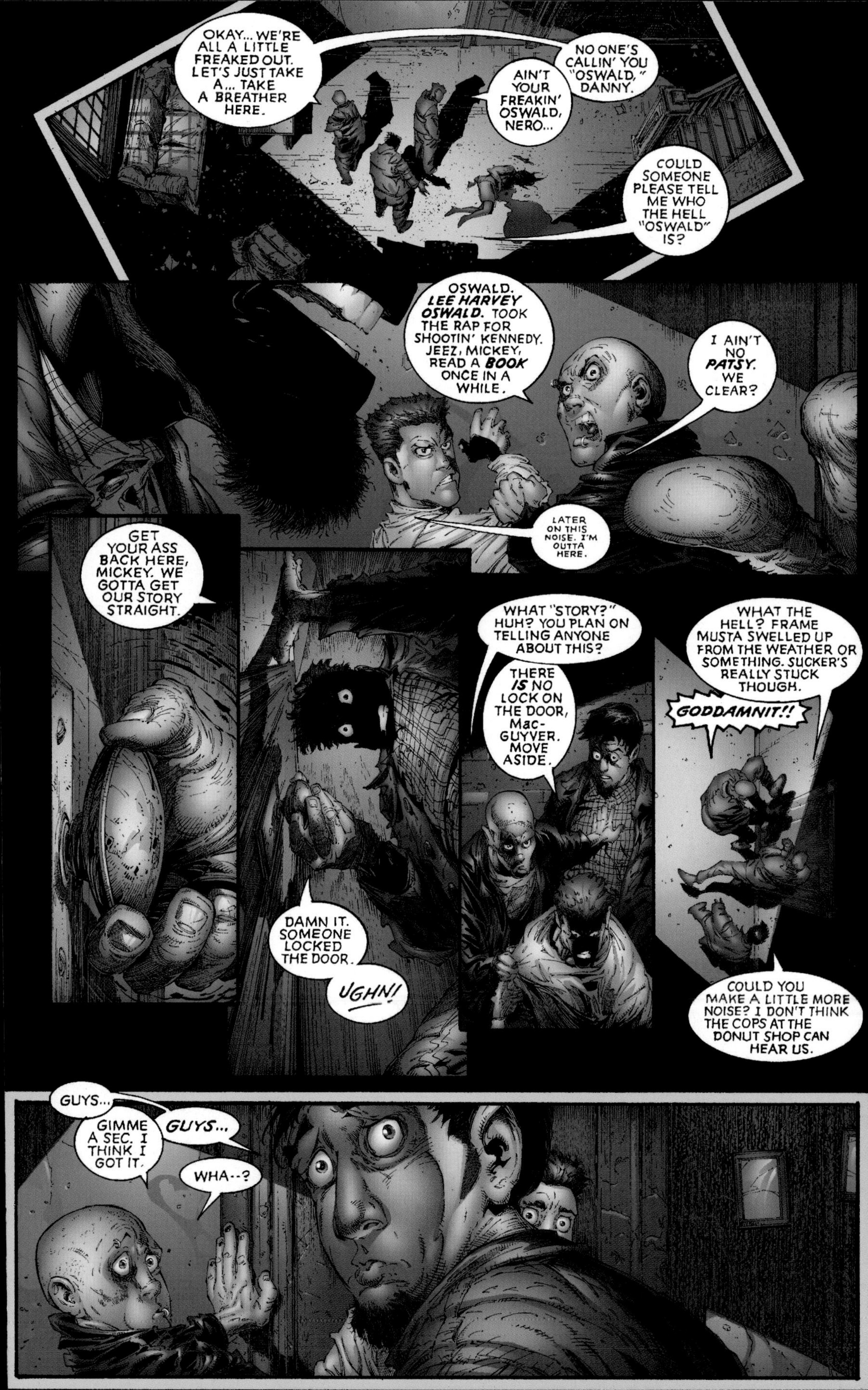
OKAY... WE'RE ALL A LITTLE FREAKED OUT. LET'S JUST TAKE A... TAKE A BREATHER HERE.
NO ONE'S CALLIN' YOU "OSWALD," DANNY.
AIN'T YOUR FREAKIN' OSWALD, NERO...
COULD SOMEONE PLEASE TELL ME WHO THE HELL "OSWALD" IS?
OSWALD. LEE HARVEY OSWALD. TOOK THE RAP FOR SHOOTIN' KENNEDY. JEEZ, MICKEY, READ A BOOK ONCE IN A WHILE.
I AIN'T NO PATSY. WE CLEAR?
LATER ON THIS NOISE. I'M OUTTA HERE.
GET YOUR ASS BACK HERE, MICKEY. WE GOTTA GET OUR STORY STRAIGHT.
DAMN IT. SOMEONE LOCKED THE DOOR.
UGHN!
WHAT "STORY?" HUH? YOU PLAN ON TELLING ANYONE ABOUT THIS?
THERE IS NO LOCK ON THE DOOR, Mac-GUYVER. MOVE ASIDE.
WHAT THE HELL? FRAME MUSTA SWELLED UP FROM THE WEATHER OR SOMETHING. SUCKER'S REALLY STUCK THOUGH.
GODDAMNIT!!
COULD YOU MAKE A LITTLE MORE NOISE? I DON'T THINK THE COPS AT THE DONUT SHOP CAN HEAR US.
GUYS...
GIMME A SEC. I THINK I GOT IT.
GUYS...
WHA--?

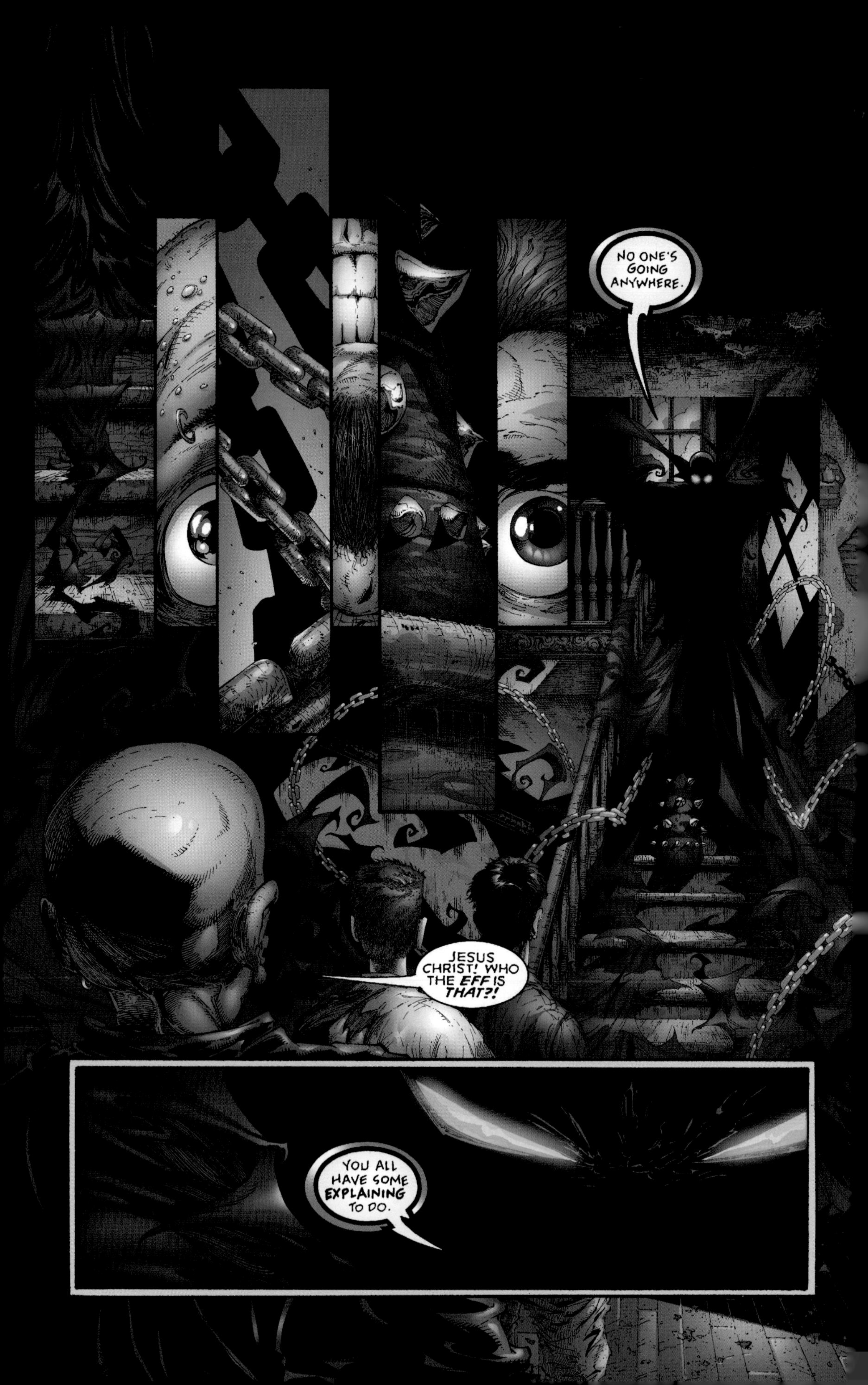
NO ONE'S GOING ANYWHERE.
JESUS CHRIST! WHO THE EFF IS THAT?!
YOU ALL HAVE SOME EXPLAINING TO DO.

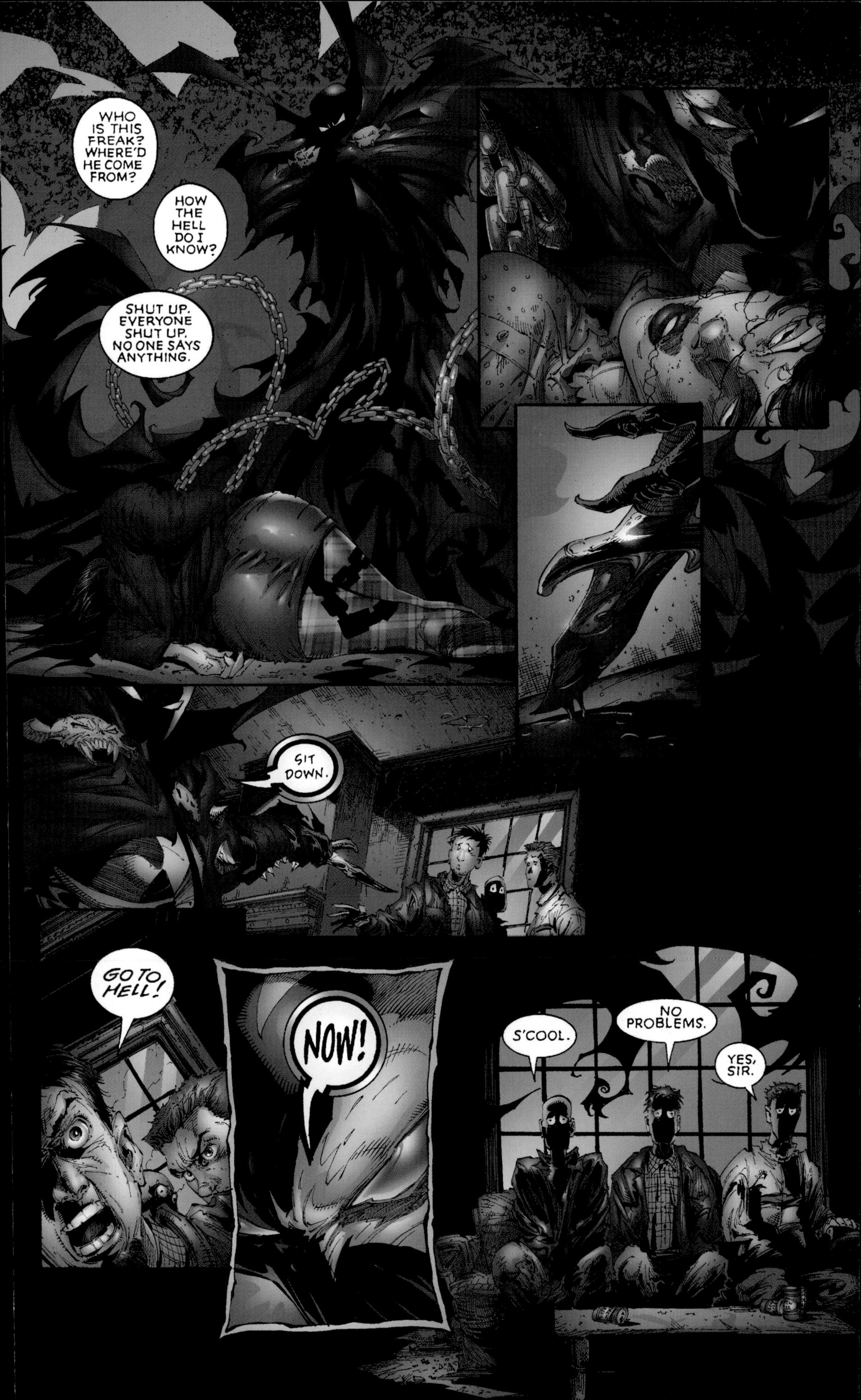
WHO IS THIS FREAK? WHERE'D HE COME FROM?
HOW THE HELL DO I KNOW?
SHUT UP. EVERYONE SHUT UP. NO ONE SAYS ANYTHING.
SIT DOWN.
GO TO HELL!
NOW!
S'COOL.
NO PROBLEMS.
YES, SIR.

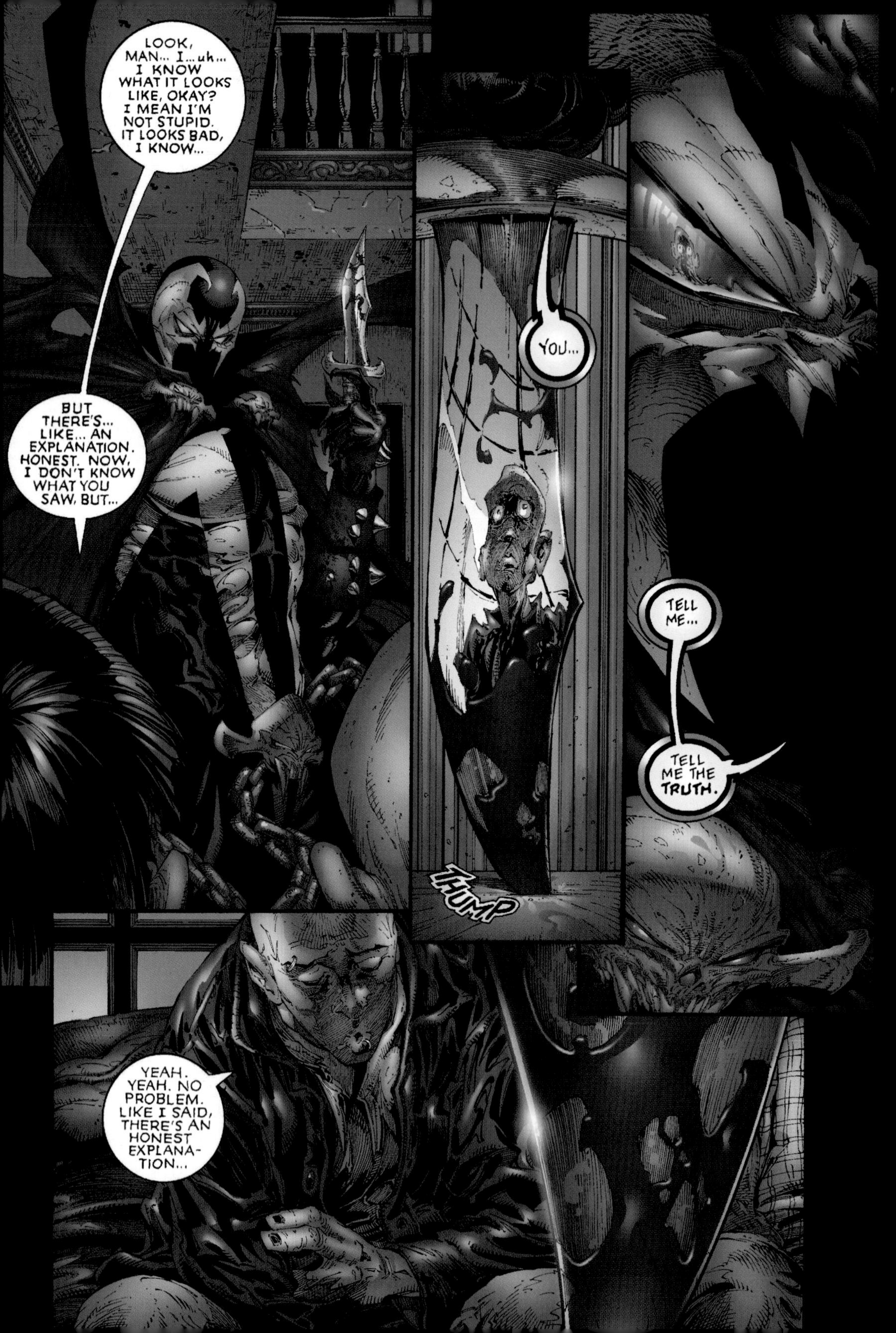
LOOK, MAN... I...uh... I KNOW WHAT IT LOOKS LIKE, OKAY? I MEAN I'M NOT STUPID. IT LOOKS BAD, I KNOW...
BUT THERE'S... LIKE... AN EXPLANATION. HONEST. NOW, I DON'T KNOW WHAT YOU SAW, BUT...
YOU...
THUMP
TELL ME...
TELL ME THE TRUTH.
YEAH. YEAH. NO PROBLEM. LIKE I SAID, THERE'S AN HONEST EXPLANATION...

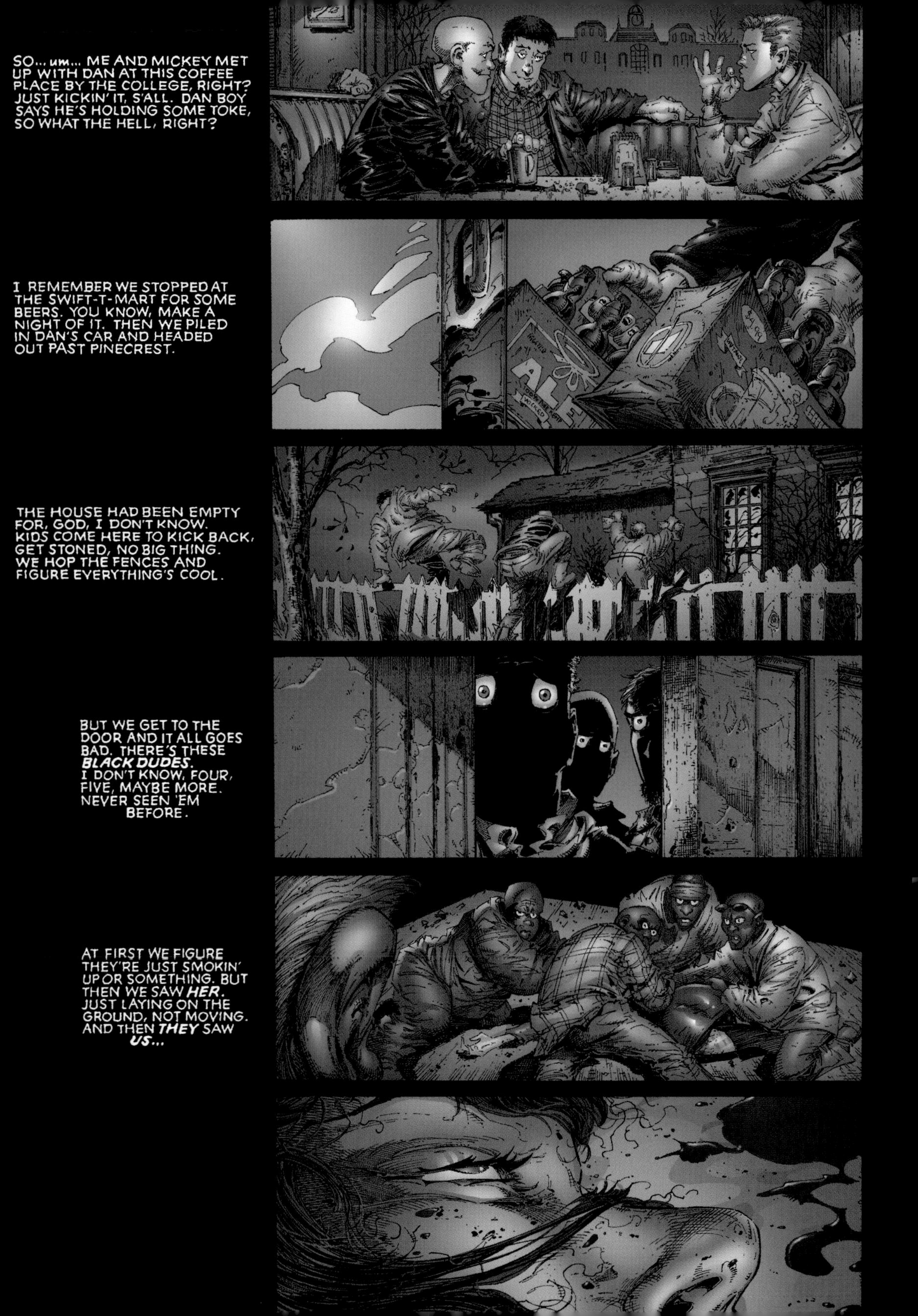
SO... um... ME AND MICKEY MET UP WITH DAN AT THIS COFFEE PLACE BY THE COLLEGE, RIGHT? JUST KICKIN' IT, S'ALL. DAN BOY SAYS HE'S HOLDING SOME TOKE, SO WHAT THE HELL, RIGHT?
I REMEMBER WE STOPPED AT THE SWIFT-T-MART FOR SOME BEERS. YOU KNOW, MAKE A NIGHT OF IT. THEN WE PILED IN DAN'S CAR AND HEADED OUT PAST PINECREST.
ALE
THE HOUSE HAD BEEN EMPTY FOR, GOD, I DON'T KNOW. KIDS COME HERE TO KICK BACK, GET STONED, NO BIG THING. WE HOP THE FENCES AND FIGURE EVERYTHING'S COOL.
BUT WE GET TO THE DOOR AND IT ALL GOES BAD. THERE'S THESE ***BLACK DUDES***. I DON'T KNOW, FOUR, FIVE, MAYBE MORE. NEVER SEEN 'EM BEFORE.
AT FIRST WE FIGURE THEY'RE JUST SMOKIN' UP OR SOMETHING. BUT THEN WE SAW ***HER***. JUST LAYING ON THE GROUND, NOT MOVING. AND THEN ***THEY*** SAW ***US***...

THINGS WENT DOWNHILL PRETTY FAST FROM THERE...

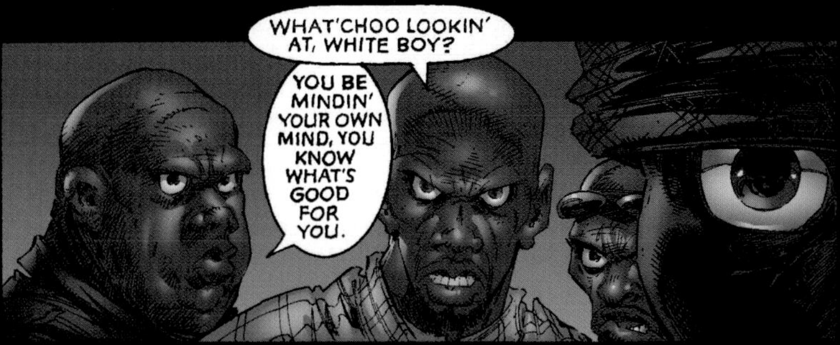
WHAT'CHOO LOOKIN' AT, WHITE BOY?
YOU BE MINDIN' YOUR OWN MIND, YOU KNOW WHAT'S GOOD FOR YOU.

AT THIS POINT, TO TELL THE TRUTH, THINGS GOT KIND OF BLURRY. I MEAN, I KNOW SOME WORDS WERE SAID...

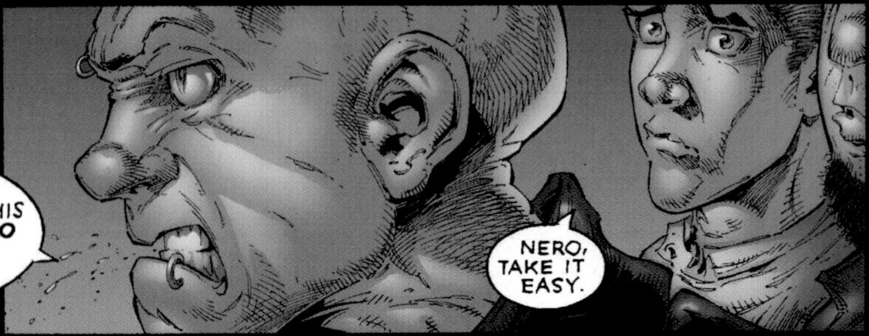
YOU'RE IN THE WRONG PART OF TOWN, DARK MEAT. THIS HERE'S A DESIGNATED "NO PIMP" ZONE. SO WHAT THE HELL YOU DOIN' IN MY HOUSE?
NERO, TAKE IT EASY.

SO SOUL BROTHER NUMBER ONE, HE TAKES A SWING AT ME. SOME CHICKENSHIT SUCKER PUNCH. CLOCKED ME IN THE JAW PRETTY GOOD.

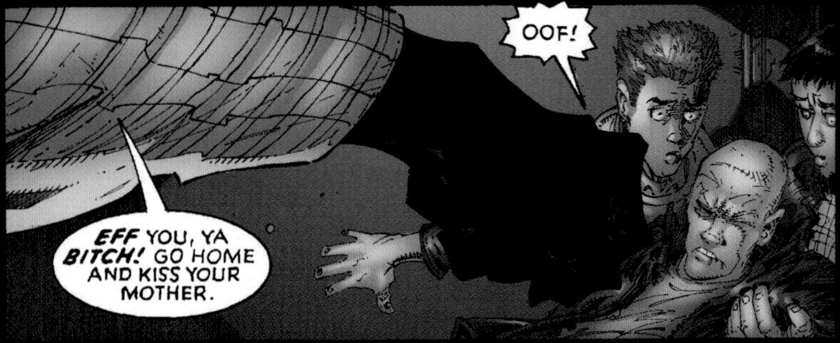
OOF!
EFF YOU, YA BITCH! GO HOME AND KISS YOUR MOTHER.

SO NOW, I'LL BE HONEST. I'M REALLY PISSED. I'M READY TO MIX IT UP. BUT BEFORE I CAN GET BACK ON MY FEET, THE SONS O' BITCHES SPLIT.

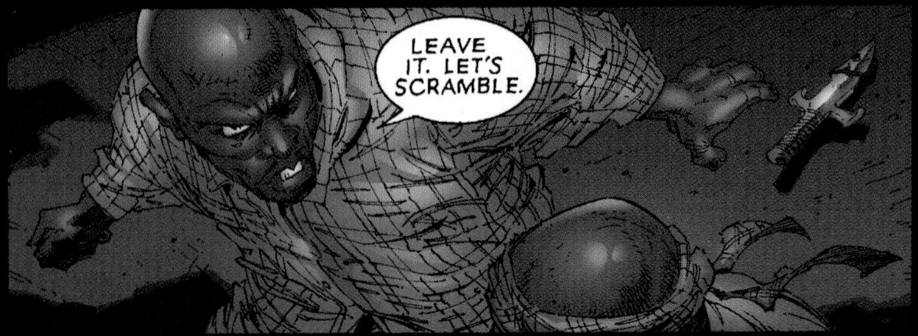
LEAVE IT. LET'S SCRAMBLE.

AN' THEY JUST LEAVE THE CHICK LYING ON THE FLOOR AND HEAD OUT THE BACK. I WANTED TO GO AFTER 'EM, BUT THE GUYS STOPPED ME.

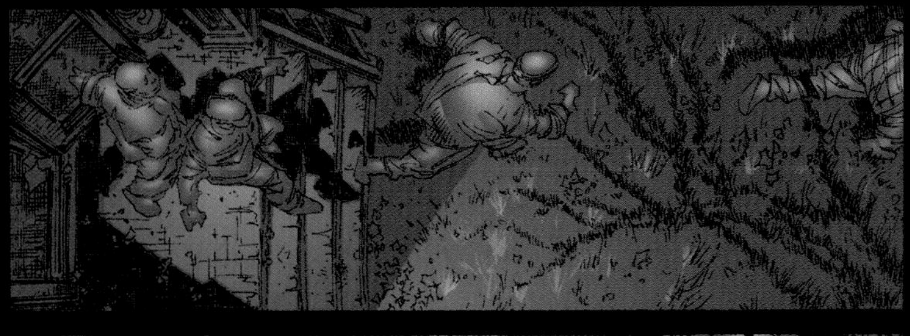

NOW AT THIS POINT, WE DON'T KNOW WHAT'S GOING ON WITH THIS... THIS ASIAN BROAD. IS SHE SICK? IS SHE STONED? PASSED OUT? TAKE A LOOK AND, JESUS CHRIST, LITTLE BITCH WAS DEAD.

THAT'S HOW WE FOUND HER. CAN'T BLAME US FOR BEING A LITTLE FREAKED.

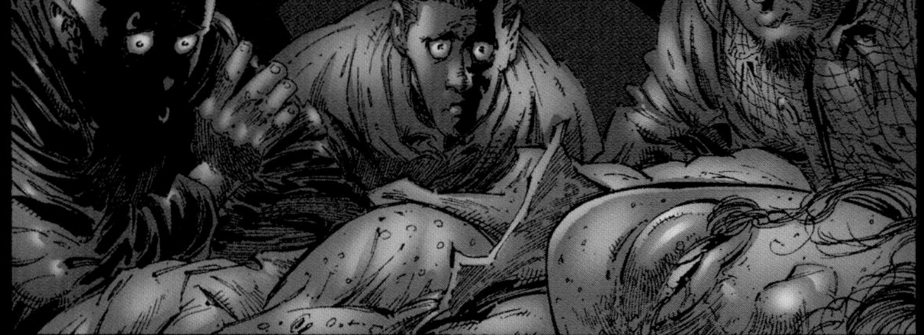

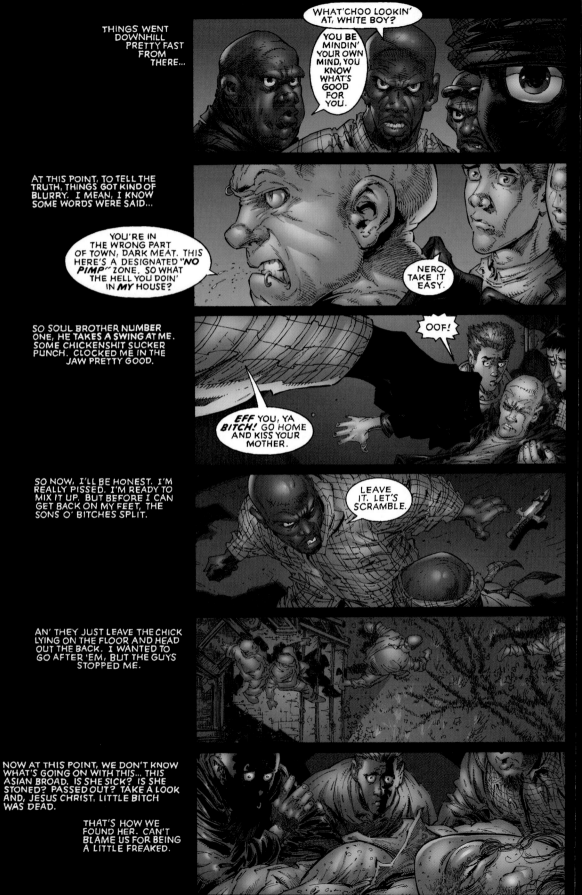

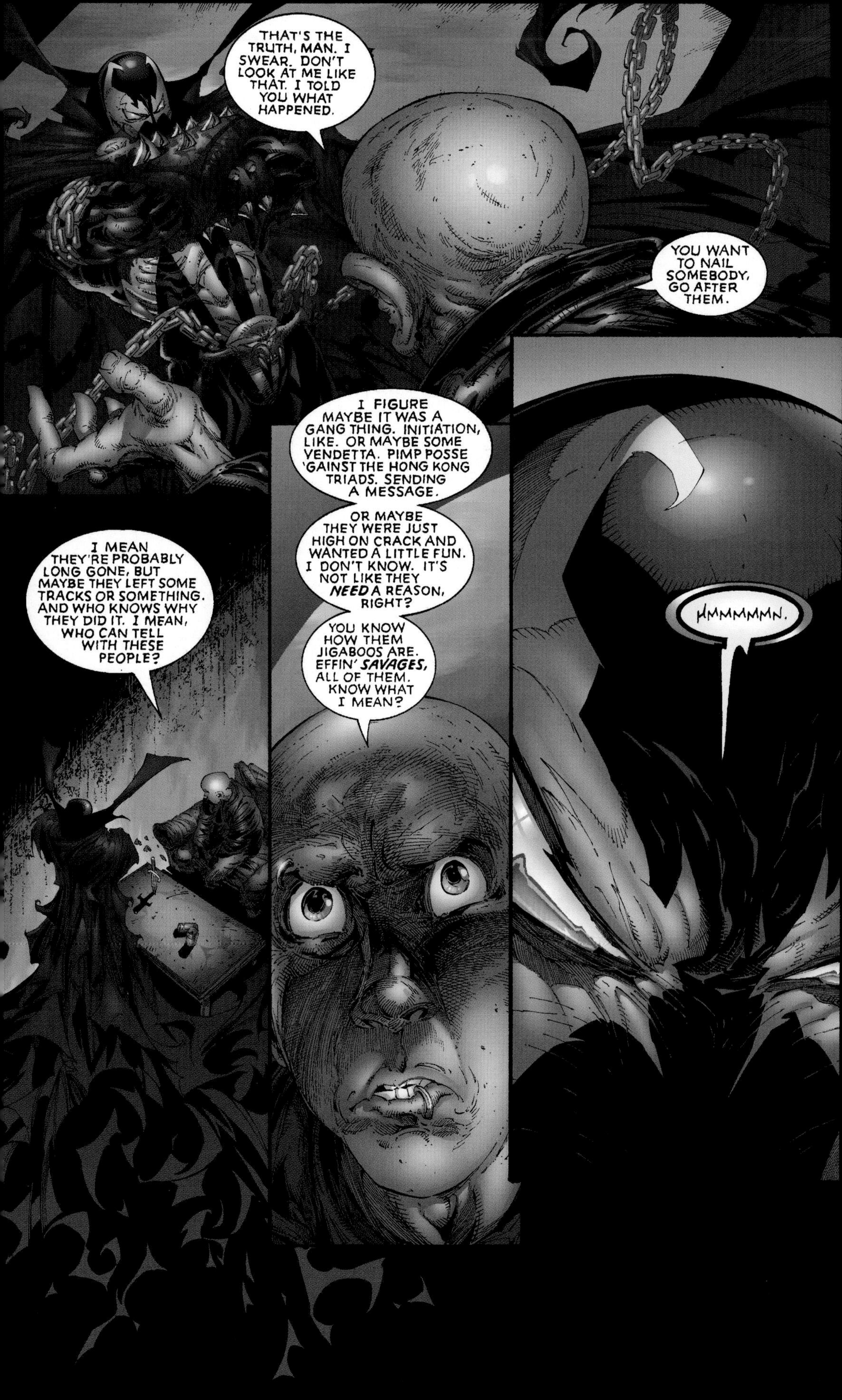
THAT'S THE TRUTH, MAN. I SWEAR. DON'T LOOK AT ME LIKE THAT. I TOLD YOU WHAT HAPPENED.
YOU WANT TO NAIL SOMEBODY, GO AFTER THEM.
I MEAN THEY'RE PROBABLY LONG GONE, BUT MAYBE THEY LEFT SOME TRACKS OR SOMETHING. AND WHO KNOWS WHY THEY DID IT. I MEAN, WHO CAN TELL WITH THESE PEOPLE?
I FIGURE MAYBE IT WAS A GANG THING. INITIATION, LIKE. OR MAYBE SOME VENDETTA. PIMP POSSE 'GAINST THE HONG KONG TRIADS. SENDING A MESSAGE.
OR MAYBE THEY WERE JUST HIGH ON CRACK AND WANTED A LITTLE FUN. I DON'T KNOW. IT'S NOT LIKE THEY *NEED* A REASON, RIGHT?
YOU KNOW HOW THEM JIGABOOS ARE. EFFIN' *SAVAGES,* ALL OF THEM. KNOW WHAT I MEAN?
HMMMMMN.

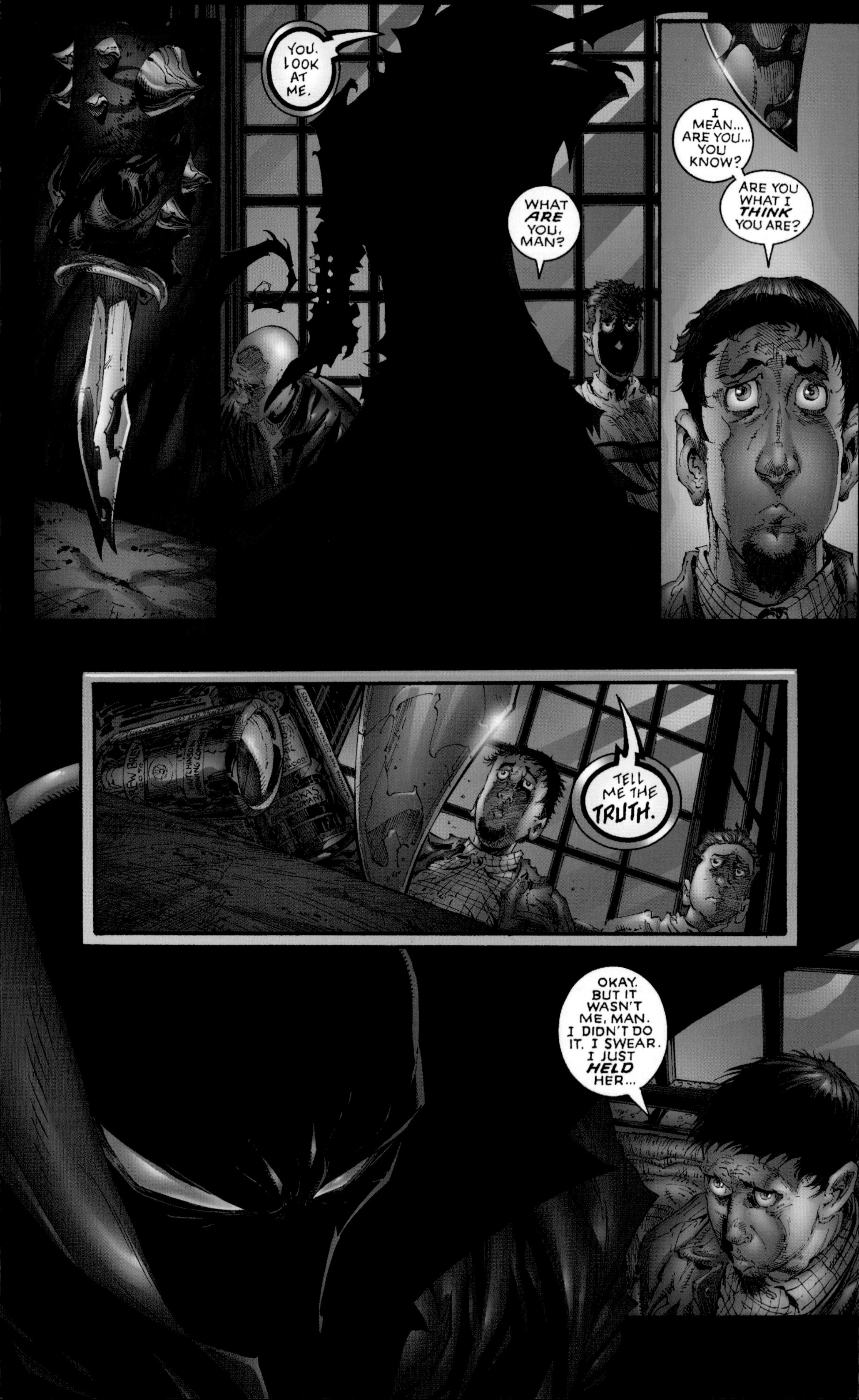
YOU. LOOK AT ME.
WHAT *ARE* YOU, MAN?
I MEAN... ARE YOU... YOU KNOW?
ARE YOU WHAT I *THINK* YOU ARE?
TELL ME THE TRUTH.
OKAY. BUT IT WASN'T ME, MAN. I DIDN'T DO IT. I SWEAR. I JUST *HELD* HER...

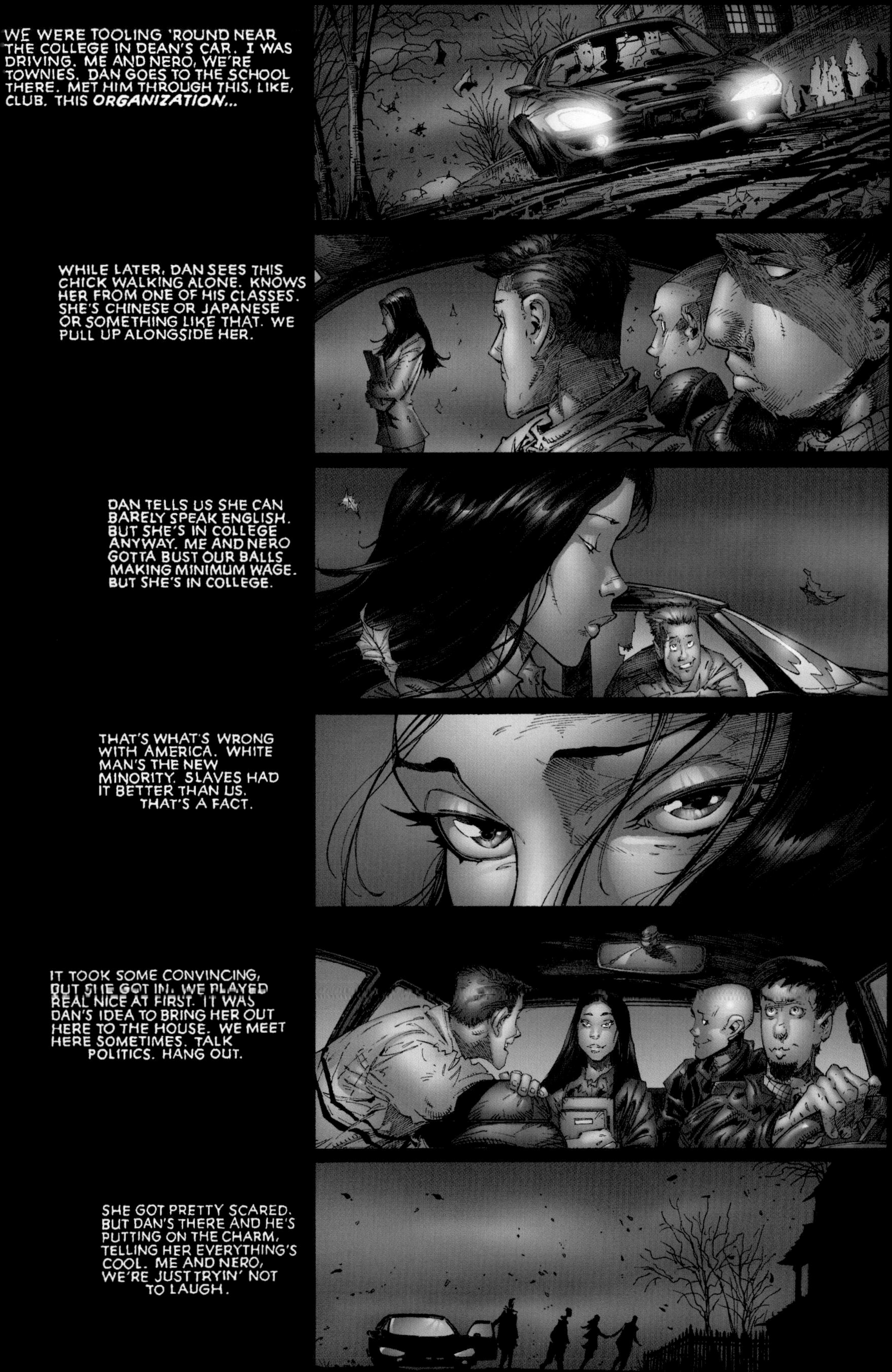
WE WERE TOOLING 'ROUND NEAR THE COLLEGE IN DEAN'S CAR. I WAS DRIVING. ME AND NERO, WE'RE TOWNIES. DAN GOES TO THE SCHOOL THERE. MET HIM THROUGH THIS, LIKE, CLUB. THIS *ORGANIZATION...*
WHILE LATER, DAN SEES THIS CHICK WALKING ALONE. KNOWS HER FROM ONE OF HIS CLASSES. SHE'S CHINESE OR JAPANESE OR SOMETHING LIKE THAT. WE PULL UP ALONGSIDE HER.
DAN TELLS US SHE CAN BARELY SPEAK ENGLISH. BUT SHE'S IN COLLEGE ANYWAY. ME AND NERO GOTTA BUST OUR BALLS MAKING MINIMUM WAGE. BUT SHE'S IN COLLEGE.
THAT'S WHAT'S WRONG WITH AMERICA. WHITE MAN'S THE NEW MINORITY. SLAVES HAD IT BETTER THAN US. THAT'S A FACT.
IT TOOK SOME CONVINCING, BUT SHE GOT IN. WE PLAYED REAL NICE AT FIRST. IT WAS DAN'S IDEA TO BRING HER OUT HERE TO THE HOUSE. WE MEET HERE SOMETIMES. TALK POLITICS. HANG OUT.
SHE GOT PRETTY SCARED. BUT DAN'S THERE AND HE'S PUTTING ON THE CHARM, TELLING HER EVERYTHING'S COOL. ME AND NERO, WE'RE JUST TRYIN' NOT TO LAUGH.

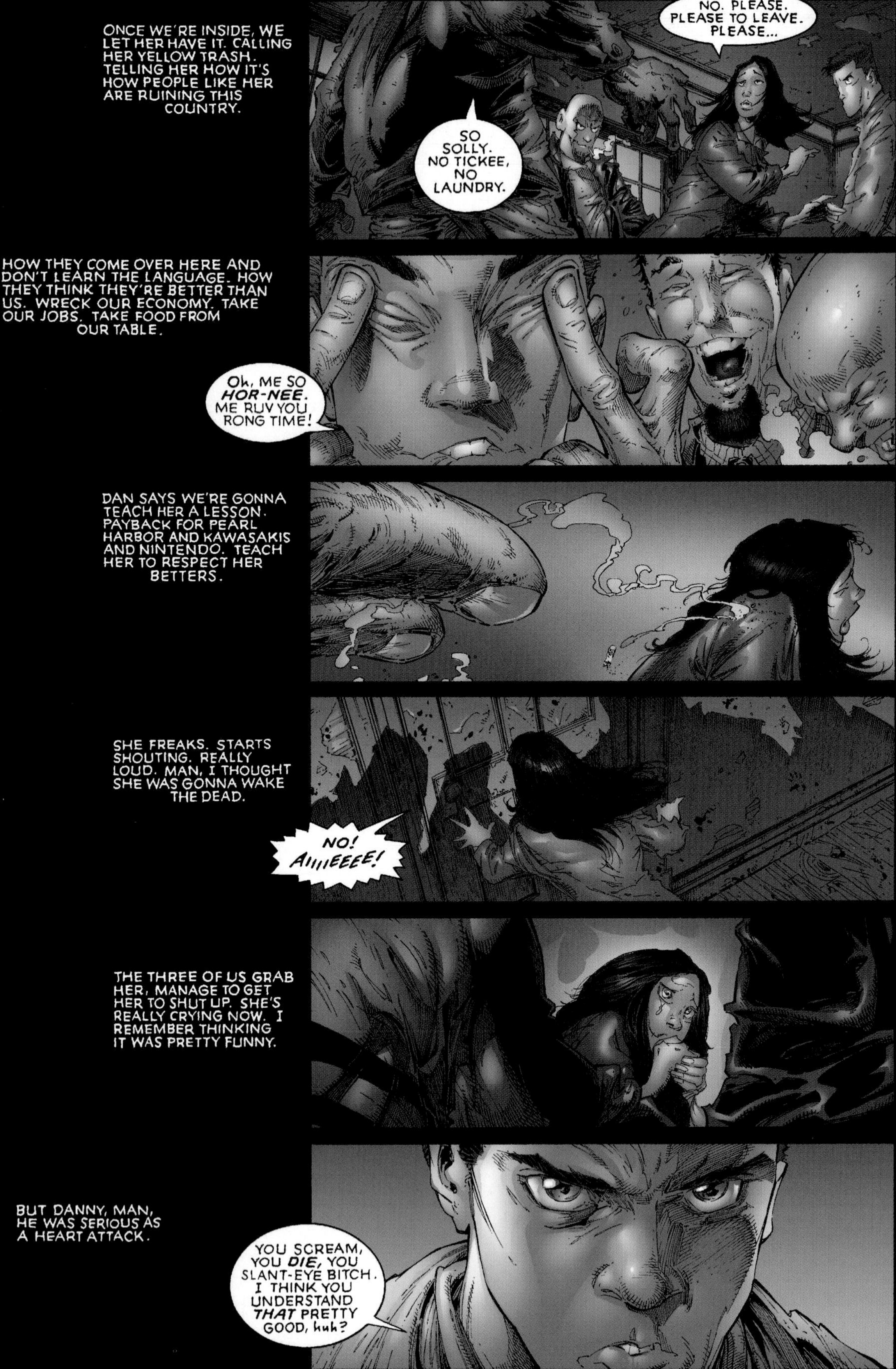
ONCE WE'RE INSIDE, WE LET HER HAVE IT. CALLING HER YELLOW TRASH. TELLING HER HOW IT'S HOW PEOPLE LIKE HER ARE RUINING THIS COUNTRY.
NO. PLEASE. PLEASE TO LEAVE. PLEASE...
SO SOLLY. NO TICKEE, NO LAUNDRY.
HOW THEY COME OVER HERE AND DON'T LEARN THE LANGUAGE. HOW THEY THINK THEY'RE BETTER THAN US. WRECK OUR ECONOMY. TAKE OUR JOBS. TAKE FOOD FROM OUR TABLE.
Oh, ME SO HOR-NEE. ME RUV YOU RONG TIME!
DAN SAYS WE'RE GONNA TEACH HER A LESSON. PAYBACK FOR PEARL HARBOR AND KAWASAKIS AND NINTENDO. TEACH HER TO RESPECT HER BETTERS.
SHE FREAKS. STARTS SHOUTING. REALLY LOUD. MAN, I THOUGHT SHE WAS GONNA WAKE THE DEAD.
NO! AIIIIEEEE!
THE THREE OF US GRAB HER, MANAGE TO GET HER TO SHUT UP. SHE'S REALLY CRYING NOW. I REMEMBER THINKING IT WAS PRETTY FUNNY.
BUT DANNY, MAN, HE WAS SERIOUS AS A HEART ATTACK.
YOU SCREAM, YOU DIE, YOU SLANT-EYE BITCH. I THINK YOU UNDERSTAND THAT PRETTY GOOD, huh?

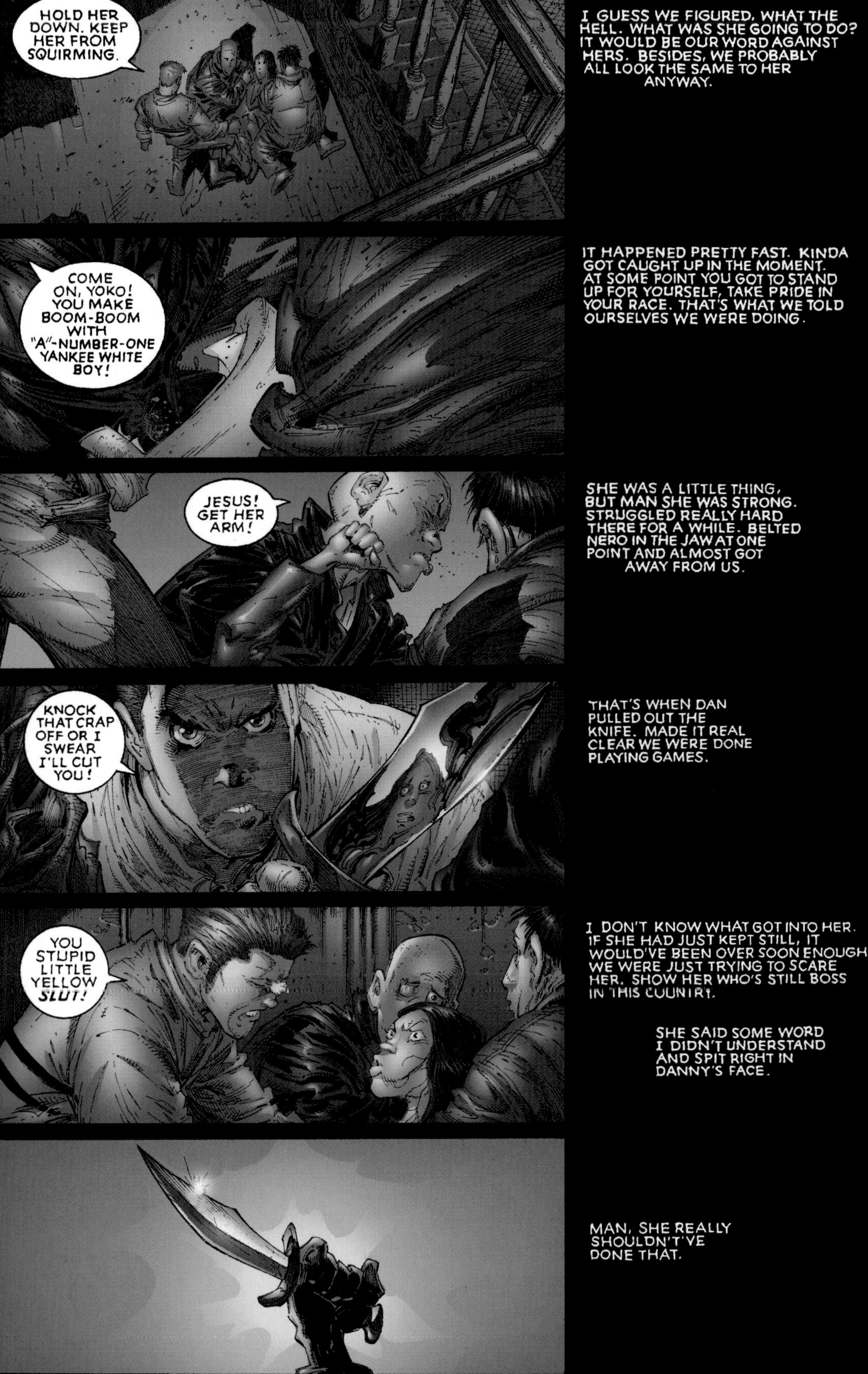
HOLD HER DOWN. KEEP HER FROM SQUIRMING.
I GUESS WE FIGURED, WHAT THE HELL. WHAT WAS SHE GOING TO DO? IT WOULD BE OUR WORD AGAINST HERS. BESIDES, WE PROBABLY ALL LOOK THE SAME TO HER ANYWAY.
COME ON, YOKO! YOU MAKE BOOM-BOOM WITH "A"-NUMBER-ONE YANKEE WHITE BOY!
IT HAPPENED PRETTY FAST. KINDA GOT CAUGHT UP IN THE MOMENT. AT SOME POINT YOU GOT TO STAND UP FOR YOURSELF, TAKE PRIDE IN YOUR RACE. THAT'S WHAT WE TOLD OURSELVES WE WERE DOING.
JESUS! GET HER ARM!
SHE WAS A LITTLE THING, BUT MAN SHE WAS STRONG. STRUGGLED REALLY HARD THERE FOR A WHILE. BELTED NERO IN THE JAW AT ONE POINT AND ALMOST GOT AWAY FROM US.
KNOCK THAT CRAP OFF OR I SWEAR I'LL CUT YOU!
THAT'S WHEN DAN PULLED OUT THE KNIFE. MADE IT REAL CLEAR WE WERE DONE PLAYING GAMES.
YOU STUPID LITTLE YELLOW SLUT!
I DON'T KNOW WHAT GOT INTO HER. IF SHE HAD JUST KEPT STILL, IT WOULD'VE BEEN OVER SOON ENOUGH WE WERE JUST TRYING TO SCARE HER. SHOW HER WHO'S STILL BOSS IN THIS COUNTRY.
SHE SAID SOME WORD I DIDN'T UNDERSTAND AND SPIT RIGHT IN DANNY'S FACE.
MAN, SHE REALLY SHOULDN'T'VE DONE THAT.

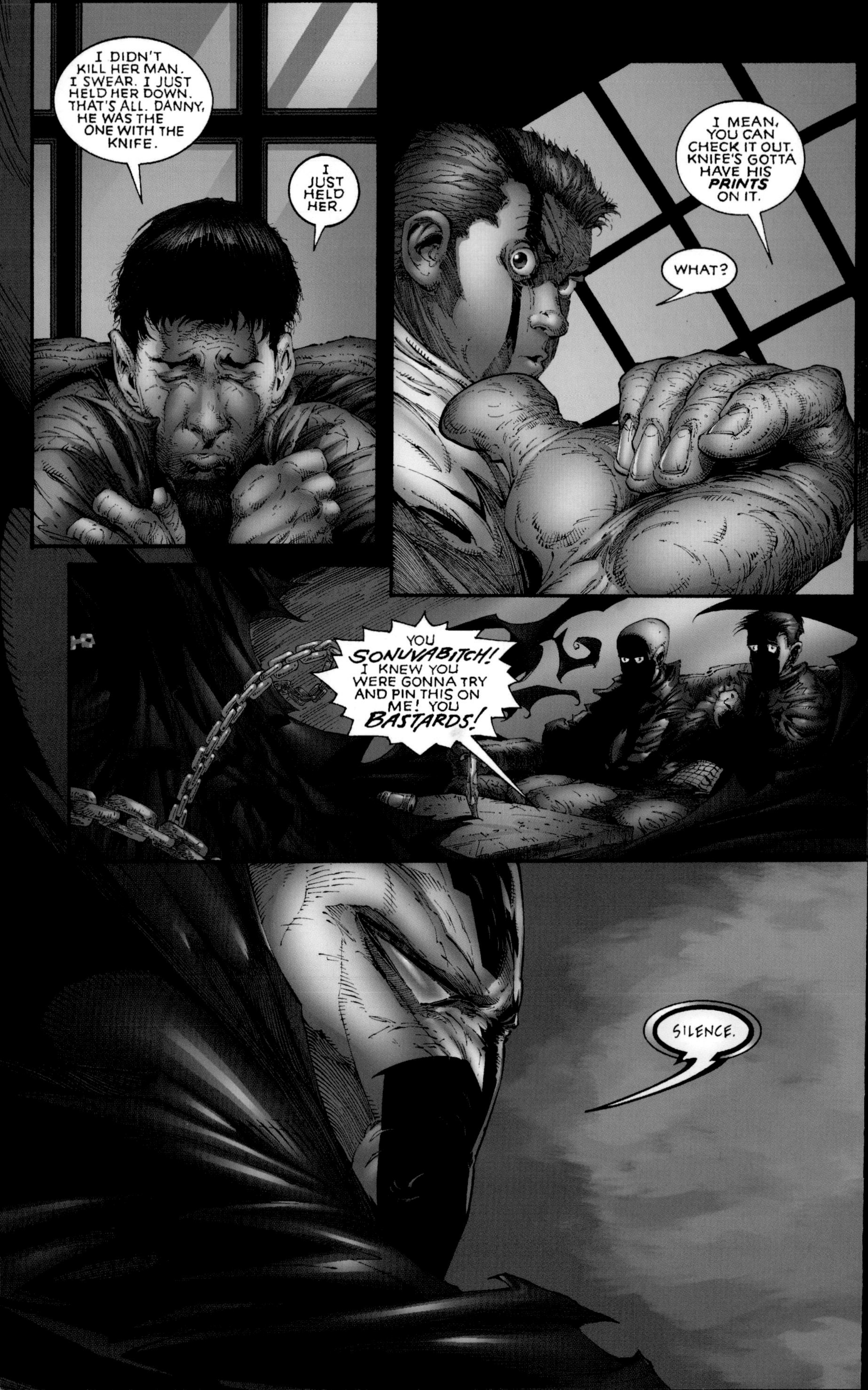
I DIDN'T KILL HER MAN. I SWEAR. I JUST HELD HER DOWN. THAT'S ALL. DANNY, HE WAS THE ONE WITH THE KNIFE.
I JUST HELD HER.
I MEAN, YOU CAN CHECK IT OUT. KNIFE'S GOTTA HAVE HIS PRINTS ON IT.
WHAT?
YOU SONUVABITCH! I KNEW YOU WERE GONNA TRY AND PIN THIS ON ME! YOU BASTARDS!
SILENCE.

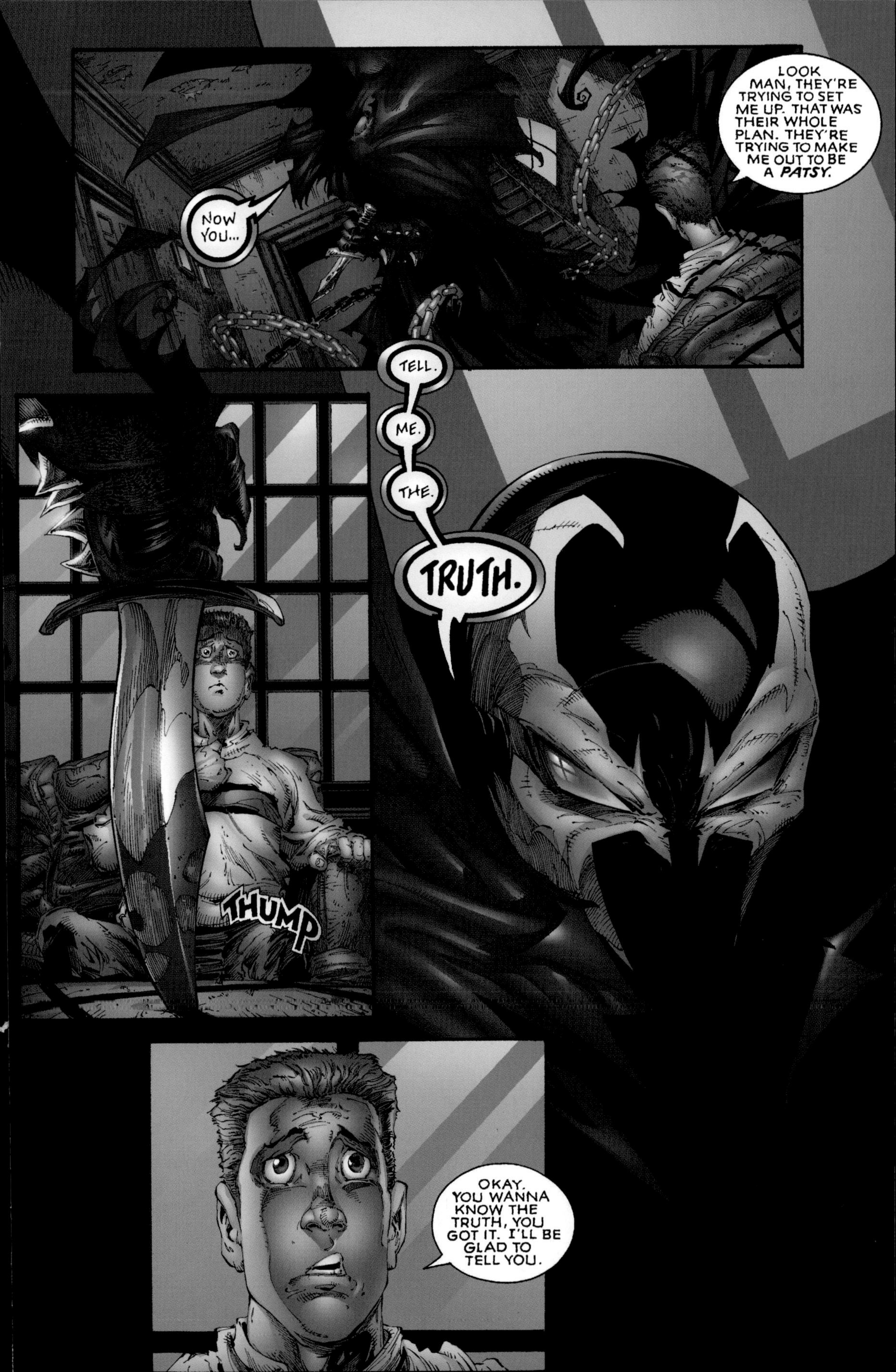
LOOK MAN, THEY'RE TRYING TO SET ME UP. THAT WAS THEIR WHOLE PLAN. THEY'RE TRYING TO MAKE ME OUT TO BE A *PATSY*.
NOW YOU...
TELL.
ME.
THE.
TRUTH.
THUMP
OKAY. YOU WANNA KNOW THE TRUTH, YOU GOT IT. I'LL BE GLAD TO TELL YOU.

YEAH, MY FINGERPRINTS ARE ON THE KNIFE. AND I'LL TELL YOU WHY. I BARELY KNOW THESE LOSERS. I'M A SOPHOMORE OVER AT THE COLLEGE. THINGS CAN BE A LITTLE TIGHT WHEN YOU'RE A STUDENT.

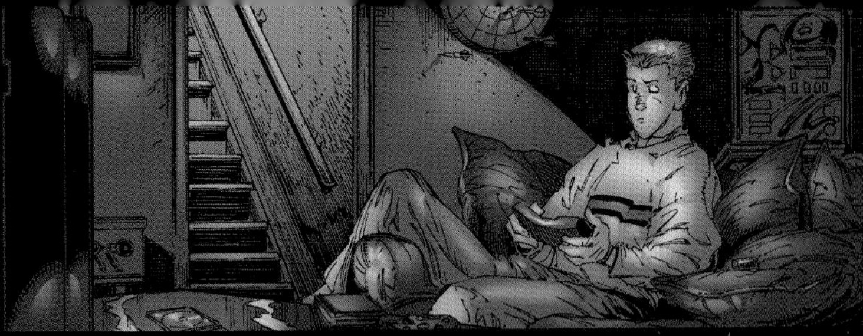

SO I DEAL A LITTLE ON THE SIDE. TO MAKE ENDS MEET. NOTHING SERIOUS, NOTHING TOO HEAVY. JUST SHIFT A LITTLE FREIGHT NOW AND THEN TO FRIENDS AND SELECT CLIENTELE.

I KEEP MY NOSE CLEAN. I'M A POLI-SCI. PLANNING TO RUN FOR SENATE SOMEDAY.

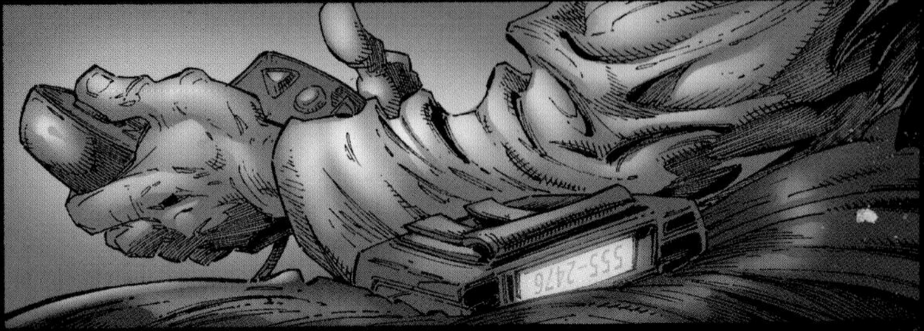
555-2476

I'M IN MY ROOM, STUDYING. I GET BEEPED. I RETURN THE CALL. IT'S MICKEY AND NERO. WE'VE DONE BUSINESS BEFORE, BUT WE'RE NOT EXACTLY BEST FRIENDS, RIGHT?

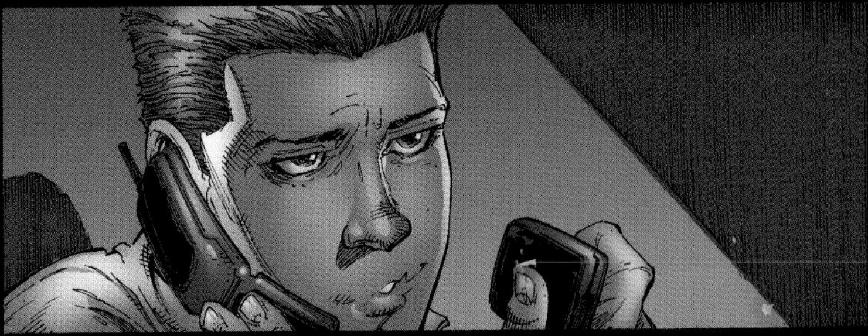

THEY ASK ME IF I'M HOLDING. I SAY YEAH. THEY SAY THEY'RE INTERESTED AND WANT ME TO BRING IT TO THEM AT SOME OLD ABANDONED HOUSE. I SAY COME AND GET IT YOURSELF. THIS AIN'T DOMINO'S.

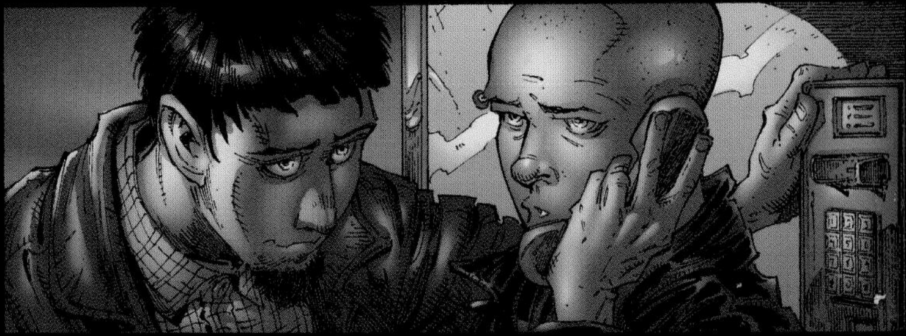

BUT THEY OFFER ME AN EXTRA HUNDRED FOR DOOR-TO-DOOR SERVICE. SO I SAY FINE. I CAN USE THE MONEY. I MEAN, DO YOU HAVE ANY IDEA WHAT TEXT BOOKS COST? IT'S A SCANDAL.

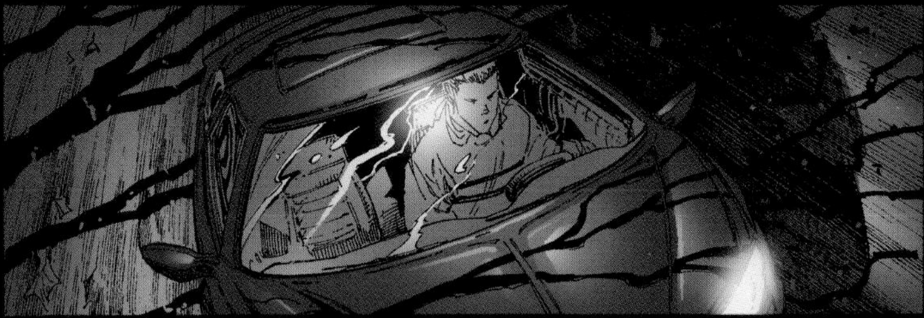

I FIND THE HOUSE OKAY AND PARK MY CAR. I TAKE A QUICK LOOK AROUND TO MAKE SURE THERE'S NO COPS OR ANYTHING. I MEAN, LIKE I SAID, I DON'T REALLY KNOW THESE GUYS TOO WELL.

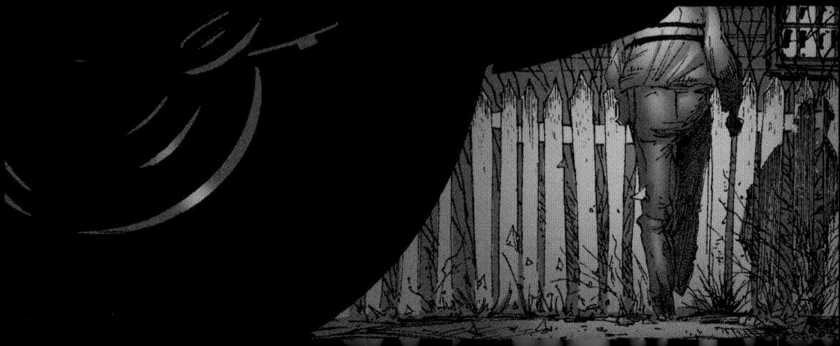

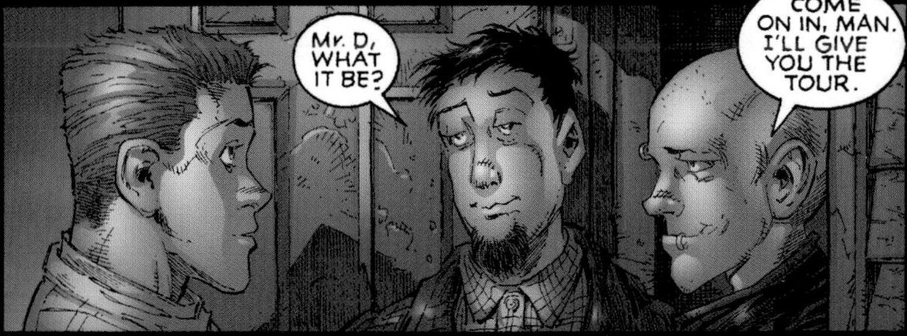
Mr. D, WHAT IT BE?
COME ON IN, MAN. I'LL GIVE YOU THE TOUR.

I GET TO THE DOOR AND EVERYTHING'S CASUAL, EVERYTHING'S FRIENDLY. THEY ASK ME INSIDE AND WE'RE ABOUT TO GET DOWN TO BUSINESS I FIGURE. BUT I WAS WRONG.

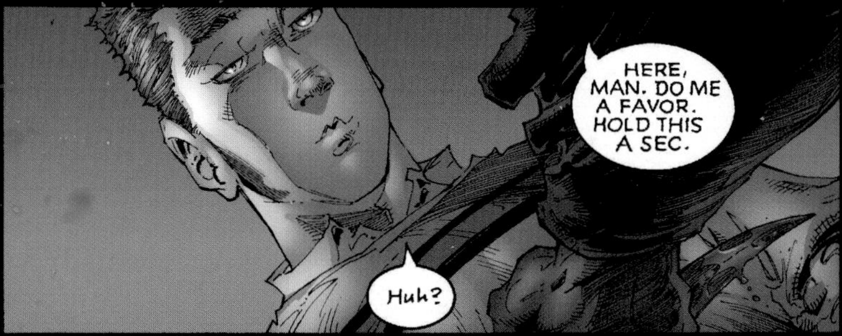
HERE, MAN. DO ME A FAVOR. HOLD THIS A SEC.
Huh?

NERO HANDS ME SOMETHING AND I TAKE IT WITHOUT THINKING, JUST BY REFLEX. I DON'T KNOW WHAT IT IS. IT'S DARK IN THERE.

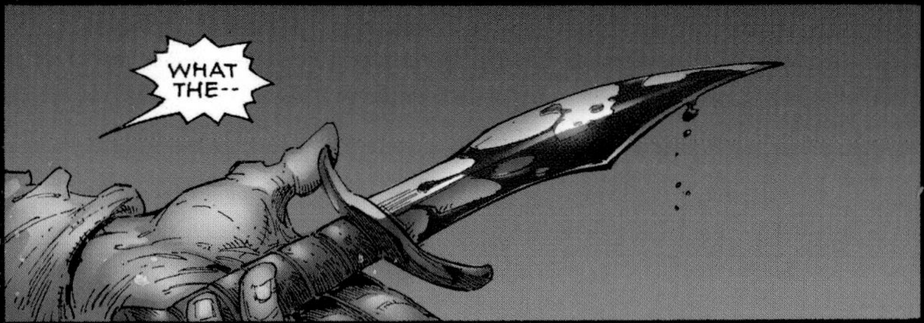
WHAT THE--

BUT THEN I SEE IT. IT'S A KNIFE. A BIG GOD-DAMN KNIFE WITH BLOOD ALL OVER IT.

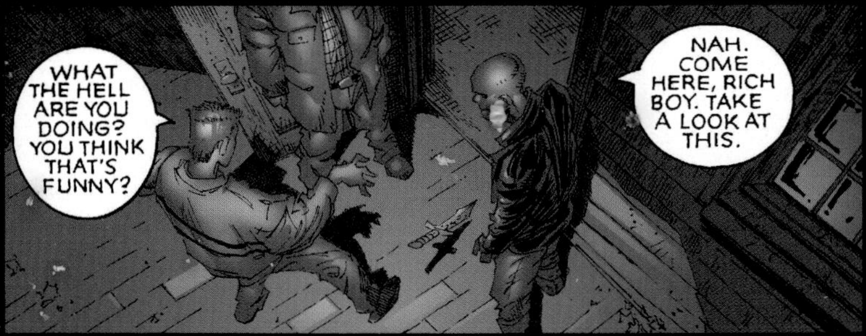
WHAT THE HELL ARE YOU DOING? YOU THINK THAT'S FUNNY?
NAH. COME HERE, RICH BOY. TAKE A LOOK AT THIS.

I DON'T HAVE THE FIRST CLUE WHAT TO THINK OF ALL THIS. I MEAN, IS THIS A JOKE? SOME KIND OF WEIRD-ASS PRANK?

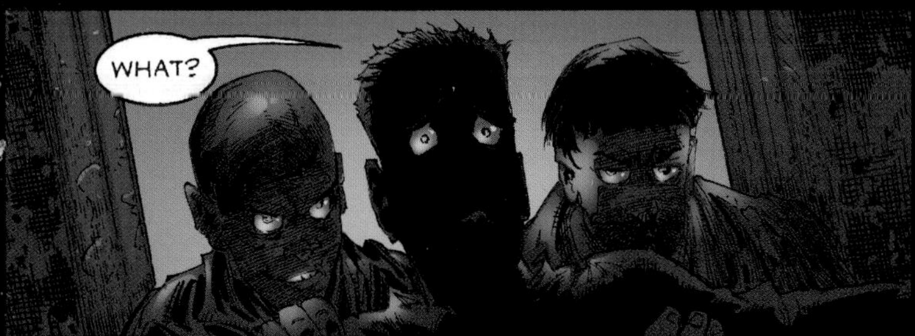
WHAT?

I MEAN IT WAS REAL BLOOD. I THOUGHT FOR A MINUTE MAYBE THEY WERE PART OF A CULT, MUTILATING ANIMALS OR SOMETHING. THEY TOOK ME IN THE OTHER ROOM.

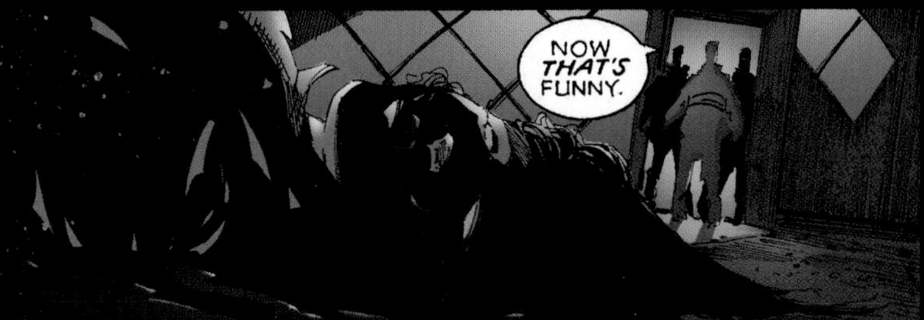
NOW *THAT'S* FUNNY.

AND THAT'S WHEN I SAW ***HER***.

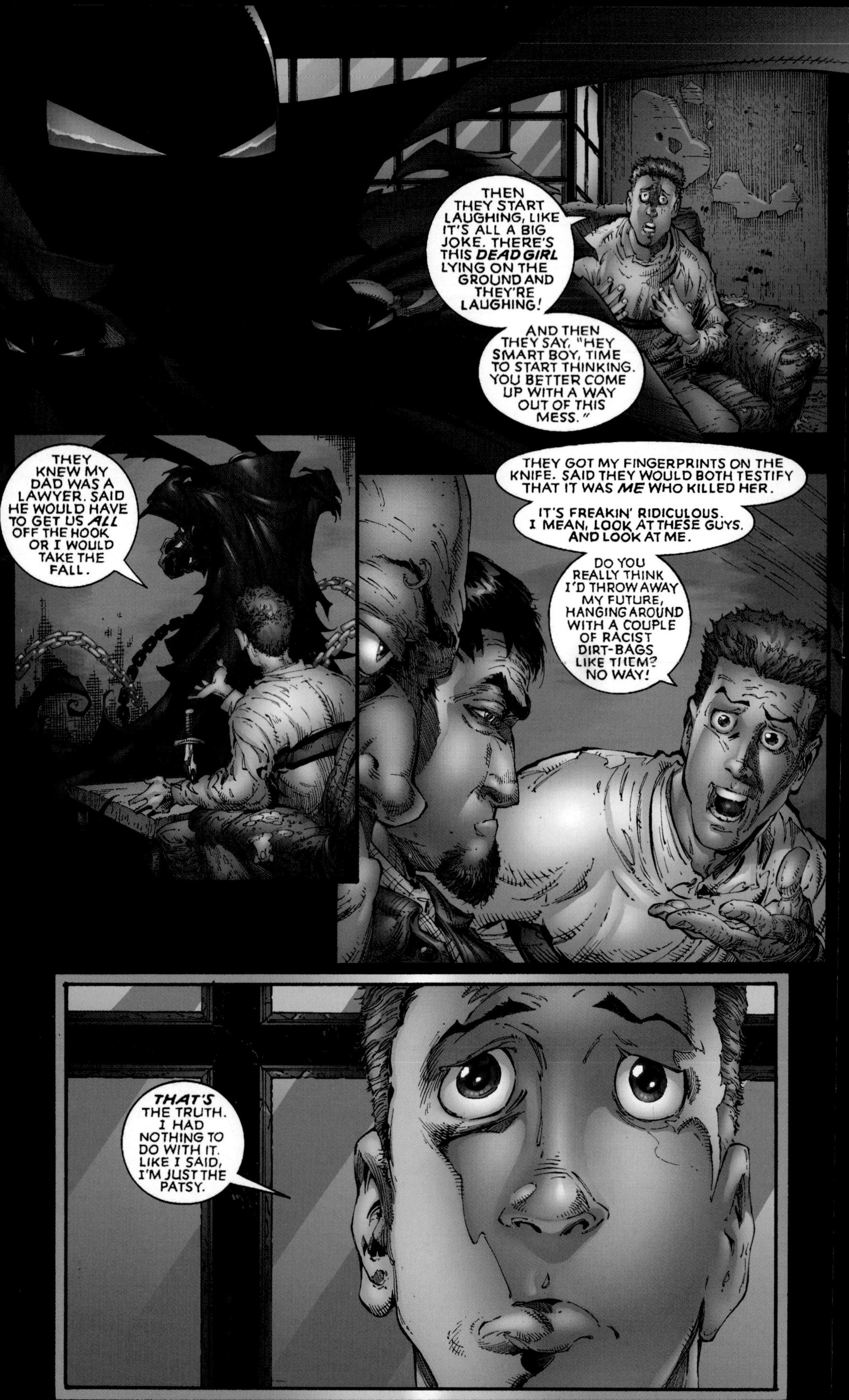
THEN THEY START LAUGHING, LIKE IT'S ALL A BIG JOKE. THERE'S THIS DEAD GIRL LYING ON THE GROUND AND THEY'RE LAUGHING!
AND THEN THEY SAY, "HEY SMART BOY, TIME TO START THINKING. YOU BETTER COME UP WITH A WAY OUT OF THIS MESS."
THEY KNEW MY DAD WAS A LAWYER. SAID HE WOULD HAVE TO GET US ALL OFF THE HOOK OR I WOULD TAKE THE FALL.
THEY GOT MY FINGERPRINTS ON THE KNIFE. SAID THEY WOULD BOTH TESTIFY THAT IT WAS ME WHO KILLED HER.
IT'S FREAKIN' RIDICULOUS. I MEAN, LOOK AT THESE GUYS. AND LOOK AT ME.
DO YOU REALLY THINK I'D THROW AWAY MY FUTURE, HANGING AROUND WITH A COUPLE OF RACIST DIRT-BAGS LIKE THEM? NO WAY!
THAT'S THE TRUTH. I HAD NOTHING TO DO WITH IT. LIKE I SAID, I'M JUST THE PATSY.

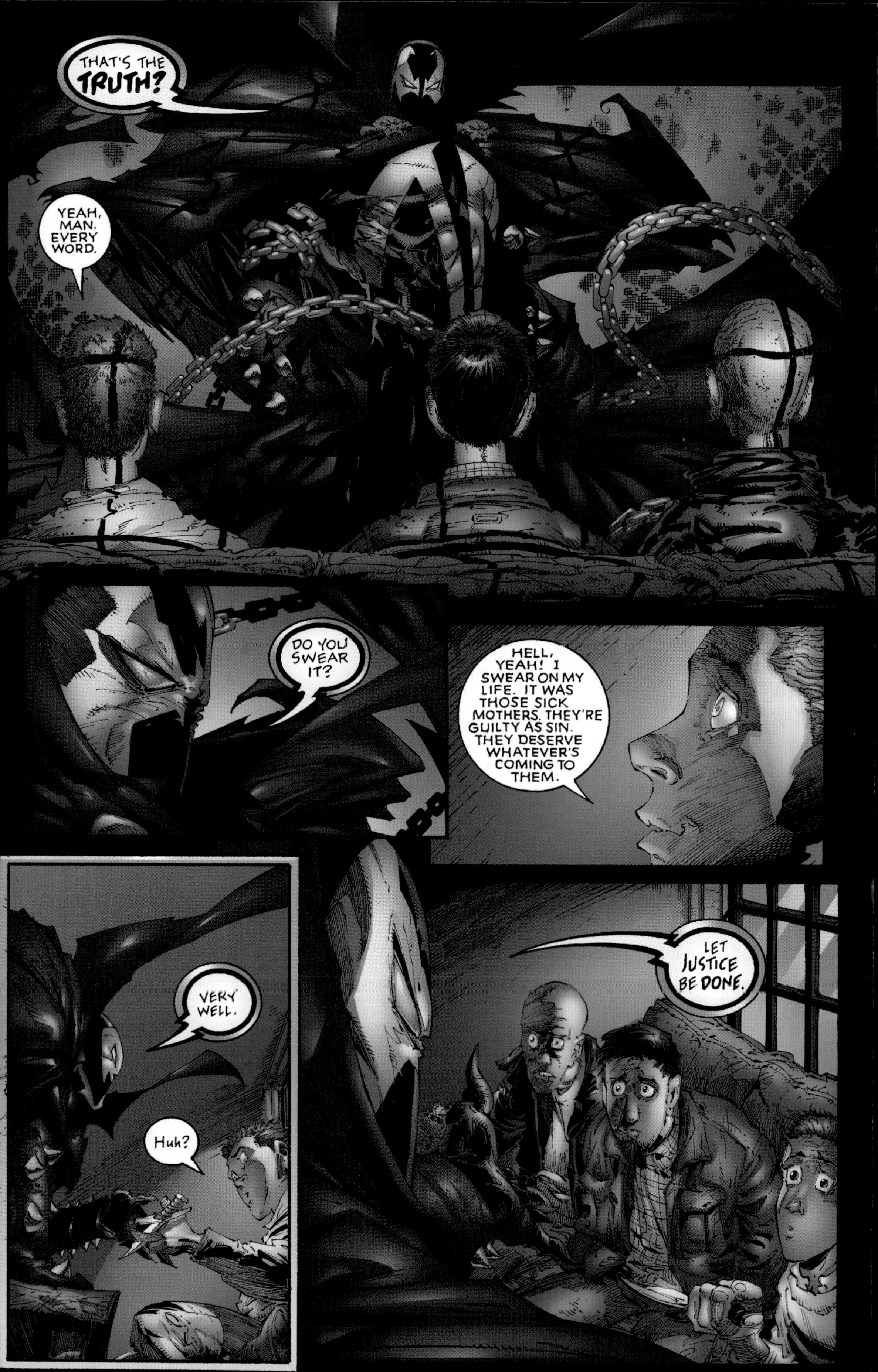
THAT'S THE TRUTH?
YEAH, MAN. EVERY WORD.
DO YOU SWEAR IT?
HELL, YEAH! I SWEAR ON MY LIFE. IT WAS THOSE SICK MOTHERS. THEY'RE GUILTY AS SIN. THEY DESERVE WHATEVER'S COMING TO THEM.
VERY WELL.
Huh?
LET JUSTICE BE DONE.

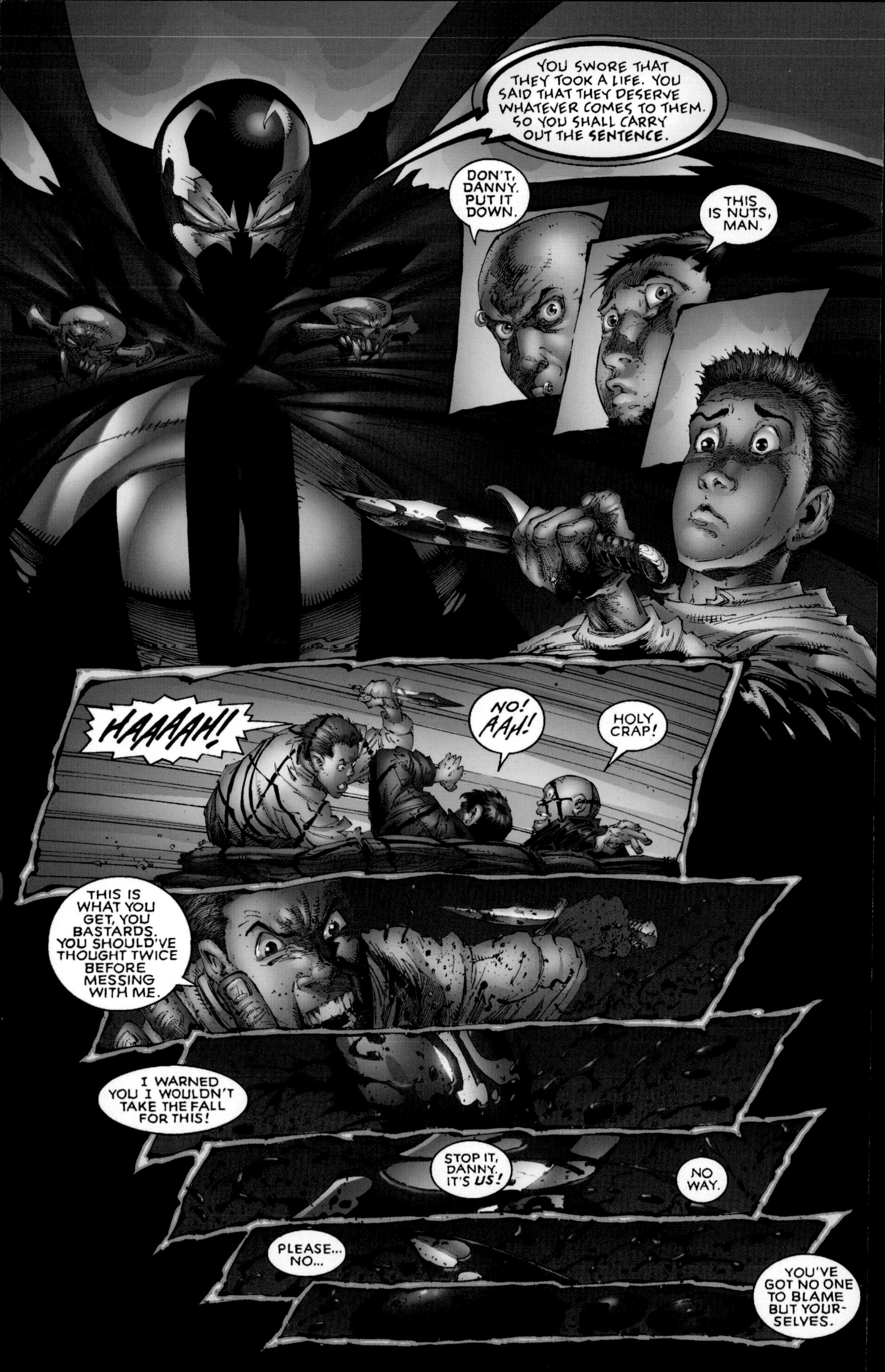
YOU SWORE THAT THEY TOOK A LIFE. YOU SAID THAT THEY DESERVE WHATEVER COMES TO THEM. SO YOU SHALL CARRY OUT THE SENTENCE.
DON'T, DANNY. PUT IT DOWN.
THIS IS NUTS, MAN.
HAAAAAH!
NO! AAH!
HOLY CRAP!
THIS IS WHAT YOU GET, YOU BASTARDS. YOU SHOULD'VE THOUGHT TWICE BEFORE MESSING WITH ME.
I WARNED YOU I WOULDN'T TAKE THE FALL FOR THIS!
STOP IT, DANNY. IT'S US!
NO WAY.
PLEASE... NO...
YOU'VE GOT NO ONE TO BLAME BUT YOUR-SELVES.

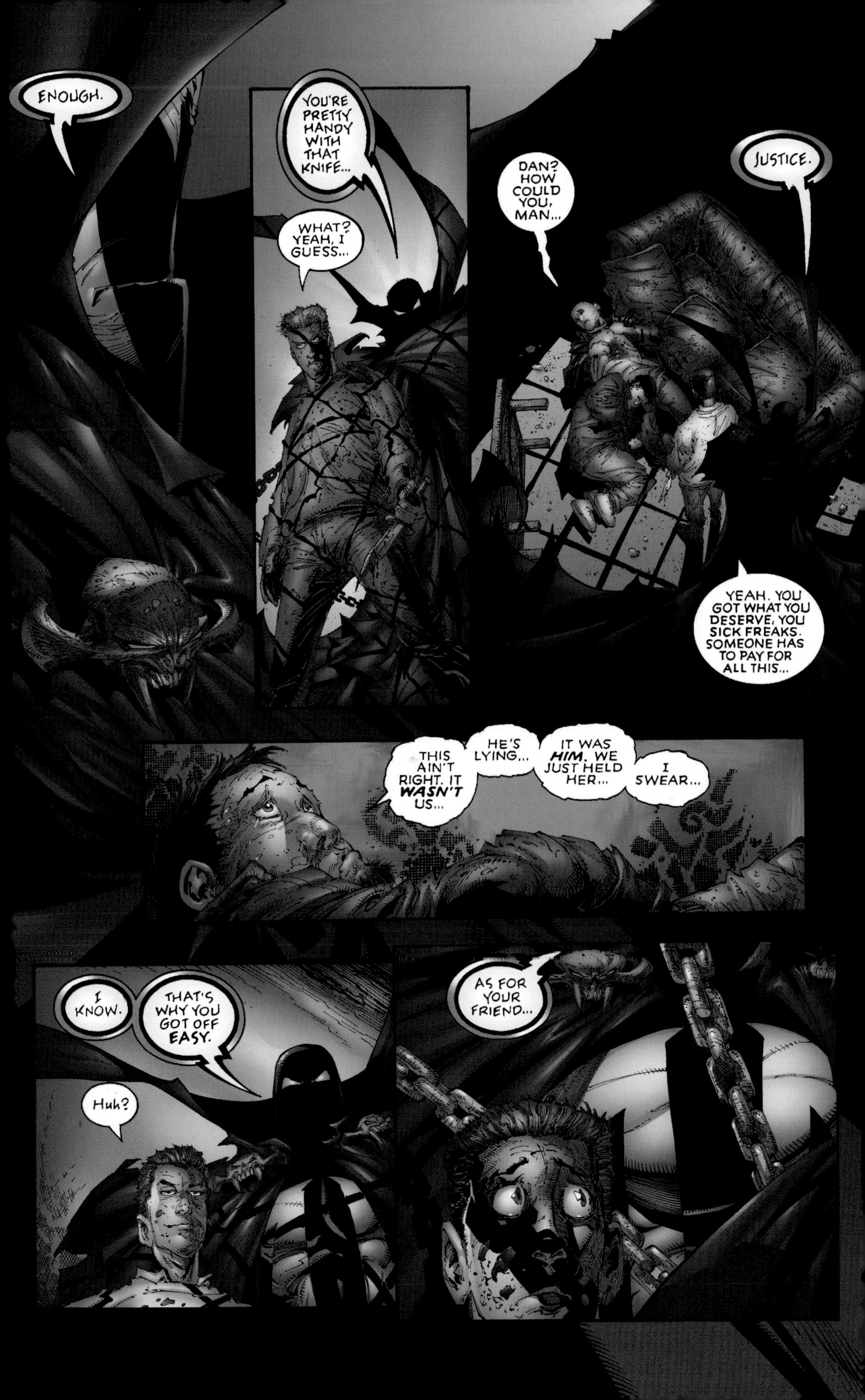
ENOUGH.
YOU'RE PRETTY HANDY WITH THAT KNIFE...
WHAT? YEAH, I GUESS...
DAN? HOW COULD YOU, MAN...
JUSTICE.
YEAH. YOU GOT WHAT YOU DESERVE, YOU SICK FREAKS. SOMEONE HAS TO PAY FOR ALL THIS...
THIS AIN'T RIGHT. IT WASN'T US...
HE'S LYING...
IT WAS HIM. WE JUST HELD HER...
I SWEAR...
I KNOW.
THAT'S WHY YOU GOT OFF EASY.
Huh?
AS FOR YOUR FRIEND...

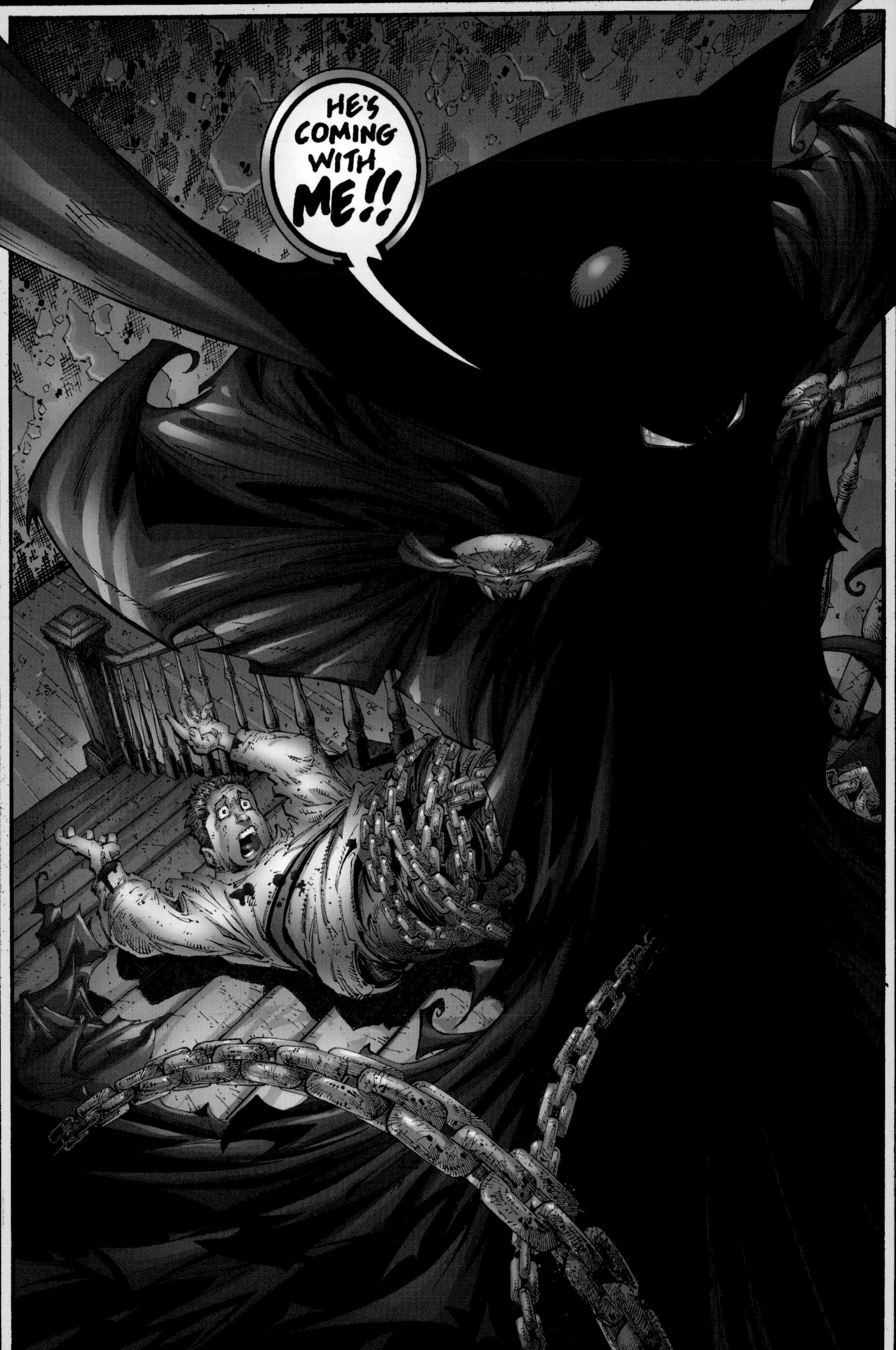
HE'S COMING WITH ME!!

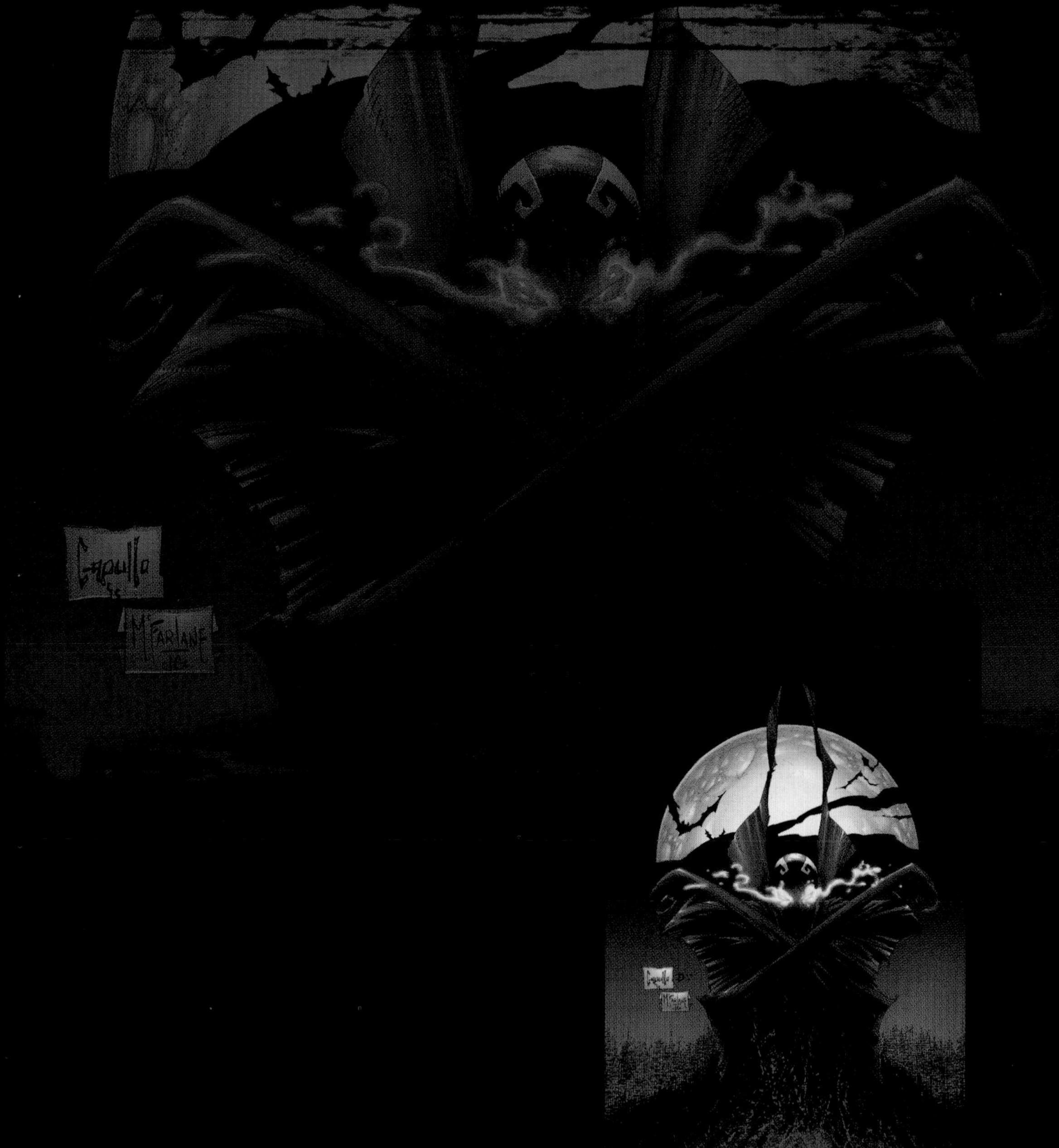

ISSUE NINETY-ONE

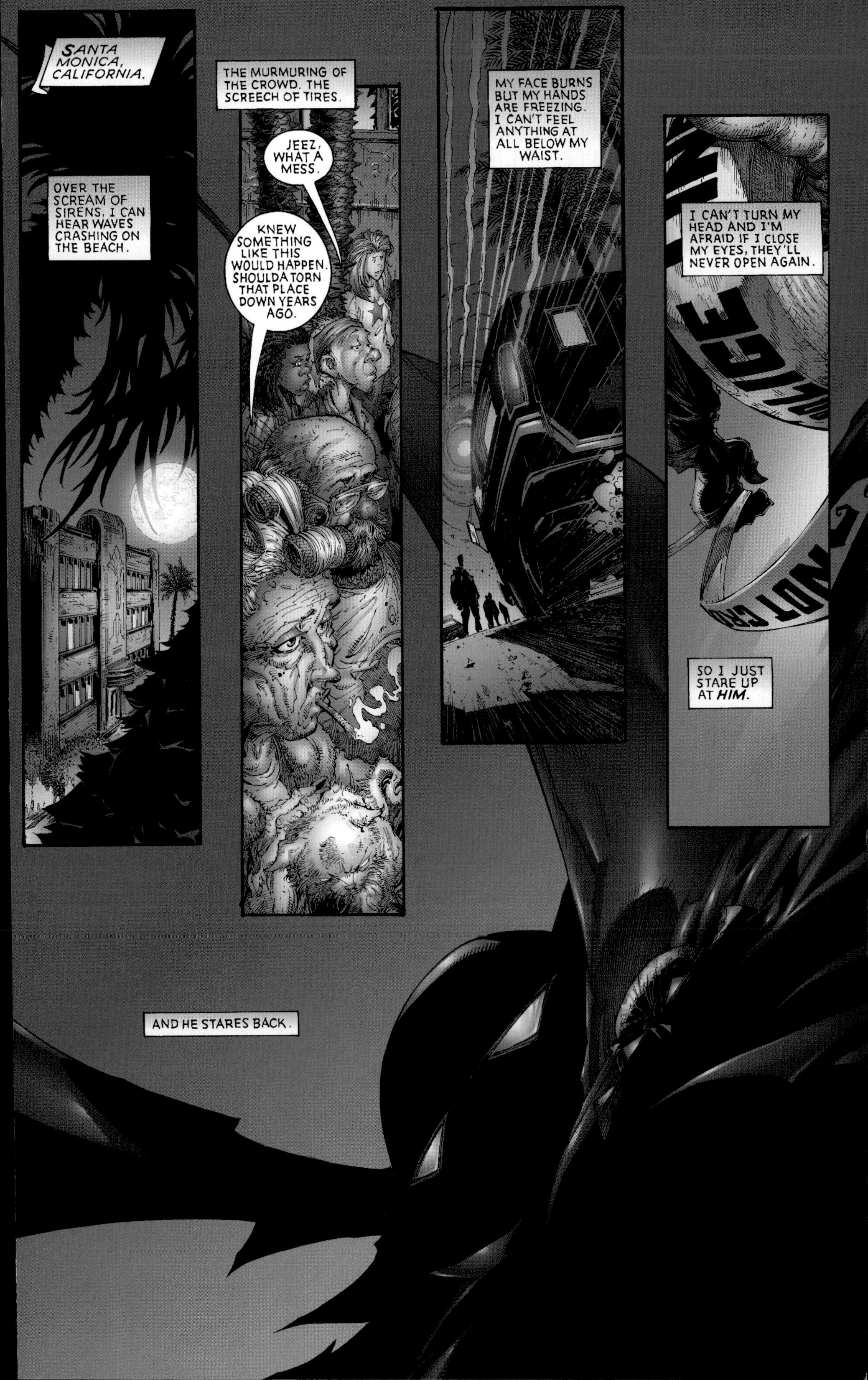
SANTA MONICA, CALIFORNIA.
OVER THE SCREAM OF SIRENS, I CAN HEAR WAVES CRASHING ON THE BEACH.
THE MURMURING OF THE CROWD. THE SCREECH OF TIRES.
JEEZ, WHAT A MESS.
KNEW SOMETHING LIKE THIS WOULD HAPPEN. SHOULDA TORN THAT PLACE DOWN YEARS AGO.
MY FACE BURNS BUT MY HANDS ARE FREEZING. I CAN'T FEEL ANYTHING AT ALL BELOW MY WAIST.
I CAN'T TURN MY HEAD AND I'M AFRAID IF I CLOSE MY EYES, THEY'LL NEVER OPEN AGAIN.
SO I JUST STARE UP AT HIM.
AND HE STARES BACK.

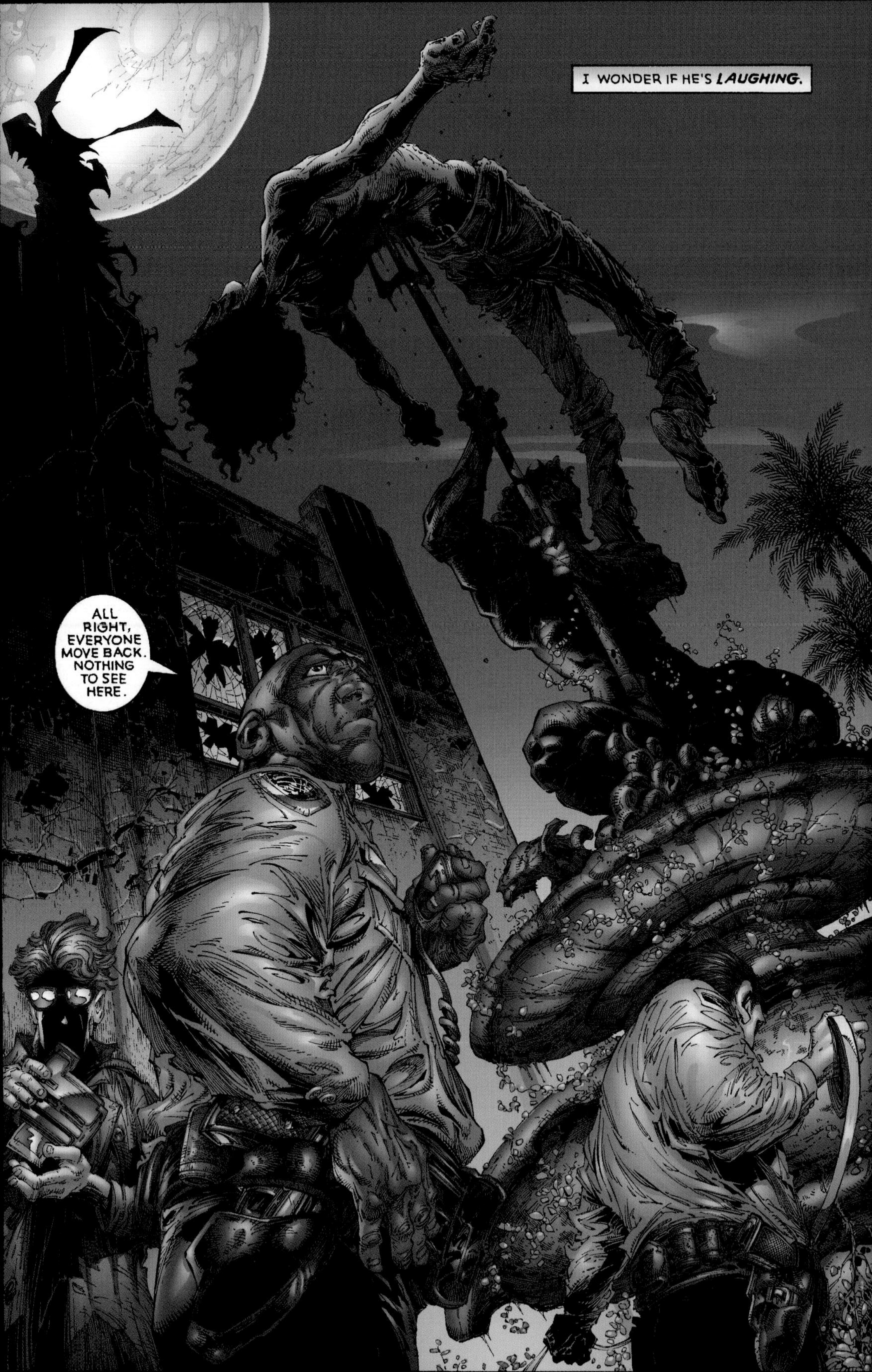
I WONDER IF HE'S LAUGHING.
ALL RIGHT, EVERYONE MOVE BACK. NOTHING TO SEE HERE.

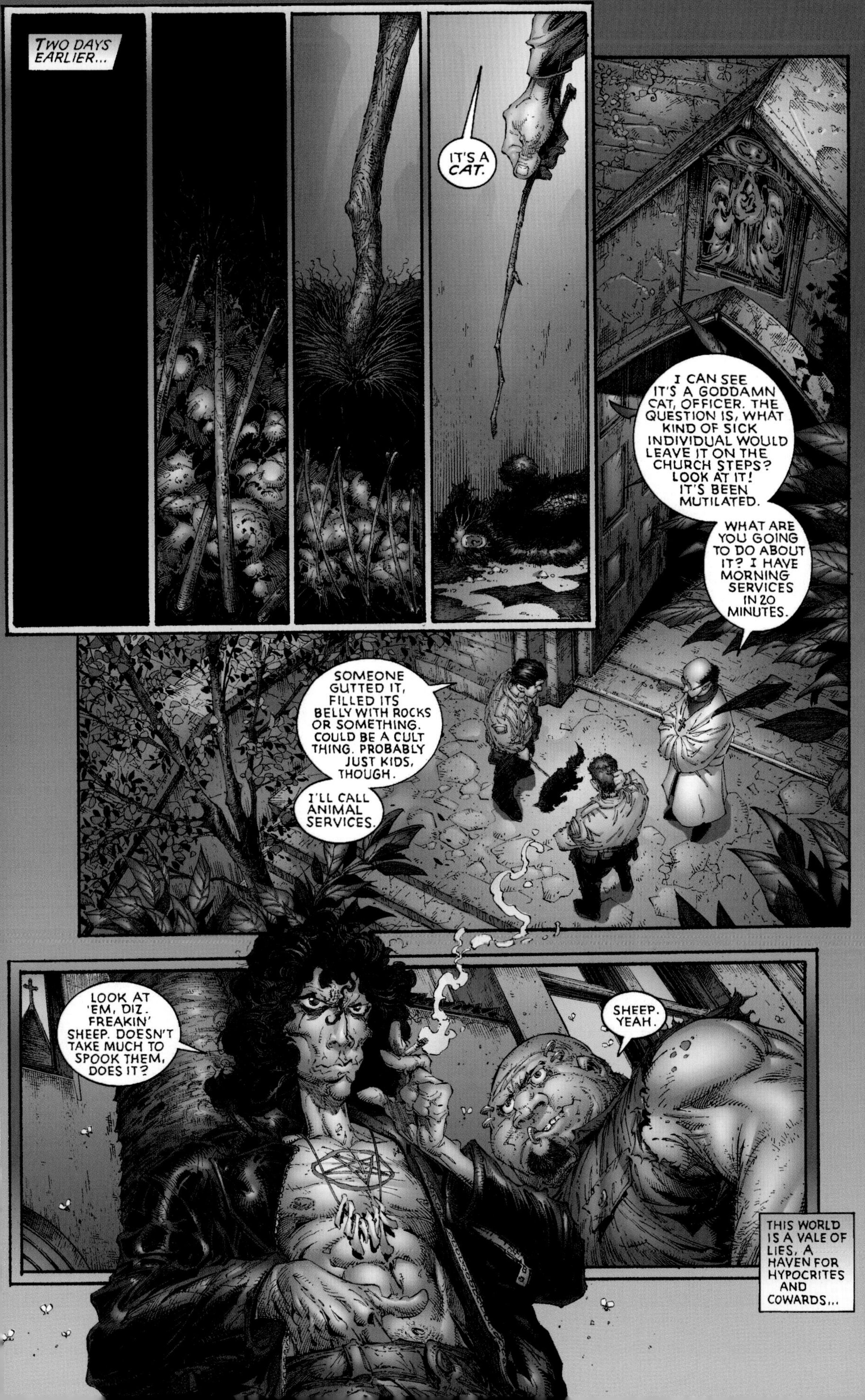
TWO DAYS EARLIER...
IT'S A CAT.
I CAN SEE IT'S A GODDAMN CAT, OFFICER. THE QUESTION IS, WHAT KIND OF SICK INDIVIDUAL WOULD LEAVE IT ON THE CHURCH STEPS? LOOK AT IT! IT'S BEEN MUTILATED.
WHAT ARE YOU GOING TO DO ABOUT IT? I HAVE MORNING SERVICES IN 20 MINUTES.
SOMEONE GUTTED IT, FILLED ITS BELLY WITH ROCKS OR SOMETHING. COULD BE A CULT THING. PROBABLY JUST KIDS, THOUGH.
I'LL CALL ANIMAL SERVICES.
LOOK AT 'EM, DIZ. FREAKIN' SHEEP. DOESN'T TAKE MUCH TO SPOOK THEM, DOES IT?
SHEEP. YEAH.
THIS WORLD IS A VALE OF LIES, A HAVEN FOR HYPOCRITES AND COWARDS...

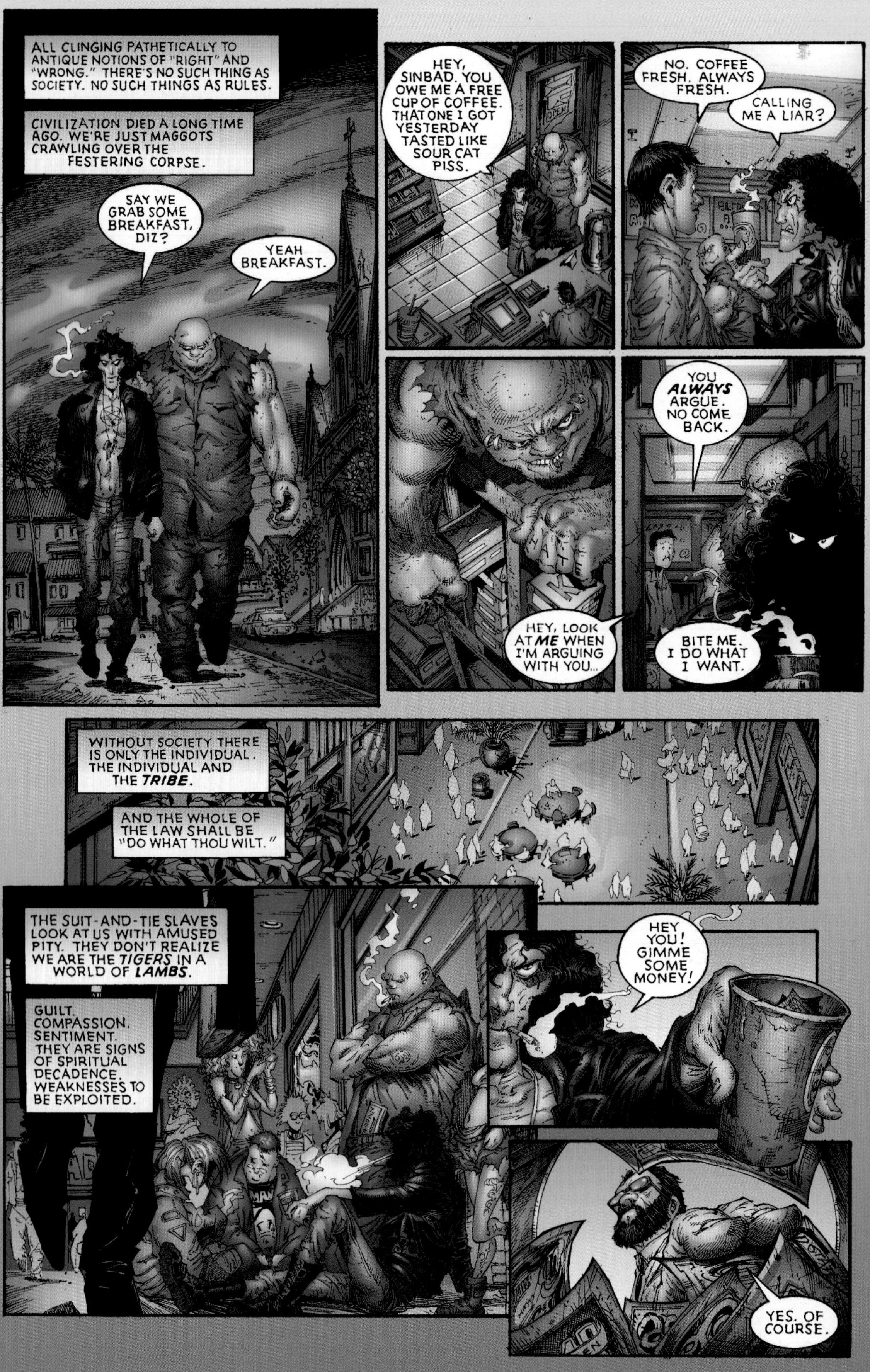

ALL CLINGING PATHETICALLY TO ANTIQUE NOTIONS OF "RIGHT" AND "WRONG." THERE'S NO SUCH THING AS SOCIETY. NO SUCH THINGS AS RULES.
CIVILIZATION DIED A LONG TIME AGO. WE'RE JUST MAGGOTS CRAWLING OVER THE FESTERING CORPSE.
SAY WE GRAB SOME BREAKFAST, DIZ?
YEAH BREAKFAST.
HEY, SINBAD. YOU OWE ME A FREE CUP OF COFFEE. THAT ONE I GOT YESTERDAY TASTED LIKE SOUR CAT PISS.
NO. COFFEE FRESH. ALWAYS FRESH.
CALLING ME A LIAR?
HEY, LOOK AT ME WHEN I'M ARGUING WITH YOU...
YOU ALWAYS ARGUE. NO COME BACK.
BITE ME. I DO WHAT I WANT.
WITHOUT SOCIETY THERE IS ONLY THE INDIVIDUAL. THE INDIVIDUAL AND THE TRIBE.
AND THE WHOLE OF THE LAW SHALL BE "DO WHAT THOU WILT."
THE SUIT-AND-TIE SLAVES LOOK AT US WITH AMUSED PITY. THEY DON'T REALIZE WE ARE THE TIGERS IN A WORLD OF LAMBS.
GUILT. COMPASSION. SENTIMENT. THEY ARE SIGNS OF SPIRITUAL DECADENCE. WEAKNESSES TO BE EXPLOITED.
HEY YOU! GIMME SOME MONEY!
YES. OF COURSE.

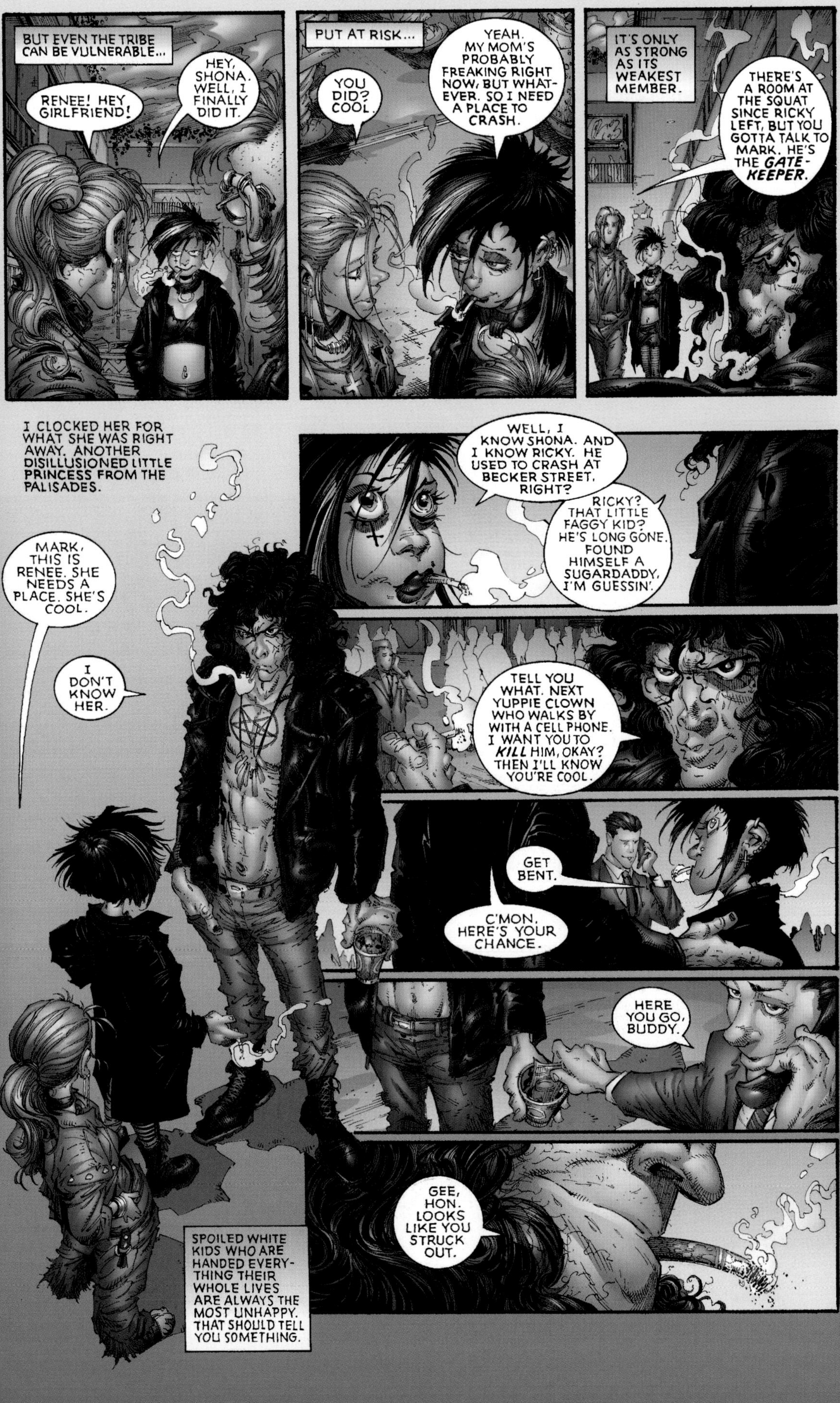
BUT EVEN THE TRIBE CAN BE VULNERABLE...
RENEE! HEY GIRLFRIEND!
HEY, SHONA. WELL, I FINALLY DID IT.
PUT AT RISK...
YOU DID? COOL.
YEAH. MY MOM'S PROBABLY FREAKING RIGHT NOW, BUT WHAT-EVER. SO I NEED A PLACE TO CRASH.
IT'S ONLY AS STRONG AS ITS WEAKEST MEMBER.
THERE'S A ROOM AT THE SQUAT SINCE RICKY LEFT, BUT YOU GOTTA TALK TO MARK. HE'S THE GATE-KEEPER.
I CLOCKED HER FOR WHAT SHE WAS RIGHT AWAY. ANOTHER DISILLUSIONED LITTLE PRINCESS FROM THE PALISADES.
MARK, THIS IS RENEE. SHE NEEDS A PLACE. SHE'S COOL.
I DON'T KNOW HER.
WELL, I KNOW SHONA. AND I KNOW RICKY. HE USED TO CRASH AT BECKER STREET, RIGHT?
RICKY? THAT LITTLE FAGGY KID? HE'S LONG GONE. FOUND HIMSELF A SUGARDADDY, I'M GUESSIN'.
TELL YOU WHAT. NEXT YUPPIE CLOWN WHO WALKS BY WITH A CELL PHONE. I WANT YOU TO KILL HIM, OKAY? THEN I'LL KNOW YOU'RE COOL.
GET BENT.
C'MON, HERE'S YOUR CHANCE.
HERE YOU GO, BUDDY.
GEE, HON. LOOKS LIKE YOU STRUCK OUT.
SPOILED WHITE KIDS WHO ARE HANDED EVERY-THING THEIR WHOLE LIVES ARE ALWAYS THE MOST UNHAPPY. THAT SHOULD TELL YOU SOMETHING.

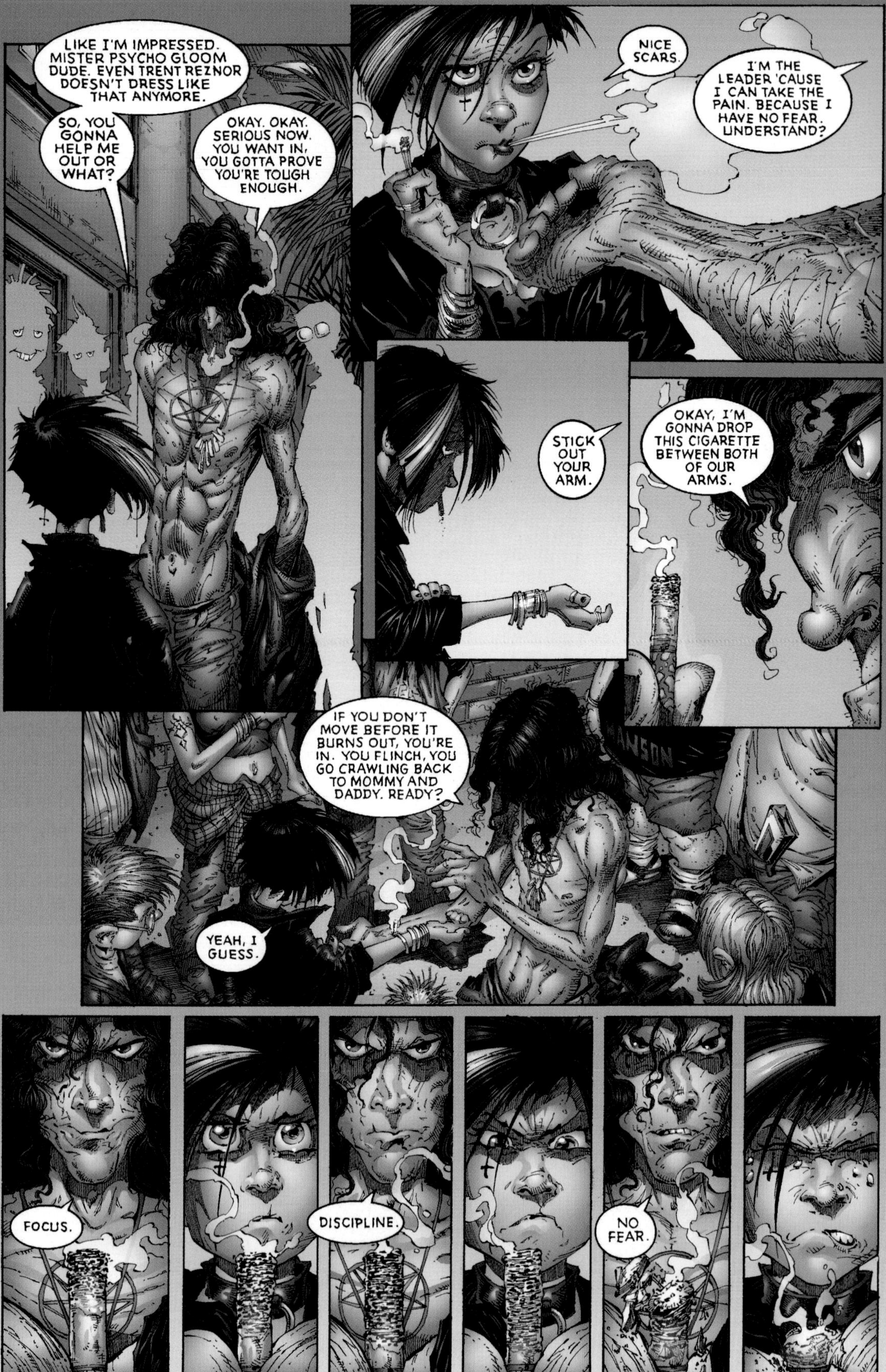
LIKE I'M IMPRESSED. MISTER PSYCHO GLOOM DUDE. EVEN TRENT REZNOR DOESN'T DRESS LIKE THAT ANYMORE.
SO, YOU GONNA HELP ME OUT OR WHAT?
OKAY. OKAY. SERIOUS NOW. YOU WANT IN, YOU GOTTA PROVE YOU'RE TOUGH ENOUGH.
NICE SCARS.
I'M THE LEADER 'CAUSE I CAN TAKE THE PAIN. BECAUSE I HAVE NO FEAR. UNDERSTAND?
STICK OUT YOUR ARM.
OKAY, I'M GONNA DROP THIS CIGARETTE BETWEEN BOTH OF OUR ARMS.
IF YOU DON'T MOVE BEFORE IT BURNS OUT, YOU'RE IN. YOU FLINCH, YOU GO CRAWLING BACK TO MOMMY AND DADDY. READY?
YEAH, I GUESS.
FOCUS.
DISCIPLINE.
NO FEAR.

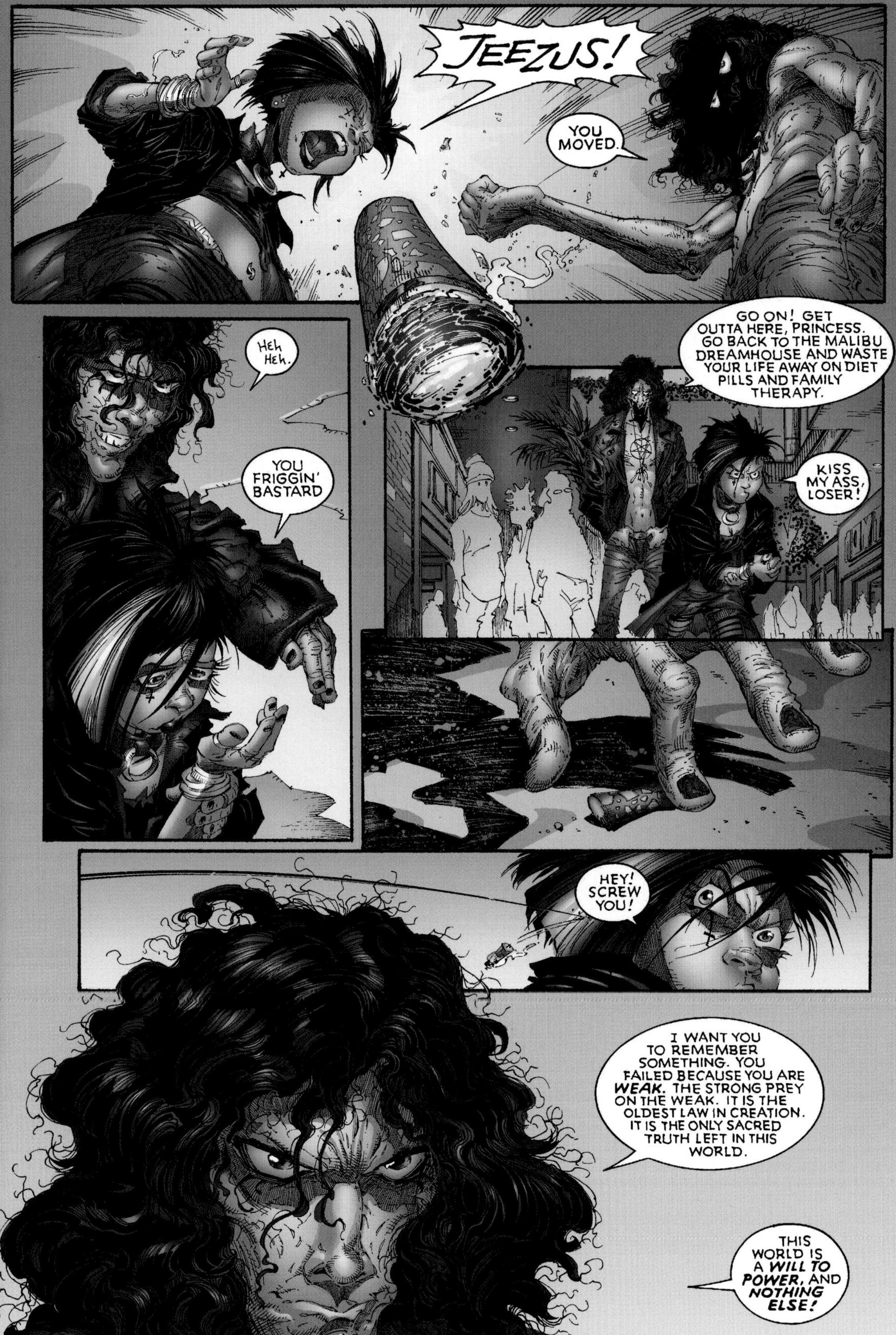
JEEZUS!
YOU MOVED.
Heh Heh.
YOU FRIGGIN' BASTARD
GO ON! GET OUTTA HERE, PRINCESS. GO BACK TO THE MALIBU DREAMHOUSE AND WASTE YOUR LIFE AWAY ON DIET PILLS AND FAMILY THERAPY.
KISS MY ASS, LOSER!
HEY! SCREW YOU!
I WANT YOU TO REMEMBER SOMETHING. YOU FAILED BECAUSE YOU ARE WEAK. THE STRONG PREY ON THE WEAK. IT IS THE OLDEST LAW IN CREATION. IT IS THE ONLY SACRED TRUTH LEFT IN THIS WORLD.
THIS WORLD IS A WILL TO POWER, AND NOTHING ELSE!

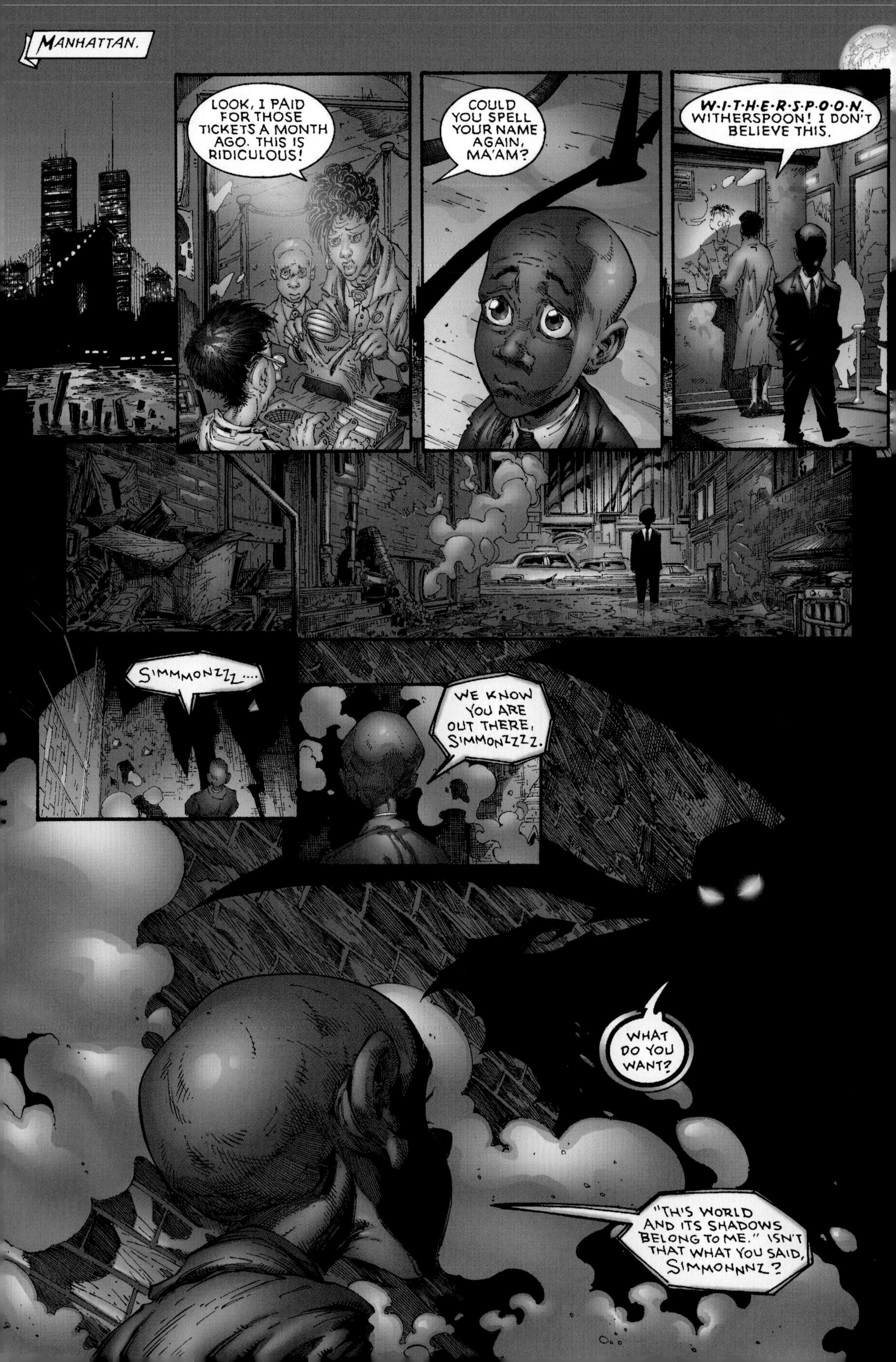
MANHATTAN.
LOOK, I PAID FOR THOSE TICKETS A MONTH AGO. THIS IS RIDICULOUS!
COULD YOU SPELL YOUR NAME AGAIN, MA'AM?
W·I·T·H·E·R·S·P·O·O·N. WITHERSPOON! I DON'T BELIEVE THIS.
SIMMMONZZZ....
WE KNOW YOU ARE OUT THERE, SIMMONZZZZ.
WHAT DO YOU WANT?
"THIS WORLD AND ITS SHADOWS BELONG TO ME." ISN'T THAT WHAT YOU SAID, SIMMONNNZ?

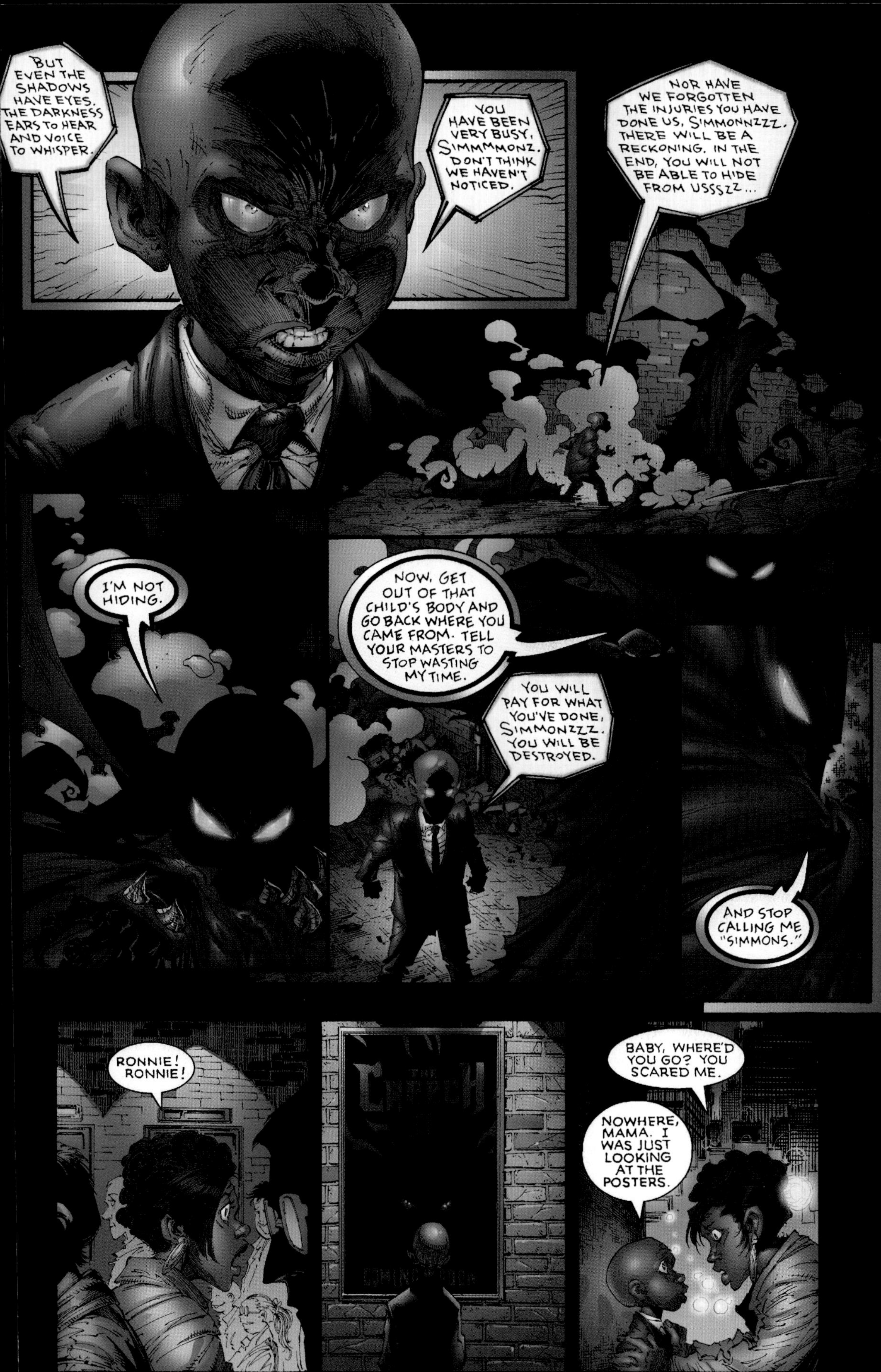
BUT EVEN THE SHADOWS HAVE EYES. THE DARKNESS EARS TO HEAR AND VOICE TO WHISPER.
YOU HAVE BEEN VERY BUSY, SIMMMMONZ. DON'T THINK WE HAVEN'T NOTICED.
NOR HAVE WE FORGOTTEN THE INJURIES YOU HAVE DONE US, SIMMONNZZZ. THERE WILL BE A RECKONING. IN THE END, YOU WILL NOT BE ABLE TO HIDE FROM USSSZZ...
I'M NOT HIDING.
NOW, GET OUT OF THAT CHILD'S BODY AND GO BACK WHERE YOU CAME FROM. TELL YOUR MASTERS TO STOP WASTING MY TIME.
YOU WILL PAY FOR WHAT YOU'VE DONE, SIMMONZZZ. YOU WILL BE DESTROYED.
AND STOP CALLING ME "SIMMONS."
RONNIE! RONNIE!
BABY, WHERE'D YOU GO? YOU SCARED ME.
NOWHERE, MAMA. I WAS JUST LOOKING AT THE POSTERS.

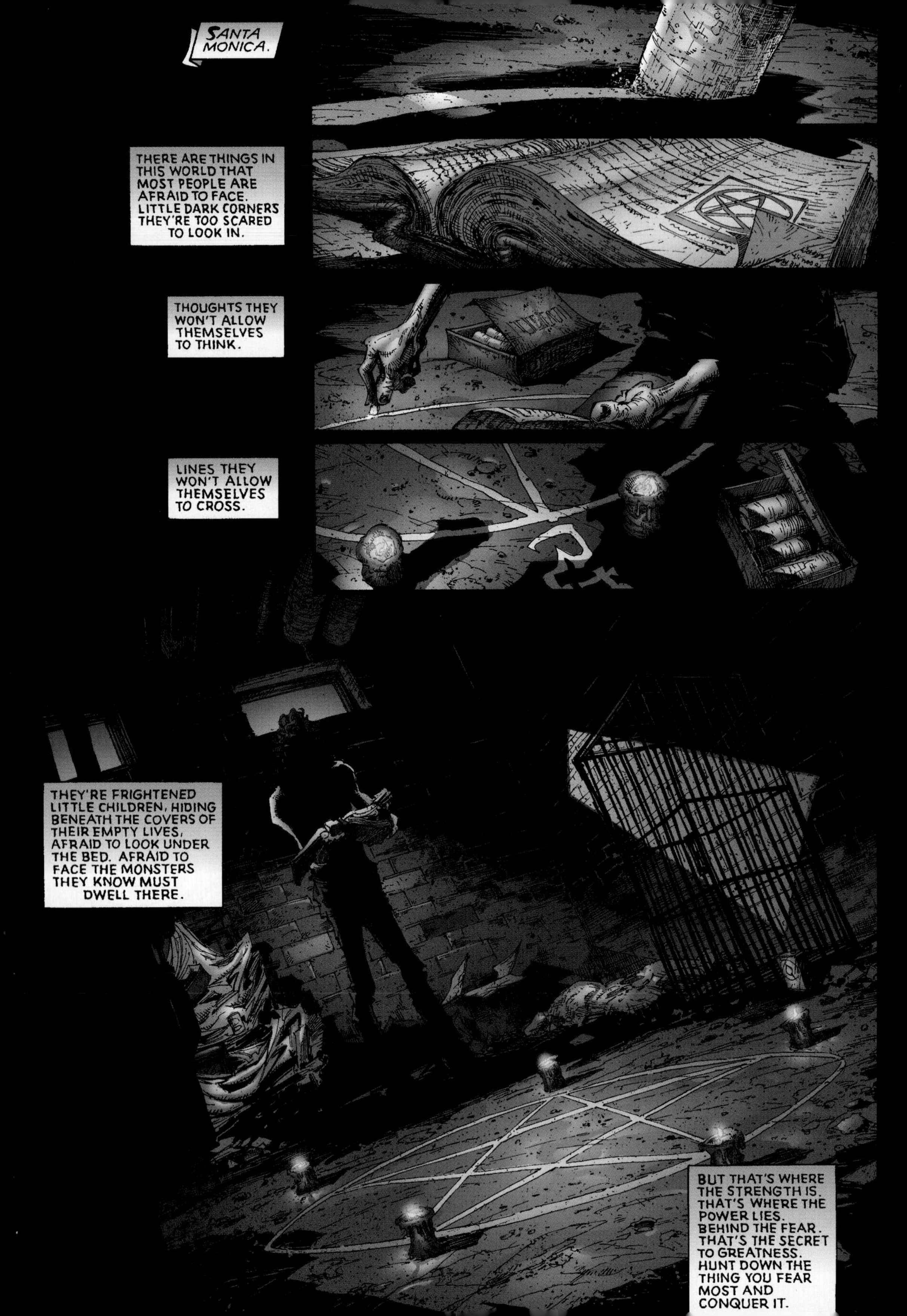
SANTA MONICA.
THERE ARE THINGS IN THIS WORLD THAT MOST PEOPLE ARE AFRAID TO FACE. LITTLE DARK CORNERS THEY'RE TOO SCARED TO LOOK IN.
THOUGHTS THEY WON'T ALLOW THEMSELVES TO THINK.
LINES THEY WON'T ALLOW THEMSELVES TO CROSS.
THEY'RE FRIGHTENED LITTLE CHILDREN, HIDING BENEATH THE COVERS OF THEIR EMPTY LIVES, AFRAID TO LOOK UNDER THE BED. AFRAID TO FACE THE MONSTERS THEY KNOW MUST DWELL THERE.
BUT THAT'S WHERE THE STRENGTH IS. THAT'S WHERE THE POWER LIES. BEHIND THE FEAR. THAT'S THE SECRET TO GREATNESS. HUNT DOWN THE THING YOU FEAR MOST AND CONQUER IT.

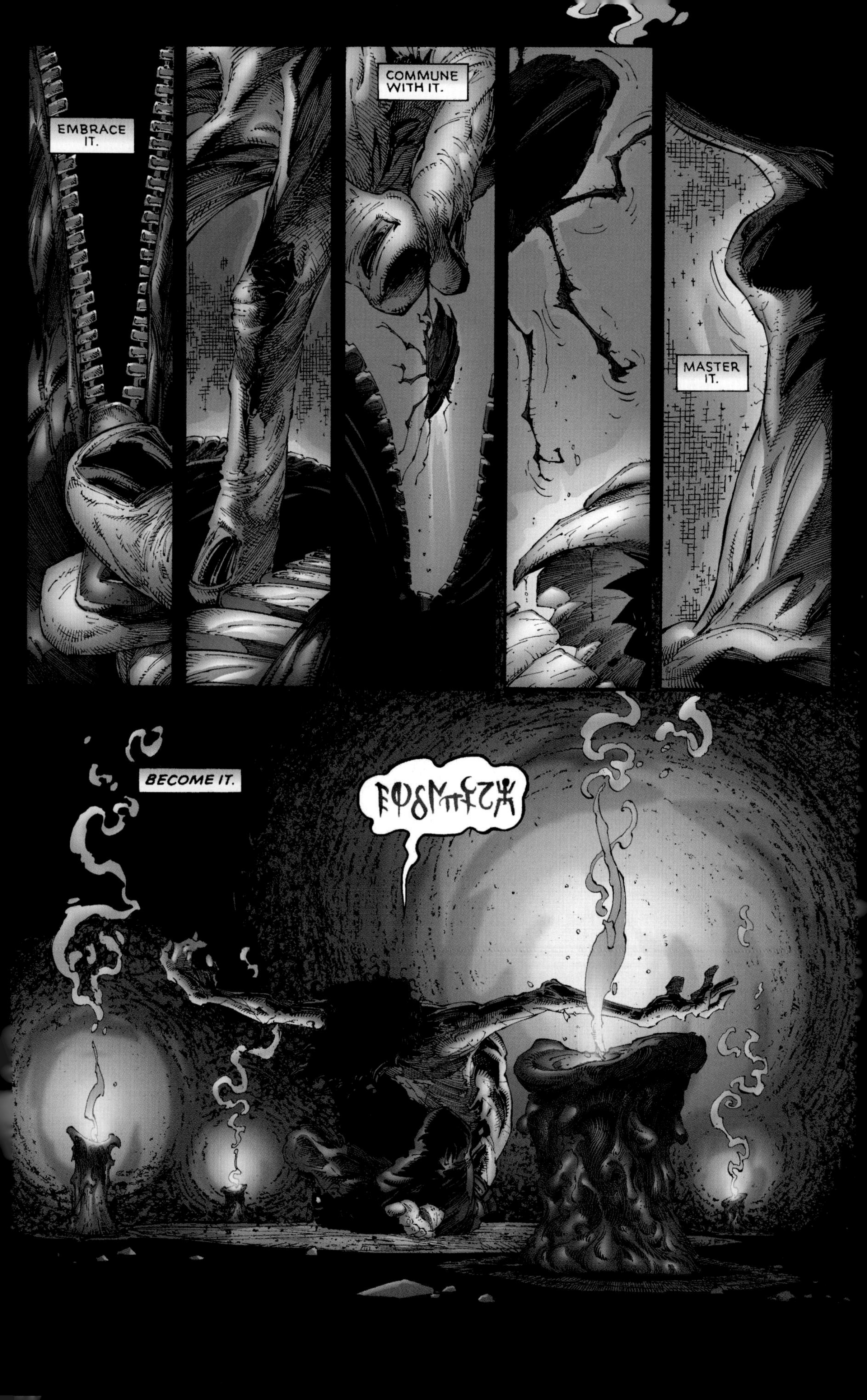
EMBRACE IT.
COMMUNE WITH IT.
MASTER IT.
BECOME IT.

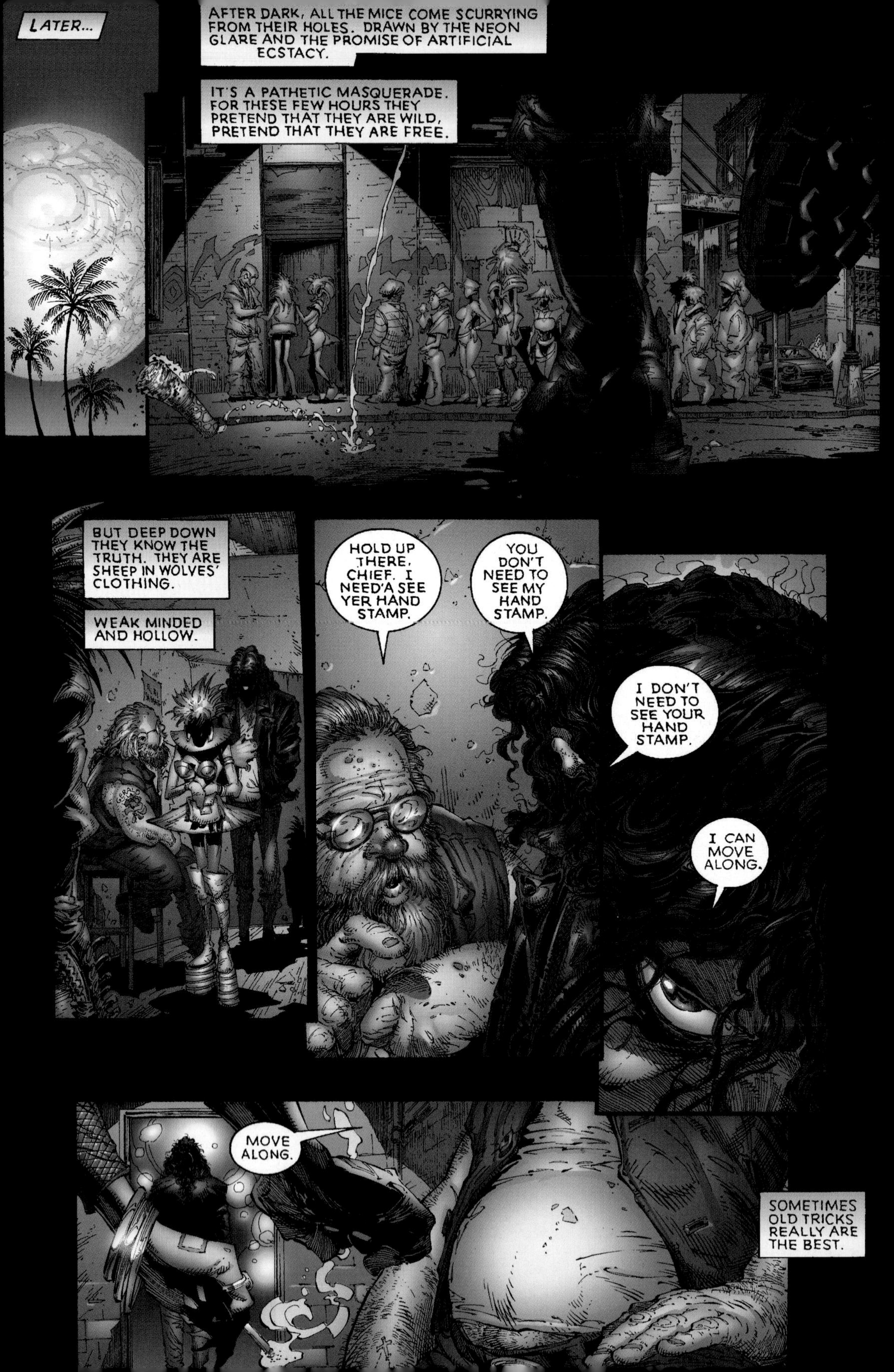
LATER...
AFTER DARK, ALL THE MICE COME SCURRYING FROM THEIR HOLES. DRAWN BY THE NEON GLARE AND THE PROMISE OF ARTIFICIAL ECSTACY.
IT'S A PATHETIC MASQUERADE. FOR THESE FEW HOURS THEY PRETEND THAT THEY ARE WILD, PRETEND THAT THEY ARE FREE.
BUT DEEP DOWN THEY KNOW THE TRUTH. THEY ARE SHEEP IN WOLVES' CLOTHING.
WEAK MINDED AND HOLLOW.
HOLD UP THERE, CHIEF. I NEED'A SEE YER HAND STAMP.
YOU DON'T NEED TO SEE MY HAND STAMP.
I DON'T NEED TO SEE YOUR HAND STAMP.
I CAN MOVE ALONG.
MOVE ALONG.
SOMETIMES OLD TRICKS REALLY ARE THE BEST.

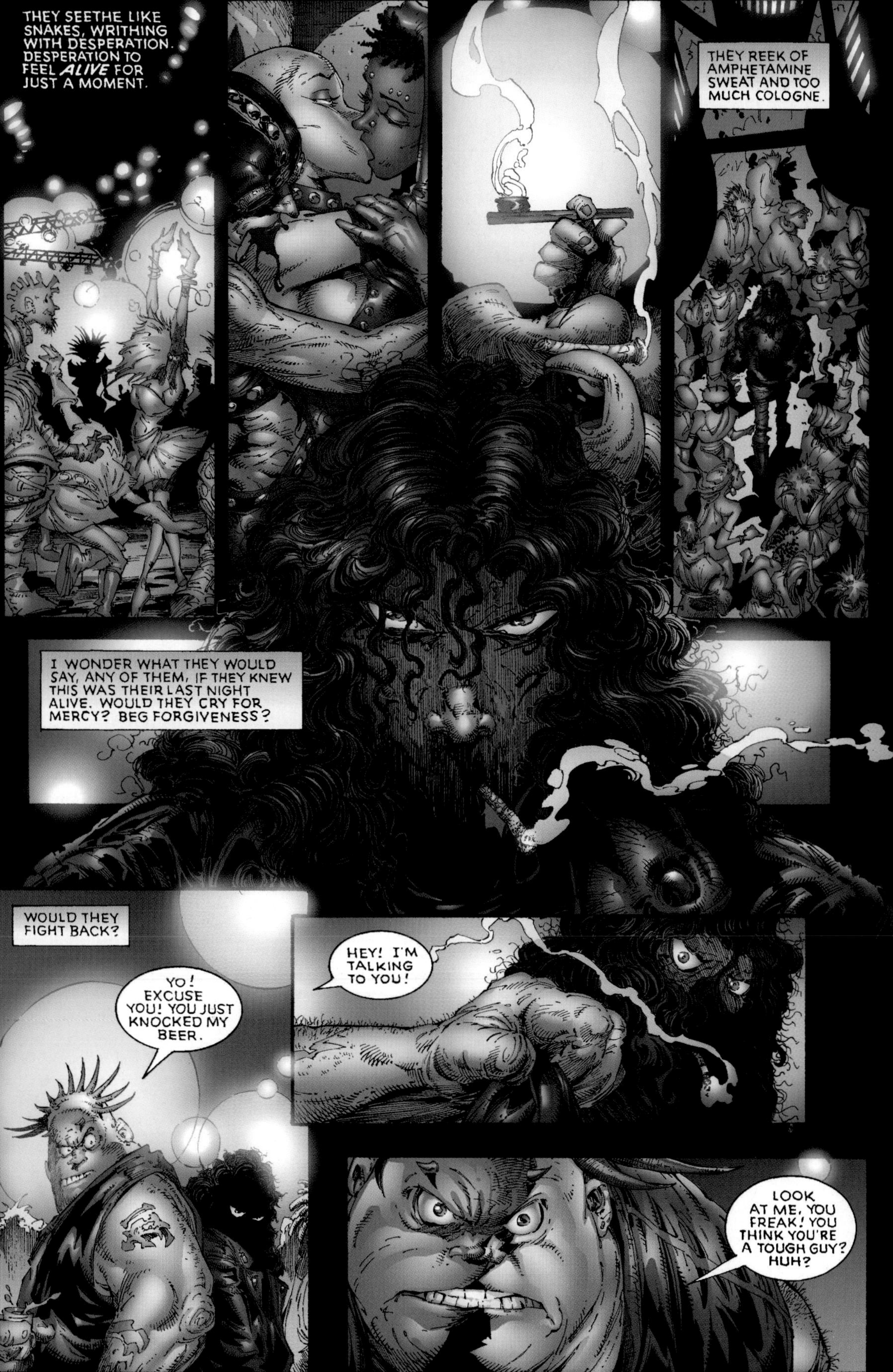
THEY SEETHE LIKE SNAKES, WRITHING WITH DESPERATION. DESPERATION TO FEEL *ALIVE* FOR JUST A MOMENT.
THEY REEK OF AMPHETAMINE SWEAT AND TOO MUCH COLOGNE.
I WONDER WHAT THEY WOULD SAY, ANY OF THEM, IF THEY KNEW THIS WAS THEIR LAST NIGHT ALIVE. WOULD THEY CRY FOR MERCY? BEG FORGIVENESS?
WOULD THEY FIGHT BACK?
YO! EXCUSE YOU! YOU JUST KNOCKED MY BEER.
HEY! I'M TALKING TO YOU!
LOOK AT ME, YOU FREAK! YOU THINK YOU'RE A TOUGH GUY? HUH?

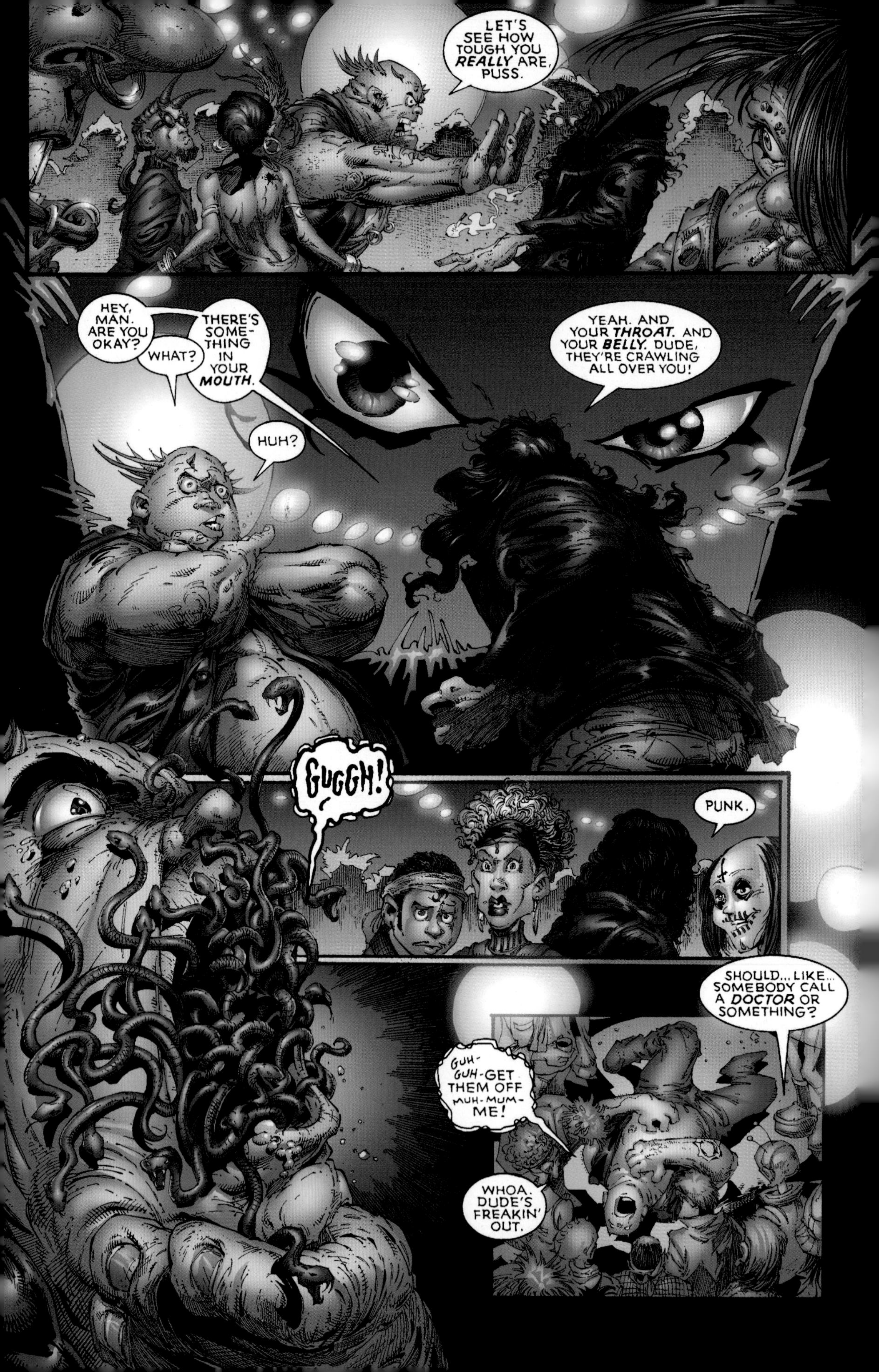
LET'S SEE HOW TOUGH YOU REALLY ARE, PUSS.
HEY, MAN. ARE YOU OKAY?
WHAT?
THERE'S SOME-THING IN YOUR MOUTH.
HUH?
YEAH. AND YOUR THROAT. AND YOUR BELLY. DUDE, THEY'RE CRAWLING ALL OVER YOU!
GUGGH!
PUNK.
SHOULD... LIKE... SOMEBODY CALL A DOCTOR OR SOMETHING?
GUH-GUH-GET THEM OFF MUH-MUM-ME!
WHOA. DUDE'S FREAKIN' OUT.

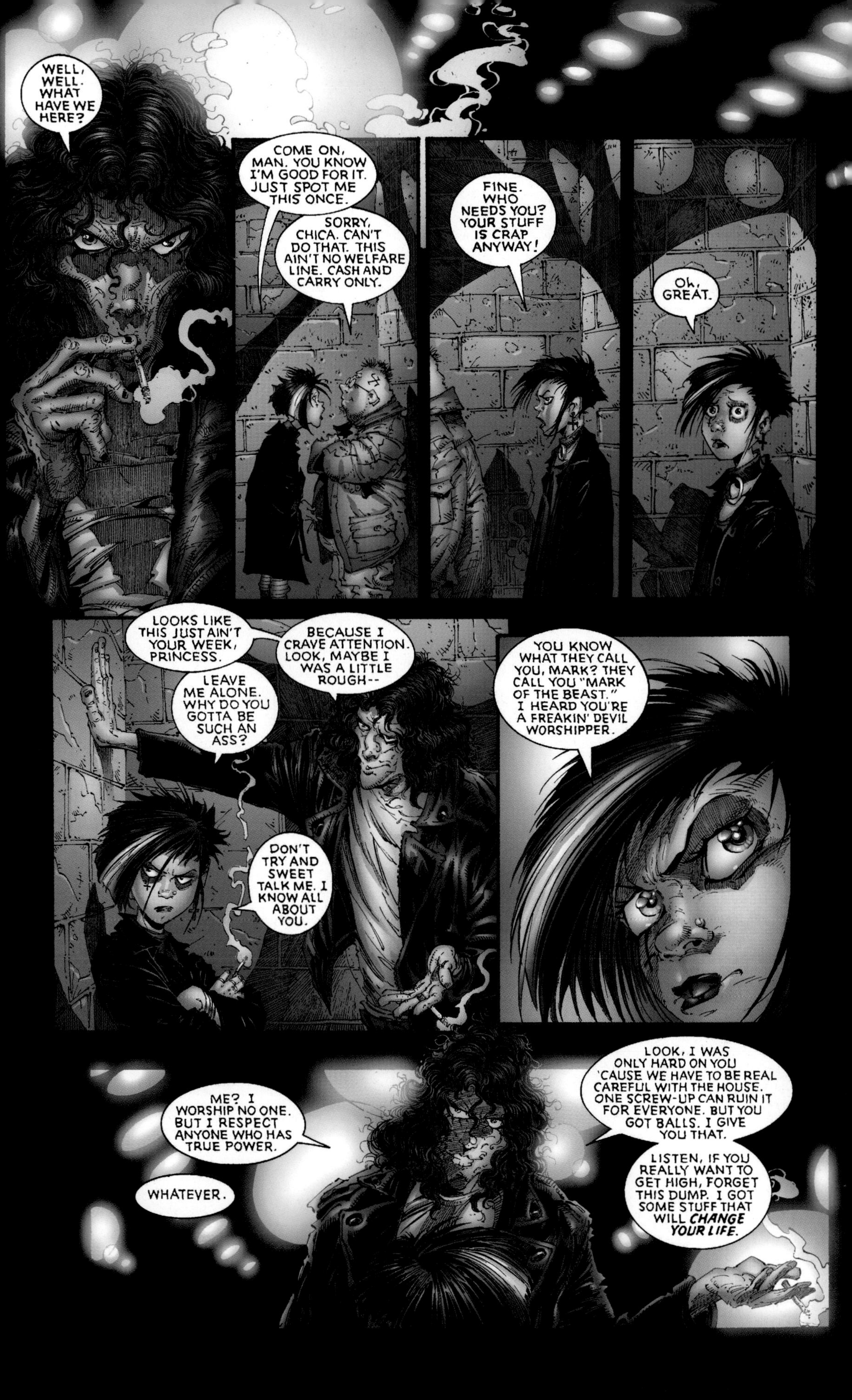
WELL, WELL. WHAT HAVE WE HERE?
COME ON, MAN. YOU KNOW I'M GOOD FOR IT. JUST SPOT ME THIS ONCE.
SORRY, CHICA. CAN'T DO THAT. THIS AIN'T NO WELFARE LINE. CASH AND CARRY ONLY.
FINE. WHO NEEDS YOU? YOUR STUFF IS CRAP ANYWAY!
Oh, GREAT.
LOOKS LIKE THIS JUST AIN'T YOUR WEEK, PRINCESS.
LEAVE ME ALONE. WHY DO YOU GOTTA BE SUCH AN ASS?
BECAUSE I CRAVE ATTENTION. LOOK, MAYBE I WAS A LITTLE ROUGH--
DON'T TRY AND SWEET TALK ME. I KNOW ALL ABOUT YOU.
YOU KNOW WHAT THEY CALL YOU, MARK? THEY CALL YOU "MARK OF THE BEAST." I HEARD YOU'RE A FREAKIN' DEVIL WORSHIPPER.
ME? I WORSHIP NO ONE. BUT I RESPECT ANYONE WHO HAS TRUE POWER.
WHATEVER.
LOOK, I WAS ONLY HARD ON YOU 'CAUSE WE HAVE TO BE REAL CAREFUL WITH THE HOUSE. ONE SCREW-UP CAN RUIN IT FOR EVERYONE. BUT YOU GOT BALLS. I GIVE YOU THAT.
LISTEN, IF YOU REALLY WANT TO GET HIGH, FORGET THIS DUMP. I GOT SOME STUFF THAT WILL CHANGE YOUR LIFE.

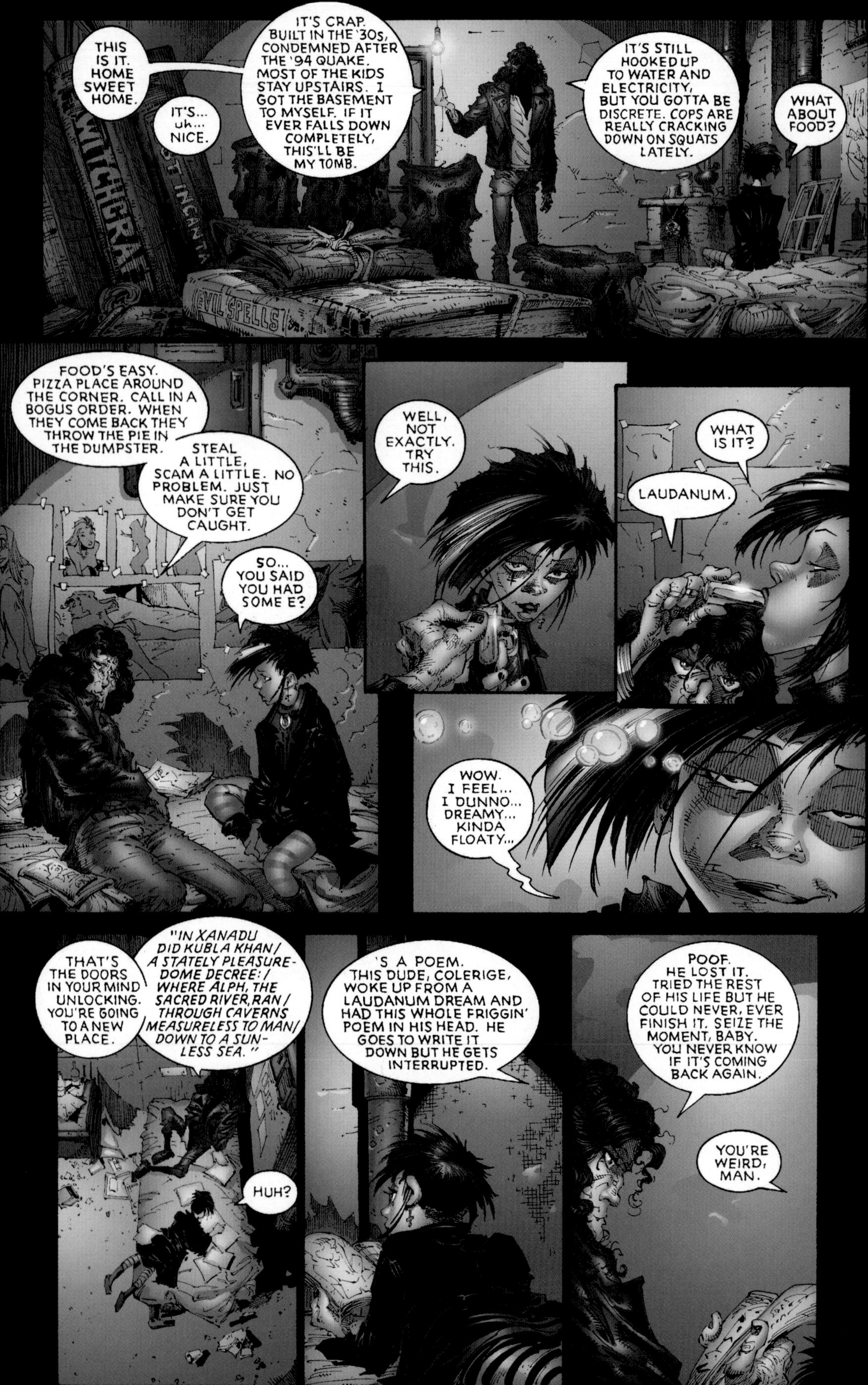
THIS IS IT. HOME SWEET HOME.
IT'S CRAP. BUILT IN THE '30S, CONDEMNED AFTER THE '94 QUAKE. MOST OF THE KIDS STAY UPSTAIRS. I GOT THE BASEMENT TO MYSELF. IF IT EVER FALLS DOWN COMPLETELY, THIS'LL BE MY TOMB.
IT'S... uh... NICE.
IT'S STILL HOOKED UP TO WATER AND ELECTRICITY, BUT YOU GOTTA BE DISCRETE. COPS ARE REALLY CRACKING DOWN ON SQUATS LATELY.
WHAT ABOUT FOOD?
WITCHCRAFT
EVIL SPELLS
FOOD'S EASY. PIZZA PLACE AROUND THE CORNER. CALL IN A BOGUS ORDER. WHEN THEY COME BACK THEY THROW THE PIE IN THE DUMPSTER.
STEAL A LITTLE, SCAM A LITTLE. NO PROBLEM. JUST MAKE SURE YOU DON'T GET CAUGHT.
SO... YOU SAID YOU HAD SOME E?
WELL, NOT EXACTLY. TRY THIS.
WHAT IS IT?
LAUDANUM.
WOW. I FEEL... I DUNNO... DREAMY... KINDA FLOATY...
THAT'S THE DOORS IN YOUR MIND UNLOCKING. YOU'RE GOING TO A NEW PLACE.
"IN XANADU DID KUBLA KHAN / A STATELY PLEASURE-DOME DECREE: / WHERE ALPH, THE SACRED RIVER, RAN / THROUGH CAVERNS MEASURELESS TO MAN / DOWN TO A SUNLESS SEA."
HUH?
'S A POEM. THIS DUDE, COLERIGE, WOKE UP FROM A LAUDANUM DREAM AND HAD THIS WHOLE FRIGGIN' POEM IN HIS HEAD. HE GOES TO WRITE IT DOWN BUT HE GETS INTERRUPTED.
POOF. HE LOST IT. TRIED THE REST OF HIS LIFE BUT HE COULD NEVER, EVER FINISH IT. SEIZE THE MOMENT, BABY. YOU NEVER KNOW IF IT'S COMING BACK AGAIN.
YOU'RE WEIRD, MAN.

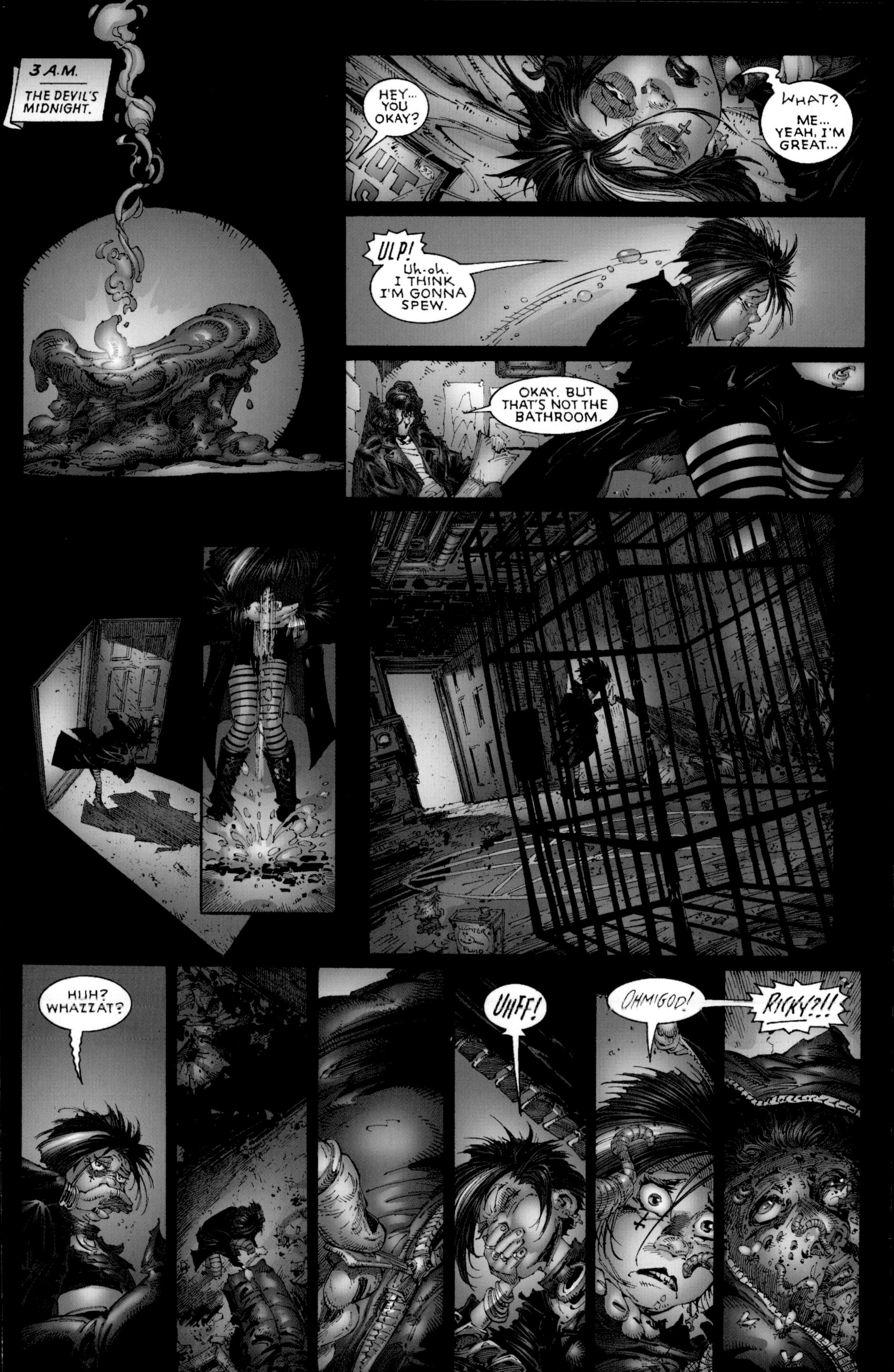
3 A.M.
THE DEVIL'S MIDNIGHT.
HEY... YOU OKAY?
WHAT? ME... YEAH, I'M GREAT...
ULP! Uh-oh. I THINK I'M GONNA SPEW.
OKAY. BUT THAT'S NOT THE BATHROOM.
HUH? WHAZZAT?
UHFF!
OHMIGOD!
RICKY?!!

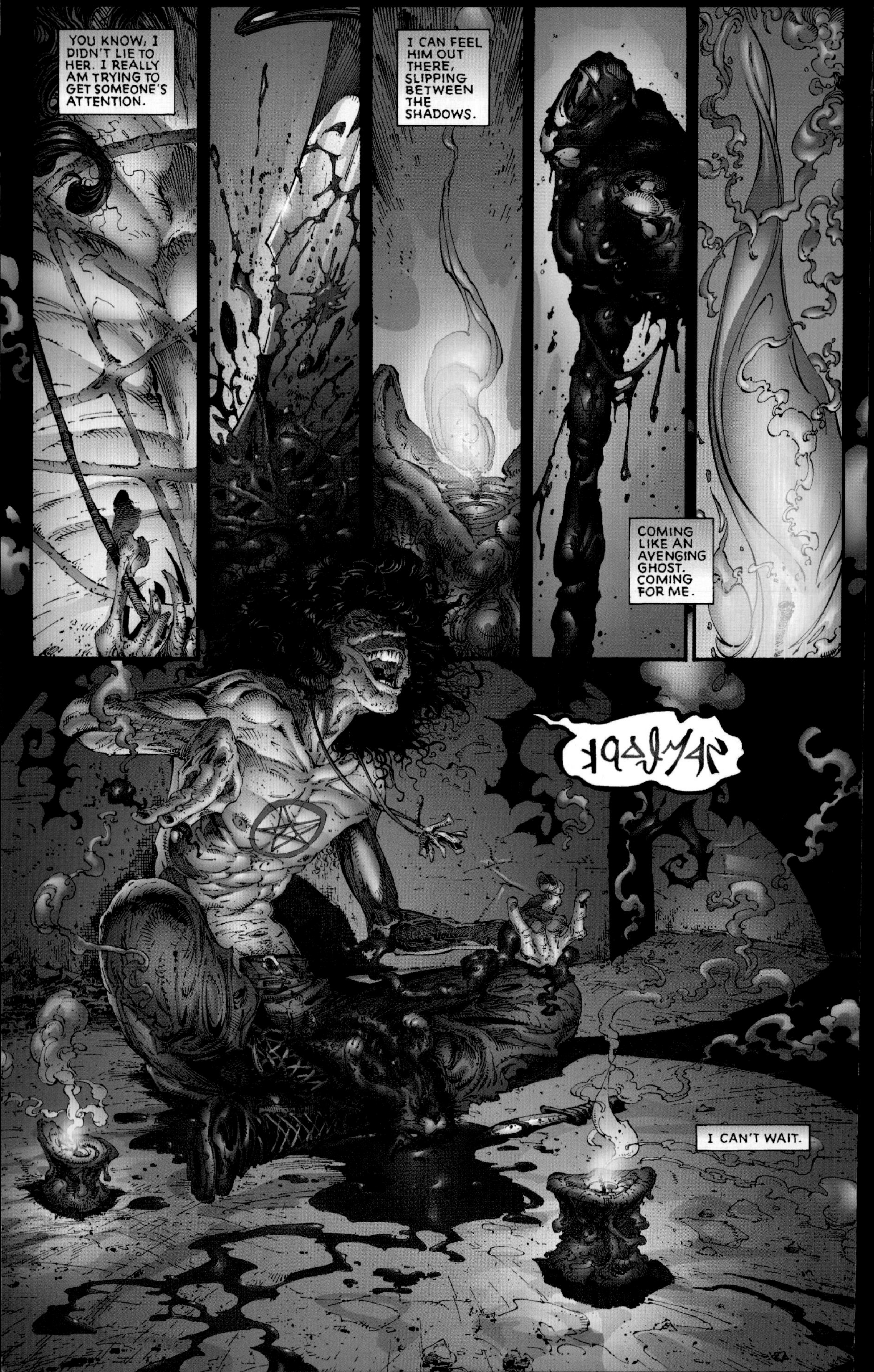
YOU KNOW, I DIDN'T LIE TO HER. I REALLY AM TRYING TO GET SOMEONE'S ATTENTION.
I CAN FEEL HIM OUT THERE, SLIPPING BETWEEN THE SHADOWS.
COMING LIKE AN AVENGING GHOST. COMING FOR ME.
I CAN'T WAIT.

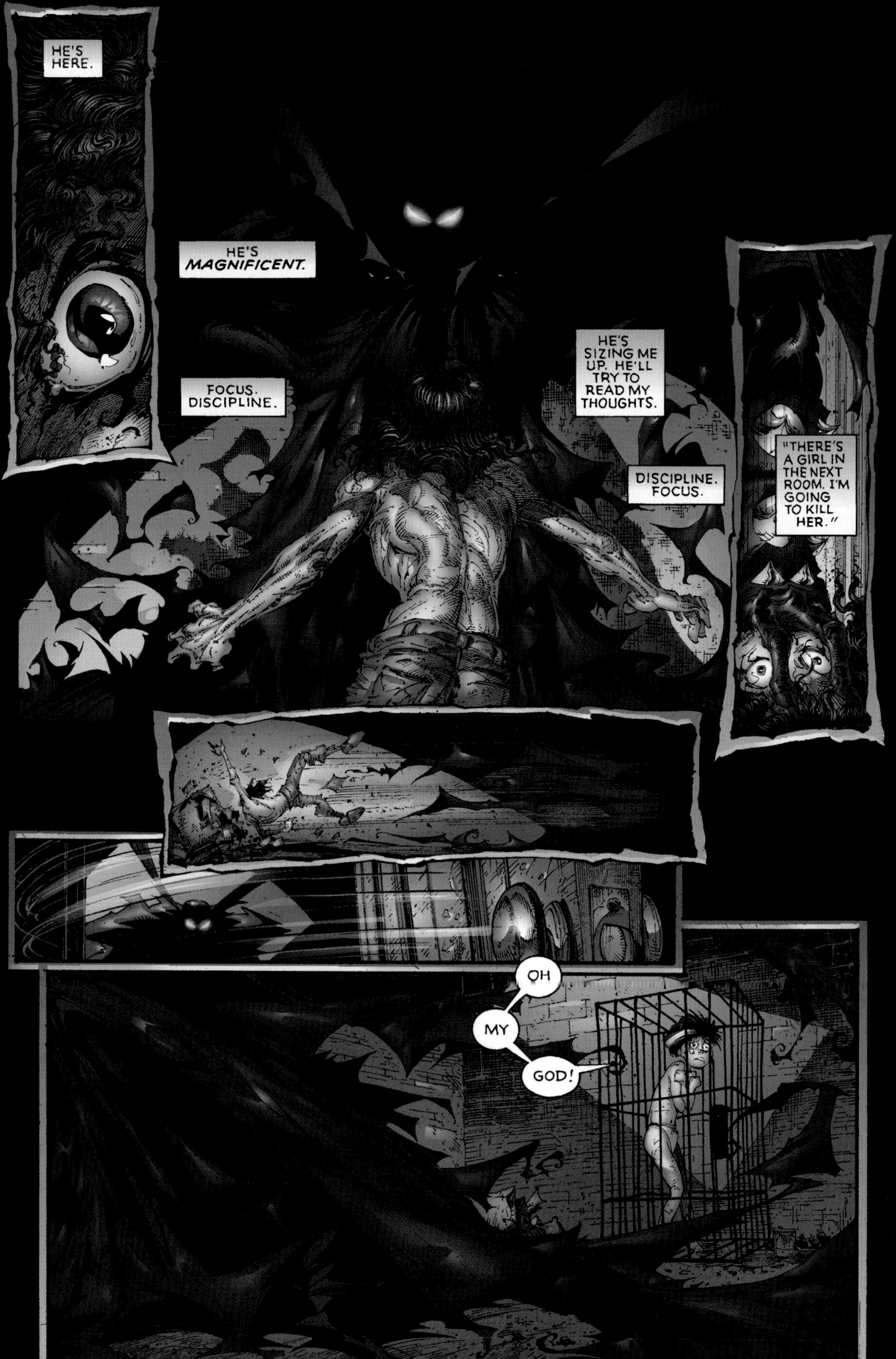

HE'S HERE.
HE'S *MAGNIFICENT.*
FOCUS. DISCIPLINE.
HE'S SIZING ME UP. HE'LL TRY TO READ MY THOUGHTS.
DISCIPLINE. FOCUS.
"THERE'S A GIRL IN THE NEXT ROOM. I'M GOING TO KILL HER."
OH
MY
GOD!

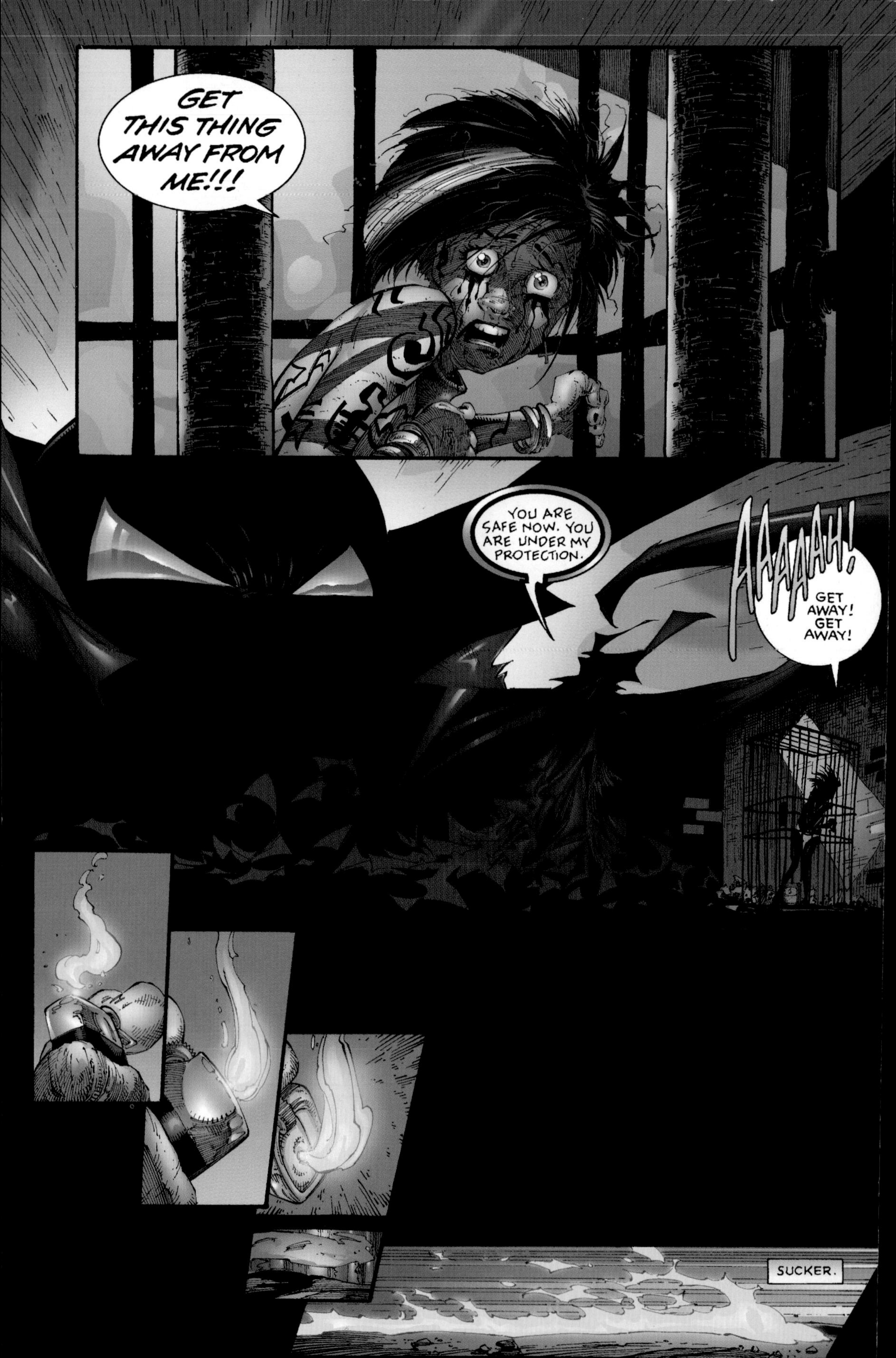
GET THIS THING AWAY FROM ME!!!
YOU ARE SAFE NOW. YOU ARE UNDER MY PROTECTION.
AAAAAH!
GET AWAY! GET AWAY!
SUCKER.

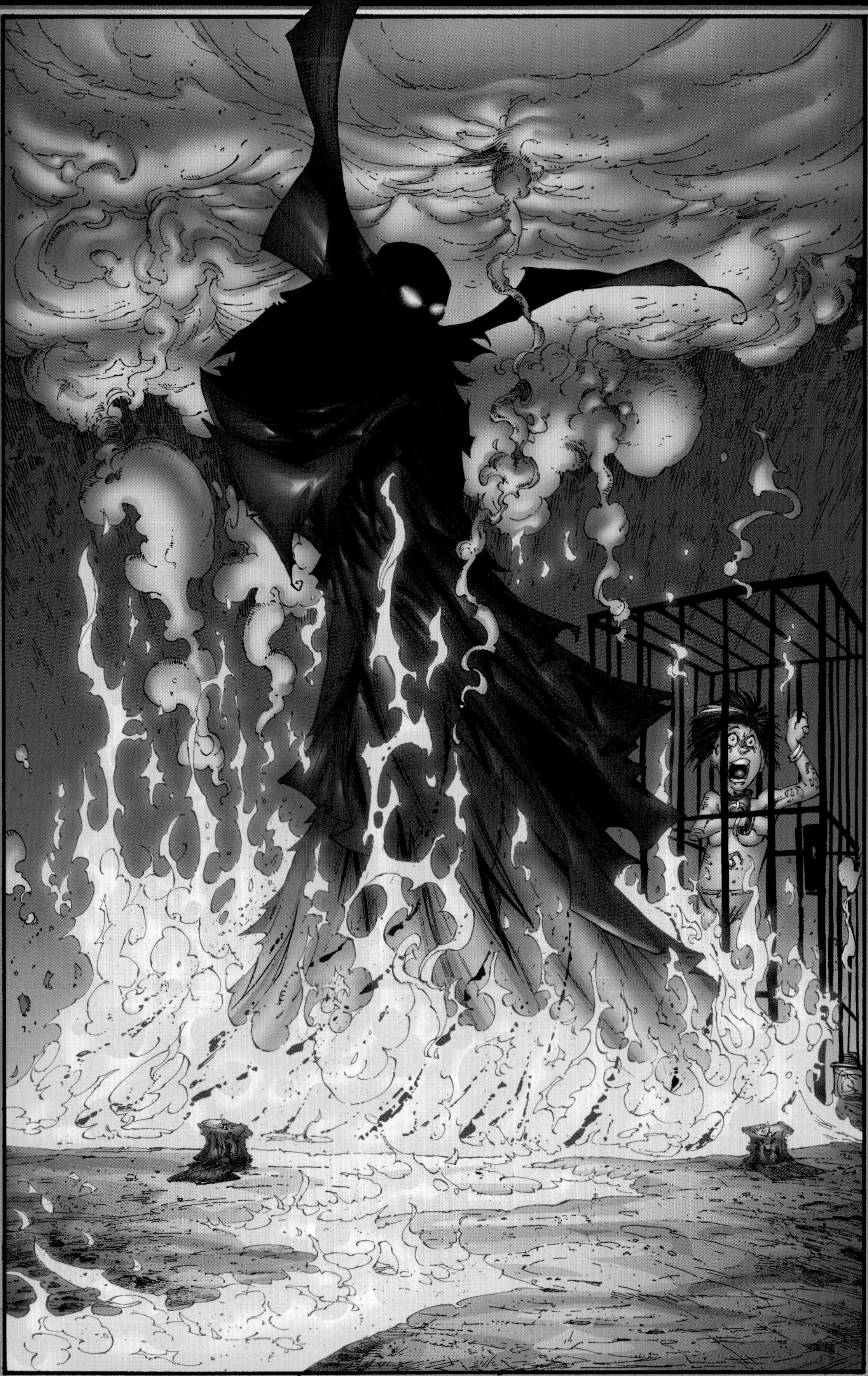

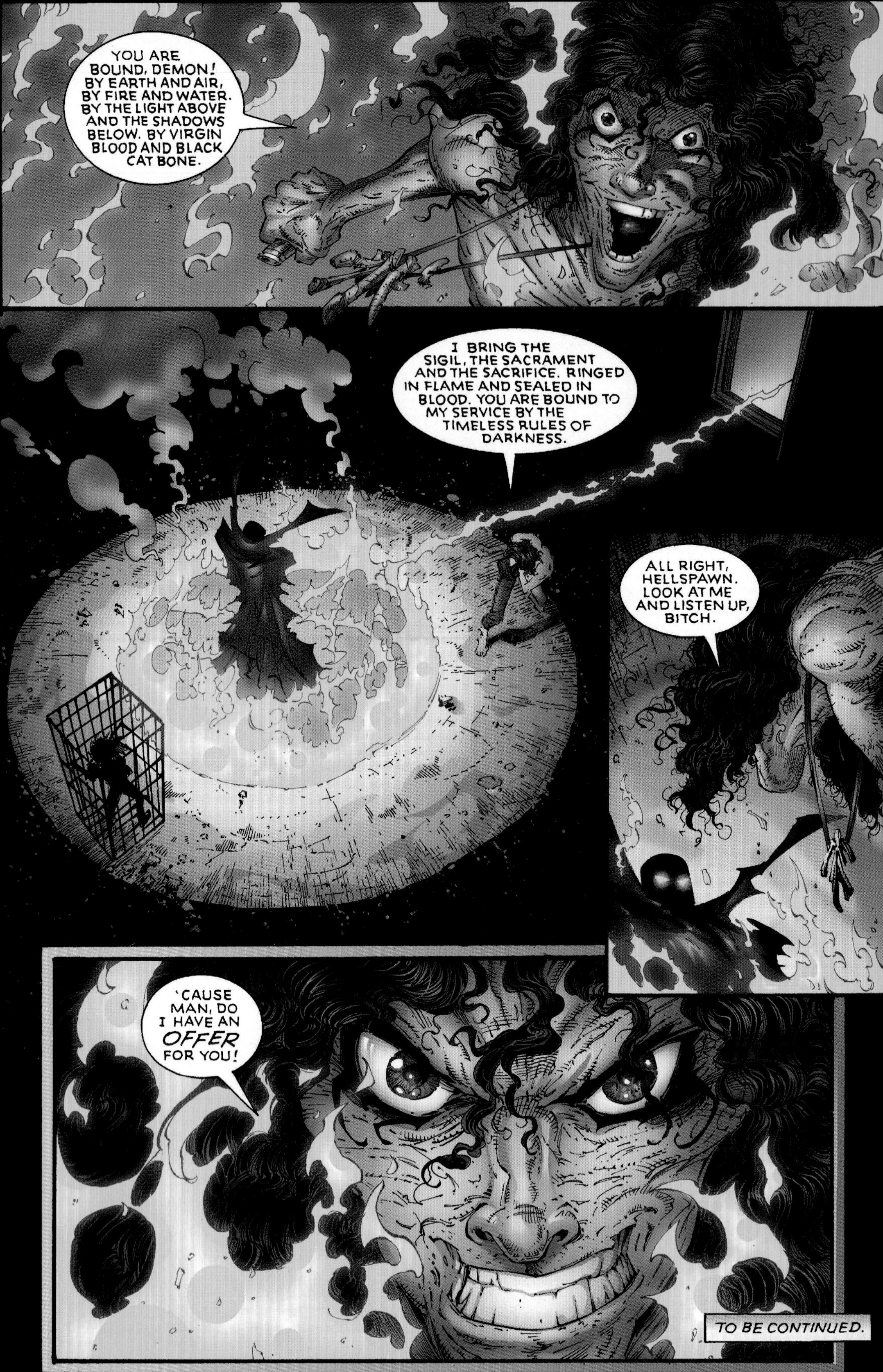
YOU ARE BOUND, DEMON! BY EARTH AND AIR, BY FIRE AND WATER. BY THE LIGHT ABOVE AND THE SHADOWS BELOW. BY VIRGIN BLOOD AND BLACK CAT BONE.
I BRING THE SIGIL, THE SACRAMENT AND THE SACRIFICE. RINGED IN FLAME AND SEALED IN BLOOD. YOU ARE BOUND TO MY SERVICE BY THE TIMELESS RULES OF DARKNESS.
ALL RIGHT, HELLSPAWN. LOOK AT ME AND LISTEN UP, BITCH.
'CAUSE MAN, DO I HAVE AN *OFFER* FOR YOU!
TO BE CONTINUED.

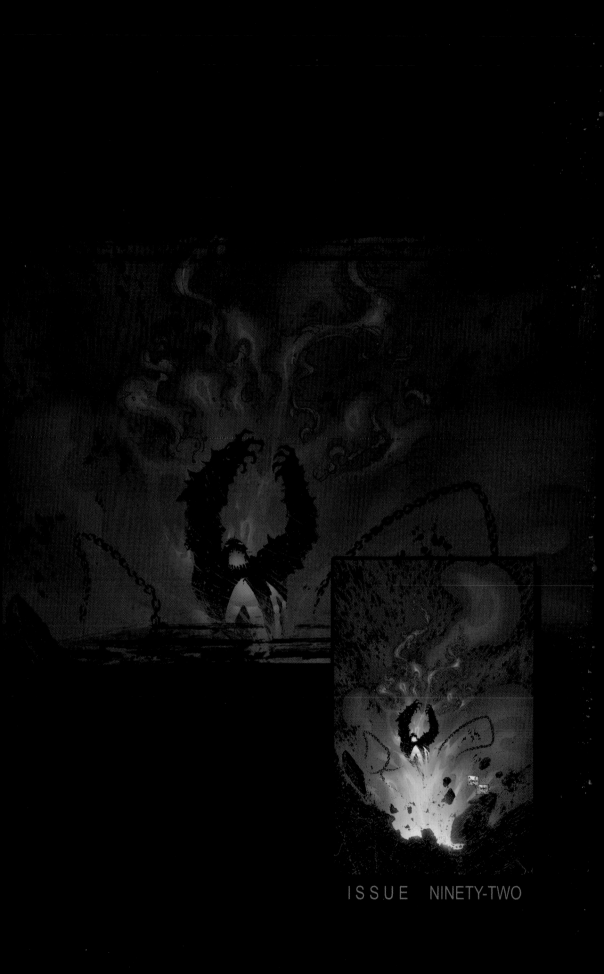

ISSUE NINETY-TWO

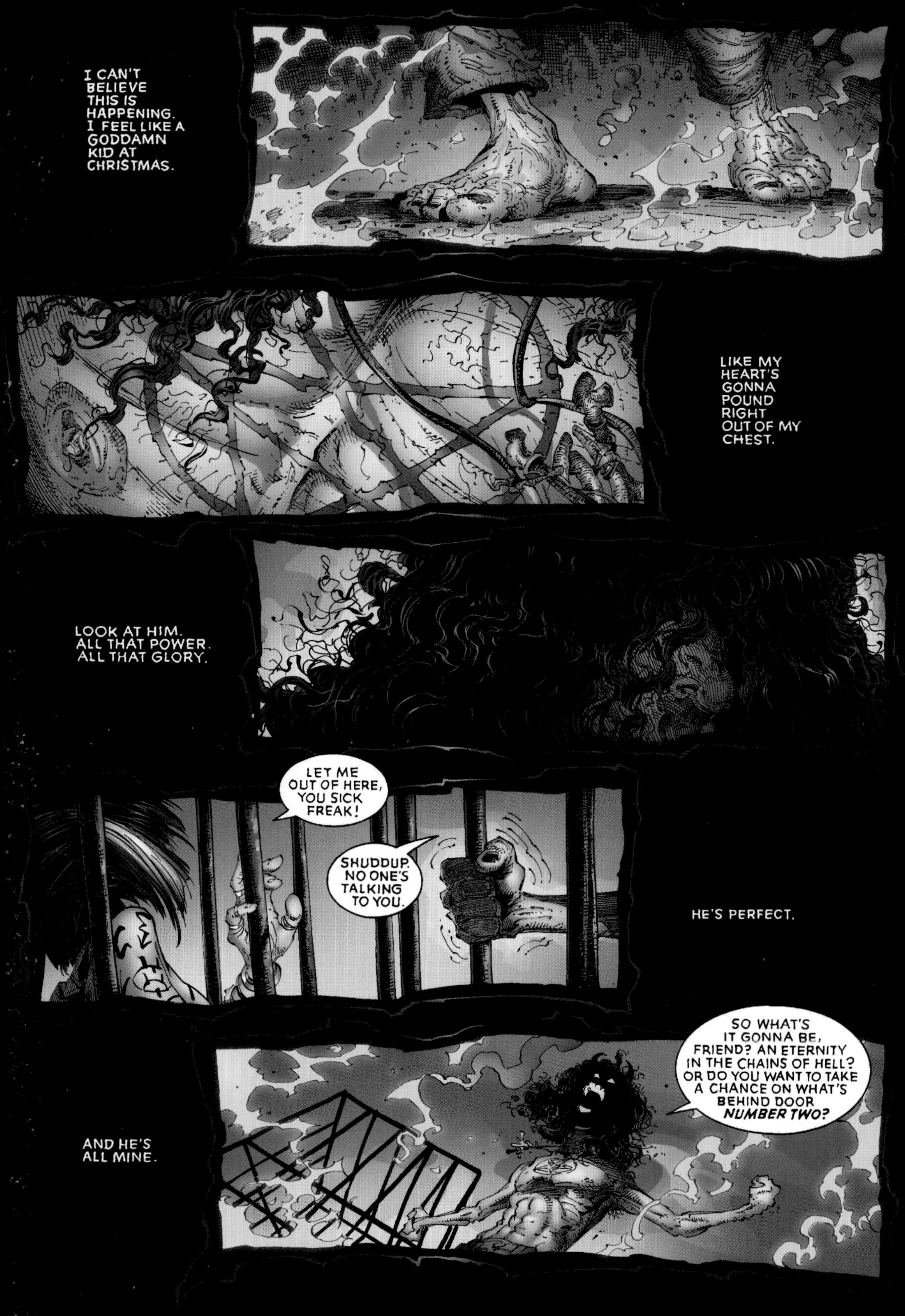

I CAN'T BELIEVE THIS IS HAPPENING. I FEEL LIKE A GODDAMN KID AT CHRISTMAS.
LIKE MY HEART'S GONNA POUND RIGHT OUT OF MY CHEST.
LOOK AT HIM. ALL THAT POWER. ALL THAT GLORY.
LET ME OUT OF HERE, YOU SICK FREAK!
SHUDDUP. NO ONE'S TALKING TO YOU.
HE'S PERFECT.
SO WHAT'S IT GONNA BE, FRIEND? AN ETERNITY IN THE CHAINS OF HELL? OR DO YOU WANT TO TAKE A CHANCE ON WHAT'S BEHIND DOOR *NUMBER TWO?*
AND HE'S ALL MINE.

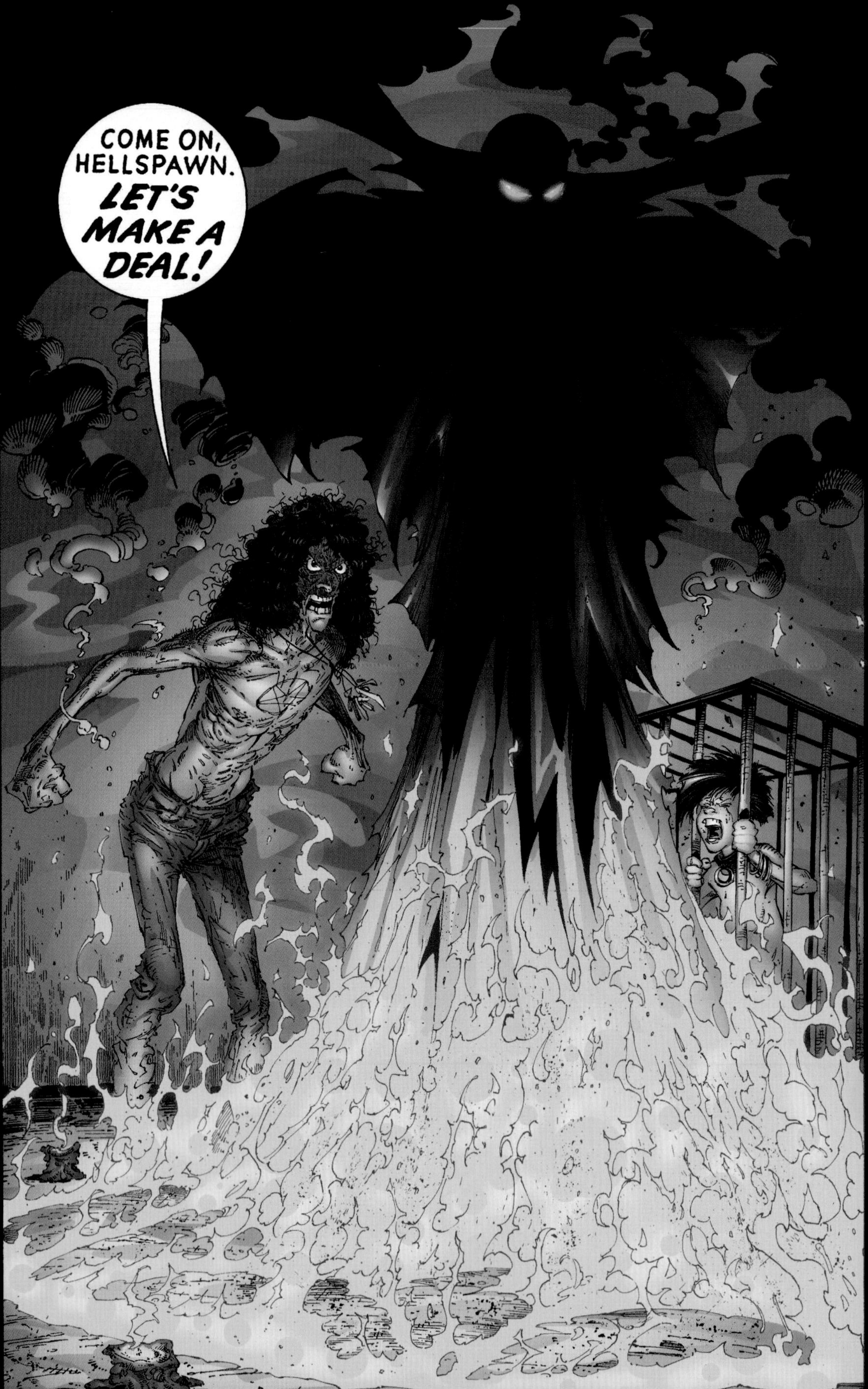
COME ON, HELLSPAWN. LET'S MAKE A DEAL!

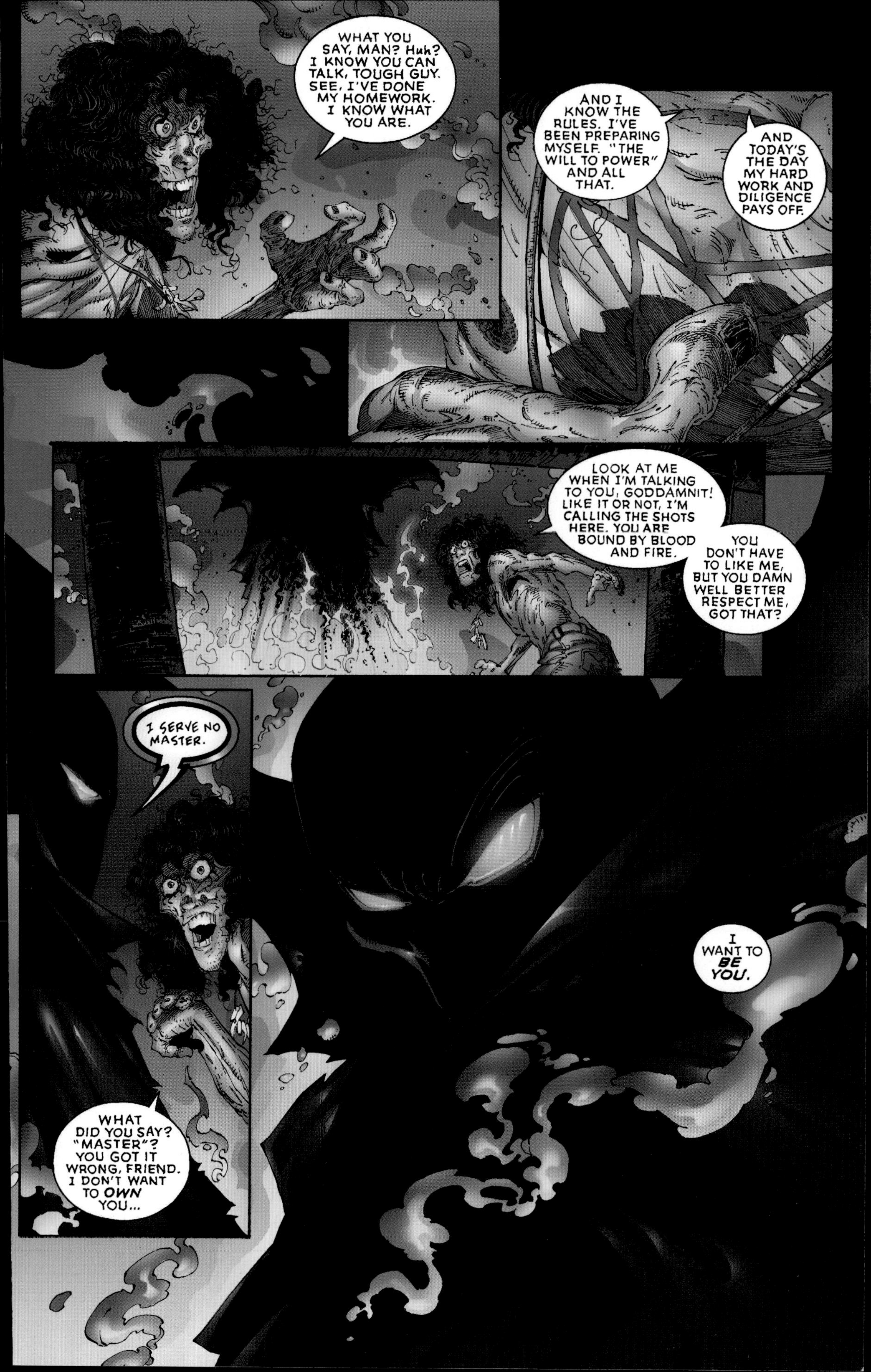
WHAT YOU SAY, MAN? Huh? I KNOW YOU CAN TALK, TOUGH GUY. SEE, I'VE DONE MY HOMEWORK. I KNOW WHAT YOU ARE.
AND I KNOW THE RULES. I'VE BEEN PREPARING MYSELF. "THE WILL TO POWER" AND ALL THAT.
AND TODAY'S THE DAY MY HARD WORK AND DILIGENCE PAYS OFF.
LOOK AT ME WHEN I'M TALKING TO YOU, GODDAMNIT! LIKE IT OR NOT, I'M CALLING THE SHOTS HERE. YOU ARE BOUND BY BLOOD AND FIRE.
YOU DON'T HAVE TO LIKE ME, BUT YOU DAMN WELL BETTER RESPECT ME, GOT THAT?
I SERVE NO MASTER.
WHAT DID YOU SAY? "MASTER"? YOU GOT IT WRONG, FRIEND. I DON'T WANT TO OWN YOU...
I WANT TO BE YOU.

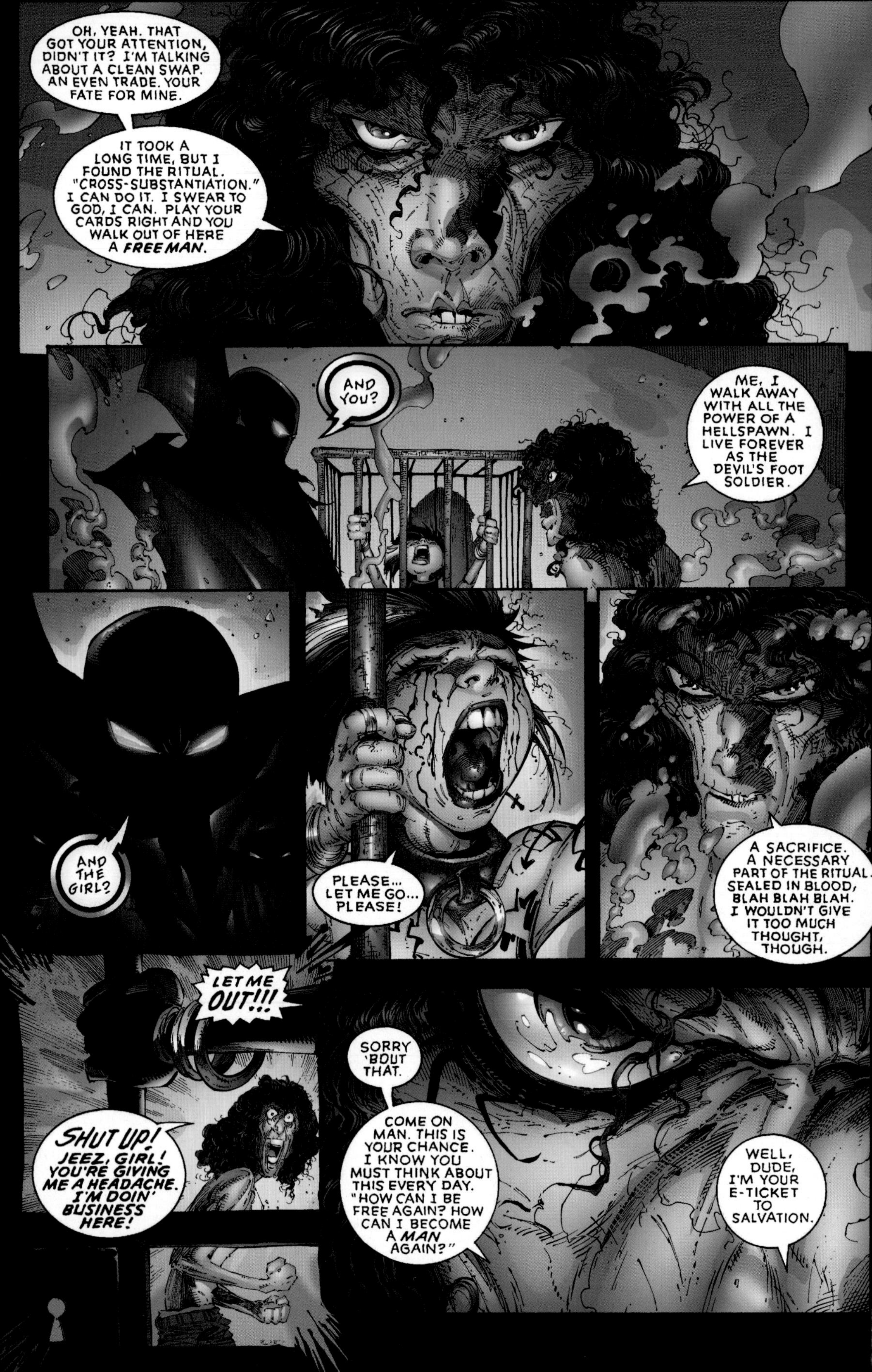

OH, YEAH. THAT GOT YOUR ATTENTION, DIDN'T IT? I'M TALKING ABOUT A CLEAN SWAP. AN EVEN TRADE. YOUR FATE FOR MINE.
IT TOOK A LONG TIME, BUT I FOUND THE RITUAL. "CROSS-SUBSTANTIATION." I CAN DO IT. I SWEAR TO GOD, I CAN. PLAY YOUR CARDS RIGHT AND YOU WALK OUT OF HERE A *FREE MAN.*
AND YOU?
ME, I WALK AWAY WITH ALL THE POWER OF A HELLSPAWN. I LIVE FOREVER AS THE DEVIL'S FOOT SOLDIER.
AND THE GIRL?
PLEASE... LET ME GO... PLEASE!
A SACRIFICE. A NECESSARY PART OF THE RITUAL. SEALED IN BLOOD, BLAH BLAH BLAH. I WOULDN'T GIVE IT TOO MUCH THOUGHT, THOUGH.
LET ME OUT!!!
SHUT UP! JEEZ, GIRL! YOU'RE GIVING ME A HEADACHE. I'M DOIN' BUSINESS HERE!
SORRY 'BOUT THAT.
COME ON MAN. THIS IS YOUR CHANCE. I KNOW YOU MUST THINK ABOUT THIS EVERY DAY. "HOW CAN I BE FREE AGAIN? HOW CAN I BECOME A *MAN* AGAIN?"
WELL, DUDE, I'M YOUR E-TICKET TO SALVATION.

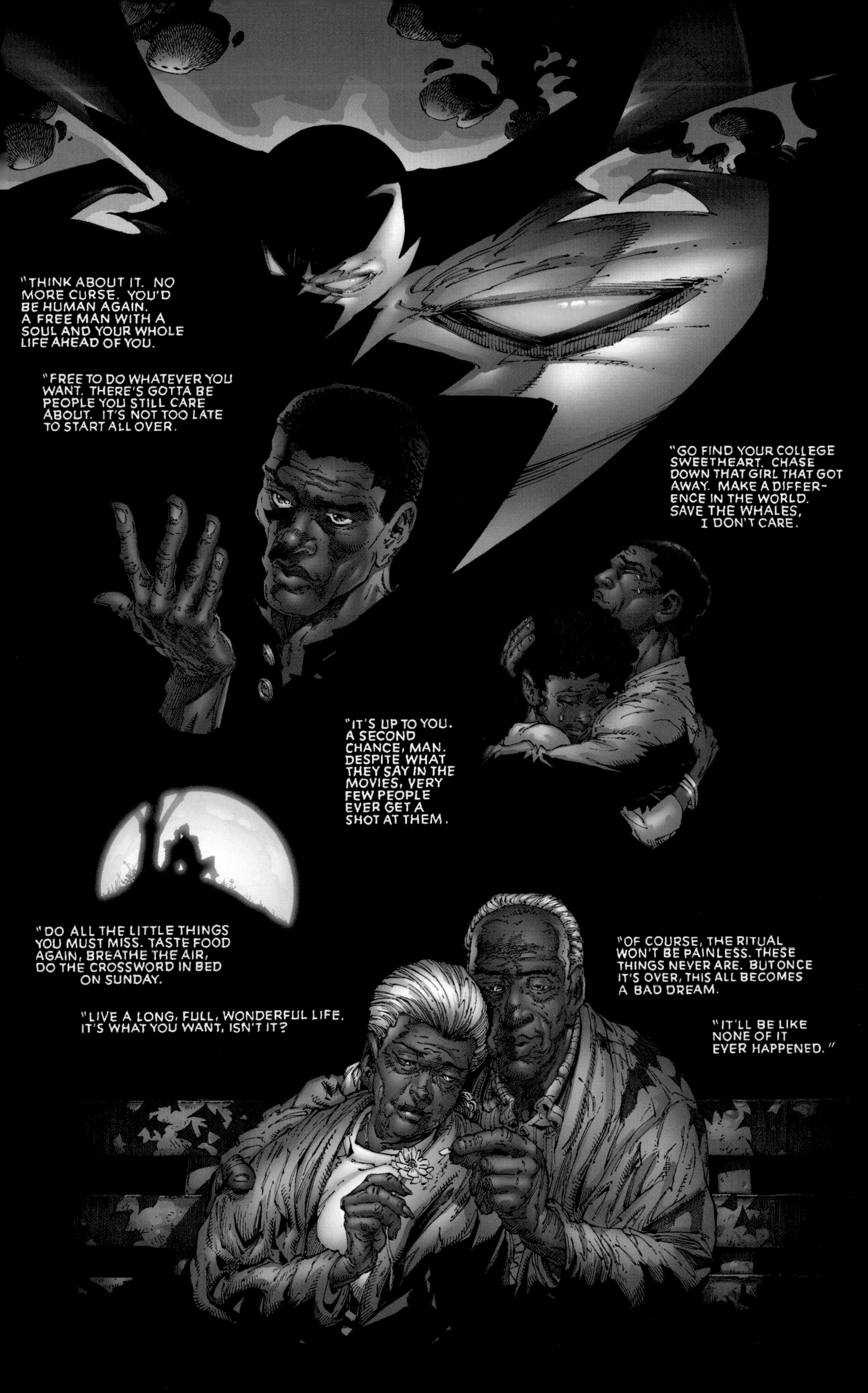
"THINK ABOUT IT. NO MORE CURSE. YOU'D BE HUMAN AGAIN. A FREE MAN WITH A SOUL AND YOUR WHOLE LIFE AHEAD OF YOU.
"FREE TO DO WHATEVER YOU WANT. THERE'S GOTTA BE PEOPLE YOU STILL CARE ABOUT. IT'S NOT TOO LATE TO START ALL OVER.
"GO FIND YOUR COLLEGE SWEETHEART. CHASE DOWN THAT GIRL THAT GOT AWAY. MAKE A DIFFERENCE IN THE WORLD. SAVE THE WHALES, I DON'T CARE.
"IT'S UP TO YOU. A SECOND CHANCE, MAN. DESPITE WHAT THEY SAY IN THE MOVIES, VERY FEW PEOPLE EVER GET A SHOT AT THEM.
"DO ALL THE LITTLE THINGS YOU MUST MISS. TASTE FOOD AGAIN, BREATHE THE AIR, DO THE CROSSWORD IN BED ON SUNDAY.
"LIVE A LONG, FULL, WONDERFUL LIFE. IT'S WHAT YOU WANT, ISN'T IT?
"OF COURSE, THE RITUAL WON'T BE PAINLESS. THESE THINGS NEVER ARE. BUT ONCE IT'S OVER, THIS ALL BECOMES A BAD DREAM.
"IT'LL BE LIKE NONE OF IT EVER HAPPENED."

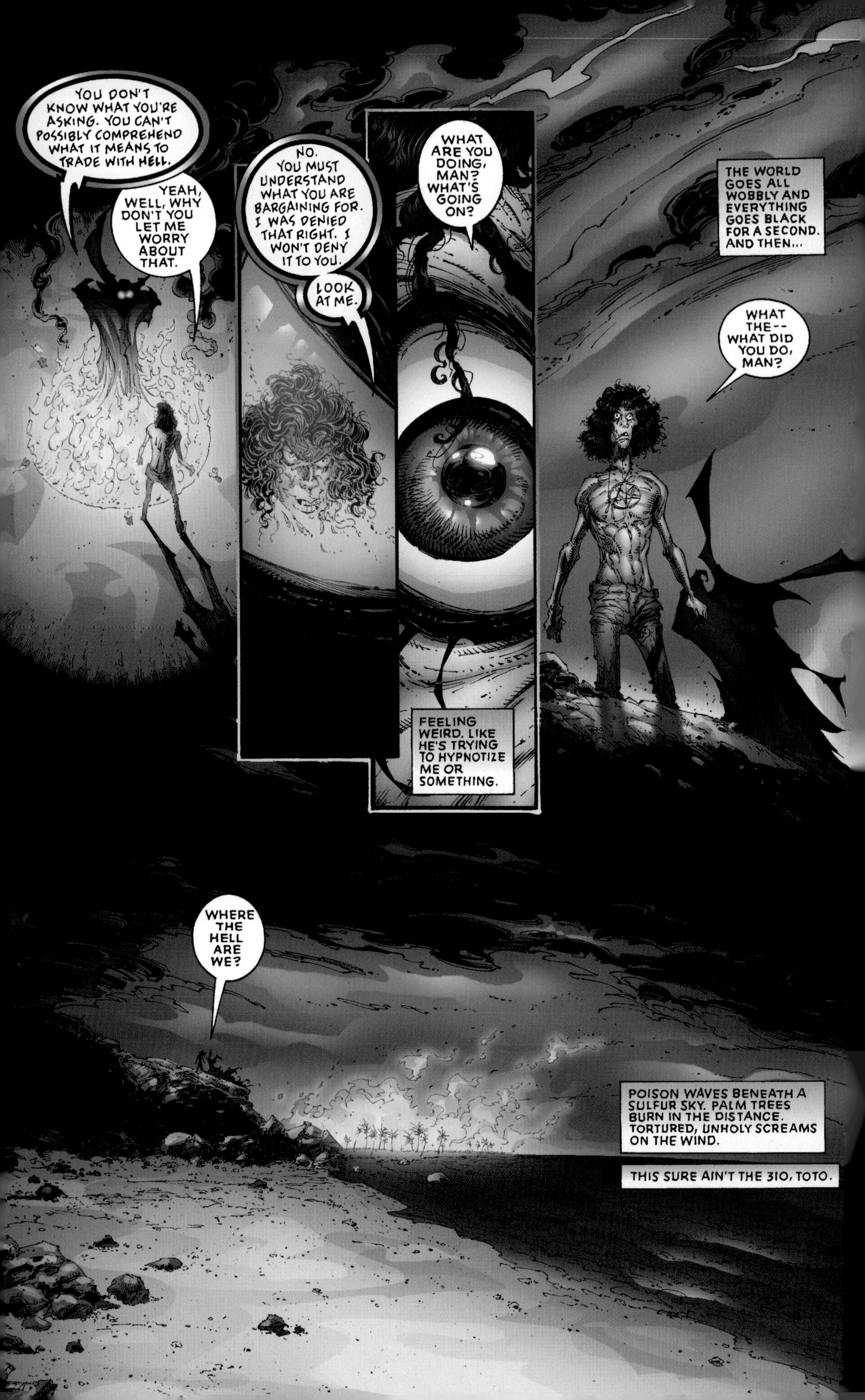
YOU DON'T KNOW WHAT YOU'RE ASKING. YOU CAN'T POSSIBLY COMPREHEND WHAT IT MEANS TO TRADE WITH HELL.
YEAH, WELL, WHY DON'T YOU LET ME WORRY ABOUT THAT.
NO. YOU MUST UNDERSTAND WHAT YOU ARE BARGAINING FOR. I WAS DENIED THAT RIGHT. I WON'T DENY IT TO YOU.
LOOK AT ME.
WHAT ARE YOU DOING, MAN? WHAT'S GOING ON?
FEELING WEIRD. LIKE HE'S TRYING TO HYPNOTIZE ME OR SOMETHING.
THE WORLD GOES ALL WOBBLY AND EVERYTHING GOES BLACK FOR A SECOND. AND THEN...
WHAT THE-- WHAT DID YOU DO, MAN?
WHERE THE HELL ARE WE?
POISON WAVES BENEATH A SULFUR SKY. PALM TREES BURN IN THE DISTANCE. TORTURED, UNHOLY SCREAMS ON THE WIND.
THIS SURE AIN'T THE 310, TOTO.

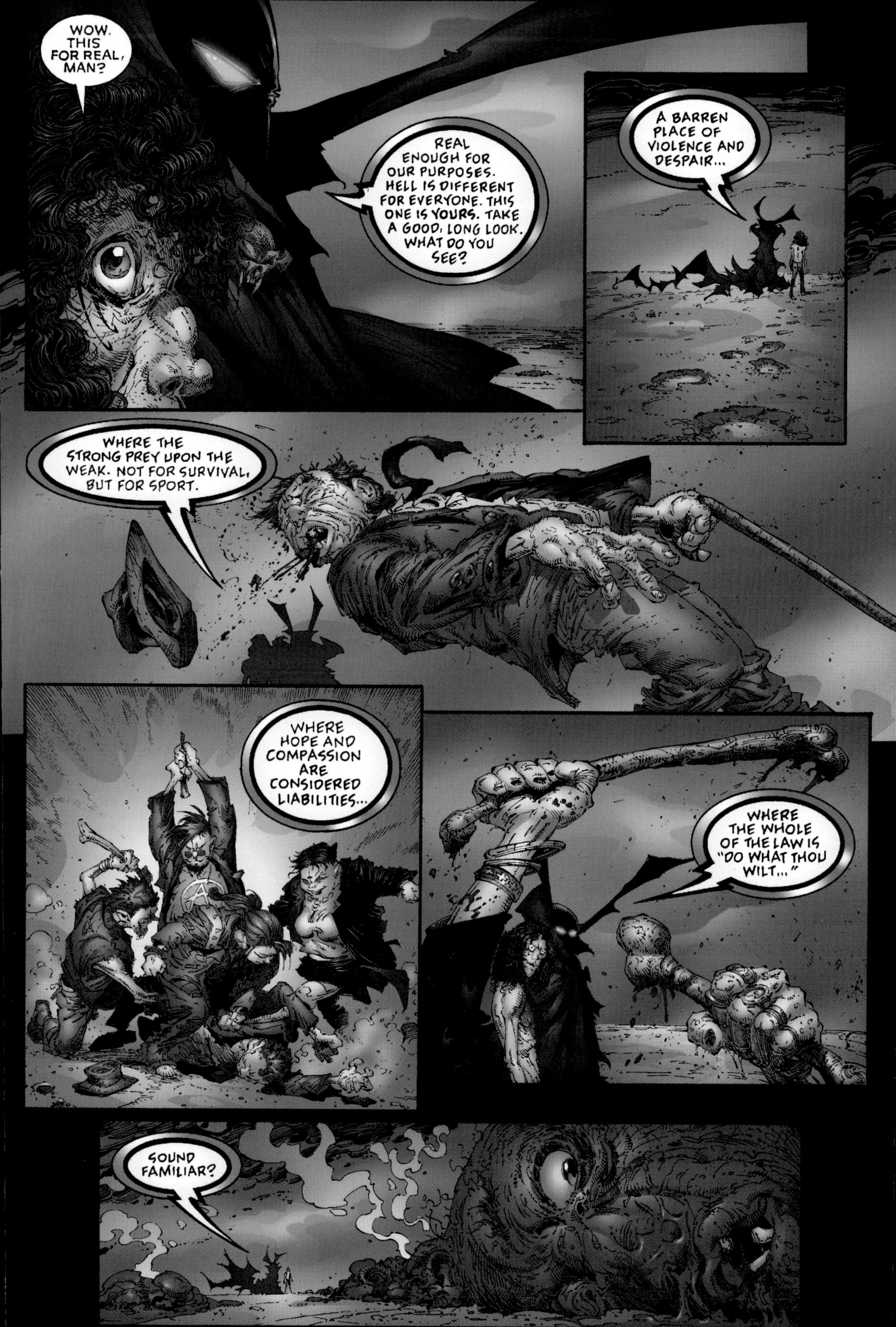
WOW. THIS FOR REAL, MAN?
REAL ENOUGH FOR OUR PURPOSES. HELL IS DIFFERENT FOR EVERYONE. THIS ONE IS YOURS. TAKE A GOOD, LONG LOOK. WHAT DO YOU SEE?
A BARREN PLACE OF VIOLENCE AND DESPAIR...
WHERE THE STRONG PREY UPON THE WEAK. NOT FOR SURVIVAL, BUT FOR SPORT.
WHERE HOPE AND COMPASSION ARE CONSIDERED LIABILITIES...
WHERE THE WHOLE OF THE LAW IS "DO WHAT THOU WILT..."
SOUND FAMILIAR?

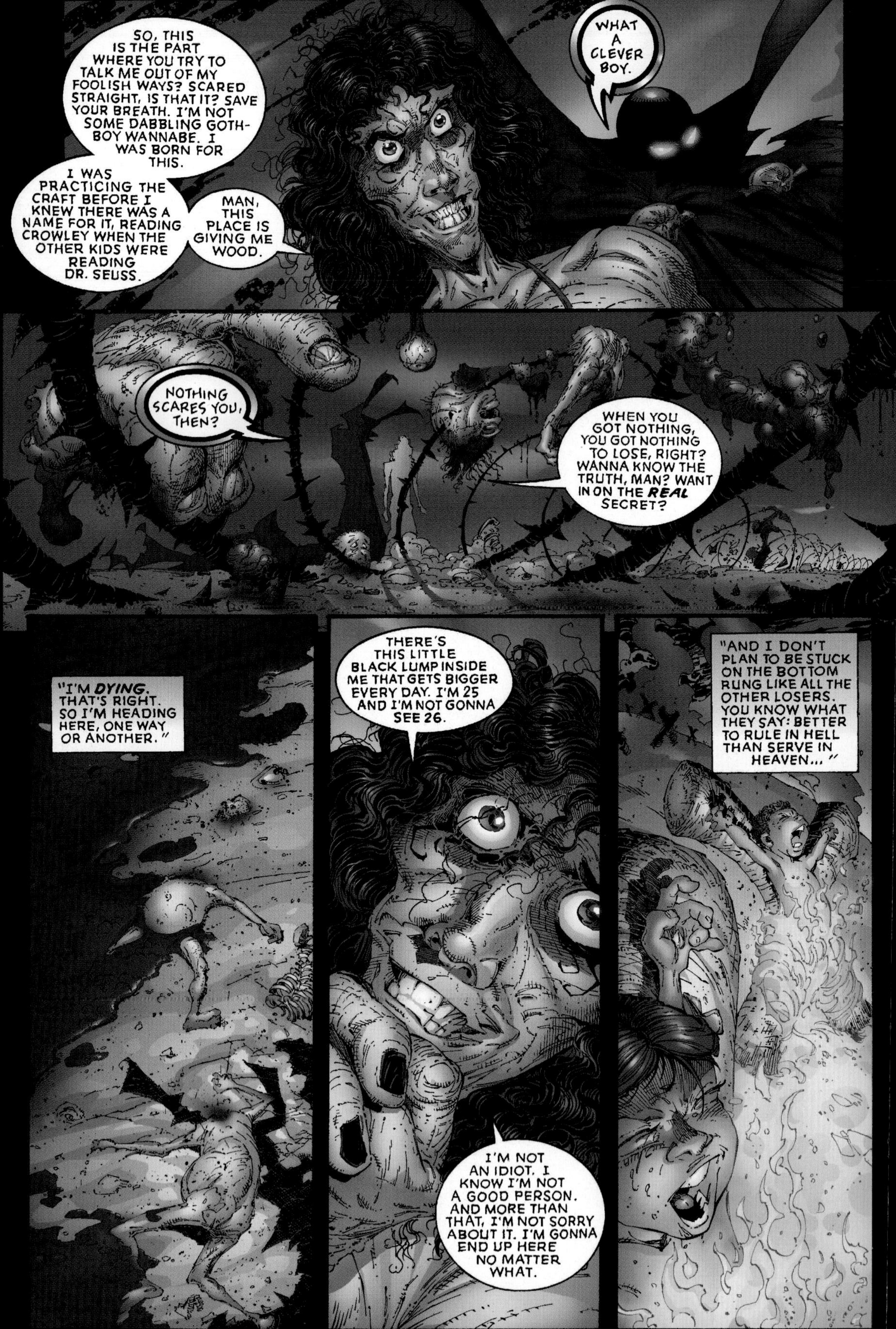
SO, THIS IS THE PART WHERE YOU TRY TO TALK ME OUT OF MY FOOLISH WAYS? SCARED STRAIGHT, IS THAT IT? SAVE YOUR BREATH. I'M NOT SOME DABBLING GOTH-BOY WANNABE. I WAS BORN FOR THIS.
WHAT A CLEVER BOY.
I WAS PRACTICING THE CRAFT BEFORE I KNEW THERE WAS A NAME FOR IT, READING CROWLEY WHEN THE OTHER KIDS WERE READING DR. SEUSS.
MAN, THIS PLACE IS GIVING ME WOOD.
NOTHING SCARES YOU, THEN?
WHEN YOU GOT NOTHING, YOU GOT NOTHING TO LOSE, RIGHT? WANNA KNOW THE TRUTH, MAN? WANT IN ON THE REAL SECRET?
"I'M DYING. THAT'S RIGHT. SO I'M HEADING HERE, ONE WAY OR ANOTHER."
THERE'S THIS LITTLE BLACK LUMP INSIDE ME THAT GETS BIGGER EVERY DAY. I'M 25 AND I'M NOT GONNA SEE 26.
I'M NOT AN IDIOT. I KNOW I'M NOT A GOOD PERSON. AND MORE THAN THAT, I'M NOT SORRY ABOUT IT. I'M GONNA END UP HERE NO MATTER WHAT.
"AND I DON'T PLAN TO BE STUCK ON THE BOTTOM RUNG LIKE ALL THE OTHER LOSERS. YOU KNOW WHAT THEY SAY: BETTER TO RULE IN HELL THAN SERVE IN HEAVEN..."

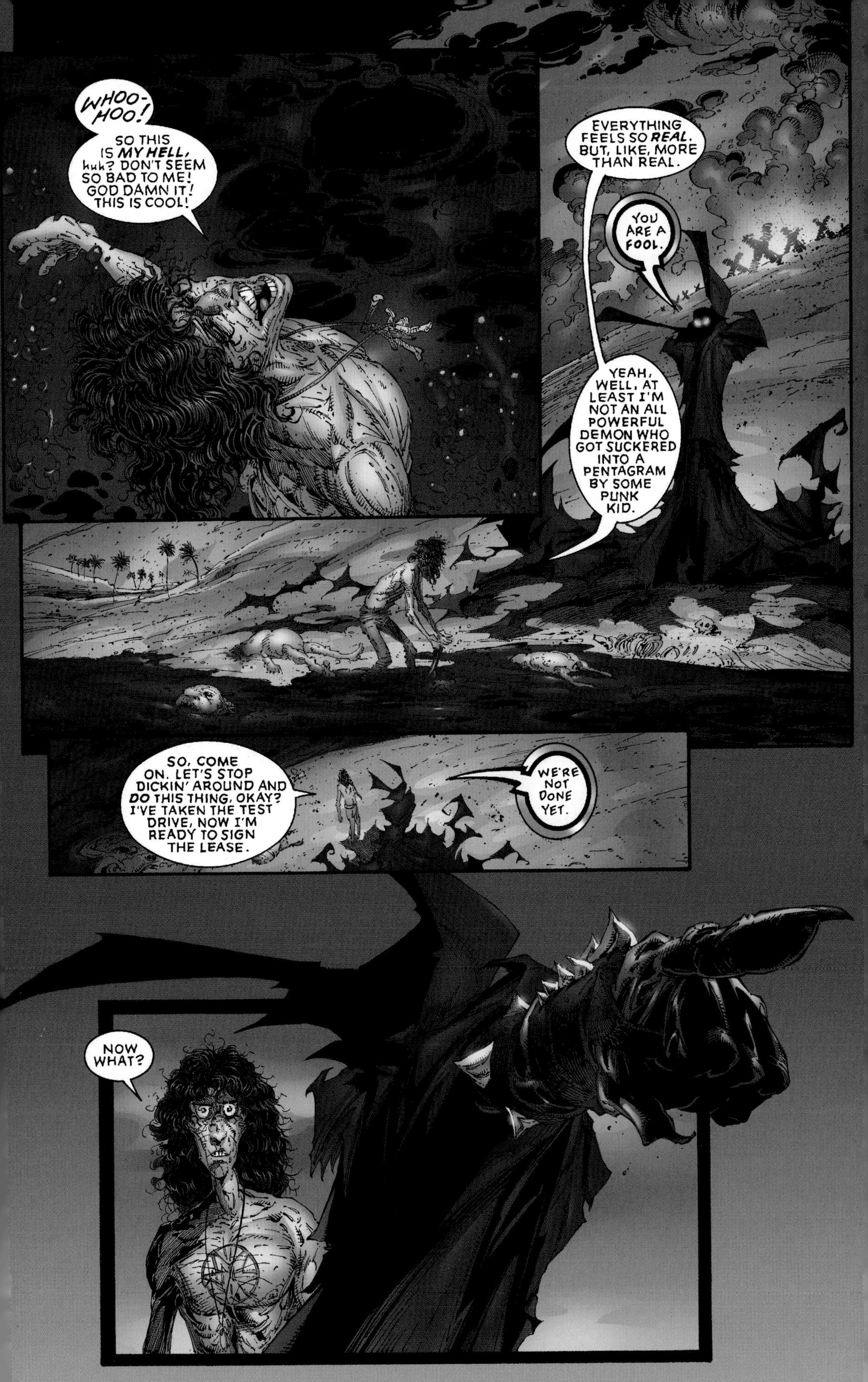
WHOO-HOO!
SO THIS IS MY HELL, huh? DON'T SEEM SO BAD TO ME! GOD DAMN IT! THIS IS COOL!
EVERYTHING FEELS SO REAL. BUT, LIKE, MORE THAN REAL.
YOU ARE A FOOL.
YEAH, WELL, AT LEAST I'M NOT AN ALL POWERFUL DEMON WHO GOT SUCKERED INTO A PENTAGRAM BY SOME PUNK KID.
SO, COME ON. LET'S STOP DICKIN' AROUND AND DO THIS THING, OKAY? I'VE TAKEN THE TEST DRIVE, NOW I'M READY TO SIGN THE LEASE.
WE'RE NOT DONE YET.
NOW WHAT?

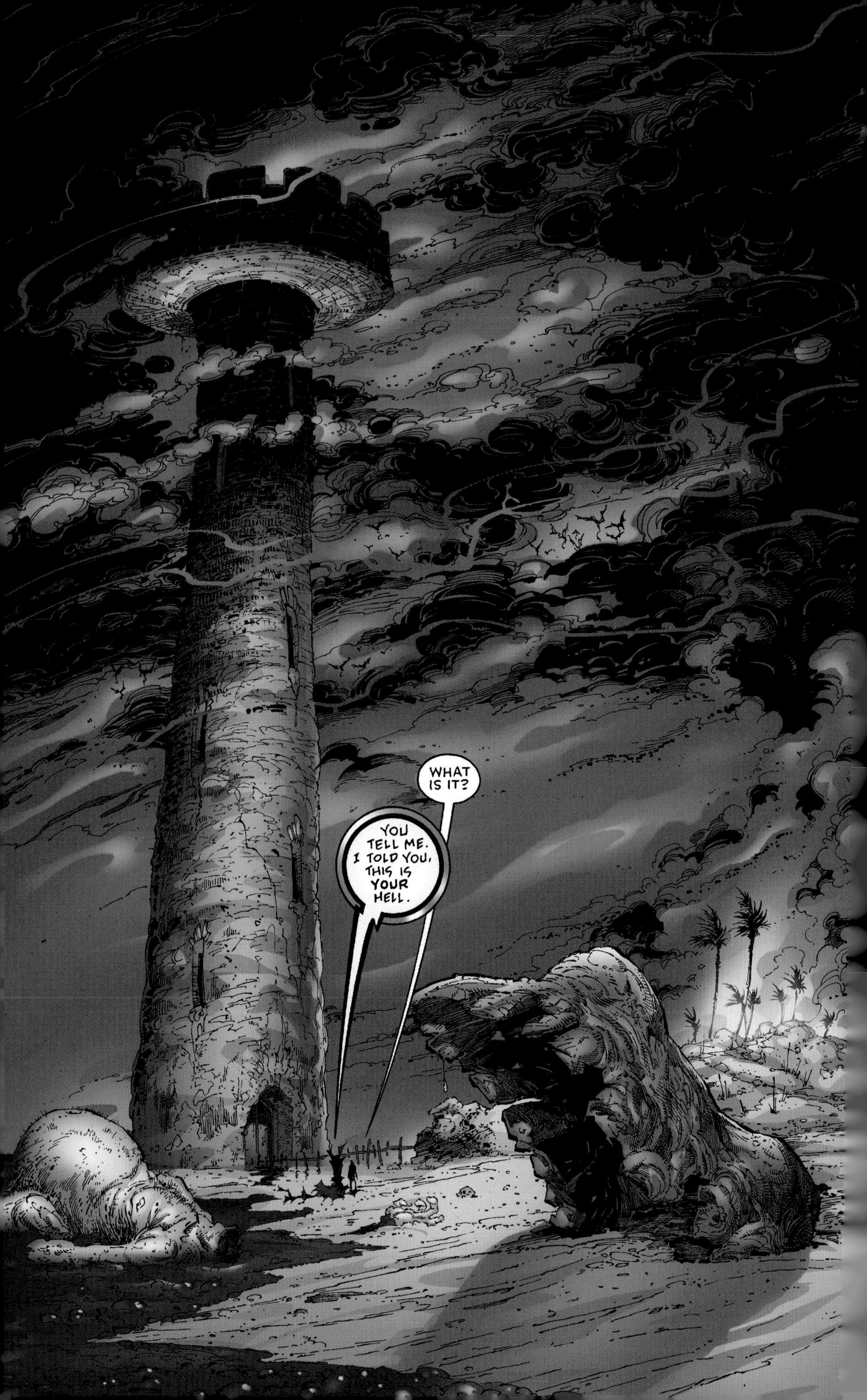
WHAT IS IT?
YOU TELL ME. I TOLD YOU, THIS IS YOUR HELL.

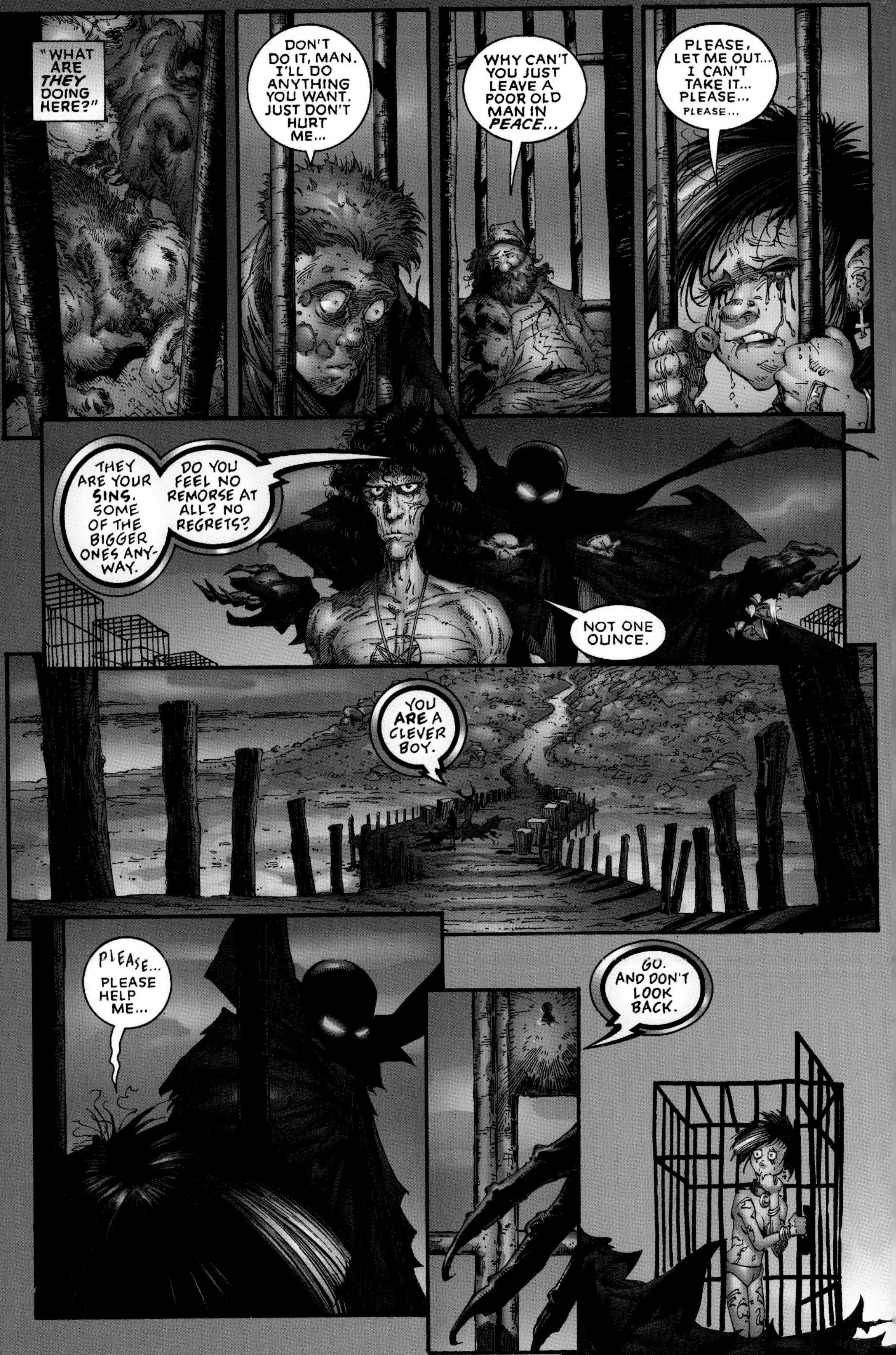
"WHAT ARE THEY DOING HERE?"
DON'T DO IT, MAN. I'LL DO ANYTHING YOU WANT. JUST DON'T HURT ME...
WHY CAN'T YOU JUST LEAVE A POOR OLD MAN IN PEACE...
PLEASE, LET ME OUT... I CAN'T TAKE IT... PLEASE... PLEASE...
THEY ARE YOUR SINS. SOME OF THE BIGGER ONES ANY-WAY.
DO YOU FEEL NO REMORSE AT ALL? NO REGRETS?
NOT ONE OUNCE.
YOU ARE A CLEVER BOY.
PLEASE... PLEASE HELP ME...
GO. AND DON'T LOOK BACK.

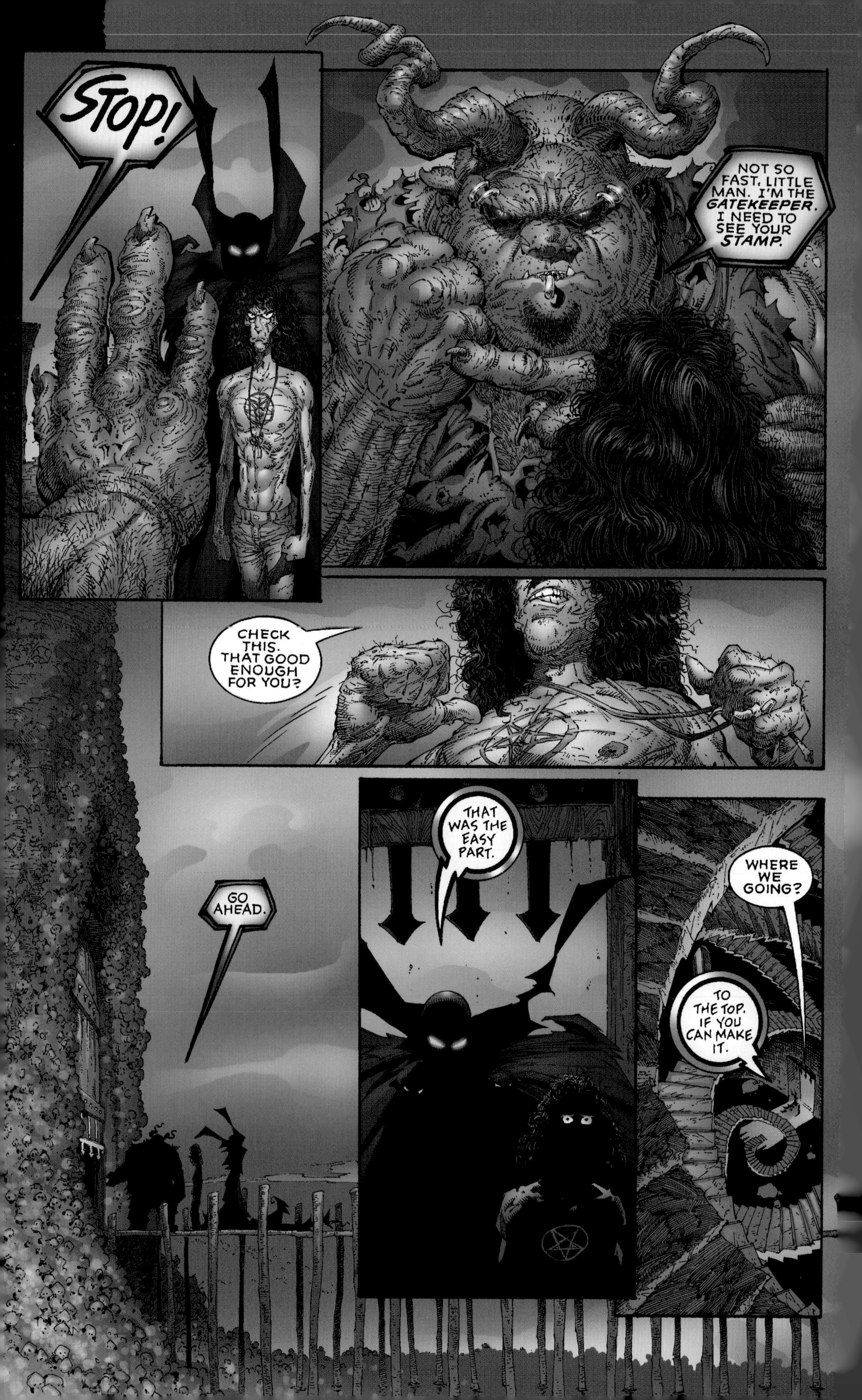
STOP!
NOT SO FAST, LITTLE MAN. I'M THE GATEKEEPER. I NEED TO SEE YOUR STAMP.
CHECK THIS. THAT GOOD ENOUGH FOR YOU?
GO AHEAD.
THAT WAS THE EASY PART.
WHERE WE GOING?
TO THE TOP. IF YOU CAN MAKE IT.

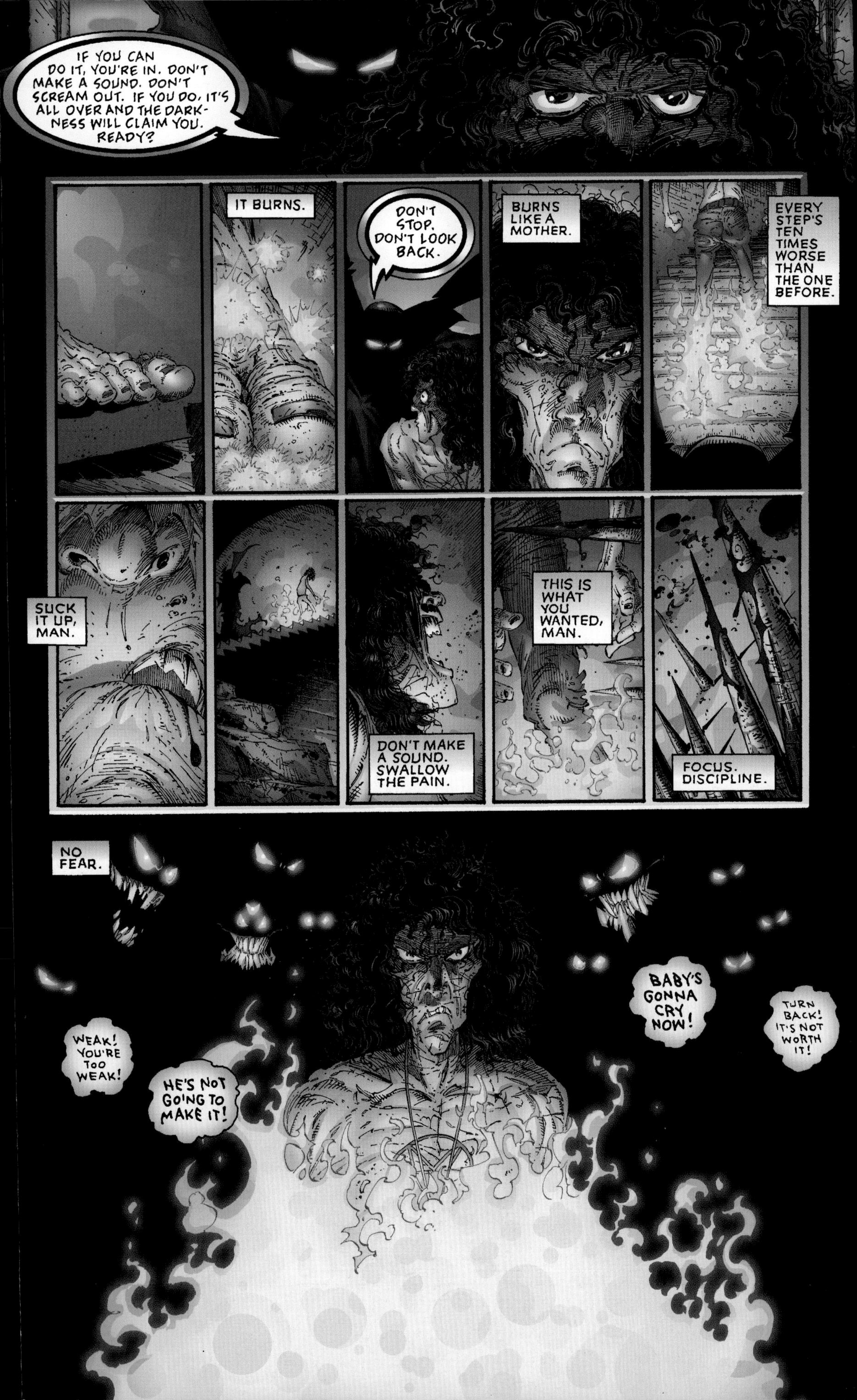
IF YOU CAN DO IT, YOU'RE IN. DON'T MAKE A SOUND. DON'T SCREAM OUT. IF YOU DO, IT'S ALL OVER AND THE DARKNESS WILL CLAIM YOU. READY?
IT BURNS.
DON'T STOP. DON'T LOOK BACK.
BURNS LIKE A MOTHER.
EVERY STEP'S TEN TIMES WORSE THAN THE ONE BEFORE.
SUCK IT UP, MAN.
DON'T MAKE A SOUND. SWALLOW THE PAIN.
THIS IS WHAT YOU WANTED, MAN.
FOCUS. DISCIPLINE.
NO FEAR.
WEAK! YOU'RE TOO WEAK!
HE'S NOT GOING TO MAKE IT!
BABY'S GONNA CRY NOW!
TURN BACK! IT'S NOT WORTH IT!

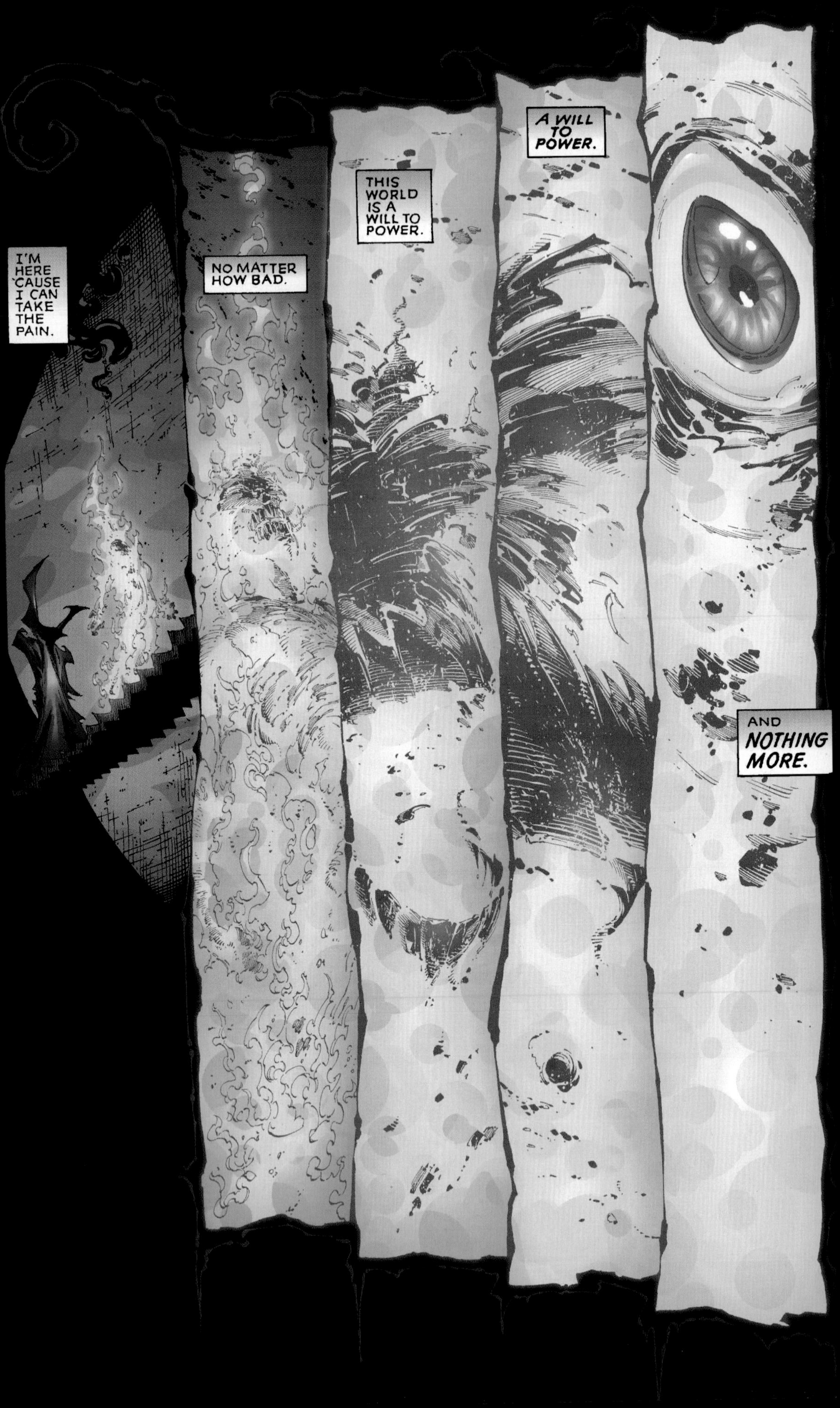

I'M HERE 'CAUSE I CAN TAKE THE PAIN.
NO MATTER HOW BAD.
THIS WORLD IS A WILL TO POWER.
A WILL TO POWER.
AND NOTHING MORE.

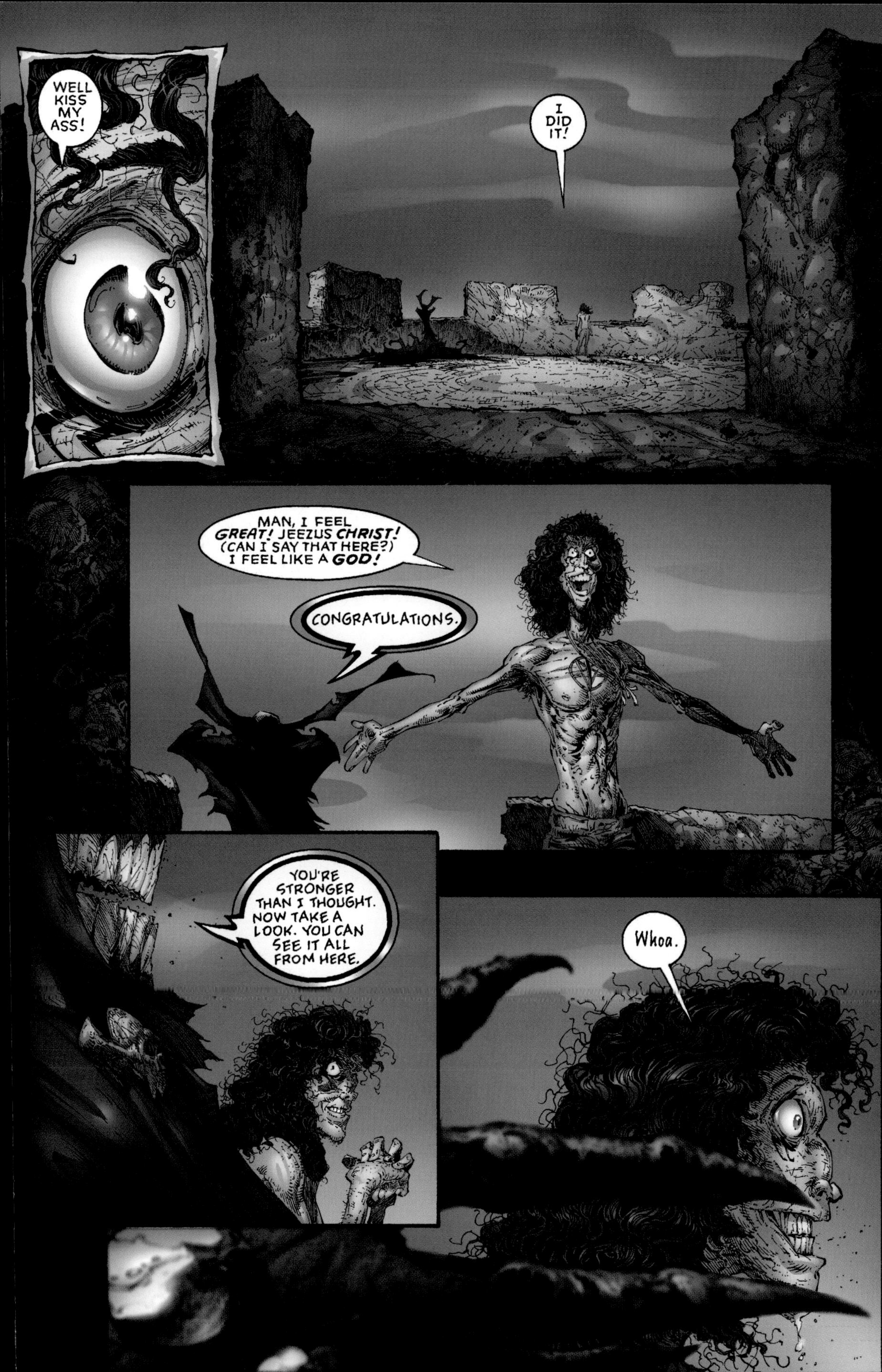
WELL KISS MY ASS!
I DID IT!
MAN, I FEEL GREAT! JEEZUS CHRIST! (CAN I SAY THAT HERE?) I FEEL LIKE A GOD!
CONGRATULATIONS.
YOU'RE STRONGER THAN I THOUGHT. NOW TAKE A LOOK. YOU CAN SEE IT ALL FROM HERE.
Whoa.

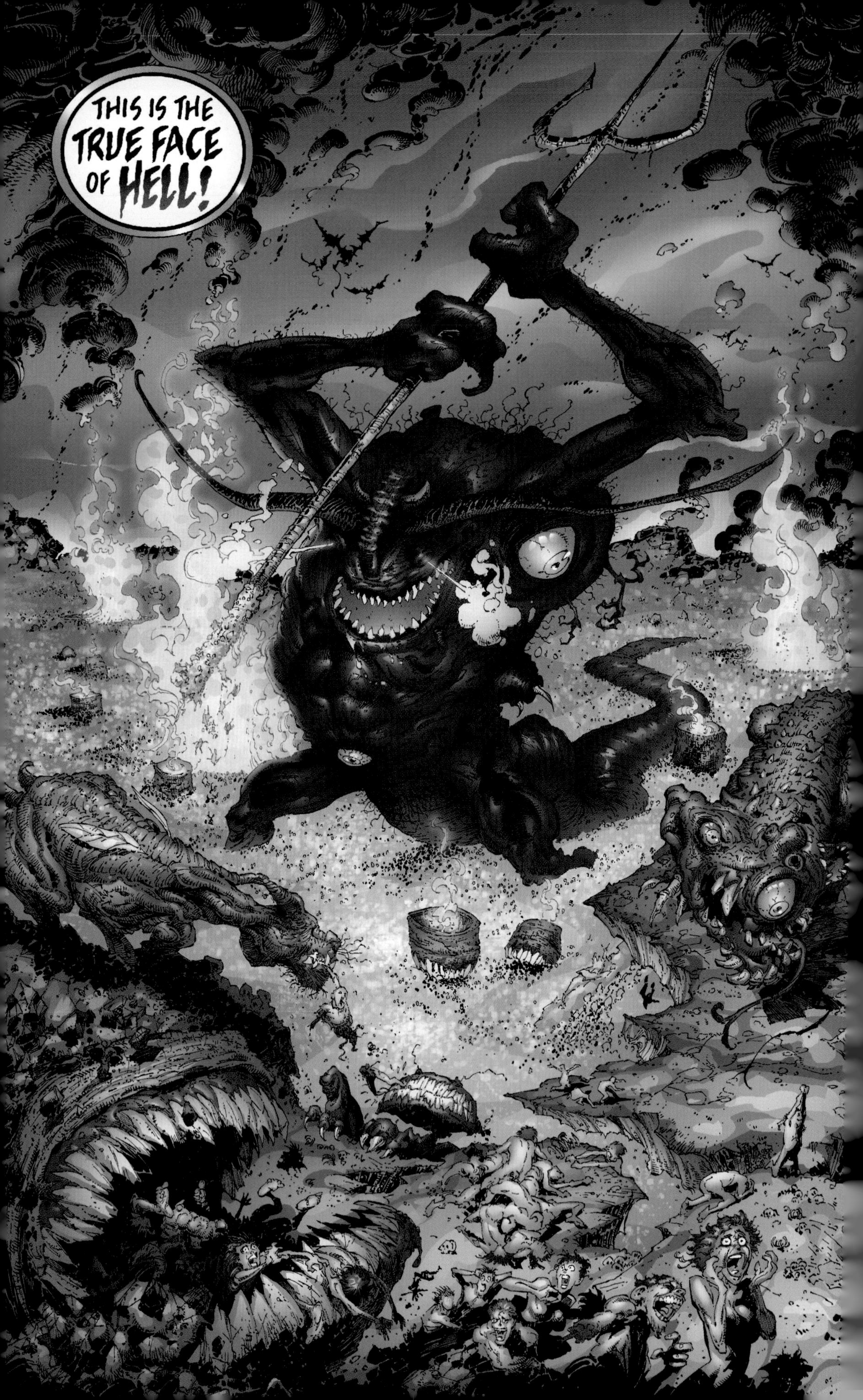
THIS IS THE TRUE FACE OF HELL!

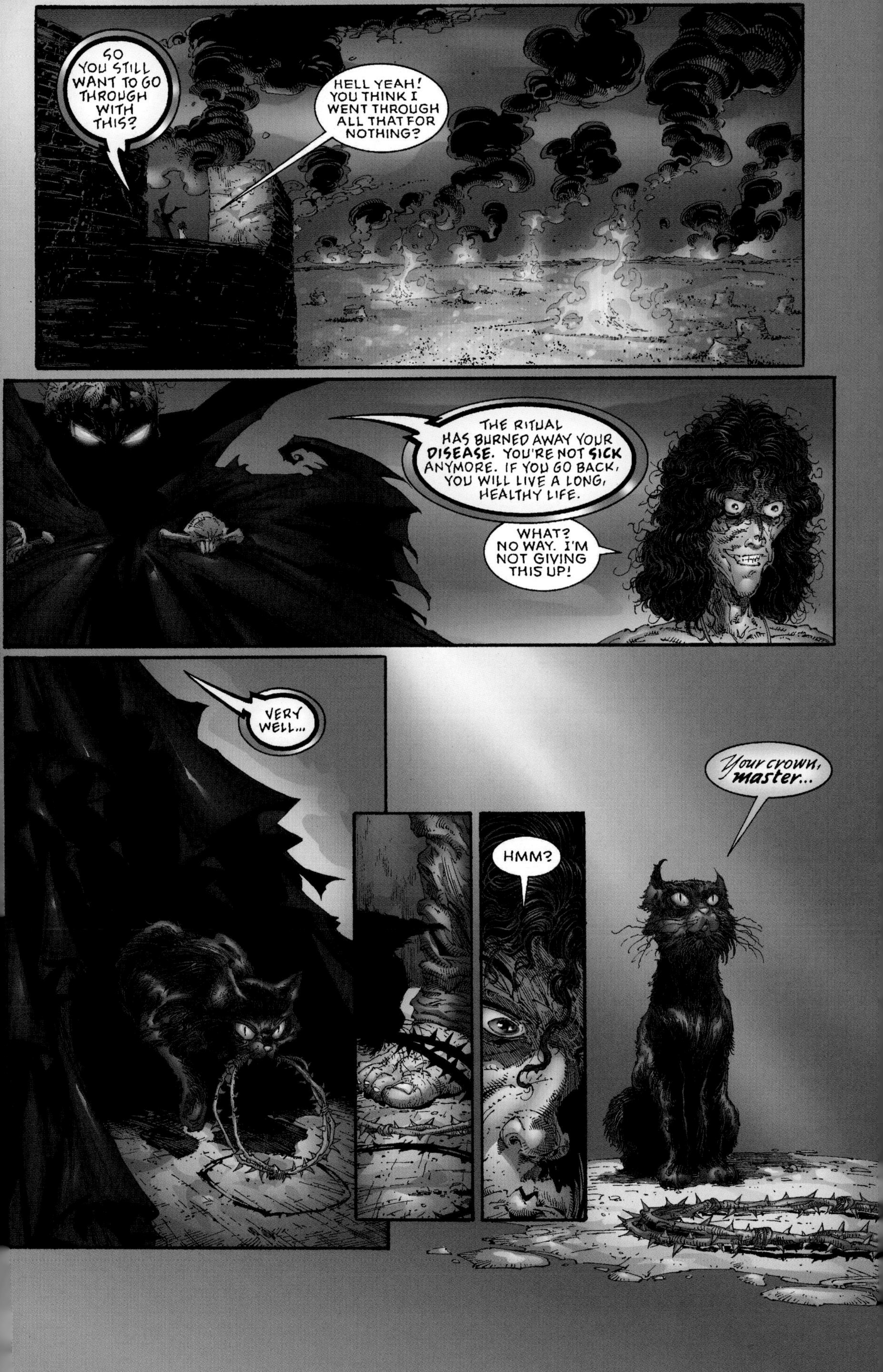
SO YOU STILL WANT TO GO THROUGH WITH THIS?
HELL YEAH! YOU THINK I WENT THROUGH ALL THAT FOR NOTHING?
THE RITUAL HAS BURNED AWAY YOUR DISEASE. YOU'RE NOT SICK ANYMORE. IF YOU GO BACK, YOU WILL LIVE A LONG, HEALTHY LIFE.
WHAT? NO WAY. I'M NOT GIVING THIS UP!
VERY WELL...
HMM?
Your crown, master...

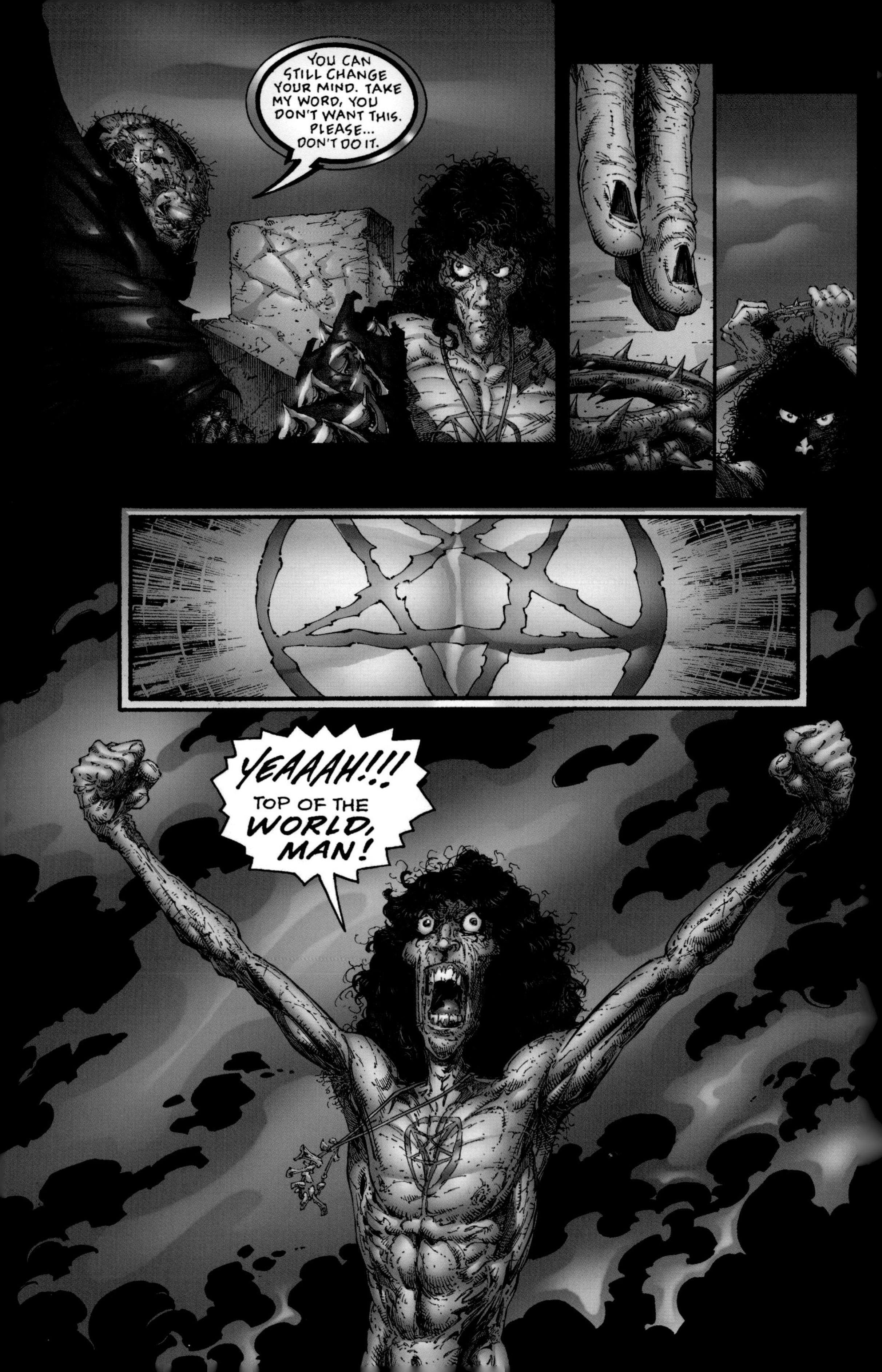
YOU CAN STILL CHANGE YOUR MIND. TAKE MY WORD, YOU DON'T WANT THIS. PLEASE... DON'T DO IT.
YEAAAH!!! TOP OF THE WORLD, MAN!

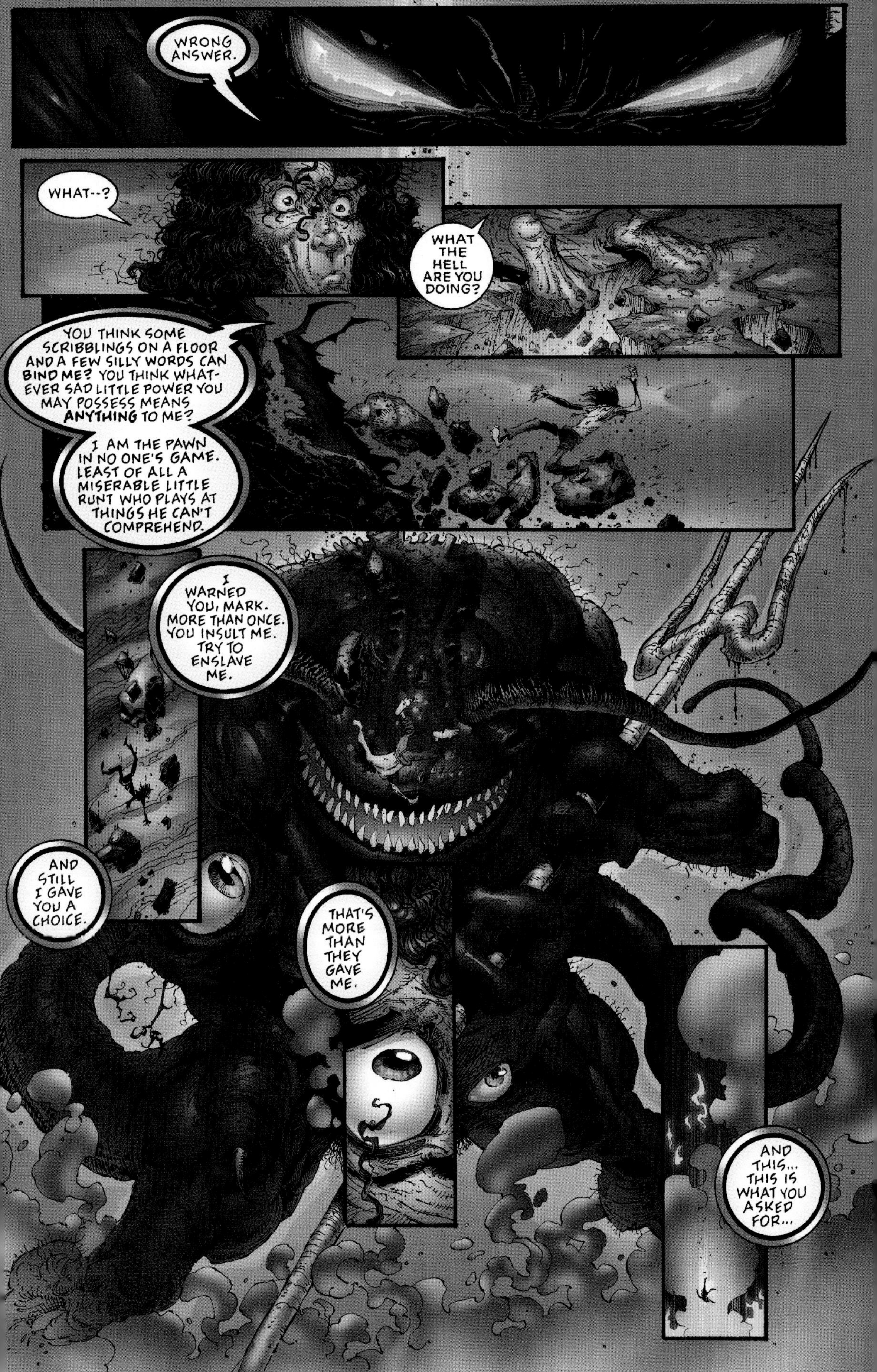
WRONG ANSWER.
WHAT--?
WHAT THE HELL ARE YOU DOING?
YOU THINK SOME SCRIBBLINGS ON A FLOOR AND A FEW SILLY WORDS CAN BIND ME? YOU THINK WHATEVER SAD LITTLE POWER YOU MAY POSSESS MEANS ANYTHING TO ME?
I AM THE PAWN IN NO ONE'S GAME. LEAST OF ALL A MISERABLE LITTLE RUNT WHO PLAYS AT THINGS HE CAN'T COMPREHEND.
I WARNED YOU, MARK. MORE THAN ONCE. YOU INSULT ME. TRY TO ENSLAVE ME.
AND STILL I GAVE YOU A CHOICE.
THAT'S MORE THAN THEY GAVE ME.
AND THIS... THIS IS WHAT YOU ASKED FOR...

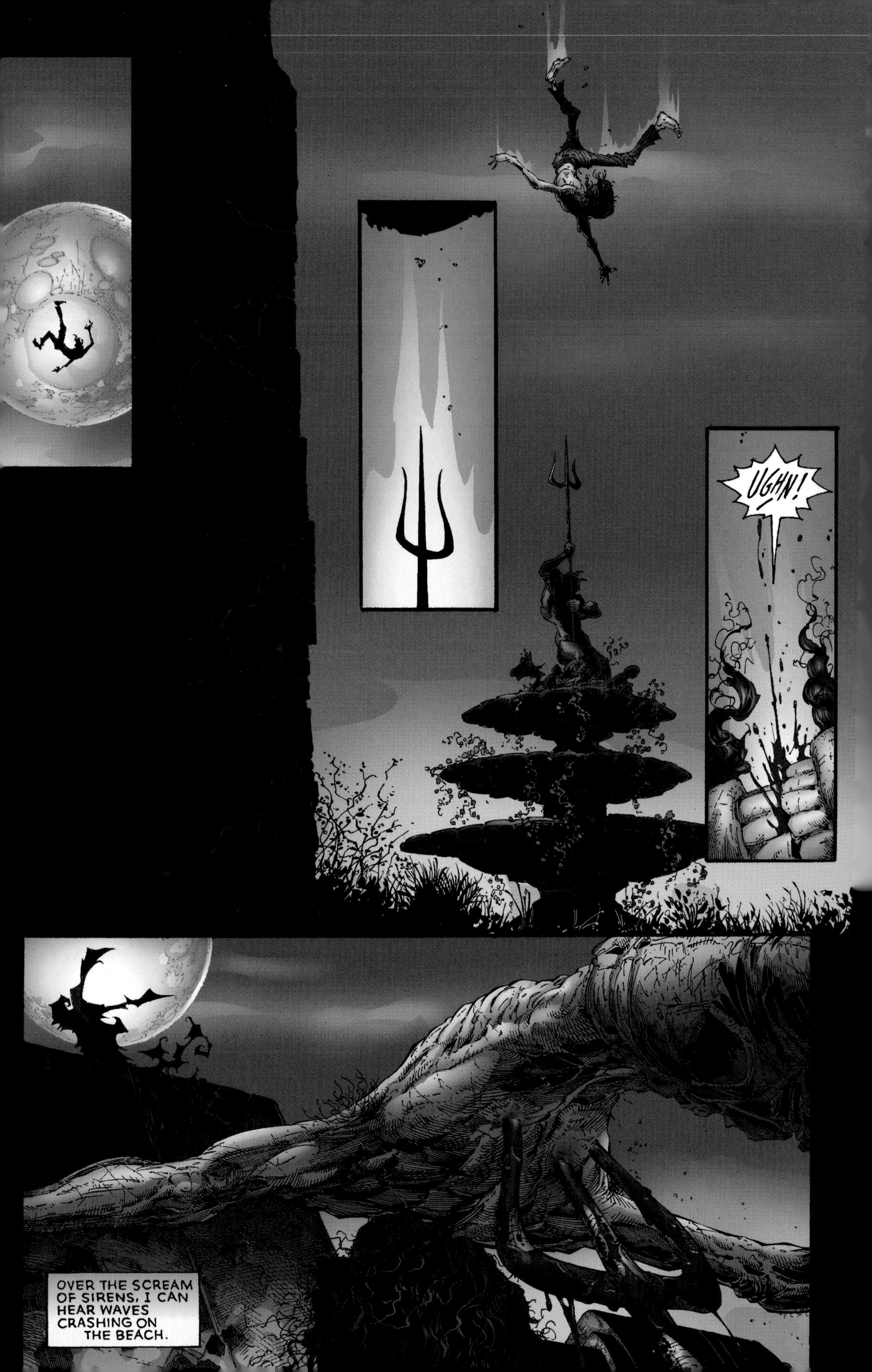
UGHN!
OVER THE SCREAM OF SIRENS, I CAN HEAR WAVES CRASHING ON THE BEACH.

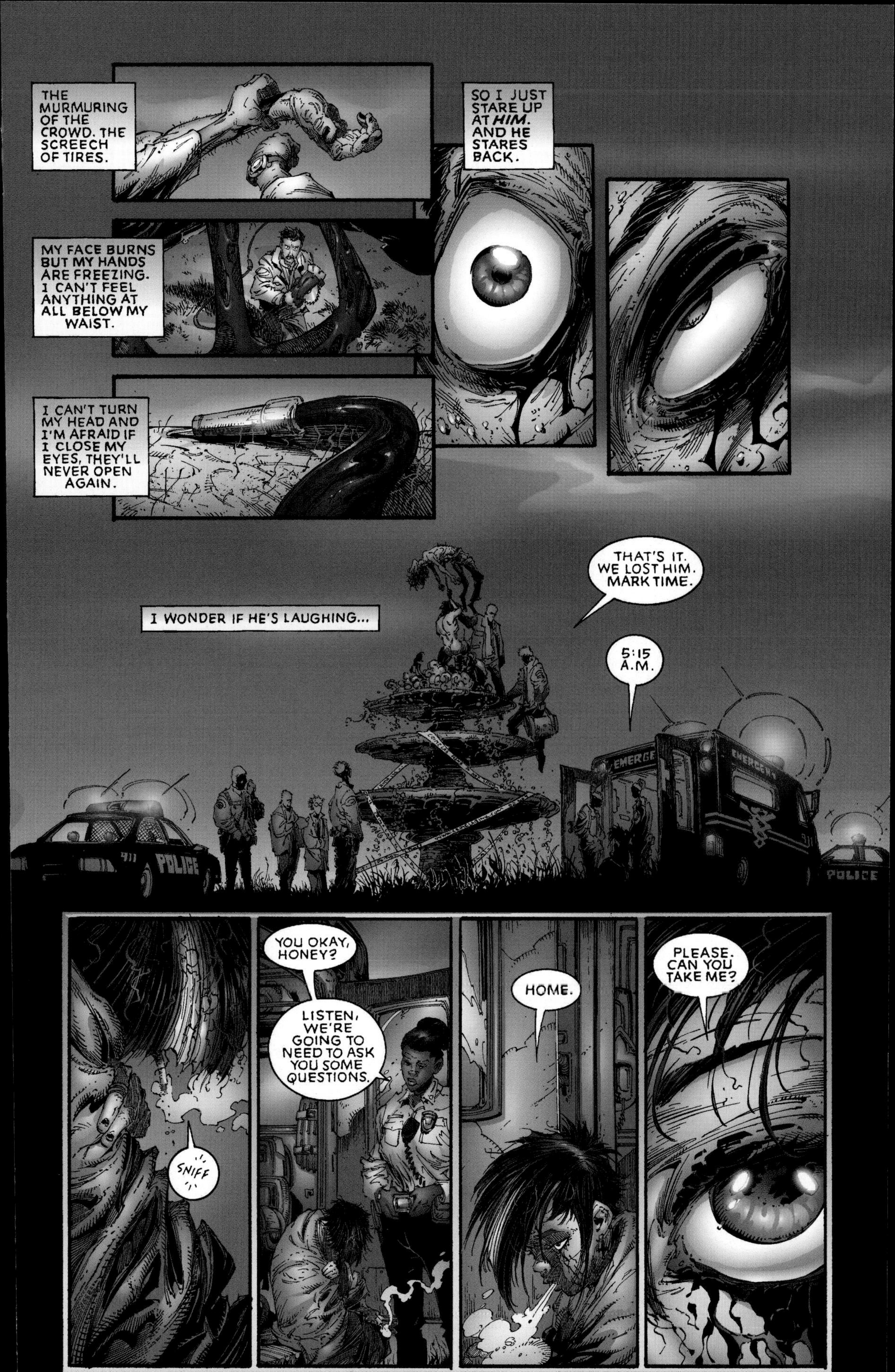
THE MURMURING OF THE CROWD. THE SCREECH OF TIRES.
MY FACE BURNS BUT MY HANDS ARE FREEZING. I CAN'T FEEL ANYTHING AT ALL BELOW MY WAIST.
I CAN'T TURN MY HEAD AND I'M AFRAID IF I CLOSE MY EYES, THEY'LL NEVER OPEN AGAIN.
SO I JUST STARE UP AT *HIM*. AND HE STARES BACK.
I WONDER IF HE'S LAUGHING...
THAT'S IT. WE LOST HIM. MARK TIME.
5:15 A.M.
POLICE
EMERGE
POLICE
SNIFF
YOU OKAY, HONEY?
LISTEN, WE'RE GOING TO NEED TO ASK YOU SOME QUESTIONS.
HOME.
PLEASE. CAN YOU TAKE ME?

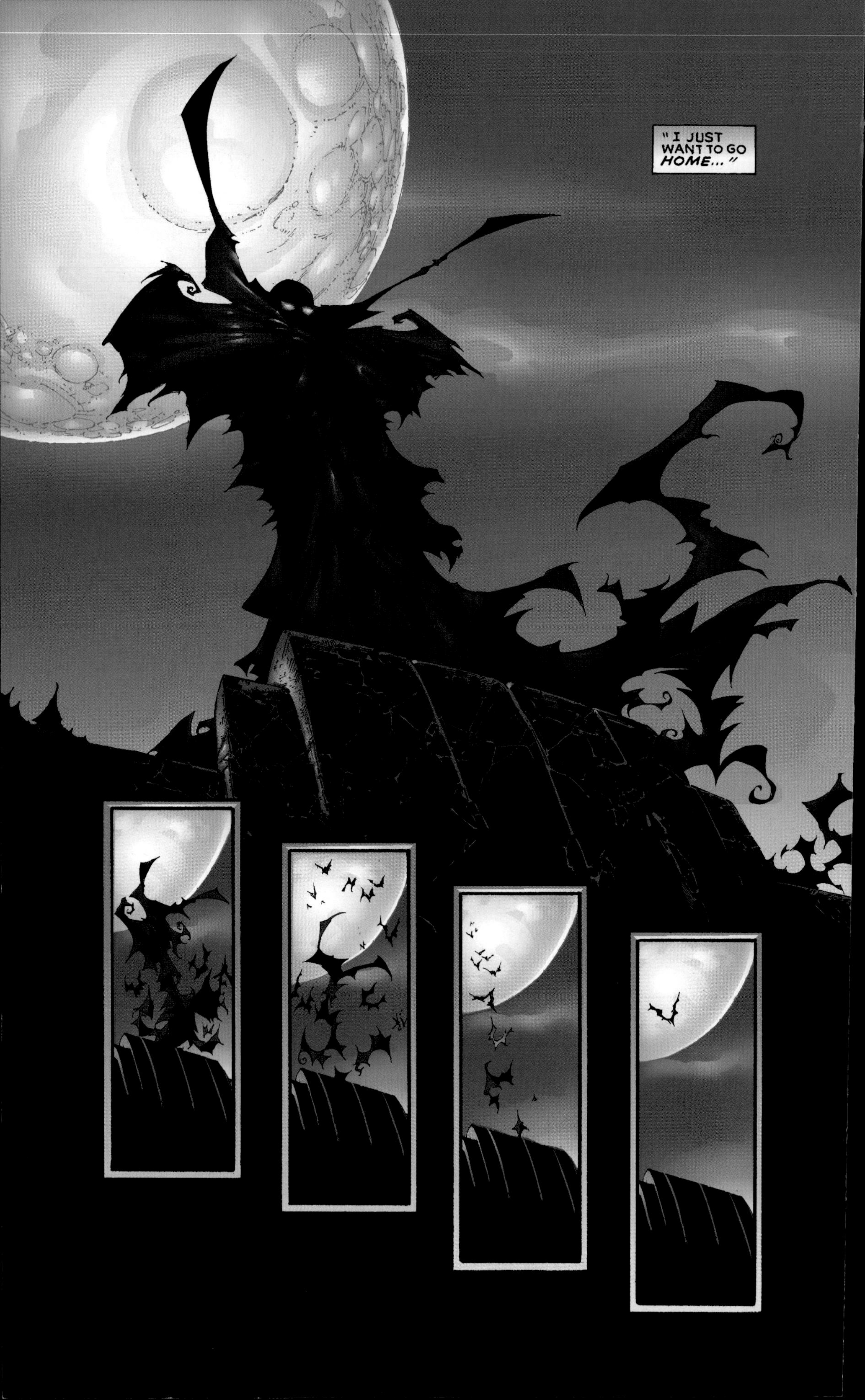
"I JUST WANT TO GO HOME..."

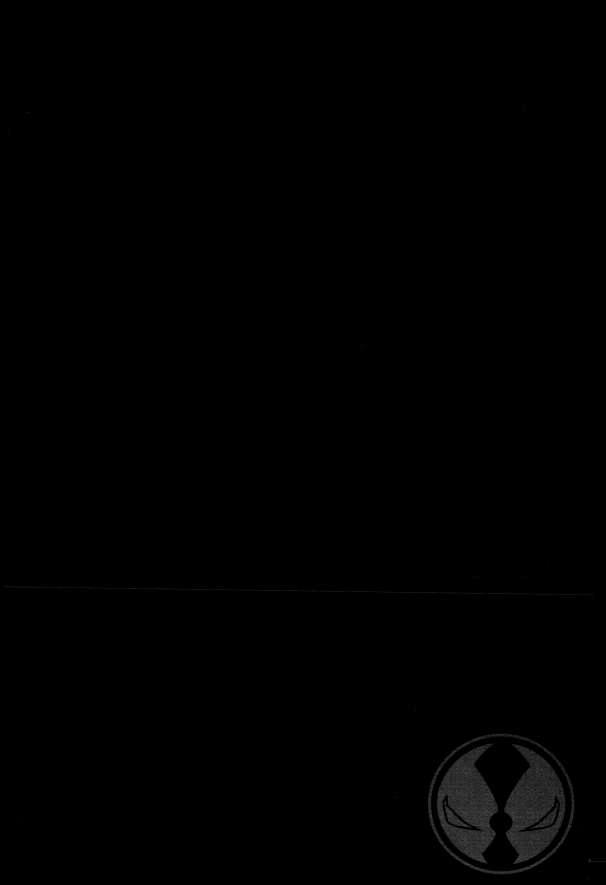

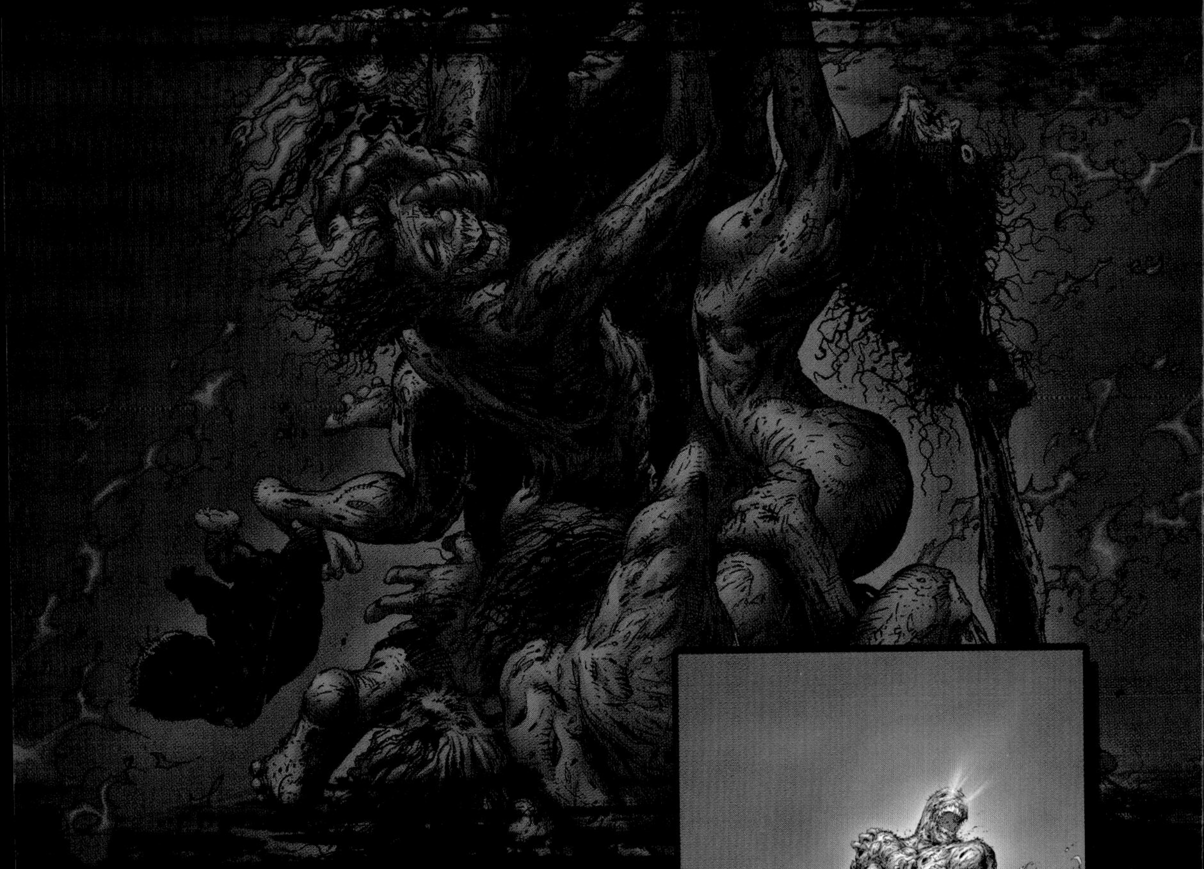

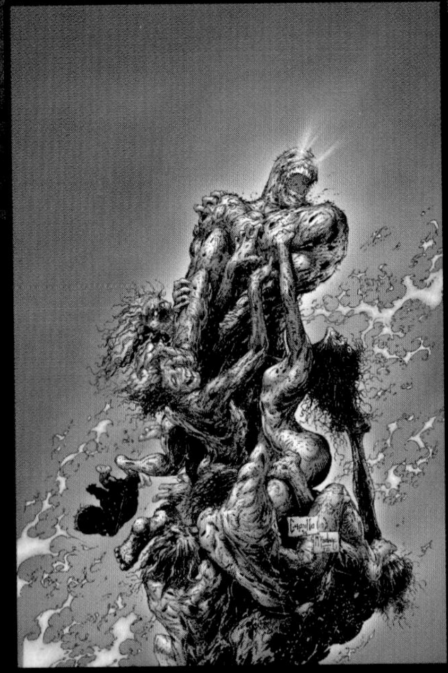

ISSUE NINETY-THREE

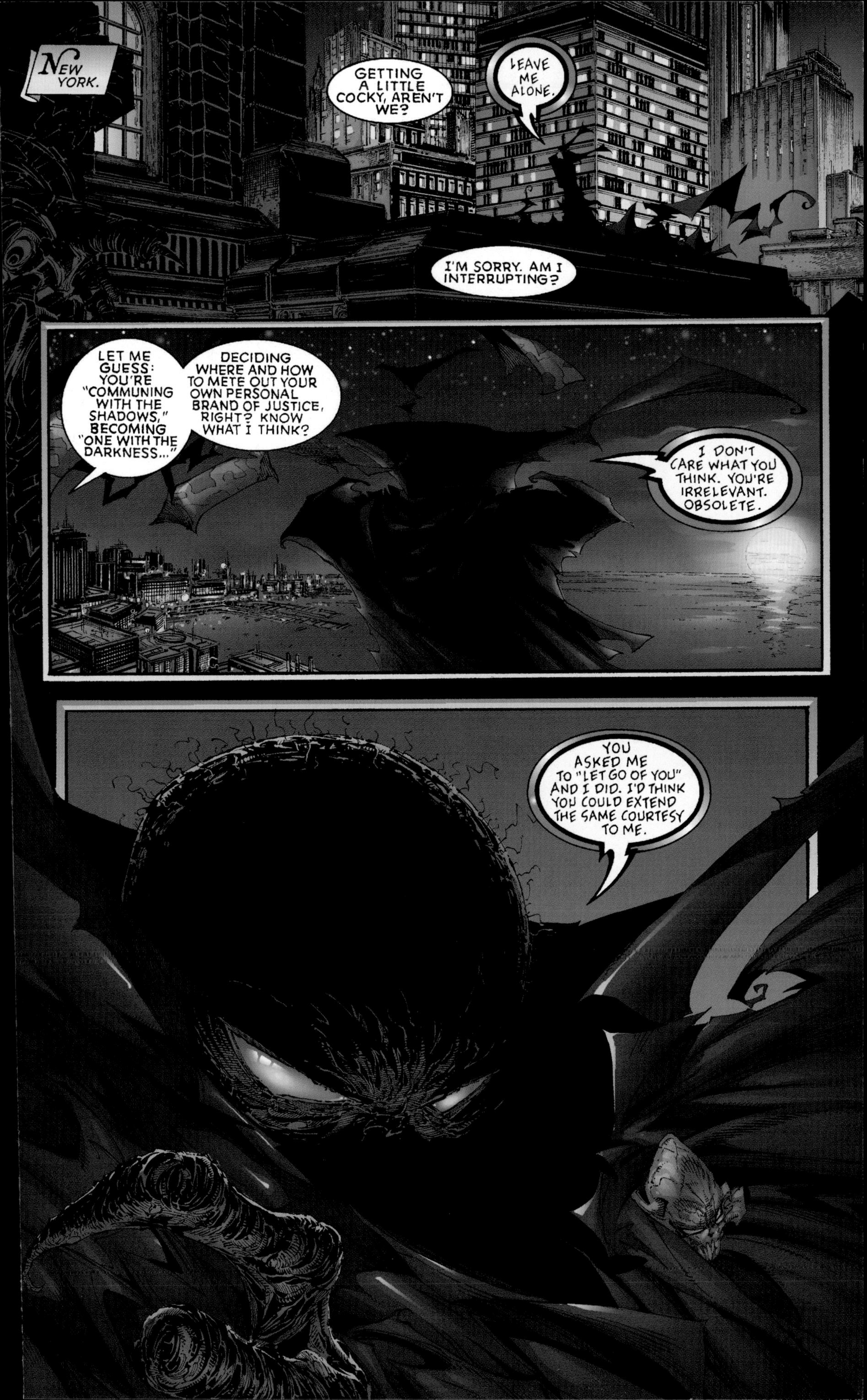
NEW YORK.
GETTING A LITTLE COCKY, AREN'T WE?
LEAVE ME ALONE.
I'M SORRY. AM I INTERRUPTING?
LET ME GUESS: YOU'RE "COMMUNING WITH THE SHADOWS," BECOMING "ONE WITH THE DARKNESS..."
DECIDING WHERE AND HOW TO METE OUT YOUR OWN PERSONAL BRAND OF JUSTICE, RIGHT? KNOW WHAT I THINK?
I DON'T CARE WHAT YOU THINK. YOU'RE IRRELEVANT. OBSOLETE.
YOU ASKED ME TO "LET GO OF YOU" AND I DID. I'D THINK YOU COULD EXTEND THE SAME COURTESY TO ME.

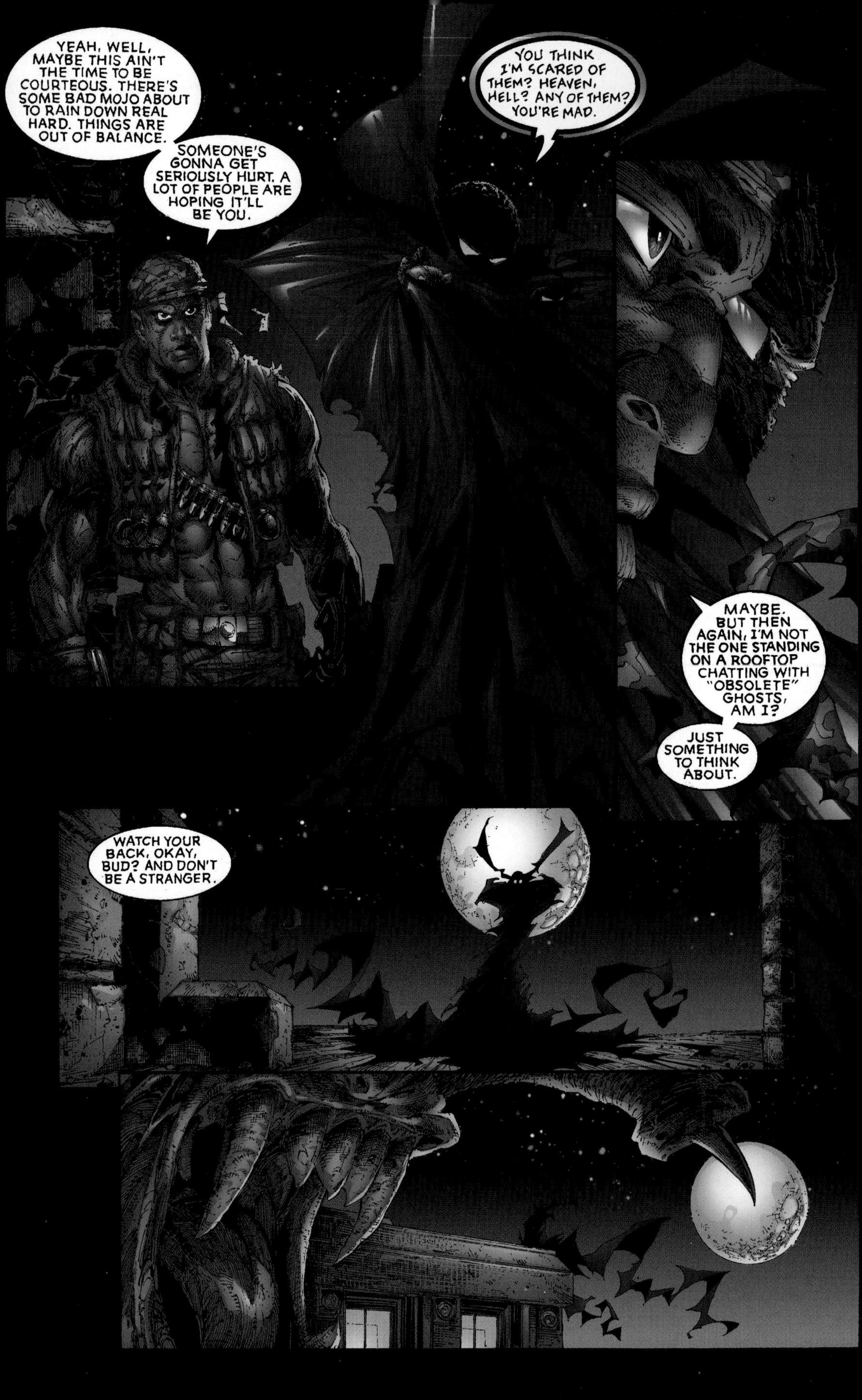
YEAH, WELL, MAYBE THIS AIN'T THE TIME TO BE COURTEOUS. THERE'S SOME BAD MOJO ABOUT TO RAIN DOWN REAL HARD. THINGS ARE OUT OF BALANCE.
SOMEONE'S GONNA GET SERIOUSLY HURT. A LOT OF PEOPLE ARE HOPING IT'LL BE YOU.
YOU THINK I'M SCARED OF THEM? HEAVEN, HELL? ANY OF THEM? YOU'RE MAD.
MAYBE. BUT THEN AGAIN, I'M NOT THE ONE STANDING ON A ROOFTOP CHATTING WITH "OBSOLETE" GHOSTS, AM I?
JUST SOMETHING TO THINK ABOUT.
WATCH YOUR BACK, OKAY, BUD? AND DON'T BE A STRANGER.

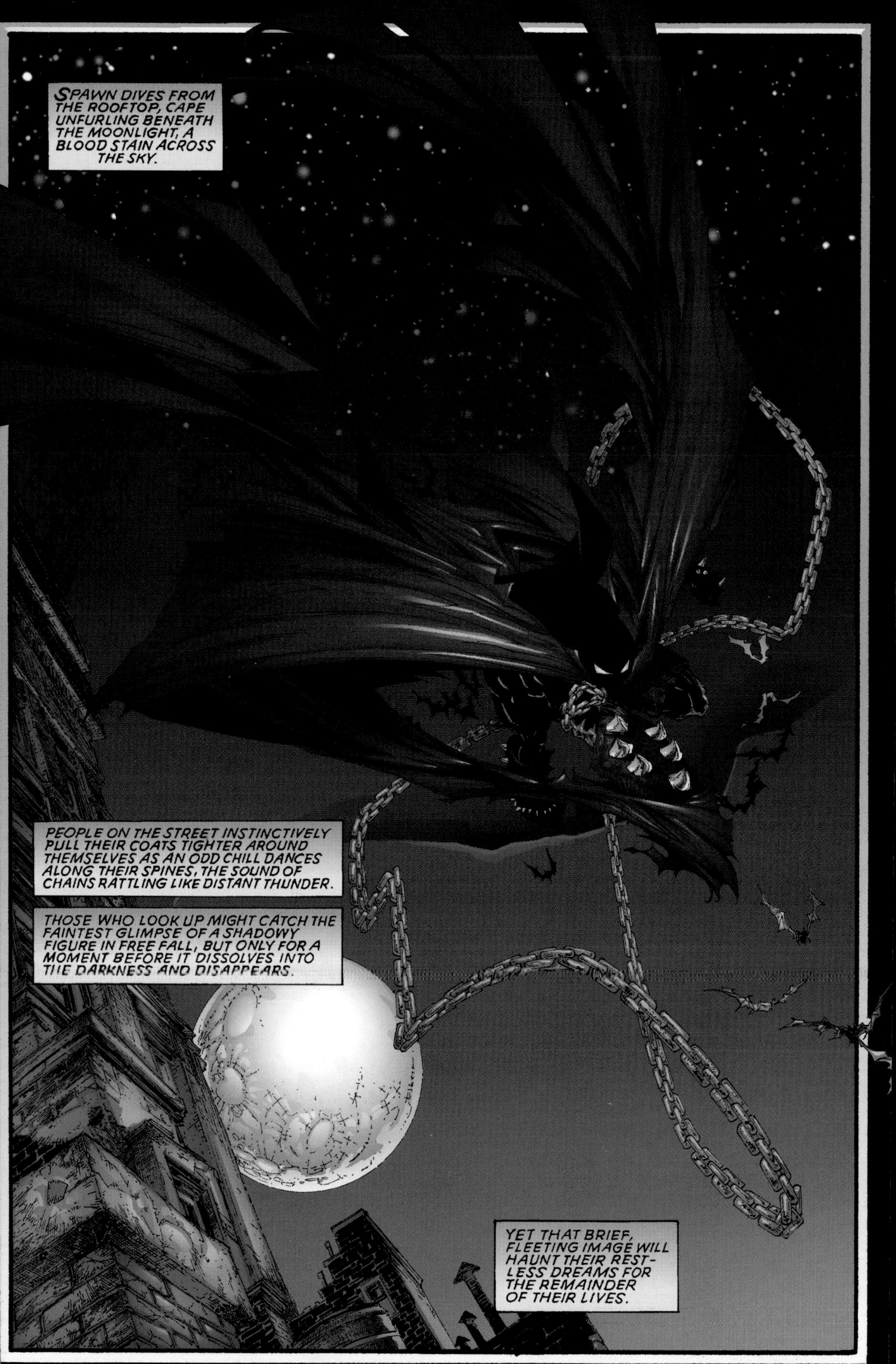
SPAWN DIVES FROM THE ROOFTOP, CAPE UNFURLING BENEATH THE MOONLIGHT, A BLOOD STAIN ACROSS THE SKY.
PEOPLE ON THE STREET INSTINCTIVELY PULL THEIR COATS TIGHTER AROUND THEMSELVES AS AN ODD CHILL DANCES ALONG THEIR SPINES, THE SOUND OF CHAINS RATTLING LIKE DISTANT THUNDER.
THOSE WHO LOOK UP MIGHT CATCH THE FAINTEST GLIMPSE OF A SHADOWY FIGURE IN FREE FALL, BUT ONLY FOR A MOMENT BEFORE IT DISSOLVES INTO THE DARKNESS AND DISAPPEARS.
YET THAT BRIEF, FLEETING IMAGE WILL HAUNT THEIR REST-LESS DREAMS FOR THE REMAINDER OF THEIR LIVES.

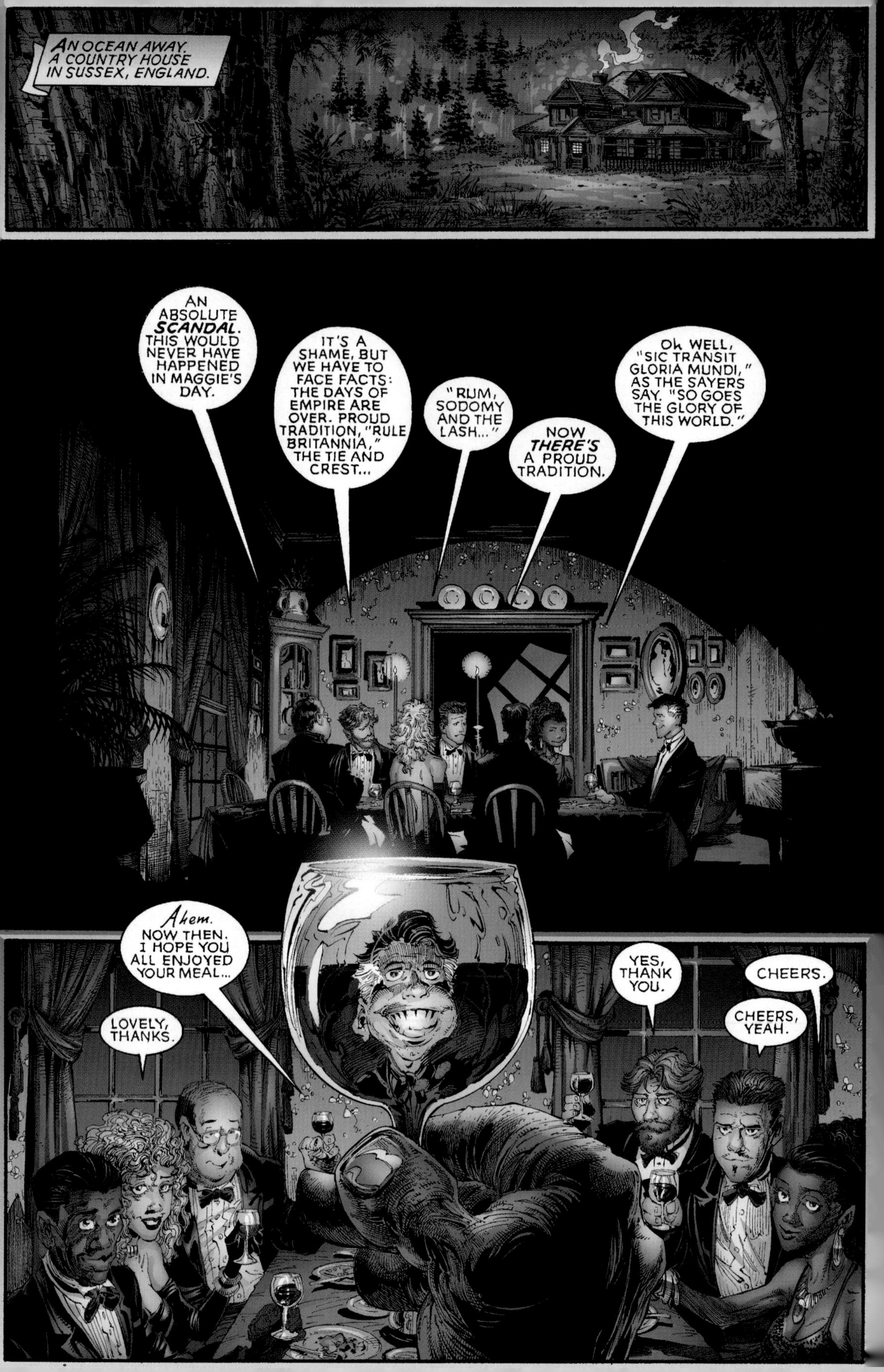
AN OCEAN AWAY. A COUNTRY HOUSE IN SUSSEX, ENGLAND.
AN ABSOLUTE SCANDAL. THIS WOULD NEVER HAVE HAPPENED IN MAGGIE'S DAY.
IT'S A SHAME, BUT WE HAVE TO FACE FACTS: THE DAYS OF EMPIRE ARE OVER. PROUD TRADITION, "RULE BRITANNIA," THE TIE AND CREST...
"RUM, SODOMY AND THE LASH..."
NOW THERE'S A PROUD TRADITION.
Oh WELL, "SIC TRANSIT GLORIA MUNDI," AS THE SAYERS SAY. "SO GOES THE GLORY OF THIS WORLD."
Ahem. NOW THEN. I HOPE YOU ALL ENJOYED YOUR MEAL...
LOVELY, THANKS.
YES, THANK YOU.
CHEERS.
CHEERS, YEAH.

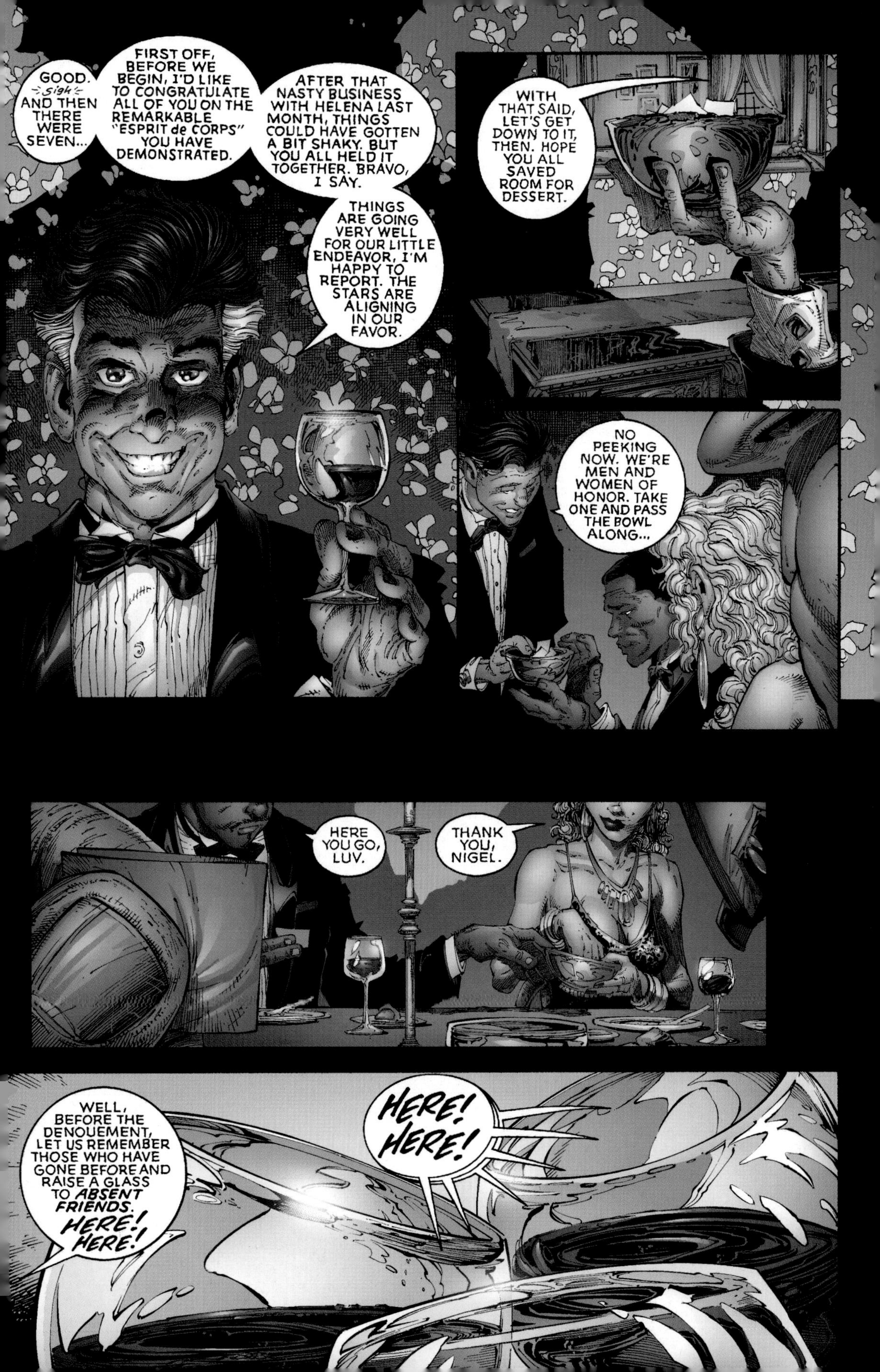
GOOD. -sigh- AND THEN THERE WERE SEVEN...
FIRST OFF, BEFORE WE BEGIN, I'D LIKE TO CONGRATULATE ALL OF YOU ON THE REMARKABLE "ESPRIT de CORPS" YOU HAVE DEMONSTRATED.
AFTER THAT NASTY BUSINESS WITH HELENA LAST MONTH, THINGS COULD HAVE GOTTEN A BIT SHAKY. BUT YOU ALL HELD IT TOGETHER. BRAVO, I SAY.
THINGS ARE GOING VERY WELL FOR OUR LITTLE ENDEAVOR, I'M HAPPY TO REPORT. THE STARS ARE ALIGNING IN OUR FAVOR.
WITH THAT SAID, LET'S GET DOWN TO IT, THEN. HOPE YOU ALL SAVED ROOM FOR DESSERT.
NO PEEKING NOW. WE'RE MEN AND WOMEN OF HONOR. TAKE ONE AND PASS THE BOWL ALONG...
HERE YOU GO, LUV.
THANK YOU, NIGEL.
WELL, BEFORE THE DENOUEMENT, LET US REMEMBER THOSE WHO HAVE GONE BEFORE AND RAISE A GLASS TO ABSENT FRIENDS. HERE! HERE!
HERE! HERE!

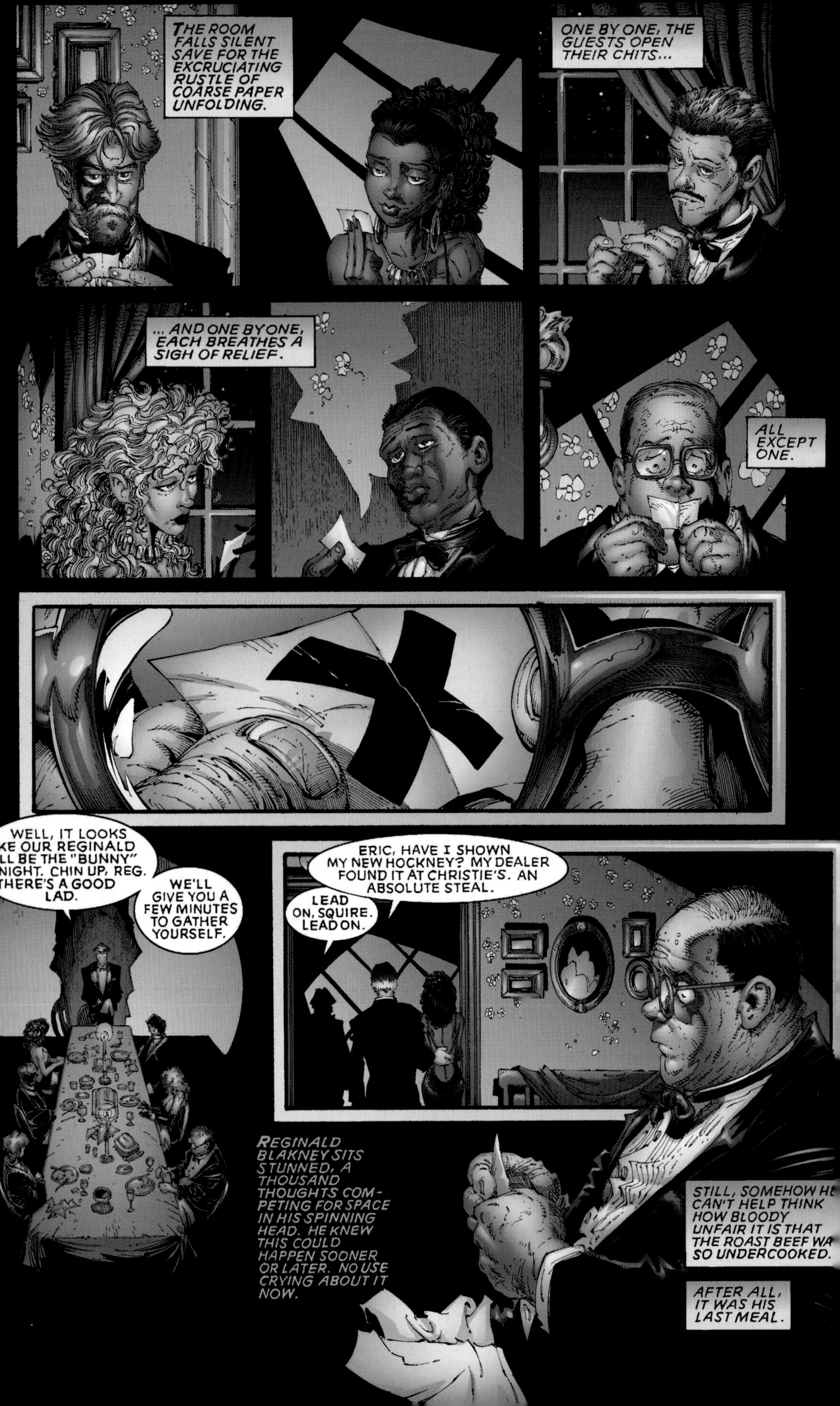
THE ROOM FALLS SILENT SAVE FOR THE EXCRUCIATING RUSTLE OF COARSE PAPER UNFOLDING.
ONE BY ONE, THE GUESTS OPEN THEIR CHITS...
...AND ONE BY ONE, EACH BREATHES A SIGH OF RELIEF.
ALL EXCEPT ONE.
WELL, IT LOOKS LIKE OUR REGINALD WILL BE THE "BUNNY" TONIGHT. CHIN UP, REG. THERE'S A GOOD LAD.
WE'LL GIVE YOU A FEW MINUTES TO GATHER YOURSELF.
ERIC, HAVE I SHOWN MY NEW HOCKNEY? MY DEALER FOUND IT AT CHRISTIE'S. AN ABSOLUTE STEAL.
LEAD ON, SQUIRE. LEAD ON.
REGINALD BLAKNEY SITS STUNNED, A THOUSAND THOUGHTS COMPETING FOR SPACE IN HIS SPINNING HEAD. HE KNEW THIS COULD HAPPEN SOONER OR LATER. NO USE CRYING ABOUT IT NOW.
STILL, SOMEHOW HE CAN'T HELP THINK HOW BLOODY UNFAIR IT IS THAT THE ROAST BEEF WAS SO UNDERCOOKED.
AFTER ALL, IT WAS HIS LAST MEAL.

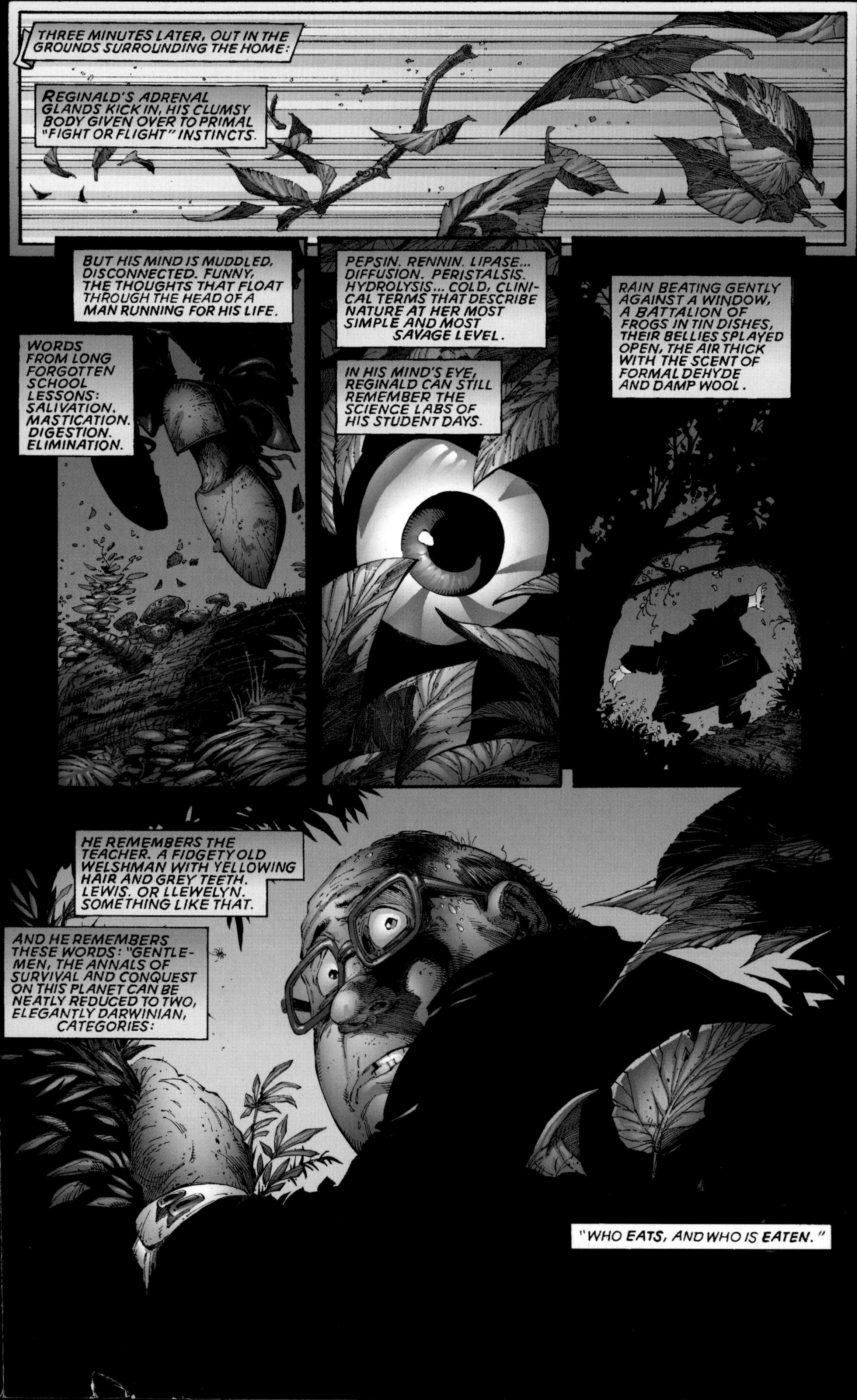

THREE MINUTES LATER, OUT IN THE GROUNDS SURROUNDING THE HOME:
REGINALD'S ADRENAL GLANDS KICK IN, HIS CLUMSY BODY GIVEN OVER TO PRIMAL "FIGHT OR FLIGHT" INSTINCTS.
BUT HIS MIND IS MUDDLED, DISCONNECTED. FUNNY, THE THOUGHTS THAT FLOAT THROUGH THE HEAD OF A MAN RUNNING FOR HIS LIFE.
WORDS FROM LONG FORGOTTEN SCHOOL LESSONS: SALIVATION. MASTICATION. DIGESTION. ELIMINATION.
PEPSIN. RENNIN. LIPASE... DIFFUSION. PERISTALSIS. HYDROLYSIS... COLD, CLINICAL TERMS THAT DESCRIBE NATURE AT HER MOST SIMPLE AND MOST SAVAGE LEVEL.
IN HIS MIND'S EYE, REGINALD CAN STILL REMEMBER THE SCIENCE LABS OF HIS STUDENT DAYS.
RAIN BEATING GENTLY AGAINST A WINDOW, A BATTALION OF FROGS IN TIN DISHES, THEIR BELLIES SPLAYED OPEN, THE AIR THICK WITH THE SCENT OF FORMALDEHYDE AND DAMP WOOL.
HE REMEMBERS THE TEACHER. A FIDGETY OLD WELSHMAN WITH YELLOWING HAIR AND GREY TEETH. LEWIS. OR LLEWELYN. SOMETHING LIKE THAT.
AND HE REMEMBERS THESE WORDS: "GENTLEMEN, THE ANNALS OF SURVIVAL AND CONQUEST ON THIS PLANET CAN BE NEATLY REDUCED TO TWO, ELEGANTLY DARWINIAN, CATEGORIES:
"WHO EATS, AND WHO IS EATEN."

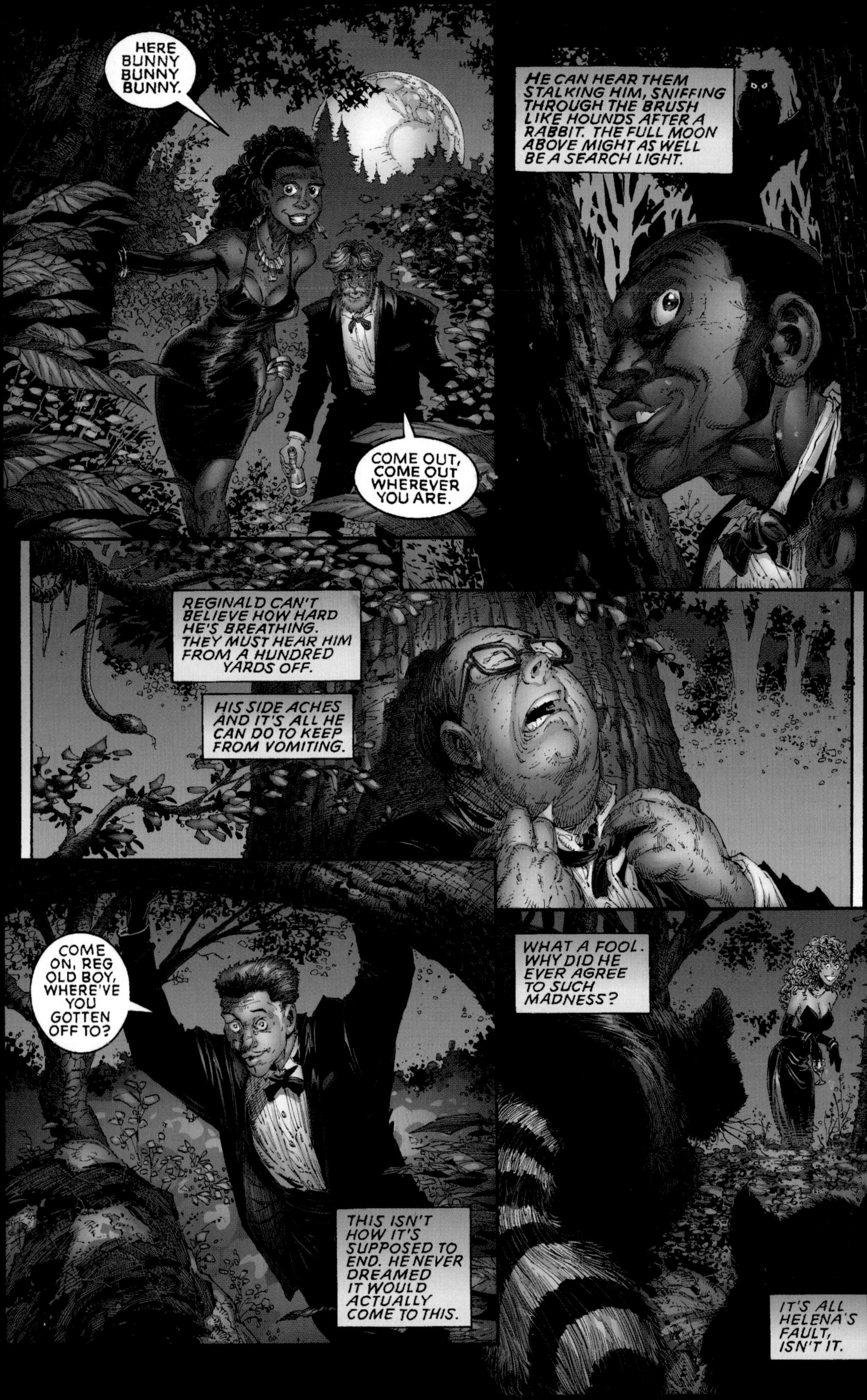
HERE BUNNY BUNNY BUNNY.
COME OUT, COME OUT WHEREVER YOU ARE.
HE CAN HEAR THEM STALKING HIM, SNIFFING THROUGH THE BRUSH LIKE HOUNDS AFTER A RABBIT. THE FULL MOON ABOVE MIGHT AS WELL BE A SEARCH LIGHT.
REGINALD CAN'T BELIEVE HOW HARD HE'S BREATHING. THEY MUST HEAR HIM FROM A HUNDRED YARDS OFF.
HIS SIDE ACHES AND IT'S ALL HE CAN DO TO KEEP FROM VOMITING.
COME ON, REG OLD BOY, WHERE'VE YOU GOTTEN OFF TO?
THIS ISN'T HOW IT'S SUPPOSED TO END. HE NEVER DREAMED IT WOULD ACTUALLY COME TO THIS.
WHAT A FOOL. WHY DID HE EVER AGREE TO SUCH MADNESS?
IT'S ALL HELENA'S FAULT, ISN'T IT.